COLLINS

CONCISE ATLAS OF THE WORLD

HarperCollins*Publishers*

Collins Concise Atlas of the World
first published 1984 by William Collins Sons & Co. Ltd.
Reprinted 1985, 1986, 1987, 1988, 1989, 1990

New Edition 1991
Maps © Collins and Collins-Longman Atlases
Illustrated section and statistics © Bartholomew

Collins is an imprint of Bartholomew,
a division of HarperCollins *Publishers*

12 Duncan Street
Edinburgh
EH9 1TA

Printed in Scotland by Bartholomew HarperCollins Manufacturing, Edinburgh

ISBN 0 00 447824 X

Photograph Credits
J. Allen Cash Photolibrary
The Hutchison Library
The Image Bank
Frank Lane Picture Library
London Docklands Development Corporation
Meteorological Department, National Centre for Atmospheric Research/National Science Foundation, USA
National Oceanic And Atmospheric Administration, USA
Panos Pictures
Science Photo Library
Spectrum Colour Library
Tropix Photographic Library
United Nations Environment Programme

FOREWORD

"The world is a beautiful book, but of little use to him who cannot read it."

This profound statement, made by the Italian playwright Carlo Goldoni over two hundred years ago, is all the more relevant today, at a time when the space age perspective of our planet heightens our awareness of the world in which we live. Daily we are exposed to media reports, transmitted instantaneously from all parts of the globe, that portray not only the physical beauty and awe-inspiring forces of the natural world, but also the human problems, the misuse of the Earth's resources, and evidence of the growing need to acknowledge the interdependence of mankind and nature. Currently too, space age technology allows man to scientifically survey our planet in the most precise detail. The mass of geographical data being collected has resulted in an information explosion so great that the non-specialist user could easily be overwhelmed. This situation calls for a convenient, clearly presented and concise source of the latest knowledge about our world suitable for everyday household use.

COLLINS CONCISE ATLAS OF THE WORLD, as its title implies, has been specially designed to meet this need. This book is a concise edition of the Collins Atlas of the World which, when published in 1983, was widely commended for its modern approach to atlas making, its clarity of presentation, the comprehensiveness of its authoritative content, and its exceptionally good value. Like its parent, this concise atlas makes available in one easily handled volume the latest findings and essential facts about our fast changing world; again presented in three self-contained but interrelated sections first under the heading of OUR PLANET EARTH there is an informative and in-depth survey of contemporary world environmental issues. Next, the WORLD ATLAS section, comprising 96 pages of newly created maps, using the most modern cartographic techniques and up-to-date sources, forms the core of this book. Finally the maps, diagrams and text of these first two sections are complemented by a detailed compendium of WORLD DATA including a comprehensive index of over 30,000 place names.

The strategy by which the content of the COLLINS ATLAS OF THE WORLD has been reduced to the practical and workmanlike proportions of this concise version has thus carefully avoided wholesale deletion of any one of these essential reference sections. Although there are slightly fewer maps, illustrated encyclopaedia spreads, and indexed place names, a fully balanced coverage of every region in the world and of the major geographical topics is maintained. Again, although the dimensions of the pages of this book are marginally smaller, the scale, area and content of the individual maps has not in any way been reduced. Similarly the presentation of the encyclopedia illustrated texts and data tables contained in this atlas has not suffered any loss of clarity or content.

In this way Collins, building on its traditions and experience of over one hundred years' innovative atlas making, provides in the CONCISE ATLAS OF THE WORLD a very useful and moderately priced new reference work that will meet most people's requirements.

Furthermore, the detailed process of research, compilation and design, together with the latest cartographic techniques and high-quality printing that have gone into its production ensure that our readers will have a most informative, stimulating and, above all, up-to-date atlas, that is especially relevant to today's needs.

The resulting COLLINS CONCISE ATLAS OF THE WORLD is, indeed, a 'beautiful book' that can be easily read - presenting us all with a platform of knowledge from which we can look critically at our fascinating world. Knowledge is the beginning of all wisdom, but finding out about our world, and ourselves in turn, can be fun too. Enjoy using this atlas.

GUIDE TO THE ATLAS

COLLINS CONCISE ATLAS OF THE WORLD consists of three self-contained but interrelated sections, as is clearly indicated in the preceding list of contents. First, under the title of OUR PLANET EARTH there is an informative and in-depth survey of contemporary world environmental issues. Next, the WORLD ATLAS section, comprising 96 pages of maps, using the most modern cartographic techniques and up-to-date sources, forms the core of this book. Finally, the maps, diagrams and text of these first two sections, are complemented by a detailed compendium of WORLD DATA.

OUR PLANET EARTH

This concise encyclopaedia section, by use of stimulating illustrations, photographs, diagrams and informative text, brings together much of the current knowledge and thinking concerning world environmental issues. The first section covers the physical environment, dealing with natural hazards and their implications for mankind, and with the detrimental effects of human activity on the natural environment. The second section covers the human environment, dealing with the exploitation of natural resources and the need to seek renewable alternatives and the continuing need to improve the quality of life for all the peoples of the world.

WORLD ATLAS

The main section of 96 pages of maps has been carefully planned and designed to meet the contemporary needs of the atlas user. Full recognition has been given to the many different purposes that currently call for map reference.

Map coverage extends to every part of the world in a balanced scheme that avoids any individual country or regional bias. Map areas are chosen to reflect the social, economic, cultural or historical importance of a particular region. Each double spread or single page map has been planned deliberately to cover an entire physical or political unit. Generous map overlaps are included to maintain continuity. Following two world maps, giving separate coverage of the main political and physical features, each of the continents is treated systematically in a subsection of its own. Apart from being listed in the contents, full coverage of all regional maps of each continent is also clearly depicted in the Key to Maps to be found on the front and back endpapers. Also at the beginning of each continental subsection, alongside a special Global View political map, all map coverage, country by country, is identified in an additional handy page index. Finally, as a further aid to the reader in locating the required area, a postage stamp key map is incorporated into the title margin of each map page.

Map projections have been chosen to reflect the different requirements of particular areas. No map can be absolutely true on account of the impossibility of representing a spheroid accurately on a flat surface without some distortion in either area, distance, direction or shape. In a general world atlas it is the equal area property that is most important to retain for comparative map studies and feature size evaluation and this principle has been followed wherever possible in this map section. As a special feature of this atlas, the Global View projections used for each continental political map have been specially devised to allow for a realistic area comparison between the land areas of each continent and also between land and sea.

Map scales, as expressions of the relationship which the distance between any two points of the map bears to the corresponding distance on the ground, are in the context of this atlas grouped into three distinct categories.

Large scales, of between 1: 1 000 000 (1 centimetre to 10 kilometres or 1 inch to 16 miles) and 1: 2 500 000 (1 centimetre to 25 kilometres or 1 inch to 40 miles), are used to cover particularly densely populated areas of Western Europe, United States, Canada and Japan, as well as a special detailed map of the Holy Land.

Medium scales, of between 1: 2 500 000 and 1: 7 500 000 are used for maps of important parts of Europe, North America, Australasia, India, China, etc.

Small scales, of less than 1: 7 500 000 (e.g. 1:10 000 000, 1: 15 000 000, 1: 25 000 000 etc.) are selected for maps of the complete world, continents, oceans, polar regions and many of the larger countries.

The actual scale at which a particular area is mapped therefore reflects its shape, size and density of detail, and as a basic principle the more detail required to be shown of an area, the greater its scale. However, throughout this atlas, map scales have been limited in number, as far as possible, in order to facilitate comparison between maps.

Map measurements give preference to the metric system which is now used in nearly every country throughout the world. All spot heights and ocean depths are shown in metres and the relief and submarine layer delineation is based on metric contour levels. However, all linear scalebar and height reference column figures are given in metric and Imperial equivalents to facilitate conversion of measurements for the non-metric reader.

Map symbols used are fully explained in the legend to be found on the first page of the World Atlas section. Careful study and frequent reference to this legend will aid in the reader's ability to extract maximum information.

Topography is shown by the combined means of precise spot heights, contouring, layer tinting and three-dimensional hill shading. Similar techniques are also used to depict the sea bed on the World Physical map and those of the oceans and polar regions.

Hydrographic features such as coastlines, rivers, lakes, swamps and canals are clearly differentiated.

Communications are particularly well represented with the contemporary importance of airports and road networks duly emphasized.

International boundaries and national capitals are fully documented and internal administrative divisions are shown with the maximum detail that the scale will allow. Boundary delineation reflects the 'de facto' rather than the 'de jure' political interpretation and where relevant an undefined or disputed boundary is distinguished. However there is no intended implication that the publishers necessarily endorse or accept the status of any political entity recorded on the maps.

Settlements are shown by a series of graded town stamps from major cities down to tiny villages.

Other features, such as notable ancient monuments, oases, national parks, oil and gas fields, are selectively included on particular maps that merit their identification.

Lettering styles used in the maps have been chosen with great care to ensure maximum legibility and clear distinction of named feature categories. The size and weight of the various typefaces reflect the relative importance of the features. Town names are graded to correspond with the appropriate town stamp.

Map place names have been selected in accordance with maintaining legibility at a given scale and at the same time striking an appropriate balance between natural and man-made features worthy of note. Name forms have been standardized according to the widely accepted principle, now well established in international reference atlases, of including place names and geographical terms in the local language of the country in question. In the case of non-Roman scripts (e.g. Arabic), transliteration and transcription have either been based on the rules recommended by the Permanent Committee on Geographical Names and the United States Board of Geographical Names, or as in the case of the adopted Pinyin transcription of Chinese names, a system officially proposed by the country concerned. The diacritical signs used in each language or transliteration have been retained on all the maps and throughout the index. However the English language reader's requirements have also been recognised in that the names of all countries, oceans, major seas and land features as well as familiar alternative name versions of important towns are presented in English.

Map sources used in the compilation of this atlas were many and varied, but always of the latest available information. At each stage of their preparation the maps were submitted to a thorough process of research and continual revision to ensure that on publication all data would be as accurate as practicable. A well-documented data bank was created to ensure consistency and validity of all information represented on the maps.

WORLD DATA

This detailed data section forms an appropriate complement to the preceding maps and illustrated texts. There are two parts, each providing a different type of essential geographical information.

World Facts and Figures Drawn from the latest available official sources, these tables present an easy reference profile of significant world physical, political and demographic as well as national data.

World Index This concluding part of the atlas list in alphabetical order all individual place names to be found on the maps, which total about 30,000. Each entry in the index is referenced to the appropriate map page number, the country or region in which the name is located and the position of the name on the map, given by its co-ordinates of latitude and longitude. A full explanation of how to use the index is to be found on page 103.

CONTENTS

V Foreword
VI Guide to the Atlas
VII Contents

OUR PLANET EARTH

VIII-IX Our Planet Earth *Introduction*
X-XI Earthquakes and Volcanoes
XII-XIII Rivers and Floods
XIV-XV Tropical Storms
XVI-XVII Drought
XVIII-XIX Deforestation
XX-XXI Desertification
XXII-XXIII Air Pollution
XXIV-XXV Land Pollution
XXVI-XXVI Water Pollution
XXVIII-XXIX Conserving Wildlife
XXX-XXXI Natural Resources
XXXII-XXXIII Energy
XXXIV-XXXV Food and Nutrition
XXXVI-XXXVII Health and Disease
XXXVIII-XXXIX Cities
XL *Postscript*

WORLD ATLAS

1 Symbols Legend

THE WORLD

2-3 The World *Political*
4-5 The World *Physical*

EUROPE

6-7 Europe *Political*
8-9 British Isles
10-11 England and Wales
12 Scotland
13 Ireland
14 The Low Countries
15 Paris Basin and Po Valley
16 Spain and Portugal
17 France
18-19 Italy and the Balkans
20-21 Central Europe
22-23 Scandinavia and Baltic Lands
24-25 U.S.S.R. in Europe

ASIA

26-27 Asia Political
28-29 Union of Soviet Socialist Republics
30-31 East Asia
32-33 East China
34 Indo - China
35 Japan
36-37 Southeast Asia
38-39 South Asia
40-41 Northern India, Pakistan and Bangladesh
42-43 Southwest Asia
44 The Levant
45 Arabia and the Horn of Africa

AFRICA

46-47 Africa *Political*
48-49 Nile Valley
50-51 Northwest Africa
52-53 West Africa
54-55 Central and East Africa
56-57 Southern Africa and Madagascar

OCEANIA

58-59 Oceania *Political*
60 New Zealand
61 Australia
62-63 Western Australia
64-65 Eastern Australia
66-67 Southeast Australia
68-69 Pacific Ocean

NORTH AMERICA

70-71 North America *Political*
72-73 Canada and Alaska
74-75 Western Canada
76-77 Eastern Canada
78-79 United States
80-81 Western United States
82-83 Central United States
84-85 Eastern United States
86-87 Central America and the Caribbean

SOUTH AMERICA

88-89 South America *Political*
90-91 South America - North
92-93 South America - South
94 South America - East
95 Atlantic Ocean
96 Polar Regions

WORLD DATA

WORLD FACTS & FIGURES

98 World Physical Data
99 World Political Data
100-102 Nations of the World

WORLD INDEX

103 Introduction/ Abbreviations
104-160 Alphabetical Index

OUR PLANET EARTH

While the earth formed about 4500 million years ago, life as we know it today has only evolved gradually over the last 45 million years. Human beings have inhabited the earth for less than half a million years, and a couple of hundred generations takes us back to the dawn of history. Within this time people have conquered the animal kingdom, learnt how to harness the forces of nature, and proliferated in such numbers that they have colonised nearly every corner of the earth. Even more stunning are the changes which have taken place within living memory. The use of electricity, nuclear fission and modern technology have now given us the power to alter the balance of life on earth.

The first astronauts reported that the earth hangs "like a blue pearl in space". Their experience has helped dispel the dangerous notion that the world is boundless in extent, with limitless resources. Ecologists have also shown that the earth is a self enclosed system in which all forms of life are interconnected. Disruption in one part of the ecosystem can have serious consequences elsewhere. It follows that all human activity has an effect on the natural environment, and that we misuse this fragile planet at our peril.

In recent years people have been putting the environment under increasing stress. Raw materials such as timber, water and minerals are beginning to run short. Pollution and the disposal of wastes are becoming critical issues, and global warming has highlighted the dangers that we face. Environmental problems have been compounded by inequalities of wealth, where rich nations control and exploit the bulk of available resources in a world in which large numbers of people are struggling for survival. Decisive and concerted action will be needed to confront the growing ecological crisis.

Despite these threats there are encouraging signs. Over the past few decades food production has more than matched the growth in population. In industry there is scope for much greater efficiency and more careful use of resources. Sustainable development holds one of the keys to the future. Improvements in social justice also offer great possibilities.

These are exciting times in which we live. In the next decade the state of the environment is set to become the most pressing issue confronting us all. The way we respond to the challenge will have a profound effect on the earth and its life support systems. We will only make balanced decisions on the basis of detailed and careful research. This illustrated encyclopaedia seeks to provide up-to-date information on the issues that confront us all.

EARTHQUAKES AND VOLCANOES

Plate boundaries, Earthquakes and Volcanoes

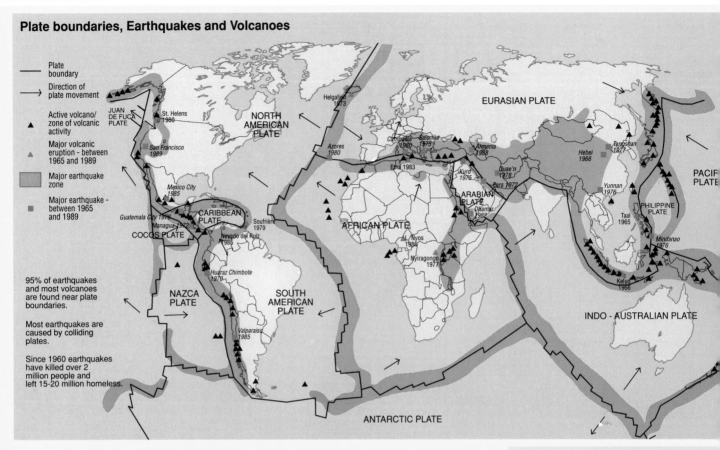

Plate boundary
Direction of plate movement
Active volcano/ zone of volcanic activity
Major volcanic eruption - between 1965 and 1989
Major earthquake zone
Major earthquake - between 1965 and 1989

JUAN DE FUCA PLATE
St. Helens 1980
San Francisco 1989
NORTH AMERICAN PLATE
Helgafjell 1973
EURASIAN PLATE
Azores 1980
Campania 1980
Salonika 1978
Armenia 1988
Etna 1983
Kurd 1975
Quae'n 1978
Pars 1972
Hebei 1966
Tangshan 1977
Yunnan 1976
PACIFIC PLATE
Mexico City 1985
Guatemala City 1976
Managua 1972
CARIBBEAN PLATE
COCOS PLATE
Soufrière 1979
Nevado del Ruiz 1985
ARABIAN PLATE
Dhamar 1982
AFRICAN PLATE
L. Nyos 1986
Nyiragongo 1977
PHILIPPINE PLATE
Taal 1965
Mindanao 1976
Kelud 1966
Huaraz Chimbote 1970
NAZCA PLATE
SOUTH AMERICAN PLATE
Valparaiso 1985
INDO - AUSTRALIAN PLATE
ANTARCTIC PLATE

95% of earthquakes and most volcanoes are found near plate boundaries.

Most earthquakes are caused by colliding plates.

Since 1960 earthquakes have killed over 2 million people and left 15-20 million homeless.

The Structure of the Earth

The earth's surface or crust forms a rigid layer of rock which varies in thickness from 6km to 40km. Beneath this there is a zone of semi-molten rock known as the aesthenosphere. Together with the upper mantle this reaches down to a depth of about 700km, below which there is the lower mantle and the core of the earth.

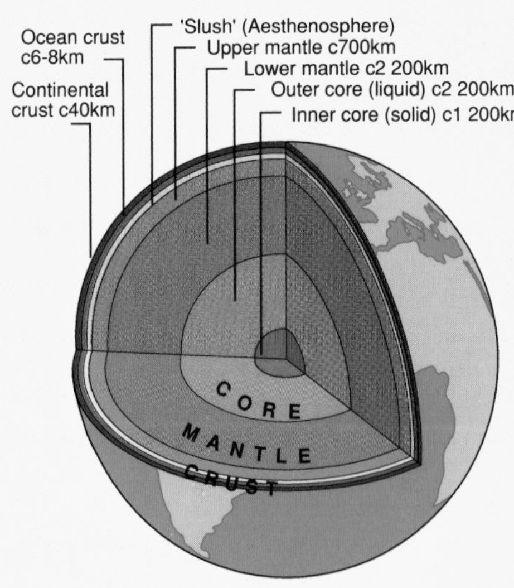

Ocean crust c6-8km
Continental crust c40km
'Slush' (Aesthenosphere)
Upper mantle c700km
Lower mantle c2 200km
Outer core (liquid) c2 200km
Inner core (solid) c1 200km
CORE
MANTLE
CRUST

The earth's interior consist of three layers - the crust on the surface, the mantle underneath and the core at the centre.

Types of Plates

The crust is broken into huge plates which fit together like the parts of a giant jigsaw. These float on the semi-molten rock below. The boundaries of the plates are marked by lines of volcanoes and earthquake activity.

There are three types of boundary:-

Diverging plates. When two plates move away from each other, molten rock wells up from the earth's core creating a ridge, eg the ridge down the Atlantic from Iceland to the Antarctic.

Converging plates. When two plates move towards each other a trench is formed as one slides beneath the other. It was a movement of this kind which created the Himalayas.

Shearing Plates. Sometimes neighbouring plates move horizontally in opposite directions from one another, eg the San Andreas fault in California

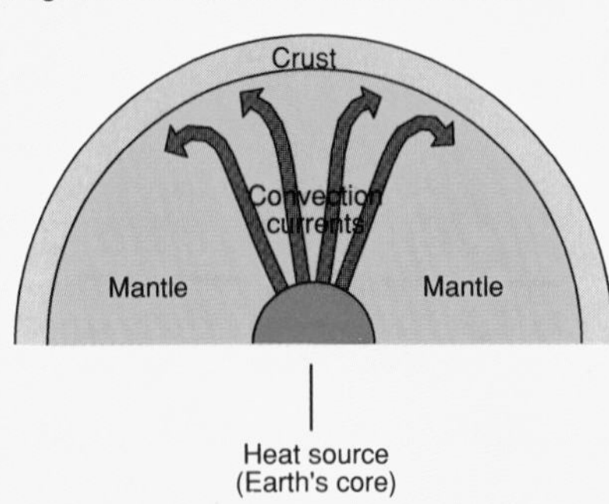

Crust
Convection currents
Mantle
Mantle
Heat source (Earth's core)

Convection and plate Movement

Plate movements cause continents to drift at about 2.5cm a year. They are carried by convection currents in the magma.

Diverging Plates

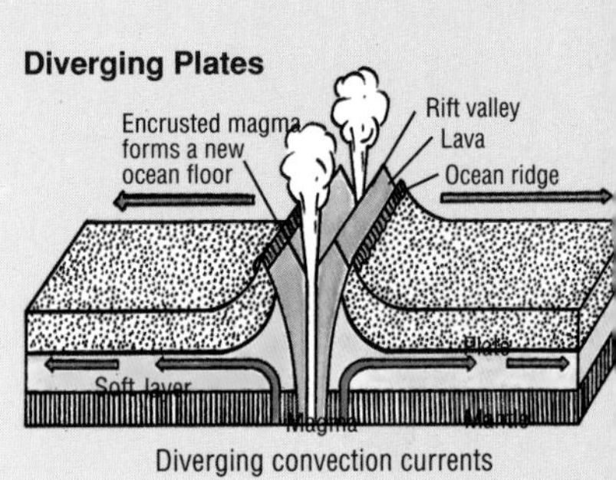

Encrusted magma forms a new ocean floor
Rift valley
Lava
Ocean ridge
Plate
Soft layer
Magma
Magma

Diverging convection currents

Converging Plates

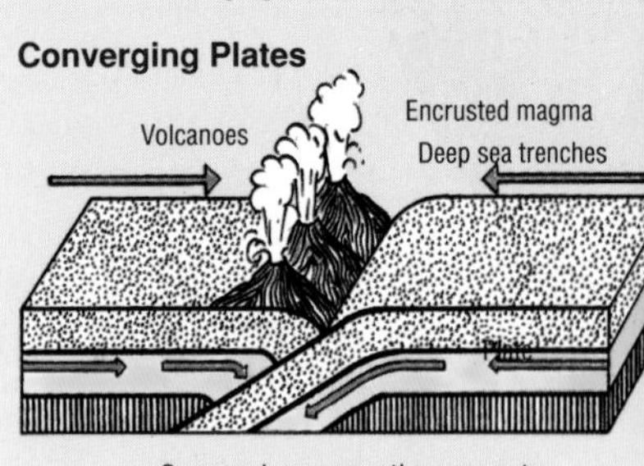

Volcanoes
Encrusted magma
Deep sea trenches
Plate

Converging convection currents

Shearing Plates

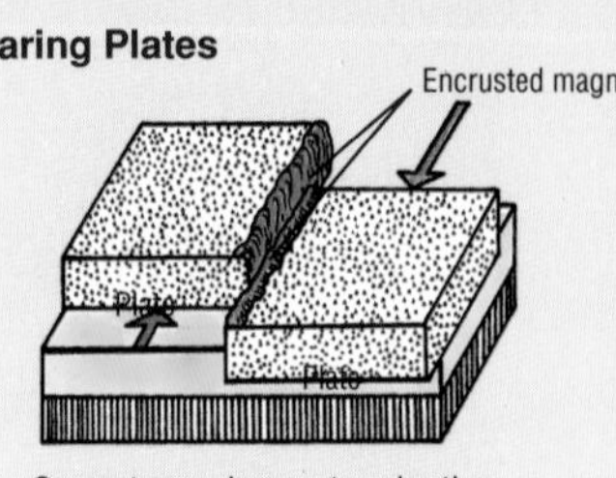

Encrusted magma
Plate
Plate

Currents moving past each other

arthquakes

ıe shock from an earthquake spreads out from a ›int known as the epicentre. The amount of mage depends, among other things, on the ›pth of the epicentre.

ıe force of an earthquake is measured on a scale vised by an American, Dr Charles Richter. Each ›p on the scale represents a tenfold increase in ›ensity.

ırts of an earthquake

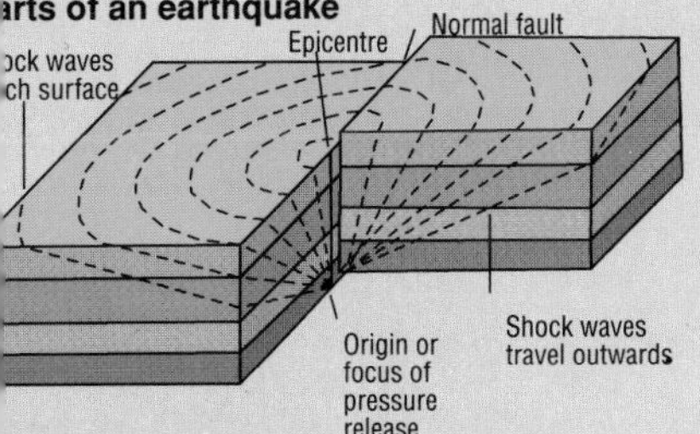

Epicentre
Normal fault
›ck waves
ch surface
Origin or focus of pressure release
Shock waves travel outwards

lajor earthquakes since 1970

DATE	COUNTRY	FORCE (Richter scale)	DEATHS
31.5.70	Peru	7.7	66 800
23.12.72	Nicaragua	6.2	5 000
4.2.76	Guatemala	7.7	22 700
27.7.76	Tangshan, China	8.2	242 000
4.3.77	Romania	7.5	1 500
16.9.78	Iran	7.7	25 000
10.10.80	Algeria	7.5	2 600
23.11.80	Italy	6.8	3 000
13.12.82	Yemen	6.0	2 000
30.10.83	Turkey	7.1	1 200
19.9.85	Mexico	8.1	25 000
7.12.88	Armenia, USSR	6.9	25 000
17.10.89	California, USA	6.9	300

The Mexican Earthquake Disaster

Devastation in Mexico City. The photo shows a multi-storey building which has completely collapsed.

Seven states were affected by the earthquake. There were thousands of deaths and injuries and over 30 000 people were made homeless.

The Mexico City Earthquake

DATE:	September 19, 1985
EPICENTRE:	65km west of the Pacific Ocean
FORCE:	8.1 (Richter scale)
AREA DEVASTATED:	803 109 sq km around Mexico City
DEATHS:	25 000
COSTS:	US $ 4 billion, including damage to buildings, public services and disruption of economic activity

STATES AFFECTED BY THE EARTHQUAKE

1. Jalisco
2. Colima
3. Michoacan
4. Guerrero
5. Mexico
6. Morelos
7. Veracruz

MEXICO CITY
1
2
3
4
5
6
EARTHQUAKE EPICENTRE

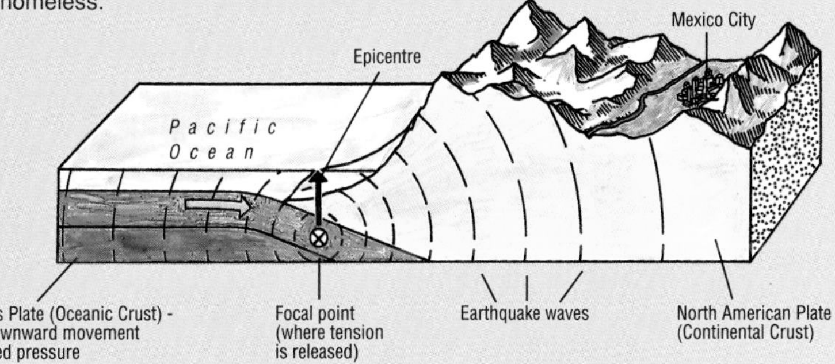

Mexico City
Epicentre
Pacific Ocean
Cocos Plate (Oceanic Crust) - Its downward movement created pressure
Focal point (where tension is released)
Earthquake waves
North American Plate (Continental Crust)

olcanoes

ıere are about 500 active volcanoes in the world. ıe majority of them are found in two main zones: 'Ring of Fire' around the Pacific Ocean and an ıst-west belt from Europe to Indonesia.

ılcanic eruptions can cause terrible damage. olten rock pours out of the vent over the ırrounding area, and rock dust and gas are own high into the atmosphere.

Mt. St. Helens Volcano

DATE:	May 18, 1980
LOCATION:	Washington, USA
EXTENT OF DEBRIS:	57 000 sq km
DEATHS:	60

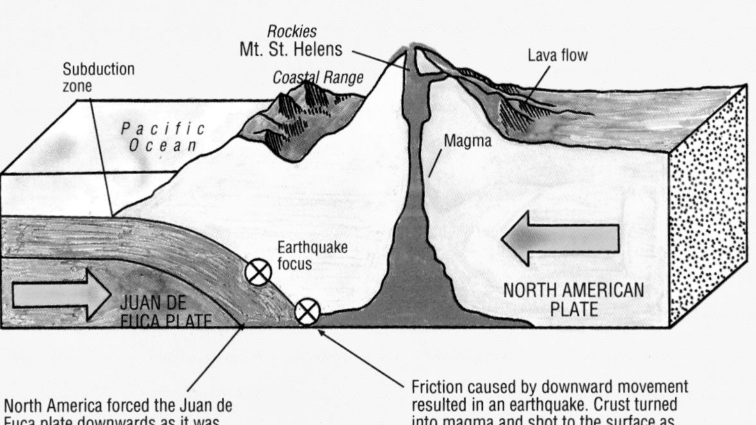

Rockies
Mt. St. Helens
Coastal Range
Lava flow
Subduction zone
Pacific Ocean
Magma
Earthquake focus
JUAN DE FUCA PLATE
NORTH AMERICAN PLATE
North America forced the Juan de Fuca plate downwards as it was moving eastwards
Friction caused by downward movement resulted in an earthquake. Crust turned into magma and shot to the surface as the temperature rose.

Mount St. Helens Eruption

The eruption of the Mount St. Helens in Washington, USA was one of the most dramatic in recent years. The explosion blew out of the side of the cone, and reduced the height of the mountain by 390m, creating a vast new crater. The blast also flattened half a million trees over a radius of 25km and blew dust high into the stratosphere across all of North America.

The volcano was in a remote area so only a small number of people were affected. It has given scientists an opportunity to find out more about what the early earth looked like. Plant life has returned quickly to the devastated areas. It seems that pockets survived in gulleys and under rocks enabling life to regenerate quickly.

How the volcano blew

1 Build up of pressure

2 Landslide caused by stress

3 Eruption released magma

Results of the eruption

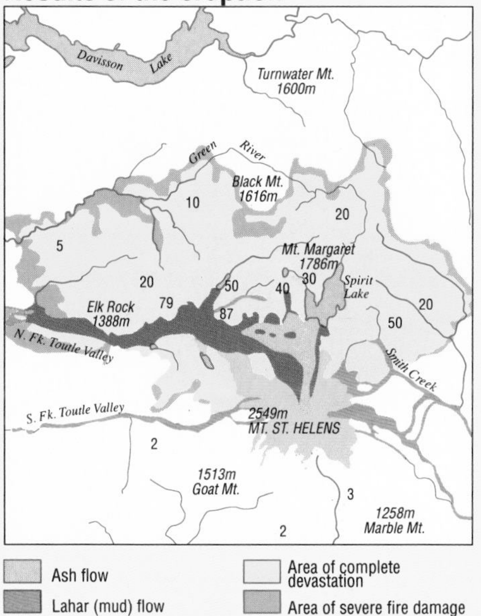

Davisson Lake
Turnwater Mt. 1600m
Green River
Black Mt. 1616m
Mt. Margaret 1786m
Spirit Lake
Elk Rock 1388m
N. Fk. Toutle Valley
S. Fk. Toutle Valley
Smith Creek
2549m MT. ST. HELENS
1513m Goat Mt.
1258m Marble Mt.
Ash flow
Lahar (mud) flow
Pyroclastic (debris) flow
Mud avalanche flow
Area of complete devastation
Area of severe fire damage
20 Ash depth (cm)

RIVERS AND FLOODS

Many important towns and cities are built on rivers. The Nile, Indus and Euphrates supported some of the earliest civilisations. The needs of agriculture, communication and trade have ensured that rivers remain important in the modern world. As population increases the demand on water resources is becoming greater. There is a pressing need for proper water management.

Major World Floods

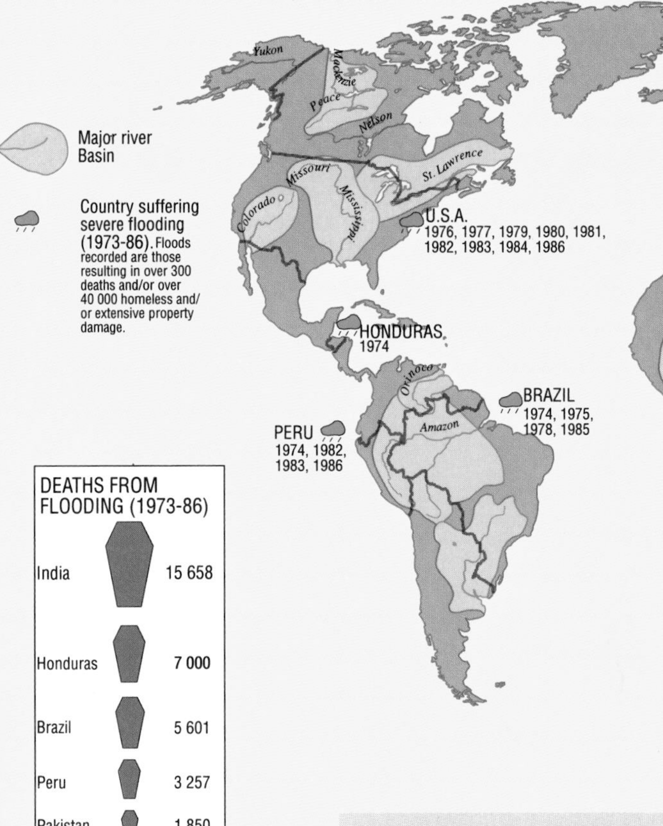

Major river Basin
Country suffering severe flooding (1973-86). Floods recorded are those resulting in over 300 deaths and/or over 40 000 homeless and/ or extensive property damage.
Yukon
Mackenzie
Peace
Nelson
Missouri
Mississippi
Colorado
St. Lawrence
U.S.A.
1976, 1977, 1979, 1980, 1981, 1982, 1983, 1984, 1986
HONDURAS
1974
Orinoco
Amazon
BRAZIL
1974, 1975, 1978, 1985
PERU
1974, 1982, 1983, 1986

DEATHS FROM FLOODING (1973-86)	
India	15 658
Honduras	7 000
Brazil	5 601
Peru	3 257
Pakistan	1 850
China	1 550
Indonesia	1 501
Bangladesh	403
Japan	335
USA	305
Mozambique	300

Figs from UNEP Data Report

Deforestation and Floods

USA
Mexico
Honduras
Peru
Brazil
Argentina
Afghanistan
Pakistan
Nepal
India
Bangladesh
Korea
Japan
China
Indonesia
Kenya
Mozambique
Rep. of South Africa

Countries experiencing severe flooding(1963-85)
- Flood(s) causing over 1 000 deaths in any one year
- Flood(s) causing over 100 deaths in any one year

Annual rates of tropical forest clearance
- 1 250 000 - 2 500 000 acres
- 125 000 - 1 250 000 acres
- 0 -125 000 acres

(Source UNEP Data)

Forests can delay the release of flood water by trapping it in their roots. When the trees are cut down the result is often soil erosion and flooding.

The Effects of Deforestation

FORESTED AREA

Ⓐ Heavy rain and water from melting snow runs down slopes and becomes trapped in the roots of trees.

Ⓑ Some fo the water evaporates, forms clouds and is carried on the wind to arid regions.

Ⓒ The water flows on towards the sea in a fairly steady flow, free of silt.

A
B
C
1
2
3

DEFORESTED AREA

① Without trees to hold it back, flood water rushes down mountain slopes.

② The swollen streams cut deep channels and carry away valuable top soil.

③ Further downstream the river channel becomes clogged with silt, causing floods.

Flooding in Bangladesh

In Bangladesh, the monsoon rains cause the rivers to flood each year. These floods are a normal part of life and help to renew the fertility of the soil. In recent years, however, the floods have become much more severe due to the clearance of forests in the Himalayas for fuelwood, farmland and logging. These floods have caused serious damage and loss of life.

Severe flooding as a result of deforestation in the Himalayas is also a problem in India. Each year it spends over a million US$ on river defences to control flooding.

SEPTEMBER 1987
- 671 dead
- 2 million homes washed away
- 4.3 million acres of land destroyed
- 3 million tonnes (10%) of rice and wheat crops lost

AUGUST 1988
- Over 3 000 dead
- 75% of country flooded
- 250 bridges and 3 520 km of road destroyed
- 3 million tonnes of rice and other crops destroyed

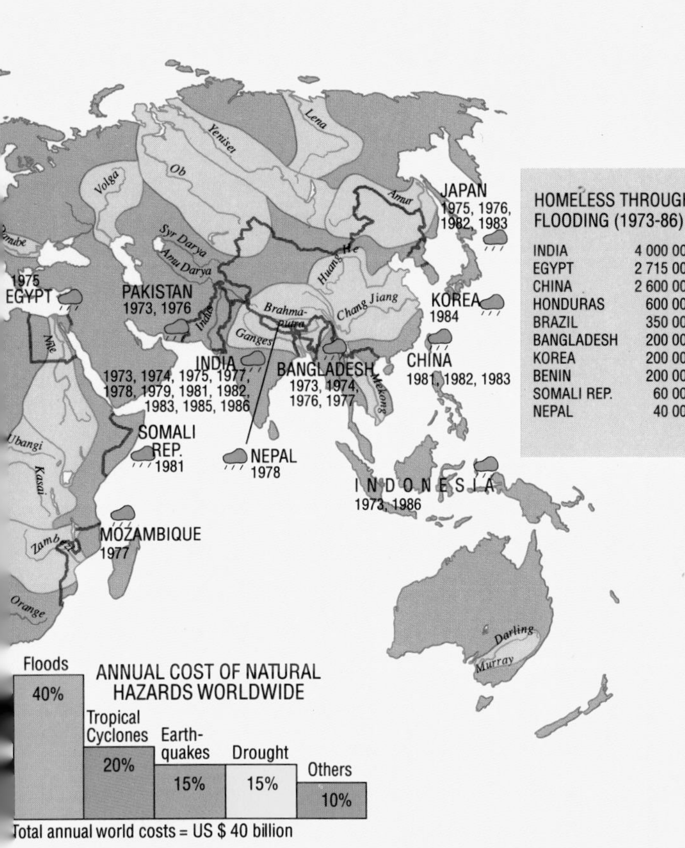

JAPAN
1975, 1976, 1982, 1983
EGYPT
1975
PAKISTAN
1973, 1976
KOREA
1984
INDIA
1973, 1974, 1975, 1977, 1978, 1979, 1981, 1982, 1983, 1985, 1986
BANGLADESH
1973, 1974, 1976, 1977
CHINA
1981, 1982, 1983
SOMALI REP.
1981
NEPAL
1978
INDONESIA
1973, 1986
MOZAMBIQUE
1977
Volga
Ob
Yenisei
Lena
Amur
Syr Darya
Amu Darya
Huang He
Chang Jiang
Indus
Brahmaputra
Ganges
Mekong
Nile
Ubangi
Kasai
Zambezi
Orange
Darling
Murray
Floods
ANNUAL COST OF NATURAL HAZARDS WORLDWIDE
40%
Tropical Cyclones
20%
Earth-quakes
15%
Drought
15%
Others
10%
Total annual world costs = US $ 40 billion

HOMELESS THROUGH FLOODING (1973-86)

INDIA	4 000 000
EGYPT	2 715 000
CHINA	2 600 000
HONDURAS	600 000
BRAZIL	350 000
BANGLADESH	200 000
KOREA	200 000
BENIN	200 000
SOMALI REP.	60 000
NEPAL	40 000

Flood Damage

Flooding causes more damage than any other environmental hazard.

While all countries in the world are affected by floods, the impact on people in developing countries is greater. The number of deaths and homes destroyed is often much higher. This is partly because they cannot afford to protect themselves, and partly because shortage of land forces them to live in vulnerable areas. In addition any loss of food crops, export crops and employment can have a devastating effect.

Controlling Floods

Around the world there are plans for dams which will control floods and generate hydro-electric power.

Examples include:

Mekong dams on the Red river
Three Gorges dam on the Chang Jiang
Narmada dam in India

The problem with all these schemes is that they will flood large areas of land and attract industry which will put pressure on environmentally sensitive areas. Often local people do not benefit from them, foreign companies and banks taking most of the profits.

Many flood control measures only deal with the symptoms. The best solutions tackle the causes as well.

Recent monsoons are bringing heavier rain than normal to northern India

TIBET

River levels rise due to heavy rain and melting snow

Forest clearance increases run-off

Unprotected soil is swept away

BHUTAN

NEPAL

Brahmaputra

The Ganges valley is one of the most densely populated areas in the world

Rivers wash away dams and bridges

BANGLADESH

INDIA

Flooding increases here due to rivers merging

Ganges

Dhaka

Silt settles in channels causing rivers to burst their banks

The Ganges discharges more water in August and September than in all the other months of the year put together

Calcutta

INDIA

MYANMA (BURMA)

Bay of Bengal

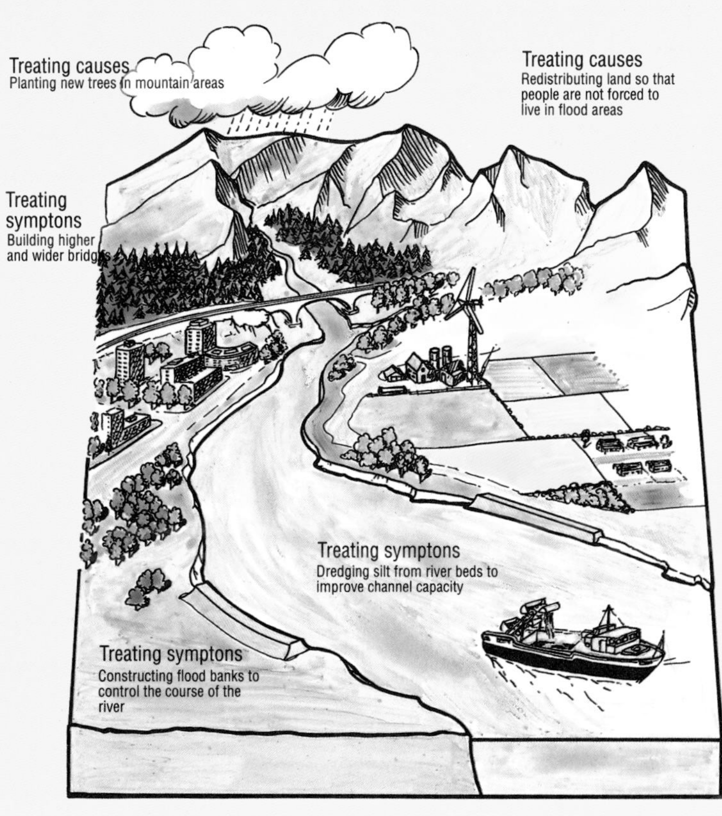

Treating causes
Planting new trees in mountain areas
Treating causes
Redistributing land so that people are not forced to live in flood areas
Treating symptons
Building higher and wider bridges
Treating symptons
Dredging silt from river beds to improve channel capacity
Treating symptons
Constructing flood banks to control the course of the river

TROPICAL STORMS

Tropical Storms

In the Tropics, intense storms form over the ocean in late summer and early autumn. The majority occur in the northern hemisphere. They are known as 'hurricanes' in the Caribbean, 'typhoons' in southeast Asia and 'cyclones' in the Bay of Bengal.

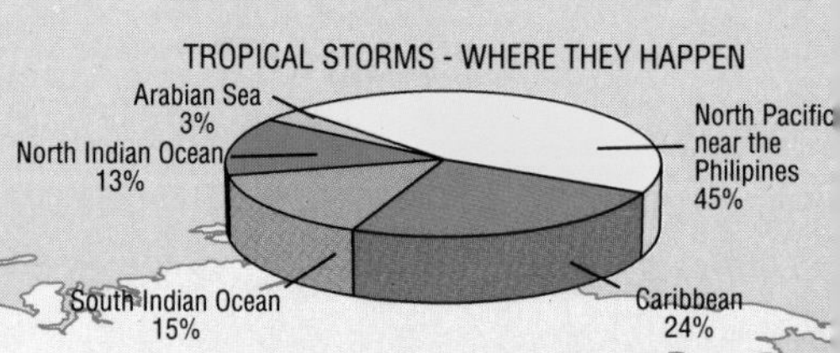

TROPICAL STORMS - WHERE THEY HAPPEN

Arabian Sea 3%
North Indian Ocean 13%
North Pacific near the Philipines 45%
South Indian Ocean 15%
Caribbean 24%

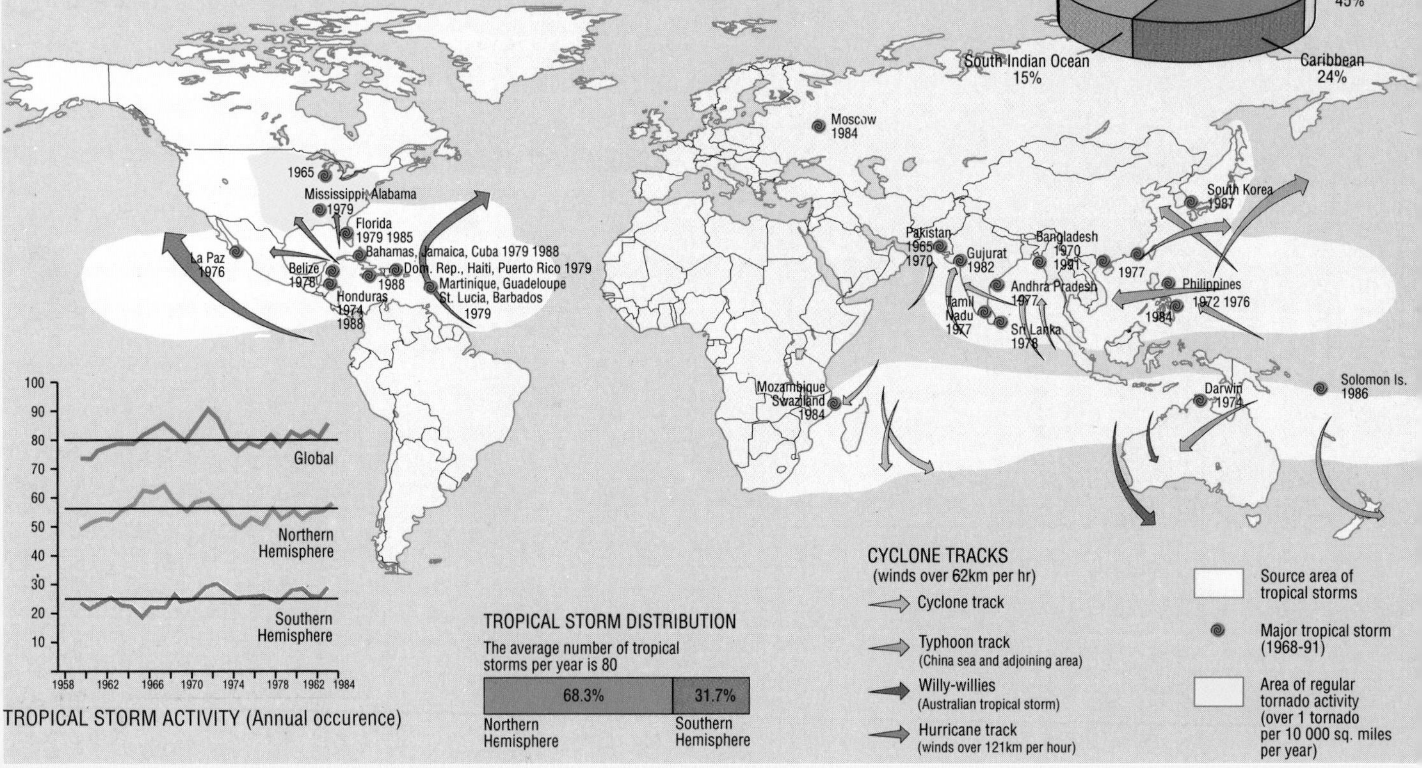

Moscow 1984
1965
Mississippi, Alabama 1979
Florida 1979 1985
Bahamas, Jamaica, Cuba 1979 1988
Dom. Rep., Haiti, Puerto Rico 1979
Martinique, Guadeloupe
St. Lucia, Barbados 1979
1988
La Paz 1976
Belize 1978
Honduras 1974 1988
Pakistan 1965 1970
Gujurat 1982
Bangladesh 1970 1991
Andhra Pradesh 1977
Tamil Nadu 1977
Sri Lanka 1978
1977
South Korea 1987
Philippines 1972 1976
1984
Mozambique Swaziland 1984
Darwin 1974
Solomon Is. 1986

TROPICAL STORM ACTIVITY (Annual occurence)

100, 90, 80, 70, 60, 50, 40, 30, 20, 10
1958 1962 1966 1970 1974 1978 1982 1984
Global
Northern Hemisphere
Southern Hemisphere

TROPICAL STORM DISTRIBUTION

The average number of tropical storms per year is 80

Northern Hemisphere	Southern Hemisphere
68.3%	31.7%

CYCLONE TRACKS (winds over 62km per hr)

- Cyclone track
- Typhoon track (China sea and adjoining area)
- Willy-willies (Australian tropical storm)
- Hurricane track (winds over 121km per hour)

- Source area of tropical storms
- Major tropical storm (1968-91)
- Area of regular tornado activity (over 1 tornado per 10 000 sq. miles per year)

The Life of a Tropical Storm

Tropical storms can only begin if sea temperatures rise to 27°C or more. This allows large quantities of moisture to evaporate into the atmosphere creating unsettled weather conditions. As the pressure drops the storm begins to spin violently and is carried along by the trade winds. The storm sucks in more moisture as it passes over the warm ocean and becomes more intense. Eventually it comes to cooler areas, or passes over land, loses energy and breaks up.

Structure of a Hurricane

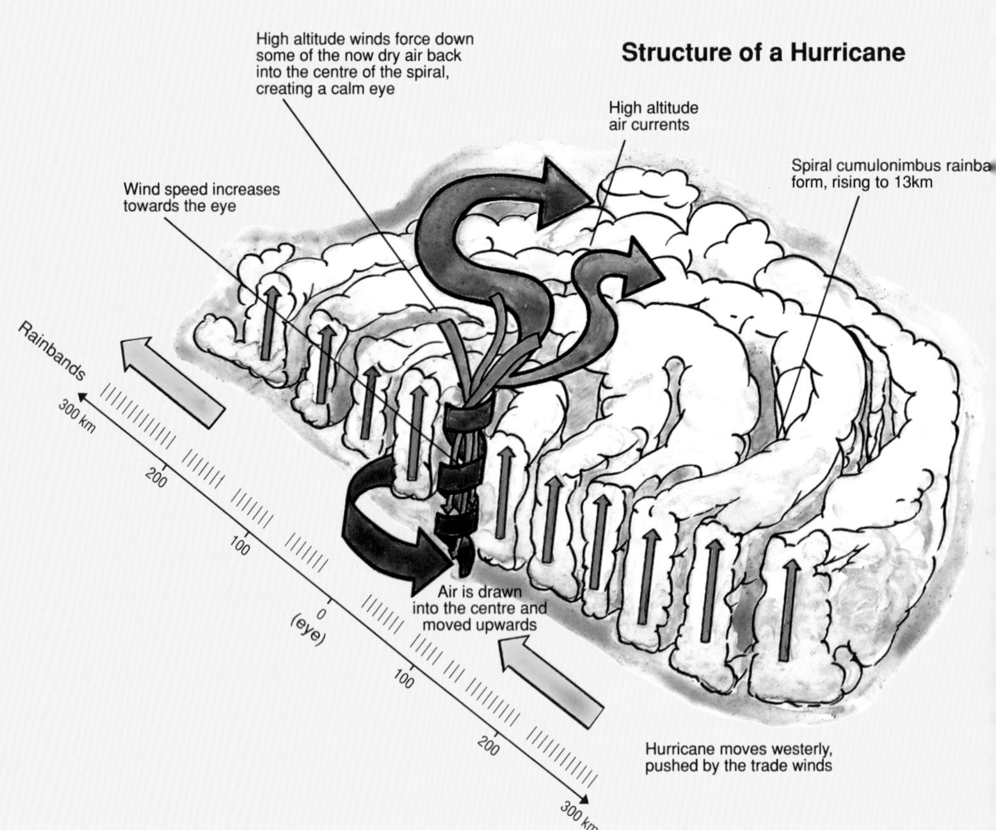
High altitude winds force down some of the now dry air back into the centre of the spiral, creating a calm eye
High altitude air currents
Spiral cumulonimbus rainba
form, rising to 13km
Wind speed increases towards the eye
Rainbands
300 km
200
100
0 (eye)
100
200
300 km
Air is drawn into the centre and moved upwards
Hurricane moves westerly, pushed by the trade winds

Structure of a Tropical Storm

At the centre of a tropical storm there is an 'eye' of calm and cloudless skies. Around it, violent winds, often in excess of 100mph, bring torrential rain that may last for several days.

Naming Tropical Storms

Since the Second World War tropical storms have been named in alphabetical order. This means you can tell from the initial letter how many there have been in a season. Typhoons often use the full range af the alphabet. Hurricanes, being less frequent, tend to only use the first half.

NORTH CAROLINA
SOUTH CAROLINA
GEORGIA
ATLANTIC OCEAN

Hurricane Hugo

First detected on the 9th September as a cluster of storms off the African coast, Hurricane Hugo developed into the strongest hurricane of 1989, sustaining wind speeds of 260km per hour. Hurricane Hugo left a trail of destruction across a number of Caribbean islands and in both North and South Carolina in the USA. The cost of the storm damage was estimated at 10 billion US dollars and 49 lives were lost.

False colour satellite image showing Hurricane Hugo as it struck the USA coast at South Carolina on 22nd September 1989.

'he Effect of Hurricanes in the Caribbean

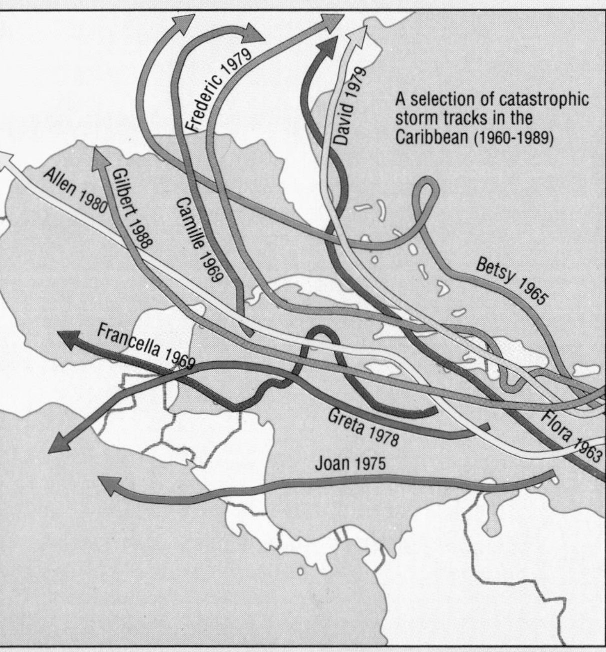

A selection of catastrophic storm tracks in the Caribbean (1960-1989)
Frederic 1979
David 1979
Allen 1980
Gilbert 1988
Camille 1969
Betsy 1965
Francella 1969
Greta 1978
Flora 1963
Joan 1975

Left on Spears

Vehicles, caught in a hurricane in Houston, Texas, dodge live power lines.

Hurricane Camille caused severe flooding in the USA. More than 300 people were killed.

ı 1988, Gilbert, the most powerful urricane ever recorded, led to a ational disaster being declared in amaica.

Hurricane David in 1979 caused widespread damage in Dominica. 1 300 people died and 100 000 were left homeless.

Hurricane Allen crossed Barbados and Jamaica causing death and destruction.

Hurricanes

Tropical storms can do terrible damage. Not only do the fierce winds tear buildings apart, but the low pressure can create a surge of seawater that floods coastal areas. The torrential rain adds to these problems.

In some parts of the world special emergency services and hurricane warning systems have been set up. It is in poorer countries that most lives are lost and the damage is worst. Here many buildings are badly constructed and people can not afford to take precautions.

Tornadoes

Tornadoes are violent whirling storms associated with rain and thunderstorms. Usually about 100 metres in width, and with only the most violent lasting longer than an hour, they are smaller and shorter lived than hurricanes. Wind speeds at the centre however can reach over 300 kph. At such high speed the tube of spinning air can cause loss of life and severe damage to property.

Tornadoes are particularly common in the Mississippi/Ohio basin where the warm humid air from the Gulf of Mexico meets the cool dry air from the north. They also occur, less frequently, in other parts of the world, including Australia and the Indian subcontinent.

DROUGHT

Drought Affected Regions

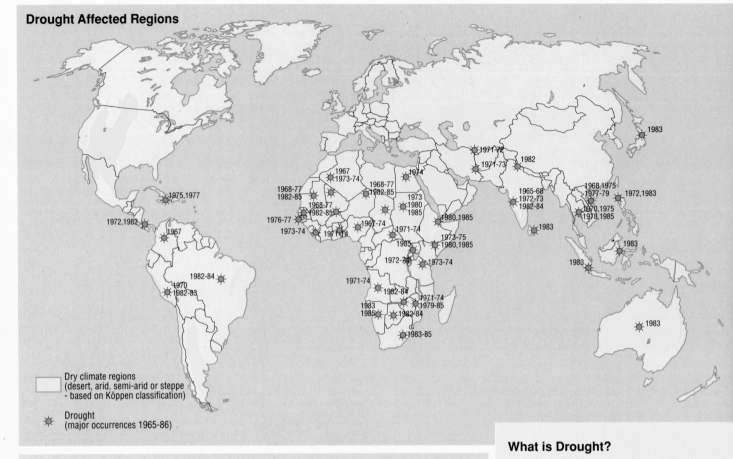

Dry climate regions (desert, arid, semi-arid or steppe - based on Köppen classification)

Drought (major occurrences 1965-86)

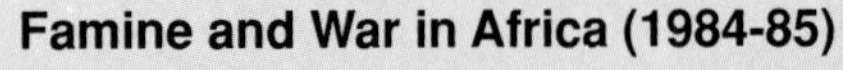

Famine and War in Africa (1984-85)

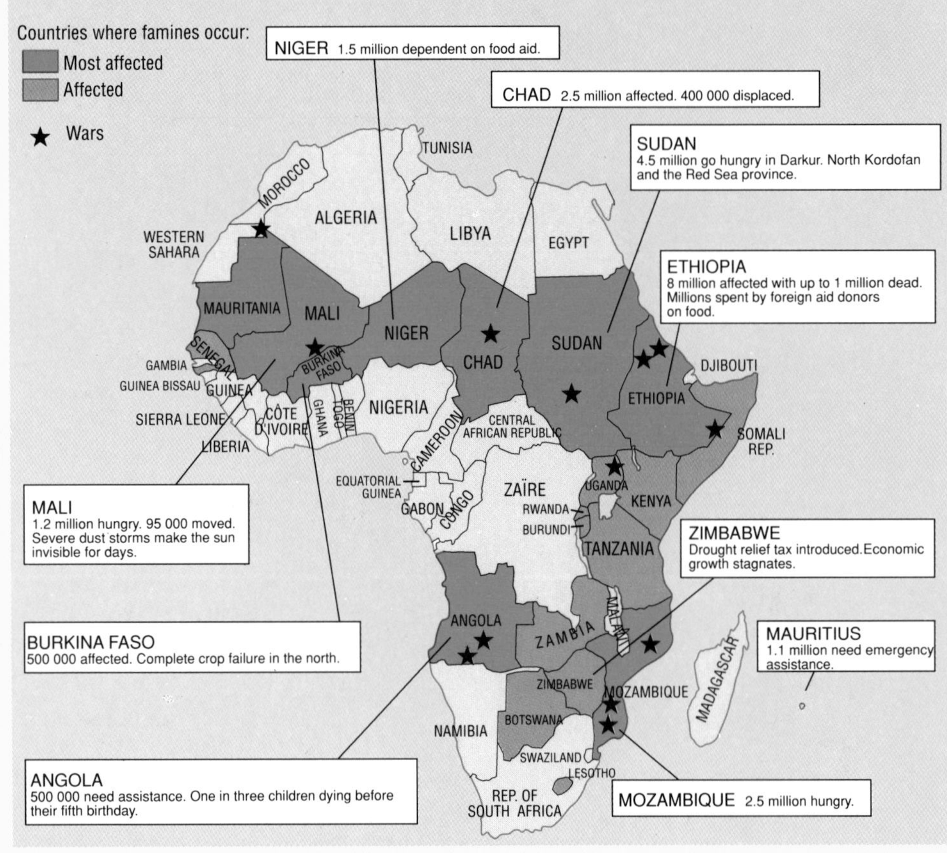
Countries where famines occur:
Most affected
Affected
Wars
NIGER 1.5 million dependent on food aid.
CHAD 2.5 million affected. 400 000 displaced.
SUDAN 4.5 million go hungry in Darkur. North Kordofan and the Red Sea province.
ETHIOPIA 8 million affected with up to 1 million dead. Millions spent by foreign aid donors on food.
MALI 1.2 million hungry. 95 000 moved. Severe dust storms make the sun invisible for days.
BURKINA FASO 500 000 affected. Complete crop failure in the north.
ZIMBABWE Drought relief tax introduced.Economic growth stagnates.
MAURITIUS 1.1 million need emergency assistance.
ANGOLA 500 000 need assistance. One in three children dying before their fifth birthday.
MOZAMBIQUE 2.5 million hungry.
TUNISIA
MOROCCO
ALGERIA
LIBYA
EGYPT
WESTERN SAHARA
MAURITANIA
MALI
NIGER
CHAD
SUDAN
ETHIOPIA
DJIBOUTI
SENEGAL
GAMBIA
GUINEA BISSAU
GUINEA
BURKINA FASO
SIERRA LEONE
LIBERIA
CÔTE D'IVOIRE
GHANA
TOGO
BENIN
NIGERIA
CAMEROON
CENTRAL AFRICAN REPUBLIC
SOMALI REP.
EQUATORIAL GUINEA
GABON
CONGO
ZAÏRE
UGANDA
KENYA
RWANDA
BURUNDI
TANZANIA
ANGOLA
ZAMBIA
MALAWI
MADAGASCAR
ZIMBABWE
MOZAMBIQUE
NAMIBIA
BOTSWANA
SWAZILAND
LESOTHO
REP. OF SOUTH AFRICA

What is Drought?

A lack of rainfall over a long period is known as drought. Droughts occur in many parts of the world but they are especially likely in places where the climate is dry and variable. Desert margins and monsoon lands suffer most.

The map shows where droughts have occurred since the mid 1960's. Africa, Southern Asia and parts of Latin America have been particularly badly affected.

Famine and War

In the last twenty years there have been wars in almost every country of Africa. These have disrupted agriculture and stopped farmers from planting and harvesting crops properly. They have also cost huge sums of money which could have been spent on land improvement schemes. These are the circumstances in which droughts are much more likely to lead to famine.

Drought in the Sahel

One of the worst droughts in the recent years has been in the Sahel. For the past 15 years rainfall has been very poor and human activities such as cutting trees and degrading the soil may have resulted in making the climate even drier.

Since 1970 rainfall in the Sahel has been well below average. No one can be certain if this is a temporary or permanent change. Scientists will need much more evidence before they can be sure what is happening to the climate.

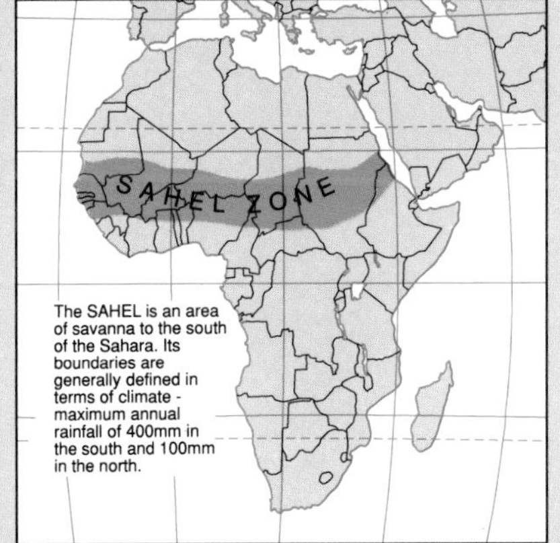
SAHEL ZONE
The SAHEL is an area of savanna to the south of the Sahara. Its boundaries are generally defined in terms of climate - maximum annual rainfall of 400mm in the south and 100mm in the north.

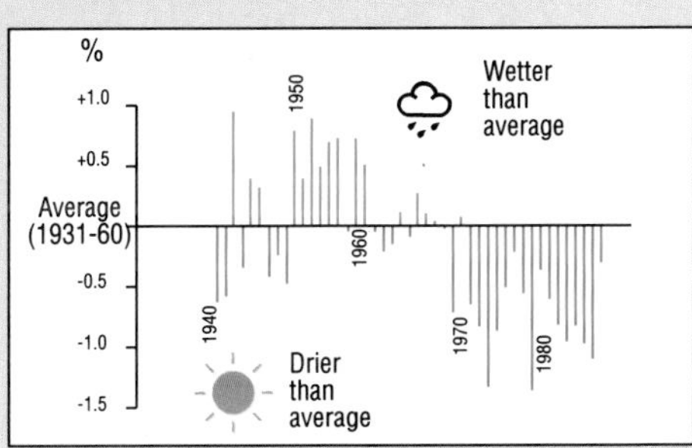
%
+1.0
+0.5
Average (1931-60)
-0.5
-1.0
-1.5
1940
1950
1960
1970
1980
Wetter than average
Drier than average

VARIATIONS IN THE ANNUAL RAINFALL AT 14 WEATHER STATIONS SINCE 1940

CARBON DIOXIDE LEVELS

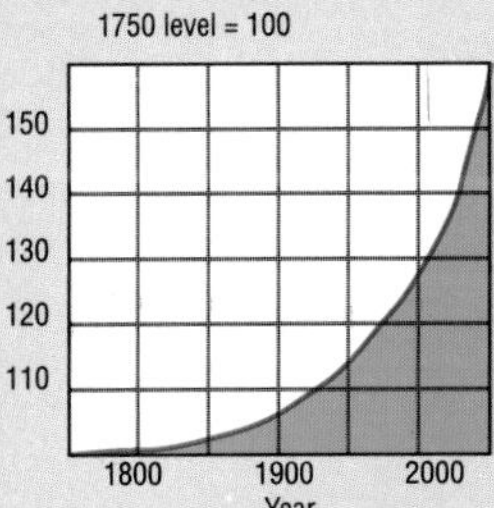
1750 level = 100
150
140
130
120
110
1800
1900
2000
Year

Some scientists believe that pollution by gases such as carbon dioxide, CO_2, is causing the earth to heat up and cause the 'greenhouse' effect.

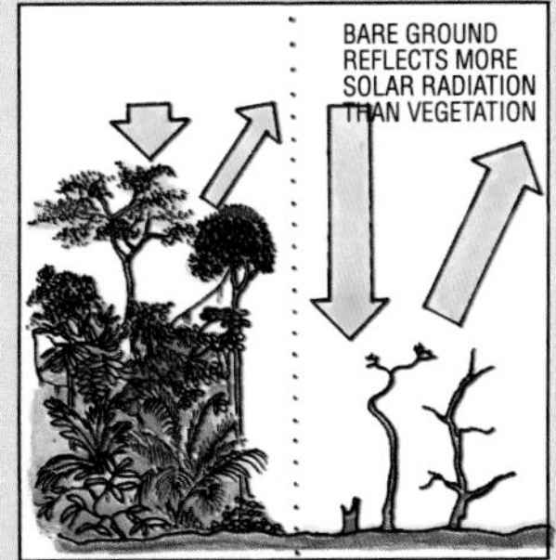
BARE GROUND REFLECTS MORE SOLAR RADIATION THAN VEGETATION

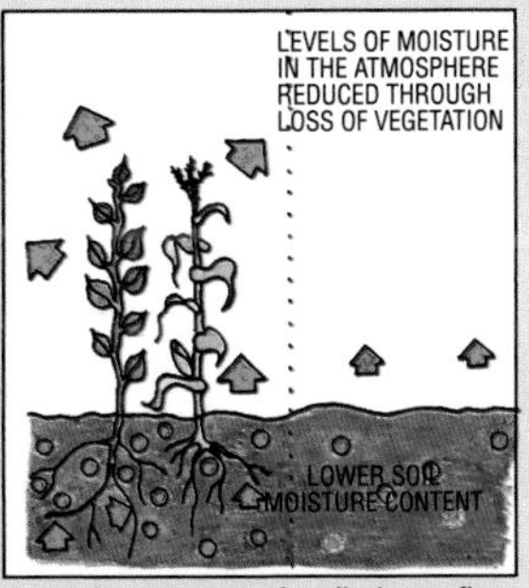
LEVELS OF MOISTURE IN THE ATMOSPHERE REDUCED THROUGH LOSS OF VEGETATION
LOWER SOIL MOISTURE CONTENT

Tree clearance increases the amount of radiation reflected from the ground. There is less evaporation and transpiration from plants, causing the climate to become drier.

Drought and Famine

Drought affects more people nowadays than any other natural disaster. The poor are especially vulnerable as they do not have the resources to protect themselves properly. Emergency food aid can help deal with the immediate food shortages.

In the longer term, famines will only be averted if people tackle the underlying causes. Land reform, fairer 'terms and trade' and peace could do much to solve the problem.

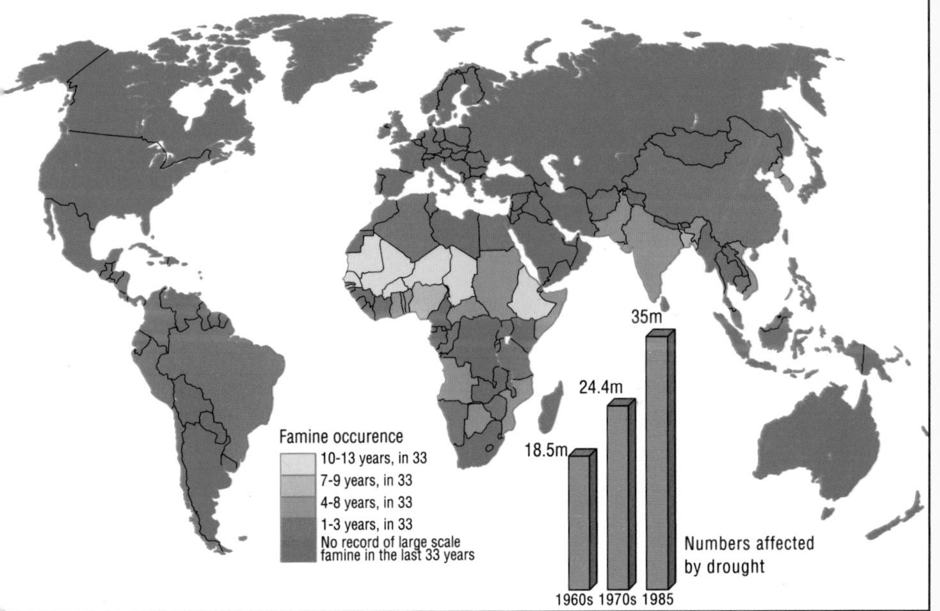
Famine occurence
10-13 years, in 33
7-9 years, in 33
4-8 years, in 33
1-3 years, in 33
No record of large scale famine in the last 33 years
18.5m
24.4m
35m
1960s
1970s
1985
Numbers affected by drought

Drought and famine in Ethiopia (1981-84)

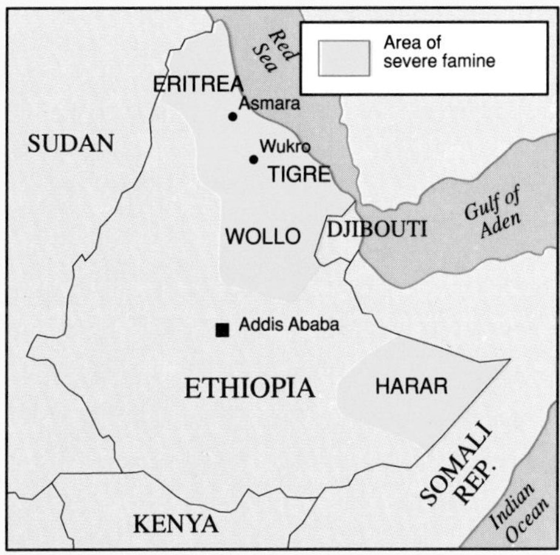
Area of severe famine
Red Sea
ERITREA
Asmara
SUDAN
Wukro
TIGRE
WOLLO
DJIBOUTI
Gulf of Aden
Addis Ababa
ETHIOPIA
HARAR
SOMALI REP.
KENYA
Indian Ocean

The famine in Ethiopia was one of the worst in the recent times. Eight million people were affected and a million lost their lives.

The famine was the result of a combination of factors:

- The population of Ethiopia is growing rapidly putting the land under pressure.
- Woods in the highlands have been cleared for fuel, leading to severe soil erosion and falling crop yields.
- In the lower areas dry grassland areas have been overgrazed.
- Since the 1960's some of the best land has been used to grow cash crops (sugar and coffee) for export.

The failure of rain for four consecutive years from 1981-1984 triggered a severe famine. However human action, not natural forces, was the underlying cause. Even at the height of the crisis, Ethiopia exported huge quantities of vegetables to Europe, while many people starved.

ECOLOGICAL CAUSES OF FAMINE	POLITICAL AND SOCIAL CAUSES OF FAMINE
increase in human population	land divided from one generation to another in small and scattered plots
forests cleared for fuel	government fails to put money into irrigation and land management schemes
animal manure used for fuel and not put back on the land	best grazing land taken from nomads to grow cash crops for export
overfarming of the grasslands	prolonged civil war costs huge sums of money
failure of the rains	countries overseas slow to give help in dealing with the famine

DEFORESTATION

Forests cover about one third of the world's land surface. Temperate and coniferous forest spreads across areas of Europe, Asia and North America. Further south, a band of tropical rainforest extending about ten degrees in latitude north and south of the equator forms the richest habitat on earth.

Temperate and coniferous forests are generally carefully managed and are quick to regrow. Rainforests take longer to grow and occupy a more fragile environment. They are also being destroyed at an alarming rate as people sell the wood and clear land for housing, crops and industry.

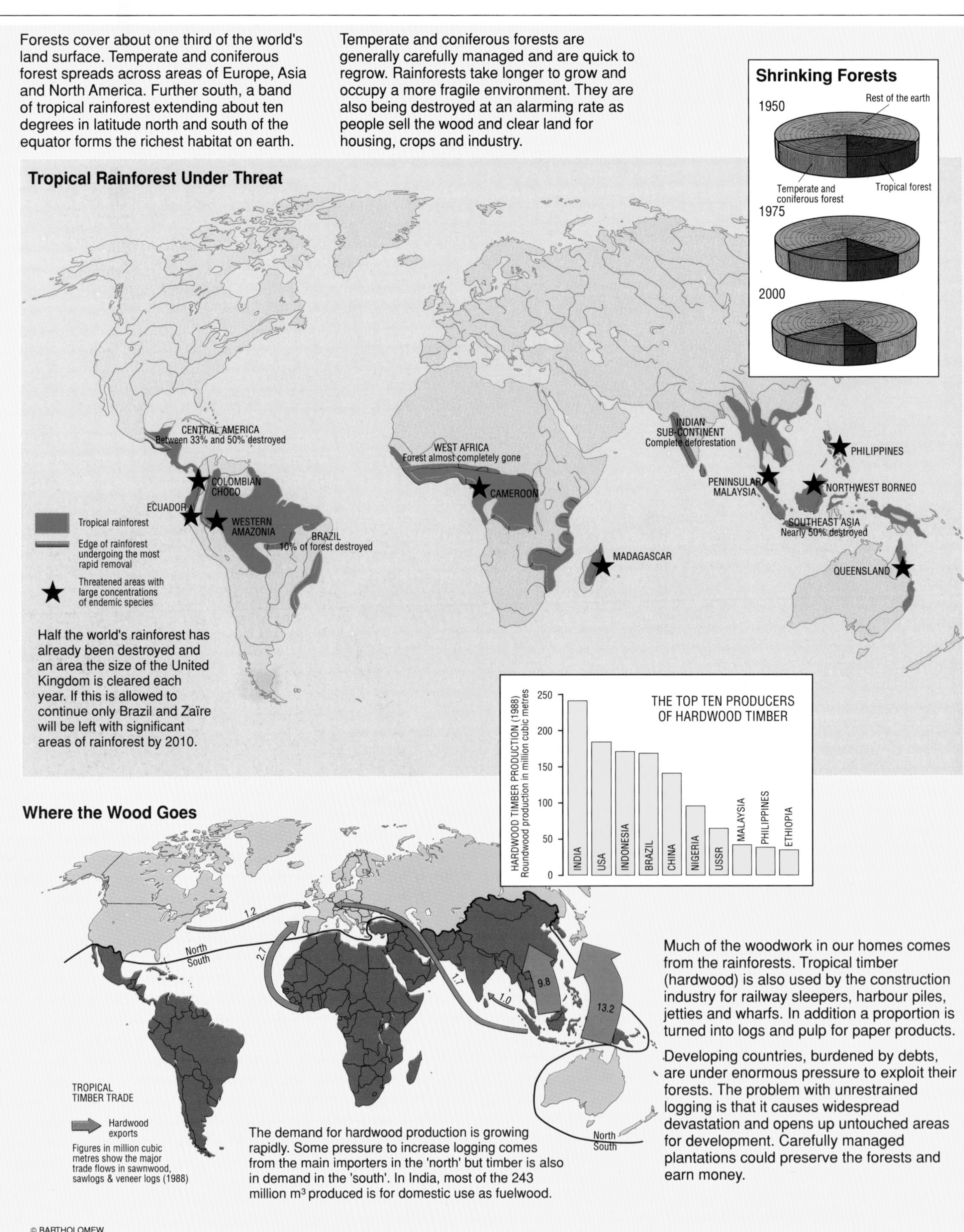

Shrinking Forests
1950
Rest of the earth
Temperate and coniferous forest
Tropical forest
1975
2000
Tropical Rainforest Under Threat
CENTRAL AMERICA
Between 33% and 50% destroyed
WEST AFRICA
Forest almost completely gone
INDIAN SUB-CONTINENT
Complete deforestation
PHILIPPINES
COLOMBIAN CHOCO
ECUADOR
WESTERN AMAZONIA
BRAZIL
10% of forest destroyed
CAMEROON
PENINSULAR MALAYSIA
NORTHWEST BORNEO
SOUTHEAST ASIA
Nearly 50% destroyed
MADAGASCAR
QUEENSLAND
Tropical rainforest
Edge of rainforest undergoing the most rapid removal
Threatened areas with large concentrations of endemic species
THE TOP TEN PRODUCERS OF HARDWOOD TIMBER
HARDWOOD TIMBER PRODUCTION (1988)
Roundwood production in million cubic metres
250
200
150
100
50
0
INDIA
USA
INDONESIA
BRAZIL
CHINA
NIGERIA
USSR
MALAYSIA
PHILIPPINES
ETHIOPIA
Where the Wood Goes
1.2
2.7
1.7
1.0
9.8
13.2
North
South
North
South
TROPICAL TIMBER TRADE
Hardwood exports
Figures in million cubic metres show the major trade flows in sawnwood, sawlogs & veneer logs (1988)

Half the world's rainforest has already been destroyed and an area the size of the United Kingdom is cleared each year. If this is allowed to continue only Brazil and Zaïre will be left with significant areas of rainforest by 2010.

Much of the woodwork in our homes comes from the rainforests. Tropical timber (hardwood) is also used by the construction industry for railway sleepers, harbour piles, jetties and wharfs. In addition a proportion is turned into logs and pulp for paper products.

Developing countries, burdened by debts, are under enormous pressure to exploit their forests. The problem with unrestrained logging is that it causes widespread devastation and opens up untouched areas for development. Carefully managed plantations could preserve the forests and earn money.

The demand for hardwood production is growing rapidly. Some pressure to increase logging comes from the main importers in the 'north' but timber is also in demand in the 'south'. In India, most of the 243 million m^3 produced is for domestic use as fuelwood.

The Real Costs of Rainforest Destruction

What we are losing?

People
In South America the rainforest is the home for tribal groups like the Yanomani. Rubber tappers also operate in many areas.

Plants
Many crops and medicines come from rainforest plants which are a unique and extremely valuable genetic resource.

Creatures
The rainforests are the richest and densest habitat on earth. They contain over half the world's insects, birds and animals.

The rainforests generally grow on very poor soils. The trees protect the soil from tropical storms and help to keep it moist during the dry season. Once the trees are cleared, the earth quickly washes away and the land, exposed to the hot sun, turns to desert.

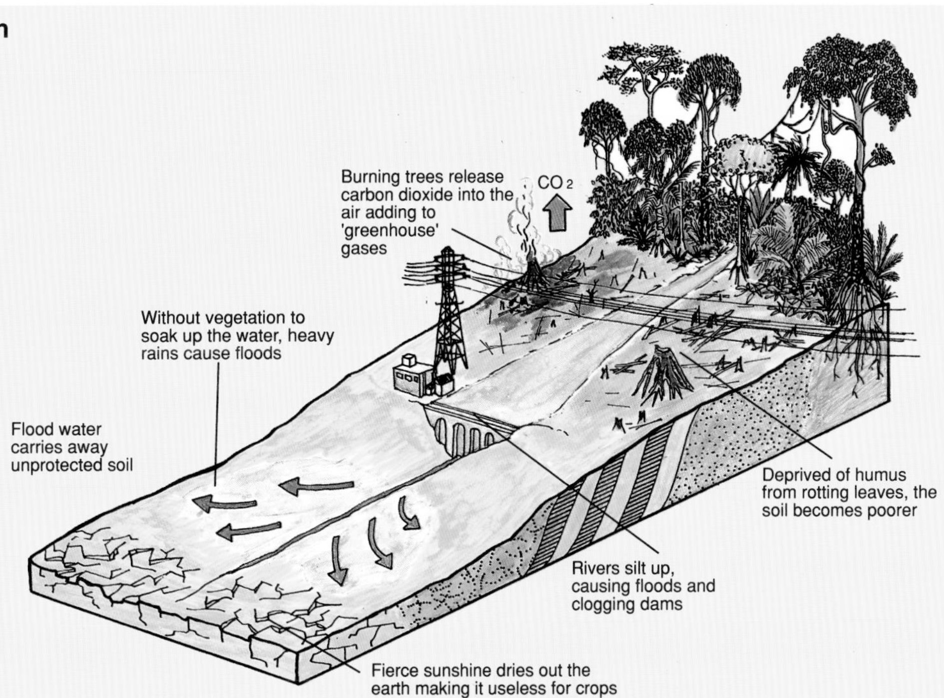

Burning trees release carbon dioxide into the air adding to 'greenhouse' gases
CO_2
Without vegetation to soak up the water, heavy rains cause floods
Flood water carries away unprotected soil
Deprived of humus from rotting leaves, the soil becomes poorer
Rivers silt up, causing floods and clogging dams
Fierce sunshine dries out the earth making it useless for crops

Deforestation in Amazonia

About a third of the world's rainforest is in Amazonia. This area mostly belongs to Brazil, but also covers parts of neighbouring countries.

Brazilians are keen to open up Amazonia and exploit its riches. They see this as a way of developing industry and paying off debts. However, many projects take little account of the destruction which causes priceless areas of rainforest to literally go up in smoke.

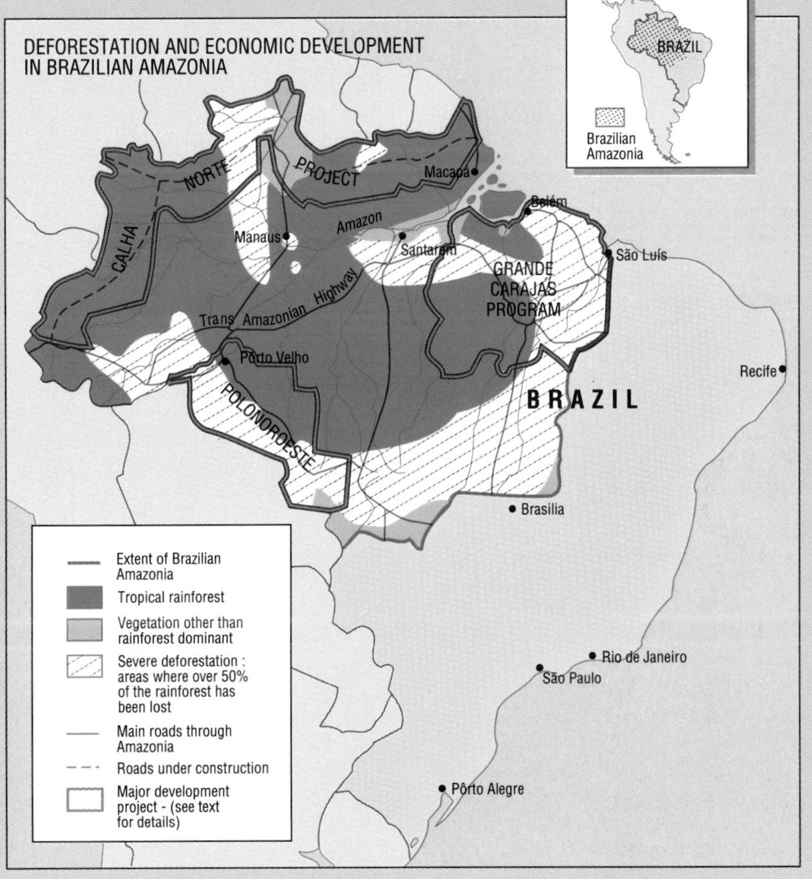

DEFORESTATION AND ECONOMIC DEVELOPMENT IN BRAZILIAN AMAZONIA
BRAZIL
Brazilian Amazonia
CALHA NORTE PROJECT
Macapá
Belém
Manaus
Amazon
Santarém
São Luís
GRANDE CARAJÁS PROGRAM
Trans Amazonian Highway
Porto Velho
POLONOROESTE
Recife
BRAZIL
Brasilia
Rio de Janeiro
São Paulo
Pôrto Alegre
Extent of Brazilian Amazonia
Tropical rainforest
Vegetation other than rainforest dominant
Severe deforestation : areas where over 50% of the rainforest has been lost
Main roads through Amazonia
Roads under construction
Major development project - (see text for details)

A huge area along the northern border of Brazil has been set aside for the Calha Norte Project. Here companies have been granted mining concessions and permission to explore for oil. Hydro-electric power stations are being built to provide power for industrial development. The dams for these schemes will flood large areas of land, threatening the homes of fifty thousand Indians.

Further south, the Grand Carajás Program involves a massive open cast iron ore mine which will be linked by rail to a special port. Huge tracts of forest will also be cleared for a bauxite mine, cash crop plantations and cattle ranches.

In the west, the Polonoroeste Development Project has allowed thousands of immigrants to flood into the area. Originally it was intended to open up the area for agriculture, but the soil is so poor it cannot sustain crops.

DEMANDS ON LAND IN BRAZILIAN AMAZONIA

	10^3 km^2	% total
Already cleared	340	10%
Area to be flooded for HEP development	150	4.4%
Forest reserves maintained for timber production	500	15%
Colonised (up to 1989)	430	13%
Total officially earmarked for development	2 100	63.5%

DESERTIFICATION

What is Desertification?

Desertification, or the spread of deserts, threatens over a third of the world's land surface. Severe deterioration and loss of soil can turn productive land into desert. Every year, an area the size of the United Kingdom is either lost or severely degraded. In some cases deserts appear to invade good land from the outside, but in fact it is deterioration of soil in the border regions which causes them to expand. By the year 2000 the situation is likely to become critical especially in the Sahel, the Andes and parts of South Asia.

At one time lush trees and shrubs surrounded this Nile valley village.

The Causes

Desertification often begins when people decide or are forced to use land in dry areas too intensively. Overcultivation, overgrazing and the clearance of trees for fuelwood combine to degrade the soil. In other places, badly damaged irrigation schemes can make the land so salty it can no longer grow crops. The diagram below shows two ways in which desertification is triggered. Once desertification is started, natural factors, such as drought accelerate the process.

Where is Desertification Taking Place?

Fertile areas on the edge of existing deserts are most at risk. Here, harsh conditions mean that the land is only just able to grow crops and needs particularly careful management. Some 850 million people live in desert border regions and the population is growing rapidly.

WORLD LAND AT RISK

Existing desert 6%
Other land 66%
Moderate 13%
Severe 12%
Very severe 3%

Land at risk of desertification

Europe 2%

In Spain, ten percent of the land is affected by severe desertification.

Southwest United States
Sahara
Turkestan
Iranian
Thar
Arabian
Somali
Atacama
Namib
Kalahari

North and South America 19%

Cattle ranching and overgrazing have degraded the soil in the western USA and parts of Mexico. Further south, unsuitable land is being cleared for crops in Brazil and Argentina.

Africa 34%

Overgrazing and the removal of trees threaten the Sahel, Mediterranean coast and southern Africa.

Two Models of Desertification

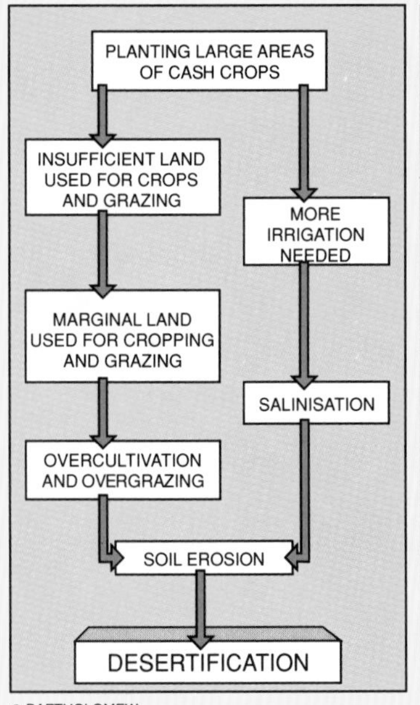
PLANTING LARGE AREAS OF CASH CROPS
INSUFFICIENT LAND USED FOR CROPS AND GRAZING
MORE IRRIGATION NEEDED
MARGINAL LAND USED FOR CROPPING AND GRAZING
SALINISATION
OVERCULTIVATION AND OVERGRAZING
SOIL EROSION
DESERTIFICATION

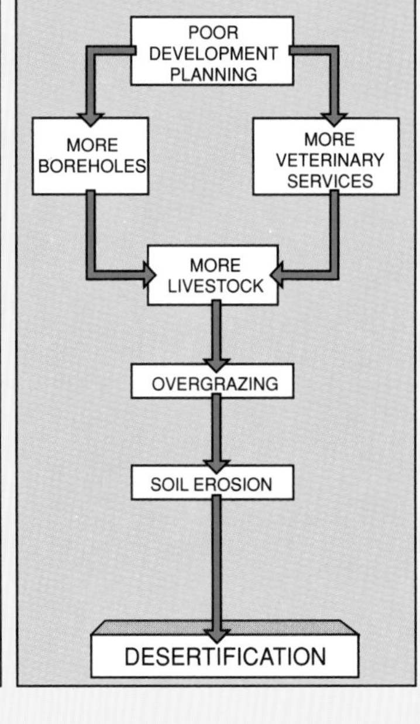
POOR DEVELOPMENT PLANNING
MORE BOREHOLES
MORE VETERINARY SERVICES
MORE LIVESTOCK
OVERGRAZING
SOIL EROSION
DESERTIFICATION

Effects of Desertification

Effects on People

Desertification is slow and insidious. Developing countries suffer most. Here, rural communities become trapped in a cycle of poverty which forces them to exploit the land beyond its capacity. This makes them very vulnerable to natural hazards, such as drought.

As crops fail and water sources dry up, people have no alternative but to leave the land. One sixth of the population of Burkina Faso fled the country in the drought of the early 1970's. In India and Brazil many victims of desertification have gone to live in the big cities, swelling the urban population.

Effects on Climate

Desertification can have a significant effect on the climate. The increase in dust prevents air from rising freely and forming clouds. In addition, the loss of vegetation reduces the amount of moisture in the air and allows temperatures to rise. Both these factors tend to make droughts worse.

Moderate desertification (Productivity reduced by up to 25%)

The removal of tree and plant cover exposes the soil. In irrigated areas, salts build up in the ground, killing crops.

ɔor irrigation schemes are causing ·sertification in the southern states of e USSR. Iran and many parts of the ddle East are also at risk.

Asia 31%

Severe desertification (Productivity reduced by 25-50%)

Dust storms and floods strip away much of the top soil. Plants struggle to survive.

Very severe desertification (Productivity reduced by over 50%)

Bare ground is baked hard in the sun and plants wither. Sand, grit and dust storms are common.

Great Australian

Australia 75%

Existing desert (Unproductive)

Most of Australia is at risk due to poor stock raising.

Combatting Desertification

There is nothing new about desertification. Before people cut them down, there were forests in the Sahara Desert which supported a good variety of wildlife. Desertification has played a role in the downfall of early civilisations, including the Roman Empire. What is new is the scale of the problem.

Human action causes desertification. By the same token it can also control and cure it. Reforestation, improved farming methods and better land use can halt the advance of the desert. There are many successful projects around the world.

- In Rajasthan, India, trees have been planted as shelter belts along roads.
- In Senegal coastal sand dunes have been stabilised.
- Lines of stones have been placed to follow the contours of the land to trap soil in fields in Burkina Faso.
- Watersheds have been terraced in Ethiopia.
- In northern China a forest 7 000 km long has been planted to protect the farmland from the Gobi Desert.

Where local people are given responsibility for the schemes and supported by their government the results have been particularly impressive. At the heart of the issue is the control of the land itself. If people feel secure and have a stake in the future they will act accordingly.

Africa - Population Affected by Desertification

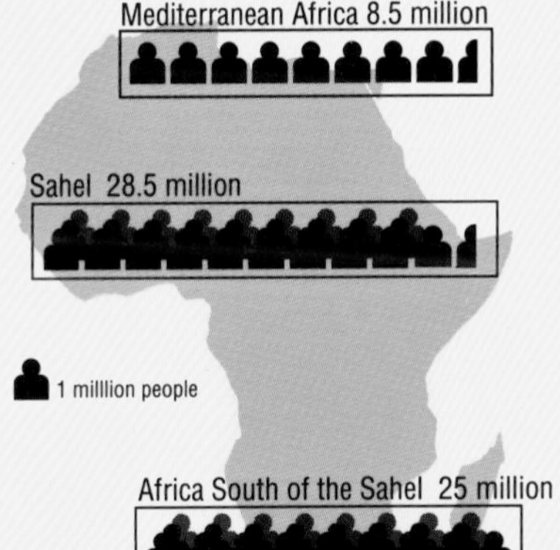
Mediterranean Africa 8.5 million
Sahel 28.5 million
1 milllion people
Africa South of the Sahel 25 million

Ɔuring the 1960's and 1970's the Sahara Ɔesert spread 100 km further south, forcing nillions of people to leave their homes.

Preventative Measures

Reforestation project ①

② Plant trees and build brushwood barriers along gullies

③ Grow tree crops on higher terraces

④ Terrace steep land

⑤ Cultivate along contours

Build bunds to control the run-off of surface water ⑥

⑦ Plant shelter belts and windbreaks using suitable indigenous trees

Stabilise sand dunes ⑧

⑨ Roate crops and interplant several crops at a time

⑩ Limit stock numbers and rotate grazing

⑪ Plant leguminous crops and allow regular fallow periods

⑫ Grow drought resistant crops in drier areas

Although we know how to halt desertification, we are not winning the battle against it. Too little money is spent on preventative measures and there is a lack of long term planning. Many people are at risk and a massive effort will be needed to avoid famine in the years ahead.

AIR POLLUTION

What is Pollution?

All damage to the environment is known as pollution. Some pollution comes from natural sources. Volcanoes, for example, release poisonous gases into the atmosphere. Most pollution, however, is caused by human activity. As world population increases and technology advances pollution problems become more severe.

Air Pollution

The earth is covered by a layer of air which extends far into space. Only the lowest few kilometres can support life. As more fumes enter the atmosphere important changes begin to occur; if we go on using the atmosphere as a dustbin the earth will eventually become uninhabitable.

Ozone Destruction

The earth is surrounded by a layer of ozone, O_3, in the stratosphere about 25km above the surface. This filters out harmful ultra-violet light from the sun which can cause skin cancer. Recently scientists have noticed that the ozone layer is getting thinner. They were particularly alarmed to discover a hole opening up over Antarctica each spring.

Ozone destruction is caused by gases known as chlorofluorocarbons, CFC's. These are used in foams, refridgerators and aerosols. In 1987 many countries undertook to reduce their use of CFC's by signing an agreement called the Montreal Protocol.

The expanding hole in the ozone layer

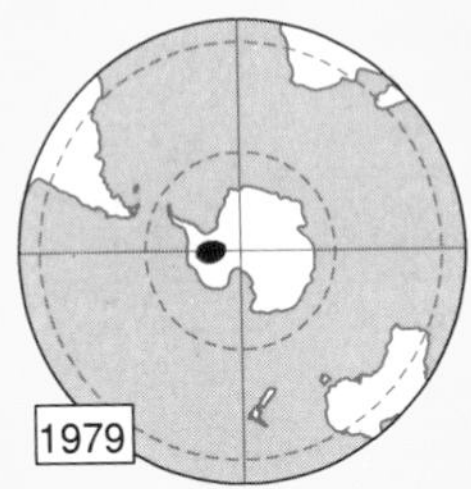
1979

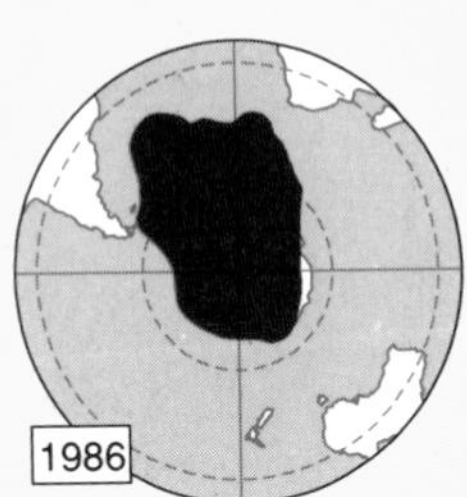
1986

Each year the hole in the ozone layer over Antarctica gets larger. Places as far away as Australia and New Zealand are affected by the reduction in the ozone layer.

Atmospheric Pollution

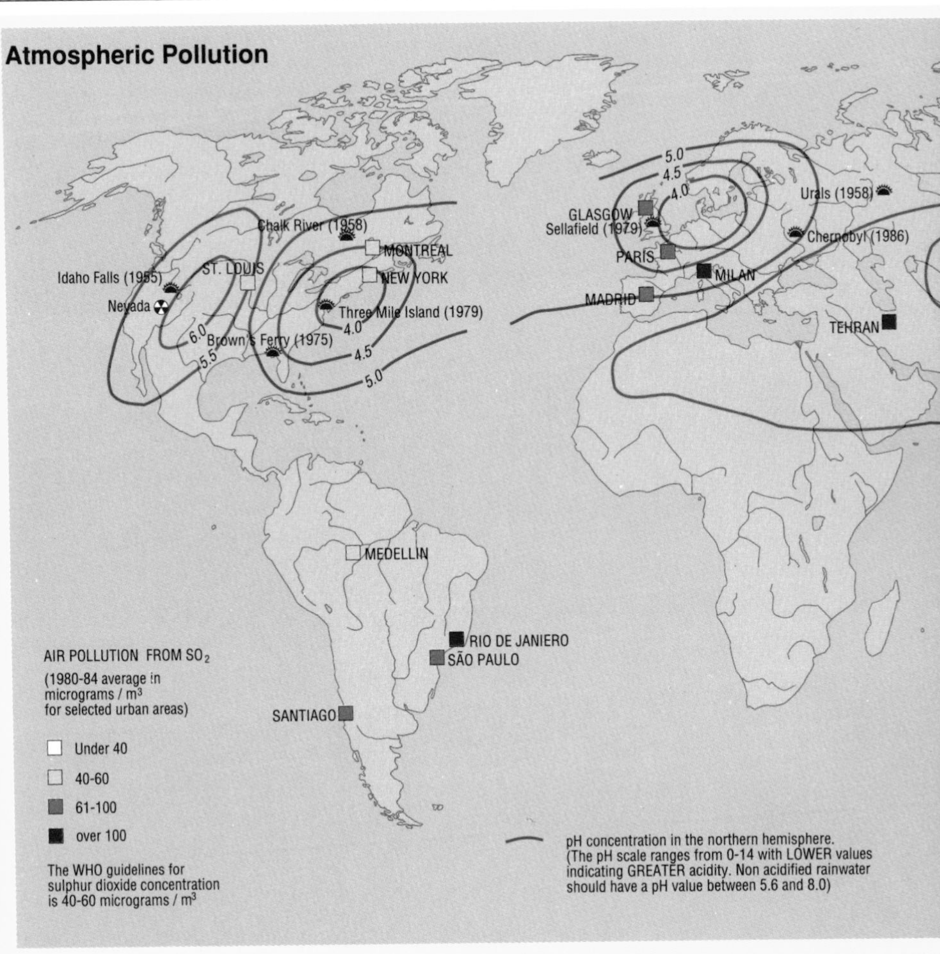
Chalk River (1958)
MONTREAL
NEW YORK
ST. LOUIS
Idaho Falls (1955)
Nevada
Three Mile Island (1979)
Brown's Ferry (1975)
6.0
5.5
5.0
4.5
4.0
GLASGOW
Sellafield (1979)
PARIS
MILAN
MADRID
Urals (1958)
Chernobyl (1986)
TEHRAN
MEDELLIN
RIO DE JANIERO
SÃO PAULO
SANTIAGO
AIR POLLUTION FROM SO_2
(1980-84 average in micrograms / m³ for selected urban areas)
Under 40
40-60
61-100
over 100
The WHO guidelines for sulphur dioxide concentration is 40-60 micrograms / m³
pH concentration in the northern hemisphere.
(The pH scale ranges from 0-14 with LOWER values indicating GREATER acidity. Non acidified rainwater should have a pH value between 5.6 and 8.0)

Global Warming

The world is now warmer than at any time since the last Ice Age. Scientists believe that in future temperatures will rise even faster. This is called global warming. Global warming is caused by a blanket of 'greenhouse gases' building up around the earth trapping heat from the sun. Carbon dioxode, CO_2, released by burning fossil fuels is one of the main causes.

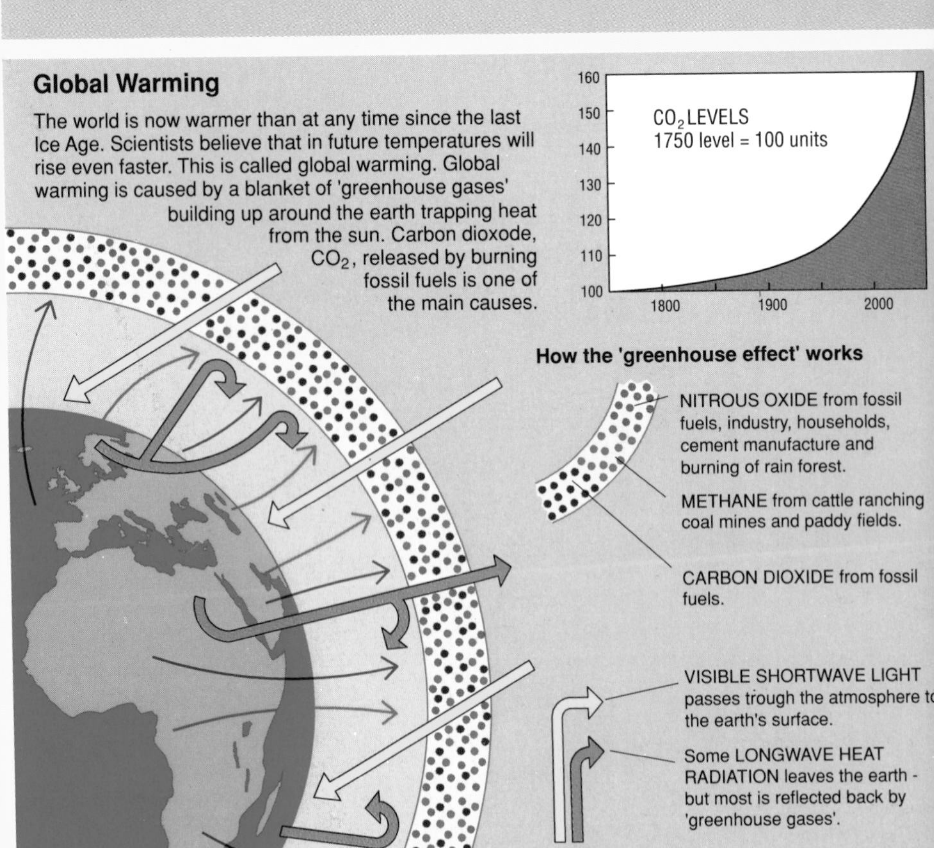
CO_2 LEVELS
1750 level = 100 units
160
150
140
130
120
110
100
1800
1900
2000
How the 'greenhouse effect' works
NITROUS OXIDE from fossil fuels, industry, households, cement manufacture and burning of rain forest.
METHANE from cattle ranching coal mines and paddy fields.
CARBON DIOXIDE from fossil fuels.
VISIBLE SHORTWAVE LIGHT passes trough the atmosphere to the earth's surface.
Some LONGWAVE HEAT RADIATION leaves the earth - but most is reflected back by 'greenhouse gases'.

mipalatinsk
SHENYANG
6.0
Xinjiang
SEOUL
TOKYO
XI'AN
4.5
5.0
CALCUTTA
HONG KONG
MANILLA
KUALA LUMPUR
SYDNEY

Current nuclear site

Major accident at nuclear power station causing air pollution from radioactive discharge

Acid Rain

Coal and oil release a mixture of gases as they burn. These gases combine with water vapour, sunlight and oxygen to form sulphuric acid and nitric acid which fall back to earth as acid rain. The effects of acid rain vary greatly, but areas with poor soil suffer most, especially in spring when melting snow pours contaminated water into rivers and lakes. One way of reducing the problem is to fit catalytic converters to cars and build flues in power stations. It would also help if we used energy more efficiently to reduce our consumption of fuel.

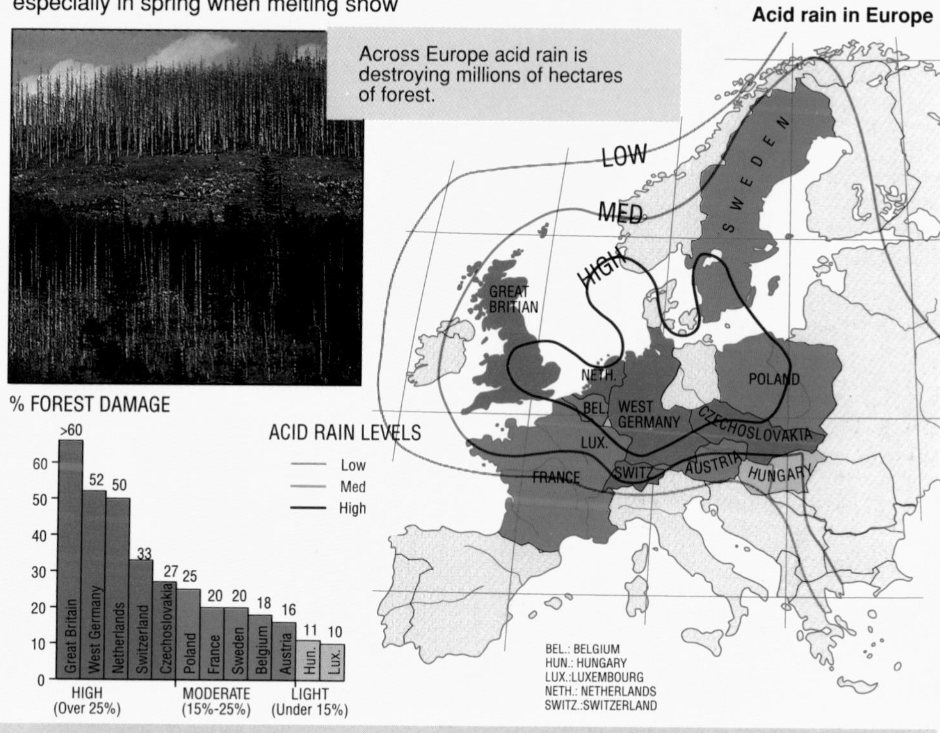

Across Europe acid rain is destroying millions of hectares of forest.
% FOREST DAMAGE
>60
52
50
33
27
25
20
20
18
16
11
10
Great Britain
West Germany
Netherlands
Switzerland
Czechoslovakia
Poland
France
Sweden
Belgium
Austria
Hun.
Lux.
HIGH (Over 25%)
MODERATE (15%-25%)
LIGHT (Under 15%)
ACID RAIN LEVELS
Low
Med
High
Acid rain in Europe
LOW
MED
HIGH
SWEDEN
GREAT BRITIAN
NETH.
BEL.
WEST GERMANY
POLAND
LUX.
CZECHOSLOVAKIA
FRANCE
SWITZ.
AUSTRIA
HUNGARY
BEL.: BELGIUM
HUN.: HUNGARY
LUX.:LUXEMBOURG
NETH.: NETHERLANDS
SWITZ.:SWITZERLAND

What might happen if the earth's surface temperature increased, on average, by 1°C.

In an attempt to tackle the problem of global warming the European Community has agreed to freeze emissions of carbon dioxide at the current levels by the year 2000.

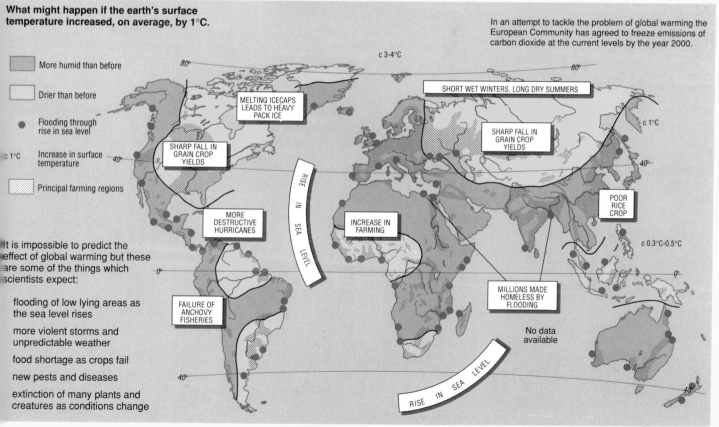

More humid than before

Drier than before

Flooding through rise in sea level

c 1°C Increase in surface temperature

Principal farming regions

c 3-4°C
MELTING ICECAPS LEADS TO HEAVY PACK ICE
SHORT WET WINTERS. LONG DRY SUMMERS
SHARP FALL IN GRAIN CROP YIELDS
SHARP FALL IN GRAIN CROP YIELDS
c 1°C
RISE IN SEA LEVEL
POOR RICE CROP
MORE DESTRUCTIVE HURRICANES
INCREASE IN FARMING
c 0.3°C-0.5°C
MILLIONS MADE HOMELESS BY FLOODING
FAILURE OF ANCHOVY FISHERIES
No data available
RISE IN SEA LEVEL

It is impossible to predict the effect of global warming but these are some of the things which scientists expect:

- flooding of low lying areas as the sea level rises
- more violent storms and unpredictable weather
- food shortage as crops fail
- new pests and diseases
- extinction of many plants and creatures as conditions change

LAND POLLUTION

Hazardous Waste - Production and Trade

Hazardous and toxic waste damages the environment and poisons people and animals. Most toxic waste comes from the chemical industry. It is produced in increasing quantities each year.

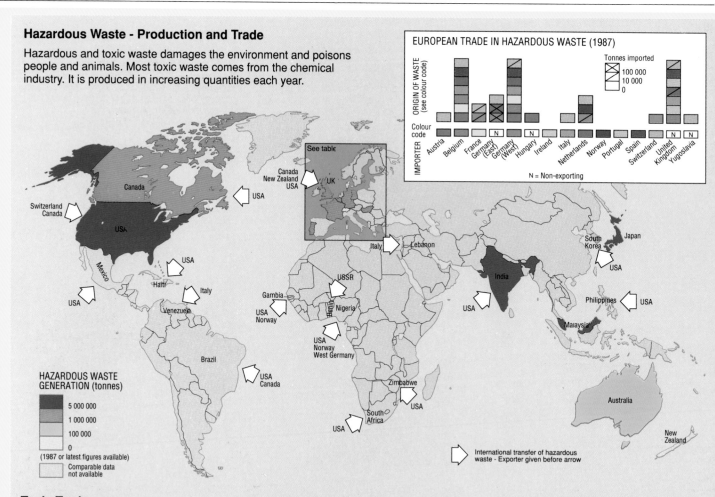

EUROPEAN TRADE IN HAZARDOUS WASTE (1987)

HAZARDOUS WASTE GENERATION (tonnes)

5 000 000
1 000 000
100 000
0
(1987 or latest figures available)
Comparable data not available

International transfer of hazardous waste - Exporter given before arrow

Toxic Trade

It is very expensive to dispose of toxic waste properly so people are looking for cheap solutions. At the moment large quantities are shipped to developing countries, often illegally. In1988, for example, 10 000 drums of hazardous waste from Italy were discovered in a yard in the port of Koko, Nigeria. They were leaking acid and poisonous chemicals but local people had no idea what they contained. Nearly forty countries have now banned toxic waste imports but the regulations are difficult to enforce.

Waste Dumping

Some 350 million tonnes of hazardous waste are produced each year and there are over 70 000 different chemicals in regular use. Many of them have never been tested for their effect on the environment and nobody knows what happens when they are mixed together.

Toxic waste dump, Czechoslovakia.

For years toxic waste has been dumped in landfill sites. If these are unlined, dangerous chemicals can seep into the soil and contaminate water supplies. The problem of indiscriminate dumping affects most industrialised countries and there are thousands of sites which need to be cleaned up.

% WASTE DISPOSAL BY LANDFILL
(selected countries - 1987 or latest figures available)

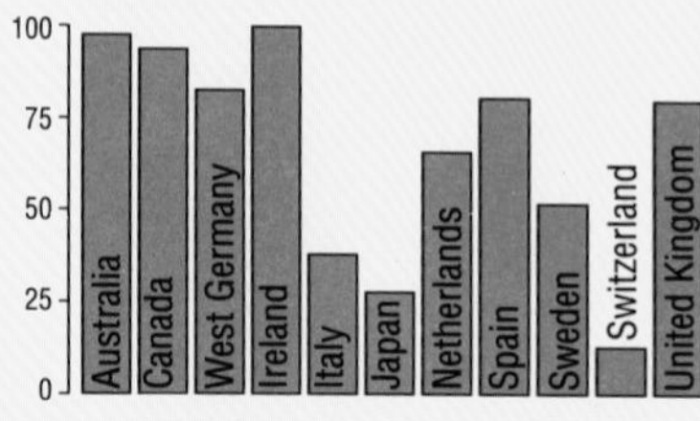
100
75
50
25
0
Australia
Canada
West Germany
Ireland
Italy
Japan
Netherlands
Spain
Sweden
Switzerland
United Kingdom

In Britain toxic waste is mixed with domestic rubbish in the controversial 'dilute and disperse' method. Many other countries favour the opposite approach and concentrate their most dangerous waste in specific places. Incineration is also increasingly favoured.

DILUTE AND DISPERSE LANDFILL DISPOSAL

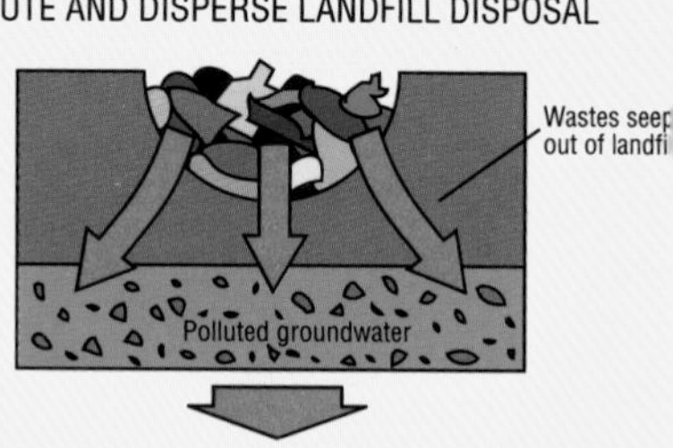
Wastes seep out of landfill
Polluted groundwater
Polluted streams and water supply

The best way of solving the problem of toxic waste is not to produce it in the first place. It is estimated that over the next decade industry could cut its production by a third. More waste could also be recycled or re-used.

.grochemicals

ɪround the world farmers are putting more ɪnd more chemicals on their land. This has ɪd to great increases in crop yields but has ˈso brought environmental problems. ɪutrients from fertilisers are polluting rivers ɪnd lakes, while residues from pesticides ave been detected in food and drinking ˈater. In addition, pesticides are losing their ffectiveness as insects develop immunity. In ɪture agrochemicals will need to be used ɪuch more selectivley.

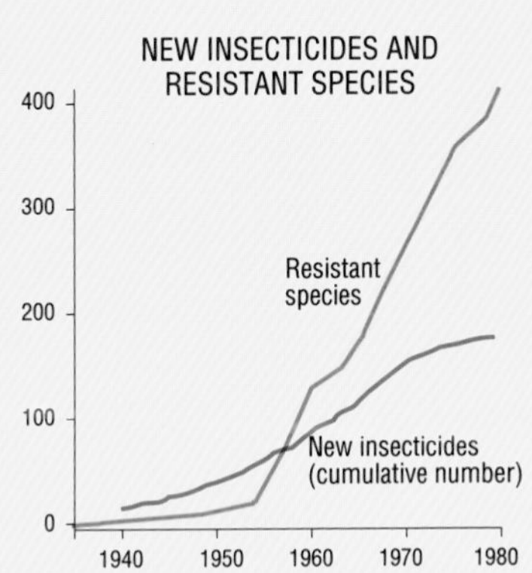

NEW INSECTICIDES AND RESISTANT SPECIES
400
300
200
100
0
1940
1950
1960
1970
1980
Resistant species
New insecticides (cumulative number)

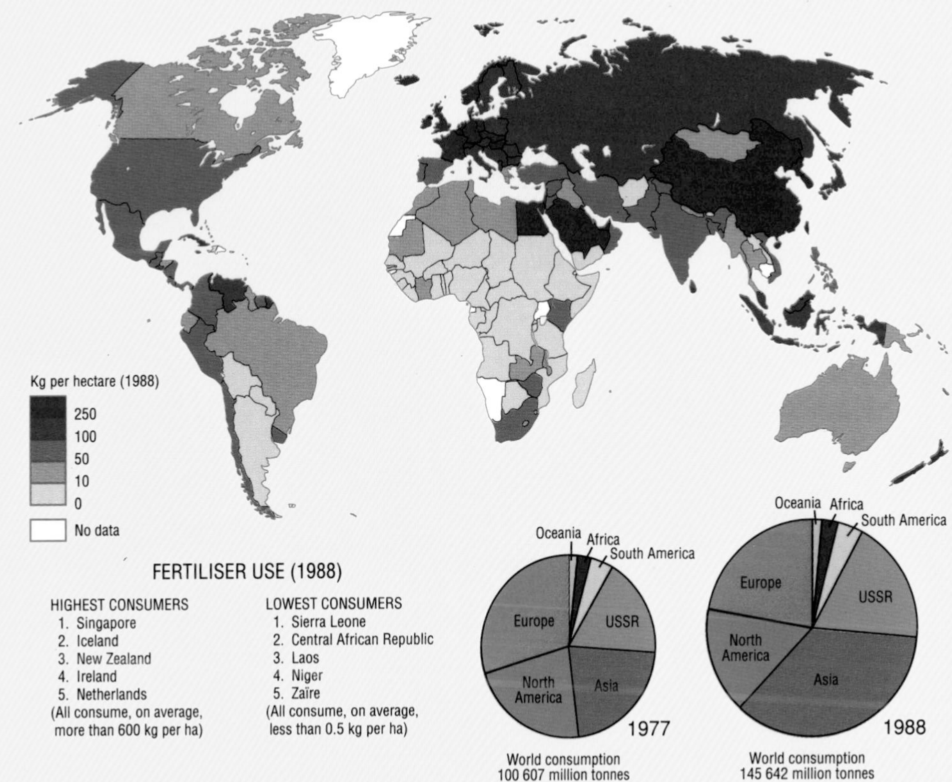

Kg per hectare (1988)
250
100
50
10
0
No data

FERTILISER USE (1988)

HIGHEST CONSUMERS	LOWEST CONSUMERS
1. Singapore	1. Sierra Leone
2. Iceland	2. Central African Republic
3. New Zealand	3. Laos
4. Ireland	4. Niger
5. Netherlands	5. Zaïre
(All consume, on average, more than 600 kg per ha)	(All consume, on average, less than 0.5 kg per ha)

Oceania Africa South America Europe USSR North America Asia 1977

World consumption 100 607 million tonnes

Oceania Africa South America Europe USSR North America Asia 1988

World consumption 145 642 million tonnes

The Aral Sea Disaster

The Aral Sea in Soviet Central Asia used to be the fourth biggest lake in the world. It supported a thriving fishing industry, mixed agriculture and many species of plants and animals. Now the Aral Sea is drying up as water is diverted to irrigate cotton crops. Unless something is done it could disappear completely over the next thirty years.

Environmental Consequences

The dry sea bed has become a desert, poisoned by salt and residues from the chemicals sprayed on the cotton crop. Huge dust storms sweep up the contaminated soil and dump it back on the fields. Deposits have been found up to 5 000 km away on the shores of the Arctic Ocean.

The climate of the region has also begun to change. The Aral Sea used to act as a battery, storing heat in the summer and releasing it in the winter. Now temperatures have become more extreme and there is less rainfall.

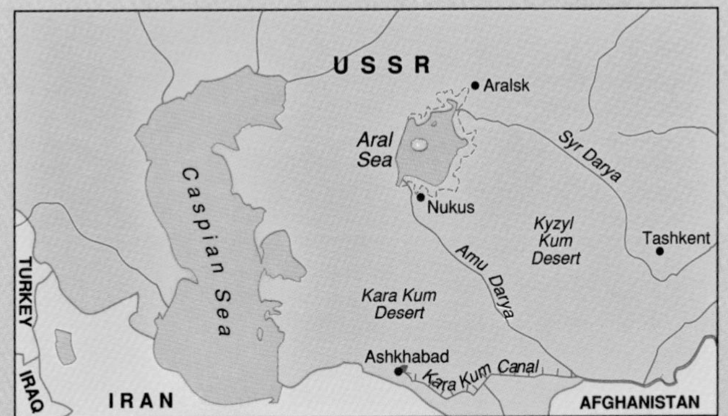

USSR
Aralsk
Aral Sea
Syr Darya
Caspian Sea
Nukus
Kyzyl Kum Desert
Tashkent
Amu Darya
Kara Kum Desert
TURKEY
IRAQ
Ashkhabad
Kara Kum Canal
IRAN
AFGHANISTAN

The location of the Aral Sea

The effect on the local community has been disasterous. Towns which used to depend on fishing are now up to 60 km from the shore. Disease and illness have multiplied among adults and one in ten babies die defore their first birthday.

ARAL SEA FACTS

- Only 4 out of 24 species of fish survive.
- The salinity of the water has increased from 10 to 27%.
- Surface area has decreased by 40% since 1960.
- 173 animal species have been cut to 38.

What could be done?

At present most of the irrigation canals leak a lot. If they were lined with plastic or concrete it would save large amounts of water. Also, the acreage under cotton could be reduced to cut down on irrigation. It will take massive changes to halt the present process and the Aral Sea will probably never be restored properly.

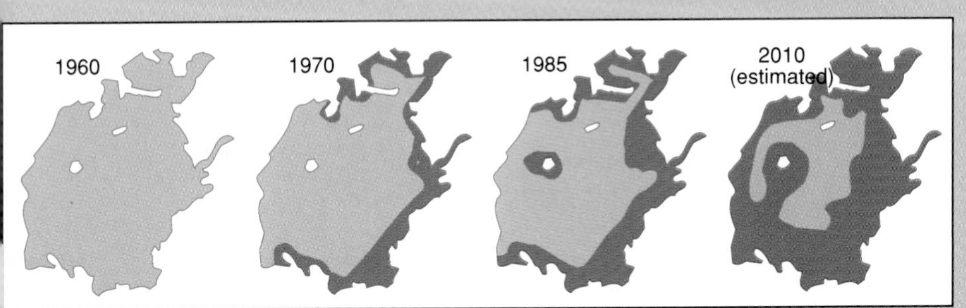

1960
1970
1985
2010 (estimated)

The changing shape of the Aral Sea

Aralsk, USSR - rusting boats lie in the wasteland that was once part of the Aral Sea.

WATER POLLUTION

The Water Budget

Seventy percent of the earth's surface is covered by water. Fresh water represents only 2.5% of the total. The rest is found in the oceans where the presence of salt makes it difficult to use.

Most of the fresh water lies deep underground or is frozen in the polar ice caps. Only a very small proportion is freely available. Nevertheless there is enough to meet our needs. The problems is that supplies are unevenly distributed around the world.

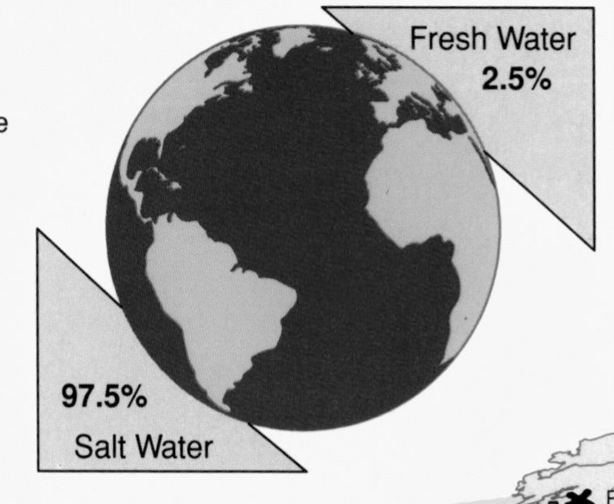

Fresh Water
2.5%
97.5%
Salt Water

Water Pollution

Water pollution is a worldwide problem. Waste from factories, farms and cities is poisoning rivers and seeping into groundwater. Lakes are particularly at risk as they allow pollutants to build up. Coastlines and shallow seas are highly vulnerable. The discharge of oil from tanker accidents and ships that wash out their tanks illegally is another problem. It is estimated that several million tonnes of oil are put into the sea each year.

Water Availability

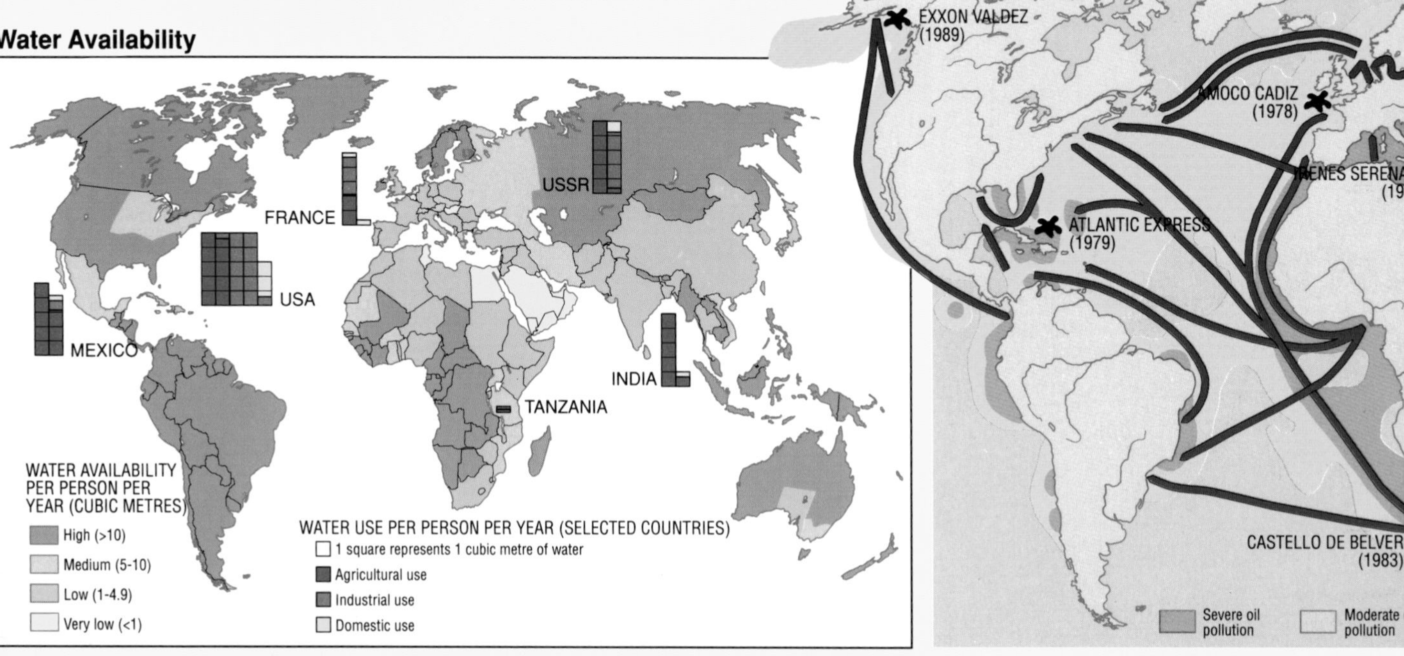

USSR
FRANCE
USA
MEXICO
INDIA
TANZANIA
WATER AVAILABILITY PER PERSON PER YEAR (CUBIC METRES)
High (>10)
Medium (5-10)
Low (1-4.9)
Very low (<1)
WATER USE PER PERSON PER YEAR (SELECTED COUNTRIES)
1 square represents 1 cubic metre of water
Agricultural use
Industrial use
Domestic use
EXXON VALDEZ (1989)
AMOCO CADIZ (1978)
IRENES SERENA
ATLANTIC EXPRESS (1979)
CASTELLO DE BELVER (1983)
Severe oil pollution
Moderate pollution

Pollution in the North Sea

North Sea Facts

- Average depth of water 95m.
- Rich variety of flora and fauna, including commercial fish stocks.
- 150 oil and gas platforms.
- 5 000 ships operating at any one time.
- Water replaced every 18 months on average.

The North Sea receives much of the pollution that is generated in north-western Europe. Some is dumped directly into the water or absorbed from the atmosphere. Rivers are the single biggest source of pollution and contribute nearly half of the total.

Pollution has begun to have a serious effect on the ecology of the North Sea. Heavy metals from industry, sewage from towns and oil from ships have all added to the problem. In 1988, large numbers of seals were killed by a mystery virus. Countries bordering the North Sea have now agreed on various measures to control pollution. A lot more still needs to be done and many people would like to see stricter controls.

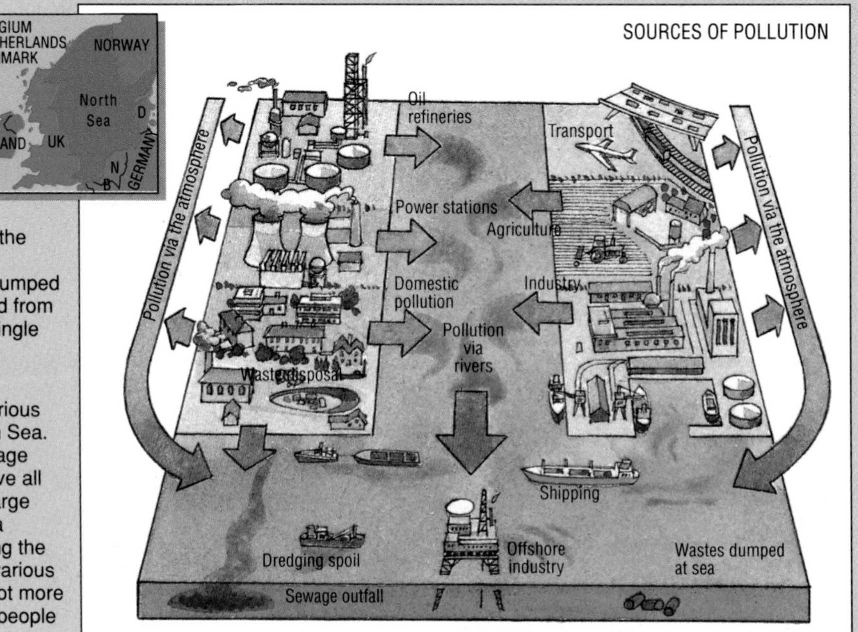

B - BELGIUM
N - NETHERLANDS
D - DENMARK
NORWAY
North Sea
IRELAND
UK
GERMANY
SOURCES OF POLLUTION
Oil refineries
Transport
Power stations
Agriculture
Domestic pollution
Industry
Pollution via rivers
Waste disposal
Pollution via the atmosphere
Shipping
Dredging spoil
Offshore industry
Wastes dumped at sea
Sewage outfall

SOURCES OF POLLUTION (1985)

Nitrogen

Total = 1 506 700 tonnes

Phosphorous

Total = 104 tonnes

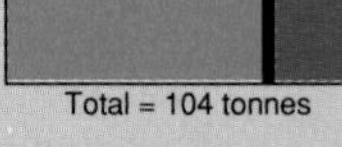

Mercury & Cadmium

Total = 409 tonnes

Copper, Lead, Zinc, Chromium, Nickel & Arsenic

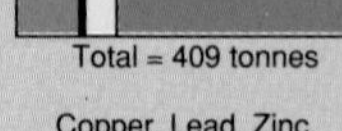

Total = 40 557 tonnes

- River Inputs
- Industrial Waste
- Sewage Sludge
- Dredging
- Atmospheric
- Direct Discharge

Source - North Sea Quality Status Report 1987

NUMBER OF ACCIDENTAL OIL SPILLS (1973-84)

70 60 50 40 30 20 10

1973 '75 '77 '79 '81 '83 1984

INDEPENDENTA (1979)

KUWAITI OILFIELDS (1991)

SEA STAR (1972)

Major oil pollution incidents (Selection 1978-91)

Main oil tanker routes

Dirty Water

In the developed world most people have access to clean piped water and mains sanitation. In developing countries however, less than half the population has access to safe water. The situation is particularly bad in rural areas. Here many people spend a great deal of time and energy collecting and carrying water.

Clean water is essential for good health. Nearly all diseases in the developing world are due to polluted water and inadequate sanitation. Simple technology and self help schemes could save millions of lives.

RURAL

URBAN

1970 1975 1980

% Population without clean water in the 'developing' countries

% Population without proper sanitation in the 'developing' countries

Access to Drinking Water

ALGERIA 88% 80% 100%

INDIA 56% 43% 80%

ECUADOR 47% 16% 75%

ZAÏRE 9% 5% 15%

KENYA 28% 21% 61%

INDONESIA 36% 30% 53%

ARGENTINA 64% 17% 72%

North South

% of population with access to safe drinking water

Over 85

50-85

15-49

Under 15

No data

Rural

Urban

Pie charts show examples of the variation in access to clean water between rural and urban population.

The Great Lakes

The Great Lakes in North America are the largest freshwater reservoir in the world. Some years ago they were threatened by large quantities of sewage and other pollution. Although this problem has been solved, the level of toxic chemicals in the water is now causing concern.

The chemicals come from a variety of sources. They are discharged into rivers, seep into the water from waste dumps, fall from the sky as toxic rain and wash off fields treated with fertilisers and pesticides. Sediments in some areas are so toxic they are unsafe to dredge. More than 360 chemicals have been identified in the Great Lakes which are the source of drinking water for 35 million people.

The International Joint Commission, which manages the Great Lakes, has designated forty two 'areas of concern' which need urgent attention. While this will help, it will not stop pollution from happening. In the longer term people need to alter their lifestyles so that they use less chemicals.

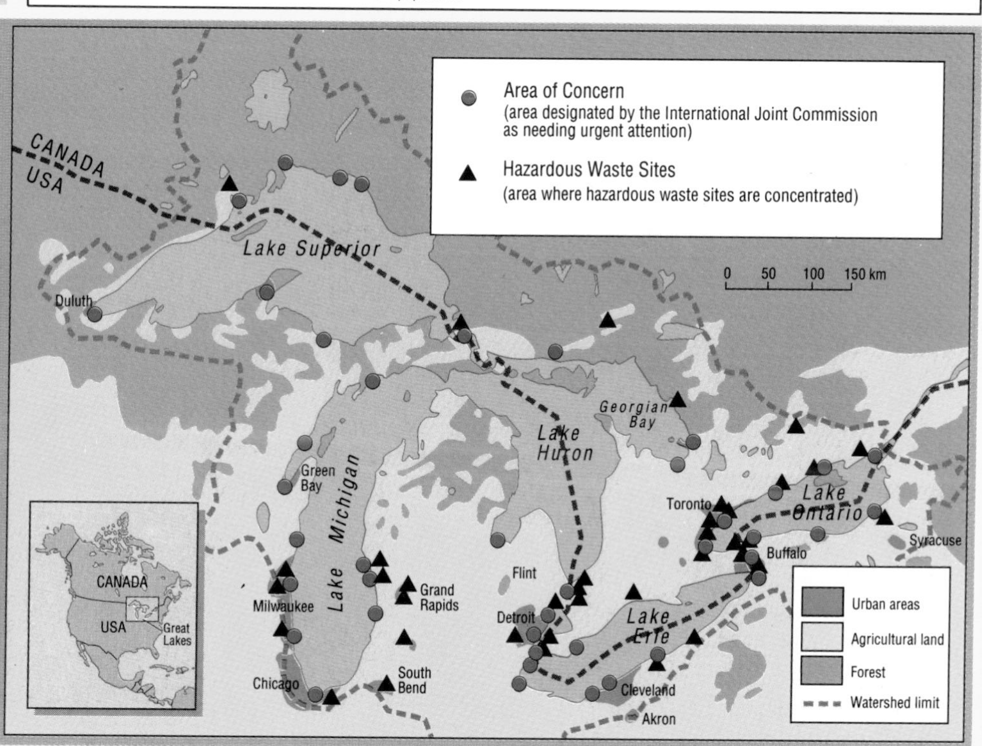

Area of Concern
(area designated by the International Joint Commission as needing urgent attention)
Hazardous Waste Sites
(area where hazardous waste sites are concentrated)
CANADA
USA
Lake Superior
Duluth
0 50 100 150 km
Georgian Bay
Lake Huron
Lake Michigan
Green Bay
Toronto
Lake Ontario
Syracuse
Buffalo
Flint
Grand Rapids
Milwaukee
Detroit
Lake Erie
Chicago
South Bend
Cleveland
Akron
Great Lakes
Urban areas
Agricultural land
Forest
Watershed limit

The Threat to Wildlife

Scientists believe there are between five and thirty million plant and animal species in the world. They estimate half of them could become extinct within the next sixty years. Thousands of plants and creatures are officially classed as endangered. There are many different threats to wildlife:

Pesticides pass through the food chain killing birds of prey and other higher forms of life

Toxic waste dumped in the sea builds up in the bodies of seals and dolphins making them vulnerable to disease

Hunting has devastated stocks of many valuable species such as elephants, whales and crocodiles

Habitat destruction has seriously affected many thousands of species as people claim new areas for farming and urban development.

Protected Areas

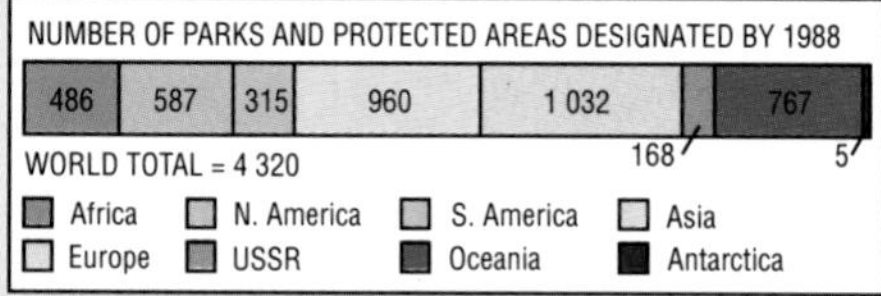

NUMBER OF PARKS AND PROTECTED AREAS DESIGNATED BY 1988
486
587
315
960
1 032
767
168
5
WORLD TOTAL = 4 320
Africa
N. America
S. America
Asia
Europe
USSR
Oceania
Antarctica

The world's first national park was created at Yellowstone in the USA in 1872. Now there are over four thousand all over the world. Many have been set up to protect areas of special wildlife and landscape value.

Endangered Wildlife

A selection of the world species at risk

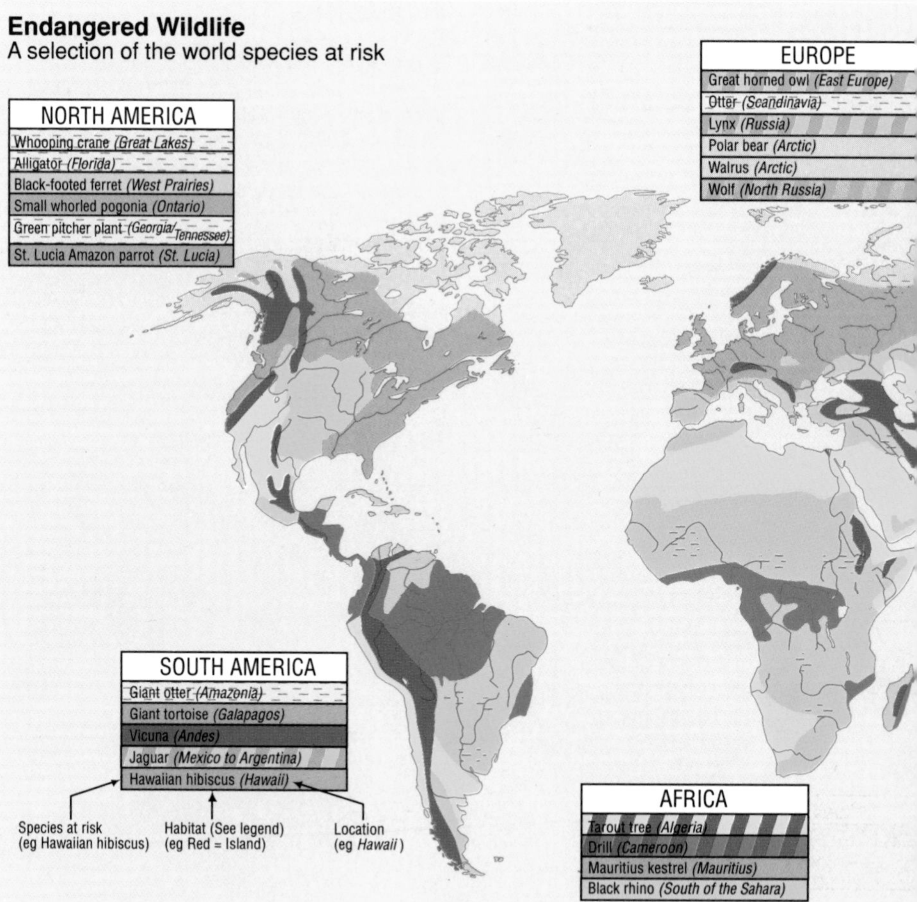

NORTH AMERICA
Whooping crane (Great Lakes)
Alligator (Florida)
Black-footed ferret (West Prairies)
Small whorled pogonia (Ontario)
Green pitcher plant (Georgia/Tennessee)
St. Lucia Amazon parrot (St. Lucia)
EUROPE
Great horned owl (East Europe)
Otter (Scandinavia)
Lynx (Russia)
Polar bear (Arctic)
Walrus (Arctic)
Wolf (North Russia)
SOUTH AMERICA
Giant otter (Amazonia)
Giant tortoise (Galapagos)
Vicuna (Andes)
Jaguar (Mexico to Argentina)
Hawaiian hibiscus (Hawaii)
Species at risk
(eg Hawaiian hibiscus)
Habitat (See legend)
(eg Red = Island)
Location
(eg Hawaii)
AFRICA
Tarout tree (Algeria)
Drill (Cameroon)
Mauritius kestrel (Mauritius)
Black rhino (South of the Sahara)

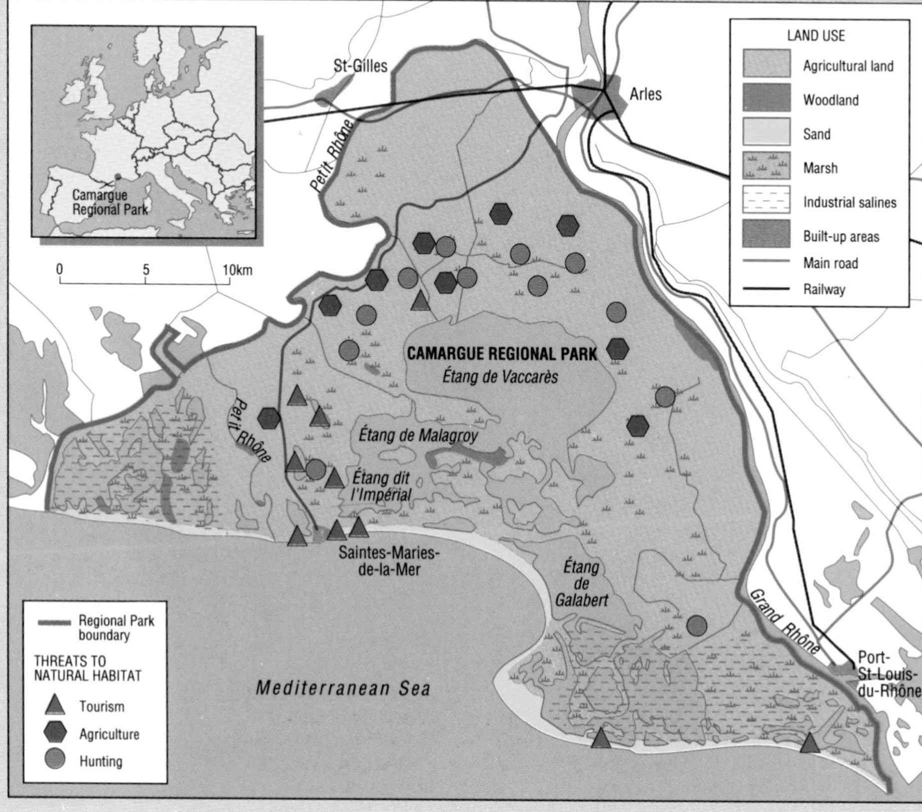

St-Gilles
Arles
Petit Rhône
Camargue Regional Park
0
5
10km
CAMARGUE REGIONAL PARK
Étang de Vaccarès
Étang de Malagroy
Étang dit l'Impérial
Saintes-Maries-de-la-Mer
Étang de Galabert
Grand Rhône
Port-St-Louis-du-Rhône
Mediterranean Sea
LAND USE
Agricultural land
Woodland
Sand
Marsh
Industrial salines
Built-up areas
Main road
Railway
Regional Park boundary
THREATS TO NATURAL HABITAT
Tourism
Agriculture
Hunting

National Parks: The Camargue Regional Park

The marshes and lakes in the Rhône delta in the Camargue in southern France form one of the mos important coastal wetlands in Europe. The area ha a complex ecology of salt steppe and freshwater lakes. It is famous for its bulls and wild horses, an is the home for many rare birds including bitterns, egrets and harriers.

Since 1942 a third of the natural habitat has been lost, mostly to agriculture, the salt industry and to create areas for hunting. Tourism is putting the are under particular pressure. Hotels and campsites have been set up and the visitors disturb the wildli Although most of the money they bring ends up in the hands of developers, some is invested in conservation and protecting wildlife.

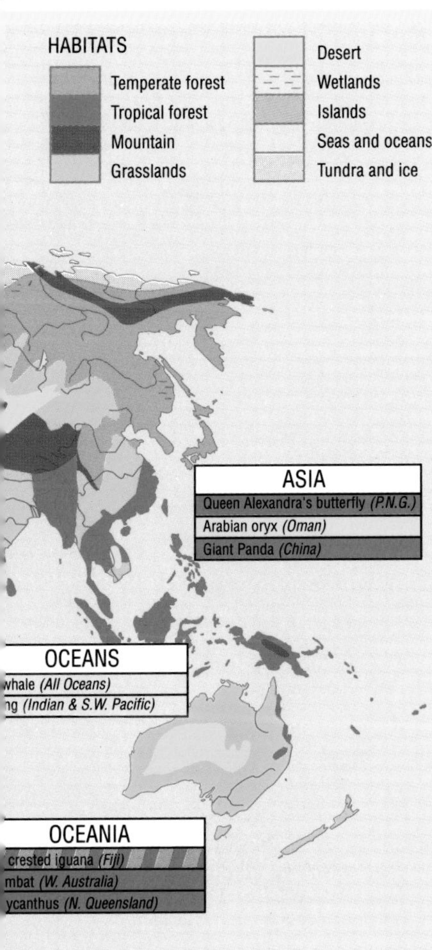
HABITATS
Temperate forest
Tropical forest
Mountain
Grasslands
Desert
Wetlands
Islands
Seas and oceans
Tundra and ice
ASIA
Queen Alexandra's butterfly (P.N.G.)
Arabian oryx (Oman)
Giant Panda (China)
OCEANS
whale (All Oceans)
ng (Indian & S.W. Pacific)
OCEANIA
crested iguana (Fiji)
mbat (W. Australia)
ycanthus (N. Queensland)

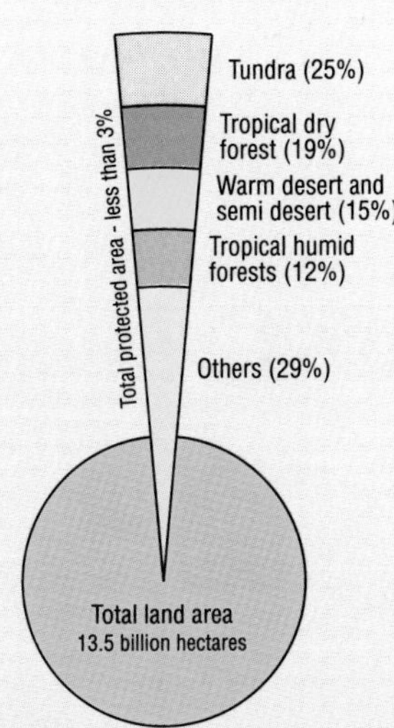
Tundra (25%)
Tropical dry forest (19%)
Warm desert and semi desert (15%)
Tropical humid forests (12%)
Others (29%)
Total protected area - less than 3%
Total land area
13.5 billion hectares

Habitat and Wildlife Protection

All over the world, wildlife is under enormous pressure. The loss of even a single species is a tragedy because it can never be recreated. As more become extinct, the environment is improverished, and unique genetic reserves are lost. Ultimately all life depends directly or indirectly on plants. The rainforests are specially important because they contain half of all known species. It seems certain that many species will disappear without ever being studied.

About 3% of the world's land surface has been made into protected areas. Major conservation initiatives have also been launched at national and international level. Some of them are shown on the maps below.

Global conventions protecting species

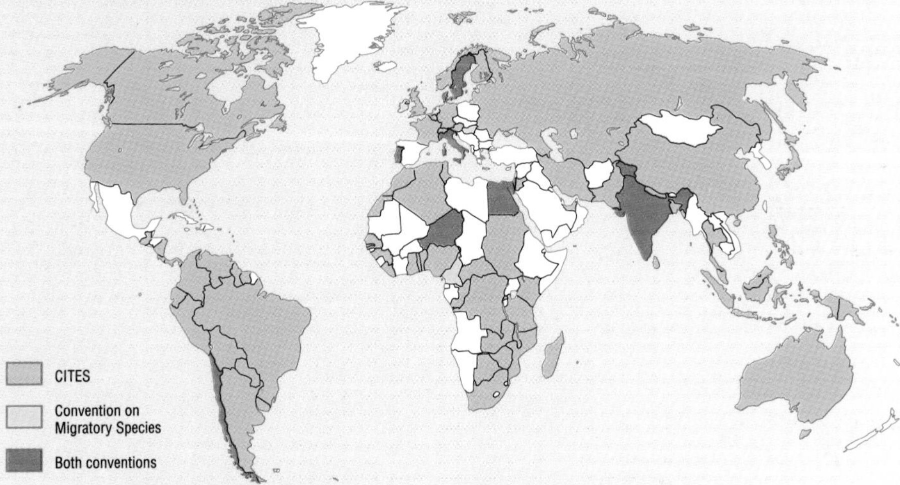
CITES
Convention on Migratory Species
Both conventions

The Convention on International Trade in Endangered Species (CITES) controls world trade in wild plants and animals. The treaty came into force in 1975 and was signed by many countries. However it has proved difficult to stop illegal trade when some countries do not support a ban.

Global conventions protecting habitat

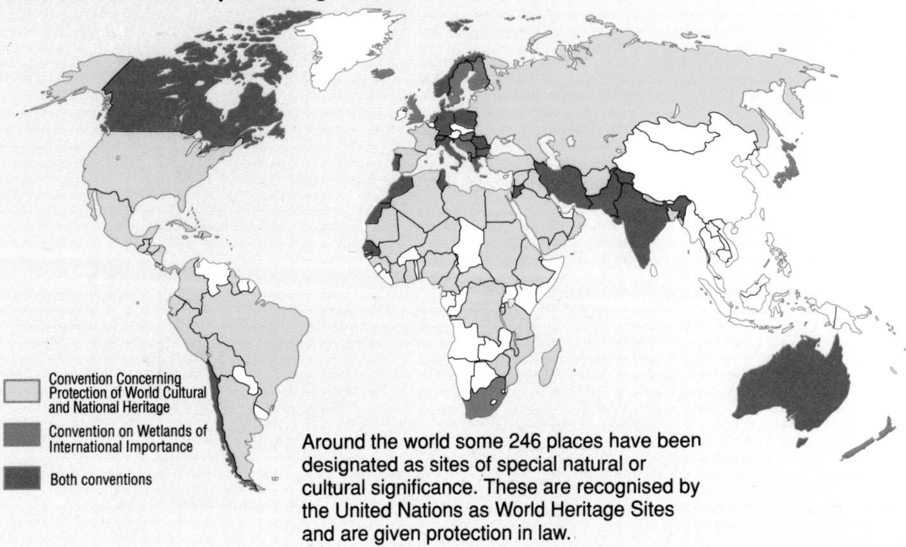
Convention Concerning Protection of World Cultural and National Heritage
Convention on Wetlands of International Importance
Both conventions

Around the world some 246 places have been designated as sites of special natural or cultural significance. These are recognised by the United Nations as World Heritage Sites and are given protection in law.

iosphere Reserves

iosphere reserves are a special kind of rotected area. They consist of a core region urrounded by a buffer zone and transitional rea. Ideally the core consists of a major cosystem that is large enough to be self ontaining.

iosphere reserves concentrate on scientific esearch and seek to involve local people herever possible. There were 267 worldwide in 988 overseen by UNESCO. One of the most uccessful is the Sierra de Manantlan Reserve Mexico where scientists are studying a wild oecies of corn.

Vildlife Ranches

n Zimbabwe the government has set up a new ildlife project called CAMPFIRE. This aims to elp local people get the most out of local esources such as trees, grazing land, water nd wildlife. Instead of trying to rear cattle on ather unsuitable farmland, some communities ow earn a living from managing wildlife.

he policy is paying dividends. It is based on the ct that wildlife is valuable and tourists, hotographers and hunters will pay good prices. AMPFIRE has succeeded by exploiting wildlife s an asset. Many plants and creatures have enefitted as a result.

NATURAL RESOURCES

What are Natural Resources?

Minerals, water, plants and animals are all natural resources. Human beings depend on exploiting them for their survival.

For thousands of years people only used natural resources in small quantities. With the growth of industry and population demand has escalated. The world now uses three times the amount of minerals that it did in1950. This is putting the environment under more and more pressure.

Renewable Resources

When we use resources we sometimes consume them completely. Many machines, for instance, burn up petrol in order to generate energy. Resources which are used up in this way are said to be non renewable. They include oil, chemicals and a variety of metals.

Other resources can be replaced. Timber, for example, is sometimes grown on plantations which are harvested at regular intervals, and is a renewable resource.

Renewable resources hold the key to the future. Sooner or later all the non renewable supplies will be used up. By contrast, we can go on using renewable resources for ever.

Exploitation of Natural Resources

Natural resources are unevenly distributed around the world. Large countries such as the USA, USSR, China and Australia have good supplies. Some smaller countries also have big reserves. Jamaica and Guinea for example, have important bauxite mines which provide the raw material for aluminium

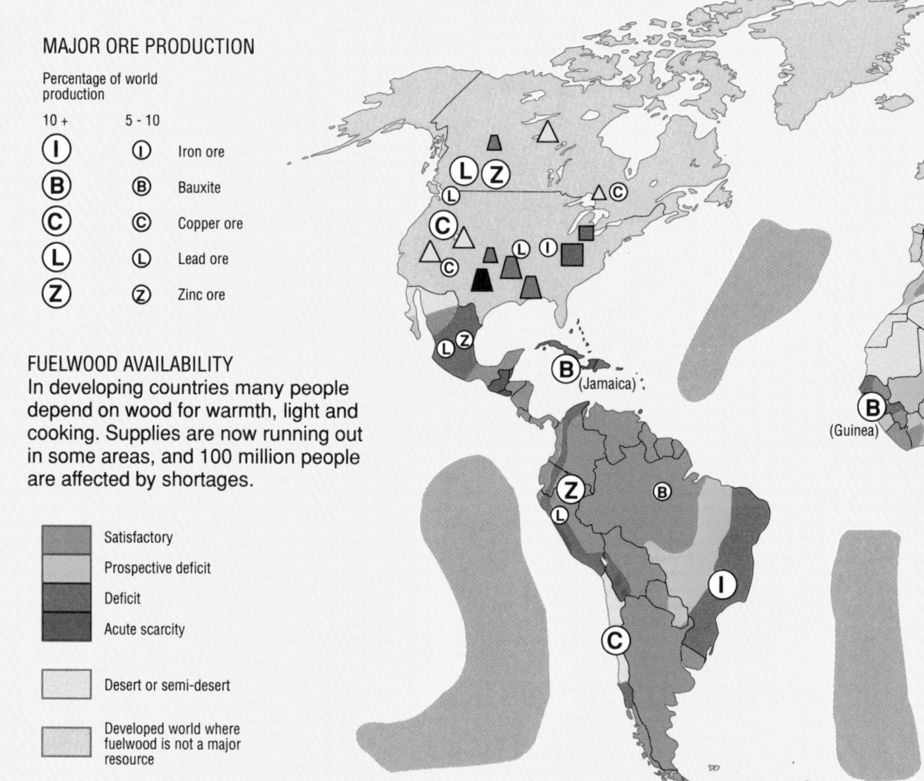
MAJOR ORE PRODUCTION
Percentage of world production
10 +
5 - 10
Iron ore
Bauxite
Copper ore
Lead ore
Zinc ore
FUELWOOD AVAILABILITY
In developing countries many people depend on wood for warmth, light and cooking. Supplies are now running out in some areas, and 100 million people are affected by shortages.
Satisfactory
Prospective deficit
Deficit
Acute scarcity
Desert or semi-desert
Developed world where fuelwood is not a major resource
(Jamaica)
(Guinea)

Environmental Issues in Mining

MIning is having a greater and greater effect on the environment. Ugly slag heaps and open pits have left scars in areas of scenic beauty. Subsidence and landslips can be a problem, but even more serious is the damage done to rivers as poisonous metals are washed into the water. This is a cause of concern in Brazil where prospectors are panning for gold in the tributaries of the Amazon.

Many countries have laws to control mining. Some old quarries have been restored to farmland or flooded to create attractive lakes.

The environmental damage caused by extensive mining.

Uranium Mining in Australia

Australia possesses about one third of the world's economic reserves of uranium.This mineral has become important in the present century as the raw material for nuclear power stations and nuclear weapons. Most of the reserves are concentrated in the Northern Territory. The decision to exploit them was highly controversial.

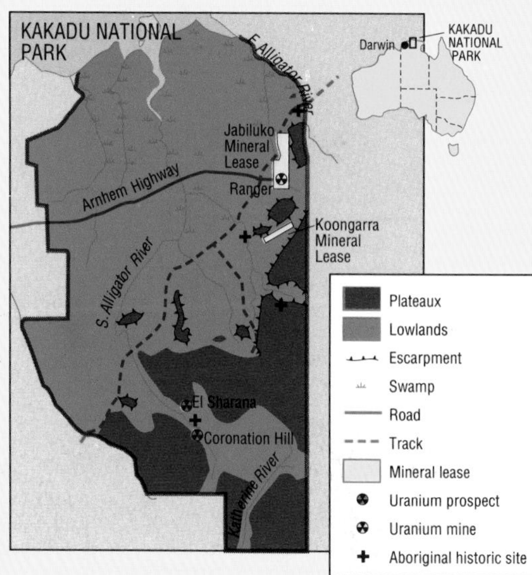
KAKADU NATIONAL PARK
Darwin
KAKADU NATIONAL PARK
E. Alligator River
Jabiluka Mineral Lease
Arnhem Highway
Ranger
Koongarra Mineral Lease
S. Alligator River
El Sharana
Coronation Hill
Katherine River
Plateaux
Lowlands
Escarpment
Swamp
Road
Track
Mineral lease
Uranium prospect
Uranium mine
Aboriginal historic site

Arguments in favour

- The mines earn money and provide employment
- Nuclear power can help solve the world's energy crisis
- Strict safeguards control how the uranium is used

Arguments against

- Nuclear power stations are not safe
- The uranium could fall into the hands of terrorists
- The mines threatened a beautiful area where Aboriginees live

In 1977 the Australian government decided to go ahead with the mines. At the same time it created a National Park in the surrounding area and agreed to give some of the profits to the Aboriginees. Despite this compromise many people are still not satisfied.

TURAL RESOURCES FROM THE OCEANS

ere are large quantities of minerals deep on the ean floor. Unfortunately these are difficult to get and exploit.

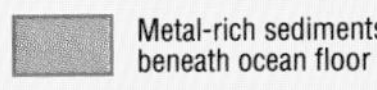
Metal-rich sediments beneath ocean floor

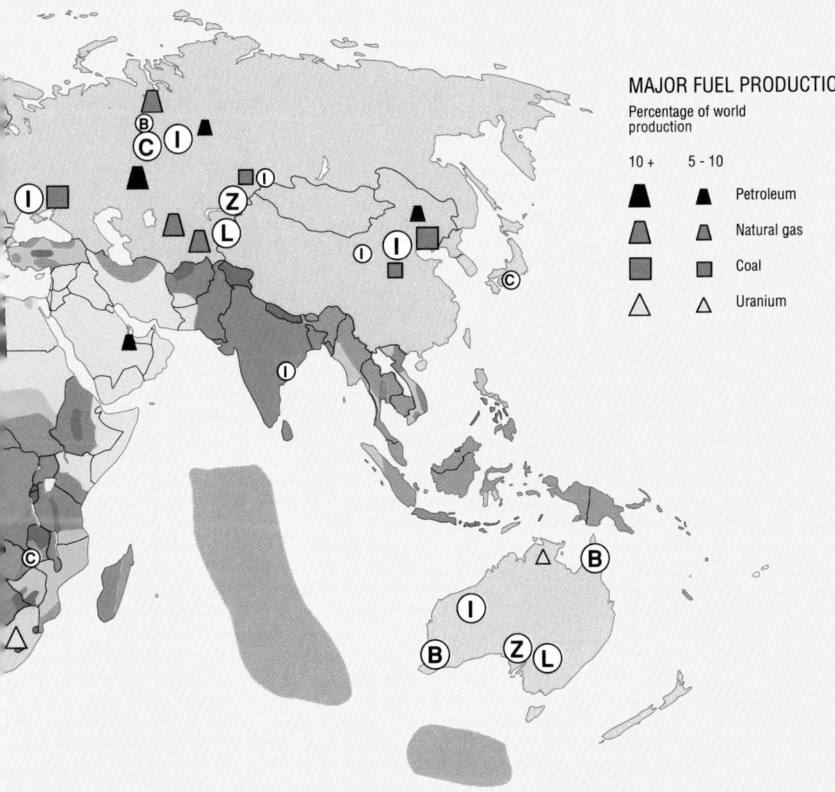
MAJOR FUEL PRODUCTION
Percentage of world production
10 +
5 - 10
Petroleum
Natural gas
Coal
Uranium

Depleting Resources

Some minerals are plentiful. Reserves of iron ore, for example, should last for 400 years at present rates of consumption. Other minerals are not so abundant and supplies may run low within our lifetime. These include diamonds, silver, gold, tin and zinc. One solution is to look for alternative materials. Another is to recycle waste products so the resources can be used again.

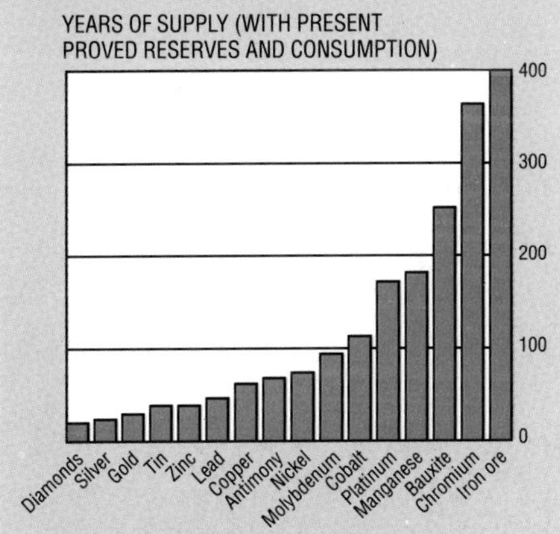
YEARS OF SUPPLY (WITH PRESENT PROVED RESERVES AND CONSUMPTION)
400
300
200
100
0
Diamonds
Silver
Gold
Tin
Zinc
Lead
Copper
Antimony
Nickel
Molybdenum
Cobalt
Platinum
Manganese
Bauxite
Chromium
Iron ore

Substitution

In the past, tin was used extensively in the canning and packaging industry. Now that supplies are becoming scarcer alternative materials are being used. Glass, plastics, steel and aluminium have all proved suitable. However, the answer is not always this simple. Manganese is essential for high grade steel and there are no substitutes for chromium and platinum.

ecycling

Most waste products can be recycled. On a omestic level, many people now sort out paper nd glass from their household rubbish. In ndustry, scrap metal provides almost half the ron needed for steel making.

ecycling not only reduces the demand on atural resources, it saves energy, conserves vater and reduces pollution. It also helps to solve the problem of waste disposal.

ecycling has enormous scope. As individuals ve can all play our part, but governments also eed to help by putting taxes on pollution and ncouraging conservation.

ENVIRONMENTAL BENEFITS OF RECYCLING

(Percentage reduction)

	ALUMINIUM	PAPER	GLASS
REDUCTION IN ENERGY USE	90-97	23-24	4-32
REDUCTION IN AIR POLLUTION	95	74	20
REDUCTION IN WATER POLLUTION	97	35	-
REDUCTION IN WATER USE	-	58	50

Recycling Aluminium Cans

Aluminium cans are cheap and easy to recycle. It takes twenty times more energy to make new aluminium from bauxite than to use scrap.

RECYCLING PROCESS

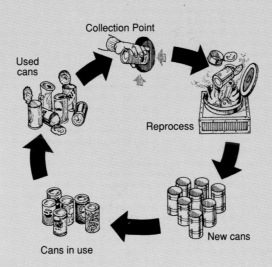

Collection Point

Used cans

Reprocess

New cans

Cans in use

In the USA nearly 80% of aluminium cans are recycled. Other countries, especially in Europe, are beginning to follow suit.

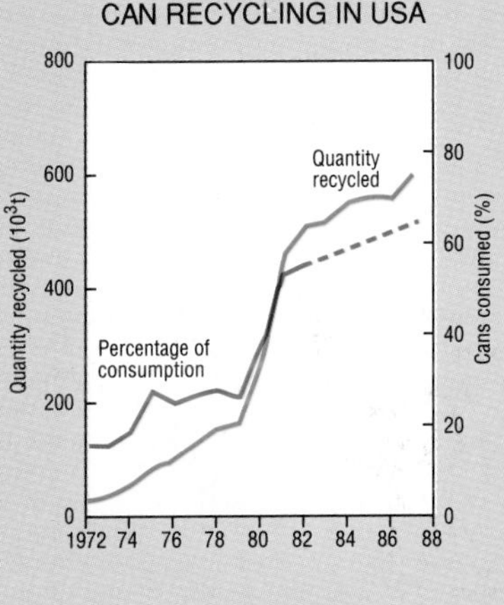
TRENDS IN ALUMINIUM CAN RECYCLING IN USA
Quantity recycled (10^3t)
Cans consumed (%)
Quantity recycled
Percentage of consumption
800
600
400
200
0
100
80
60
40
20
0
1972 74 76 78 80 82 84 86 88

The Energy Problem

We depend on energy for almost everything that we do. Factories, farms, houses and vehicles all need power to make them work.

It was the discovery of new sources of power - chiefly wind, water and coal - which fuelled the Industrial Revolution. Since 1945 the boom in world economic activity has been based largely on oil.

Fossil fuels - coal, oil and gas - provide most of the world's energy. Consumption is very uneven. USA, Western Europe and Japan use nearly three quarters of the total. Africa and South Asia use only small quantities.

Fumes from fossil fuels are responsible for many pollution problems and are major factors in acid rain and global warming. This is one reason why plans to save energy are receiving so much attention. Energy conservation would also help to conserve supplies.

WORLD ENERGY PRODUCTION

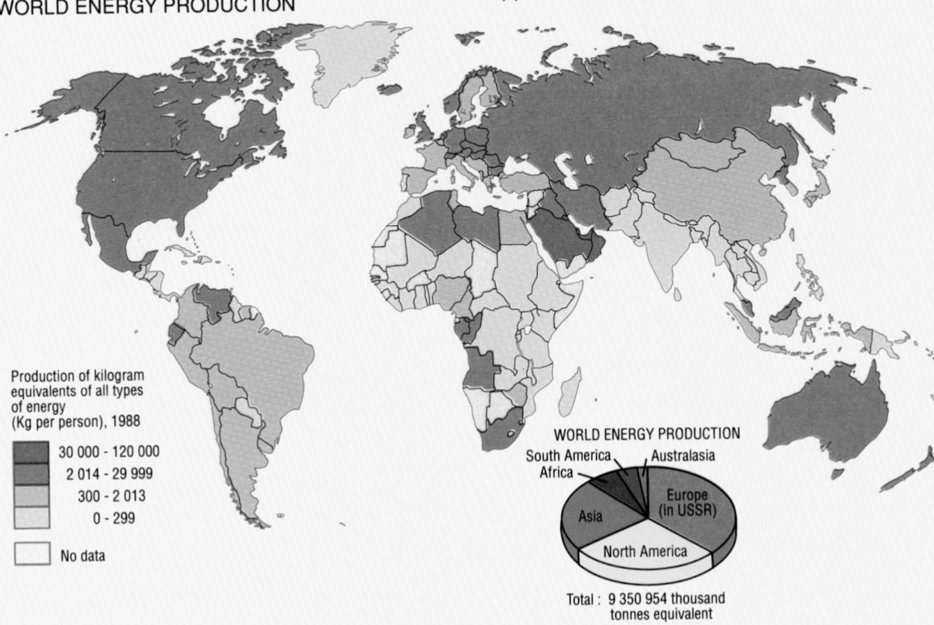
Production of kilogram equivalents of all types of energy (Kg per person), 1988
30 000 - 120 000
2 014 - 29 999
300 - 2 013
0 - 299
No data
WORLD ENERGY PRODUCTION
South America
Australasia
Africa
Europe (in USSR)
Asia
North America
Total : 9 350 954 thousand tonnes equivalent

WORLD ENERGY CONSUMPTION

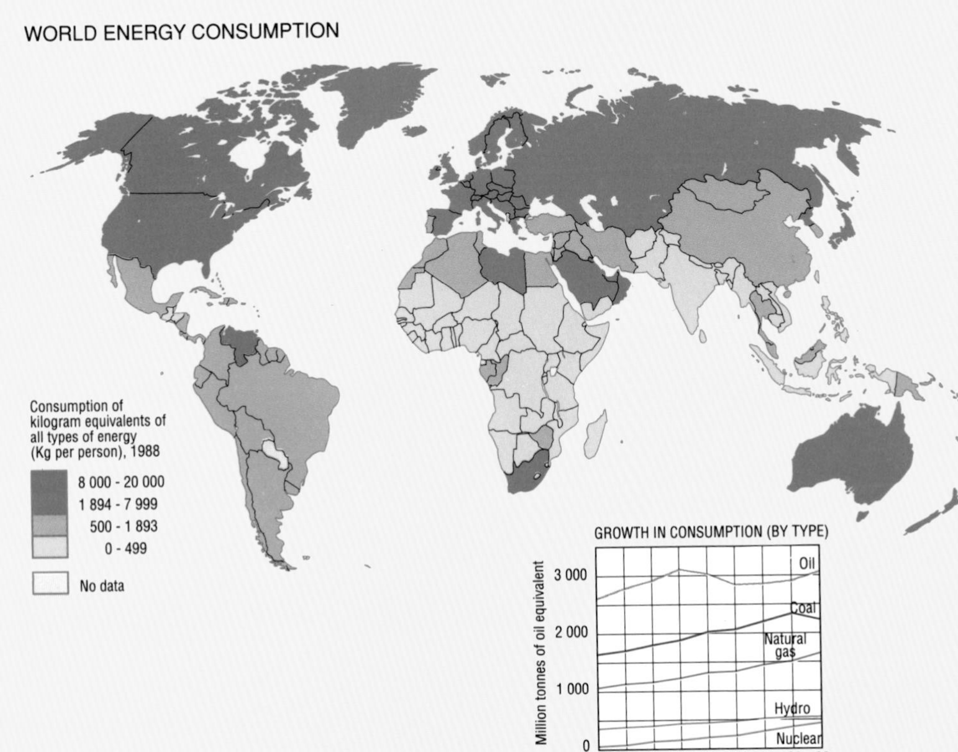
Consumption of kilogram equivalents of all types of energy (Kg per person), 1988
8 000 - 20 000
1 894 - 7 999
500 - 1 893
0 - 499
No data
GROWTH IN CONSUMPTION (BY TYPE)
Million tonnes of oil equivalent
3 000
2 000
1 000
0
1972 74 76 78 80 82 84 86 88
Oil
Coal
Natural gas
Hydro
Nuclear

Fuel Reserves

Fossil fuels will not last forever. It took a million years to create the fuel we now burn every twelve months. At present rates of consumption the known supplies of oil will be used up in about 45 years. Coal is much more plentiful and will last for several centuries.

WORLD RESERVES (BY TYPE), 1989

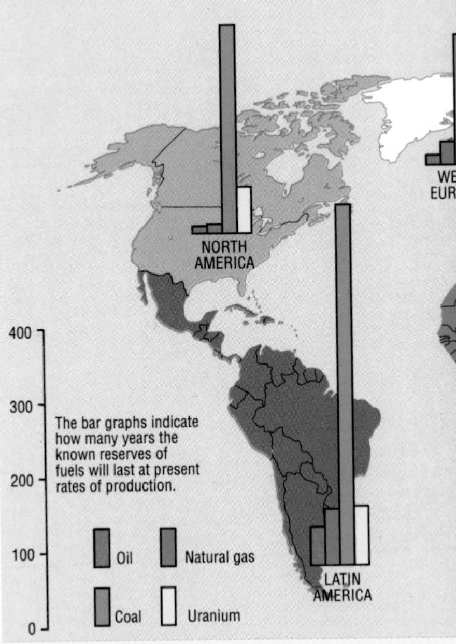
NORTH AMERICA
LATIN AMERICA
WEST EURO
400
300
200
100
0
The bar graphs indicate how many years the known reserves of fuels will last at present rates of production.
Oil
Natural gas
Coal
Uranium

Nuclear Energy

At one time nuclear power appeared to offer almost limitless supplies of cheap and clean electricity. However, there have always been doubts. There was the problem of disposing of nuclear waste and there was the risk of accidents. The catastrophe at Chernobyl in 1986, which spread radiation across the whole of Europe, made the dangers abundantly clear. We now know that electricity from nuclear power is expensive compared to electricity from coal.

In 1989 there were 426 commercial nuclear reactors producing one sixth of the world's electricity. The map shows the number of reactors in the European Community. Countries like France and the UK have invested heavily in nuclear power. Others, like Denmark, Ireland and Greece have never become involved.

NUCLEAR POWER IN THE EC

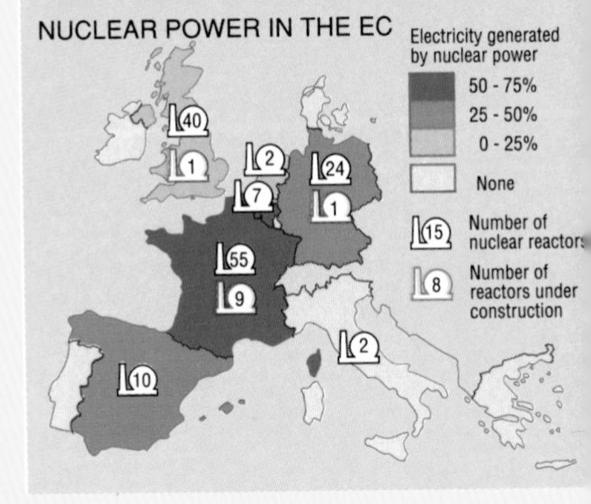
Electricity generated by nuclear power
50 - 75%
25 - 50%
0 - 25%
None
Number of nuclear reactors
Number of reactors under construction
40
1
2
24
7
1
55
9
2
10

e search for new supplies will almost certainly sult in valuable new finds. In addition, velopments in technology will make it ssible to exploit reserves that are currently economic. The disadvantage is that many of se are likely to be in remote areas and ficult to extract.

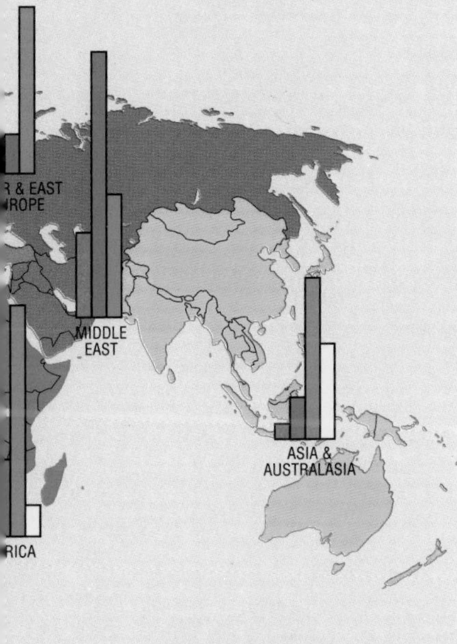

R & EAST
ROPE
MIDDLE
EAST
ASIA &
AUSTRALASIA
RICA

Renewable Energy

Fossil fuels are likely to become more expensive as they get scarcer, and nuclear power is surrounded by questions. The alternative is to harness renewable energy from natural sources. This has the added advantage of avoiding the problem of air pollution.

Hydro Power
Hydro power works by storing water in dams to drive turbines. It now provides more than a fifth of the world's electricity. One of the drawbacks of hydro power is that the dams flood good farmland and in hot countries encourage the spread of waterborne diseases.

Solar Power
The simplest way of using the sun's rays is to heat water and buildings. Solar power can be converted into electricity using reflectors. The most promising areas are in the tropics where solar radiation is highest.

Solar panels for powering a borehole pump, Somali Republic.

Geothermal Power
Hot rocks beneath the earth's surface are a valuable source of energy. Most houses in Iceland are heated with water from underground reservoirs. In the UK experiments are being undertaken in Cornwall and Southampton.

Wind Power *see below*

Wave Power
The motion of the waves can be used to generate electricity. It is estimated that half the UK's supplies could come from an area off northwest Scotland. Much more research is needed but the world's first wave power scheme is operating off the coast of Norway.

A tidal barrage on the River Rance, Brittany, France.

Tidal Power
Dams can trap sea water as it rises and falls with the tide. Estuaries make the best sites as they have a large tidal range. A dam on the Severn estuary could generate 5% of the UK's electricity but would cause ecological problems.

Biomass Power
Rotting waste matter from plants and animals produces methane which can be collected in tanks and used as fuel. In some places special power stations run on crop waste. India, Malaysia, the Philippines and the USA, for example, have power stations which burn rice husks.

Wind Power in the United Kingdom

LOCATION OF UK
WIND DEVELOPMENTS
Turbines connected to the grid
Turbines under construction
Possible wind farm locations
Susetter Hill Shetland
Burgar Hill Orkney
Eaglesham
Langdon Common
Ovenden Moor
Offshore Norfolk
Capel Cynon
Carmarthen Bay
Ilfracombe
Richborough
Cold Northcott
Treculliacks

Modern wind turbines can harness the power of the wind, much as windmills did in the past. Coasts and mountains are the best sites as the turbines need winds of over 25km per hour to make them work. Unfortunately, as shown on the map, these coincide with many of the UK's most scenic areas. Off shore locations might provide a solution.

A wind turbine in operation at Burgar Hill, Orkney.

Ovenden Moor Wind Farm

At Ovenden Moor in West Yorkshire, a local company plans to build a wind farm with 35 turbines. The turbines will be about 30 metres high and painted so they blend in with the landscape. The site is on windy moorland remote from towns and villages.

Some people are worried about how the scheme will affect the landscape. They are also concerned about the disruption to a peaceful part of the country. A proposed wind farm in mid Wales has met with similar objections.

LOCATION MAP OF PROPOSED SITE

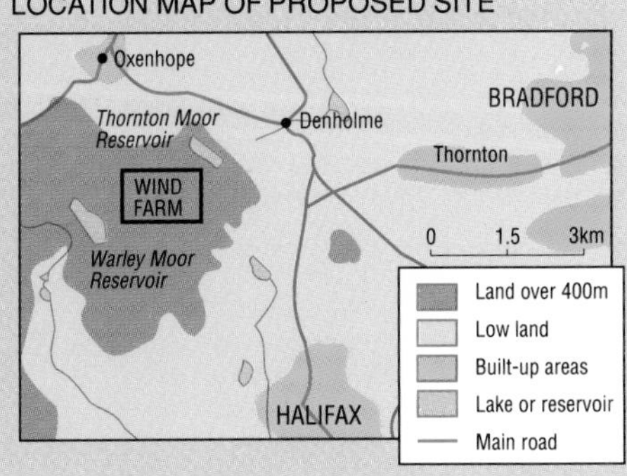

Oxenhope
Thornton Moor Reservoir
Denholme
BRADFORD
Thornton
WIND FARM
0
1.5
3km
Warley Moor Reservoir
HALIFAX
Land over 400m
Low land
Built-up areas
Lake or reservoir
Main road

FOOD AND NUTRITION

Food Supply - A Problem of Poverty

There is enough food to feed all the people in the world. Production has more than doubled since the 1950's. Yet despite this, one person in five suffers from serious hunger. Most of the victims live in developing countries. They are either unable to grow the food they need, or too poor to buy it.

Queueing for food - Ethiopian famine

Thousands of people died in the Ethiopian famine of 1984, yet there was plenty of food in the area for those who could afford it.

Who Gets the Food?

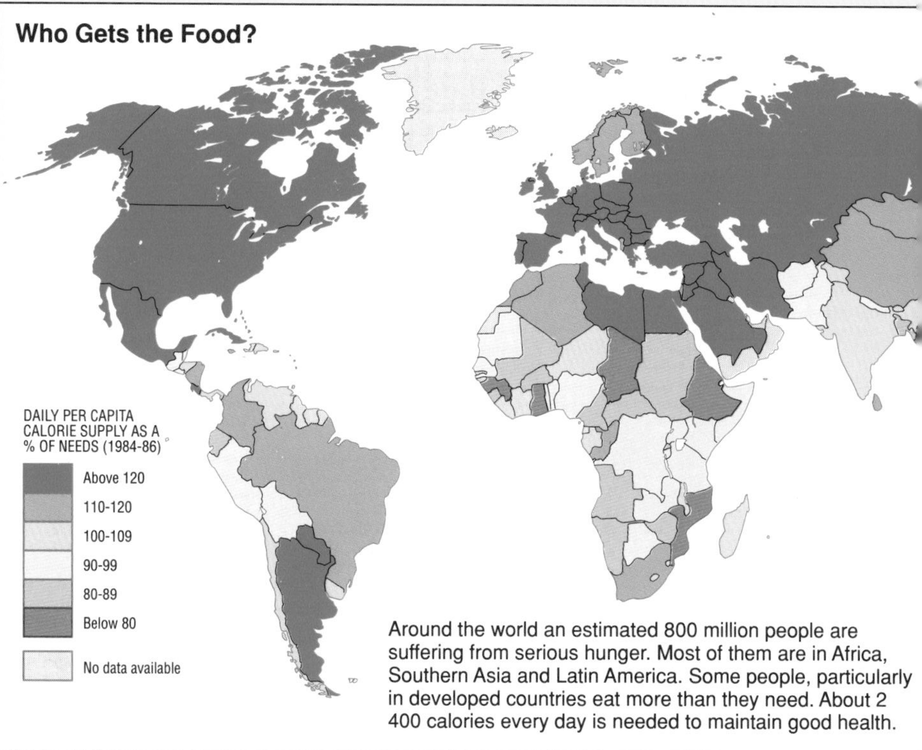
DAILY PER CAPITA CALORIE SUPPLY AS A % OF NEEDS (1984-86)
Above 120
110-120
100-109
90-99
80-89
Below 80
No data available

Around the world an estimated 800 million people are suffering from serious hunger. Most of them are in Africa, Southern Asia and Latin America. Some people, particularly in developed countries eat more than they need. About 2 400 calories every day is needed to maintain good health.

The Real Causes of Hunger

Land Ownership

Farmland is distributed very unevenly. A few rich people and transnational companies own huge tracts but millions of peasants are landless and cannot support themselves.

Subsistence farmer on poor land

Cash Crops

Some of the poorest countries in the world rely on selling cash crops, such as sugar and tea, to pay off their debts and buy machinery. These crops are grown on the best land, forcing local farmers to go elsewhere.

Natural Disasters

Natural disasters such as floods and famines seem inevitable. In fact they can be made worse by short-sighted farming and forestry policies.

Diet

More than a third of the grain in the world goes to feed animals. World hunger could be reduced immediately if some of this was fed directly to humans.

Mistaken Policies

In developing countries some governments supply city dwellers with cheap food. This keeps prices down and means that farmers have no incentive to grow more than they need for themselves.

War

War has disrupted agriculture in many parts of the developing world. The result is disasterous. Crops are left unharvested, villages abandoned and refugees flood into the cities.

Subsidies

In North America and Western Europe governments subsidise farmers. This causes surpluses, pushes prices down on world markets and forces people in poorer countries to overuse their land in order to survive. Food aid can have a similar effect. The photo below shows 'surplus' tomatoes being dumped on a farm in Italy.

Zimbabwe - Improving Food Security

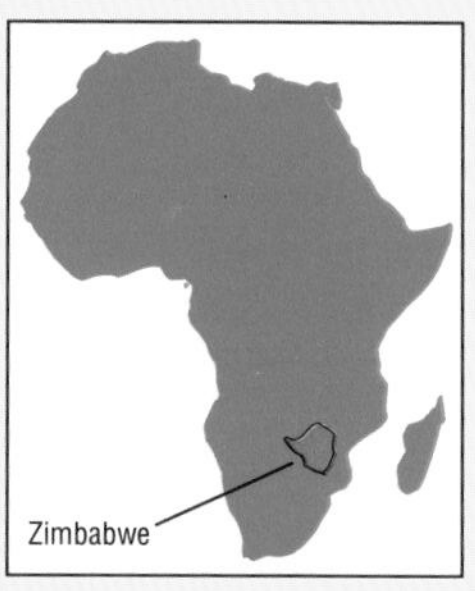
Zimbabwe

Since becoming independent in 1980, Zimbabwe has made agriculture one of its main priorities. The government has encouraged small farmers and reduced dependence on cash crops.

The measures taken include:

- redistributing land from large estates
- improving the status of women, many of whom run farms
- making more loans available
- promoting research into seeds and fertilisers
- putting up the price of crops

Advances in Agriculture

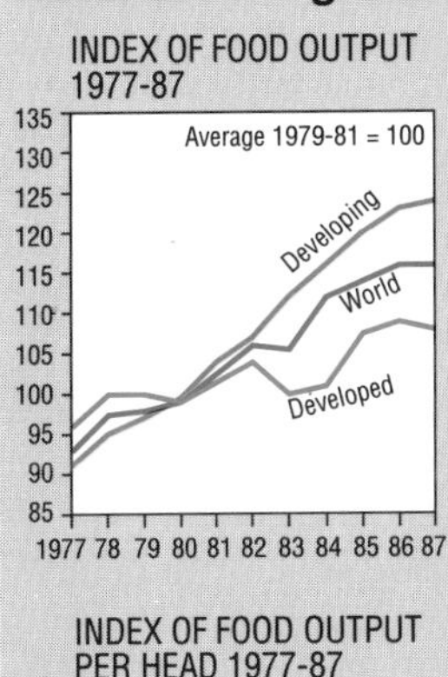
INDEX OF FOOD OUTPUT 1977-87
Average 1979-81 = 100
Developing
World
Developed
135
130
125
120
115
110
105
100
95
90
85
1977 78 79 80 81 82 83 84 85 86 87

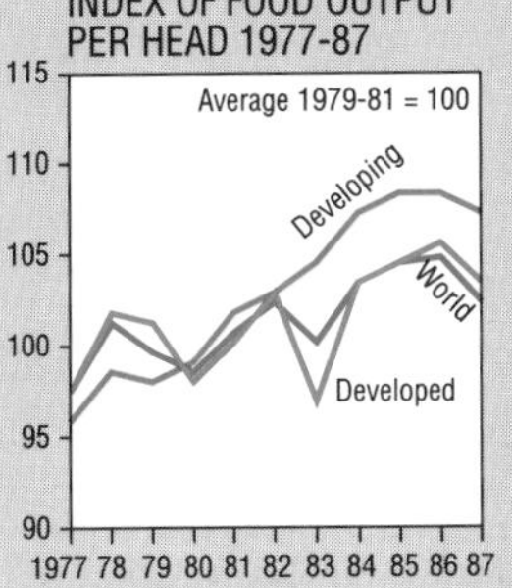
INDEX OF FOOD OUTPUT PER HEAD 1977-87
Average 1979-81 = 100
Developing
World
Developed
115
110
105
100
95
90
1977 78 79 80 81 82 83 84 85 86 87

Remarkable changes have been made in agriculture over the last fifty years. Using new seeds and fertilisers, bumper crops have been produced in many parts of the world. The most dramatic results have been in Latin America and Asia. Here many countries have doubled production of three main cereal crops - wheat, rice and maize. This is known as the Green Revolution.

The graphs to the left show how food output in developing countries has increased dramatically since 1980 compared to the developed world. In the last few years however, the increase in output has tailed off. Since 1986, it has not kept pace with population growth.

The Green Revolution has only been achieved at a cost. The new seeds are expensive and can be vulnerable to disease. Fertilisers and pesticides are also expensive and cause pollution and soil degradation. For these reasons attention is now switching to organic methods which have been used with remarkable success by the Chinese.

Under this system crop wastes are recycled, weeds are kept down by biological methods and soil is conserved through terracing and forestry. Instead of trying to control natural forces, organic farming works with them. As the environment comes under more and more pressure, this approach appears increasingly attractive.

PROBLEMS OF ADVANCED AGRICULTURE

POLLUTION • Agrochemicals reach and pollute water system
PESTICIDE POISONING • Toxins build up in wildlife feeding on sprayed crops (and accumulate up the food chain) • Farm workers may suffer effects of harmful chemicals
CONCENTRATION OF LAND OWNERSHIP • New methods are more capital intensive and suited to farming large areas - small farms lose out
DEPLETION OF GROUNDWATER STOCKS • New crop varieties require vast amounts of water for irrigation
EROSION AND DESERTIFICATION • Monoculture, deforestation, ploughing and overcropping all encourage erosion
RESEARCH BIAS • Research often funded by companies who produce and sell new hybrids and agrochemicals • Traditional crops and farming methods rarely considered
LOSS OF GENETIC DIVERSITY • Wide variety of traditional crops replaced by a few new hybrids • Increase in use of monoculture

omen working the land

his policy has proved highly successful, articularly in cereal production. While most f Africa suffers from food shortages, imbabwe has produced record harvests. Iot only is the country self sufficient, it also xports a surplus.

ROP YIELD - CEREALS

CEREALS	(a) 1964-66	1974-76	(b) 1984-86	a ›› b change
WORLD	1 549	1 952	2 552	65%
AFRICA	845	1 004	1 077	28%
ZIMBABWE	897	1 412	1 460	63%

ield in kg per hectare

Unequal Shares

In rich countries many people eat more than they need. Elsewhere people go hungry. It is one of the scandals of modern times that poor nations, where people are starving, export food to nations that have too much.

The map shows the pattern of food and trade around the world. What it doesn't show is the vast differences within countries. Some sections of the population have access to many more resources than others. Even in a poor country a few rich people live very well indeed.

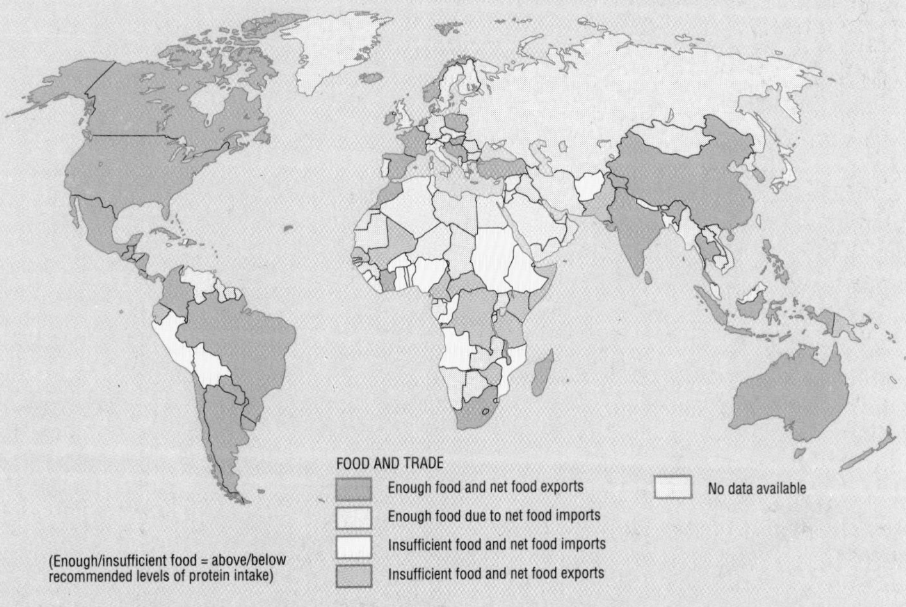
FOOD AND TRADE
Enough food and net food exports
Enough food due to net food imports
Insufficient food and net food imports
Insufficient food and net food exports
No data available
(Enough/insufficient food = above/below recommended levels of protein intake)

Improved methods of food farming are unlikely to solve the food crisis on their own. What are needed are political and economic reforms. Many developing countries are forced to sell cash crops to pay off their debts while people starve at home. Not only is this morally wrong, it is putting the environment under untold stress.

HEALTH AND DISEASE

Health for all?

We tend to take good health for granted. Yet we have only to become ill, to realise health is fundamental to our lives.
There is no simple way of measuring the health of a nation. One approach is to compare statistics. These show that in some rich countries people can expect to live nearly twice as long as in poor ones. Clearly health is very unevenly distributed around the world.

Taking and Saving Life

% of GNP spent on health and defence

0 10 20 30

Health / Defence

POOREST COUNTRIES

- MALI
- BURKINA FASO
- NEPAL
- MYANMA (BURMA)
- BANGLADESH

MODERATELY POOR COUNTRIES

- YEMEN
- BOLIVIA
- ZIMBABWE
- PARAGUAY
- THAILAND

RICH COUNTRIES

- USA
- NEW ZEALAND
- ITALY
- UNITED KINGDOM
- FINLAND

(Source : UNICEF)

0 10 20 30

Most countries spend more on their armed forces than on medical services. This suggests that they rate the protection of territory higher than the health of their inhabitants.

DEATHS FROM WANT 1945-83

1 skull represents 1 million deaths

DEATHS FROM WAR 1945-83

Two million people have died in wars since 1945. Lack of food, water and sanitation have caused nearly twenty times that number of deaths.

Diseases of the Rich and Poor

In the rich countries of the 'North' most people can expect to live to a ripe old age. The most common diseases are heart disease and cancer, often brought on by stress, lack of exercise, smoking and bad diet. In the poor countries of the 'South' people are likely to die much earlier. Lack of food (malnutrition) and dirty water are the cause of many illnesses. Children are especially vulnerable.

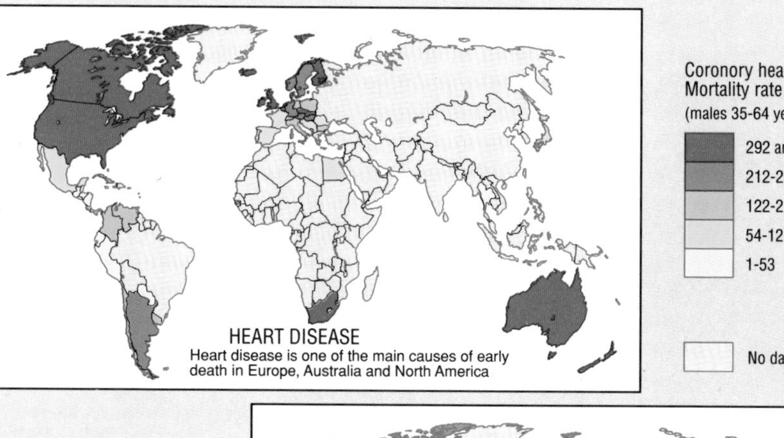

HEART DISEASE
Heart disease is one of the main causes of early death in Europe, Australia and North America

Coronory heart disease-Mortality rate per 100 000 (males 35-64 years)

- 292 and over
- 212-291
- 122-211
- 54-121
- 1-53

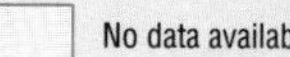

No data available

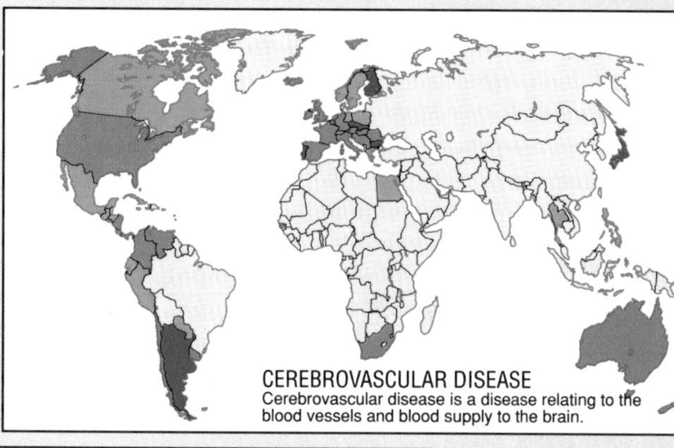

Cerebrovascular disease-Mortality rate per 100 000 (males 35-64 years)

- 105 and over
- 64-104
- 18-63

No data available

CEREBROVASCULAR DISEASE
Cerebrovascular disease is a disease relating to the blood vessels and blood supply to the brain.

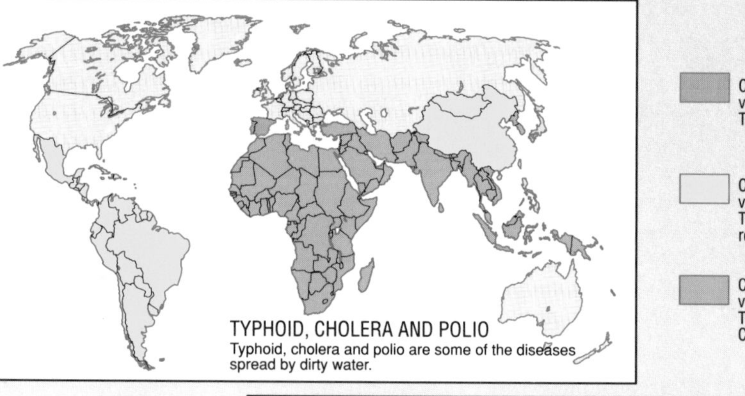

- Countries where vaccination against Typhoid recommended
- Countries where vaccination against Typhoid and Polio recommended
- Countries where vaccination against Typhoid, Polio and Cholera recommended

TYPHOID, CHOLERA AND POLIO
Typhoid, cholera and polio are some of the diseases spread by dirty water.

Based on daily per capita protein requirement (76grams)

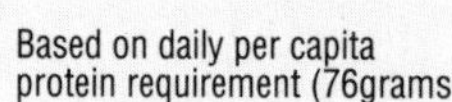

- Above recommended daily protein intake
- Below recommended daily protein intake

No data available

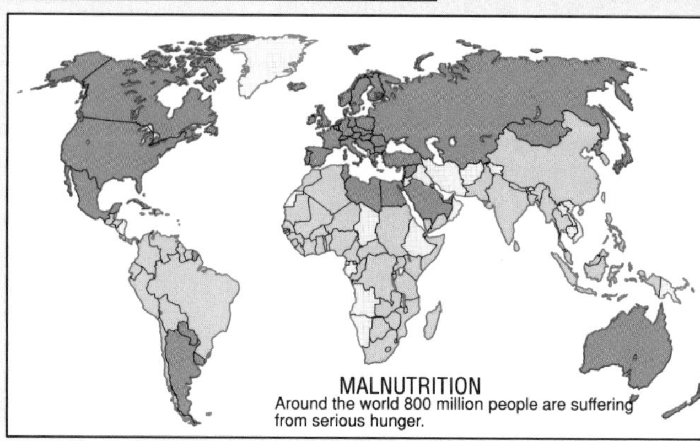

MALNUTRITION
Around the world 800 million people are suffering from serious hunger.

Malaria

Malaria is a disease caused by a parasite and is spread from person to person by a mosquito. Half the world's population is at risk from malaria and 800 million suffer from it each year. Africa and the tropics are the worst affected. Recently cases have also been reported in the eastern Mediterranean.

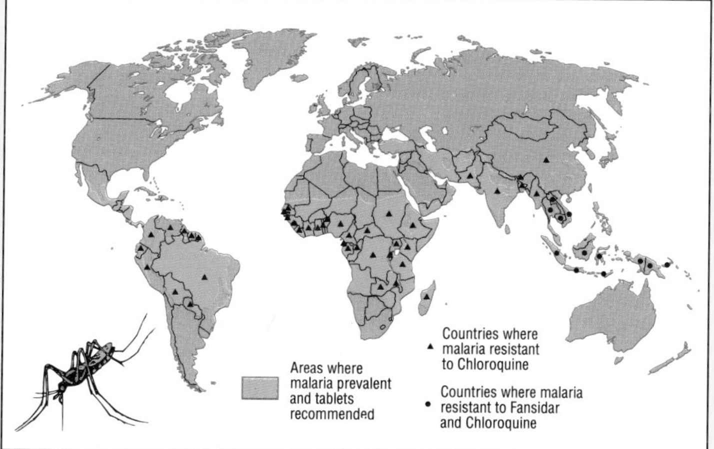

Areas where malaria prevalent and tablets recommended
▲ Countries where malaria resistant to Chloroquine
• Countries where malaria resistant to Fansidar and Chloroquine

Bilharzia

Bilharzia is an infection of the blood stream by parasites. It is carried by snails living in water and is passed to humans through dirty water. It affects 200 million people around the world sapping the energy of those who are infected.

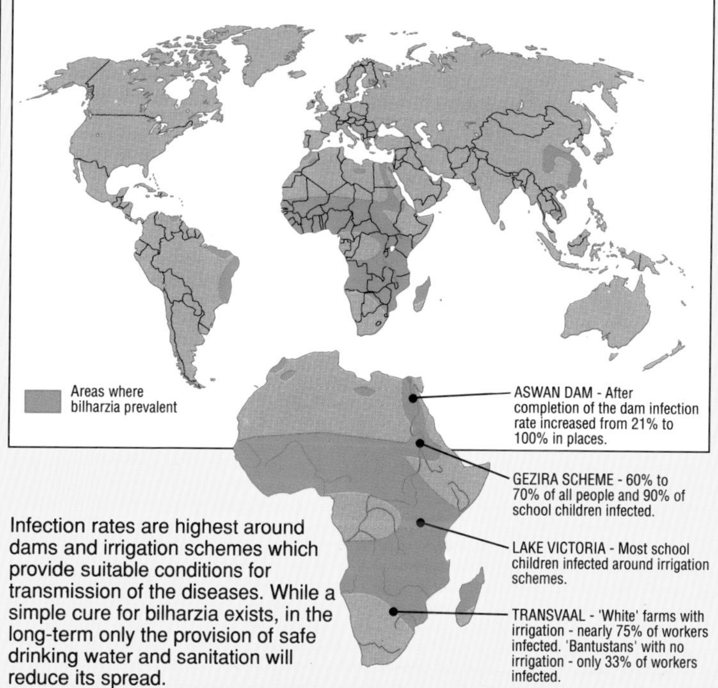

Areas where bilharzia prevalent
ASWAN DAM - After completion of the dam infection rate increased from 21% to 100% in places.
GEZIRA SCHEME - 60% to 70% of all people and 90% of school children infected.
LAKE VICTORIA - Most school children infected around irrigation schemes.
TRANSVAAL - 'White' farms with irrigation - nearly 75% of workers infected. 'Bantustans' with no irrigation - only 33% of workers infected.

Infection rates are highest around dams and irrigation schemes which provide suitable conditions for transmission of the diseases. While a simple cure for bilharzia exists, in the long-term only the provision of safe drinking water and sanitation will reduce its spread.

Health Care

It is often more effective to put money into keeping people healthy than spending it on curing diseases. In the 'North' this means getting people to changes their life styles. Smoking, over-eating and the consumption of sugar, salt, fatty foods and alcohol are the main problems. Advertising campaigns can help spread the message.

In the 'South' most diseases are spread by dirty water. Better supplies and improved sanitation could save many lives. Better education and community health workers are also very effective. As it is, most governments spend their money on hospitals, doctors and expensive drugs. The diagram below shows how this only benefits a minority of people, most of them city dwellers.

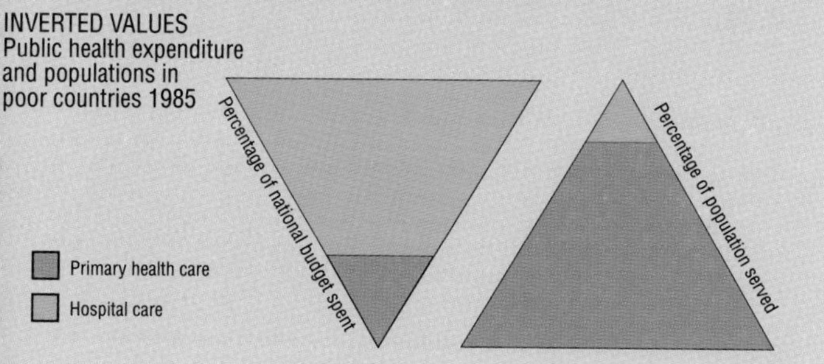

INVERTED VALUES
Public health expenditure and populations in poor countries 1985
Percentage of national budget spent
Percentage of population served
Primary health care
Hospital care

The Bilharzia Cycle

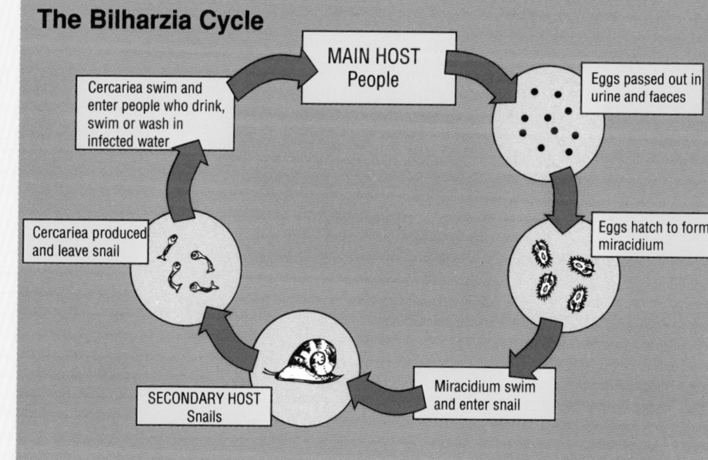

MAIN HOST
People
Eggs passed out in urine and faeces
Eggs hatch to form miracidium
Miracidium swim and enter snail
SECONDARY HOST
Snails
Cercariea produced and leave snail
Cercariea swim and enter people who drink, swim or wash in infected water

ORT

Every year five million children under the age of five die from dehydration caused by diarrhoea. A cheap and simple treatment has now been discovered which could save many of these lives. Known as Oral Rehydration Therapy (ORT), it consists of a mixture of sugar, water and salts. The challenge is to show parents how to use it. Already it may be preventing a million deaths a year.

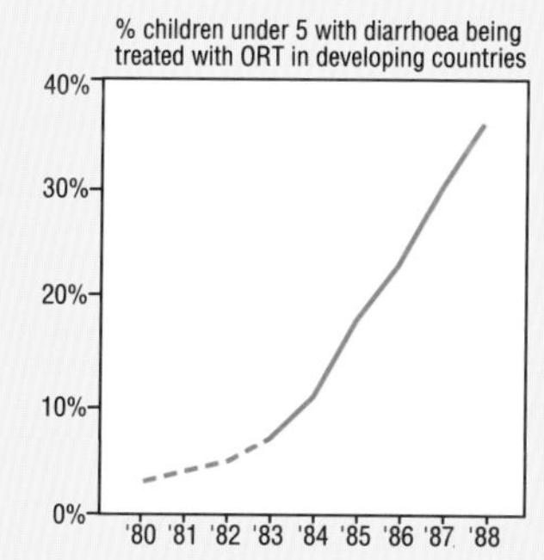

% children under 5 with diarrhoea being treated with ORT in developing countries
40%
30%
20%
10%
0%
'80 '81 '82 '83 '84 '85 '86 '87 '88

Primary Health Care

Many other diseases which affect poor countries can be treated without great expense. Immunisation, better education and simple methods of treatment could make an enormous difference. This approach, which works through the family and community, is known as primary health care.

The fight against disease

Some diseases have been eliminated. Smallpox, for example, has disappeared through vaccination. After the war great progress was made in controlling malaria. However the mosquito and bilharzia could increase if global warming is a reality.

CITIES

The Growth of Cities

Cities were first built in the Middle East about 8 000 years ago. Here, the development of settled agriculture provided enough surplus food to support an urban population.

Today cities play a crucial role in human affairs. Athens, Rome and Venice, for example are famous for their contribution to European civilisation and culture. Administration and government is also organised from cities which explains their political importance.

The largest cities have vast populations. About 18 million people live in New York and Mexico City has now almost 20 million inhabitants. By the year 2000 over half the world's population will be living in urban areas. This rapid expansion of cities in the developing world is causing a crisis.

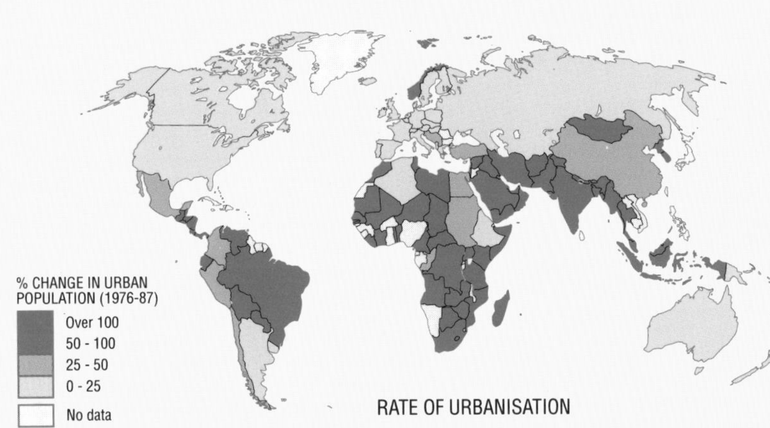

% CHANGE IN URBAN POPULATION (1976-87)
Over 100
50 - 100
25 - 50
0 - 25
No data
RATE OF URBANISATION

The World's Largest Cities

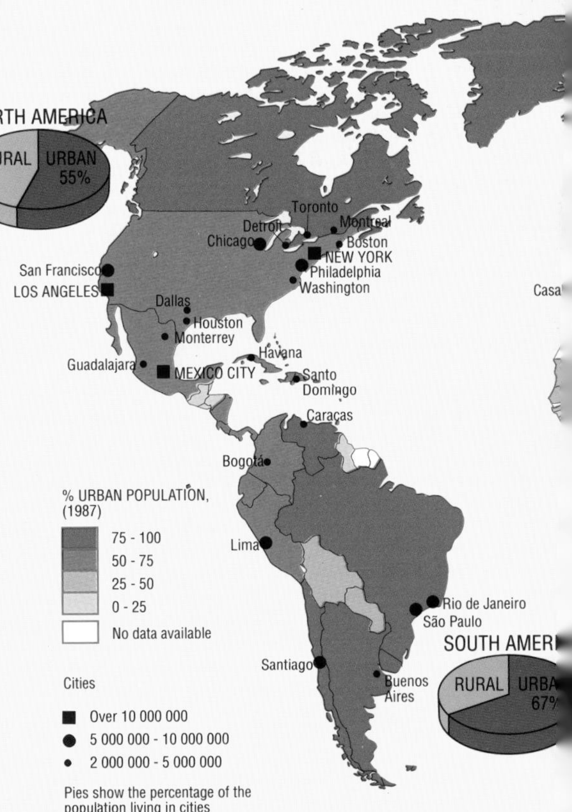

NORTH AMERICA
RURAL
URBAN 55%
Toronto
Montreal
Boston
Detroit
Chicago
NEW YORK
Philadelphia
Washington
San Francisco
LOS ANGELES
Dallas
Houston
Monterrey
Havana
Guadalajara
MEXICO CITY
Santo Domingo
Caracas
Bogotá
Lima
Rio de Janeiro
São Paulo
Santiago
Buenos Aires
SOUTH AMERI
RURAL
URBA 67%
% URBAN POPULATION, (1987)
75 - 100
50 - 75
25 - 50
0 - 25
No data available
Cities
Over 10 000 000
5 000 000 - 10 000 000
2 000 000 - 5 000 000
Pies show the percentage of the population living in cities

Planned Growth?

Developing World : Jakarta

Jakarta is one of the largest cities in the world. Almost half the population has no proper job but survives by providing services for others. This has created an underclass of people living in miserable shanties that sprawl along the surrounding roads. The population increases by a million every three years. Coping with such huge numbers is an immense challenge for the city authorities.

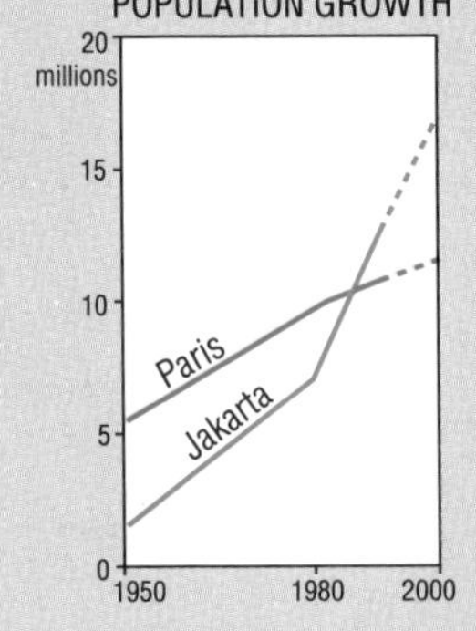

POPULATION GROWTH
20 millions
15
10
5
0
1950
1980
2000
Paris
Jakarta

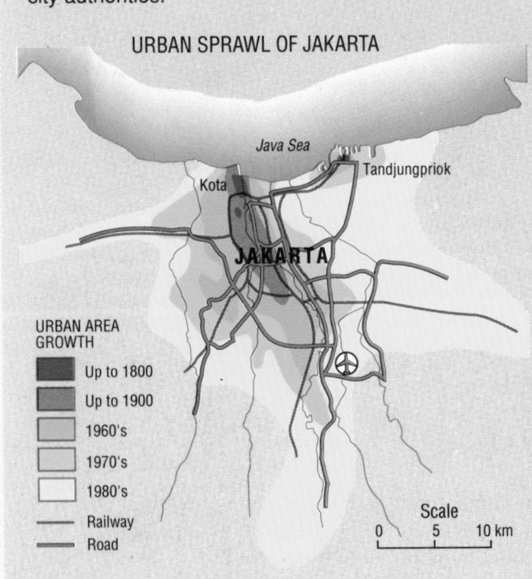

URBAN SPRAWL OF JAKARTA
Java Sea
Kota
Tandjungpriok
JAKARTA
URBAN AREA GROWTH
Up to 1800
Up to 1900
1960's
1970's
1980's
Railway
Road
Scale
0
5
10 km

Sprawling slums of suburban Jakarta

Developed World : Paris

Paris is another large city. It suffers from overcrowding, traffic congestion and poor housing. To tackle these problems, new buildings have been put up in the historic centre, satellite towns established round the edge and transport systems improved. These measures have helped to protect the city and maintain the quality of life for the people who live there.

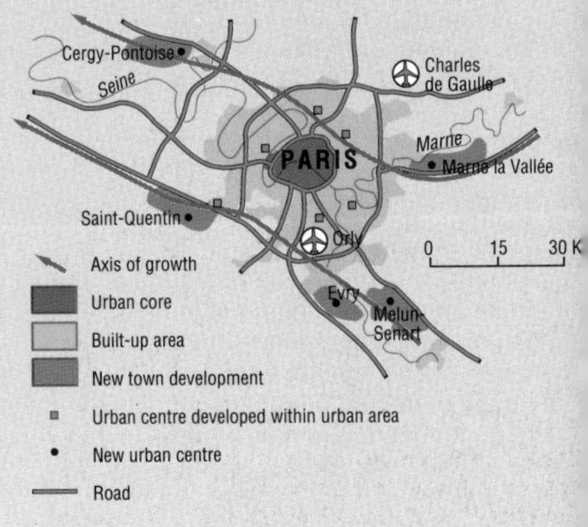

URBAN GROWTH PLAN FOR PARIS
Cergy-Pontoise
Seine
Charles de Gaulle
Marne
Marne la Vallée
PARIS
Saint-Quentin
Orly
Evry
Melun-Senart
0
15
30 K
Axis of growth
Urban core
Built-up area
New town development
Urban centre developed within urban area
New urban centre
Road

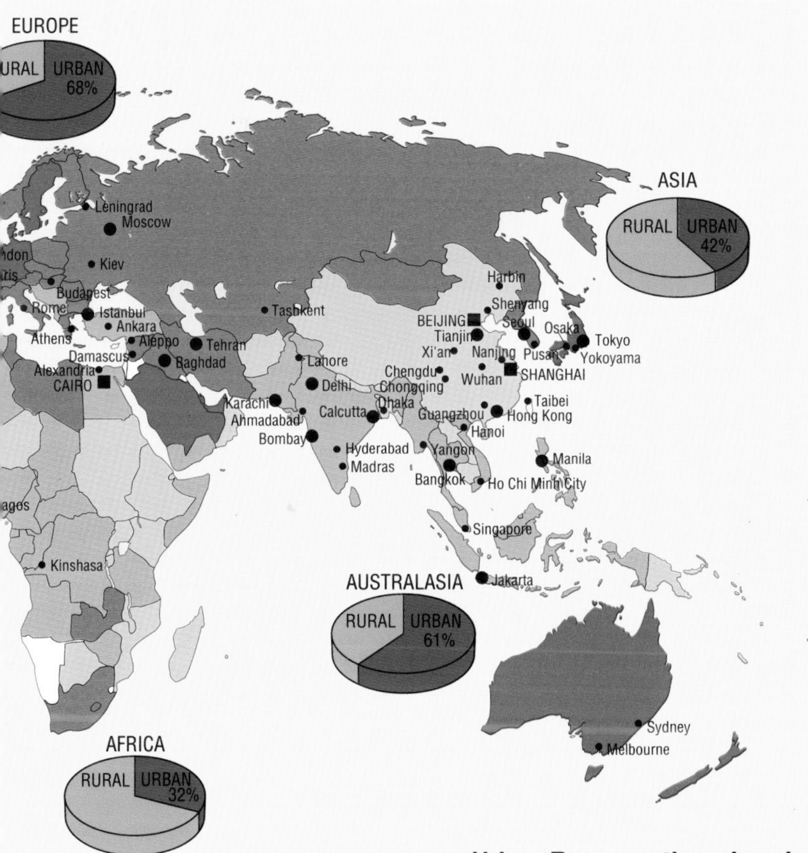
EUROPE
URAL URBAN 68%
ASIA
RURAL URBAN 42%
AUSTRALASIA
RURAL URBAN 61%
AFRICA
RURAL URBAN 32%
Leningrad
Moscow
Kiev
Budapest
Rome
Istanbul
Ankara
Athens
Aleppo
Tehran
Damascus
Baghdad
Alexandria
CAIRO
Tashkent
Lahore
Delhi
Karachi
Ahmadabad
Bombay
Calcutta
Dhaka
Hyderabad
Madras
Kinshasa
BEIJING
Tianjin
Xi'an
Chengdu
Chongqing
Nanjing
Wuhan
Harbin
Shenyang
Seoul
Pusan
Osaka
Tokyo
Yokoyama
SHANGHAI
Taibei
Guangzhou
Hong Kong
Hanoi
Yangon
Bangkok
Ho Chi Minh City
Manila
Singapore
Jakarta
Sydney
Melbourne

Why do People come to Cities?

People come to cities for a variety of reasons. Some are attracted by the bright lights, greater freedom, better living conditions and the prospect of work. Others are driven off the land by wars, famines and development schemes.

This mixture of forces, which both encourages people to move and drives them forward, is known as the 'push-pull' process. It affects almost every country in the developing world.

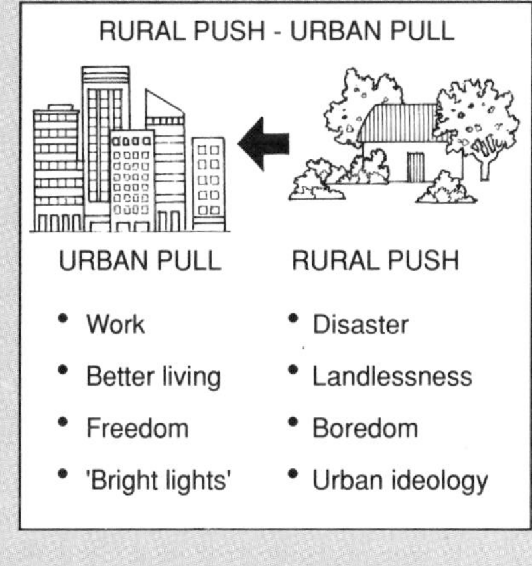
RURAL PUSH - URBAN PULL
URBAN PULL
• Work
• Better living
• Freedom
• 'Bright lights'
RURAL PUSH
• Disaster
• Landlessness
• Boredom
• Urban ideology

Urban Problems

Since 1950 the number of people living in cities has almost tripled.

Housing
All big cities have homeless people. In the developing world over half the city dwellers live in shanties where dirty water and poor sanitation cause disease. A quarter of all slum children die before the age of five.

Transport
Cities are busy, congested places and it is difficult to get about. In Athens traffic fumes are eating away the historic buildings.

Waste
New York produces so much garbage it has run out of places to dispose of it. Human sewage has helped make the Mediterranean the dirtiest sea in the world.

Resources
As they grow, cities cover valuable farmland, and make huge demands on the surrounding countryside for food, water and energy. Due to the shortage of firewood, Delhi is supplied from forests 700 km away.

Welfare
Overcrowding, noise and stress can have an adverse effect on the health of city dwellers. Levels of violent crime also tend to be higher.

Careful planning can help to provide better housing and services for city dwellers. Governments around the world could take a lead in tackling these issues.

Urban Regeneration : London Docklands

The London Docklands stretch down the Thames from Tower Bridge. A large community depended on the docks, but during the 1960's trade began to decline. This was due, to some extent to changing patterns of trade, larger ships, labour disputes, and poor management. By 1981 all the docks had closed.

People had different ideas about what to do. One suggestion was to try and halt the job losses. The alternative, adopted by the government, was to attract new companies to the area. An airport and light railway to the centre of London were built to encourage them.

The population of the area has now begun to increase. Fifteen thousand new homes have been built and a major office centre opened at Canary Wharfe. This may benefit newcomers but local people question if it has helped the old community.

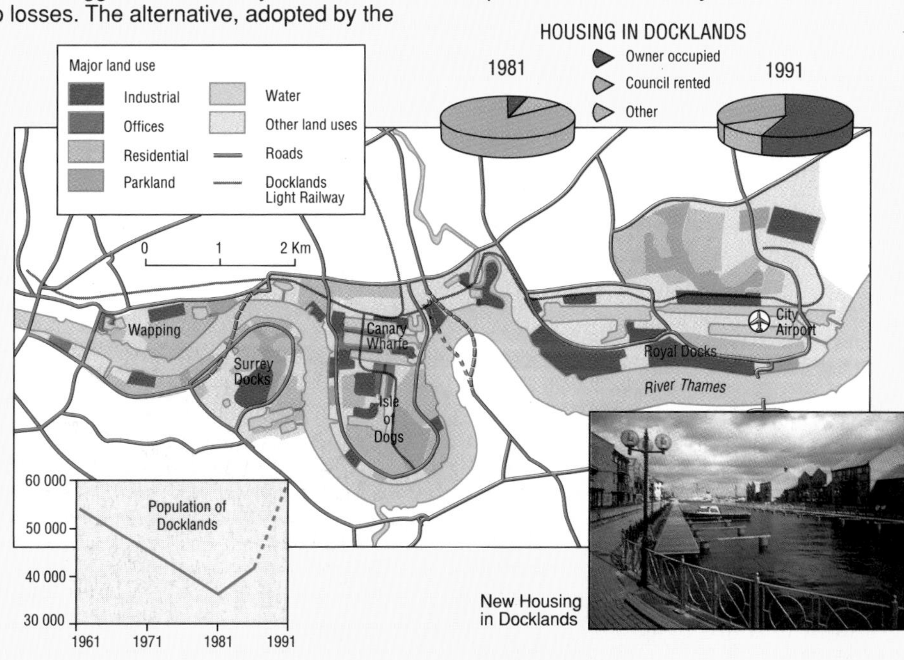
HOUSING IN DOCKLANDS
1981
1991
Owner occupied
Council rented
Other
Major land use
Industrial
Offices
Residential
Parkland
Water
Other land uses
Roads
Docklands Light Railway
0
1
2 Km
Wapping
Surrey Docks
Canary Wharfe
Isle of Dogs
Royal Docks
City Airport
River Thames
Population of Docklands
60 000
50 000
40 000
30 000
1961
1971
1981
1991

New Housing in Docklands

HEALING THE WOUNDS

Environmental problems are often complex and interconnected. Deforestation in the Himalayas, for example, is contributing to flooding in Bangladesh; pollution from factories in north west Europe is threatening fish stocks in the North Sea, and the debt crisis is forcing many developing countries to overuse their farmland.

Natural processes usually follow predictable patterns, but on occasions extreme events such as droughts, floods and earthquakes can pose a major threat in certain parts of the world. Often human activity has tended to exacerbate these natural hazards. Deforestation and overgrazing, for example, makes fragile environments even more vulnerable.

Economic activity has had a major impact on the environment, especially in the last fifty years. It is largely responsible for land, air and sea pollution and this is leading to widespread environmental degradation. The accumulation of pollutants is now reaching crisis proportions, and the nuclear accident at Chernobyl illustrated how a single incident can affect an entire continent. It is clear that major problems such as acid rain and global warming can only be solved by international action.

As world population has grown and living standards improve, there has been an increasing demand for raw materials. Yet the earth's resources are finite and need to be carefully conserved. One solution is to make use of sustainable sources such as renewable energy. Another is to recycle waste and use material more economically.

Concern has also been focused on contrasts in human welfare. In developing countries large numbers of people are trapped by poverty. Bad housing, lack of food, poor education and disease create a cycle of deprivation. Not only is this indefensible on humanitarian grounds, it is also putting the environment under unnecessary stress.

The world is undergoing an urban revolution, and everywhere people are moving into cities. The sheer pressure of numbers is threatening to swamp improvements in living conditions, and as populations continue to grow the difficulties increase. Development could help to alleviate these problems. However, the present pattern of world trade favours a few rich nations at the expense of the rest. A fairer world would be better for us all.

The environment crisis is a pressing concern. We need to ensure that economic growth is based on sustainable technologies. We need to address the problem of poverty and give genuine respect to human rights. The earth is the only home we have. Either we look after it properly, or we risk setting in motion a train of events that we will be unable to control.

WORLD ATLAS

SYMBOLS

Relief

Land contour
▲ 8848 Spot height (metres)
Pass
Permanent ice cap

Feet	Relief	Metres
16404		5000
9843		3000
6562		2000
3281		1000
1640		500
656		200
0	Land Dep.	Sea Level
656		200
13123		4000
22966		7000

Hydrography

Submarine contour
▼11034 Ocean depth (metres)
(217) Lake level (metres)
Reef
River
Intermittent river
Falls
Dam
Gorge
Canal
Lake/Reservoir
Intermittent lake
Marsh/Swamp

Communications

Tunnel Main railway
Main airport
Track

Road representation varies with the scale category.

Principal road	1:1M-1:2½M
Other main road	1:1M-1:2½M
Principal road	1:2½M-1:7½M
Other main road	1:2½M-1:7½M
Principal road	1:7½M or smaller

Administration

International boundary
Undefined/Disputed international boundary
Internal division : First order
Internal division : Second order
National capitals

Settlement

Each settlement is given a town stamp according to its relative importance and scale category.

1:1M-1:2½M	1:2½M-1:7½M	1:7½M or smaller
Major City	Major City	Major City
City	City	City
Large Town	Large Town	Large Town
Town	Town	Town
Small Town	Small Town	–
Village	–	–

Urban area (1:1M-1:2½M only)

The size of type used for each settlement is graded to correspond with the appropriate town stamp.

Other features

Ancient monument
Oasis
National Park
Oil field
Gas field
Oil/Gas pipeline

Lettering

Various styles of lettering are used-each one representing a different type of feature.

ALPS	Physical feature	KENYA	Country name
Red Sea	Hydrographic feature	IOWA	Internal division
Paris	Settlement name	*(Fr.)*	Territorial administration

THE WORLD : Political

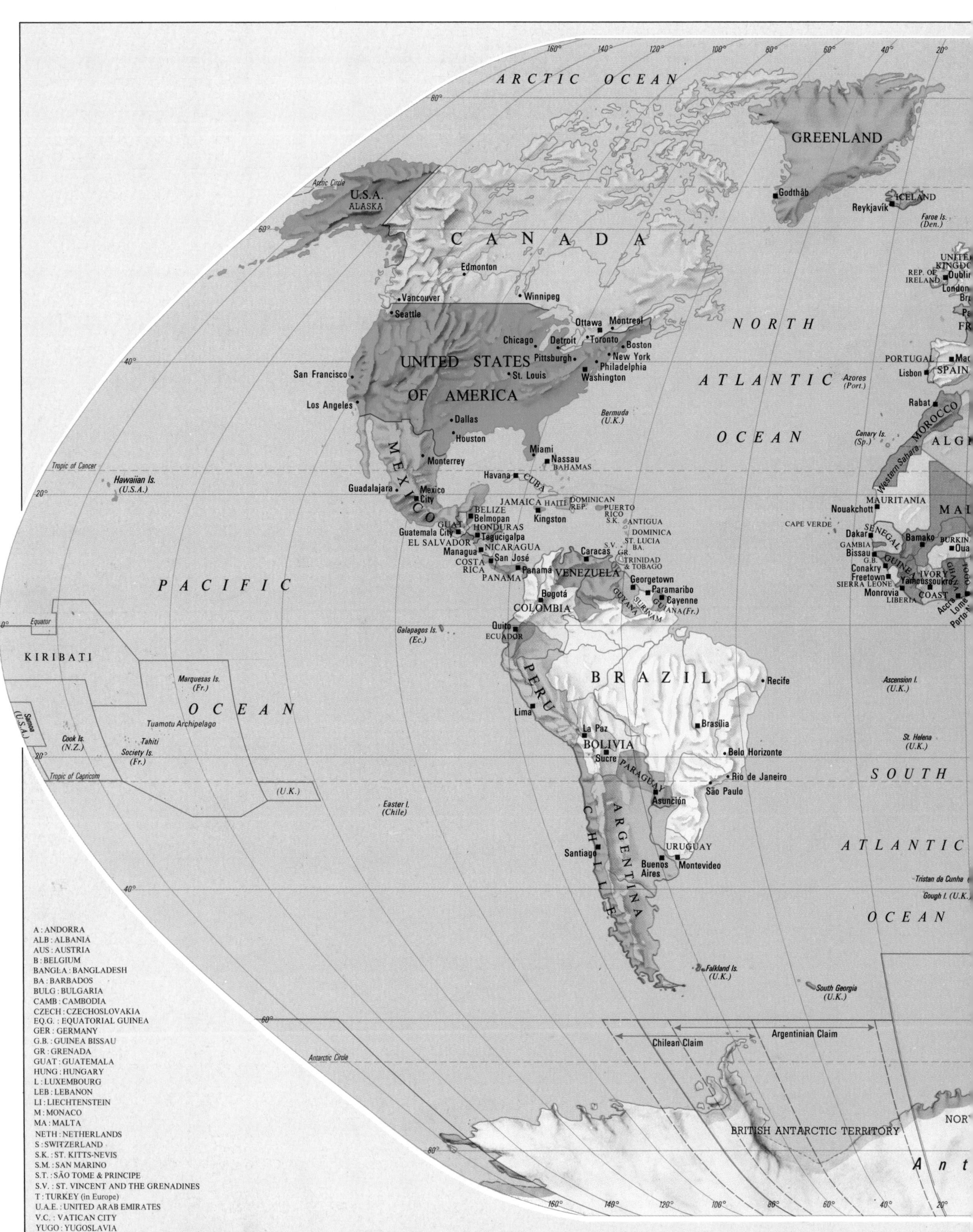

ARCTIC OCEAN
GREENLAND
Godthåb
ICELAND
Reykjavík
Faroe Is. (Den.)
Arctic Circle
U.S.A.
ALASKA
CANADA
Edmonton
Winnipeg
Vancouver
Seattle
Ottawa
Montreal
Toronto
Chicago
Detroit
Boston
Pittsburgh
New York
Philadelphia
Washington
St. Louis
UNITED STATES OF AMERICA
San Francisco
Los Angeles
Dallas
Houston
Miami
Nassau
BAHAMAS
Bermuda (U.K.)
NORTH ATLANTIC OCEAN
Azores (Port.)
REP. OF IRELAND
PORTUGAL
Lisbon
SPAIN
Rabat
MOROCCO
Canary Is. (Sp.)
Western Sahara
MAURITANIA
Nouakchott
CAPE VERDE
Dakar
SENEGAL
GAMBIA
Bamako
Bissau
G.B.
GUINEA
Conakry
Freetown
SIERRA LEONE
Monrovia
LIBERIA
IVORY COAST
Yamoussoukro
GHANA
Accra
Lomé
Porto-Novo
Tropic of Cancer
Hawaiian Is. (U.S.A.)
MEXICO
Monterrey
Guadalajara
Mexico City
Havana
CUBA
JAMAICA
HAITI
DOMINICAN REP.
PUERTO RICO
Kingston
S.K.
ANTIGUA
DOMINICA
ST. LUCIA
S.V.
BA.
GR.
TRINIDAD & TOBAGO
BELIZE
Belmopan
GUAT.
Guatemala City
HONDURAS
Tegucigalpa
EL SALVADOR
NICARAGUA
Managua
COSTA RICA
San José
PANAMA
Panamá
Caracas
VENEZUELA
Georgetown
Paramaribo
Cayenne
GUYANA
SURINAM
GUIANA (Fr.)
Bogotá
COLOMBIA
Quito
ECUADOR
Galapagos Is. (Ec.)
PACIFIC OCEAN
Equator
KIRIBATI
Marquesas Is. (Fr.)
Tuamotu Archipelago
Samoa (U.S.A.)
Cook Is. (N.Z.)
Tahiti
Society Is. (Fr.)
Tropic of Capricorn
(U.K.)
Easter I. (Chile)
BRAZIL
Recife
PERU
Lima
La Paz
BOLIVIA
Sucre
Brasília
Belo Horizonte
Rio de Janeiro
São Paulo
PARAGUAY
Asunción
CHILE
ARGENTINA
Santiago
URUGUAY
Buenos Aires
Montevideo
Ascension I. (U.K.)
St. Helena (U.K.)
SOUTH ATLANTIC OCEAN
Tristan da Cunha
Gough I. (U.K.)
Falkland Is. (U.K.)
South Georgia (U.K.)
Chilean Claim
Argentinian Claim
Antarctic Circle
BRITISH ANTARCTIC TERRITORY
160°
140°
120°
100°
80°
60°
40°
20°
0°
A : ANDORRA
ALB : ALBANIA
AUS : AUSTRIA
B : BELGIUM
BANGLA : BANGLADESH
BA : BARBADOS
BULG : BULGARIA
CAMB : CAMBODIA
CZECH : CZECHOSLOVAKIA
EQ.G. : EQUATORIAL GUINEA
GER : GERMANY
G.B. : GUINEA BISSAU
GR : GRENADA
GUAT : GUATEMALA
HUNG : HUNGARY
L : LUXEMBOURG
LEB : LEBANON
LI : LIECHTENSTEIN
M : MONACO
MA : MALTA
NETH : NETHERLANDS
S : SWITZERLAND
S.K. : ST. KITTS-NEVIS
S.M. : SAN MARINO
S.T. : SÃO TOME & PRINCIPE
S.V. : ST. VINCENT AND THE GRENADINES
T : TURKEY (in Europe)
U.A.E. : UNITED ARAB EMIRATES
V.C. : VATICAN CITY
YUGO : YUGOSLAVIA

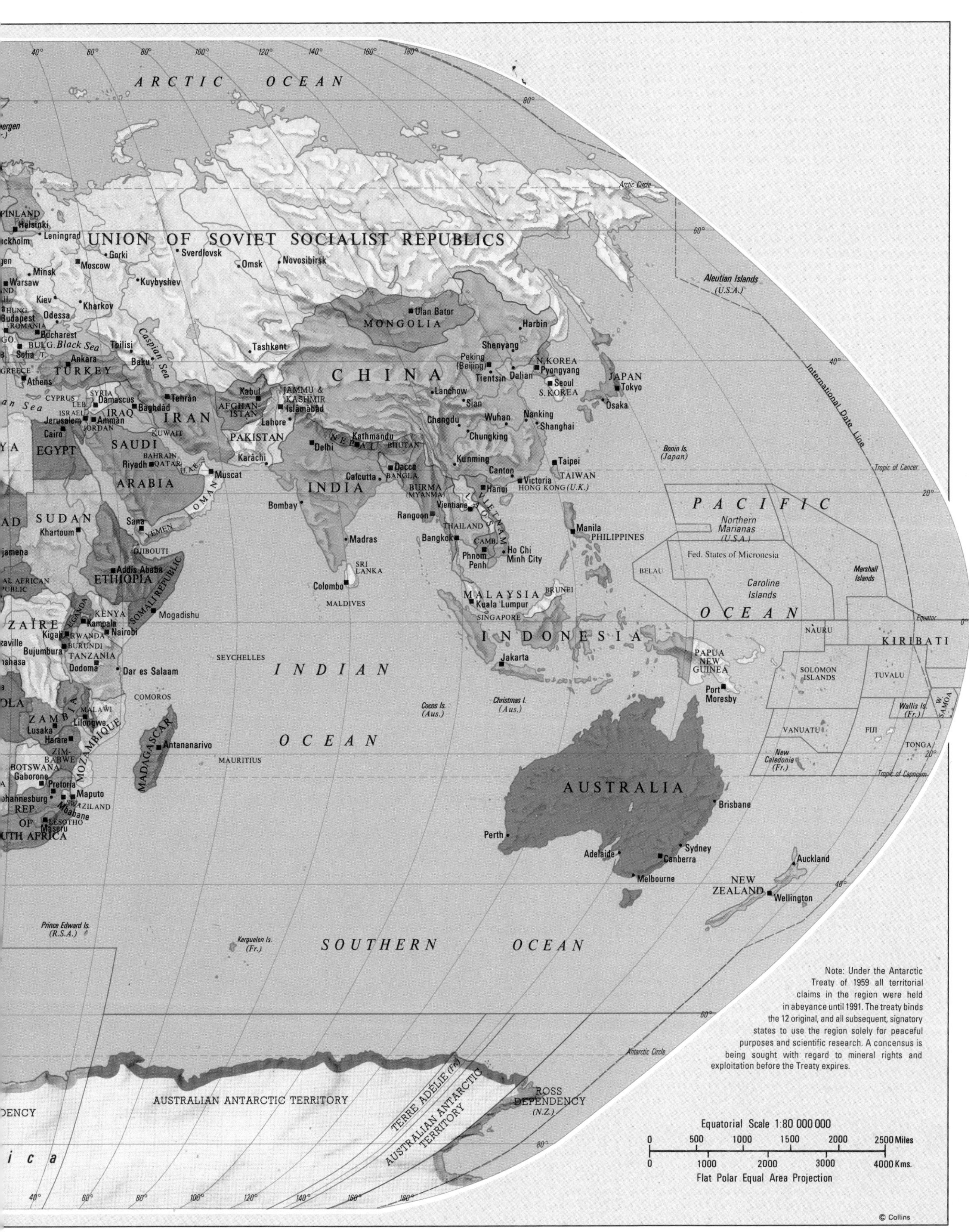

ARCTIC OCEAN
UNION OF SOVIET SOCIALIST REPUBLICS
FINLAND
Helsinki
Leningrad
Gorki
Sverdlovsk
Moscow
Omsk
Novosibirsk
Minsk
Warsaw
Kuybyshev
Kiev
Kharkov
Budapest
Odessa
ROMANIA
Bucharest
BULG.
Black Sea
Sofia
Tbilisi
Caspian Sea
Tashkent
Baku
GREECE
Athens
TURKEY
Ankara
CYPRUS
SYRIA
Damascus
LEB.
ISRAEL
Jerusalem
Amman
JORDAN
Baghdad
IRAQ
Tehran
IRAN
Kabul
AFGHANISTAN
JAMMU & KASHMIR
Islamabad
Lahore
PAKISTAN
Karachi
Cairo
EGYPT
KUWAIT
SAUDI ARABIA
BAHRAIN
QATAR
Riyadh
U.A.E.
Muscat
OMAN
YEMEN
Sana
SUDAN
Khartoum
DJIBOUTI
Addis Ababa
ETHIOPIA
SOMALI REPUBLIC
Mogadishu
KENYA
Nairobi
UGANDA
Kampala
ZAÏRE
Kigali
RWANDA
BURUNDI
Bujumbura
TANZANIA
Dodoma
Dar es Salaam
SEYCHELLES
COMOROS
MALAWI
Lilongwe
ZAMBIA
Lusaka
Harare
ZIMBABWE
MOZAMBIQUE
MADAGASCAR
Antananarivo
MAURITIUS
BOTSWANA
Gaborone
Pretoria
Maputo
Johannesburg
SWAZILAND
Mbabane
LESOTHO
Maseru
REP. OF SOUTH AFRICA
Prince Edward Is. (R.S.A.)
MONGOLIA
Ulan Bator
Harbin
Shenyang
Peking (Beijing)
Tientsin
Dalian
N. KOREA
Pyongyang
Seoul
S. KOREA
JAPAN
Tokyo
Osaka
CHINA
Lanchow
Sian
Chengdu
Wuhan
Nanking
Shanghai
Chungking
Kunming
Canton
Victoria
HONG KONG (U.K.)
Taipei
TAIWAN
NEPAL
Kathmandu
BHUTAN
Delhi
INDIA
Calcutta
Dacca
BANGLA.
BURMA (MYANMA)
Hanoi
Vientiane
LAOS
VIETNAM
Rangoon
THAILAND
Bangkok
CAMB.
Phnom Penh
Ho Chi Minh City
Bombay
Madras
SRI LANKA
Colombo
MALDIVES
Manila
PHILIPPINES
MALAYSIA
Kuala Lumpur
BRUNEI
SINGAPORE
INDONESIA
Jakarta
INDIAN OCEAN
Cocos Is. (Aus.)
Christmas I. (Aus.)
Kerguelen Is. (Fr.)
Aleutian Islands (U.S.A.)
International Date Line
Bonin Is. (Japan)
PACIFIC OCEAN
Northern Marianas (U.S.A.)
Fed. States of Micronesia
BELAU
Marshall Islands
Caroline Islands
NAURU
KIRIBATI
PAPUA NEW GUINEA
Port Moresby
SOLOMON ISLANDS
TUVALU
W. SAMOA
Wallis Is. (Fr.)
VANUATU
FIJI
TONGA
New Caledonia (Fr.)
AUSTRALIA
Brisbane
Perth
Sydney
Adelaide
Canberra
Melbourne
Auckland
NEW ZEALAND
Wellington
SOUTHERN OCEAN
Arctic Circle
Tropic of Cancer
Equator
Tropic of Capricorn
Antarctic Circle
AUSTRALIAN ANTARCTIC TERRITORY
TERRE ADÉLIE (Fr.)
ROSS DEPENDENCY (N.Z.)
Note: Under the Antarctic Treaty of 1959 all territorial claims in the region were held in abeyance until 1991. The treaty binds the 12 original, and all subsequent, signatory states to use the region solely for peaceful purposes and scientific research. A concensus is being sought with regard to mineral rights and exploitation before the Treaty expires.
Equatorial Scale 1:80 000 000
0 500 1000 1500 2000 2500 Miles
0 1000 2000 3000 4000 Kms.
Flat Polar Equal Area Projection
© Collins

THE WORLD : Physical

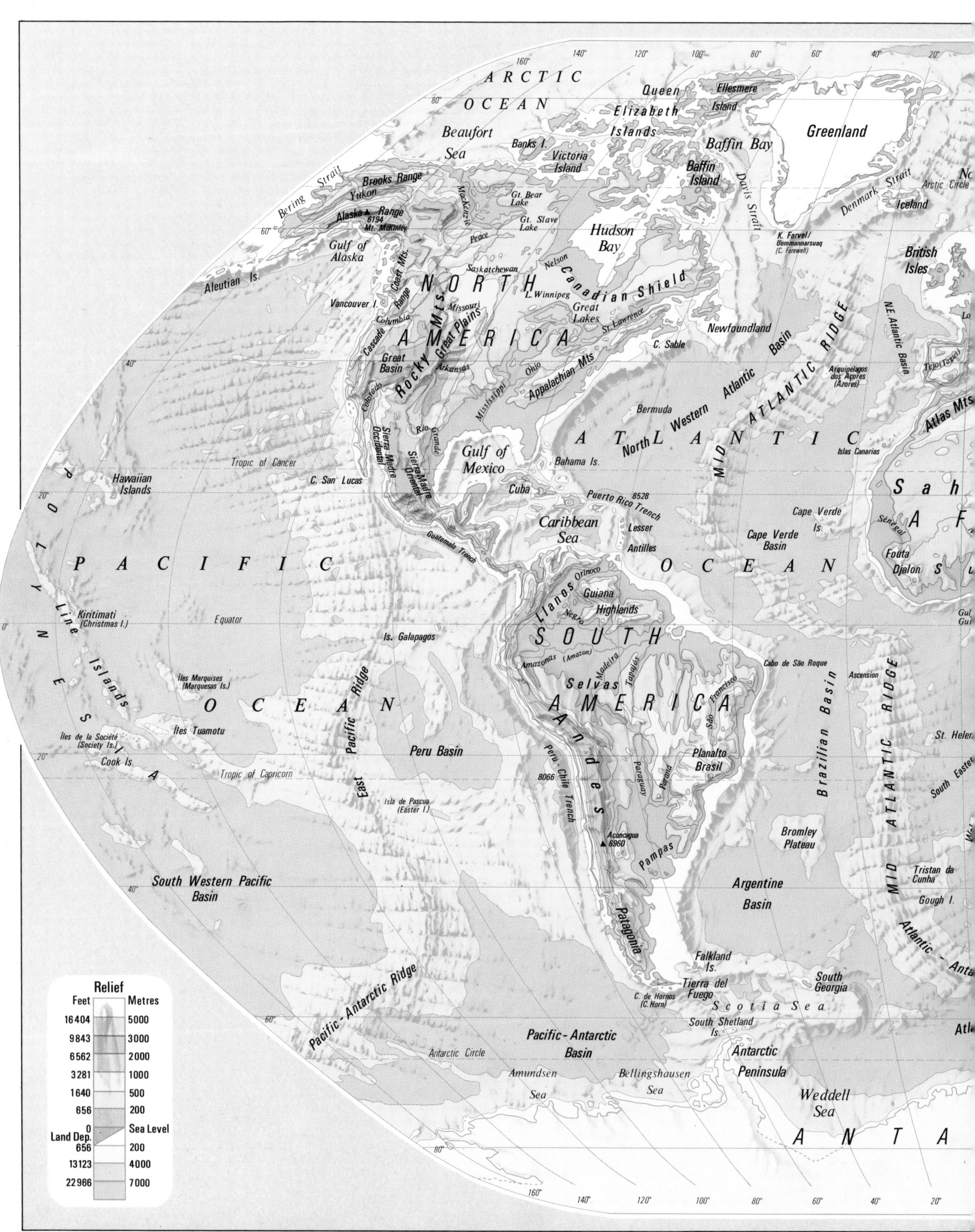

ARCTIC OCEAN
Beaufort Sea
Banks I.
Victoria Island
Queen Elizabeth Islands
Ellesmere Island
Greenland
Baffin Bay
Baffin Island
Davis Strait
Denmark Strait
Iceland
Arctic Circle
Bering Strait
Brooks Range
Yukon
Alaska Range
6194 Mt. McKinley
Mackenzie
Gt. Bear Lake
Gt. Slave Lake
Hudson Bay
K. Farvel/ Uummannarsuaq (C. Farewell)
Gulf of Alaska
Peace
Saskatchewan
Nelson
Canadian Shield
Aleutian Is.
Coast Mts.
Vancouver I.
NORTH AMERICA
L. Winnipeg
Great Lakes
St. Lawrence
Missouri
Columbia
Cascade Range
Great Plains
Rocky Mts.
Great Basin
Arkansas
Ohio
Appalachian Mts
Mississippi
Colorado
Newfoundland
C. Sable
British Isles
N.E. Atlantic Basin
Tejo (Tagus)
Arquipélagos dos Açores (Azores)
Atlas Mts
Bermuda
North Western Atlantic Basin
MID ATLANTIC RIDGE
NORTH ATLANTIC OCEAN
Islas Canarias
Sierra Madre Occidental
Sierra Madre Oriental
Rio Grande
Gulf of Mexico
Bahama Is.
Tropic of Cancer
C. San Lucas
Hawaiian Islands
Cuba
8528 Puerto Rico Trench
Caribbean Sea
Lesser Antilles
Cape Verde Is.
Cape Verde Basin
Sénégal
Fouta Djalon
Guatemala Trench
PACIFIC OCEAN
POLYNESIA
Orinoco
Llanos
Guiana Highlands
Negro
Kiritimati (Christmas I.)
Line Islands
Equator
Is. Galapagos
SOUTH AMERICA
Amazonas (Amazon)
Madeira
Tapajós
Selvas
Cabo de São Roque
Ascension
Îles Marquises (Marquesas Is.)
Pacific Ridge
São Francisco
Îles Tuamotu
Îles de la Société (Society Is.)
Cook Is.
Peru Basin
Andes
Planalto Brasil
Brazilian Basin
St. Helena
Tropic of Capricorn
East Pacific Ridge
8066 Peru-Chile Trench
Paraguay
Paraná
Isla de Pascua (Easter I.)
Aconcagua 6960
Pampas
Bromley Plateau
Tristan da Cunha
Gough I.
South Western Pacific Basin
Argentine Basin
Patagonia
Falkland Is.
Tierra del Fuego
C. de Hornos (C. Horn)
South Georgia
Scotia Sea
Pacific-Antarctic Ridge
South Shetland Is.
Pacific-Antarctic Basin
Antarctic Circle
Antarctic Peninsula
Amundsen Sea
Bellingshausen Sea
Weddell Sea
ANTA
Relief
Feet
Metres
16404 5000
9843 3000
6562 2000
3281 1000
1640 500
656 200
0 Sea Level
Land Dep.
656 200
13123 4000
22966 7000

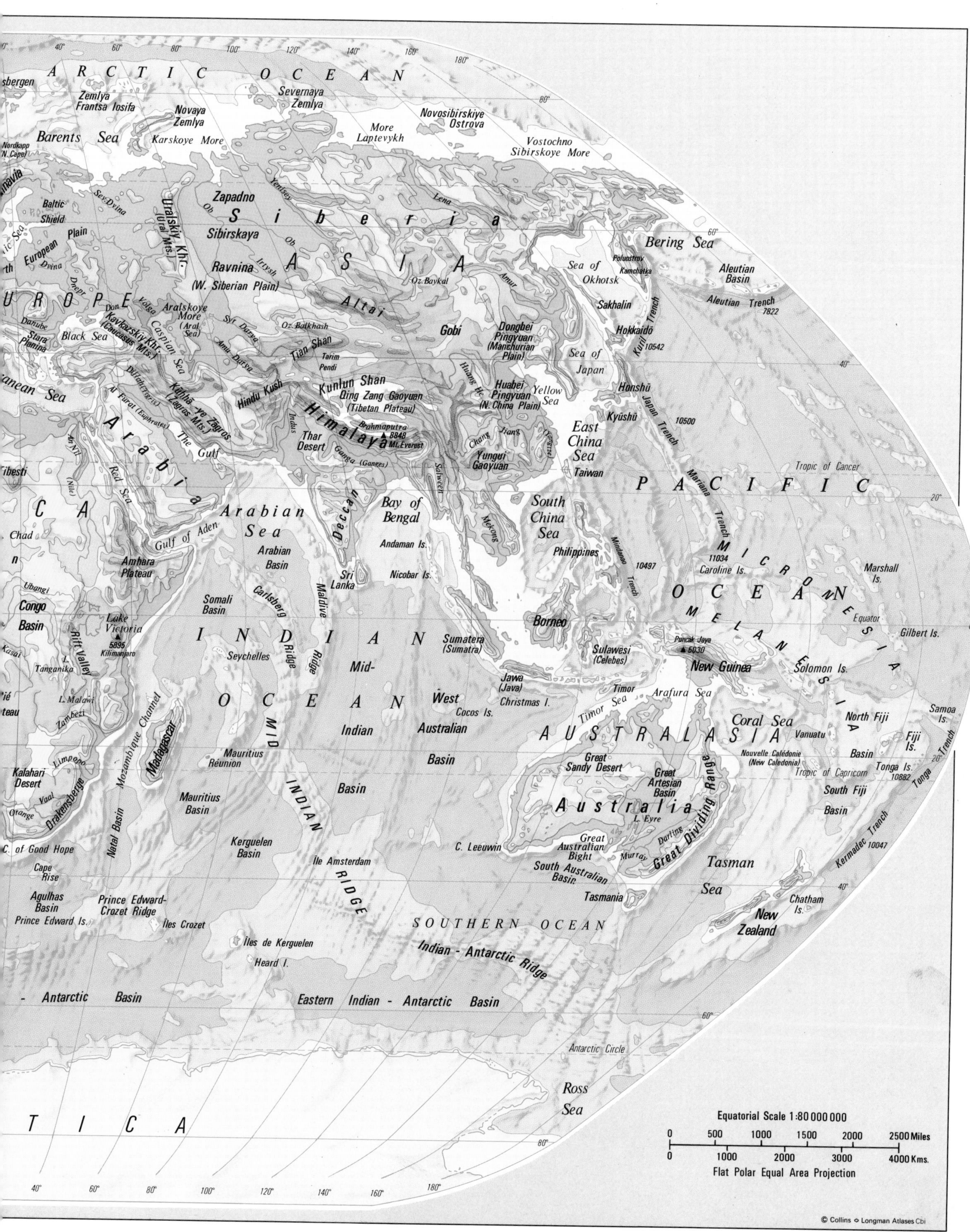
ARCTIC OCEAN
Severnaya Zemlya
Zemlya Frantsa Iosifa
Novaya Zemlya
Novosibirskiye Ostrova
Barents Sea
Karskoye More
More Laptevykh
Vostochno Sibirskoye More
Baltic Shield
European Plain
Zapadno Sibirskaya Ravnina (W. Siberian Plain)
Siberia
Uralskiy Khr. (Ural Mts.)
ASIA
EUROPE
Bering Sea
Sea of Okhotsk
Aleutian Basin
Aleutian Trench
Sakhalin
Hokkaidō
Kuril Trench
Altai
Gobi
Dongbei Pingyuan (Manchurian Plain)
Sea of Japan
Aralskoye More (Aral Sea)
Caspian Sea
Black Sea
Kavkazskiy Khr. (Caucasus Mts.)
Tian Shan
Oz. Balkhash
Oz. Baykal
Hindu Kush
Kunlun Shan
Qing Zang Gaoyuan (Tibetan Plateau)
Himalaya
Mt. Everest
Huabei Pingyuan (N. China Plain)
Yellow Sea
Honshū
Kyūshū
Japan Trench
East China Sea
Mediterranean Sea
Kūhhā-ye Zāgros (Zagros Mts.)
The Gulf
Arabia
Thar Desert
Yungui Gaoyuan
Taiwan
PACIFIC
Red Sea
Arabian Sea
Deccan
Bay of Bengal
South China Sea
Mariana Trench
Gulf of Aden
Amhara Plateau
Arabian Basin
Andaman Is.
Philippines
MICRONESIA
Caroline Is.
Marshall Is.
Sri Lanka
Nicobar Is.
Somali Basin
Carlsberg Ridge
Maldive Ridge
OCEANIA
MELANESIA
Congo Basin
Lake Victoria
Kilimanjaro
Rift Valley
Borneo
Gilbert Is.
INDIAN
Sumatera (Sumatra)
Sulawesi (Celebes)
Puncak Jaya
New Guinea
Solomon Is.
Seychelles
Mid-
Jawa (Java)
Timor
Arafura Sea
OCEAN
West
Cocos Is.
Christmas I.
Timor Sea
Coral Sea
North Fiji
Samoa Is.
Mozambique Channel
Madagascar
Indian
Australian
AUSTRALASIA
Vanuatu
Fiji Is.
Mauritius
Réunion
Basin
Great Sandy Desert
Great Artesian Basin
Nouvelle Calédonie (New Caledonia)
Tropic of Capricorn
Tonga Is.
Tonga Trench
Kalahari Desert
Drakensberge
Mauritius Basin
MID INDIAN RIDGE
Australia
L. Eyre
Great Dividing Range
South Fiji Basin
Natal Basin
C. of Good Hope
Kerguelen Basin
Île Amsterdam
C. Leeuwin
Great Australian Bight
South Australian Basin
Murray
Darling
Tasman Sea
Kermadec Trench
Cape Rise
Agulhas Basin
Prince Edward-Crozet Ridge
Prince Edward Is.
Îles Crozet
Tasmania
Chatham Is.
New Zealand
SOUTHERN OCEAN
Îles de Kerguelen
Heard I.
Indian - Antarctic Ridge
Antarctic Basin
Eastern Indian - Antarctic Basin
Antarctic Circle
Ross Sea
ANTARCTICA
Tropic of Cancer
Equator
Equatorial Scale 1:80 000 000
0 500 1000 1500 2000 2500 Miles
0 1000 2000 3000 4000 Kms.
Flat Polar Equal Area Projection

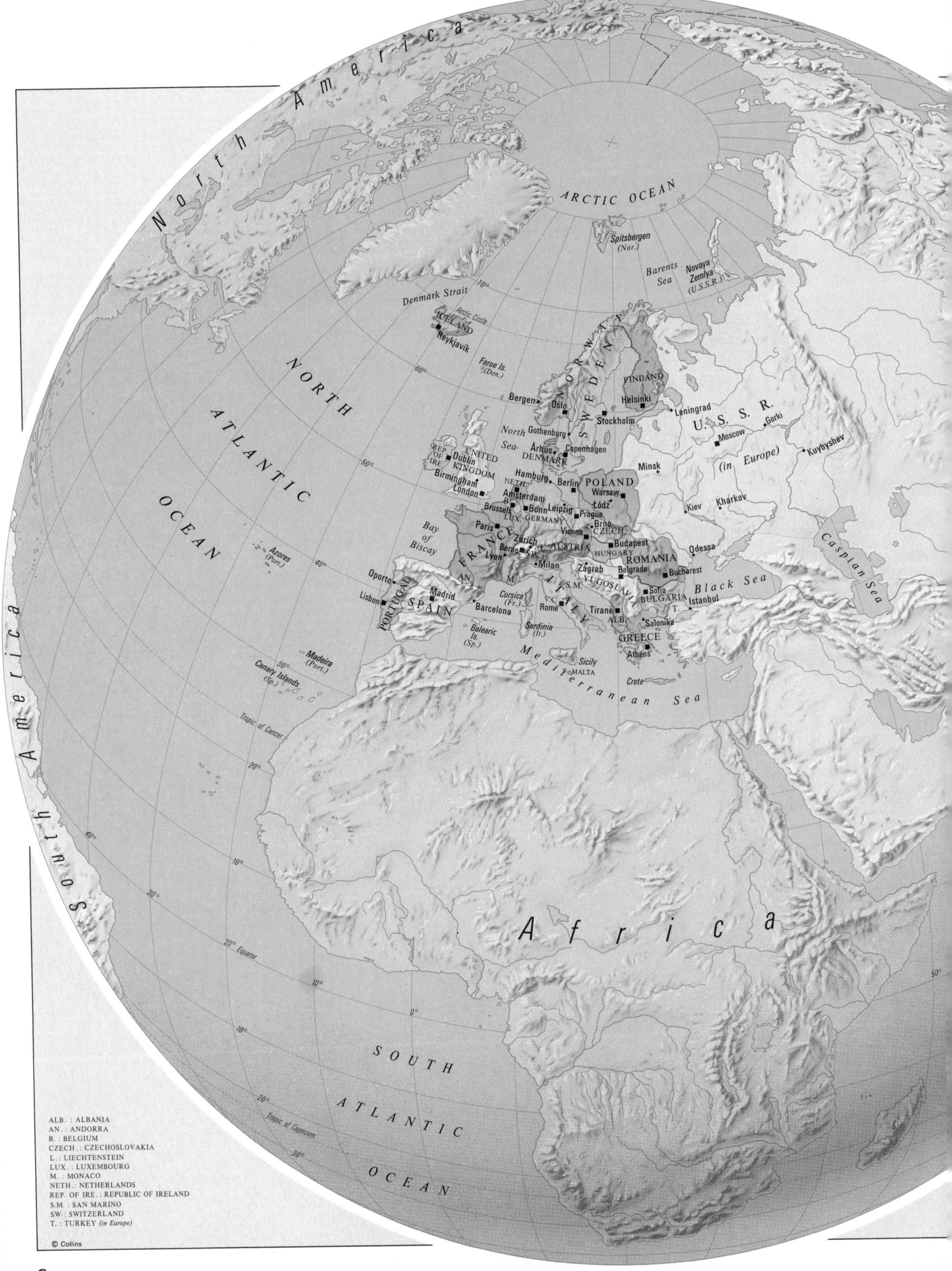
North America
South America
Africa
ARCTIC OCEAN
NORTH ATLANTIC OCEAN
SOUTH ATLANTIC OCEAN
Spitsbergen (Nor.)
Barents Sea
Novaya Zemlya (U.S.S.R.)
Denmark Strait
Arctic Circle
ICELAND
Reykjavík
Faroe Is. (Den.)
NORWAY
SWEDEN
FINLAND
Bergen
Oslo
Stockholm
Helsinki
Leningrad
U. S. S. R. (in Europe)
Moscow
Gorki
Kuybyshev
Minsk
Kiev
Kharkov
Odessa
Gothenburg
Århus
Copenhagen
DENMARK
North Sea
REP. OF IRE.
Dublin
UNITED KINGDOM
Birmingham
London
Hamburg
Berlin
POLAND
Warsaw
Łódź
NETH.
Amsterdam
B.
Brussels
Bonn
Leipzig
Prague
LUX.
GERMANY
Brno
CZECH.
Vienna
AUSTRIA
Budapest
HUNGARY
ROMANIA
Bucharest
Paris
FRANCE
Zürich
Berne
L.
SW.
Lyon
Milan
Zagreb
Belgrade
YUGOSLAVIA
S.M.
M.
AN.
Bay of Biscay
Azores (Port.)
Oporto
Lisbon
PORTUGAL
Madrid
SPAIN
Barcelona
Corsica (Fr.)
V.C.
Rome
ITALY
Sardinia (It.)
Balearic Is. (Sp.)
Tirane
ALB.
Sofia
BULGARIA
Istanbul
T.
Salonika
GREECE
Athens
Black Sea
Caspian Sea
Sicily
MALTA
Crete
Mediterranean Sea
Madeira (Port.)
Canary Islands (Sp.)
Tropic of Cancer
Equator
Tropic of Capricorn
ALB.: ALBANIA
AN.: ANDORRA
B.: BELGIUM
CZECH.: CZECHOSLOVAKIA
L.: LIECHTENSTEIN
LUX.: LUXEMBOURG
M.: MONACO
NETH.: NETHERLANDS
REP. OF IRE.: REPUBLIC OF IRELAND
S.M.: SAN MARINO
SW.: SWITZERLAND
T.: TURKEY (in Europe)

EUROPE

COUNTRY	PAGE
ALBANIA	19
ANDORRA	17
AUSTRIA	20
BELGIUM	14
BULGARIA	19
CZECHOSLOVAKIA	20-21
DENMARK	23
FINLAND	24; 22-23
FRANCE	17; 15
GERMANY	20; 14
GREECE	19
HUNGARY	20-21
ICELAND	22
IRELAND, REPUBLIC OF	13
ITALY	18-19; 15
LIECHTENSTEIN	20
LUXEMBOURG	14
MALTA	18
MONACO	15
NETHERLANDS	14
NORWAY	22-23
POLAND	20-21
PORTUGAL	16
ROMANIA	21
SAN MARINO	15
SPAIN	16
SWEDEN	22-23
SWITZERLAND	20
U.S.S.R. (IN EUROPE)	24-25
UNITED KINGDOM	8-9; 10-11; 12; 13
YUGOSLAVIA	18-19

a

INDIAN OCEAN

BRITISH ISLES

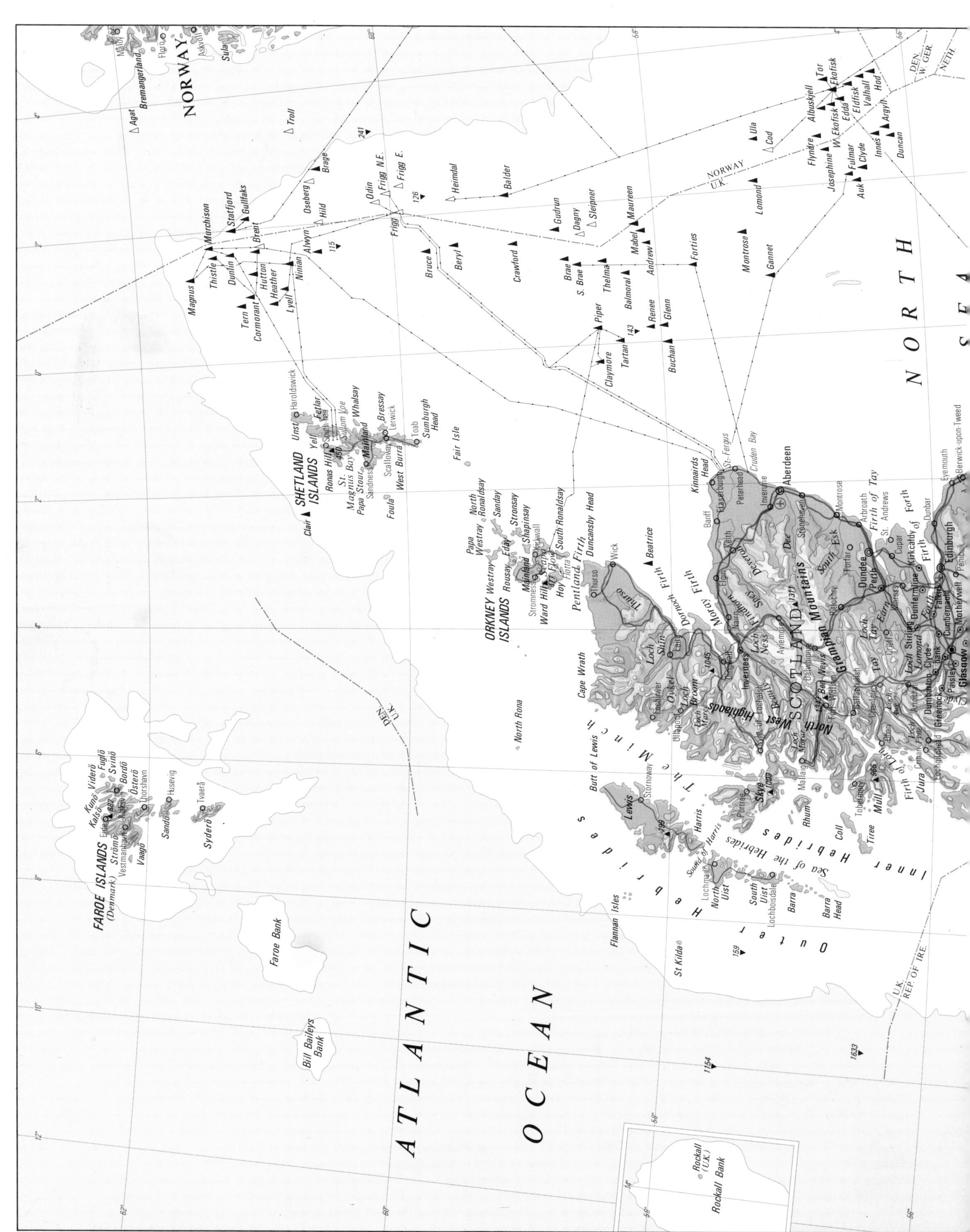

NORWAY
NORTH SEA
ATLANTIC OCEAN
SCOTLAND
SHETLAND ISLANDS
ORKNEY ISLANDS
FAROE ISLANDS (Denmark)
Faroe Bank
Bill Baileys Bank
Rockall (U.K.)
Rockall Bank
Outer Hebrides
Inner Hebrides
Sea of the Hebrides
The Minch
Grampian Mountains
North West Highlands
Pentland Firth
Moray Firth
Dornoch Firth
Firth of Tay
Firth of Forth
Firth of Lorn
Cape Wrath
Butt of Lewis
Lewis
Harris
Sound of Harris
North Uist
South Uist
Barra
Barra Head
St Kilda
Flannan Isles
North Rona
Skye
Rhum
Coll
Tiree
Mull
Jura
Fair Isle
Foula
Unst
Yell
Fetlar
Whalsay
Bressay
Mainland
Sumburgh Head
Kinnairds Head
Duncansby Head
Aberdeen
Dundee
Perth
Edinburgh
Glasgow
Inverness
Stornoway
Thurso
Wick
Kirkwall
Lerwick
Thorshavn
Berwick-upon-Tweed
Magnus
Thistle
Murchison
Statfjord
Gullfaks
Brent
Dunlin
Hutton
Heather
Lyell
Ninian
Alwyn
Tern
Cormorant
Oseberg
Hild
Brage
Troll
Agat
Frigg
Frigg N.E.
Frigg E.
Odin
Heimdal
Balder
Bruce
Beryl
Crawford
Gudrun
Dagny
Sleipner
Brae
S. Brae
Thelma
Balmoral
Andrew
Mabel
Maureen
Forties
Piper
Claymore
Tartan
Renee
Glenn
Buchan
Beatrice
Montrose
Gannet
Lomond
Ula
Cod
Albuskjell
Tor
Ekofisk
W. Ekofisk
Edda
Eldfisk
Valhall
Hod
Flyndre
Josephine
Fulmar
Auk
Clyde
Innes
Argyll
Duncan
Clair
NORWAY
U.K.
DEN.
W. GER.
NETH.
U.K.
REP. OF IRE.

ENGLISH CHANNEL
Bristol Channel
WALES
Cambrian Mts.
Cardigan Bay
Carmarthen Bay
Lyme Bay
Baie de la Seine
Baie de la Somme
Strait of Dover
Passage de la Déroute
FRANCE
CHANNEL ISLANDS
Alderney
Guernsey
Jersey
St. Helier
Sark
Isles of Scilly
St. Mary's
St. Martin's
Land's End
Lizard Pt.
Mount's Bay
Same Scale
London
Birmingham
Bristol
Cardiff
Swansea
Newport
Plymouth
Exeter
Torquay
Southampton
Portsmouth
Bournemouth
Brighton
Hastings
Eastbourne
Dover
Folkestone
Canterbury
Ramsgate
Margate
Southend-on-Sea
Ipswich
Colchester
Chelmsford
Cambridge
Peterborough
Northampton
Bedford
Luton
Oxford
Reading
Swindon
Gloucester
Cheltenham
Worcester
Hereford
Coventry
Wolverhampton
Salisbury
Weymouth
Taunton
Yeovil
Bath
St. Austell
Truro
Falmouth
Penzance
Barnstaple
Dartmoor Forest
Exmoor Forest
Bodmin Moor
New Forest
ISLE OF WIGHT
Isle of Portland
Bill of Portland
Chesil Beach
The Needles
St. Catherine's Pt.
Selsey Bill
Beachy Hd.
Dungeness
North Foreland
Orford Ness
Isle of Sheppey
Foulness I.
Cotswold Hills
Chiltern Hills
Mendip Hills
Salisbury Plain
Vale of Pewsey
North Downs
South Downs
The Weald
Romney Marsh
Brecon Beacons
Black Mts.
Hartland Pt.
Lundy
St. Govan's Head
St. David's Head
Start Pt.
Berry Hd.
Rame Hd.
Dodman Pt.
Cherbourg
Le Havre
Caen
Rouen
Dieppe
Boulogne
C. Gris-Nez
C. de la Hague
Pte. de Barfleur
Lisieux
Évreux
Coutances
MANCHE
CALVADOS
EURE
SEINE MARITIME
CORNWALL
DEVON
DORSET
SOMERSET
WILTSHIRE
HAMPSHIRE
SURREY
KENT
ESSEX
SUFFOLK
AVON
GWENT
DYFED
POWYS
OXFORDSHIRE
BERKSHIRE
GLOUCESTERSHIRE
WARWICKSHIRE
NORTHAMPTONSHIRE
CAMBRIDGESHIRE
© Collins - Longman Atlases

SCOTLAND

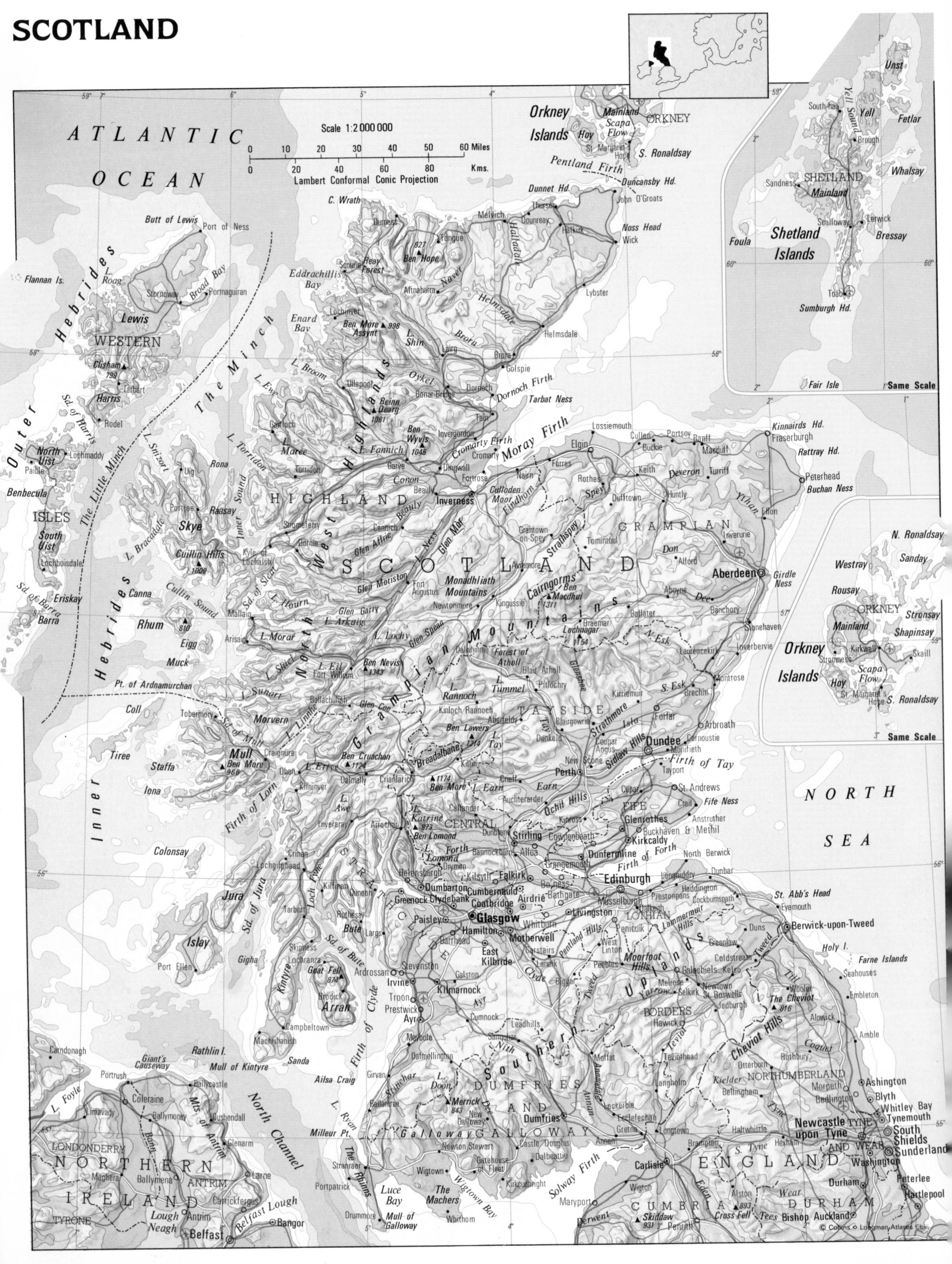

ATLANTIC OCEAN
Scale 1:2 000 000
Lambert Conformal Conic Projection
Miles
Kms.
Orkney Islands
Shetland Islands
Outer Hebrides
Inner Hebrides
The Minch
The Little Minch
Pentland Firth
Moray Firth
HIGHLAND
GRAMPIAN
TAYSIDE
CENTRAL
FIFE
LOTHIAN
BORDERS
STRATHCLYDE
DUMFRIES AND GALLOWAY
SCOTLAND
WESTERN ISLES
North West Highlands
Grampian Mountains
Southern Uplands
NORTH SEA
North Channel
Firth of Clyde
Firth of Forth
Firth of Tay
Firth of Lorn
Solway Firth
Lewis
Harris
North Uist
Benbecula
South Uist
Barra
Skye
Rhum
Eigg
Muck
Coll
Tiree
Mull
Iona
Colonsay
Jura
Islay
Arran
Kintyre
Ben Nevis 1343
Ben Macdhui 1311
Cairngorms
Monadhliath Mountains
Inverness
Aberdeen
Dundee
Perth
Stirling
Edinburgh
Glasgow
Falkirk
Dunfermline
Kirkcaldy
Ayr
Kilmarnock
Dumfries
Carlisle
Fort William
Oban
Stornoway
Wick
Thurso
John O'Groats
Elgin
Peterhead
Fraserburgh
Kirkwall
Lerwick
NORTHERN IRELAND
Belfast
Lough Neagh
ENGLAND
NORTHUMBERLAND
CUMBRIA
DURHAM
TYNE AND WEAR
Newcastle upon Tyne
Sunderland
Berwick-upon-Tweed
Cheviot Hills
Same Scale
© Collins - Longman Atlases

IRELAND

Relief
Feet
Metres
3281
1000
1640
500
656
200
328
100
0
Sea Level
66
20
164
50
328
100
656
200
ATLANTIC OCEAN
IRISH SEA
North Channel
St. George's Channel
REPUBLIC OF IRELAND
NORTHERN IRELAND
SCOTLAND
WALES
ISLE OF MAN
DONEGAL
LONDONDERRY
ANTRIM
TYRONE
FERMANAGH
ARMAGH
DOWN
MONAGHAN
SLIGO
LEITRIM
CAVAN
LOUTH
MAYO
ROSCOMMON
LONGFORD
MEATH
WESTMEATH
DUBLIN
GALWAY
OFFALY
KILDARE
WICKLOW
LAOIS
CLARE
TIPPERARY
KILKENNY
CARLOW
WEXFORD
LIMERICK
KERRY
CORK
WATERFORD
Malin Head
Tory I.
Tory Sound
Bloody Foreland
Melmore Pt.
Inishowen Pen.
Slieve Snaght
Carndonagh
Errigal Mtn.
Derryveagh Mts.
Aran I.
Gweebarra Bay
Loughros More Bay
Glen Hd.
Malin More
Blue Stack Mts.
Croaghnameal
Killybegs
Donegal
Donegal Bay
Ballyshannon
Bundoran
L. Derg
Lower Lough Erne
Upper Lough Erne
L. Foyle
Londonderry
Strabane
Sperrin Mts.
Mullaghmore
Omagh
Enniskillen
Belfast
Lisburn
Bangor
Newtownards
Strangford L.
Ards Peninsula
Portaferry
Mourne Mts.
Slieve Donard
Dundrum Bay
Newry
Lough Neagh
Larne
Ballymena
Coleraine
Portrush
Rathlin I.
Fair Head
Ballycastle
Islay
Port Ellen
Gigha
Kintyre
Mull of Kintyre
Campbeltown
Arran
Goat Fell
Firth of Clyde
Ayr
Girvan
Ailsa Craig
Stranraer
Luce Bay
Mull of Galloway
Dundalk
Dundalk Bay
Carlingford L.
Drogheda
Boyne
Navan
Balbriggan
Skerries
Lambay I.
Howth Head
Dublin
Dublin Bay
Dun Laoghaire
Bray
Greystones
Wicklow
Wicklow Head
Wicklow Mts.
Lugnaquilla Mtn.
Arklow
Kilmichael Pt.
Cahore Pt.
Wexford
Wexford Bay
Rosslare
Greenore Pt.
Carnsore Pt.
Saltee Is.
Hook Head
Waterford
Waterford Harbour
New Ross
Dungarvan
Youghal
Cork
Cork Harbour
Kinsale
Old Head of Kinsale
Galley Hd.
Clear I.
C. Clear
Sherkin I.
Mizen Hd.
Dunmanus B.
Bantry Bay
Bantry
Dursey Head
Coulagh B.
Bolus Hd.
Bray Hd.
Macgillycuddy's Reeks
Carrauntoohil
Killarney
Dingle Bay
Dingle
Brandon Mtn.
Brandon Pt.
Tralee
Tralee Bay
Kerry Head
Shannon Estuary
Loop Head
Kilkee
Limerick
Shannon
Ennis
Slieve Callan
Liscannor B.
Hags Head
Aran Is.
Inishmore
Inishmaan
Inisheer
Galway Bay
Galway
Lough Corrib
L. Mask
L. Carra
Connemara
Maamturk Mts.
Clifden
Slyne Head
Mannin Bay
Bertraghboy Bay
Kilkieran Bay
Killary Harbour
Inishbofin
Inishturk
Clew Bay
Westport
Achill I.
Blacksod Bay
Mullet Pen.
Belmullet
Erris Head
Downpatrick Head
Killala Bay
Ballina
Nephin Beg
Lough Conn
Sligo
Sligo Bay
Lough Ree
Athlone
Lough Derg
Slieve Bloom Mts.
Galtymore
Galty Mts.
Knockmealdown Mts.
Comeragh Mts.
Clonmel
Kilkenny
Carlow
Barrow
Nore
Slaney
Suir
Blackwater
Liffey
Scale 1: 2 000 000
0 10 20 30 40 Miles
0 20 40 60 Kms.
Lambert Conformal Conic Projection
© Collins ◇ Longman Atlases Cbiii

THE LOW COUNTRIES

Scale 1:2 000 000

0 10 20 30 40 50 60 Miles

0 20 40 60 80 Kms.

Conic Projection

Relief

Feet	Metres
16 404	5000
9843	3000
6562	2000
3281	1000
1640	500
656	200
0	Sea Level
Land Dep. 656	200
13123	4000
22966	7000

NORTH SEA

NETHERLANDS

BELGIUM

GERMANY

FRANCE

LUXEMBOURG

PARIS BASIN AND PO VALLEY

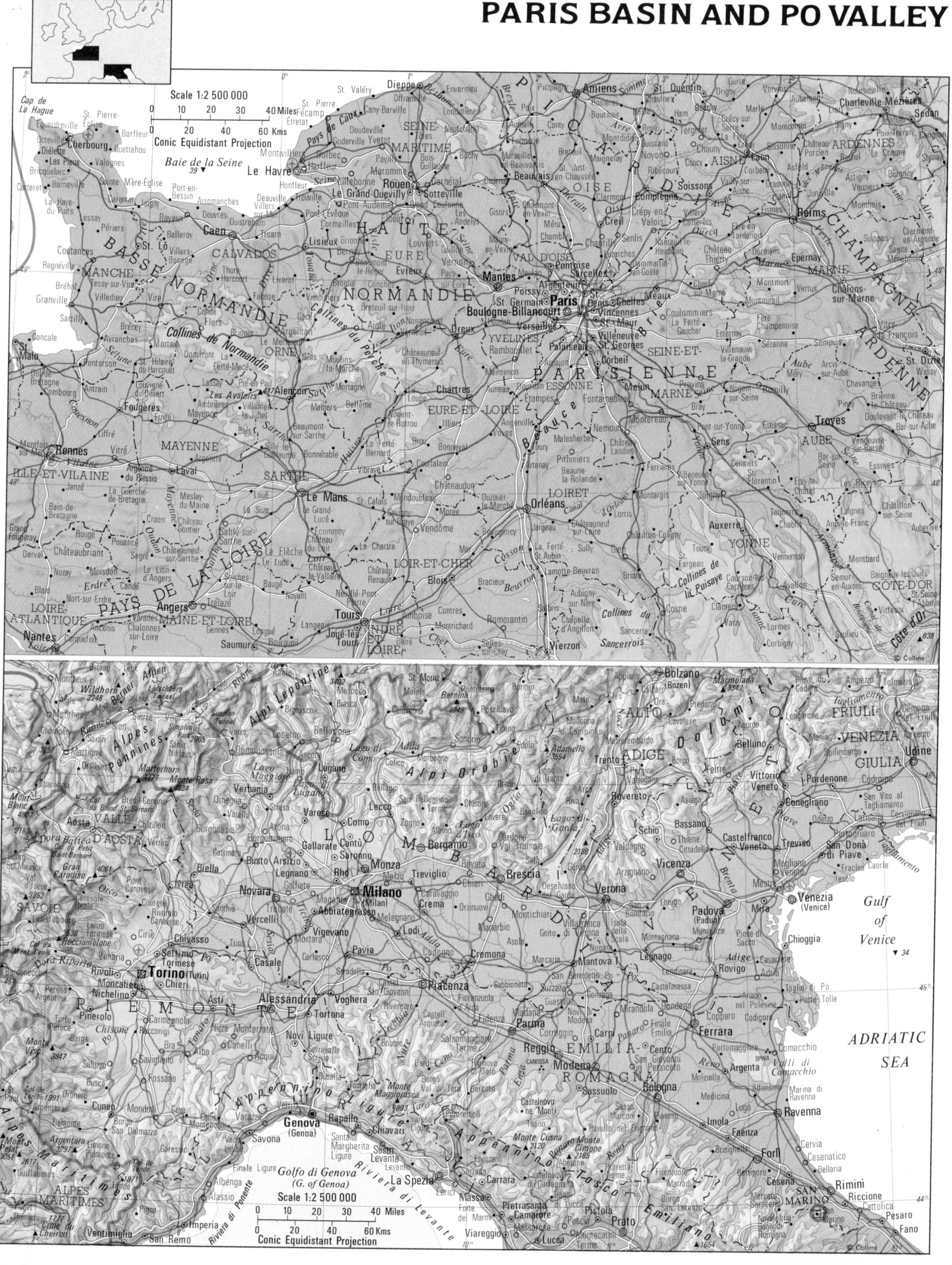

Scale 1:2 500 000
0 10 20 30 40 Miles
0 20 40 60 Kms
Conic Equidistant Projection
Cap de La Hague
Baie de la Seine
Cherbourg
Le Havre
Dieppe
Amiens
St. Quentin
Charleville-Mézières
Sedan
Rouen
Caen
Lisieux
Évreux
Beauvais
Compiègne
Soissons
Laon
Reims
Épernay
Châlons-sur-Marne
Paris
Versailles
Boulogne-Billancourt
Meaux
Melun
Troyes
Sens
Auxerre
Chartres
Orléans
Le Mans
Alençon
Laval
Rennes
St. Malo
Angers
Nantes
Tours
Blois
Vierzon
Saumur
BASSE NORMANDIE
HAUTE NORMANDIE
PICARDIE
CHAMPAGNE ARDENNE
PARISIENNE
PAYS DE LA LOIRE
CALVADOS
MANCHE
EURE
ORNE
OISE
AISNE
ARDENNES
MARNE
AUBE
YONNE
LOIRET
LOIR-ET-CHER
EURE-ET-LOIRE
SARTHE
MAYENNE
ILLE-ET-VILAINE
LOIRE-ATLANTIQUE
MAINE-ET-LOIRE
INDRE ET LOIRE
CÔTE-D'OR
SEINE-MARITIME
YVELINES
ESSONNE
VAL D'OISE
SEINE-ET-MARNE
Collines de Normandie
Collines du Perche
Collines de la Puisaye
Beauce
Brie
Seine
Loire
Marne
Bolzano (Bozen)
Trento
Udine
Belluno
Vicenza
Verona
Padova (Padua)
Venezia (Venice)
Treviso
Chioggia
Gulf of Venice
ADRIATIC SEA
Milano (Milan)
Bergamo
Brescia
Monza
Como
Varese
Novara
Vercelli
Torino (Turin)
Alessandria
Asti
Cuneo
Genova (Genoa)
Golfo di Genova (G. of Genoa)
Riviera di Ponente
Riviera di Levante
La Spezia
Savona
Pavia
Piacenza
Cremona
Mantova
Parma
Reggio
Modena
Bologna
Ferrara
Ravenna
Forlì
Rimini
SAN MARINO
Lucca
Pistoia
Prato
Sion
Lugano
Aosta
Matterhorn 4477
Monte Rosa 4634
Mont Blanc 4807
Gran Paradiso 4061
Monte Viso 3847
Marmolada 3342
Alpes Pennines
Alpi Lepontine
Alpi Orobie
Dolomiti
Alpes Maritimes
Appennino Ligure
Appennino Tosco-Emiliano
LOMBARDIA
PIEMONTE
VALLE D'AOSTA
ALTO ADIGE
VENETO
FRIULI-VENEZIA GIULIA
EMILIA-ROMAGNA
LIGURIA
SAVOIE
Lago Maggiore
Lago di Como
Lago di Garda
Po
Adige
© Collins

SPAIN AND PORTUGAL

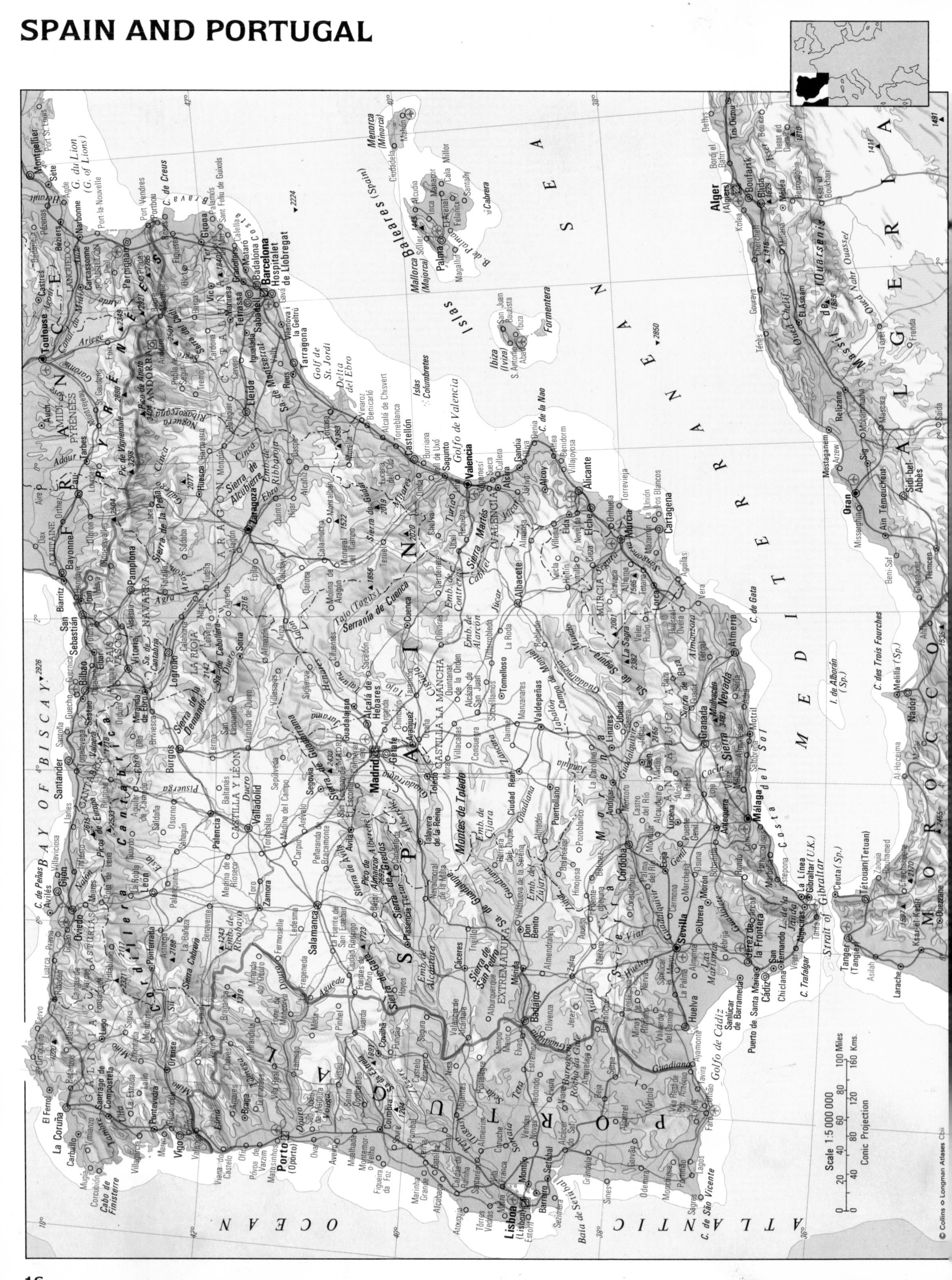

BAY OF BISCAY
MEDITERRANEAN SEA
ATLANTIC OCEAN
SPAIN
PORTUGAL
FRANCE
ALGERIA
MOROCCO
Islas Baleares (Spain)
Mallorca (Majorca)
Menorca (Minorca)
Ibiza (Iviza)
Formentera
Madrid
Barcelona
Valencia
Sevilla
Lisboa (Lisbon)
Porto (Oporto)
Zaragoza
Bilbao
Málaga
Granada
Córdoba
Alicante
Murcia
Cartagena
Alger (Algers)
Oran
Tanger (Tangier)
Strait of Gibraltar
Gibraltar (U.K.)
Ceuta (Sp.)
Melilla (Sp.)
Toulouse
Montpellier
Cordillera Cantábrica
Sierra Morena
Sierra Nevada
Scale 1:5 000 000
Conic Projection
100 Miles
160 Kms.
© Collins • Longman Atlases Cbii

FRANCE
GERMANY
SWITZERLAND
BELGIUM
ITALIA
SPAIN
ANDORRA
MONACO
English Channel
Bay of Biscay
Golfe de Gascogne
(G. of Gascony)
Mediterranean Sea
Ligurian Sea
G. du Lion
(Gulf of Lions)
Corse
(Corsica)
(Fr.)
Channel Islands
(U.K.)
Massif Central
Paris
Lyon
Marseille
Bordeaux
Toulouse
Nantes
Scale 1: 5 000 000
0 20 40 60 80 100 Miles
0 40 80 120 160 Kms.
Conic Projection
© Collins ◇ Longman Atlases Cbi

ITALY AND THE BALKANS

Relief
Feet
Metres
16404
5000
9843
3000
6562
2000
3281
1000
1640
500
656
200
0
Land Dep.
Sea Level
656
200
13123
4000
22966
7000
FRANCE
SWITZ
ALPS
AUSTRIA
SLOVENIJA
ALGERIA
TUNISIA
MALTA
LIGURIAN SEA
TYRRHENIAN SEA
MEDITERRANEAN SEA
ADRIATIC
Gulf of Venice
G. du Lion (G. of Lions)
Golfo di Genova (Gulf of Genoa)
Strait of Bonifacio
Malta Channel
Corse (Corsica) (Fr.)
Sardegna (Sardinia) (Italy)
Sicilia (Sicily)
Menorca
Elba
Ischia
Capri
I. Eolie
Pantelleria (Italy)
Lampedusa (Italy)
Ustica (Italy)
Isole Ponziane
Milano (Milan)
Torino (Turin)
Genova (Genoa)
Venezia (Venice)
Firenze (Florence)
Roma (Rome)
Napoli (Naples)
Palermo
Catania
Messina
Cagliari
Sassari
Bologna
Verona
Trieste
Ljubljana
Rijeka
Marseille
Lyon
Nice
Monaco
Grenoble
Montpellier
Tunis
Annaba
Constantine
Valletta
Genève (Geneva)
PIEMONTE
LOMBARDIA
TOSCANA
UMBRIA
MARCHE
LAZIO
ABRUZZI
MOLISE
CAMPANIA
ROMAGNA
VENETO
TRENTINO-ALTO ADIGE
FRIULI-VENEZIA GIULIA
PROVENCE
CÔTE D'AZUR
AUVERGNE
RHÔNE-ALPES
LANGUEDOC-ROUSSILLON
Alpes Maritimes
Dolomiti
Monts de Constantine
Monts de la Medjerda
Mt. Blanc 4807
Matterhorn 4477
Mt. Rosa 4634
Gran Paradiso 4061
Mt. Etna 3340
Vesuvio 1277
Stromboli 926

HUNGARY
ROMANIA
U.S.S.R.
YUGOSLAVIA
BULGARIA
ALBANIA
GREECE
TURKEY
SRBIJA (SERBIA)
BOSNA I HERCEGOVINA
CRNA GORA (MONTENEGRO)
MAKEDONIJA (MACEDONIA)
BLACK SEA
AEGEAN SEA
IONIAN SEA
SEA
Kritikón Pélagos (Sea of Crete)
Marmara Denizi (Sea of Marmara)
Str. of Otranto
Iónioi Nísoi (Ionian Is.)
Voriai Sporádhes (N. Sporades)
Kikládhes (Cyclades)
Dhodhekánisos (Dodecanese)
Delta Dunării (Mouths of the Danube)
Carpaţii Meridionali (Transylvanian Alps)
Stara Planina (Balkan Mts.)
Rhodopi Planina
Pindhos Óros (Pindus Mts.)
Wallachia
Ludogorie
Dobrudja
Dunărea
Danube
Iron Gate
Beograd (Belgrade)
Bucureşti (Bucharest)
Sofiya (Sofia)
Tiranë
Athínai (Athens)
Istanbul
Skopje
Sarajevo
Thessaloníki
Izmir
Bursa
Varna
Burgas
Constanţa
Plovdiv
Szeged
Arad
Timişoara
Craiova
Ruse
Novi Sad
Niš
Dubrovnik
Pátrai
Kríti (Crete)
Ródhos (Rhodes)
Kérkira (Corfu)
Lésvos
Khíos
Sámos
Límnos
Thásos
Évvoia (Euboea)
Kefallinía
Zákinthos
Scale 1:5 250 000
50 100 150 200 Miles
50 100 150 200 250 300 Kms.
Conic Projection
© Collins ◇ Longman Atlases Cbii

CENTRAL EUROPE

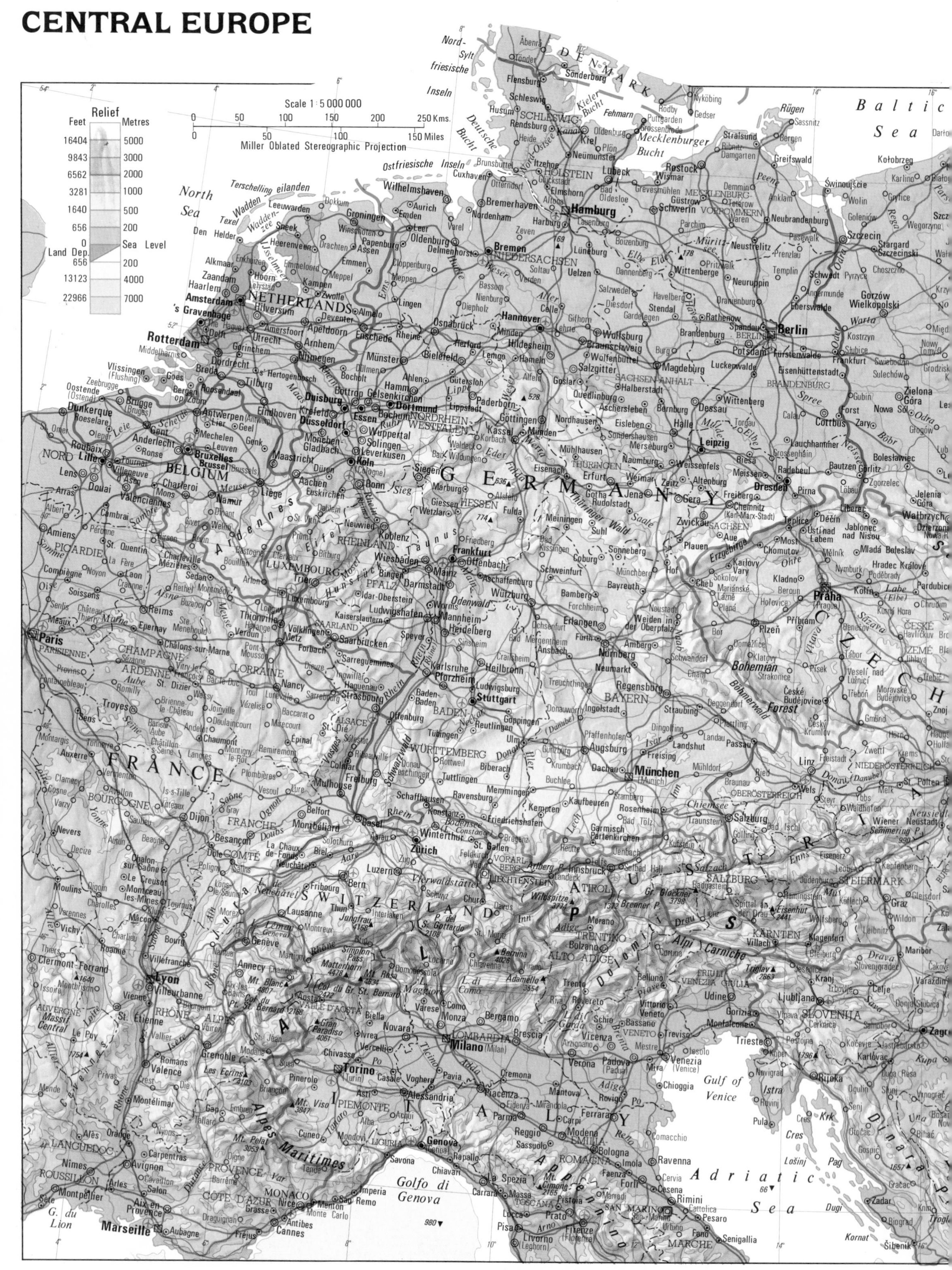

Relief
Feet
Metres
16404
5000
9843
3000
6562
2000
3281
1000
1640
500
656
200
0
Sea Level
Land Dep.
656
200
13123
4000
22966
7000
Scale 1 : 5 000 000
0 50 100 150 200 250 Kms.
0 50 100 150 Miles
Miller Oblated Stereographic Projection
North Sea
Baltic Sea
DENMARK
NETHERLANDS
BELGIUM
LUXEMBOURG
GERMANY
FRANCE
SWITZERLAND
AUSTRIA
ITALY
CZECH
LIECHTENSTEIN
SLOVENIJA
Adriatic Sea
Gulf of Venice
Golfo di Genova
G. du Lion
Nordfriesische Inseln
Ostfriesische Inseln
Deutsche Bucht
Kieler Bucht
Mecklenburger Bucht
Amsterdam
Rotterdam
's Gravenhage
Bruxelles
Antwerpen
Luxembourg
Paris
Lyon
Marseille
Berlin
Hamburg
Bremen
Hannover
Dortmund
Essen
Düsseldorf
Köln
Frankfurt
Stuttgart
München
Nürnberg
Leipzig
Dresden
Praha
Wien
Zürich
Bern
Genève
Milano
Torino
Genova
Venezia
Bologna
Firenze
Ljubljana
Zagreb
Szczecin
Salzburg
Innsbruck
Graz
Linz
Ardennes
Alpes Maritimes
Appennino
Bohemian Forest
Dolomiti
Alpi Carniche
Mt. Blanc 4807
Matterhorn 4478
Jungfrau 4158
Gr. Glockner 3798
Rhein
Donau
Elbe
Oder
Weser
Rhône
Po
MONACO
SAN MARINO

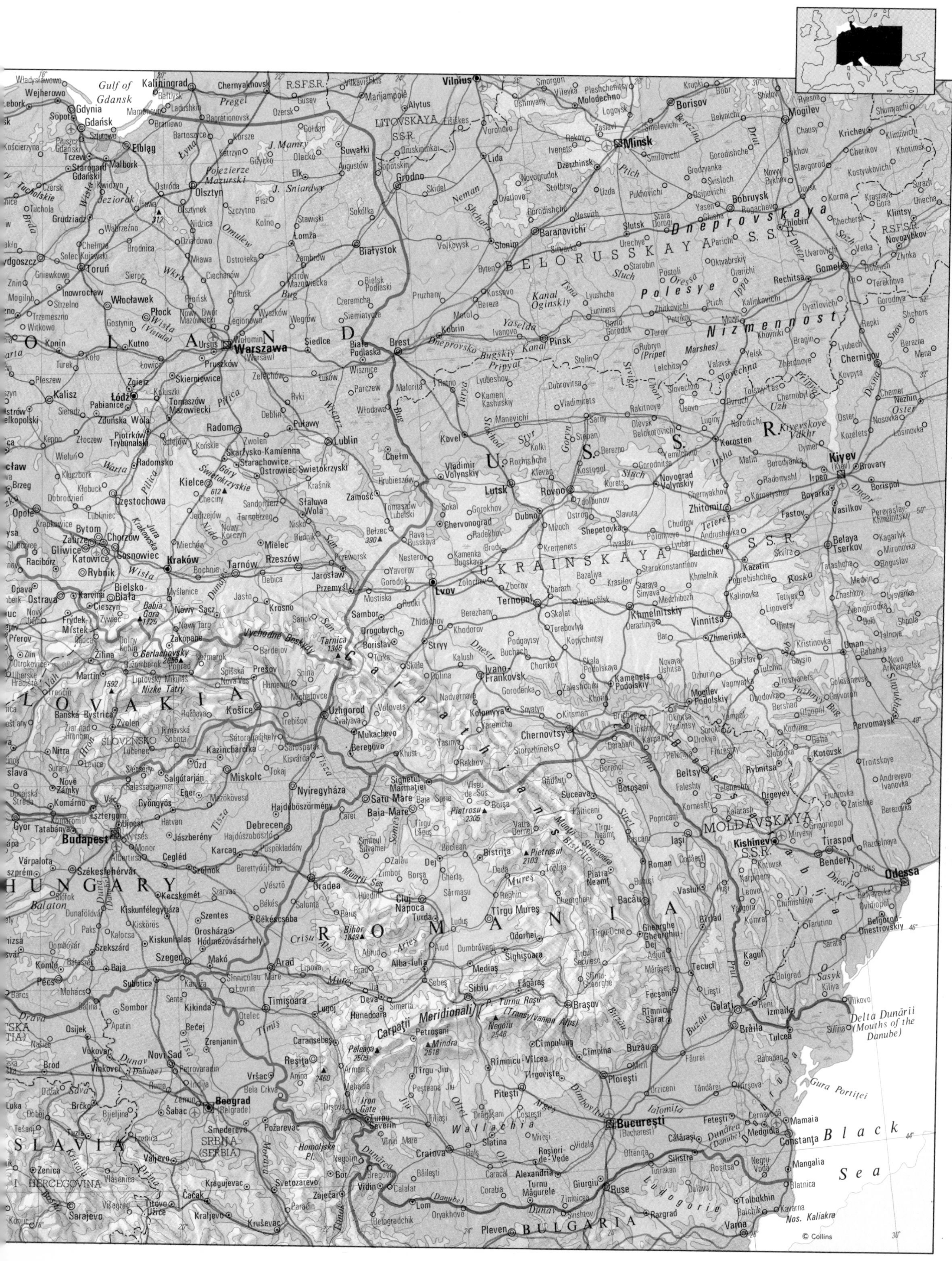

Gulf of Gdansk
Kaliningrad
Gdynia
Gdańsk
Elbląg
Malbork
Olsztyn
Toruń
Włocławek
Płock
Warszawa
(Warsaw)
Łódź
Radom
Lublin
Kielce
Częstochowa
Kraków
Tarnów
Rzeszów
Katowice
Białystok
Vilnius
Grodno
Minsk
Borisov
Mogilev
Bobruysk
Gomel
Baranovichi
Pinsk
Brest
Kovel
Lutsk
Rovno
Zhitomir
Kiyev
Chernigov
Lvov
Ternopol
Ivano Frankovsk
Chernovtsy
Khmelnitskiy
Vinnitsa
Uzhgorod
Košice
Miskolc
Budapest
Debrecen
Szeged
Kecskemét
Cluj Napoca
Oradea
Arad
Timişoara
Sibiu
Braşov
Iaşi
Bacău
Galaţi
Brăila
Ploieşti
Bucureşti
(Bucharest)
Constanţa
Craiova
Kishinev
Odessa
Izmail
Beograd
(Belgrade)
Novi Sad
Sarajevo
Pleven
Varna
Ruse
P O L A N D
H U N G A R Y
R O M A N I A
B U L G A R I A
S L O V A K I A
B E L O R U S S K A Y A S. S. R.
U K R A I N S K A Y A S. S. R.
MOLDAVSKAYA S.S.R.
LITOVSKAYA S.S.R.
R.S.F.S.R.
U. S. S. R.
Carpathians
Carpaţii Meridionali
(Transylvanian Alps)
Polesye
Dneprovskaya
Nizmennost
(Pripet Marshes)
Wisła
Dnepr
Dnestr
Prut
Dunărea
(Danube)
Tisza
Black Sea
Delta Dunării
(Mouths of the Danube)
Wallachia
Balaton
© Collins

SCANDINAVIA AND BALTIC LANDS

ICELAND
on the same scale
© Collins
FAROE IS.
(Denmark)
on the same scale
Scale 1: 5 000 000
0 20 40 60 80 100 Miles
0 40 80 120 160 Kms.
Conic Projection
Relief
Feet Metres
16404 5000
9843 3000
6562 2000
3281 1000
1640 500
656 200
0 Sea Level
Land Dep. 656 200
13123 4000
22966 7000
ATLANTIC
OCEAN
Arctic Circle
Vatnajökull
Reykjavik
Vesterålen
Lofoten
Tromsö
Trondheim
Östersund
Umeå
Luleå
Oulu
Rovaniemi
Vaasa
FINNMARK
NORRBOTTEN
VÄSTERBOTTEN
NORDLAND

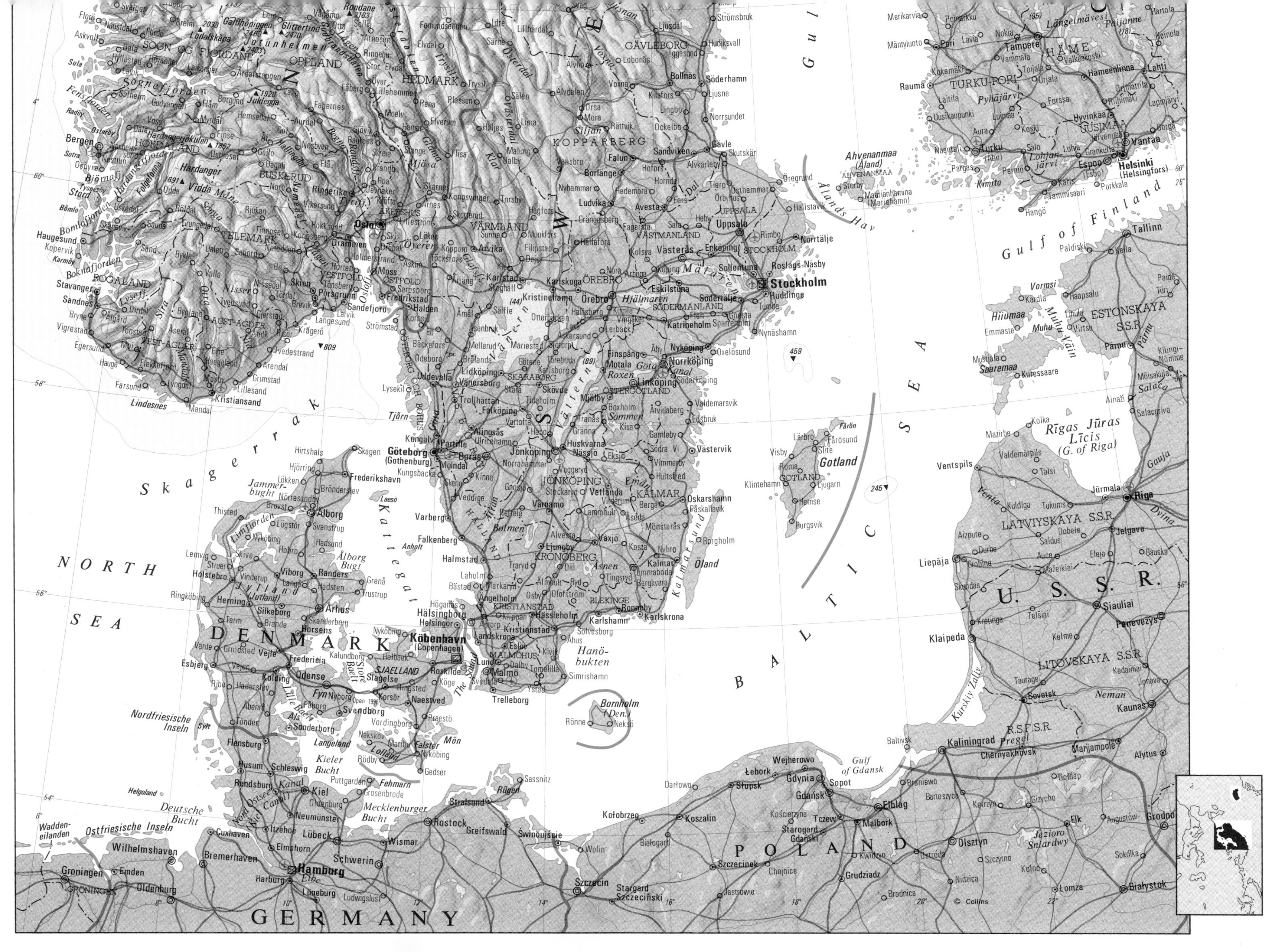

NORTH SEA
BALTIC SEA
Skagerrak
Kattegat
Gulf of Finland
Rīgas Jūras Līcis (G. of Riga)
Gulf of Gdansk
Ålands Hav
GERMANY
POLAND
DENMARK
U.S.S.R.
ESTONSKAYA S.S.R.
LATVIYSKAYA S.S.R.
LITOVSKAYA S.S.R.
Stockholm
Oslo
Göteborg (Gothenburg)
København (Copenhagen)
Helsinki (Helsingfors)
Tallinn
Riga
Gdańsk
Hamburg
Szczecin
Kaliningrad
Kaunas
Bergen
Stavanger
Kristiansand
Malmö
Uppsala
Västerås
Örebro
Norrköping
Linköping
Jönköping
Turku
Tampere
Gotland
Öland
Bornholm (Den.)
Saaremaa
Hiiumaa
Sjælland
Fyn
Lolland
Falster
Rügen
Fehmarn
Vänern
Vättern
Mälaren
Hjälmaren
Lindesnes
Mandal
Göteborg och Bohus
© Collins

U.S.S.R. IN EUROPE

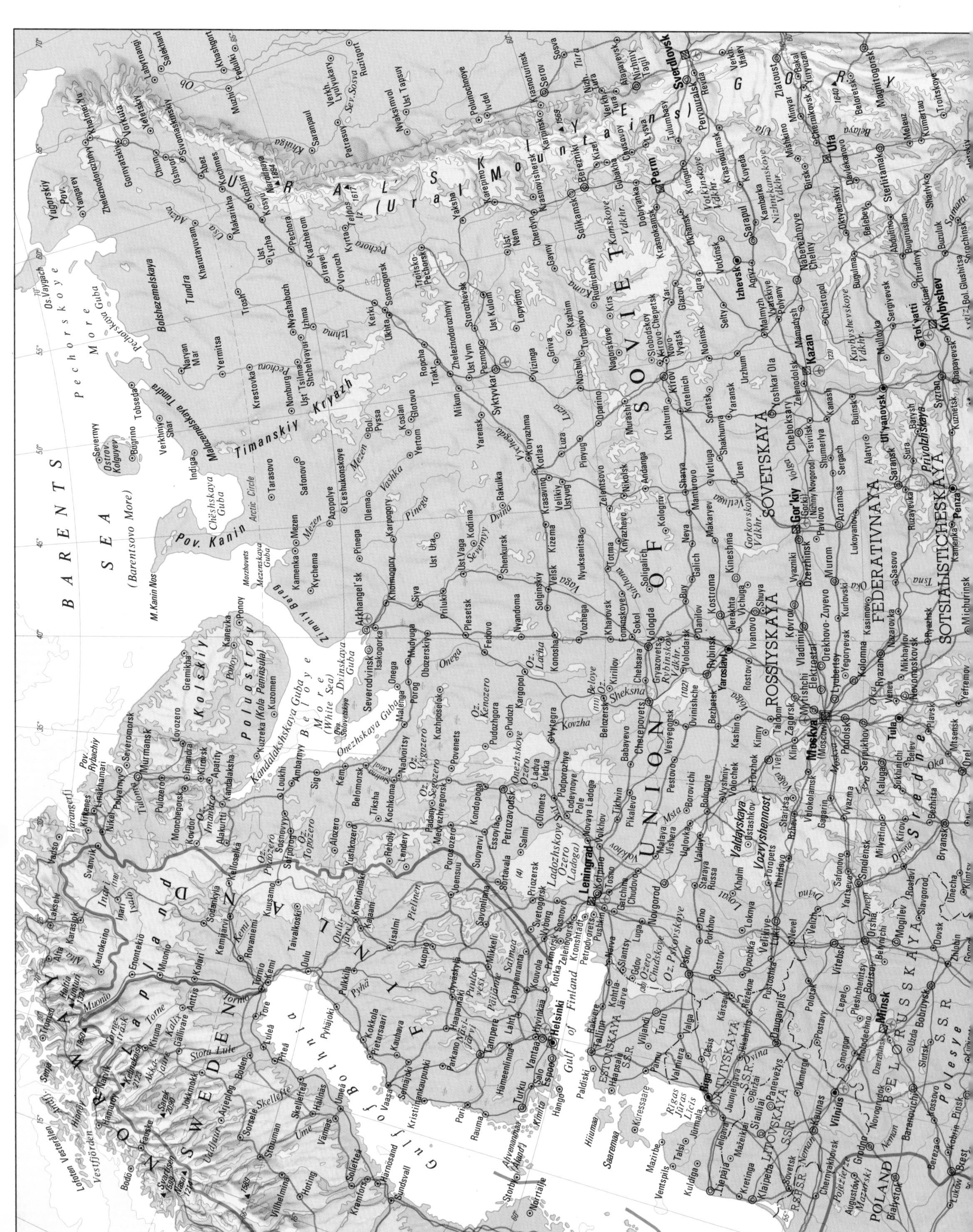

BARENTS SEA
(Barentsovo More)
Pechorskoye More
Pechorskaya Guba
Beloye More
(White Sea)
Gulf of Finland
Gulf of Bothnia
Rigas Juras Licis
UNION OF SOVIET SOCIALIST REPUBLICS
ROSSIYSKAYA SOVETSKAYA FEDERATIVNAYA SOTSIALISTICHESKAYA
ESTONSKAYA S.S.R.
LATVIYSKAYA S.S.R.
LITOVSKAYA S.S.R.
BELORUSSKAYA S.S.R.
FINLAND
SWEDEN
NORWAY
POLAND
Lappland
Poluostrov Kolskiy
(Kola Peninsula)
Ural'skiye Gory
(Ural Mountains)
Timanskiy Kryazh
Pov. Kanin
Ostrov Kolguyev
Valdayskaya Vozvyshennost
Privolzhskaya Vozvyshennost
Sredne Russkaya
Polesye
Ladozhskoye Ozero
(Ladoga)
Onezhskoye Ozero
Moskva
(Moscow)
Leningrad
Helsinki
Riga
Tallinn
Vilnius
Minsk
Kaunas
Arkhangel'sk
Murmansk
Gor'kiy
Kazan
Kuybyshev
Sverdlovsk
Perm
Ufa
Izhevsk
Kirov
Yaroslavl
Vologda
Syktyvkar
Petrozavodsk
Ul'yanovsk
Tula
Smolensk
Penza

SOCIALIST REPUBLICS
UKRAINSKAYA S.S.R.
MOLDAVSKAYA S.S.R.
KAZAKHSKAYA S.S.R.
GRUZINSKAYA S.S.R.
ARMYANSKAYA S.S.R.
AZERBAYDZHANSKAYA S.S.R.
TURKMENSKAYA
ROMANIA
BULGARIA
TURKEY
CYPRUS
SYRIA
LEBANON
IRAQ
IRAN
BLACK SEA
CASPIAN SEA
MEDITERRANEAN SEA
Azovskoye More (Sea of Azov)
Krym (Crimea)
Delta Dunării (Mouths of the Danube)
Prikaspiyskaya Nizmennost (Caspian Depression)
Plato Ustyurt
Kavkazskiy Khrebet
(Caucasus Mts)
Kuzey Anadolu Dağlari
Anadolu (Anatolia)
Toros Dağlari
Mesopotamia
Al Jazīrah
Reshteh-ye Kūhhā-ye Alborz (Elburz Mts)
Bucureşti (Bucharest)
Istanbul
Ankara
Izmir
Bursa
Konya
Adana
Kishinev
Odessa
Kiyev (Kiev)
Kharkov
Donetsk
Dnepropetrovsk
Zaporozhye
Krivoy Rog
Rostov
Volgograd
Astrakhan
Guryev
Krasnodar
Tbilisi
Yerevan
Baku
Tabrīz
Tehrān
Eşfahān
Baghdād
Dimashq (Damascus)
Ḩalab (Aleppo)
Bayrūt (Beirut)
Levkosia (Nicosia)
Scale 1:10 000 000
0 100 200 300 Miles
0 100 200 300 400 Kms.
Conic Projection
© Collins

North America
ARCTIC OCEAN
International Date Line
Bering Strait
Europe
UNION OF SOVIET SOCIALIST REPUBLICS
Sea of Okhotsk
Sverdlovsk
Omsk
Novosibirsk
Black Sea
Caspian Sea
Aral Sea
Tbilisi
Baku
Tashkent
Ankara
TURKEY
CYPRUS
Nicosia
LEB.
Beirut
SYRIA
Damascus
JOR.
Ammān
Jerusalem
IRAQ
Baghdād
Tehrān
IRAN
AFGHANISTAN
Kābul
Islāmābād
JAMMU AND KASHMIR
Kuwait
SAUDI ARABIA
Red Sea
BAH.
Manāmah
Riyadh
QAT.
Doha
U.A.E.
OMAN
Muscat
Sana
YEMEN
PAKISTAN
Lahore
Karāchi
Delhi
NEPAL
Kathmandu
BHU.
Thimbu
Kānpur
Ahmadābād
BANGLA.
Dacca
Calcutta
INDIA
Arabian Sea
Bombay
Hyderābād
Bangalore
Madras
Bay of Bengal
Andaman Islands (Ind.)
Nicobar Islands (Ind.)
SRI LANKA
Colombo
MALDIVES
Socotra (Yemen)
Africa
MONGOLIA
Ulan Bator
Harbin
Changchun
Shenyang
Fushun
Anshan
N. KOREA
Pyongyang
Seoul
S. KO
Taegu
Pusan
Kitakyu
Dalian
Peking (Beijing)
Tientsin
Taiyuan
Tsinan
Tsingtao
Lanchow
Chengchow
Sian
Nanking
Shanghai
East China Sea
CHINA
Wuhan
Chengdu
Chungking
Kunming
Taipei
TAIWAN
Canton
Victoria
HONG KONG (U.K.)
Hanoi
Hainan
BURMA (MYANMA)
Vientiane
LAOS
VIETNAM
Rangoon
THAILAND
Bangkok
CAMBODIA
Phnom Penh
Ho Chi Minh
South China Sea
Luzon
Manila
Bandar Seri Begawan
BRUNEI
Kuala Lumpur
MALAYSIA
Singapore
SINGAPORE
Sumatra
Borneo
Sulaw
INDON
Jakarta
Java
Surabaya
Bandung
INDIAN OCEAN
Equator
Tropic of Capricorn
Kerguelen (Fr.)
50°
60°
70°
80°
90°
20°
10°
10°
20°
30°
40°
50°
BAH. : BAHRAIN
BANGLA. : BANGLADESH
BHU. : BHUTAN
IS. : ISRAEL
JOR. : JORDAN
K. : KUWAIT
LEB. : LEBANON
N. KOREA : NORTH KOREA
QAT. : QATAR
S. KOREA : SOUTH KOREA
T : TURKEY (European)
U.A.E. : UNITED ARAB EMIRATES
© Collins

ASIA

COUNTRY	PAGE
AFGHANISTAN	26; 38; 40
BAHRAIN	43
BANGLADESH	41
BHUTAN	41
BRUNEI	36
BURMA	34
CAMBODIA	34
CHINA	30-31; 32-33
CYPRUS	44
HONG KONG	33
INDIA	38-39; 40-41
INDONESIA	36-37
IRAN	43
IRAQ	42-43
ISRAEL	44
JAPAN	35
JORDAN	42; 44
KUWAIT	43
LAOS	34
LEBANON	44
MACAU	33
MALAYSIA	36
MALDIVES	38
MONGOLIA	30-31; 32
NEPAL	41
NORTH KOREA	31
OMAN	38
PAKISTAN	38; 40
PHILIPPINES	36-37
QATAR	43
SAUDI ARABIA	45; 42-43
SINGAPORE	36
SOUTH KOREA	31
SRI LANKA	39
SYRIA	42; 44
TAIWAN	33
THAILAND	34
TURKEY	42
U.S.S.R.	28-29
UNITED ARAB EMIRATES	43
VIETNAM	34
YEMEN	45

U.S.S.R.

UNION OF SOVIET
ROSSIYSKAYA S.F.S.R.
UKRAINSKAYA S.S.R.
KAZAKHSKAYA S.S.R.
UZBEKSKAYA S.S.R.
TURKMENSKAYA S.S.R.
KIRGIZSKAYA S.S.R.
TADZHIKSKAYA S.S.R.
AZERBAYDZHANSKAYA S.S.R.
NORWAY
SWEDEN
FINLAND
POLAND
GERMANY
CZECHOSLOVAKIA
HUNGARY
ROMANIA
DENMARK
TURKEY
IRAQ
IRAN
AFGHANISTAN
XINJIANG UYGUR
BARENTS SEA
BALTIC SEA
BLACK SEA
CASPIAN SEA
KARSKOYE MORE
Novaya Zemlya
Zemlya Frantsa Iosifa (Franz Josef Land)
Gulf of Bothnia
G. of Finland
Beloye More (White Sea)
Azovskoye More (Sea of Azov)
Aral'skoye More (Aral Sea)
Ozero Balkhash
Zapadno-Sibirskaya Ravnina (West Siberian Plain)
Prikaspiyskaya Nizmennost' (Caspian Depression)
Kazakhskiy Melkosopochnik
Peski Karakumy
Peski Kyzyl Kum
Plato Ustyurt
Moskva
Leningrad
Kiyev
Minsk
Riga
Vil'nius
Kishinev
Tbilisi
Yerevan
Baku
Alma-Ata
Tashkent
Frunze
Dushanbe
Ashkhabad
Novosibirsk
Omsk
Sverdlovsk
Chelyabinsk
Kuybyshev
Gor'kiy
Kazan
Perm
Ufa
Volgograd
Rostov
Kharkov
Odessa
Donetsk
Dnepropetrovsk
Karaganda
Samarkand
Tehran
Stockholm
Oslo
Helsinki
Warszawa
Berlin
Praha
Scale I : 20 000 000
Conic Projection
Miles
Kms.
© Collins - Longman Atlases

Relief
Feet
Metres
16404
5000
9843
3000
6562
2000
3281
1000
1640
500
656
200
0
Sea Level
Land Dep.
656
200
13123
4000
22966
7000
Bering Str.
O. Vrangelya (Wrangel I.)
Proliv Longa
Chukotskiy Poluostrov
Vankarem
Anadyrskiy Zaliv
Arctic Circle
Pevek
O. Ayon
Ambarchik
Bilibino
Yeropol
Anadyr
Koryakskiy Khrebet
Machevna
Markovo
Nizhne Kolymsk
Omolon
Kamenskoye
BERING SEA
VOSTOCHNO SIBIRSKOYE MORE
Novosibirskiye Ostrova
O. Novaya Sibir
O. Bol. Lyakhovskiy
O. Kotel'nyy
Proliv Dmitriya Lapteva
MORE LAPTEVYKH
Yanskiy Zaliv
O. Komsomolets
O. Oktyabr'skoy Revolyutsii
Severnaya Zemlya
O. Bol'shevik
Proliv Vil'kitskogo
M. Chelyuskin
Poluostrov Taymyr
Gory Byrranga
Ozero Taymyr
Khatangskiy Zaliv
Nordvik
Olenëkskiy Zaliv
Ust Olenëk
Tiksi
Kokuora
Kazachye
Yercha
Kondakovo
Srednekolymsk
Indigirka
Kolyma
Khatanga
Anabar
Volochanka
Bulun
Khrebet Cherskogo
G. Pobeda
Khonu
G. Chën
Verkhoyansk
Verkhoyanskiy Khrebet
Balygychan
Gizhiga
Penzhinskaya Guba
Gizhiginskaya Guba
Kichiga
O. Karaginskiy
Palana
Khrebet Kolymskiy
Orotukan
Seimchan
Sanga-Talon
Viliga-Kushka
Magadan
Ust-Omchug
Oymyakon
Dzhelinde
Dzhardzhan
Lena
Olenëk
Kamen
Putorana
Yessey
Sredne
Zhigansk
Sibirskoye
Ploskogor'ye
(Central Siberian Plateau)
Tigil
Uka
Poluostrov Kamchatka
Ust Kamchatsk
Klyuchevskaya
Zhupanovo
Petropavlovsk Kamchatskiy
Opala
Kirovskiy
SEA OF OKHOTSK
SOCIALIST REPUBLICS
RESPUBLIKA
SOTSIALISTICHESKAYA
Atara
Aldan
Okhotskiy Perevoz
Okhotsk
Markha
Nyurba
Vilyuysk
Vilyuy
Suntar
Yakutsk
Amga
Ust'Maya
Tura
Tunguska
Simenga
Tuoy-Khaya
Khrebet Dzhugdzhur
Topko
Ayan
Nelkan
Aim
Buyaga
Olekminsk
Baykit
Mutoray
Aldan
Chagda
Shantarskiy Ostrova
Okha
Vitim
Mama
Yenyuka
Olekma
Chulman
Golets Skalistyy
Stanovoy Khrebet
Chumikan
Tugur
Nikolayevsk-na-Amure
Susanino
Aleksandrovsk Sakhalinskiy
Sakhalin
Poronaysk
Kuril'skiye Ostrova
Nizh. Tunguska
Podkamennaya Tunguska
Kezhma
Angara
Yeniseysk
Kirensk
Chuna
Kondratyevo
Muya
Kalakan
Ust-Tungir
Tyndinskiy
Skovorodino
Zeya
Ekimchan
Sofiysk
Amgun
Uglegorsk
Yuzhno Sakhalinsk
Tatarskiy Proliv
Kansk
Nevanka
Ust Kut
Nizhneangarsk
Bagdarin
Yablonovyy Khrebet
Ushumun
Norsk
Komsomolsk na-Amure
Sovetskaya Gavan
La Perouse Str.
Tayshet
Bratsk
Ust'-Ilga
Bratsk Vdkhr.
Bol'shoy Onguren
Barguzin
Vitim
Shilka
Gulian
Svobodnyy
Chegdomyn
Zavitinsk
Birobidzhan
Khabarovsk
Nizhneudinsk
Tulun
Zima
Sretensk
Amur
Blagoveshchensk
Wakkanai
Asahikawa
Asahi-dake
Cheremkhovo
Angarsk
Irkutsk
Ozero Baykal
Ulan-Ude
Chita
Aihui
HEILONGJIANG
Amurzet
Fuyuan
Bikin
Sikhote Alin
Hokkaidō
Otaru
Sapporo
Hakodate
Amgu
Munku Sardyk
Petrovsk Zabaykal'skiy
Aginskoye
Olovyannaya
Borzya
Oroqen Zizhiqi
Bei'an
Yichun
Shuangyashan
Rudnaya Pristan
Hövsgöl Nuur
Kyakhta
Altanbulag
Khapcheranga
Manzhouli
Hailar
Hulun Nur
Fuyu
Qiqihar
Hailun
Suihua
Lesozavodsk
Oz. Khanka
Xingkai Hu
Erzin
Mörön
Selenge Mörön
Darhan
Harbin
Acheng
Jixi
Ussuriysk
Olga
Vladivostok
Nakhodka
Aomori
Hachinohe
Bulgan
Ulaanbaatar (Ulan Bator)
Kerulen
Tamsagbulag
Da Hinggan Ling
Da'an
Mudanjiang
Akita
Morioka
Uliastay
Altay
Tuul Gol
Baicheng
JILIN
Jilin
Kraskino
SEA OF JAPAN
Sendai
Yamagata
Niigata
MONGOLIA
CHINA
Changchun
Shuangliao
Siping
Kaiyuan
Mandalgovĭ
Saynshand
Hexigten Qi
Tieling
Fushun
NEI MONGGOL
Erenhot
Qagan Nur
LIAONING
Shenyang
Anshan
Hüngnam
NORTH KOREA
Wŏnsan
Toyama
Tokyo
Honshū
Kanazawa
Yokohama
Fuji san
Dalandzadgad
Weichang
Jinzhou
Dandong
Pyŏngyang
Nagoya
Huade
HEBEI
Jinxi
Liaodong Wan
Huang Hai
SOUTH KOREA
Kyōto
Ōsaka
Kōbe
Guyang
Jining
Zhangjiakou
Xingcheng
Dalian (Lüda)
Nampo
Sŏul (Seoul)
Inch'on
Baotou
Hohhot
Beijing (Peking)
Ejin Qi
Hanggin Houqi

EAST ASIA

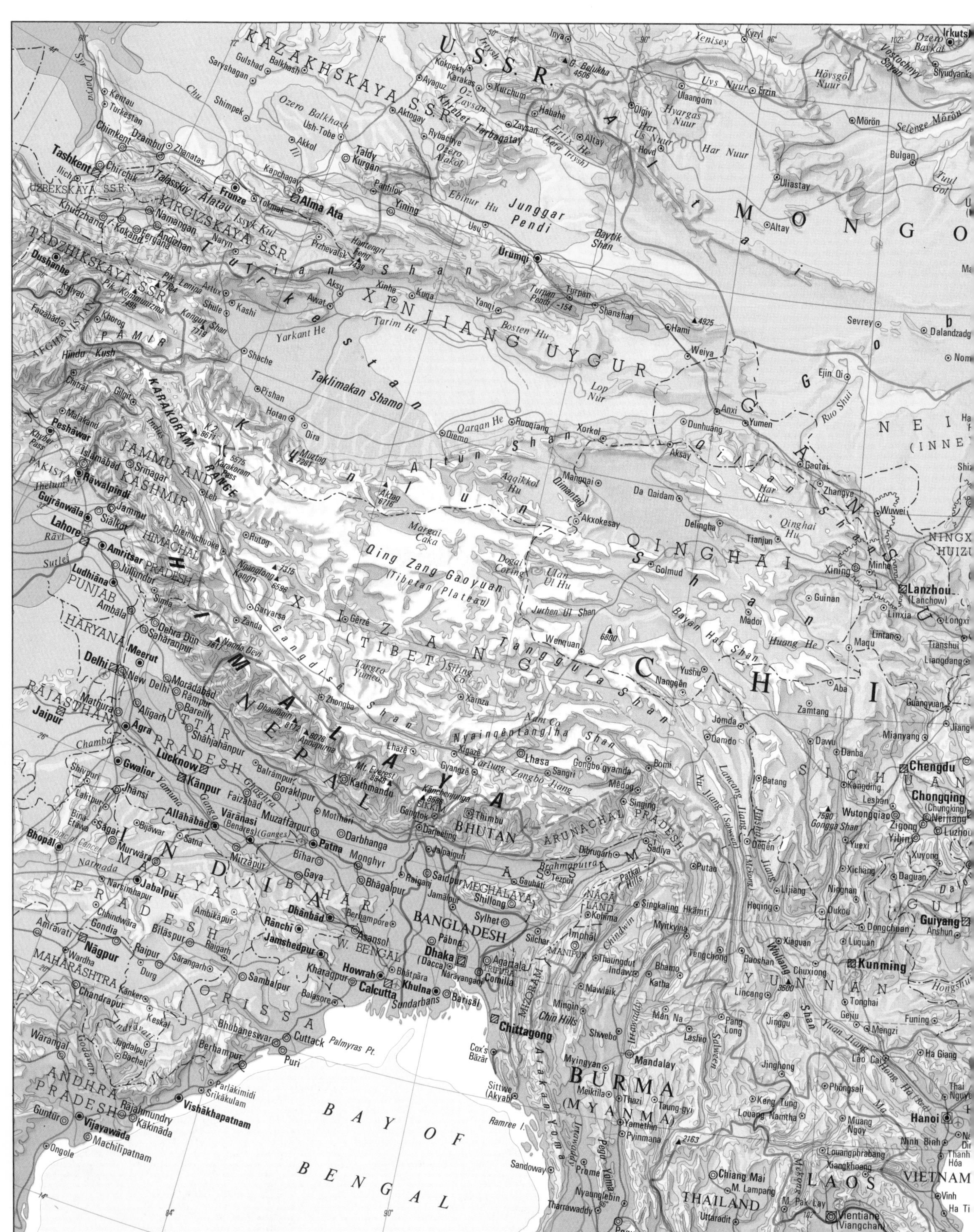

KAZAKHSKAYA S.S.R.
U.S.S.R.
Inya
Yenisey
Kyzyl
Irkutsk
Ozero Baykal
Vostochnyy Sayan
Slyudyanka
Hövsgöl Nuur
Uvs Nuur
Erzin
Ulaangom
Hyargas Nuur
Mörön
Selenge Mörön
Bulgan
Tuul Gol
Har Nuur
Hovd
Ölgiy
Altay
Uliastay
MONGOLIA
Gobi
Kokpekty
Karakas
Oz. Zaysan
Kurchum
G. Belukha 4506
Khrebet Tarbagatay
Zaysan
Habahe
Ertix He (Irtysh)
Ayaguz
Aktogay
Balkhash
Gulshad
Sarysahgan
Ozero Balkhash
Ush-Tobe
Akkol
Ili
Rybach'ye
Ozero Alakol
Taldy Kurgan
Kapchagay
Panfilov
Alma Ata
Chu
Shimpek
Syr Darya
Kentau
Turkestan
Chimkent
Dzhambul
Zhanatas
Tashkent
Chirchik
Ilich
UZBEKSKAYA S.S.R.
Talasskiy Alatau
Frunze
Tokmak
Issyk Kul
KIRGIZSKAYA S.S.R.
Khudzhand
Kokand
Namangan
Fergana
Andizhan
Naryn
Przhevalsk
Hantengri Feng 7439
Yining
Ebinur Hu
Junggar Pendi
Usu
Baytik Shan
Ürümqi
TADZHIKSKAYA S.S.R.
Dushanbe
Kulyab
Faizabad
Khorog
Pik Lenina 7134
Pik Kommunizma 7495
PAMIR
AFGHANISTAN
Hindu Kush
Artux
Shule
Kashi
Kongur Shan 7719
Aksu
Awat
Xinhe
Kuqa
Yanqi
Turpan Pendi -154
Turpan
Shanshan
Hami
4925
Tian Shan
XINJIANG UYGUR
Tarim He
Yarkant He
Bosten Hu
Shache
Turkestan
Taklimakan Shamo
Pishan
Hotan
Qira
Lop Nur
Weiya
Ejin Qi
Anxi
Yumen
Dunhuang
Ruo Shui
NEI
Qarqan He
Qiemo
Ruoqiang
Xorkol
Altun Shan
Aksay
Qilian Shan
GANSU
Gaotai
Zhangye
Wuwei
Chitral
Gilgit
Malakand
Peshawar
Khyber Pass
KARAKORAM
K2 8611
Indus
Muztag 7282
Karakoram Pass 5575
Islamabad
Rawalpindi
PAKISTAN
JAMMU AND KASHMIR
Srinagar
Jhelum
Gujranwala
Jammu
Sialkot
Lahore
Ravi
Leh
Kunlun Shan
Aktag 6716
Aqqikkol Hu
Mangnai
Qimantag
Da Qaidam
Akxokesay
Delingha
Tianjun
Qinghai Hu
Har Hu
QINGHAI
Xining
Minhe
Lanzhou (Lanchow)
Golmud
Rutog
Margai Caka
Dogai Coring
Ulan Ul Hu
Qing Zang Gaoyuan (Tibetan Plateau)
Amritsar
Jullundur
Ludhiana
Sutlej
PUNJAB
HIMACHAL PRADESH
Dharmshala
Mount Kailas
Kangri 7315
6596
Simla
Ambala
HARYANA
Dehra Dun
Saharanpur
Nanda Devi 7817
Gar
Zanda
Garyarsa
Gêrzê
XIZANG (TIBET)
Gangdise Shan
Tangra Yumco
Siling Co
Jurhen Ul Shan
Wenquan
6600
Tanggula Shan
Bayan Har Shan
Madoi
Huang He
Guinan
Linxia
Maqu
Lintan
Tianshui
Longxi
Liangdang
Delhi
New Delhi
Meerut
Moradabad
Rampur
Bareilly
Aligarh
Mathura
Agra
RAJASTHAN
Jaipur
UTTAR PRADESH
Shahjahanpur
Lucknow
Kanpur
Chambal
Gwalior
Jhansi
Yamuna
Shivpuri
Lalitpur
Bina-Etawa
Bhopal
Sagar
Narmada
Dhaulagiri 8172
Annapurna 8078
NEPAL
HIMALAYA
Zhongba
Xainza
Nam Co
Lhazê
Xigazê
Gyangzê
Lhasa
Sangri
Yarlung Zangbo Jiang
Nyainqêntanglha Shan
Gongbo'gyamda
Mêdog
Bomi
Nu Jiang
Lancang Jiang
Jinsha Jiang
Yushu
Nangqên
Jomda
Qamdo
Batang
Zamtang
Aba
Dawu
Danba
Mianyang
Guangyuan
Chengdu
SICHUAN
Kangding
Leshan
Chongqing (Chungking)
Neijiang
Zigong
Yibin
Luzhou
Gongga Shan 7590
Wutongqiao
Balrampur
Gorakhpur
Faizabad
Ghaghra
Kathmandu
Mt. Everest 8848
Kanchenjunga 8586
Gangtok
SIKKIM
Thimbu
BHUTAN
ARUNACHAL PRADESH
Darjeeling
Jalpaiguri
Allahabad
Varanasi (Benares)
Ganges
Muzaffarpur
Motihari
Darbhanga
Patna
Monghyr
Bihar
Gaya
Bhagalpur
Raiganj
Saidpur
MEGHALAYA
Shillong
Gauhati
Tezpur
Dibrugarh
Sadiya
Brahmaputra
ASSAM
Patkai Hills
Putao
Dêqên
Lijiang
Xichang
Yuexi
Ningnan
Daguan
Xuyong
Bijawar
Satna
Murwara
Mirzapur
MADHYA PRADESH
INDIA
BIHAR
Jabalpur
Narsimhapur
Ambikapur
Chhindwara
Gondia
Bilaspur
Amravati
Nagpur
Wardha
MAHARASHTRA
Raipur
Durg
Sarangarh
Raigarh
Kanker
Chandrapur
Dhanbad
Ranchi
Jamshedpur
Asansol
Berhampore
W. BENGAL
BANGLADESH
Jamalpur
Sylhet
Pabna
Dhaka (Dacca)
Agartala
TRIPURA
Narayanganj
Comilla
Howrah
Bhatpara
Kharagpur
Calcutta
Khulna
Barisal
Sundarbans
Sambalpur
Balasore
ORISSA
Keskal
Indravati
Bhubaneswar
Cuttack
Palmyras Pt.
Jagdalpur
Bacheli
Berhampur
Puri
Warangal
Godavari
ANDHRA PRADESH
Parlakimidi
Srikakulam
Vishakhapatnam
Rajahmundry
Kakinada
Guntur
Vijayawada
Machilipatnam
Ongole
BAY OF BENGAL
NAGA LAND
Kohima
Singkaling Hkamti
Imphal
MANIPUR
Silchar
Chindwin
Myitkyina
Thaungdut
Indaw
Bhamo
Katha
Mawlaik
MIZORAM
Chittagong
Cox's Bazar
Mingin
Chin Hills
Man Na
Shwebo
Mandalay
Lashio
Pang Long
Salween
Myingyan
Meiktila
Thazi
Taunggyi
BURMA (MYANMA)
Sittwe (Akyab)
Ramree I.
Arakan Yoma
Yamethin
Pyinmana
2163
Irrawaddy
Pegu Yoma
Sandoway
Prome
Nyaunglebin
Tharrawaddy
Pegu
Tengchong
Baoshan
Xiaguan
Chuxiong
Heqing
Dukou
Luquan
Dongchuan
Kunming
YUNNAN
Lincang
3500
Jinggu
Tonghai
Gejiu
Mengzi
Funing
Hongshui He
Guiyang
Anshun
Yuan Jiang
Lao Cai
Ha Giang
Jinghong
Phôngsali
Keng Tung
Louang Namtha
Muang Ngoy
Louangphrabang
Xiangkhoang
Hanoi
Ninh Binh
Thanh Hoa
Vinh
Ha Tinh
VIETNAM
LAOS
Mekong
Chiang Mai
M. Lampang
THAILAND
Uttaradit
M. Pak Lay
Vientiane (Viangchan)
CHINA

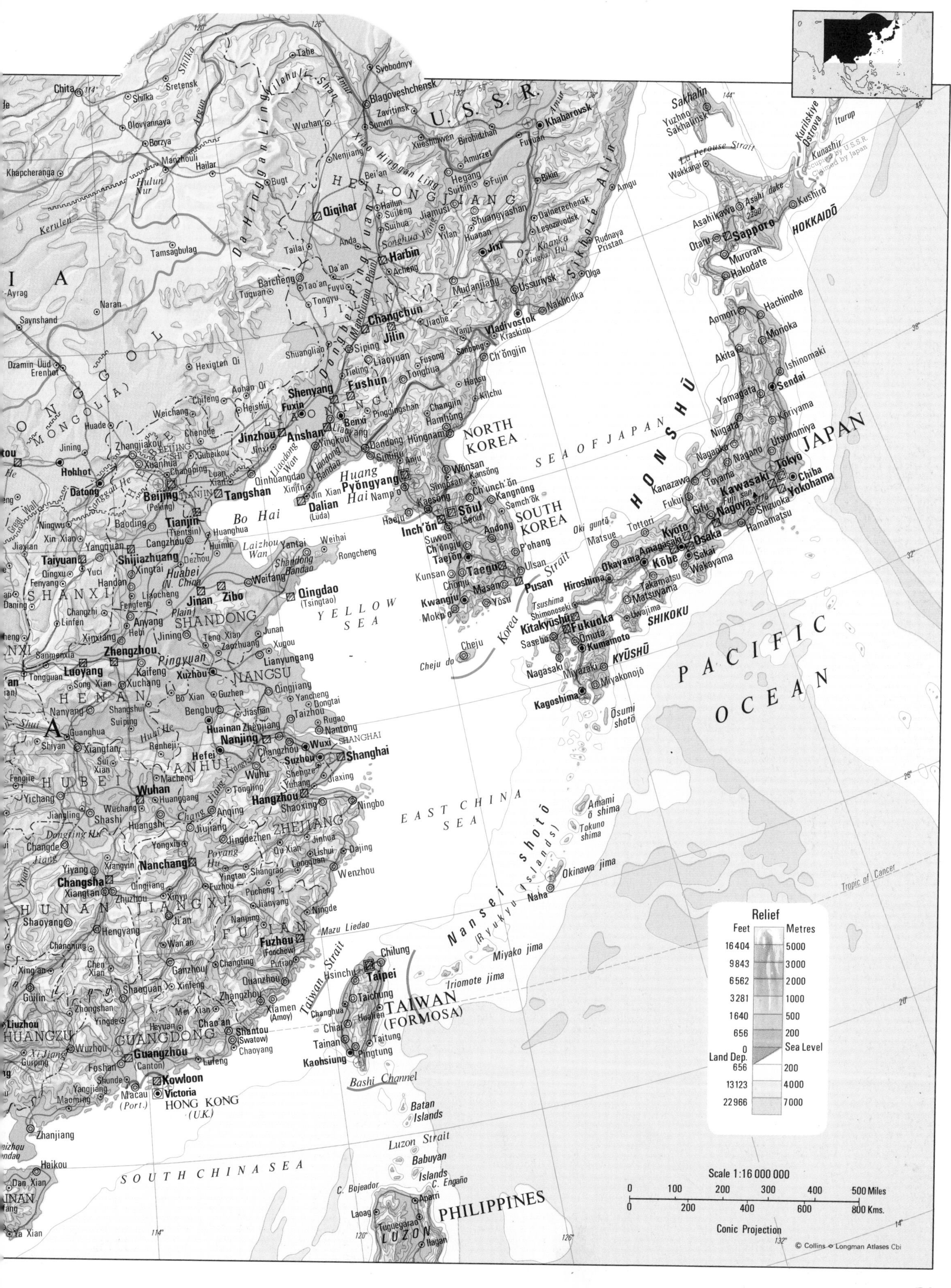

U. S. S. R.
HEILONGJIANG
JILIN
LIAONING
MONGOLIA
NEI MONGOL
NORTH KOREA
SOUTH KOREA
JAPAN
HONSHŪ
HOKKAIDŌ
SHIKOKU
KYŪSHŪ
SEA OF JAPAN
YELLOW SEA
EAST CHINA SEA
SOUTH CHINA SEA
PACIFIC OCEAN
Bo Hai
Huang Hai
TAIWAN (FORMOSA)
HONG KONG (U.K.)
PHILIPPINES
LUZON
SHANDONG
HENAN
ANHUI
HUBEI
HUNAN
JIANGXI
ZHEJIANG
FUJIAN
GUANGDONG
SHANXI
JIANGSU
Chita
Blagoveshchensk
Khabarovsk
Vladivostok
Nakhodka
Ussuriysk
Sakhalin
Yuzhno Sakhalinsk
La Perouse Strait
Kurilskiye Ostrova
Iturup
Kunashir
Occupied by U.S.S.R. Claimed by Japan
Wakkanai
Asahikawa
Sapporo
Otaru
Muroran
Hakodate
Kushiro
Aomori
Hachinohe
Morioka
Akita
Sendai
Ishinomaki
Yamagata
Kōriyama
Niigata
Utsunomiya
Nagano
Tokyo
Chiba
Yokohama
Kawasaki
Shizuoka
Hamamatsu
Nagoya
Gifu
Kanazawa
Toyama
Fukui
Kyoto
Osaka
Kōbe
Sakai
Wakayama
Amagasaki
Okayama
Hiroshima
Matsue
Tottori
Takamatsu
Matsuyama
Uwajima
Kitakyūshū
Shimonoseki
Fukuoka
Sasebo
Nagasaki
Omuta
Kumamoto
Miyazaki
Miyakonojō
Kagoshima
Ōsumi shotō
Amami ō shima
Tokuno shima
Okinawa jima
Naha
Nansei shotō (Ryukyu Islands)
Miyako jima
Iriomote jima
Tropic of Cancer
Harbin
Qiqihar
Changchun
Jilin
Shenyang
Fushun
Anshan
Benxi
Fuxin
Jinzhou
Dandong
Dalian (Lüda)
Beijing (Peking)
Tianjin (Tientsin)
Tangshan
Qinhuangdao
Zhangjiakou
Hohhot
Datong
Taiyuan
Shijiazhuang
Jinan
Zibo
Qingdao (Tsingtao)
Yantai
Weifang
Zhengzhou
Luoyang
Kaifeng
Xuzhou
Nanjing
Shanghai
Suzhou
Wuxi
Hangzhou
Hefei
Wuhan
Nanchang
Changsha
Fuzhou (Foochow)
Xiamen (Amoy)
Shantou (Swatow)
Guangzhou (Canton)
Kowloon
Victoria
Macau (Port.)
Zhanjiang
Haikou
Taipei
Chilung
Hsinchu
Taichung
Tainan
Kaohsiung
Taiwan Strait
Bashi Channel
Batan Islands
Luzon Strait
Babuyan Islands
P'yŏngyang
Wŏnsan
Hamhŭng
Sŏul (Seoul)
Inch'ŏn
Taejŏn
Taegu
Pusan
Kwangju
Mokp'o
Cheju do
Korea Strait
Tsushima
Relief
Feet
Metres
16404
5000
9843
3000
6562
2000
3281
1000
1640
500
656
200
0
Sea Level
Land Dep.
656
200
13123
4000
22966
7000
Scale 1:16 000 000
0
100
200
300
400
500 Miles
0
200
400
600
800 Kms.
Conic Projection
© Collins-Longman Atlases

EAST CHINA

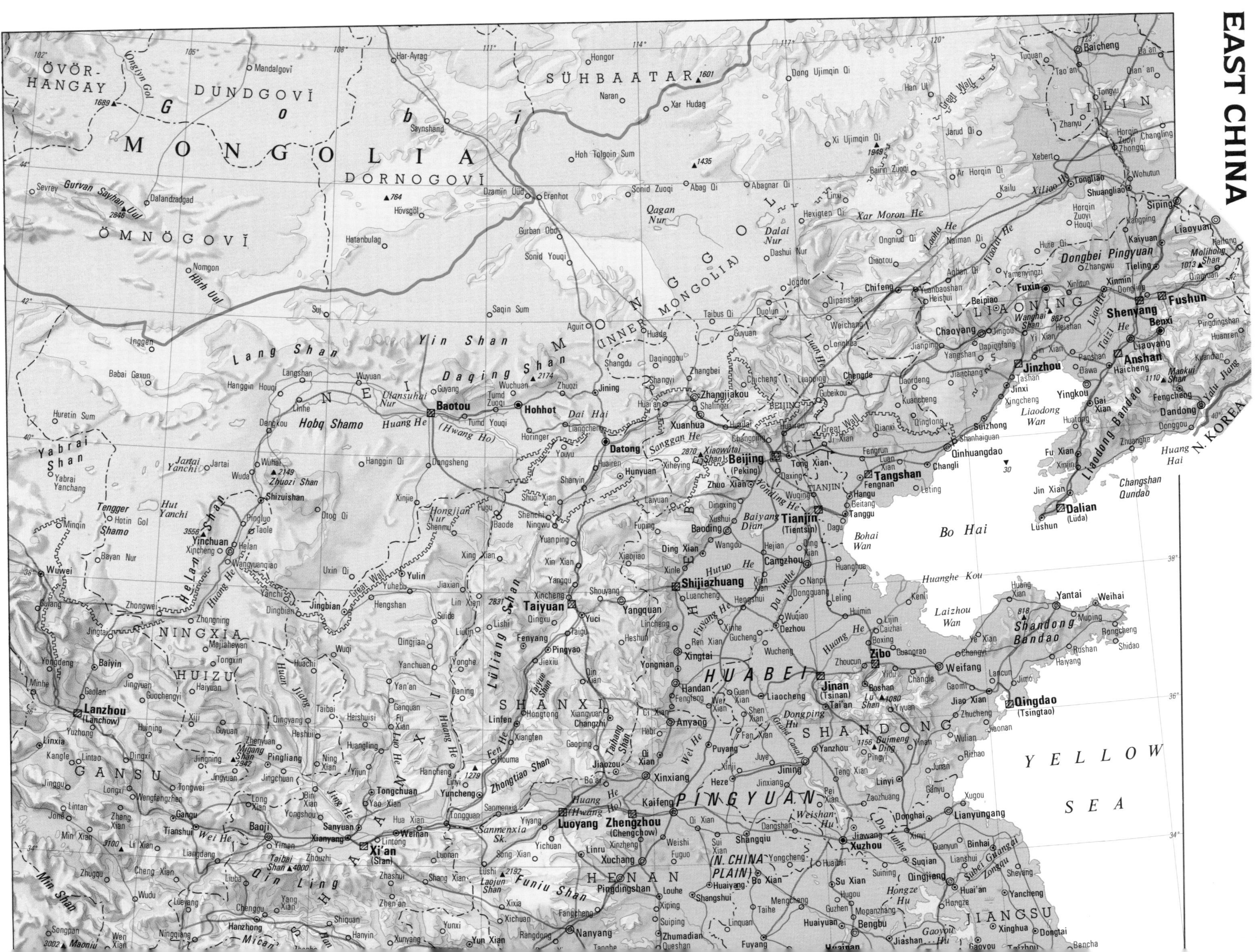

YELLOW SEA
Bo Hai
Bohai Wan
Laizhou Wan
Liaodong Wan
Liaodong Bandao
Shandong Bandao
N.KOREA
JILIN
LIAONING
SHANDONG
HUABEI PINGYUAN
(N. CHINA PLAIN)
SHANXI
HENAN
JIANGSU
GANSU
NINGXIA HUIZU
MONGOLIA
NEI MONGOL
(INNER MONGOLIA)
SÜHBAATAR
DORNOGOVĬ
DUNDGOVĬ
ÖMNÖGOVĬ
ÖVÖR-HANGAY
Gobi
Beijing
(Peking)
Tianjin
(Tientsin)
Shijiazhuang
Taiyuan
Jinan
(Tsinan)
Qingdao
(Tsingtao)
Dalian
(Lüda)
Shenyang
Anshan
Fushun
Hohhot
Baotou
Datong
Zhengzhou
(Chengchow)
Luoyang
Kaifeng
Xi'an
(Sian)
Lanzhou
(Lanchow)
Yinchuan
Tangshan
Zhangjiakou
Huang He
Yin Shan
Taihang Shan
Lüliang Shan
Qin Ling
Helan Shan
Great Wall
Grand Canal

CHINA
SICHUAN
Sichuan Pendi (Red Basin)
HUBEI
HUNAN
JIANGXI
ZHEJIANG
FUJIAN
GUANGDONG
GUIZHOU
YUNNAN
GUANGXI ZHUANGZU
HAINAN
TAIWAN (FORMOSA)
HONG KONG (U.K.)
VIETNAM
LAOS
PHILIPPINES
LUZON
SOUTH CHINA SEA
Gulf of Tongking
Taiwan Strait
Bashi Channel
Luzon Strait
Tropic of Cancer
Chengdu
Chongqing (Chungking)
Wuhan
Changsha
Nanchang
Hangzhou
Shanghai
Fuzhou (Foochow)
Guangzhou (Canton)
Kowloon
Victoria
Macau (Port.)
Guiyang
Nanning
Hanoi
Haiphong
Haikou
Taipei
Kaohsiung
Xiamen (Amoy)
Shantou (Swatow)
Quemoy
Matsu Liehtao
Penghu Liehtao
Relief
Feet
Metres
16404
5000
9843
3000
6562
2000
3281
1000
1640
500
656
200
0
Sea Level
Land Dep.
656
200
13123
4000
22966
7000
Scale 1:7 500 000
0 50 100 150 200 Miles
0 100 200 300 Kms.
Conic Projection
© Collins - Longman Atlases

INDO-CHINA

INDIA
BANGLA-DESH
BURMA (MYANMA)
CHINA
LAOS
VIETNAM
THAILAND
CAMBODIA (KAMPUCHEA)
INDONESIA
PENINSULAR MALAYSIA
BAY OF BENGAL
ANDAMAN SEA
Gulf of Martaban
Gulf of Thailand
Gulf of Tongking
Andaman Islands (India)
Nicobar Islands (India)
Mergui Archipelago
Isthmus of Kra
HAINAN
YUNNAN
GUANGXI ZHUANGZU
GUIZHOU
SHAN
Shan Plateau
Irrawaddy Delta
Ten Degree Channel
Great Coco
Little Coco
North
Middle
South
Port Blair
Little Andaman
Car Nicobar
Great Nicobar
Preparis
Cheduba I.
Ramree I.
C. Negrais
Chittagong
Shillong
Gauhati
Sylhet
Imphal
Kohima
Sittwe (Akyab)
Mandalay
Rangoon (Yangon)
Moulmein
Tavoy
Mergui
Kunming
Guiyang
Nanning
Liuzhou
Guilin
Zhanjiang
Haikou
Hanoi
Haiphong
Vientiane (Viangchan)
Luang Phrabang
Chiang Mai
Bangkok (Krung Thep)
Thonburi
Phnom Penh
Ho Chi Minh (Saigon)
Vung Tau
Da Nang
Hue
Nha Trang
Cam Ranh
Da Lat
Songkhla
Nakhon Si Thammarat
Phuket
Kota Bharu
Kuala Trengganu
George Town
Butterworth
Banda Aceh
Lhokseumawe
Ko Samui
Ko Chang
Phu Quoc
Con Son
Mui Ca Mau
Tonle Sap
Tropic of Cancer
Scale 1:10 000 000
0 100 200 300 Miles
0 100 200 300 400 500 Kms.
Conic Projection
Relief
Feet Metres
16404 5000
9843 3000
6562 2000
3281 1000
1640 500
656 200
0 Sea Level
Land Dep. 656 200
13123 4000
22966 7000
© Collins • Longman Atlases Cbi

JAPAN
CHINA
U.S.S.R.
NORTH KOREA
SOUTH KOREA
SEA OF JAPAN
PACIFIC OCEAN
Sea of Okhotsk
HOKKAIDŌ
Wakkanai
Rebun jima
Rishiri tō
Teshio
Uryu ko
Nayoro
Abashiri wan
Kunashir
Occupied by U.S.S.R. Claimed by Japan
Kitami
Rumoi
Asahikawa
Asahi dake
Fukagawa
Sunagawa
Kussharo ko
Shibecha
Nemuro
Nemuro kaikyō
Kamui misaki
Ishikari wan
Otaru
Sapporo
Shikotsu ko
Yūbari
Obihiro
Kushiro
Urahoro
Hidaka Sammyaku
Tomakomai
Noboribetsu
Setana
Uchiura wan
Muroran
Urakawa
Erimo misaki
Okushiri tō
Kameda
Hakodate
Ō shima
Matsumae
Tsugaru kaikyō
Shiriya saki
Mutsu
Mutsu wan
Aomori
Towada ko
Misawa
Hirosaki
Hachinohe
Ōdate
Noshiro
Mi saki
Oga
Akita
Tazawa ko
Morioka
Miyako
Honjō
Hanamaki
Kamaishi
Ōfunato
Mizusawa
Tobi shima
Chokai zan
Sakata
Tsuruoka
TŌHOKU
Ishinomaki
Furukawa
Ojika Hantō
Awa shima
Hajiki saki
Ryōtsu
Sado
Yamagata
Sendai
Nanyō
Shiroishi
Niigata
Iide yama
Fukushima
Sanjo
Aizuwakamatsu
Nagaoka
Kōriyama
Hekura jima
Suzu misaki
Wajima
Suzu
Joetsu
Shirakawa
Iwaki
Nanao
Himi
Toyama wan
Takaoka
Toyama
Nagano
Kanazawa
Komatsu
Yatsuo
Yariga take
Matsumoto
Takayama
Maebashi
Takasaki
Utsunomiya
Kiryū
Ashikaga
Hitachi
Mito
Nakaminato
Tsuchiura
Kumagaya
Gyōda
Kawagoe
Kawaguchi
Funabashi
Tōkyō
Chiba
Kawasaki
Yokohama
Inubō saki
Fukui
Wakasa wan
Tsuruga
Ontake san
Shirane san
Kōfu
Sagamihara
Atsugi
Fuji san
Hiratsuka
Yokosuka
Odawara
Numazu
Shimizu
Shizuoka
Ō shima
Kasumi
Matsue
Izumo
Yonago
Tottori
Maizuru
Ōgaki
Gifu
Mino
Ichinomiya
Nagoya
Yokkaichi
Kyōto
Amagasaki
Himeji
Akashi
Kōbe
Ōsaka
Sakai
Higashiōsaka
Tsu
Okazaki
Toyohashi
Hamamatsu
Matsusaka
Ise
Wakayama
Owase
Shingū
Shiono zaki
Kii suidō
Kii sanchi
Nii shima
Kōzu shima
Miyake jima
Mikura jima
Gōtsu
CHUGOKU
Chūgoku sanchi
Masuda
Okayama
Kurashiki
Fukuyama
Hiroshima
Kure
Takamatsu
Harima nada
Hagi
Yamaguchi
Iwakuni
Tokuyama
Shimonoseki
Ube
Kitakyūshū
Suō nada
Imabari
Niihama
Matsuyama
Yoshino
Tokushima
Anan
Muroto
SHIKOKU
Shikoku sanchi
Iyo nada
Uwajima
Kōchi
Tosa wan
Ashizuri zaki
Iki shima
Fukuoka
Saga
Nakatsu
Sasebo
Nagasaki
Kurume
Beppu
Ōita
Ōmuta
Kuju san
Bungo suidō
Kumamoto
Yatsushiro
Nobeoka
Kyūshū sanchi
KYŪSHŪ
Shimo jima
Minamata
Sendai
Miyazaki
Miyakonojō
Koshikijima retto
Kagoshima
Kanoya
Ibusuki
Kagoshima wan
Ōsumi kaikyō
Tanega shima
Yaku shima
Kuchino shima
Oki guntō
Tsushima
Ullŭng do
Samch'ŏk
P'ohang
Kamp'o
Ulsan
Taejin
Yŏndŏk
Ch'ŏngjin
Nanam
Kilchu
Kimch'aek
Tanch'ŏn
Musan
Hoeryŏng
Sŏnbong
Najin
Aoji
Yanji
Wangqing
Hunchun
Jingpo Hu
Ussuriysk
Artem
Vladivostok
Suchan
Nakhodka
Sudzukhe
Valentin
Olga
Tetyukhe Pristan
Sikhote Alin
Zaliv Petra Velikogo
Relief
Feet
Metres
16404
5000
9843
3000
6562
2000
3281
1000
1640
500
656
200
0
Sea Level
Land Dep.
656
200
13123
4000
22966
7000
Scale 1:7 500 000
0
50
100
150 Miles
0
50
100
150
200 Kms.
Conic Projection
© Collins ◇ Longman Atlases Cbii
Kantō sanchi
SAITAMA
Higashimatsuyama
Chichibu
Ageo
Kazo
Kōnosu
Mizukaidō
Kasukabe
Toride
Ryūgasaki
Ōmiya
Urawa
Sayama
Niiza
Kashiwa
Narita
Matsudo
Ichikawa
Higashimurayama
Kodaira
Tachikawa
Hachiōji
Fuchū
Chōfu
Machida
Yamato
Kisarazu
Ichihara
Mobara
Tōkyō wan
KANAGAWA
Hadano
CHIBA
Ina
Komagane
Nirasaki
Enzan
Yamanashi
Ōtsuki
Tsuru
Fuji-yoshida
YAMANASHI
Kiso sammyaku
Akaishi sammyaku
NAGANO
Iida
GIFU
Mino-kamo
Kakamigahara
Mizunami
Ena
Inuyama
Kōnan
Tajimi
Toki
Komaki
Seto
Kasugai
Hikone
Inazawa
Tsushima
Biwa ko
Omi-hachiman
Yōkaichi
Moriyama
Ōtsu
Kusatsu
SHIGA
Kuwana
Tōkai
Ōbu
Anjō
Toyota
Kariya
Handa
Tokoname
Suzuka
Kameyama
MIE
Ueno
Ise-wan
AICHI
Shinshiro
Hekinan
Gamagōri
Toyokawa
Atsumi-wan
Tahara
Atsumi-hantō
Irago-suidō
Enshū-nada
Tenryū
Hamakita
Shimada
Fujieda
Yaizu
Kakegawa
Fukuroi
Iwata
Sagara
Omae-zaki
Suruga-wan
SHIZUOKA
Sakuma
Fujinomiya
Gotemba
Fuji
Mishima
Atami
Chigasaki
Fujisawa
Kamakura
Zushi
Miura
Uraga-suidō
Bōsō-hantō
Katsuura
Kamo
Tateyama
Nojima-zaki
Sagami-nada
Ōshima
Itō
Izu-hantō
Shimoda
Irō-zaki
Takarazuka
Ibaraki
Takatsuki
Miki
Itami
Suita
Nishinomiya
Neyagawa
Daitō
Nara
Yao
Matsubara
Yamato-takada
Habikino
Izumi
Izumi-ōtsu
Kishiwada
Izumi-sano
Sennan
Kaizuka
Kawachi-nagano
Gojō
Hashimoto
Ōsaka-wan
NARA
ŌSAKA
KINKI
Toba
Shima-hantō
Ago
Shima
Scale 1:2 500 000
0
20
40
60 Miles
0
20
40
60
80 Kms.
Conic Projection
© Collins

SOUTHEAST ASIA

BURMA
(MYANMA)
THAILAND
LAOS
VIETNAM
CAMBODIA
(KAMPUCHEA)
CHINA
HAINAN
MALAYSIA
BRUNEI
SINGAPORE
INDONESIA
SOUTH CHINA SEA
ANDAMAN SEA
INDIAN OCEAN
LAUT JAWA
(JAVA SEA)
Gulf of Tongking
Gulf of Thailand
Gulf of Martaban
Strait of Malacca
Andaman Islands (India)
Nicobar Islands (India)
Ten Degree Channel
Irrawaddy Delta
Mergui Archipelago
Isthmus of Kra
Mekong Delta
SUMATERA
BORNEO
KALIMANTAN
JAWA
(JAVA)
SARAWAK
SABAH
PENINSULAR MALAYSIA
Bangka
Belitung
Kep. Riau
Lingga
Singkep
Natuna Besar
Kep. Anambas
Mentawai
Siberut
Nias
Simeulue
Madura
Bali
Lombok
Nusa Tenggara
Paracel Is.
Spratly
Christmas I. (Austl.)
Java Trench
Rangoon (Yangon)
Bangkok
Krung Thep
Hanoi
Haiphong
Vientiane (Viangchan)
Phnom Penh
Ho Chi Minh (Saigon)
Kuala Lumpur
Singapore
Jakarta
Bandung
Semarang
Surabaya
Palembang
Medan
Padang
Pekanbaru
Jambi
Pontianak
Banjarmasin
Balikpapan
Samarinda
Kuching
Bandar Seri Begawan
Kota Kinabalu
Nanning
Guangzhou (Canton)
Kowloon
HONG KONG
Victoria (U.K.)
Macau (Port.)
Haikou
Da Nang
Hue
Nha Trang
Chiang Mai
Moulmein
George Town
Ipoh
Equator
Scale 1:15 000 000
0 100 200 300 400 500 Miles
0 200 400 600 800 Kms
Bonne Projection
© Collins-Longman Atlases Cbi

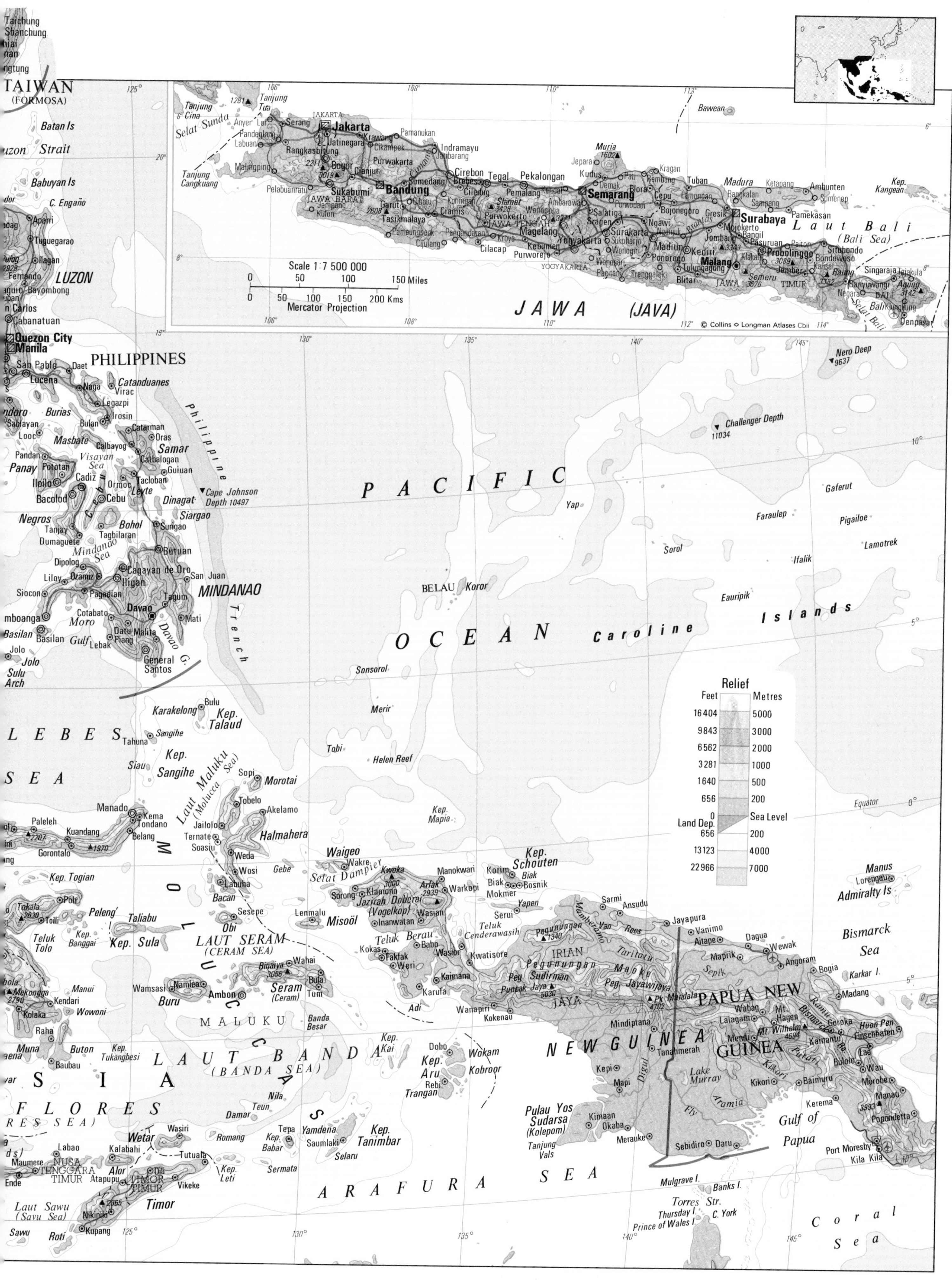

TAIWAN
(FORMOSA)
Batan Is
Luzon Strait
Babuyan Is
C. Engaño
Aparri
Tuguegarao
Ilagan
LUZON
Bayombong
Cabanatuan
Quezon City
Manila
PHILIPPINES
San Pablo
Lucena
Daet
Naga
Catanduanes
Virac
Legazpi
Irosin
Burias
Bulan
Masbate
Catarman
Oras
Samar
Calbayog
Catbalogan
Guiuan
Visayan Sea
Pandan
Panay
Iloilo
Cadiz
Bacolod
Ormoc
Tacloban
Leyte
Cebu
Negros
Tanjay
Dumaguete
Bohol
Tagbilaran
Dinagat
Siargao
Surigao
Mindanao Sea
Dipolog
Butuan
Liloy
Ozamiz
Cagayan de Oro
San Juan
Iligan
Siocon
Pagadian
Tagum
MINDANAO
Cotabato
Davao
Moro Gulf
Mati
Basilan
Jolo
Sulu Arch
Datu Piang
Malita
Lebak
General Santos
Davao G.
Philippine Trench
Cape Johnson Depth 10497
Selat Sunda
Tanjung Cina
Tanjung Tua
Anyer
Pandeglang
Labuan
Serang
JAKARTA
Jakarta
Jatinegara
Krawang
Pamanukan
Cikampek
Indramayu
Jatibarang
Rangkasbitung
Bogor
Purwakarta
Malingping
Sukabumi
Cianjur
Tanjung Cangkuang
Pelabuanratu
JAWA BARAT
Bandung
Cirebon
Brebes
Tegal
Pekalongan
Sumedang
Cibatu
Kuningan
Ciledug
Pemalang
Garut
Tasikmalaya
Ciamis
Slamet 3428
Purwokerto
JAWA TENGAH
Wonosobo
Kendal
Semarang
Ambarawa
Pangandaran
Cilacap
Kroya
Kebumen
Purworejo
Magelang
Salatiga
Sragen
Yogyakarta
YOGYAKARTA
Surakarta
Sukoharjo
Wonogiri
Wonosari
Pacitan
Muria 1602
Jepara
Kudus
Demak
Pati
Kragan
Rembang
Tuban
Blora
Cepu
Purwodadi
Ngawi
Bojonegoro
Lamongan
Gresik
Madiun
Ponorogo
Kediri
Trenggalek
Tulungagung
Blitar
Malang
JAWA
Jombang
Mojokerto
Bangil
Pasuruan
Surabaya
Madura
Bangkalan
Sampang
Ketapang
Pamekasan
Sumenep
Ambunten
Bawean
Kep. Kangean
Laut Bali
(Bali Sea)
Probolinggo
Situbondo
Bondowoso
Jember
Semeru 3676
TIMUR
Raung 3332
Banyuwangi
Singaraja
Tejakula
Agung 3142
BALI
Negara
Klungkung
Denpasar
Selat Bali
Scale 1:7 500 000
0 50 100 150 Miles
0 50 100 150 200 Kms
Mercator Projection
JAWA (JAVA)
© Collins ◇ Longman Atlases Cbii
PACIFIC OCEAN
Nero Deep 9637
Challenger Depth 11034
Gaferut
Yap
Faraulep
Pigailoe
Sorol
Lamotrek
Ifalik
BELAU
Koror
Eauripik
Caroline Islands
Sonsorol
Merir
Tobi
Helen Reef
Kep. Mapia
Equator
Relief
Feet
Metres
16404 5000
9843 3000
6562 2000
3281 1000
1640 500
656 200
0 Sea Level
Land Dep.
656 200
13123 4000
22966 7000
CELEBES SEA
Karakelong
Bulu
Kep. Talaud
Tahuna
Sangihe
Siau
Kep. Sangihe
Laut Maluku (Molucca Sea)
Sopi
Morotai
Tobelo
Akelamo
Manado
Kema
Tondano
Belang
Jailolo
Ternate
Soasiu
Halmahera
Paleleh
Kuandang
Gorontalo
Weda
Wosi
Gebe
Kep. Togian
Labuha
Bacan
Poh
Peleng
Taliabu
Kep. Banggai
Kep. Sula
Sesepe
Obi
Teluk Tolo
LAUT SERAM
(CERAM SEA)
Wahai
Seram
(Ceram)
Bula
Tum
Mekongga 2790
Kendari
Manui
Wowoni
Kolaka
Wamsasi
Namlea
Buru
Ambon
MALUKU
Banda Besar
Raha
Muna
Buton
Baubau
Kep. Tukangbesi
LAUT BANDA
(BANDA SEA)
MOLUCCAS
FLORES SEA
Teun
Nila
Damar
Wetar
Wasiri
Romang
Kep. Babar
Tepa
Yamdena
Saumlaki
Selaru
Kep. Tanimbar
Labao
Maumere
NUSA TENGGARA TIMUR
Ende
Kalabahi
Alor
Atapupu
Dili
TIMOR TIMUR
Tutuala
Kep. Leti
Vikeke
Sermata
Timor
Laut Sawu
(Savu Sea)
Sawu
Nikiniki
Kupang
Roti
Waigeo
Wakre
Selat Dampier
Kwoka 3000
Sorong
Klamono
Jazirah Doberai
(Vogelkop)
Arfak 2939
Manokwari
Warkopi
Inanwatan
Wasian
Lenmalu
Misoöl
Teluk Berau
Babo
Kokas
Fakfak
Weri
Wasior
Kaimana
Karufa
Adi
Kep. Schouten
Korim
Biak
Bosnik
Mokmer
Yapen
Serui
Teluk Cenderawasih
Kwatisore
Sarmi
Ansudu
Mamberamo
Van Rees
Pegunungan
Jayapura
Vanimo
Aitape
IRIAN
Taritatu
Pegunungan Sudirman
Maoke
Peg. Jayawijaya
Puncak Jaya 5030
JAYA
Pk. 4702
Mandala
Wanapiri
Kokenau
Mindiptana
Tanahmerah
NEW GUINEA
Kepi
Mapi
Digul
Pulau Yos Sudarsa
(Kolepom)
Kimaan
Okaba
Merauke
Tanjung Vals
Kep. Kai
Dobo
Kep. Aru
Wokam
Kobroor
Rebi
Trangan
ARAFURA SEA
Dagua
Wewak
Maprik
Sepik
Angoram
Bogia
Karkar I.
Madang
PAPUA NEW GUINEA
Wabag
Mt. Hagen
Laiagam
Mendi
Mt. Wilhelm 4694
Goroka
Kainantu
Huon Pen.
Finschhafen
Lae
Bulolo
Wau
Lake Murray
Aramia
Fly
Kikori
Baimuru
Sebidiro
Daru
Morobe
Manau 3993
Kerema
Popondetta
Gulf of Papua
Port Moresby
Kila Kila
Manus
Lorengau
Admiralty Is
Bismarck Sea
Mulgrave I.
Banks I.
Torres Str.
Thursday I.
Prince of Wales I.
C. York
Coral Sea

SOUTH ASIA

U.S.S.R.
AFGHANISTAN
IRAN
PAKISTAN
IRAQ
SAUDI ARABIA
OMAN
YEMEN
QATAR
BAHRAIN
UNITED ARAB EMIRATES
INDIA
MALDIVES
THE GULF
ARABIAN SEA
INDIAN OCEAN
Gulf of Oman
Str. of Hormuz
Tropic of Cancer
Dasht-e Kavīr
Dasht-e Lūt
Hindu Kush
Karakoram Range
Thar Desert
(Gt. Indian Desert)
Rann of Kachchh
G. of Kachchh
Gulf of Khambhat
Western Ghats
Sulaimān Range
Toba Kākar Range
Central Makrān Range
Makrān Coast Range
Rīgestān
Ar Rub' al Khālī
(Rub' al Khali)
Najd
Al Jāfūrah
Wahiba Sands
Lakshadweep Is.
(India)
Suquṭrá (Socotra)
(Yemen)
Kābol (Kabul)
Islāmābād
Karāchi
Tehrān
Eṣfahān
(Isfahan)
Al Kuwayt
(Kuwait)
Masqaṭ
(Muscat)
Ad Dawḥah
(Doha)
Abū Ẓaby
(Abu Dhabi)
Dubayy
(Dubai)
Bombay
Ahmadābād
Lahore
Quetta
Hyderābād
Pune
Thiruvananthapuram
(Trivandrum)
© Collins ◇ Longman Atlases Cbi

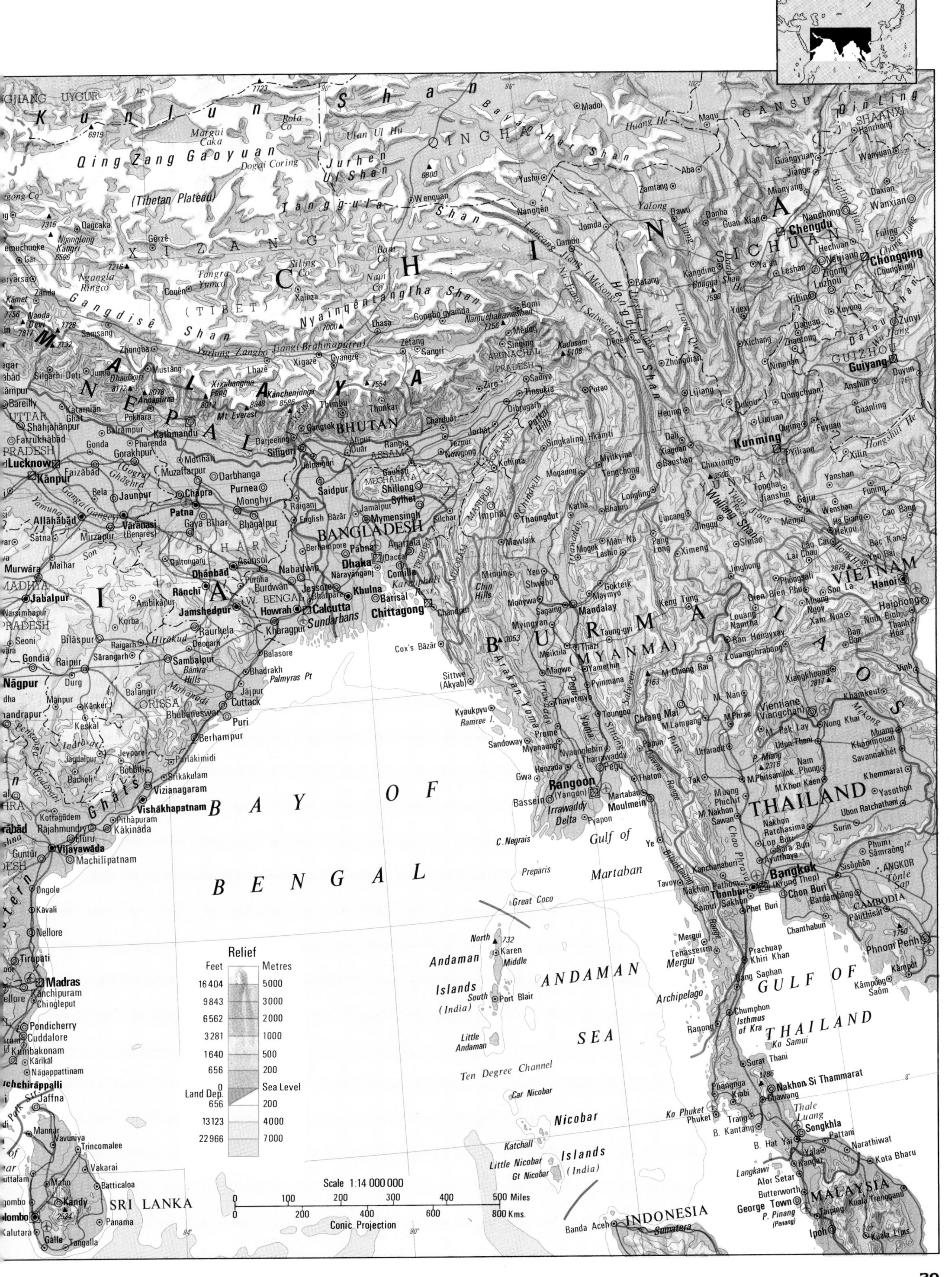

Kunlun Shan
Qing Zang Gaoyuan
(Tibetan Plateau)
Tanggula Shan
XIZANG
(TIBET)
CHINA
Gangdisê Shan
Nyainqêntanglha Shan
Yarlung Zangbo Jiang (Brahmaputra)
Bayan Har Shan
QINGHAI
GANSU
SHAANXI
Qin Ling
SICHUAN
YUNNAN
GUIZHOU
Hengduan Shan
Lancang Jiang (Mekong)
Nu Jiang (Salween)
Chengdu
Chongqing
(Chungking)
Kunming
Guiyang
Lhasa
Mt Everest
Kanchenjunga
Annapurna
Dhaulagiri
HIMALAYA
NEPAL
Kathmandu
BHUTAN
Thimbu
SIKKIM
Gangtok
ASSAM
MEGHALAYA
ARUNACHAL PRADESH
NAGALAND
MANIPUR
MIZORAM
TRIPURA
BANGLADESH
Dhaka
Chittagong
Khulna
Calcutta
Howrah
W. BENGAL
BIHAR
Patna
Vārānasi
(Benares)
Lucknow
Kānpur
Allahābād
UTTAR PRADESH
MADHYA PRADESH
Jabalpur
Nāgpur
ORISSA
Bhubaneswar
Cuttack
Sundarbans
INDIA
Vishākhapatnam
Vijayawāda
Madras
Pondicherry
Tiruchirāppalli
Jaffna
Trincomalee
SRI LANKA
Kandy
Colombo
Galle
BAY OF BENGAL
ANDAMAN SEA
Andaman Islands
(India)
Port Blair
Little Andaman
Ten Degree Channel
Car Nicobar
Nicobar Islands
(India)
Great Coco
Preparis
Gulf of Martaban
BURMA
(MYANMA)
Mandalay
Rangoon
(Yangon)
Irrawaddy Delta
Moulmein
Arakan Yoma
Pegu Yoma
Chin Hills
Sittwe
(Akyab)
Ramree I.
C. Negrais
Mergui Archipelago
Isthmus of Kra
THAILAND
Bangkok
(Krung Thep)
Thonburi
Chiang Mai
GULF OF THAILAND
Ko Samui
Phuket
Songkhla
Hat Yai
LAOS
Vientiane
(Viangchan)
Luangphrabang
VIETNAM
Hanoi
Haiphong
CAMBODIA
Phnom Penh
ANGKOR
Tônlé Sap
MALAYSIA
George Town
P. Pinang
(Penang)
Ipoh
Kota Bharu
INDONESIA
Sumatera
Banda Aceh
Relief
Feet
Metres
16404
5000
9843
3000
6562
2000
3281
1000
1640
500
656
200
0
Sea Level
Land Dep.
656
200
13123
4000
22966
7000
Scale 1:14 000 000
0
100
200
300
400
500 Miles
0
200
400
600
800 Kms.
Conic Projection

NORTHERN INDIA, PAKISTAN AND BANGLADESH

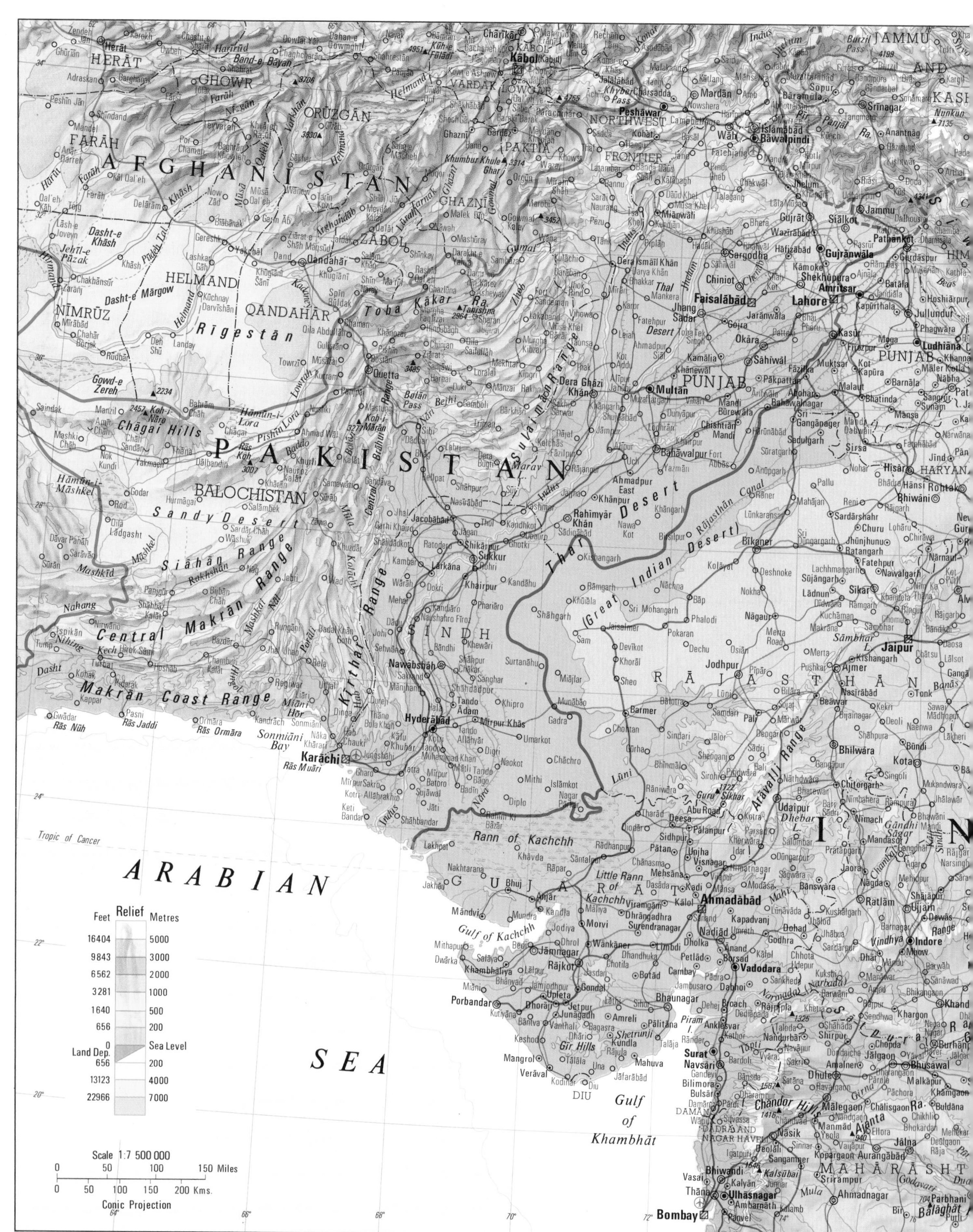
A F G H A N I S T A N
P A K I S T A N
ARABIAN
SEA
HERĀT
GHOWR
ORŪZGĀN
FARĀH
HELMAND
NĪMRŪZ
QANDAHĀR
ZĀBOL
GHAZNĪ
PAKTIA
LOWGAR
VARDAK
KĀBOL
NORTHWEST FRONTIER
BALOCHISTAN
PUNJAB
SINDH
PUNJAB
HARYANA
RĀJASTHĀN
GUJARAT
JAMMU AND KASHMIR
MAHĀRĀSHTRA
DIU
DAMAN
DADRA AND NAGAR HAVELI
Herāt
Kābol
Peshāwar
Islāmābād
Rawalpindi
Lahore
Amritsar
Faisalābād
Multān
Quetta
Sukkur
Hyderābād
Karāchi
Ahmadābād
Vadodara
Surat
Bombay
Jaipur
Jodhpur
Bīkaner
Indore
Ludhiāna
Jullundur
Srīnagar
Jammu
Gujrānwāla
Sargodha
Bahāwalpur
Rājkot
Jāmnagar
Bhāvnagar
Nāsik
Thar Desert
(Great Indian Desert)
Rann of Kachchh
Little Rann of Kachchh
Gulf of Kachchh
Gulf of Khambhāt
Sonmiāni Bay
Makrān Coast Range
Central Makrān Range
Siāhān Range
Chāgai Hills
Toba Kākar Ra.
Sulaimān Range
Kīrthar Range
Arāvalli Range
Vindhya Range
Sandy Desert
Rīgestān
Dasht-e Mārgow
Tropic of Cancer
Indus
Helmand
Relief
Feet
Metres
16404
5000
9843
3000
6562
2000
3281
1000
1640
500
656
200
0
Sea Level
Land Dep.
656
200
13123
4000
22966
7000
Scale 1:7 500 000
0
50
100
150 Miles
0
50
100
150
200 Kms.
Conic Projection

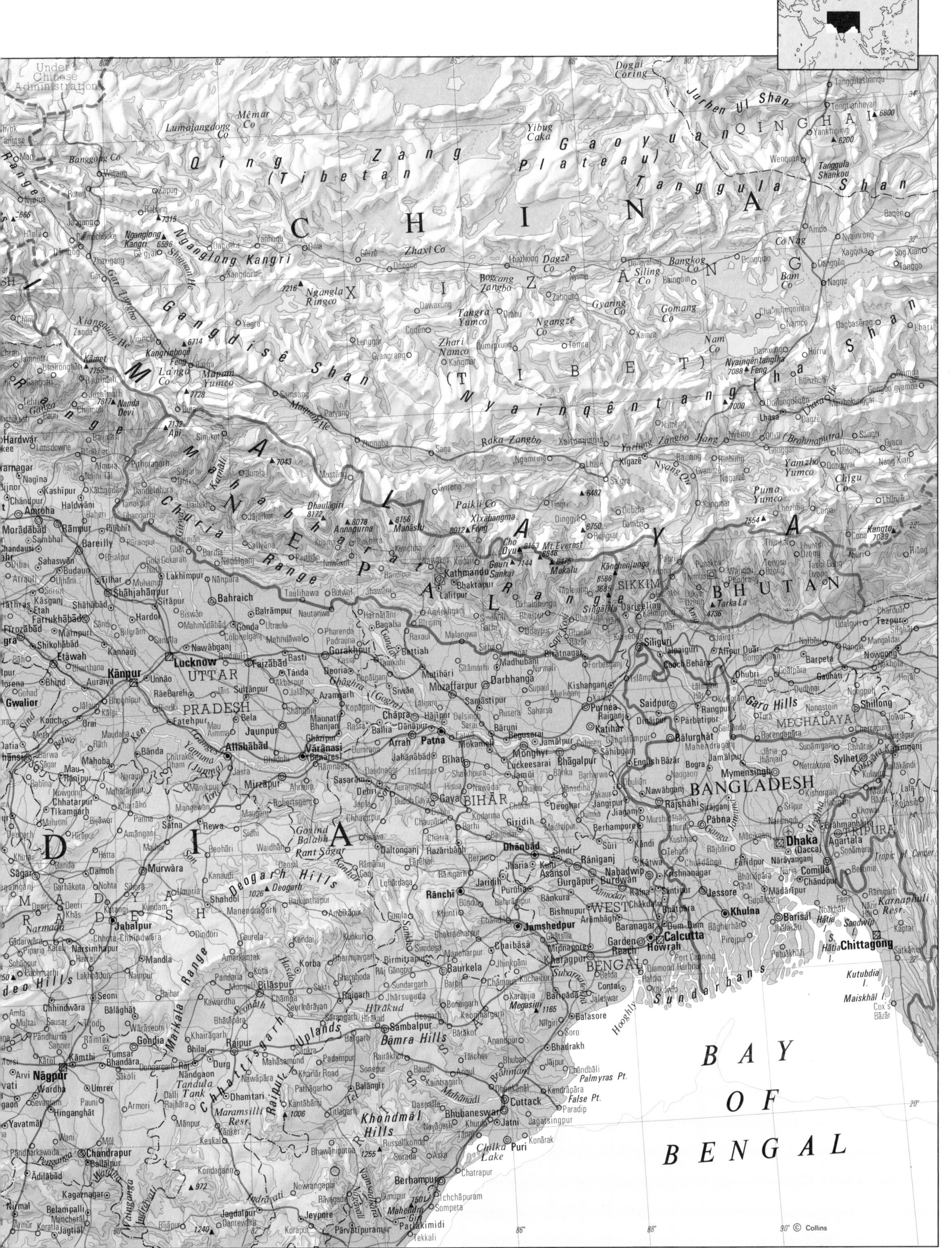

Under Chinese Administration
C H I N A
Qing Zang Gaoyuan (Tibetan Plateau)
X I Z A N G (T I B E T)
Q I N G H A I
Jurhen Ul Shan
Tanggula Shan
Nyainqêntanglha Shan
Gangdisê Shan
Nganglong Kangri
H I M A L A Y A
Mahabharat Range
Churia Range
N E P A L
SIKKIM
B H U T A N
BANGLADESH
MEGHALAYA
TRIPURA
I N D I A
UTTAR PRADESH
BIHAR
WEST BENGAL
M A D H Y A P R A D E S H
Garo Hills
Deogarh Hills
Maikala Range
Chhattisgarh Uplands
Bāmra Hills
Khondmāl Hills
Sundarbans
Zhaxi Co
Mt. Everest 8848
Kānchenjunga 8586
Makalu 8475
Dhaulāgiri 8172
Annapurna 8078
Manāslu 8156
Nanda Devi 7817
Kāmet 7756
Lhasa
Xigazê
Kathmandu
Thimbu
Darjeeling
Siliguri
Lucknow
Kānpur
Allahābād
Vārānasi (Benares)
Patna
Gaya
Dhānbād
Rānchi
Jamshedpur
Calcutta
Howrah
Dhaka (Dacca)
Chittagong
Shillong
Gauhati
Jabalpur
Nāgpur
Raipur
Bilāspur
Sambalpur
Cuttack
Bhubaneswar
Puri
Chilka Lake
Berhampur
Gwalior
Bareilly
Tropic of Cancer
B A Y O F B E N G A L
© Collins

SOUTHWEST ASIA

BLACK SEA
GREECE
AEGEAN SEA
TURKEY
CYPRUS
MEDITERRANEAN SEA
LEBANON
SYRIA
ISRAEL
JORDAN
EGYPT
LIBYA
SUDAN
RED SEA
Thessaloníki
Athínai (Athens)
Istanbul
Bursa
Balikesir
İzmir
Ankara
Konya
Antalya
Adana
Kayseri
Sivas
Malatya
Diyarbakir
Gaziantep
Samsun
Trabzon
Erzurum
Halab (Aleppo)
Ḥimş
Dimashq (Damascus)
Bayrūt (Beirut)
Tel Aviv-Yafo
Yerushalayim (Jerusalem)
'Ammān
Al Iskandarīyah (Alexandria)
Al Qāhirah (Cairo)
Al Jīzah
Bûr Sa'îd (Port Said)
As Suways (Suez)
Aswân
Al Madīnah (Medina)
Kríti (CRETE)
Ródhos (Rhodes)
Scale 1:9 000 000
0 50 100 150 200 250 Miles
0 100 200 300 400 Kms.
Conic Projection
Tropic of Cancer

THE LEVANT

Relief
Feet
Metres
16404
5000
9843
3000
6562
2000
3281
1000
1640
500
656
200
0
Sea Level
Land Dep.
656
200
13123
4000
22966
7000
Scale 1:3 500 000
0
20
40
60
80
100 Miles
0
50
100
150 Kms.
Polyconic Projection
M E D I T E R R A N E A N
S E A
CYPRUS
Lefkosía (Nicosia)
Ammókhostos (Famagusta)
Lárnax (Lárnaca)
Lemesós (Limassol)
Néa Páfos (Paphos)
Troödos
Ólimbos 1952
Akr. Apostólou Andréa
Akr. Akámas
Akr. Pidálion
Akr. Gátas
Kólpos Mórfou
Kólpos Ammókhostou
Al Lādhiqīyah (Latakia)
Ḩamāh
Ḩimş
Ţarţūs
Ţarābulus (Tripoli)
LEBANON
Bayrūt (Beirut)
Şaydā (Sidon)
Şūr (Tyre)
Qurnat as Sawdā 3066
Dimashq (Damascus)
SYRIA
Golan Heights
Yam Kinneret (L. Tiberias)
Hefa (Haifa)
ISRAEL
Netanya
Tel Aviv-Yafo
Rishon LeZiyyon
Ashdod
Ashqelon
Gaza Strip
Ghazzah (Gaza)
Yerushalayim (Jerusalem)
West Bank
Dead Sea
Al Khalīl (Hebron)
Be'er Sheva'
Nābulus
Irbid
Az Zarqā'
'Ammān
JORDAN
Al Karak
Ma'ān
Al 'Aqabah
Elat
HaNegev (Negev)
PETRA
Gulf of Aqaba
SAUDI ARABIA
Ḩismá
J. al Lawz 2580
J. Dabbāgh 2350
Tabūk
Al Iskandarīyah (Alexandria)
Damanhūr
Rashīd
Dumyāţ
Būr Sa'īd (Port Said)
Buḩayrat al Manzilah
Buḩayrat al Burullus
Ţanţā
Al Manşūrah
Az Zaqāzīq
Al Ismā'īlīyah
Qanāt as Suways (Suez Canal)
Al Buḩayrah al Murrah al Kubrá (Great Bitter Lake)
Al Jīzah
Al Qāhirah (Cairo)
PYRAMIDS
MEMPHIS
As Suways (Suez)
Mamarra Mitla (Mitla Pass)
Al 'Arīsh
Sabkhat al Bardawīl
Wādī an Naţrūn
Birkat Qārūn
Al Fayyūm
Banī Suwayf
Al Minyā
Mallawī
E G Y P T
Aş Şaḩrā' ash Sharqīyah
(Arabian or Eastern Desert)
Khalīj as Suways (Gulf of Suez)
Shibh Jazīrat Sīnā' (Sinai Peninsula)
Jabal at Tīh
J. Mūsá 2285
J. Kātrīnā 2637
Sharm ash Shaykh
Ra's Muḩammad
Jazīrat Tīrān
Maḑīq Jūbāl (Str. of Jubal)
RED SEA
© Collins – Longman Atlases

ARABIA AND THE HORN OF AFRICA

Relief

Feet	Metres
16404	5000
9843	3000
6562	2000
3281	1000
1640	500
656	200
0	Sea Level
Land Dep.	
656	200
13123	4000
22966	7000

Scale 1:15 000 000

0 100 200 300 Miles

0 100 200 300 400 500 Kms

Lambert Zenithal Equal Area Projection

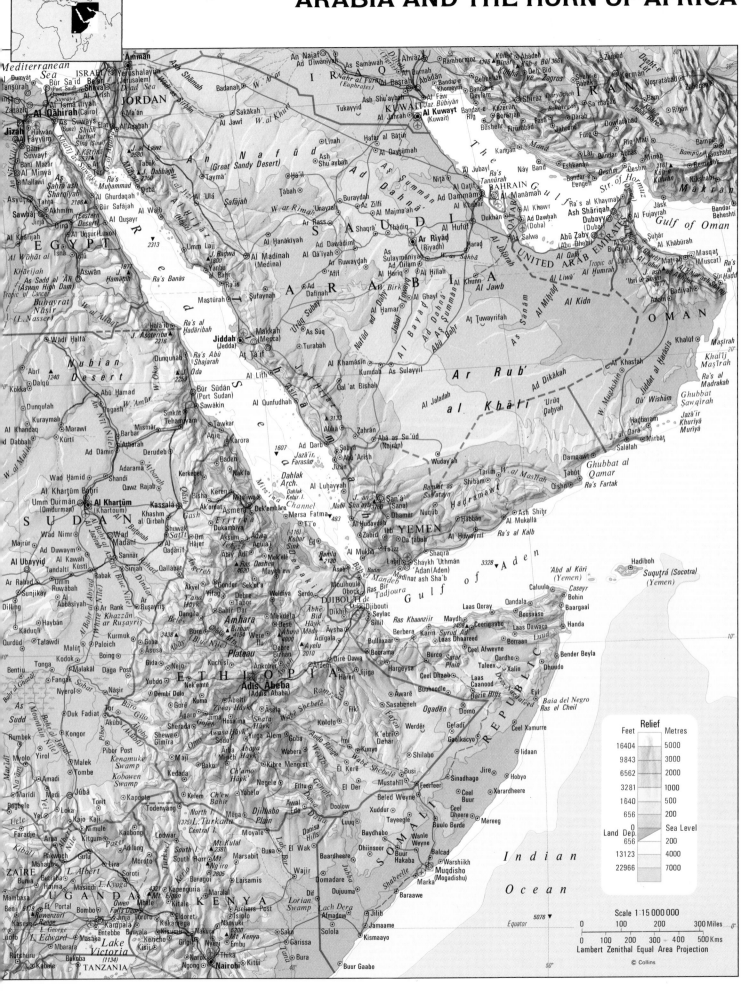

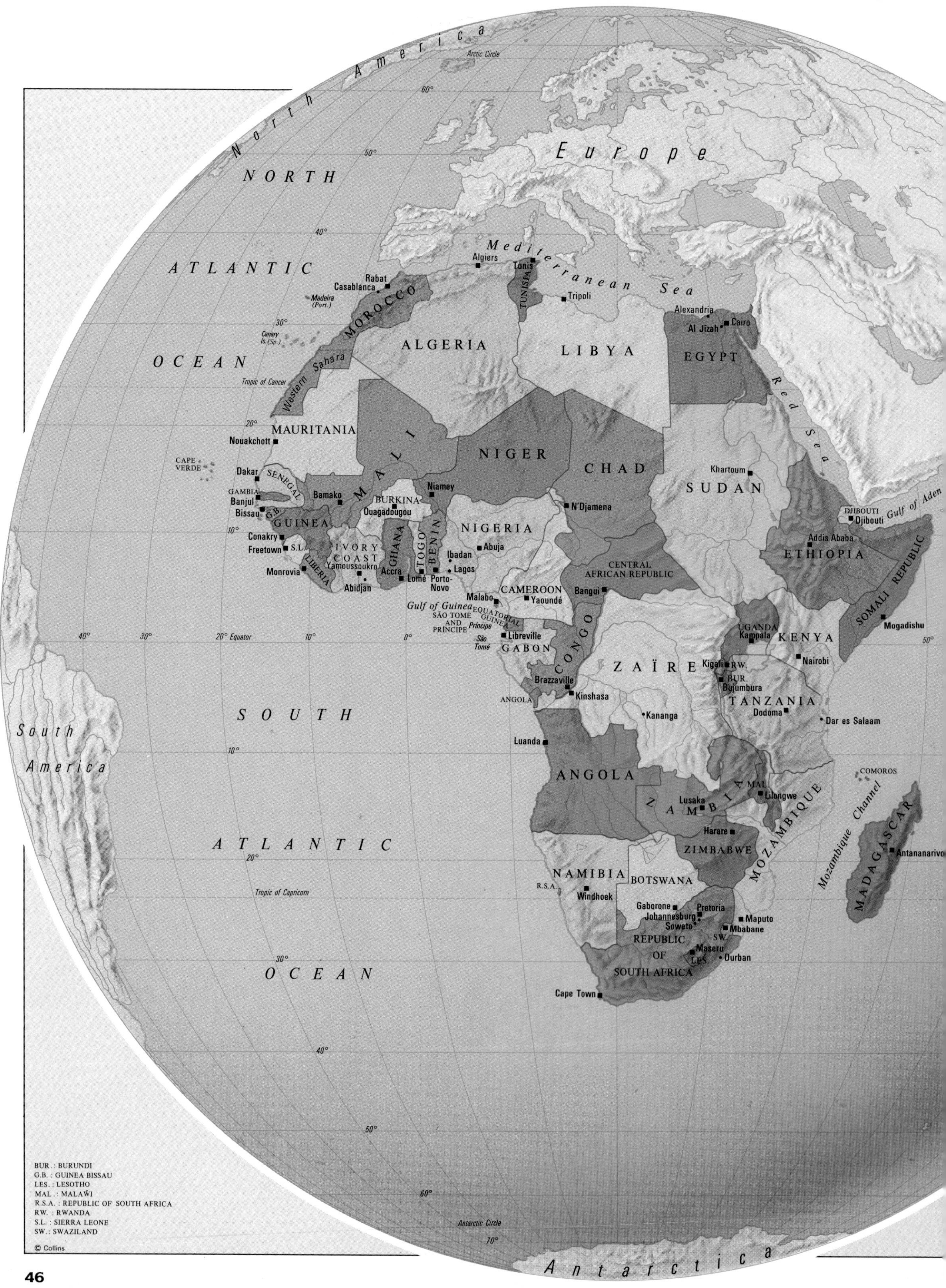
North America
Arctic Circle
Europe
NORTH
ATLANTIC
OCEAN
Mediterranean Sea
Algiers
Tunis
Tripoli
Rabat
Casablanca
Madeira (Port.)
Canary Is. (Sp.)
MOROCCO
TUNISIA
ALGERIA
LIBYA
Alexandria
Al Jizah
Cairo
EGYPT
Western Sahara
Tropic of Cancer
Red Sea
MAURITANIA
Nouakchott
CAPE VERDE
MALI
NIGER
CHAD
SUDAN
Khartoum
Dakar
SENEGAL
GAMBIA
Banjul
Bissau
G.B.
GUINEA
Bamako
Niamey
BURKINA
Ouagadougou
N'Djamena
DJIBOUTI
Djibouti
Gulf of Aden
Conakry
Freetown
S.L.
IVORY COAST
Yamoussoukro
GHANA
TOGO
BENIN
NIGERIA
Abuja
Ibadan
Lagos
Addis Ababa
ETHIOPIA
SOMALI REPUBLIC
Monrovia
LIBERIA
Abidjan
Accra
Lomé
Porto-Novo
CENTRAL AFRICAN REPUBLIC
Bangui
CAMEROON
Yaoundé
Malabo
Gulf of Guinea
EQUATORIAL GUINEA
SÃO TOMÉ AND PRÍNCIPE
Príncipe
São Tomé
Libreville
GABON
CONGO
UGANDA
Kampala
KENYA
Mogadishu
Nairobi
Equator
ZAÏRE
Kigali
RW.
BUR.
Bujumbura
Brazzaville
Kinshasa
ANGOLA
TANZANIA
Dodoma
Dar es Salaam
Kananga
SOUTH
South America
Luanda
ANGOLA
COMOROS
ZAMBIA
Lusaka
MAL.
Lilongwe
MOZAMBIQUE
Mozambique Channel
MADAGASCAR
Antananarivo
Harare
ZIMBABWE
ATLANTIC
NAMIBIA
BOTSWANA
R.S.A.
Windhoek
Tropic of Capricorn
Gaborone
Pretoria
Johannesburg
Soweto
Maputo
Mbabane
SW.
REPUBLIC OF SOUTH AFRICA
Maseru
LES.
Durban
OCEAN
Cape Town
Antarctic Circle
Antarctica
BUR.: BURUNDI
G.B.: GUINEA BISSAU
LES.: LESOTHO
MAL.: MALAWI
R.S.A.: REPUBLIC OF SOUTH AFRICA
RW.: RWANDA
S.L.: SIERRA LEONE
SW.: SWAZILAND
© Collins

AFRICA

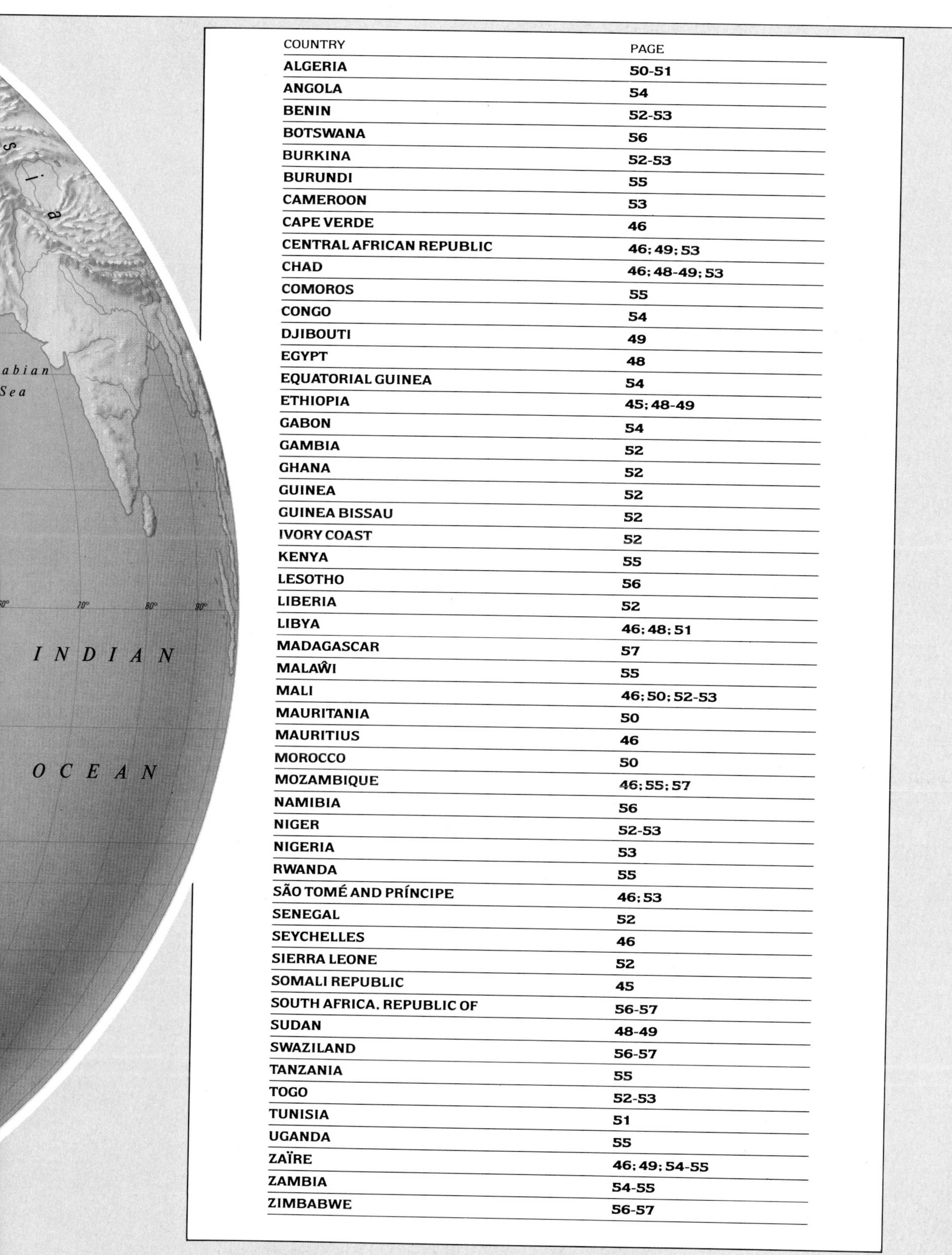
abian
Sea
60°
70°
80°
90°
INDIAN
OCEAN

COUNTRY	PAGE
ALGERIA	50-51
ANGOLA	54
BENIN	52-53
BOTSWANA	56
BURKINA	52-53
BURUNDI	55
CAMEROON	53
CAPE VERDE	46
CENTRAL AFRICAN REPUBLIC	46; 49; 53
CHAD	46; 48-49; 53
COMOROS	55
CONGO	54
DJIBOUTI	49
EGYPT	48
EQUATORIAL GUINEA	54
ETHIOPIA	45; 48-49
GABON	54
GAMBIA	52
GHANA	52
GUINEA	52
GUINEA BISSAU	52
IVORY COAST	52
KENYA	55
LESOTHO	56
LIBERIA	52
LIBYA	46; 48; 51
MADAGASCAR	57
MALAŴI	55
MALI	46; 50; 52-53
MAURITANIA	50
MAURITIUS	46
MOROCCO	50
MOZAMBIQUE	46; 55; 57
NAMIBIA	56
NIGER	52-53
NIGERIA	53
RWANDA	55
SÃO TOMÉ AND PRÍNCIPE	46; 53
SENEGAL	52
SEYCHELLES	46
SIERRA LEONE	52
SOMALI REPUBLIC	45
SOUTH AFRICA, REPUBLIC OF	56-57
SUDAN	48-49
SWAZILAND	56-57
TANZANIA	55
TOGO	52-53
TUNISIA	51
UGANDA	55
ZAÏRE	46; 49; 54-55
ZAMBIA	54-55
ZIMBABWE	56-57

NILE VALLEY

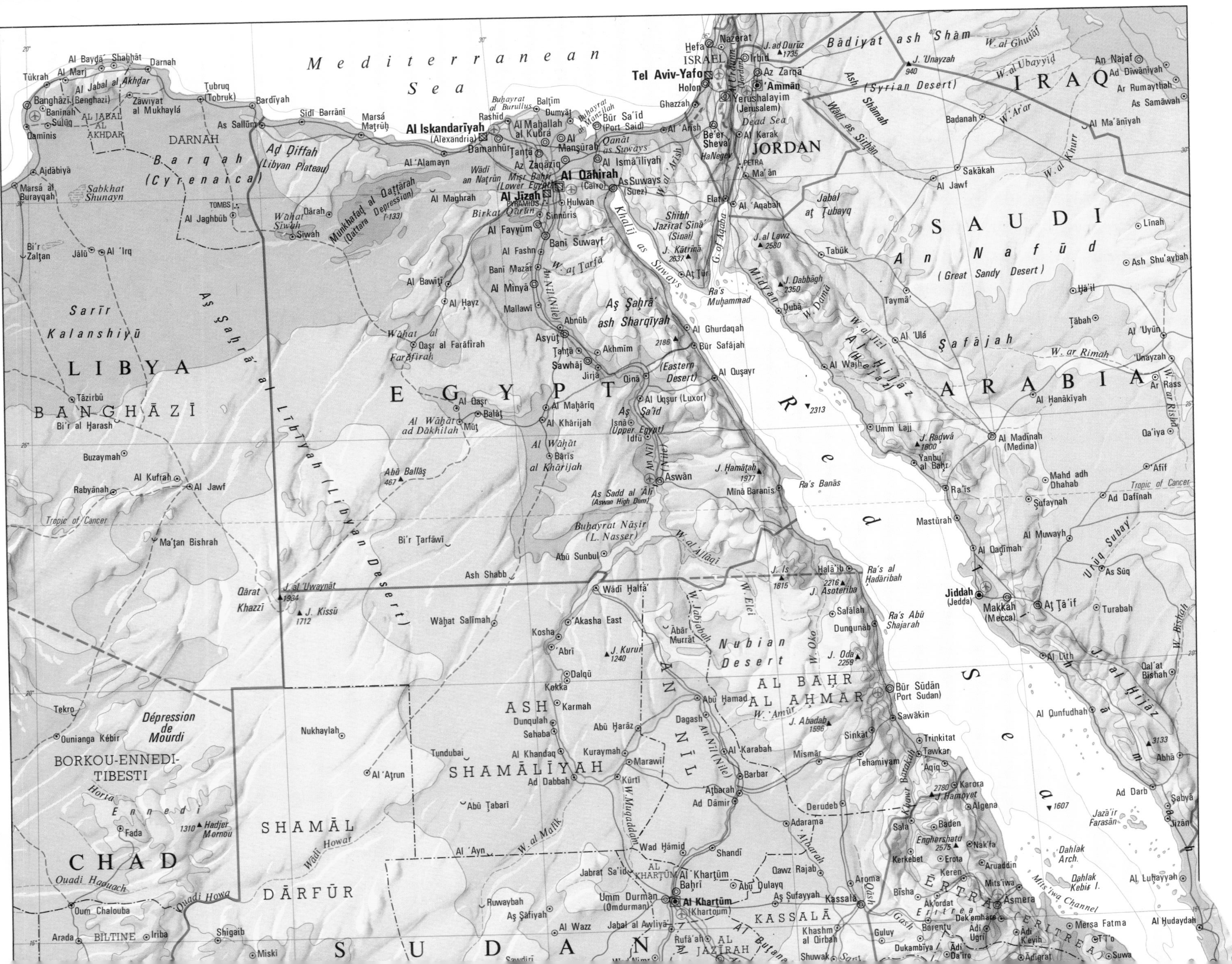

Mediterranean Sea
Red Sea
EGYPT
LIBYA
SUDAN
CHAD
SAUDI ARABIA
IRAQ
JORDAN
ISRAEL
ERITREA
Al Qāhirah (Cairo)
Al Iskandarīyah (Alexandria)
Al Jīzah
Būr Sa'īd (Port Said)
As Suways (Suez)
Aswān
Al Uqşur (Luxor)
Al Kharţūm (Khartoum)
Umm Durmān (Omdurman)
Būr Sūdān (Port Sudan)
Jiddah (Jedda)
Makkah (Mecca)
Al Madīnah (Medina)
'Ammān
Yerushalayim (Jerusalem)
Tel Aviv-Yafo
Banghāzī (Benghazi)
Asmera
Khalīj as Suways
G. of Aqaba
An Nīl (Nile)
Buhayrat Nāşir (L. Nasser)
Nubian Desert
Aş Şaḩrā' ash Sharqīyah (Eastern Desert)
Aş Şaḩrā' al Lībīyah (Libyan Desert)
An Nafūd (Great Sandy Desert)
Al Ḩijāz (Hejaz)
Shibh Jazīrat Sīnā' (Sinai)
Munkhafad al Qaţţārah (Qattara Depression)
Ad Diffah (Libyan Plateau)
Barqah (Cyrenaica)
Sarīr Kalanshiyū
Tropic of Cancer

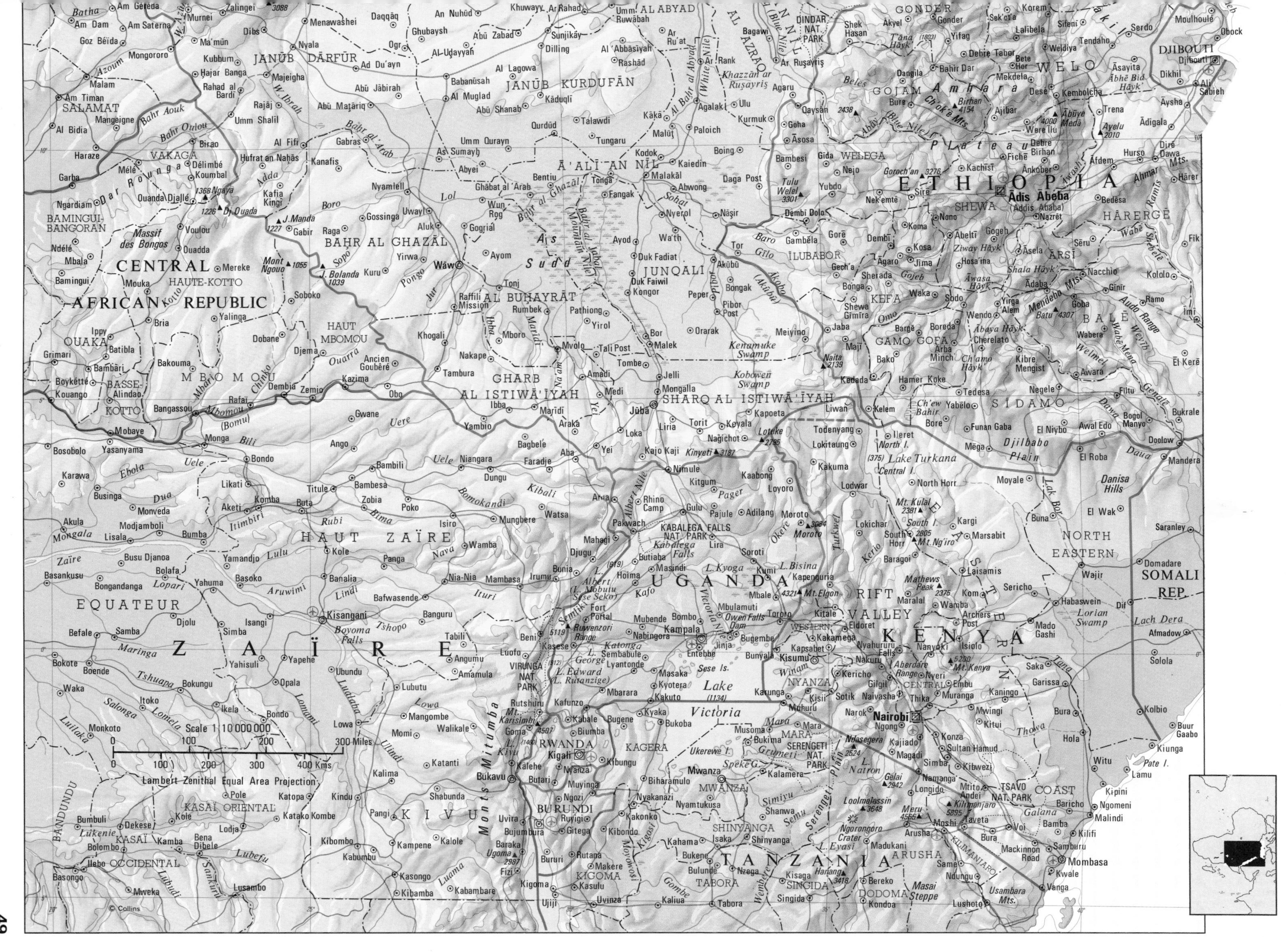
ETHIOPIA
DJIBOUTI
SOMALI REP.
KENYA
UGANDA
TANZANIA
RWANDA
BURUNDI
ZAÏRE
CENTRAL AFRICAN REPUBLIC
Ādis Ābeba
Nairobi
Kampala
Mombasa
Kisangani
Lake Victoria
Lake Turkana
Scale 1:10 000 000
Lambert Zenithal Equal Area Projection
0 100 200 300 Miles
0 100 200 300 400 Kms
© Collins

NORTHWEST AFRICA

Scale 1:10 000 000
0 100 200 300 Miles
0 100 200 300 400 Kms.
Lambert Zenithal Equal Area Projection
Feet
Metres
16404
5000
9843
3000
6562
2000
3281
1000
1640
500
656
200
0
Sea Level
Land Dep.
656
200
13123
4000
22966
7000
Metres
ATLANTIC
OCEAN
Arquipélago da Madeira (Madeira Is.) (Port.)
Funchal
Madeira
Porto Santo
Islas Canarias (Sp.) (Canary Is.)
La Palma
Tenerife
Santa Cruz de Tenerife
Gomera
Hierro
Las Palmas de Gran Canaria
Gran Canaria
Lanzarote
Arrecife
Fuerteventura
C. Juby
Tarfaya
SPAIN
Jerez de la Frontera
Golfo de Cádiz
Cádiz
Málaga
Sierra Nevada
Almería
C. de Gata
Algeciras
Gibraltar (U.K.)
Strait of Gibraltar
Tanger (Tangier)
Ceuta (Sp.)
Tétouan (Tetuan)
Asilah
Larache
Chechaouene
Al-Hoceima
Melilla (Sp.)
Nador
Oujda
Souk-el-Arba-du-Rharb
Ksar-el-Kebir
Ouezzane
Kenitra
Salé
Rabat
Sidi Kacem
Fès
Taza
Mohammedia
Casablanca
Khemisset
Meknès
Sefrou
Jerada
El Jadida
Berrechid
Azrou
Sidi Smaïl
Settat
Khouribga
Oued Zem
Khenifra
MOROCCO
Moyen Atlas
Oued Moulouya
Hauts Plateaux
Tendrara
Bou Arfa
Safi
Oued Oum er Rbia
Beni Mellal
El-Kelâa-des-Srarhna
Oued Tensift
Marrakech
Aït-Ourir
Toubkal 4165
Haut Atlas
Er Rachidia
Boudenib
Essaouira
Tamanar
J. Aoulime 3555
C. Rhir
Tamri
Agadir
Oued Sous
Taroudannt
Ouarzazate
Tazenakht
Jbel Sarho
Jbel Bani
Erfoud
Rissani
Hamada du Guir
Béchar
Abadla
Igli
Beni Abbès
Oued Saoura
Oued Namous
Tagounit
Tiznit
Tafraout
Oued Zemoul
Sidi Ifni
Bou-Izakarn
Goulimime
Tarhjicht
Tiglit
Oued Drâa
Hamada du Drâa
Tabelbala
Hamada Tounassine
Tindouf
Sebkha de Tindouf
Sbaa
El Aaiún (Laâyoune)
Hamada
Mahbès
Saguia el Hamra
Lemsid
Cabo Bojador
Bu Craa
Semara
Bordj Flye Ste. Marie
El Eglab
Chenachane
Reggane
Aïn ben Tili
Bir Mogrein
Western Sahara
Guelta Zemmur
Sebjet Agsumal
Tourassine
TIRIS ZEMMOUR
Sebkhet Oumm ed Droûs Telli
Oued el-Ma
El Mreïti
Chegga
Erg Chech
Poste Weygand
Dakhla
Tropic of Cancer
Sebkhet Oumm ed Droûs Guebli
Tni Haïa
Terhazza
Aguêraktem
Fdérik
Zouîrât
Kediet Ijill 915
Bir Zreïgat
Taoudenni
Tanezrouft
Poste Maurice Cortier (Bidon Cinq)
Tichla
Oued Atui
Nouadhibou
C. Blanc
Choum
Passe de Ouarane
ADRAR
Ouadane
Ouarane
El Djouf
El Khnâchîch
Bîr Ounâne
Erg i-n Sâkâne
DAKHLET NOUADHIBOU
INCHIRI
Atar
MAURITANIA
El Ouassi
Tessalit
Akjoujt
C. Timiris
Sebkha de Ndrhamcha
El Mreyyé
TOMBOUCTOU
Mabrouk
HODH ECH CHARGUI
Bouraga
Araouane
Nouakchott
Tidjikdja 420
TAGANT
Tichît
Tagant
Trarza
TRARZA
Boutilimit
Moudjéria
Azaouâd
MALI
Vallée du Tilemsi
Anefis
Mederdra
Aleg
Boumdeit
Tamchaket
HODH EL GHARBI
Oualâta
Tombouctou (Timbuktu)
Bamba
Bourem
BRAKNA
Rosso
Bogué
Kiffa
Ayoûn el 'Atroûs
L. Faguibine
Gourma-Rharous
Tondibi
Dagana
Podor
L. de Guiers
Mbagne
Kaédi
ASSABA
Néma
Goundam
Diré
Niger
GHARBI
St. Louis
Louga
GORGOL
Sénégal
Mbout
Timbédra
Niout
Niafounké
Doro
Gao
Dahra
Linguère
Pouté
Matam
Kankossa
KOUMBISALEH
Ansongo
GUIDIMAKA
Karakoro
Gossi
Tivaouane
SENEGAL
Namari
MOPTI
Fafa
Dakar
Thiès
Bakel
Yélimané
Nioro
Nara
SÉGOU
Hombori
Douentza
Labbeza
Diourbel
KAYES
BAMAKO
© Collins

Alger (Algiers)
Boufarik
Blida
Médéa
El Asnam
Tizi-Ouzou
Bouira
Bejaïa
Jijel
Skikda
Annaba
Bordj Bou Arreridj
Sétif
El Eulma
Guelma
Constantine
Monts du Hodna
Aïn Beïda
Ksar el Boukhari
Tiaret
Bou Saâda
Barika
Batna
Khenchela
Tébessa
Biskra
Djelfa
Aflou
Laghouat
Chott Melrhir
Oued Ittel
Oued el Attar
El Oued
Touggourt
Hassi er Rmel
Ghardaïa
Ouargla
Hassi Messaoud
Fort Lallemand
El Golea
Oued Mya
Fort Miribel
Hassi bel Guebbour
Grand Erg Oriental
Bordj Omar Driss
Miliana
I-n-Salah
Amguid
Illizi
Tassili-n-Ajjer
Tadjmout
Arak
Oued Irharrhar
Garet el Djenoun
2327
Azao
2158
Zaouatallaz
Djanet
I-n-Eker
Ideles
I-n-Amguel
Ahaggar
2918
Tahat
2132
Djebel Serkout
2306
Oued Tafassasset
Tit
Abalessa
Tamanrasset
Silet
Amsel
Oued Tadjetaret
Oued Ti-n-Tarabine
Tassili oua-n-Ahaggar
Admer
Anou Ti-n Elhaoua
Tassili
Menzel Bourguiba
Bizert (Bizerte)
C. Bon
Tunis
La Goulette
Tabarka
Béja
Hammam Lif
Nabeul
Souk Ahras
El Kef
Enfida
G. de Hammamet
Msaken
Sousse
Ouenza
El Kairouan
Monastir
El Mahdia
Ra's Kaboudia
1378
Djebel Mrhila
El Kasserine
Îles Kerkenna
Sfax
Gafsa
El Metlaoui
Tozeur
Nefta
Chott Djerid
Kebili
G. de Gabès
Gabès
Île de Djerba
Médenine
TUNISIA
Ksar Rhilane
Dehibat
Sicilia (Sicily)
Catania
Siracusa
Ragusa
C. Passero
MALTA
Valletta
Lampedusa (Italy)
Mediterranean Sea
Kalámai
GREECE
Akr. Akrítas
Akr. Taínaron
Ţarābulus (Tripoli)
Zuwārah
AZ ZĀWIYAH
ṬARĀBULUS
Qaşr al Qarābūllī
Al Khums
Zlīţan
Al Qaşabāt
Mişrātah
Gharyān
Al Jawsh
Nālūt
Jādū
Banī Walīd
W. Sawfajjin
Mizdah
Qaryat al Qaddāḩīyah
AL KHUMS
Sabkhat Tāwurghā'
Khalīj Surt (Gulf of Sidra)
Bu'ayrāt al Ḩasūn
Surt
As Sulţān
Sīnāwin
Ţarābulus (Tripolitania)
An Nawfalīyah
Ra's al Unūf
Al 'Uqaylah
Marsá al Burayqah
Ajdābiyā
Sabkhat Shunayn
Banghāzī (Benghazi)
Banīnah
Qamīnis
Sulūq
Tūkrah
Al Marj
Al Bayḑā'
Shaḩḩāt
Al Jabal al Akhḑar
AL JABAL AL AKHḑAR
Fort Saint
Ghadāmis
Dirj
GHARYĀN
MIŞRĀTAH
Abyār ash Shuwayrif
Waddān
Hūn
Marādah
Bi'r Zalţan
Jālū
Al 'Irq
Jabal as Sawdā'
Zillah
SABHĀ
Şaḩrā' Awbārī
Birāk
Al Harūj al Aswad
Sarīr Kalanshiyū
Samnū
Sabhā
LIBYA
Awbārī
W. Irauen
Ghaddūwah
Tmassah
Zawīlah
Al 'Uwaynāt
Ḩamādat Marzūq
W. Barjūj
Marzūq
Tāzirbū
BANGHĀZĪ
Bi'r al Ḩarash
AWBĀRĪ
Wāw al Kabīr
Ghāt
Al Qaţrūn
Şaḩrā' Marzūq
Buzaymah
Şaḩrā' Rabyānah (Rebiana Sand Sea)
Rabyānah
Tajarḩī
Sarīr Tibastī
Tropic of Cancer
I-n-Ezzane
Toummo
SAHARA
Plateau du Djado
Plateau du Tchigai
Djado
Aozou
Bette
2286
Bardaï
Tarso Ouri
3150
Ouri
Wour
3265
Tibesti
3325
Tarso Ahon
3415
Emi Koussi
Zouar
Ténéré du Tafassasset
Séguédine
1994
Mt. Gréboun
Tekro
Gouro
Ounianga Kébir
AGADEZ
Aney
Iferouâne
1795
Aïr (Azbine)
Sidaouet
In Abbangarit
Teguidda I-n-Tessoum
Agadez
I-n-Gall
Vallée de l'Azaouak
Bilma
Grand Erg de Bilma
BORKOU-ENNEDI-TIBESTI
Enneri Yoo
Aïn Galakka
Largeau
Horta
Fada
CHAD
Bodélé
Ouadi Haouach
NIGER
DIFFA
Koro Toro
Bahr el Ghazal
Oum Chalouba
TAHOUA
Tegouma
508
ZINDER
Tanout
KANEM
Nokou
Zigey
BATHA
Arada
BILTINE
Biltine

WEST AFRICA

Western Sahara
TIRIS ZEMMOUR
MAURITANIA
SENEGAL
GAMBIA
GUINEA BISSAU
GUINEA
SIERRA LEONE
LIBERIA
IVORY COAST
(CÔTE D'IVOIRE)
BURKINA
GHANA
MALI
ATLANTIC
OCEAN
DAKHLET NOUADHIBOU
INCHIRI
ADRAR
TAGANT
TRARZA
BRAKNA
ASSABA
GUIDIMAKA
HODH EL GHARBI
HODH ECH CHARGUI
TOMBOUCTOU
MOPTI
KAYES
SÉGOU
BAMAKO
SIKASSO
Nouakchott
Nouadhibou
Dakar
Banjul
Bissau
Conakry
Freetown
Monrovia
Bamako
Abidjan
Accra
Ouagadougou
Tombouctou (Timbuktu)
Relief
Feet
Metres
16404
5000
9843
3000
6562
2000
3281
1000
1640
500
656
200
0
Sea Level
Land Dep.
656
200
13123
4000
22966
7000
Scale 1:10 000 000
0
100
200
300 Miles
0
100
200
300
400 Kms.
Lambert Azimuthal Equal Area Projection

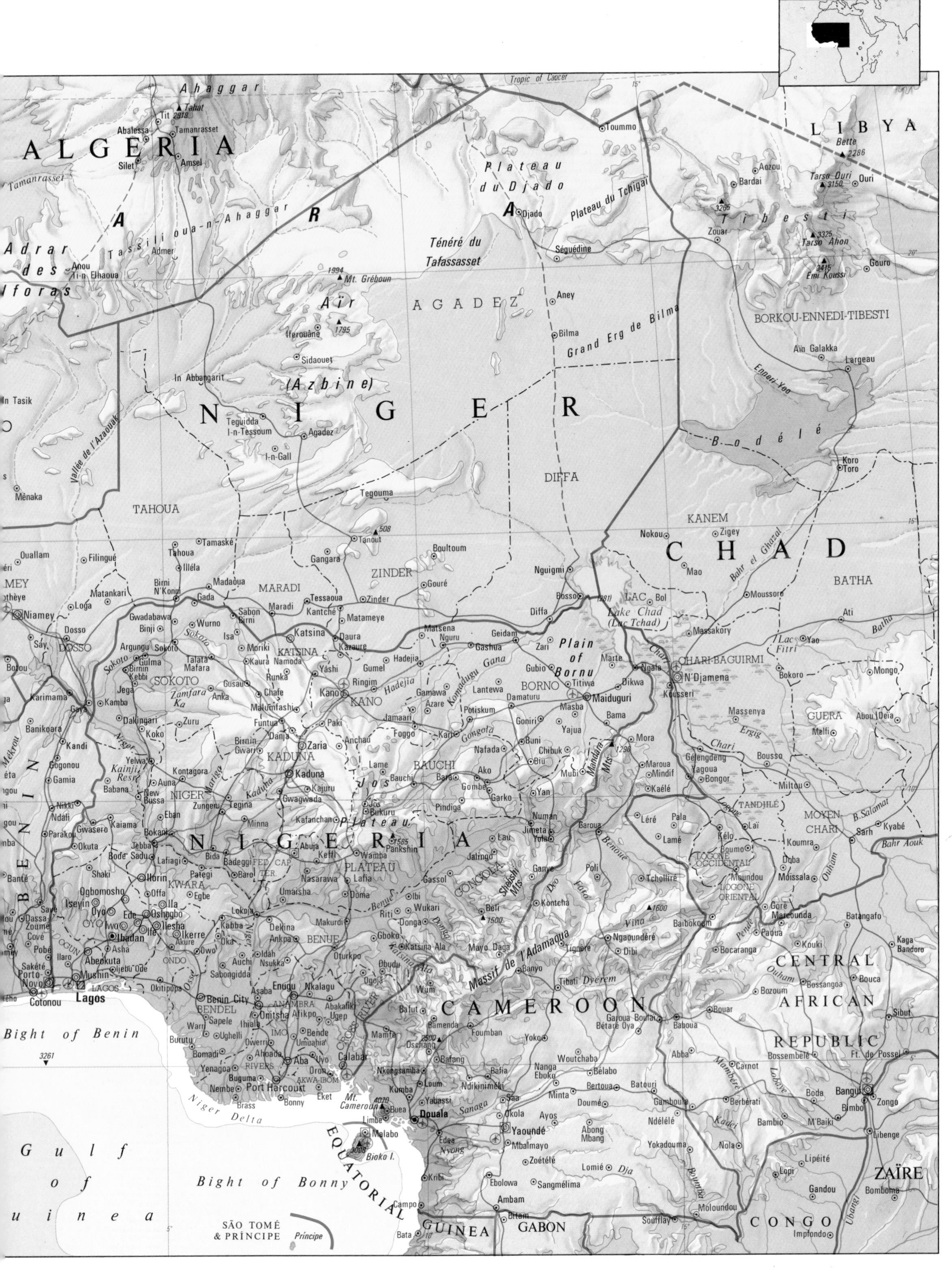

ALGERIA
LIBYA
NIGER
CHAD
NIGERIA
CAMEROON
CENTRAL AFRICAN REPUBLIC
CONGO
ZAÏRE
GABON
EQUATORIAL GUINEA
SÃO TOMÉ & PRÍNCIPE
BENIN
Tropic of Cancer
Ahaggar
Tassili oua-n-Ahaggar
Adrar des Iforas
Plateau du Djado
Plateau du Tchigaï
Ténéré du Tafassasset
Aïr (Azbine)
Grand Erg de Bilma
Tibesti
Tarso Ahon
Emi Koussi
Bodélé
Enneri Yoo
BORKOU-ENNEDI-TIBESTI
AGADEZ
TAHOUA
ZINDER
MARADI
DIFFA
KANEM
BATHA
LAC
Lake Chad (Lac Tchad)
Plain of Bornu
CHARI-BAGUIRMI
GUERA
TANDJILÉ
MOYEN CHARI
LOGONE OCCIDENTAL
LOGONE ORIENTAL
SOKOTO
KATSINA
KANO
BORNO
BAUCHI
KADUNA
NIGER
KWARA
PLATEAU
GONGOLA
BENUE
OYO
OGUN
ONDO
LAGOS
BENDEL
ANAMBRA
IMO
RIVERS
AKWA-IBOM
CROSS RIVER
FED. CAP. TER.
Jos Plateau
Mandara Mts
Shebshi Mts
Massif de l'Adamaoua
Niger Delta
Bight of Benin
Bight of Bonny
Gulf of Guinea
Bioko I.
Príncipe
Mt. Cameroun
Niamey
Agadez
Zinder
Maradi
Tahoua
Bilma
Djado
Largeau
N'Djamena
Kousseri
Maiduguri
Kano
Katsina
Sokoto
Kaduna
Zaria
Jos
Abuja
Ilorin
Ibadan
Abeokuta
Lagos
Cotonou
Porto-Novo
Benin City
Onitsha
Enugu
Aba
Port Harcourt
Calabar
Douala
Yaoundé
Malabo
Garoua
Ngaoundéré
Moundou
Sarh
Bangui
Berbérati
Bouar
Bossangoa
Tamanrasset
Bardai
Aozou

CENTRAL AND EAST AFRICA

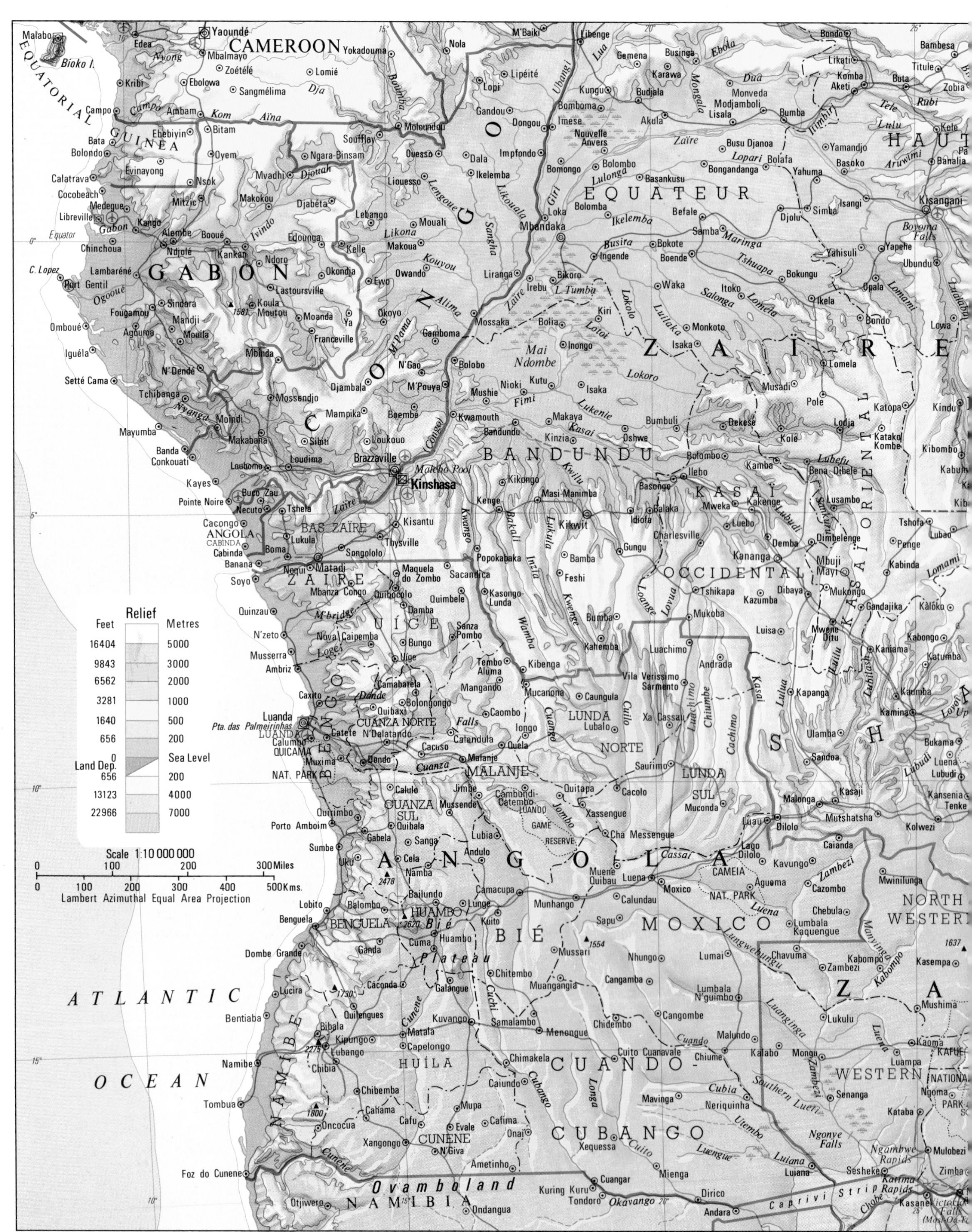

Relief
Feet
Metres
16404
5000
9843
3000
6562
2000
3281
1000
1640
500
656
200
0
Sea Level
Land Dep.
656
200
13123
4000
22966
7000
Scale 1:10 000 000
0
100
200
300 Miles
0
100
200
300
400
500 Kms.
Lambert Azimuthal Equal Area Projection
ATLANTIC
OCEAN
CAMEROON
EQUATORIAL GUINEA
GABON
CONGO
ZAÏRE
ANGOLA
NAMIBIA
EQUATEUR
BANDUNDU
KASAÏ OCCIDENTAL
KASAÏ ORIENTAL
SHABA
HAUT ZAÏRE
BAS ZAÏRE
CABINDA
ZAIRE
UÍGE
CUANZA NORTE
LUANDA
BENGO
MALANJE
LUNDA NORTE
LUNDA SUL
CUANZA SUL
BENGUELA
HUAMBO
BIÉ
MOXICO
HUÍLA
NAMIBE
CUNENE
CUANDO - CUBANGO
NORTH WESTERN
WESTERN
ZAMBIA
Ovamboland
Caprivi Strip
Malabo
Bioko I.
Yaoundé
Edea
Mbalmayo
Zoétélé
Lomié
Kribi
Ebolowa
Sangmélima
Campo
Ambam
Bitam
Ebebiyin
Bata
Bolondo
Oyem
Evinayong
Calatrava
Nsok
Cocobeach
Medegue
Mitzic
Libreville
Kango
Alembe
Booué
Equator
Chinchoua
Ndjolé
Kankan
Ndoro
C. Lopez
Port Gentil
Lambaréné
Lastoursville
Koula Moutou
Sindara
Fougamou
Mandji
Moanda
Franceville
Omboué
Agouma
Mouila
Iguéla
Mbinda
N'Dendé
Setté Cama
Tchibanga
Mossendjo
Mayumba
Moindi
Makabana
Banda
Conkouati
Loubomo
Loudima
Kayes
Pointe Noire
Buco Zau
Necuto
Tshela
Cacongo
Cabinda
Banana
Boma
Lukula
Songololo
Soyo
Noqui
Matadi
Mbanza Congo
Quinzau
N'zeto
Musserra
Ambriz
Caxito
Luanda
Pta. das Palmeirinhas
Catete
Calumbo
Quicama
Muxima
NAT. PARK
Porto Amboim
Quitimbo
Sumbe
Gabela
Quibala
Uku
Cela
Lobito
Benguela
Balombo
Dombe Grande
Lucira
Bentiaba
Namibe
Bibala
Lubango
Chibia
Tombua
Chibemba
Oncocua
Foz do Cunene
Otjiwero
Yokadouma
Nola
M'Baiki
Libenge
Lipéité
Lopi
Gandou
Dongou
Impfondo
Moloundou
Souffley
Ngara-Binsam
Ouesso
Dala
Ikelemba
Mvadhi
Makokou
Djabéta
Liouesso
Lebango
Mouali
Edounga
Kelle
Makoua
Okondja
Ewo
Owando
Liranga
Okoyo
Mossaka
Gamboma
N'Gao
Bolobo
M'Pouya
Djambala
Mampika
Boembé
Sibiti
Loukouo
Brazzaville
Kinshasa
Malebo Pool
Kisantu
Thysville
Mbandaka
Bikoro
Irebu
L. Tumba
Mai Ndombe
Inongo
Mushie
Kwamouth
Bandundu
Kikongo
Kenge
Masi-Manimba
Kikwit
Gungu
Popokabaka
Kasongo-Lunda
Feshi
Bamba
Bumba
Kahemba
Kibenga
Tembo Aluma
Mangando
Mucanona
Caungula
Lubalo
Xa Cassau
Saurimo
Cacolo
Quitapa
Xassengue
Muconda
Cha Messengue
Dilolo
Luena
Moxico
Calundau
Munhango
Camacupa
Kuito
Huambo
Cuma
Chitembo
Muangangia
Caconda
Galangue
Kuvango
Matala
Capelongo
Menongue
Chimakela
Caiundo
Mupa
Cafu
Evale
Cafima
Xangongo
N'Giva
Ametinho
Cuangar
Kuring Kuru
Tondoro
Dirico
Andara
Ondangua
Gemena
Businga
Karawa
Kungu
Budjala
Bomboma
Imese
Akula
Nouvelle Anvers
Bomongo
Bolombo
Basankusu
Bolomba
Loka
Ingende
Bokote
Boende
Waka
Itoko
Monkoto
Isaka
Bolia
Kiri
Nioki
Kutu
Isaka
Makaya
Kinzia
Oshwe
Bumbuli
Dekese
Mweka
Kakenge
Ilebo
Basongo
Idiofa
Charlesville
Luebo
Demba
Kananga
Tshikapa
Dibaya
Kazumba
Mukoba
Luisa
Luachimo
Andrada
Bondo
Bambesa
Likati
Titule
Komba
Aketi
Buta
Zobia
Monveda
Modjamboli
Lisala
Bumba
Kole
Yamandjo
Banalia
Busu Djanoa
Bolafa
Basoko
Bongandanga
Yahuma
Kisangani
Isangi
Simba
Djolu
Befale
Samba
Boyoma Falls
Yahisuli
Yapehe
Ubundu
Bokungu
Opala
Ikela
Bondo
Lowa
Lomela
Musadi
Pole
Katopa
Kindu
Lodja
Katako Kombe
Kibombo
Kole
Kamba
Bena Dibele
Lusambo
Tshofa
Lubao
Dimbelenge
Penge
Mbuji Mayi
Kabinda
Mukongo
Gandajika
Kaloko
Mwene Ditu
Kabongo
Kaniama
Katumba
Kapanga
Kaumba
Kamina
Ulamba
Bukama
Sandoa
Luena
Lubudi
Kasaji
Malonga
Kansenia
Tenke
Mutshatsha
Kolwezi
Lago Dilolo
Kavungo
Caianda
Mwinilunga
CAMEIA NAT. PARK
Cazombo
Aguema
Chebula
Lumbala Kaquengue
Chavuma
Zambezi
Kabompo
Kasempa
Mushima
Lukulu
Nhungo
Lumai
Cangamba
Lumbala N'guimbo
Cangombe
Chidembo
Malundo
Cuito Cuanavale
Chiume
Kalabo
Mongu
Kaoma
Luampa
Senanga
Mavinga
Neriquinha
Kataba
Ngonye Falls
Ngambwe Rapids
Mulobezi
Luiana
Sesheke
Katima Rapids
Kasane
Victoria Falls
Mussende
Lubia
Andulo
Bailundo
Lunge
Sapu
Mussari
Xequessa
Mienga
Cutato
Calandula
Cacuso
Malanje
Quela
Iongo
Caombo
Dondo
Calulo
N'Dalatando
Quibaxi
Bolongongo
Camabatela
Bungo
Uíge
Sanza Pombo
Damba
Quimbele
Maquela do Zombo
Sacandica
Quibocolo
Nova Caipemba
Quilengues
Kipungo
Cahama
Chipindo
Lubango
Nyong
Dja
Kom
Aïna
Ivindo
Ogooué
Nyanga
Likouala
Sangha
Ubangi
Lua
Mongala
Ebola
Dua
Tele
Rubi
Aruwimi
Lulu
Itimbiri
Lopori
Lulonga
Ikelemba
Busira
Maringa
Tshuapa
Salonga
Lomela
Luilaka
Lomami
Lualaba
Lukenie
Kasai
Kwilu
Kwango
Bakali
Lukula
Inzia
Kwenge
Wamba
Loange
Lovua
Luachimo
Chiumbe
Cachimo
Lulua
Sankuru
Lubefu
Lubudi
Lubilash
Lufira
Cuango
Cuilo
Lukenie
Lotoi
Lokolo
Lokoro
Fimi
Alima
Kouyou
Likona
Lengoue
Djouah
M'Pama
Congo
Zaïre
M'bridge
Loge
Dande
Cuanza
Jombo
Cassai
Zambezi
Lungwebungu
Luanginga
Cuando
Cubia
Southern Lueti
Luena
Luengue
Utembo
Cuito
Cubango
Longa
Cuchi
Cunene
Okavango
Chobe
Kabompo
Manyinga
Plateau
Bié
Huambo
Sanga
Camacupa
Calomo
Namba
2478
2620
1554
1730
2275
1800
1581
1637

UGANDA
KENYA
RIFT VALLEY
NORTH EASTERN
EASTERN
CENTRAL
NYANZA
WESTERN
COAST
SOMALI REP
TANZANIA
KAGERA
MARA
MWANZA
SHINYANGA
ARUSHA
KIGOMA
TABORA
SINGIDA
DODOMA
TANGA
RUKWA
MBEYA
IRINGA
MOROGORO
PWANI
MTWARA
RUVUMA
RWANDA
BURUNDI
MALAWI
MOZAMBIQUE
NIASSA
CABO DELGADO
NAMPULA
ZAMBEZIA
TETE
SOFALA
MANICA
ZIMBABWE
NORTHERN
LUAPULA
COPPERBELT
CENTRAL
EASTERN
COMOROS
MADAGASCAR
INDIAN OCEAN
Mozambique Channel
Lake Turkana
Lake Victoria
L. Rukwa
Lake Mweru
Lake Bangweulu
Lake Kariba
Albert L.
L. George
L. Edward
L. Kyoga
L. Natron
L. Eyasi
L. Manyara
L. Malawi
L. Chilwa
L. Chiuta
Pemba I.
Zanzibar I.
Mafia I.
Pate I.
Njazídja (Grande Comore)
Mwali (Mohéli)
Nzwani (Anjouan)
Île Mayotte (Fr.)
Juan de Nova
Nairobi
Kampala
Dodoma
Dar es Salaam
Mombasa
Kigali
Bujumbura
Muqdisho (Mogadishu)
Harare
Ndola
Zanzibar
Tanga
Moroni
Lilongwe
Blantyre
Mt. Kenya 5200
Kilimanjaro 5895
Mt. Elgon 4321
Mt. Meru 4565
Ruwenzori Range 5119
Equator
© Collins Longman Atlases Cbi

SOUTHERN AFRICA AND MADAGASCAR

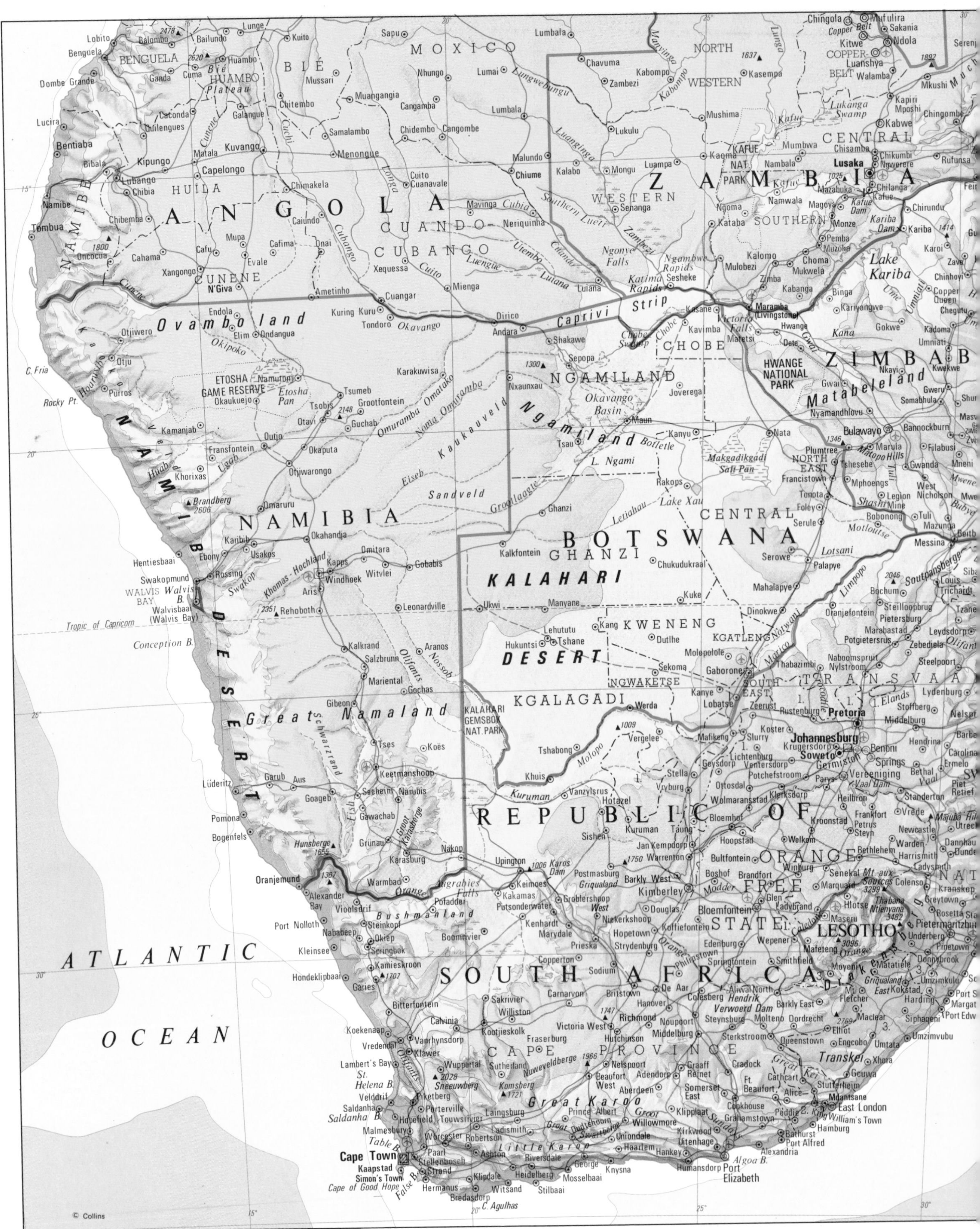
ANGOLA
ZAMBIA
NAMIBIA
BOTSWANA
ZIMBAB
REPUBLIC OF SOUTH AFRICA
LESOTHO
ATLANTIC
OCEAN
KALAHARI
DESERT
NAMIB DESERT
Great Namaland
Great Karoo
Little Karoo
Ovamboland
Ngamiland
Caprivi Strip
Okavango Basin
Makgadikgadi Salt Pan
Lake Kariba
L. Ngami
Lake Xau
Tropic of Capricorn
Conception B.
Rocky Pt.
C. Fria
Cape of Good Hope
C. Agulhas
Algoa B.
Saldanha B.
Table B.
False B.
ETOSHA GAME RESERVE
KALAHARI GEMSBOK NAT. PARK
HWANGE NATIONAL PARK
KAFUE NAT. PARK
ORANGE FREE STATE
TRANSVAAL
CAPE PROVINCE
Transkei
Matabeleland
Lusaka
Pretoria
Johannesburg
Soweto
Bulawayo
Windhoek
Gaborone
Kimberley
Bloemfontein
Maseru
Cape Town
Kaapstad
Port Elizabeth
East London
Walvis Bay
Lüderitz
Swakopmund
Benguela
Lobito
Namibe
Lubango
Tsumeb
Maun
Francistown
Livingstone
Pietermaritzburg
Upington
Oranjemund
Port Nolloth
Mafikeng
Ndola
Kitwe
Chingola
Mufulira
Kariba
Victoria Falls
Keetmanshoop
Rehoboth
Gobabis
Ghanzi
Serowe
Mahalapye
Pietersburg
Welkom
Kroonstad
Grahamstown
Mossel Baai
Knysna
Queenstown
Umtata
Cunene
Okavango
Orange
Limpopo
Zambezi
Molopo
Nossob
Fish
Olifants
Vaal
Kafue
Cuando
Cubango
Cuito
Chobe
Brandberg 2606
Thabana Ntlenyana 3482
Mt. aux Sources 3299
© Collins

INDIAN
OCEAN
Mozambique Channel
MOZAMBIQUE
MADAGASCAR
NIASSA
CABO DELGADO
NAMPULA
ZAMBEZIA
SOPALA
INHAMBANE
GAZA
MAPUTO
Tropic of Capricorn
Tj. Bobaomby
Antsiranana
Nosy Be
Ambilobe
Vohimarina
Andoany
Ambanja
Massif de Tsaratanana
2876
Sambava
Anorotsangana
Analalava
Bealanana
Antsohihy
Antalaha
Befandriana
Maroantsetra
Mandritsara
Mahajanga
Port-Bergé
Mitsinjo
Soalala
Marovoay
Mampikony
Mananara
Tj. Masoala
Tanjona Vilanandro
Ambato Boeni
Besalampy
Tsaratanana
Maevatanana
Soanierana-Ivongo
Nosy Boraha
Juan de Nova
Ambodifototra
Fenoarivo Atsinanana
Tambohorano
Kandreho
Morafenobe
Andriba
L. Alaotra
Maintirano
Ambatondrazaka
Ankazobe
Toamasina
Antsalova
Fenoarivo
Fihaonana
Anjozorobe
Tsiroanomandidy
Ambohidratrimo
Arivonimamo
Manjakandriana
Vohibinany
Anivorano
Andevoranto
Miarinarivo
Soavinandriana
Antananarivo (Tananarive)
2643
Faratsiho
Ambatolampy
Vatomandry
Miandrivazo
Belo-sur-Tsiribihina
Mandoto
Betafo
Berevo
Antsirabé
Mahanoro
Morondava
Malaimbandy
Mahabo
Fandriana
Marolambo
Ambatofinandrahana
Ambositra
Nosy-Varika
Mandabe
Ambohimanga du Sud
Ambohimahasoa
Manja
Massif du Makay
Fianarantsoa
Mananjary
Morombe
Tanjona Ankaboa
Ambalavao
Ifanadiana
Beroroha
Ankaramena
Fort Carnot
Befandriana
1761
Manakara
Ankazoabo
Ihosy
Ivohibe
Vohipeno
Ranohira
Vondrozo
Manombo
Farafangana
Toliara
Tongobory
Iakoro
Betroka
Vangaindrano
Benenitra
Betioky
Midongy-Sud
Tsivory
Bekily
Manantenina
Ampanihy
Tranoroa
1956
Behara
Androka
Tsihombé
Tôlânaro
Ambovombe
Tj. Vohimena
Metangula
Maniamba
Nkhotakota
Guerro
Lichinga
Namecala
Ancuabe
Pemba
Kasungu
Montepuez
Mecufi
Mponela
Marrupa
Balama
Nungo
Ocua
Lurio
Dowa
Ft. Maguire
Chaonde
Chipata
Salima
Belem
Maua
Namapa
Simuco
Katete
Mchinji
Lilongwe
Massangulo
Vatiua
Lalaua
Intute
Memba
Dedza
Mangochi
Imala
Nacala
Furancungo
Ulongwe
Ncheu
Balaka
Cuamba
Malema
Ribaué
Mossuril
Moçambique
Chinga
Nampula
Meconta
Mogincual
Chipera
Cabora Bassa Dam
Casula
Matope
Zomba
Gurué
Alto Molocue
Blantyre
Namarroi
Nametil
Namaponda
Magué
Moatize
Mulanje Mts
3000
Mutala
Tete
Chikwawa
Milange
Erego
Gilé
Angoche
Chióco
Lugela
Chiromo
Moma
Mt. Darwin
Tambara
Nsanje
Mocuba
Nyamapanda
Moebase
Chemba
Shamva
Mungari
Pebane
Murewa
Mutoko
Sena
Namacurra
Vila da Maganja
Maringue
Chindio
Quelimane
Macheke
Inyangani
2592
Mopêia Velha
Inhaminga
Marromeu
Rusape
Luabo
Wedza
Mazamba
Chinde
Mutare
Manica
Conceição
Chimoio
Buhera
Machece
Mt. Binga
2436
Dondo
Chimanimani
Beira
Chipinge
Nova Sofala
Espungabera
Gorongosa
Bartolomeu Dias
Macobere
Maave
Massangena
Inhassoro
I. do Bazaruto
Vilanculos
Mapinhane
Chigubo
Nhachengue
Pomene
Massinga
Mabalane
Cubo
Homoine
Morrumbene
Massingir
Inhambane
Estivane
C. das Correntes
Marão
Inharrime
Jangamo
Chibuto
Nhacoongo
Chicomo
Quissico
Magude
Macia
Chidenguele
Xai-Xai
Manhiça
Marracuene
Maputo
Bela Vista
Zitundo
Mseleni
St. Lucia
Relief
Feet
Metres
16404
5000
9843
3000
6562
2000
3281
1000
1640
500
656
200
0
Sea Level
Land Dep.
656
200
13123
4000
22966
7000
Independent homelands numbered on map
1. BOPHUTHATSWANA
2. CISKEI
3. TRANSKEI
4. VENDA
Scale 1:10 000 000
0
100
200
300 Miles
0
100
200
300
400
500 Kms.
Lambert Azimuthal Equal Area Projection
15°
20°
25°
30°
35°
40°
45°
50°

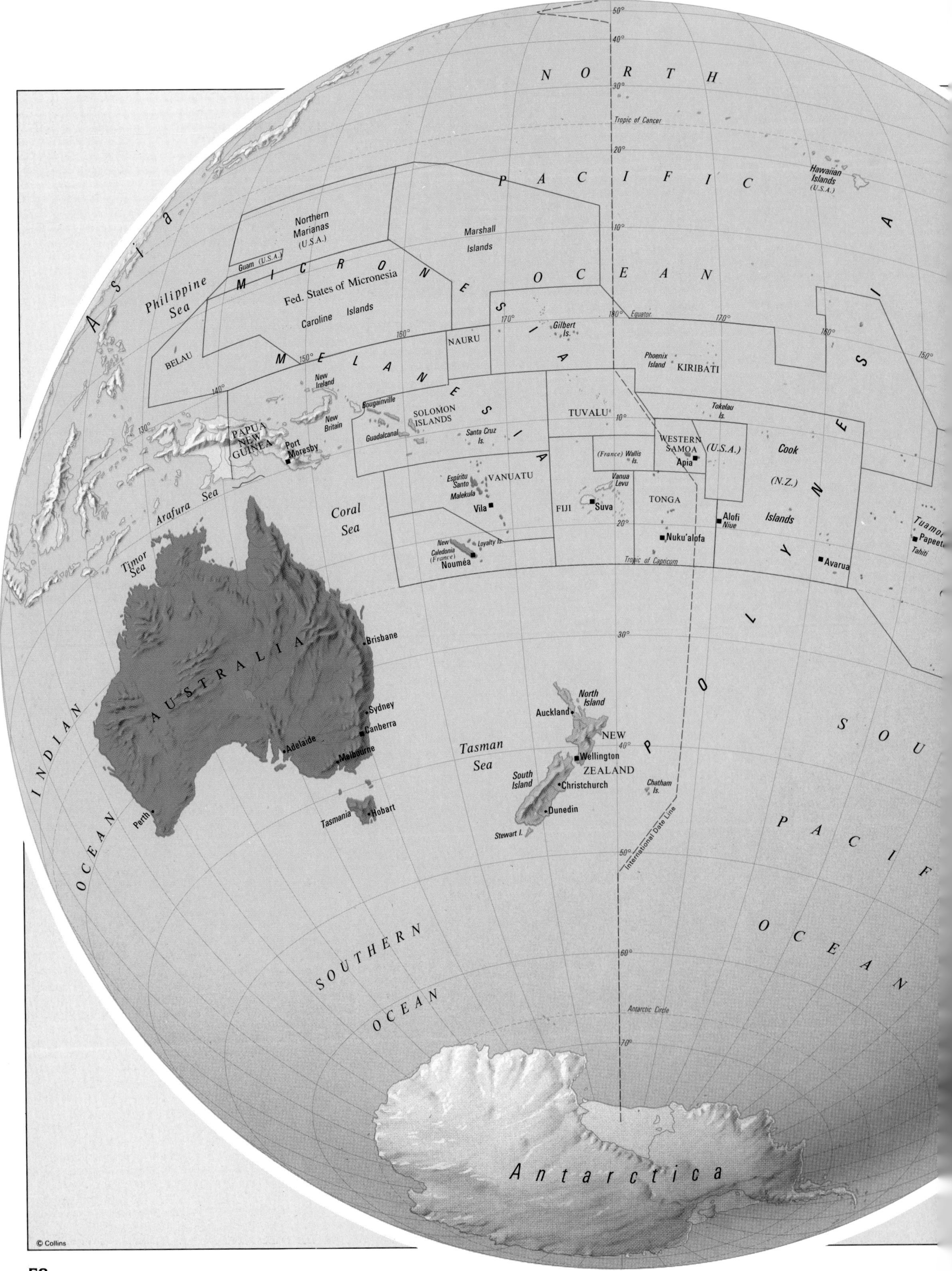
NORTH PACIFIC OCEAN
Tropic of Cancer
Hawaiian Islands (U.S.A.)
Asia
Philippine Sea
Northern Marianas (U.S.A.)
Guam (U.S.A.)
MICRONESIA
Marshall Islands
Fed. States of Micronesia
Caroline Islands
BELAU
NAURU
Gilbert Is.
Equator
MELANESIA
New Ireland
New Britain
Bougainville
SOLOMON ISLANDS
Guadalcanal
Santa Cruz Is.
Phoenix Island
KIRIBATI
Tokelau Is.
TUVALU
PAPUA NEW GUINEA
Port Moresby
(France) Wallis Is.
WESTERN SAMOA
Apia
(U.S.A.)
Cook (N.Z.) Islands
POLYNESIA
Espiritu Santo
Malekula
VANUATU
Vila
Vanua Levu
FIJI
Suva
TONGA
Alofi
Niue
Nuku'alofa
Arafura Sea
Coral Sea
Timor Sea
New Caledonia (France)
Loyalty Is.
Nouméa
Tropic of Capricorn
Avarua
Tuamot
Papeet
Tahiti
AUSTRALIA
Brisbane
Sydney
Canberra
Adelaide
Melbourne
Perth
Tasmania
Hobart
INDIAN OCEAN
Tasman Sea
North Island
Auckland
NEW ZEALAND
Wellington
South Island
Christchurch
Dunedin
Stewart I.
Chatham Is.
International Date Line
SOUTH PACIFIC OCEAN
SOUTHERN OCEAN
Antarctic Circle
Antarctica
© Collins

OCEANIA

COUNTRY	PAGE
AUSTRALIA	**61; 62-63; 64-65; 66-67**
FIJI	**68**
KIRIBATI	**68-69**
NAURU	**68**
NEW ZEALAND	**60**
PAPUA NEW GUINEA	**68; 61**
SOLOMON ISLANDS	**68**
TONGA	**69**
TUVALU	**68**
VANUATU	**68**
WESTERN SAMOA	**68**

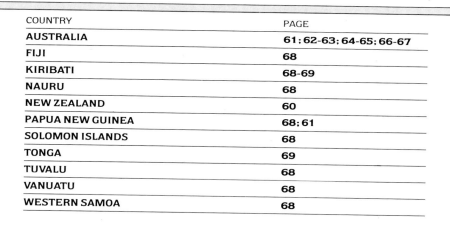

Oceania as a continental name is used for the area extending from Australia in the west, to the most easterly island of Polynesia and from New Zealand in the south, to the Hawaiian Islands in the north. Australasia is that portion of Oceania which lies between the equator and 47°S but in general the term is not often used because of confusion with Australia the country name.

North America
140°
130°
120°
110°
100°
Marquesas Is.
(U.K.)
Easter I.
(Chile)

NEW ZEALAND

Relief

Feet	Metres
16 404	5000
9843	3000
6562	2000
3281	1000
1640	500
656	200
0	Sea Level
Land Dep. 656	200
13123	4000
22966	7000

TASMAN SEA

PACIFIC OCEAN

NORTH ISLAND

SOUTH ISLAND

North Cape
Ninety Mile Beach
Doubtless Bay
Bay of Islands
C. Brett
Kaitaia
Mangonui
Rawene
Paihia
Kaikohe
Hikurangi
NORTHLAND
Whangarei
Dargaville
Bream Bay
Waipu
Gt. Barrier I.
Kaipara Harbour
Warkworth
Hauraki Gulf
Helensville
Coromandel
Coromandel Peninsula
Takapuna
Auckland
Manukau
Manukau Harbour
AUCKLAND
Whitianga
Thames
Pukekohe
Waiuku
Waikato
Mayor I.
Bay of Plenty
Paeroa
Waihi
Huntly
Morrinsville
Matakana I.
Hamilton
Ngaruawahia
Tauranga
Cambridge
Matamata
Te Kaha
Hicks Bay
East Cape
Hikurangi 1754
Tikitiki
Whakatane
Rotorua
BAY OF PLENTY
Waipiro
Kawhia
Te Awamutu
Te Kuiti
WAIKATO
Tokoroa
Putaruru
Kawerau
Opotiki
Matawai
North Taranaki Bight
Bennydale
Lake Taupo
Taupo
Murupara
GISBORNE
Tolaga Bay
Ormond
Gisborne
Mokau
Raukumara Ra.
Huiarau Ra.
Taumarunui
New Plymouth
Waitara
Ngauruhoe 2291
Turangi
Waiotapu
Mt. Egmont 2518
Inglewood
Stratford
Ruapehu 2797
Kaimanawa Mts.
HAWKES BAY
Wairoa
Waikokopu
Mahia Peninsula
Opunake
TARANAKI
Eltham
Waiouru
Ngaruroro
Hawke Bay
Bay View
Napier
Hawera
Patea
MANAWATU
Taihape
Mangaweka
Ruahine Ra.
Hastings
Wanganui
WANGANUI
Marton
Waipawa
Waipukurau
Feilding
Dannevirke
Palmerston North
Woodville
Foxton
Levin
Pahiatua
Eketahuna
Kapiti I.
Paraparaumu
Otaki
WELLINGTON
Masterton
Carterton
Porirua
Upper Hutt
Lower Hutt
Wellington
Cook Strait
C. Palliser
Cape Farewell
Collingwood
Golden Bay
D'Urville I.
Takaka
Tasman Mts.
Tasman Bay
Karamea Bight
Karamea
Motueka
Nelson
Picton
Richmond
Havelock
Tapawera
Wairau
Granity
Blenheim
Westport
Buller
Murchison
Seddon
Cape Foulwind
Cape Campbell
Inangahua
NELSON-MARLBOROUGH
Reefton
Mt. Travers 2338
Kaikoura Ra.
Clarence
Greymouth
Ahaura
Lewis Pass
Hanmer Springs
Kaikoura
Kumara
Brunner
Hokitika
Waiau
Ross
Otira
Arthur's Pass
Cheviot
Whataroa
Waipara
Pegasus Bay
Okarito
Rangiora
Kaiapoi
Fox Glacier
SOUTHERN ALPS
WEST COAST
Springfield
Waimakariri
Christchurch
Darfield
Rakaia
Lincoln
Mt. Cook 3764
Akaroa
Banks Peninsula
CANTERBURY
Ashburton
Leeston
Okuru
L. Pukaki
L. Tekapo
Cascade Pt.
Fairlie
Geraldine
Twizel
Canterbury Bight
Mt. Aspiring 3027
L. Wanaka
L. Hawea
Timaru
Omarama
Otematata
Homer Tunnel
Milford Sound
Dunstan Mts.
Kurow
Waitaki
Waimate
Wanaka
Arrowtown
Queenstown
Cromwell
Naseby
Pukeuri
L. Te Anau
L. Wakatipu
Clyde
Alexandra
Ranfurly
Oamaru
Garvie Mts.
OTAGO
Kingston
Te Anau
Palmerston
Waikouaiti
L. Manapouri
Roxburgh
Mossburn
SOUTHLAND
Port Chalmers
Otago Peninsula
Resolution I.
Lumsden
Lawrence
Mosgiel
Dunedin
Clutha
Tapanui
Ohai
Nightcaps
Cameron Mts.
Winton
Clinton
Tuatapere
Gore
Puysegur Pt.
Edendale
Balclutha
Mataura
Riverton
Invercargill
Owaka
Foveaux Strait
Fortrose
Bluff
Ruapuke I.
980
Stewart I.
Halfmoon Bay
Southwest Cape

Scale 1:6 000 000

0 50 100 150 Miles

0 50 100 150 200 Kms.

Conic Projection

INDONESIA
PAPUA NEW GUINEA
NEW GUINEA
LAUT BANDA
(BANDA SEA)
LAUT FLORES
(FLORES SEA)
ARAFURA SEA
TIMOR SEA
CORAL SEA
Gulf of Carpentaria
Great Barrier Reef
NORTHERN TERRITORY
QUEENSLAND
WESTERN AUSTRALIA
SOUTH AUSTRALIA
NEW SOUTH WALES
VICTORIA
TASMANIA
AUST. CAP. TER.
Great Australian Bight
SOUTHERN OCEAN
TASMAN SEA
Bass Strait
Torres Strait
Solomon Sea
Bismarck Sea
Great Sandy Desert
Gibson Desert
Great Victoria Desert
Simpson Desert
Nullarbor Plain
Great Artesian Basin
Great Dividing Range
Macdonnell Ranges
Musgrave Ranges
Perth
Adelaide
Melbourne
Sydney
Brisbane
Darwin
Hobart
Canberra
Alice Springs
Port Moresby
Scale 1:20 000 000
0 100 200 300 400 500 Miles
0 200 400 600 800 Kms.
Lambert Azimuthal Equal Area Projection
© Collins ◇ Longman Atlases Cbi

WESTERN AUSTRALIA

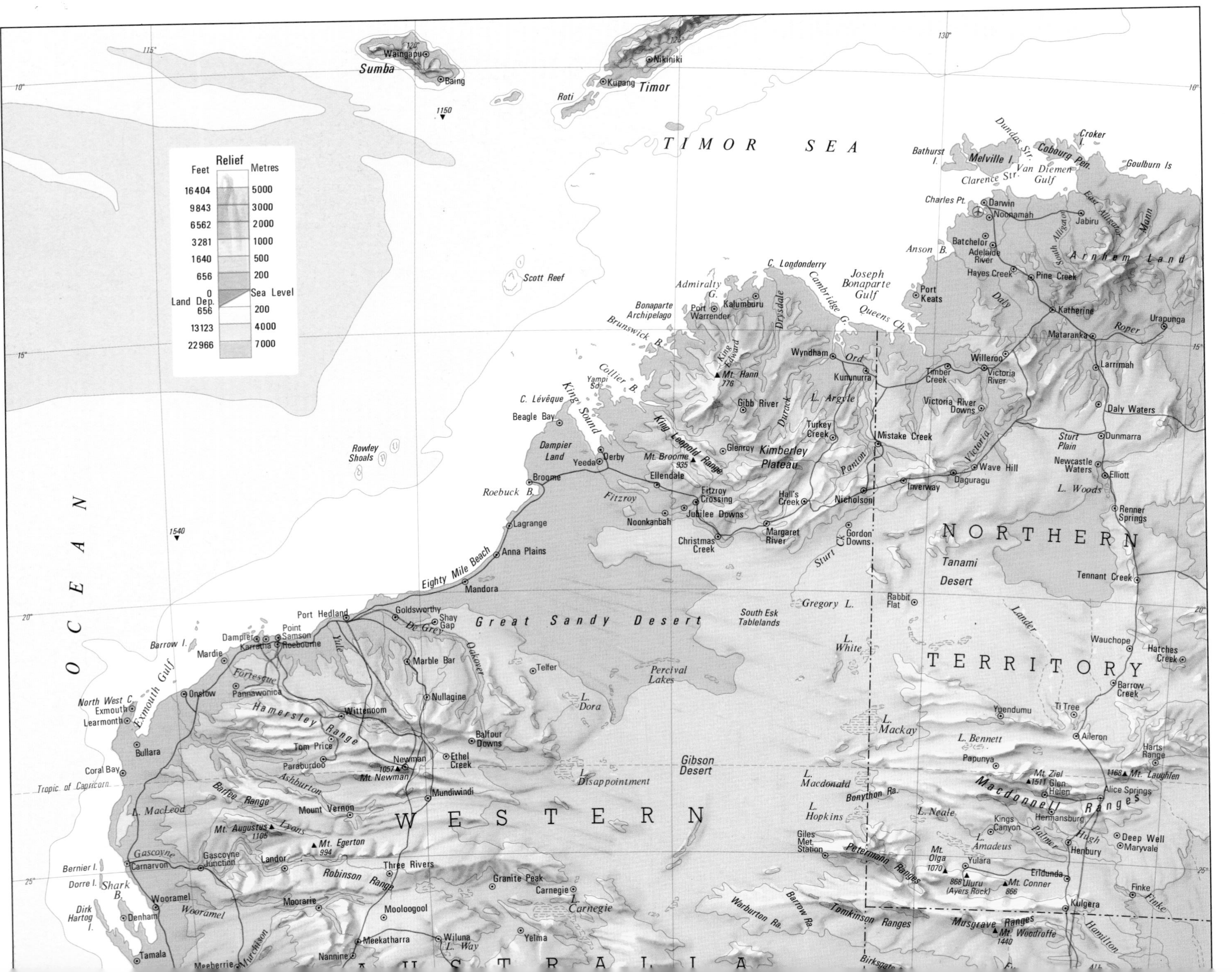

TIMOR SEA
OCEAN
Sumba
Waingapu
Baing
Timor
Kupang
Nikiniki
Roti
1150
Scott Reef
Rowley Shoals
1540
Bathurst I.
Melville I.
Dundas Str.
Cobourg Pen.
Croker I.
Goulburn Is
Van Diemen Gulf
Clarence Str.
Charles Pt.
Darwin
Noonamah
Jabiru
East Alligator
South Alligator
Mann
Arnhem Land
Batchelor
Adelaide River
Hayes Creek
Pine Creek
Anson B.
Port Keats
Daly
Katherine
Mataranka
Roper
Urapunga
Larrimah
Daly Waters
Dunmarra
Sturt Plain
Newcastle Waters
Elliott
L. Woods
Renner Springs
Tennant Creek
C. Londonderry
Joseph Bonaparte Gulf
Cambridge G.
Queens Ch.
Admiralty G.
Port Warrender
Kalumburu
Drysdale
Bonaparte Archipelago
Brunswick B.
King Edward
Mt. Hann
776
Wyndham
Ord
Kununurra
Timber Creek
Willeroo
Victoria River
Victoria River Downs
Collier B.
Yampi Sd.
C. Lévêque
King Sound
Beagle Bay
Gibb River
L. Argyle
Durack
Turkey Creek
Mistake Creek
Dampier Land
Yeeda
Derby
Mt. Broome
935
King Leopold Range
Glenroy
Kimberley Plateau
Panton
Victoria
Wave Hill
Daguragu
Inverway
Broome
Ellendale
Roebuck B.
Fitzroy
Fitzroy Crossing
Hall's Creek
Nicholson
Noonkanbah
Jubilee Downs
Christmas Creek
Margaret River
Gordon Downs
Sturt Ck.
Lagrange
Anna Plains
Eighty Mile Beach
Mandora
NORTHERN TERRITORY
Tanami Desert
Port Hedland
Goldsworthy
Shay Gap
De Grey
Great Sandy Desert
South Esk Tablelands
Gregory L.
Rabbit Flat
Lander
Wauchope
Hatches Creek
Barrow I.
Dampier
Karratha
Point Samson
Roebourne
Yule
Mardie
Marble Bar
Oakover
Telfer
Percival Lakes
L. White
Fortescue
Pannawonica
Exmouth Gulf
North West C.
Exmouth
Learmonth
Onslow
Nullagine
L. Dora
Barrow Creek
Ti Tree
Yuendumu
Hamersley Range
Wittenoom
Tom Price
Balfour Downs
L. Mackay
Aileron
L. Bennett
Bullara
Coral Bay
Tropic of Capricorn
Paraburdoo
Ashburton
Newman
1057
Mt. Newman
Ethel Creek
L. Disappointment
Gibson Desert
L. Macdonald
Bonython Ra.
Papunya
Mt. Ziel
1511
Glen Helen
Harts Range
1168
Mt. Laughlen
Alice Springs
Macdonnell Ranges
Barlee Range
Mundiwindi
L. MacLeod
Mount Vernon
WESTERN
L. Hopkins
L. Neale
Hermansburg
Kings Canyon
Mt. Augustus
1105
Lyons
Mt. Egerton
994
Giles Met. Station
Petermann Ranges
L. Amadeus
Palmer
Hugh
Henbury
Deep Well
Maryvale
Gascoyne
Carnarvon
Gascoyne Junction
Landor
Three Rivers
Mt. Olga
1070
Yulara
Erldunda
Bernier I.
Dorre I.
Shark B.
Robinson Range
Granite Peak
Carnegie
L. Carnegie
868
Uluru (Ayers Rock)
Mt. Conner
866
Finke
Wooramel
Moorarie
Warburton Ra.
Barrow Ra.
Tomkinson Ranges
Kulgera
Dirk Hartog I.
Denham
Mooloogool
Musgrave Ranges
Mt. Woodroffe
1440
Hamilton
Meekatharra
Wiluna
L. Way
Yelma
Tamala
Murchison
Nannine
Meeberrie
Birksgate
AUSTRALIA
Relief
Feet
Metres
16404
9843
6562
3281
1640
656
0
Land Dep.
656
13123
22966
5000
3000
2000
1000
500
200
Sea Level
200
4000
7000

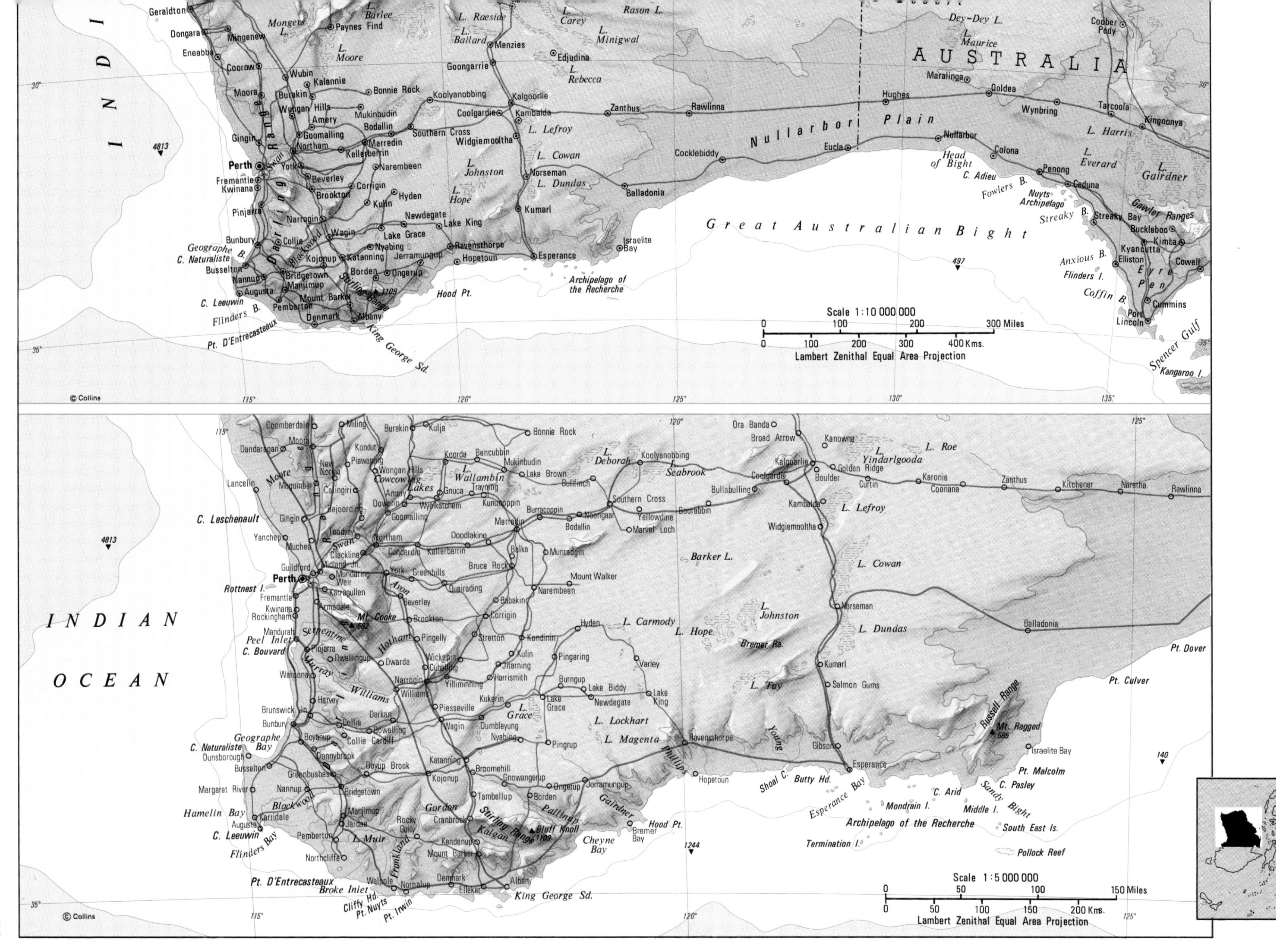
AUSTRALIA
Nullarbor Plain
Great Australian Bight
INDIAN OCEAN
Perth
Fremantle
Kalgoorlie
Coolgardie
Esperance
Albany
Bunbury
Geraldton
Eucla
Ceduna
Port Lincoln
Archipelago of the Recherche
King George Sd.
C. Leeuwin
C. Naturaliste
Geographe Bay
Stirling Range
Scale 1:10 000 000
0 100 200 300 Miles
0 100 200 300 400 Kms.
Lambert Zenithal Equal Area Projection
Scale 1:5 000 000
0 50 100 150 Miles
0 50 100 150 200 Kms.
Lambert Zenithal Equal Area Projection
© Collins

EASTERN AUSTRALIA

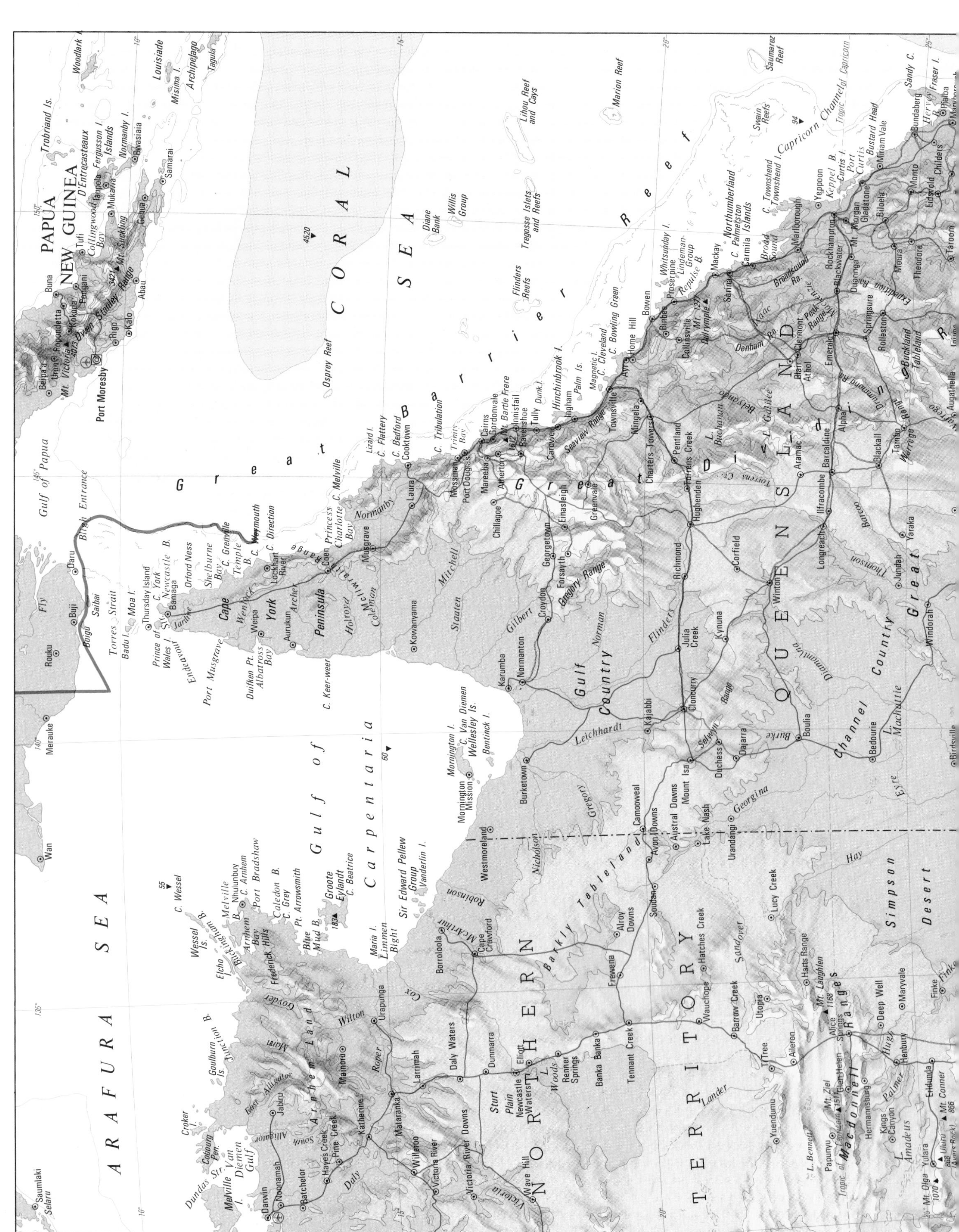

PAPUA NEW GUINEA
Port Moresby
Owen Stanley Range
Gulf of Papua
Torres Strait
Thursday Island
Cape York Peninsula
Gulf of Carpentaria
ARAFURA SEA
CORAL SEA
Great Barrier Reef
QUEENSLAND
NORTHERN TERRITORY
Arnhem Land
Darwin
Katherine
Tennant Creek
Alice Springs
Macdonnell Ranges
Simpson Desert
Barkly Tableland
Gulf Country
Channel Country
Great Dividing Range
Cairns
Cooktown
Townsville
Mackay
Rockhampton
Bundaberg
Mount Isa
Cloncurry
Longreach
Normanton
Burketown
Weipa
Groote Eylandt
Mornington I.
Wellesley Is.
Capricorn Channel
Tropic of Capricorn
Whitsunday I.
Hinchinbrook I.
Fraser I.

SOUTH AUSTRALIA
NEW SOUTH WALES
VICTORIA
TASMANIA
TASMAN SEA
Great Australian Bight
Bass Strait
Great Victoria Desert
Sturt Desert
Flinders Ranges
Gawler Ranges
Lake Eyre (North)
L. Eyre (South)
L. Torrens
L. Gairdner
L. Frome
L. Gregory
L. Blanche
L. Callabonna
Spencer Gulf
Gulf St. Vincent
Kangaroo I.
King I.
Flinders I.
Furneaux Group
Cape Barren I.
Brisbane
Sydney
Canberra
Melbourne
Adelaide
Hobart
Newcastle
Wollongong
Gosford
Geelong
Launceston
Broken Hill
Mildura
Wagga Wagga
Albury
Dubbo
Bathurst
Goulburn
Bendigo
Ballarat
Port Augusta
Port Pirie
Whyalla
Port Lincoln
Mount Gambier
Darling
Murray
Murrumbidgee
Lachlan
Macquarie
Mt. Kosciusko 2228
COMMONWEALTH TERRITORY
Relief
Feet
Metres
16404 5000
9843 3000
6562 2000
3281 1000
1640 500
656 200
0 Sea Level
Land Dep. 656 200
13123 4000
22966 7000
Scale 1:10 000 000
0 50 100 150 200 250 Miles
0 100 200 300 400 Kms.
Lambert Zenithal Equal Area Projection
© Collins

SOUTHEAST AUSTRALIA

SOUTH AUSTRALIA
Lake Eyre (North)
L. Eyre (South)
Madigan Gulf
Koolkootinnie L.
L. Kalamurra
Mungeranie
L. Kittakittaooloo
L. Warrakalanna
L. Hope
Cooper Creek
Etadunna
L. Gregory
L. Florence
Clayton
L. Blanche
Strzelecki Creek
Sturt Desert
Grey Range
Bransby
Bulloo Downs
Bulloo
Naryilco
Caryapundy Swamp
Arckaringa
Mount Willoughby
Evelyn Cr.
Peake Cr.
Neales
Warrina
George
L. Conway
Lora Cr.
Duff Creek
Douglas Cr.
Anna Creek
William Creek
L. Cadibarrawirracanna
Irrapatana
Strangways
Stuart Range
Coober Pedy
Wooring
Warriner Cr.
Beresford
Mulcorina
Bopeechee
Wangianna
Marree
Mount Hopeless
Callabonna Creek
Tilcha
Hawker Gate
Tibooburra
Milparinka
L. Ulenia
The Salt Lake
Bootra
Cobham Lake
Yancannia
Lake Callabonna
Moolawatana
Old Moolawatana
L. Phillipson
L. Woorong
L. Wirrida
Ingomar
McDouall Peak
The Twins
Stuart Creek
Curdlawidny Lagoon
Ediacara
Farina
Lyndhurst
Leigh Creek
Frome
Wooltana
Mt. Serle 933
Balcanoona
Lake Frome
L. Elder
Morden
Tongo
Packsaddle
Peri L.
White Cliffs
Mulgathing
Mount Eba
Andamooka
Roxby Downs
Lake Torrens
Bon Bon
Warburton Range
L. Labyrinth
Lyons
Malbooma
Tarcoola
Wilgena
Kingoonya
L. Younghusband
L. Hanson
L. Hart
Arcoona
Beltana
1128 Mt. Hack
Blinman
Parachilna
Flinders Ranges
Eurinilla
Noonthorangee Ra.
Tarella
Marra
Mount Murchison
Wilcannia
Coondambo
Wirraminna
L. Harris
Yerda
Woomera
Pimba
Wirrappa
Island Lagoon
Pernatty Lagoon
Moralana
Edeowie
Wilpena
St. Mary Peak 1165
Frome Downs
Erudina
Pasmore
Curnamona
Benagerie
Mulyungarie
Barrier Range
474 Mt. Robe
Euriowie
Mootwingee
Little Topar
Yanco Glen
Silverton
Broken Hill
Lake Everard
Lake Gairdner
Woocalla
L. Dutton
Bookaloo
Willochra
Hawker
Siccus
Kalabity
Cockburn
Mingary
Box Tank
Talyawalka
Darling
Nyngyndery
L. Macfarlane
Hesso
Cradock
Belton
Baratta
Waukaringa
Florina
Olary
Burta
Menindee L.
Menindee
Cawndilla L.
Victoria
Ratcatchers L.
L. Acraman
Wandana
Ceduna
Puntabie
Yardea
Nonning
Gawler Ranges
Port Augusta
Quorn
967 Mt. Brown
Hammond
Carrieton
Yunta
Mannahill
Radium Hill
Mutooroo
Tandou L.
Sayers Lake
Darnick
Wirrulla
Cungena
Smoky Bay
Streaky Bay
L. Gilles
Iron Knob
Mt. Remarkable
960
Orroroo
Booleroo Centre
Paratoo
Manunda Creek
Lilydale
Oakvale
Oakbank
Coombah
Mindona L.
Moornanyah L.
Poochera
Minnipa
Buckleboo
Iron Baron
Whyalla
Port Germein
Wirrabara
Laura
Peterborough
Popilta L.
Travellers L.
Pooncarie
Wudinna
Kyancutta
Koongawa
Kimba
Port Pirie
Jamestown
Crystal Br.
Gladstone
Mt. Bryan 932
Port Kenny
C. Radstock
Talia
Anxious Bay
Balumbah
Waddikee
477 Darke Pk.
Cleve
Cowell
Redhill
Spalding
Broughton
Burra
Anabranch
Canopus
Burtundy
Hatfield
Polda
Lock
Bramfield
Elliston
Flinders I.
Investigator Group
Sheringa
Eyre Peninsula
Karkoo
Franklin Harbour
Arno Bay
Port Broughton
Snowtown
Bute
Brinkworth
Clare
Robertstown
Morgan
Wallaroo
Kadina
Moonta
Kulpara
Watervale
Eudunda
Balaklava
Riverton
Kapunda
Waikerie
Renmark
Paringa
Yamba
Murray
L. Victoria
Wentworth
Dareton
Buronga
Merbein
Mildura
Red Cliffs
Pitarpunga L.
Benanee
Port Neill
Spencer Gulf
Cockaleechie
Mount Hope
Coffin Bay
Cummins
Tumby Bay
Sir Joseph Banks Group
Port Victoria
Maitland
Port Wakefield
Ardrossan
Hamley Br.
Truro
Blanchetown
Yinkanie
Barmera
Berri
Loxton
Merigur
Euston
Robinvale
Balranald
Nowingi
Hattah
Yungera
Coffin Bay Pen.
Wangary
Port Lincoln
Whidbey Isles
Hardwicke Bay
Yorke Pen.
Minlaton
Yorketown
Gulf St. Vincent
Elizabeth
Gawler
Adelaide
Cambrai
Mannum
Wanbi
Malpas
Meribah
Alawoona
Mindarie
Peebinga
Ouyen
Annuello
Kulwin
Manangatang
Kyalite
C. Carnot
Sleaford B.
Thistle I.
Gambier I.
Edithburgh
Sturt Bay
Mt. Barker
Mt. Lofty Ranges
Murray Bridge
Tailem Bend
Borrika
Karoonda
Pinnaroo
Underbool
Cowangie
Patchewollock
Murrayville
Chinkapook
Nyah West
Swan Hill
L. Tyrrell
C. Spencer
Marion Bay
Willunga
Strathalbyn
Wellington
Parrakie
Lameroo
Sea Lake
Ultima
Lake Boga
Investigator Strait
Rapid Bay
Goolwa
Victor Harbor
L. Alexandrina
L. Albert
Tyrrell
Kerang
Koondrook
Kingscote
Backstairs Pass.
Encounter Bay
Coonalpyn
Hopetoun
Yaapeet
Quambatook
Cape Borda
Parndana
Kangaroo I.
Penneshaw
Tintinara
Rainbow
Beulah
Birchip
Wycheproof
Charlton
Avoca
Loddon
Vivonne Bay
C. du Couëdic
C. Gantheaume
The Coorong
Younghusband Pen.
Keith
Wirrega
L. Hindmarsh
Yanac
Jeparit
Bordertown
Kaniva
Nhill
Warracknabeal
Donald
Wedderburn
Wolseley
Serviceton
Dimboola
Marnoo
St. Arnaud
Goroke
Horsham
Murtoa
Lubeck
Lacepede Bay
Padthaway
Frances
Kybybolite
Wimmera
Navarre
Dunolly
Kingston S.E.
C. Jaffa
Naracoorte
Apsley
Toolondo
Rocklands Resr.
Grampians
Stawell
L. Lonsdale
Avoca
Maryborough
Lucindale
Struan
Edenhope
Glenelg
Robe
C. Dombey
L. Hawdon North
Coonawarra
Balmoral
1167 Mt. William
Ararat
Clunes
Daylesford
L. George
Penola
Casterton
Coleraine
Dunkeld
Beaufort
Beachport
Millicent
Glencoe
Hamilton
Lake Bolac
L. Bolac
Buninyong
Ballarat
Meredith
L. Bonney
Glenburnie
Merino
Penshurst
Lismore
Mount Gambier
Port MacDonnell
Dartmoor
Macarthur
Cressy
Nelson
Heywood
Mortlake
Camperdown
L. Corangamite
C. Northumberland
Discovery Bay
Koroit
Terang
Cobden
Colac
C. Bridgewater
Portland
Port Fairy
Warrnambool
Timboon
C. Nelson
Peterborough
Port Campbell
Otway Ra.
Apollo Bay
C. Otway
Q U
N E
V I C

Brisbane
Sandgate
Ipswich
Beenleigh
Southport
Surfer's Paradise
Beaudesert
Coolangatta
Tweed Heads
Murwillumbah
McPherson Range
Darling Downs
Cunnamulla
Murra Murra
Fernlee
Nindigully
Talwood
Toobeah
Goondiwindi
Inglewood
Warwick
Killarney
Dirranbandi
Thallon
Boggabilla
Cottonvale
Stanthorpe
Texas
Ballandean
Wallangarra
Woodenbong
Kyogle
Nimbin
Mullumbimby
C. Byron
Byron Bay
Lismore
Ballina
Casino
Tabulam
Drake
Tenterfield
Coraki
Woodburn
Evans Hd.
Richmond Range
Bundaleer
Tego
Tinnenburra
Hebel
Culgoa
Weir
Macintyre
Whalan
Mungindi
Weemelah
Garah
Gil Gil
New Angledool
Goodooga
Barringun
Enngonia
Weilmoringle
Warrego
Cuttaburra
Yantabulla
Lightning Ridge
Birrie
Bokhara
Narran
Warrambool
Narran L.
Collerina
Ford's Bridge
Goombalie
N. Bourke
Bourke
Brewarrina
Walgett
Collarenebri
Gwydir
Moomin Cr.
Rowena
Pian
Ashley
Moree
Croppa Creek
Yetman
Dumaresq
Bonshaw
Ashford
Emmaville
Deepwater
Mt. Capoompeta
Severn
Clarence
Warialda
Gravesend
Delungra
Inverell
Bingara
Bellata
Glen Innes
Mann
Wooded Bluff
Yamba
Maclean
Grafton
Nymboida
Corindi
Woolgoolga
Tingha
Burren Jc.
Wee Waa
Narrabri
Namoi
Pilliga
Narrabri West
Mt. Kaputar
Nandewar Range
Barraba
Bundarra
Guyra
New England Ra.
Boyd
Mt. Hyland
Round Mt.
Dorrigo
Coff's Harbour
Sawtell
Urunga
Bellingen
Point Lookout
Armidale
Uralla
Nambucca Heads
Macksville
Bellbrook
Tarcoon
Gongolgon
Macquarie
Marra
Carinda
Castlereagh
Bogan
Bourindal
Byrock
Louth
Yanda
Macquarie Marshes
Quambone
Marthaguy Cr.
Gwabegar
Baradine
Kenebri
Coonamble
Boggabri
Gunnedah
Curlewis
L. Keepit
Manilla
Bendemeer
Moonbi Ra.
Walcha
Tamworth
Macleay
Smoky Cape
Kempsey
Smithtown
Crescent Head
Coolabah
Mount Drysdale
Girilambone
Canonba
Gulargambone
Bugaldie
Coonabarabran
Mullaley
Warrumbungle Range
Tambar Springs
Premer
Quirindi
Werris Creek
Nundle
Black Sugarloaf Mt.
Nowendoc
Tia
Wauchope
Port Macquarie
Comboyne
Laurieton
Kendall
Harrington
Cobar
Canbelego
Hermidale
Nyngan
Mt. Nurri
Mullengudgery
Curban
Collie
Gilgandra
Mendooran
Binnaway
Bundella
Blackville
Liverpool Ra.
Murrurundi
Manning
Wingham
Taree
Old Bar
Tuncurry
Forster
Gloucester
Barrington Tops
Buckambool Mt.
Crowl Cr.
Nymagee
Nevertire
Warren
Trangie
Coolah
Talbragar
Dunedoo
Cassilis
Merriwa
Wingen
Scone
Aberdeen
Muswellbrook
Tottenham
Albert
Narromine
Dubbo
Goolma
Gulgong
Denman
Singleton
Dungog
Stroud
Bulahdelah
Myall L.
Hunter
Gilgunnia
Bobadah
Tarran Hills
Yellow Mt.
Tomingley
Wellington
Mudgee
Rylstone
Kandos
Mt. Coricudgy
Maitland
Port Stephens
Nelson Bay
Raymond Terrace
Kurri Kurri
Cessnock
Wallsend
Newcastle
Belmont
L. Macquarie
Morisset
Wyong
Gosford
Broken Bay
Manly
Sydney
Botany Bay
Sutherland
Parramatta
Liverpool
Penrith
Hornsby
Windsor
Colo
Glen Davis
SOUTH WALES
PACIFIC OCEAN
TASMAN SEA
Mount Hope
Matakana
Tullamore
Peak Hill
Yeoval
Cumnock
Stuart Town
Sofala
Hill End
Turon
Trundle
Condobolin
Bogan Gate
Parkes
Molong
Trida
Billabong
Roto
Euabalong
Lake Cargelligo
Eugowra
Manildra
Orange
Bathurst
Portland
Lithgow
Blue Mts.
Lachlan
Hillston
Naradhan
Burcher
Forbes
L. Cowal
Canowindra
Blayney
Oberon
Katoomba
Jenolan Caves
L. Burragorang
Rankins Springs
Ungarie
West Wyalong
Marsden
Gooloogong
Caragabal
Grenfell
Cowra
Wyangala Resr.
Abercrombie
Cocoparra Range
Goolgowi
Wyalong
Bribbaree
Koorawatha
Young
Murringo
Crookwell
Picton
Campbelltown
Bulli
Wollongong
Port Kembla
Shellharbour
Kiama
Gerringong
Mittagong
Bowral
Moss Vale
Gunbar
Yenda
Barellan
Barmedman
Ariah Park
Bland
Carrathool
Griffith
Wumbulgal
Ardlethan
Leeton
Yanco
Temora
Stockinbingal
Cootamundra
Boorowa
Murrumburrah
Galong
Darlington Pt.
Narrandera
Coleambally
Ganmain
Coolamon
Junee
Burrinjuck Resr.
Yass
Gunning
Goulburn
Bomaderry
Nowra
Morundah
Murrumbidgee
Kywong
Gundagai
Wagga Wagga
Burrinjuck
L. George
Tarago
Pt. Perpendicular
Jervis Bay
COMMONWEALTH TERRITORY
Urana
Jerilderie
Lockhart
The Rock
Tarcutta
Tumut
Canberra
AUST. CAPITAL TERRITORY
Queanbeyan
Shoalhaven
Milton
Ulladulla
Braidwood
Deniliquin
Oaklands
Urana
Henty
Adelong
Batlow
Rand
Mt. Bimberi
Captains Flat
Nelligen
Finley
Berrigan
Walla Walla
Culcairn
Holbrook
Tumbarumba
Batemans Bay
Burrewarra Pt.
Tocumwal
Cobram
Corowa
Albury
L. Hume
Jingellic
Murray
Bredbo
Moruya
Numurkah
Yarrawonga
Wodonga
Corryong
Adaminaby
Bunyan
Cooma
Bodalla
Narooma
C. Dromedary
Bermagui
Shepparton
Mooroopna
Bowser
Chiltern
Tallangatta
Mt. Townsend
Mt. Kosciusko
Eucumbene
Berridale
Jindabyne
Snowy Mts.
Cobargo
Nimmitabel
Bega
Tathra
Merimbula
Cathcart
Bombala
Eden
Twofold Bay
Murchison
Wangaratta
Beechworth
Dartmouth Resr.
Myrtleford
Benalla
Tatong
Ovens
Bright
Mount Beauty
Mt. Bogong
Euroa
Whitfield
Nagambie
Mt. Hotham
Seymour
Mansfield
Mt. Buller
Mt. Howitt
Omeo
Mt. Bowen
Delegate
Bendoc
Disaster Bay
Yea
Alexandra
Lake Eildon
Tambo
Ensay
Dargo
Macalister
Mitchell
Bruthen
Genoa
Cann River
C. Howe
Mallacoota
Mallacoota Inlet
Orbost
Marlo
Rame Hd.
C. Everard
Whittlesea
Healesville
Yarra
Warburton
Upper Yarra Resr.
Noojee
Melbourne
Bairnsdale
Lakes Entrance
Ninety Mile Beach
Dandenong
Pakenham
Cranbourne
Warragul
Moe
Maffra
Stratford
Sale
Rosedale
Traralgon
Morwell
Yarram
Korumburra
Leongatha
Hastings
French I.
Woodside
Wonthaggi
Inverloch
Toora
Foster
Port Albert
Corner Inlet
Venus Bay
C. Liptrap
Waratah Bay
Mt. La Trobe
Wilsons Promontory
Relief
Feet
Metres
16404
5000
9843
3000
6562
2000
3281
1000
1640
500
656
200
0
Sea Level
Land Dep.
656
200
13123
4000
22966
7000
Scale 1 : 5 000 000
0 25 50 75 100 125Miles
0 50 100 150 200Kms.
Lambert Zenithal Equal Area Projection
© Collins

PACIFIC OCEAN

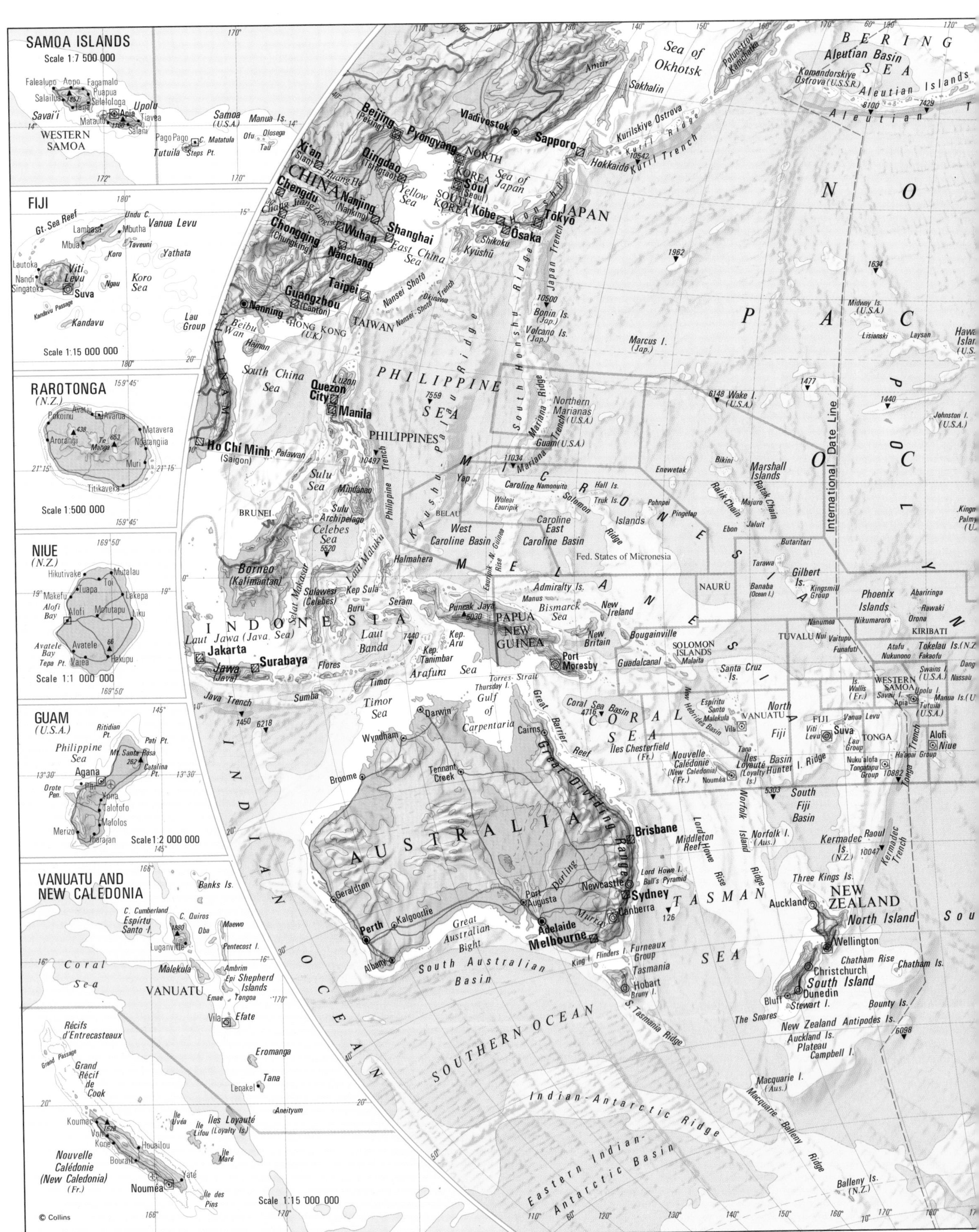

SAMOA ISLANDS
Scale 1:7 500 000
Savai'i
Upolu
Apia
WESTERN SAMOA
Samoa (U.S.A.)
Manua Is.
Pago Pago
Tutuila
FIJI
Vanua Levu
Viti Levu
Suva
Koro Sea
Kandavu
Lau Group
Scale 1:15 000 000
RAROTONGA
(N.Z.)
Avarua
Scale 1:500 000
NIUE
(N.Z.)
Alofi
Scale 1:1 000 000
GUAM
(U.S.A.)
Philippine Sea
Agana
Scale 1:2 000 000
VANUATU AND NEW CALEDONIA
Espíritu Santo I.
Coral Sea
VANUATU
Vila
Efate
Eromanga
Tana
Îles Loyauté (Loyalty Is.)
Nouvelle Calédonie (New Caledonia) (Fr.)
Nouméa
Scale 1:15 000 000
© Collins
Sea of Okhotsk
BERING SEA
Aleutian Basin
Aleutian Islands
Sakhalin
Vladivostok
Sapporo
Hokkaidō
Kuril Trench
Beijing (Peking)
Pyongyang
NORTH KOREA
Sea of Japan
Soul (Seoul)
SOUTH KOREA
JAPAN
Tōkyō
Ōsaka
Kōbe
Xi'an
Qingdao
CHINA
Chengdu
Nanjing
Wuhan
Shanghai
Chongqing (Chungking)
Nanchang
Yellow Sea
East China Sea
Taipei
TAIWAN
Guangzhou (Canton)
Nanning
HONG KONG (U.K.)
Hainan
South China Sea
VIETNAM
Ho Chí Minh (Saigon)
Quezon City
Manila
PHILIPPINES
PHILIPPINE SEA
Bonin Is. (Jap.)
Volcano Is. (Jap.)
Marcus I. (Jap.)
Northern Marianas (U.S.A.)
Guam (U.S.A.)
Mariana Trench
Wake I. (U.S.A.)
Midway Is. (U.S.A.)
International Date Line
Marshall Islands
Caroline Islands
Fed. States of Micronesia
MICRONESIA
PACIFIC OCEAN
POLYNESIA
MELANESIA
Sulu Sea
Celebes Sea
BRUNEI
Borneo (Kalimantan)
Sulawesi (Celebes)
Halmahera
INDONESIA
Jakarta
Jawa (Java)
Surabaya
Laut Banda
Arafura Sea
Timor Sea
PAPUA NEW GUINEA
Port Moresby
Bismarck Sea
Admiralty Is.
New Ireland
New Britain
Bougainville
SOLOMON ISLANDS
Guadalcanal
NAURU
Gilbert Is.
KIRIBATI
Phoenix Islands
TUVALU
Tokelau Is. (N.Z.)
WESTERN SAMOA
Apia
VANUATU
FIJI
Suva
TONGA
Nuku'alofa
Alofi
Niue
Tonga Trench
Kermadec Is. (N.Z.)
Kermadec Trench
CORAL SEA
Gulf of Carpentaria
Darwin
Wyndham
Cairns
Great Barrier Reef
Great Dividing Range
Tennant Creek
Broome
AUSTRALIA
Brisbane
Newcastle
Sydney
Canberra
Melbourne
Adelaide
Port Augusta
Geraldton
Perth
Kalgoorlie
Albany
Great Australian Bight
South Australian Basin
Tasmania
Hobart
Norfolk I. (Aus.)
Lord Howe I.
TASMAN SEA
Three Kings Is.
NEW ZEALAND
Auckland
North Island
Wellington
Christchurch
South Island
Dunedin
Chatham Is.
Chatham Rise
Bounty Is.
Antipodes Is.
Auckland Is.
Campbell I.
Macquarie I. (Aus.)
INDIAN OCEAN
Java Trench
SOUTHERN OCEAN
Indian-Antarctic Ridge
South Tasmania Ridge
Macquarie-Balleny Ridge
Eastern Indian-Antarctic Basin
Balleny Is. (N.Z.)

HAWAIIAN ISLANDS
(U.S.A.)
Scale 1:10 000 000
KIRITIMATI (CHRISTMAS I.)
(Kiribati)
Scale 1:2 500 000
TONGA
Scale 1:7 500 000
MARQUESAS ISLANDS
(France)
Scale 1:10 000 000
EASTER ISLAND
(Chile)
Scale 1:1 000 000
SOCIETY ISLANDS
(France)
Scale 1:7 500 000
TAHITI
(France)
Scale 1:2 500 000
CANADA
UNITED STATES OF AMERICA
MEXICO
Gulf of Mexico
CARIBBEAN SEA
VENEZUELA
COLOMBIA
ECUADOR
PERU
CHILE
ARGENTINA
Peru Basin
East Pacific Ridge
Pacific-Antarctic Ridge
Pacific-Antarctic Basin
Tropic of Cancer
Equator
Tropic of Capricorn
Antarctic Circle
Scale 1:60 000 000
0 200 400 600 800 1000 Miles
0 400 800 1200 1600 Kms
Modified Zenithal Equidistant Projection

Asia
Europe
ARCTIC OCEAN
Bering Strait
ALASKA
U.S.A.
Anchorage
Ellesmere I.
GREENLAND
Parry Islands
Baffin Bay
Baffin Island
Victoria Island
Denmark Strait
Arctic Circle
Godthåb/Nuuk
Hudson Bay
International Date Line
CANADA
Edmonton
Newfoundland
Vancouver
Seattle
Winnipeg
Québec
Montreal
Ottawa
Toronto
Boston
Portland
UNITED STATES OF AMERICA
Hamilton
Buffalo
Paterson
Newark
New York
Milwaukee
Detroit
Cleveland
Chicago
Pittsburgh
Baltimore
Philadelphia
Washington
Indianapolis
Cincinnati
St. Louis
Kansas City
Denver
San Francisco
San Jose
Los Angeles
San Bernardino
San Diego
Tijuana
Atlanta
Dallas
Houston
New Orleans
Ciudad Juárez
Miami
Bermuda (U.K.)
NORTH PACIFIC OCEAN
Honolulu
Hawaiian Islands (U.S.A.)
I. de Guadalupe (Mex.)
Tropic of Cancer
Gulf of Mexico
BAHAMAS
MEXICO
Monterrey
Havana
CUBA
Santiago de Cuba
HAITI
DOM. REP.
Port-au-Prince
Santo Domingo
JAMAICA
Kingston
Caribbean Sea
León
Guadalajara
Mexico City
Is. de Revilla Gigedo (Mex.)
Belmopan
BELIZE
Guatemala City
GUA.
HONDURAS
Tegucigalpa
San Salvador
EL SAL.
NICARAGUA
Managua
COSTA RICA
San José
PANAMA
Panamá
Equator
Tropic of Capricorn
SOUTH PACIFIC OCEAN
50°
40°
30°
20°
10°
10°
20°
30°
180°
170°
160°
150°
140°
130°
120°
110°
100°
90°

DOM. REP.: DOMINICAN REPUBLIC
EL SAL.: EL SALVADOR
GUA.: GUATEMALA
ST.V. AND G.: ST.VINCENT AND THE GRENADINES

NORTH AMERICA

COUNTRY	PAGE
ANTIGUA	87
BAHAMAS	87
BARBADOS	87
BELIZE	87
CANADA	72-73; 74-75; 76-77
COSTA RICA	87
CUBA	87
DOMINICA	87
DOMINICAN REPUBLIC	87
EL SALVADOR	86-87
GREENLAND	96; 73
GRENADA	87
GUATEMALA	86-87
HAITI	87
HONDURAS	87
JAMAICA	87
MEXICO	86-87
NICARAGUA	87
PANAMA	87
PUERTO RICO	87
ST. KITTS – NEVIS	87
ST. LUCIA	87
ST. VINCENT AND THE GRENADINES	87
UNITED STATES	78-79; 80-81; 82-83; 84-85

Africa

TH

ATLANTIC

OCEAN

20°

30°

40°

ARBADOS

th

rica

CANADA AND ALASKA

U.S.S.R.
BERING SEA
Bering Str.
St. Lawrence I.
St. Matthew I.
Nunivak I.
Norton Sound
Kotzebue Sound
BEAUFORT SEA
Brooks Range
Endicott Mts.
De Long Mts.
Baird Mts.
A L A S K A (U.S.A.)
Kuskokwim Mts.
Alaska Range
Mt. McKinley 6194
Aleutian Range
Alaska Pen.
Bristol Bay
Shelikof Strait
Kodiak I.
Shumagin Is.
Unimak I.
Cook Inlet
Gulf of Alaska
Mt. St. Elias 5489
Mt. Logan 6050
Mt. Fairweather 4670
Alexander Archipelago
Baranof I.
Chichagof I.
Pr. of Wales I.
Dixon Entrance
Queen Charlotte Islands
Hecate Str.
Qn. Charlotte Str.
Vancouver Island
P A C I F I C O C E A N
Barrow
Wainwright
Point Hope
C. Lisburne
Kotzebue
Nome
Teller
Noorvik
Umiat
Prudhoe Bay
C. Halkett
Bethel
Kwiguk
Unalakleet
Galena
Tanana
Hughes
Bettles
Allakaket
Nenana
College
Fairbanks
Fort Yukon
Beaver
Healy
Talkeetna
Willow
Palmer
Anchorage
Whittier
Seward
Homer
Seldovia
Kodiak
Valdez
Cordova
Copper Center
Tanacross
Northway
Yakutat
Skagway
Haines
Juneau
Sitka
Wrangell
Ketchikan
Y U K O N
Whitehorse
Carcross
Dawson
Mayo Landing
Keno Hill
Carmacks
Old Crow
Watson Lake
Mackenzie Mts.
Selwyn Mts.
Ogilvie Mts.
British Mts.
Richardson Mts.
Martin Pt.
Banks Island
Victoria Island
Prince Patrick I.
McClure Strait
Amundsen Gulf
Franklin Bay
Coronation Gulf
C. Bathurst
C. Kellett
Tuktoyaktuk
Inuvik
Aklavik
Fort McPherson
Arctic Red River
Fort Good Hope
Norman Wells
Fort Franklin
Fort Norman
Gt. Bear Lake
Port Radium
Wrigley
Fort Simpson
Fort Providence
Fort Liard
Yellowknife
Rae
Gt. Slave Lake
Hay River
Fort Resolution
Fort Smith
Fort Reliance
Snowdrift
Discovery
N O R T H W E S T T E R R I T O R I E S
INUVIK
FORT SMITH
B R I T I S H C O L U M B I A
A L B E R T A
SASKATCHEWAN
R O C K Y M O U N T A I N S
Coast Mountains
Cassiar Mountains
Stikine
Telegraph Creek
Atlin
Teslin
Stewart
Hazelton
Prince Rupert
Kitimat
Bella Coola
Prince George
Quesnel
Williams Lake
Mt. Waddington 4042
Port Alice
Courtenay
Nanaimo
Ladysmith
Squamish
Vancouver
Victoria
Lillooet
Clinton
Kamloops
Revelstoke
Vernon
Kelowna
Penticton
Nelson
Trail
Cranbrook
Fort Nelson
Fort St. John
Dawson Creek
Hudson Hope
Grande Prairie
Peace River
McLennan
Lesser Slave Lake
Athabasca
Mt. Robson 3954
Jasper
Edmonton
Leduc
Wetaskiwin
Red Deer
Lacombe
Camrose
Stettler
Vegreville
Vermilion
Lloydminster
Banff
Calgary
Drumheller
Hanna
Bassano
Brooks
Medicine Hat
Lethbridge
Crowsnest Pass 1357
Kicking Horse Pass 1622
Yellowhead Pass
Fort Vermilion
Fort Chipewyan
Fort McMurray
Fort Mackay
L. Athabasca
Uranium City
Birch Mts.
Caribou Mts.
Saskatoon
North Battleford
Prince Albert
La Ronge
Swift Current
Maple Creek
Moose Jaw
Regina
W A S H I N G T O N
Seattle
Tacoma
Bellingham
Port Angeles
C. Flattery
Aberdeen
Astoria
Longview
Mt. Rainier 4392
Yakima
Richland
Spokane
Sandpoint
Wallace
Oroville
Portland
Salem
Albany
Eugene
North Bend
C. Blanco
La Grande
Baker
Blue Mountains
O R E G O N
Harney Basin
Grants Pass
Klamath Falls
Crescent City
Mt. Shasta 4317
C. Mendocino
Eureka
CALIFORNIA
N E V A D A
UTAH
I D A H O
Boise
Moscow
Grangeville
Salmon River Mts.
Borah Pk. 3857
Twin Falls
Shoshone
Pocatello
Idaho Falls
Grand Teton 4196
M O N T A N A
Missoula
Helena
Great Falls
Havre
Shelby
Butte
Bozeman
Billings
Roundup
Miles City
Glasgow
Fort Peck Resr.
Yellowstone
W Y O M I N G
Sheridan
Buffalo
Casper
Lusk
Relief
Feet Metres
16404 5000
9843 3000
6562 2000
3281 1000
1640 500
656 200
0 Sea Level
Land Dep.
656 200
13123 4000
22966 7000
Scale 1 : 17 000 000
0 100 200 300 400 500 Miles
0 100 200 300 400 500 600 700 800 Kms.
Bonne Projection

GREENLAND
ATLANTIC
OCEAN
Kong Christian den IX Land
Kong Frederik den VI Kyst
Mt. Forel 3360
Baffin Bay
Davis Strait
Labrador Sea
Baffin Island
Devon Island
Ellesmere Island
Axel Heiberg I.
Somerset Island
Cornwallis I.
Bylot I.
Lancaster Sound
Jones Sd.
Nares Strait
Thule/Qaanaaq
Upernavik
Nunavik
Disko
Godthåb/Nuuk
Christianshåb/Qasigiannguit
Søndrestrømfjord/Kangerlussuaq
Holsteinsborg/Sisimiut
Sukkertoppen/Maniitsoq
Fiskenaesset/Qeqertarsuatsiaat
Frederikshåb/Paamiut
Ivigtut/Ivittuut
Julianehåb/Qaqortoq
K. Farvel/Uummannarsuaq (C. Farewell)
Angmagssalik/Tasiilaq
Arctic Circle
Resolute
Pond Inlet
Clyde
C. Dyer
Padloping Island
Penny Highland 2591
Pangnirtung
Cumberland Sound
Cumberland Pen.
Frobisher Bay
Hall Pen.
Lake Harbour
Resolution Island
Foxe Basin
Foxe Channel
Foxe Peninsula
Prince Charles I.
Melville Peninsula
Igloolik Island
Hall Lake
Repulse Bay
Pelly Bay
Spence Bay
Gjoa Haven
Boothia Peninsula
Gulf of Boothia
Cape Dorchester
Cape Dorset
Amadjuak
Nettilling L.
Southampton Island
Coral Harbour
Wager Bay
Baker Lake
Chesterfield Inlet
Rankin Inlet
Whale Cove
Eskimo Point
KEEWATIN
NORTH WEST TERRITORIES
Hudson Strait
Akpatok I.
C. Chidley
Coats I.
Mansel I.
Ivujivik
Salluit
Kangiqsujuaq
Quaqtaq
Kangirsuk
Péninsule D'Ungava
Ungava Bay
Kuujjuaq
Port-Nouveau Québec
Hebron
Nutak
Nain
Hopedale
C. Harrison
Indian Harbour
Rigolet
Cartwright
Battle Harbour
C. Bauld
St. Anthony
NEWFOUNDLAND
Labrador
Smallwood Resr.
Schefferville
North West River
Churchill
Labrador City
Wabush City
Hudson Bay
Ottawa Is.
Belcher Is.
King George Is.
Churchill
C. Churchill
C. Tatnam
Port Nelson
York Factory
Fort Severn
Winisk
C. Henrietta Maria
James Bay
Akimiski I.
Fort Albany
Moosonee
CANADA
ONTARIO
QUÉBEC
MANITOBA
Newfoundland
Gander
Bonavista
Carbonear
St. John's
Placentia
Trepassey
C. Race
Corner Brook
Grand Falls
Channel-Port-aux-Basques
St. Pierre and Miquelon (Fr.)
Gulf of St. Lawrence
Cabot Str.
Cape Breton I.
Sydney
Port Hawkesbury
Sable I.
Île d'Anticosti
Sept Îles
Gaspé
PR. EDWARD I.
Charlottetown
NEW BRUNSWICK
NOVA SCOTIA
Halifax
Truro
Moncton
Saint John
Fredericton
Yarmouth
C. Sable
Bay of Fundy
Chicoutimi-Jonquière
Québec
Trois-Rivières
Montreal
Sherbrooke
Ottawa
Kingston
Toronto
Hamilton
London
Windsor
Detroit
Sudbury
North Bay
Timmins
Thunder Bay
Sault Sainte Marie
Winnipeg
L. Winnipeg
L. Superior
L. Huron
L. Michigan
L. Erie
L. Ontario
Duluth
Minneapolis
St. Paul
Milwaukee
Chicago
Toledo
Cleveland
Buffalo
Rochester
Syracuse
Albany
Pittsburgh
Philadelphia
New York
Baltimore
Hartford
Providence
Boston
C. Cod
Portland
Long Island
UNITED STATES OF AMERICA

WESTERN CANADA

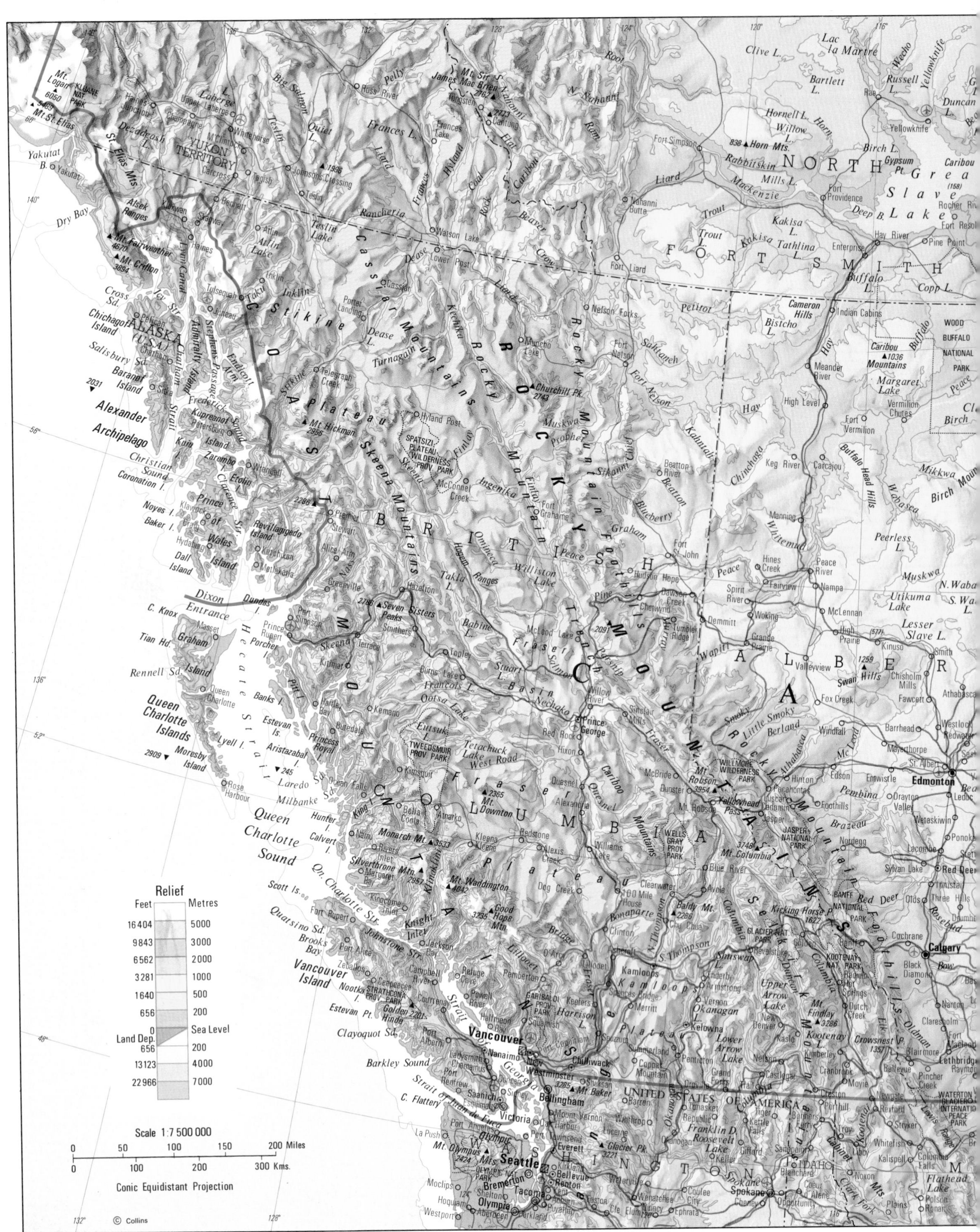

Relief
Feet
Metres
16404
5000
9843
3000
6562
2000
3281
1000
1640
500
656
200
0
Sea Level
Land Dep.
656
200
13123
4000
22966
7000
Scale 1:7 500 000
0
50
100
150
200 Miles
0
100
200
300 Kms.
Conic Equidistant Projection
© Collins
YUKON TERRITORY
ALASKA (U.S.A.)
B R I T I S H
C O L U M B I A
A L B E R T A
N O R T H
F O R T S M I T H
UNITED STATES OF AMERICA
W A S H I N G T O N
IDAHO
Vancouver
Victoria
Seattle
Edmonton
Calgary
Prince George
Prince Rupert
Whitehorse
Yellowknife
Spokane
Bellingham
Tacoma
Olympia
Kamloops
Kelowna
Great Slave Lake
Queen Charlotte Islands
Vancouver Island
Alexander Archipelago
Queen Charlotte Sound
Hecate Strait
Dixon Entrance
Strait of Juan de Fuca
Strait of Georgia
Rocky Mountains
Coast Mountains
Cassiar Mountains
Skeena Mountains
Mackenzie Mountains
Fraser Plateau
Mt. Logan 6050
Mt. Robson 3954
Mt. Waddington 4042
Mt. Fairweather 4670
Yellowhead Pass
Kicking Horse P.
Wood Buffalo National Park
Jasper National Park
Banff National Park
Glacier Nat. Park
Kootenay Nat. Park
Wells Gray Prov. Park
Tweedsmuir Prov. Park
Strathcona Prov. Park
Garibaldi Prov. Park
Spatsizi Plateau Wilderness Prov. Park
Kluane Nat. Park
Willmore Wilderness Park
Waterton Glacier International Peace Park
Fort Nelson
Fort St. John
Dawson Creek
Grande Prairie
Peace River
Fort Liard
Fort Simpson
Fort Providence
Hay River
Watson Lake
Liard
Peace
Fraser
Columbia
Skeena
Stikine
Finlay
Athabasca
Mackenzie
Williston Lake
Lesser Slave L.
Kootenay L.
Okanagan Lake
Rocky Mountain Trench
Cariboo Mountains
Monashee Mts.
Selkirk Mts.
Purcell Mts.
Columbia Mountains
Stikine Plateau
Kamloops Plateau
Nechako Basin
Mt. Baker 3285
Mt. Olympus 2424
Glacier Pk. 3221

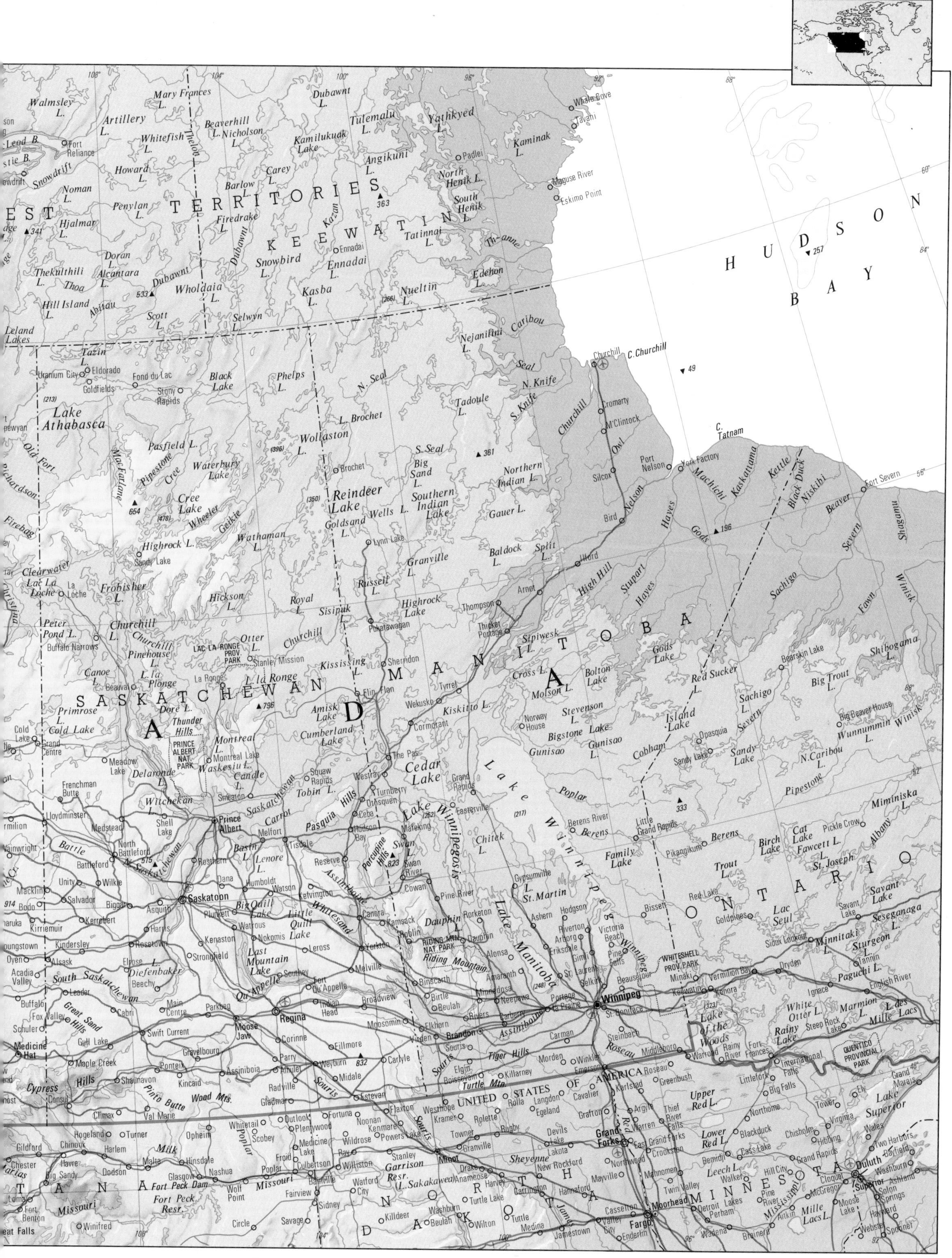

TERRITORIES
KEEWATIN
HUDSON BAY
SASKATCHEWAN
MANITOBA
ONTARIO
UNITED STATES OF AMERICA
MINNESOTA
NORTH DAKOTA
MONTANA
Walmsley L.
Mary Frances L.
Dubawnt L.
Artillery L.
Beaverhill L.
Nicholson L.
Tulemalu L.
Yathkyed L.
Whitefish L.
Kamilukuak Lake
Kaminak L.
Whale Cove
Tavani
Fort Reliance
Angikuni L.
Padlei
Howard L.
Carey L.
Barlow L.
North Henik L.
South Henik L.
Maguse River
Eskimo Point
Noman L.
Penylan L.
Firedrake L.
Hjalmar L.
Tatinnai L.
Ennadai
Doran L.
Alcantara L.
Snowbird L.
Ennadai L.
Thekulthili L.
Dubawnt
Wholdaia L.
Kasba L.
Nueltin L.
Edehon L.
Hill Island L.
Scott L.
Selwyn L.
Leland Lakes
Tazin L.
Nejanilini L.
Caribou
Churchill
C. Churchill
Uranium City
Eldorado
Fond du Lac
Black Lake
Phelps L.
N. Seal
Seal
N. Knife
Goldfields
Stony Rapids
Lake Athabasca
L. Brochet
Tadoule L.
S. Knife
Cromarty
M'Clintock
Wollaston L.
Pasfield L.
S. Seal
C. Tatnam
Port Nelson
York Factory
Old Fort
Pipestone
Cree
Waterbury Lake
Brochet
Big Sand L.
Northern Indian L.
Silcox
Owl
Machichi
Kaskattama
Kettle
Fort Severn
Black Duck
Niskibi
MacFarlane
Cree Lake
Reindeer Lake
Southern Indian Lake
Gauer L.
Nelson
Bird
Hayes
Gods
Beaver
Severn
Shagamu
Wheeler
Geikie
Goldsand L.
Wells L.
Highrock L.
Wathaman L.
Lynn Lake
Baldock L.
Split L.
Sandy Lake
Granville L.
Ilford
Clearwater
Lac La Loche
La Loche
Frobisher L.
Russell L.
High Hill
Stupart
Sachigo
Winisk
Hickson L.
Royal L.
Sisipuk L.
Highrock Lake
Thompson
Arnot
Fawn
Peter Pond L.
Churchill L.
Pukatawagan
Thicket Portage
Sipiwesk L.
Buffalo Narrows
Pinehouse L.
Otter L.
LAC LA RONGE PROV. PARK
Stanley Mission
Sherridon
Kississing L.
Gods Lake
Bearskin Lake
Shibogama L.
Canoe L.
La Ronge
L. la Ronge
Cross L.
Bolton Lake
Red Sucker L.
Big Trout L.
Beauval
L. la Plonge
Flin Flon
Tyrrel
Molson L.
Sachigo L.
Primrose L.
Doré L.
Amisk Lake
Wekusko
Kiskitto L.
Stevenson L.
Island Lake
Big Beaver House
Cold Lake
Thunder Hills
Norway House
Bigstone Lake
Opasquia
Wunnummin L.
Grand Centre
PRINCE ALBERT NAT. PARK
Montreal L.
Cumberland Lake
Cormorant
Gunisao L.
Cobham
Sandy Lake
N. Caribou L.
Meadow Lake
Delaronde L.
Waskesiu L.
Candle L.
The Pas
Cedar Lake
Squaw Rapids
Westray
Grand Rapids
Pipestone
Frenchman Butte
Tobin L.
Turnberry
Lake Winnipeg
Poplar
Smeaton
Witchekan L.
Saskatchewan
Hills
Lake Winnipegosis
Easterville
Ompsquen
Lloydminster
Medstead
Shell Lake
Prince Albert
Carrot
Pasquia Hills
Ceba
Mafeking
Berens River
Little Grand Rapids
Pickle Crow
Miminiska L.
Melfort
Tisdale
Hudson Bay
Berens
Birch Lake
Cat Lake
Albany
North Battleford
Battle
Basin L.
Lenore L.
Swan L.
Chitek L.
Pikangikum
Fawcett L.
Battleford
Rosthern
Porcupine Hills
Reserve
Swan River
Family Lake
St. Joseph L.
Macklin
Unity
Wilkie
Dana
Humboldt
Assiniboine
Gypsumville
Trout L.
Saskatoon
Watson
Kelvington
Cowan
Pine River
St. Martin
Red Lake
Savant Lake
Bodo
Salvador
Biggar
Asquith
Big Quill Lake
Little Quill Lake
Whitesand
Canora
Dauphin L.
Ashern
Hodgson
Bissett
Goldpines
Lac Seul
Seseganaga L.
Kerrobert
Plunkett
Watrous
Kamsack
Rorketon
Riverton
Kirriemuir
Harris
Kenaston
Nokomis
Roblin
Dauphin
Victoria Beach
Kindersley
Rosetown
Leross
Yorkton
RIDING MTN. NAT. PARK
Lake Manitoba
Arborg
Sioux Lookout
Minnitaki L.
Sturgeon L.
Alsask
Elrose
L. Diefenbaker
Strongfield
Last Mountain Lake
Melville
Riding Mountain
Alonsa
Eriksdale
Gimli
Pine Falls
WHITESHELL PROV. PARK
Dryden
Tannin
Acadia Valley
Beechy
Southey
Amaranth
St. Laurent
Selkirk
Beausejour
Minaki
Vermilion Bay
Paguchi L.
South Saskatchewan
Leader
Qu'Appelle
Fort Qu'Appelle
Binscarth
Minnedosa
Winnipeg
Keewatin
Kenora
Ignace
English River
Buffalo
Great Sand Hills
Cabri
Main Centre
Parkbeg
Indian Head
Broadview
Birtle
Neepawa
Portage la Prairie
White Otter L.
Marmion L.
L. des Mille Lacs
Fox Valley
Moose Jaw
Regina
Moosomin
Elkhorn
Carberry
St. Boniface
Lake of the Woods
Schuler
Swift Current
Corinne
Brandon
Rivers
Steinbach
Rainy Lake
Steep Rock Lake
Medicine Hat
Gull Lake
Fillmore
Virden
Carman
Rainy River
Fort Frances
Gravelbourg
Parry
Carlyle
Souris
Tiger Hills
Morden
Winkler
Roseau
Middleboro
Warroad
International Falls
QUETICO PROVINCIAL PARK
Maple Creek
Ponteix
Weyburn
Midale
Elgin
Boissevain
Killarney
Emerson
Assiniboia
Ambulet
Kincaid
Radville
Estevan
Turtle Mtn.
Cypress Hills
Shaunavon
Pinto Butte
Wood Mts.
Gladmar
Flaxton
Westhope
Rolla
Langdon
Cavalier
Karlstad
Greenbush
Upper Red L.
Littlefork
Big Falls
Grand Marais
Lake Superior
Consul
Climax
Val Marie
Whitetail
Outlook
Fortuna
Noonan
Kramer
Rolette
Egeland
Grafton
Argyle
Warren
Thief River Falls
Northome
Tower
Ely
Hogeland
Turner
Opheim
Scobey
Plentywood
Kenmare
Powers Lake
Towner
Rugby
Devils Lake
Grand Forks
East Grand Forks
Crookston
Lower Red L.
Blackduck
Chisholm
Virginia
Hibbing
Wales
Two Harbors
Gildford
Chinook
Harlem
Milk
Hinsdale
Poplar
Medicine Lake
Wildrose
Ray
Stanley
Minot
Granville
Sheyenne
Lakota
Bemidji
Cass Lake
Grand Rapids
Duluth
Superior
Chester
Havre
Big Sandy
Dodson
Malta
Glasgow
Nashua
Fort Peck Dam
Froid
Culbertson
Williston
Garrison Resr. (L. Sakakawea)
Drake
New Rockford
Northwood
Mahnomen
Leech L.
Hill City
Washburn
Ashland
Wolf Point
Missouri
Bainville
Watford City
Anamoose
Harvey
Carrington
Mayville
Twin Valley
Pine River
McGregor
Cloquet
Fort Peck Resr.
Fairview
Sidney
Turtle Lake
Hannaford
Casselton
Moorhead
Fargo
Detroit Lakes
Perham
Mississippi
Moose Lake
Solon Springs
Fort Benton
Great Falls
Winifred
Circle
Savage
Killdeer
Washburn
Beulah
Wilton
Tuttle
Medina
Jamestown
Valley City
Enderlin
Wadena
Brainerd
Aitkin
Mille Lacs L.
Hayward
Webster
Spooner
James
Red
Souris
Turtle Mtn.

EASTERN CANADA

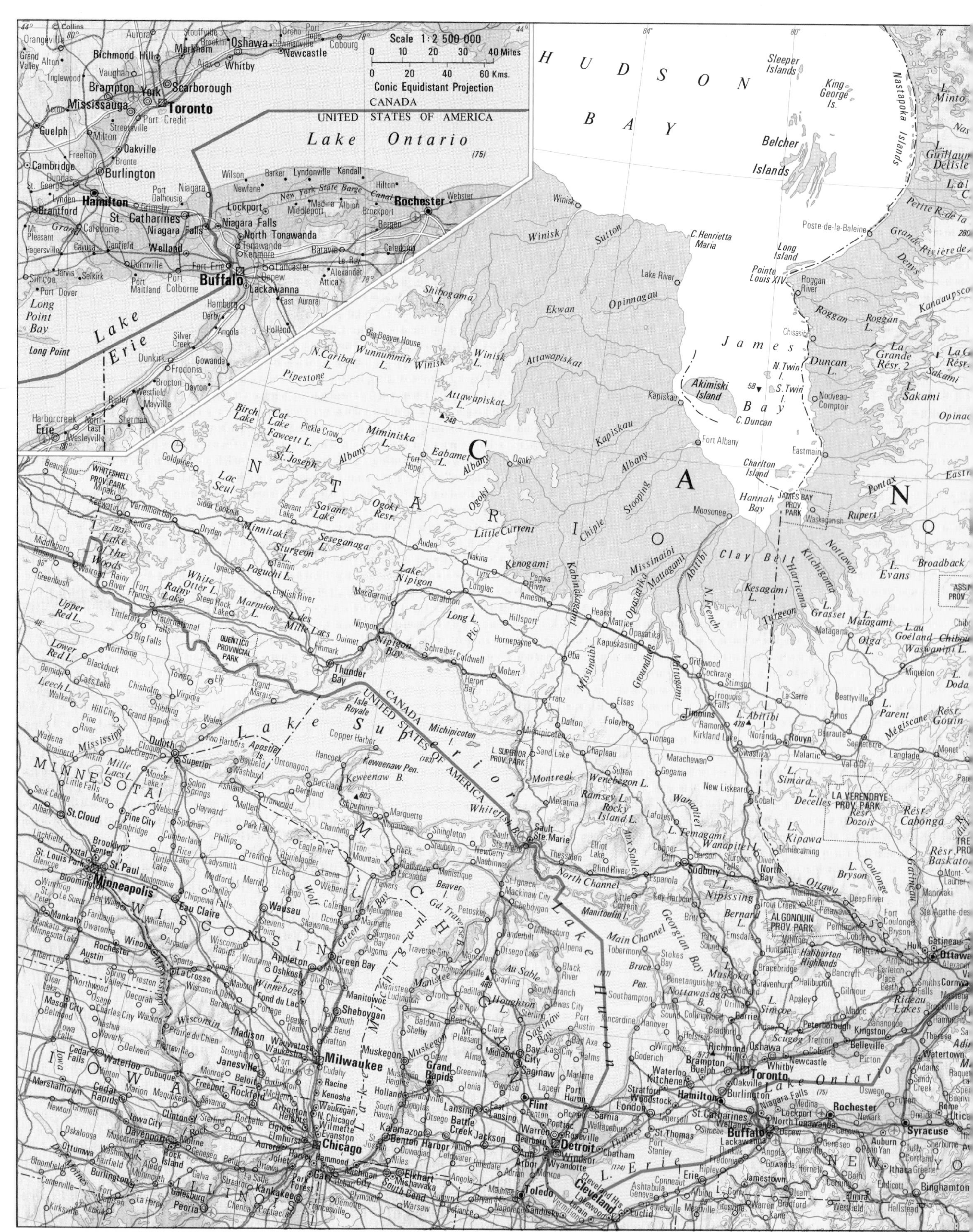

© Collins
Scale 1: 2 500 000
0 10 20 30 40 Miles
0 20 40 60 Kms.
Conic Equidistant Projection
CANADA
UNITED STATES OF AMERICA
Lake Ontario
Lake Erie
Toronto
Oshawa
Scarborough
Mississauga
Brampton
Hamilton
Burlington
St. Catharines
Niagara Falls
Buffalo
Rochester
Lockport
North Tonawanda
Lackawanna
Welland
Guelph
Oakville
Cambridge
Brantford
Long Point Bay
Long Point
Erie
HUDSON BAY
Belcher Islands
Sleeper Islands
King George Is.
Nastapoka Islands
James Bay
Akimiski Island
Charlton Island
Hannah Bay
JAMES BAY PROV. PARK
ONTARIO
C.Henrietta Maria
Winisk
Sutton
Ekwan
Opinnagau
Attawapiskat
Kapiskau
Albany
Fort Albany
Moosonee
Clay Belt
Ogoki
Kenogami
Lake Nipigon
Nipigon Bay
Thunder Bay
Lake Superior
Isle Royale
Michipicoten I.
Sault Ste. Marie
North Channel
Manitoulin I.
Georgian Bay
Lake Huron
Lake Michigan
Lake Erie
Lake of the Woods
Lac Seul
Rainy Lake
Kenora
Dryden
Timmins
Kirkland Lake
Rouyn
Sudbury
North Bay
Lake Nipissing
ALGONQUIN PROV. PARK
LA VERENDRYE PROV. PARK
Ottawa
Kingston
Peterborough
Barrie
London
Windsor
Detroit
Toledo
Cleveland
Flint
Saginaw
Lansing
Grand Rapids
Milwaukee
Chicago
Green Bay
Madison
Minneapolis
St. Paul
Duluth
Superior
MINNESOTA
WISCONSIN
MICHIGAN
IOWA
ILLINOIS
NEW YORK
Syracuse
Binghamton

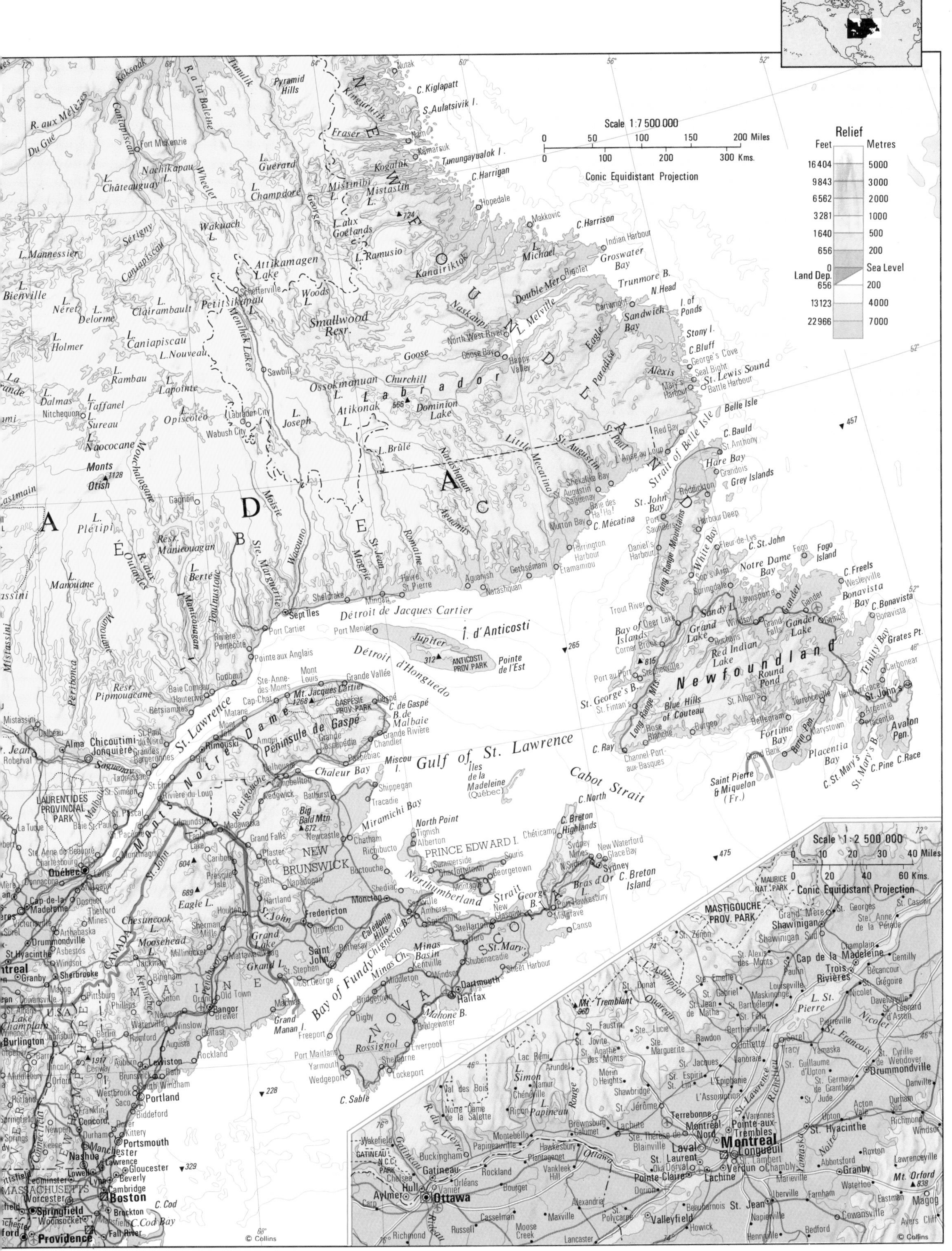

Scale 1:7 500 000
0 50 100 150 200 Miles
0 100 200 300 Kms.
Conic Equidistant Projection
Relief
Feet Metres
16 404 5000
9843 3000
6562 2000
3281 1000
1640 500
656 200
0 Sea Level
Land Dep.
656 200
13123 4000
22966 7000
Labrador
Newfoundland
Gulf of St. Lawrence
Cabot Strait
Strait of Belle Isle
Détroit de Jacques Cartier
Détroit d'Honguedo
Î. d'Anticosti
Péninsule de Gaspé
Chaleur Bay
Bay of Fundy
Northumberland Strait
NEW BRUNSWICK
PRINCE EDWARD I.
C. Breton Island
Îles de la Madeleine (Québec)
Saint Pierre & Miquelon (Fr.)
Smallwood Resr.
Lake Melville
Sept Îles
Québec
Halifax
Fredericton
Saint John
Charlottetown
St. John's
Bangor
Portland
Boston
Providence
Chicoutimi-Jonquière
Scale 1: 2 500 000
0 10 20 30 40 Miles
0 20 40 60 Kms.
Conic Equidistant Projection
Montréal
Ottawa
Laval
Longueuil
Trois Rivières
Shawinigan
Drummondville
St. Hyacinthe
Granby
Valleyfield
St. Jean
© Collins

UNITED STATES

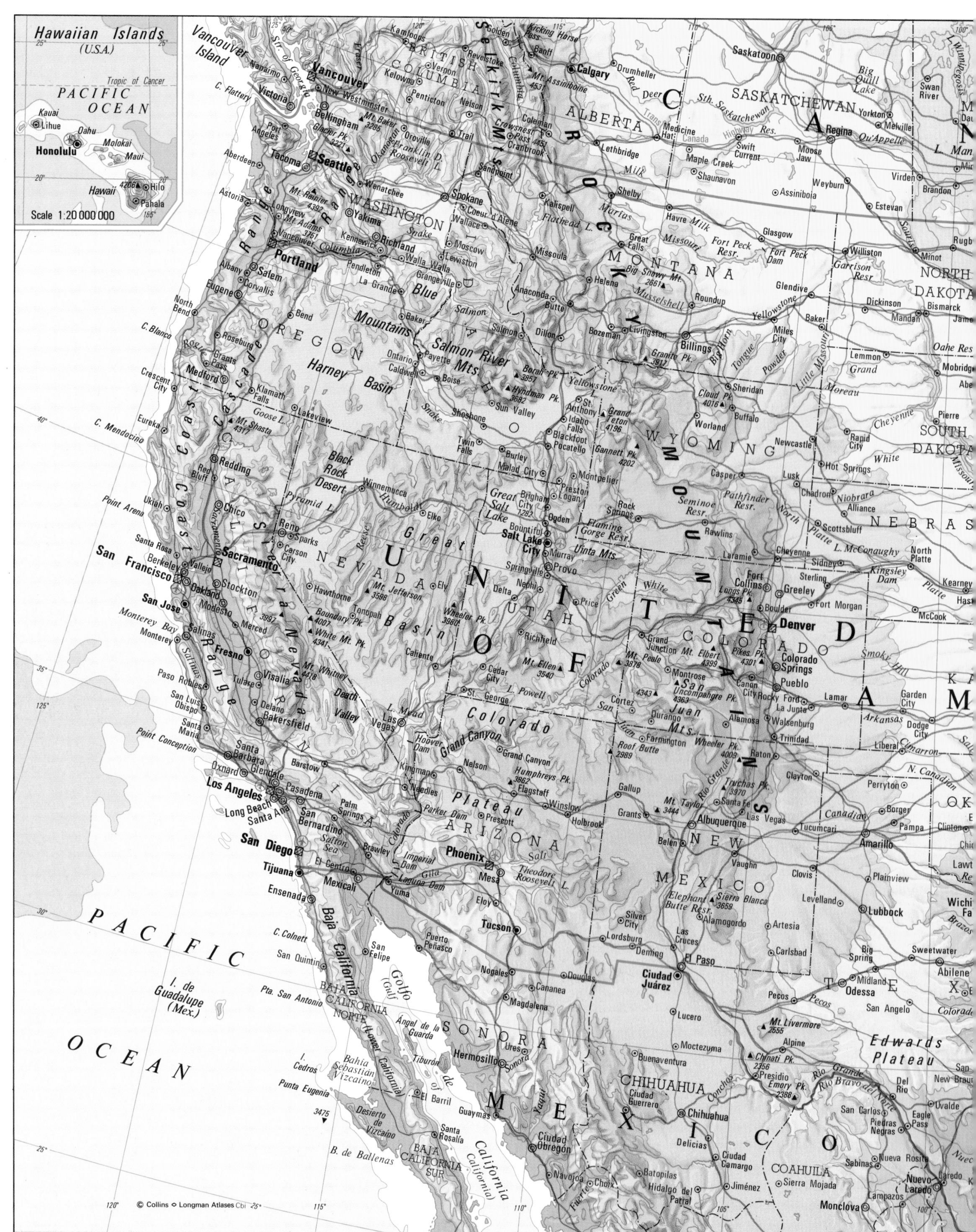

Hawaiian Islands
(U.S.A.)
Tropic of Cancer
PACIFIC
OCEAN
Kauai
Lihue
Oahu
Honolulu
Molokai
Maui
Hawaii
4206
Hilo
Pahala
Scale 1:20 000 000
Vancouver Island
BRITISH COLUMBIA
Vancouver
Victoria
New Westminster
Kamloops
Kelowna
Penticton
Calgary
Banff
Drumheller
ALBERTA
Medicine Hat
Lethbridge
Saskatoon
SASKATCHEWAN
Regina
Swift Current
Maple Creek
Moose Jaw
Yorkton
Melville
Weyburn
Brandon
Virden
Estevan
C A N
Seattle
Tacoma
Bellingham
Mt. Baker 3285
Aberdeen
Astoria
Port Angeles
C. Flattery
WASHINGTON
Spokane
Yakima
Richland
Mt. Rainier 4392
Mt. Adams 3751
Wenatchee
Walla Walla
Portland
Salem
Eugene
Corvallis
Albany
OREGON
Bend
Medford
Klamath Falls
Harney Basin
C. Blanco
Crescent City
Eureka
C. Mendocino
Mt. Shasta 4317
Redding
Red Bluff
Chico
Point Arena
Ukiah
Sacramento
San Francisco
Oakland
Berkeley
Santa Rosa
San Jose
Stockton
Modesto
Merced
Fresno
Monterey Bay
Monterey
Salinas
Visalia
Bakersfield
Paso Robles
San Luis Obispo
Santa Maria
Point Conception
Santa Barbara
Oxnard
Los Angeles
Glendale
Pasadena
Long Beach
Santa Ana
San Bernardino
Palm Springs
San Diego
Tijuana
Mexicali
El Centro
Ensenada
Salton Sea
Coast Range
Cascade Range
Sierra Nevada
Mt. Whitney 4418
Death Valley
Las Vegas
Reno
Sparks
Carson City
NEVADA
Great Basin
Black Rock Desert
Winnemucca
Elko
Ely
Hawthorne
Tonopah
Boundary Pk. 4007
White Mt. Pk. 4341
Mt. Jefferson 3598
Wheeler Pk. 3980
IDAHO
Boise
Lewiston
Moscow
Coeur d'Alene
Sandpoint
Twin Falls
Pocatello
Idaho Falls
Blackfoot
Burley
Salmon River Mts
Borah Pk. 3857
Hyndman Pk. 3682
Sun Valley
Blue Mountains
MONTANA
Missoula
Helena
Butte
Great Falls
Billings
Bozeman
Livingston
Kalispell
Shelby
Havre
Glasgow
Miles City
Glendive
Granite Pk. 3917
Fort Peck Resr.
Big Snowy Mt. 2661
WYOMING
Yellowstone
Grand Teton 4196
Gannett Pk. 4202
Casper
Sheridan
Cloud Pk. 4016
Worland
Rock Springs
Rawlins
Laramie
Cheyenne
Lusk
Newcastle
UTAH
Great Salt Lake
Ogden
Salt Lake City
Provo
Logan
Brigham City
Uinta Mts.
Flaming Gorge Resr.
Richfield
Cedar City
St. George
L. Powell
Mt. Ellen 3540
Mt. Peale 3878
COLORADO
Denver
Boulder
Fort Collins
Greeley
Colorado Springs
Pueblo
Grand Junction
Mt. Elbert 4399
Pikes Pk. 4301
Longs Pk. 4345
Montrose
Durango
Alamosa
Trinidad
Lamar
Sterling
Fort Morgan
San Juan Mts.
Uncompahgre Pk. 4363
ARIZONA
Phoenix
Tucson
Flagstaff
Mesa
Yuma
Kingman
Prescott
Winslow
Nogales
Douglas
Grand Canyon
Humphreys Pk. 3862
Colorado Plateau
Hoover Dam
L. Mead
Theodore Roosevelt L.
NEW MEXICO
Albuquerque
Santa Fe
Las Vegas
Gallup
Farmington
Roswell
Raton
Clovis
Las Cruces
Alamogordo
Silver City
Deming
Lordsburg
Carlsbad
Artesia
Truchas Pk. 3970
Wheeler Pk. 4009
Sierra Blanca 3659
Elephant Butte Resr.
TEXAS
El Paso
Amarillo
Lubbock
Odessa
Midland
Abilene
San Angelo
Pecos
Alpine
Del Rio
Laredo
Sweetwater
Plainview
Mt. Livermore 2555
Chinati Pk. 2356
Emory Pk. 2388
Edwards Plateau
Rio Grande
NORTH DAKOTA
Williston
Minot
Dickinson
Bismarck
Mandan
SOUTH DAKOTA
Rapid City
Pierre
Hot Springs
NEBRASKA
Scottsbluff
Alliance
North Platte
Kearney
McCook
Sidney
KANSAS
Garden City
Dodge City
Liberal
Rocky Mountains
UNITED STATES
MEXICO
Ciudad Juárez
Chihuahua
CHIHUAHUA
Hermosillo
Guaymas
Ciudad Obregón
Navojoa
Los Mochis
Delicias
Ciudad Camargo
Jiménez
Hidalgo del Parral
Monclova
Nuevo Laredo
Piedras Negras
Sabinas
COAHUILA
SONORA
BAJA CALIFORNIA NORTE
BAJA CALIFORNIA SUR
Golfo de California
Cananea
Magdalena
Puerto Peñasco
San Felipe
San Quintin
C. Colnett
Punta Eugenia
I. Cedros
Bahía Sebastián Vizcaíno
Desierto de Vizcaíno
Santa Rosalía
B. de Ballenas
I. de Guadalupe (Mex.)
PACIFIC OCEAN
© Collins ◇ Longman Atlases

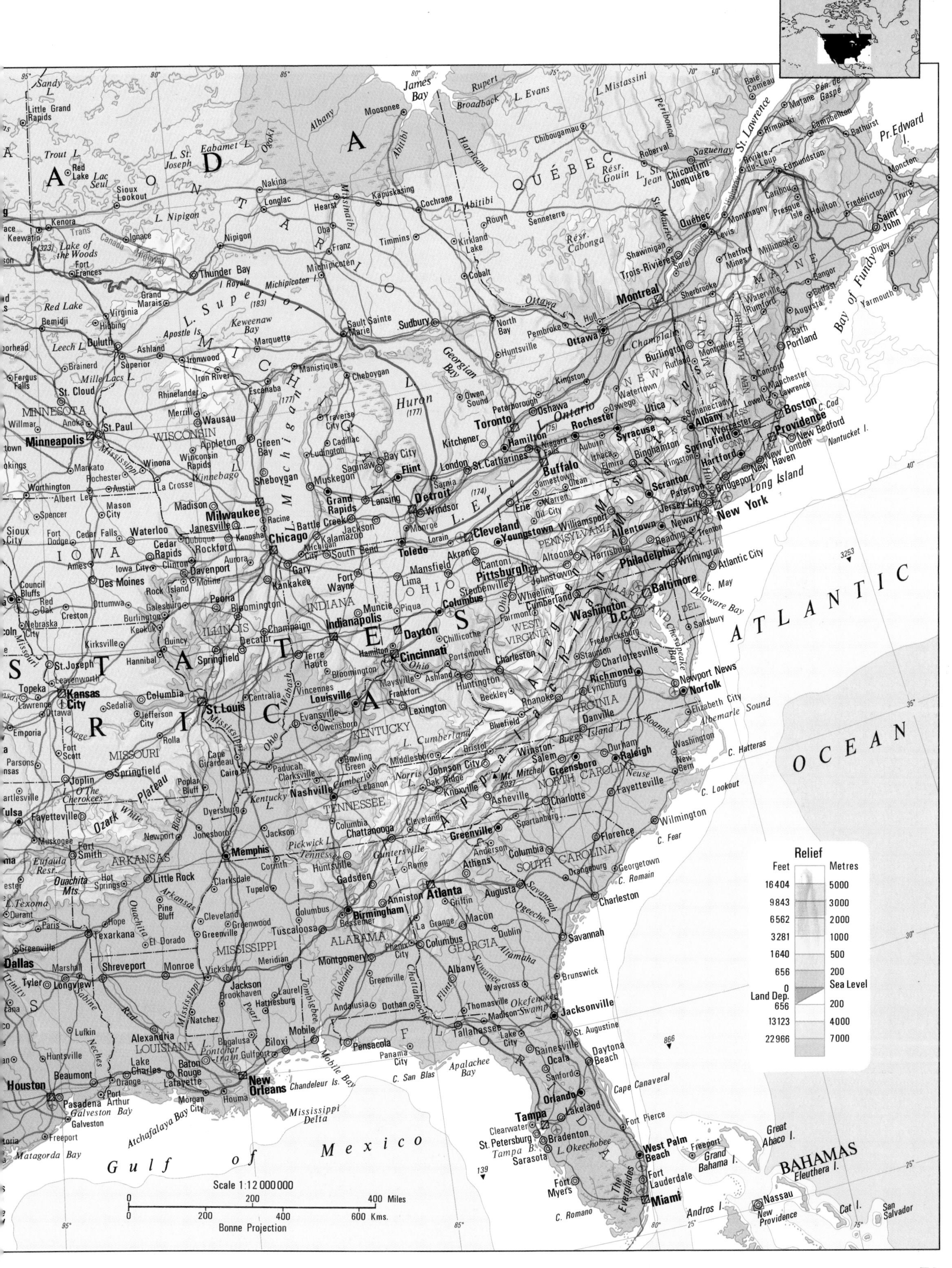
C A N A D A
O N T A R I O
Q U É B E C
U N I T E D S T A T E S O F A M E R I C A
James Bay
Moosonee
Albany
Rupert
Broadback
L. Evans
L. Mistassini
Chibougamau
Baie Comeau
Matane
Pén. de Gaspé
Rimouski
Campbellton
Bathurst
Pr. Edward I.
St. Lawrence
Peribonca
Roberval
Saguenay
Chicoutimi Jonquière
Rivière-du-Loup
Edmundston
Moncton
Truro
Little Grand Rapids
Sandy L.
Trout L.
Red Lake
Lac Seul
L. St. Joseph
Eabamet L.
Ogoki
Sioux Lookout
Nakina
Longlac
L. Nipigon
Hearst
Kapuskasing
Cochrane
L. Abitibi
Abitibi
Harricana
Rouyn
Senneterre
Résr. Gouin
L. St. Jean
St. Maurice
Québec
Lévis
Montmagny
Caribou
Presque Isle
Houlton
Fredericton
Saint John
Kenora
Keewatin
Lake of the Woods
Fort Frances
Trans Canada Highway
Ignace
Nipigon
Thunder Bay
I. Royale
Oba
Franz
Missinaibi
Timmins
Kirkland Lake
Résr. Cabonga
Shawinigan
Trois-Rivières
Sorel
Thetford Mines
Millinocket
Michipicoten
Michipicoten I.
Cobalt
Sherbrooke
M A I N E
Bangor
Belfast
Bay of Fundy
Digby
Yarmouth
Red Lake
Virginia
Hibbing
Grand Marais
L. Superior
Keweenaw Bay
Apostle Is.
Sault Sainte Marie
Sudbury
North Bay
Ottawa
Pembroke
Hull
Montreal
Waterville
Rumford
Augusta
Bath
Portland
Bemidji
Leech L.
Duluth
Ashland
Marquette
Superior
Ironwood
Iron River
Brainerd
Fergus Falls
Mille Lacs L.
St. Cloud
Rhinelander
Escanaba
Manistique
Cheboygan
Georgian Bay
Huntsville
L. Champlain
Burlington
Rutland
Montpelier
Kingston
Watertown
Concord
Manchester
Lawrence
Lowell
MINNESOTA
Willmar
Anoka
St. Paul
Minneapolis
Merrill
Wausau
WISCONSIN
Appleton
Green Bay
Traverse City
L. Huron
Owen Sound
Peterborough
Oshawa
Toronto
L. Ontario
Rochester
Oswego
Utica
Schenectady
Albany
Boston
C. Cod
Worcester
Providence
New Bedford
Nantucket I.
Mankato
Rochester
Austin
Winona
Wisconsin Rapids
L. Winnebago
La Crosse
Cadillac
Ludington
Saginaw
Bay City
Flint
Kitchener
Hamilton
St. Catharines
Niagara Falls
Buffalo
Syracuse
Auburn
Ithaca
Elmira
Binghamton
Kingston
Springfield
Hartford
New London
New Haven
Bridgeport
Long Island
Worthington
Albert Lea
Mason City
Madison
Milwaukee
Sheboygan
Muskegon
Grand Rapids
Lansing
London
Sarnia
Detroit
Windsor
L. Erie
Jamestown
Olean
Scranton
Paterson
Jersey City
New York
Spencer
Sioux City
Fort Dodge
Cedar Falls
Waterloo
Janesville
Racine
Kenosha
Chicago
Battle Creek
Jackson
Kalamazoo
Monroe
Toledo
Lorain
Cleveland
Youngstown
Erie
Warren
Oil City
Williamsport
Allentown
Newark
Trenton
Reading
IOWA
Dubuque
Cedar Rapids
Rockford
Aurora
Michigan City
South Bend
Akron
Canton
PENNSYLVANIA
Harrisburg
Philadelphia
Wilmington
Atlantic City
Ames
Iowa City
Clinton
Davenport
Moline
Rock Island
Gary
Mansfield
Pittsburgh
Altoona
Johnstown
Des Moines
Council Bluffs
Red Oak
Kankakee
Fort Wayne
Lima
OHIO
Steubenville
Wheeling
Cumberland
Baltimore
C. May
Delaware Bay
Ottumwa
Galesburg
Peoria
Bloomington
Muncie
Piqua
Columbus
Washington D.C.
DEL.
Salisbury
Creston
Burlington
Keokuk
INDIANA
Indianapolis
Fairmont
WEST VIRGINIA
Nebraska City
Champaign
Dayton
ILLINOIS
Decatur
Quincy
Chillicothe
Fredericksburg
Chesapeake Bay
ATLANTIC OCEAN
Kirksville
Hannibal
Springfield
Terre Haute
Hamilton
Cincinnati
Portsmouth
Charleston
Staunton
Charlottesville
St. Joseph
Topeka
Leavenworth
Kansas City
Columbia
Bloomington
Vincennes
Maysville
Ashland
Huntington
Richmond
Lynchburg
Newport News
Norfolk
Lawrence
Ottawa
Sedalia
Jefferson City
St. Louis
Centralia
Wabash
Louisville
Frankfort
Lexington
Beckley
Roanoke
VIRGINIA
Elizabeth City
Albemarle Sound
Emporia
Osage
Rolla
Evansville
Owensboro
KENTUCKY
L. Cumberland
Bluefield
Danville
Buggs Island L.
Roanoke
Fort Scott
MISSOURI
Cape Girardeau
Cairo
Bowling Green
Middlesboro
Bristol
Winston-Salem
Durham
Raleigh
Washington
C. Hatteras
Parsons
Springfield
Paducah
Clarksville
Johnson City
Mt. Mitchell 2037
Greensboro
New Bern
Neuse
Joplin
L. O' The Cherokees
Poplar Bluff
Nashville
Lebanon
Norris L.
Oak Ridge
Knoxville
NORTH CAROLINA
Fayetteville
C. Lookout
Tulsa
Fayetteville
Ozark Plateau
Kentucky L.
TENNESSEE
Asheville
Charlotte
Wilmington
Dyersburg
Columbia
Cleveland
Spartanburg
Muskogee
Fort Smith
Newport
Jonesboro
Jackson
Chattanooga
Greenville
Florence
C. Fear
Eufaula Resr.
ARKANSAS
Memphis
Pickwick L.
Tennessee
Guntersville L.
Anderson
Columbia
Athens
SOUTH CAROLINA
Georgetown
C. Romain
Ouachita Mts.
Hot Springs
Little Rock
Corinth
Huntsville
Rome
Gadsden
Orangeburg
L. Texoma
Durant
Clarksdale
Tupelo
Atlanta
Augusta
Charleston
Paris
Hope
Pine Bluff
Cleveland
Greenwood
Greenville
Columbus
Anniston
Birmingham
Bessemer
Griffin
Macon
Ogeechee
Texarkana
El Dorado
Tuscaloosa
ALABAMA
La Grange
Columbus
GEORGIA
Dublin
Savannah
Greenville
Dallas
Marshall
Shreveport
Monroe
MISSISSIPPI
Meridian
Montgomery
Phenix City
Altamaha
Tyler
Longview
Vicksburg
Jackson
Brookhaven
Laurel
Hattiesburg
Greenville
Albany
Waycross
Brunswick
Sabine
Natchez
Andalusia
Dothan
Thomasville
Okefenokee Swamp
Madison
Jacksonville
Lufkin
Alexandria
Mobile
Tallahassee
Lake City
St. Augustine
LOUISIANA
Bogalusa
L. Pontchartrain
Gulfport
Biloxi
Pensacola
Panama City
Gainesville
Ocala
Daytona Beach
Huntsville
Lake Charles
Baton Rouge
Lafayette
New Orleans
Chandeleur Is.
Mobile Bay
C. San Blas
Apalachee Bay
Sanford
Beaumont
Orange
Houston
Pasadena
Port Arthur
Galveston Bay
Galveston
Morgan City
Houma
Atchafalaya Bay
Mississippi Delta
Orlando
Cape Canaveral
Tampa
Lakeland
Clearwater
St. Petersburg
Tampa B.
Bradenton
Sarasota
Fort Pierce
L. Okeechobee
Freeport
Matagorda Bay
Gulf of Mexico
West Palm Beach
Freeport
Grand Bahama I.
Great Abaco I.
BAHAMAS
Eleuthera I.
Fort Myers
The Everglades
Fort Lauderdale
Miami
Andros I.
Nassau
New Providence
Cat I.
San Salvador
C. Romano
3253
866
139
Scale 1:12 000 000
0 200 400 Miles
0 200 400 600 Kms.
Bonne Projection
Relief
Feet
Metres
16404 5000
9843 3000
6562 2000
3281 1000
1640 500
656 200
0 Sea Level
Land Dep.
656 200
13123 4000
22966 7000
95°
90°
85°
80°
75°
70°
65°
50°
45°
40°
35°
30°
25°

WESTERN UNITED STATES

CANADA
SASKATCHEWAN
ALBERTA
BRITISH COLUMBIA
NORTH DAKOTA
SOUTH DAKOTA
NEBRASKA
MONTANA
WYOMING
COLORADO
UTAH
IDAHO
NEVADA
WASHINGTON
OREGON
ROCKY MOUNTAINS
Bighorn Mountains
Great Salt Lake
Columbia Plateau
Coast Ranges
Seattle
Portland
Vancouver
Billings
Boise
Salt Lake City
Denver
Sacramento
San Francisco
Reno
Spokane
Great Falls
Missoula
Fort Collins
Greeley
Pueblo
Colorado Springs

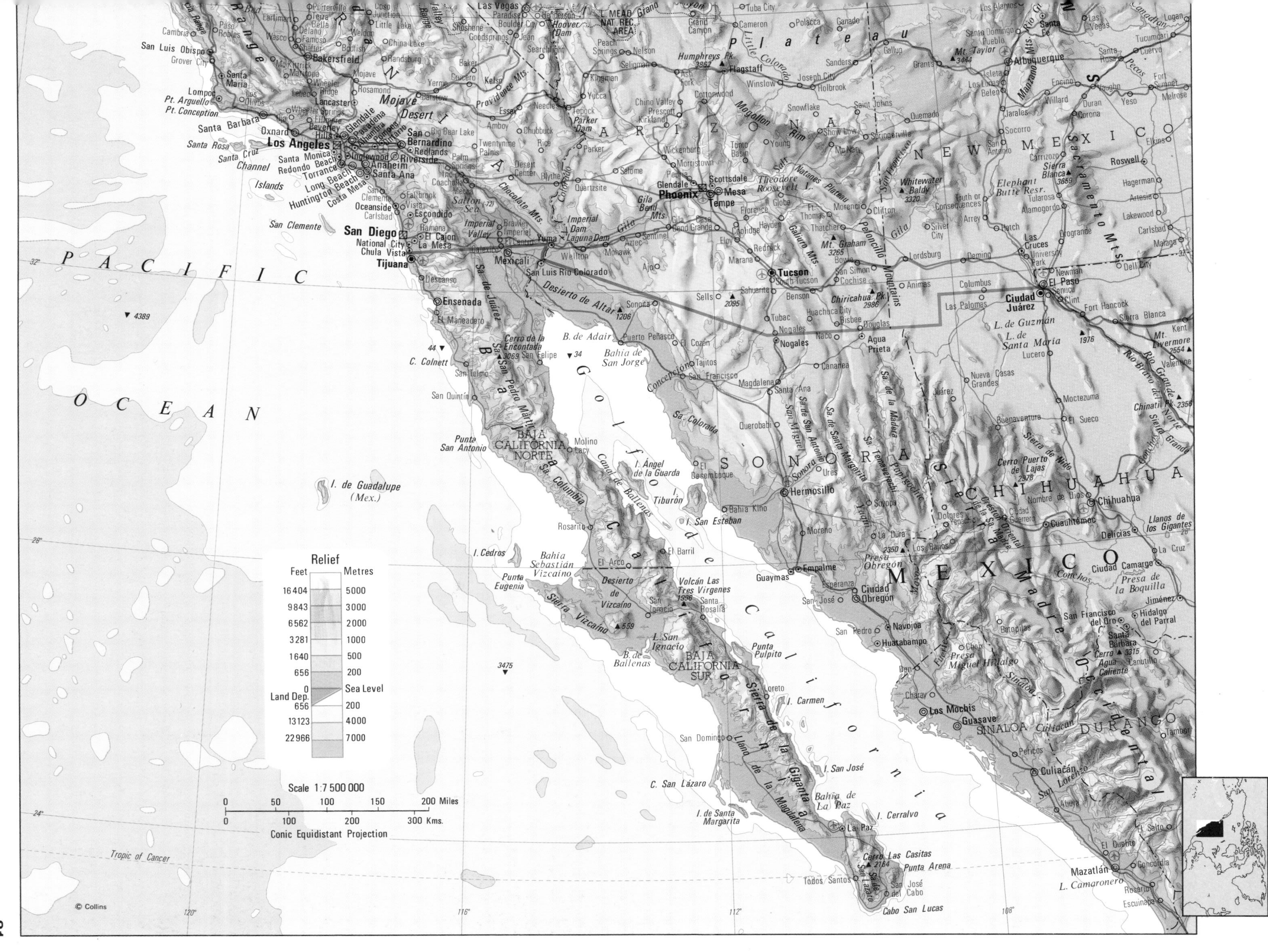
PACIFIC OCEAN
Golfo de California
NEW MEXICO
ARIZONA
SONORA
CHIHUAHUA
MEXICO
SINALOA
DURANGO
BAJA CALIFORNIA NORTE
BAJA CALIFORNIA SUR
Sierra Madre Occidental
Mojave Desert
Desierto de Altar
Sierra de la Giganta
Llano de la Magdalena
Los Angeles
San Diego
Tijuana
Mexicali
Ensenada
Phoenix
Tucson
Nogales
Hermosillo
Guaymas
Ciudad Obregón
Los Mochis
Culiacán
Mazatlán
Chihuahua
Ciudad Juárez
El Paso
Albuquerque
Las Cruces
La Paz
Cabo San Lucas
Santa Rosalía
Loreto
I. de Guadalupe (Mex.)
I. Cedros
I. Tiburón
I. Ángel de la Guarda
Tropic of Cancer
Relief
Feet
Metres
16404 5000
9843 3000
6562 2000
3281 1000
1640 500
656 200
0 Sea Level
Land Dep. 656 200
13123 4000
22966 7000
Scale 1:7 500 000
0 50 100 150 200 Miles
0 100 200 300 Kms.
Conic Equidistant Projection
© Collins

CENTRAL UNITED STATES

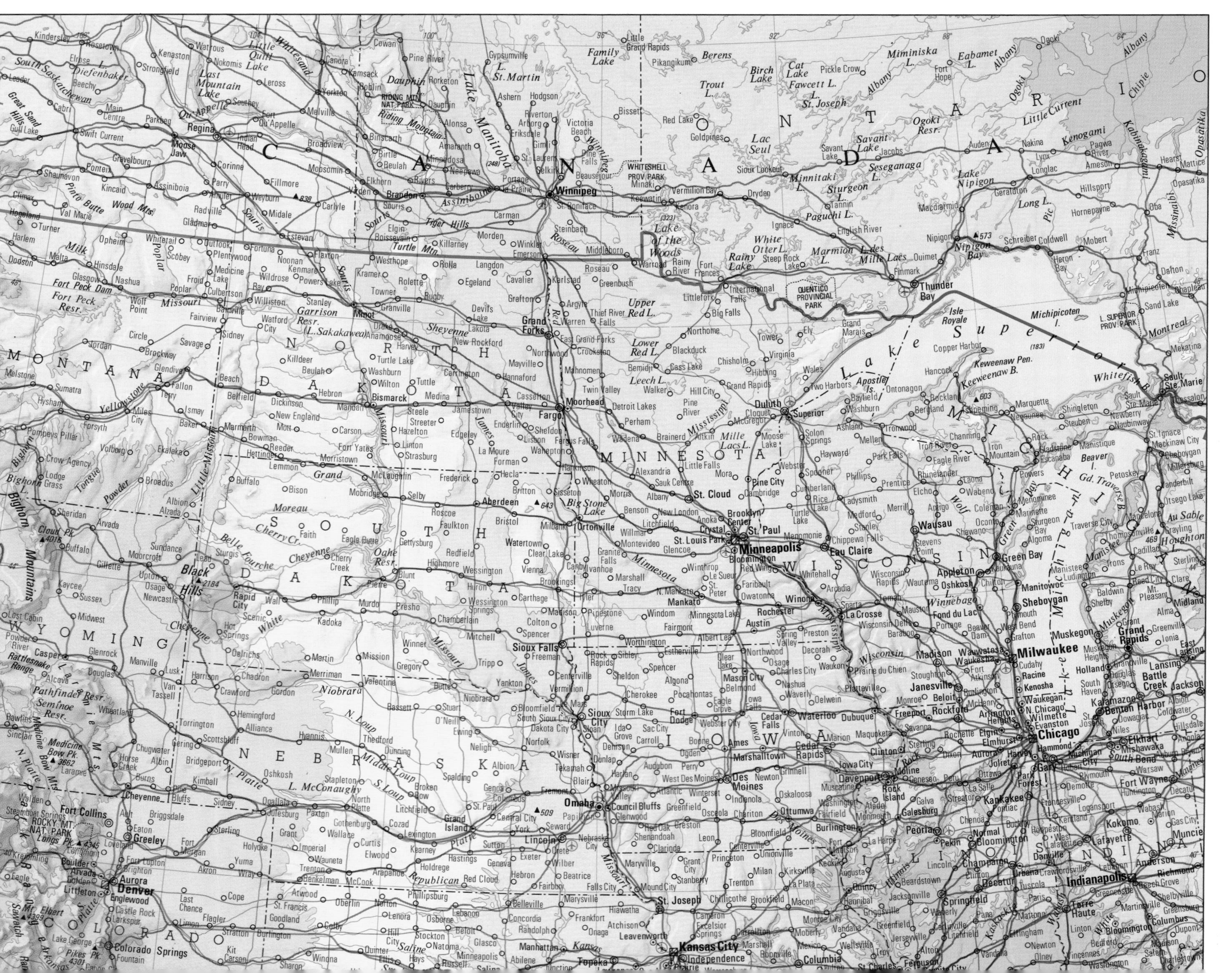

CANADA
ONTARIO
MONTANA
NORTH DAKOTA
SOUTH DAKOTA
WYOMING
NEBRASKA
COLORADO
MINNESOTA
WISCONSIN
MICHIGAN
IOWA
ILLINOIS
INDIANA
Lake Superior
Lake Michigan
Lake Manitoba
Lake of the Woods
Lake Nipigon
Bighorn Mountains
Black Hills
Regina
Winnipeg
Thunder Bay
Duluth
Superior
Fargo
Moorhead
Bismarck
Minot
Grand Forks
Aberdeen
St. Cloud
Minneapolis
St. Paul
Eau Claire
Wausau
Green Bay
Milwaukee
Madison
Chicago
Grand Rapids
Sioux Falls
Sioux City
Des Moines
Cedar Rapids
Omaha
Lincoln
Kansas City
St. Joseph
Topeka
Denver
Aurora
Colorado Springs
Fort Collins
Greeley
Indianapolis
Springfield
Peoria

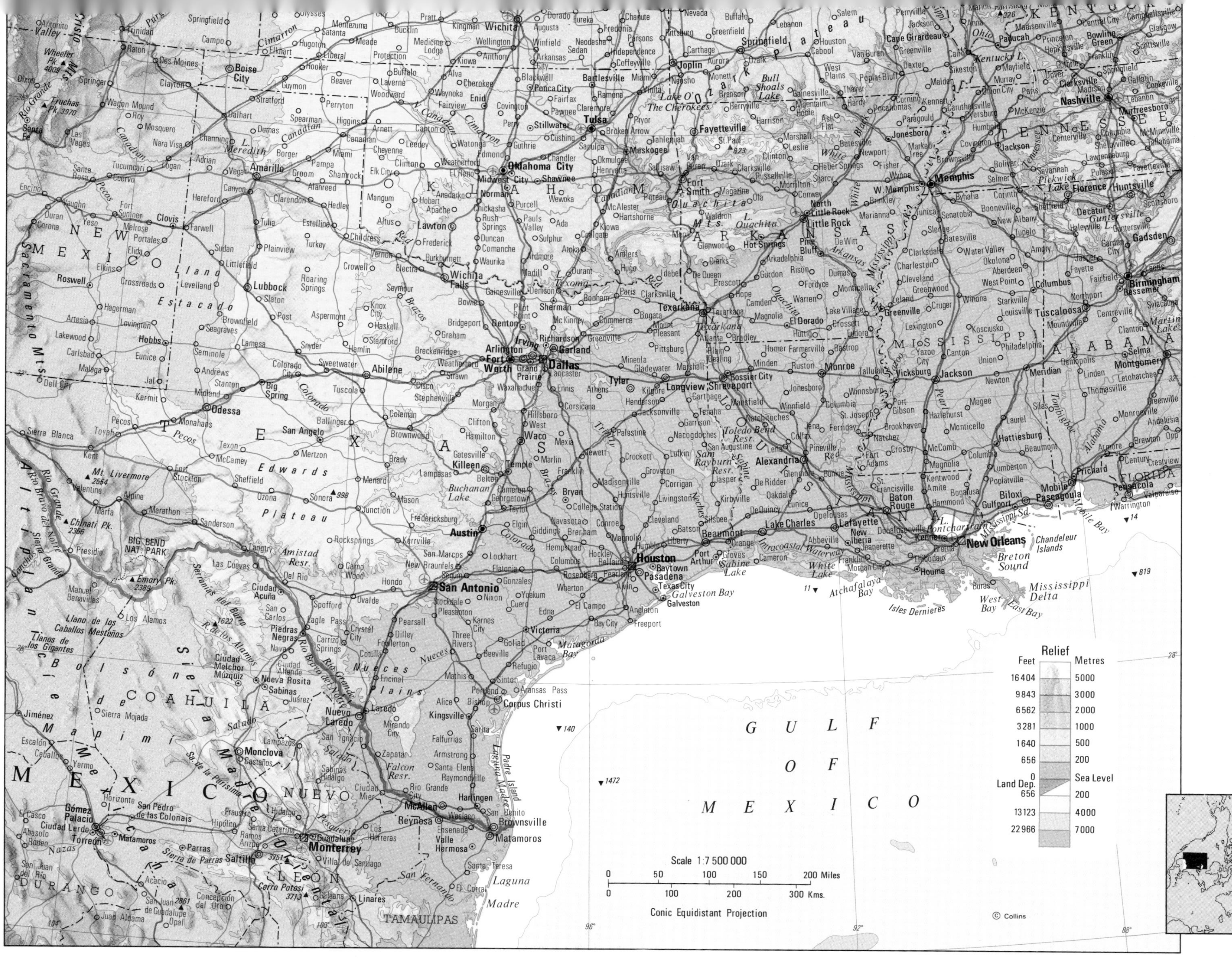
Relief
Feet
Metres
16404
5000
9843
3000
6562
2000
3281
1000
1640
500
656
200
0
Sea Level
Land Dep.
656
200
13123
4000
22966
7000
Scale 1:7 500 000
0
50
100
150
200 Miles
0
100
200
300 Kms.
Conic Equidistant Projection
© Collins
GULF OF MEXICO
TEXAS
OKLAHOMA
ARKANSAS
LOUISIANA
MISSISSIPPI
ALABAMA
TENNESSEE
NEW MEXICO
MEXICO
COAHUILA
NUEVO LEÓN
TAMAULIPAS
DURANGO
Houston
Dallas
San Antonio
Austin
New Orleans
Memphis
Oklahoma City
Monterrey

EASTERN UNITED STATES

C A N A D A
Q U É B E C
O N T A R I O
MAINE
NEW BRUNSWICK
NEW YORK
PENNSYLVANIA
MICHIGAN
WISCONSIN
ILLINOIS
INDIANA
OHIO
MASSACHUSETTS
CONNECTICUT
Lake Superior
Lake Huron
Lake Erie
Lake Ontario
Lake Michigan
Georgian Bay
St. Lawrence
Bay of Fundy
Long Island
Montreal
Québec
Ottawa
Toronto
Boston
New York
Philadelphia
Baltimore
Washington D.C.
Pittsburgh
Cleveland
Detroit
Chicago
Milwaukee
Buffalo
Rochester
Syracuse
Albany
Portland
Providence
Hartford
Indianapolis
Columbus
Cincinnati
Dayton
Toledo
Flint
Thunder Bay
Sudbury
Hamilton
London

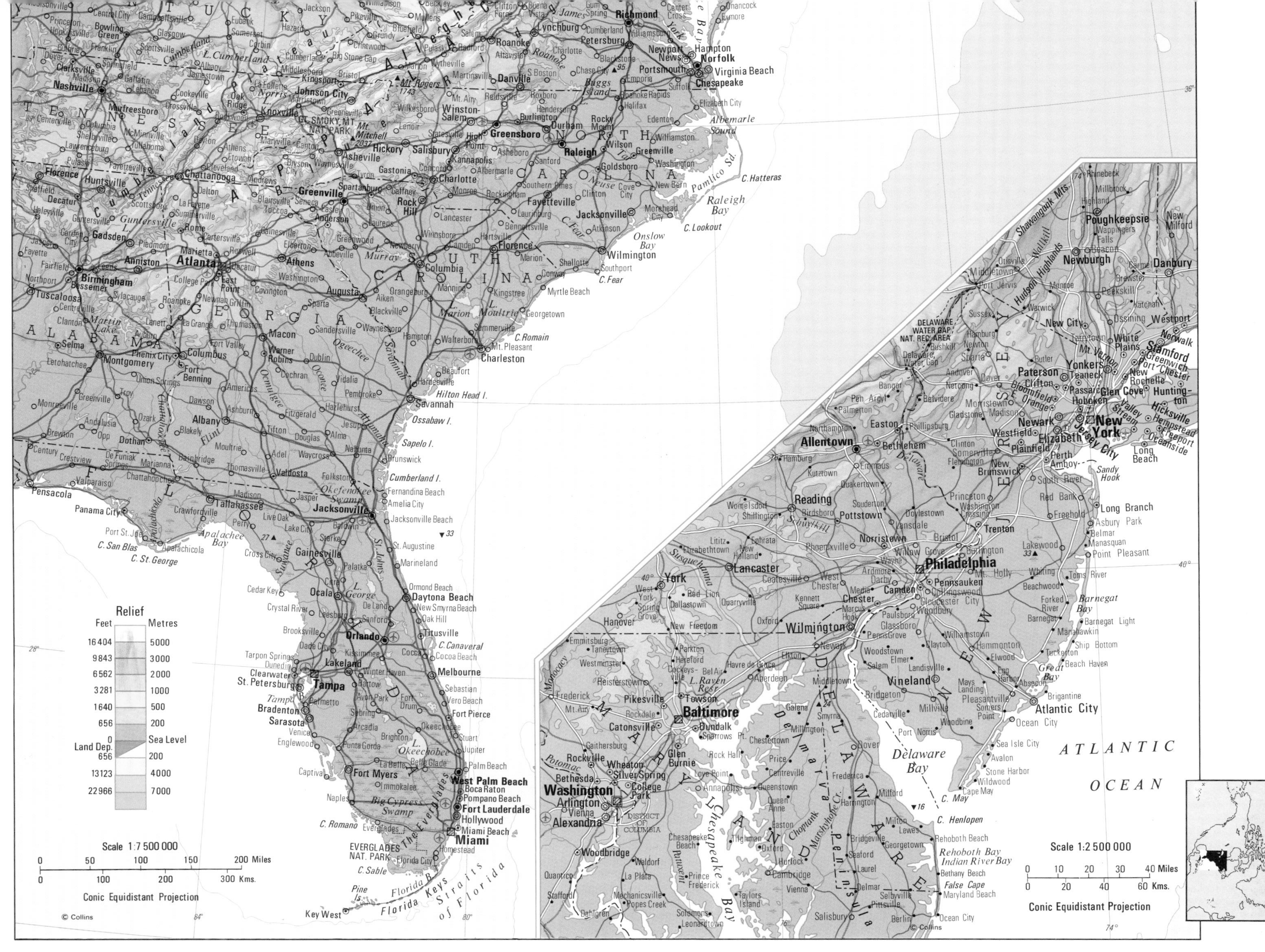

ATLANTIC OCEAN
Relief
Feet Metres
16404 5000
9843 3000
6562 2000
3281 1000
1640 500
656 200
0 Sea Level
Land Dep.
656 200
13123 4000
22966 7000
Scale 1:7 500 000
0 50 100 150 200 Miles
0 100 200 300 Kms.
Conic Equidistant Projection
© Collins
Scale 1:2 500 000
0 10 20 30 40 Miles
0 20 40 60 Kms.
Conic Equidistant Projection
NORTH CAROLINA
SOUTH CAROLINA
GEORGIA
ALABAMA
TENNESSEE
FLORIDA
MARYLAND
DELAWARE
NEW JERSEY
Delmarva Peninsula
Chesapeake Bay
Delaware Bay
New York
Philadelphia
Baltimore
Washington
Wilmington
Trenton
Newark
Jersey City
Atlantic City
Allentown
Reading
Lancaster
York
Richmond
Norfolk
Virginia Beach
Raleigh
Charlotte
Columbia
Charleston
Savannah
Atlanta
Jacksonville
Orlando
Tampa
Miami
Birmingham
Nashville
Montgomery
Tallahassee
Pensacola
Key West
C. Hatteras
C. Lookout
C. Fear
C. Canaveral
C. Sable
C. May
C. Henlopen
Straits of Florida
Florida Keys

CENTRAL AMERICA AND THE CARIBBEAN

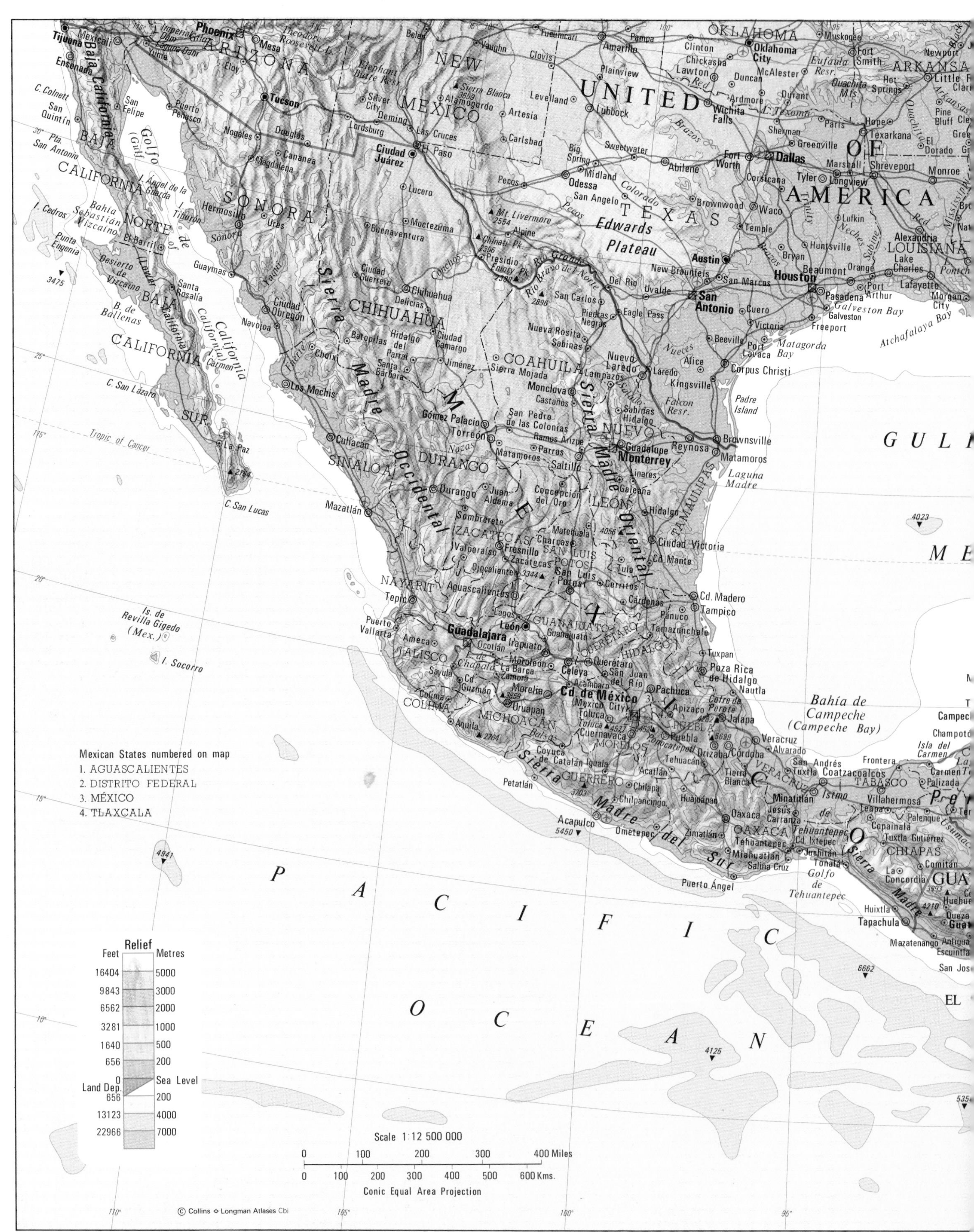

UNITED STATES OF AMERICA
OKLAHOMA
ARKANSAS
LOUISIANA
TEXAS
NEW MEXICO
ARIZONA
Edwards Plateau
MEXICO
BAJA CALIFORNIA NORTE
BAJA CALIFORNIA SUR
SONORA
CHIHUAHUA
COAHUILA
NUEVO LEÓN
TAMAULIPAS
SINALOA
DURANGO
ZACATECAS
SAN LUIS POTOSÍ
NAYARIT
JALISCO
GUANAJUATO
QUERÉTARO
HIDALGO
COLIMA
MICHOACÁN
MORELOS
PUEBLA
GUERRERO
OAXACA
VERACRUZ
TABASCO
CHIAPAS
Sierra Madre Occidental
Sierra Madre Oriental
Sierra Madre del Sur
Golfo de California (Gulf of California)
Bahía de Campeche (Campeche Bay)
Golfo de Tehuantepec
Istmo de Tehuantepec
Is. de Revilla Gigedo (Mex.)
I. Socorro
Tropic of Cancer
PACIFIC OCEAN
GULF OF MEXICO
Phoenix
Tucson
Ciudad Juárez
El Paso
Chihuahua
Hermosillo
Dallas
Fort Worth
Houston
San Antonio
Austin
Oklahoma City
Monterrey
Guadalajara
Cd. de México (Mexico City)
Puebla
Veracruz
Acapulco
Mexican States numbered on map
1. AGUASCALIENTES
2. DISTRITO FEDERAL
3. MÉXICO
4. TLAXCALA
Relief
Feet | Metres
16404 | 5000
9843 | 3000
6562 | 2000
3281 | 1000
1640 | 500
656 | 200
0 | Sea Level
Land Dep.
656 | 200
13123 | 4000
22966 | 7000
Scale 1:12 500 000
0 100 200 300 400 Miles
0 100 200 300 400 500 600 Kms.
Conic Equal Area Projection
© Collins ◇ Longman Atlases Cbi

ATLANTIC OCEAN
CARIBBEAN SEA
CUBA
JAMAICA
HAITI
DOMINICAN REP.
PUERTO RICO (U.S.A.)
BAHAMAS
Greater Antilles
Lesser Antilles
HONDURAS
NICARAGUA
COSTA RICA
PANAMA
COLOMBIA
VENEZUELA
BELIZE
Gulf of Honduras
Straits of Florida
Yucatan Channel
Windward Passage
Netherlands Antilles
Tropic of Cancer
Same Scale

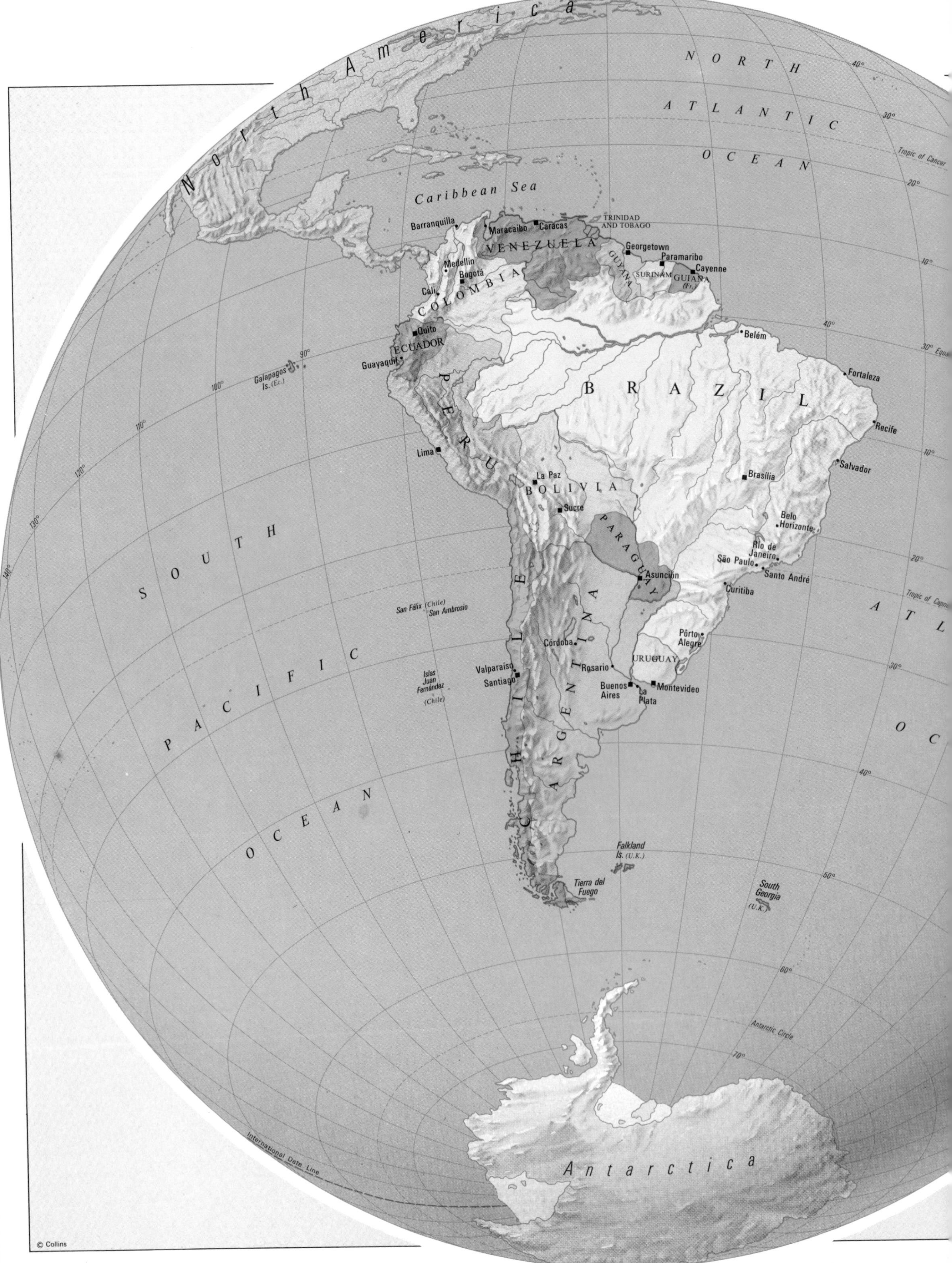
North America
NORTH ATLANTIC OCEAN
Caribbean Sea
Barranquilla
Maracaibo
Caracas
TRINIDAD AND TOBAGO
VENEZUELA
Georgetown
GUYANA
Paramaribo
SURINAM
Cayenne
GUIANA (Fr.)
Medellín
Bogotá
Cali
COLOMBIA
Quito
ECUADOR
Guayaquil
Galapagos Is. (Ec.)
Belém
Fortaleza
BRAZIL
Recife
PERU
Lima
Salvador
La Paz
Brasília
BOLIVIA
Sucre
PARAGUAY
Belo Horizonte
Rio de Janeiro
São Paulo
Santo André
Asunción
Curitiba
SOUTH PACIFIC OCEAN
San Félix (Chile)
San Ambrosio
Tropic of Cancer
Tropic of Capricorn
Equator
ATLANTIC OCEAN
Pôrto Alegre
Córdoba
URUGUAY
Rosario
Valparaíso
Santiago
Islas Juan Fernández (Chile)
Buenos Aires
La Plata
Montevideo
CHILE
ARGENTINA
Falkland Is. (U.K.)
Tierra del Fuego
South Georgia (U.K.)
Antarctic Circle
International Date Line
Antarctica

SOUTH AMERICA

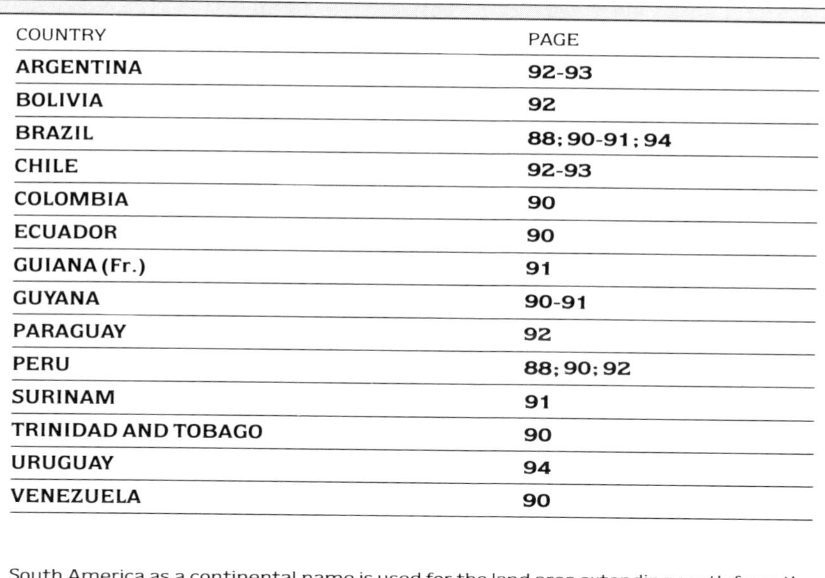

COUNTRY	PAGE
ARGENTINA	**92-93**
BOLIVIA	**92**
BRAZIL	**88; 90-91; 94**
CHILE	**92-93**
COLOMBIA	**90**
ECUADOR	**90**
GUIANA (Fr.)	**91**
GUYANA	**90-91**
PARAGUAY	**92**
PERU	**88; 90; 92**
SURINAM	**91**
TRINIDAD AND TOBAGO	**90**
URUGUAY	**94**
VENEZUELA	**90**

South America as a continental name is used for the land area extending south from the Isthmus of Panama to Cape Horn and lying between 34°W and 82°W. Latin America is a term widely used to cover those parts of the Americas where Spanish, or Portuguese as in Brazil, are the adopted national languages, and thus refers to an area that includes all of South America, Central America, Mexico and the Caribbean, except for the few English, French and Dutch speaking countries and dependencies.

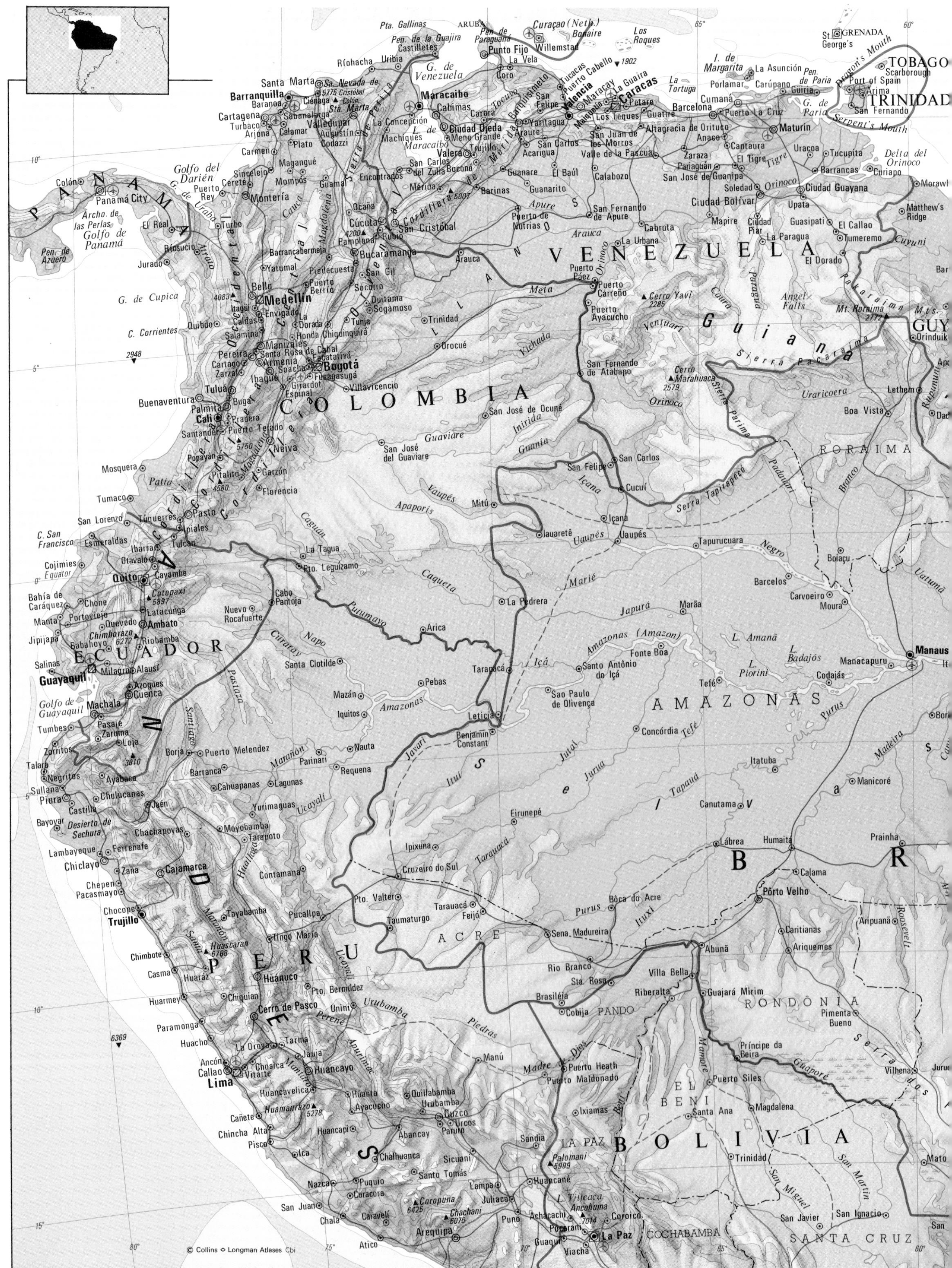

Pta. Gallinas
ARUBA
Curaçao (Neth.)
Bonaire
Los Roques
Pen. de la Guajira
Castilletes
Pen. de Paraguaná
Punto Fijo
Willemstad
La Vela
Coro
Ríohacha
Uribia
G. de Venezuela
Santa Marta
Barranquilla
Baranoa
Ciénaga
Cartagena
Turbaco
Arjona
Sabanalarga
Valledupar
Calamar
Maracaibo
Cabimas
Ciudad Ojeda
Mene Grande
L. de Maracaibo
Machiques
La Concepción
Carora
Tocuyo
Tucacas
Puerto Cabello
Valencia
Maracay
La Guaira
Caracas
Petare
Los Teques
San Felipe
Yaritagua
Araure
Acarigua
Barquisimeto
San Carlos
Valera
Trujillo
Boconó
Guanare
El Baúl
Valle de la Pascua
Calabozo
Barinas
Mérida
Guanarito
Apure
San Fernando de Apure
Puerto de Nutrias
Cabruta
Arauca
La Urbana
I. de Margarita
La Asunción
La Tortuga
Porlamar
Carúpano
Cumaná
Barcelona
Puerto La Cruz
Güiria
Pen. de Paria
G. de Paria
Dragon's Mouth
Serpent's Mouth
TOBAGO
Scarborough
Port of Spain
Arima
San Fernando
TRINIDAD
St. George's
GRENADA
Altagracia de Orituco
Anaco
Maturín
Zaraza
Pariaguán
El Tigre
Cantaura
San José de Guanipa
Tigre
Uracoa
Tucupita
Delta del Orinoco
Barrancas
Curiapo
Soledad
Orinoco
Ciudad Guayana
Ciudad Bolívar
Upata
Mapire
Ciudad Piar
Guasipati
El Callao
Tumeremo
La Paragua
El Dorado
Cuyuni
Matthew's Ridge
Morawhanna
Golfo del Darién
G. de Urabá
Colón
PANAMÁ
Panamá City
Archo. de las Perlas
Golfo de Panamá
Pen. de Azuero
El Real
Turbo
Riosucio
Jurado
Carmen
Sincelejo
Magangué
Mompós
Cereté
Montería
Puerto Rey
Plato
Codazzi
Guamal
Encontrados
Ocaña
Cúcuta
Rubio
San Cristóbal
Pamplona
Barrancabermeja
Bucaramanga
Yarumal
Piedecuesta
San Gil
Socorro
Puerto Berrío
Bello
Medellín
Itagüí
Envigado
Duitama
Sogamoso
Tunja
La Dorada
Honda
Chiquinquirá
Caldas
Salamina
Manizales
Santa Rosa de Cabal
Facatativá
Pereira
Cartago
Armenia
Soacha
Bogotá
Zarzal
Ibagué
Fusagasugá
Girardot
Espinal
Villavicencio
G. de Cupica
C. Corrientes
Quibdó
Tuluá
Buenaventura
Palmira
Buga
Cali
Pradera
Santander
Puerto Tejada
Popayán
Neiva
Pitalito
Garzón
Florencia
Mosquera
Patía
Tumaco
San Lorenzo
Túquerres
Pasto
Ipiales
Tulcán
C. San Francisco
Esmeraldas
Ibarra
Otavalo
Cojimíes
Equator
Quito
Cayambe
Cotopaxi
Latacunga
Bahía de Caráquez
Chone
Portoviejo
Quevedo
Manta
Ambato
Jipijapa
Babahoyo
Chimborazo
Riobamba
ECUADOR
Salinas
Guayaquil
Milagro
Alausí
Azogues
Cuenca
Golfo de Guayaquil
Machala
Pasaje
Zaruma
Tumbes
Loja
Zorritos
Talara
Negritos
Ayabaca
Sullana
Piura
Chulucanas
Castilla
Jaén
Bayóvar
Desierto de Sechura
Chachapoyas
Moyobamba
Tarapoto
Lambayeque
Ferreñafe
Chiclayo
Zaña
Cajamarca
Chepen
Pacasmayo
Chocope
Trujillo
Tayabamba
Contamana
Chimbote
Huascarán
Casma
Huaraz
Huánuco
Tingo María
Pucallpa
Huarmey
Chiquián
Cerro de Pasco
Pto. Bermúdez
Paramonga
Huacho
Ancón
Callao
Lima
La Oroya
Tarma
Jauja
Huancayo
Chosica
Vitarte
Huancavelica
Huamanrazo
Huanta
Ayacucho
Cañete
Chincha Alta
Pisco
Ica
Huancapi
Abancay
Cuzco
Urubamba
Quillabamba
Chalhuanca
Sicuani
Santo Tomás
Nazca
Puquio
Coracora
Coropuna
Chachani
San Juan
Chala
Caravelí
Arequipa
Atico
Juliaca
Puno
Lampa
Huancané
L. Titicaca
Achacachi
Ancohuma
Coroico
Pucarani
La Paz
Guaqui
Viacha
COCHABAMBA
SANTA CRUZ
Palomani
LA PAZ
Sandia
BOLIVIA
EL BENI
Santa Ana
Trinidad
Magdalena
Puerto Siles
San Javier
San Ignacio
San Martín
San Miguel
PANDO
Cobija
Brasiléia
Rio Branco
Sta. Rosa
Villa Bella
Riberalta
Guajará Mirim
RONDÔNIA
Pimenta Bueno
Príncipe da Beira
Vilhena
Guaporé
Abunã
Pôrto Velho
Calama
Ariquemes
Caritianas
Aripuanã
Humaitá
Lábrea
Prainha
Manicoré
Canutama
ACRE
Sena Madureira
Tarauacá
Feijó
Taumaturgo
Pto. Valter
Cruzeiro do Sul
Ipixuna
Eirunepé
Bôca do Acre
Purus
Ituxi
Madre de Dios
Puerto Heath
Puerto Maldonado
Manú
Piedras
Urubamba
Unini
Perené
Apurímac
Mantaro
Ucayali
Huallaga
Marañón
Santiago
Pastaza
Curaray
Napo
Putumayo
Caquetá
Caguán
Apaporis
Vaupés
Guaviare
Vichada
Meta
Inírida
Guainía
Iça
Içana
Uaupés
Marié
Japurá
Amazonas (Amazon)
Juruá
Jutaí
Itui
Javari
Tefé
Tapauá
Madeira
Negro
Branco
Uatumã
Cabo Pantoja
Nuevo Rocafuerte
Arica
Santa Clotilde
Pebas
Mazán
Iquitos
Leticia
Tarapacá
Benjamin Constant
Nauta
Requena
Parinari
Borja
Puerto Melendez
Barranca
Cahuapanas
Lagunas
Yurimaguas
La Tagua
Pto. Leguízamo
La Pedrera
Mitú
Iauaretê
Içana
Uaupés
Tapurucuara
Barcelos
Carvoeiro
Moura
Maraã
Fonte Boa
Santo Antônio do Içá
Sao Paulo de Olivença
Tefé
Codajás
Manacapuru
Manaus
L. Amanã
L. Badajós
L. Piorini
AMAZONAS
Concórdia
Itatuba
COLOMBIA
VENEZUELA
PERU
Trinidad
Orocué
San José de Ocuné
San José del Guaviare
Puerto Páez
Puerto Carreño
Puerto Ayacucho
San Fernando de Atabapo
Cerro Yaví
Cerro Marahuaca
Ventuari
Caura
Paragua
Angel Falls
Mt. Roraima
Guiana
Sierra Pacaraima
Sierra Parima
Uraricoera
Orinoco
San Carlos
San Felipe
Cucuí
Serra Tapirapecó
Padauari
RORAIMA
Boa Vista
Lethem
Rupununi
Orinduik
Pakaraima Mts.
Cordillera de Mérida
Sierra de Perijá
Cordillera Occidental
Cordillera Central
Cordillera Oriental
Cauca
Magdalena
Apure
Arauca
Llanos
Serra dos Parecis

Relief
Feet
Metres
16404
5000
9843
3000
6562
2000
3281
1000
1640
500
656
200
0
Sea Level
Land Dep.
656
200
13123
4000
Scale 1:12 500 000
0
100
200
300
400
500 Miles
0
100
200
300
400
500
600
700
800 Kms.
Lambert Azimuthal Equal Area Projection
Paramaribo
Nieuw Nickerie
Albina
St. Laurent du Maroni
Afobaka
W. J. Van Blommestein Meer
Cayenne
Kaw
C. Orange
SURINAM
GUIANA
(Fr.)
St. Georges
Camopi
Oyapock
Tumuc Humac Mts.
Amapá
AMAPÁ
C. Norte
Serra do Navio
Araguari
Merirumã
Pto. Grande
Macapá
Estuario do Rio Amazonas (Amazon Delta)
Ilha Caviana
Mazagão
Chaves
I. Grande do Gurupá
I. de Marajó
Salinópolis
Bragança
Capanema
Icoraci
Belém
Viseu
Óbidos
Monte Alegre
Prainha
Gurupá
Pôrto de Moz
Amazonas (Amazon)
Muaná
Abaetetuba
Acará
Turiaçu
Cururupu
Juruti
LITIGATED AREA
Parintins
Santarém
Belterra
Cametá
Baião
Guimarães
São Luís
Altamira
Xingu
Tocantins
Rosário
Tutóia
Parnaíba
Viana
Itapecuru Mirim
Camocim
Granja
PARÁ
Tucuruí
Capim
Gurupi
Represa de Tucuruí
Sobral
Antônio Bezerra
Fortaleza
Parangaba
Caroatá
Codó
Piracuruca
Itaituba
Iriri
Bacabal
Pedreiras
União
Ipu
Baturité
Caxias
Campo Maior
Aracati
Bacabal
Marabá
Imperatriz
Teresina
CEARÁ
Crateús
Areia Branca
Barra do Corda
Colinas
Mossoró
Macau
Tocantinópolis
MARANHÃO
Senador Pompeu
Açu
Natal
Pôrto Franco
Amarante
RIO GRANDE DO NORTE
Represa da Boa Esperança
Floriano
Iguatu
Caicó
Carolina
Loreto
Oeiras
Sousa
Riachão
Uruçui
Pombal
Picos
Cajàzeiras
Patos
Guarabira
João Pessoa
Crato
Juàzeiro do Norte
Campina Grande
PIAUÍ
Serra Talhada
Sapé
Itabaiana
Conceição do Araguaia
São João do Piauí
Paulistana
Salgueiro
PERNAMBUCO
Caruaru
Olinda
Recife
Araguacema
Sta. Filomena
Pedro Afonso
Arcoverde
Belo Jardim
Palmares
Petrolina
Garanhuns
Barreiros
Remanso
Juàzeiro
Paulo Afonso
Palmeira dos Índios
Viçosa
Rio Largo
TOCANTINS
Pto. Nacional
Parnaguá
Represa de Sobradinho
Senhor do Bonfim
ALAGOAS
Maceió
Arapiraca
Sta. Isabel do Morro
Xique Xique
Barra
Queimadas
Itapicuru
Propriá
SERGIPE
Penedo
Jacobina
Aracaju
Planalto
Peixe
BAHIA
Estância
Serrinha
Pedrinhas
Barreiras
Ibotirama
Paraná
Campos Belos
Feira de Santana
Alagoinhas
Cachoeira
Santo Amaro
Brasil
(Brazilian Highlands)
Maragogipe
Nazaré
Salvador
Valença
Carinhanha
Posse
Niquelândia
Brumado
Jequié
Ipiaú
Uruaçu
Aruanã
Vitória da Conquista
Ibicaraí
Ilhéus
Itabuna
GOIÁS
DIST. FED.
Brasília
Formosa
Goiás
Januária
Monte Azul
MINAS GERAIS
Itapetinga
Anápolis
Luziânia
Goiânia
Salto da Divisa
Canavieiras
Pouso Alegre
Serra Formosa
Ronuro
MATO GROSSO
Planalto do Mato Grosso
Diamantino
Culuene
Cuiabá
Aragarças
Rondonópolis
Alto Araguaia
Equator

SOUTH AMERICA – SOUTH

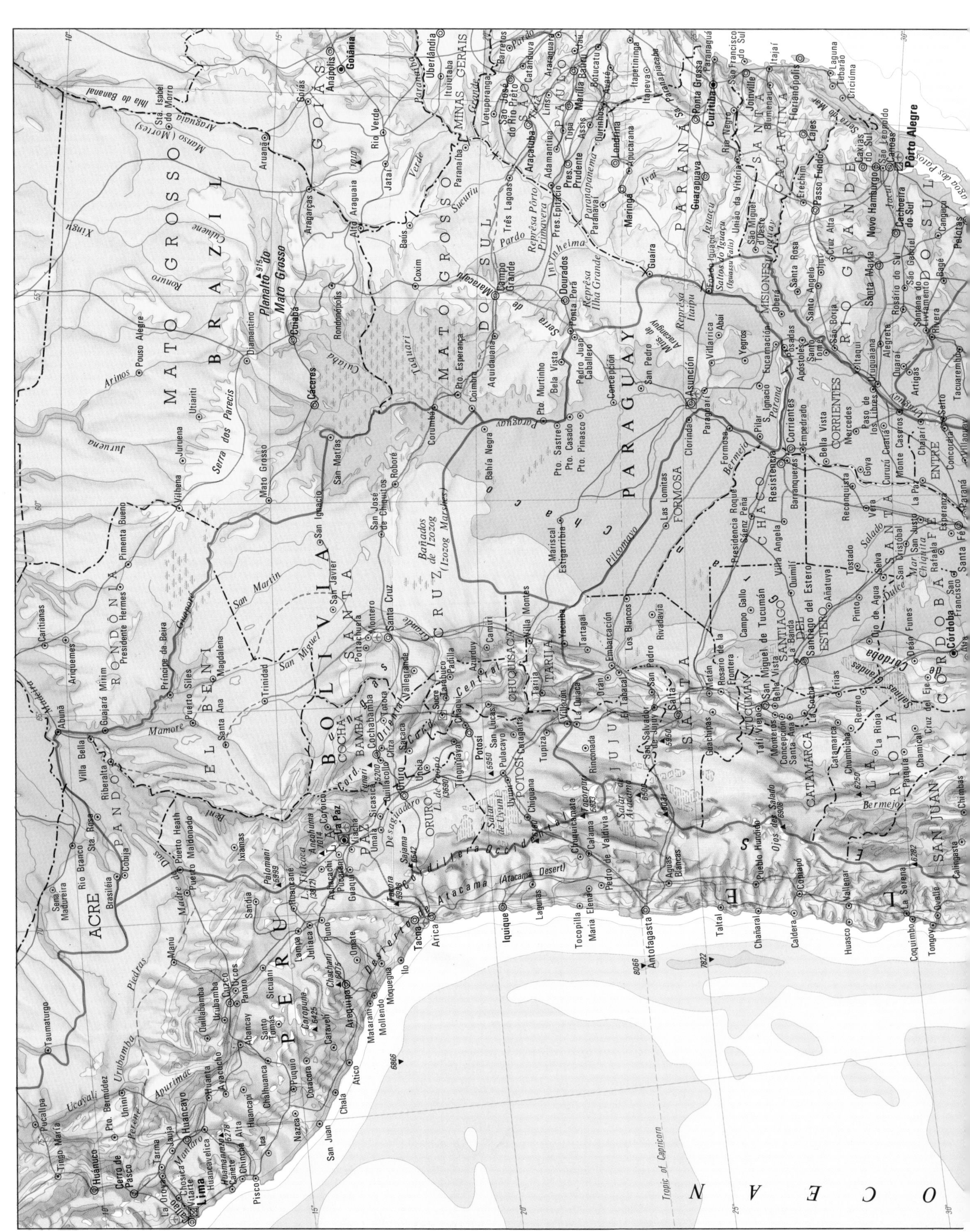

O C E A N
B R A Z I L
MATO GROSSO
GOIÁS
MINAS GERAIS
SÃO PAULO
PARANÁ
SANTA CATARINA
RIO GRANDE DO SUL
MATO GROSSO DO SUL
RONDÔNIA
ACRE
P E R U
B O L I V I A
PARAGUAY
CHACO
FORMOSA
SALTA
JUJUY
TUCUMÁN
CATAMARCA
SANTIAGO DEL ESTERO
SANTA FE
CÓRDOBA
CORRIENTES
ENTRE RIOS
MISIONES
LA RIOJA
SAN JUAN
EL BENI
PANDO
LA PAZ
COCHABAMBA
SANTA CRUZ
ORURO
POTOSÍ
CHUQUISACA
TARIJA
Lima
La Paz
Asunción
Pôrto Alegre
Curitiba
Goiânia
Córdoba
Antofagasta
Iquique
Arica
Cuzco
Arequipa
Tropic of Capricorn

PACIFIC
SOUTH ATLANTIC OCEAN
ARGENTINA
CHILE
URUGUAY
BRAZIL
MENDOZA
LUIS
LA PAMPA
BUENOS AIRES
NEUQUÉN
RÍO NEGRO
CHUBUT
SANTA CRUZ
Patagonia
Santiago
Buenos Aires
Montevideo
La Plata
Río de la Plata (R. Plate)
Bahía Samborombón
Mar del Plata
Bahía Blanca
Valdivia
Golfo San Matías
Golfo Nuevo
Golfo San Jorge
Comodoro Rivadavia
Bahía Grande
Tierra del Fuego
Estrecho de Magallanes
Cabo de Hornos (Cape Horn)
Falkland Is. (U.K.) (Islas Malvinas)
West Falkland
East Falkland
Stanley
Falkland Sound
I. de los Estados (Staten I.)
Relief
Feet
Metres
16404 5000
9843 3000
6562 2000
3281 1000
1640 500
656 200
0 Sea Level
Land Dep. 656 200
13123 4000
22966 7000
Scale 1 : 12 500 000
0 100 200 300 400 Miles
0 200 400 600 Kms.
Lambert Azimuthal Equal Area Projection
© Collins ◇ Longman Atlases Cbi 55°
CORRIENTES
SANTA FÉ
ENTRE RÍOS
RIO GRANDE DO SUL
Rosario
Paraná
Scale 1:7 500 000
0 40 80 Miles
0 40 80 120 Kms.
© Collins

SOUTH AMERICA – EAST

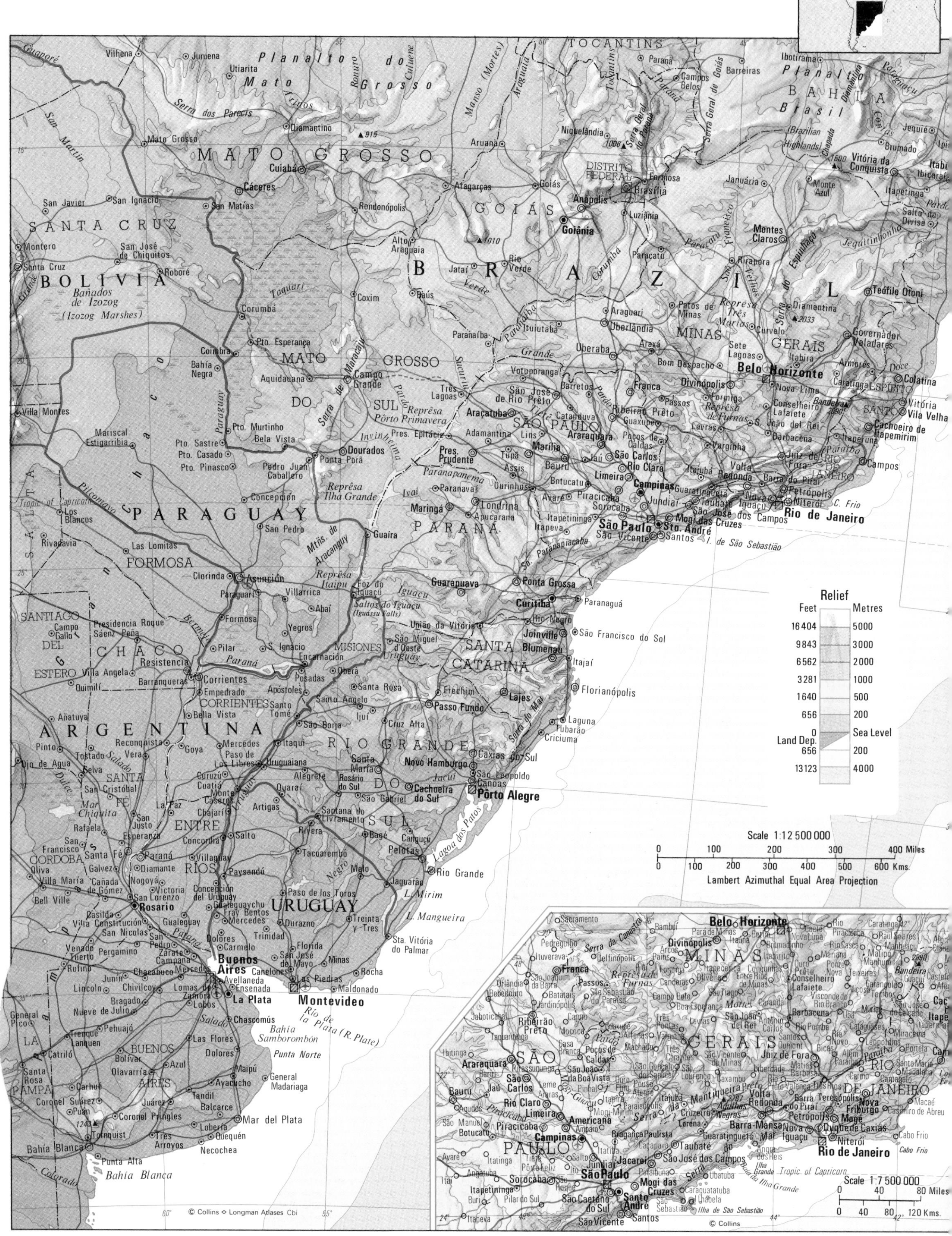

Relief
Feet
Metres
16404
5000
9843
3000
6562
2000
3281
1000
1640
500
656
200
0
Sea Level
Land Dep.
656
200
13123
4000
Scale 1:12 500 000
0
100
200
300
400 Miles
0
100
200
300
400
500
600 Kms.
Lambert Azimuthal Equal Area Projection
Scale 1:7 500 000
0
40
80 Miles
0
40
80
120 Kms.
© Collins ◇ Longman Atlases Cbi
© Collins
B R A Z I L
BOLIVIA
PARAGUAY
ARGENTINA
URUGUAY
MATO GROSSO
MATO GROSSO DO SUL
GOIÁS
DISTRITO FEDERAL
MINAS GERAIS
SÃO PAULO
PARANÁ
SANTA CATARINA
RIO GRANDE DO SUL
RIO DE JANEIRO
ESPÍRITO SANTO
BAHIA
TOCANTINS
SANTA CRUZ
FORMOSA
CHACO
SANTIAGO DEL ESTERO
SANTA FÉ
CORRIENTES
MISIONES
ENTRE RIOS
CORDOBA
BUENOS AIRES
LA PAMPA
SALTA
Planalto do Mato Grosso
Planalto da Bahia Brasil (Brazilian Highlands)
Bañados de Izozog (Izozog Marshes)
Tropic of Capricorn
Brasília
Goiânia
Belo Horizonte
Rio de Janeiro
São Paulo
Curitiba
Pôrto Alegre
Montevideo
Buenos Aires
La Plata
Asunción
Campo Grande
Cuiabá
Florianópolis
Vitória
Campinas
Santos
Rosario
Corrientes
Mar del Plata
Bahía Blanca
Río de la Plata (R. Plate)
Lagoa dos Patos

ATLANTIC OCEAN

BERMUDA (U.K.)
Scale 1:1 000 000
CANARY ISLANDS (Spain)
Scale 1:10 000 000
MADEIRA ISLANDS
Scale 1:4 000 000 (Portugal)
ASCENSION (U.K.)
Scale 1:1 000 000
ST. HELENA (U.K.)
Scale 1:1 000 000
TRISTAN DA CUNHA (U.K.)
Scale 1:1 000 000
NORTH ATLANTIC OCEAN
SOUTH ATLANTIC OCEAN
MID ATLANTIC RIDGE
Sargasso Sea
Caribbean Sea
Scotia Sea
Argentine Basin
Cape Basin
Agulhas Basin
Brazilian Basin
Atlantic-Indian-Antarctic Basin
Atlantic-Antarctic Ridge
Walvis Ridge
Scale 1:60 000 000
0 500 1000 1500 Miles
0 500 1000 1500 2000 2500 Kms.
Zenithal Equal-Area Projection
© Collins

POLAR REGIONS

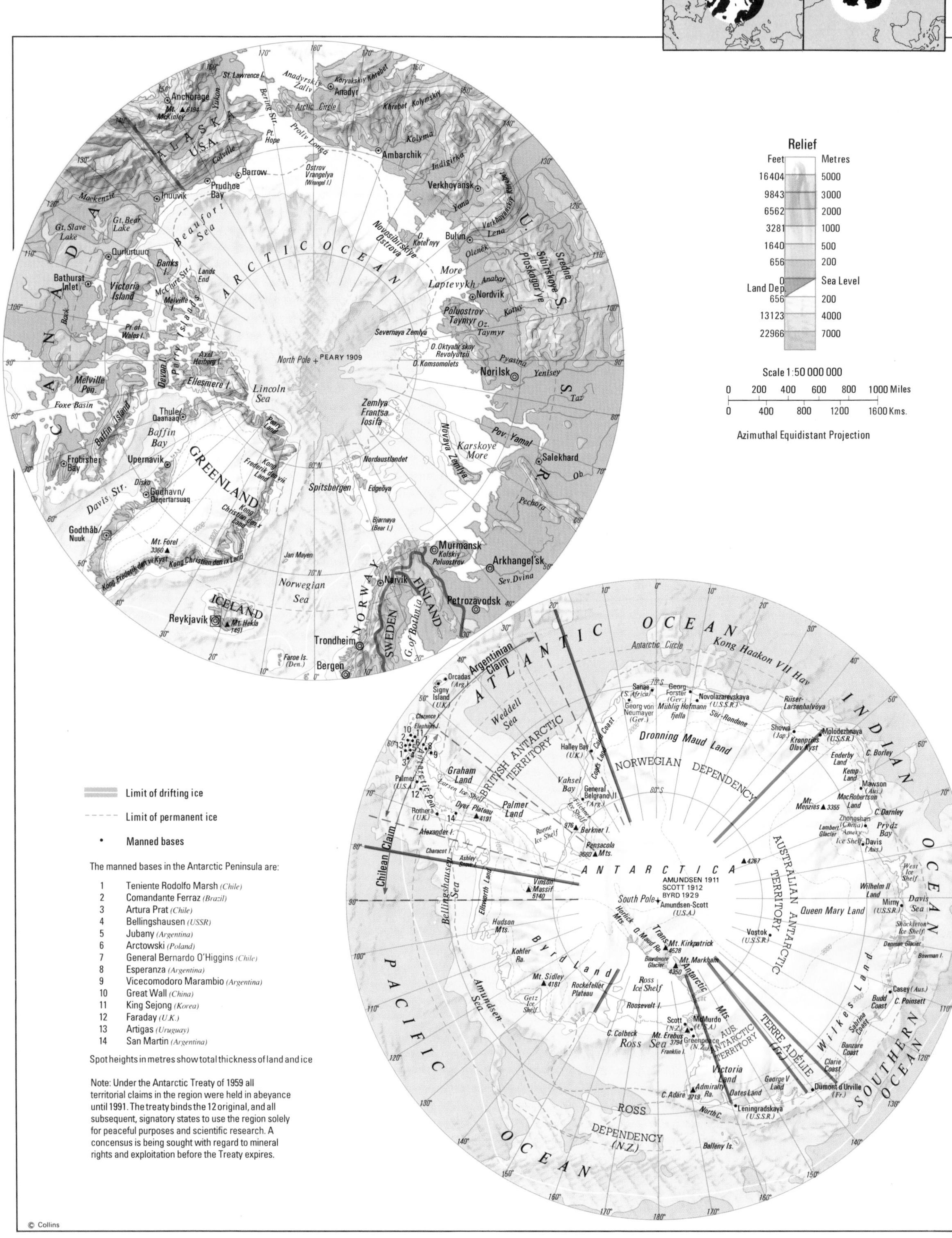

Relief
Feet
Metres
16404
5000
9843
3000
6562
2000
3281
1000
1640
500
656
200
0
Sea Level
Land Dep.
656
200
13123
4000
22966
7000
Scale 1:50 000 000
0 200 400 600 800 1000 Miles
0 400 800 1200 1600 Kms.
Azimuthal Equidistant Projection
Limit of drifting ice
Limit of permanent ice
Manned bases
The manned bases in the Antarctic Peninsula are:
1 Teniente Rodolfo Marsh (Chile)
2 Comandante Ferraz (Brazil)
3 Artura Prat (Chile)
4 Bellingshausen (USSR)
5 Jubany (Argentina)
6 Arctowski (Poland)
7 General Bernardo O'Higgins (Chile)
8 Esperanza (Argentina)
9 Vicecomodoro Marambio (Argentina)
10 Great Wall (China)
11 King Sejong (Korea)
12 Faraday (U.K.)
13 Artigas (Uruguay)
14 San Martin (Argentina)
Spot heights in metres show total thickness of land and ice
Note: Under the Antarctic Treaty of 1959 all territorial claims in the region were held in abeyance until 1991. The treaty binds the 12 original, and all subsequent, signatory states to use the region solely for peaceful purposes and scientific research. A concensus is being sought with regard to mineral rights and exploitation before the Treaty expires.
ARCTIC OCEAN
North Pole
PEARY 1909
GREENLAND
ICELAND
CANADA
ALASKA
U.S.A.
U.S.S.R.
NORWAY
SWEDEN
FINLAND
ATLANTIC OCEAN
INDIAN OCEAN
PACIFIC OCEAN
SOUTHERN OCEAN
ROSS OCEAN
ANTARCTICA
South Pole
AMUNDSEN 1911
SCOTT 1912
BYRD 1929
BRITISH ANTARCTIC TERRITORY
NORWEGIAN DEPENDENCY
AUSTRALIAN ANTARCTIC TERRITORY
TERRE ADÉLIE (Fr.)
ROSS DEPENDENCY (N.Z.)
Argentinian Claim
Chilean Claim

WORLD DATA

Part 1

WORLD FACTS AND FIGURES 98-102

WORLD PHYSICAL DATA 98

WORLD POLITICAL DATA 99

NATIONS OF THE WORLD 100-102

Part 2

WORLD INDEX 103-160

WORLD PHYSICAL DATA

Earth's Dimensions

Superficial area	510 066 000 km^2
Land surface	148 326 000 km^2
Water surface	361 740 000 km^2
Equatorial circumference	40 075 km
Meridional circumference	40 007 km
Volume	1 083 230x10^6 km^3
Mass	5.976x10^{21} tonnes

Oceans and Sea Areas

Pacific Ocean	165 384 000 km^2
Atlantic Ocean	82 217 000 km^2
Indian Ocean	73 481 000 km^2
Arctic Ocean	14 056 000 km^2
Mediterranean Sea	2 505 000 km^2
South China Sea	2 318 000 km^2
Bering Sea	2 269 000 km^2
Caribbean Sea	1 943 000 km^2
Gulf of Mexico	1 544 000 km^2
Okhotskoye More (Sea of Okhotsk)	1 528 000 km^2
East China Sea	1 248 000 km^2
Hudson Bay	1 233 000 km^2
Sea of Japan	1 008 000 km^2
North Sea	575 000 km^2
Black Sea	461 000 km^2

River Lengths

An Nīl (Nile) ; Africa	6695 km
Amazonas (Amazon) ; South America	6516 km
Chang Jiang (Yangtze) ; Asia	6380 km
Mississippi - Missouri; North America	6020 km
Ob-Irtysh; Asia	5570 km
Huang He (Hwang Ho) ; Asia	5464 km
Zaïre; Africa	4667 km
Mekong; Asia	4425 km
Amur; Asia	4416 km
Lena; Asia	4400 km
Mackenzie; North America	4250 km
Yenisey; Asia	4090 km
Niger; Africa	4030 km
Murray - Darling; Oceania	3750 km
Volga; Europe	3688 km

Lake and Inland Sea Areas

Some areas are subject to seasonal variations.

Caspian Sea; U.S.S.R. / Iran	371 795 km^2
Lake Superior; U.S.A. / Canada	83 270 km^2
Lake Victoria; East Africa	69 485 km^2
Lake Huron; U.S.A. / Canada	60 700 km^2
Lake Michigan; U.S.A.	58 016 km^2
Aralskoye More (Aral Sea) ; U.S.S.R.	36 500 km^2
Lake Tanganyika; East Africa	32 893 km^2
Great Bear Lake; Canada	31 792 km^2
Ozero Baykal (Lake Baikal) ; U.S.S.R.	30 510 km^2
Great Slave Lake; Canada	28 930 km^2
Lake Erie; U.S.A. / Canada	25 667 km^2
Lake Winnipeg; Canada	24 514 km^2
Lake Malaŵi; Malaŵi / Mozambique	22 490 km^2
Lake Ontario; U.S.A. / Canada	19 529 km^2
Ladozhskoye Ozero (Lake Ladoga) ; U.S.S.R.	18 390 km^2

The Continents

Asia	43 608 000 km^2
Africa	30 355 000 km^2
North America	25 349 000 km^2
South America	17 611 000 km^2
Antarctica	13 338 500 km^2
Europe	10 498 000 km^2
Oceania	8 547 000 km^2

Island Areas

Greenland; Arctic / Atlantic Ocean	2 175 597 km^2
New Guinea; Indonesia / Papua New Guinea	808 510 km^2
Borneo; Malaysia / Indonesia / Brunei	757 050 km^2
Madagascar; Indian Ocean	594 180 km^2
Sumatera (Sumatra) ; Indonesia	524 100 km^2
Baffin Island; Canada	476 068 km^2
Honshū; Japan	230 455 km^2
Great Britain; United Kingdom	229 867 km^2
Ellesmere Island; Canada	212 688 km^2
Victoria Island; Canada	212 199 km^2
Sulawesi (Celebes) ; Indonesia	189 040 km^2
South Island; New Zealand	150 461 km^2
Jawa (Java) ; Indonesia	134 045 km^2
North Island; New Zealand	114 688 km^2
Cuba; Caribbean Sea	114 525 km^2

Mountain Heights (Selected)

Everest; Nepal / China	8848 m
K2; Jammu & Kashmir / China	8611 m
Kānchenjunga; Nepal / India	8586 m
Dhaulāgiri; Nepal	8167 m
Annapurna; Nepal	8091 m
Aconcagua; Argentina	6960 m
Ojos del Salado; Argentina / Chile	6908 m
McKinley; Alaska U.S.A.	6194 m
Logan; Canada	5951 m
Kilimanjaro; Tanzania	5895 m
Elbrus; U.S.S.R.	5642 m
Kenya; Kenya	5200 m
Vinson Massif; Antarctica	5139 m
Puncak Jaya; Indonesia	5030 m
Blanc; France / Italy	4807 m

Volcanoes (Selected)

	Last Eruption	Height
Cameroun; Cameroon	1922	4070 m
Cotopaxi; Ecuador	1975	5897 m
Elbrus; U.S.S.R.	extinct	5642 m
Erebus; Antarctica	1979	3794 m
Etna; Sicilia, Italy	1983	3340 m
Fuji san (Fujiyama) ; Japan	extinct	3776 m
Hekla; Iceland	1981	1491 m
Kilimanjaro; Tanzania	extinct	5895 m
Mauna Loa; Hawaii	1978	4171 m
Ngauruhoe; New Zealand	1975	2291 m
Popocatépetl; Mexico	1920	5452 m
St. Helens; U.S.A.	1981	2949 m
Stromboli; Italy	1975	926 m
Tristan da Cunha; Atlantic Ocean	1962	2160 m
Vesuvio (Vesuvius) ; Italy	1944	1277 m

National Areas

Union of Soviet Socialist Republics; Asia / Europe	22 402 000 km^2
Canada; North America	9 922 385 km^2
China; Asia	9 596 961 km^2
United States; North America	9 363 123 km^2
Brazil; South America	8 511 965 km^2
Australia; Oceania	7 686 848 km^2
India; Asia	3 166 830 km^2
Argentina; South America	2 766 889 km^2
Sudan; Africa	2 505 813 km^2
Saudi Arabia; Asia	2 400 900 km^2
Algeria; Africa	2 381 741 km^2
Zaïre; Africa	2 345 409 km^2
Greenland; North America	2 175 600 km^2
Mexico; North America	1 972 547 km^2
Indonesia; Asia	1 919 445 km^2
Libya; Africa	1 759 540 km^2
Iran; Asia	1 648 000 km^2
Mongolia; Asia	1 565 000 km^2
Peru; South America	1 285 216 km^2
Chad; Africa	1 284 000 km^2

National Populations

China; Asia	1 114 311 000
India; Asia	811 817 000
Union of Soviet Socialist Republics; Asia / Europe	286 717 000
United States; North America	249 928 000
Indonesia; Asia	179 136 000
Brazil; South America	147 404 000
Japan; Asia	123 116 000
Pakistan; Asia	108 678 000
Bangladesh; Asia	106 507 000
Nigeria; Africa	104 957 000
Mexico; North America	84 275 000
Germany; Europe	78 620 000
Vietnam; Asia	64 412 000
Philippines; Asia	60 097 000
Italy; Europe	57 557 000
United Kingdom; Europe	57 205 000
Turkey; Asia / Europe	56 741 000
France; Europe	56 160 000
Thailand; Asia	55 448 000
Egypt; Africa	53 080 000

World Cities

Ciudad de México (Mexico City) ; Mexico	19 396 000
New York; United States	17 931 000
Tōkyō; Japan	15 911 000
Cairo; Egypt	13 000 000
São Paulo; Brazil	13 000 000
Shanghai; China	12 500 000
Los Angeles; United States	10 232 000
Buenos Aires; Argentina	9 970 000
Sŏul (Seoul) ; South Korea	9 646 000
Rio de Janeiro; Brazil	9 500 000
Beijing (Peking) ; China	9 470 000
Calcutta; India	9 160 000
London; United Kingdom	9 055 000
Moskva (Moscow) ; U.S.S.R.	8 967 000
Paris; France	8 706 000

Major International Organisations

United Nations - On December 1990 the United Nations had 160 members. Independent States not represented include Liechtenstein, Monaco, Nauru, North Korea, San Marino, South Korea, Switzerland, Taiwan, Tonga.

Commonwealth

Antigua	Australia	Bahamas	Bangladesh
Barbados	Belize	Botswana	Brunei
Canada	Cyprus	Dominica	Fiji
Gambia	Ghana	Grenada	Guyana
Hong Kong	India	Jamaica	Kenya
Kiribati	Lesotho	Malaŵi	Malaysia
Maldives	Malta	Mauritius	Nauru
New Zealand	Nigeria	Pakistan	Papua New Guinea
St. Kitts & Nevis	St. Lucia	St. Vincent	Seychelles
Sierra Leone	Singapore	Solomon Islands	Sri Lanka
Swaziland	Tanzania	Tonga	Trinidad & Tobago
Tuvalu	Uganda	United Kingdom	Vanuatu
Western Samoa	Zambia	Zimbabwe	

OAU - Organisation of African Unity

Algeria	Angola	Benin	Botswana
Burkina	Burundi	Cameroon	Cape Verde
Central African Rep.	Chad	Comoros	Congo
Djibouti	Egypt	Equatorial Guinea	Ethiopia
Gabon	Gambia	Ghana	Guinea
Guinea Bissau	Ivory Coast	Kenya	Lesotho
Liberia	Libya	Madagascar	Malaŵi
Mali	Mauritania	Mauritius	Mozambique
Namibia	Niger	Nigeria	Rwanda
São Tomé & Príncipe	Senegal	Seychelles	Sierra Leone
Somali Rep.	Sudan	Swaziland	Tanzania
Togo	Tunisia	Uganda	Western Sahara
Zaïre	Zambia	Zimbabwe	

OAS - Organisation of American States

Antigua	Argentina	Bahamas	Barbados
Bolivia	Brazil	Chile	Colombia
Costa Rica	Dominica	Dominican Rep.	Ecuador
El Salvador	Grenada	Guatemala	Haiti
Honduras	Jamaica	Mexico	Nicaragua
Panama	Paraguay	Peru	St. Kitts & Nevis
St. Lucia	St. Vincent	Surinam	Trinidad & Tobago
United States	Uruguay	Venezuela	

EEC - European Economic Community

Belgium	Denmark	France	Germany
Greece	Ireland	Italy	Luxembourg
Netherlands	Portugal	Spain	United Kingdom

EFTA - European Free Trade Association

Austria	Finland (assoc.)	Iceland	Norway
Sweden	Switzerland		

COMECON - Council for Mutual Economic Assistance

Bulgaria	Cuba	Czechoslovakia	Hungary
Mongolia	Poland	Romania	U.S.S.R.
Vietnam	Yugoslavia (assoc.)		

Note: as of January 1991 COMECON is to be gradually dismantled. It will be replaced by a new body called the Organisation for International Economic Co-operation (OIEC).

ASEAN - Association of Southeast Asian Nations

Brunei	Indonesia	Malaysia	Philippines
Singapore	Thailand		

ECOWAS - Economic Community of West African States

Benin	Burkina	Cape Verde	Gambia
Ghana	Guinea	Guinea Bissau	Ivory Coast
Liberia	Mali	Mauritania	Niger
Nigeria	Senegal	Sierra Leone	Togo

CARICOM - Caribbean Community and Common Market

Antigua	Bahamas	Barbados	Belize
Dominica	Grenada	Guyana	Jamaica
Montserrat	St. Kitts & Nevis	St. Lucia	St. Vincent
Trindad & Tobago			

NATIONS OF THE WORLD

COUNTRY	AREA sq. km.	POPULATION total	per sq. km.	FORM OF GOVERNMENT	CAPITAL CITY	MAIN LANGUAGES	CURRENCY
AFGHANISTAN	647,497	15,814,000	24	republic	Kābol	Pushtu, Dari (Persian)	afghani
ALBANIA	28,748	3,202,000	111	socialist republic	Tiranë	Albanian	lek
ALGERIA	2,381,741	24,597,000	10	republic	Alger (Algiers)	Arabic	dinar
ANDORRA	453	50,000	110	principality	Andorra	Catalan	French franc, Spanish peseta
ANGOLA	1,246,700	9,747,000	8	people's republic	Luanda	Portuguese	kwanza
ANTIGUA AND BARBUDA	442	85,000	192	constitutional monarchy	St John's	English	East Caribbean dollar
ARGENTINA	2,766,889	31,929,000	12	federal republic	Buenos Aires	Spanish	austral
AUSTRALIA	7,686,848	16,807,000	2	monarchy (federal)	Canberra	English	dollar
AUSTRIA	83,849	7,618,000	91	federal republic	Wien (Vienna)	German	schilling
BAHAMAS	13,935	249,000	18	constitutional monarchy	Nassau	English	dollar
BAHRAIN	622	489,000	786	emirate	Al Manāmah	Arabic	dinar
BANGLADESH	143,998	106,507,000	740	republic	Dhaka	Bengali	taka
BARBADOS	431	256,000	594	constitutional monarchy	Bridgetown	English	dollar
BELGIUM	30,513	9,883,000	324	constitutional monarchy	Bruxelles/Brussel (Brussels)	French, Dutch, German	franc
BELIZE	22,965	180,000	8	constitutional monarchy	Belmopan	English	dollar
BENIN	112,622	4,591,000	41	republic	Porto-Novo	French	CFA franc
BHUTAN	47,000	1,483,000	32	monarchy (Indian protection)	Thimbu	Dzongkha	Indian rupee, nguitrum
BOLIVIA	1,098,581	7,193,000	7	republic	La Paz/Sucre	Spanish	bolivano
BOTSWANA	600,372	1,256,000	2	republic	Gaborone	English, Tswana	pula
BRAZIL	8,511,965	147,404,000	17	federal republic	Brasília	Portuguese	cruzado
BRUNEI	5,765	249,000	43	sultanate	Bandar Seri Begawan	Malay	dollar
BULGARIA	110,912	8,981,000	81	people's republic	Sofiya (Sofia)	Bulgarian	lev
BURKINA	274,200	8,798,000	32	republic	Ouagadougou	French	CFA franc
BURMA	676,552	38,541,000	57	federal republic	Rangoon	Burmese	kyat
BURUNDI	27,834	5,302,000	190	republic	Bujumbura	French, Kirundi	franc
CAMBODIA	181,035	8,055,000	44	republic	Phnom Penh	Cambodian, Khmer	riel
CAMEROON	475,442	11,540,000	24	republic	Yaoundé	French, English	CFA franc
CANADA	9,976,139	26,248,000	3	monarchy (federal)	Ottawa	English, French	dollar
CAPE VERDE	4,033	368,000	91	republic	Praia	Portuguese, Creole	escudo
CENTRAL AFRICAN REPUBLIC	622,984	2,740,000	4	republic	Bangui	French, Sango	CFA franc
CHAD	1,284,000	5,538,000	4	republic	N'Djamena	French	CFA franc
CHILE	756,945	12,961,000	17	republic	Santiago	Spanish	peso
CHINA	9,596,961	1,114,311,000	116	people's republic	Beijing (Peking)	Mandarin	yuan
COLOMBIA	1,138,914	30,241,000	27	republic	Bogotá	Spanish	peso
COMOROS	2,171	484,000	223	federal republic	Moroni	Comoran, Arabic, French	CFA franc
CONGO	342,000	1,940,000	6	republic	Brazzaville	French	CFA franc
COSTA RICA	50,700	2,922,000	58	republic	San José	Spanish	colon
CUBA	114,524	10,594,000	93	people's republic	La Habana (Havana)	Spanish	peso
CYPRUS	9,251	694,000	75	republic	Levkosía (Nicosia)	Greek	pound
CZECHOSLOVAKIA	127,869	15,651,000	122	federal republic	Praha (Prague)	Czech, Slovak	koruna
DENMARK	43,069	5,132,000	119	constitutional monarchy	København (Copenhagen)	Danish	krone
DJIBOUTI	22,000	456,000	21	republic	Djibouti	French, Somali, Afar	franc
DOMINICA	751	81,000	108	republic	Roseau	English, French	East Caribbean dollar
DOMINICAN REPUBLIC	48,734	7,018,000	144	republic	Santo Dominigo	Spanish	peso
ECUADOR	283,561	10,490,000	37	republic	Quito	Spanish	sucre
EGYPT	1,001,449	53,080,000	53	republic	Al Qāhirah (Cairo)	Arabic	pound
EL SALVADOR	21,041	5,207,000	247	republic	San Salvador	Spanish	colón
EQUATORIAL GUINEA	28,051	341,000	12	republic	Malabo	Spanish	CFA franc
ETHIOPIA	1,221,900	50,774,000	42	people's republic	Ādīs Ābeba (Addis Ababa)	Amharic	birr
FIJI	18,274	727,000	40	republic	Suva	English, Fijian, Hindustani	dollar
FINLAND	337,032	4,962,000	15	republic	Helsinki	Finnish, Swedish	markka
FRANCE	547,026	56,160,000	103	republic	Paris	French	franc
GABON	267,667	1,206,000	5	republic	Libreville	French	CFA franc
GAMBIA	11,295	835,000	74	republic	Banjul	English	dalasi
GERMANY	356,755	78,620,000	220	federal republic	Berlin/Bonn	German	mark
GHANA	238,537	14,566,000	61	republic	Accra	English	cedi
GREECE	131,944	9,983,000	76	republic	Athínai (Athens)	Greek	drachma
GREENLAND	2,175,600	56,000	0	overseas territory (Denmark)	Godthåb/Nuuk	Danish, Greenlandic	krone

COUNTRY	AREA sq. km.	POPULATION total	POPULATION per sq. km.	FORM OF GOVERNMENT	CAPITAL CITY	MAIN LANGUAGES	CURRENCY
GRENADA	344	97,000	282	constitutional monarchy	St George's	English	East Caribbean dollar
GUATEMALA	108,889	8,935,000	82	republic	Guatemala	Spanish	quetzal
GUIANA	91,000	90,000	1	overseas department (France)	Cayenne	French	franc
GUINEA	245,857	5,071,000	21	republic	Conakry	French	franc
GUINEA BISSAU	36,125	943,000	26	republic	Bissau	Portuguese	peso
GUYANA	214,969	1,023,000	5	republic	Georgetown	English	dollar
HAITI	27,750	5,609,000	202	republic	Port-au-Prince	French, Creole	goude
HONDURAS	112,088	4,951,000	44	republic	Tegucigalpa	Spanish	lempira
HONG KONG	1,045	5,681,000	5436	colony (U.K.)		English, Chinese	dollar
HUNGARY	93,030	10,563,000	114	republic	Budapest	Magyar	forint
ICELAND	103,000	250,000	2	republic	Reykjavik	Icelandic	króna
INDIA	3,287,590	811,817,000	247	republic	New Delhi	Hindi	rupee
INDONESIA	1,904,569	179,136,000	94	republic	Jakarta	Bahasa Indonesia	rupiah
IRAN	1,648,000	55,208,000	34	Islamic republic	Tehrān	Persian	rial
IRAQ	434,924	16,278,000	37	republic	Baghdād	Arabic	dinar
IRELAND, REPUBLIC OF	70,283	3,515,000	50	republic	Dublin	English, Irish	punt
ISRAEL	20,770	4,566,000	220	republic	Yerushalayim (Jerusalem)	Hebrew	shekel
ITALY	301,225	57,557,000	191	republic	Roma (Rome)	Italian	lira
IVORY COAST	322,463	12,097,000	38	republic	Yamoussoukro	French	CFA franc
JAMAICA	10,991	2,392,000	218	constitutional monarchy	Kingston	English	dollar
JAPAN	372,313	123,116,000	331	monarchy	Tōkyō	Japanese	yen
JORDAN	97,740	4,102,000	42	monarchy	'Ammān	Arabic	dinar
KENYA	582,646	24,872,000	43	republic	Nairobi	Swahili, English	shilling
KIRIBATI	886	64,000	72	republic	Tarawa	English, Gilbertese (I-Kiribati)	Australian dollar
KUWAIT	17,818	2,048,000	115	emirate	Al Kuwayt (Kuwait)	Arabic	dinar
LAOS	236,800	3,972,000	17	people's republic	Vientiane (Viangchan)	Lao	new kip
LEBANON	10,400	2,897,000	279	republic	Bayrūt (Beirut)	Arabic	pound
LESOTHO	30,355	1,700,000	56	monarchy	Maseru	English, Sesotho	maluti
LIBERIA	111,369	2,508,000	23	republic	Monrovia	English	dollar
LIBYA	1,759,540	4,385,000	2	republic (jamahiriya)	Tarābulus (Tripoli)	Arabic	dinar
LIECHTENSTEIN	157	28,000	178	constitutional monarchy	Vaduz	German	Swiss franc
LUXEMBOURG	2,586	378,000	146	constitutional monarchy	Luxembourg	Letzeburgish, French, German	franc
MADAGASCAR	587,041	9,985,000	17	republic	Antananarivo	Malagasy	Malagasy franc
MALAWI	118,484	8,022,000	68	republic	Lilongwe	English, Chichewa	kwacha
MALAYSIA	329,749	16,942,000	51	constitutional monarchy	Kuala Lumpur	Malay	ringgit
MALDIVES	298	206,000	691	republic	Malé	Divehi	rufiya
MALI	1,240,000	7,960,000	6	republic	Bamako	French, Bambara	CFA franc
MALTA	316	350,000	1108	republic	Valletta	Maltese, English	pound
MAURITANIA	1,030,700	1,969,000	2	republic	Nouakchott	French, Arabic	ouguiya
MAURITIUS	2,045	1,068,000	522	constitutional monarchy	Port-Louis	English, Creole	rupee
MEXICO	1,972,547	84,275,000	43	federal republic	Ciudad de México (Mexico City)	Spanish	peso
MONACO	2	28,000	18667	constitutional monarchy	Monaco	French	French franc
MONGOLIA	1,565,000	2,043,000	1	people's republic	Ulaanbaatar (Ulan Bator)	Mongol	tugrik
MOROCCO	446,550	24,521,000	55	monarchy	Rabat	Arabic	dirham
MOZAMBIQUE	801,590	15,326,000	19	people's republic	Maputo	Portuguese	metical
NAMIBIA	824,292	1,817,000	2	republic	Windhoek	Afrikaans, English	Namibian dollar
NAURU	21	8,000	381	republic	Nauru	Nauruan, English	Australian dollar
NEPAL	140,797	18,442,000	131	monarchy	Kātmāndu	Nepali	rupee
NETHERLANDS	40,844	14,891,000	365	constitutional monarchy	Amsterdam	Dutch	guilder
NEW ZEALAND	268,676	3,389,000	13	constitutional monarchy	Wellington	English	dollar
NICARAGUA	130,000	3,384,000	26	republic	Managua	Spanish	córdoba
NIGER	1,267,000	7,250,000	6	republic	Niamey	French	CFA franc
NIGERIA	923,768	104,957,000	114	federal republic	Abuja	English	naira
NORTH KOREA	120,538	22,418,000	186	people's republic	Pyŏngyang	Korean	won
NORWAY	324,219	4,227,000	13	constitutional monarchy	Oslo	Norwegian	krone
OMAN	212,457	1,422,000	7	sultanate	Masqaţ (Muscat)	Arabic	rial
PAKISTAN	803,943	108,678,000	135	federal republic	Islāmābād	Urdu, Punjabi, English	rupee
PANAMA	77,082	2,370,000	31	republic	Panamá	Spanish	balbao

NATIONS OF THE WORLD

COUNTRY	AREA sq. km.	POPULATION total	per sq. km.	FORM OF GOVERNMENT	CAPITAL CITY	MAIN LANGUAGES	CURRENCY
PAPUA NEW GUINEA	461,691	3,593,000	8	constitutional monarchy	Port Moresby	English, Pidgin, Motu	kina
PARAGUAY	406,752	4,157,000	10	republic	Asunción	Spanish, Guaraní	guaraní
PERU	1,285,216	21,792,000	17	republic	Lima	Spanish	inti
PHILIPPINES	300,000	60,097,000	200	republic	Manila	Pilipino	peso
POLAND	312,677	37,931,000	121	republic	Warszawa (Warsaw)	Polish	zloty
PORTUGAL	92,082	10,467,000	114	republic	Lisboa (Lisbon)	Portuguese	escudo
PUERTO RICO	8,897	3,293,000	370	commonwealth (U.S.A.)	San Juan	Spanish, English	dollar
QATAR	11,000	422,000	38	emirate	Ad Dawḩah (Doha)	Arabic	riyal
ROMANIA	237,500	23,152,000	97	republic	Bucureşti (Bucharest)	Romanian	leu
RWANDA	26,338	6,989,000	265	republic	Kigali	Kinyarwanda, French	franc
ST KITTS-NEVIS	266	49,000	184	constitutional monarchy	Basseterre	English	East Caribbean dollar
ST LUCIA	616	148,000	240	constitutional monarchy	Castries	English, French	East Caribbean dollar
ST VINCENT AND THE GRENADINES	389	113,000	290	constitutional monarchy	Kingstown	English	East Caribbean dollar
SAN MARINO	61	23,000	377	republic	San Marino	Italian	Italian lira
SÃO TOMÉ AND PRINCIPE	964	116,000	120	republic	São Tomé	Portuguese, Creole	dobra
SAUDI ARABIA	2,149,690	14,435,000	7	monarchy	Ar Riyāḑ (Riyadh)	Arabic	riyal
SENEGAL	196,192	7,113,000	36	republic	Dakar	French	CFA franc
SEYCHELLES	280	67,000	239	republic	Victoria	English, French	rupee
SIERRA LEONE	71,740	3,516,000	49	republic	Freetown	English	leone
SINGAPORE	602	2,704,000	4492	republic	Singapore	Malay, English, Chinese, Tamil	dollar
SOLOMON ISLANDS	28,446	299,000	11	constitutional monarchy	Honiara	English	dollar
SOMALI REPUBLIC	637,657	7,339,000	12	republic	Muqdisho	Arabic, Italian, English, Somali	shilling
SOUTH AFRICA, REPUBLIC OF	1,221,037	34,492,000	28	federal republic	Cape Town (Kaapstad)/Pretoria	Afrikaans, English	rand
SOUTH KOREA	98,484	42,380,000	430	republic	Sŏul (Seoul)	Korean	won
SPAIN	504,782	39,248,000	78	constitutional monarchy	Madrid	Spanish	peseta
SRI LANKA	65,610	16,806,000	256	republic	Colombo	Sinhala, Tamil	rupee
SUDAN	2,505,813	24,484,000	10	republic	Al Kharţūm (Khartoum)	Arabic	pound
SURINAM	163,265	397,000	2	republic	Paramaribo	Dutch, English	guilder
SWAZILAND	17,363	681,000	39	monarchy	Mbabane	English, Siswati	lilangeni
SWEDEN	449,964	8,541,000	19	constitutional monarchy	Stockholm	Swedish	krona
SWITZERLAND	41,288	6,647,000	161	federal republic	Bern (Berne)	German, French, Italian, Romansh	franc
SYRIA	185,180	11,719,000	63	republic	Dimashq (Damascus)	Arabic	pound
TAIWAN	35,961	19,900,000	553	republic	Taipei	Mandarin	dollar
TANZANIA	945,087	24,802,000	26	republic	Dodoma	Swahili	shilling
THAILAND	514,000	54,448,000	106	monarchy	Bangkok (Krung Thep)	Thai	baht
TOGO	56,785	3,296,000	58	republic	Lomé	French	CFA franc
TONGA	699	95,000	136	monarchy	Nuku'alofa	Tongan, English	pa anga
TRINIDAD AND TOBAGO	5,130	1,212,000	236	republic	Port of Spain	English	dollar
TUNISIA	163,610	7,465,000	46	republic	Tunis	Arabic	dinar
TURKEY	780,576	56,741,000	73	republic	Ankara	Turkish	lira
TUVALU	24	7,000	292	constitutional monarchy	Funafuti	Tuvalu, English	Australian dollar
U.S.S.R.	22,402,200	286,717,000	13	federal socialist republic	Moskva (Moscow)	Russian	rouble
UGANDA	236,036	17,804,000	75	republic	Kampala	English	new shilling
UNITED ARAB EMIRATES	83,600	1,546,000	18	self-governing union		Arabic	dirham
UNITED KINGDOM	244,046	57,205,000	234	constitutional monarchy	London	English	pound
UNITED STATES OF AMERICA	9,372,614	249,928,000	27	federal republic	Washington	English	dollar
URUGUAY	176,215	3,077,000	17	republic	Montevideo	Spanish	peso
VANUATU	14,763	143,000	10	republic	Vila	English, French	vatu
VENEZUELA	912,050	19,246,000	21	federal republic	Caracas	Spanish	bolívar
VIETNAM	329,556	64,412,000	195	people's republic	Hanoi	Vietnamese	dong
WESTERN SAMOA	2,842	168,000	59	constitutional monarchy	Apia	Samoan, English	tala
YEMEN	527,968	11,619,439	22	republic	Şan'ā	Arabic	rial
YUGOSLAVIA	255,804	23,764,000	93	socialist federal republic	Beograd (Belgrade)	Serbo-Croat, Macedonian, Slovene	dinar
ZAÏRE	2,345,409	34,491,000	15	republic	Kinshasa	French, Lingala	zaïre
ZAMBIA	752,614	7,804,000	10	republic	Lusaka	English	kwacha
ZIMBABWE	390,580	9,122,000	23	republic	Harare	English	dollar

Introduction to World Index

The index includes an alphabetical list of all names appearing on the maps in the World Atlas section. Each entry indicates the country or region of the world in which the name is located. This is followed by a page reference and finally the name's location on the map, given by latitude and longitude co-ordinates. Most features are indexed to the largest scale map on which they appear, however when the name applies to countries or other extensive features it is generally indexed to the map on which it appears in its entirety. Areal features are generally indexed using co-ordinates which indicate the centre of the feature. The latitude and longitude indicated for a point feature gives the location of the point on the map. In the case of rivers the mouth or confluence is always taken as the point of reference.

Names in the index are generally in the local language and where a conventional English version exists, this is cross referenced to the entry in the local language. Names of features which extend across the boundaries of more than one country are usually named in English if no single official name exists. Names in languages not written in the Roman alphabet have been transliterated using the official system of the country if one exists, e.g. Pinyin system for China, otherwise the systems recognised by the United States Board on Geographical Names have been used.

Names abbreviated on the maps are given in full in the Index. Abbreviations are used for both geographical terms and administrative names in the Index. All abbreviations used in the Index are listed below.

Abbreviations of Geographical Terms

b., **B.**	bay, Bay
c., **C.**	cape, Cape
d.	internal division e.g county, region, state
des.	desert
est.	estuary
f.	physical feature e.g. valley, plain, geographic district or region
g., G.	gulf, Gulf
i., I., **is.**, Is.	island, Island, islands, Islands
l., L.	lake, Lake
mtn., Mtn.	mountain, Mountain
mts., Mts.	mountains, Mountains
pen., Pen.	peninsula, Peninsula
Pt.	Point
r.	river
resr., Resr.	reservoir, Reservoir
Sd.	Sound
str., Str.	strait, Strait

Abbreviations of Country / Administrative Names

Afghan.	Afghanistan
A.H. Prov.	Alpes de Haut Provence
Ala.	Alabama
Alas.	Alaska
Alta.	Alberta
Ariz.	Arizona
Ark.	Arkansas
Baja Calif. Norte	Baja California Norte
Baja Calif. Sur	Baja California Sur
Bangla.	Bangladesh
B.C.	British Columbia
B.S.S.R.	Belorusskaya Sovetskaya Sotsialisticheskaya Respublika
B.-Würt	Baden-Württemberg
Calif.	California
C.A.R.	Central African Republic
Char. Mar.	Charente Maritime
Colo.	Colorado
Conn.	Connecticut
C.P.	Cape Province
Czech.	Czechoslovakia
D.C.	District of Colombia
Del.	Delaware
Dom. Rep.	Dominican Republic
Equat. Guinea	Equatorial Guinea
Eth.	Ethiopia
Fla.	Florida
Ga.	Georgia
Guang. Zhuang	Guangxi Zhuangzu
H.-Gar.	Haute Garonne
Himachal P.	Himachal Pradesh
H. Zaïre	Haut Zaïre
Ill.	Illinois
Ind.	Indiana
Kans.	Kansas
K. Occidental	Kasai Occidental
K. Oriental	Kasai Oriental
Ky.	Kentucky
La.	Louisiana
Liech.	Liechtenstein
Lit. S.S.R.	Litovskaya Sovetskaya Sotsialisticheskaya Respublika
Lux.	Luxembourg
Madhya P.	Madhya Pradesh
Man.	Manitoba
Mass.	Massachusetts
Md.	Maryland
Mich.	Michigan
Minn.	Minnesota
Miss.	Mississippi
Mo.	Missouri
Mont.	Montana
M.-Pyr.	Midi-Pyrénées
M.S.S.R.	Moldavskaya Sovetskaya Sotsialisticheskaya Respublika
N.B.	New Brunswick
N.C.	North Carolina
N. Dak.	North Dakota
Nebr.	Nebraska
Neth.	Netherlands
Nev.	Nevada
Nfld.	Newfoundland
N.H.	New Hampshire
N. Ireland	Northern Ireland
N.J.	New Jersey
N. Korea	North Korea
N. Mex	New Mexico
Nschn.	Niedersachsen
N.S.W.	New South Wales
N. Trönd.	North Tröndelag
N.T.	Northern Territory
N.-Westfålen	Nordrhein-Westfalen
N.W.T.	Northwest Territories
N.Y.	New York State
O.F.S.	Orange Free State
Okla.	Oklahoma
Ont.	Ontario
Oreg.	Oregon
P.E.I.	Prince Edward Island
Penn.	Pennsylvania
Phil.	Philippines
P.N.G.	Papua New Guinea
Poit.-Char.	Poitou-Charente
Pyr. Or.	Pyrénées Orientales
Qld.	Queensland
Que.	Québec
Raj.	Rājasthān
Rep. of Ire.	Republic of Ireland
Rhein.-Pfalz	Rheinland-Pfalz
R.I.	Rhode Island
R.S.A.	Republic of South Africa
R.S.F.S.R.	Rossiyskaya Sovetskaya Federativnaya Sotsialisticheskaya Respublika
S.A.	South Australia
Sask.	Saskatchewan
S.C.	South Carolina
Sch.-Hol.	Schleswig-Holstein
S. Dak.	South Dakota
S. Korea	South Korea
S. Mar.	Seine Maritime
Sogn og Fj.	Sogn og Fjordane
Somali Rep.	Somali Republic
Switz.	Switzerland
Tas.	Tasmania
Tenn.	Tennessee
Tex.	Texas
T.G.	Tarn-et-Garonne
Tk. S.S.R.	Turkmenskaya Sovetskaya Sotsialisticheskaya Respublika
Trans.	Transvaal
U.A.E.	United Arab Emirates
U.K.	United Kingdom
Ukr. S.S.R.	Ukrainskaya Sovetskaya Sotsialisticheskaya Respublika
U.S.A.	United States of America
U.S.S.R.	Union of Soviet Socialist Republics
Uttar P.	Uttar Pradesh
Va.	Virginia
Vic.	Victoria
Vt.	Vermont
W.A.	Western Australia
Wash.	Washington
W. Bengal	West Bengal
Wisc.	Wisconsin
W. Sahara	Western Sahara
W. Va.	West Virginia
Wyo.	Wyoming
Xin Uygur	Xinjiang Uygur
Yugo.	Yugoslavia

A

Aachen Germany 14 50.46N 6.06E
A 'âlî an Nîl d. Sudan 49 9.35N 31.05E
Aalsmeer Neth. 14 52.17N 4.46E
Aalst Belgium 14 50.57N 4.03E
Äänekoski Finland 22 62.36N 25.44E
Aarau Switz. 20 47.24N 8.04E
Aardenburg Neth. 14 51.16N 3.26E
Aare r. Switz. 20 47.37N 8.13E
Aarschot Belgium 14 50.59N 4.50E
Aba China 39 32.55N101.42E
Aba Nigeria 53 5.06N 7.21E
Aba Zaïre 49 3.52N 30.14E
Abā as Su'ūd Saudi Arabia 45 17.28N 44.06E
Abadab, Jabal mtn. Sudan 48 18.53N 35.59E
Ābādān Iran 43 30.21N 48.15E
Abadan, Jazīreh-ye i. Iran 43 30.10N 48.30E
Ābādeh Iran 43 31.10N 52.40E
Abadla Algeria 50 31.01N 2.44W
Abaetetuba Brazil 91 1.45S 48.54W
Abagnar Qi China 32 43.58N116.02E
Abag Qi China 32 43.53N114.33E
Abaí Paraguay 92 26.01S 55.57W
Abajo Peak mtn. U.S.A. 80 37.51N109.28W
Abakaliki Nigeria 53 6.17N 8.04E
Abakan U.S.S.R. 29 53.43N 91.25E
Abalessa Algeria 51 22.54N 4.50E
Abancay Peru 92 13.35S 72.55W
Abariringa i. Kiribati 68 2.50S171.40W
Ābār Murrāt wells Sudan 48 21.03N 32.55E
Abasolo Mexico 83 25.18N104.40W
Abau P.N.G. 64 10.10S148.40E
Abāy r. Ethiopia see Azraq, Al Baḩr al r. r. Sudan 48
Abay U.S.S.R. 28 49.40N 72.47E
Ābaya Hāyk' l. Ethiopia 49 6.20N 37.55E
Abba C.A.R. 53 5.20N 15.11E
Abbeville France 17 50.06N 1.51E
Abbeville La. U.S.A. 83 29.58N 92.08W
Abbeville S.C. U.S.A. 85 34.10N 82.23W
Abbiategrasso Italy 15 45.24N 8.54E
Abbotsbury U.K. 11 50.40N 2.36W
Abbotsford Canada 77 45.27N 72.55W
Abbottābād Pakistan 40 34.09N 73.13E
'Abd al Kūrī i. Yemen 45 12.12N 52.13E
Abdulino U.S.S.R. 24 53.42N 53.40E
Abéché Chad 48 13.49N 20.49E
Ābeltī Ethiopia 49 8.10N 37.37E
Abengourou Ivory Coast 52 6.42N 3.27W
Åbenrå Denmark 23 55.02N 9.26E
Abeokuta Nigeria 53 7.10N 3.26E
Aberayron U.K. 11 52.15N 4.16W
Abercrombie r. Australia 67 33.50S149.10E
Aberdare U.K. 11 51.43N 3.27W
Aberdare Range mts. Kenya 55 0.20S 36.40E
Aberdeen Australia 67 32.10S150.54E
Aberdeen R.S.A. 56 32.28S 24.03E
Aberdeen U.K. 12 57.08N 2.07W
Aberdeen Md. U.S.A. 85 39.30N 76.10W
Aberdeen Miss. U.S.A. 83 33.49N 88.33W
Aberdeen Ohio U.S.A. 84 38.39N 83.46W
Aberdeen S. Dak. U.S.A. 82 45.28N 98.29W
Aberdeen Wash. U.S.A. 80 46.59N123.50W
Aberdovey U.K. 11 52.33N 4.03W
Aberfeldy U.K. 12 56.37N 3.54W
Abergavenny U.K. 11 51.49N 3.01W
Abersoch U.K. 10 52.50N 4.31W
Aberystwyth U.K. 11 52.25N 4.06W
Abetone Italy 15 44.08N 10.40E
Abez U.S.S.R. 24 66.33N 61.51E
Abhā Saudi Arabia 48 18.13N 42.30E
Abhar Iran 43 36.09N 49.13E
Ābhē Bid Hāyk' l. Ethiopia 49 11.06N 41.50E
Abidjan Ivory Coast 52 5.19N 4.01W
Abilene Kans. U.S.A. 82 38.55N 97.13W
Abilene Tex. U.S.A. 83 32.27N 99.44W
Abingdon U.K. 11 51.40N 1.17W
Abisko Sweden 22 68.20N 18.51E
Abitau r. Canada 75 59.53N109.03W
Abitibi r. Canada 76 51.03N 80.55W
Abitibi, L. Canada 76 48.42N 79.45W
Ābiy Ādī Ethiopia 49 13.36N 39.00E
Abnūb Egypt 42 27.16N 31.09E
Åbo see Turku Finland 23
Abohar India 40 30.08N 74.12E
Abomey Benin 53 7.14N 2.00E
Abong Mbang Cameroon 53 3.59N 13.12E
Abou Deïa Chad 53 11.20N 19.20E
Aboyne U.K. 12 57.05N 2.48W
Abrantes Portugal 16 39.28N 8.12W
'Abrī Sudan 48 20.48N 30.20E
Abring Jammu & Kashmir 40 33.42N 76.35E
Abrud Romania 21 46.17N 23.04E
Abruzzi d. Italy 18 42.05N 13.45E
Absaroka Range mts. U.S.A. 80 44.45N109.50W
Absecon U.S.A. 85 39.26N 74.30W
Abū 'Arīsh Saudi Arabia 45 16.58N 42.50E
Abū Baḩr f. Saudi Arabia 45 21.30N 48.15E
Abū Ballāş hill Egypt 48 24.26N 27.39E
Abu Dhabi see Abū Z̧aby U.A.E. 43
Abū Dharbah Egypt 44 28.29N 33.20E
Abū Dulayq Sudan 48 15.54N 33.49E
Abū Ḩamad Sudan 48 19.32N 33.19E
Abū Ḩarāz Sudan 48 19.04N 32.07E
A1 Buḩayrāt d. Sudan 49 6.50N 29.40E
Abuja Nigeria 53 9.12N 7.11E
Abū Jābirah Sudan 49 11.04N 26.51E
Abū Kabīr Egypt 44 30.44N 31.40E
Abū Kamāl Syria 42 34.27N 40.55E
Abū Madd, Ra's c. Saudi Arabia 42 24.50N 37.07E
Abū Maţāriq Sudan 49 10.58N 26.17E
Abunā Brazil 90 9.41S 65.20W
Abū Qurqāş Egypt 44 27.56N 30.50E
Abu Road town India 40 24.29N 72.47E
Abū Shajarah, Ra's c. Sudan 48 21.04N 37.14E
Abū Shanab Sudan 49 10.47N 29.32E
Abū Sulţān Egypt 44 30.25N 32.19E
Abū Sunbul Egypt 42 22.18N 31.40E
Abū Ţabarī well Sudan 48 17.35N 28.31E
Abū Ţarafah Jordan 44 30.00N 35.56E
Abū Tīj Egypt 42 27.06N 31.17E
Abuya Mexico 81 24.16N107.01W
Ābuyē Mēda mtn. Ethiopia 49 10.28N 39.44E
Abū Zabad Sudan 49 12.21N 29.15E
Abū Z̧aby U.A.E. 43 24.27N 54.23E
Abū Zanīmah Egypt 44 29.03N 33.06E
Abwong Sudan 49 9.07N 32.12E
Åby Sweden 23 58.40N 16.11E
Abyaḑ Sudan 48 13.46N 26.28E
Abyaḑ, Al Baḩr al r. Sudan 48 15.38N 32.31E
Abyār ash Shuwayrif wells Libya 51 29.59N 14.16E
Abyei Sudan 49 9.36N 28.26E
Acacio Mexico 83 24.50N102.44W
Acadia Valley town Canada 75 51.08N110.13W
Acámbaro Mexico 86 20.01N101.42W
Acapulco Mexico 86 16.51N 99.56W
Acará Brazil 91 1.57S 48.11W
Acarigua Venezuela 90 9.35N 69.12W
Acatlán Mexico 86 18.12N 98.02W
Accra Ghana 52 5.33N 0.15W
Accrington U.K. 10 53.46N 2.22W
Aceh d. Indonesia 36 4.00N 97.30E
Acevedo Argentina 93 33.46S 60.27W
Achacachi Bolivia 92 16.03S 68.43W
Achalpur India 41 21.16N 77.31E
Achar Uruguay 93 32.25S 56.10W
Acheng China 31 45.32N126.59E
Achill I. Rep. of Ire. 13 53.57N 10.00W
Āchin Afghan. 40 34.08N 70.42E
Achinsk U.S.S.R. 28 56.10N 90.10E
Acklin's I. Bahamas 87 22.30N 74.10W
Aconcagua mtn. Argentina 92 32.39S 70.00W
Açores, Arquipélago dos is. Atlantic Oc. 95 38.30N 28.00W
Acqui Italy 15 44.41N 8.28E
Acraman, L. Australia 66 32.02S135.26E
Acre d. Brazil 90 8.50S 71.30W
Acton Canada 76 43.37N 80.02W
Acton Vale Canada 77 45.39N 72.34W
Açu Brazil 91 5.35S 36.57W
Acuña Argentina 93 29.54S 57.57W
Ada U.S.A. 83 34.46N 96.41W
Ādaba Ethiopia 49 7.07N 39.20E
Adair, Bahía de b. Mexico 81 31.30N113.50W
Adair, C. Canada 73 71.24N 71.13W
Adam Oman 45 22.23N 57.32E
Adamantina Brazil 94 21.42S 51.04W
Adamaoua, Massif de l' mts. Cameroon / Nigeria 53 7.05N 12.00E
Adamello mtn. Italy 15 46.10N 10.35E
Adaminaby Australia 67 36.04S148.42E
Adamintina Brazil 92 21.42S 51.04W
Adams N.Y. U.S.A. 84 43.49N 76.01W
Adams, Mt. U.S.A. 80 46.12N121.28W
'Adan Yemen 45 12.50N 45.00E
Adana Turkey 42 37.00N 35.19E
Adapazari Turkey 42 40.45N 30.23E
Adarama Sudan 48 17.05N 34.54E
Adare, C. Antarctica 96 71.30S171.00E
Adavale Australia 64 25.55S144.36E
Adda r. Italy 15 45.08N 9.55E
Ad Dab'ah Egypt 42 31.02N 28.26E
Ad Dabbah Sudan 48 18.03N 30.57E
Ad Dafīnah Saudi Arabia 42 23.18N 41.58E
Ad Dahnā' des. Saudi Arabia 43 26.00N 47.00E
Ad Dāmir Sudan 48 17.35N 33.58E
Ad Dammām Saudi Arabia 43 26.23N 50.08E
Ad Darb Saudi Arabia 48 17.44N 42.15E
Ad Dawādimī Saudi Arabia 43 24.29N 44.23E
Ad Dawḩah Qatar 43 25.15N 51.34E
Ad Diffah f. Africa 42 30.45N 26.00E
Ad Dikākah f. Saudi Arabia 45 19.25N 51.30E
Ad Dilam Saudi Arabia 43 23.59N 47.10E
Ad Dīmās Syria 44 33.35N 36.05E
Addis Ababa see Ādīs Ābeba Ethiopia 49
Ad Dīwānīyah Iraq 43 31.59N 44.57E
Ad Du'ayn Sudan 49 11.26N 26.09E
Ad Duwaym Sudan 48 14.00N 32.19E
Adel U.S.A. 85 31.07N 83.27W
Adelaide Australia 66 34.56S138.36E
Adelaide Pen. Canada 73 68.09N 97.45W
Adelaide River town Australia 62 13.14S131.06E
Adelong Australia 67 35.21S148.04E
Aden see 'Adan Yemen 45
Aden, G. of Indian Oc. 45 13.00N 50.00E
Adendorp R.S.A. 56 32.18S 24.31E
Adi i. Indonesia 37 4.10S133.10E
Ādī Da'iro Ethiopia 48 14.27N 38.16E
Adieu, C. Australia 63 31.59S132.09E
Ādīgala Ethiopia 49 10.25N 42.17E
Adige r. Italy 15 45.10N 12.20E
Ādīgrat Ethiopia 48 14.18N 39.31E
Ādī K'eyih Ethiopia 48 14.49N 39.23E
Ādilābād India 41 19.40N 78.32E
Adilang Uganda 55 2.44N 33.28E
Adin U.S.A. 80 41.12N120.57W
Adirondack Mts. U.S.A. 84 44.00N 74.00W
Ādīs Ābeba Ethiopia 49 9.03N 38.42E
Ādī Ugrī Ethiopia 48 14.55N 38.53E
Adiyaman Turkey 42 37.46N 38.15E
Adjud Romania 21 46.04N 27.11E
Admer well Algeria 51 20.23N 5.27E
Admiralty G. Australia 62 14.20S125.50E
Admiralty I. U.S.A. 74 57.50N134.30W
Admiralty Is. P.N.G. 37 2.30S147.20E
Admiralty Range mts. Antarctica 96 72.00S164.00E
Adour r. France 17 43.28N 1.35W
Adra Spain 16 36.43N 3.03W
Adrano Italy 18 37.39N 14.49E
Adrar d. Mauritania 50 21.00N 10.00W
Adrar des Iforas mts. Mali / Algeria 51 20.00N 2.30E
Adraskan Afghan. 40 33.39N 62.16E
Adria Italy 15 45.03N 12.03E
Adrian Mich. U.S.A. 84 41.55N 84.01W
Adrian Mo. U.S.A. 82 38.24N 94.21W
Adrian Tex. U.S.A. 83 35.16N102.40W
Adriatic Sea Med. Sea 18 42.30N 16.00E
Ādwa Ethiopia 48 14.12N 38.56E
Adzopé Ivory Coast 52 6.07N 3.49W
Adzwa r. U.S.S.R. 24 66.30N 59.30E
Aegean Sea Med. Sea 19 39.00N 25.00E
Āfdem Ethiopia 49 9.26N 41.02E
Afghanistan Asia 40 32.45N 65.00E
'Afif Saudi Arabia 42 23.53N 42.59E
Afikpo Nigeria 53 5.53N 7.55E
Afjord Norway 22 63.57N 10.12E
Aflou Algeria 51 34.07N 2.06E
Afmadow Somali Rep. 55 0.27N 42.05E
Afobaka Surinam 91 5.00N 55.05W
Afognak I. U.S.A. 72 58.15N152.30W
Afonso Cláudio Brazil 94 20.05S 41.06W
Afsluitdijk f. Neth. 14 53.04N 5.11E
'Afula Israel 44 32.36N 35.17E
Afyon Turkey 42 38.46N 30.32E
Agadez Niger 53 17.00N 7.56E
Agadez d. Niger 53 19.25N 11.00E
Agadir Morocco 50 30.26N 9.36W
Agalak Sudan 49 11.01N 32.42E
Agana Guam 37 13.28N144.45E
Agapa U.S.S.R. 29 71.29N 86.16E
Agar India 40 23.42N 76.01E
Āgaro Ethiopia 49 7.50N 36.40E
Agartala India 41 23.49N 91.16E
Agaru Sudan 49 10.59N 34.44E
Agboville Ivory Coast 52 5.55N 4.15W
Agde France 17 43.19N 3.28E
Agen France 17 44.12N 0.38E
Ageo Japan 35 35.58N139.36E
Agger r. Germany 14 50.45N 7.06E
Aghada Rep. of Ire. 13 51.50N 8.13W
Agia India 41 26.05N 90.32E
Aginskoye U.S.S.R. 29 51.10N114.32E
Agnew Australia 63 28.01S120.30E
Ago Japan 35 34.17N136.48E
Agordo Italy 15 46.17N 12.02E
Agouma Gabon 54 1.33S 10.08E
Āgra India 41 27.11N 78.01E
Agra r. Spain 16 42.12N 1.43W
Agraciada Uruguay 93 33.48S 58.15W
Agreda Spain 16 41.51N 1.55W
Agri r. Italy 19 40.13N 16.45E
Agri Turkey 42 39.44N 43.04E
Agri Dagi mtn. Turkey 43 39.45N 44.15E
Agrigento Italy 18 37.19N 13.36E
Agrihan i. Mariana Is. 37 18.44N145.39E
Agropoli Italy 18 40.21N 15.00E
Agryz U.S.S.R. 24 56.30N 53.00E
Agsumal, Sebjet f. W. Sahara 50 24.21N 12.52W
Agua Caliente, Cerro mtn. Mexico 81 26.27N106.12W
Aguanish Canada 77 50.16N 62.10W
Aguanus r. Canada 77 50.12N 62.10W
Agua Prieta Mexico 81 31.18N109.34W
Aguas Blancas Chile 92 24.13S 69.50W
Aguascalientes Mexico 86 21.51N102.18W
Aguascalientes d. Mexico 86 22.00N102.00W
Agudos Brazil 94 22.27S 49.03W
Águeda r. Spain 16 41.00N 6.56W
Aguelhok Mali 50 19.28N 0.52E
Aguema Angola 54 12.03S 21.52E
Aguêraktem well Mali 50 23.07N 6.12W
Aguilar de Campóo Spain 16 42.47N 4.15W
Águilas Spain 16 37.25N 1.35W
Aguit China 32 41.42N113.20E
Āgula'i Ethiopia 48 13.42N 39.35E
Agulhas, C. R.S.A. 56 34.50S 20.00E
Agulhas Basin f. Indian Oc. 95 43.00S 25.00E
Agulhas Negras mtn. Brazil 94 22.20S 44.43W
Agung, Gunung mtn. Indonesia 37 8.20S115.28E
Ahaggar f. Algeria 51 23.36N 5.50E
Ahar Iran 43 38.25N 47.07E
Ahaura New Zealand 60 42.21S171.33E
Ahaus Germany 14 52.04N 7.01E
Ahklun Mts. U.S.A. 72 59.15N161.00W
Ahlen Germany 14 51.47N 7.52E
Ahmadābād India 40 23.02N 72.37E
Aḩmadī Iran 43 27.56N 56.42E
Ahmadnagar India 40 19.05N 74.44E
Ahmadpur East Pakistan 40 29.09N 71.16E
Ahmadpur Siāl Pakistan 40 30.41N 71.46E
Ahmad Wāl Pakistan 40 29.25N 65.56E
Ahmar Mts. Ethiopia 49 9.15N 41.00E
Ahoada Nigeria 53 5.06N 6.39E
Ahr r. Germany 14 50.34N 7.16E
Ahram Iran 43 28.52N 51.16E
Ahraura India 41 25.01N 83.01E
Aḩsā', Wāḩat al oasis Saudi Arabia 43 25.37N 49.40E
Ähtäri Finland 22 62.34N 24.06E
Åhus Sweden 23 55.55N 14.17E
Ahvāz Iran 43 31.17N 48.44E
Ahvenanmaa d. Finland 23 60.15N 20.00E
Ahvenanmaa is. Finland 23 60.15N 20.00E
Aichi d. Japan 35 35.02N137.15E
Aigle Switz. 15 46.19N 6.58E
Aigues-Mortes France 17 43.34N 4.11E
Aiken U.S.A. 85 33.34N 81.44W
Aileron Australia 64 22.38S133.20E
Ailette r. France 14 49.35N 3.09E
Ailsa Craig i. U.K. 12 55.15N 5.07W
Aim U.S.S.R. 29 58.50N134.15E
Aimorés Brazil 94 19.30S 41.04W
Ain r. France 17 45.47N 5.12E
Aïna r. Gabon 54 0.38N 12.47E
Ainaži U.S.S.R. 23 57.52N 24.21E
Aïn Beïda Algeria 51 35.50N 7.27E
Aïn ben Tili Mauritania 50 26.00N 9.32W
Aïn Galakka Chad 51 18.04N 18.24E
Aïn Sefra Algeria 50 32.45N 0.35W
Aïr mts. Niger 53 18.30N 8.30E
Airdrie U.K. 12 55.52N 3.59W
Aire France 17 43.39N 0.15W
Aire r. France 15 49.19N 4.49E
Aire r. U.K. 10 53.42N 0.54W
Aisne d. France 15 49.30N 3.30E
Aisne r. France 15 49.27N 2.51E
Aitape P.N.G. 37 3.10S142.17E
Aitkin U.S.A. 82 46.32N 93.43W
Aït Ourir Morocco 50 31.38N 7.42W
Aitutaki Atoll Cook Is. 69 18.52S159.46W
Aiud Romania 21 46.19N 23.44E
Aix-en-Provence France 17 43.31N 5.27E
Aix-les-Bains France 17 45.42N 5.55E
Aíyina i. Greece 19 37.43N 23.30E
Aíyion Greece 19 38.15N 22.05E
Aizpute U.S.S.R. 23 56.43N 21.38E
Ajaccio France 17 41.55N 8.43E
Ajanta Range mts. India 40 20.15N 75.30E
Ajax Canada 76 43.51N 79.02W
Ajdābiyā Libya 48 30.46N 20.14E
Ajibar Ethiopia 49 10.41N 38.37E
'Ajlūn Jordan 44 32.20N 35.45E
'Ajmah, Jabal al f. Egypt 44 29.12N 33.58E
'Ajmān U.A.E. 43 25.23N 55.26E
Ajmer India 40 26.27N 74.38E
Ajnāla India 40 31.51N 74.47E
Ajo U.S.A. 81 32.22N112.52W
Akaishi sammyaku mts. Japan 35 35.20N138.10E
Akámas, Akrotírion c. Cyprus 44 35.06N 32.17E
Akaroa New Zealand 60 43.50S172.59E
'Akasha East Sudan 48 21.05N 30.43E
Akashi Japan 35 34.38N134.59E
Akbarpur India 41 26.25N 82.33E
Akbulak U.S.S.R. 25 51.00N 55.40E
Akelamo Indonesia 37 1.35N129.40E
Akershus d. Norway 23 60.00N 11.10E
Aketi Zaïre 54 2.46N 23.51E
Akhaltsikhe U.S.S.R. 42 41.37N 42.59E
Akhḑar, Al Jabal al mts. Libya 48 32.30N 21.30E
Akhḑar, Al Jabal al mts. Oman 43 23.10N 57.25E
Akhḑar, Wādī r. Egypt 44 28.42N 33.41E
Akhḑar, Wādī al r. Saudi Arabia 44 28.30N 36.48E
Akhelóös Greece 19 38.20N 21.04E
Akhisar Turkey 19 38.54N 27.49E
Akhmīm Egypt 42 26.34N 31.44E
Akhtyrka U.S.S.R. 25 50.19N 34.54E
Akimiski I. Canada 76 53.00N 81.20W
Akita Japan 31 39.44N140.05E
Akjoujt Mauritania 50 19.44N 14.26W
Akkajaure l. Sweden 22 67.40N 17.30E
'Akko Israel 44 32.55N 35.04E
Akkol U.S.S.R. 30 45.04N 75.39E
Aklavik Canada 72 68.12N135.00W
Ako Nigeria 53 10.19N 10.48E
Ākobo r. Ethiopia 49 8.30N 33.15E
Akola India 40 20.44N 77.00E
Āk'ordat Ethiopia 48 15.35N 37.55E
Akot India 40 21.11N 77.04E
Akpatok I. Canada 73 60.30N 68.30W
Akranes Iceland 22 64.19N 22.05W
Akron Colo. U.S.A. 82 40.10N103.13W
Akron Ohio U.S.A. 84 41.04N 81.31W
Akrotíri Cyprus 44 34.36N 32.57E
Aksaray Turkey 42 38.22N 34.02E
Aksarka U.S.S.R. 28 66.31N 67.50E
Aksay China 30 39.28N 94.15E
Aksay U.S.S.R. 25 51.24N 52.11E
Akşehir Turkey 42 38.22N 31.24E
Aksu China 30 42.10N 80.00E
Āksum Ethiopia 48 14.08N 38.48E
Aktag mtn. China 30 36.45N 84.40E
Aktogay U.S.S.R. 30 46.59N 79.42E
Aktyubinsk U.S.S.R. 25 50.16N 57.13E
Akūbū Sudan 49 7.47N 33.01E
Akūbū r. see Ākobo r. Sudan 49
Akula Zaïre 54 2.22N 20.11E
Akure Nigeria 53 7.14N 5.08E
Akureyri Iceland 22 65.41N 18.04W
Akuse Ghana 52 6.04N 0.12E
Akwa-Ibom d. Nigeria 53 4.45N 7.50E
Akxokesay China 30 36.48N 91.06E
Akyab see Sittwe Burma 34
Akyel Ethiopia 49 12.30N 37.04E
Ål Norway 23 60.38N 8.34E
Alabama d. U.S.A. 85 32.50N 87.00W
Alabama r. U.S.A. 83 31.08N 87.57W
Al 'Abbāsīyah Sudan 49 14.27N 33.31E
Ālādāgh, Kūh-e mts. Iran 43 37.15N 57.30E
Alagoas d. Brazil 91 9.30S 37.00W
Alagoinhas Brazil 91 12.09S 38.21W
Alagón Spain 16 41.46N 1.12W
Alakol, Ozero l. U.S.S.R. 30 46.00N 81.40E
Alakurtti U.S.S.R. 24 67.00N 30.23E
Al 'Alamayn Egypt 42 30.49N 28.57E
Al 'Amārah Iraq 43 31.52N 47.50E
Al Āmirīyah Egypt 44 31.01N 29.48E
Alamogordo U.S.A. 81 32.54N105.57W
Alamos, Rio de los r. Mexico 83 27.53N101.12W
Alamosa U.S.A. 80 37.28N105.52W
Åland is. see Ahvenanmaa is. Finland 23
Ålands Hav sea Finland 23 60.00N 19.30E
Alanreed U.S.A. 83 35.14N100.45W
Alanya Turkey 42 36.32N 32.02E
Alaotra, Lac l. Madagascar 57 17.30S 48.30E
Alapayevsk U.S.S.R. 24 57.55N 61.42E
Alappuzha India 38 9.30N 76.22E
Al 'Aqabah Jordan 44 29.32N 35.00E
Al 'Aramah f. Saudi Arabia 43 25.30N 46.30E
Alarcón, Embalse de resr. Spain 16 39.36N 2.10W
Al 'Arīsh Egypt 44 31.08N 33.48E
Alaşehir Turkey 19 38.22N 28.29E
Alaska d. U.S.A. 72 65.00N153.00W
Alaska, G. of U.S.A. 72 58.45N145.00W
Alaska Pen. U.S.A. 72 56.00N160.00W
Alaska Range mts. U.S.A. 72 62.10N152.00W
Alassio Italy 15 44.00N 8.10E
Al 'Atīqah Lebanon 44 33.42N 35.27E
Al 'Aţrun Sudan 48 18.11N 26.36E
Alatyr U.S.S.R. 24 54.51N 46.35E
Alausí Ecuador 90 2.00S 78.50W
Alavus Finland 22 62.35N 23.37E
Alawoona Australia 66 34.44S140.33E
Al 'Ayn wells Sudan 48 16.36N 29.19E
Al 'Ayyāţ Egypt 44 29.37N 31.15E
Alazani r. U.S.S.R. 43 41.06N 46.40E
Alba Italy 15 44.42N 8.02E
Albacete Spain 16 39.00N 1.52W
Al Bad' Saudi Arabia 44 28.29N 35.02E
Al Badārī Egypt 42 26.59N 31.25E
Al Bahnasā Egypt 44 28.32N 30.39E
Al Baḩr al Aḩmar d. Sudan 48 19.30N 35.30E
Alba-Iulia Romania 21 46.04N 23.33E
Albania Europe 19 41.00N 20.00E
Albany Australia 63 34.57S117.54E
Albany r. Canada 76 52.10N 82.00W
Albany Ga. U.S.A. 85 31.37N 84.10W
Albany Ky. U.S.A. 85 36.42N 85.08W
Albany Minn. U.S.A. 82 45.38N 94.34W
Albany N.Y. U.S.A. 84 42.39N 73.45W
Albany Oreg. U.S.A. 80 44.38N123.06W
Al Başrah Iraq 43 30.33N 47.50E
Al Bāţinah f. Oman 43 24.25N 56.50E
Albatross B. Australia 64 12.45S141.43E
Al Batrūn Lebanon 44 34.16N 35.40E
Al Bawīţī Egypt 42 28.21N 25.52E
Al Bayāḑ f. Saudi Arabia 45 22.00N 47.00E
Al Bayḑā' Libya 51 32.46N 21.43E
Albemarle Sd. U.S.A. 79 36.10N 76.00W
Albenga Italy 15 44.03N 8.13E
Alberche r. Spain 16 40.00N 4.45W
Alberga Australia 65 27.12S135.28E
Alberga r. Australia 65 27.12S135.28E
Albermarle U.S.A. 85 35.21N 80.12W
Albermarle Sd. U.S.A. 85 36.03N 76.12W
Albert Australia 67 32.21S147.33E
Albert France 14 50.02N 2.38E
Albert, L. Australia 66 35.38S139.17E
Albert, L. Uganda / Zaïre 55 1.45N 31.00E
Alberta d. Canada 74 54.00N115.00W
Alberti Argentina 93 35.01S 60.16W
Albertirsa Hungary 21 47.15N 19.38E
Albert Kanaal canal Belgium 14 51.00N 5.15
Albert Lea U.S.A. 82 43.39N 93.22W
Albert Nile r. Uganda 55 3.30N 32.00E
Alberton Canada 77 46.49N 64.04W
Albi France 17 43.56N 2.08E
Al Bidia Chad 49 10.33N 20.13E
Albin U.S.A. 80 41.26N104.08W
Albina Surinam 91 5.30N 54.03W
Albino Italy 15 45.46N 9.47E
Albion Mich. U.S.A. 84 42.14N 84.45W
Albion Mont. U.S.A. 80 45.11N104.15W
Albion Nebr. U.S.A. 82 41.42N 98.00W
Albion N.Y. U.S.A. 76 43.15N 78.12W
Albion Penn. U.S.A. 84 41.53N 80.22W
Al Bi'r Saudi Arabia 44 28.52N 36.15E
Alborán, Isla de i. Spain 16 35.55N 3.10W
Ålborg Denmark 23 57.03N 9.56E
Ålborg Bugt b. Denmark 23 56.45N 10.30E
Alborz, Reshteh-ye Kūhhā-ye mts. Iran 43 36.00N 52.30E
Albuquerque U.S.A. 81 35.05N106.40W
Al Buraymī U.A.E. 43 24.15N 55.45E
Al Burj Egypt 44 31.35N 30.59E
Alburquerque Spain 16 39.13N 6.59W
Albury Australia 67 36.03S146.53E
Al Buţanah f. Sudan 48 14.50N 34.30E
Alby Sweden 22 62.30N 15.25E
Alcácer do Sal Portugal 16 38.22N 8.30W
Alcalá de Chisvert Spain 16 40.19N 0.13E
Alcalá de Henares Spain 16 40.28N 3.22W
Alcalá la Real Spain 16 37.28N 3.55W
Alcamo Italy 18 37.59N 12.58E
Alcañiz Spain 16 41.03N 0.09W
Alcántara, Embalse de resr. Spain 16 39.4 6.25W
Alcantara L. Canada 75 60.57N108.09W
Alcaudete Spain 16 37.35N 4.05W
Alcázar de San Juan Spain 16 39.24N 3.12
Alcira Spain 16 39.10N 0.27W
Alcobaça Portugal 16 39.33N 8.59W
Alcova U.S.A. 80 42.35N106.34W
Alcoy Spain 16 38.42N 0.29W
Alcubierre, Sierra de mts. Spain 16 41.40N 0.20W
Alcudia Spain 16 39.51N 3.09E
Aldan U.S.S.R. 29 58.44N125.22E
Aldan r. U.S.S.R. 29 63.30N130.00E
Aldeburgh U.K. 11 52.09N 1.35E
Alderney i. U.K. 11 49.42N 2.11W
Aldershot U.K. 11 51.15N 0.47W
Alderson Canada 75 50.20N111.25W
Aldridge U.K. 11 52.36N 1.55W
Aledo U.S.A. 82 41.12N 90.45W
Aleg Mauritania 50 17.03N 13.55W
Alegre Brazil 94 20.44S 41.30W
Alegrete Brazil 93 29.46S 55.46W
Aleksandrov Gay U.S.S.R. 25 50.08N 48.3

ndrovsk Sakhalinskiy U.S.S.R. 29 N142.12E
e Gabon 54 0.03N 10.57E
araíba Brazil 94 21.49S 42.36W
n France 15 48.25N 0.05E
haha Channel Hawaiian Is. 69 N156.00W
see Halab Syria 42
France 17 42.05N 9.30E
rance 17 44.08N 4.05E
ndria Italy 15 44.54N 8.37E
d Norway 22 62.28N 6.11E
n Basin Bering Sea 68 57.00N179.00E
n Is U.S.A. 68 52.00N176.00W
n Range mts. U.S.A. 72 N156.00W
n Trench Pacific Oc. 68 N176.00W
der U.S.A. 76 42.54N 78.16W
der Archipelago is. U.S.A. 74 N134.30W
nder Bay town R.S.A. 56 28.36S 16.26E
der I. Antarctica 96 72.00S 70.00W
dra Australia 67 37.12S145.14E
dra New Zealand 60 45.14S169.26E
dria B.C. Canada 74 52.35N122.27W
dria Ont. Canada 77 45.18N 74.39W
dria see Al Iskandarīyah Egypt 44
dria Romania 21 43.58N 25.20E
dria R.S.A. 56 33.39S 26.24E
dria La. U.S.A. 83 31.18N 92.27W
dria Minn. U.S.A. 82 45.53N 95.22W
dria Va. U.S.A. 85 38.48N 77.03W
drina, L. Australia 66 35.26S139.10E
droúpolis Greece 19 40.50N 25.53E
r. Canada 77 52.32N 56.08W
Creek town Canada 74 52.05N123.20W
U.S.S.R. 28 52.32N 82.45E
t Egypt 44 28.46N 30.53E
Spain 16 42.11N 1.45W
hir Sudan 49 13.38N 25.21E
hn Egypt 44 28.49N 30.54E
Iraq 43 29.57N 48.30E
yūm Egypt 44 29.19N 30.50E
Germany 20 51.59N 9.50E
s Brazil 94 21.28S 45.48W
Sudan 49 10.03N 25.01E
r. Greece 19 37.37N 21.27E
ine Italy 15 44.30N 12.03E
U.K. 12 57.14N 2.42W
ayrah U.A.E. 43 25.10N 56.20E
J.S.S.R. 28 49.49N 57.16E
Norway 23 58.46N 5.51E
bir Sudan 49 13.43N 29.49E
iras Spain 16 36.08N 5.27W
nesí Spain 16 39.11N 0.27W
a Ethiopia 48 16.20N 38.34E
Algeria 51 36.50N 3.00E
a Africa 50 28.00N 2.00E
ayl Saudi Arabia 43 22.36N 46.19E
ro Italy 18 40.33N 8.20E
urdaqah Egypt 42 27.14N 33.50E
s see Alger Algeria 51
B. R.S.A. 56 33.50S 26.00E
na U.S.A. 82 44.36N 87.27W
na U.S.A. 82 43.04N 94.14W
quin Prov. Park Canada 76 45.27N 8W
ta Uruguay 93 32.25S 57.23W
jar al Gharbī mts. Oman 43 24.00N 0E
jar ash Sharqī mts. Oman 43 22.45N 5E
na Spain 16 37.51N 1.25W
mād des. Saudi Arabia 42 31.45N 39.00E
mar Saudi Arabia 43 22.26N 46.12E
nbra U.S.A. 81 34.06N118.08W
midīyah Syria 44 34.43N 35.56E
nākīyah Saudi Arabia 42 24.53N 40.30E
rīq Saudi Arabia 43 23.37N 46.31E
rūj al Aswad hills Libya 51 27.00N 10E
sakah Syria 42 36.29N 40.45E
wāmidīyah Egypt 44 29.54N 31.15E
yz Egypt 42 28.02N 28.39E
āz f. Saudi Arabia 42 26.00N 37.30E
llah Iraq 43 32.28N 44.29E
llah Saudi Arabia 43 23.30N 46.51E
rmil Lebanon 44 34.25N 36.23E
ceima Morocco 50 35.15N 3.55W
daydah Yemen 48 14.50N 42.58E
fūf Saudi Arabia 43 25.20N 49.34E
mrah des. U.A.E. 43 22.45N 55.10E
saynīyah Egypt 44 30.52N 31.55E
waymī Yemen 45 14.05N 47.44E
ād, Kūh-e mtn. Iran 43 34.09N 50.48E
mon r. Greece 19 40.30N 22.38E
nte Spain 16 38.21N 0.29W
R.S.A. 56 32.47S 26.49E
U.S.A. 83 27.45N 98.04W
Arm Canada 74 55.29N129.31W
Springs town Australia 64 42S133.52E
rh India 41 27.53N 78.05E
darz Iran 43 33.25N 49.38E
q, Kūh-e mtn. Iran 43 31.27N 51.43E
a r. Congo 54 1.36S 16.35E
ao C.A.R. 49 5.02N 21.13E
sås Sweden 23 57.56N 12.31E
r Pakistan 40 29.23N 70.55E
r Duār India 41 26.29N 89.44E
r Janūbī Pakistan 40 30.13N 71.18E
ippa U.S.A. 84 40.30N 80.16W
q Libya 51 29.05N 15.48E
abieh Djibouti 49 11.09N 42.42E
kandarīyah Egypt 44 31.13N 29.55E
mā'īlīyah Egypt 44 30.36N 32.15E
al North R.S.A. 56 30.41S 26.41E

Al Jabal al Akhḑar *d.* Libya **51** 32.00N 21.30E
Al Jafr Jordan **44** 30.16N 36.11E
Al Jāfūrah *des.* Saudi Arabia **43** 24.40N 50.20E
Al Jaghbūb Libya **48** 29.45N 24.31E
Al Jahrah Kuwait **43** 29.20N 47.41E
Al Jaladah *f.* Saudi Arabia **45** 18.30N 46.25E
Al Jawārah Oman **38** 18.55N 57.17E
Al Jawb *f.* Saudi Arabia **43** 23.00N 50.00E
Al Jawf Libya **48** 24.12N 23.18E
Al Jawf Saudi Arabia **42** 29.49N 39.52E
Al Jawsh Libya **51** 32.00N 11.40E
Al Jazīrah *f.* Iraq **42** 35.00N 41.00E
Al Jazīrah *d.* Sudan **48** 14.35N 33.30E
Al Jazīrah *f.* Sudan **48** 14.25N 33.00E
Al Jifārah Saudi Arabia **43** 23.59N 45.11E
Al Jīzah Egypt **44** 30.01N 31.12E
Al Jubayl Saudi Arabia **43** 27.59N 49.40E
Al Junaynah Sudan **49** 13.27N 22.27E
Aljustrel Portugal **16** 37.55N 8.10W
Al Karabah Sudan **48** 18.33N 33.42E
Al Karak Jordan **44** 31.11N 35.42E
Al Kawah Sudan **49** 13.44N 32.30E
Al Khābūr *r.* Syria **42** 35.07N 40.30E
Al Khābūrah Oman **43** 23.58N 57.10E
Al Khalīl Jordan **44** 31.32N 35.06E
Al Khamāsīn Saudi Arabia **45** 20.29N 44.49E
Al Khandaq Sudan **48** 18.36N 30.34E
Al Khānkah Egypt **44** 30.12N 31.21E
Al Khārijah Egypt **42** 25.26N 30.33E
Al Kharṭūm Sudan **48** 15.33N 32.35E
Al Kharṭūm *d.* Sudan **48** 15.45N 32.30E
Al Kharṭūm Baḩrī Sudan **48** 15.39N 32.34E
Al Khasfah *well* Oman **45** 19.45N 54.19E
Al Khawr Qatar **43** 25.39N 51.32E
Al Khirbah as Samrā' Jordan **44** 32.11N 36.10E
Al Khubar Saudi Arabia **43** 26.18N 50.06E
Al Khufayfīyah Saudi Arabia **43** 24.55N 44.42E
Al Khums Libya **51** 32.39N 14.16E
Al Khums *d.* Libya **51** 31.20N 14.10E
Al Khunn Saudi Arabia **43** 23.18N 49.15E
Al Kidn *des.* Saudi Arabia **43** 22.20N 54.20E
Al Kiswah Syria **44** 33.21N 36.14E
Alkmaar Neth. **14** 52.37N 4.44E
Al Kufrah Libya **48** 24.14N 23.15E
Al Kuntillah Egypt **44** 30.00N 34.41E
Al Kūt Iraq **43** 32.30N 45.51E
Al Kuwayt Kuwait **43** 29.20N 48.00E
Al Labwah Lebanon **44** 34.11N 36.21E
Al Lādhiqīyah Syria **44** 35.31N 35.47E
Al Lagowa Sudan **49** 11.24N 29.08E
Allāhābād India **41** 25.27N 81.51E
Allakaket U.S.A. **72** 66.30N152.45W
Allanche France **17** 45.14N 2.56E
'Allāqī, Wādī al *r.* Egypt **42** 22.55N 33.02E
Allegheny *r.* U.S.A. **84** 40.27N 80.00W
Allegheny Mts. U.S.A. **84** 38.30N 80.00W
Allen, Lough Rep. of Ire. **13** 54.07N 8.04W
Allentown U.S.A. **85** 40.37N 75.30W
Aller *r.* Germany **20** 52.57N 9.11E
Alliance Nebr. U.S.A. **82** 42.06N102.52W
Allier *r.* France **17** 46.58N 3.04E
Al Līṭānī *r.* Lebanon **44** 33.22N 35.14E
Al Līth Saudi Arabia **48** 20.09N 40.16E
Al Līwā' *f.* U.A.E. **45** 23.00N 54.00E
Alloa U.K. **12** 56.07N 3.49W
Allos France **17** 44.14N 6.38E
Al Luḩayyah Yemen **48** 15.43N 42.42E
Alluitsup-Paa *see* Sydpröven Greenland **73**
Alma Canada **77** 48.32N 71.40W
Alma Ga. U.S.A. **85** 31.33N 82.29W
Alma Mich. U.S.A. **84** 43.23N 84.40W
Al Ma'ānīyah *well* Iraq **42** 30.44N 43.00E
Alma-Ata U.S.S.R. **30** 43.19N 76.55E
Almadén Spain **16** 38.47N 4.50W
Al Madīnah Saudi Arabia **42** 24.30N 39.35E
Al Madīnah al Fikrīyah Egypt **44** 27.56N 30.49E
Al Mafraq Jordan **44** 32.20N 36.12E
Al Maghrah *well* Egypt **42** 30.14N 28.56E
Almagor Israel **44** 32.55N 35.36E
Al Maḩallah al Kubrá Egypt **44** 30.59N 31.12E
Al Maḩārīq Egypt **42** 25.37N 30.39E
Al Maḩmūdīyah Egypt **44** 31.10N 30.30E
Al Majma'ah Saudi Arabia **43** 25.52N 45.25E
Al Manāmah Bahrain **43** 26.12N 50.36E
Almanor U.S.A. **80** 40.15N121.08W
Almansa Spain **16** 38.52N 1.06W
Al Manshāh Egypt **42** 26.28N 31.48E
Al Manṣūrah Egypt **44** 31.03N 31.23E
Al Manzil Jordan **44** 31.03N 36.01E
Al Manzilah Egypt **44** 31.10N 31.56E
Almanzor, Pico de *mtn.* Spain **16** 40.20N 5.22W
Almanzora *r.* Spain **16** 37.16N 1.49W
Al Marj Libya **48** 32.30N 20.50E
Al Maṭarīyah Egypt **44** 31.12N 32.02E
Al Matnah Sudan **48** 13.47N 35.03E
Al Mawṣil Iraq **42** 36.21N 43.08E
Al Mayādīn Syria **42** 35.01N 40.28E
Almazán Spain **16** 41.29N 2.31W
Al Mazra'ah Jordan **44** 31.16N 35.31E
Almeirim Portugal **16** 39.12N 8.37W
Almelo Neth. **14** 52.21N 6.40E
Almendralejo Spain **16** 38.41N 6.26W
Almería Spain **16** 36.50N 2.26W
Älmhult Sweden **23** 56.33N 14.08E
Al Midhnab Saudi Arabia **43** 25.52N 44.15E
Al Miḩrāḑ *des.* Saudi Arabia **43** 20.00N 52.30E
Al Minyā Egypt **44** 28.06N 30.45E
Al Mismīyah Syria **44** 33.08N 36.24E
Almonte Spain **16** 37.16N 6.31W
Almora India **41** 29.37N 79.40E
Al Mudawwarah Jordan **44** 29.20N 36.00E
Al Muglad Sudan **49** 11.02N 27.44E
Al Muḩarraq Bahrain **43** 26.16N 50.38E
Al Mukallā Yemen **45** 14.34N 49.09E

Al Mukhā Yemen **49** 13.19N 43.15E
Almuñécar Spain **16** 36.44N 3.41W
Al Muwayh Saudi Arabia **42** 22.41N 41.37E
Alnwick U.K. **10** 55.25N 1.41W
Alofi Niue **68** 19.03S169.55W
Alofi B. Niue **68** 19.02S169.55W
Alónnisos *i.* Greece **19** 39.08N 23.50E
Alonsa Canada **75** 50.50N 99.00W
Alor *i.* Indonesia **37** 8.20S124.30E
Alor Setar Malaysia **36** 6.06N100.23E
Alozero U.S.S.R. **24** 65.02N 31.10E
Alpena U.S.A. **84** 45.04N 83.27W
Alpes Maritimes *mts.* France **17** 44.07N 7.08E
Alpha Australia **64** 23.39S146.38E
Alphen Neth. **14** 52.08N 4.40E
Alpine U.S.A. **83** 30.22N103.40W
Alps *mts.* Europe **17** 46.00N 7.30E
Al Qaḑārif Sudan **48** 14.02N 35.24E
Al Qaḑīmah Saudi Arabia **48** 22.21N 39.09E
Al Qafā' *des.* U.A.E. **43** 23.30N 53.30E
Al Qāhirah Egypt **44** 30.03N 31.15E
Al Qā'īyah Saudi Arabia **42** 24.18N 43.30E
Al Qā'īyah *well* Saudi Arabia **43** 26.27N 45.35E
Al Qalībah Saudi Arabia **42** 28.24N 37.42E
Al Qanāṭir al Khayrīyah Egypt **44** 30.12N 31.08E
Al Qanṭarah Egypt **44** 30.52N 32.20E
Al Qaryatayn Syria **44** 34.13N 37.13E
Al Qaṣabāt Libya **51** 32.35N 14.03E
Al Qaṣr Egypt **42** 25.43N 28.54E
Al Qaṣṣāṣīn Egypt **44** 30.34N 31.56E
Al Qaṭīf Saudi Arabia **43** 26.31N 50.00E
Al Qaṭrānah Jordan **44** 31.15N 36.03E
Al Qaṭrūn Libya **51** 24.56N 14.38E
Al Qayṣūmah Saudi Arabia **43** 28.20N 46.07E
Al Qunayṭirah Syria **44** 33.08N 35.49E
Al Qunfudhah Saudi Arabia **48** 19.08N 41.05E
Al Qurnah Iraq **43** 31.00N 47.26E
Al Quṣaymah Egypt **44** 30.40N 34.22E
Al Quṣayr Egypt **42** 26.06N 34.17E
Al Qūṣīyah Egypt **42** 27.26N 30.49E
Al Quṭayfah Syria **44** 33.44N 36.36E
Alroy Downs *town* Australia **64** 19.18S136.04E
Als *i.* Denmark **23** 54.59N 9.55E
Alsace *d.* France **17** 48.25N 7.40E
Alsask Canada **75** 51.23N109.59W
Alsasua Spain **16** 42.54N 2.10W
Älsborg *d.* Sweden **23** 58.00N 12.20E
Alsek Ranges *mts.* Canada **74** 59.21N137.05W
Alsfeld Germany **20** 50.45N 9.16E
Alsten *i.* Norway **22** 65.55N 12.35E
Alston U.K. **12** 54.48N 2.26W
Alta Norway **22** 70.00N 23.15E
Alta *r.* Norway **22** 69.50N 23.30E
Altafjorden *est.* Norway **22** 70.10N 23.00E
Alta Gracia Argentina **92** 31.40S 64.26W
Altagracia de Orituco Venezuela **90** 9.54N 66.24W
Altai *mts.* Mongolia **30** 46.30N 93.30E
Altamaha *r.* U.S.A. **85** 31.19N 81.17W
Altamira Brazil **91** 3.12S 52.12W
Altamont Oreg. U.S.A. **80** 42.12N121.44W
Altamura Italy **19** 40.50N 16.32E
Altar, Desierto de *des.* Mexico **81** 31.50N114.15W
Altavista U.S.A. **85** 37.07N 79.18W
Altay China **30** 47.48N 88.07E
Altay Mongolia **30** 46.20N 97.00E
Altea Spain **16** 38.37N 0.03W
Altenburg Germany **20** 50.59N 12.27E
Altenkirchen Germany **14** 50.41N 7.40E
Altiplanicie Mexicana *mts.* Mexico **83** 29.00N105.00W
Altnaharra U.K. **12** 58.16N 4.26W
Alto Araguaia Brazil **91** 17.19S 53.10W
Alto Molocue Mozambique **55** 15.38S 37.42E
Alton Canada **76** 43.52N 80.04W
Alton U.K. **11** 51.08N 0.59W
Alton U.S.A. **82** 38.55N 90.10W
Altona Germany **20** 53.32N 9.56E
Altoona U.S.A. **84** 40.30N 78.24W
Altun Shan *mts.* China **30** 38.10N 87.50E
Altus U.S.A. **83** 34.38N 99.20W
Al Ubayyiḑ Sudan **49** 13.11N 30.13E
Al Uḑayyah Sudan **49** 12.03N 28.17E
Aluk Sudan **49** 8.26N 27.32E
Al 'Ulá Saudi Arabia **42** 26.39N 37.58E
Al 'Uqaylah Libya **51** 30.16N 19.12E
Al Uqṣur Egypt **42** 25.41N 32.24E
Al Urduun *r.* Asia **44** 31.47N 35.31E
Al 'Uwaynah *well* Saudi Arabia **43** 26.46N 48.13E
Al 'Uwaynāt Libya **51** 25.48N 10.33E
Al 'Uyūn Saudi Arabia **43** 26.32N 43.41E
Alva U.S.A. **83** 36.48N 98.40W
Alvarado Mexico **86** 18.49N 95.46W
Älvdalen Sweden **23** 61.14N 14.02E
Alvesta Sweden **23** 56.54N 14.33E
Älvho Sweden **23** 61.30N 14.46E
Alvin U.S.A. **83** 29.25N 95.15W
Älvkarleby Sweden **23** 60.34N 17.27E
Älvsbyn Sweden **22** 65.39N 20.59E
Al Wajh Saudi Arabia **42** 26.16N 36.28E
Al Wakrah Qatar **43** 25.09N 51.36E
Alwar India **40** 27.34N 76.36E
Al Wazz Sudan **48** 15.01N 30.10E
Al Yamāmah Saudi Arabia **43** 24.11N 47.21E
Alyaty U.S.S.R. **43** 39.59N 49.20E
Alytus U.S.S.R. **21** 54.24N 24.03E
Alzada U.S.A. **80** 45.01N104.26W
Alzette *r.* Lux. **14** 49.52N 6.07E
Amadeus, L. Australia **62** 24.50S130.45E
Amadi Sudan **49** 5.31N 30.20E
Amadjuak Canada **73** 64.00N 72.50W
Amadjuak L. Canada **73** 65.00N 71.00W
Amagasaki Japan **35** 34.43N135.25E
Åmål Sweden **23** 59.03N 12.42E

Amaliás Greece **19** 37.48N 21.21E
Amalner India **40** 21.03N 75.04E
Amami ō shima *i.* Japan **31** 28.20N129.30E
Amamula Zaïre **55** 0.17S 27.49E
Amanā, L. Brazil **90** 2.35S 64.40W
Amānganj India **41** 24.26N 80.02E
Amangeldy U.S.S.R. **28** 50.12N 65.11E
Amapá Brazil **91** 2.00N 50.50W
Amapá *d.* Brazil **91** 2.00N 52.00W
Amarante Brazil **91** 6.14S 42.51W
Amaranth Canada **75** 50.36N 98.43W
Amareleja Portugal **16** 38.12N 7.13W
Amares Portugal **16** 41.38N 8.21W
Amarillo U.S.A. **83** 35.13N101.49W
Amar Jadīd Sudan **48** 14.28N 25.14E
Amarkantak India **41** 22.40N 81.45E
Amaro, Monte *mtn.* Italy **18** 42.06N 14.04E
Amasya Turkey **42** 40.37N 35.50E
Amazon *r. see* Amazonas *r.* Brazil **91**
Amazonas *d.* Brazil **90** 4.50S 64.00W
Amazonas *r.* Brazil **91** 2.00S 52.00W
Amazonas, Estuario do Rio *f.* Brazil **91** 0.00 50.30W
Amazon Delta *see* Amazonas, Estuario do Rio *f.* Brazil **91**
Amb Pakistan **40** 34.19N 72.51E
Ambāla India **40** 30.23N 76.46E
Ambalavao Madagascar **57** 21.50S 46.56E
Ambam Cameroon **53** 2.25N 11.16E
Ambarawa Indonesia **37** 7.12S110.30E
Ambarchik U.S.S.R. **29** 69.39N162.27E
Ambarnāth India **40** 19.11N 73.10E
Ambarnyy U.S.S.R. **24** 65.59N 33.53E
Ambato Ecuador **90** 1.18S 78.36W
Ambato-Boeni Madagascar **57** 16.28S 46.43E
Ambatofinandrahana Madagascar **57** 20.33S 46.48E
Ambatolampy Madagascar **57** 19.23S 47.25E
Ambatondrazaka Madagascar **57** 17.50S 48.25E
Amberg Germany **20** 49.27N 11.52E
Ambergris Cay *i.* Belize **87** 18.00N 87.58W
Ambidédi Mali **52** 14.35N 11.47W
Ambikāpur India **41** 23.07N 83.12E
Ambilobe Madagascar **57** 13.12S 49.04E
Amble U.K. **10** 55.20N 1.34W
Ambleside U.K. **10** 54.26N 2.58W
Ambodifototra Madagascar **57** 16.59S 49.52E
Ambohidratrimo Madagascar **57** 18.50S 47.26E
Ambohimahasoa Madagascar **57** 21.07S 47.13E
Ambohimanga du Sud Madagascar **57** 20.52S 47.36E
Amboise France **15** 47.25N 1.00E
Ambon Indonesia **37** 4.50S128.10E
Ambositra Madagascar **57** 20.31S 47.15E
Ambovombe Madagascar **57** 25.11S 46.05E
Amboy U.S.A. **81** 34.33N115.44W
Ambrières France **15** 48.24N 0.38W
Ambrim *i.* Vanuatu **68** 16.15S168.10E
Ambriz Angola **54** 7.54S 13.12E
Ambunten Indonesia **37** 6.55S113.45E
Am Dam Chad **49** 12.46N 20.29E
Amderma U.S.S.R. **28** 69.44N 61.35E
Amdo China **41** 32.22N 91.07E
Ameca Mexico **86** 20.33N104.02W
Ameland *i.* Neth. **14** 53.28N 5.48E
Amelia City U.S.A. **85** 30.37N 81.27W
Americana Brazil **94** 22.44S 47.19W
American Falls Resr. U.S.A. **80** 43.00N113.00W
American Fork U.S.A. **80** 40.23N111.48W
Americus U.S.A. **85** 32.04N 84.14W
Amersfoort Neth. **14** 52.10N 5.23E
Amery Australia **63** 31.09S117.05E
Ames U.S.A. **82** 42.02N 93.37W
Ameson Canada **76** 49.50N 84.35W
Ametinho Angola **54** 17.20S 17.20E
Amga U.S.S.R. **29** 60.51N131.59E
Amga *r.* U.S.S.R. **29** 62.40N135.20E
Am Géréda Chad **49** 12.52N 21.10E
Amgu U.S.S.R. **31** 45.48N137.36E
Amguid Algeria **51** 26.26N 5.22E
Amgun *r.* U.S.S.R. **29** 53.10N139.47E
Amhara Plateau *f.* Ethiopia **49** 11.00N 38.00E
Amherst Canada **77** 45.49N 64.14W
Amiata *mtn.* Italy **18** 42.53N 11.37E
Amiens France **15** 49.54N 2.18E
Amīr Chāh *well* Pakistan **40** 29.13N 62.28E
Amisk L. Canada **75** 54.35N102.13W
Amistad Resr. U.S.A. **83** 29.34N101.15W
Amite U.S.A. **83** 30.44N 90.33W
Amla India **41** 21.56N 78.07E
Amlekhganj Nepal **41** 27.17N 85.00E
Åmli Norway **23** 58.47N 8.30E
Amlwch U.K. **10** 53.24N 4.21W
'Ammān Jordan **44** 31.57N 35.56E
Ammanford U.K. **11** 51.48N 4.00W
Ammassalik Greenland **73** 65.40N 38.00W
Ammókhostos Cyprus **44** 35.07N 33.57E
Ammókhostou, Kólpos *b.* Cyprus **44** 35.12N 34.05E
Amo *r.* India **41** 25.58N 89.36E
Āmol Iran **43** 36.26N 52.24E
Amorgós *i.* Greece **19** 36.50N 25.55E
Amory U.S.A. **83** 33.59N 88.29W
Amos Canada **76** 48.35N 78.05W
Amoy *see* Xiamen China **33**
Ampala Honduras **87** 13.16N 87.39W
Ampanihy Madagascar **57** 24.42S 44.45E
Amparo Brazil **94** 22.44S 46.44W
Ampezzo Italy **15** 46.25N 12.48E
Amqui Canada **77** 48.28N 67.26W
Amrāvati India **41** 20.56N 77.45E
Amreli India **40** 21.37N 71.14E
Amritsar India **40** 31.38N 74.53E
Amroha India **41** 28.55N 78.28E

Am Saterna Chad **49** 12.26N 21.25E
Amsel Algeria **51** 22.37N 5.26E
Amstelveen Neth. **14** 52.18N 4.51E
Amsterdam Neth. **14** 52.22N 4.54E
Amsterdam N.Y. U.S.A. **84** 42.57N 74.11W
Am Timan Chad **49** 11.02N 20.17E
Amu Darya *r.* U.S.S.R. **28** 43.50N 59.00E
Amulet Canada **75** 49.40N104.45W
Amundsen G. Canada **72** 70.30N122.00W
Amundsen Sea Antarctica **96** 72.00S120.00W
Amuntai Indonesia **36** 2.24S115.14E
Amur *r.* U.S.S.R. **29** 53.17N140.00E
'Amūr, Wādī *r.* Sudan **48** 18.56N 33.34E
Amurzet U.S.S.R. **31** 47.50N131.05E
Anabar *r.* U.S.S.R. **29** 72.40N113.30E
Anabranch *r.* Australia **66** 34.08S141.46E
Anaco Venezuela **90** 9.27N 64.28W
Anaconda U.S.A. **80** 46.08N112.57W
Anadarko U.S.A. **83** 35.04N 98.15W
Anadolu *f.* Turkey **42** 38.00N 35.00E
Anadyr U.S.S.R. **29** 64.40N177.32E
Anadyr *r.* U.S.S.R. **29** 65.00N176.00E
Anadyrskiy Zaliv *g.* U.S.S.R. **29** 64.30N177.50W
Anáfi *i.* Greece **19** 36.21N 25.50E
Anaheim U.S.A. **81** 33.51N117.57W
Analalava Madagascar **57** 14.38S 47.45E
Anambas, Kepulauan *is.* Indonesia **36** 3.00N106.10E
Anambra *d.* Nigeria **53** 6.20N 7.25E
Anamoose U.S.A. **82** 47.53N100.15W
Anamur Turkey **42** 36.06N 32.49E
Ānand India **40** 22.34N 72.56E
Anandpur India **41** 21.16N 86.13E
Anantapur India **38** 14.41N 77.36E
Anantnāg Jammu & Kashmir **40** 33.44N 75.09E
Anápolis Brazil **91** 16.19S 48.58W
Anapú *r.* Brazil **91** 1.53S 50.53W
Anār Iran **43** 30.54N 55.18E
Anārak Iran **43** 33.20N 53.42E
Anār Darreh Afghan. **40** 32.46N 61.39E
Anatolia *f. see* Anadolu *f.* Turkey **42**
Anatone U.S.A. **80** 46.08N117.09W
Añatuya Argentina **92** 28.26S 62.48W
Ancenis France **15** 47.21N 1.10W
Anchau Nigeria **53** 11.00N 8.23E
Anchorage U.S.A. **72** 61.10N150.00W
Ancien Goubéré C.A.R. **49** 5.51N 26.46E
Ancohuma *mtn.* Bolivia **92** 16.05S 68.36W
Ancón Peru **90** 11.50S 77.10W
Ancona Italy **18** 43.37N 13.33E
Ancuabe Mozambique **55** 13.00S 39.50E
Ancud Chile **93** 41.05S 73.50W
Ancy-le-Franc France **15** 47.46N 4.10E
Anda China **31** 46.25N125.20E
Andalsnes Norway **22** 62.33N 7.43E
Andalucía *d.* Spain **16** 37.36N 4.30W
Andalusia U.S.A. **85** 31.20N 86.30W
Andaman Is. India **34** 12.00N 92.45E
Andaman Sea Indian Oc. **34** 10.00N 95.00E
Andamooka Australia **66** 30.27S137.12E
Andanga U.S.S.R. **24** 59.11N 45.44E
Andara Namibia **56** 18.04S 21.26E
Andelot France **17** 48.15N 5.18E
Andenes Norway **22** 69.18N 16.10E
Andenne Belgium **14** 50.29N 5.04E
Anderlecht Belgium **14** 50.51N 4.18E
Andernach Germany **14** 50.25N 7.24E
Anderson *r.* Canada **72** 69.45N129.00W
Anderson Ind. U.S.A. **84** 40.05N 85.41W
Anderson S.C. U.S.A. **85** 34.30N 82.39W
Andes *mts.* S. America **93** 32.40S 70.00W
Andevoranto Madagascar **57** 18.57S 49.06E
Andfjorden *est.* Norway **22** 68.55N 16.00E
Andhra Pradesh *d.* India **39** 17.00N 79.00E
Andikíthira *i.* Greece **19** 35.52N 23.18E
Andizhan U.S.S.R. **30** 40.48N 72.23E
Andoany Madagascar **57** 13.25S 48.16E
Andong S. Korea **31** 36.37N128.44E
Andorra *town* Andorra **17** 42.30N 1.31E
Andorra Europe **17** 42.30N 1.32E
Andover U.K. **11** 51.13N 1.29W
Andover N.J. U.S.A. **85** 40.59N 74.45W
Andöy *i.* Norway **22** 69.05N 15.40E
Andrada Angola **54** 7.41S 21.22E
Andrews N.C. U.S.A. **85** 35.13N 83.49W
Andrews Tex. U.S.A. **83** 32.19N102.33W
Andreyevo-Ivanovka U.S.S.R. **21** 47.28N 30.29E
Andria Italy **18** 41.13N 16.18E
Andriba Madagascar **57** 17.36S 46.55E
Androka Madagascar **57** 25.02S 44.05E
Andropov U.S.S.R. **24** 58.01N 38.52E
Ándros Greece **19** 37.50N 24.57E
Ándros *i.* Greece **19** 37.50N 24.50E
Andros I. Bahamas **87** 24.25N 78.00W
Andros Town Bahamas **87** 24.43N 77.47W
Andrushevka U.S.S.R. **21** 50.00N 28.59E
Andújar Spain **16** 38.02N 4.03W
Andulo Angola **54** 11.28S 16.43E
Anefis I-n-Darane Mali **52** 17.57N 0.35E
Anegada *i.* B.V.Is. **87** 18.46N 64.24W
Aného Togo **53** 6.17N 1.40E
Aneityum *i.* Vanuatu **68** 20.12S169.45E
Añelo Argentina **93** 38.20S 68.45W
Aneto, Pico de *mtn.* Spain **16** 42.40N 0.19E
Aney Niger **53** 19.24N 12.56E
Angara *r.* U.S.S.R. **29** 58.00N 93.00E
Angarsk U.S.S.R. **29** 52.31N103.55E
Angaston Australia **65** 34.30S139.03E
Angatuba Brazil **94** 23.27S 48.25W
Ånge Sweden **22** 62.31N 15.40E
Ángel de la Guarda, Isla *i.* Mexico **81** 29.20N113.25W
Angel Falls *f.* Venezuela **90** 5.55N 62.30W
Ängelholm Sweden **23** 56.15N 12.50E
Angels Camp U.S.A. **80** 38.04N120.32W
Ångereb *r.* Ethiopia **49** 13.45N 36.40E

Ängerman r. Sweden 22 63.00N 17.43E
Angermünde Germany 20 53.01N 14.00E
Angers France 15 47.29N 0.32W
Angerville France 15 48.19N 2.00E
Ångesån r. Sweden 22 66.22N 22.58E
Angikuni L. Canada 75 62.00N100.00W
Angkor ruins Cambodia 34 13.30N103.50E
Anglesey i. U.K. 10 53.16N 4.25W
Angleton U.S.A. 83 29.10N 95.26W
Ango Zaïre 49 4.02N 25.52E
Angoche Mozambique 57 16.10S 39.57E
Angol Chile 93 37.48S 72.43W
Angola Africa 54 11.00S 18.00E
Angola Ind. U.S.A. 84 41.38N 85.01W
Angola N.Y. U.S.A. 84 42.39N 79.02W
Angoram P.N.G. 37 4.04S144.04E
Angoulême France 17 45.40N 0.10E
Angra dos Reis Brazil 94 22.59S 44.17W
Ang Thong Thailand 34 14.35N100.25E
Anguilla i. Leeward Is. 87 18.14N 63.05W
Angul India 41 20.51N 85.06E
Angumu Zaïre 55 0.10S 27.38E
Anholt i. Denmark 23 56.42N 11.34E
Anholt Germany 14 51.51N 6.26E
Anh Son Vietnam 34 18.54N105.18E
Anhua China 33 28.24N111.13E
Anhui d. China 33 32.00N117.00E
Aniak U.S.A. 72 61.32N159.40W
Animas U.S.A. 81 31.57N108.48W
Anin Burma 34 15.40N 97.46E
Anina Romania 21 45.05N 21.51E
Anivorano Madagascar 57 18.44S 48.58E
Anjad India 40 22.02N 75.03E
Anjangaon India 40 21.10N 77.18E
Anjār India 40 23.08N 70.01E
Anjō Japan 35 34.57N137.05E
Anjouan see Nzwani i. Comoros 55
Anjozorobe Madagascar 57 18.24S 47.52E
Anju N. Korea 31 39.36N125.42E
Anka Nigeria 53 12.06N 5.56E
Ankang China 32 32.38N109.12E
Ankara Turkey 42 39.55N 32.50E
Ankaramena Madagascar 57 21.57S 46.39E
Ankazoabo Madagascar 57 22.18S 44.31E
Ankazobe Madagascar 57 18.21S 47.07E
Anklam Germany 20 53.51N 13.41E
Anklesvar India 40 21.38N 72.59E
Ānkober Ethiopia 49 9.30N 39.44E
Ankpa Nigeria 53 7.26N 7.38E
Anlong China 33 25.06N105.31E
Anlu China 33 31.15N113.40E
Anna U.S.A. 83 37.28N 89.15W
Annaba Algeria 51 36.55N 7.47E
An Nabk Syria 44 34.02N 36.43E
Anna Creek town Australia 66 28.50S136.07E
An Nafūd des. Saudi Arabia 42 28.40N 41.30E
An Najaf Iraq 43 31.59N 44.19E
An Nakhl Egypt 44 29.55N 33.45E
Annam Highlands see Annamitique, Chaîne mts. Laos / Vietnam 34
Annamitique, Chaîne mts. Laos / Vietnam 34 17.00N106.00E
Annan U.K. 12 54.59N 3.16W
Annan r. U.K. 12 54.58N 3.16W
Annandale f. U.K. 12 55.12N 3.25W
Anna Plains Australia 62 19.18S121.34E
Annapolis U.S.A. 85 38.59N 76.30W
Annapurna mtn. Nepal 41 28.34N 83.50E
An Naqīrah well Saudi Arabia 43 27.53N 48.15E
Ann Arbor U.S.A. 84 42.18N 83.43W
An Nāşirīyah Iraq 43 31.04N 46.16E
An Nawfalīyah Libya 51 30.47N 17.50E
Annecy France 17 45.54N 6.07E
An Nīl d. Sudan 48 18.30N 33.10E
An Nīl al Abyad d. Sudan 49 13.10N 32.00E
An Nīl al Azraq d. Sudan 49 13.00N 34.00E
Anniston U.S.A. 85 33.38N 85.50W
Annobón i. Equat. Guinea 95 1.25S 5.36E
Annonay France 17 45.15N 4.40E
Annuello Australia 66 34.52S142.54E
An Nuhūd Sudan 49 12.42N 28.26E
Anoka U.S.A. 82 45.11N 93.20W
Anorotsangana Madagascar 57 13.56S 47.55E
Anou Ti-n Elhaoua well Algeria 51 20.02N 2.55E
Anpu China 33 21.27N110.01E
Anqing China 33 30.40N117.03E
Ansbach Germany 20 49.18N 10.36E
Anshan China 32 41.06N122.58E
Anshun China 33 26.11N105.50E
Anson B. Australia 62 13.10S130.00E
Ansongo Mali 52 15.40N 0.30E
Anstruther U.K. 12 56.14N 2.42W
Ansudu Indonesia 37 2.11S139.22E
Antakya Turkey 42 36.12N 36.10E
Antalaha Madagascar 57 14.53S 50.16E
Antalya Turkey 42 36.53N 30.42E
Antalya Körfezi g. Turkey 42 36.38N 31.00E
Antananarivo Madagascar 57 18.55S 47.31E
Antarctica 96
Antarctic Pen. f. Antarctica 95 65.00S 64.00W
Antas Brazil 91 10.20S 38.20W
Antequera Spain 16 37.01N 4.34W
Anthony U.S.A. 83 37.09N 89.02W
Antibes France 17 43.35N 7.07E
Anticosti, Île d' i. Canada 77 49.20N 63.00W
Anticosti Prov. Park Canada 77 49.20N 63.00W
Antifer, Cap d' c. France 15 49.41N 0.10E
Antigo U.S.A. 82 45.09N 89.09W
Antigua Guatemala 86 14.33N 90.42W
Antigua i. Leeward Is. 87 17.09N 61.49W
Anti-Lebanon mts. see Sharqī, Al Jabal ash mts. Lebanon 44
Antipodes Is. Pacific Oc. 68 49.42S178.50E
Antlers U.S.A. 83 34.14N 95.47W
Antofagasta Chile 92 23.39S 70.24W
Antônio Bezerra Brazil 91 3.44S 38.35W
Antônio Carlos Brazil 94 21.18S 43.48W
Antonito U.S.A. 80 37.05N106.00W
Antrain France 15 48.28N 1.30W
Antrim U.K. 13 54.43N 6.14W
Antrim d. U.K. 13 54.58N 6.20W
Antrim, Mts. of U.K. 13 55.00N 6.10W
Antsalova Madagascar 57 18.40S 44.37E
Antsirabé Madagascar 57 19.51S 47.02E
Antsiranana Madagascar 57 12.16S 49.17E
Antsohihy Madagascar 57 14.52S 47.59E
Anttis Sweden 22 67.16N 22.52E
Antwerp see Antwerpen Belgium 14
Antwerpen Belgium 14 51.13N 4.25E
Antwerpen d. Belgium 14 51.16N 4.45E
Anūpgarh India 40 29.11N 73.12E
Anvik U.S.A. 72 62.38N160.20W
Anxi Fujian China 33 25.03N118.13E
Anxi Gansu China 30 40.32N 95.57E
Anxious B. Australia 66 33.25S134.35E
Anyama Ivory Coast 52 5.30N 4.03W
Anyang China 32 36.05N114.20E
Anyer Lor Indonesia 37 6.02S105.57E
Anyi China 33 28.50N115.32E
Anyuan China 33 25.09N115.21E
Anyue China 33 30.09N105.18E
Anzhero-Sudzhensk U.S.S.R. 28 56.10N 86.10E
Anzio Italy 18 41.27N 12.37E
Ao Ban Don b. Thailand 34 9.00N 99.20E
Aohan Qi China 32 42.23N119.59E
Aomori Japan 31 40.50N140.43E
Aopo W. Samoa 68 13.29S172.30W
Aosta Italy 15 45.43N 7.19E
Aoulef Algeria 50 26.58N 1.05E
Aoulime, Jbel mtn. Morocco 50 30.48N 8.50W
Aozou Chad 53 21.49N 17.25E
Apache U.S.A. 83 34.54N 98.22W
Apalachee B. U.S.A. 85 30.00N 84.13W
Apalachicola U.S.A. 85 29.43N 85.01W
Apalachicola r. U.S.A. 85 29.44N 84.59W
Apaporis r. Colombia 90 1.40S 69.20W
Aparri Phil. 37 18.22N121.40E
Apatin Yugo. 19 45.40N 18.59E
Apatity U.S.S.R. 24 67.32N 33.21E
Apeldoorn Neth. 14 52.13N 5.57E
Api mtn. Nepal 41 30.01N 80.56E
Apia W. Samoa 68 13.48S171.45W
Apizaco Mexico 86 19.25N 98.09W
Apoka Uganda 49 3.42N 33.38E
Apollo Bay town Australia 66 38.45S143.40E
Apostle Is. U.S.A. 82 46.50N 90.30W
Apóstoles Argentina 92 27.55S 55.45W
Apostólou Andréa, Akrotírion c. Cyprus 44 35.40N 34.35E
Apoteri Guyana 90 4.02N 58.32W
Appalachian Mts. U.S.A. 84 41.00N 77.00W
Appennino mts. Italy 18 42.00N 13.30E
Appennino Ligure mts. Italy 15 44.30N 9.00E
Appennino Tosco-Emiliano mts. Italy 15 44.05N 11.00E
Appiano Italy 15 46.28N 11.15E
Appingedam Neth. 14 53.18N 6.52E
Appleby U.K. 10 54.35N 2.29W
Appleton U.S.A. 82 44.16N 88.25W
Apsheronsk U.S.S.R. 25 44.26N 39.45E
Apsheronskiy Poluostrov pen. U.S.S.R. 43 40.28N 50.00E
Apsley Australia 66 36.58S141.08E
Apsley Canada 76 44.45N 78.06W
Apucarana Brazil 94 23.34S 51.28W
Apure r. Venezuela 90 7.40N 66.30W
Apurimac r. Peru 90 10.43S 73.55W
Aqaba, G. of Asia 44 28.45N 34.45E
Aqabat al Ḩijāzīyah Jordan 44 29.40N 35.55E
'Aqdā Iran 43 32.25N 33.38E
'Aqiq Sudan 48 18.14N 38.12E
Aqqikkol Hu l. China 30 35.44N 81.34E
Aquidauana Brazil 92 20.27S 55.45W
Aquila Mexico 86 18.30N103.50W
Aquitaine d. France 17 44.40N 0.00
'Arab, Baḩr al r. Sudan 49 9.12N 29.28E
Arabābād Iran 43 33.02N 57.41E
'Arabah, Wādī r. Egypt 44 29.07N 32.40E
Arabian Sea Asia 38 16.00N 65.00E
Araç Turkey 42 41.14N 33.20E
Aracaju Brazil 91 10.54S 37.07W
Aracanguy, Montañas de mts. Paraguay 92 24.00S 55.50W
Aracati Brazil 91 4.32S 37.45W
Araçatuba Brazil 94 21.12S 50.24W
Arad Romania 21 46.12N 21.19E
Arada Chad 51 15.01N 20.40E
Arafura Sea Austa. 64 9.00S133.00E
Aragarças Brazil 91 15.55S 52.12W
Aragats mtn. U.S.S.R. 43 40.32N 44.11E
Aragón d. Spain 16 41.25N 1.00W
Aragón r. Spain 16 42.20N 1.45W
Araguacema Brazil 91 8.50S 49.34W
Araguaia r. Brazil 91 5.20S 48.30W
Araguari Brazil 94 18.38S 48.13W
Araguari r. Brazil 91 1.15N 50.05W
Arak Algeria 51 25.18N 3.45E
Arāk Iran 43 34.06N 49.44E
Araka Sudan 49 4.16N 30.21E
Arakan d. Burma 34 19.00N 94.15E
Arakan Yoma mts. Burma 34 19.30N 94.30E
Araks r. U.S.S.R. 43 40.00N 48.28E
Aral Sea see Aralskoye More sea U.S.S.R. 28
Aralsk U.S.S.R. 28 46.56N 61.43E
Aralskoye More sea U.S.S.R. 28 45.00N 60.00E
Aralsor, Ozero l. U.S.S.R. 25 49.00N 48.40E
Aramac Australia 64 22.59S145.14E
Arāmbāgh India 41 22.53N 87.47E
Aramia r. P.N.G. 37 8.00S143.20E
Aranda de Duero Spain 16 41.40N 3.41W
Aran I. Rep. of Ire. 13 53.07N 9.38W
Aran Is. Rep. of Ire. 13 53.07N 9.38W
Aranjuez Spain 16 40.02N 3.37W
Aranos Namibia 56 24.09S 19.09E
Aransas Pass town U.S.A. 83 27.54N 97.09W
Araouane Mali 52 18.53N 3.31W
Arapahoe U.S.A. 82 40.18N 99.54W
Arapey Uruguay 93 30.58S 57.30W
Arapey Grande r. Uruguay 93 30.55S 57.49W
Arapiraca Brazil 91 9.45S 36.40W
Arapkir Turkey 42 39.03N 38.29E
'Ar'ar, Wādī r. Iraq 42 32.00N 42.30E
Araraquara Brazil 94 21.46S 48.08W
Araras Brazil 94 22.20S 47.23W
Ararat Australia 66 37.20S143.00E
Ararat mtn. see Ağri Daği mtn. Turkey 43
Aras r. Turkey see Araks r. U.S.S.R. 42
Arauca Colombia 90 7.04N 70.41W
Arauca r. Venezuela 90 7.05N 70.45W
Araure Venezuela 90 9.36N 69.15W
Arāvalli Range mts. India 40 25.00N 73.45E
Araxá Brazil 94 19.37S 46.50W
Araxes r. Iran see Araks r. U.S.S.R. 43
Ārba Minch' Ethiopia 49 6.02N 37.40E
Arbatax Italy 18 39.56N 9.41E
Arboga Sweden 23 59.24N 15.50E
Arborg Canada 75 50.55N 97.15W
Arbroath U.K. 12 56.34N 2.35W
Arcachon France 17 44.40N 1.11W
Arcadia Fla. U.S.A. 85 27.12N 81.52W
Arcadia Wisc. U.S.A. 82 44.15N 91.30W
Arcata U.S.A. 80 40.52N124.05W
Archer r. Australia 64 13.28S141.41E
Archers Post Kenya 55 0.42N 37.40E
Arcis-sur-Aube France 15 48.32N 4.08E
Arckaringa r. Australia 66 27.56S134.45E
Arco Italy 15 45.55N 10.53E
Arco U.S.A. 80 43.38N113.18W
Arcoona Australia 66 31.06S137.19E
Arcos Brazil 94 20.12S 45.30W
Arcos Spain 16 36.45N 5.45W
Arcoverde Brazil 91 8.23S 37.00W
Arctic Bay town Canada 73 73.05N 85.20W
Arctic Ocean 96
Arctic Red r. Canada 72 67.26N133.48W
Arctic Red River town Canada 72 67.27N133.46W
Arda r. Greece 19 41.39N 26.30E
Ardabīl Iran 43 38.15N 48.18E
Ardahan Turkey 42 41.08N 42.41E
Årdalstangen Norway 23 61.14N 7.43E
Ardara Rep. of Ire. 13 54.46N 8.25W
Ard aş Şawwān f. Jordan 44 30.45N 37.15E
Ardèche r. France 17 44.31N 4.40E
Ardee Rep. of Ire. 9 53.51N 6.33W
Ardennes mts. Belgium 14 50.10N 5.30E
Ardennes d. France 15 49.40N 4.40E
Ardennes, Canal des France 15 49.26N 4.02E
Ardestān Iran 43 33.22N 52.25E
Ardfert Rep. of Ire. 13 52.20N 9.48W
Ardila r. Portugal 16 38.10N 7.30W
Ardlethan Australia 67 34.20S146.53E
Ardmore Rep. of Ire. 13 51.58N 7.43W
Ardmore Okla. U.S.A. 83 34.10N 97.08W
Ardmore Penn. U.S.A. 85 40.01N 75.18W
Ardnamurchan, Pt. of U.K. 12 56.44N 6.14W
Ardrossan Australia 66 34.25S137.55E
Ardrossan U.K. 12 55.38N 4.49W
Ards Pen. U.K. 13 54.30N 5.30W
Åre Sweden 22 63.25N 13.05E
Arecibo Puerto Rico 87 18.29N 66.44W
Areia Branca Brazil 91 4.56S 37.07W
Arena, Pt. U.S.A. 78 38.58N123.44W
Arena, Punta c. Mexico 81 23.32N109.30W
Arendal Norway 23 58.27N 8.48E
Arequipa Peru 90 16.25S 71.32W
Arès France 17 44.47N 1.08W
Arévalo Spain 16 41.03N 4.43W
Arezzo Italy 18 43.27N 11.52E
Arfak mtn. Indonesia 37 1.30S133.50E
Arganda Spain 16 40.19N 3.26W
Argelès-sur-Mer France 17 42.33N 3.01E
Argens r. France 17 43.10N 6.45E
Argenta Italy 15 44.37N 11.50E
Argentan France 15 48.45N 0.01W
Argentera Italy 15 44.24N 6.57E
Argentera mtn. Italy 15 44.10N 7.18E
Argenteuil France 15 48.57N 2.15E
Argentia Canada 77 47.18N 53.59W
Argentina S. America 93 36.00S 63.00W
Argentine Basin f. Atlantic Oc. 95 40.00S 40.00W
Argentino, L. Argentina 93 50.15S 72.25W
Argenton France 17 46.36N 1.30E
Argentré France 15 48.05N 0.39W
Argentré du Plessis France 15 48.03N 1.08W
Argeş r. Romania 19 44.13N 26.22E
Arghandāb r. Afghan. 40 31.27N 64.23E
Árgos Greece 19 37.37N 22.45E
Argostólion Greece 19 38.10N 20.30E
Arguello, Pt. U.S.A. 81 34.35N120.39W
Argun r. U.S.S.R. 31 53.30N121.48E
Argungu Nigeria 53 12.45N 4.35E
Argyle U.S.A. 82 48.20N 96.49W
Ar Horqin Qi China 32 43.45N120.00E
Århus Denmark 23 56.09N 10.13E
Ariah Park town Australia 67 34.20S147.10E
Ariano Italy 18 41.04N 15.00E
Ariano nel Polesine Italy 15 44.56N 12.07E
Aribinda Burkina 52 14.17N 0.52W
Arica Chile 92 18.29S 70.20W
Arica Colombia 90 2.07S 71.46W
Arid, C. Australia 63 33.58S123.05E
Arieş r. Romania 21 46.26N 23.59E
Ārifwāla Pakistan 40 30.17N 73.04E
Arīḩā Al Quds Jordan 44 31.51N 35.27E
Arima Trinidad 90 10.38N 61.17W
Arinos r. Brazil 91 10.20S 57.35W
Aripuanã Brazil 90 9.10S 60.38W
Aripuanã r. Brazil 90 5.05S 60.30W
Ariquemes Brazil 90 9.56S 63.04W
Aris Namibia 56 22.48S 17.10E
Arisaig U.K. 12 56.55N 5.51W
'Arīsh, Wādī al r. Egypt 44 31.09N 33.49E
Aristazabal I. Canada 74 52.40N129.10W
Arivonimamo Madagascar 57 19.01S 47.15E
Ariza Spain 16 41.19N 2.03W
Arizona d. U.S.A. 78 34.00N112.00W
Årjäng Sweden 23 59.23N 12.08E
Arjeplog Sweden 22 66.00N 17.58E
Arjona Colombia 90 10.14N 75.22W
Arkadelphia U.S.A. 83 34.07N 93.04W
Arkaig, Loch U.K. 12 56.58N 5.08W
Arkansas d. U.S.A. 83 34.20N 92.00W
Arkansas r. U.S.A. 83 33.48N 91.04W
Arkansas City U.S.A. 83 37.04N 97.02W
Arkhangel'sk U.S.S.R. 24 64.32N 41.10E
Árki i. Greece 19 37.22N 26.45E
Arklow Rep. of Ire. 13 52.47N 6.10W
Arkville U.S.A. 84 42.09N 74.37W
Arlberg Pass Austria 20 47.00N 10.05E
Arles France 17 43.41N 4.38E
Arlington Colo. U.S.A. 80 38.20N103.19W
Arlington Oreg. U.S.A. 80 45.16N120.13W
Arlington Tex. U.S.A. 83 32.44N 97.07W
Arlington Va. U.S.A. 85 38.52N 77.05W
Arlington Heights town U.S.A. 82 42.06N 88.00W
Arlon Belgium 14 49.41N 5.49E
Armadale Australia 63 32.10S115.57E
Armagh U.K. 13 54.21N 6.41W
Armagh d. U.K. 13 54.16N 6.35W
Armançon r. France 15 47.57N 3.30E
Armavir U.S.S.R. 25 44.59N 41.10E
Armenia Colombia 90 4.32N 75.40W
Armenia f. Iran / Turkey / U.S.S.R. 43 40.00N 44.30E
Armenia see Armyanskaya S.S.R. d. U.S.S.R. 43
Armeniş Romania 21 45.12N 22.19E
Armentières France 14 50.41N 2.53E
Armidale Australia 67 30.32S151.40E
Armori India 41 20.28N 79.59E
Armstrong Canada 74 50.25N119.10W
Armstrong U.S.A. 83 26.55N 97.47W
Ārmūr India 41 18.48N 78.17E
Armyanskaya S.S.R. d. U.S.S.R. 43 40.00N 45.00E
Arnaud r. Canada 73 60.00N 69.45W
Årnes Norway 23 60.09N 11.28E
Arnett U.S.A. 83 36.08N 99.46W
Arnhem Neth. 14 52.00N 5.55E
Arnhem, C. Australia 64 12.10S137.00E
Arnhem B. Australia 64 12.20S136.12E
Arnhem Land f. Australia 64 13.10S134.30E
Arno r. Italy 18 43.43N 10.17E
Arno Bay town Australia 66 33.54S136.34E
Arnot Canada 75 55.46N 96.41W
Arnprior Canada 76 45.26N 76.21W
Arnsberg Germany 14 51.24N 8.03E
Aroma Sudan 48 15.49N 36.08E
Arona Italy 15 45.46N 8.34E
Arorangi Rarotonga Cook Is. 68 21.13S159.49W
Arpajon France 15 48.35N 2.15E
Arra Ivory Coast 52 6.42N 3.57W
Arrah India 41 25.34N 84.40E
Ar Rahad Sudan 49 12.43N 30.39E
Ar Ramādī Iraq 42 33.27N 43.19E
Ar Ramthā Jordan 44 32.34N 36.00E
Arran i. U.K. 12 55.35N 5.14W
Ar Rank Sudan 49 11.45N 32.48E
Ar Raqqah Syria 42 35.57N 39.03E
Arras France 14 50.17N 2.46E
Ar Rass Saudi Arabia 42 25.54N 43.30E
Ar Rastān Syria 44 34.55N 36.44E
Arrecife Canary Is. 50 28.57N 13.32W
Arrecifes Argentina 93 34.05S 60.05W
Arrey U.S.A. 81 32.51N107.19W
Ar Riyāḑ Saudi Arabia 43 24.39N 46.44E
Arrochar U.K. 12 56.12N 4.44W
Arromanches France 15 49.20N 0.38W
Arrow, Lough Rep.of Ire. 13 54.03N 8.20W
Arrowsmith, Pt. Australia 64 13.18S136.24E
Arrowtown New Zealand 60 44.56S168.50E
Arroyo Feliciano r. Argentina 93 31.06S 59.53W
Arroyo Villimanca r. Argentina 93 35.36S 59.05W
Ar Ru'at Sudan 49 12.21N 32.17E
Ar Rub' al Khālī des. Saudi Arabia 38 20.20N 52.30E
Ar Rubayqī Egypt 44 30.10N 31.46E
Ar Rumaythah Iraq 43 31.32N 45.12E
Ar Ruşayriş Sudan 49 11.51N 34.23E
Ar Ruţbah Iraq 42 33.03N 40.18E
Ar Ruwayḑah Saudi Arabia 43 23.46N 44.46E
Ārsī d. Ethiopia 49 7.50N 39.50E
Ársos Cyprus 44 34.50N 32.46E
Árta Greece 19 39.10N 20.57E
Artemovsk U.S.S.R. 25 48.35N 38.00E
Artenay France 15 48.05N 1.53E
Artesia U.S.A. 81 32.51N104.24W
Arthabaska Canada 77 46.02N 71.55W
Arthal Jammu & Kashmir 40 33.16N 76.11E
Arthington Liberia 52 6.35N 10.45W
Arthur's Pass New Zealand 60 42.50S171.45E
Artigas Uruguay 93 30.24S 56.28W
Artillery L. Canada 75 63.09N107.52W
Artois f. France 14 50.16N 2.50E
Artux China 30 39.40N 76.10E
Artvin Turkey 42 41.12N 41.48E
Aru, Kepulauan is. Indonesia 37 6.00S134.30E
Arua Uganda 55 3.02N 30.56E
Aruaddin Ethiopia 48 16.16N 38.46E
Aruanã Brazil 91 14.54S 51.05W
Aruba i. Neth. Ant. 87 12.30N 70.00W
Arucas Canary Is. 95 28.08N 15.32W
Arun r. U.K. 9 50.48N 0.32W
Arunachal Pradesh d. India 39 28.40N 94.60E
Arundel Canada 77 45.58N 74.37W
Arusha Tanzania 55 3.21S 36.40E
Arusha d. Tanzania 55 4.00S 37.00E
Aruwimi r. Zaïre 54 1.20N 23.36E
Arvada Colo. U.S.A. 80 39.50N105.05W
Arvada Wyo. U.S.A. 80 44.39N105.05W
Arvagh Rep. of Ire. 13 53.56N 7.35W
Arvi India 41 20.59N 78.14E
Arvidsjaur Sweden 22 65.35N 19.07E
Arvika Sweden 23 59.39N 12.36E
Arzamas U.S.S.R. 24 55.24N 43.48E
Arzgir U.S.S.R. 25 45.24N 44.04E
Arzignano Italy 15 45.31N 11.20E
Asaba Nigeria 53 6.12N 6.44E
Asadābād Afghan. 40 34.52N 71.09E
Asahi dake mtn. Japan 31 43.42N142.54E
Asahikawa Japan 31 43.50N142.20E
Asansol India 41 23.41N 86.59E
Åsarna Sweden 22 62.40N 14.20E
Āsayita Ethiopia 49 11.33N 41.30E
Asbestos Canada 77 45.46N 71.57W
Asbury Park U.S.A. 85 40.14N 74.00W
Ascension i. Atlantic Oc. 95 7.57S 14.22W
Aschaffenburg Germany 20 49.58N 9.10E
Aschendorf Germany 14 53.03N 7.20E
Aschersleben Germany 20 51.46N 11.28E
Ascoli Piceno Italy 18 42.52N 13.36E
Ascona Switz. 15 46.09N 8.46E
Āseb Ethiopia 49 13.01N 42.47E
Åseda Sweden 23 57.10N 15.20E
Asedjrad Algeria 51 24.42N 1.40E
Āsela Ethiopia 49 7.59N 39.08E
Åsele Sweden 22 64.10N 17.20E
Åsenbruk Sweden 23 58.54N 12.40E
Asenovgrad Bulgaria 19 42.00N 24.53E
Åseral Norway 23 58.37N 7.25E
Asfeld France 15 49.27N 4.05E
Asha Nigeria 53 7.07N 3.43E
Ashanti d. Ghana 52 6.30N 1.30W
Ashbourne Rep. of Ire. 13 53.31N 6.25W
Ashburn U.S.A. 85 31.42N 83.41W
Ashburton r. Australia 62 21.15S115.00E
Ashburton New Zealand 60 43.54S171.46E
Ashby de la Zouch U.K. 11 52.45N 1.29W
Ashcroft Canada 74 50.40N121.20W
Ashdod Israel 44 31.48N 34.38E
Asheboro U.S.A. 85 35.42N 79.50W
Ashern Canada 75 51.11N 98.21W
Asheville U.S.A. 85 35.35N 82.35W
Ashewat Pakistan 40 31.22N 68.32E
Ash Flat town U.S.A. 83 36.12N 91.38W
Ashford Australia 67 29.19S151.07E
Ashford Kent U.K. 11 51.08N 0.53E
Ash Fork U.S.A. 81 35.13N112.29W
Ashington U.K. 10 55.11N 1.34W
Ashiya Japan 35 34.43N135.17E
Ashkhabad U.S.S.R. 43 37.58N 58.24E
Ashland Ky. U.S.A. 84 38.28N 82.40W
Ashland Oreg. U.S.A. 80 42.12N122.42W
Ashland Wisc. U.S.A. 82 46.35N 90.53W
Ashley Australia 67 29.19S149.52E
Ashley U.S.A. 82 38.20N 89.10W
Ashley Snow I. Antarctica 96 72.30S 77.00
Ashmūn Egypt 44 30.18N 30.59E
Ashoknagar India 41 24.34N 77.43E
Ashqelon Israel 44 31.40N 34.35E
Ash Shabb well Egypt 48 22.19N 29.46E
Ash Shallūfah Egypt 44 30.07N 32.34E
Ash Shāmah des. Saudi Arabia 42 31.20N 38.00E
Ash Shamālīyah d. Sudan 48 19.30N 29.50E
Ash Shāmīyah des. Iraq 43 30.30N 45.30E
Ash Shāriqah U.A.E. 43 25.20N 55.26E
Ash Sharmah Saudi Arabia 44 28.01N 35.14
Ash Shawbak Jordan 44 30.33N 35.35E
Ash Shaykh Faḑl Egypt 44 28.29N 30.50E
Ash Shaykh 'Ibādah Egypt 44 27.48N 30.52
Ash Shaykh Miskīn Syria 44 32.49N 36.09E
Ash Shiḩr Yemen 45 14.45N 49.36E
Ash Shu'aybab Iraq 43 30.30N 47.40E
Ash Shu'aybah Saudi Arabia 42 27.53N 42.43E
Ash Shumlūl Saudi Arabia 43 26.29N 47.20
Ashta India 40 23.01N 76.43E
Ashtabula U.S.A. 84 41.53N 80.47W
Ashton R.S.A. 56 33.49S 20.04E
Ashton U.S.A. 80 44.04N111.27W
'Āsī r. Lebanon 44 34.37N 36.30E
Asiago Italy 15 45.52N 11.30E
Asilah Morocco 50 35.32N 6.00W
Asinara i. Italy 18 41.04N 8.18E
Asinara, Golfo dell' g. Italy 18 41.00N 8.32
'Asīr f. Saudi Arabia 45 19.00N 42.00E
Aska India 41 19.36N 84.39E
Askeaton Rep. of Ire. 13 52.36N 9.00W
Askersund Sweden 23 58.53N 14.54E
Askim Norway 23 59.35N 11.10E
Askvoll Norway 23 61.21N 5.04E
Āsmera Ethiopia 48 15.20N 38.58E
Åsnen l. Sweden 23 56.38N 14.42E
Asola Italy 15 45.13N 10.24E
Āsosa Ethiopia 49 10.03N 34.32E
Asoteriba, Jabal mtn. Sudan 48 21.51N 36.30E
Aspen U.S.A. 80 39.11N106.49W
Aspermont U.S.A. 83 33.08N100.14W
Aspiring, Mt. New Zealand 60 44.20S168.
Asquith Canada 75 52.08N107.13W
Assaba d. Mauritania 50 16.40N 11.40W
As Sadd al 'Ālī dam Egypt 48 23.59N 32.5
Aş Şaff Egypt 44 29.34N 31.17E
As Saffānīyah Saudi Arabia 43 28.00N 48.
Aş Şāfiyah Sudan 48 15.31N 30.07E
Aş Şa'īd f. Egypt 42 25.30N 32.00E

ş Şāliḩīyah Egypt 44 30.47N 31.59E
s Sallūm Egypt 42 31.31N 25.09E
s Salţ Jordan 44 32.03N 35.44E
s Salwa Saudi Arabia 43 24.44N 50.50E
ssam d. India 39 26.30N 93.00E
s Samāwah Iraq 43 31.18N 45.18E
s Sanām f. Saudi Arabia 45 22.00N 51.10E
ş Şarafand Lebanon 44 33.27N 35.18E
s Sarīrīyah Egypt 44 28.20N 30.45E
ssebroek Belgium 14 51.11N 3.16E
ssen Neth. 14 53.00N 6.34E
s Sinbillāwayn Egypt 44 30.53N 31.27E
ssiniboia Canada 75 49.38N105.59W
ssiniboine r. Canada 75 49.53N 97.08W
ssinica Prov. Park Canada 76 50.24N 75.00W
ssis Brazil 94 22.37S 50.25W
s Sudd Sudan 49 7.50N 30.00E
ş Şufayyah Sudan 48 15.30N 34.42E
s Sulaymānīyah Iraq 43 35.32N 45.27E
s Sulaymānīyah Saudi Arabia 43 24.10N 47.20E
s Sulayyil Saudi Arabia 45 20.27N 45.34E
Sulţān Libya 51 31.07N 17.09E
Sumayḩ Sudan 49 9.49N 27.39E
Şummān f. Saudi Arabia 43 27.00N 47.00E
Sūq Saudi Arabia 48 21.55N 42.02E
Suwaydā' Syria 44 32.43N 36.33E
Suways Egypt 44 29.59N 32.33E
ti Italy 15 44.54N 8.13E
tipálaia i. Greece 19 36.35N 26.25E
storga Spain 16 42.30N 6.02W
storia U.S.A. 80 46.11N123.50W
storp Sweden 23 56.08N 12.57E
strakhan U.S.S.R. 25 46.22N 48.00E
sträsk Sweden 22 64.38N 20.00E
sturias d. Spain 16 43.20N 6.00W
unción Paraguay 94 25.15S 57.40W
swân Egypt 42 24.05N 32.56E
swan High Dam see As Sadd al 'Ālī Egypt 42
yûţ Egypt 42 27.14N 31.07E
acama, Desierto des. S. America 92 20.00S 69.00W
acama, Salar de f. Chile 92 23.30S 68.46W
acama Desert see Atacama, Desierto des. S. America 92
afu Pacific Oc. 68 8.40S172.40W
akpamé Togo 53 7.34N 1.14E
ami Japan 35 35.05N139.04E
apupu Indonesia 37 9.00S124.51E
ar Mauritania 50 20.32N 13.08W
ara U.S.S.R. 29 63.10N129.10E
asu U.S.S.R. 28 48.42N 71.38E
barah Sudan 48 17.42N 33.59E
barah r. Sudan 48 17.40N 33.58E
chafalaya B. U.S.A. 83 29.25N 91.20W
chison U.S.A. 82 39.34N 95.07W
Belgium 14 50.38N 3.45E
abasca Canada 74 54.45N113.20W
abasca r. Canada 75 58.40N110.50W
abasca, L. Canada 75 59.07N110.00W
ea Rep. of Ire. 13 52.28N 9.19W
enry Rep. of Ire. 13 53.18N 8.45W
ens see Athínai Greece 19
ens Ga. U.S.A. 85 33.57N 83.24W
ens Tenn. U.S.A. 85 35.27N 84.38W
ens Tex. U.S.A. 83 32.12N 95.51W
erton Australia 64 17.15S145.29E
ínai Greece 19 37.59N 23.42E
lone Rep. of Ire. 13 53.26N 7.57W
oll, Forest of U.K. 12 56.50N 3.55W
os mtn. Greece 19 40.09N 24.19E
Thamad Egypt 44 29.40N 34.18E
Chad 53 13.11N 18.20E
co Peru 90 16.12S 73.37W
konak L. Canada 77 52.40N 64.30W
maono Tahiti 69 17.46S149.28W
arsk U.S.S.R. 25 51.55N 45.00E
inson U.S.A. 85 34.33N 78.12W
anta Ga. U.S.A. 85 33.45N 84.23W
anta Tex. U.S.A. 83 33.07N 94.10W
antic Iowa U.S.A. 82 41.24N 95.01W
antic-Antarctic Ridge f. Atlantic Oc. 95 .00S 0.00
antic City U.S.A. 85 39.22N 74.26W
antic-Indian-Antarctic Basin f. .Oc./Ind.Oc. 95 61.00S 0.00
antic Ocean 95
s Saharien mts. Algeria 51 34.00N 2.00E
n Canada 74 59.31N133.41W
n L. Canada 74 59.26N133.45W
ore U.S.A. 83 31.02N 87.29W
arko Canada 74 52.25N126.00W
osen Norway 23 61.44N 10.49E
ka U.S.A. 83 34.23N 96.08W
uat mtn. Laos 34 16.03N107.17E
uguia Portugal 16 39.20N 9.20W
k r. Iran see Atrek r. Asia 43
n r. Sweden 23 56.53N 12.30E
o r. Colombia 90 8.15N 76.58W
auli India 41 28.02N 78.17E
k r. Asia 43 37.23N 54.00E
igi Japan 35 35.27N139.22E
ami-hantō pen. Japan 35 34.40N137.20E
ami-wan b. Japan 35 34.45N137.10E
afilah Jordan 44 30.52N 35.36E
ā'if Saudi Arabia 48 21.15N 40.21E
all Syria 44 33.36N 36.18E
pu Laos 36 14.51N106.56E
r, Oued el wadi Algeria 51 33.23N 5.12E
wapiskat r. Canada 76 53.00N 82.30W
wapiskat L. Canada 76 52.20N 88.00W
ayrīyah Egypt 44 30.39N 30.46E
ndorn Germany 14 51.07N 7.54E
a N.Y. U.S.A. 76 42.52N 78.17W
ny France 15 49.29N 4.35E
amagen L. Canada 77 55.00N 66.38W
borough U.K. 11 52.31N 1.01E

Aţ Ţubayq mts. Saudi Arabia 42 29.30N 37.15E
Aţ Ţunayb Jordan 44 31.48N 35.56E
Aţ Ţūr Egypt 44 28.14N 33.36E
At Ţuwayrifah well Saudi Arabia 45 21.30N 49.35E
Atucha Argentina 93 33.58S 59.17W
Atuel r. Argentina 93 36.15S 66.55W
Atui, Uad wadi Mauritania 50 20.03N 15.35W
Atui I. Cook Is. 69 20.00S158.07W
Atuona Îs. Marquises 69 9.48S139.02W
Åtvidaberg Sweden 23 58.12N 16.00E
Atwater U.S.A. 80 37.21N120.36W
Atwood U.S.A. 82 39.48N101.03W
Aubagne France 17 43.17N 5.35E
Aube d. France 15 48.15N 4.05E
Aube r. France 15 48.30N 3.37E
Aubenton France 15 49.50N 4.12E
Auberive France 15 47.47N 5.03E
Aubigny-sur-Nère France 15 47.29N 2.26E
Aubin France 17 44.32N 2.14E
Auburn Ala. U.S.A. 85 32.38N 85.38W
Auburn Calif. U.S.A. 80 38.54N121.04W
Auburn Ind. U.S.A. 84 41.22N 85.02W
Auburn Maine U.S.A. 84 44.06N 70.14W
Auburn N.Y. U.S.A. 84 42.57N 76.34W
Auburn Wash. U.S.A. 80 47.18N122.13W
Aubusson France 17 45.57N 2.11E
Auce U.S.S.R. 23 56.28N 22.53E
Auch France 17 43.40N 0.36E
Auchi Nigeria 53 7.05N 6.16E
Auchterarder U.K. 12 56.18N 3.43W
Auckland New Zealand 60 36.55S174.45E
Auckland d. New Zealand 60 36.45S174.45E
Auckland Is. Pacific Oc. 68 50.35S166.00E
Aude r. France 17 43.13N 2.20E
Auden Canada 76 50.17N 87.54W
Audo Range mts. Ethiopia 49 6.30N 41.30E
Audubon U.S.A. 82 41.43N 94.55W
Aue Germany 20 50.35N 12.42E
Augathella Australia 64 25.48S146.35E
Augrabies Falls f. R.S.A. 56 28.33S 20.27E
Augsburg Germany 20 48.21N 10.54E
Augusta Australia 63 34.19S115.09E
Augusta Italy 18 37.13N 15.13E
Augusta Ga. U.S.A. 85 33.29N 82.00W
Augusta Ill. U.S.A. 82 40.14N 90.56W
Augusta Kans. U.S.A. 83 37.41N 96.58W
Augusta Maine U.S.A. 84 44.19N 69.47W
Augustín Codazzi Colombia 90 10.01N 73.10W
Augustów Poland 21 53.51N 22.59E
Augustus, Mt. Australia 62 24.20S116.49E
Aulla Italy 15 44.12N 9.58E
Aulnay France 17 46.02N 0.22W
Aulne r. France 17 48.30N 4.11W
Aulnoye-Aymeries France 14 50.13N 3.50E
Ault U.S.A. 80 40.35N104.44W
Aumale France 15 49.46N 1.45E
Aumont-Aubrac France 17 44.43N 3.17E
Auna Nigeria 53 10.11N 4.46E
Auneau France 15 48.27N 1.46E
Aura Finland 23 60.36N 22.34E
Auraiya India 41 26.28N 79.31E
Aurangābād Bihār India 41 24.45N 84.22E
Aurangābād Mahār India 40 19.53N 75.20E
Aurdal Norway 23 60.56N 9.24E
Aure Norway 22 63.16N 8.34E
Aurich Germany 14 53.28N 7.29E
Aurillac France 17 44.56N 2.26E
Aurora Canada 76 44.00N 79.28W
Aurora Colo. U.S.A. 80 39.44N104.52W
Aurora Ill. U.S.A. 82 41.45N 88.20W
Aurora Mo. U.S.A. 83 36.58N 93.43W
Aursunden l. Norway 22 62.37N 11.40E
Aurukun Australia 64 13.20S141.42E
Aus Namibia 56 26.41S 16.14E
Au Sable r. U.S.A. 84 44.27N 83.21W
Aust-Agder d. Norway 23 58.50N 8.20E
Austin Minn. U.S.A. 82 43.40N 92.59W
Austin Nev. U.S.A. 80 39.30N117.04W
Austin Penn. U.S.A. 84 41.38N 78.05W
Austin Tex. U.S.A. 83 30.16N 97.45W
Austin, L. Australia 62 27.40S118.00E
Austral Downs town Australia 64 20.28S137.55E
Australia Austa. 61
Australian Alps mts. Australia 65 36.30S148.30E
Australian Antarctic Territory Antarctica 96 73.00S 90.00E
Australian Capital Territory d. Australia 67 35.30S149.00E
Austral Ridge Pacific Oc. 69 24.00S148.00W
Austria Europe 20 47.30N 14.00E
Austvågöy i. Norway 22 68.20N 14.40E
Autun France 17 46.58N 4.18E
Auvergne d. France 17 45.20N 3.00E
Auxerre France 15 47.48N 3.35E
Aux Sables r. Canada 76 46.13N 82.04W
Auzances France 17 46.02N 2.29E
Ava Burma 34 21.49N 95.57E
Avallon France 15 47.30N 3.54E
Avaloirs, Les hills France 15 48.28N 0.07W
Avalon U.S.A. 85 39.06N 74.43W
Avalon Pen. Canada 77 47.00N 53.15W
Avanos Turkey 42 38.44N 34.51E
Avaré Brazil 94 23.06S 48.57W
Avarua Rarotonga Cook Is. 68 21.12S159.46W
Avatele Niue 68 19.06S169.55W
Avatele B. Niue 68 19.05S169.56W
Avatiu Rarotonga Cook Is. 68 21.12S159.47W
Aveiro Portugal 16 40.40N 8.35W
Avellaneda Argentina 93 34.40S 58.20W
Avellino Italy 18 40.55N 14.46E
Aversa Italy 18 40.58N 14.12E
Avery U.S.A. 80 47.15N115.49W
Avesnes France 14 50.08N 3.57E

Avesta Sweden 23 60.09N 16.12E
Aveyron r. France 17 44.09N 1.10E
Avezzano Italy 18 42.03N 13.26E
Aviemore U.K. 12 57.12N 3.50W
Avignon France 17 43.56N 4.48E
Ávila Spain 16 40.39N 4.42W
Ávila, Sierra de mts. Spain 16 40.35N 5.08W
Avilés Spain 16 43.35N 5.57W
Avoca r. Australia 66 35.56S143.44E
Avoca Vic. Australia 66 37.04S143.29E
Avola Canada 74 51.45N119.19W
Avon r. Australia 63 31.40S116.07E
Avon d. U.K. 11 51.35N 2.40W
Avon r. Avon U.K. 9 51.30N 2.43W
Avon r. Dorset U.K. 11 50.43N 1.45W
Avon r. Glos. U.K. 11 52.00N 2.10W
Avon Downs town Australia 64 20.05S137.30E
Avonmouth U.K. 11 51.30N 2.42W
Avon Park town U.S.A. 85 27.36N 81.30W
Avranches France 15 48.42N 1.21W
Avre r. France 15 49.53N 2.20E
Awal Edo Ethiopia 49 4.14N 40.39E
Awara Ethiopia 49 5.30N 40.00E
Åwarē Ethiopia 45 8.15N 44.10E
Āwasa Hāyk' l. Ethiopia 49 7.05N 38.25E
Āwash r. Ethiopia 49 11.45N 41.05E
Awaso Ghana 52 6.20N 2.22W
Awat China 30 40.38N 80.22E
Awbārī Libya 51 26.35N 12.46E
Awbārī d. Libya 51 25.10N 12.45E
Awbārī, Şaḩrā' des. Libya 51 27.30N 11.30E
Awdah, Hawr al l. Iraq 43 31.36N 46.53E
Awe, Loch U.K. 12 56.18N 5.24W
Axarfjördhur est. Iceland 22 66.10N 16.30W
Axat France 17 42.48N 2.14E
Axel Heiberg I. Canada 73 79.30N 90.00W
Axim Ghana 52 4.53N 2.14W
Axiós r. Greece 19 40.31N 22.43E
Axminster U.K. 11 50.47N 3.01W
Ayabaca Peru 90 4.40S 79.53W
Ayachi, Ari n' mtn. Morocco 50 32.29N 4.57W
Ayacucho Argentina 93 37.10S 58.30W
Ayacucho Peru 90 13.10S 74.15W
Ayaguz U.S.S.R. 30 47.59N 80.27E
Ayamonte Spain 16 37.12N 7.24W
Ayan U.S.S.R. 29 56.29N138.00E
Aydin Turkey 42 37.52N 27.50E
Ayelu mtn. Ethiopia 49 10.04N 40.46E
Ayers Cliff town Canada 77 45.10N 72.03W
Ayers Rock see Uluru Australia 64
Áyios Evstrátios i. Greece 19 39.30N 25.00E
Aylesbury U.K. 11 51.48N 0.49W
Aylmer Que. Canada 77 45.23N 75.51W
Aylmer L. Canada 72 64.05N108.30W
Aylsham U.K. 10 52.48N 1.16E
'Ayn, Wādī al r. Oman 43 22.18N 55.35E
'Ayn Dāllah well Egypt 42 27.19N 27.20E
Ayod Sudan 49 8.07N 31.26E
Ayom Sudan 49 7.52N 28.23E
Ayon, Ostrov i. U.S.S.R. 29 70.00N169.00E
Ayos Cameroon 53 3.55N 12.30E
'Ayoûn el' Atroûs Mauritania 50 16.40N 9.37W
Ayr Australia 64 19.35S147.24E
Ayr U.K. 12 55.28N 4.37W
Ayr r. U.K. 12 55.28N 4.38W
Ayre, Pt. of U.K. 10 54.25N 4.22W
Āysha Ethiopia 49 10.46N 42.37E
Ayutthaya Thailand 34 14.20N100.40E
Ayvalik Turkey 19 39.19N 26.42E
Azamgarh India 41 26.04N 83.11E
Azao mtn. Algeria 51 25.12N 8.08E
Azaouâd des. Mali 52 18.00N 3.00W
Azaouak, Vallée de l' f. Mali 53 16.00N 3.40E
Azare Nigeria 53 11.40N 10.08E
Azbine mts. see Aïr mts. Niger 53
Azerbaydzhanskaya S.S.R. d. U.S.S.R. 43 40.10N 47.50E
Azogues Ecuador 90 2.35S 78.00W
Azopolye U.S.S.R. 24 65.15N 45.18E
Azores is. see Açores, Arquipélago dos is. Atlantic Oc. 95
Azoum r. Chad 49 10.53N 20.15E
Azov, Sea of see Azovskoye More U.S.S.R. 25
Azovskoye More sea U.S.S.R. 25 46.00N 36.30E
Azraq, Al Baḩr al r. Sudan 48 15.38N 32.31E
Azrou Morocco 50 33.27N 5.14W
Aztec U.S.A. 81 32.48N113.26W
Azua Dom. Rep. 87 18.29N 70.44W
Azuaga Spain 16 38.16N 5.40W
Azuero, Península de pen. Panama 87 7.30N 80.30W
Azul Argentina 93 36.46S 59.50W
'Azūm, Wādī r. Sudan see Azoum r. Chad 49
Azurduy Bolivia 92 19.59S 64.29W
Az Zāb al Kabīr r. Iraq 43 35.37N 43.20E
Az Zāb aş Şaghīr r. Iraq 43 35.15N 43.27E
Az Zabdānī Syria 44 33.43N 36.05E
Az Zahrān Saudi Arabia 43 26.18N 50.08E
Az Zaqāzīq Egypt 44 30.36N 31.30E
Az Zarqā' Jordan 44 32.04N 36.05E
Az Zarqā' r. Jordan 44 32.08N 35.32E
Az Zāwiyah d. Libya 51 32.40N 12.10E
Azzel Matti, Sebkha f. Algeria 50 26.00N 0.55E
Az Zilfi Saudi Arabia 43 26.15N 44.50E
Az Zrārīyah Lebanon 44 33.21N 35.20E

B

Baan Baa Australia 67 30.28S149.58E
Baardheere Somali Rep. 55 2.18N 42.18E
Baargaal Somali Rep. 45 11.18N 51.07E
Baarle-Hertog Neth. 14 51.26N 4.56E
Babadag Romania 21 44.54N 28.43E
Babahoyo Ecuador 90 1.53S 79.31W
Babai Gaxun China 32 40.30N104.43E
Babakin Australia 63 32.11S117.58E
Babana Nigeria 53 10.26N 3.51E
Babanka U.S.S.R. 21 48.41N 30.30E
Babanūsah Sudan 49 11.20N 27.48E
Babar, Kepulauan is. Indonesia 37 8.00S129.30E
Babayevo U.S.S.R. 24 59.24N 35.50E
B'abdā Lebanon 44 33.50N 35.31E
Babia Gora mtn. Czech./Poland 21 49.38N 19.38E
Babina India 41 25.15N 78.28E
Babine L. Canada 74 54.48N126.00W
Babo Indonesia 37 2.33S133.25E
Bābol Iran 43 36.32N 52.42E
Baboua C.A.R. 53 5.49N 14.51E
Babuyan Channel Phil. 33 18.40N121.30E
Babuyan Is. Phil. 37 19.20N121.30E
Babylon ruins Iraq 43 32.33N 44.25E
Bacabal Maranhão Brazil 91 4.15S 44.45W
Bacabal Para Brazil 91 5.20S 56.45W
Bacău Romania 21 46.32N 26.59E
Baccarat France 17 48.27N 6.45E
Bacchus Marsh town Australia 66 37.41S144.27E
Bacharach Germany 14 50.03N 7.48E
Bacheli India 39 18.40N 81.16E
Bachelina U.S.S.R. 28 57.45N 67.20E
Back r. Canada 73 66.37N 96.00W
Bac Kan Vietnam 33 22.06N105.57E
Bäckefors Sweden 23 58.48N 12.10E
Backstairs Passage str. Australia 66 35.42S138.05E
Bac Lieu Vietnam 34 9.16N105.45E
Bac Ninh Vietnam 34 21.10N106.04E
Bacolod Phil. 37 10.38N122.58E
Bac Phan f. Vietnam 34 22.00N105.00E
Bac Quang Vietnam 33 22.30N104.52E
Badagara India 38 11.36N 75.35E
Badajós, Lago l. Brazil 90 3.15S 62.47W
Badajoz Spain 16 38.53N 6.58W
Badal Khān Goth Pakistan 40 26.31N 67.06E
Badalona Spain 16 41.27N 2.15E
Badanah Saudi Arabia 42 30.59N 41.02E
Bad Axe U.S.A. 84 43.49N 82.59W
Baddo r. Pakistan 40 28.15N 65.00E
Badeggi Nigeria 53 9.04N 6.09E
Bad Ems Germany 14 50.21N 7.42E
Baden Austria 20 48.01N 16.14E
Baden Ethiopia 48 17.00N 38.00E
Baden-Baden Germany 20 48.45N 8.15E
Baden-Württemberg d. Germany 20 48.30N 9.00E
Badgastein Austria 20 47.07N 13.09E
Bad Godesberg Germany 14 50.41N 7.09E
Bad Honnef Germany 14 50.39N 7.13E
Badīn Pakistan 40 24.39N 68.50E
Bad Ischl Austria 20 47.43N 13.38E
Badīyah Oman 45 22.27N 58.48E
Bādiyat ash Shām des. Asia 42 32.00N 39.00E
Bad Kissingen Germany 20 50.12N 10.04E
Bad Kreuznach Germany 14 49.51N 7.52E
Bad Mergentheim Germany 20 49.30N 9.46E
Bad Münstereifel Germany 14 50.34N 6.47E
Badnera India 41 20.52N 77.44E
Bad Neuenahr-Ahrweiler Germany 14 50.33N 7.07E
Bad Oldesloe Germany 20 53.48N 10.22E
Badong China 33 31.02N110.20E
Badou Togo 52 7.37N 0.37E
Badoumbé Mali 52 13.42N 10.09W
Badrīnāth India 41 30.44N 79.29E
Bad Tölz Germany 20 47.46N 11.34E
Badu Australia 64 10.07S142.08E
Bad Wildungen Germany 20 51.07N 9.07E
Baerami Australia 67 32.23S150.30E
Baeza Spain 16 37.57N 3.25W
Bafang Cameroon 53 5.11N 10.12E
Bafatá Guinea Bissau 52 12.09N 14.38W
Baffin Canada 73 66.00N 72.00W
Baffin B. Canada 73 74.00N 70.00W
Baffin I. Canada 73 68.50N 70.00W
Bafia Cameroon 53 4.39N 11.14E
Bafing r. Mali 52 14.48N 12.10W
Bafoulabé Mali 52 13.49N 10.50W
Bāfq Iran 43 31.35N 55.21E
Bafra Turkey 42 41.34N 35.56E
Bafut Cameroon 53 6.06N 10.02E
Bafwasende Zaïre 55 1.09N 27.12E
Bagaha India 41 27.06N 84.05E
Bagamoyo Tanzania 55 6.26S 38.55E
Bagasra India 40 21.29N 70.57E
Bagawi Sudan 49 12.19N 34.21E
Bagbele Zaïre 49 4.21N 29.17E
Bagdarin U.S.S.R. 29 54.28N113.38E
Bagé Brazil 94 31.22S 54.06W
Baggy Pt. U.K. 11 51.08N 4.15W
Baghdād Iraq 43 33.20N 44.26E
Bāgherhāt Bangla. 41 22.40N 89.48E
Bagheria Italy 18 38.05N 13.30E
Baghlān Afghan. 38 36.11N 68.44E
Baghrān Khowleh Afghan. 40 33.01N 64.58E
Bagni di Lucca Italy 15 44.01N 10.35E
Bagnois-sur-Cèze France 17 44.10N 4.37E
Bagodar India 41 24.05N 85.52E
Bagoé r. Mali 52 12.34N 6.30W
Bagolino Italy 15 45.49N 10.28E

Bagrationovsk U.S.S.R. 21 54.26N 20.38E
Baguio Phil. 37 16.25N120.37E
Bāh India 41 26.53N 78.36E
Bahamas C. America 87 24.15N 76.00W
Bahāwalnagar Pakistan 40 29.59N 73.16E
Bahāwalpur Pakistan 40 29.24N 71.41E
Baheri India 41 28.47N 79.30E
Bahi Tanzania 55 5.59S 35.15E
Bahia d. Brazil 91 12.30S 42.30W
Bahía, Islas de la is. Honduras 87 16.10N 86.30W
Bahía Blanca Argentina 94 38.45S 62.15W
Bahía de Caráquez Ecuador 90 0.40S 80.25W
Bahía Kino Mexico 81 28.50N111.55W
Bahía Laura Argentina 93 48.18S 66.30W
Bahía Negra Paraguay 94 20.15S 58.12W
Bahir Dar Ethiopia 49 11.35N 37.28E
Bahraich India 41 27.35N 81.36E
Bahrain Asia 43 26.00N 50.35E
Baḩr al Ghazāl d. Sudan 49 8.00N 26.30E
Bahrām Chāh Afghan. 40 29.26N 64.03E
Bahr Aouk r. C.A.R. 53 8.50N 18.50E
Bahr el Ghazal r. Chad 53 12.26N 15.25E
Bahr Salamat r. Chad 53 9.30N 18.10E
Bāhū Kalāt Iran 43 25.42N 61.28E
Baia-Mare Romania 21 47.40N 23.35E
Baião Brazil 91 2.41S 49.41W
Baia Sprie Romania 21 47.40N 23.42E
Baïbokoum Chad 53 7.46N 15.43E
Baicheng China 32 45.40N122.52E
Baie Comeau Canada 77 49.13N 68.10W
Baie des Ha! Ha! town Canada 77 50.56N 58.58W
Baie St. Paul town Canada 77 47.27N 70.30W
Baigneux-les-Juifs France 15 47.31N 4.39E
Baihar India 41 22.06N 80.33E
Baijnāth India 41 29.55N 79.37E
Baikunthapur India 41 23.15N 82.33E
Băileşti Romania 21 44.02N 23.21E
Bailleul France 14 50.44N 2.44E
Bailundo Angola 54 12.13S 15.46E
Baimuru P.N.G. 37 7.30S144.49E
Bainang China 41 29.10N 89.15E
Bainbridge U.S.A. 85 30.54N 84.33W
Bain-de-Bretagne France 15 47.50N 1.41W
Baing Indonesia 62 10.15S120.34E
Baingoin China 41 31.45N 89.50E
Bāir Jordan 44 30.46N 36.41E
Bā'ir, Wādī r. Jordan 44 31.10N 36.55E
Baird Mts. U.S.A. 72 67.35N161.30W
Bairin Zuoqi China 32 43.59N119.11E
Bairnsdale Australia 67 37.51S147.38E
Bais France 15 48.15N 0.22W
Baise r. France 17 44.15N 0.20E
Baisha China 33 19.13N109.26E
Baiyang Dian l. China 32 38.55N116.00E
Baiyin China 32 36.40N104.15E
Baja Hungary 21 46.12N 18.58E
Baja California pen. Mexico 81 28.40N114.40W
Baja California Norte d. Mexico 81 29.45N115.30W
Baja California Sur d. Mexico 81 26.00N113.00W
Bakal U.S.S.R. 24 54.58N 58.45E
Bakali r. Zaïre 54 3.58S 17.10E
Bakel Senegal 52 14.54N 12.26W
Baker Calif. U.S.A. 81 35.16N116.04W
Baker Mont. U.S.A. 80 46.22N104.17W
Baker Oreg. U.S.A. 80 44.47N117.50W
Baker, Mt. U.S.A. 80 48.47N121.49W
Baker I. U.S.A. 74 55.20N133.36W
Baker Lake town Canada 73 64.20N 96.10W
Bakersfield U.S.A. 81 35.23N119.01W
Bâ Kêv Cambodia 34 13.42N107.12E
Bako Ethiopia 49 5.50N 36.40E
Bako Ivory Coast 52 9.08N 7.40W
Bakouma C.A.R. 49 5.42N 22.47E
Baku U.S.S.R. 43 40.22N 49.53E
Bala Senegal 52 14.01N 13.08W
Bala U.K. 10 52.54N 3.36W
Balabac i. Phil. 36 7.57N117.01E
Balabac Str. Malaysia/Phil. 36 7.30N117.00E
Ba'labakk Lebanon 44 34.00N 36.12E
Bālāghāt India 41 21.48N 80.11E
Bālāghāt Range mts. India 40 19.00N 76.30E
Balaguer Spain 16 41.50N 0.50E
Balaka Malaŵi 55 15.00S 34.56E
Balaka Zaïre 54 4.51S 19.57E
Balaklava Australia 66 34.08S138.24E
Balaklava U.S.S.R. 25 44.31N 33.35E
Balakovo U.S.S.R. 24 52.04N 47.46E
Balama Mozambique 55 13.19S 38.35E
Bālā Morghāb Afghan. 43 35.34N 63.20E
Balāngīr India 41 20.43N 83.29E
Balarāmpur India 41 23.07N 86.13E
Balashov U.S.S.R. 25 51.30N 43.10E
Balasore India 41 21.30N 86.56E
Balassagyarmat Hungary 21 48.05N 19.18E
Balāţ Egypt 42 25.33N 29.16E
Balaton l. Hungary 21 46.55N 17.50E
Balboa Panama 87 8.37N 79.33W
Balbriggan Rep. of Ire. 13 53.36N 6.12W
Balcad Somali Rep. 45 2.22N 45.25E
Balcarce Argentina 93 37.52S 58.15W
Balchik Bulgaria 21 43.24N 28.10E
Balclutha New Zealand 60 46.16S169.46E
Baldock L. Canada 75 56.33N 97.57W
Baldwin Fla. U.S.A. 85 30.18N 81.59W
Baldwin Mich. U.S.A. 84 43.54N 85.50W
Baldwin Penn. U.S.A. 84 40.23N 79.58W
Baldy Mt. Canada 74 51.28N120.02W
Balē Ethiopia 49 6.30N 40.45E
Baleanoona Australia 66 30.33S139.22E
Baleares, Islas is. Spain 16 39.30N 2.30E
Baleine, Grande rivière de la r. Canada 76 55.20N 77.40W

Baleine, Petite rivière de la *r.* Canada **76** 56.00N 76.45W
Balfate Honduras **87** 15.48N 86.25W
Balfour Downs *town* Australia **62** 22.57S120.46E
Bali India **40** 25.50N 74.05E
Bali *d.* Indonesia **37** 8.45S114.56E
Bali *i.* Indonesia **37** 8.20S115.07E
Bali, Laut *sea* Indonesia **37** 7.30S115.15E
Bali, Selat *str.* Indonesia **37** 8.21S114.30E
Balikesir Turkey **19** 39.38N 27.51E
Balīkh *r.* Syria **42** 35.58N 39.05E
Balikpapan Indonesia **36** 1.15S116.50E
Bali Sea *see* Bali, Laut Indonesia **37**
Balkan Mts. *see* Stara Planina *mts.* Bulgaria **19**
Balkhash U.S.S.R. **30** 46.51N 75.00E
Balkhash, Ozero *l.* U.S.S.R. **30** 46.40N 75.00E
Ballachulish U.K. **12** 56.40N 5.08W
Balladonia Australia **63** 32.27S123.51E
Ballālpur India **41** 19.50N 79.22E
Ballandean Australia **67** 28.39S151.50E
Ballantrae U.K. **12** 55.06N 5.01W
Ballarat Australia **66** 37.36S143.58E
Ballard, L. Australia **63** 29.27S120.55E
Ballater U.K. **12** 57.03N 3.03W
Ballenas, Bahía de *b.* Mexico **81** 26.45N113.25W
Ballenas, Canal de *str.* Mexico **81** 29.10N113.30W
Balleny Is. Antarctica **96** 66.30S163.00E
Balleroy France **15** 49.11N 0.50W
Ballia India **41** 25.45N 84.10E
Ballina Australia **67** 28.50S153.37E
Ballina Rep. of Ire. **13** 54.08N 9.10W
Ballinasloe Rep. of Ire. **13** 53.20N 8.15W
Ballingeary Rep. of Ire. **13** 51.50N 9.15W
Ballinger U.S.A. **83** 31.44N 99.57W
Ball's Pyramid *i.* Pacific Oc. **68** 31.45S159.15E
Ballybay Rep. of Ire. **13** 54.08N 6.56W
Ballycastle U.K. **13** 55.12N 6.15W
Ballyclare U.K. **13** 54.45N 6.00W
Ballyconnell Rep. of Ire. **13** 54.06N 7.37W
Ballydehob Rep. of Ire. **13** 51.34N 9.28W
Ballydonegan Rep. of Ire. **13** 51.38N 10.04W
Ballygar Rep. of Ire. **13** 53.32N 8.20W
Ballygawley U.K. **13** 54.28N 7.03W
Ballykelly U.K. **13** 55.03N 7.00W
Ballymena U.K. **13** 54.52N 6.17W
Ballymoney U.K. **13** 55.04N 6.31W
Ballyquintin Pt. U.K. **13** 54.40N 5.30W
Ballyragget Rep. of Ire. **13** 52.47N 7.21W
Ballyshannon Rep. of Ire. **13** 54.30N 8.11W
Ballyvaughan Rep.of Ire. **13** 53.06N 9.09W
Ballyvourney Rep. of Ire. **13** 51.57N 9.10W
Balmoral Australia **66** 37.17S141.50E
Balochistān *d.* Pakistan **40** 28.30N 65.00E
Balochistan *f.* Pakistan **38** 28.00N 66.00E
Balombo Angola **54** 12.20S 14.45E
Balonne *r.* Australia **67** 28.30S148.20E
Bālotra India **40** 25.50N 72.14E
Balrāmpur India **41** 27.26N 82.11E
Balranald Australia **66** 34.37S143.37E
Balş Romania **21** 44.21N 24.06E
Balsas *r.* Brazil **91** 9.00S 48.10W
Balsas *r.* Mexico **86** 18.10N102.05W
Balta U.S.S.R. **21** 47.58N 29.39E
Baltanás Spain **16** 41.56N 4.15W
Baltasar Brum Uruguay **93** 30.44S 57.19W
Baltic Sea Europe **23** 57.00N 20.00E
Balṭîm Egypt **44** 31.34N 31.05E
Baltimore Md. U.S.A. **85** 39.17N 76.37W
Baltiysk U.S.S.R. **23** 54.39N 19.55E
Balumbah Australia **66** 33.16S136.14E
Bālurghāt India **41** 25.13N 88.46E
Balygychan U.S.S.R. **29** 63.55N154.12E
Balykshi U.S.S.R. **25** 47.04N 51.55E
Bām Iran **43** 29.07N 58.20E
Bama Nigeria **53** 11.35N 13.40E
Bamaga Australia **64** 10.52S142.23E
Bamako Mali **52** 12.40N 7.59W
Bamako *d.* Mali **52** 12.40N 7.55W
Bamba Kenya **55** 3.33S 39.32E
Bamba Mali **52** 17.05N 1.23W
Bamba Zaïre **54** 5.45S 18.23E
Bambari C.A.R. **49** 5.45N 20.40E
Bamberg Germany **20** 49.54N 10.53E
Bambesa Zaïre **54** 3.27N 25.43E
Bambesi Ethiopia **49** 9.45N 34.40E
Bambili Zaïre **54** 3.34N 26.07E
Bambio C.A.R. **53** 3.55N 16.57E
Bambuí Brazil **94** 20.01S 45.59W
Bam Co *l.* China **41** 31.30N 91.10E
Bamenda Cameroon **53** 5.55N 10.09E
Bāmīān Afghan. **40** 34.50N 67.50E
Bamingui C.A.R. **49** 7.34N 20.11E
Bamingui Bangoran *d.* C.A.R. **49** 8.30N 20.30E
Bampton Devon U.K. **11** 51.00N 3.29W
Bampūr Iran **43** 27.13N 60.29E
Bampūr *r.* Iran **43** 27.18N 59.02E
Bāmra Hills India **41** 21.20N 84.30E
Banaba *i.* Kiribati **68** 0.52S169.35E
Banagher Rep. of Ire. **13** 53.12N 8.00W
Banalia Zaïre **54** 1.33N 25.23E
Banamba Mali **52** 13.29N 7.22W
Banana Zaïre **54** 5.55S 12.27E
Bananal, Ilha do *f.* Brazil **91** 11.30S 50.15W
Ban Aranyaprathet Thailand **34** 13.43N102.31E
Banās *r.* India **40** 25.54N 76.45E
Banâs, Ra's *c.* Egypt **42** 23.54N 35.48E
Ban Ban Laos **34** 19.38N103.34E
Banbridge U.K. **13** 54.21N 6.17W
Ban Bua Chum Thailand **34** 15.15N101.15E
Banbury U.K. **11** 52.04N 1.21W
Banchory U.K. **12** 57.03N 2.30W
Bancroft Canada **76** 45.03N 77.51W
Band Afghan. **40** 33.17N 68.39E
Banda Gabon **54** 3.47S 11.04E
Banda Madhya P. India **41** 24.03N 78.57E
Bānda Uttar P. India **41** 25.29N 80.20E
Banda, Laut *sea* Indonesia **37** 5.00S128.00E
Banda Aceh Indonesia **36** 5.35N 95.20E
Banda Besar *i.* Indonesia **37** 4.30S129.55E
Bānda Dāūd Shāh Pakistan **40** 33.16N 71.11E
Bandama *r.* Ivory Coast **52** 5.10N 4.59W
Bandar 'Abbās Iran **43** 27.10N 56.15E
Bandar Beheshtī Iran **43** 25.17N 60.41E
Bandar-e Anzalī Iran **43** 37.26N 49.29E
Bandar-e Deylam Iran **43** 30.05N 50.11E
Bandar-e Khomeynī Iran **43** 30.26N 49.03E
Bandar-e-Lengeh Iran **43** 26.34N 54.53E
Bandar-e Rīg Iran **43** 29.30N 50.40E
Bandar-e Torkeman Iran **43** 36.55N 54.05E
Bandar Seri Begawan Brunei **36** 4.56N114.58E
Banda Sea *see* Banda, Laut *sea* Indonesia **37**
Bandawe Malaŵi **55** 11.57S 34.11E
Bandeira *mtn.* Brazil **94** 20.25S 41.45W
Bāndhi Pakistan **40** 26.36N 68.18E
Bandiagara Mali **52** 14.12N 3.29W
Bāndīkūi India **40** 27.03N 76.34E
Bandīpur Nepal **41** 27.56N 84.25E
Bandipura Jammu & Kashmir **40** 34.25N 74.39E
Bandirma Turkey **19** 40.22N 28.00E
Bandon Rep. of Ire. **13** 51.45N 8.45W
Bandon *r.* Rep. of Ire. **13** 51.43N 8.38W
Bandundu Zaïre **54** 3.20S 17.24E
Bandundu *d.* Zaïre **54** 4.00S 18.30E
Bandung Indonesia **37** 6.57S107.34E
Banes Cuba **87** 20.59N 75.24W
Banff Canada **74** 51.10N115.34W
Banff U.K. **12** 57.40N 2.31W
Banff Nat. Park Canada **74** 51.30N116.15W
Banfora Burkina **52** 10.36N 4.45W
Bangalore India **38** 12.58N 77.35E
Bangassou C.A.R. **49** 4.50N 23.07E
Banggai, Kepulauan *is.* Indonesia **37** 1.30S123.10E
Banggi *i.* Malaysia **36** 7.17N117.12E
Banggong Co *l.* China **41** 33.45N 79.15E
Banghāzī Libya **51** 32.07N 20.05E
Banghāzī *d.* Libya **51** 25.40N 21.00E
Bangil Indonesia **37** 7.34S112.47E
Bangka *i.* Indonesia **36** 2.20S106.10E
Bangkalan Indonesia **37** 7.05S112.44E
Bangkog Co *l.* China **41** 31.45N 89.30E
Bangkok Thailand **34** 13.44N100.30E
Bangladesh Asia **41** 24.30N 90.00E
Bangor Rep. of Ire. **13** 54.09N 9.44W
Bangor *Down* U.K. **13** 54.40N 5.41W
Bangor *Gwynnedd* U.K. **10** 53.13N 4.09W
Bangor Maine U.S.A. **84** 44.49N 68.47W
Bangor Penn. U.S.A. **85** 40.52N 75.13W
Bang Saphan Thailand **34** 11.14N 99.31E
Bangui C.A.R. **53** 4.23N 18.37E
Bangui Phil. **33** 18.33N120.45E
Banguru Zaïre **55** 0.30N 27.10E
Bangweulu, L. Zambia **55** 11.15S 29.45E
Banhā Egypt **44** 30.28N 31.11E
Ban Hat Yai Thailand **34** 7.10N100.28E
Ban Houayxay Laos **34** 20.21N100.32E
Bani *r.* Mali **52** 14.30N 4.15W
Bani, Jbel *mtn.* Morocco **50** 30.00N 8.00W
Banikoara Benin **53** 11.21N 2.25E
Banī Mazār Egypt **44** 28.29N 30.48E
Banīnah Libya **51** 32.05N 20.16E
Banī Suwayf Egypt **44** 29.05N 31.05E
Banī Walīd Libya **51** 31.46N 13.59E
Bāniyās Syria **44** 35.09N 35.58E
Banja Luka Yugo. **19** 44.47N 17.10E
Banjarmasin Indonesia **36** 3.22S114.36E
Banjul Gambia **52** 13.28N 16.39W
Bānka India **41** 24.53N 86.55E
Banka Banka Australia **64** 18.48S134.01E
Ban Kan Vietnam **34** 22.08N105.49E
Ban Kantang Thailand **34** 7.25N 99.35E
Bankasse Mali **52** 14.01N 3.29W
Banks I. B.C. Canada **74** 53.25N130.10W
Banks I. N.W.T. Canada **72** 73.00N122.00W
Banks Is. Vanuatu **68** 13.50S167.30E
Banks Pen. New Zealand **60** 43.45S173.10E
Banks Str. Australia **65** 40.37S148.07E
Bānkura India **41** 23.15N 87.04E
Ban-m'drack Vietnam **34** 12.45N108.50E
Bann *r.* U.K. **13** 55.10N 6.46W
Ban Na San Thailand **34** 8.53N 99.17E
Bannockburn U.K. **12** 56.06N 3.55W
Bannockburn Zimbabwe **56** 20.16S 29.51E
Bannu Pakistan **40** 32.59N 70.36E
Ban Pak Phraek Thailand **34** 8.13N100.13E
Bānsda India **40** 20.45N 73.22E
Banská Bystrica Czech. **21** 48.44N 19.07E
Bānswāra India **40** 23.33N 74.27E
Bantaeng Indonesia **36** 5.32S119.58E
Banté Benin **53** 8.26N 1.54E
Bantry Rep. of Ire. **13** 51.41N 9.27W
Bantry B. Rep. of Ire. **13** 51.40N 9.40W
Bāntva India **40** 21.29N 70.05E
Banyak, Kepulauan *is.* Indonesia **36** 2.15N 97.10E
Banyo Cameroon **53** 6.47N 11.50E
Banyuwangi Indonesia **37** 8.12S114.22E
Banzare Coast *f.* Antarctica **96** 66.30S125.00E
Baode China **32** 39.00N111.05E
Baoding China **32** 38.50N115.26E
Bao Ha Vietnam **33** 22.10N104.22E
Baoji China **32** 34.20N107.17E
Baojing China **33** 28.43N109.37E
Bao-Loc Vietnam **34** 11.30N107.54E
Baoshan China **39** 25.07N 99.08E
Baotou China **32** 40.35N109.59E
Baoulé *r.* Mali **52** 13.47N 10.45W
Bāp India **40** 27.23N 72.21E
Bapaume France **14** 50.07N 2.51E
Baqên China **41** 31.56N 94.00E
Ba'qūbah Iraq **43** 33.45N 44.38E
Bar Albania **19** 42.05N 19.06E
Bar U.S.S.R. **21** 49.05N 27.40E
Bara Nigeria **53** 10.24N 10.43E
Baraawe Somali Rep. **55** 1.02N 44.02E
Barabinsk U.S.S.R. **28** 55.20N 78.18E
Baraboo U.S.A. **82** 43.28N 89.50W
Baracoa Cuba **87** 20.23N 74.31W
Baradero Argentina **93** 33.50S 59.30W
Baradine Australia **67** 30.56S149.05E
Baradine *r.* Australia **67** 30.17S148.27E
Baragoi Kenya **49** 1.47N 36.47E
Bārah Sudan **49** 13.42N 30.22E
Barahona Dom. Rep. **87** 18.13N 71.07W
Baraka Zaïre **55** 4.09S 29.05E
Barakī Barak Afghan. **40** 33.56N 68.55E
Bārākot India **41** 21.33N 85.01E
Bāramūla Jammu & Kashmir **40** 34.12N 74.21E
Bārān India **40** 25.06N 76.31E
Baranagar India **41** 22.38N 88.22E
Baranoa Colombia **90** 10.50N 74.55W
Baranof I. U.S.A. **74** 57.00N135.00W
Baranovichi U.S.S.R. **24** 53.09N 26.00E
Baratta Australia **66** 32.01S139.10E
Barbacena Brazil **94** 21.13S 43.47W
Barbados Lesser Antilles **87** 13.20N 59.40W
Barbar Sudan **48** 18.01N 33.59E
Barbastro Spain **16** 42.02N 0.07E
Barberton R.S.A. **56** 25.46S 31.02E
Barbezieux France **17** 45.28N 0.09W
Barbil India **41** 22.06N 85.20E
Barbuda *i.* Leeward Is. **87** 17.41N 61.48W
Barcaldine Australia **64** 23.31S145.15E
Barcellona Italy **18** 38.10N 15.13E
Barcelona Spain **16** 41.25N 2.10E
Barcelona Venezuela **90** 10.08N 64.43W
Barcelos Brazil **90** 0.59S 62.58W
Barcoo *r.* Australia **64** 25.30S142.50E
Barcs Hungary **21** 45.58N 17.28E
Bardai Chad **53** 21.21N 16.56E
Bardejov Czech. **21** 49.18N 21.16E
Bardi Italy **15** 44.38N 9.44E
Bardia Nepal **41** 28.18N 81.23E
Bardīyah Libya **48** 31.46N 25.06E
Bardnovichi U.S.S.R. **21** 53.09N 26.00E
Bardoli India **40** 21.07N 73.07E
Bardsey *i.* U.K. **10** 52.45N 4.48W
Bardu Norway **22** 68.54N 18.20E
Bardufoss Norway **22** 69.00N 18.30E
Bareilly India **41** 28.21N 79.25E
Barellan Australia **67** 34.17S146.34E
Barengapāra India **41** 25.14N 90.14E
Barentsovo More *see* Barents Sea Arctic Oc. **24**
Barents Sea Arctic Oc. **24** 73.00N 40.00E
Barentu Ethiopia **48** 15.04N 37.37E
Barfleur France **15** 49.40N 1.15W
Barga China **41** 30.51N 81.20E
Bargarh India **41** 21.20N 83.37E
Barge Ethiopia **49** 6.15N 37.00E
Barge Italy **15** 44.43N 7.20E
Barghanak Afghan. **40** 33.56N 62.26E
Barguzin U.S.S.R. **29** 53.40N109.35E
Barham Australia **66** 35.37S144.10E
Barharwa India **41** 24.52N 87.47E
Barhi India **41** 24.18N 85.25E
Bāri Madhya P. India **41** 23.03N 78.05E
Bāri Rāj. India **41** 26.39N 77.36E
Bari Italy **19** 41.08N 16.52E
Baricho Kenya **55** 3.07S 39.47E
Barika Algeria **51** 35.25N 5.19E
Barīm *i.* Yemen **45** 12.40N 43.24E
Barinas Venezuela **90** 8.36N 70.15W
Baripāda India **41** 21.56N 86.43E
Bariri Brazil **94** 22.04S 48.41W
Bâris Egypt **42** 24.40N 30.36E
Bari Sādri India **40** 24.25N 74.28E
Barisāl Bangla. **41** 22.42N 90.22E
Barisan, Pegunungan *mts.* Indonesia **36** 3.30S102.30E
Barito *r.* Indonesia **36** 3.35S114.35E
Barjūj, Wādī Libya **51** 26.03N 12.50E
Barker U.S.A. **76** 43.20N 78.33W
Barker L. Australia **63** 31.45S120.05E
Bārkhān Pakistan **40** 29.54N 69.31E
Barking U.K. **11** 51.32N 0.05E
Barkley Sd. Canada **74** 48.53N125.20W
Barkly East R.S.A. **56** 30.58S 27.33E
Barkly Tableland *f.* Australia **64** 19.00S136.40E
Barkly West R.S.A. **56** 28.32S 24.29E
Bar-le-Duc France **17** 48.46N 5.10E
Barlee, L. Australia **63** 29.30S119.30E
Barlee Range *mts.* Australia **62** 23.40S116.00E
Barletta Italy **18** 41.20N 16.15E
Barlow L. Canada **75** 62.00N103.00W
Barmedman Australia **67** 34.08S147.25E
Barmer India **40** 25.45N 71.23E
Barmera Australia **66** 34.15S140.31E
Barm Fīrūz, Kūh-e *mtn.* Iran **43** 30.21N 52.00E
Barmouth U.K. **10** 52.44N 4.03W
Barnagar India **40** 23.03N 75.22E
Barnāla India **40** 30.22N 75.33E
Barnard Castle *town* U.K. **10** 54.33N 1.55W
Barnato Australia **67** 31.38S144.59E
Barnaul U.S.S.R. **28** 53.21N 83.15E
Barnegat U.S.A. **85** 39.45N 74.13W
Barnegat B. U.S.A. **85** 39.52N 74.07W
Barnegat Light U.S.A. **85** 39.46N 74.06W
Barnet U.K. **11** 51.39N 0.11W
Barneveld Neth. **14** 52.10N 5.39E
Barneville France **15** 49.23N 1.45W
Barneys L. Australia **66** 33.16S144.13E
Barnsley U.K. **10** 53.33N 1.29W
Barnstaple U.K. **11** 51.05N 4.03W
Baro *r.* Ethiopia **49** 8.26N 33.13E
Baro Nigeria **53** 8.37N 6.19E
Barpeta India **41** 26.19N 91.00E
Barqah *f.* Libya **48** 31.00N 23.00E
Barquisimeto Venezuela **90** 10.03N 69.18W
Barra Brazil **91** 11.06S 43.15W
Barra *i.* U.K. **12** 56.59N 7.28W
Barra, Sd. of U.K. **12** 57.04N 7.20W
Barraba Australia **67** 30.24S152.36E
Barra do Corda Brazil **91** 5.30S 45.15W
Barra do Piraí Brazil **94** 22.28S 43.49W
Barra Head U.K. **8** 56.47N 7.36W
Barra Mansa Brazil **94** 22.35S 44.12W
Barranca Peru **90** 4.50S 76.40W
Barrancabermeja Colombia **90** 7.06N 73.54W
Barrancas Venezuela **90** 8.45N 62.13W
Barrancos Portugal **16** 38.10N 7.01W
Barranqueras Argentina **94** 27.30S 58.55W
Barranquilla Colombia **90** 11.10N 74.50W
Barraute Canada **76** 48.26N 77.39W
Barre U.S.A. **84** 44.12N 72.30W
Barreiras Brazil **91** 12.09S 44.58W
Barreiro Portugal **16** 38.40N 9.05W
Barreiros Brazil **91** 8.49S 35.12W
Barrême France **20** 43.57N 6.22E
Barretos Brazil **94** 20.37S 48.38W
Barrhead Canada **74** 54.10N114.24W
Barrhead U.K. **12** 55.47N 4.24W
Barrie Canada **76** 44.22N 79.42W
Barrier Range *mts.* Australia **66** 31.25S141.25E
Barrington Tops *mts.* Australia **67** 32.30S151.28E
Barringun Australia **67** 29.01S145.43E
Barron U.S.A. **80** 48.44N120.43W
Barrow *r.* Rep. of Ire. **13** 52.17N 7.00W
Barrow U.S.A. **72** 71.16N156.50W
Barrow Creek *town* Australia **64** 21.32S133.53E
Barrow I. Australia **62** 21.40S115.27E
Barrow-in-Furness U.K. **10** 54.08N 3.15W
Barrow Range *mts.* Australia **62** 26.04S127.28E
Barry U.K. **11** 51.23N 3.19W
Barstow U.S.A. **81** 34.54N117.01W
Bar-sur-Aube France **15** 48.14N 4.43E
Bar-sur-Seine France **15** 48.07N 4.22E
Bartica Guyana **90** 6.24N 58.38W
Bartin Turkey **42** 41.37N 32.20E
Bartle Frere, Mt. Australia **64** 17.23S145.49E
Bartlesville U.S.A. **83** 36.45N 95.59W
Bartlett L. Canada **74** 63.05N118.20W
Bartolomeu Dias Mozambique **57** 21.10S 35.09E
Barton-upon-Humber U.K. **10** 53.41N 0.27W
Bartoszyce Poland **21** 54.16N 20.49E
Bartow U.S.A. **85** 27.54N 81.51W
Bāruni India **41** 25.29N 85.59E
Barwāh India **40** 22.16N 76.03E
Barwāni India **40** 22.02N 74.54E
Barwa Sāgar India **41** 25.23N 78.44E
Barwon *r.* Australia **67** 30.00S148.05E
Barysh U.S.S.R. **24** 53.40N 47.09E
Basāl Pakistan **40** 33.33N 72.15E
Basankusu Zaïre **54** 1.12N 19.50E
Basavilbaso Argentina **93** 32.20S 58.52W
Basel Switz. **20** 47.33N 7.36E
Bashi Channel Taiwan/Phil. **33** 21.30N121.00E
Basilan Phil. **37** 6.40N121.59E
Basilan *i.* Phil. **37** 6.40N122.10E
Basildon U.K. **11** 51.34N 0.25E
Basilicata *d.* Italy **18** 40.30N 16.20E
Basin U.S.A. **80** 44.23N108.02W
Basingstoke U.K. **11** 51.15N 1.05W
Basin L. Canada **75** 52.38N105.18W
Baskatong, Résr. Canada **76** 46.48N 75.50W
Basmat India **40** 19.19N 77.10E
Bāsoda India **41** 23.51N 77.56E
Basoko Zaïre **49** 1.20N 23.30E
Basongo Zaïre **49** 4.23S 20.28E
Bassano Canada **74** 50.48N112.20W
Bassano Italy **15** 45.46N 11.44E
Bassari Togo **52** 9.12N 0.18E
Bassein Burma **34** 16.46N 94.45E
Basse-Kotto *d.* C.A.R. **49** 5.00N 21.30E
Basse Normandie *d.* France **15** 49.00N 0.00
Basse Santa Su Gambia **52** 13.23N 14.15W
Basse-Terre Guadeloupe **87** 16.00N 61.43W
Bassett U.S.A. **82** 42.35N 99.32W
Bass Str. Australia **65** 39.45S146.00E
Bassum Germany **20** 52.51N 8.43E
Båstad Sweden **23** 56.26N 12.51E
Bastak Iran **43** 27.15N 54.26E
Bastelica France **17** 42.00N 9.03E
Basti India **41** 26.48N 82.43E
Bastia France **17** 42.41N 9.26E
Bastogne Belgium **14** 50.00N 5.43E
Bastrop U.S.A. **83** 32.47N 91.55W
Basyūn Egypt **44** 30.57N 30.49E
Bas Zaïre *d.* Zaïre **54** 5.15S 14.00E
Bata Equat. Guinea **54** 1.51N 9.49E
Batabanó, Golfo de *g.* Cuba **87** 23.15N 82.30W
Batāla India **40** 31.48N 75.13E
Batalha Portugal **16** 39.39N 8.50W
Batang China **39** 30.02N 99.01E
Batangafo C.A.R. **53** 7.27N 18.11E
Batangas Phil. **37** 13.46N121.01E
Batan Is. Phil. **37** 20.50N121.55E
Bátaszék Hungary **21** 46.12N 18.44E
Batatais Brazil **94** 20.54S 47.37W
Batavia U.S.A. **76** 43.00N 78.11W
Bataysk U.S.S.R. **25** 47.09N 39.46E
Batchelor Australia **64** 13.04S131.01E
Bătdâmbâng Cambodia **34** 13.06N103.12E
Batemans Bay *town* Australia **67** 35.55S150.09E
Batesville Ark. U.S.A. **83** 35.46N 91.39W
Batesville Miss. U.S.A. **83** 34.18N 90.00W
Bath Canada **77** 46.31N 67.37W
Bath U.K. **11** 51.22N 2.22W
Bath Maine U.S.A. **84** 43.55N 69.49W
Bath N.Y. U.S.A. **84** 42.20N 77.19W
Batha *d.* Chad **53** 14.30N 18.30E
Batha *r.* Chad **53** 12.47N 17.34E
Baṭḥā, Wādī al *r.* Oman **43** 20.01N 59.39E
Bathgate U.K. **12** 55.44N 3.38W
Bathurst Australia **67** 33.27S149.35E
Bathurst Canada **77** 47.36N 65.39W
Bathurst R.S.A. **56** 33.30S 26.48E
Bathurst, C. Canada **72** 70.30N128.00W
Bathurst I. Australia **62** 11.45S130.15E
Bathurst I. Canada **73** 76.00N100.00W
Bathurst Inlet *town* Canada **72** 66.48N108.00W
Batibla C.A.R. **49** 5.56N 21.09E
Batié Burkina **52** 9.42N 2.53W
Batina Yugo. **21** 45.51N 18.51E
Batley U.K. **10** 53.43N 1.38W
Batlow Australia **67** 35.32S148.10E
Batman Turkey **42** 37.52N 41.07E
Batna Algeria **51** 35.35N 6.11E
Baton Rouge U.S.A. **83** 30.23N 91.11W
Batopilas Mexico **81** 27.00N107.45W
Batouri Cameroon **53** 4.26N 14.27E
Batson U.S.A. **83** 30.15N 94.37W
Batticaloa Sri Lanka **39** 7.43N 81.42E
Battle *r.* Canada **75** 52.43N108.15W
Battle U.K. **11** 50.55N 0.30E
Battle Creek *town* U.S.A. **84** 42.20N 85.11W
Battleford Canada **75** 52.45N108.15W
Battle Harbour Canada **77** 52.17N 55.35W
Batu *mtn.* Ethiopia **49** 6.55N 39.46E
Batu, Kepulauan *is.* Indonesia **36** 0.30S 98.2
Batumi U.S.S.R. **42** 41.37N 41.36E
Batu Pahat Malaysia **36** 1.50N102.48E
Baturaja Indonesia **36** 4.10S104.10E
Baturité Brazil **91** 4.20S 38.53W
Bat Yam Israel **44** 32.01N 34.45E
Baubau Indonesia **37** 5.30S122.37E
Bauchi Nigeria **53** 10.16N 9.50E
Bauchi *d.* Nigeria **53** 10.40N 10.00E
Baudh India **41** 20.50N 84.19E
Baugé France **15** 47.33N 0.06W
Bauld, C. Canada **77** 51.38N 55.25W
Bauru Brazil **94** 22.19S 49.07W
Baús Brazil **94** 18.19S 53.10W
Bauska U.S.S.R. **23** 56.24N 24.14E
Bautzen Germany **20** 51.11N 14.29E
Bavay France **14** 50.18N 3.48E
Bawean *i.* Indonesia **37** 5.50S112.39E
Bawku Ghana **52** 11.05N 0.13W
Bayamo Cuba **87** 20.23N 76.39W
Bayamón Puerto Rico **87** 18.24N 66.10W
Bāyan, Band-e *mts.* Afghan. **40** 34.20N 65.0
Bayāna India **40** 26.54N 77.17E
Bayan Har Shan *mts.* China **30** 34.00N 97.2
Bayan Nur China **32** 38.14N103.56E
Bayburt Turkey **42** 40.15N 40.16E
Bay City Mich. U.S.A. **84** 43.35N 83.52W
Bay City Tex. U.S.A. **83** 28.59N 95.58W
Baydaratskaya Guba *b.* U.S.S.R. **28** 70.00N 66.00E
Baydhabo Somali Rep. **55** 3.08N 43.34E
Bayern *d.* Germany **20** 48.30N 11.30E
Bayeux France **15** 49.16N 0.42W
Bayfield U.S.A. **82** 46.49N 90.49W
Baykal, Ozero *l.* U.S.S.R. **30** 53.30N100.00E
Baykit U.S.S.R. **29** 61.45N 96.22E
Baykonyr U.S.S.R. **28** 47.50N 66.03E
Bay of Plenty *d.* New Zealand **60** 38.00S177.10E
Bayombong Phil. **37** 16.27N121.10E
Bayonne France **17** 43.30N 1.28W
Bayovar Peru **90** 5.50S 81.03W
Bayreuth Germany **20** 49.56N 11.35E
Bayrūt Lebanon **44** 33.52N 35.30E
Baytik Shan *mts.* China **30** 45.15N 90.50E
Baytown U.S.A. **83** 29.44N 94.58W
Bay View New Zealand **60** 39.26S176.52E
Baza Spain **16** 37.30N 2.45W
Baza, Sierra de *mts.* Spain **16** 37.15N 2.45W
Bazaliya U.S.S.R. **21** 49.42N 26.29E
Bazaruto, Ilha do *i.* Mozambique **57** 21.40S 35.28E
Bazas France **17** 44.26N 0.13W
Bazdār Pakistan **40** 26.21N 65.03E
Bazhong China **33** 31.51N106.42E
Bazmān Iran **43** 27.48N 60.12E
Bazmān, Kūh-e *mtn.* Iran **43** 28.06N 60.00E
Beach U.S.A. **82** 46.55N103.52W
Beach Haven U.S.A. **85** 39.34N 74.14W
Beachport Australia **66** 37.29S140.01E
Beachwood U.S.A. **85** 39.56N 74.12W
Beachy Head U.K. **11** 50.43N 0.15E
Beacon U.S.A. **85** 41.30N 73.58W
Beagle Bay *town* Australia **62** 16.58S122.4
Bealanana Madagascar **57** 14.33S 48.44E
Beardstown U.S.A. **82** 40.01N 90.26W
Bear I. *see* Bjørnøya *i.* Arctic Oc. **96**
Bear L. U.S.A. **80** 42.00N111.20W
Bearskin Lake *town* Canada **75** 53.58N 91.02W
Beas *r.* India **40** 31.10N 75.00E
Beatrice U.S.A. **82** 40.16N 96.44W
Beatrice, C. Australia **64** 14.15S136.59E
Beatton *r.* Canada **74** 56.15N120.45W
Beatton River *town* Canada **74** 57.26N121.20W
Beatty U.S.A. **80** 36.54N116.46W
Beattyville Canada **76** 48.53N 77.10W
Beauce *f.* France **15** 48.22N 1.50E
Beaudesert Australia **67** 27.58S153.01E

Beaufort Australia 66 37.28S143.28E
Beaufort U.S.A. 85 32.26N 80.40W
Beaufort Sea N. America 72 72.00N141.00W
Beaufort West R.S.A. 56 32.20S 22.34E
Beaugency France 15 47.47N 1.38E
Beauharnois Canada 77 45.19N 73.52W
Beaulieu r. Canada 74 62.03N113.11W
Beauly U.K. 12 57.29N 4.29W
Beauly r. U.K. 12 57.29N 4.25W
Beaumaris U.K. 10 53.16N 4.07W
Beaumetz-lès-Loges France 14 50.15N 2.36E
Beaumont Belgium 14 50.14N 4.16E
Beaumont Miss. U.S.A. 83 31.11N 88.55W
Beaumont Tex. U.S.A. 83 30.05N 94.06W
Beaumont-le-Roger France 15 49.05N 0.47E
Beaumont-sur-Sarthe France 15 48.13N 0.07E
Beaune France 17 47.02N 4.50E
Beaune-la-Rolande France 15 48.04N 2.26E
Beaupréau France 17 47.12N 0.59W
Beauséjour Canada 75 50.04N 96.33W
Beauvais France 15 49.26N 2.05E
Beauval Canada 75 55.09N107.35W
Beauvoir France 17 46.55N 2.01W
Beaver r. N.W.T. Canada 74 59.43N124.16W
Beaver r. Ont. Canada 75 55.55N 87.50W
Beaver Alaska U.S.A. 72 66.22N147.24W
Beaver Okla. U.S.A. 83 36.49N100.31W
Beaver Dam town U.S.A. 82 43.28N 88.50W
Beaverhill L. Alta. Canada 74 53.27N112.32W
Beaverhill L. N.W.T. Canada 75 63.02N104.22W
Beaver I. U.S.A. 84 45.42N 85.28W
Beāwar India 40 26.06N 74.19E
ebedouro Brazil 94 20.54S 48.31W
ebington U.K. 10 53.23N 3.01W
écancour Canada 77 46.20N 72.26W
eccles U.K. 11 52.27N 1.33E
ečej Yugo. 21 45.37N 20.03E
échar Algeria 50 31.37N 2.13W
eckley U.S.A. 85 37.46N 81.12W
eckum Germany 14 51.45N 8.02E
eclean Romania 21 47.11N 24.10E
édarieux France 17 43.35N 3.10E
edēsa Ethiopia 49 8.50N 40.45E
edford Canada 77 45.07N 72.59W
edford U.K. 11 52.08N 0.29W
edford U.S.A. 84 38.51N 86.30W
edford, C. Australia 64 15.14S145.21E
edford Levels f. U.K. 11 52.35N 0.08W
edfordshire d. U.K. 11 52.04N 0.28W
edi India 40 22.30N 70.02E
edlington U.K. 10 55.08N 1.34W
edourie Australia 64 24.21S139.28E
eech Grove U.S.A. 84 39.42N 86.06W
eechworth Australia 67 36.23S146.42E
eenleigh Australia 67 27.43S153.09E
e'er Menuha Israel 44 30.19N 35.08E
e'er Sheva' Israel 44 31.15N 34.47E
eerta Neth. 14 53.12N 7.07E
eeston U.K. 10 52.55N 1.11W
eeville U.S.A. 83 28.24N 97.45W
efale Zaïre 54 0.27N 21.01E
efandriana Madagascar 57 15.16S 48.32E
efandriana Madagascar 57 22.06S 43.54E
eg, Lough U.K. 13 54.47N 6.29W
ega Australia 67 36.41S149.50E
egamganj India 41 23.36N 78.20E
ègles France 17 44.48N 0.32W
egna r. Norway 23 60.32N 10.00E
egusarai India 41 25.25N 86.08E
ehara Madagascar 57 25.00S 46.25E
ehbehān Iran 43 30.35N 50.17E
ei'an China 31 48.17N126.33E
eihai China 33 21.29N109.09E
ei Jiang r. China 33 23.19N112.51E
eijing China 32 39.55N116.25E
eijing d. China 32 40.00N116.30E
eijing Shi d. China 31 40.15N116.30E
eilen Neth. 14 52.51N 6.31E
inn Dearg mtn. U.K. 12 57.47N 4.55W
ipa'a P.N.G. 64 8.30S146.35E
ipiao China 32 41.47N120.40E
ira Mozambique 57 19.49S 34.52E
irut see Bayrūt Lebanon 44
itang China 32 39.06N117.43E
itbridge Zimbabwe 56 22.10S 30.01E
iuş Romania 21 46.40N 22.21E
ja Portugal 16 38.01N 7.52W
ja Tunisia 51 36.44N 9.11E
jaïa Algeria 51 36.45N 5.05E
jar Spain 16 40.24N 5.45W
jestān Iran 43 34.32N 58.08E
jhi r. Pakistan 40 29.47N 67.58E
oording Australia 63 31.22S116.30E
kés Hungary 21 46.46N 21.08E
késcsaba Hungary 21 46.41N 21.06E
kily Madagascar 57 24.13S 45.19E
la India 41 25.56N 81.59E
la Pakistan 40 26.14N 66.19E
labo Cameroon 53 5.00N 13.20E
la Crkva Yugo. 21 44.54N 21.26E
Air U.S.A. 85 39.32N 76.21W
alcázar Spain 16 38.35N 5.10W
ampalli India 41 19.02N 79.30E
ang Indonesia 37 0.58N124.56E
au Pacific Oc. 37 7.00N134.25E
a Vista Brazil 92 22.05S 56.22W
a Vista Mozambique 57 26.20S 32.41E
aya r. U.S.S.R. 28 55.40N 52.30E
aya Glina U.S.S.R. 25 46.04N 40.54E
aya Tserkov U.S.S.R. 21 49.49N 30.10E
cher Is. Canada 76 56.00N 79.00W
coo U.K. 13 54.18N 7.53W
da India 41 22.05N 87.21E
ebey U.S.S.R. 24 54.05N 54.07E
ed Weyne Somali Rep. 45 4.47N 45.12E
ém Brazil 91 1.27S 48.29W
Belem Mozambique 57 14.11S 35.59E
Belén Uruguay 93 30.47S 57.47W
Belen U.S.A. 81 34.40N106.46W
Belén, Cuchilla de mts. Uruguay 93 30.49S 56.28W
Beles r. Ethiopia 45 11.10N 35.10E
Belev U.S.S.R. 24 53.50N 36.08E
Belfast U.K. 13 54.36N 5.57W
Belfast Maine U.S.A. 84 44.27N 69.01W
Belfast Lough U.K. 13 54.42N 5.45W
Belfield U.S.A. 82 46.53N103.12W
Belfort France 17 47.38N 6.52E
Belfry U.S.A. 80 45.09N109.01W
Belgaum India 38 15.54N 74.36E
Belgium Europe 14 51.00N 4.30E
Belgorod U.S.S.R. 25 50.38N 36.36E
Belgorod-Dnestrovskiy U.S.S.R. 21 46.10N 30.19E
Belgrade see Beograd Yugo. 21
Beli Nigeria 53 7.53N 10.59E
Belitung i. Indonesia 36 3.00S108.00E
Belize Belize 87 17.29N 88.20W
Belize C. America 87 17.00N 88.30W
Belka Australia 63 31.45S118.09E
Bellac France 17 46.07N 1.04E
Bella Coola Canada 74 52.25N126.40W
Bellagio Italy 15 45.59N 9.15E
Bellaire Tex. U.S.A. 83 29.44N 95.03W
Bellaria Italy 15 44.09N 12.28E
Bellary India 38 15.11N 76.54E
Bellata Australia 67 29.55S149.50E
Bella Unión Uruguay 93 30.15S 57.35W
Bella Vista Corrientes Argentina 92 28.30S 59.00W
Bella Vista Tucuman Argentina 92 27.02S 65.19W
Bellbrook Australia 67 30.48S152.30E
Bellefontaine U.S.A. 84 40.22N 83.45W
Belle Fourche r. U.S.A. 82 44.26N102.19W
Belle Glade U.S.A. 85 26.41N 80.41W
Belle Île France 17 47.20N 3.10W
Belle Isle Canada 77 51.55N 55.20W
Belle Isle, Str. of Canada 77 51.35N 56.30W
Bellême France 15 48.22N 0.34E
Belleoram Canada 77 47.32N 55.28W
Belleville Canada 76 44.10N 77.22W
Belleville Kans. U.S.A. 82 39.49N 97.38W
Bellevue Canada 74 49.35N114.22W
Bellevue Idaho U.S.A. 80 43.28N114.16W
Bellevue Penn. U.S.A. 84 40.32N 80.08W
Bellevue Wash. U.S.A. 80 47.37N122.12W
Belle Yella Liberia 52 7.24N 10.09W
Bellingen Australia 67 30.28S152.43E
Bellingham U.K. 10 55.09N 2.15W
Bellingham U.S.A. 80 48.46N122.29W
Bellingshausen Sea Antarctica 96 70.00S 88.00W
Bellinzona Switz. 15 46.11N 9.02E
Bello Colombia 90 6.20N 75.41W
Bellpat Pakistan 40 28.59N 68.00E
Belluno Italy 15 46.09N 12.13E
Bell Ville Argentina 93 32.35S 62.41W
Belmar U.S.A. 85 40.11N 74.01W
Bélmez Spain 16 38.17N 5.17W
Belmond U.S.A. 82 42.51N 93.37W
Belmont Australia 67 33.02S151.40E
Belmopan Belize 87 17.25N 88.46W
Belmullet Rep. of Ire. 13 54.14N 10.00W
Belogradchik Bulgaria 21 43.38N 22.41E
Belo Horizonte Brazil 94 19.45S 43.54W
Beloit Kans. U.S.A. 82 39.28N 98.06W
Beloit Wisc. U.S.A. 82 42.31N 89.02W
Belo Jardim Brazil 91 8.22S 36.22W
Belokorovichi U.S.S.R. 21 51.04N 28.00E
Belomorsk U.S.S.R. 24 64.34N 34.45E
Belonia India 41 23.15N 91.27E
Beloretsk U.S.S.R. 24 53.59N 58.20E
Belorusskaya S.S.R. d. U.S.S.R. 21 53.30N 28.00E
Beloye More sea U.S.S.R. 24 65.30N 38.00E
Beloye Ozero l. U.S.S.R. 24 60.12N 37.45E
Belozersk U.S.S.R. 24 60.00N 37.49E
Belper U.K. 10 53.02N 1.29W
Beltana Australia 66 30.40S138.27E
Belterra Brazil 91 2.38S 54.57W
Belton Australia 66 32.12S138.45E
Belton U.S.A. 83 31.04N 97.28W
Beltsy U.S.S.R. 21 47.45N 27.59E
Belukha, Gora mtn. U.S.S.R. 30 49.48N 86.40E
Belvidere U.S.A. 85 40.49N 75.05W
Belyando r. Australia 64 21.38S146.50E
Belyayevka U.S.S.R. 21 46.30N 30.12E
Belynichi U.S.S.R. 21 54.00N 29.42E
Belyy, Ostrov U.S.S.R. 28 73.10N 70.45E
Belyy Yar U.S.S.R. 28 58.28N 85.03E
Bełżec Poland 21 50.24N 23.26E
Bemaraha, Plateau du mts. Madagascar 57 20.00S 45.15E
Bemarivo r. Madagascar 57 15.27S 47.40E
Bemidji U.S.A. 82 47.29N 94.53W
Bena Dibele Zaïre 54 4.07S 22.50E
Benagerie Australia 66 31.30S140.21E
Benalla Australia 67 36.35S145.58E
Benanee Australia 66 34.32S142.56E
Benares see Vārānasi India 41
Benavente Spain 16 42.00N 5.40W
Benbecula i. U.K. 12 57.26N 7.18W
Bencha China 32 32.31N120.53E
Ben Cruachan mtn. U.K. 12 56.26N 5.18W
Bencubbin Australia 63 30.48S117.52E
Bend U.S.A. 80 44.03N121.19W
Bende Nigeria 53 5.34N 7.37E
Bendel d. Nigeria 53 6.10N 6.00E
Bendemeer Australia 67 30.52S151.10E
Bender Beyla Somali Rep. 45 9.30N 50.30E
Bendery U.S.S.R. 21 46.50N 29.29E
Bendigo Australia 66 36.48S144.21E
Bendoc Australia 67 37.10S148.55E
Bendorf Germany 14 50.26N 7.34E
Bénéna Mali 52 13.09N 4.17W
Benenitra Madagascar 57 23.27S 45.05E
Benešov Czech. 20 49.45N 14.22E
Benevento Italy 18 41.07N 14.46E
Bengal, B. of Indian Oc. 41 20.00N 90.00E
Bengbu China 32 32.53N117.26E
Benghazi see Banghāzī Libya 51
Bengkulu Indonesia 36 3.46S102.16E
Bengo d. Angola 54 9.00S 13.40E
Benguela Angola 54 12.34S 13.24E
Benguela d. Angola 54 12.45S 14.00E
Ben Hope mtn. U.K. 12 58.24N 4.36W
Beni r. Bolivia 92 10.23S 65.24W
Beni Zaïre 55 0.29N 29.27E
Beni Abbes Algeria 50 30.08N 2.10W
Benicarló Spain 16 40.25N 0.25E
Benidorm Spain 16 38.33N 0.09W
Beni-Mellal Morocco 50 32.22N 6.29W
Benin Africa 53 9.00N 2.30E
Benin, Bight of Africa 53 5.30N 3.00E
Benin City Nigeria 53 6.19N 5.41E
Beni Saf Algeria 50 35.19N 1.23W
Benjamin Constant Brazil 90 4.22S 70.02W
Benkelman U.S.A. 82 40.03N101.32W
Ben Lawers mtn. U.K. 12 56.33N 4.14W
Ben Lomond mtn. U.K. 12 56.12N 4.38W
Ben Macdhui mtn. U.K. 12 57.04N 3.40W
Ben More mtn. Central U.K. 12 56.23N 4.31W
Ben More mtn. Strath. U.K. 12 56.26N 6.02W
Ben More Assynt mtn. U.K. 12 58.07N 4.52W
Bennett Canada 74 59.49N135.01W
Bennett, L. Australia 64 22.50S131.01E
Bennettsville U.S.A. 85 34.36N 79.40W
Ben Nevis mtn. U.K. 12 56.48N 5.00W
Benneydale New Zealand 60 38.31S175.21E
Benoni R.S.A. 56 26.12S 28.18E
Bénoué r. Cameroon see Benue r. Nigeria 53
Benson Ariz. U.S.A. 81 31.58N110.18W
Benson Minn. U.S.A. 82 45.19N 95.36W
Bentiaba Angola 54 14.19S 12.23E
Bentinck I. Australia 64 17.04S139.30E
Bentiu Sudan 49 9.14N 29.50E
Benton U.S.A. 82 38.01N 88.54W
Benton Harbor U.S.A. 84 42.07N 86.27W
Benue d. Nigeria 53 7.20N 8.00E
Benue r. Nigeria 53 7.52N 6.45E
Ben Wyvis mtn. U.K. 12 57.40N 4.35W
Benxi China 32 41.21N123.47E
Beograd Yugo. 21 44.49N 20.28E
Beohāri India 41 24.03N 81.23E
Beowawe U.S.A. 80 40.35N116.29W
Berat Albania 19 40.42N 19.59E
Berau, Teluk b. Indonesia 37 2.20S133.00E
Berbera Somali Rep. 45 10.28N 45.02E
Berbérati C.A.R. 53 4.19N 15.51E
Berceto Italy 15 44.31N 9.59E
Berchem Belgium 14 50.48N 3.32E
Berck France 17 50.25N 1.36E
Bercu France 14 50.32N 3.15E
Berdichev U.S.S.R. 21 49.54N 28.39E
Berdsk U.S.S.R. 28 54.51N 82.51E
Berdyansk U.S.S.R. 25 46.45N 36.47E
Beregovo U.S.S.R. 21 48.13N 22.39E
Bereko Tanzania 55 4.27S 35.43E
Berens r. Canada 75 52.21N 97.02W
Berens River town Canada 75 52.22N 97.02W
Beresford Australia 66 29.14S136.40E
Berettyóújfalu Hungary 21 47.14N 21.32E
Berevo Madagascar 57 19.44S 44.58E
Bereza U.S.S.R. 21 52.32N 25.00E
Berezhany U.S.S.R. 21 49.27N 24.56E
Berezina r. U.S.S.R. 21 54.10N 28.10E
Berezna U.S.S.R. 21 51.34N 31.46E
Berezniki U.S.S.R. 24 59.26N 56.49E
Berezno U.S.S.R. 21 51.00N 26.41E
Berezovka U.S.S.R. 21 47.12N 30.56E
Berezovo U.S.S.R. 28 63.58N 65.00E
Berga Spain 16 42.06N 1.48E
Berga Sweden 23 57.14N 16.03E
Bergama Turkey 19 39.08N 27.10E
Bergamo Italy 15 45.42N 9.40E
Bergen Germany 20 54.25N 13.26E
Bergen Neth. 14 52.40N 4.41E
Bergen Norway 23 60.23N 5.20E
Bergen U.S.A. 76 43.05N 77.57W
Bergen op Zoom Neth. 14 51.30N 4.17E
Bergerac France 17 44.50N 0.29E
Bergheim Germany 14 50.58N 6.39E
Berghem Neth. 14 51.46N 5.32E
Bergisch Gladbach Germany 14 50.59N 7.10E
Bergkamen Germany 14 51.35N 7.39E
Bergkvara Sweden 23 56.23N 16.05E
Bergland U.S.A. 84 46.36N 89.33W
Bergues France 14 50.58N 2.21E
Bergum Neth. 14 53.14N 5.59E
Berhampore India 41 24.06N 88.15E
Berhampur India 41 19.19N 84.47E
Bering Sea N. America/Asia 72 65.00N170.00W
Bering Str. U.S.S.R./U.S.A. 72 65.00N170.00W
Berislav U.S.S.R. 25 46.51N 33.26E
Berja Spain 16 36.50N 2.56W
Berkåk Norway 22 62.48N 10.03E
Berkel r. Neth. 14 52.10N 6.12E
Berkeley U.S.A. 80 37.57N122.18W
Berkner I. Antarctica 96 79.30S 50.00W
Berkshire d. U.K. 11 51.25N 1.03W
Berkshire Downs hills U.K. 11 51.32N 1.36W
Berland r. Canada 74 54.00N116.50W
Berlin Germany 20 52.32N 13.25E
Berlin d. Germany 20 52.30N 13.20E
Berlin Md. U.S.A. 85 38.20N 75.13W
Berlin N.H. U.S.A. 84 44.29N 71.10W
Bermagui Australia 67 36.28S150.03E
Bermejo r. San Juan Argentina 92 31.40S 67.15W
Bermejo r. Tucumán Argentina 92 26.47S 58.30W
Bermo India 41 23.47N 85.57E
Bermuda Atlantic Oc. 95 32.18N 64.45W
Bermuda Rise f. Atlantic Oc. 95 34.00N 60.00W
Bern Switz. 20 46.57N 7.26E
Bernard L. Canada 76 45.44N 79.24W
Bernay France 15 48.06N 0.36E
Bernburg Germany 20 51.48N 11.44E
Berne see Bern Switz. 17
Bernier I. Australia 62 24.51S113.09E
Bernina mtn. Italy/Switz. 15 46.22N 9.57E
Bernkastel Germany 14 49.55N 7.05E
Beroroha Madagascar 57 21.41S 45.10E
Beroun Czech. 20 49.58N 14.04E
Berrechid Morocco 50 33.17N 7.35W
Berri Australia 66 34.17S140.36E
Berridale Australia 67 36.21S148.51E
Berrigan Australia 67 35.41S145.48E
Berry Head U.K. 11 50.24N 3.28W
Berryville Ark. U.S.A. 83 36.22N 93.34W
Bersenbrück Germany 14 52.36N 7.58E
Bershad U.S.S.R. 21 48.20N 29.30E
Berté, Lac l. Canada 77 50.47N 68.30W
Berthierville Canada 77 46.05N 73.10W
Bertinoro Italy 15 44.09N 12.08E
Bertoua Cameroon 53 4.34N 13.42E
Bertraghboy B. Rep. of Ire. 13 53.23N 9.52W
Berwick-upon-Tweed U.K. 10 55.46N 2.00W
Besalampy Madagascar 57 16.45S 44.30E
Besançon France 17 47.14N 6.02E
Bessarabia f. U.S.S.R. 21 46.30N 28.40E
Bessemer U.S.A. 85 33.22N 87.00W
Betafo Madagascar 57 19.50S 46.51E
Betanzos Spain 16 43.17N 8.13W
Bétaré Oya Cameroon 53 5.34N 14.09E
Bete Hor Ethiopia 49 11.40N 39.00E
Bethal R.S.A. 56 26.26S 29.27E
Bethany Beach town U.S.A. 85 38.31N 75.04W
Bethel Alas. U.S.A. 72 60.48N161.46W
Bethesda U.S.A. 85 38.59N 77.06W
Bethlehem R.S.A. 56 28.13S 28.18E
Bethlehem U.S.A. 85 40.36N 75.22W
Béthune France 14 50.32N 2.38E
Béthune r. France 15 49.53N 1.09E
Betim Brazil 94 19.55S 44.07W
Betioky Madagascar 57 23.42S 44.22E
Betroka Madagascar 57 23.16S 46.06E
Bet She'an Israel 44 32.30N 35.30E
Bet Shemesh Israel 44 31.45N 35.00E
Betsiamites Canada 77 48.56N 68.38W
Betsiboka r. Madagascar 57 16.03S 46.36E
Bette mtn. Libya 51 22.00N 19.12E
Bettiah India 41 26.48N 84.30E
Bettles U.S.A. 72 66.53N151.51W
Betūl India 41 21.55N 77.54E
Betwa r. India 41 25.55N 80.12E
Betws-y-Coed U.K. 9 53.05N 3.48W
Betzdorf Germany 14 50.48N 7.54E
Beulah Australia 66 35.59S142.26E
Beulah Canada 75 50.16N101.02W
Beulah U.S.A. 82 47.16N101.47W
Beuvron r. France 15 47.29N 3.31E
Beverley Australia 63 32.06S116.56E
Beverley U.K. 10 53.52N 0.26W
Beverley Hills town U.S.A. 81 34.04N118.26W
Beverly Mass. U.S.A. 84 42.33N 70.53W
Beverwijk Neth. 14 52.29N 4.40E
Bewcastle Fells hills U.K. 10 55.05N 2.50W
Bexhill U.K. 11 50.51N 0.29E
Bexley U.K. 11 51.26N 0.10E
Beyla Guinea 52 8.42N 8.39W
Beyneu U.S.S.R. 25 45.16N 55.04E
Beypazari Turkey 42 40.10N 31.56E
Beyşehir Gölü l. Turkey 42 37.47N 31.30E
Bezhanovo Bulgaria 19 43.13N 24.26E
Bezhetsk U.S.S.R. 24 57.49N 36.40E
Bezhitsa U.S.S.R. 24 53.19N 34.17E
Béziers France 17 43.21N 3.13E
Bhadohi India 41 25.25N 82.34E
Bhādra India 40 29.07N 75.10E
Bhadrakh India 41 21.04N 86.30E
Bhāg Pakistan 40 29.02N 67.49E
Bhāgalpur India 41 25.15N 87.00E
Bhāi Pheru Pakistan 40 31.12N 73.57E
Bhaironghāti India 41 31.01N 78.53E
Bhaisa India 41 19.06N 77.58E
Bhakkar Pakistan 40 31.38N 71.04E
Bhaktapur Nepal 41 27.42N 85.27E
Bhalwāl Pakistan 40 32.16N 72.54E
Bhamo Burma 34 24.10N 97.30E
Bhandāra India 41 21.10N 79.39E
Bhānvad India 40 21.56N 69.47E
Bharatpur India 41 27.13N 77.29E
Bharthana India 41 26.45N 79.14E
Bhātāpāra India 41 21.44N 81.56E
Bhatewar India 40 24.40N 74.05E
Bhātiāpāra Ghāt Bangla. 41 23.12N 89.42E
Bhatinda India 40 30.13N 74.56E
Bhatkal India 38 13.58N 74.34E
Bhātpāra India 41 22.52N 88.24E
Bhaunagar India 40 21.46N 72.09E
Bhawāni Mandi India 40 24.25N 75.50E
Bhawānipatna India 41 19.54N 83.10E
Bhera Pakistan 40 32.29N 72.55E
Bhikangaon India 40 21.52N 75.57E
Bhilai India 41 21.13N 81.26E
Bhilwāra India 40 25.21N 74.38E
Bhima r. India 38 16.30N 77.10E
Bhind India 41 26.34N 78.48E
Bhinmāl India 40 25.00N 72.15E
Bhiwandi India 40 19.18N 73.04E
Bhiwāni India 40 28.47N 76.08E
Bhognīpur India 41 26.12N 79.48E
Bhojpur Nepal 41 27.11N 87.02E
Bhokardan India 40 20.16N 75.46E
Bhopāl India 41 23.16N 77.24E
Bhor India 38 18.12N 73.53E
Bhuban India 41 20.53N 85.50E
Bhubaneswar India 41 20.15N 85.50E
Bhuj India 40 23.16N 69.40E
Bhusāwal India 40 21.03N 75.46E
Bhutan Asia 41 27.15N 91.00E
Bia, Phou mtn. Laos 34 18.59N103.11E
Biābānak Afghan. 40 32.11N 64.11E
Biak Indonesia 37 1.10S136.05E
Biak i. Indonesia 37 0.55S136.00E
Biała Podlaska Poland 21 52.02N 23.06E
Białogard Poland 20 54.00N 16.00E
Białystok Poland 21 53.09N 23.10E
Biankouma Ivory Coast 52 7.51N 7.34W
Biaora India 40 23.55N 76.54E
Biarritz France 17 43.29N 1.33W
Biasca Switz. 15 46.22N 8.58E
Bibā Egypt 44 28.56N 30.59E
Bibala Angola 54 14.46S 13.21E
Biberach Germany 20 48.20N 9.30E
Bic Canada 77 48.22N 68.42W
Bicas Brazil 94 21.44S 43.04W
Bicester U.K. 11 51.53N 1.09W
Bida Nigeria 53 9.06N 5.59E
Bīdar India 38 17.54N 77.33E
Biddeford U.S.A. 84 43.30N 70.26W
Bideford U.K. 11 51.01N 4.13W
Bidon Cinq see Poste Maurice Cortier Algeria 50
Bi Doup mtn. Vietnam 34 12.05N108.40E
Bié d. Angola 54 12.30S 17.30E
Biel Switz. 17 47.09N 7.16E
Bielefeld Germany 20 52.02N 8.32E
Biella Italy 15 45.34N 8.03E
Bielsko-Biała Poland 21 49.49N 19.02E
Bielsk Podlaski Poland 21 52.47N 23.12E
Bien Hoa Vietnam 34 10.58N106.50E
Bienville, Lac l. Canada 77 55.05N 72.40W
Bié Plateau f. Angola 54 13.00S 16.00E
Big Bald Mtn. Canada 77 47.12N 66.25W
Big Bear Lake town U.S.A. 81 34.15N116.53W
Big Beaver House town Canada 76 52.59N 89.50W
Big Belt Mts. U.S.A. 80 46.40N111.25W
Big Bend Nat. Park U.S.A. 83 29.12N103.12W
Bigbury B. U.K. 11 50.15N 3.56W
Big Cypress Swamp f. U.S.A. 85 26.10N 81.38W
Big Falls town U.S.A. 82 48.12N 93.48W
Biggar Canada 75 52.04N107.59W
Biggar U.K. 12 55.38N 3.31W
Bighorn r. U.S.A. 80 46.09N107.28W
Bighorn L. U.S.A. 80 45.06N108.08W
Bighorn Mts. U.S.A. 80 44.00N107.30W
Bight, Head of b. Australia 65 31.29S131.16E
Bignasco Switz. 15 46.20N 8.36E
Bignona Senegal 52 12.48N 16.18W
Big Pine U.S.A. 80 37.10N118.17W
Big Piney U.S.A. 80 42.32N110.07W
Big Quill L. Canada 75 51.55N104.22W
Big Salmon Canada 72 61.53N134.55W
Big Salmon r. Canada 74 61.52N134.56W
Big Sand L. Canada 75 57.45N 99.42W
Big Sandy U.S.A. 80 48.11N110.07W
Big Smoky Valley f. U.S.A. 80 38.30N117.15W
Big Snowy Mtn. U.S.A. 80 46.50N109.30W
Big Spring town U.S.A. 83 32.15N101.28W
Big Stone Gap town U.S.A. 85 36.52N 82.46W
Bigstone L. Canada 75 53.42N 95.44W
Big Stone L. U.S.A. 82 45.25N 96.40W
Big Sur U.S.A. 81 36.15N121.48W
Big Timber U.S.A. 80 45.50N109.57W
Big Trout L. Canada 75 53.40N 90.00W
Bihać Yugo. 18 44.49N 15.53E
Bihār India 41 25.11N 85.31E
Bihār d. India 41 24.30N 86.00E
Biharamulo Tanzania 55 2.34S 31.20E
Bihor mtn. Romania 21 46.26N 22.43E
Bihu China 33 28.21N119.47E
Bijagós, Arquipélago dos is. Guinea Bissau 52 11.30N 16.00W
Bijainagar India 40 25.56N 74.38E
Bijaipura India 41 24.46N 77.48E
Bijāpur India 38 16.52N 75.47E
Bijāpur India 41 18.48N 80.49E
Bijār Iran 43 35.52N 47.39E
Bijāwar India 41 24.38N 79.30E
Bijbān Chāh Pakistan 40 26.54N 64.42E
Bijeljina Yugo. 19 44.45N 19.13E
Bijeypur India 40 26.03N 77.22E
Bijie China 33 27.28N105.20E
Bijnor India 41 29.22N 78.08E
Bikaner India 40 28.42N 73.25E
Bikin U.S.S.R. 31 46.52N134.15E
Bikini i. Pacific Oc. 68 11.35N165.23E
Bikoro Zaïre 54 0.45S 18.09E
Bilāra India 40 26.10N 73.42E
Bilāspur Himachal P. India 40 31.19N 76.45E
Bilāspur Madhya P. India 41 22.05N 82.09E
Bilauktaung Range mts. Thailand 34 13.00N 99.15E
Bilbao Spain 16 43.15N 2.56W
Bilbays Egypt 44 30.25N 31.34E
Bilecik Turkey 42 40.10N 29.59E
Bilgrām India 41 27.11N 80.02E
Bili r. Zaïre 49 4.09N 22.29E
Bilibino U.S.S.R. 29 68.02N166.15E
Bilimora India 40 20.45N 72.57E
Billabong Creek r. Australia 66 35.04S144.06E
Bill Baileys Bank f. Atlantic Oc. 8 60.45N 10.30W
Billingham U.K. 10 54.36N 1.18W
Billings U.S.A. 80 45.47N108.27W

Bill of Portland *c.* U.K. **11** 50.32N 2.28W
Bilma Niger **51** 18.41N 12.56E
Biloela Australia **64** 24.24S150.30E
Biloxi U.S.A. **83** 30.24N 88.53W
Bilqās Qism Awwal Egypt **44** 31.14N 31.22E
Biltine Chad **51** 14.32N 20.55E
Biltine *d.* Chad **51** 15.00N 21.00E
Bilto Norway **22** 69.26N 21.35E
Bima *r.* Zaïre **54** 3.24N 25.10E
Bimberi, Mt. Australia **67** 35.40S148.47E
Bimbo C.A.R. **53** 4.15N 18.33E
Bīna-Etāwa India **41** 24.11N 78.11E
Binaiya *mtn.* Indonesia **37** 3.10S129.30E
Bīnālūd, Kūh-e *mts.* Iran **43** 36.15N 59.00E
Binbee Australia **64** 20.20S147.55E
Binche Belgium **14** 50.25N 4.10E
Bindki India **41** 26.02N 80.36E
Bindura Zimbabwe **57** 17.18S 31.20E
Binga Zimbabwe **56** 17.38S 27.19E
Binga, Mt. Zimbabwe **57** 19.47S 33.03E
Bingara Australia **67** 29.51S150.38E
Bingen Germany **14** 49.58N 7.55E
Bingerville Ivory Coast **52** 5.20N 3.53W
Bingham U.K. **10** 52.57N 0.57W
Bingham U.S.A. **84** 45.03N 69.53W
Binghamton U.S.A. **84** 42.08N 75.54W
Bingkor Malaysia **36** 5.26N116.15E
Bingöl Turkey **25** 38.54N 40.29E
Bingol Dağlari *mtn.* Turkey **42** 39.21N 41.22E
Binhai China **32** 34.00N119.55E
Binh Dinh Vietnam **34** 13.53N109.07E
Binjai Indonesia **36** 3.37N 98.25E
Binji Nigeria **53** 13.12N 4.55E
Binnaway Australia **67** 31.32S149.23E
Binscarth Canada **75** 50.37N101.16W
Bintan *i.* Indonesia **36** 1.10N104.30E
Bintulu Malaysia **36** 3.12N113.01E
Bin Xian China **32** 35.02N108.04E
Binyang China **33** 23.12N108.48E
Binzert Tunisia **51** 37.17N 9.51E
Biograd Yugo. **18** 43.56N 15.27E
Bioko I. Equat. Guinea **53** 3.25N 8.45E
Bīr India **40** 18.59N 75.46E
Bir, Ras *c.* Djibouti **45** 11.59N 43.25E
Bi'r Abū 'Uwayqilah *well* Egypt **44** 30.50N 34.07E
Bi'r ad Dakhal *well* Egypt **44** 28.40N 32.24E
Birāk Libya **51** 27.32N 14.17E
Bi'r al Harash *well* Libya **51** 25.30N 22.06E
Bi'r al Jidy *well* Egypt **44** 30.13N 33.03E
Bi'r al Jufayr *well* Egypt **44** 30.49N 32.40E
Bi'r al 'Udayd *well* Egypt **44** 28.59N 34.05E
Birao C.A.R. **49** 10.17N 22.47E
Bi'r aş Şafrā' *well* Egypt **44** 28.46N 34.20E
Bi'r ath Thamadah *well* Egypt **44** 30.10N 33.28E
Birātnagar Nepal **41** 26.18N 87.17E
Bi'r Buerāt *well* Egypt **44** 28.59N 32.10E
Bi'r Bukhayt *well* Egypt **44** 29.13N 32.17E
Birch *r.* Canada **74** 58.30N112.15W
Birchip Australia **66** 35.59S142.59E
Birch L. N.W.T. Canada **74** 62.04N116.33W
Birch L. Ont. Canada **76** 51.24N 92.20W
Birch Mts. Canada **74** 57.30N112.30W
Bird Canada **75** 56.30N 94.13W
Birdsboro U.S.A. **85** 40.16N 75.48W
Birdsville Australia **64** 25.54S139.22E
Birecik Turkey **42** 37.03N 37.59E
Bīrganj Nepal **41** 27.01N 84.54E
Birhan *mtn.* Ethiopia **49** 11.00N 37.50E
Bi'r Hasanah *well* Egypt **44** 30.29N 33.47E
Bi'r Hooker *well* Egypt **44** 30.23N 30.20E
Bīrjand Iran **43** 32.54N 59.10E
Bi'r Jifjafah *well* Egypt **44** 30.28N 33.11E
Birk, Wādī *r.* Saudi Arabia **43** 24.08N 47.35E
Birkenfeld Rhein.-Pfalz Germany **14** 49.39N 7.10E
Birkenhead U.K. **10** 53.24N 3.01W
Birksgate Range *mts.* Australia **62** 27.10S129.45E
Bi'r Kusaybah *well* Egypt **44** 22.41N 29.55E
Bîrlad Romania **21** 46.14N 27.40E
Bi'r Lahfān *well* Egypt **44** 31.01N 33.52E
Birmingham U.K. **11** 52.30N 1.55W
Birmingham Ala. U.S.A. **85** 33.30N 86.55W
Birmitrapur India **41** 22.24N 84.46E
Bir Mogreïn Mauritania **50** 25.14N 11.35W
Birni Benin **53** 9.59N 1.34E
Birnin Gwari Nigeria **53** 11.02N 6.47E
Birnin Kebbi Nigeria **53** 12.30N 4.11E
Birni N'Konni Niger **53** 13.49N 5.19E
Birobidzhan U.S.S.R. **31** 48.49N132.54E
Bîr Ounâne *well* Mali **50** 21.02N 3.18W
Birr Rep. of Ire. **13** 53.06N 7.56W
Birrie *r.* Australia **67** 29.43S146.37E
Birsilpur India **40** 28.11N 72.15E
Birsk U.S.S.R. **24** 55.28N 55.31E
Bi'r Tābah *well* Egypt **44** 29.30N 34.53E
Bi'r Ţarfāwī *well* Egypt **48** 22.55N 28.53E
Birtle Canada **75** 50.32N101.02W
Bi'r Umm Sa'īd *well* Egypt **44** 29.40N 33.34E
Bi'r Umm 'Umayyid *well* Egypt **44** 27.53N 32.30E
Biržai U.S.S.R. **24** 56.10N 24.48E
Bi'r Zalţan *well* Libya **51** 28.27N 19.46E
Bir Zreigat Mauritania **50** 22.27N 8.53W
Bisalpur India **41** 28.18N 79.48E
Bisbee U.S.A. **81** 31.27N109.55W
Biscay, B. of France **17** 45.30N 4.00W
Bisceglie Italy **19** 41.14N 16.31E
Bisha Ethiopia **48** 15.28N 37.34E
Bishnupur India **41** 23.05N 87.19E
Bishop Calif. U.S.A. **80** 37.22N118.24W
Bishop Tex. U.S.A. **83** 27.35N 97.48W
Bishop Auckland U.K. **10** 54.40N 1.40W
Bishop's Stortford U.K. **11** 51.53N 0.09E
Bisina, L. Uganda **55** 1.35N 34.08E
Biskra Algeria **51** 34.48N 5.40E
Bismarck U.S.A. **82** 46.48N100.47W
Bismarck Range *mts.* P.N.G. **37** 6.00S145.00E
Bismarck Sea Pacific Oc. **37** 4.00S146.30E
Bison U.S.A. **82** 45.31N102.28W
Bīsotūn Iran **43** 34.22N 47.29E
Bispgården Sweden **22** 63.02N 16.40E
Bissau Guinea Bissau **52** 11.52N 15.39W
Bissett Canada **75** 51.02N 95.40W
Bissikrima Guinea **52** 10.50N 10.58W
Bistcho L. Canada **74** 59.45N118.50W
Bistriţa Romania **21** 47.08N 24.30E
Bistriţa *r.* Romania **21** 46.30N 26.54E
Biswān India **41** 27.30N 81.00E
Bitam Gabon **54** 2.05N 11.30E
Bitburg Germany **14** 49.58N 6.31E
Bitéa, Ouadi *wadi* Chad **49** 13.11N 20.10E
Bitlis Turkey **42** 38.23N 42.04E
Bitola Yugo. **19** 41.02N 21.21E
Bitter Creek *town* U.S.A. **80** 41.31N109.27W
Bitterfontein R.S.A. **56** 31.02S 18.14E
Bitterroot Range *mts.* U.S.A. **80** 47.06N115.10W
Biu Nigeria **53** 10.36N 12.11E
Biumba Rwanda **55** 1.38S 30.02E
Biwa ko *l.* Japan **35** 35.10N136.00E
Biyalā Egypt **44** 31.11N 31.13E
Biysk U.S.S.R. **28** 52.35N 85.16E
Bizerte *see* Binzert Tunisia **51**
Bjelovar Yugo. **19** 45.54N 16.51E
Bjorli Norway **23** 62.16N 8.13E
Björna Sweden **22** 63.32N 18.36E
Bjørnafjorden *est.* Norway **23** 60.06N 5.22E
Bjørnøya *i.* Arctic Oc. **96** 74.30N 19.00E
Black *r.* Ark. U.S.A. **83** 35.38N 91.19W
Black *r. see* Đà *r.* Vietnam **34**
Blackall Australia **64** 24.25S145.28E
Blackburn U.K. **10** 53.44N 2.30W
Black Diamond Canada **74** 50.45N114.14W
Black Duck *r.* Canada **75** 56.51N 89.02W
Blackduck U.S.A. **82** 47.44N 94.33W
Blackfoot U.S.A. **80** 43.11N112.20W
Black Hills U.S.A. **82** 44.00N104.00W
Black L. Canada **75** 59.10N105.20W
Black Mtn. U.K. **11** 51.52N 3.50W
Black Mts. U.K. **11** 51.52N 3.09W
Blackpool U.K. **10** 53.48N 3.03W
Black River *town* Jamaica **87** 18.02N 77.52W
Black River *town* Mich. U.S.A. **84** 44.51N 83.21W
Black Rock *town* U.S.A. **80** 38.41N112.59W
Black Rock Desert U.S.A. **80** 41.10N119.00W
Black Sand Desert U.S.S.R. **43** 37.45N 60.00E
Black Sea Europe **21** 44.00N 30.00E
Blacksod B. Rep. of Ire. **13** 54.04N 10.00W
Blackstone U.S.A. **85** 37.05N 78.02W
Black Sugarloaf Mt. Australia **67** 31.24S151.34E
Blackville Australia **67** 31.34S150.10E
Blackville U.S.A. **85** 33.22N 81.17W
Black Volta *r.* Ghana **52** 8.14N 2.11W
Blackwater Australia **64** 23.34S148.53E
Blackwater *r.* Waterford Rep. of Ire. **13** 51.58N 7.52W
Blackwater *r.* U.K. **9** 54.31N 6.36W
Blackwell U.S.A. **83** 36.48N 97.17W
Blackwood *r.* Australia **63** 34.15S115.10E
Blaenau Ffestiniog U.K. **10** 53.00N 3.57W
Blagoevgrad Bulgaria **19** 42.02N 23.04E
Blagoveshchensk U.S.S.R. **31** 50.19N127.30E
Blain France **15** 47.29N 1.46W
Blair U.S.A. **82** 41.33N 96.08W
Blair Athol Australia **64** 22.42S147.33E
Blair Atholl U.K. **12** 56.46N 3.51W
Blairgowrie U.K. **12** 56.36N 3.21W
Blairmore Canada **74** 49.40N114.25W
Blairsville Ga. U.S.A. **85** 34.52N 83.52W
Blakely U.S.A. **85** 31.22N 84.58W
Blanc, Cap *c.* Mauritania **52** 20.44N 17.05W
Blanc, Mont *mtn.* Europe **17** 45.50N 6.52E
Blanca, Bahía *b.* Argentina **93** 39.20S 62.00W
Blanca, Sierra *mtn.* U.S.A. **81** 33.23N105.48W
Blanchard U.S.A. **80** 48.01N116.59W
Blanche, L. Australia **66** 29.15S139.40E
Blanchetown Australia **66** 34.21S139.38E
Blanco, C. Argentina **93** 47.12S 65.20W
Blanco, C. Costa Rica **87** 9.36N 85.06W
Blanco, C. U.S.A. **80** 42.50N124.34W
Bland *r.* Australia **67** 33.42S147.30E
Blandford Forum U.K. **11** 50.52N 2.10W
Blankenberge Belgium **14** 51.18N 3.08E
Blansko Czech. **20** 49.22N 16.39E
Blantyre Malaŵi **55** 15.46S 35.00E
Blarney Rep. of Ire. **13** 51.56N 8.34W
Blatnica Bulgaria **21** 43.42N 28.31E
Blavet *r.* France **17** 47.43N 3.18W
Blaye France **17** 45.08N 0.40W
Blayney Australia **67** 33.32S149.19E
Blednaya, Gora *mtn.* U.S.S.R. **28** 76.23N 65.08E
Bleiburg Austria **20** 46.35N 14.48E
Blekinge *d.* Sweden **23** 56.20N 15.00E
Blenheim New Zealand **60** 41.32S173.58E
Bléré France **15** 47.20N 0.59E
Blerick Neth. **14** 51.22N 6.08E
Bletchley U.K. **11** 51.59N 0.45W
Blida Algeria **51** 36.30N 2.50E
Bligh Entrance Australia **64** 9.18S144.10E
Blind River *town* Canada **76** 46.15N 83.00W
Blinman Australia **66** 31.05S138.11E
Blitar Indonesia **37** 8.06S112.12E
Blitta Togo **53** 8.23N 1.06E
Bloemfontein R.S.A. **56** 29.07S 26.14E
Bloemhof R.S.A. **56** 27.37S 25.34E
Blois France **15** 47.36N 1.20E
Blönduós Iceland **22** 65.39N 20.18W
Bloody Foreland *c.* Rep. of Ire. **13** 55.09N 8.17W
Bloomfield Iowa U.S.A. **82** 40.45N 92.25W
Bloomfield Nebr. U.S.A. **82** 42.36N 97.39W
Bloomfield N.J. U.S.A. **85** 40.48N 74.12W
Bloomington Ill. U.S.A. **82** 40.29N 89.00W
Bloomington Ind. U.S.A. **84** 39.10N 86.31W
Bloomington Minn. U.S.A. **82** 44.50N 93.17W
Bloomsburg U.S.A. **84** 41.00N 76.27W
Blora Indonesia **37** 6.55S111.29E
Blueberry *r.* Canada **74** 56.45N120.49W
Bluefield U.S.A. **85** 37.14N 81.17W
Bluefields Nicaragua **87** 12.00N 83.49W
Blue Hills of Couteau Canada **77** 47.59N 57.43W
Blue Mts. Australia **67** 33.16S150.19E
Blue Mts. U.S.A. **80** 45.30N118.15W
Blue Mud B. Australia **64** 13.26S135.56E
Blue Nile *r. see* Azraq, Al Baḩr al *r.* Sudan **48**
Bluenose L. Canada **72** 68.30N119.35W
Blue River *town* Canada **74** 52.05N119.09W
Blue Stack Mts. Rep. of Ire. **13** 54.44N 8.09W
Bluff New Zealand **60** 46.38S168.21E
Bluff U.S.A. **80** 37.17N109.33W
Bluff, C. Canada **77** 52.48N 55.53W
Bluff Knoll *mtn.* Australia **63** 34.25S118.15E
Blumenau Brazil **94** 26.55S 49.07W
Blunt U.S.A. **82** 44.31N 99.59W
Blyth Northum. U.K. **10** 55.07N 1.29W
Blythe U.S.A. **81** 33.37N114.36W
Bö Nordland Norway **22** 68.38N 14.35E
Bö Telemark Norway **23** 59.25N 9.04E
Bo Sierra Leone **52** 7.58N 11.45W
Boa Esperança Brazil **94** 21.03S 45.37W
Boa Esperança, Reprêsa da *resr.* Brazil **91** 6.45S 44.15W
Bo'ai Henan China **32** 35.10N113.04E
Boane Mozambique **57** 26.02S 32.19E
Boa Vista Brazil **90** 2.51N 60.43W
Bobadah Australia **67** 32.18S146.42E
Bobadilla Spain **16** 37.02N 4.44W
Bobbili India **39** 18.34N 83.22E
Bobbio Italy **15** 44.46N 9.23E
Bobo-Dioulasso Burkina **52** 11.11N 4.18W
Bobonong Botswana **56** 21.59S 28.29E
Bóbr *r.* Poland **20** 52.04N 15.04E
Bobr U.S.S.R. **21** 54.19N 29.18E
Bobruysk U.S.S.R. **21** 53.08N 29.10E
Bôca do Acre Brazil **90** 8.45S 67.23W
Bocaranga C.A.R. **53** 7.01N 15.35E
Boca Raton U.S.A. **85** 26.22N 80.05W
Bochnia Poland **21** 49.58N 20.26E
Bocholt Germany **14** 51.49N 6.37E
Bochum Germany **14** 51.28N 7.11E
Bochum R.S.A. **56** 23.12S 29.12E
Bockum-Hövel Germany **14** 51.42N 7.41E
Boconó Venezuela **90** 9.17N 70.17W
Boda C.A.R. **53** 4.19N 17.26E
Bodalla Australia **67** 36.05S150.03E
Bodallin Australia **63** 31.22S118.52E
Bodélé *f.* Chad **53** 16.50N 17.10E
Boden Sweden **22** 65.50N 21.42E
Bodensee *l.* Europe **20** 47.40N 9.30E
Bode Sadu Nigeria **53** 8.57N 4.49E
Bodfish U.S.A. **81** 35.36N118.30W
Bodmin U.K. **11** 50.28N 4.44W
Bodmin Moor U.K. **11** 50.53N 4.35W
Bodo Canada **75** 52.11N110.04W
Bodö Norway **22** 67.18N 14.26E
Bodrum Turkey **42** 37.03N 27.28E
Boembé Congo **54** 2.59S 15.34E
Boende Zaïre **54** 0.15S 20.49E
Boffa Guinea **52** 10.12N 14.02W
Bogale Burma **34** 16.17N 95.24E
Bogalusa U.S.A. **83** 30.47N 89.52W
Bogan *r.* Australia **67** 30.00S146.20E
Bogan Gate *town* Australia **67** 33.08S147.50E
Bogata U.S.A. **83** 33.28N 95.13W
Bogcang Zangbo *r.* China **41** 31.50N 87.25E
Bogenfels Namibia **56** 27.26S 15.22E
Boggabilla Australia **67** 28.36S150.21E
Boggabri Australia **67** 30.42S150.02E
Boggeragh Mts. Rep. of Ire. **13** 52.03N 8.53W
Bogia P.N.G. **37** 4.16S145.00E
Bognes Norway **22** 68.15N 16.00E
Bognor Regis U.K. **11** 50.47N 0.40W
Bog of Allen *f.* Rep. of Ire. **13** 53.17N 7.00W
Bogol Manyo Ethiopia **49** 4.32N 41.32E
Bogong, Mt. Australia **67** 36.45S147.21E
Bogor Indonesia **36** 6.34S106.45E
Bogotá Colombia **90** 4.38N 74.05W
Bogra Bangla. **41** 24.51N 89.22E
Bogué Mauritania **50** 16.35N 14.16W
Boguslav U.S.S.R. **21** 49.32N 30.52E
Bo Hai *b.* China **32** 38.30N119.30E
Bohain France **14** 49.59N 3.28E
Bohai Wan *b.* China **32** 38.30N117.55E
Bohemian Forest *see* Böhmerwald *mts.* Germany **20**
Bohin Somali Rep. **45** 11.42N 51.17E
Böhmerwald *mts.* Germany **20** 49.20N 13.10E
Bohol *i.* Phil. **37** 9.45N124.10E
Boiaçu Brazil **90** 0.27S 61.46W
Boigu *i.* Australia **64** 9.16S142.12E
Boing Sudan **49** 9.58N 33.44E
Bois, Lac des *l.* Canada **72** 66.40N125.15W
Boise U.S.A. **80** 43.37N116.13W
Boise City U.S.A. **83** 36.44N102.31W
Bois-Guillaume France **15** 49.28N 1.08E
Boissevain Canada **75** 49.15N100.00W
Boizenburg Germany **20** 53.22N 10.43E
Bojador, Cabo *c.* W. Sahara **50** 26.08N 14.30W
Bojeador, C. Phil. **33** 18.30N120.36E
Bojnūrd Iran **43** 37.28N 57.20E
Bojonegoro Indonesia **37** 7.06S111.50E
Bokani Nigeria **53** 9.27N 5.13E
Boké Guinea **52** 10.57N 14.13W
Bokhara *r.* Australia **67** 29.55S146.42E
Boknafjorden *est.* Norway **23** 59.10N 5.35E
Bokoro Chad **53** 12.17N 17.04E
Bokote Zaïre **54** 0.05S 20.08E
Bokpyin Burma **34** 11.16N 98.46E
Bokungu Zaïre **54** 0.44S 22.28E
Bol Chad **53** 13.27N 14.40E
Bolac Lake *town* Australia **66** 37.42S142.50E
Bolafa Zaïre **54** 1.23N 22.06E
Bolama Guinea Bissau **52** 11.35N 15.30W
Bolān *r.* Pakistan **40** 29.05N 67.45E
Bolanda, Jabal *mtn.* Sudan **49** 7.44N 25.28E
Bolān Pass Pakistan **40** 29.45N 67.35E
Bolbec France **15** 49.34N 0.28E
Bole Ghana **52** 9.03N 2.23W
Bolesławiec Poland **20** 51.16N 15.34E
Bolgatanga Ghana **52** 10.42N 0.52W
Bolgrad U.S.S.R. **21** 45.42N 28.40E
Bolia Zaïre **54** 1.36S 18.23E
Bolívar Argentina **93** 36.14S 61.07W
Bolivar Tenn. U.S.A. **83** 35.16N 88.59W
Bolivia S. America **92** 17.00S 65.00W
Bollnäs Sweden **23** 61.21N 16.25E
Bollon Australia **65** 28.02S147.28E
Bollstabruk Sweden **22** 62.59N 17.42E
Bolmen *l.* Sweden **23** 56.55N 13.40E
Bolobo Zaïre **54** 2.10S 16.17E
Bologna Italy **15** 44.30N 11.20E
Bologoye U.S.S.R. **24** 57.58N 34.00E
Bolomba Zaïre **54** 0.30N 19.13E
Bolombo Zaïre **54** 3.59S 21.22E
Bolondo Equat. Guinea **54** 1.40N 9.38E
Bolongongo Angola **54** 8.28S 15.16E
Bolovens, Plateau des *f.* Laos **34** 15.10N106.30E
Bolsena, Lago di *l.* Italy **18** 42.36N 11.55E
Bolshaya Glushitsa U.S.S.R. **24** 52.28N 50.30E
Bolshaya Pyssa U.S.S.R. **24** 64.11N 48.44E
Bolsherechye U.S.S.R. **28** 56.07N 74.40E
Bol'shevik, Ostrov *i.* U.S.S.R. **29** 78.30N102.00E
Bolshezemelskaya Tundra *f.* U.S.S.R. **24** 67.00N 56.10E
Bolshoy Atlym U.S.S.R. **28** 62.17N 66.30E
Bol'shoy Balkhan, Khrebet *mts.* U.S.S.R. **43** 39.38N 54.30E
Bol'shoy Irgiz *r.* U.S.S.R. **24** 52.00N 47.20E
Bol'shoy Lyakhovskiy, Ostrov *i.* U.S.S.R. **29** 73.30N142.00E
Bol'shoy Onguren U.S.S.R. **29** 53.40N107.40E
Bolshoy Uzen *r.* U.S.S.R. **25** 49.00N 49.40E
Bolsover U.K. **10** 53.14N 1.18W
Bolton U.K. **10** 53.35N 2.26W
Bolton L. Canada **75** 54.16N 95.47W
Bolu Turkey **42** 40.45N 31.38E
Bolus Head Rep. of Ire. **13** 51.47N 10.20W
Bolvadin Turkey **42** 38.43N 31.02E
Bolzano Italy **15** 46.30N 11.20E
Boma Zaïre **54** 5.50S 13.03E
Bomaderry Australia **67** 34.21S150.34E
Bomadi Nigeria **53** 5.13N 6.01E
Bombala Australia **67** 36.55S149.16E
Bombay India **40** 18.58N 72.50E
Bombo Uganda **45** 0.35N 32.32E
Bomboma Zaïre **54** 2.25N 18.54E
Bom Despacho Brazil **94** 19.46S 45.15W
Bomi China **30** 29.50N 95.45E
Bomi Hills Liberia **52** 7.01N 10.38W
Bömlafjorden *est.* Norway **23** 59.39N 5.20E
Bömlo *i.* Norway **23** 59.46N 5.13E
Bomokandi *r.* Zaïre **55** 3.37N 26.09E
Bomongo Zaïre **54** 1.30N 18.21E
Bomu *r.* Zaïre *see* Mbomou *r.* C.A.R. **49**
Bon, Cap *c.* Tunisia **51** 37.05N 11.03E
Bonaigarh India **41** 21.50N 84.57E
Bonaire *i.* Neth. Antilles **90** 12.15N 68.27W
Bonanza U.S.A. **80** 40.01N109.11W
Bonaparte *r.* Canada **74** 50.46N121.17W
Bonaparte Archipelago *is.* Australia **62** 14.17S125.18E
Bonar-Bridge *town* U.K. **12** 57.53N 4.21W
Bonavista Canada **77** 48.39N 53.07W
Bonavista, C. Canada **77** 48.42N 53.05W
Bonavista B. Canada **77** 48.45N 53.20W
Bon Bon Australia **66** 30.26S135.28E
Bondeno Italy **15** 44.53N 11.25E
Bondo *Equateur* Zaïre **54** 3.47N 23.45E
Bondo *Haut-Zaïre* Zaïre **54** 1.22S 23.53E
Bondoukou Ivory Coast **52** 8.03N 2.15W
Bondowoso Indonesia **37** 7.54S113.50E
Bone, Teluk *b.* Indonesia **37** 4.00S120.50E
Bo'ness U.K. **12** 56.01N 3.36W
Bonga Ethiopia **49** 7.17N 36.15E
Bongaigaon India **41** 26.28N 90.34E
Bongak Sudan **49** 7.27N 33.14E
Bongandanga Zaïre **54** 1.28N 21.03E
Bongor Chad **53** 10.18N 15.20E
Bongos, Massif des *mts.* C.A.R. **49** 8.20N 21.35E
Bongouanou Ivory Coast **52** 6.44N 4.10W
Bonham U.S.A. **83** 33.35N 96.11W
Bonifacio, Str. of Med. Sea **18** 41.18N 9.10E
Bonin Is. Japan **68** 27.00N142.10E
Bonn Germany **14** 50.44N 7.06E
Bonners Ferry U.S.A. **80** 48.41N116.18W
Bonnétable France **15** 48.11N 0.26E
Bonneval France **15** 48.11N 1.24E
Bonneville Salt Flats *f.* U.S.A. **80** 40.45N113.52W
Bonney, L. Australia **66** 37.47S140.23E
Bonnie Rock *town* Australia **63** 30.32S118.21E
Bonny Nigeria **53** 4.25N 7.10E
Bonny, Bight of Africa **53** 2.58N 7.00E
Bonnyville Canada **75** 54.16N110.44W
Bonshaw Australia **67** 29.08S150.53E
Bontang Indonesia **36** 0.05N117.31E
Bonthe Sierra Leone **52** 7.32N 12.30W
Bonython Range *mts.* Australia **62** 23.51S129.00E
Bookaloo Australia **66** 31.56S137.21E
Boola Guinea **52** 8.22N 8.41W
Booleroo Centre Australia **66** 32.53S138.2
Booligal Australia **67** 33.54S144.54E
Boom Belgium **14** 51.07N 4.21E
Boomrivier R.S.A. **56** 29.34S 20.26E
Boone U.S.A. **82** 42.04N 93.53W
Booneville U.S.A. **83** 34.39N 88.34W
Boonville Mo. U.S.A. **82** 38.58N 92.44W
Boonville N.Y. U.S.A. **84** 43.29N 75.20W
Boorabbin Australia **63** 31.14S120.21E
Boorama Somali Rep. **45** 9.58N 43.07E
Boorindal Australia **67** 30.23S146.11E
Booroorban Australia **67** 34.56S144.46E
Boorowa Australia **67** 34.26S148.48E
Boort Australia **66** 36.08S143.46E
Boosaaso Somali Rep. **45** 11.13N 49.08E
Boothia, G. of Canada **73** 70.00N 90.00W
Boothia Pen. Canada **73** 70.30N 95.00W
Bootra Australia **66** 30.00S143.00E
Booué Gabon **54** 0.00 11.58E
Bopeechee Australia **66** 29.36S137.23E
Bophuthatswana Africa **56** 27.00S 23.30E
Boppard Germany **14** 50.13N 7.35E
Boquilla, Presa de la *l.* Mexico **81** 27.30N105.30W
Bor Czech. **20** 49.43N 12.47E
Bor Sudan **49** 6.12N 31.33E
Bor Yugo. **19** 44.05N 22.07E
Bora Bora *i.* Îs. de la Société **69** 16.30S151.45W
Borah Peak *mtn.* U.S.A. **80** 44.08N113.38W
Borås Sweden **23** 57.43N 12.55E
Borāzjān Iran **43** 29.14N 51.12E
Borba Brazil **90** 4.24S 59.35W
Borda Cape *town* Australia **66** 35.44S136.3
Bordeaux France **17** 44.50N 0.34W
Borden Australia **63** 34.05S118.16E
Borden I. Canada **72** 78.30N111.00W
Borden Pen. Canada **73** 73.00N 83.00W
Borders *d.* U.K. **12** 55.30N 2.53W
Bordertown Australia **66** 36.18S140.49E
Bordheyri Iceland **22** 65.12N 21.06W
Bordighera Italy **15** 43.46N 7.39E
Bordj Bou Arreridj Algeria **51** 36.04N 4.46E
Bordj Flye Sainte Marie Algeria **50** 27.17N 2.59W
Bordj Omar Driss Algeria **51** 28.09N 6.49E
Bordö *i.* Faroe Is. **22** 62.10N 7.13W
Bore Ethiopia **49** 4.40N 37.40E
Boreda Ethiopia **49** 6.32N 37.48E
Borgå Finland **23** 60.24N 25.40E
Borga Sweden **22** 64.49N 15.05E
Börgefjell *mtn.* Norway **22** 65.20N 13.45E
Börgefjell Nat. Park Norway **22** 65.00N 13.58E
Borger Neth. **14** 52.57N 6.46E
Borger U.S.A. **83** 35.39N101.24W
Borgholm Sweden **23** 56.53N 16.39E
Borghorst Germany **14** 52.08N 7.27E
Borgo Italy **15** 46.03N 11.27E
Borgomanero Italy **15** 45.42N 8.28E
Borgo San Dalmazzo Italy **15** 44.20N 7.30E
Borgo San Lorenzo Italy **15** 43.57N 11.23E
Borgosesia Italy **15** 45.43N 8.16E
Borgo Val di Taro Italy **15** 44.29N 9.46E
Borgund Norway **23** 61.03N 7.49E
Borislav U.S.S.R. **21** 49.18N 23.28E
Borisoglebsk U.S.S.R. **25** 51.23N 42.02E
Borisov U.S.S.R. **21** 54.09N 28.30E
Borispol U.S.S.R. **21** 50.21N 30.59E
Borja Peru **90** 4.20S 77.40W
Borken Germany **14** 51.50N 6.52E
Borkou-Ennedi-Tibesti *d.* Chad **51** 18.15N 20.00E
Borkum Germany **14** 53.34N 6.41E
Borkum *i.* Germany **14** 53.35N 6.45E
Borlänge Sweden **23** 60.29N 15.25E
Borley, C. Antarctica **96** 66.15S 55.00E
Bormio Italy **15** 46.28N 10.22E
Borndiep *g.* Neth. **14** 53.28N 5.35E
Borneo *i.* Asia **36** 1.00N114.00E
Bornheim Germany **14** 50.45N 7.00E
Bornholm *i.* Denmark **23** 55.10N 15.00E
Borno *d.* Nigeria **53** 12.20N 12.40E
Bornu, Plain of *f.* Nigeria **53** 12.30N 13.00E
Boro *r.* Sudan **49** 8.52N 26.11E
Borodyanka U.S.S.R. **21** 50.38N 29.59E
Boromo Burkina **52** 11.43N 2.53W
Borotou Ivory Coast **52** 8.46N 7.30W
Boroughbridge U.K. **10** 54.06N 1.23W
Borovichi U.S.S.R. **24** 58.22N 34.00E
Borraan Somali Rep. **45** 10.10N 48.48E
Borrika Australia **66** 35.00S140.05E
Borroloola Australia **64** 16.04S136.17E
Borşa Romania **21** 46.56N 23.40E
Borşa Romania **21** 47.39N 24.40E
Borsad India **40** 22.25N 72.54E
Borth U.K. **11** 52.29N 4.03W
Borūjerd Iran **43** 33.54N 48.47E
Bory Tucholskie *f.* Poland **21** 53.45N 17.30E
Borzhomi U.S.S.R. **25** 41.49N 43.23E
Borzna U.S.S.R. **25** 51.15N 32.25E
Borzya U.S.S.R. **29** 50.24N116.35E
Bosa Italy **18** 40.18N 8.29E
Bosanska Gradiška Yugo. **19** 45.09N 17.15E
Bosanski Novi Yugo. **20** 45.03N 16.23E
Boscastle U.K. **11** 50.42N 4.42W
Bose China **33** 23.58N106.32E
Boshan China **32** 36.29N117.50E
Boshof R.S.A. **56** 28.32S 25.12E
Bosna *r.* Yugo. **19** 45.04N 18.27E
Bosna i Hercegovina *d.* Yugo. **19** 44.00N 18.10E
Bosnik Indonesia **37** 1.09S136.14E
Bosobolo Zaïre **49** 4.11N 19.54E
Bōsō-hantō *pen.* Japan **35** 35.08N140.00E
Bosporus *str. see* İstanbul Boğazi *str.* Turkey **19**

ssangoa C.A.R. 53 6.27N 17.21E
ssembélé C.A.R. 53 5.10N 17.44E
ssier City U.S.A. 83 32.31N 93.43W
sso Niger 53 13.43N 13.19E
stān Pakistan 40 30.26N 67.02E
sten Hu *l.* China 30 42.00N 87.00E
ston U.K. 10 52.59N 0.02W
ston U.S.A. 84 42.21N 71.04W
ād India 40 22.10N 71.40E
tany B. Australia 67 34.04S151.08E
ev *mtn.* Bulgaria 19 42.43N 24.55E
evgrad Bulgaria 19 42.55N 23.57E
hnia, G. of Europe 22 63.30N 20.30E
letle *r.* Botswana 56 21.06S 24.47E
oşani Romania 21 47.44N 26.41E
ou Burkina 53 12.47N 2.02E
ange *mtn.* Belgium 14 50.30N 6.04E
ro Ivory Coast 52 7.51N 5.19W
swana Africa 56 22.00S 24.15E
trop Germany 14 51.31N 6.55E
ucatu Brazil 94 22.52S 48.30W
aflé Ivory Coast 52 7.01N 5.47W
aké Ivory Coast 52 7.42N 5.00W
ar C.A.R. 53 5.58N 15.35E
Arfa Morocco 50 32.30N 1.59W
ca C.A.R. 53 6.30N 18.21E
choir France 15 49.45N 2.41E
denib Morocco 50 31.57N 4.38W
farik Algeria 51 36.36N 2.54E
ugainville *i.* Pacific Oc. 68 6.00S155.00E
gouni Mali 52 11.25N 7.28W
illon Belgium 14 49.48N 5.03E
ira Algeria 51 36.23N 3.54E
-Izakarn Morocco 50 29.09N 9.44W
ulder Australia 63 30.55S121.32E
ulder U.S.A. 82 40.01N105.17W
ulder City U.S.A. 81 35.59N114.50W
ulia Australia 64 22.54S139.54E
ulogne France 17 50.43N 1.37E
ulogne-Billancourt France 15 48.50N 2.15E
ultoum Niger 53 14.45N 10.25E
umba *r.* Cameroon 53 2.00N 15.10E
umdeit Mauritania 50 17.26N 9.50W
umo Chad 53 9.01N 16.24E
una Ivory Coast 52 9.19N 2.53W
undary Peak *mtn.* U.S.A. 80
7.51N118.21W
undiali Ivory Coast 52 9.30N 6.31W
untiful U.S.A. 80 40.53N111.53W
unty Is. Pacific Oc. 68 48.00S178.30E
uraga *well* Mali 52 19.00N 3.36W
urail N. Cal. 68 21.34S165.30E
urem Mali 52 16.59N 0.20W
urg France 17 46.12N 5.13E
urganeuf France 17 45.57N 1.44E
urges France 17 47.05N 2.23E
urget Canada 77 45.26N 75.09W
urg Madame France 17 42.26N 1.55E
urgogne *d.* France 17 47.10N 4.20E
urgogne, Canal de France 15 47.58N 3.30E
urgoin France 17 45.35N 5.17E
urgueil France 15 47.17N 0.10E
urke Australia 67 30.09S145.59E
urnemouth U.K. 11 50.43N 1.53W
u Saâda Algeria 51 35.12N 4.11E
ussac France 17 46.22N 2.13E
usso Chad 53 10.32N 16.45E
utilimit Mauritania 50 17.33N 14.42W
uvard, C. Australia 63 32.40S115.34E
uvetöya *i.* Atlantic Oc. 95 54.26S 3.24E
vill U.S.A. 80 46.51N116.24W
vril Argentina 93 31.22S 59.25W
w *r.* Canada 74 51.10N115.00W
welling Australia 63 33.25S116.27E
wen Australia 64 20.00S148.15E
wen, Mt. Australia 67 37.11S148.34E
wie Ariz. U.S.A. 81 32.19N109.29W
wie Tex. U.S.A. 83 33.34N 97.51W
w Island *town* Canada 75 49.52N111.22W
wling Green U.S.A. 85 37.00N 86.29W
wling Green, C. Australia 64
9.19S146.25E
wman U.S.A. 82 46.11N103.24W
wman I. Antarctica 96 65.00S104.00E
wmanville Canada 76 43.55N 78.41W
wral Australia 67 34.30S150.24E
wser Australia 67 36.19S146.23E
xholm Sweden 23 58.12N 15.03E
Xian China 32 33.50N115.46E
xing China 32 37.08N118.05E
x Tank Australia 66 32.13S142.17E
xtel Neth. 14 51.36N 5.20E
yabat Turkey 42 41.27N 34.45E
yang China 33 28.59N116.42E
yanup Australia 63 33.29S115.40E
yarka U.S.S.R. 21 50.20N 30.26E
yd *r.* Australia 67 29.51S152.25E
ykétté C.A.R. 49 5.28N 20.50E
yle Rep. of Ire. 13 53.58N 8.19W
yne *r.* Rep. of Ire. 13 53.43N 6.17W
yoma Falls *f.* Zaïre 54 0.18N 25.32E
yup Brook Australia 63 33.50S116.22E
zca Ada *i.* Turkey 19 39.49N 26.03E
zen *see* Bolzano Italy 15
zeman U.S.A. 80 45.41N111.02W
zoum C.A.R. 53 6.16N 16.22E
Italy 15 44.42N 7.51E
abant *d.* Belgium 14 50.47N 4.30E
ač *i.* Yugo. 19 43.20N 16.38E
acadale, Loch U.K. 12 57.22N 6.30W
acebridge Canada 76 45.02N 79.19W
acieux France 15 47.33N 1.33E
äcke Sweden 22 62.44N 15.30E
ad Romania 19 46.06N 22.48E
adano *r.* Italy 19 40.23N 16.52E
adenton U.S.A. 85 27.29N 82.33W
adford Canada 76 44.07N 79.34W
adford U.K. 10 53.47N 1.45W
Bradford Penn. U.S.A. 84 41.58N 78.39W
Bradley U.S.A. 83 33.06N 93.39W
Bradworthy U.K. 11 50.54N 4.22W
Brady U.S.A. 83 31.08N 99.20W
Braemar U.K. 12 57.01N 3.24W
Braga Portugal 16 41.32N 8.26W
Bragado Argentina 93 35.10S 60.30W
Bragança Brazil 91 1.03S 46.46W
Bragança Portugal 16 41.47N 6.46W
Bragança Paulista Brazil 94 22.59S 46.32W
Bragin U.S.S.R. 21 51.49N 30.16E
Brāhmanbāria Bangla. 41 23.59N 91.07E
Brāhmani *r.* India 41 20.39N 86.46E
Brahmaputra *r.* Asia 41 23.50N 89.45E
Braidwood Australia 67 35.27S149.50E
Brăila Romania 21 45.18N 27.58E
Brainerd U.S.A. 79 46.20N 94.10W
Braintree U.K. 11 51.53N 0.32E
Brakna *d.* Mauritania 50 17.00N 13.20W
Brålanda Sweden 23 58.34N 12.22E
Bramfield Australia 66 33.37S134.59E
Brampton Canada 76 43.41N 79.46W
Brampton U.K. 10 54.56N 2.43W
Bramsche Germany 14 52.26N 7.59E
Branco *r.* Brazil 90 1.00S 62.00W
Brandberg *mtn.* Namibia 56 21.08S 14.35E
Brandbu Norway 23 60.28N 10.30E
Brande Denmark 23 55.57N 9.07E
Brandenburg Germany 20 52.25N 12.34E
Brandenburg *d.* Germany 20 52.15N 13.10E
Brandfort R.S.A. 56 28.41S 26.27E
Brandon Canada 75 49.50N 99.57W
Brandon Mtn. Rep. of Ire. 13 52.14N 10.15W
Brandon Pt. Rep. of Ire. 13 52.17N 10.11W
Braniewo Poland 21 54.24N 19.50E
Bransby Australia 66 28.40S142.00E
Branson U.S.A. 83 36.39N 93.13W
Brantas *r.* Indonesia 37 7.13S112.45E
Brantford Canada 76 43.08N 80.16W
Bras d'Or L. Canada 77 45.52N 60.50W
Brasil, Planalto *mts.* Brazil 91 17.02S 50.00W
Brasiléia Brazil 90 11.00S 68.44W
Brasília Brazil 91 15.45S 47.57W
Braşov Romania 21 45.40N 25.35E
Brass Nigeria 53 4.20N 6.15E
Brasschaat Belgium 14 51.18N 4.28E
Bratislava Czech. 21 48.10N 17.10E
Bratsk U.S.S.R. 29 56.20N101.15E
Bratsk Vodokhranilishche *resr.* U.S.S.R. 29
54.40N103.00E
Bratslav U.S.S.R. 21 48.49N 28.51E
Braunau Austria 20 48.15N 13.02E
Braunschweig Germany 20 52.15N 10.30E
Braunton U.K. 11 51.06N 4.09W
Bravo del Norte, Rio *r.* Mexico *see* Rio Grande
r. Mexico/U.S.A. 83
Brawley U.S.A. 81 32.59N115.31W
Bray France 15 48.25N 3.14E
Bray Rep. of Ire. 13 53.12N 6.07W
Bray Head Kerry Rep. of Ire. 13 51.53N
10.26W
Brazeau *r.* Canada 74 52.55N115.15W
Brazilian Basin *f.* Atlantic Oc. 95 15.00S
25.00W
Brazilian Highlands *see* Brasil, Planalto *mts.*
Brazil 91
Brazos *r.* U.S.A. 83 28.53N 95.23W
Brazzaville Congo 54 4.14S 15.10E
Brčko Yugo. 21 44.53N 18.48E
Brda *r.* Poland 21 53.07N 18.08E
Breadalbane *f.* U.K. 12 56.30N 4.20W
Bream B. New Zealand 60 36.00S174.30E
Brebes Indonesia 37 6.54S109.00E
Brécey France 15 48.44N 1.10W
Brechin U.K. 12 56.44N 2.40W
Breckenridge U.S.A. 83 32.45N 98.54W
Breckland *f.* U.K. 11 52.28N 0.40E
Břeclav Czech. 20 48.46N 16.53E
Brecon U.K. 11 51.57N 3.23W
Brecon Beacons *mts.* U.K. 11 51.53N 3.27W
Breda Neth. 14 51.35N 4.46E
Bredasdorp R.S.A. 56 34.31S 20.03E
Bredbo Australia 67 35.57S149.10E
Bregenz Austria 20 47.31N 9.46E
Bregovo Bulgaria 19 44.08N 22.39E
Bréhal France 15 48.53N 1.30W
Breidhafjördhur *est.* Iceland 22 65.15N
23.00W
Breim Norway 23 61.44N 6.25E
Brekstad Norway 22 63.42N 9.40E
Bremangerland *i.* Norway 23 61.51N 5.02E
Bremen Germany 20 53.05N 8.48E
Bremer Bay *town* Australia 63 34.21S119.20E
Bremerhaven Germany 20 53.33N 8.35E
Bremer Range *mts.* Australia 63
32.40S120.55E
Bremerton U.S.A. 80 47.34N122.38W
Brenham U.S.A. 83 30.10N 96.24W
Brenner Pass Italy/Austria 20 47.00N 11.30E
Breno Italy 15 45.57N 10.18E
Brent Canada 76 46.00N 78.24W
Brenta *r.* Italy 15 45.25N 12.15E
Brentwood U.K. 11 51.38N 0.18E
Brescia Italy 15 45.33N 10.12E
Breskens Neth. 14 51.24N 3.34E
Bressay *i.* U.K. 12 60.08N 1.05W
Bressuire France 17 46.50N 0.28W
Brest France 17 48.23N 4.30W
Brest U.S.S.R. 21 52.08N 23.40E
Bretagne *d.* France 17 48.15N 2.30W
Breteuil France 15 49.38N 2.18E
Breteuil-sur-Iton France 15 48.50N 0.55E
Breton Sd. U.S.A. 83 29.30N 89.30W
Brett, C. New Zealand 60 35.15S174.20E
Breuil-Cervinia Italy 15 45.56N 7.38E
Brevik Norway 23 59.04N 9.42E
Brewarrina Australia 67 29.57S147.54E
Brewer U.S.A. 84 44.48N 68.46W
Brewster N.Y. U.S.A. 85 41.24N 73.37W
Brewton U.S.A. 85 31.07N 87.04W
Brezovo Bulgaria 19 42.20N 25.06E
Bria C.A.R. 49 6.32N 21.59E
Briançon France 17 44.53N 6.39E
Briare France 15 47.38N 2.44E
Bribbaree Australia 67 34.07S147.51E
Brichany U.S.S.R. 21 48.20N 27.01E
Bricquebec France 15 49.28N 1.38W
Bride U.K. 10 54.23N 4.24W
Bridge *r.* Canada 74 50.50N122.40W
Bridgend U.K. 11 51.30N 3.35W
Bridgeport Calif. U.S.A. 80 38.10N119.13W
Bridgeport Conn. U.S.A. 84 41.12N 73.12W
Bridgeport Nebr. U.S.A. 82 41.40N103.06W
Bridgeport Tex. U.S.A. 83 33.13N 97.45W
Bridger U.S.A. 80 45.18N108.55W
Bridgeton U.S.A. 85 39.26N 75.14W
Bridgetown Australia 63 33.57S116.08E
Bridgetown Barbados 87 13.06N 59.37W
Bridgetown Canada 77 44.51N 65.18W
Bridgetown Rep. of Ire. 13 52.14N 6.33W
Bridgeville U.S.A. 85 38.45N 75.36W
Bridgewater Canada 77 44.23N 64.31W
Bridgewater, C. Australia 66 38.25S141.28E
Bridgnorth U.K. 11 52.33N 2.25W
Bridgwater U.K. 11 51.08N 3.00W
Bridlington U.K. 10 54.06N 0.11W
Brie *f.* France 15 48.40N 3.20E
Brienne-le-Château France 15 48.24N 4.32E
Brig Switz. 15 46.19N 8.00E
Brigantine U.S.A. 85 39.24N 74.22W
Brigg U.K. 10 53.33N 0.30W
Briggsdale U.S.A. 82 40.38N104.20W
Brigham City U.S.A. 80 41.31N112.01W
Bright Australia 67 36.42S146.58E
Brighton U.K. 11 50.50N 0.09W
Brighton Colo. U.S.A. 80 39.59N104.49W
Brighton Fla. U.S.A. 85 27.13N 81.06W
Brikama Gambia 52 13.15N 16.39W
Brindisi Italy 19 40.38N 17.57E
Brinkley U.S.A. 83 34.53N 91.12W
Brinkworth Australia 66 33.42S138.24E
Brionne France 15 49.12N 0.43E
Briouze France 15 48.42N 0.22W
Brisbane Australia 67 27.30S153.00E
Brisighella Italy 15 44.13N 11.46E
Bristol U.K. 11 51.26N 2.35W
Bristol Penn. U.S.A. 85 40.06N 74.52W
Bristol S.Dak. U.S.A. 82 45.21N 97.45W
Bristol Tenn. U.S.A. 85 36.33N 82.11W
Bristol B. U.S.A. 72 58.00N158.50W
Bristol Channel U.K. 11 51.17N 3.20W
British Antarctic Territory Antarctica 96
70.00S 50.00W
British Columbia *d.* Canada 74
55.00N125.00W
British Mts. Canada 72 69.00N140.20W
British Virgin Is. C. America 87 18.30N
64.30W
Britstown R.S.A. 56 30.34S 23.30E
Britt Canada 76 45.46N 80.35W
Britton U.S.A. 82 45.48N 97.45W
Brive France 17 45.09N 1.32E
Briviesca Spain 16 42.33N 3.19W
Brixham U.K. 11 50.24N 3.31W
Brno Czech. 20 49.11N 16.39E
Broach India 40 21.42N 72.58E
Broad Arrow Australia 63 30.32S121.20E
Broad B. U.K. 12 58.15N 6.15W
Broadback *r.* Canada 76 51.20N 78.50W
Broadford Australia 67 37.16S145.03E
Broadmere Australia 64 25.30S149.30E
Broad Sd. Australia 64 22.20S149.50E
Broadsound Range *mts.* Australia 64
22.30S149.30E
Broadus U.S.A. 80 45.27N105.25W
Broadview Canada 75 50.20N102.30W
Broadway U.K. 11 52.02N 1.51W
Brochet Canada 75 57.53N101.40W
Brochet, L. Canada 75 58.36N101.35W
Brockport U.S.A. 76 43.13N 77.56W
Brockton U.S.A. 84 42.05N 71.01W
Brockville Canada 84 44.35N 75.41W
Brockway Mont. U.S.A. 80 47.15N105.45W
Brocton U.S.A. 76 42.23N 79.27W
Brod Hrvatska Yugo. 21 45.09N 18.02E
Brodeur Pen. Canada 73 73.00N 88.00W
Brodick U.K. 12 55.34N 5.09W
Brodnica Poland 21 53.16N 19.23E
Brody U.S.S.R. 21 50.05N 25.08E
Broglie France 15 49.01N 0.32E
Broke Inlet Australia 63 34.55S116.25E
Broken Arrow U.S.A. 83 36.03N 95.48W
Broken B. Australia 67 33.34S151.18E
Broken Bow U.S.A. 82 41.24N 99.38W
Broken Hill *town* Australia 66 31.57S141.30E
Bromley U.K. 11 51.24N 0.02E
Bromley Plateau *f.* Atlantic Oc. 95 30.00S
34.00W
Bromsgrove U.K. 9 52.20N 2.03W
Brönderslev Denmark 23 57.16N 9.58E
Brong-Ahafo *d.* Ghana 52 7.45N 1.30W
Brönnöysund Norway 22 65.30N 12.10E
Bronte Canada 76 43.23N 79.43W
Brooke's Point *town* Phil. 36 8.50N117.52E
Brookfield U.S.A. 82 39.47N 93.04W
Brookhaven U.S.A. 83 31.35N 90.26W
Brookings Oreg. U.S.A. 80 42.03N124.17W
Brookings S.Dak. U.S.A. 82 44.19N 96.48W
Brooklin Canada 76 43.57N 78.57W
Brooklyn Center U.S.A. 82 45.05N 93.20W
Brooks Canada 72 50.35N111.53W
Brooks B. Canada 74 50.15N127.55W
Brooks Range *mts.* U.S.A. 72 68.50N152.00W
Brooksville U.S.A. 85 28.34N 82.24W
Brookton Australia 63 32.22S117.01E
Broom, Loch U.K. 12 57.52N 5.07W
Broome Australia 62 17.58S122.15E
Broome, Mt. Australia 62 17.21S125.23E
Broomehill *town* Australia 63 33.50S117.35E
Brora U.K. 12 58.01N 3.52W
Brora *r.* U.K. 12 58.00N 3.51W
Brosna *r.* Rep.of Ire. 13 53.13N 7.58W
Brothers U.S.A. 80 43.49N120.36W
Brou France 15 48.13N 1.11E
Brough England U.K. 10 54.32N 2.19W
Brough Scotland U.K. 12 60.29N 1.12W
Broughton *r.* Australia 66 33.21S137.46E
Broughton in Furness U.K. 10 54.17N 3.12W
Brouwershaven Neth. 14 51.44N 3.53E
Brovary U.S.S.R. 21 50.30N 30.45E
Brovst Denmark 23 57.06N 9.32E
Brown, Mt. Australia 66 32.33S138.02E
Brownfield U.S.A. 83 33.11N102.16W
Browning U.S.A. 80 48.34N113.01W
Brownsburg Canada 77 45.41N 74.25W
Brownsville Tenn. U.S.A. 83 35.36N 89.15W
Brownsville Tex. U.S.A. 83 25.54N 97.30W
Brownwood U.S.A. 83 31.43N 98.59W
Bruay-en-Artois France 14 50.29N 2.36E
Bruce Pen. Canada 76 44.50N 81.20W
Bruce Rock *town* Australia 63 31.52S118.09E
Bruges *see* Brugge Belgium 14
Brugge Belgium 14 51.13N 3.14E
Brühl Germany 14 50.50N 6.55E
Brûlé, Lac *l.* Canada 77 52.17N 63.52W
Brumadinho Brazil 94 20.09S 44.11W
Brumado Brazil 91 14.13S 41.40W
Brunei Asia 36 4.56N114.58E
Brünen Germany 14 51.45N 6.41E
Brunflo Sweden 22 63.04N 14.50E
Brunner New Zealand 60 42.28S171.12E
Brunsbüttel Germany 20 53.44N 9.05E
Brunssum Neth. 14 50.57N 5.59E
Brunswick Ga. U.S.A. 85 31.09N 81.30W
Brunswick Maine U.S.A. 84 43.55N 69.58W
Brunswick B. Australia 62 15.05S125.00E
Brunswick Junction Australia 63
33.15S115.45E
Bruny I. Australia 65 43.15S147.16E
Brusilovka U.S.S.R. 25 50.39N 54.59E
Brussel *see* Bruxelles Belgium 14
Brussels *see* Bruxelles Belgium 14
Bruthen Australia 67 37.44S147.49E
Bruton U.K. 11 51.06N 2.28W
Bruxelles Belgium 14 50.50N 4.23E
Bryan Ohio U.S.A. 84 41.30N 84.34W
Bryan Tex. U.S.A. 83 30.40N 96.22W
Bryan, Mt. Australia 66 33.26S138.27E
Bryansk U.S.S.R. 24 53.15N 34.09E
Bryne Norway 23 58.44N 5.39E
Bryson Canada 76 45.41N 76.37W
Bryson, Lac *l.* Canada 76 46.19N 77.27W
Bryson City U.S.A. 85 35.26N 83.27W
Brzeg Poland 21 50.52N 17.27E
Bsharrī Lebanon 44 34.15N 36.00E
Bua *r.* Malaŵi 55 12.42S 34.15E
Bua Yai Thailand 34 15.34N102.24E
Bu'ayrāt al Ḥasūn Libya 51 31.24N 15.44E
Buba Guinea Bissau 52 11.36N 14.55W
Būbiyān, Jazīrat *i.* Kuwait 45 29.45N 48.15E
Bubye *r.* Zimbabwe 56 22.18S 31.00E
Bucak Turkey 42 37.28N 30.36E
Bucaramanga Colombia 90 7.08N 73.10W
Buchach U.S.S.R. 21 49.09N 25.20E
Buchanan Liberia 52 5.57N 10.02W
Buchanan, L. Australia 64 21.28S145.52E
Buchanan L. U.S.A. 83 30.48N 98.25W
Buchan Ness *c.* U.K. 12 57.28N 1.47W
Buchans Canada 77 48.49N 56.52W
Bucharest *see* Bucureşti Romania 21
Buchloe Germany 20 48.02N 10.44E
Buchy France 15 49.35N 1.22E
Buckambool Mt. Australia 67 31.55S145.40E
Buckhaven and Methil U.K. 10 56.11N 3.03W
Buckie U.K. 12 57.40N 2.58W
Buckingham Canada 77 45.35N 75.25W
Buckingham U.K. 11 52.00N 0.59W
Buckingham B. Australia 64 12.10S135.46E
Buckinghamshire *d.* U.K. 11 51.50N 0.48W
Buckland Tableland *f.* Australia 64
25.00S148.00E
Buckleboo Australia 66 32.55S136.12E
Buckley U.S.A. 82 40.35N 88.04W
Bucklin U.S.A. 83 37.33N 99.38W
Buco Zau Angola 54 4.46S 12.34E
Bucquoy France 14 50.09N 2.43E
Bu Craa W. Sahara 50 26.21N 12.57W
Buctouche Canada 77 46.28N 64.43W
Bucureşti Romania 21 44.25N 26.06E
Bucyrus U.S.A. 84 40.47N 82.57W
Bud Norway 22 62.54N 6.56E
Budapest Hungary 21 47.30N 19.03E
Budaun India 41 28.03N 79.07E
Budda Australia 66 31.12S144.16E
Budd Coast *f.* Antarctica 96 67.00S112.00E
Buddh Gaya India 41 24.42N 84.59E
Bude U.K. 11 50.49N 4.33W
Bude B. U.K. 11 50.50N 4.40W
Budennovsk U.S.S.R. 25 44.50N 44.10E
Budjala Zaïre 54 2.38N 19.48E
Buea Cameroon 53 4.09N 9.13E
Buenaventura Colombia 90 3.54N 77.02W
Buenaventura Mexico 81 29.51N107.29W
Buena Vista U.S.A. 85 37.44N 79.22W
Buenos Aires Argentina 93 34.40S 58.25W
Buenos Aires *d.* Argentina 93 36.30S 59.00W
Buenos Aires, L. Argentina/Chile 93 46.35S
72.00W
Buffalo Canada 75 50.49N110.42W
Buffalo *r.* Canada 74 60.55N115.00W
Buffalo Mo. U.S.A. 83 37.39N 93.06W
Buffalo N.Y. U.S.A. 84 42.52N 78.55W
Buffalo Okla. U.S.A. 83 36.50N 99.38W
Buffalo S.Dak. U.S.A. 82 45.35N103.33W
Buffalo Wyo. U.S.A. 80 44.21N106.42W
Buffalo Head Hills Canada 74 57.25N115.55W
Buffalo L. Canada 74 60.10N115.30W
Buffalo Narrows *town* Canada 75
55.51N108.30W
Bug *r.* Poland 21 52.29N 21.11E
Buga Colombia 90 3.53N 76.17W
Bugaldie Australia 67 31.02S149.08E
Bugembe Uganda 55 0.26N 33.16E
Bugene Tanzania 55 1.34S 31.07E
Buggs Island L. U.S.A. 85 36.35N 78.28W
Bugrino U.S.S.R. 24 68.45N 49.15E
Bugt China 31 48.45N121.58E
Bugulma U.S.S.R. 24 54.32N 52.46E
Buguma Nigeria 53 4.43N 6.53E
Buguruslan U.S.S.R. 24 53.36N 52.30E
Buhera Zimbabwe 57 19.21S 31.25E
Buhuşi Romania 21 46.43N 26.41E
Builth Wells U.K. 11 52.09N 3.24W
Buinsk U.S.S.R. 24 54.58N 48.15E
Bu'in-Sofīā Iran 43 35.51N 46.02E
Buitenpost Neth. 14 53.15N 6.09E
Buji P.N.G. 64 9.07S142.26E
Bujumbura Burundi 55 3.22S 29.21E
Bukama Zaïre 54 9.16S 25.52E
Bukavu Zaïre 55 2.30S 28.49E
Bukene Tanzania 55 4.13S 32.52E
Bukhara U.S.S.R. 43 39.47N 64.26E
Buki U.S.S.R. 21 49.02N 30.29E
Bukima Tanzania 55 1.48S 33.25E
Bukittinggi Indonesia 36 0.18S100.20E
Bukoba Tanzania 55 1.20S 31.49E
Bukrale Ethiopia 49 4.30N 42.03E
Bukuru Nigeria 53 9.48N 8.52E
Būl, Kūh-e *mtn.* Iran 43 30.48N 52.45E
Bula Indonesia 37 3.07S130.27E
Bulahdelah Australia 67 32.25S152.13E
Bulan Phil. 37 12.40N123.53E
Bulandshahr India 41 28.24N 77.51E
Bulawayo Zimbabwe 56 20.10S 28.43E
Buldāna India 40 20.32N 76.11E
Buldern Germany 14 51.52N 7.21E
Bulgan Mongolia 30 48.34N103.12E
Bulgaria Europe 19 42.30N 25.00E
Bullabulling Australia 63 31.05S120.52E
Bullara Australia 62 22.40S114.03E
Bullaxaar Somali Rep. 45 10.23N 44.27E
Buller *r.* New Zealand 60 41.45S171.35E
Buller, Mt. Australia 67 37.11S146.26E
Bullfinch Australia 63 30.59S119.06E
Bulli Australia 67 34.20S150.55E
Bull Mts. U.S.A. 80 46.05N109.00W
Bulloo *r.* Australia 66 28.43S142.27E
Bulloo Downs *town* Australia 66
28.30S142.45E
Bull Shoals L. U.S.A. 83 36.30N 92.50W
Bulolo P.N.G. 37 7.13S146.35E
Bulsār India 40 20.38N 72.56E
Bultfontein R.S.A. 56 28.17S 26.09E
Bulu Indonesia 37 4.34N126.45E
Bulu, Gunung *mtn.* Indonesia 36 3.00N116.00E
Bulun U.S.S.R. 29 70.50N127.20E
Bulunde Tanzania 55 4.19S 32.57E
Bumba Bandundu Zaïre 54 6.55S 19.16E
Bumba Equateur Zaïre 54 2.15N 22.32E
Bumbuli Zaïre 54 3.25S 20.30E
Buna Kenya 55 2.49N 39.27E
Buna P.N.G. 64 8.40S148.25E
Bunbury Australia 63 33.20S115.34E
Buncrana Rep. of Ire. 13 55.08N 7.27W
Bundaberg Australia 64 24.50S152.21E
Bundaleer Australia 67 28.39S146.31E
Bundarra Australia 67 30.11S151.04E
Bunde Germany 14 53.12N 7.16E
Bundella Australia 67 31.35S149.59E
Būndi India 40 25.27N 75.39E
Bundoran Rep. of Ire. 13 54.28N 8.17W
Būndu India 41 23.11N 85.35E
Bungay U.K. 11 52.27N 1.26E
Bungo Angola 54 7.26S 15.23E
Bungu Tanzania 55 7.37S 39.07E
Buni Nigeria 53 11.20N 11.59E
Bunia Zaïre 55 1.30N 30.10E
Buninyong Australia 66 37.41S143.58E
Bunkie U.S.A. 83 30.57N 92.11W
Bunyala Kenya 45 0.07N 34.00E
Bunyan Australia 67 36.11S149.09E
Buol Indonesia 37 1.12N121.28E
Buqayq Saudi Arabia 43 25.55N 49.40E
Bura Coast Kenya 55 3.30S 38.19E
Bura Coast Kenya 55 1.09S 39.55E
Burakin Australia 63 30.30S117.08E
Burang China 41 30.16N 81.11E
Buras U.S.A. 83 29.21N 89.32W
Buraydah Saudi Arabia 43 26.18N 43.58E
Burcher Australia 67 33.32S147.18E
Burco Somali Rep. 45 9.30N 45.30E
Burdur Turkey 25 37.44N 30.17E
Burdwān India 41 23.15N 87.51E
Bure Ethiopia 49 10.40N 37.04E
Burg Germany 20 52.17N 11.51E
Burgas Bulgaria 19 42.30N 27.29E
Burgenland *d.* Austria 20 47.30N 16.20E
Burgeo Canada 77 47.36N 57.34W
Burgess Hill U.K. 11 50.57N 0.07W
Burgos Spain 16 42.21N 3.41W
Burgsteinfurt Germany 14 52.09N 7.21E
Burgsvik Sweden 23 57.03N 18.16E
Burhānpur India 40 21.18N 76.14E
Buri Brazil 94 23.46S 48.39W
Burias *i.* Phil. 37 12.50N123.10E
Burica, Punta *c.* Panama 87 8.05N 82.50W
Burin Pen. Canada 77 47.00N 55.40W
Buriram Thailand 34 14.59N103.08E
Burkburnett U.S.A. 83 34.06N 98.34W
Burke *r.* Australia 64 23.12S139.33E
Burketown Australia 64 17.44S139.22E
Burkina Africa 52 12.30N 2.00W

Burley U.S.A. **80** 42.32N113.48W
Burlington Canada **76** 43.19N 79.48W
Burlington Iowa U.S.A. **82** 40.49N 91.14W
Burlington Kans. U.S.A. **82** 38.12N 95.45W
Burlington N.C. U.S.A. **85** 36.05N 79.27W
Burlington N.J. U.S.A. **85** 40.04N 74.49W
Burlington Vt. U.S.A. **84** 44.29N 73.13W
Burlington Wisc. U.S.A. **82** 42.41N 88.17W
Burma Asia **34** 21.45N 97.00E
Burngup Australia **63** 33.00S118.39E
Burnham-on-Crouch U.K. **11** 51.37N 0.50E
Burnham-on-Sea U.K. **11** 51.15N 3.00W
Burnie Australia **65** 41.03S145.55E
Burnley U.K. **10** 53.47N 2.15W
Burns Oreg. U.S.A. **80** 43.35N119.03W
Burns Wyo. U.S.A. **80** 41.11N104.21W
Burnside *r.* Canada **72** 66.51N108.04W
Burns Lake *town* Canada **74** 54.20N125.45W
Buronga Australia **66** 34.08S142.11E
Burra Australia **66** 33.40S138.57E
Burracoppin Australia **63** 31.22S118.30E
Burragorang, L. Australia **67** 33.58S150.27E
Burren Junction Australia **67** 30.08S148.59E
Burrewarra Pt. Australia **67** 35.56S150.12E
Burriana Spain **16** 39.54N 0.05W
Burrinjuck Australia **67** 35.01S148.33E
Burrinjuck Resr. Australia **67** 35.00S148.40E
Burro, Serranías del *mts.* Mexico **83** 29.20N102.00W
Burry Port U.K. **11** 51.41N 4.17W
Bursa Turkey **19** 40.11N 29.04E
Būr Safājah Egypt **42** 26.44N 33.56E
Būr Sa'īd Egypt **44** 31.17N 32.18E
Būr Sūdān Sudan **48** 19.39N 37.01E
Burta Australia **66** 32.30S141.05E
Būr Tawfīq Egypt **44** 29.57N 32.34E
Burton upon Trent U.K. **10** 52.58N 1.39W
Burtundy Australia **66** 33.45S142.22E
Buru *i.* Indonesia **37** 3.30S126.30E
Burullus, Buḥayrat al *l.* Egypt **44** 31.30N 30.45E
Burundi Africa **55** 3.00S 30.00E
Bururi Burundi **55** 3.58S 29.35E
Burutu Nigeria **53** 5.20N 5.31E
Bury G.M. U.K. **10** 53.36N 2.19W
Bury St. Edmunds U.K. **11** 52.15N 0.42E
Burzil Jammu & Kashmir **40** 34.52N 75.07E
Burzil Pass Jammu & Kashmir **40** 34.54N 75.06E
Busalla Italy **15** 44.34N 8.57E
Busca Italy **15** 44.31N 7.29E
Būsh Egypt **44** 29.09N 31.07E
Būshehr Iran **43** 28.57N 50.52E
Bushkill U.S.A. **85** 41.06N 75.00W
Bushmanland *f.* R.S.A. **56** 29.25S 19.40E
Busi Ethiopia **45** 5.30N 44.30E
Busigny France **14** 50.03N 3.29E
Businga Zaïre **54** 3.16N 20.55E
Busira *r.* Zaïre **54** 0.05N 18.18E
Buskerud Norway **23** 60.20N 9.00E
Buṣrá ash Shām Syria **44** 32.30N 36.29E
Busselton Australia **63** 33.43S115.15E
Bussum Neth. **14** 52.17N 5.10E
Bustard Head *c.* Australia **64** 24.02S151.48E
Busto Arsizio Italy **15** 45.37N 8.51E
Busu Djanoa Zaïre **54** 1.42N 21.23E
Buta Zaïre **54** 2.50N 24.50E
Butari Rwanda **55** 2.38S 29.43E
Butaritari *i.* Kiribati **68** 3.07N172.48E
Bute Australia **66** 33.24S138.01E
Bute *i.* U.K. **12** 55.51N 5.07W
Bute, Sd. of U.K. **12** 55.44N 5.10W
Butedale Canada **74** 53.12N128.45W
Butiaba Uganda **55** 1.48N 31.15E
Butler Mo. U.S.A. **83** 38.16N 94.20W
Butler N.J. U.S.A. **85** 41.00N 74.21W
Buton *i.* Indonesia **37** 5.00S122.50E
Butte Mont. U.S.A. **80** 46.00N112.32W
Butte Nebr. U.S.A. **82** 42.58N 98.51W
Butterworth Malaysia **36** 5.24N100.22E
Buttevant Rep. of Ire. **13** 52.14N 8.41W
Butt of Lewis *c.* U.K. **12** 58.31N 6.15W
Butty Head Australia **63** 33.52S121.35E
Butuan Phil. **37** 8.56N125.31E
Butwal Nepal **41** 27.42N 83.28E
Buuhoodle Somali Rep. **45** 8.16N 46.24E
Buulo Berdi Somali Rep. **45** 3.52N 45.40E
Buur Gaabo Somali Rep. **49** 1.10S 41.50E
Buur Hakaba Somali Rep. **55** 2.43N 44.10E
Buxton U.K. **10** 53.16N 1.54W
Buy U.S.S.R. **24** 58.23N 41.27E
Buyaga U.S.S.R. **29** 59.42N126.59E
Buynaksk U.S.S.R. **25** 42.48N 47.07E
Büyük Menderes *r.* Turkey **19** 37.30N 27.05E
Buzachi, Poluostrov *pen.* U.S.S.R. **25** 45.00N 51.55E
Buzancy France **15** 49.30N 4.59E
Buzău Romania **21** 45.10N 26.49E
Buzău *r.* Romania **21** 45.24N 27.48E
Buzaymah Libya **51** 24.55N 22.02E
Buzi *r.* Mozambique **57** 19.52S 34.00E
Buzuluk U.S.S.R. **24** 52.49N 52.19E
Bwasiaia P.N.G. **64** 10.06S150.48E
Byala Bulgaria **19** 42.53N 27.55E
Byam Martin I. Canada **72** 75.15N104.00W
Bydgoszcz Poland **21** 53.16N 17.33E
Byemoor Canada **74** 52.00N112.17W
Bygland Norway **23** 58.48N 7.50E
Byhalia U.S.A. **83** 34.52N 89.41W
Bykhov U.S.S.R. **21** 53.30N 30.15E
Bykle Norway **23** 59.21N 7.20E
Bylot I. Canada **73** 73.00N 78.30W
Byrd Land *f.* Antarctica **96** 79.30S125.00W
Byrock Australia **67** 30.40S146.25E
Byron, C. Australia **67** 28.37S153.40E
Byron Bay *town* Australia **67** 28.43S153.34E
Byrranga, Gory *mts.* U.S.S.R. **29** 74.50N101.00E
Byske Sweden **22** 64.57N 21.12E
Byske *r.* Sweden **22** 64.57N 21.13E
Byten U.S.S.R. **21** 52.50N 25.28E
Bytom Poland **21** 50.22N 18.54E
Bzipi U.S.S.R. **25** 43.15N 40.24E

C

Ca *r.* Vietnam **33** 18.47N105.40E
Caballos Mesteños, Llano de los *f.* Mexico **83** 28.15N104.00W
Cabanatuan Phil. **37** 15.30N120.58E
Cabimas Venezuela **90** 10.26N 71.27W
Cabinda Angola **54** 5.34S 12.12E
Cabinet Mts. U.S.A. **80** 48.08N115.46W
Cabo Delgado *d.* Mozambique **55** 12.30S 39.00E
Cabo Frio *town* Brazil **94** 22.51S 42.03W
Cabonga, Résr. Canada **76** 47.35N 76.40W
Cabool U.S.A. **83** 37.07N 92.06W
Caboolture Australia **65** 27.05S152.57E
Cabo Pantoja Peru **90** 1.00S 75.10W
Cabot Str. Canada **77** 47.20N 59.30W
Cabras Italy **18** 39.56N 8.32E
Cabrera *i.* Spain **16** 39.08N 2.56E
Cabrera, Sierra *mts.* Spain **16** 42.10N 6.30W
Cabri Canada **75** 50.37N108.28W
Cabriel *r.* Spain **16** 39.13N 1.07W
Cabruta Venezuela **90** 7.40N 66.16W
Čačak Yugo. **21** 43.53N 20.21E
Caçapava Brazil **94** 23.05S 45.40W
Cáceres Brazil **91** 16.05S 57.40W
Cáceres Spain **16** 39.29N 6.23W
Cacharí Argentina **93** 36.23S 59.29W
Cachimo *r.* Zaïre **54** 7.02S 21.13E
Cachoeira Brazil **91** 12.35S 38.59W
Cachoeira do Sul Brazil **94** 30.03S 52.52W
Cachoeiro de Itapemirim Brazil **94** 20.51S 41.07W
Cacín *r.* Spain **16** 37.10N 4.01W
Cacine Guinea **52** 11.08N 14.57W
Cacolo Angola **54** 10.09S 19.15E
Caconda Angola **54** 13.46S 15.06E
Cacongo Angola **54** 5.11S 12.10E
Cacuso Angola **54** 9.26S 15.43E
Čadca Czech. **21** 49.26N 18.48E
Cader Idris *mtn.* U.K. **11** 52.40N 3.55W
Cadí, Serra del *mts.* Spain **16** 42.12N 1.35E
Cadibarrawirracanna, L. Australia **66** 28.52S135.27E
Cadillac U.S.A. **84** 44.15N 85.23W
Cadiz Phil. **37** 10.57N123.18E
Cádiz Spain **16** 36.32N 6.18W
Cádiz, Golfo de *g.* Spain **16** 37.00N 7.10W
Cadomin Canada **74** 53.02N117.20W
Cadoux Australia **63** 30.47S117.05E
Caen France **15** 49.11N 0.22W
Caernarfon U.K. **10** 53.08N 4.17W
Caernarfon B. U.K. **10** 53.05N 4.25W
Caerphilly U.K. **11** 51.34N 3.13W
Caeté Brazil **94** 19.54S 43.37W
Cafima Angola **54** 16.34S 16.30E
Cafu Angola **54** 16.30S 15.14E
Cagayan de Oro Phil. **37** 8.29N124.40E
Cagliari Italy **18** 39.14N 9.07E
Cagliari, Golfo di *g.* Italy **18** 39.07N 9.15E
Cagnes France **15** 43.40N 7.09E
Caguán *r.* Colombia **90** 0.08S 74.18W
Caguas Puerto Rico **87** 18.08N 66.00W
Cahama Angola **54** 16.16S 14.23E
Caha Mts. Rep. of Ire. **13** 51.44N 9.45W
Caherciveen Rep. of Ire. **13** 51.51N 10.14W
Cahir Rep. of Ire. **13** 52.23N 7.56W
Cahora Bassa Dam Mozambique **55** 15.36S 32.41E
Cahore Pt. Rep. of Ire. **13** 52.34N 6.12W
Cahors France **17** 44.28N 0.26E
Cahuapanas Peru **90** 5.15S 77.00W
Caianda Angola **54** 11.02S 23.29E
Caibarién Cuba **87** 22.31N 79.28W
Caicó Brazil **91** 6.25S 37.04W
Caicos Is. Turks & Caicos Is. **87** 21.30N 72.00W
Caird Coast *f.* Antarctica **96** 75.00S 20.00W
Cairngorms *mts.* U.K. **12** 57.04N 3.30W
Cairns Australia **64** 16.51S145.43E
Cairo *see* Al Qāhirah Egypt **44**
Cairo Ill. U.S.A. **83** 37.01N 89.09W
Cairo Montenotte Italy **15** 44.24N 8.16E
Caiundo Angola **54** 15.43S 17.30E
Caiwarro Australia **67** 28.38S144.45E
Caizhai China **32** 37.20N118.10E
Caizi Hu *l.* China **33** 30.50N117.06E
Cajamarca Peru **90** 7.09S 78.32W
Cajàzeiras Brazil **91** 6.52S 38.31W
Çajuru Brazil **94** 21.15S 47.18W
Čakovec Yugo. **20** 46.23N 16.26E
Calabar Nigeria **53** 4.56N 8.22E
Calabozo Venezuela **90** 8.58N 67.28W
Calabria *d.* Italy **19** 39.00N 16.30E
Calafat Romania **21** 43.59N 22.57E
Calafate Argentina **93** 50.20S 72.16W
Calahorra Spain **16** 42.18N 1.58W
Calais France **17** 50.57N 1.52E
Calama Brazil **90** 8.03S 62.53W
Calama Chile **92** 22.30S 68.55W
Calamar Colombia **90** 10.15N 74.55W
Calamian Group *is.* Phil. **37** 12.00N120.05E
Cala Millor Spain **16** 39.35N 3.22E
Calamocha Spain **16** 40.54N 1.18W
Calapan Phil. **37** 13.23N121.10E
Călăraşi Romania **21** 44.11N 27.21E
Calatayud Spain **16** 41.21N 1.39W
Calatrava Equat. Guinea **54** 1.09N 9.24E
Calau Germany **20** 51.45N 13.56E
Calayan *i.* Phil. **33** 19.20N121.25E
Calbayog Phil. **37** 12.04N124.58E
Calcutta India **41** 22.32N 88.22E
Caldaro Italy **15** 46.25N 11.14E
Caldas Colombia **90** 6.05N 75.36W
Caldas da Rainha Portugal **16** 39.24N 9.08W
Caldera Chile **92** 27.04S 70.50W
Caldwell Idaho U.S.A. **80** 43.40N116.41W
Caldwell Ohio U.S.A. **84** 39.44N 81.32W
Caledon *r.* R.S.A. **56** 30.27S 26.12E
Caledon B. Australia **64** 12.58S136.52E
Caledonia Canada **76** 43.04N 79.56W
Caledonia Hills Canada **77** 45.40N 65.00W
Calella Spain **16** 41.37N 2.40E
Calexico Mexico **81** 32.40N115.30W
Calf of Man *i.* U.K. **10** 54.03N 4.49W
Calgary Canada **74** 51.00N114.10W
Cali Colombia **90** 3.24N 76.30W
Caliente U.S.A. **80** 37.37N114.31W
California *d.* U.S.A. **80** 37.29N119.58W
California, G. of *see* California, Golfo de *g.* Mexico **86**
California, Golfo de *g.* Mexico **81** 28.00N112.00W
Calingasta Argentina **92** 31.15S 69.30W
Calingiri Australia **63** 31.07S116.27E
Callabonna, L. Australia **66** 29.47S140.07E
Callabonna Creek *r.* Australia **66** 29.37S140.08E
Callander U.K. **12** 56.15N 4.13W
Callao Peru **92** 12.05S 77.08W
Caloocan Phil. **37** 14.38N120.58E
Caloundra Australia **65** 26.47S153.08E
Caltagirone Italy **18** 37.14N 14.30E
Caltanissetta Italy **18** 37.30N 14.05E
Calulo Angola **54** 10.05S 14.56E
Calumbo Angola **54** 9.08S 13.24E
Calumet Canada **77** 45.39N 74.41W
Calundau Angola **54** 12.05S 19.10E
Caluula Somali Rep. **45** 11.58N 50.48E
Calvados *d.* France **15** 49.10N 0.30W
Calvert I. Canada **74** 51.30N128.00W
Calvi France **17** 42.34N 8.44E
Calvinia R.S.A. **56** 31.29S 19.44E
Cam *r.* U.K. **11** 52.34N 0.21E
Camabatela Angola **54** 8.20S 15.29E
Camacupa Angola **54** 12.01S 17.22E
Camagüey Cuba **87** 21.25N 77.55W
Camagüey, Archipiélago de Cuba **87** 22.30N 78.00W
Camaiore Italy **15** 43.56N 10.18E
Camarès France **17** 43.49N 2.53E
Camaret-sur-Mer France **17** 48.16N 4.37W
Camarón, C. Honduras **87** 15.59N 85.00W
Camaronero, Laguna *l.* Mexico **81** 23.00N106.07W
Camarones Argentina **93** 44.45S 65.40W
Camas U.S.A. **80** 45.35N122.24W
Cambay India **40** 22.18N 72.37E
Camberley U.K. **11** 51.21N 0.45W
Cambodia Asia **34** 12.45N105.00E
Camborne U.K. **11** 50.12N 5.19W
Cambrai Australia **66** 34.39S139.17E
Cambrai France **17** 50.10N 3.14E
Cambria U.S.A. **81** 35.34N121.05W
Cambrian Mts. U.K. **11** 52.33N 3.33W
Cambridge Canada **76** 43.22N 80.19W
Cambridge New Zealand **60** 37.53S175.29E
Cambridge U.K. **11** 52.13N 0.08E
Cambridge Idaho U.S.A. **80** 44.34N116.41W
Cambridge Mass. U.S.A. **84** 42.22N 71.06W
Cambridge Md. U.S.A. **85** 38.34N 76.04W
Cambridge Minn. U.S.A. **82** 45.31N 93.14W
Cambridge Bay *town* Canada **72** 69.09N105.00W
Cambridge G. Australia **62** 15.00S128.05E
Cambridgeshire *d.* U.K. **11** 52.15N 0.05E
Cambundi-Catembo Angola **54** 10.09S 17.35E
Camden U.K. **11** 51.33N 0.10W
Camden Ark. U.S.A. **83** 33.35N 92.50W
Camden N.J. U.S.A. **85** 39.57N 75.07W
Camden S.C. U.S.A. **85** 34.16N 80.36W
Cameia Nat. Park Angola **54** 12.00S 21.30E
Camelford U.K. **11** 50.37N 4.41W
Cameron Ariz. U.S.A. **81** 35.51N111.25W
Cameron La. U.S.A. **83** 29.48N 93.19W
Cameron Mo. U.S.A. **82** 39.44N 94.14W
Cameron Tex. U.S.A. **83** 30.51N 96.59W
Cameron Hills Canada **74** 59.48N118.00W
Cameron Mts. New Zealand **60** 45.50S167.00E
Cameroon Africa **53** 6.00N 12.30E
Cameroun, Mont *mtn.* Cameroon **53** 4.20N 9.05E
Cametá Brazil **91** 2.12S 49.30W
Camiri Bolivia **92** 20.03S 63.31W
Camocim Brazil **91** 2.55S 40.50W
Camooweal Australia **64** 19.55S138.07E
Camopi Guiana **91** 3.12N 52.15W
Campana Argentina **93** 34.10S 58.57W
Campana, Isla *i.* Chile **93** 48.25S 75.20W
Campania *d.* Italy **18** 41.00N 14.30E
Campbell, C. New Zealand **60** 41.45S174.15E
Campbell I. Pacific Oc. **68** 52.30S169.02E
Campbellpore Pakistan **40** 33.46N 72.22E
Campbell River *town* Canada **74** 50.05N125.20W
Campbellsville U.S.A. **85** 37.20N 85.21W
Campbellton Canada **77** 48.00N 66.40W
Campbelltown Australia **67** 34.04S150.49E
Campbell Town Australia **67** 41.55S147.30E
Campbeltown U.K. **12** 55.25N 5.36W
Campeche Mexico **86** 19.50N 90.30W
Campeche *d.* Mexico **86** 19.00N 90.00W
Campeche, Bahía de *b.* Mexico **86** 19.30N 94.00W
Campeche B. *see* Campeche, Bahía de *b.* Mexico **86**
Camperdown Australia **66** 38.15S143.14E
Cam Pha Vietnam **34** 21.07N107.19E
Campina Grande Brazil **91** 7.15S 35.50W
Campinas Brazil **94** 22.54S 47.06W
Campo Cameroon **53** 2.22N 9.50E
Campo *r.* Cameroon **54** 2.21N 9.51E
Campo U.S.A. **83** 37.06N102.35W
Campobasso Italy **18** 41.34N 14.39E
Campo Belo Brazil **94** 20.52S 45.16W
Campo Gallo Argentina **92** 26.35S 62.50W
Campo Grande Brazil **92** 20.24S 54.35W
Campo Maior Brazil **91** 4.50S 42.12W
Campo Maior Portugal **16** 39.01N 7.04W
Campos Brazil **94** 21.45S 41.18W
Campos Belos Brazil **91** 13.09S 47.03W
Campos do Jordão Brazil **94** 23.28S 46.10W
Camp Wood U.S.A. **83** 29.40N100.01W
Cam Ranh Vietnam **34** 11.54N109.14E
Camrose Canada **74** 53.00N112.50W
Canada N. America **72** 60.00N105.00W
Cañada de Gómez Argentina **92** 32.49S 61.25W
Canadian U.S.A. **83** 35.55N100.23W
Canadian *r.* U.S.A. **83** 35.27N 95.03W
Çanakkale Turkey **19** 40.09N 26.26E
Çanakkale Boğazi *str.* Turkey **19** 40.15N 26.30E
Canal du Midi France **17** 43.18N 2.00E
Cananea Mexico **81** 30.57N110.18W
Canarias, Islas *is.* Atlantic Oc. **50** 28.00N 15.00W
Canary Is. *see* Canarias, Islas *is.* Atlantic Oc. **50**
Canastra, Serra da *mts.* Brazil **94** 20.05S 46.30W
Canaveral, C. U.S.A. **85** 28.27N 80.32W
Canavieiras Brazil **91** 15.44S 38.58W
Canbelego Australia **67** 31.33S146.19E
Canberra Australia **67** 35.18S149.08E
Canby Calif. U.S.A. **80** 41.27N120.52W
Canby Minn. U.S.A. **82** 44.43N 96.16W
Cancale France **15** 48.40N 1.50W
Cancon France **17** 44.32N 0.38E
Candé France **15** 47.34N 1.02W
Candeias Brazil **94** 20.44S 45.18W
Candeleda Spain **16** 40.10N 5.14W
Candle L. Canada **75** 53.50N105.18W
Canelli Italy **15** 44.43N 8.17E
Canelones Uruguay **93** 34.32S 56.17W
Cañete Peru **90** 13.00S 76.30W
Canfield Canada **76** 42.59N 79.43W
Cangamba Angola **54** 13.40S 19.50E
Cangas de Narcea Spain **16** 43.11N 6.33W
Cangkuang, Tanjung *c.* Indonesia **37** 6.45S105.15E
Cangombe Angola **54** 14.27S 20.00E
Canguçu Brazil **92** 31.24S 52.41W
Cangwu China **33** 23.27N111.17E
Cangzhou China **32** 38.15N116.58E
Caniapiscau *r.* Canada **77** 57.40N 69.30W
Caniapiscau, Lac *l.* Canada **77** 54.10N 69.55W
Çankiri Turkey **42** 40.35N 33.37E
Canna *i.* U.K. **12** 57.03N 6.30W
Cannes France **17** 43.33N 7.00E
Cannich U.K. **12** 57.20N 4.45W
Cannock U.K. **11** 52.42N 2.02W
Cann River *town* Australia **67** 37.35S149.06E
Canõas Brazil **94** 29.55S 51.10W
Canoe L. Canada **75** 55.11N108.15W
Canonba Australia **67** 31.19S147.22E
Canon City U.S.A. **80** 38.27N105.14W
Canopus Australia **66** 33.30S140.57E
Canora Canada **75** 51.37N102.26W
Canossa *site* Italy **15** 44.35N 10.27E
Canowindra Australia **67** 33.34S148.30E
Canso Canada **77** 45.20N 61.00W
Cantabria *d.* Spain **16** 43.10N 4.15W
Cantabria, Sierra de *mts.* Spain **16** 42.40N 2.30W
Cantábrica, Cordillera *mts.* Spain **16** 42.55N 5.10W
Cantagalo Brazil **94** 21.59S 42.22W
Cantaura Venezuela **90** 9.22N 64.24W
Canterbury *d.* New Zealand **60** 43.30S172.00E
Canterbury U.K. **11** 51.17N 1.05E
Canterbury Bight New Zealand **60** 44.15S172.00E
Can Tho Vietnam **34** 10.03N105.40E
Canton *see* Guangzhou China **33**
Canton Miss. U.S.A. **83** 32.37N 90.02W
Canton N.C. U.S.A. **85** 35.33N 82.51W
Canton Ohio U.S.A. **84** 40.48N 81.23W
Canton Okla. U.S.A. **83** 36.03N 98.35W
Cantù Italy **15** 45.44N 9.08E
Cantua Creek *town* U.S.A. **81** 36.30N120.19W
Cantung Canada **74** 62.00N128.09W
Cañuelas Argentina **93** 35.03S 58.44W
Canumã *r.* Brazil **90** 3.55S 59.10W
Canutama Brazil **90** 6.32S 64.20W
Canutillo Mexico **81** 26.21N105.25W
Cany-Barville France **15** 49.47N 0.38E
Canyon Tex. U.S.A. **83** 34.59N101.55W
Canyon Wyo. U.S.A. **80** 44.43N110.32W
Cao Bang Vietnam **33** 22.37N106.18E
Caombo Angola **54** 8.45S 16.50E
Caorle Italy **15** 45.36N 12.53E
Capanema Brazil **91** 1.08S 47.07W
Cap-Chat Canada **77** 48.56N 66.53W
Cap-de-la-Madeleine *town* Canada **77** 46.22N 72.32W
Cape Barren I. Australia **65** 40.25S148.15E
Cape Basin *f.* Atlantic Oc. **95** 38.00S 10.00E
Cape Breton Highlands Canada **77** 46.45N 60.45W
Cape Breton I. Canada **77** 46.00N 60.30W
Cape Coast *town* Ghana **52** 5.10N 1.13W
Cape Cod B. U.S.A. **84** 41.50N 70.17W
Cape Crawford *town* Australia **64** 16.38S135.43E
Cape Dyer *town* Canada **73** 66.30N 61.20W
Cape Girardeau *town* U.S.A. **83** 37.19N 89.32W
Cape Johnson Depth Pacific Oc. **37** 10.20N127.20E
Capellen Lux. **14** 49.39N 5.59E
Capelongo Angola **54** 14.55S 15.03E
Cape May *town* U.S.A. **85** 38.56N 74.55W
Cape Province *d.* R.S.A. **56** 31.30S 23.30E
Cape Town R.S.A. **56** 33.55S 18.27E
Cape Verde Atlantic Oc. **95** 16.00N 24.00W
Cape Verde Basin *f.* Atlantic Oc. **95** 15.00N 35.00W
Cape York Pen. Australia **64** 12.40S142.20E
Cap-Haïtien *town* Haiti **87** 19.47N 72.17W
Capim *r.* Brazil **91** 1.40S 47.47W
Capoompeta, Mt. Australia **67** 29.22S151.59E
Cappoquin Rep. of Ire. **13** 52.09N 7.52W
Capraia *i.* Italy **18** 43.03N 9.50E
Caprera *i.* Italy **18** 41.48N 9.27E
Capri *i.* Italy **18** 40.33N 14.13E
Caprivi Strip *f.* Namibia **56** 17.50S 23.10E
Captains Flat Australia **67** 35.34S149.28E
Captiva U.S.A. **85** 26.31N 82.12W
Caqueta *r.* Colombia **90** 1.20S 70.50W
Caracal Romania **21** 44.08N 24.18E
Caracas Venezuela **90** 10.35N 66.56W
Caragabal Australia **67** 33.49S147.46E
Caraguatatuba Brazil **94** 23.39S 45.26W
Carandaí Brazil **94** 20.55S 43.46W
Carangola Brazil **94** 20.44S 42.03W
Caransebeş Romania **21** 45.25N 22.13E
Caratasca, Laguna de *b.* Honduras **87** 15.10N 84.00W
Caratinga Brazil **94** 19.50S 42.06W
Caravaca Spain **16** 38.06N 1.51W
Caravaggio Italy **15** 45.30N 9.38E
Caravelí Peru **90** 15.45S 73.25W
Carballo Spain **16** 43.13N 8.41W
Carbenyabba Creek *r.* Australia **66** 29.02S143.28E
Carberry Canada **75** 49.52N 99.20W
Carbonara, Capo *c.* Italy **18** 39.06N 9.32E
Carbondale Ill. U.S.A. **83** 37.44N 89.13W
Carbondale Penn. U.S.A. **84** 41.35N 75.30W
Carbonear Canada **77** 47.45N 53.14W
Carbonia Italy **18** 39.11N 8.32E
Carcajou Canada **74** 57.47N117.06W
Carcassonne France **17** 43.13N 2.21E
Carcross Canada **74** 60.13N134.45W
Cárdenas Cuba **87** 23.02N 81.12W
Cárdenas Mexico **86** 22.00N 99.40W
Cardenete Spain **16** 39.46N 1.42W
Cardiff U.K. **11** 51.28N 3.11W
Cardigan U.K. **11** 52.06N 4.41W
Cardigan B. U.K. **11** 52.30N 4.30W
Cardona Spain **16** 41.56N 1.40E
Cardona Uruguay **93** 33.53S 57.23W
Cardwell Australia **64** 18.21S146.04E
Carei Romania **21** 47.42N 22.28E
Carentan France **15** 49.18N 1.14W
Carey U.S.A. **80** 43.18N113.56W
Carey, L. Australia **63** 29.05S122.15E
Carey L. Canada **75** 62.12N102.55W
Carhaix France **17** 48.16N 3.35W
Carhué Argentina **93** 37.11S 62.45W
Caribbean Sea C. America **87** 15.00N 75.00W
Cariboo Mts. Canada **74** 53.00N121.00W
Caribou *r.* Man. Canada **75** 59.20N 94.44W
Caribou *r.* N.W.T. Canada **74** 61.27N125.45W
Caribou U.S.A. **84** 46.52N 68.01W
Caribou Is. Canada **74** 61.55N113.15W
Caribou Mts. Canada **74** 59.12N115.40W
Carignan France **15** 49.38N 5.10E
Carinda Australia **67** 30.29S147.45E
Carinhanha Brazil **91** 14.18S 43.47W
Carini Italy **18** 38.08N 13.11E
Caritianas Brazil **90** 9.25S 63.06W
Carleton Place Canada **76** 45.08N 76.09W
Carlingford Rep. of Ire. **13** 54.03N 6.12W
Carlingford Lough Rep. of Ire. **13** 54.03N 6.09W
Carlinville U.S.A. **82** 39.17N 89.52W
Carlisle U.K. **10** 54.54N 2.55W
Carlos Reyles Uruguay **93** 33.03S 56.29W
Carlow Rep. of Ire. **12** 52.50N 6.46W
Carlow *d.* Rep. of Ire. **13** 52.43N 6.50W
Carlsbad Calif. U.S.A. **81** 33.10N117.21W
Carlsbad N.Mex. U.S.A. **81** 32.25N104.14W
Carlyle Canada **75** 49.38N102.16W
Carmacks Canada **72** 62.04N136.21W
Carmagnola Italy **15** 44.51N 7.43E
Carman Canada **75** 49.32N 98.00W
Carmarthen U.K. **11** 51.52N 4.20W
Carmarthen B. U.K. **11** 52.30N 4.30W
Carmaux France **17** 44.03N 2.09E
Carmel U.S.A. **85** 41.26N 73.41W
Carmel Head U.K. **10** 53.24N 4.35W
Carmelo Uruguay **93** 34.00S 58.17W
Carmen Colombia **90** 9.46N 75.06W
Carmen Mexico **86** 18.38N 91.50W
Carmen Uruguay **93** 33.15S 56.01W
Carmen, Isla *i.* Mexico **81** 25.55N111.10W
Carmen, Isla del *i.* Mexico **86** 18.35N 91.40W
Carmen de Areco Argentina **93** 34.20S 59.50W
Carmen de Patagones Argentina **93** 40.48S 63.00W
Carmi U.S.A. **82** 38.05N 88.11W
Carmichael U.S.A. **80** 38.38N121.19W
Carmila Australia **64** 21.55S149.25E
Carmo Brazil **94** 21.56S 42.37W
Carmody, L. Australia **63** 32.27S119.20E
Carmona Spain **16** 37.28N 5.38W

Carnac France **17** 47.35N 3.05W
Carnarvon Australia **62** 24.53S113.40E
Carnarvon R.S.A. **56** 30.58S 22.07E
Carndonagh Rep. of Ire. **13** 55.15N 7.15W
Carnegie Australia **62** 25.43S122.59E
Carnegie, L. Australia **62** 26.15S123.00E
Carnew Rep. of Ire. **13** 52.43N 6.31W
Carniche, Alpi *mts.* Austria/Italy **18** 46.40N 12.48E
Car Nicobar *i.* India **34** 9.11N 92.45E
Carnot C.A.R. **53** 4.59N 15.56E
Carnot, C. Australia **66** 34.57S135.38E
Carnoustie U.K. **12** 56.30N 2.44W
Carnsore Pt. Rep. of Ire. **13** 52.10N 6.21W
Carolina Brazil **91** 7.20S 47.25W
Carolina Puerto Rico **87** 18.23N 65.57W
Carolina R.S.A. **56** 26.04S 30.07E
Caroline I. Kiribati **69** 10.00S150.30W
Caroline Is. Pacific Oc. **37** 7.50N145.00E
Caroline-Solomon Ridge Pacific Oc. **68** 8.00N150.00E
Caroní *r.* Venezuela **90** 8.20N 62.42W
Carora Venezuela **90** 10.12N 70.07W
Carp Canada **77** 45.21N 76.02W
Carpathians *mts.* Europe **21** 48.45N 23.45E
Carpaţii Meridionali *mts.* Romania **21** 45.35N 24.40E
Carpentaria, G. of Australia **64** 14.00S139.00E
Carpentras France **17** 44.03N 5.03E
Carpi Italy **15** 44.47N 10.53E
Carpio Spain **16** 41.13N 5.07W
Carquefou France **15** 47.18N 1.30W
Carra, Lough Rep. of Ire. **13** 53.41N 9.15W
Carrara Italy **15** 44.04N 10.06E
Carrathool Australia **67** 34.25S145.24E
Carrauntoohil *mtn.* Rep. of Ire. **13** 52.00N 9.45W
Carrickfergus U.K. **13** 54.43N 5.49W
Carrickmacross Rep. of Ire. **13** 53.58N 6.43W
Carrick-on-Shannon Rep. of Ire. **13** 53.57N 8.06W
Carrick-on-Suir Rep. of Ire. **13** 52.21N 7.26W
Carrieton Australia **66** 32.28S138.34E
Carrington U.S.A. **82** 47.27N 99.08W
Carrizo Springs *town* U.S.A. **83** 28.31N 99.52W
Carrizozo U.S.A. **81** 33.38N105.53W
Carroll U.S.A. **82** 42.04N 94.52W
Carrollton Mo. U.S.A. **82** 39.22N 93.30W
Carrot *r.* Canada **75** 53.50N101.17W
Carrowmore Lough Rep. of Ire. **13** 54.11N 9.47W
Carrum Australia **67** 38.05S145.08E
Carşamba Turkey **42** 41.13N 36.43E
Carşamba *r.* Turkey **42** 37.52N 31.48E
Carson U.S.A. **82** 46.25N101.34W
Carson City U.S.A. **80** 39.10N119.46W
Carstairs U.K. **12** 55.42N 3.41W
Cartagena Colombia **90** 10.24N 75.33W
Cartagena Spain **16** 37.36N 0.59W
Cartago Colombia **90** 4.45N 75.55W
Cartago Costa Rica **87** 9.50N 83.52W
Carter U.S.A. **80** 41.27N110.25W
Carteret France **15** 49.22N 1.48W
Cartersville U.S.A. **85** 34.09N 84.49W
Carterton New Zealand **60** 41.01S175.31E
Carthage Mo. U.S.A. **83** 37.11N 94.19W
Carthage S.Dak. U.S.A. **82** 44.10N 97.43W
Carthage Tex. U.S.A. **83** 32.09N 94.20W
Cartwright Canada **77** 53.50N 56.45W
Caruarú Brazil **91** 8.15S 35.55W
Carúpano Venezuela **90** 10.39N 63.14W
Caruthersville U.S.A. **83** 36.11N 89.39W
Carvin France **14** 50.30N 2.58E
Carvoeiro Brazil **90** 1.24S 61.59W
Caryapundy Swamp Australia **66** 29.00S142.36E
Casablanca Morocco **50** 33.39N 7.35W
Casa Branca Brazil **94** 21.45S 47.06W
Casa Grande U.S.A. **81** 32.53N111.45W
Casale Italy **15** 45.08N 8.27E
Casarano Italy **19** 40.00N 18.10E
Cascade Idaho U.S.A. **80** 44.31N116.02W
Cascade Mont. U.S.A. **80** 47.16N111.42W
Cascade Pt. New Zealand **60** 44.01S168.22E
Cascade Range *mts.* U.S.A. **80** 46.15N121.00W
Caserta Italy **18** 41.06N 14.21E
Caseyr *c.* Somali Rep. **45** 11.48N 51.22E
Cashel Tipperary Rep. of Ire. **13** 52.31N 7.54W
Casilda Argentina **93** 33.03S 61.10W
Casimiro de Abreu Brazil **94** 22.28S 42.12W
Casino Australia **67** 28.50S153.02E
Casma Peru **90** 9.30S 78.20W
Caspe Spain **16** 41.14N 0.03W
Casper U.S.A. **80** 42.51N106.19W
Caspian Depression *see* Prikaspiyskaya Nizmennost *ost* U.S.S.R. **25**
Caspian Sea U.S.S.R. **25** 42.00N 51.00E
Cassai *r.* Angola **54** 10.38S 22.15E
Cassano allo Ionio Italy **19** 39.47N 16.20E
Cass City U.S.A. **84** 43.37N 83.11W
Casselman Canada **77** 45.19N 75.05W
Casselton U.S.A. **82** 46.54N 97.13W
Cassiar Canada **74** 59.16N129.40W
Cassiar Mts. Canada **74** 59.00N129.00W
Cassilis Australia **67** 32.01S149.59E
Cass Lake *town* U.S.A. **82** 47.22N 94.35W
Castaños Mexico **83** 26.48N101.26W
Castelfranco Veneto Italy **15** 45.40N 11.55E
Casteljaloux France **17** 44.19N 0.06W
Castell' Arquato Italy **15** 44.51N 9.52E
Castelli Argentina **93** 36.07S 57.50W
Castellón Spain **16** 39.59N 0.03W
Castelmassa Italy **15** 45.01N 11.18E
Castelnovo ne'Monti Italy **15** 44.26N 10.24E
Castelnuovo di Garfagnana Italy **15** 44.06N 10.24E
Castelo Brazil **94** 20.33S 41.14W
Castelo Branco Portugal **16** 39.50N 7.30W
Castel San Giovanni Italy **15** 45.04N 9.26E
Castelvetrano Italy **18** 37.41N 12.47E
Casterton Australia **66** 37.35S141.25E
Castets France **17** 43.53N 1.09W
Castilla Peru **90** 5.16S 80.36W
Castilla la Mancha *d.* Spain **16** 40.00N 3.45W
Castilla y León *d.* Spain **16** 41.50N 4.15W
Castilletes Colombia **90** 11.55N 71.20W
Castlebar Rep. of Ire. **13** 53.52N 9.19W
Castleblayney Rep. of Ire. **13** 54.08N 6.46W
Castle Douglas U.K. **12** 54.56N 3.56W
Castleford U.K. **10** 53.43N 1.21W
Castlegar Canada **74** 49.20N117.40W
Castlegate U.S.A. **80** 39.44N110.52W
Castle Harbour *b.* Bermuda **95** 32.20N 64.40W
Castleisland Rep. of Ire. **13** 52.13N 9.28W
Castlemaine Australia **66** 37.05S144.19E
Castlerea Rep. of Ire. **13** 53.45N 8.30W
Castlereagh *r.* Australia **67** 30.12S147.32E
Castle Rock *town* Colo. U.S.A. **80** 39.22N104.51W
Castle Rock *town* Wash. U.S.A. **80** 46.17N122.54W
Castletown U.K. **10** 54.04N 4.38W
Castletownshend Rep. of Ire. **13** 51.32N 9.12W
Castres France **17** 43.36N 2.14E
Castries St. Lucia **87** 14.01N 60.59W
Castro Chile **93** 42.30S 73.46W
Castro del Río Spain **16** 37.41N 4.29W
Casula Mozambique **55** 15.26S 33.32E
Cataguases Brazil **94** 21.23S 42.39W
Çatalca Turkey **19** 41.09N 28.29E
Catalina Pt. Guam **68** 13.31N144.55E
Cataluña *d.* Spain **16** 42.00N 2.00E
Catamarca Argentina **92** 28.30S 65.45W
Catamarca *d.* Argentina **92** 27.45S 67.00W
Catanduanes *i.* Phil. **37** 13.45N124.20E
Catanduva Brazil **94** 21.03S 49.00W
Catania Italy **18** 37.31N 15.05E
Catanzaro Italy **19** 38.55N 16.35E
Catarman Phil. **37** 12.28N124.50E
Catbalogan Phil. **37** 11.46N124.55E
Catete Angola **54** 9.09S 13.40E
Cathcart Australia **67** 36.49S149.25E
Cathcart R.S.A. **56** 32.17S 27.08E
Cat I. Bahamas **87** 24.33N 75.36W
Cat L. Canada **76** 51.40N 91.50W
Catoche, C. Mexico **87** 21.38N 87.08W
Catonsville U.S.A. **85** 39.16N 76.44W
Catriló Argentina **93** 36.23S 63.24W
Catterick U.K. **10** 54.23N 1.38W
Cattolica Italy **15** 43.58N 12.44E
Catuane Mozambique **57** 26.49S 32.17E
Cauca *r.* Colombia **90** 8.57N 74.30W
Caucasus Mts. *see* Kavkazskiy Khrebet *mts.* U.S.S.R. **25**
Caudry France **17** 50.07N 3.22E
Caungula Angola **54** 8.26S 18.35E
Cauquenes Chile **93** 35.58S 72.21W
Caura *r.* Venezuela **90** 7.38N 64.53W
Cavaillon France **17** 43.50N 5.02E
Cavalese Italy **15** 46.17N 11.26E
Cavalier U.S.A. **82** 48.48N 97.37W
Cavally *r.* Ivory Coast **52** 4.25N 7.39W
Cavan Rep. of Ire. **13** 54.00N 7.22W
Cavan *d.* Rep. of Ire. **13** 53.58N 7.10W
Cavarzere Italy **15** 45.08N 12.05E
Caviana, Ilha *i.* Brazil **91** 0.02N 50.00W
Cawndilla L. Australia **66** 32.30S142.18E
Caxambu Brazil **94** 21.59S 44.54W
Caxias Brazil **91** 4.53S 43.20W
Caxias do Sul Brazil **94** 29.14S 51.10W
Caxito Angola **54** 8.32S 13.38E
Cayambe Ecuador **90** 0.03N 78.08W
Cayenne Guiana **91** 4.55N 52.18W
Cayman Brac *i.* Cayman Is. **87** 19.44N 79.48W
Cayman Is. C. America **87** 19.00N 81.00W
Cayman Trough Carib. Sea **95** 18.00N 8.00W
Cayuga Canada **76** 42.56N 79.51W
Cazères France **17** 43.13N 1.05E
Cazombo Angola **54** 11.54S 22.56E
Ceara *d.* Brazil **91** 4.50S 39.00W
Ceba Canada **75** 53.07N102.14W
Ceballos Mexico **83** 26.32N104.09W
Cebollera, Sierra de *mts.* Spain **16** 41.58N 2.30W
Cebu Phil. **37** 10.17N123.56E
Cebu *i.* Phil. **37** 10.15N123.45E
Cecina Italy **18** 43.18N 10.30E
Cedar City U.S.A. **78** 37.40N113.04W
Cedar Falls *town* U.S.A. **82** 42.32N 92.27W
Cedar Key U.S.A. **85** 29.08N 83.03W
Cedar L. Canada **75** 53.20N100.00W
Cedar Rapids *town* U.S.A. **82** 41.59N 91.40W
Cedarville U.S.A. **85** 39.20N 75.12W
Cedros, Isla *i.* Mexico **81** 28.10N115.15W
Ceduna Australia **66** 32.07S133.42E
Ceel Afweyne Somali Rep. **45** 9.55N 47.14E
Ceel Buur Somali Rep. **45** 4.40N 46.40E
Ceel Dhaab Somali Rep. **45** 8.58N 46.38E
Ceel Dheere Somali Rep. **45** 3.55N 47.10E
Ceel Xamurre Somali Rep. **45** 7.11N 48.55E
Ceepeecee Canada **74** 49.52N126.42W
Ceerigaabo Somali Rep. **45** 10.40N 47.20E
Cefalù Italy **18** 38.01N 14.03E
Cegléd Hungary **21** 47.10N 19.48E
Cela Angola **54** 11.26S 15.05E
Celaya Mexico **86** 20.32N100.48W
Celebes *i. see* Sulawesi *i.* Indonesia **37**
Celebes Sea Indonesia **37** 3.00N122.00E
Celina U.S.A. **84** 40.34N 84.35W
Celje Yugo. **18** 46.15N 15.16E
Celle Germany **20** 52.37N 10.05E
Cemaes Head U.K. **11** 52.08N 4.42W
Cenderawasih, Teluk *b.* Indonesia **37** 2.20S135.50E
Ceno *r.* Italy **15** 44.41N 10.05E
Center Cross U.S.A. **85** 37.48N 76.48W
Centerville Iowa U.S.A. **82** 40.43N 92.52W
Centerville S.Dak. U.S.A. **82** 43.07N 96.58W
Centerville Tenn. U.S.A. **85** 35.45N 87.29W
Cento Italy **15** 44.43N 11.17E
Central *d.* Botswana **56** 21.45S 26.15E
Central *d.* Ghana **52** 5.30N 1.10W
Central *d.* Kenya **55** 0.30S 37.00E
Central *d.* U.K. **12** 56.10N 4.20W
Central *d.* Zambia **56** 14.30S 29.30E
Central, Cordillera *mts.* Bolivia **92** 18.30S 65.00W
Central, Cordillera *mts.* Colombia **90** 5.00N 75.20W
Central Brāhui Range *mts.* Pakistan **40** 29.15N 67.15E
Central City Ky. U.S.A. **85** 37.17N 87.08W
Central City Nebr. U.S.A. **82** 41.07N 98.00W
Central I. Kenya **55** 3.30N 36.02E
Centralia Ill. U.S.A. **82** 38.32N 89.08W
Centralia Wash. U.S.A. **80** 46.43N122.58W
Central Makrān Range *mts.* Pakistan **40** 26.30N 65.00E
Central Siberian Plateau *see* Sredne Sibirskoye Ploskogor'ye *f.* U.S.S.R. **29**
Centre *d.* Burkina **52** 11.50N 1.10W
Centre *d.* France **17** 47.40N 1.45E
Centre Est *d.* Burkina **52** 11.20N 0.10W
Centre Nord *d.* Burkina **52** 13.30N 1.00W
Centre Ouest *d.* Burkina **52** 12.00N 2.20W
Centreville Ala. U.S.A. **85** 32.57N 87.08W
Centreville Md. U.S.A. **85** 39.03N 76.04W
Century Fla. U.S.A. **85** 30.59N 87.18W
Cepu Indonesia **37** 7.07S111.35E
Ceram *i. see* Seram *i.* Indonesia **37**
Ceram Sea *see* Seram, Laut *sea* Pacific Oc. **37**
Ceres U.S.A. **80** 37.35N120.57W
Ceresole Reale Italy **15** 45.26N 7.15E
Cereté Colombia **90** 8.54N 75.51W
Cerignola Italy **18** 41.17N 15.53E
Cérilly France **17** 46.37N 2.50E
Cerisiers France **15** 48.08N 3.29E
Cerknica Yugo. **18** 45.48N 14.22E
Cernavodă Romania **21** 44.20N 28.02E
Cerralvo, Isla *i.* Mexico **81** 24.17N109.52W
Cerritos Mexico **86** 22.26N100.17W
Cerro de Pasco Peru **90** 10.43S 76.15W
Cervera Lérida Spain **16** 41.40N 1.16E
Cervia Italy **15** 44.15N 12.22E
Cervignano del Friuli Italy **15** 45.49N 13.20E
Cervo Spain **16** 43.40N 7.24W
Cesena Italy **15** 44.08N 12.15E
Cesenatico Italy **15** 44.12N 12.24E
Cēsis U.S.S.R. **24** 57.18N 25.15E
České Budějovice Czech. **20** 49.00N 14.30E
České Zemé *d.* Czech. **20** 49.50N 15.50E
Český Krumlov Czech. **20** 48.49N 14.19E
Cessnock Australia **67** 32.51S151.21E
Cetinje Yugo. **19** 42.24N 18.55E
Ceuta Spain **16** 35.53N 5.19W
Ceva Italy **15** 44.23N 8.01E
Cévennes *mts.* France **17** 44.25N 4.05E
Ceyhan Turkey **42** 37.02N 35.48E
Ceyhan *r.* Turkey **42** 36.54N 34.58E
Chablis France **15** 47.47N 3.48E
Chacabuco Argentina **93** 34.38S 60.29W
Chachani *mtn.* Peru **90** 16.12S 71.32W
Chachapoyas Peru **90** 6.13S 77.54W
Chāchro Pakistan **40** 25.07N 70.15E
Chaco *d.* Argentina **92** 26.30S 60.00W
Chad, L. Africa **53** 13.30N 14.00E
Chadron U.S.A. **82** 42.50N103.02W
Chafe Nigeria **53** 11.56N 6.55E
Chāgai Pakistan **40** 29.18N 64.42E
Chāgai Hills Pakistan **40** 29.10N 63.35E
Chagda U.S.S.R. **29** 58.44N130.38E
'Chaghcharān Afghan. **40** 34.32N 65.15E
Cha'gyüngoinba China **41** 31.10N 90.42E
Chahār Borjak Afghan. **40** 30.17N 62.03E
Chāh Sandan *well* Pakistan **40** 28.59N 63.27E
Chaibāsā India **41** 22.34N 85.49E
Chainat Thailand **34** 15.10N100.10E
Chaiyaphum Thailand **34** 15.46N101.57E
Chajarí Argentina **93** 30.45S 57.59W
Chākāi India **41** 24.34N 86.24E
Chākdaha India **41** 23.05N 88.31E
Chake Chake Tanzania **55** 5.13S 39.46E
Chakhānsūr Afghan. **40** 31.10N 62.04E
Chakradharpur India **41** 22.42N 85.38E
Chakwāl Pakistan **40** 32.56N 72.52E
Chala Peru **90** 15.48S 74.20W
Chaleur B. Canada **77** 48.00N 65.45W
Chalhuanca Peru **90** 14.20S 73.10W
Chālisgaon India **40** 20.28N 75.01E
Challans France **17** 46.51N 1.52W
Challenger Depth Pacific Oc. **37** 11.19N142.15E
Challis U.S.A. **80** 44.30N114.14W
Chalonnes-sur-Loire France **15** 47.21N 0.46W
Châlons-sur-Marne France **15** 48.58N 4.22E
Chalon-sur-Saône France **17** 46.47N 4.51E
Cham Germany **20** 49.13N 12.41E
Chama U.S.A. **80** 36.54N106.35W
Chama Zambia **55** 11.09S 33.10E
Chaman Pakistan **40** 30.55N 66.27E
Chamba India **40** 32.34N 76.08E
Chambal *r.* India **41** 26.29N 79.15E
Chamberlain U.S.A. **82** 43.49N 99.20W
Chambersburg U.S.A. **84** 39.56N 77.39W
Chambéry France **17** 45.34N 5.55E
Chambeshi Zambia **55** 10.57S 31.04E
Chambeshi *r.* Zambia **55** 11.15S 30.37E
Chambly Canada **77** 45.27N 73.17W
Chambly France **15** 49.10N 2.15E
Chamburi Kalāt Pakistan **40** 26.09N 64.43E
Cha Messengue Angola **54** 11.04S 18.56E
Chamical Argentina **92** 30.22S 66.19W
Ch'amo Hāyk' *l.* Ethiopia **49** 5.49N 37.35E
Chamoli India **41** 30.24N 79.21E
Chamonix France **17** 45.55N 6.52E
Chāmpa India **41** 22.03N 82.39E
Champagne Canada **74** 60.47N136.29W
Champagne-Ardenne *d.* France **14** 49.42N 4.30E
Champaign U.S.A. **82** 40.07N 88.14W
Champdoré, Lac *l.* Canada **77** 55.55N 65.50W
Champéry Switz. **15** 46.10N 6.52E
Champlain Canada **77** 46.27N 72.21W
Champlain, L. U.S.A. **84** 44.45N 73.15W
Champotón Mexico **86** 19.21N 90.43W
Chāmpua India **41** 22.05N 85.40E
Chañaral Chile **92** 26.21S 70.37W
Chānasma India **40** 23.43N 72.07E
Chandausi India **41** 28.27N 78.46E
Chāndbāli India **41** 20.46N 86.49E
Chandeleur Is. U.S.A. **83** 29.48N 88.51W
Chandīgarh India **40** 30.44N 76.47E
Chandīgarh *d.* India **40** 30.45N 76.45E
Chāndil India **41** 22.58N 86.03E
Chandler Canada **77** 48.21N 64.41W
Chandler U.S.A. **83** 35.42N 96.53W
Chāndor Hills India **40** 20.30N 74.00E
Chāndpur Bangla. **41** 23.13N 90.39E
Chāndpur Bangla. **39** 22.08N 91.55E
Chāndpur India **41** 29.09N 78.16E
Chandrapur India **41** 19.57N 79.18E
Chāndvad India **40** 20.20N 74.15E
Chānf Iran **43** 26.40N 60.31E
Chang, Ko *i.* Thailand **34** 12.04N102.23E
Changchun China **32** 43.51N125.15E
Changde China **33** 29.00N111.35E
Changfeng China **33** 32.27N117.09E
Changhua Jiang *r.* China **33** 19.20N108.38E
Chang Jiang *r.* China **33** 31.40N121.15E
Changjin N. Korea **31** 40.21N127.20E
Changle China **32** 36.42N118.49E
Changli China **32** 39.43N119.08E
Changling China **32** 44.16N123.58E
Changning China **33** 26.24N112.24E
Changping China **32** 40.12N116.12E
Changsha China **33** 28.09N112.59E
Changshan China **33** 28.57N118.31E
Changshan Qundao *is.* China **32** 39.20N123.00E
Changshou China **33** 29.50N107.02E
Changshu China **33** 31.48N120.52E
Changshun China **33** 25.59N106.25E
Changting China **33** 25.42N116.20E
Changyi China **32** 36.51N119.23E
Changzhi China **32** 36.10N113.00E
Changzhou China **33** 31.46N119.58E
Channel Is. U.K. **11** 49.28N 2.13W
Channel Is. U.S.A. **81** 34.00N120.00W
Channel-Port-aux-Basques *town* Canada **77** 47.35N 59.11W
Channing Mich. U.S.A. **84** 46.08N 88.06W
Channing Tex. U.S.A. **83** 35.41N102.20W
Chantada Spain **16** 42.36N 7.46W
Chanthaburi Thailand **34** 12.35N102.05E
Chantilly France **15** 49.12N 2.28E
Chanute U.S.A. **83** 37.41N 95.27W
Chao'an China **33** 23.40N116.32E
Chao Hu *l.* China **33** 31.32N117.30E
Chaonde Mozambique **57** 13.43S 40.31E
Chao Phraya *r.* Thailand **34** 13.34N100.35E
Chao Xian China **33** 31.36N117.52E
Chaoyang Guangdong China **33** 23.25N116.31E
Chaoyang Liaoning China **32** 41.35N120.20E
Chapada das Mangabeiras *mts.* Brazil **91** 10.00S 46.30W
Chapada Diamantina Brazil **94** 13.30S 42.30W
Chapala, Lago de *l.* Mexico **86** 20.00N103.00W
Chapayevo U.S.S.R **25** 50.12N 51.09E
Chapayevsk U.S.S.R. **24** 52.58N 49.44E
Chapelle-d'Angillon France **15** 47.22N 2.26E
Chapicuy Uruguay **93** 31.39S 57.54W
Chapleau Canada **76** 47.50N 83.24W
Chāpra India **41** 25.46N 84.45E
Chaqui Bolivia **92** 19.36S 65.32W
Characot I. Antarctica **96** 70.00S 75.00W
Charay Mexico **81** 26.01N108.50W
Charcas Mexico **86** 23.08N101.07W
Chard U.K. **11** 50.52N 2.59W
Chardūār India **41** 26.52N 92.46E
Chardzhou U.S.S.R. **43** 39.09N 63.34E
Charente *r.* France **17** 45.57N 1.00W
Chari *r.* Chad **53** 13.00N 14.30E
Chari-Baguirmi *d.* Chad **53** 12.20N 15.30E
Chārīkār Afghan. **40** 35.01N 69.11E
Charing U.K. **11** 51.12N 0.49E
Chariton U.S.A. **82** 41.01N 93.19W
Charleroi Belgium **14** 50.25N 4.27E
Charlesbourg Canada **77** 46.52N 71.16W
Charles City U.S.A. **82** 43.04N 92.40W
Charles Pt. Australia **62** 12.23S130.37E
Charleston Miss. U.S.A. **83** 34.00N 90.04W
Charleston S.C. U.S.A. **85** 32.48N 79.58W
Charleston W.Va. U.S.A. **84** 38.23N 81.40W
Charlestown Rep. of Ire. **13** 53.57N 8.48W
Charlestown Ind. U.S.A. **84** 38.28N 85.40W
Charlesville Zaïre **54** 5.27S 20.58E
Charleville Australia **64** 26.25S146.13E
Charleville-Mézières France **15** 49.46N 4.43E
Charlieu France **17** 46.10N 4.10E
Charlotte N.C. U.S.A. **85** 35.03N 80.50W
Charlotte Va. U.S.A. **85** 37.03N 78.44W
Charlottesville U.S.A. **85** 38.02N 78.29W
Charlottetown Canada **77** 46.14N 63.08W
Charlton Australia **66** 36.18S143.27E
Charlton I. Canada **76** 52.00N 79.30W
Charly-sur-Marne France **15** 48.58N 3.17E
Charolles France **17** 46.26N 4.17E
Chārsadda Pakistan **40** 34.09N 71.44E
Charters Towers Australia **64** 20.05S146.16E
Chartres France **15** 48.27N 1.30E
Chascomús Argentina **93** 35.35S 58.00W
Chase City U.S.A. **85** 36.59N 78.30W
Châteaubriant France **15** 47.43N 1.22W
Château-du-Loir France **15** 47.42N 0.25E
Châteaudun France **15** 48.04N 1.20E
Château Gontier France **15** 47.50N 0.42W
Châteauguay, Lac *l.* Canada **77** 56.27N 70.05W
Château Landon France **15** 48.09N 2.42E
Château-la-Vallière France **15** 47.33N 0.19E
Châteauneuf-en-Thymerais France **15** 48.35N 1.15E
Châteauneuf-sur-Loire France **15** 47.52N 2.14E
Chateauneuf-sur-Sarthe France **15** 47.41N 0.30W
Château-Porcien France **15** 49.32N 4.15E
Château Renault France **15** 47.35N 0.55E
Châteauroux France **17** 46.49N 1.41E
Château-Thierry France **15** 49.03N 3.24E
Châtelet Belgium **14** 50.24N 4.32E
Châtellerault France **17** 46.49N 0.33E
Chatham N.B. Canada **77** 47.02N 65.28W
Chatham Ont. Canada **76** 42.24N 82.11W
Chatham U.K. **11** 51.23N 0.32E
Chatham Alas. U.S.A. **74** 57.30N135.00W
Chatham Is. Pacific Oc. **68** 44.00S176.35W
Chatham Rise Pacific Oc. **68** 43.30S178.00W
Chatham Str. U.S.A. **74** 57.30N134.45W
Châtillon Italy **15** 45.45N 7.37E
Châtillon-Coligny France **15** 47.50N 2.51E
Châtillon-sur-Seine France **15** 47.52N 4.35E
Chatra India **41** 24.13N 84.52E
Chatrapur India **41** 19.21N 84.59E
Chātsu India **40** 26.36N 75.57E
Chattahoochee U.S.A. **85** 30.42N 84.51W
Chattahoochee *r.* U.S.A. **85** 30.52N 84.57W
Chattanooga U.S.A. **85** 35.02N 85.18W
Chatteris U.K. **11** 52.27N 0.03E
Chauk Burma **34** 20.52N 94.50E
Chaulnes France **15** 49.49N 2.48E
Chaumont France **17** 48.07N 5.08E
Chaumont-en-Vexin France **15** 49.16N 1.53E
Chaungwabyin Burma **34** 13.41N 98.22E
Chauny France **15** 49.37N 3.13E
Chaupāran India **41** 24.23N 85.15E
Chau Phu Vietnam **34** 10.42N105.03E
Chausy U.S.S.R. **21** 53.49N 30.57E
Chavanges France **15** 48.31N 4.34E
Chaves Brazil **91** 0.10S 49.55W
Chaves Portugal **16** 41.44N 7.28W
Chavuma Zambia **54** 13.04S 22.43E
Chawang Thailand **34** 8.25N 99.32E
Cheb Czech. **20** 50.04N 12.20E
Cheboksary U.S.S.R. **24** 56.08N 47.12E
Cheboygan U.S.A. **84** 45.40N 84.28W
Chebsara U.S.S.R. **24** 59.14N 38.59E
Chebula Angola **54** 12.27S 23.49E
Chech, Erg *des.* Mali/Algeria **50** 24.30N 2.30W
Chechaouene Morocco **50** 35.10N 5.16W
Chechersk U.S.S.R. **21** 52.54N 30.54E
Checiny Poland **21** 50.48N 20.28E
Cheduba I. Burma **34** 18.50N 93.35E
Chegdomyn U.S.S.R. **29** 51.09N133.01E
Chegga *well* Mauritania **50** 25.30N 5.46W
Chegutu Zimbabwe **56** 18.09S 30.07E
Chehalis U.S.A. **80** 46.40N122.58W
Cheil, Ras el *c.* Somali Rep. **45** 7.45N 49.48E
Cheiron, Cime du *mtn.* France **15** 43.49N 6.58E
Cheju S. Korea **31** 33.31N126.29E
Cheju do *i.* S. Korea **31** 33.20N126.30E
Cheleken U.S.S.R. **43** 39.26N 53.11E
Chelforó Argentina **93** 39.04S 66.33W
Chelif, Oued *r.* Algeria **51** 36.15N 2.05E
Chelkar U.S.S.R. **28** 47.48N 59.39E
Chelles France **15** 48.53N 2.36E
Chełm Poland **21** 51.10N 23.28E
Chelmer *r.* U.K. **9** 51.43N 0.40E
Chelmsford U.K. **11** 51.44N 0.28E
Chełmża Poland **21** 53.12N 18.37E
Chelsea Canada **77** 45.29N 75.48W
Cheltenham U.K. **11** 51.53N 2.07W
Chelva Spain **16** 39.45N 1.00W
Chelyabinsk U.S.S.R. **28** 55.10N 61.25E
Chelyuskin, Mys *c.* U.S.S.R. **29** 77.20N106.00E
Chemainus Canada **74** 48.55N123.48W
Chemba Mozambique **55** 17.11S 34.53E
Chemnitz Germany **20** 50.50N 12.55E
Chemult U.S.A. **80** 43.13N121.47W
Chēn, Gora *mtn.* U.S.S.R. **29** 65.30N141.20E
Chenāb *r.* Pakistan **40** 29.23N 71.02E
Chenachane Algeria **50** 26.00N 4.15W
Chénéville Canada **77** 45.53N 75.03W
Cheney U.S.A. **80** 47.29N117.34W
Chengchow *see* Zhengzhou China **32**
Chengde China **32** 41.00N117.52E
Chengdu China **33** 30.41N104.05E
Chenggu China **32** 33.10N107.22E
Chenghai China **33** 23.31N116.43E
Chengkou China **33** 31.58N108.48E
Chengmai China **33** 19.44N109.59E
Cheng Xian China **32** 33.42N105.36E
Chenoa U.S.A. **82** 40.44N 88.43W
Chen Xian China **33** 25.45N113.00E
Chepen Peru **90** 7.15S 79.20W
Chepstow U.K. **11** 51.38N 2.40W
Cher *r.* France **15** 47.12N 2.04E
Cherbourg France **15** 49.38N 1.37W
Cherdyn U.S.S.R. **24** 60.25N 55.22E

Cherelato Ethiopia 49 6.00N 38.10E
Cheremkhovo U.S.S.R. 29 53.08N 103.01E
Cherepovets U.S.S.R. 24 59.05N 37.55E
Chergui, Chott ech *f.* Algeria 51 34.21N 0.30E
Cherikov U.S.S.R. 21 53.35N 31.23E
Cherkassy U.S.S.R. 25 49.27N 32.04E
Cherkessk U.S.S.R. 25 44.14N 42.05E
Cherkovitsa Bulgaria 19 43.41N 24.49E
Cherlak U.S.S.R. 28 54.10N 74.52E
Chernigov U.S.S.R. 21 51.30N 31.18E
Chernikovsk U.S.S.R. 24 54.51N 56.06E
Chernobyl U.S.S.R. 21 51.17N 30.15E
Chernovtsy U.S.S.R. 21 48.19N 25.52E
Chernyakhov U.S.S.R. 21 50.30N 28.38E
Chernyakhovsk U.S.S.R. 23 54.38N 21.49E
Cherokee Iowa U.S.A. 82 42.45N 95.33W
Cherokee Okla. U.S.A. 83 36.45N 98.21W
Cherquenco Chile 93 38.41S 72.00W
Cherrapunji India 41 25.18N 91.42E
Cherry Creek *r.* U.S.A. 82 44.36N 101.30W
Cherry Creek *town* Nev. U.S.A. 80 39.54N 113.53W
Cherry Creek *town* S.Dak. U.S.A. 82 44.36N 101.26W
Cherskogo, Khrebet *mts.* U.S.S.R. 29 65.50N 143.00E
Chertkovo U.S.S.R. 25 49.22N 40.12E
Chertsey U.K. 11 51.23N 0.27W
Chervonograd U.S.S.R. 21 50.25N 24.10E
Cherwell *r.* U.K. 11 51.44N 1.15W
Chesapeake Va. U.S.A. 85 36.43N 76.15W
Chesapeake B. U.S.A. 84 38.40N 76.25W
Chesapeake Beach *town* U.S.A. 85 38.41N 76.32W
Chesham U.K. 11 51.43N 0.38W
Cheshire *d.* U.K. 10 53.14N 2.30W
Chëshskaya Guba *g.* U.S.S.R. 24 67.20N 46.30E
Chesht-e Sharif Afghan. 40 34.21N 63.44E
Chesil Beach *f.* U.K. 11 50.37N 2.33W
Chester U.K. 10 53.12N 2.53W
Chester Mont. U.S.A. 80 48.31N 110.58W
Chester Penn. U.S.A. 85 39.51N 75.21W
Chesterfield U.K. 10 53.14N 1.26W
Chesterfield, Îles *is.* N. Cal. 68 20.00S 159.00E
Chesterfield Inlet *town* Canada 73 63.00N 91.00W
Chestertown Md. U.S.A. 85 39.13N 76.04W
Chesuncook L. U.S.A. 84 46.00N 69.20W
Chéticamp Canada 77 46.38N 61.01W
Chetumal Mexico 87 18.30N 88.17W
Chetumal B. Mexico 87 18.30N 88.00W
Chetwynd Canada 74 55.45N 121.45W
Cheviot New Zealand 60 42.49S 173.16E
Cheviot U.S.A. 84 39.10N 84.32W
Ch'ew Bahir *l.* Ethiopia 49 4.40N 36.50E
Cheyenne *r.* U.S.A. 82 44.40N 101.15W
Cheyenne Okla. U.S.A. 83 35.37N 99.40W
Cheyenne Wyo. U.S.A. 80 41.08N 104.49W
Cheyne B. Australia 63 34.35S 118.50E
Chhabra India 40 24.40N 76.50E
Chhātak Bangla. 41 25.02N 91.40E
Chhatarpur Bihār India 41 24.23N 84.11E
Chhatarpur Madhya P. India 41 24.54N 79.36E
Chhattisgarh *f.* India 41 21.00N 82.00E
Chhindwāra India 41 22.04N 78.56E
Chhota-Chhindwāra India 41 23.03N 79.29E
Chhota Udepur India 40 22.19N 74.01E
Chiali Taiwan 33 23.10N 120.11E
Chiang Mai Thailand 34 18.48N 98.59E
Chiapas *d.* Mexico 86 16.30N 93.00W
Chiari Italy 15 45.32N 9.56E
Chiavari Italy 15 44.19N 9.19E
Chiavenna Italy 15 46.19N 9.24E
Chiba Japan 35 35.36N 140.07E
Chiba *d.* Japan 35 35.10N 140.00E
Chibemba Angola 56 15.43S 14.07E
Chibia Angola 54 15.10S 13.32E
Chibougamau Canada 76 49.56N 74.24W
Chibougamau Lac *l.* Canada 76 49.50N 74.20W
Chibougamau Prov. Park Canada 77 49.25N 73.50W
Chibuk Nigeria 53 10.52N 12.50E
Chibuto Mozambique 57 24.41S 33.32E
Chicago U.S.A. 82 41.50N 87.45W
Chichagof I. U.S.A. 72 57.55N 135.45W
Chicheng China 32 40.52N 115.50E
Chichester U.K. 11 50.50N 0.47W
Chichibu Japan 35 35.59N 139.05E
Chickasha U.S.A. 83 35.02N 97.58W
Chiclana Spain 16 36.26N 6.09W
Chiclayo Peru 90 6.47S 79.47W
Chico *r.* Chubut Argentina 93 43.45S 66.10W
Chico *r.* Santa Cruz Argentina 93 50.03W 68.35W
Chico U.S.A. 80 39.44N 121.50W
Chicomo Mozambique 57 24.33S 34.11E
Chicoutimi-Jonquière Canada 77 48.26N 71.06W
Chicualacuala Mozambique 57 22.06S 31.42E
Chidambaram India 39 11.24N 79.42E
Chidembo Angola 54 14.34S 19.17E
Chidenguele Mozambique 57 24.54S 34.13E
Chidley, C. Canada 73 60.30N 65.00W
Chiemsee *l.* Germany 20 47.55N 12.30E
Chiengi Zambia 55 8.42S 29.07E
Chieri Italy 15 45.01N 7.49E
Chieti Italy 18 42.22N 14.12E
Chifeng China 32 42.13N 118.56E
Chigasaki Japan 35 35.19N 139.24E
Chignecto B. Canada 77 45.35N 64.45W
Chiguana Bolivia 92 21.05S 67.58W
Chigubo Mozambique 57 22.38S 33.18E
Chigu Co *l.* China 41 28.40N 91.50E
Chihuahua Mexico 81 28.38N 106.05W
Chihuahua *d.* Mexico 81 28.40N 106.00W
Chiili U.S.S.R. 28 44.10N 66.37E
Chikhli India 40 20.21N 76.15E
Chikumbi Zambia 55 15.14S 28.21E
Chikwawa Malaŵi 55 16.00S 34.54E
Chil *r.* Iran 43 25.12N 61.30E
Chilanga Zambia 56 15.33S 28.17E
Chilapa Mexico 86 17.38N 99.11W
Chilcoot U.S.A. 80 39.49N 120.08W
Childers Australia 64 25.14S 152.17E
Childress U.S.A. 83 34.25N 100.13W
Chile S. America 92 32.30S 71.00W
Chile Basin Pacific Oc. 69 34.20S 80.00W
Chile Chico Chile 93 46.33S 71.44W
Chilka L. India 41 19.46N 85.20E
Chilko L. Canada 72 51.20N 124.05W
Chillagoe Australia 64 17.09S 144.32E
Chillán Chile 93 36.36S 72.07W
Chillicothe Mo. U.S.A. 82 39.48N 93.33W
Chillicothe Ohio U.S.A. 84 39.20N 82.59W
Chilliwack Canada 74 49.10N 122.00W
Chiloé, Isla de *i.* Chile 93 43.00S 73.00W
Chilonga Zambia 55 12.02S 31.17E
Chilpancingo Mexico 86 17.33N 99.30W
Chiltern Australia 67 36.11S 146.36E
Chiltern Hills U.K. 11 51.40N 0.53W
Chilton U.S.A. 82 44.04N 88.10W
Chilumba Malaŵi 55 10.25S 34.18E
Chilwa, L. Malaŵi 55 15.15S 35.45E
Chimakela Angola 54 15.12S 16.58E
Chimanimani Zimbabwe 57 19.48S 32.52E
Chimay Belgium 14 50.03N 4.20E
Chimbas Argentina 92 31.28S 68.30W
Chimborazo *mtn.* Ecuador 90 1.29S 78.52W
Chimbote Peru 90 9.04S 78.34W
Chimishliya U.S.S.R. 21 46.30N 28.50E
Chimkent U.S.S.R. 30 42.16N 69.05E
Chimoio Mozambique 57 19.04S 33.29E
Chin *d.* Burma 34 22.00N 93.30E
China Asia 30 33.00N 103.00E
China Lake *town* U.S.A. 81 35.46N 117.39W
Chinandega Nicaragua 87 12.35N 87.10W
Chinati Peak U.S.A. 81 29.57N 104.29W
Chincha Alta Peru 90 13.25S 76.07W
Chinchaga *r.* Canada 74 58.50N 118.20W
Chinchilla Australia 65 26.44S 150.39E
Chinchón Spain 16 40.09N 3.26W
Chinchoua Gabon 54 0.00 9.48E
Chincoteague U.S.A. 85 37.55N 75.23W
Chinde Mozambique 57 18.37S 36.24E
Chindio Mozambique 55 17.46S 35.23E
Chindwin *r.* Burma 34 21.30N 95.12E
Chinga Mozambique 55 15.14S 38.40E
Chingleput India 39 12.42N 79.59E
Chingola Zambia 55 12.29S 27.53E
Chingombe Zambia 55 14.25S 29.56E
Chingshui Taiwan 33 24.15N 120.35E
Chin Hills Burma 34 22.30N 93.30E
Chinhoyi Zimbabwe 56 17.22S 30.10E
Chini India 41 31.32N 78.15E
Chiniot Pakistan 40 31.43N 72.59E
Chinjan Pakistan 40 30.34N 67.58E
Chinkapook Australia 66 35.11S 142.57E
Chinko *r.* C.A.R. 49 4.50N 23.53E
Chinle U.S.A. 81 36.09N 109.33W
Chinon France 17 47.10N 0.15E
Chinook U.S.A. 80 48.35N 109.14W
Chino Valley *town* U.S.A. 81 34.45N 112.27W
Chinsali Zambia 55 10.33S 32.05E
Chintheche Malaŵi 55 11.50S 34.13E
Chiny Belgium 14 49.45N 5.20E
Chiôco Mozambique 55 16.27S 32.49E
Chioggia Italy 15 45.13N 12.17E
Chipata Zambia 55 13.37S 32.40E
Chipera Mozambique 55 15.20S 32.35E
Chipie *r.* Canada 76 51.25N 83.20W
Chipinge Zimbabwe 57 20.12S 32.38E
Chippenham U.K. 11 51.27N 2.07W
Chippewa Falls *town* U.S.A. 82 44.56N 91.24W
Chipping Norton U.K. 11 51.56N 1.32W
Chiquian Peru 90 10.10S 77.00W
Chiquinquirá Colombia 90 5.37N 73.50W
Chir *r.* U.S.S.R. 25 48.34N 42.53E
Chirāwa India 40 28.15N 75.38E
Chirchik U.S.S.R. 30 41.28N 69.31E
Chiredzi Zimbabwe 57 21.03S 31.39E
Chiredzi *r.* Zimbabwe 57 21.10S 31.50E
Chiricahua Peak *mtn.* U.S.A. 81 31.52N 109.20W
Chiriquí *mtn.* Panama 87 8.49N 82.38W
Chiriquí, Laguna de *b.* Panama 87 9.00N 82.00W
Chiromo Malaŵi 55 16.28S 35.10E
Chirripó *mtn.* Costa Rica 87 9.31N 83.30W
Chirundu Zimbabwe 56 16.04S 28.51E
Chisamba Zambia 56 14.58S 28.23E
Chisasibi Canada 76 53.50N 79.00W
Chishan Taiwan 33 22.53N 120.29E
Chisholm U.S.A. 82 47.29N 92.53W
Chisholm Mills Canada 74 54.55N 114.09W
Chishtiān Mandi Pakistan 40 29.48N 72.52E
Chishui China 33 28.29N 105.38E
Chisone *r.* Italy 15 44.49N 7.25E
Chistopol U.S.S.R. 24 55.25N 50.38E
Chita U.S.S.R. 31 52.03N 113.35E
Chitek L. Canada 75 52.25N 99.20W
Chitembo Angola 54 13.33S 16.47E
Chitipa Malaŵi 55 9.41S 33.19E
Chitorgarh India 40 24.53N 74.38E
Chitrakūt Dham India 41 25.11N 80.52E
Chitrāl Pakistan 38 35.52N 71.58E
Chittagong Bangla. 41 22.20N 91.50E
Chittoor India 39 13.13N 79.06E
Chiumbe *r.* Zaïre 54 6.37S 21.04E
Chiume Angola 54 15.08S 21.11E
Chiuta, L. Malaŵi/Mozambique 55 14.45S 35.50E
Chivasso Italy 15 45.11N 7.53E
Chivhu Zimbabwe 56 19.01S 30.53E
Chivilcoy Argentina 93 34.52S 60.02W
Chiwanda Tanzania 55 11.21S 34.55E
Chobe *d.* Botswana 56 18.30S 25.15E
Chobe *r.* Namibia/Botswana 56 17.48S 25.12E
Chobe Swamp *f.* Namibia 56 18.20S 23.40E
Chocolate Mts. U.S.A. 81 33.20N 115.15W
Chocope Peru 90 7.47S 79.12W
Choele-Choel Argentina 93 39.15S 65.30W
Chōfu Japan 35 35.39N 139.33E
Chohtan India 40 25.29N 71.04E
Choix Mexico 81 26.43N 108.17W
Chojnice Poland 21 53.42N 17.32E
Ch'ok'ē Mts. Ethiopia 49 11.00N 37.30E
Cholet France 17 47.04N 0.53W
Cholon Vietnam 34 10.40N 106.30E
Choluteca Honduras 87 13.16N 87.11W
Choma Zambia 55 16.51S 27.04E
Chomu India 40 27.10N 75.44E
Chomutov Czech. 20 50.28N 13.25E
Chon Buri Thailand 34 13.20N 101.02E
Chone Ecuador 90 0.44S 80.04W
Chong'an China 33 27.46N 118.01E
Ch'ŏngjin N. Korea 31 41.55N 129.50E
Ch'ŏngju S. Korea 31 36.39N 127.31E
Chŏng Kal Cambodia 34 13.57N 103.35E
Chongming *i.* China 33 31.36N 121.33E
Chongqing China 33 29.31N 106.35E
Chongren China 33 27.44N 116.02E
Chŏnju S. Korea 31 35.50N 127.05E
Chonos, Archipelago de los *is.* Chile 93 45.00S 74.00W
Cho Oyu *mtn.* China/Nepal 41 28.06N 86.40E
Chopda India 40 21.15N 75.18E
Choptank *r.* U.S.A. 85 38.38N 76.13W
Chorley U.K. 10 53.39N 2.39W
Chorokh *r.* U.S.S.R. 25 41.36N 41.35E
Chortkov U.S.S.R. 21 49.01N 25.42E
Chorzów Poland 21 50.19N 18.56E
Chosica Peru 90 11.55S 76.38W
Chos Malal Argentina 93 37.20S 70.15W
Choszczno Poland 20 53.10N 15.26E
Choteau U.S.A. 80 47.49N 112.11W
Chotila India 40 22.25N 71.11E
Choum Mauritania 50 21.10N 13.00W
Chowchilla U.S.A. 80 37.07N 120.16W
Christchurch New Zealand 60 43.33S 172.40E
Christchurch U.K. 11 50.44N 1.47W
Christian Sd. U.S.A. 74 55.56N 134.40W
Christianshåb Greenland 73 68.50N 51.00W
Christie B. Canada 75 62.32N 111.10W
Christina *r.* Canada 75 56.40N 111.03W
Christmas Creek *town* Australia 62 18.55S 125.56E
Christmas I. Indian Oc. 36 10.30S 105.40E
Christmas I. *see* Kiritimati *i.* Kiribati 69
Chrudim Czech. 20 49.57N 15.48E
Chu *r.* U.S.S.R. 30 42.30N 76.10E
Chuādānga Bangla. 41 23.38N 88.51E
Chubbuck U.S.A. 81 34.22N 115.20W
Chūbu *d.* Japan 35 35.25N 137.40E
Chubut *d.* Argentina 93 44.00S 68.00W
Chubut *r.* Argentina 93 43.18S 65.06W
Chu Chua Canada 74 51.22N 120.10W
Chudleigh U.K. 11 50.35N 3.36W
Chudnov U.S.S.R. 21 50.05N 28.01E
Chudovo U.S.S.R. 24 59.10N 31.41E
Chudskoye, Ozero *l.* U.S.S.R. 24 58.30N 27.30E
Chugwater U.S.A. 80 41.46N 104.49W
Chuiquimula Guatemala 87 15.52N 89.50W
Chukai Malaysia 36 4.16N 103.24E
Chukotskiy Poluostrov *pen.* U.S.S.R. 29 66.00N 174.30W
Chukudukraal Botswana 56 22.30S 23.22E
Chula Vista U.S.A. 81 32.39N 117.05W
Chulman U.S.S.R. 29 56.54N 124.55E
Chulucanas Peru 90 5.08S 80.00W
Chulym U.S.S.R. 28 55.09N 80.59E
Chum U.S.S.R. 24 67.05N 63.15E
Chumbicha Argentina 92 28.50S 66.18W
Chumikan U.S.S.R. 29 54.40N 135.15E
Chumphon Thailand 34 10.34N 99.15E
Chuna *r.* U.S.S.R. 29 58.00N 94.00E
Ch'unch'ŏn S. Korea 31 37.53N 127.45E
Chungking *see* Chongqing China 33
Chunya Tanzania 55 8.31S 33.28E
Chuquicamata Chile 92 22.20S 68.56W
Chuquisaca *d.* Bolivia 92 21.00S 64.00W
Chur Switz. 17 46.52N 9.32E
Churchill Canada 75 58.46N 94.10W
Churchill *r.* Man. Canada 75 58.47N 94.12W
Churchill *r.* Nfld. Canada 77 53.20N 60.11W
Churchill, C. Canada 75 58.46N 93.12W
Churchill L. Canada 75 55.55N 108.20W
Churchill Peak *mtn.* Canada 74 58.10N 125.10W
Church Stretton U.K. 11 52.32N 2.49W
Churia Range *mts.* Nepal 41 28.40N 81.30E
Churu India 40 28.18N 74.57E
Chusovoy U.S.S.R. 24 58.18N 57.50E
Chu Xian China 32 32.25N 118.15E
Chuxiong China 39 25.03N 101.33E
Chu Yang Sin *mtn.* Vietnam 34 12.25N 108.25E
Ciamis Indonesia 37 7.20S 108.21E
Cianjur Indonesia 37 6.50S 107.09E
Cibatu Indonesia 37 7.10S 107.59E
Ciechanów Poland 21 52.53N 20.38E
Ciego de Avila Cuba 87 21.51N 78.47W
Ciénaga Colombia 90 11.11N 74.15W
Cienfuegos Cuba 87 22.10N 80.27W
Cieszyn Poland 21 49.45N 18.38E
Cieza Spain 16 38.14N 1.25W
Cifuentes Spain 16 40.47N 2.37W
Cigüela *r.* Spain 16 39.47N 3.00W
Cijara, Embalse de *resr.* Spain 16 39.20N 4.50W
Cijulang Indonesia 37 7.44S 108.30E
Cikampek Indonesia 37 6.21S 107.25E
Cilacap Indonesia 37 7.44S 109.00E
Ciledug Indonesia 37 6.56S 108.43E
Cili China 33 29.24N 111.04E
Cimanuk *r.* Indonesia 37 6.20S 108.12E
Cimarron U.S.A. 83 37.48N 100.21W
Cimarron *r.* U.S.A. 83 36.10N 96.17W
Cimone, Monte *mtn.* Italy 15 44.12N 10.42E
Cîmpina Romania 19 45.08N 25.44E
Cîmpulung Romania 19 45.16N 25.03E
Cinca *r.* Spain 16 41.22N 0.20E
Cincinnati U.S.A. 84 39.10N 84.30W
Ciney Belgium 14 50.17N 5.06E
Cinto, Monte *mtn.* France 17 42.23N 8.57E
Cipolletti Argentina 93 38.56S 67.59W
Circle U.S.A. 80 47.25N 105.35W
Circleville Ohio U.S.A. 84 39.36N 82.57W
Circleville Utah U.S.A. 80 38.10N 112.16W
Cirebon Indonesia 37 6.46S 108.33E
Cirencester U.K. 11 51.43N 1.59W
Ciriè Italy 15 45.14N 7.36E
Cirò Marina Italy 19 39.22N 17.08E
Cisco U.S.A. 83 32.23N 98.59W
Ciskei Africa 56 32.45S 27.00E
Citra U.S.A. 85 29.24N 82.06W
Cittadella Italy 15 45.39N 11.47E
Cittanova Italy 18 38.21N 16.05E
Ciudad Acuña Mexico 83 29.18N 100.55W
Ciudad Allende Mexico 83 28.20N 100.51W
Ciudad Bolívar Venezuela 90 8.06N 63.36W
Ciudad Camargo Mexico 81 27.40N 105.10W
Ciudad de México Mexico 86 19.25N 99.10W
Ciudadela Spain 16 40.00N 3.50E
Ciudad Guayana Venezuela 90 8.22N 62.40W
Ciudad Guerrero Mexico 86 28.33N 107.28W
Ciudad Guzmán Mexico 86 19.41N 103.29W
Ciudad Ixtepec Mexico 86 16.32N 95.10W
Ciudad Jiménez Mexico 81 27.08N 104.55W
Ciudad Juárez Mexico 81 31.44N 106.29W
Ciudad Lerdo Mexico 83 25.32N 103.32W
Ciudad Madero Mexico 86 22.19N 97.50W
Ciudad Mante Mexico 86 22.44N 98.57W
Ciudad Melchor Múzquiz Mexico 83 27.53N 101.31W
Ciudad Mier Mexico 83 26.26N 99.09W
Ciudad Obregón Mexico 81 27.29N 109.56W
Ciudad Ojeda Venezuela 90 10.05N 71.17W
Ciudad Piar Venezuela 90 7.27N 63.19W
Ciudad Real Spain 16 38.59N 3.55W
Ciudad Rodrigo Spain 16 40.36N 6.33W
Ciudad Victoria Mexico 86 23.43N 99.10W
Civitanova Italy 18 43.19N 13.40E
Civitavecchia Italy 18 42.06N 11.48E
Civray France 17 46.09N 0.18E
Çivril Turkey 42 38.18N 29.43E
Ci Xian China 32 36.22N 114.23E
Cizre Turkey 42 37.21N 42.11E
Clackline Australia 63 31.43S 116.31E
Clacton on Sea U.K. 11 51.47N 1.10E
Clairambault, Lac *l.* Canada 77 54.45N 69.22W
Claire, L. Canada 74 58.30N 112.00W
Clamecy France 15 47.27N 3.31E
Clanton U.S.A. 85 32.50N 86.38W
Clara Rep. of Ire. 13 53.21N 7.37W
Clare N.S.W. Australia 66 33.27S 143.55E
Clare S.A. Australia 66 33.50S 138.38E
Clare *d.* Rep. of Ire. 13 52.52N 8.55W
Clare *r.* Rep. of Ire. 13 53.17N 9.04W
Clare U.S.A. 84 43.49N 84.47W
Clare I. Rep. of Ire. 13 53.48N 10.00W
Claremore U.S.A. 83 36.19N 95.36W
Claremorris Rep. of Ire. 13 53.44N 9.00W
Clarence *r.* Australia 67 29.25S 153.02E
Clarence *r.* New Zealand 60 42.10S 173.55E
Clarence I. Antarctica 96 61.30S 53.50W
Clarence Str. Australia 62 12.00S 131.00E
Clarence Str. U.S.A. 74 55.40N 132.10W
Clarendon U.S.A. 83 34.56N 100.53W
Claresholm Canada 74 50.00N 113.45W
Clarie Coast *f.* Antarctica 96 67.00S 133.00E
Clarinda U.S.A. 82 40.44N 95.02W
Clark, L. U.S.A. 72 60.15N 154.15W
Clarke I. Australia 65 40.30S 148.10E
Clark Fork *r.* U.S.A. 80 48.09N 116.15W
Clarksburg U.S.A. 84 39.16N 80.22W
Clarksdale U.S.A. 83 34.12N 90.34W
Clarkston U.S.A. 80 46.26N 117.02W
Clarksville Ark. U.S.A. 83 35.28N 93.28W
Clarksville Tenn. U.S.A. 85 36.31N 87.21W
Clarksville Tex. U.S.A. 83 33.37N 95.03W
Clary France 14 50.05N 3.21E
Clayoquot Sd. Canada 74 49.11N 126.08W
Clayton *r.* Australia 66 29.06S 137.59E
Clayton Idaho U.S.A. 80 44.16N 114.25W
Clayton N.J. U.S.A. 85 39.39N 75.06W
Clayton N.Mex. U.S.A. 83 36.27N 103.11W
Clear, C. Rep. of Ire. 9 51.25N 9.32W
Clearfield Utah U.S.A. 80 41.07N 112.01W
Clear I. Rep. of Ire. 13 51.26N 9.30W
Clear L. U.S.A. 80 39.02N 122.50W
Clear Lake *town* Iowa U.S.A. 82 43.08N 92.23W
Clear Lake *town* S.Dak. U.S.A. 82 44.45N 96.41W
Clearwater Canada 74 51.38N 120.02W
Clearwater *r.* Canada 75 56.40N 109.30W
Clearwater U.S.A. 85 27.57N 82.48W
Clearwater Mts. U.S.A. 80 46.00N 115.30W
Cle Elum U.S.A. 80 47.12N 120.56W
Cleethorpes U.K. 10 53.33N 0.02W
Clermont Australia 64 22.49S 147.39E
Clermont France 15 49.23N 2.24E
Clermont-en-Argonne France 15 49.05N 5.05E
Clermont-Ferrand France 17 45.47N 3.05E
Clervaux Lux. 14 50.04N 6.01E
Cles Italy 15 46.22N 11.02E
Cleve Australia 66 33.37S 136.32E
Clevedon U.K. 11 51.26N 2.52W
Cleveland *d.* U.K. 10 54.37N 1.08W
Cleveland Miss. U.S.A. 83 33.45N 90.50W
Cleveland Ohio U.S.A. 84 41.30N 81.41W
Cleveland Tenn. U.S.A. 85 35.10N 84.51W
Cleveland Tex. U.S.A. 83 30.21N 95.05W
Cleveland, C. Australia 64 19.11S 147.01E
Cleveland Heights *town* U.S.A. 84 41.30N 81.34W
Cleveland Hills U.K. 10 54.25N 1.10W
Cleveleys U.K. 10 53.52N 3.01W
Clew B. Rep. of Ire. 13 53.50N 9.47W
Clifden Rep. of Ire. 13 53.29N 10.02W
Cliffy Head Australia 63 34.58S 116.24E
Clifton Ariz. U.S.A. 81 33.03N 109.18W
Clifton N.J. U.S.A. 85 40.53N 74.08W
Clifton Tex. U.S.A. 83 31.47N 97.35W
Clifton Forge U.S.A. 85 37.49N 79.49W
Climax Canada 75 49.13N 108.23W
Clint U.S.A. 81 31.35N 106.14W
Clinton B.C. Canada 74 51.05N 121.35W
Clinton New Zealand 60 46.13S 169.23E
Clinton Ark. U.S.A. 83 35.36N 92.38W
Clinton Ill. U.S.A. 82 40.10N 88.57W
Clinton Iowa U.S.A. 82 41.51N 90.12W
Clinton Mo. U.S.A. 82 38.22N 93.46W
Clinton N.C. U.S.A. 85 35.00N 78.20W
Clinton N.J. U.S.A. 85 40.38N 74.55W
Clinton Okla. U.S.A. 83 35.31N 98.59W
Clintwood U.S.A. 85 37.09N 82.30W
Clipperton *i.* Pacific Oc. 69 10.17N 109.13W
Clisham *mtn.* U.K. 12 57.58N 6.50W
Clive L. Canada 74 63.13N 118.54W
Cliza Bolivia 92 17.36S 65.56W
Cloghan Offaly Rep. of Ire. 13 53.13N 7.54W
Clogher Head Kerry Rep. of Ire. 13 52.09N 10.28W
Clonakilty Rep. of Ire. 13 51.37N 8.54W
Cloncurry Australia 64 20.42S 140.30E
Clones Rep. of Ire. 13 54.11N 7.16W
Clonmel Rep. of Ire. 13 52.21N 7.44W
Clonroche Rep. of Ire. 13 52.27N 6.45W
Cloppenburg Germany 14 52.52N 8.02E
Cloquet U.S.A. 82 46.43N 92.28W
Clorinda Argentina 92 25.20S 57.40W
Cloud Peak *mtn.* U.S.A. 80 44.25N 107.10W
Cloughton U.K. 10 54.20N 0.27W
Cloverdale U.S.A. 80 38.48N 123.01W
Clovis Calif. U.S.A. 80 36.49N 119.42W
Clovis N.Mex. U.S.A. 83 34.24N 103.12W
Clowne U.K. 10 53.18N 1.16W
Cluj-Napoca Romania 21 46.47N 23.37E
Clunes Australia 66 37.16S 143.47E
Cluny France 17 46.26N 4.39E
Clusone Italy 15 45.53N 9.57E
Clutha *r.* New Zealand 60 46.18S 169.05E
Clwyd *d.* U.K. 10 53.07N 3.20W
Clwyd *r.* U.K. 10 53.19N 3.30W
Clyde Canada 73 70.30N 68.30W
Clyde New Zealand 60 45.11S 169.19E
Clyde *r.* U.K. 12 55.58N 4.53W
Clydebank U.K. 12 55.53N 4.23W
Coachella U.S.A. 81 33.41N 116.10W
Coahuila *d.* Mexico 83 27.40N 102.00W
Coal *r.* Canada 74 59.39N 126.57W
Coalgate U.S.A. 83 34.32N 96.13W
Coalinga U.S.A. 81 36.09N 120.21W
Coalville U.K. 11 52.43N 1.21W
Coast *d.* Kenya 55 3.00S 39.30E
Coast Mts. Canada 74 55.00N 129.00W
Coast Range *mts.* U.S.A. 80 42.40N 123.30W
Coatbridge U.K. 12 55.52N 4.02W
Coatesville U.S.A. 85 39.59N 75.49W
Coats I. Canada 73 62.30N 83.00W
Coats Land *f.* Antarctica 96 77.00S 25.00W
Coatzacoalcos Mexico 86 18.10N 94.25W
Cobalt Canada 76 47.25N 79.42W
Cobán Guatemala 86 15.28N 90.20W
Cobar Australia 67 31.32S 145.51E
Cobargo Australia 67 36.24S 149.52E
Cobden Australia 66 38.21S 143.07E
Cobden Canada 76 45.38N 76.53W
Cobh Rep. of Ire. 13 51.50N 8.18W
Cobham L. Australia 66 30.09S 142.05E
Cobija Bolivia 92 11.02S 68.44W
Cobourg Canada 76 43.58N 78.10W
Cobourg Pen. Australia 64 11.20S 132.15E
Cobram Australia 67 35.56S 145.40E
Cobre U.S.A. 80 41.07N 114.25W
Cobue Mozambique 55 12.10S 34.50E
Coburg Germany 20 50.15N 10.58E
Coburg I. Canada 73 76.00N 79.25W
Cochabamba Bolivia 92 17.24S 66.09W
Cochabamba *d.* Bolivia 92 17.30S 65.40W
Cochem Germany 14 50.08N 7.10E
Cochise U.S.A. 81 32.06N 109.56W
Cochran U.S.A. 85 32.22N 83.21W
Cochrane Alta. Canada 74 51.11N 114.30W
Cochrane Ont. Canada 76 49.00N 81.00W
Cochrane Chile 93 47.20S 72.30W
Cockaleechie Australia 66 34.07S 135.53E
Cockburn Australia 66 32.05S 141.00E
Cockburnspath U.K. 12 55.56N 2.22W
Cockeysville U.S.A. 85 39.29N 76.39W
Cocklebiddy Australia 63 32.02S 126.05E
Coco *r.* Honduras 87 14.58N 83.15W
Coco, Isla del *i.* Pacific Oc. 69 5.32N 87.04W
Cocoa U.S.A. 85 28.21N 80.46W
Cocoa Beach *town* U.S.A. 85 28.19N 80.36W
Cocobeach Gabon 54 0.59N 9.36E
Cocoparra Range *mts.* Australia 67 34.00S 146.00E
Cod, C. U.S.A. 84 41.42N 70.15W
Codăeşti Romania 21 46.52N 27.46E
Codajás Brazil 90 3.55S 62.00W
Codigoro Italy 15 44.49N 12.08E
Codó Brazil 91 4.28S 43.51W

gno Italy **15** 45.09N 9.42E
oipo Italy **15** 45.58N 12.59E
U.S.A. **80** 44.32N109.03W
Australia **64** 13.56S143.12E
feld Germany **14** 51.55N 7.13E
r d'Alene U.S.A. **78** 47.40N116.46W
orden Neth. **14** 52.39N 6.45E
eyville U.S.A. **83** 37.02N 93.37W
n B. Australia **66** 34.27S135.19E
n Bay Pen. Australia **66** 34.30S135.14E
s Harbour Australia **67** 30.19S153.05E
e de Perote *mtn.* Mexico **86** 19.30N
0W
inas *r.* Italy **18** 40.57N 8.50E
ac France **17** 45.42N 0.19W
es U.S.A. **84** 42.46N 73.42W
na Australia **66** 35.47S144.15E
a, Isla de *i.* Panama **87** 7.23N 81.45W
ique Chile **93** 45.35S 72.08W
batore India **38** 11.00N 76.57E
bra Brazil **94** 19.55S 57.47W
bra Portugal **16** 40.12N 8.25W
Spain **16** 36.40N 4.45W
nies Ecuador **90** 0.20N 80.00W
ville U.S.A. **80** 42.05N110.57W
c Australia **66** 38.22S143.38E
tina Brazil **94** 19.35S 40.37W
eck, C. Antarctica **96** 77.20S159.00W
y U.S.A. **82** 39.24N101.03W
hester U.K. **11** 51.54N 0.55E
L. Canada **75** 54.33N110.05W
Lake *town* Canada **75** 54.27N110.10W
stream U.K. **12** 55.39N 2.15W
water U.S.A. **84** 41.57N 85.01W
well Canada **76** 48.45N 86.30W
ambally Australia **67** 34.48S145.53E
man *r.* Australia **64** 15.06S141.38E
man Tex. U.S.A. **83** 31.50N 99.26W
man Wisc. U.S.A. **82** 45.04N 88.02W
nso R.S.A. **56** 28.43S 29.49E
raine Australia **66** 37.36S141.42E
raine U.K. **13** 55.08N 6.40W
sberg R.S.A. **56** 30.43S 25.05E
ax U.S.A. **83** 31.31N 92.42W
ong India **41** 25.16N 87.13E
o Italy **15** 46.08N 9.22E
na Mexico **86** 19.14N103.41W
na *d.* Mexico **86** 19.05N104.00W
nas Brazil **91** 6.02S 44.14W
i. U.K. **12** 56.38N 6.34W
arenebri Australia **67** 29.33S148.36E
ege U.S.A. **72** 64.54N147.55W
ege Park *town* Ga. U.S.A. **85** 33.39N
28W
ege Park *town* Md. U.S.A. **85** 39.00N
55W
ege Station *town* U.S.A. **83** 30.37N
21W
erina Australia **67** 29.22S146.32E
ie N.S.W. Australia **67** 31.41S148.22E
ie W.A. Australia **63** 33.21S116.09E
ie Cardiff Australia **63** 33.27S116.09E
ier B. Australia **62** 16.10S124.15E
ingswood U.S.A. **85** 39.55N 75.04W
ingwood Canada **76** 44.29N 80.13W
ingwood New Zealand **60** 40.41S172.41E
ingwood B. P.N.G. **64** 9.20S149.30E
insville Australia **64** 20.34S147.51E
in Top *mtn.* U.K. **13** 54.58N 6.08W
on Rep. of Ire. **13** 53.47N 6.30W
ooney Rep. of Ire. **13** 54.11N 8.29W
mar France **17** 48.05N 7.21E
menar Viejo Spain **16** 40.39N 3.46W
ne *r.* Essex U.K. **11** 51.50N 0.59E
nett, C. Mexico **86** 31.00N116.20W
nett, Cabo *c.* Mexico **81** 31.00N116.20W
o *r.* Australia **67** 33.26S150.53E
ogne *see* Köln Germany **14**
ombia S. America **90** 4.00N 72.30W
ombian Basin *f.* Carib. Sea **95** 14.00N
.00W
ombo Sri Lanka **39** 6.55N 79.52E
ón Argentina **93** 32.15S 58.10W
ón Panama **90** 9.21N 79.54W
ona Australia **65** 31.38S132.05E
onelganj India **41** 27.08N 81.42E
onia del Sacramento Uruguay **93** 34.28S
.51W
onia Las Heras Argentina **93** 46.33S
.57W
onia Lavelleja Uruguay **93** 31.06S 57.01W
onsay *i.* U.K. **12** 56.04N 6.13W
orado *r.* Argentina **93** 39.50S 62.02W
orado *d.* U.S.A. **80** 39.07N105.27W
orado *r.* Ariz. U.S.A. **81** 31.45N114.40W
orado *r.* Tex. U.S.A. **83** 28.36N 95.58W
orado City U.S.A. **83** 32.24N100.52W
orado Plateau *f.* U.S.A. **81** 36.30N108.00W
orado Springs *town* U.S.A. **80**
.50N104.49W
ton S.Dak. U.S.A. **82** 43.47N 96.56W
umbia *r.* U.S.A. **80** 46.15N124.05W
umbia La. U.S.A. **83** 32.06N 92.05W
umbia Miss. U.S.A. **83** 31.15N 89.56W
umbia Mo. U.S.A. **82** 38.57N 92.20W
umbia S.C. U.S.A. **85** 34.00N 81.00W
umbia Tenn. U.S.A. **85** 35.37N 87.02W
umbia, Mt. Canada **74** 52.08N117.20W
lumbia, Sierra *mts.* Mexico **81**
.30N114.50W
umbia Basin *f.* U.S.A. **80** 46.55N117.36W
umbia Falls *town* U.S.A. **80**
.23N114.11W
umbia Plateau *f.* U.S.A. **80**
.00N117.30W
umbretes, Islas *is.* Spain **16** 39.50N 0.40E
umbus Ga. U.S.A. **85** 32.28N 84.59W
umbus Ind. U.S.A. **84** 39.12N 85.57W
Columbus Miss. U.S.A. **83** 33.30N 88.25W
Columbus Mont. U.S.A. **80** 45.38N109.15W
Columbus Nebr. U.S.A. **82** 41.25N 97.22W
Columbus N.Mex. U.S.A. **81** 31.50N107.38W
Columbus Ohio U.S.A. **84** 39.59N 83.03W
Columbus Tex. U.S.A. **83** 29.42N 96.33W
Colville *r.* U.S.A. **72** 70.06N151.30W
Colwyn Bay *town* U.K. **10** 53.18N 3.43W
Comacchio Italy **15** 44.42N 12.11E
Comacchio, Valli di *b.* Italy **15** 44.38N 12.06E
Comai China **41** 28.28N 91.33E
Comanche U.S.A. **83** 34.22N 97.58W
Comayagua Honduras **87** 14.30N 87.39W
Comblain-au-Pont Belgium **14** 50.29N 5.32E
Combles France **14** 50.01N 2.52E
Combourg France **15** 48.25N 1.45W
Comboyne Australia **67** 31.35S152.27E
Comeragh Mts. Rep. of Ire. **13** 52.17N 7.34W
Comilla Bangla. **41** 23.28N 91.10E
Comitán Mexico **86** 16.15N 92.08W
Commentry France **17** 46.17N 2.44E
Commerce U.S.A. **83** 33.15N 95.54W
Commonwealth Territory *d.* Australia **67**
35.00S151.00E
Como Italy **15** 45.48N 9.04E
Como, Lago di *l.* Italy **15** 46.05N 9.17E
Comodoro Rivadavia Argentina **93** 45.50S
67.30W
Comorin, C. India **38** 8.04N 77.35E
Comoros Africa **55** 12.15S 44.00E
Compiègne France **15** 49.24N 2.50E
Cona China **41** 27.59N 91.59E
Co Nag *l.* China **41** 32.00N 91.15E
Conakry Guinea **52** 9.30N 13.43W
Concarneau France **17** 47.53N 3.55W
Conceição Mozambique **57** 18.45S 36.10E
Conceição do Araguaia Brazil **91** 8.15S
49.17W
Concepción Argentina **92** 27.20S 65.36W
Concepción Chile **93** 36.50S 73.03W
Concepción *r.* Mexico **81** 30.32N112.59W
Concepción Paraguay **92** 23.22S 57.26W
Concepción del Oro Mexico **83**
24.38N101.25W
Concepción del Uruguay Argentina **93** 32.30S
58.14W
Conception, Pt. U.S.A. **81** 34.27N120.27W
Conception B. Namibia **56** 23.53S 14.28E
Conches France **15** 48.58N 0.58E
Conchillas Uruguay **93** 34.15S 58.04W
Conchos *r.* Mexico **81** 29.32N104.25W
Concord N.C. U.S.A. **85** 35.25N 80.34W
Concord N.H. U.S.A. **84** 43.12N 71.32W
Concordia Argentina **93** 31.24S 58.02W
Concórdia Brazil **90** 4.35S 66.35W
Concordia Mexico **81** 23.17N106.04W
Concordia U.S.A. **82** 39.34N 97.39W
Condé France **15** 48.51N 0.33W
Condé-sur-l'Escaut France **14** 50.28N 3.35E
Condobolin Australia **67** 33.03S147.11E
Condom France **17** 43.58N 0.22E
Conegliano Italy **15** 45.53N 12.18E
Confolens France **17** 46.01N 0.40E
Conghua China **33** 23.33N113.34E
Congleton U.K. **10** 53.10N 2.12W
Congo Africa **54** 1.00S 16.00E
Congo *r. see* Zaïre *r.* Zaïre **54**
Congonhas Brazil **94** 20.30S 43.53W
Coningsby U.K. **10** 53.07N 0.09W
Coniston U.K. **10** 54.22N 3.06W
Conkouati Congo **54** 4.00S 11.16E
Conn, Lough Rep. of Ire. **13** 54.01N 9.15W
Connah's Quay *town* U.K. **10** 53.13N 3.03W
Conneaut U.S.A. **84** 41.58N 80.34W
Connecticut *d.* U.S.A. **84** 41.45N 72.45W
Connecticut *r.* U.S.A. **84** 41.17N 72.21W
Connellsville U.S.A. **84** 40.01N 79.35W
Connemara *f.* Rep. of Ire. **13** 53.32N 9.56W
Conner, Mt. Australia **64** 25.35S131.49E
Conon *r.* U.K. **12** 57.33N 4.33W
Conrad U.S.A. **80** 48.10N111.57W
Conroe U.S.A. **83** 30.19N 95.27W
Conselheiro Lafaiete Brazil **94** 20.40S
43.48W
Consett U.K. **10** 54.52N 1.50W
Con Son *is.* Vietnam **34** 8.45N106.38E
Constance, L. *see* Bodensee Europe **20**
Constanța Romania **19** 44.10N 28.31E
Constantina Spain **16** 37.54N 5.36W
Constantine Algeria **51** 36.22N 6.38E
Constitución Chile **93** 35.20S 72.25W
Constitución Uruguay **93** 31.05S 57.50W
Consuegra Spain **16** 39.28N 3.43W
Consul Canada **75** 49.21N109.30W
Contact U.S.A. **80** 41.48N114.46W
Contai India **41** 21.47N 87.45E
Contamana Peru **90** 7.19S 75.00W
Contas *r.* Brazil **91** 14.15S 39.00W
Contreras, Embalse de *resr.* Spain **16** 39.32N
1.30W
Contres France **15** 47.25N 1.26E
Contwoyto L. Canada **72** 65.42N110.50W
Conty France **15** 49.44N 2.09E
Conway Ark. U.S.A. **83** 35.05N 92.26W
Conway N.H. U.S.A. **84** 43.59N 71.07W
Conway S.C. U.S.A. **85** 33.51N 79.04W
Conway, L. Australia **66** 28.17S135.35E
Conwy *r.* U.K. **9** 53.17N 3.49W
Coober Pedy Australia **66** 29.01S134.43E
Cooch Behār India **41** 26.19N 89.26E
Cook, C. Canada **72** 50.08N127.55W
Cook, Mt. New Zealand **60** 43.45S170.12E
Cooke, Mt. Australia **63** 32.26S116.18E
Cookeville U.S.A. **85** 36.10N 85.30W
Cookhouse R.S.A. **56** 32.44S 25.47E
Cook Inlet U.S.A. **72** 60.30N152.00W
Cook Is. Pacific Oc. **68** 15.00S160.00W
Cookstown U.K. **13** 54.39N 6.46W
Cook Str. New Zealand **60** 41.15S174.30E
Cooktown Australia **64** 15.29S145.15E
Coolabah Australia **67** 31.02S146.45E
Coolah Australia **67** 31.48S149.45E
Coolamara Australia **66** 31.59S143.42E
Coolamon Australia **67** 34.48S147.12E
Coolangatta Australia **67** 28.10S153.26E
Coolgardie Australia **63** 31.01S121.12E
Coolidge U.S.A. **81** 32.59N111.31W
Cooma Australia **67** 36.15S149.07E
Coombah Australia **66** 32.58S141.39E
Coomberdale Australia **63** 30.29S116.03E
Coonabarabran Australia **67** 31.16S149.18E
Coonalpyn Australia **66** 35.41S139.52E
Coonamble Australia **67** 30.55S148.26E
Coonana Australia **63** 31.01S123.05E
Coonawarra Australia **66** 37.16S140.50E
Coondambo Australia **66** 31.07S135.20E
Cooper Creek *r.* Australia **66** 28.33S137.46E
Coorow Australia **63** 29.53S116.01E
Coos Bay *town* U.S.A. **80** 43.22N124.13W
Cootamundra Australia **67** 34.41S148.03E
Cootehill Rep. of Ire. **13** 54.05N 7.05W
Copainalá Mexico **86** 17.05N 93.12W
Copán *ruins* Honduras **87** 14.52N 89.10W
Cope U.S.A. **80** 39.40N102.51W
Copenhagen *see* København Denmark **23**
Copiapó Chile **92** 27.22S 70.20W
Copparo Italy **15** 44.54N 11.49E
Copperbelt *d.* Zambia **56** 13.00S 28.00E
Copper Belt *f.* Zambia **55** 12.40S 28.00E
Copper Center U.S.A. **72** 61.58N145.19W
Copper Cliff *town* Canada **76** 46.28N 81.04W
Copper Harbor U.S.A. **84** 47.28N 87.54W
Coppermine *r.* Canada **72** 67.54N115.10W
Coppermine *see* Qurlurtuuq *town* Canada **72**
Copper Mountain *town* Canada **74**
49.20N120.30W
Copper Queen Zimbabwe **56** 17.31S 29.20E
Copperton R.S.A. **56** 30.00S 22.15E
Copp L. Canada **74** 60.14N114.40W
Coqên China **41** 31.13N 85.12E
Coquet *r.* U.K. **10** 55.21N 1.35W
Coquille U.S.A. **80** 43.11N124.11W
Coquimbo Chile **92** 29.58S 71.21W
Corabia Romania **19** 43.45N 24.29E
Coracora Peru **90** 15.02S 73.48W
Coraki Australia **67** 23.00S153.17E
Coral Bay *town* Australia **62** 23.02S113.48E
Coral Harbour *town* Canada **73** 64.10N
83.15W
Coral Sea Pacific Oc. **64** 14.30S149.30E
Coral Sea Basin Pacific Oc. **68**
14.00S152.00E
Corangamite, L. Australia **66** 38.10S143.25E
Corbeil France **15** 48.37N 2.29E
Corbeny France **15** 49.28N 3.49E
Corbigny France **15** 47.15N 3.40E
Corbin U.S.A. **85** 36.58N 84.06W
Corby U.K. **11** 52.29N 0.41W
Corcubión Spain **16** 42.56N 9.12W
Córdoba Argentina **92** 31.25S 64.10W
Córdoba *d.* Argentina **92** 30.30S 64.30W
Córdoba Mexico **86** 18.55N 96.55W
Córdoba Spain **16** 37.53N 4.46W
Córdoba, Sierras de *mts.* Argentina **92** 30.30S
64.40W
Cordova U.S.A. **72** 60.33N139.44W
Corentyne *r.* Guyana **91** 5.10N 57.20W
Corfield Australia **64** 21.43S143.22E
Corfu *i. see* Kérkira *i.* Greece **19**
Coricudgy, Mt. Australia **67** 32.51S150.25E
Corigliano Italy **19** 39.36N 16.31E
Corindi Australia **67** 30.00S153.21E
Corinne Canada **75** 50.04N104.40W
Corinth Miss. U.S.A. **83** 34.56N 88.31W
Corinto Nicaragua **87** 12.29N 87.14W
Cork Rep. of Ire. **13** 51.54N 8.28W
Cork *d.* Rep. of Ire. **13** 52.00N 8.40W
Cork Harbour *est.* Rep. of Ire. **13** 51.50N
8.17W
Cormeilles France **15** 49.15N 0.23E
Cormorant Canada **75** 54.14N100.35W
Corner Brook *town* Canada **77** 48.57N 57.57W
Corner Inlet *b.* Australia **67** 38.43S146.20E
Corning Ark. U.S.A. **83** 36.24N 90.35W
Corning N.Y. U.S.A. **84** 42.09N 77.04W
Corno, Monte *mtn.* Italy **18** 42.29N 13.33E
Cornwall Canada **76** 45.02N 74.45W
Cornwall *d.* U.K. **11** 50.26N 4.40W
Cornwallis I. Canada **73** 75.00N 95.00W
Coro Venezuela **90** 11.27N 69.41W
Coroatá Brazil **91** 4.08S 44.08W
Coroico Bolivia **92** 16.10S 67.44W
Coromandel New Zealand **60** 36.46S175.30E
Coromandel Pen. New Zealand **60**
36.45S175.30E
Corona U.S.A. **81** 34.15N105.36W
Coronation G. Canada **72** 68.00N112.00W
Coronation I. U.S.A. **74** 55.52N134.20W
Coronda Argentina **93** 31.55S 60.55W
Coronel Chile **93** 37.01S 73.08W
Coronel Brandsen Argentina **93** 35.10S
58.15W
Coronel Pringles Argentina **93** 37.56S 61.25W
Coronel Suárez Argentina **93** 37.30S 61.52W
Coropuna *mtn.* Peru **90** 15.31S 72.45W
Corowa Australia **67** 36.00S146.20E
Corozal Belize **87** 18.23N 88.23W
Corpus Christi U.S.A. **83** 27.48N 97.24W
Correggio Italy **15** 44.46N 10.47E
Correntes, Cabo das *c.* Mozambique **57**
24.11S 35.35E
Corrib, Lough Rep. of Ire. **13** 53.26N 9.14W
Corrientes Argentina **92** 27.30S 58.48W
Corrientes *d.* Argentina **92** 28.00S 57.00W
Corrientes, Cabo *c.* Colombia **90** 5.30N
77.34W
Corrigan U.S.A. **83** 31.00N 94.50W
Corrigin Australia **63** 32.21S117.52E
Corry U.S.A. **84** 41.56N 79.39W
Corryong Australia **67** 36.11S147.58E
Corse *d.* France **17** 42.00N 9.10E
Corse *i.* France **17** 42.00N 9.10E
Corse, Cap *c.* France **17** 43.00N 9.21E
Corsham U.K. **11** 51.25N 2.11W
Corsica *i. see* Corse *i.* France **17**
Corsicana U.S.A. **83** 32.06N 96.28W
Corte France **17** 42.18N 9.08E
Cortegana Spain **16** 37.55N 6.49W
Cortez Colo. U.S.A. **80** 37.21N108.35W
Cortez Nev. U.S.A. **80** 40.09N116.38W
Cortina Italy **18** 46.32N 12.08E
Cortland N.Y. U.S.A. **84** 42.36N 76.11W
Cortona Italy **18** 43.16N 11.59E
Coruche Portugal **16** 38.58N 8.31W
Çoruh Nehri *r.* Turkey *see* Chorokh. *r.* U.S.S.R.
42
Çorum Turkey **42** 40.31N 34.57E
Corumbá Brazil **92** 19.00S 57.27W
Corumbá *r.* Brazil **94** 18.15S 48.55W
Corvallis U.S.A. **80** 44.34N123.16W
Corwen U.K. **10** 52.59N 3.23W
Cosenza Italy **18** 39.17N 16.14E
Cosne France **15** 47.25N 2.55E
Coso Junction U.S.A. **81** 36.03N117.58W
Cosson *r.* France **15** 47.30N 1.15E
Costa Brava *f.* Spain **16** 41.30N 3.00E
Costa del Sol *f.* Spain **16** 36.30N 4.00W
Costa Mesa U.S.A. **81** 33.39N117.55W
Costa Rica C. America **87** 10.00N 84.00W
Costeşti Romania **19** 44.40N 24.53E
Cotabato Phil. **37** 7.14N124.15E
Cotagaita Bolivia **92** 20.50S 65.41W
Côte d'Azur *f.* France **17** 43.20N 6.45E
Côte d'Ivoire *see* Ivory Coast Africa **52**
Côte-d'Or *d.* France **15** 47.30N 4.50E
Côte d'Or *f.* France **15** 47.10N 4.50E
Cotonou Benin **53** 6.24N 2.31E
Cotopaxi *mtn.* Ecuador **90** 0.40S 78.28W
Cotswold Hills U.K. **11** 51.50N 2.00W
Cottage Grove U.S.A. **80** 43.48N123.03W
Cottbus Germany **20** 51.43N 14.21E
Cottonvale Australia **67** 28.32S151.57E
Cottonwood U.S.A. **81** 34.45N112.01W
Cotulla U.S.A. **83** 28.26N 99.14W
Coucy France **15** 49.31N 3.19E
Couer d'Alene U.S.A. **80** 47.41N117.00W
Couesnon *r.* France **15** 48.37N 1.31W
Coulagh B. Rep. of Ire. **13** 51.42N 10.00W
Coulee City U.S.A. **80** 47.37N119.17W
Coulommiers France **15** 48.49N 3.05E
Coulonge *r.* Canada **76** 45.51N 76.46W
Council U.S.A. **72** 64.55N163.44W
Council Bluffs U.S.A. **82** 41.16N 95.52W
Coupar Angus U.K. **12** 56.33N 3.17W
Courson-les-Carrières France **15** 47.36N
3.30E
Courtalain France **15** 48.05N 1.09E
Courtenay Canada **74** 49.41N125.00W
Courtrai *see* Kortrijk Belgium **14**
Coutances France **15** 49.03N 1.29W
Coutras France **17** 45.02N 0.07W
Couvin Belgium **14** 50.03N 4.30E
Cové Benin **53** 7.16N 2.20E
Cove City U.S.A. **85** 35.11N 77.20W
Coventry U.K. **11** 52.25N 1.31W
Covilhã Portugal **16** 40.17N 7.30W
Covington Ga. U.S.A. **85** 33.35N 83.52W
Covington Ky. U.S.A. **84** 39.04N 84.30W
Covington Okla. U.S.A. **83** 36.18N 97.35W
Covington Tenn. U.S.A. **83** 35.34N 89.38W
Covington Va. U.S.A. **85** 37.48N 80.01W
Cowal, L. Australia **67** 33.36S147.22E
Cowan Canada **75** 52.05N100.45W
Cowan, L. Australia **63** 32.00S122.00E
Cowangie Australia **66** 35.14S141.28E
Cowansville Canada **77** 45.12N 72.45W
Cowcowing Lakes Australia **63**
31.01S117.18E
Cowdenbeath U.K. **12** 56.07N 3.21W
Cowell Australia **66** 33.41S136.55E
Cowes Australia **67** 38.27S145.15E
Cowes U.K. **11** 50.45N 1.18W
Cowra Australia **67** 33.50S148.45E
Cox *r.* Australia **64** 15.19S135.25E
Coxim Brazil **92** 18.28S 54.37W
Cox's Bāzār Bangla. **41** 21.26N 91.59E
Coyuca de Catalán Mexico **86**
18.20N100.39W
Cozad U.S.A. **82** 40.52N 99.59W
Cozes France **17** 45.35N 0.50W
Cozumel, Isla de *i.* Mexico **87** 20.30N 87.00W
Cradock Australia **66** 31.59S138.34E
Cradock R.S.A. **56** 32.10S 25.35E
Craig Alas. U.S.A. **74** 55.29N133.09W
Craig Colo. U.S.A. **80** 40.31N107.33W
Craigavon U.K. **13** 54.28N 6.25W
Craignure U.K. **12** 56.28N 5.42W
Craigsville U.S.A. **85** 38.04N 79.23W
Crail U.K. **12** 56.16N 2.38W
Crailsheim Germany **20** 49.09N 10.06E
Craiova Romania **19** 44.18N 23.46E
Cranbourne Australia **67** 38.07S145.19E
Cranbrook Australia **63** 34.15S117.32E
Cranbrook Canada **74** 49.30N115.46W
Crane U.S.A. **80** 43.25N118.34W
Cranston U.S.A. **84** 41.47N 71.26W
Craon France **15** 47.50N 0.58W
Craonne France **15** 49.27N 3.46E
Crater L. U.S.A. **80** 42.56N122.06W
Crateús Brazil **91** 5.10S 40.39W
Crati *r.* Italy **19** 39.43N 16.29E
Crato Amazonas Brazil **90** 7.25S 63.00W
Crato Ceará Brazil **91** 7.10S 39.25W
Craughwell Rep. of Ire. **13** 53.14N 8.44W
Crawford U.S.A. **82** 42.41N103.25W
Crawfordsville U.S.A. **84** 40.03N 86.54W
Crawfordville U.S.A. **85** 30.12N 84.21W
Crawley U.K. **11** 51.07N 0.10W
Crazy Mts. U.S.A. **80** 46.08N110.20W
Crécy France **17** 50.15N 1.53E
Crécy-sur-Serre France **15** 49.42N 3.37E
Cree *r.* Canada **75** 59.00N105.47W
Creede U.S.A. **80** 37.51N106.56W
Cree L. Canada **75** 57.30N106.30W
Creil France **15** 49.16N 2.29E
Crema Italy **15** 45.22N 9.41E
Cremona Italy **15** 45.08N 10.03E
Crépy France **15** 49.36N 3.31E
Crépy-en-Valois France **15** 49.14N 2.54E
Cres *i.* Yugo. **18** 44.50N 14.20E
Cres *town* Yugo. **18** 44.58N 14.25E
Crescent U.S.A. **80** 43.29N121.41W
Crescent City U.S.A. **80** 41.45N124.12W
Crescent Head *town* Australia **67**
31.10S152.59E
Crespo Argentina **93** 32.02S 60.20W
Cressy Australia **66** 38.02S143.38E
Crest France **17** 44.44N 5.02E
Creston Canada **74** 49.10N116.31W
Creston Iowa U.S.A. **82** 41.04N 94.22W
Creston Oriental de la Sierra Madre *mts.*
Mexico **81** 28.40N107.50W
Crestview U.S.A. **85** 30.44N 86.34W
Creswick Australia **66** 37.25S143.54E
Crete *i. see* Kríti *i.* Greece **19**
Crete U.S.A. **82** 40.38N 96.58W
Crete, Sea of *see* Kritikón Pélagos *sea* Greece
19
Creus, Cabo de *c.* Spain **16** 42.20N 3.19E
Creuse *r.* France **17** 47.00N 0.35E
Crewe U.K. **10** 53.06N 2.28W
Crianlarich U.K. **12** 56.23N 4.37W
Criccieth U.K. **10** 52.55N 4.15W
Criciúma Brazil **94** 28.40S 49.23W
Crieff U.K. **12** 56.23N 3.52W
Crillon, Mt. U.S.A. **74** 58.39N137.14W
Crimea *pen. see* Krym *pen.* U.S.S.R. **25**
Crinan U.K. **12** 56.06N 5.34W
Cristóbal Colón *mtn.* Colombia **90** 10.53N
73.48W
Crişu Alb *r.* Romania **21** 46.42N 21.17E
Crna *r.* Yugo. **19** 41.33N 21.58E
Crna Gora *d.* Yugo. **19** 43.00N 19.30E
Croaghnameal *mtn.* Rep. of Ire. **13** 54.40N
7.57W
Croatia *d. see* Hrvatska *d.* Yugo. **19**
Crockett U.S.A. **83** 31.19N 95.28W
Crocodile *r.* Trans. R.S.A. **56** 24.11S 26.48E
Croker I. Australia **64** 11.12S132.32E
Cromarty Canada **75** 58.03N 94.09W
Cromarty U.K. **12** 57.40N 4.02W
Cromarty Firth *est.* U.K. **12** 57.41N 4.10W
Cromer U.K. **10** 52.56N 1.18E
Cromwell New Zealand **60** 45.03S169.14E
Crooked I. Bahamas **87** 22.45N 74.00W
Crookhaven Rep. of Ire. **13** 51.29N 9.45W
Crookston U.S.A. **82** 47.47N 96.37W
Crookwell Australia **67** 34.27S149.28E
Croom Rep. of Ire. **13** 52.31N 8.43W
Croppa Creek *town* Australia **67**
29.08S150.20E
Crosby U.K. **10** 54.11N 4.34W
Crosby U.S.A. **83** 31.17N 91.04W
Cross City U.S.A. **85** 29.39N 83.09W
Crossett U.S.A. **83** 33.08N 91.58W
Cross Fell *mtn.* U.K. **10** 54.43N 2.28W
Cross L. Canada **75** 54.45N 97.30W
Cross River *d.* Nigeria **53** 5.45N 8.25E
Crossroads U.S.A. **83** 33.30N103.21W
Cross Sd. U.S.A. **74** 58.10N136.30W
Crossville U.S.A. **85** 35.57N 85.02W
Crotone Italy **19** 39.05N 17.06E
Crow *r.* Canada **74** 59.41N124.20W
Crow Agency U.S.A. **80** 45.36N107.27W
Crowell U.S.A. **83** 33.59N 99.43W
Crowl Creek *r.* Australia **67** 31.58S144.53E
Crowsnest Pass Canada **74** 49.40N114.40W
Croyde U.K. **11** 51.07N 4.13W
Croyden Australia **61** 18.12S142.14E
Croydon Australia **64** 18.12S142.14E
Croydon U.K. **11** 51.23N 0.06W
Crucero U.S.A. **81** 35.03N116.10W
Cruger U.S.A. **83** 33.14N 90.14W
Cruz, Cabo *c.* Cuba **87** 19.52N 77.44W
Cruz Alta Brazil **94** 28.38S 53.38W
Cruz del Eje Argentina **92** 30.44S 64.49W
Cruzeiro Brazil **94** 22.33S 44.59W
Cruzeiro do Sul Brazil **90** 7.40S 72.39W
Crystal U.S.A. **82** 45.00N 93.25W
Crystal Brook *town* Australia **66**
33.21S138.13E
Crystal City U.S.A. **83** 28.41N 99.50W
Crystal River *town* U.S.A. **85** 28.54N 82.36W
Csorna Hungary **21** 47.37N 17.16E
Csurgó Hungary **21** 46.16N 17.06E
Cuamba Mozambique **55** 14.48S 36.32E
Cuando *r.* Angola **56** 18.30S 23.32E
Cuando-Cubango *d.* Angola **56** 16.00S 20.00E
Cuangar Angola **54** 17.34S 18.39E
Cuango *r. see* Kwango *r.* Zaïre **54**
Cuanza *r.* Angola **54** 9.20S 13.09E
Cuanza Norte *d.* Angola **54** 8.45S 15.00E
Cuanza Sul *d.* Angola **54** 11.00S 15.00E
Cua Rao Vietnam **34** 19.16N104.27E
Cuaró Uruguay **93** 30.37S 56.54W
Cuaró *r.* Uruguay **93** 30.15S 57.01W
Cuauhtémoc Mexico **81** 28.25N106.52W
Cuba C. America **87** 22.00N 79.00W
Cuba U.S.A. **81** 36.01N107.04W
Cuballing Australia **63** 32.50S117.07E
Cubango *r. see* Okavango *r.* Angola **54**
Cubia *r.* Angola **54** 16.00S 21.46E

Cubo Mozambique 57 23.48S 33.55E
Cuchi r. Angola 56 15.23S 17.12E
Cuckfield U.K. 11 51.00N 0.08W
Cucuí Brazil 90 1.12N 66.50W
Cúcuta Colombia 90 7.55N 72.31W
Cudahy U.S.A. 82 42.57N 87.52W
Cuddalore India 39 11.43N 79.46E
Cue Australia 62 27.25S117.54E
Cuenca Ecuador 90 2.54S 79.00W
Cuenca Spain 16 40.04N 2.07W
Cuenca, Serranía de mts. Spain 16 40.25N 2.00W
Cuernavaca Mexico 86 18.57N 99.15W
Cuero U.S.A. 83 29.06N 97.18W
Cuervo U.S.A. 81 35.02N104.24W
Cuiabá Brazil 91 15.32S 56.05W
Cuiabá r. Brazil 92 18.00S 57.25W
Cuidado, Punta c. I. de Pascua 69 27.08S109.19W
Cuillin Hills U.K. 12 57.12N 6.13W
Cuilo r. see Kwilu r. Zaïre 54
Cuito r. Angola 54 18.01S 20.50E
Cuito Cuanavale Angola 56 15.11S 19.11E
Culbertson U.S.A. 80 48.09N104.31W
Culcairn Australia 67 35.40S147.03E
Culemborg Neth. 14 51.57N 5.14E
Culgoa r. Australia 67 29.56S146.20E
Culiacán Mexico 81 24.48N107.24W
Culiacán r. Mexico 81 24.30N107.31W
Cullen U.K. 12 57.41N 2.50W
Cullera Spain 16 39.10N 0.15W
Cullin Sd. U.K. 12 57.03N 6.13W
Culloden Moor U.K. 12 57.29N 3.55W
Culpeper U.S.A. 84 38.28N 77.53W
Culuene r. Brazil 91 12.56S 52.51W
Culver, Pt. Australia 63 32.52S124.41E
Cuma Angola 54 12.52S 15.05E
Cumaná Venezuela 90 10.29N 64.12W
Cumberland r. U.S.A. 85 37.09N 88.25W
Cumberland Ky. U.S.A. 85 36.58N 82.59W
Cumberland Md. U.S.A. 84 39.39N 78.46W
Cumberland Va. U.S.A. 85 37.31N 78.16W
Cumberland Wisc. U.S.A. 82 45.32N 92.01W
Cumberland, C. Vanuatu 68 14.39S166.37E
Cumberland, L. U.S.A. 85 36.45N 84.51W
Cumberland I. U.S.A. 85 30.51N 81.27W
Cumberland L. Canada 75 54.02N102.17W
Cumberland Pen. Canada 73 66.50N 64.00W
Cumberland Plateau f. U.S.A. 85 36.00N 85.00W
Cumberland Sd. Canada 73 65.00N 65.30W
Cumbernauld U.K. 12 55.57N 4.00W
Cumbria d. U.K. 10 54.30N 3.00W
Cumbrian Mts. U.K. 10 54.32N 3.05W
Cuminá r. Brazil 91 1.30S 56.00W
Cummins Australia 66 34.16S135.44E
Cumnock Australia 67 32.56S148.46E
Cumnock U.K. 12 55.27N 4.15W
Cunderdin Australia 63 31.39S117.15E
Cunene d. Angola 54 16.00S 16.00E
Cunene r. Angola 54 17.15S 11.50E
Cuneo Italy 15 44.22N 7.32E
Cungena Australia 66 32.33S134.40E
Cunnamulla Australia 67 28.04S145.40E
Cuokkaraš'ša mtn. Norway 22 69.57N 24.32E
Cuorgnè Italy 15 45.23N 7.39E
Cupar U.K. 12 56.19N 3.01W
Cupica, Golfo de g. Colombia 90 6.35N 77.25W
Curaçao i. Neth. Antilles 90 12.15N 69.00W
Curacautín Chile 93 38.26S 71.53W
Curaco r. Argentina 93 38.49S 65.01W
Curanilahue Chile 93 37.28S 73.21W
Curaray r. Peru 90 2.20S 74.05W
Curban Australia 67 31.33S148.36E
Curdlawidny L. Australia 66 30.16S136.20E
Cure r. France 15 47.40N 3.41E
Curiapo Venezuela 90 8.33N 61.05W
Curicó Chile 93 34.59S 71.14W
Curitiba Brazil 94 25.24S 49.16W
Curlewis Australia 67 31.08S150.16E
Curnamona Australia 66 31.40S139.35E
Currane, Lough Rep. of Ire. 13 51.50N 10.07W
Currant U.S.A. 80 38.44N115.30W
Curranyalpa Australia 67 30.57S144.33E
Currie Australia 65 39.56S143.52E
Currie U.S.A. 80 40.17N114.44W
Curtin Australia 63 30.50S122.05E
Curtis U.S.A. 82 40.38N100.31W
Curtis I. Australia 64 23.38S151.09E
Curuá r. Brazil 91 5.23S 54.22W
Cururupu Brazil 91 1.50S 44.52W
Curuzú Cuatiá Argentina 93 29.50S 58.05W
Curvelo Brazil 94 18.45S 44.27W
Cushendall U.K. 13 55.06N 6.05W
Cushing U.S.A. 83 35.59N 96.46W
Cusna, Monte mtn. Italy 15 44.17N 10.23E
Cut Bank U.S.A. 80 48.38N112.20W
Cuttaburra Creek r. Australia 67 29.18S145.00E
Cuttack India 41 20.30N 85.50E
Cuxhaven Germany 20 53.52N 8.42E
Cuyuni r. Guyana 90 6.24N 58.38W
Cuzco Peru 90 13.32S 71.57W
Cwmbran U.K. 11 51.39N 3.01W
Cyclades is. see Kikládhes is. Greece 19
Cynthiana U.S.A. 84 38.22N 84.18W
Cypress Hills Canada 75 49.40N109.30W
Cyprus Asia 44 35.00N 33.00E
Cyrenaica f. see Barqah f. Libya 48
Czechoslovakia Europe 20 49.30N 15.00E
Czeremcha Poland 21 52.32N 23.15E
Czersk Poland 21 53.48N 18.00E
Częstochowa Poland 21 50.49N 19.07E

D

Dà r. Vietnam 34 21.20N105.24E
Da'an China 32 45.30N124.18E
Ḑab'ah Jordan 44 31.36N 36.04E
Dabakala Ivory Coast 52 8.19N 4.24W
Daba Shan mts. China 33 32.00N109.00E
Dabat Ethiopia 49 12.58N 37.48E
Dabbāgh, Jabal mtn. Saudi Arabia 44 27.51N 35.43E
Dabhoi India 40 22.11N 73.26E
Dabie Shan mts. China 33 31.15N115.20E
Dabola Guinea 52 10.48N 11.02W
Dabra India 41 25.54N 78.20E
Dabu Jiangxi China 33 26.47N116.04E
Dacca see Dhaka Bangla. 41
Dachau Germany 20 48.15N 11.26E
Dadanawa Guyana 90 2.30N 59.30W
Dade City U.S.A. 85 28.23N 82.11W
Dādhar Pakistan 40 29.28N 67.39E
Dādra & Nagar Haveli d. India 40 20.05N 73.00E
Dādu Pakistan 40 26.44N 67.47E
Dadu He r. China 39 28.47N104.40E
Daet Phil. 37 14.07N122.58E
Dagali Norway 23 60.25N 8.27E
Dagana Senegal 52 16.28N 15.35W
Daga Post Sudan 49 9.12N 33.58E
Dagash Sudan 48 19.22N 33.24E
Dagu China 32 38.58N117.40E
Dagua P.N.G. 37 3.25S143.20E
Daguan China 30 27.44N103.53E
Dagupan Phil. 37 16.02N120.21E
Daguragu Australia 62 17.33S130.30E
Dagzê China 41 29.45N105.45E
Dagzê Co l. China 41 31.45N 87.50E
Dahan-e Qowmghī Afghan. 40 34.28N 66.31E
Da Hinggan Ling mts. China 31 50.00N122.10E
Dahlak Archipelago is. Ethiopia 48 15.45N 40.30E
Dahlak Kebir I. Ethiopia 48 15.38N 40.11E
Dahlem Germany 20 50.23N 6.33E
Dahlgren U.S.A. 85 38.20N 77.03W
Dahra Senegal 52 15.21N 15.29W
Dahujiang China 33 26.06N114.58E
Dahūk Iraq 42 36.52N 43.00E
Daḩy, Nafūd ad f. Saudi Arabia 45 22.00N 45.25E
Ḑaḩyah, 'Urūq f. Yemen 45 18.45N 51.15E
Dai Hai l. China 32 40.31N112.43E
Dailekh Nepal 41 28.50N 81.43E
Daimiel Spain 16 39.05N 3.35W
Daitō Japan 35 34.42N135.38E
Daiyun Shan mtn. China 33 25.41N118.11E
Dājal Pakistan 40 29.33N 70.23E
Dajarra Australia 64 21.42S139.31E
Dajing China 33 28.25N121.10E
Dakar Senegal 52 14.38N 17.27W
Dakhal, Wādī ad r. Egypt 44 28.49N 32.45E
Dākhilah, Al Wāḩāt ad oasis Egypt 42 25.30N 28.10E
Dakhla W. Sahara 50 23.43N 15.57W
Dakhlet Nouadhibou d. Mauritania 50 20.30N 16.00W
Dakingari Nigeria 53 11.40N 4.06E
Dakota City U.S.A. 82 42.25N 96.25W
Dakovica Yugo. 19 42.23N 20.25E
Dal r. Sweden 23 60.38N 17.27E
Dala Congo 54 1.40N 16.39E
Dalaba Guinea 52 10.47N 12.12W
Dalai Nur l. China 32 43.27N116.25E
Dalandzadgad Mongolia 32 43.30N104.18E
Da Lat Vietnam 34 11.56N108.25E
Dālbandin Pakistan 40 28.53N 64.25E
Dalbeattie U.K. 12 54.55N 3.49W
Dalby Australia 65 27.11S151.12E
Dalby Sweden 23 55.40N 13.20E
Dale Hordaland Norway 23 60.35N 5.49E
Dale Sogn og Fj. Norway 23 61.22N 5.24E
Dalen Norway 23 59.27N 8.00E
Dalhart U.S.A. 83 36.04N102.31W
Dalhousie Canada 77 48.04N 66.23W
Dalhousie Jammu & Kashmir 40 32.32N 75.59E
Dali China 30 25.42N100.11E
Dalian China 32 38.49N121.48E
Dalkeith U.K. 12 55.54N 3.04W
Dallas Oreg. U.S.A. 80 44.55N123.19W
Dallas Tex. U.S.A. 83 32.47N 96.48W
Dallastown U.S.A. 85 39.54N 76.39W
Dall I. U.S.A. 74 55.00N133.00W
Dalli Rajhāra India 41 20.35N 81.04E
Dalmally U.K. 12 56.25N 4.58W
Dalmas, Lac l. Canada 77 53.27N 71.50W
Dalmellington U.K. 12 55.19N 4.24W
Dalnerechensk U.S.S.R. 31 45.55N133.45E
Daloa Ivory Coast 52 6.56N 6.28W
Dalou Shan mts. China 33 28.25N107.15E
Dalqū Sudan 48 20.07N 30.35E
Dalrymple, Mt. Australia 64 21.02S148.38E
Dalsingh Sarai India 41 25.40N 85.50E
Dalton Canada 76 48.10N 84.00W
Dalton U.S.A. 85 34.46N 84.59W
Daltonganj India 41 24.02N 84.04E
Dalupiri i. Phil. 33 19.05N121.13E
Dalvik Iceland 22 65.58N 18.28W
Dalwhinnie U.K. 12 56.56N 4.15W
Daly r. Australia 62 13.20S130.19E
Daly City U.S.A. 80 37.42N122.29W
Daly Waters town Australia 64 16.15S133.22E
Damā, Wādī r. Saudi Arabia 42 27.04N 35.48E
Damān India 40 20.25N 72.51E
Damān d. India 40 20.10N 73.00E
Damanhūr Egypt 44 31.03N 30.28E
Damar i. Indonesia 37 7.10S128.30E
Damascus see Dimashq Syria 44
Damaturu Nigeria 53 11.49N 11.50E
Damāvand, Qolleh-ye mtn. Iran 43 35.47N 52.04E
Damba Angola 54 6.44S 15.17E
Damen i. China 33 27.58N121.05E
Dāmghān Iran 43 36.09N 54.22E
Damiaoshan China 33 24.43N109.15E
Daming Shan mts. China 33 23.23N108.30E
Dammartin-en-Goële France 15 49.03N 2.41E
Dāmodar r. India 41 22.17N 88.05E
Damoh India 41 23.50N 79.27E
Damongo Ghana 52 9.06N 1.48W
Dampier Australia 62 20.40S116.42E
Dampier, Selat str. Pacific Oc. 37 0.30S130.50E
Dampier Land Australia 62 17.20S123.00E
Damqawt Yemen 45 16.34N 52.50E
Damxung China 41 30.32N 91.06E
Dana Canada 75 52.18N105.42W
Danané Ivory Coast 52 7.21N 8.10W
Da Nang Vietnam 34 16.04N108.13E
Dānāpur India 41 25.38N 85.03E
Danba China 30 30.57N101.55E
Danbury Conn. U.S.A. 85 41.24N 73.26W
Dand Afghan. 40 31.37N 65.41E
Dandaragan Australia 63 30.40S115.42E
Dande r. Angola 54 8.30S 13.23E
Dandeldhura Nepal 41 29.17N 80.36E
Dandenong Australia 67 37.59S145.14E
Dandong China 32 40.10N124.25E
Danger Is. Cook Is. 68 10.53S165.49W
Dangila Ethiopia 49 11.18N 36.54E
Dangqên China 41 31.41N 91.51E
Dangriga Belize 87 16.58N 88.13W
Dangshan China 32 34.25N116.24E
Dangyang China 33 30.52N111.40E
Daniel U.S.A. 80 42.52N110.04W
Daniel's Harbour Canada 77 50.14N 57.35W
Danilov U.S.S.R. 24 58.10N 40.12E
Daning China 32 36.32N110.47E
Danisa Hills Kenya 55 3.10N 39.37E
Danja Nigeria 53 11.29N 7.30E
Danlí Honduras 87 14.02N 86.30W
Dannenberg Germany 20 53.06N 11.05E
Dannevirke New Zealand 60 40.12S176.08E
Dannhauser R.S.A. 56 28.00S 30.03E
Dansville U.S.A. 84 42.34N 77.41W
Dantewāra India 41 18.54N 81.21E
Danube r. Europe 21 45.26N 29.38E
Danube, Mouths of the see Dunării, Delta f. Romania 21
Danville Canada 77 45.47N 72.01W
Danville Ill. U.S.A. 82 40.09N 87.37W
Danville Ky. U.S.A. 85 37.40N 84.49W
Danville Va. U.S.A. 85 36.34N 79.25W
Dan Xian China 33 19.30N109.35E
Daordeng China 32 40.47N119.05E
Daosa India 40 26.53N 76.20E
Daoukro Ivory Coast 52 7.10N 3.58W
Dao Xian China 33 25.32N111.35E
Daozhen China 33 28.46N107.45E
Dapango Togo 52 10.51N 0.15E
Dapingfang China 32 41.25N120.07E
Da Qaidam China 30 37.44N 95.08E
Daqinggou China 32 41.22N114.13E
Daqing Shan mts. China 32 41.00N111.00E
Daqqāq Sudan 49 12.56N 26.58E
Daqq-e Patargān f. Iran 43 33.30N 60.40E
Dar'ā Syria 44 32.37N 36.06E
Dārāb Iran 43 28.45N 54.34E
Darāban Pakistan 40 31.44N 70.20E
Darabani Romania 21 48.11N 26.35E
Darakht-e Yahyá Afghan. 40 31.50N 68.08E
Dārān Iran 43 33.00N 50.27E
Darband, Kūh-e mtn. Iran 43 31.33N 57.08E
Darbhanga India 41 26.10N 85.54E
Darby Mont. U.S.A. 80 46.01N114.11W
Darby Penn. U.S.A. 85 39.54N 75.15W
D'Arcy Canada 74 50.33N122.32W
Dardanelles see Çanakkale Boğazi str. Turkey 19
Dar es Salaam Tanzania 55 6.51S 39.18E
Dar es Salaam d. Tanzania 55 6.45S 39.10E
Dareton Australia 66 34.04S142.04E
Darfield New Zealand 60 43.29S172.07E
Dargan Ata U.S.S.R. 28 40.30N 62.10E
Dargaville New Zealand 60 35.57S173.53E
Dargo Australia 67 37.30S147.16E
Darhan Mongolia 30 49.34N106.23E
Darie Hills Somali Rep. 45 8.15N 47.25E
Darién, Golfo del g. Colombia 90 9.20N 77.30W
Darjeeling India 41 27.02N 88.16E
Darkan Australia 63 33.19S116.42E
Darke Peak mtn. Australia 66 33.28S136.12E
Darling r. Australia 66 34.05S141.57E
Darling Downs f. Australia 65 28.00S149.45E
Darling Range mts. Australia 63 32.00S116.30E
Darlington U.K. 10 54.33N 1.33W
Darlington Point town Australia 67 34.36S146.01E
Darlowe Poland 20 54.26N 16.23E
Darmstadt Germany 20 49.52N 8.30E
Darnah Libya 48 32.45N 22.39E
Darnah d. Libya 48 31.30N 23.30E
Darnétal France 15 49.27N 1.09E
Darnick Australia 66 32.55S143.39E
Darnley, C. Antarctica 96 68.00S 69.00E
Daroca Spain 16 41.09N 1.25W
Darreh Gaz Iran 43 37.22N 59.08E
Dar Rounga f. C.A.R. 49 9.25N 21.30E
Dartmoor Australia 66 37.58S141.19E
Dartmoor Forest hills U.K. 11 50.33N 3.55W
Dartmouth Canada 77 44.40N 63.34W
Dartmouth U.K. 11 50.21N 3.35W
Dartmouth Resr. Australia 67 36.36S147.38E
Dartry Mts. Rep. of Ire. 13 54.23N 8.25W
Daru P.N.G. 64 9.04S143.12E
Darvaza U.S.S.R. 28 40.12N 58.24E
Darvel, Teluk b. Malaysia 36 4.40N118.30E
Darwen U.K. 10 53.42N 2.29W
Dārwha India 41 20.19N 77.46E
Darwin Australia 64 12.23S130.44E
Daryācheh-ye Bakhtegān l. Iran 43 29.20N 54.05E
Daryācheh-ye Namak l. Iran 43 34.45N 51.36E
Daryācheh-ye Orūmīyeh l. Iran 43 37.40N 45.28E
Daryācheh-ye Sīstān f. Iran 43 31.00N 61.15E
Darya Khān Pakistan 40 31.48N 71.06E
Daryāpur India 40 20.56N 77.20E
Dasāda India 40 23.19N 71.50E
Dasht r. Pakistan 40 25.10N 61.40E
Dashte-e Mārgow des. Afghan. 43 30.45N 63.00E
Dasht-e Kavīr des. Iran 43 34.40N 55.00E
Dasht-e Lūt des. Iran 43 31.30N 58.00E
Dashui Nur China 32 42.45N116.47E
Daspalla India 41 20.21N 84.51E
Dassa-Zoumé Benin 53 7.50N 2.13E
Dastgardān Iran 43 34.19N 56.51E
Dastjerd Iran 43 34.33N 50.15E
Datia India 41 25.40N 78.28E
Datong China 32 40.10N113.15E
Datteln Germany 14 51.40N 7.20E
Datu, Tanjung c. Malaysia 36 2.00N109.30E
Datu Piang Phil. 37 7.02N124.30E
Daua r. Kenya see Dawa r. Ethiopia 49
Dāud Khel Pakistan 40 32.53N 71.34E
Daudnagar India 41 25.02N 84.24E
Daugavpils U.S.S.R. 24 55.52N 26.31E
Daun Germany 14 50.11N 6.50E
Dauphin Canada 75 51.09N100.03W
Dauphiné, Alpes du mts. France 17 44.35N 5.45E
Dauphin L. Canada 75 51.17N 99.48W
Daura Nigeria 53 13.05N 8.18E
Dāvangere India 38 14.30N 75.52E
Davao Phil. 37 7.05N125.38E
Davao G. Phil. 37 6.30N126.00E
Daveluyville Canada 77 46.12N 72.08W
Davenport U.S.A. 82 41.32N 90.36W
Daventry U.K. 11 52.16N 1.10W
David Panama 87 8.26N 82.26W
David-Gorodok U.S.S.R. 21 52.04N 27.10E
Davis U.S.A. 80 38.33N121.44W
Davis Creek town U.S.A. 80 41.44N120.24W
Davis Sea Antarctica 96 66.00S 90.00E
Davis Str. N. America 73 66.00N 58.00W
Davlekanovo U.S.S.R. 24 54.12N 55.00E
Davos Switz. 20 46.47N 9.50E
Dawa China 32 40.58N122.00E
Dawa r. Ethiopia 49 4.11N 42.06E
Dawaxung China 41 31.26N 85.06E
Dawlish U.K. 11 50.34N 3.28W
Dawna Range mts. Burma 34 17.00N 98.00E
Dawson Canada 72 64.04N139.24W
Dawson U.S.A. 85 31.47N 84.27W
Dawson Creek town Canada 74 55.45N120.15W
Dawson Range f. Canada 72 62.40N139.00W
Dawu China 30 31.00N101.09E
Dax France 17 43.43N 1.03W
Daxian China 33 31.10N107.28E
Daxing China 32 39.44N116.20E
Daylesford Australia 66 37.22S144.12E
Dayman r. Uruguay 93 31.25S 58.00W
Dayong Hunan China 33 29.06N110.24E
Dayr az Zawr Syria 42 35.20N 40.08E
Dayton N.Y. U.S.A. 76 42.25N 78.58W
Dayton Ohio U.S.A. 84 39.45N 84.10W
Dayton Tenn. U.S.A. 85 35.30N 85.01W
Dayton Wash. U.S.A. 80 46.19N117.59W
Daytona Beach town U.S.A. 85 29.11N 81.01W
Dayu China 33 25.24N114.22E
Da Yunhe canal China 32 39.10N117.12E
Dazhu China 33 30.50N107.12E
De Aar R.S.A. 56 30.39S 24.01E
Dead Sea Jordan 44 31.25N 35.30E
Deal U.K. 11 51.13N 1.25E
De'an China 33 29.20N115.46E
Deán Funes Argentina 92 30.25S 64.20W
Dearborn U.S.A. 84 42.18N 83.14W
Dease r. Canada 74 59.54N128.30W
Dease Arm b. Canada 72 66.52N119.37W
Dease L. Canada 74 58.05N130.04W
Death Valley f. U.S.A. 81 36.30N117.00W
Death Valley town U.S.A. 81 36.18N116.25W
Death Valley Nat. Monument U.S.A. 80 36.30N117.00W
Deauville France 15 49.21N 0.04E
Debar Yugo. 19 41.31N 20.31E
Debica Poland 21 50.04N 21.24E
Deblin Poland 21 51.35N 21.50E
Deborah, L. Australia 63 30.45S119.07E
Debre Birhan Ethiopia 49 9.40N 39.33E
Debrecen Hungary 21 47.30N 21.37E
Debre Tabor Ethiopia 49 11.50N 38.05E
Decatur Ala. U.S.A. 85 34.36N 87.00W
Decatur Ga. U.S.A. 85 33.45N 84.17W
Decatur Ill. U.S.A. 82 39.51N 89.32W
Decatur Ind. U.S.A. 84 40.50N 84.57W
Deccan f. India 38 18.30N 77.30E
Decelles, Lac l. Canada 76 47.40N 78.10W
Dechu India 40 26.47N 72.20E
Děčín Czech. 20 50.48N 14.15E
Decize France 20 46.50N 3.27E
De Cocksdorp Neth. 14 53.12N 4.52E
Decorah U.S.A. 82 43.18N 91.48W
Deda Romania 21 46.57N 24.53E
Dédi Ivory Coast 52 8.34N 3.33W
Dediāpada India 40 21.35N 73.40E
Dedza Malaŵi 55 14.20S 34.24E
Dee r. D. and G. U.K. 12 54.50N 4.05W
Dee r. Grampian U.K. 12 57.07N 2.04W
Dee r. Wales U.K. 10 53.13N 3.05W
Deep B. Canada 74 61.15N116.35W
Deep River town Canada 76 46.04N 77.29W
Deepwater Australia 67 29.26S151.51E
Deep Well Australia 64 24.25S134.05E
Deer Lake town Canada 77 49.07N 57.35W
Deer Lodge U.S.A. 80 46.24N112.44W
Deesa India 40 24.15N 72.10E
Deeth U.S.A. 80 41.04N115.18W
Deex Nugaaleed r. Somali Rep. 45 7.58N 49.52E
Defiance U.S.A. 84 41.17N 84.21W
De Funiak Springs town U.S.A. 85 30.41N 86.08W
Deggendorf Germany 20 48.51N 12.59E
De Grey r. Australia 62 20.12S119.11E
Deh Bīd Iran 43 30.38N 53.12E
Dehej India 40 21.42N 72.35E
Dehibat Tunisia 51 32.01N 10.42E
Dehra Dūn India 41 30.19N 78.02E
Dehri India 41 24.52N 84.11E
Deh Shū Afghan. 40 30.28N 63.25E
Dehua China 33 25.30N118.14E
Deinze Belgium 14 50.59N 3.32E
Dej Romania 21 47.08N 23.55E
Deje Sweden 23 59.36N 13.28E
Dejiang China 33 28.19N108.05E
Dek'emhāre Ethiopia 48 15.05N 39.02E
Dekese Zaïre 54 3.25S 21.24E
Dekina Nigeria 53 7.43N 7.04E
De Land U.S.A. 85 29.02N 81.18W
Delano U.S.A. 81 35.41N119.15W
Delārām Afghan. 40 32.11N 63.25E
Delaronde L. Canada 75 54.05N107.05W
Delaware d. U.S.A. 85 39.10N 75.30W
Delaware r. U.S.A. 85 39.20N 75.25W
Delaware town U.S.A. 84 40.18N 83.06W
Delaware B. U.S.A. 85 39.05N 75.15W
Delaware Water Gap town U.S.A. 85 40.59N 75.09W
Delaware Water Gap Nat. Recreation Area U.S.A. 85 41.07N 75.06W
Delegate Australia 67 37.03S148.58E
Delfinópolis Brazil 94 20.21S 46.51W
Delft Neth. 14 52.01N 4.23E
Delfzijl Neth. 14 53.20N 6.56E
Delgado, C. Mozambique 55 10.45S 40.38E
Delhi India 40 28.40N 77.13E
Delhi d. India 40 28.37N 77.10E
Delicias Mexico 81 28.13N105.28W
Délimbé C.A.R. 49 9.53N 22.37E
Delingha China 30 37.16N 97.12E
Dell City U.S.A. 81 31.56N105.12W
Delmar U.S.A. 85 38.27N 75.34W
Delmarva Pen. U.S.A. 85 38.48N 75.47W
Delmenhorst Germany 20 53.03N 8.37E
De Long Mts. U.S.A. 72 68.20N162.00W
Delorme, Lac l. Canada 77 54.40N 69.50W
Delphos U.S.A. 84 40.50N 84.21W
Del Rio U.S.A. 83 29.22N100.54W
Delta Colo. U.S.A. 80 38.44N108.04W
Delta Utah U.S.A. 80 39.21N112.35W
Delungra Australia 67 29.38S150.50E
Demak Indonesia 37 6.53S110.40E
Demba Zaïre 54 5.28S 22.14E
Dembi Ethiopia 49 8.05N 36.27E
Dembia C.A.R. 49 5.07N 24.25E
Dembī Dolo Ethiopia 49 8.30N 34.48E
Demer r. Belgium 14 50.59N 4.42E
Deming U.S.A. 81 32.16N107.45W
Demmin Germany 20 53.54N 13.02E
Demmitt Canada 74 55.20N119.50W
Demonte Italy 15 44.19N 7.17E
Demopolis U.S.A. 83 32.31N 87.50W
Demotte U.S.A. 84 41.07N 87.14W
Dêmqog China 41 32.43N 79.29E
Denain France 14 50.20N 3.24E
Denakil f. Ethiopia 49 13.00N 41.00E
Denbigh U.K. 10 53.11N 3.25W
Den Burg Neth. 14 53.03N 4.47E
Dendermonde Belgium 14 51.01N 4.07E
Dendre r. Belgium 14 51.01N 4.07E
Dengkou China 32 40.18N106.59E
Deng Xian China 32 32.44N112.00E
Denham Australia 62 25.54S113.35E
Denham Range mts. Australia 64 21.55S147.46E
Den Helder Neth. 14 52.58N 4.46E
Denia Spain 16 38.51N 0.07E
Deniliquin Australia 67 35.33S144.58E
Denison Iowa U.S.A. 82 42.01N 95.21W
Denison Tex. U.S.A. 83 33.45N 96.33W
Denizli Turkey 42 37.46N 29.05E
Denman Australia 67 32.23S150.42E
Denmark Australia 63 34.54S117.25E
Denmark Europe 23 55.50N 10.00E
Denmark Str. Greenland / Iceland 95 66.00N 25.00W
Den Oever Neth. 14 52.56N 5.01E
Denpasar Indonesia 37 8.40S115.14E
Denton Mont. U.S.A. 80 47.19N109.57W
Denton Tex. U.S.A. 83 33.13N 97.08W
D'Entrecasteaux, Pt. Australia 63 34.50S116.00E
D'Entrecasteaux, Recifs reef N. Cal. 68 18.00S163.10E
D'Entrecasteaux Is. P.N.G. 64 9.30S150.40E
Denver U.S.A. 80 39.43N105.01W
Denys r. Canada 76 55.05N 77.22W
Deo r. Cameroon 53 8.33N 12.45E
Deogarh mtn. India 41 23.32N 82.16E
Deogarh Madhya P. India 41 24.33N 78.15E
Deogarh Orissa India 41 21.32N 84.44E
Deogarh Rāj. India 40 25.32N 73.54E
Deogarh Hills India 41 23.45N 82.30E

Deoghar India 41 24.29N 86.42E
Deolāli India 40 19.57N 73.50E
Deoli India 40 25.45N 75.23E
Deori India 41 23.08N 78.41E
Deoria India 41 26.31N 83.47E
Deori Khās India 41 23.24N 79.01E
Deosil India 41 23.42N 82.15E
De Peel f. Belgium 14 51.30N 5.50E
Depew U.S.A. 84 42.54N 78.41W
Dêqên China 30 28.45N 98.58E
De Queen U.S.A. 83 34.02N 94.21W
De Quincy U.S.A. 83 30.27N 93.26W
Dera Bugti Pakistan 40 29.02N 69.09E
Dera Ghāzi Khān Pakistan 40 30.03N 70.38E
Dera Ismāīl Khān Pakistan 40 31.50N 70.54E
Derazhnya U.S.S.R. 21 49.18N 27.28E
Derbent U.S.S.R. 43 42.03N 48.18E
Derby Tas. Australia 65 41.08S147.47E
Derby W.A. Australia 62 17.19S123.38E
Derby U.K. 10 52.55N 1.28W
Derby N.Y. U.S.A. 76 42.41N 78.58W
Derbyshire d. U.K. 10 52.55N 1.28W
Derg, Lough Donegal Rep. of Ire. 13 54.37N 7.55W
Derg, Lough Tipperary Rep. of Ire. 13 52.57N 8.18W
De Ridder U.S.A. 83 30.51N 93.17W
Dernieres, Isles is. U.S.A. 83 29.02N 90.47W
Déroute, Passage de la str. France/U.K. 11 49.10N 1.45W
Derrynasaggart Mts. Rep. of Ire. 13 51.58N 9.15W
Derryveagh Mts. Rep. of Ire. 13 55.00N 8.07W
Derudeb Sudan 48 17.32N 36.06E
Derval France 15 47.40N 1.40W
Derwent r. Cumbria U.K. 10 54.38N 3.34W
Derwent r. Derbys. U.K. 9 52.52N 1.19W
Derwent r. N. Yorks. U.K. 10 53.44N 0.57W
Desaguadero r. Bolivia 92 18.24S 67.05W
Desappointement, Îles du is. Pacific Oc. 69 14.02S141.24W
Descanso Mexico 81 32.14N116.58W
Deschutes r. U.S.A. 80 45.38N120.54W
Desē Ethiopia 49 11.05N 39.41E
Deseado Argentina 93 47.39S 65.20W
Deseado r. Argentina 93 47.45S 65.50W
Desenzano del Garda Italy 15 45.28N 10.32E
Deserta Grande is. Madeira Is. 95 32.32N 16.30W
Desert Center U.S.A. 81 33.44N115.25W
Deshnoke India 40 27.48N 73.21E
Des Moines r. U.S.A. 82 40.22N 91.26W
Des Moines Iowa U.S.A. 82 41.35N 93.37W
Des Moines N.Mex. U.S.A. 80 36.46N103.50W
Desna r. U.S.S.R. 21 50.32N 30.37E
De Soto U.S.A. 83 38.08N 90.33W
Dessau Germany 20 51.51N 12.15E
Dete Zimbabwe 56 18.39S 26.49E
Detroit U.S.A. 84 42.23N 83.05W
Detroit Lakes town U.S.A. 82 46.49N 95.51W
Deūlgaon Rāja India 40 20.01N 76.02E
Deurne Belgium 14 51.13N 4.26E
Deurne Neth. 14 51.29N 5.44E
Deutsche Bucht b. Germany 20 54.00N 8.15E
Deva Romania 21 45.54N 22.55E
Deventer Neth. 14 52.15N 6.10E
Deveron r. U.K. 12 57.40N 2.30W
Devikot India 40 26.42N 71.12E
Devil's Bridge U.K. 11 52.23N 3.50W
Devils Lake town U.S.A. 82 48.07N 98.59W
Devin Bulgaria 19 41.44N 24.24E
Devizes U.K. 11 51.21N 2.00W
Devon d. U.K. 11 50.50N 3.40W
Devon I. Canada 73 75.00N 86.00W
Devonport Australia 65 41.09S146.16E
Devrez r. Turkey 42 41.07N 34.25E
Dewās India 40 22.58N 76.04E
De Witt U.S.A. 83 34.18N 91.20W
Dewsbury U.K. 10 53.42N 1.38W
Dexter Mo. U.S.A. 83 36.48N 89.57W
Deyang China 33 31.05N104.18E
Dey-Dey L. Australia 65 29.12S131.02E
Dez r. Iran 43 31.38N 48.54E
Dezadeash L. Canada 74 60.28N136.58W
Dezfūl Iran 43 32.24N 48.27E
Dezhou China 32 37.23N116.16E
Dezh Shāhpūr Iran 43 35.31N 46.10E
Dhahab Egypt 44 28.30N 34.31E
Dhahran see Az̧ Z̧ahrān Saudi Arabia 43
Dhaka Bangla. 41 23.43N 90.25E
Dhamār Yemen 45 14.33N 44.24E
Dhamtari India 41 20.41N 81.34E
Dhānbād India 41 23.48N 86.27E
Dhandhuka India 40 22.22N 71.59E
Dhangarhi Nepal 41 28.41N 80.38E
Dhankuta Nepal 41 26.59N 87.21E
Dhār India 40 22.36N 75.18E
Dharampur India 40 20.32N 73.11E
Dharān Bāzār Nepal 41 26.49N 87.17E
Dharangaon India 40 21.01N 75.16E
Dhāri India 40 21.20N 71.01E
Dharmābād India 41 18.54N 77.51E
Dharmjaygarh India 41 22.28N 83.13E
Dharmsāla India 40 32.13N 76.19E
Dhārni India 40 21.33N 76.53E
Dhaulāgiri mtn. Nepal 41 28.42N 83.31E
Dhebar L. India 40 24.16N 74.00E
Dhenkānāl India 41 20.40N 85.36E
Dhiinsoor Somali Rep. 45 2.28N 43.00E
Dhodhekánisos is. Greece 19 37.00N 27.00E
Dholka India 40 22.43N 72.28E
Dholpur India 41 26.42N 77.54E
Dhorāji India 40 21.44N 70.27E
Dhrāngadhra India 40 22.59N 71.28E
Dhrol India 40 22.34N 70.25E
Dhubri India 41 26.02N 89.58E
Dhule India 40 20.54N 74.47E
Dhuliān India 41 24.41N 87.58E
Dhuudo Somali Rep. 45 9.20N 50.14E
Dialakoro Mali 52 12.18N 7.54W
Diamante Argentina 93 32.05S 60.35W
Diamantina r. Australia 64 26.45S139.10E
Diamantina Brazil 94 18.17S 43.37W
Diamantina, Chapada hills Brazil 91 13.00S 42.30W
Diamantino Brazil 94 14.25S 56.29W
Diamond Harbour India 41 22.12N 88.12E
Diana's Peak mtn. St. Helena 95 15.58S 5.42W
Dianbai China 33 21.30N111.01E
Diane Bank is. Australia 64 15.50S149.48E
Dianjiang China 33 30.14N107.27E
Diapaga Burkina 53 12.04N 1.48E
Dibai India 41 28.13N 78.15E
Dibaya Zaïre 54 6.31S 22.57E
Dibi Cameroon 53 7.09N 13.43E
Dibrugarh India 39 27.29N 94.56E
Dibs Sudan 49 14.18N 24.23E
Dickinson U.S.A. 82 46.53N102.47W
Dicle r. Turkey see Dijlah r. Asia 42
Didcot U.K. 11 51.36N 1.14W
Didiéni Mali 52 14.05N 7.50W
Didwāna India 40 27.24N 74.34E
Die France 17 44.45N 5.23E
Diefenbaker, L. Canada 75 51.00N106.55W
Diekirch Lux. 14 49.52N 6.10E
Diélette France 15 49.33N 1.52W
Diéma Mali 52 14.32N 9.03W
Diemen Neth. 14 52.22N 4.58E
Diemuchuoke Jammu & Kashmir 41 32.42N 79.29E
Dien Bien Phu Vietnam 34 21.23N103.02E
Diepholz Germany 20 52.35N 8.21E
Dieppe France 15 49.55N 1.05E
Dierdorf Germany 14 50.33N 7.38E
Dieren Neth. 14 52.03N 6.06E
Dierks U.S.A. 83 34.07N 94.01W
Diesdorf Germany 20 52.45N 10.52E
Diest Belgium 14 50.59N 5.03E
Dieuze France 17 48.49N 6.43E
Dif Kenya 55 1.04N 40.57E
Diffa Niger 53 13.19N 12.35E
Diffa d. Niger 53 16.00N 13.00E
Dig India 40 27.28N 77.25E
Digby Canada 77 44.30N 65.47W
Dighton U.S.A. 82 38.29N100.28W
Digne France 17 44.05N 6.14E
Digoin France 17 46.29N 3.59E
Digras India 41 20.07N 77.43E
Digri Pakistan 40 25.10N 69.07E
Digul r. Indonesia 37 7.10S139.08E
Dijlah r. Asia 43 31.00N 47.27E
Dijle r. Belgium 14 51.02N 4.25E
Dijon France 17 47.20N 5.02E
Dikhil Djibouti 49 11.06N 42.22E
Dikili Turkey 19 39.05N 26.52E
Dikirnis Egypt 44 31.05N 31.35E
Dikodougou Ivory Coast 52 9.00N 5.45W
Diksmuide Belgium 14 51.01N 2.52E
Dikwa Nigeria 53 12.01N 13.55E
Dili Indonesia 37 8.35S125.35E
Dilley U.S.A. 83 28.40N 99.10W
Dilling Sudan 49 12.03N 29.39E
Dillingham U.S.A. 72 59.02N158.29W
Dillon U.S.A. 80 45.13N112.38W
Dilolo Zaïre 54 10.39S 22.20E
Dimashq Syria 44 33.30N 36.19E
Dimbelenge Zaïre 54 5.32S 23.04E
Dimbokro Ivory Coast 52 6.43N 4.46W
Dimboola Australia 66 36.27S142.02E
Dîmbovița r. Romania 21 44.13N 26.22E
Dimitrovgrad Bulgaria 19 42.01N 25.34E
Dimona Israel 44 31.04N 35.01E
Dinagat i. Phil. 37 10.15N125.30E
Dinājpur Bangla. 41 25.38N 88.38E
Dinan France 17 48.27N 2.02W
Dinant Belgium 14 50.16N 4.55E
Dinar Turkey 42 38.05N 30.09E
Dīnār, Kūh-e mtn. Iran 43 30.45N 51.39E
Dinara Planina mts. Yugo. 20 44.00N 16.30E
Dindar r. Sudan 48 14.06N 33.40E
Dindar Nat. Park Sudan 49 12.00N 35.00E
Dindigul India 38 10.23N 78.00E
Dindori India 41 22.57N 81.05E
Dinga Pakistan 40 25.26N 67.10E
Dingbian China 32 37.36N107.38E
Dinggyê China 41 28.18N 88.06E
Dingle Rep. of Ire. 13 52.09N 10.17W
Dingle B. Rep. of Ire. 13 52.05N 10.12W
Dingolfing Germany 20 48.38N 12.31E
Dinguiraye Guinea 52 11.19N 10.49W
Dingwall U.K. 12 57.35N 4.26W
Dingxi China 32 35.33N104.32E
Ding Xian China 32 38.30N115.00E
Dingxing China 32 39.17N115.46E
Dinokwe Botswana 56 23.24S 26.40E
Dinuba U.S.A. 81 36.32N119.23W
Diö Sweden 23 56.38N 14.13E
Diodār India 40 24.06N 71.47E
Dioïla Mali 52 12.30N 6.49W
Diourbel Senegal 52 14.30N 16.10W
Diplo Pakistan 40 24.28N 69.35E
Dipolog Phil. 37 8.34N123.28E
Dirdal Norway 23 58.47N 6.14E
Diré Mali 52 16.16N 3.24W
Direction, C. Australia 64 12.51S143.32E
Dirē Dawa Ethiopia 49 9.35N 41.50E
Dirico Angola 54 17.58S 20.40E
Dirj Libya 51 30.09N 10.26E
Dirk Hartog I. Australia 62 25.50S113.00E
Dirranbandi Australia 67 28.35S148.10E
Disappointment, L. Australia 62 23.30S122.55E
Disaster B. Australia 67 37.20S149.58E
Discovery Canada 72 63.10N113.58W
Discovery B. Australia 66 38.12S141.07E
Disko i. Greenland 73 69.45N 53.00W
Diss U.K. 11 52.23N 1.06E
District of Columbia d. U.S.A. 85 38.55N 77.00W
Distrito Federal d. Brazil 91 15.45S 47.50W
Distrito Federal d. Mexico 86 19.20N 99.10W
Disūq Egypt 44 31.09N 30.39E
Diu India 40 20.42N 70.59E
Diu d. India 40 20.45N 70.59E
Diver Canada 76 46.44N 79.30W
Dives r. France 15 49.19N 0.05W
Divinópolis Brazil 94 20.08S 44.55W
Divnoye U.S.S.R. 25 45.55N 43.21E
Divo Ivory Coast 52 5.48N 5.15W
Divriği Turkey 42 39.23N 38.06E
Dīwāl Qol Afghan. 40 34.19N 67.54E
Dixcove Ghana 52 4.49N 1.57W
Dixie U.S.A. 80 45.34N115.28W
Dixon Ill. U.S.A. 82 41.50N 89.29W
Dixon N.Mex. U.S.A. 81 36.12N105.33W
Dixon Entrance str. U.S.A./Canada 74 54.25N132.30W
Diyālā r. Iraq 43 33.13N 44.33E
Diyarbakir Turkey 42 37.55N 40.14E
Dja r. Cameroon 54 1.38N 16.03E
Djabéta Gabon 54 0.45N 14.00E
Djado Niger 53 21.00N 12.20E
Djado, Plateau du f. Niger 53 22.00N 12.30E
Djambala Congo 54 2.33S 14.38E
Djanet Algeria 51 24.34N 9.29E
Djelfa Algeria 51 34.40N 3.15E
Djema C.A.R. 49 6.03N 25.19E
Djénne Mali 52 13.55N 4.31W
Djerba, Île de i. Tunisia 51 33.48N 10.54E
Djerid, Chott f. Tunisia 51 33.42N 8.26E
Djibo Burkina 52 14.09N 1.38W
Djibouti Africa 49 12.00N 42.50E
Djibouti town Djibouti 49 11.35N 43.11E
Djilbabo Plain f. Ethiopia 49 4.00N 39.10E
Djolu Zaïre 54 0.35N 22.28E
Djouah r. Gabon 54 1.16N 13.12E
Djougou Benin 53 9.40N 1.47E
Djugu Zaïre 55 1.55N 30.31E
Djúpivogur Iceland 22 64.41N 14.16W
Dmitriya Lapteva, Proliv str. U.S.S.R. 29 73.00N142.00E
Dnepr r. U.S.S.R. 21 50.00N 31.00E
Dneprodzerzhinsk U.S.S.R. 25 48.30N 34.37E
Dnepropetrovsk U.S.S.R. 25 48.29N 35.00E
Dneprovskaya Nizmennost f. U.S.S.R. 21 52.30N 29.45E
Dneprovsko-Bugskiy Kanal U.S.S.R. 21 52.03N 25.35E
Dnestr r. U.S.S.R. 21 46.21N 30.20E
Dno U.S.S.R. 24 57.50N 30.00E
Doba Chad 53 8.40N 16.50E
Dobane C.A.R. 49 6.24N 24.42E
Dobele U.S.S.R. 23 56.37N 23.16E
Dobo Indonesia 37 5.46S134.13E
Doboj Yugo. 21 44.44N 18.02E
Dobrodzień Poland 21 50.44N 18.27E
Dobruja f. Romania 21 44.30N 28.15E
Dobrush U.S.S.R. 21 52.24N 31.19E
Dobryanka U.S.S.R. 24 58.30N 56.26E
Dobzha China 41 28.28N 88.13E
Doce r. Brazil 94 19.32S 39.57W
Docking U.K. 10 52.55N 0.39E
Doda Jammu & Kashmir 40 33.08N 75.34E
Doda, Lac l. Canada 76 49.24N 75.14W
Dodecanese is. see Dhodhekánisos is. Greece 19
Dodge City U.S.A. 83 37.45N100.01W
Dodman Pt. U.K. 11 50.13N 4.48W
Dodoma Tanzania 55 6.10S 35.40E
Dodoma d. Tanzania 55 6.00S 36.00E
Dodson U.S.A. 80 48.24N108.15W
Doetinchem Neth. 14 51.57N 6.17E
Dogai Coring l. China 39 34.30N 89.00E
Dog Creek town Canada 74 51.35N122.14W
Dogger Bank f. North Sea 9 54.45N 2.00E
Doğubayazit Turkey 43 39.32N 44.08E
Do'gyaling China 41 31.58N 88.24E
Doha see Ad Dawḩah Qatar 43
Dohad India 40 22.50N 74.16E
Dohhi India 41 24.32N 84.54E
Doilungdêqên China 41 30.06N 90.32E
Dokkum Neth. 14 53.20N 6.00E
Dokri Pakistan 40 27.23N 68.06E
Dolbeau Canada 77 48.53N 72.14W
Dol-de-Bretagne France 15 48.33N 1.45W
Dole France 17 47.05N 5.30E
Dolgellau U.K. 11 52.44N 3.53W
Dolina U.S.S.R. 21 49.00N 23.59E
Dolinskaya U.S.S.R. 25 48.06N 32.46E
Dollard b. Germany 14 53.20N 7.10E
Dolný Kubín Czech. 21 49.12N 19.17E
Dolomiti mts. Italy 15 46.25N 11.50E
Dolores Argentina 93 36.19S 57.40W
Dolores Mexico 81 28.53N108.27W
Dolores Uruguay 93 33.33S 58.13W
Dolores U.S.A. 80 37.28N108.30W
Dolphin and Union Str. Canada 72 69.20N118.00W
Doma Nigeria 53 8.23N 8.21E
Domadare Somali Rep. 49 1.48N 41.13E
Domažlice Czech. 20 49.27N 12.56E
Dombås Norway 23 62.05N 9.08E
Dombe Grande Angola 54 13.00S 13.06E
Dombey, C. Australia 66 37.12S139.43E
Dombóvár Hungary 21 46.23N 18.08E
Domburg Neth. 14 51.35N 3.31E
Domfront France 15 48.36N 0.39W
Dominica Windward Is. 87 15.30N 61.30W
Dominican Republic C. America 87 18.00N 70.00W
Dominion L. Canada 77 52.40N 61.42W
Dommel r. Neth. 14 51.44N 5.17E
Domo Ethiopia 45 7.54N 46.52E
Domodossola Italy 15 46.07N 8.17E
Domuyo mtn. Argentina 93 36.37S 70.28W
Don Mexico 81 26.26N109.02W
Don r. England U.K. 10 53.41N 0.50W
Don r. Scotland U.K. 12 57.10N 2.05W
Don r. U.S.S.R. 25 47.06N 39.16E
Donaghadee U.K. 13 54.39N 5.33W
Donald Australia 66 36.25S143.04E
Donaldsonville U.S.A. 83 30.06N 90.59W
Donau r. Germany see Danube r. Europe 20
Donaueschingen Germany 20 47.57N 8.29E
Donauwörth Germany 20 48.44N 10.48E
Don Benito Spain 16 38.57N 5.52W
Doncaster U.K. 10 53.31N 1.09W
Dondaicha India 40 21.20N 74.34E
Dondo Angola 54 9.40S 14.25E
Dondo Mozambique 57 19.39S 34.39E
Donegal Rep. of Ire. 13 54.39N 8.06W
Donegal d. Rep. of Ire. 13 54.52N 8.00W
Donegal B. Rep. of Ire. 13 54.32N 8.18W
Donegal Pt. Rep. of Ire. 13 52.43N 9.38W
Donetsk U.S.S.R. 25 48.00N 37.50E
Donga Nigeria 53 7.45N 10.05E
Donga r. Nigeria 53 8.20N 10.00E
Dongara Australia 63 29.15S114.56E
Dongargarh India 41 21.12N 80.44E
Dongbei Pingyuan f. China 32 42.30N123.00E
Dongchuan China 30 26.10N103.02E
Dongco China 41 32.07N 84.35E
Dongfang China 33 19.05N108.39E
Donggala Indonesia 36 0.48S119.45E
Donggou China 32 39.52N124.08E
Dongguang China 32 37.53N116.32E
Donghai China 32 34.35N118.49E
Donghai i. China 33 21.02N110.25E
Dong Hoi Vietnam 34 17.32N106.35E
Dong Jiang r. China 33 23.00N113.33E
Dongkalang Indonesia 37 0.12N120.07E
Dongling China 32 41.44N123.32E
Dongou Congo 54 2.05N 18.00E
Dongping Hu l. China 32 35.55N116.15E
Dongqiao China 41 31.57N 90.30E
Dongsheng China 32 39.49N109.59E
Dongtai China 32 32.42N120.26E
Dongting Hu l. China 33 29.10N113.00E
Dongtou i. China 33 27.50N121.08E
Dong Ujimqin Qi China 32 45.33N116.50E
Dongxi China 33 28.42N106.40E
Dongxing China 33 21.33N107.58E
Donington U.K. 10 52.55N 0.12W
Donja Stubica Yugo. 20 45.59N 15.58E
Dönna i. Norway 22 66.05N 12.30E
Donnacona Canada 77 46.40N 71.47W
Donnybrook Australia 63 33.34S115.47E
Donnybrook R.S.A. 56 29.55S 29.51E
Doodlakine Australia 63 31.41S117.23E
Doolow Somali Rep. 45 4.13N 42.08E
Doon, Loch U.K. 12 55.15N 4.23W
Dora, L. Australia 62 22.05S122.55E
Dora Baltea r. Italy 15 45.11N 8.05E
Doran L. Canada 75 61.13N108.06W
Dora Riparia r. Italy 15 45.05N 7.44E
Dorchester U.K. 11 50.52N 2.28W
Dorchester, C. Canada 73 65.29N 77.30W
Dordogne r. France 17 45.03N 0.34W
Dordrecht Neth. 14 51.48N 4.40E
Dordrecht R.S.A. 56 31.22S 27.02E
Dore, Mont mtn. France 17 45.32N 2.49E
Doré L. Canada 75 54.46N107.17W
Dori Burkina 52 14.03N 0.02W
Dorion Canada 77 45.23N 74.03W
Dorking U.K. 11 51.14N 0.20W
Dormagen Germany 14 51.05N 6.50E
Dormans France 15 49.04N 3.38E
Dornie U.K. 12 57.16N 5.31W
Dornoch U.K. 12 57.52N 4.02W
Dornoch Firth est. U.K. 12 57.50N 4.04W
Dornogovi d. Mongolia 32 44.00N110.00E
Dornum Germany 14 53.39N 7.26E
Doro Mali 52 16.09N 0.51W
Dorohoi Romania 21 47.57N 26.24E
Dörpen Germany 14 52.58N 7.20E
Dorre I. Australia 62 25.08S113.06E
Dorrigo Australia 67 30.20S152.41E
Dorris U.S.A. 80 41.58N121.55W
Dorset d. U.K. 11 50.48N 2.25W
Dorset, C. Canada 73 64.10N 76.40W
Dorsten Germany 14 51.38N 6.58E
Dortmund Germany 14 51.32N 7.27E
Dortmund-Ems Kanal Germany 14 52.20N 7.30E
Dorval Canada 77 45.27N 73.44W
Dos Bahías, C. Argentina 93 44.55S 65.32W
Dosquet Canada 77 46.28N 71.32W
Dosso Niger 53 13.03N 3.10E
Dosso d. Niger 53 13.00N 3.15E
Dossor U.S.S.R. 25 47.31N 53.01E
Dothan U.S.A. 85 31.12N 85.25W
Douai France 14 50.22N 3.05E
Douako Guinea 52 9.45N 10.08W
Douala Cameroon 53 4.05N 9.43E
Douarnenez France 17 48.05N 4.20W
Double Mer g. Canada 77 54.05N 59.00W
Doubs r. France 17 46.57N 5.03E
Doubtless B. New Zealand 60 35.10S173.30E
Doudeville France 15 49.43N 0.48E
Douentza Mali 52 14.58N 2.48W
Douglas R.S.A. 56 29.03S 23.45E
Douglas U.K. 10 54.09N 4.29W
Douglas Ariz. U.S.A. 81 31.21N109.33W
Douglas Ga. U.S.A. 85 31.30N 82.54W
Douglas Mich. U.S.A. 84 42.38N 86.13W
Douglas Wyo. U.S.A. 80 42.45N105.24W
Douglas Creek r. Australia 66 28.35S136.50E
Doulaincourt France 17 48.19N 5.12E
Doulevant-le-Château France 15 48.23N 4.55E
Doumé Cameroon 53 4.13N 13.30E
Douna Mali 52 12.40N 6.00W
Dounreay U.K. 12 58.35N 3.42W
Dourados Brazil 92 22.09S 54.52W
Dourdan France 15 48.32N 2.01E
Douro r. Portugal 16 41.10N 8.40W
Douvres France 15 49.17N 0.23W
Dove r. Derbys. U.K. 10 52.50N 1.35W
Dover U.K. 11 51.07N 1.19E
Dover Del. U.S.A. 85 39.10N 75.32W
Dover N.H. U.S.A. 84 43.12N 70.56W
Dover N.J. U.S.A. 85 40.53N 74.34W
Dover Ohio U.S.A. 84 40.32N 81.30W
Dover Tenn. U.S.A. 85 36.30N 87.50W
Dover, Pt. Australia 63 32.32S125.30E
Dover, Str. of U.K. 11 51.00N 1.30E
Dovey r. U.K. 11 52.33N 3.56W
Dovrefjell mts. Norway 23 62.06N 9.25E
Dovsk U.S.S.R. 21 53.07N 30.29E
Dowa Malaŵi 55 13.40S 33.55E
Dowagiac U.S.A. 84 41.58N 86.06W
Dowerin Australia 63 31.15S117.00E
Dowlatābād Iran 43 28.19N 56.40E
Dowlat Yār Afghan. 40 34.33N 65.47E
Down d. U.K. 13 54.20N 6.00W
Downey U.S.A. 80 42.26N112.07W
Downham Market U.K. 11 52.36N 0.22E
Downpatrick U.K. 13 54.21N 5.43W
Downpatrick Head Rep. of Ire. 13 54.20N 9.22W
Downton, Mt. Canada 74 52.42N124.51W
Dowra Rep. of Ire. 13 54.11N 8.02W
Doylestown U.S.A. 85 40.19N 75.08W
Dozois, Résr. Canada 76 47.30N 77.00W
Drâa, Hamada du f. Algeria 50 29.00N 6.00W
Drâa, Oued wadi Morocco 50 28.40N 11.06W
Drachten Neth. 14 53.05N 6.06E
Drăgăşani Romania 21 44.40N 24.16E
Dragoman, Pasul pass Bulgaria/Yugo. 19 42.56N 22.52E
Dragon's Mouth str. Trinidad 90 11.00N 61.35W
Dragovishtitsa Bulgaria 19 42.22N 22.39E
Draguignan France 17 43.32N 6.28E
Drake Australia 67 28.55S152.24E
Drake U.S.A. 82 47.55N100.23W
Drakensberg mts. R.S.A./Lesotho 56 30.00S 29.05E
Drake Passage str. Atlantic Oc. 95 59.00S 65.00W
Dráma Greece 19 41.09N 24.11E
Drammen Norway 23 59.44N 10.15E
Drās Jammu & Kashmir 40 34.27N 75.46E
Drau r. Austria see Drava r. Yugo. 20
Drava r. Yugo. 21 45.34N 18.56E
Drayton Valley town Canada 74 53.25N114.58W
Drenthe d. Neth. 14 52.52N 6.30E
Dresden Germany 20 51.03N 13.45E
Dreux France 15 48.44N 1.23E
Driftwood Canada 76 49.08N 81.23W
Drin r. Albania 19 41.45N 19.34E
Drina r. Yugo. 21 44.53N 19.20E
Dröbak Norway 23 59.39N 10.39E
Drogheda Rep. of Ire. 13 53.42N 6.23W
Drogobych U.S.S.R. 21 49.10N 23.30E
Droitwich U.K. 11 52.16N 2.10W
Drokiya U.S.S.R. 21 48.07N 27.49E
Dromedary, C. Australia 67 36.18S150.15E
Dronero Italy 15 44.28N 7.22E
Dronfield U.K. 10 53.18N 1.29W
Dronne r. France 17 45.02N 0.09W
Dronning Maud Land f. Antarctica 96 74.00S 10.00E
Drumheller Canada 74 51.25N112.40W
Drum Hills Rep. of Ire. 13 52.03N 7.42W
Drummond Range mts. Australia 64 23.30S147.15E
Drummondville Canada 77 45.53N 72.30W
Drummore U.K. 12 54.41N 4.54W
Druskininkai U.S.S.R. 21 53.48N 23.58E
Drut r. U.S.S.R. 21 53.03N 30.42E
Drvar Yugo. 20 44.22N 16.24E
Dry B. U.S.A. 74 59.08N138.25W
Dryden Canada 76 49.47N 92.50W
Drymen U.K. 12 56.04N 4.27W
Drysdale r. Australia 62 13.59S126.51E
Dschang Cameroon 53 5.28N 10.02E
Dua r. Zaïre 54 3.12N 20.55E
Du'an China 33 24.01N108.06E
Duaringa Australia 64 23.42S149.40E
Ḑubā Saudi Arabia 42 27.21N 35.40E
Dubai see Dubayy U.A.E. 43
Dubawnt r. Canada 73 62.50N102.00W
Dubawnt L. Canada 75 63.04N101.42W
Dubayy U.A.E. 43 25.13N 55.17E
Dubbo Australia 67 32.16S148.41E
Dubica Yugo. 20 45.11N 16.48E
Dublin Rep. of Ire. 13 53.21N 6.18W
Dublin d. Rep. of Ire. 13 53.20N 6.18W
Dublin U.S.A. 85 32.31N 82.54W
Dublin B. Rep. of Ire. 13 53.20N 6.09W
Dubno U.S.S.R. 21 50.28N 25.40E
Dubois Idaho U.S.A. 80 44.10N112.14W
Du Bois Penn. U.S.A. 84 41.07N 78.46W
Dubovka U.S.S.R. 25 49.04N 44.48E
Dubréka Guinea 52 9.50N 13.32W
Dubrovitsa U.S.S.R. 21 51.38N 26.40E
Dubrovnik Yugo. 19 42.40N 18.07E
Dubuque U.S.A. 82 42.30N 90.41W
Duchesne U.S.A. 80 40.10N110.24W
Duchess Australia 64 21.22S139.52E
Ducie I. Pacific Oc. 69 24.40S124.48W
Du Couëdic, C. Australia 66 36.00S136.10E
Dudhnai India 41 25.59N 90.44E
Dudinka U.S.S.R. 29 69.27N 86.13E
Dudley U.K. 11 52.30N 2.05W
Dudna r. India 40 19.07N 76.54E
Duékoué Ivory Coast 52 6.50N 7.22W
Duero r. Spain see Douro r. Portugal 16

Duff Creek *town* Australia 66 28.28S135.51E
Dufftown U.K. 12 57.27N 3.09W
Duga Resa Yugo. 20 45.27N 15.30E
Dugi *i.* Yugo. 20 44.04N 15.00E
Du Gué *r.* Canada 77 57.20N 70.48W
Duifken Pt. Australia 64 12.33S141.38E
Duisburg Germany 14 51.26N 6.45E
Duitama Colombia 90 5.50N 73.01W
Duiveland *i.* Neth. 14 51.39N 4.00E
Dujuuma Somali Rep. 55 1.14N 42.37E
Dukambīya Ethiopia 48 14.42N 37.30E
Duk Fadiat Sudan 49 7.45N 31.25E
Duk Faiwil Sudan 49 7.30N 31.29E
Dukhān Qatar 43 25.24N 50.47E
Duki Pakistan 40 30.09N 68.34E
Dukou China 30 26.33N101.44E
Dukye Dzong Bhutan 41 27.20N 89.30E
Dulce *r.* Argentina 92 30.40S 62.00W
Duleek Rep. of Ire. 13 53.39N 6.24W
Dülmen Germany 14 51.49N 7.17E
Dulovo Bulgaria 21 43.49N 27.09E
Duluth U.S.A. 82 46.47N 92.06W
Dūmā Syria 44 33.33N 36.24E
Dumaguete Phil. 37 9.20N123.18E
Dumai Indonesia 36 1.41N101.27E
Dumaran *i.* Phil. 36 10.33N119.50E
Dumaresq *r.* Australia 67 28.40S150.28E
Dumaring Indonesia 36 1.36N118.12E
Dumas Ark. U.S.A. 83 33.53N 91.29W
Dumas Tex. U.S.A. 83 35.52N101.58W
Dumbarton U.K. 12 55.57N 4.35W
Dumbleyung Australia 63 33.18S117.42E
Dumbrăveni Romania 21 46.14N 24.35E
Dum-Dum India 41 22.35N 88.24E
Dumfries U.K. 12 55.04N 3.37W
Dumfries and Galloway *d.* U.K. 12 55.05N 3.40W
Dumka India 41 24.16N 87.15E
Dumraon India 41 25.33N 84.09E
Dumyāṭ Egypt 44 31.26N 31.48E
Duna *r.* Hungary *see* Danube *r.* Europe 21
Dunaföldvár Hungary 21 46.48N 18.55E
Dunajec *r.* Poland 21 50.15N 20.44E
Dunajská Streda Czech. 21 48.01N 17.35E
Dunany Pt. Rep. of Ire. 13 53.51N 6.15W
Dunărea *r.* Romania *see* Danube *r.* Europe 21
Dunării, Delta *f.* Romania 21 45.05N 29.45E
Dunav *r.* Bulgaria *see* Danube *r.* Europe 21
Dunav *r.* Yugo. *see* Danube *r.* Europe 21
Dunbar U.K. 12 56.00N 2.31W
Dunblane U.K. 12 56.12N 3.59W
Dunboyne Rep. of Ire. 13 53.26N 6.30W
Duncan Canada 74 48.45N123.40W
Duncan *r.* Canada 74 50.11N116.57W
Duncan U.S.A. 83 34.30N 97.57W
Duncan, C. Canada 76 52.40N 80.48W
Duncan L. N.W.T. Canada 74 62.51N113.58W
Duncan L. Que. Canada 76 53.35N 77.55W
Duncansby Head U.K. 12 58.39N 3.01W
Dundalk Rep. of Ire. 13 54.01N 6.25W
Dundalk U.S.A. 85 39.15N 76.31W
Dundalk B. Rep. of Ire. 13 53.55N 6.17W
Dundas Canada 76 43.16N 79.58W
Dundas, L. Australia 63 32.35S121.50E
Dundas I. Canada 74 54.33N130.50W
Dundas Str. Australia 64 11.20S131.35E
Dundee R.S.A. 56 28.09S 30.14E
Dundee U.K. 12 56.28N 3.00W
Dundgovi *d.* Mongolia 32 45.00N106.00E
Dundrum U.K. 13 54.16N 5.51W
Dundrum B. U.K. 13 54.12N 5.46W
Dunedin New Zealand 60 45.52S170.30E
Dunedin U.S.A. 85 28.02N 82.47W
Dunedoo Australia 67 32.00S149.25E
Dunfermline U.K. 12 56.04N 3.29W
Dungannon U.K. 13 54.31N 6.47W
Düngarpur India 40 23.50N 73.43E
Dungarvan Rep. of Ire. 13 52.06N 7.39W
Dungeness *c.* U.K. 11 50.55N 0.58E
Dungiven U.K. 13 54.56N 6.56W
Dungog Australia 67 32.24S151.46E
Dungu Zaïre 55 3.40N 28.40E
Dunhuang China 30 40.00N 94.40E
Dunkeld Qld. Australia 66 26.55S148.00E
Dunkeld Vic. Australia 66 37.40S142.23E
Dunkeld U.K. 12 56.34N 3.36W
Dunkerque France 14 51.02N 2.23E
Dunk I. Australia 64 17.56S146.10E
Dunkirk *see* Dunkerque France 14
Dunkirk U.S.A. 84 42.29N 79.21W
Dunkwa Central Ghana 52 5.59N 1.45W
Dun Laoghaire Rep. of Ire. 13 53.17N 6.09W
Dunlap U.S.A. 82 41.51N 95.36W
Dunleer Rep. of Ire. 13 53.49N 6.24W
Dunmahon Rep. of Ire. 13 52.09N 7.23W
Dunmarra Australia 64 16.37S133.22E
Dunmore U.S.A. 84 41.25N 75.38W
Dunnet Head U.K. 12 58.40N 3.23W
Dunning U.S.A. 82 41.50N100.06W
Dunnville Canada 76 42.54N 79.36W
Dunolly Australia 66 36.50S143.45E
Dunoon U.K. 12 55.57N 4.57W
Dunqulah Sudan 48 19.10N 30.29E
Dunqunāb Sudan 48 21.06N 37.05E
Duns U.K. 12 55.47N 2.20W
Dunsborough Australia 63 33.37S115.06E
Dunshaughlin Rep. of Ire. 13 53.30N 6.34W
Dunstable U.K. 11 51.53N 0.32W
Dunstan Mts. New Zealand 60 44.45S169.45E
Dunster Canada 74 53.08N119.50W
Dunyāpur Pakistan 40 29.48N 71.44E
Duolun China 32 42.09N116.21E
Duong Dong Vietnam 34 10.12N103.57E
Dupont U.S.A. 84 38.53N 85.30W
Duque de Caxias Brazil 94 22.47S 43.18W
Du Quoin U.S.A. 83 38.01N 89.14W
Duran U.S.A. 81 34.28N105.24W
Durance *r.* France 17 43.55N 4.48E
Durango Mexico 86 24.01N104.00W
Durango *d.* Mexico 83 24.30N104.00W
Durango Spain 16 43.13N 2.40W
Durango U.S.A. 80 37.16N107.53W
Durant U.S.A. 83 34.00N 96.23W
Durazno Uruguay 93 33.22S 56.31W
Durban R.S.A. 56 29.50S 30.59E
Durbe U.S.S.R. 23 56.35N 21.21E
Dureji Pakistan 40 25.53N 67.18E
Düren Germany 14 50.48N 6.30E
Durg India 41 21.11N 81.17E
Durgāpur India 41 23.29N 87.20E
Durham U.K. 10 54.47N 1.34W
Durham *d.* U.K. 10 54.42N 1.45W
Durham N.C. U.S.A. 85 36.00N 78.54W
Durham N.H. U.S.A. 84 43.08N 70.56W
Durham Sud Canada 77 45.39N 72.19W
Durlston Head *c.* U.K. 11 50.35N 1.58W
Durmitor *mtn.* Yugo. 19 43.08N 19.03E
Durness U.K. 12 58.33N 4.45W
Durrës Albania 19 41.19N 19.27E
Durrow Rep. of Ire. 13 52.51N 7.25W
Dursey Head Rep. of Ire. 13 51.35N 10.15W
Durūz, Jabal ad *mtn.* Syria 44 32.42N 36.42E
D'Urville I. New Zealand 60 40.45S173.50E
Dushak U.S.S.R. 28 37.13N 60.01E
Dushan China 33 25.50N107.30E
Dushanbe U.S.S.R. 30 38.38N 68.51E
Duskotna Bulgaria 19 42.52N 27.10E
Düsseldorf Germany 14 51.13N 6.47E
Dutch Creek *town* Canada 74 50.18N115.58W
Dutlhe Botswana 56 23.55S 23.47E
Dutton, L. Australia 66 31.49S137.08E
Duvno Yugo. 21 43.43N 17.14E
Duxun China 33 23.57N117.37E
Duyun China 33 26.12N107.29E
Dvina *r.* U.S.S.R. 28 57.03N 24.02E
Dvinskaya Guba *b.* U.S.S.R. 24 64.40N 39.30E
Dwarda Australia 63 32.45S116.23E
Dwārka India 40 22.14N 68.58E
Dwellingup Australia 63 32.42S116.04E
Dyatlovichi U.S.S.R. 21 52.08N 30.49E
Dyatlovo U.S.S.R. 21 53.28N 25.28E
Dyer, C. Canada 73 67.45N 61.45W
Dyérem *r.* Cameroon 53 6.36N 13.10E
Dyer Plateau Antarctica 96 70.00S 65.00W
Dyersburg U.S.A. 83 36.03N 89.23W
Dyfed *d.* U.K. 11 52.00N 4.17W
Dykh Tau *mtn.* U.S.S.R. 25 43.04N 43.10E
Dymer U.S.S.R. 21 50.50N 30.20E
Dyulevo Bulgaria 19 42.22N 27.10E
Dyultydag *mtn.* U.S.S.R. 43 41.55N 46.52E
Dzamïn Üüd Mongolia 32 43.50N111.53E
Dzerzhinsk B.S.S.R. U.S.S.R. 21 53.40N 27.01E
Dzerzhinsk R.S.F.S.R. U.S.S.R. 24 56.15N 43.30E
Dzhambul U.S.S.R. 30 42.50N 71.25E
Dzhankoy U.S.S.R. 25 45.42N 34.23E
Dzhardzhan U.S.S.R. 29 68.49N124.08E
Dzhelinde U.S.S.R. 29 70.09N114.00E
Dzhetygara U.S.S.R. 28 52.14N 61.10E
Dzhezkazgan U.S.S.R. 28 47.48N 67.24E
Dzhizak U.S.S.R. 28 40.06N 67.45E
Dzhugdzhur, Khrebet *mts.* U.S.S.R. 29 57.30N138.00E
Dzhurin U.S.S.R. 21 48.40N 28.16E
Działdowo Poland 21 53.15N 20.10E
Dzierzoniów Poland 20 50.44N 16.39E
Dzodze Ghana 52 6.14N 1.00E

E

Eabamet L. Canada 76 51.30N 88.00W
Eads U.S.A. 82 38.29N102.47W
Eagle *r.* Canada 77 53.35N 57.25W
Eagle U.S.A. 82 39.39N106.50W
Eagle Butte *town* U.S.A. 82 45.00N101.14W
Eagle Grove U.S.A. 82 42.40N 93.54W
Eagle L. U.S.A. 84 46.17N 69.20W
Eagle Lake *town* U.S.A. 84 47.02N 68.36W
Eagle Pass *town* U.S.A. 83 28.43N100.30W
Eagle River *town* U.S.A. 82 45.55N 89.15W
Ealing U.K. 11 51.31N 0.20W
Earlimart U.S.A. 81 35.53N119.16W
Earn *r.* U.K. 12 56.21N 3.18W
Earn, Loch U.K. 12 56.23N 4.12W
Easingwold U.K. 10 54.08N 1.11W
Easky Rep. of Ire. 13 54.17N 8.58W
Easley U.S.A. 85 34.50N 82.34W
East Alligator *r.* Australia 64 12.25S132.58E
East Anglian Heights *hills* U.K. 11 52.03N 0.15E
East Aurora U.S.A. 76 42.46N 78.37W
East B. U.S.A. 83 29.30N 94.35W
Eastbourne U.K. 11 50.46N 0.18E
East C. New Zealand 60 37.45S178.30E
East Caroline Basin Pacific Oc. 68 3.00N147.00E
East China Sea Asia 31 29.00N125.00E
East Dereham U.K. 9 52.40N 0.57E
Easter I. *see* Pascua, Isla de *i.* Pacific Oc. 69
Eastern *d.* Ghana 52 6.20N 0.45W
Eastern *d.* Kenya 55 0.00 38.00E
Eastern Desert *see* Sharqīyah, Aş Şaḩrā' ash *des.* Egypt 44
Eastern Ghāts *mts.* India 39 16.30N 80.30E
Easterville Canada 75 53.06N 99.53W
East Falkland *i.* Falkland Is. 93 51.45W 58.50W
East Grand Forks U.S.A. 82 47.56N 96.55W
East Grinstead U.K. 11 51.08N 0.01W
East Ilsley U.K. 11 51.33N 1.15W
East Kilbride U.K. 12 55.46N 4.09W
East Lansing U.S.A. 84 42.45N 84.30W
Eastleigh U.K. 11 50.58N 1.21W
East London R.S.A. 56 33.00S 27.54E
Eastmain Canada 76 52.15N 78.30W
Eastmain *r.* Canada 76 52.15N 78.30W
Eastman Canada 77 45.18N 72.19W
Easton Md. U.S.A. 85 38.46N 76.04W
Easton Penn. U.S.A. 85 40.41N 75.13W
Easton Wash. U.S.A. 80 47.14N121.11W
East Orange U.S.A. 85 40.46N 74.14W
East Pacific Ridge Pacific Oc. 69 15.00S112.00W
East Point *town* U.S.A. 85 33.41N 84.29W
East Retford U.K. 10 53.19N 0.55W
East St. Louis U.S.A. 82 38.34N 90.04W
East Sussex *d.* U.K. 11 50.56N 0.12E
Eaton U.S.A. 82 40.32N104.42W
Eau Claire U.S.A. 82 44.50N 91.30W
Eau-Claire, Lac à l' *l.* Canada 76 56.10N 74.30W
Eauripik *i.* Caroline Is. 37 6.42N143.04E
Eauripik-N. Guinea Rise Pacific Oc. 68 2.00N141.00E
Eban Nigeria 53 9.41N 4.54E
Ebbw Vale U.K. 11 51.47N 3.12W
Ebebiyin Equat. Guinea 54 2.09N 11.20E
Eberswalde Germany 20 52.50N 13.50E
Ebinur Hu *l.* China 30 45.00N 83.00E
Ebola *r.* Zaïre 49 3.20N 20.57E
Eboli Italy 18 40.37N 15.04E
Ebolowa Cameroon 54 2.56N 11.11E
Ebon *i.* Pacific Oc. 68 4.38N168.43E
Ebony Namibia 56 22.05S 15.15E
Ebro *r.* Spain 16 40.43N 0.54E
Ebro, Delta del *f.* Spain 16 40.43N 0.54E
Ecclefechan U.K. 10 55.03N 3.18W
Echeng China 33 30.26N114.00E
Echternach Lux. 14 49.49N 6.25E
Echuca Australia 67 36.10S144.20E
Écija Spain 16 37.33N 5.04W
Écommoy France 15 47.50N 0.16E
Ecuador S. America 90 1.40S 79.00W
Ēd Ethiopia 48 13.52N 41.40E
Ed Sweden 23 58.55N 11.55E
Edam Neth. 14 52.30N 5.02E
Eday *i.* U.K. 8 59.11N 2.47W
Eddrachillis B. U.K. 12 58.17N 5.15W
Eddystone Pt. Australia 65 40.58S148.12E
Ede Neth. 14 52.03N 5.40E
Ede Nigeria 53 7.45N 4.26E
Edea Cameroon 54 3.47N 10.15E
Edehon L. Canada 75 60.25N 97.15W
Eden Australia 67 37.04S149.54E
Eden *r.* Cumbria U.K. 10 54.57N 3.02W
Eden U.S.A. 80 42.03N109.26W
Edenburg R.S.A. 56 29.44S 25.55E
Edendale New Zealand 60 46.19S168.47E
Edenderry Rep. of Ire. 13 53.21N 7.05W
Edenhope Australia 66 37.04S141.20E
Edenton U.S.A. 85 36.04N 76.39W
Edeowie Australia 66 31.28S138.29E
Eder *r.* Germany 20 51.13N 9.27E
Ederny U.K. 13 54.32N 7.40W
Edgeley U.S.A. 82 40.07N 98.43W
Edgeöya *i.* Arctic Oc. 96 77.45N 22.30E
Edgeworthstown Rep. of Ire. 13 53.42N 7.38W
Édhessa Greece 19 40.47N 22.03E
Ediacara Australia 66 30.18S137.50E
Edina Liberia 52 6.01N 10.10W
Edinburgh U.K. 12 55.57N 3.13W
Edirne Turkey 19 41.40N 26.35E
Edithburgh Australia 66 35.06S137.44E
Edjudina Australia 63 29.48S122.23E
Edmond U.S.A. 83 35.39N 97.29W
Edmonton Canada 74 53.30N113.30W
Edmundston Canada 77 47.22N 68.20W
Edna U.S.A. 83 28.59N 96.39W
Edo *r.* Japan 35 35.37N139.53E
Edolo Italy 15 46.11N 10.20E
Edounga Gabon 54 0.03S 13.43E
Edremit Turkey 19 39.35N 27.02E
Edsbruk Sweden 23 58.02N 16.28E
Edson Canada 74 53.35N116.26W
Edward, L. Uganda/Zaïre 55 0.30S 29.30E
Edwards Plateau *f.* U.S.A. 83 31.20N101.00W
Eeklo Belgium 14 51.11N 3.34E
Eel *r.* U.S.A. 80 40.40N124.20W
Efate *i.* Vanuatu 68 17.40S168.25E
Effingham U.S.A. 82 39.07N 88.33W
Egaña Argentina 93 36.57S 59.06W
Egbe Nigeria 53 8.13N 5.31E
Egeland U.S.A. 82 48.38N 99.10W
Eger Hungary 21 47.54N 20.23E
Egersund Norway 23 58.27N 6.00E
Egerton, Mt. Australia 62 24.44S117.40E
Egg Harbor U.S.A. 85 39.32N 74.39W
Egmont, Mt. New Zealand 60 39.20S174.05E
Egridir Turkey 42 37.52N 30.51E
Egridir Gölü *l.* Turkey 42 38.04N 30.55E
Egypt Africa 48 26.00N 30.00E
Eiao *i.* Is. Marquises 69 8.00S140.40W
Éibar Spain 16 43.11N 2.28W
Eidsvåg Norway 22 62.47N 8.03E
Eidsvold Australia 64 25.23S151.08E
Eifel *f.* Germany 14 50.10N 6.45E
Eigg *i.* U.K. 12 56.53N 6.09W
Eighty Mile Beach *f.* Australia 62 19.00S121.00E
Eil, Loch U.K. 12 56.51N 5.12W
Eildon, L. Australia 67 37.10S146.00E
Einasleigh Australia 64 18.31S144.05E
Eindhoven Neth. 14 51.26N 5.30E
Eirunepé Brazil 90 6.40S 69.52W
Eiseb *r.* Namibia 56 20.26S 20.05E
Eisenach Germany 20 50.59N 10.19E
Eisenerz Austria 20 47.33N 14.53E
Eisenhut *mtn.* Austria 20 47.00N 13.45E
Eisenhüttenstadt Germany 20 52.09N 14.41E
Eišiškes U.S.S.R. 21 54.09N 24.55E
Eisleben Germany 20 51.32N 11.33E
Eitort Germany 14 50.46N 7.27E
Ejde Faroe Is. 8 62.03N 7.06W
Ejin Qi China 30 41.50N100.50E
Ejura Ghana 52 7.24N 1.20W
Ekalaka U.S.A. 80 45.53N104.33W
Eket Nigeria 53 4.39N 7.56E
Eketahuna New Zealand 60 40.39S175.44E
Ekibastuz U.S.S.R. 28 51.45N 75.22E
Ekimchan U.S.S.R. 29 53.09N133.00E
Eksjö Sweden 23 57.40N 14.47E
Ekträsk Sweden 22 64.29N 19.50E
Ekuku Zaïre 54 0.42S 21.38E
Ekwan *r.* Canada 76 53.30N 84.00W
El Aaiún W. Sahara 50 27.09N 13.12W
Elands *r.* Trans. R.S.A. 56 24.52S 29.20E
El Arco Mexico 81 28.00N113.25W
El Arenal Spain 16 39.30N 2.45E
El Asnam Algeria 51 36.10N 1.20E
Elat Israel 44 29.33N 34.56E
Elâzig Turkey 42 38.41N 39.14E
Elba *i.* Italy 18 42.47N 10.17E
El Barril Mexico 81 28.22N113.00W
Elbasan Albania 19 41.07N 20.04E
El Baúl Venezuela 90 8.59N 68.16W
Elbe *r.* Germany 20 53.33N 10.00E
El Beni *d.* Bolivia 92 14.00S 65.30W
Elbert, Mt. U.S.A. 82 39.07N106.27W
Elberton U.S.A. 85 34.05N 82.54W
Elbeuf France 15 49.17N 1.01E
Elbistan Turkey 42 38.14N 37.11E
Elbląg Poland 21 54.10N 19.25E
Elbrus *mtn.* U.S.S.R. 25 43.21N 42.29E
Elburg Neth. 14 52.27N 5.50E
Elburz Mts. *see* Alborz, Reshteh-ye Kūhhā-ye *ye* Iran 43
El Cajon U.S.A. 81 32.48N116.58W
El Callao Venezuela 90 7.18N 61.48W
El Campo U.S.A. 83 29.12N 96.16W
El Casco Mexico 83 25.34N104.35W
El Centro U.S.A. 81 32.48N115.34W
Elche Spain 16 38.16N 0.41W
Elcho U.S.A. 82 45.26N 89.11W
Elcho I. Australia 64 11.55S135.45E
El Corral Mexico 83 25.09N 97.58W
El Cozón Mexico 81 31.18N112.29W
El Cuy Argentina 93 39.57S 68.20W
Elda Spain 16 38.29N 0.47W
Elde *r.* Germany 20 53.17N 12.40E
El Der Ethiopia 45 5.08N 43.08E
Elder, L. Australia 66 30.39S140.13E
El Desemboque Mexico 81 29.30N112.27W
El Djouf *des.* Mauritania 50 20.30N 7.30W
Eldon U.S.A. 82 38.21N 93.35W
Eldorado Canada 75 59.35N108.30W
El Dorado Ark. U.S.A. 83 33.13N 92.40W
El Dorado Kans. U.S.A. 83 37.49N 96.52W
El Dorado Venezuela 90 6.45N 61.37W
Eldoret Kenya 55 0.31N 35.17E
Electra U.S.A. 83 34.02N 98.55W
El Eglab *f.* Algeria 50 26.30N 4.15W
Elei, Wādi Sudan 48 22.04N 34.27E
Eleja U.S.S.R. 23 56.26N 23.42E
Elektrostal U.S.S.R. 24 55.46N 38.30E
Elephant Butte Resr. U.S.A. 81 33.19N107.10W
Elephant I. Antarctica 96 61.00S 55.00W
El Eulma Algeria 51 36.09N 5.41E
Eleuthera I. Bahamas 87 25.15N 76.20W
Elevtheroúpolis Greece 19 40.55N 24.16E
El Ferrol Spain 16 43.29N 8.14W
Elgå Norway 23 62.11N 11.07E
Elgin Canada 75 49.26N100.15W
Elgin U.K. 12 57.39N 3.20W
Elgin Ill. U.S.A. 82 42.03N 88.19W
Elgin Nev. U.S.A. 80 37.21N114.30W
Elgin Oreg. U.S.A. 80 45.34N117.55W
Elgin Tex. U.S.A. 83 30.21N 97.22W
El Golea Algeria 51 30.34N 2.53E
Elgon, Mt. Kenya/Uganda 55 1.07N 34.35E
Elida U.S.A. 83 33.57N103.39W
Elim Namibia 56 17.47S 15.30E
Elista U.S.S.R. 25 46.18N 44.14E
Elizabeth Australia 66 34.45S138.39E
Elizabeth N.J. U.S.A. 85 40.40N 74.13W
Elizabeth W.Va. U.S.A. 84 39.04N 81.24W
Elizabeth City U.S.A. 85 36.18N 76.16W
Elizabethtown Ky. U.S.A. 85 37.41N 85.51W
Elizabethtown Penn. U.S.A. 85 40.09N 76.36W
El Jadida Morocco 50 33.16N 8.30W
Elk *r.* Canada 74 49.10N115.14W
Elk Poland 21 53.50N 22.22E
El Kairouan Tunisia 51 35.41N 10.07E
El Kasserine Tunisia 51 35.11N 8.48E
Elk City U.S.A. 83 35.25N 99.25W
El Kef Tunisia 51 36.11N 8.43E
El-Kelâa-des-Srarhna Morocco 50 32.02N 7.23W
Ēl Kerē Ethiopia 49 5.48N 42.10E
Elkhart Ind. U.S.A. 82 41.52N 85.56W
Elkhart Kans. U.S.A. 83 37.00N101.54W
El Khnâchich *f.* Mali 52 21.50N 3.45W
Elkhorn Canada 75 49.58N101.14W
Elkhovo Bulgaria 19 42.10N 26.35E
Elkins N.Mex. U.S.A. 81 33.41N104.04W
Elkins W.Va. U.S.A. 84 38.55N 79.51W
Elko U.S.A. 80 40.50N115.46W
Elkton Md. U.S.A. 85 39.36N 75.50W
Elleker Australia 63 34.55S117.40E
Ellen, Mt. U.S.A. 78 38.06N110.50W
Ellendale Australia 62 17.56S124.48E
Ellensburg U.S.A. 80 47.00N120.32W
Ellesmere I. Canada 73 78.00N 82.00W
Ellesmere Port U.K. 10 53.17N 2.55W
Elliot R.S.A. 56 31.19S 27.49E
Elliot Lake *town* Canada 76 46.35N 82.35W
Elliott Australia 64 17.33S133.31E
Ellis U.S.A. 82 38.56N 99.34W
Elliston Australia 66 33.39S134.55E
Ellon U.K. 12 57.22N 2.05W
Ellora India 40 20.01N 75.10E
El Mahdia Tunisia 51 35.30N 11.04E
Elmali Turkey 42 36.43N 29.56E
El Maneadero Mexico 81 31.45N116.35W
Elmer U.S.A. 85 39.36N 75.10W
El Metlaoui Tunisia 51 34.20N 8.24E
Elmhurst U.S.A. 82 41.54N 87.56W
Elmina Ghana 52 5.07N 1.21W
Elmira U.S.A. 84 42.06N 76.49W
Elmore Australia 67 36.30S144.40E
El Mreiti *well* Mauritania 50 23.29N 7.52W
El Mreyyé *f.* Mauritania 50 19.30N 7.00W
Elmshorn Germany 20 53.46N 9.40E
El Niybo Ethiopia 49 4.32N 39.59E
El Ouassi *well* Mali 52 20.23N 0.12E
El Oued Algeria 51 33.20N 6.53E
Eloy U.S.A. 81 32.45N111.33W
El Paso U.S.A. 81 31.45N106.29W
El Portal U.S.A. 80 37.41N119.47W
El Quelite Mexico 81 23.32N106.28W
El Real Panama 87 8.06N 77.42W
El Reno U.S.A. 83 35.32N 97.57W
El Roba Kenya 55 3.57N 40.01E
Elrose Canada 75 51.13N108.01W
El Salto Mexico 81 23.47N105.22W
El Salvador C. America 87 13.30N 89.00W
Elsas Canada 76 48.32N 82.55W
Elsdorf Germany 14 50.56N 6.35E
Elsinore U.S.A. 80 38.41N112.09W
El Sueco Mexico 81 29.54N106.24W
El Tabacal Argentina 92 23.15S 64.14W
El Tigre Venezuela 90 8.44N 64.18W
Elton, Ozero *l.* U.S.S.R. 25 49.10N 46.34E
El Turbio Argentina 93 51.41S 72.05W
Elūru India 39 16.45N 81.10E
Elvas Portugal 16 38.53N 7.10W
Elvdal Norway 23 61.38N 11.56E
Elverum Norway 23 60.53N 11.34E
Elvira Argentina 93 35.15S 59.30W
El Wak Kenya 55 2.45N 40.52E
Elwood Nebr. U.S.A. 82 40.36N 99.52W
Elwood N.J. U.S.A. 85 39.35N 74.43W
Ely U.K. 9 52.24N 0.16E
Ely Minn. U.S.A. 82 47.53N 91.52W
Ely Nev. U.S.A. 80 39.15N114.53W
Elyria U.S.A. 84 41.22N 82.06W
Emae *i.* Vanuatu 68 17.04S168.24E
Emāmshahr Iran 43 36.25N 55.00E
Emån *r.* Sweden 23 57.08N 16.30E
Emba U.S.S.R. 28 48.47N 58.05E
Emba *r.* U.S.S.R. 25 46.38N 53.00E
Embarcación Argentina 92 23.15S 64.10W
Embleton U.K. 10 55.30N 1.37W
Embrun France 17 44.34N 6.30E
Embu Kenya 55 0.32S 37.28E
Emden Germany 14 53.23N 7.13E
Emerald Australia 64 23.32S148.10E
Emerson Canada 75 49.00N 97.12W
Emi Koussi *mtn.* Chad 53 19.58N 18.30E
Emilia-Romagna *d.* Italy 15 44.35N 11.00E
Emlichheim Germany 14 52.37N 6.50E
Emmaboda Sweden 23 56.38N 15.32E
Emmaste U.S.S.R. 23 58.42N 22.36E
Emmaus U.S.A. 85 40.32N 75.30W
Emmaville Australia 67 29.25S151.39E
Emmeloord Neth. 14 52.43N 5.46E
Emmen Neth. 14 52.48N 6.55E
Emmerich Germany 14 51.49N 6.16E
Emmett U.S.A. 80 43.52N116.30W
Emmitsburg U.S.A. 85 39.42N 77.20W
Emory Peak *mtn.* U.S.A. 83 29.13N103.17W
Empalme Mexico 81 27.58N110.51W
Empangeni R.S.A. 57 28.45S 31.54E
Empedrado Argentina 92 27.59S 58.47W
Emporia Kans. U.S.A. 82 38.24N 96.11W
Emporia Va. U.S.A. 85 36.42N 77.33W
Ems *r.* Germany 14 53.14N 7.25E
Emsdale Canada 76 45.28N 79.18W
Emsdetten Germany 14 52.14N 7.32E
Ems-Jade Kanal Germany 14 53.28N 7.40E
Emyvale Rep. of Ire. 13 54.20N 6.59W
Enard B. U.K. 12 58.05N 5.20W
Encarnación Paraguay 94 27.20S 55.50W
Enchi Ghana 52 5.53N 2.48W
Encinal U.S.A. 83 28.02N 99.21W
Encino U.S.A. 81 34.39N105.28W
Encontada, Cerro de la *mtn.* Mexico 81 27.03N112.31W
Encontrados Venezuela 90 9.03N 72.14W
Encounter B. Australia 66 35.35S138.44E
Ende Indonesia 37 8.51S121.40E
Endeavour Str. Australia 64 10.50S142.15E
Enderbury I. Kiribati 68 3.08S171.05W
Enderby Canada 74 50.35N119.10W
Enderby Land *f.* Antarctica 96 67.00S 53.00E
Enderlin U.S.A. 82 46.37N 97.36W
Endicott U.S.A. 84 42.06N 76.03W
Endicott Arm *f.* U.S.A. 74 57.38N133.22W
Endicott Mts. U.S.A. 72 68.00N152.00W
Endola Namibia 56 17.37S 15.50E
Eneabba Australia 63 29.48S115.16E
Enewetak *i.* Pacific Oc. 68 11.30N162.15E
Enfida Tunisia 51 36.08N 10.22E
Enfield U.K. 11 51.40N 0.05W
Engaño, C. Phil. 37 18.30N122.20E
Engcobo R.S.A. 56 31.39S 28.01E
'En Gedi Israel 44 31.28N 35.23E
Engels U.S.S.R. 25 51.30N 46.07E
Enggano *i.* Indonesia 36 5.20S102.15E
Enghershatu *mtn.* Ethiopia 48 16.40N 38.20E
Enghien Belgium 14 50.42N 4.02E
England U.K. 10 53.00N 2.00W

Englewood Colo. U.S.A. **80** 39.39N104.59W
Englewood Fla. U.S.A. **85** 26.58N 82.21W
English Bāzār India **41** 25.00N 88.09E
English Channel U.K. **11** 50.15N 1.00W
English River *town* Canada **76** 49.20N 91.00W
Enid U.S.A. **83** 36.19N 97.48W
Enkhuizen Neth. **14** 52.42N 5.17E
Enköping Sweden **23** 59.38N 17.04E
Enna Italy **18** 37.34N 14.15E
Ennadai Canada **75** 61.08N100.53W
Ennadai L. Canada **75** 61.00N101.00W
Ennedi *f.* Chad **48** 17.15N 22.00E
Enneri Yoo *wadi* Chad **53** 19.24N 16.38E
Enngonia Australia **67** 29.20S145.53E
Ennis Rep. of Ire. **13** 52.51N 9.00W
Ennis U.S.A. **83** 32.20N 96.38W
Enniscorthy Rep. of Ire. **13** 52.30N 6.35W
Enniskillen U.K. **13** 54.21N 7.40W
Ennistymon Rep. of Ire. **13** 52.56N 9.18W
Enns *r.* Austria **20** 48.14N 14.22E
Enontekiö Finland **22** 68.23N 23.38E
Enping China **33** 22.11N112.18E
Ensay Australia **67** 37.24S147.52E
Enschede Neth. **14** 52.13N 6.54E
Ensenada Argentina **93** 34.51S 57.55W
Ensenada Baja Calif. Norte Mexico **81** 31.52N116.37W
Ensenada Nuevo León Mexico **83** 25.56N 97.50W
Enshi China **33** 30.18N109.29E
Enshū-nada *sea* Japan **35** 34.30N137.30E
Entebbe Uganda **55** 0.08N 32.29E
Enterprise Canada **74** 60.47N115.45W
Entre Ríos *d.* Argentina **93** 32.10S 59.00W
Entre Rios de Minas Brazil **94** 20.39S 44.06W
Entwistle Canada **74** 53.30N115.00W
Enugu Nigeria **53** 6.20N 7.29E
Envermeu France **15** 49.53N 1.15E
Envigado Colombia **90** 6.09N 75.35W
Enza *r.* Italy **15** 44.54N 10.31E
Enzan Japan **35** 35.42N138.44E
Eolie, Isole *is.* Italy **18** 38.35N 14.45E
Epe Neth. **14** 52.21N 5.59E
Epernay France **15** 49.02N 3.58E
Ephraim U.S.A. **80** 39.22N111.35W
Ephrata Penn. U.S.A. **85** 40.11N 76.10W
Ephrata Wash. U.S.A. **80** 47.19N119.33W
Epi *i.* Vanuatu **68** 16.43S168.15E
Épila Spain **16** 41.36N 1.17W
pinal France **17** 48.10N 6.28E
pping U.K. **11** 51.42N 0.07E
psom U.K. **11** 51.20N 0.16W
pte *r.* France **15** 49.04N 1.37E
quateur *d.* Zaïre **54** 0.00 21.00E
quatorial Guinea Africa **54** 2.00N 10.00E
querdreville France **15** 49.40N 1.40W
ra, Ozero *l.* U.S.S.R. **25** 47.38N 45.18E
raclea Italy **15** 45.35N 12.40E
rciyaş Daği *mtn.* Turkey **42** 38.33N 35.25E
rdre *r.* France **15** 47.27N 1.34W
rebus, Mt. Antarctica **96** 77.40S167.20E
rechim Brazil **94** 27.35S 52.15W
reğli Konya Turkey **42** 37.30N 34.02E
reğli Zonguldak Turkey **42** 41.17N 31.26E
renhot China **32** 43.48N112.00E
rer *r.* Ethiopia **45** 7.35N 42.05E
rfoud Morocco **50** 31.28N 4.10W
rft *r.* Germany **14** 51.12N 6.45E
rfurt Germany **20** 50.58N 11.02E
rgani Turkey **42** 38.17N 39.44E
rgene *r.* Turkey **19** 41.02N 26.22E
rgig *r.* Chad **53** 11.30N 15.30E
rica Neth. **14** 52.44N 6.56E
rie U.S.A. **84** 42.07N 80.05W
rie, L. Canada/U.S.A. **76** 42.15N 81.00W
riksdale Canada **75** 50.52N 98.06W
riskay *i.* U.K. **12** 57.04N 7.17W
ritrea *f.* Ethiopia **48** 15.30N 38.00E
ritrea *see* Ērtra *d.* Ethiopia **48**
kelenz Germany **14** 51.05N 6.18E
langen Germany **20** 49.36N 11.02E
ldunda Australia **64** 25.14S133.12E
melo Neth. **14** 52.19N 5.38E
melo R.S.A. **56** 26.30S 29.59E
ne *r.* Rep. of Ire. **9** 54.30N 8.17W
née France **15** 48.18N 0.56W
ode India **38** 11.21N 77.43E
omanga *i.* Vanuatu **68** 18.45S169.05E
ota Ethiopia **48** 16.13N 37.57E
Rachidia Morocco **50** 31.58N 4.25W
rego Mozambique **55** 16.02S 37.11E
rigal Mtn. Rep. of Ire. **13** 55.02N 8.08W
ris Head Rep. of Ire. **13** 54.19N 10.00W
tix He *r.* U.S.S.R. **30** 48.00N 84.20E
tra *d.* Ethiopia **48** 15.30N 39.00E
udina Australia **66** 31.30S139.23E
vy-le-Châtel France **15** 48.02N 3.55E
zgebirge *mts.* Germany **20** 50.30N 12.50E
zin U.S.S.R. **30** 50.16N 95.14E
zincan Turkey **42** 39.44N 39.30E
zurum Turkey **42** 39.57N 41.17E
bjerg Denmark **23** 55.28N 8.27E
bo *see* Espoo Finland **23**
calante U.S.A. **80** 37.47N111.36W
calón Mexico **83** 26.45N104.20W
canaba U.S.A. **84** 45.47N 87.04W
ch Lux. **14** 49.31N 5.59E
chweiler Germany **14** 50.49N 6.16E
condido *r.* Nicaragua **87** 11.58N 83.45W
condido U.S.A. **81** 33.07N117.05W
cuinapa Mexico **81** 22.51N105.48W
cuintla Guatemala **86** 14.18N 90.47W
ens Germany **14** 53.40N 7.40E
fahān Iran **43** 32.42N 51.40E
her U.K. **11** 51.23N 0.22W
kanān Iran **43** 27.10N 53.38E
howe R.S.A. **56** 28.53S 31.29E
r. N. Yorks. U.K. **10** 54.29N 0.37W
Eskifjördhur *town* Iceland **22** 65.05N 14.00W
Eskilstuna Sweden **23** 59.22N 16.30E
Eskimo Point *town* Canada **75** 61.10N 94.03W
Eskişehir Turkey **42** 39.46N 30.30E
Esla *r.* Spain **16** 41.29N 6.03W
Eslāmābād-e-Gharb Iran **43** 34.08N 46.35E
Eslöv Sweden **23** 55.50N 13.20E
Esmeraldas Ecuador **90** 0.56N 79.40W
Espanola Canada **76** 46.15N 81.46W
Espe U.S.S.R. **28** 43.50N 74.10E
Esperance Australia **63** 33.49S121.52E
Esperance B. Australia **63** 33.51S121.53E
Esperanza Argentina **93** 31.30S 61.00W
Esperanza Mexico **81** 27.35N109.56W
Espinal Colombia **90** 4.08N 75.00W
Espinhaço, Serra do *mts.* Brazil **94** 17.15S 43.10W
Espírito Santo *d.* Brazil **94** 20.00S 40.30W
Espíritu Santo I. Vanuatu **68** 15.50S166.50E
Espoo Finland **23** 60.13N 24.40E
Espungabera Mozambique **57** 20.28S 32.48E
Esquel Argentina **93** 42.55S 71.20W
Esquimalt Canada **74** 48.30N123.23W
Esquina Argentina **93** 30.00S 59.30W
Essaouira Morocco **50** 31.30N 9.47W
Essen Germany **14** 51.27N 6.57E
Essequibo *r.* Guyana **90** 6.30N 58.40W
Essex *d.* U.K. **11** 51.46N 0.30E
Essex U.S.A. **81** 34.45N115.15W
Essonne *d.* France **15** 48.36N 2.20E
Essoyes France **15** 48.04N 4.32E
Essoyla U.S.S.R. **24** 61.47N 33.11E
Es Suki Sudan **49** 13.24N 33.55E
Est *d.* Burkina **52** 12.45N 0.25E
Est, Pointe de l' *c.* Canada **77** 49.08N 61.41W
Estacado, Llano *f.* U.S.A. **83** 33.30N102.40W
Estados, Isla de los *i.* Argentina **93** 54.45S 64.00W
Eşṭahbānāt Iran **43** 29.05N 54.03E
Estância Brazil **91** 11.15S 37.28W
Estand, Kūh-e *mtn.* Iran **43** 31.18N 60.03E
Este Italy **15** 45.14N 11.39E
Estelline U.S.A. **83** 34.33N100.26W
Estepona Spain **16** 36.26N 5.09W
Esternay France **15** 48.44N 3.34E
Estevan Canada **75** 49.07N103.05W
Estevan Is. Canada **74** 53.03N129.38W
Estevan Pt. Canada **74** 49.23N126.33W
Estherville U.S.A. **82** 43.24N 94.50W
Estissac France **15** 48.16N 3.49E
Estivane Mozambique **57** 24.07S 32.38E
Eston U.K. **10** 54.34N 1.07W
Estonskaya S.S.R. *d.* U.S.S.R. **23** 58.35N 24.35E
Estoril Portugal **16** 38.42N 9.23W
Estrela, Serra da *mts.* Portugal **16** 40.20N 7.40W
Estremoz Portugal **16** 38.50N 7.35W
Esztergom Hungary **21** 47.48N 18.45E
Étables France **17** 48.37N 2.50W
Etadunna Australia **66** 28.43S138.38E
Etah India **41** 27.38N 78.40E
Etamamiou Canada **77** 50.16N 59.58W
Étampes France **15** 48.26N 2.10E
Étaples France **17** 50.31N 1.39E
Etāwah India **41** 26.46N 79.02E
Ethel Creek *town* Australia **62** 23.05S120.14E
Ethiopia Africa **49** 9.00N 39.00E
Etive, Loch U.K. **12** 56.27N 5.15W
Etna, Monte *mtn.* Italy **18** 37.43N 14.59E
Etolin I. U.S.A. **74** 56.10N132.30W
Etosha Game Res. Namibia **56** 18.50S 15.40E
Etosha Pan *f.* Namibia **56** 18.50S 16.20E
Etowah U.S.A. **85** 35.20N 84.30W
Étretat France **15** 49.42N 0.12E
Ettelbrück Lux. **14** 49.51N 6.06E
Eua *i.* Tonga **69** 21.23S174.55W
Euabalong Australia **67** 33.07S146.28E
Eubank U.S.A. **85** 37.16N 84.40W
Euboea *see* Évvoia *i.* Greece **19**
Eucla Australia **63** 31.40S128.51E
Euclid U.S.A. **84** 41.34N 81.33W
Eucumbene, L. Australia **67** 36.05S148.45E
Eudora U.S.A. **83** 33.07N 91.16W
Eudunda Australia **66** 34.09S139.04E
Eufaula Resr. U.S.A. **79** 35.15N 95.35W
Eugene U.S.A. **80** 44.02N123.05W
Eugenia, Punta *c.* Mexico **81** 27.50N115.03W
Eugowra Australia **67** 33.24S148.25E
Eunice La. U.S.A. **83** 30.30N 92.25W
Eunice N.Mex. U.S.A. **83** 32.26N103.09W
Eupen Belgium **14** 50.38N 6.04E
Euphrates *r. see* Nahr al Furāt *r.* Asia **43**
Eurdon U.S.A. **83** 33.55N 93.09W
Eure *d.* France **15** 49.10N 1.00E
Eure *r.* France **15** 48.18N 1.12E
Eure et Loire *d.* France **15** 48.30N 1.30E
Eureka Calif. U.S.A. **80** 40.47N124.09W
Eureka Kans. U.S.A. **83** 37.49N 96.17W
Eureka Nev. U.S.A. **80** 39.31N115.58W
Eureka Utah U.S.A. **80** 39.57N112.07W
Eurinilla *r.* Australia **66** 30.50S140.01E
Euriowie Australia **66** 31.22S141.42E
Euroa Australia **67** 36.46S145.35E
Europa, Picos de *mts.* Spain **16** 43.10N 4.40W
Euskirchen Germany **14** 50.40N 6.47E
Euston Australia **66** 34.34S142.49E
Eutsuk L. Canada **74** 53.20N126.45W
Evale Angola **54** 16.24S 15.50E
Evans, Lac *l.* Canada **76** 50.50N 77.00W
Evans Head *c.* Australia **67** 29.06S153.25E
Evanston Ill. U.S.A. **82** 42.02N 87.41W
Evanston Wyo. U.S.A. **80** 41.16N110.58W
Evansville U.S.A. **84** 38.00N 87.33W
Evelyn Creek *r.* Australia **66** 28.20S134.50E
Everard, C. Australia **67** 37.50S149.16E
Everard, L. Australia **66** 31.25S135.05E
Everard Range *mts.* Australia **65** 27.05S132.28E
Everest, Mt. China/Nepal **41** 27.59N 86.56E
Everett Wash. U.S.A. **80** 47.59N122.13W
Everglades U.S.A. **85** 25.52N 81.23W
Everglades Nat. Park U.S.A. **85** 25.27N 80.53W
Evesham U.K. **11** 52.06N 1.57W
Evijärvi Finland **22** 63.22N 23.29E
Evinayong Equat. Guinea **54** 1.27N 10.34E
Evje Norway **23** 58.36N 7.51E
Évora Portugal **16** 38.34N 7.54W
Évreux France **15** 49.03N 1.11E
Évry France **15** 48.38N 2.27E
Évvoia *i.* Greece **19** 38.30N 23.50E
Ewe, Loch U.K. **12** 57.48N 5.38W
Ewing U.S.A. **82** 42.16N 98.21W
Ewo Congo **54** 0.48S 14.47E
Excelsior Springs *town* U.S.A. **82** 39.20N 94.13W
Exe *r.* U.K. **11** 50.40N 3.28W
Exeter U.K. **11** 50.43N 3.31W
Exeter Nebr. U.S.A. **82** 40.39N 97.27W
Exmoor Forest *hills* U.K. **11** 51.08N 3.45W
Exmore U.S.A. **85** 37.32N 75.49W
Exmouth Australia **62** 21.54S114.10E
Exmouth U.K. **11** 50.37N 3.24W
Exmouth G. Australia **62** 22.00S114.20E
Expedition Range *mts.* Australia **64** 24.30S149.05E
Extremadura *d.* Spain **16** 39.00N 6.00W
Exuma Is. Bahamas **87** 24.00N 76.00W
Eyasi, L. Tanzania **55** 3.40S 35.00E
Eye U.K. **11** 52.19N 1.09E
Eyemouth U.K. **12** 55.52N 2.05W
Eygurande France **17** 45.40N 2.26E
Eyjafjördhur *est.* Iceland **22** 65.54N 18.15W
Eyl Somali Rep. **45** 8.00N 49.51E
Eyrarbakki Iceland **22** 63.52N 21.09W
Eyre *r.* Australia **64** 26.40S139.00E
Eyre, L. Australia **66** 28.30S137.25E
Eyre Pen. Australia **66** 34.00S135.45E
Ezequil Ramos Mexia, Embalse *resr.* Argentina **93** 39.20S 69.00W

F

Faaone Tahiti **69** 17.40S149.18W
Fåberg Norway **23** 61.10N 10.22E
Fåborg Denmark **23** 55.06N 10.15E
Fabriano Italy **18** 43.20N 12.54E
Facatativá Colombia **90** 4.48N 74.32W
Facundo Argentina **93** 45.19S 69.59W
Fada Chad **48** 17.14N 21.33E
Fada-N'Gourma Burkina **52** 12.03N 0.22E
Faenza Italy **15** 44.17N 11.52E
Fafa Mali **52** 15.20N 0.43E
Fafen *r.* Ethiopia **45** 6.07N 44.20E
Fagamalo W. Samoa **68** 13.24S172.22W
Făgăraş Romania **21** 45.51N 24.58E
Fagernes Norway **23** 60.59N 9.17E
Fagersta Sweden **23** 60.00N 15.47E
Faguibine, Lac *l.* Mali **52** 16.45N 3.54W
Fagus Egypt **44** 30.44N 31.47E
Fā'id Egypt **44** 30.19N 32.19E
Fairbanks U.S.A. **72** 64.50N147.50W
Fairborn U.S.A. **84** 39.48N 84.03W
Fairbury U.S.A. **82** 40.08N 97.11W
Fairfax U.S.A. **83** 36.34N 96.42W
Fairfield Ala. U.S.A. **85** 33.29N 86.59W
Fairfield Calif. U.S.A. **80** 38.15N122.03W
Fairfield Ill. U.S.A. **82** 38.22N 88.23W
Fairfield Iowa U.S.A. **82** 40.56N 91.57W
Fair Head U.K. **13** 55.13N 6.09W
Fair Isle U.K. **12** 59.32N 1.38W
Fairlie New Zealand **60** 44.06S170.50E
Fairmont Minn. U.S.A. **82** 43.39N 94.28W
Fairmont W.Va. U.S.A. **84** 39.28N 80.08W
Fairview Canada **74** 56.05N118.25W
Fairview Mont. U.S.A. **80** 47.51N104.03W
Fairview Okla. U.S.A. **83** 36.16N 98.29W
Fairview Utah U.S.A. **80** 39.38N111.26W
Fairweather, Mt. U.S.A. **74** 59.00N137.30W
Faisalābād Pakistan **40** 31.25N 73.05E
Faith U.S.A. **82** 45.02N102.02W
Faizābād India **41** 26.47N 82.08E
Fajr, Wādī *r.* Saudi Arabia **42** 30.00N 38.25E
Fakaofo Pacific Oc. **68** 9.30S171.15W
Fakenham U.K. **10** 52.50N 0.51E
Fakfak Indonesia **37** 2.55S132.17E
Falaise France **15** 48.54N 0.11W
Falam Burma **34** 22.58N 93.45E
Falcarragh Rep. of Ire. **13** 55.08N 8.06W
Falcone, Capo del *c.* Italy **18** 40.57N 8.12E
Falcon Resr. U.S.A. **83** 26.37N 99.11W
Falealupo W. Samoa **68** 13.29S172.47W
Falémé *r.* Senegal **52** 14.55N 12.00W
Faleshty U.S.S.R. **21** 47.30N 27.45E
Falfurrias U.S.A. **83** 27.14N 98.09W
Falkenberg Sweden **23** 56.54N 12.28E
Falkirk U.K. **12** 56.00N 3.48W
Falkland Is. Atlantic Oc. **93** 51.45W 59.00W
Falkland Sd. *str.* Falkland Is. **93** 51.45W 59.25W
Falköping Sweden **23** 58.10N 13.31E
Fallbrook U.S.A. **81** 33.23N117.15W
Fallon U.S.A. **80** 46.50N105.07W
Fall River *town* U.S.A. **84** 41.43N 71.08W
Falls City U.S.A. **82** 40.03N 95.36W
Falmouth U.K. **11** 50.09N 5.05W
False B. R.S.A. **56** 34.10S 18.40E
False C. U.S.A. **85** 38.29N 74.59W
False Pt. India **41** 20.22N 86.52E
Falster *i.* Denmark **23** 54.48N 11.58E
Fălticeni Romania **21** 47.28N 26.18E
Falun Sweden **23** 60.36N 15.38E
Famagusta *see* Ammókhostos Cyprus **44**
Family L. Canada **75** 51.54N 95.30W
Famoso U.S.A. **81** 35.36N119.14W
Fandriana Madagascar **57** 20.14S 47.23E
Fangak Sudan **49** 9.04N 30.53E
Fangcheng China **32** 33.16N112.59E
Fangdou Shan *mts.* China **33** 30.36N108.45E
Fang Xian China **33** 32.04N110.47E
Fanjing Shan *mtn.* China **33** 27.57N108.50E
Fannich, Loch U.K. **12** 57.38N 5.00W
Fanning I. *see* Tabuaeran *i.* Kiribati **69**
Fano Italy **15** 43.50N 13.01E
Fan Xian China **32** 35.59N115.31E
Faradje Zaïre **55** 3.45N 29.43E
Faradofay Madagascar **57** 25.02S 47.00E
Farafangana Madagascar **57** 22.49S 47.50E
Farāfirah, Wāḥāt al *oasis* Egypt **42** 27.15N 28.10E
Farāh Afghan. **40** 32.22N 62.07E
Farāh *d.* Afghan. **40** 33.00N 62.00E
Farāh *r.* Afghan. **40** 31.29N 61.24E
Faranah Guinea **52** 10.01N 10.47W
Farasān, Jazā'ir *is.* Saudi Arabia **48** 16.48N 41.54E
Faratsiho Madagascar **57** 19.24S 46.57E
Faraulep *is.* Northern Marianas **37** 8.36N144.33E
Fareara, Pt. Tahiti **69** 17.52S149.39W
Fareham U.K. **11** 50.52N 1.11W
Farewell, C. *see* Farvel, Kap *c.* Greenland **73**
Farewell, C. New Zealand **60** 40.30S172.35E
Fargo U.S.A. **82** 46.52N 96.48W
Faribault U.S.A. **82** 44.18N 93.16W
Farīdpur Bangla. **41** 23.36N 89.50E
Farim Guinea Bissau **52** 12.30N 15.09W
Farina Australia **66** 30.05S138.20E
Farkwa Tanzania **55** 5.26S 35.15E
Farmerville U.S.A. **83** 32.47N 92.24W
Farmington Mo. U.S.A. **83** 37.47N 90.25W
Farmington N.Mex. U.S.A. **80** 36.44N108.12W
Farnborough U.K. **11** 51.17N 0.46W
Farne Is. U.K. **10** 55.38N 1.36W
Farnham Canada **77** 45.17N 72.59W
Farnham U.K. **11** 51.13N 0.49W
Faro Brazil **91** 2.11S 56.44W
Faro Portugal **16** 37.01N 7.56W
Faroe Bank *f.* Atlantic Oc. **8** 61.00N 9.00W
Faroe Is. Europe **8** 62.00N 7.00W
Fårön *i.* Sweden **23** 57.56N 19.08E
Fårösund Sweden **23** 57.52N 19.03E
Farrell U.S.A. **84** 41.13N 80.31W
Farrukhābād India **41** 27.24N 79.34E
Fársala Greece **19** 39.17N 22.22E
Fārsī Afghan. **40** 33.47N 63.15E
Farsund Norway **23** 58.05N 6.48E
Fartak, Ra's *c.* Yemen **45** 15.38N 52.15E
Farvel, Kap *c.* Greenland **73** 60.00N 44.20W
Farwell U.S.A. **83** 34.23N103.02W
Fasā Iran **43** 28.55N 53.38E
Fastov U.S.S.R. **21** 50.08N 29.59E
Fatehābād India **40** 29.31N 75.28E
Fatehjang Pakistan **40** 33.34N 72.39E
Fatehpur Rāj. India **40** 27.59N 74.57E
Fatehpur Uttar P. India **41** 25.56N 80.48E
Fatehpur Pakistan **40** 31.10N 71.13E
Fatehpur Sīkri India **41** 27.06N 77.40E
Fatick Senegal **52** 14.19N 16.27W
Fatu Hiva *i.* Is. Marquises **69** 10.27S138.39W
Fatwā India **41** 25.31N 85.19E
Faulkton U.S.A. **82** 45.02N 99.08W
Făurei Romania **21** 45.04N 27.15E
Fauske Norway **22** 67.17N 15.25E
Favara Italy **18** 37.19N 13.40E
Favignana *i.* Italy **18** 37.57N 12.19E
Fawcett Canada **74** 54.34N114.06W
Fawcett L. Canada **76** 51.20N 91.46W
Fawn *r.* Canada **75** 55.20N 88.20W
Faxaflói *b.* Iceland **22** 64.30N 22.50W
Faxe *r.* Sweden **22** 63.15N 17.15E
Fayette U.S.A. **85** 33.42N 87.50W
Fayetteville Ark. U.S.A. **83** 36.04N 94.10W
Fayetteville N.C. U.S.A. **85** 35.03N 78.53W
Fayetteville Tenn. U.S.A. **85** 35.08N 86.33W
Fāzilka India **40** 30.24N 74.02E
Fāzilpur Pakistan **40** 29.18N 70.27E
Fdérik Mauritania **50** 22.30N 12.30W
Feale *r.* Rep. of Ire. **13** 52.28N 9.37W
Fear, C. U.S.A. **85** 33.50N 77.58W
Fécamp France **15** 49.45N 0.23E
Federación Argentina **93** 31.00S 57.55W
Federal Argentina **93** 30.55S 58.45W
Federal Capital Territory *d.* Nigeria **53** 8.50N 7.00E
Federal States of Micronesia Pacific Oc. **68** 10.00N155.00E
Fedovo U.S.S.R. **24** 62.22N 39.21E
Fedulki U.S.S.R. **24** 65.00N 66.10E
Feeagh, Lough Rep. of Ire. **13** 53.56N 9.35W
Feerfeer Somali Rep. **45** 5.07N 45.07E
Fehmarn *i.* Germany **20** 54.30N 11.05E
Feia, Lagoa *l.* Brazil **94** 22.00S 41.20W
Feijó Brazil **90** 8.09S 70.21W
Feilding New Zealand **60** 40.10S175.25E
Feira Zambia **55** 15.30S 30.27E
Feira de Santana Brazil **91** 12.17S 38.53W
Felanitx Spain **16** 39.27N 3.08E
Feldkirch Austria **20** 47.15N 9.38E
Felixstowe U.K. **11** 51.58N 1.20E
Feltre Italy **15** 46.01N 11.54E
Femunden *l.* Norway **23** 62.12N 11.52E
Femundsenden Norway **23** 61.55N 11.55E
Fengcheng Jiangxi China **33** 28.10N115.45E
Fengcheng Liaoning China **32** 40.29N124.00E
Fengfeng China **32** 36.35N114.28E
Fenggang China **33** 27.58N107.47E
Fengjie China **33** 31.02N109.31E
Fengnan China **32** 39.30N117.58E
Fengpin Taiwan **33** 23.36N121.31E
Fengrun China **32** 39.51N118.08E
Fen He *r.* China **32** 35.30N110.38E
Feni Bangla. **41** 23.01N 91.20E
Fenoarivo Madagascar **57** 18.26S 46.34E
Fenoarivo Atsinanana Madagascar **57** 17.22S 49.25E
Fensfjorden *est.* Norway **23** 60.51N 4.50E
Fenton U.S.A. **84** 42.48N 83.42W
Fenwick U.S.A. **85** 38.14N 80.36W
Fenyang China **32** 37.10N111.40E
Feodosiya U.S.S.R. **25** 45.03N 35.23E
Ferdows Iran **43** 34.00N 58.10E
Fère-Champenoise France **15** 48.45N 3.59E
Fère-en-Tardenois France **15** 48.12N 3.31E
Fergana U.S.S.R. **30** 40.23N 71.19E
Fergus Falls *town* U.S.A. **82** 46.17N 96.04W
Ferguson U.S.A. **82** 38.46N 90.19W
Fergusson I. P.N.G. **64** 9.30S150.40E
Ferkéssédougou Ivory Coast **52** 9.30N 5.10W
Fermanagh *d.* U.K. **13** 54.21N 7.40W
Fermo Italy **18** 43.09N 13.43E
Fermoselle Spain **16** 41.19N 6.24W
Fermoy Rep. of Ire. **13** 52.08N 8.17W
Fernandina Beach *town* U.S.A. **85** 30.40N 81.26W
Fernando de Noronha *i* Atlantic Oc. **95** 3.50S 32.25W
Fernlee Australia **67** 28.12S147.05E
Ferrara Italy **15** 44.49N 11.38E
Ferreñafe Peru **90** 6.42S 79.45W
Ferret, Cap *c.* France **17** 44.42N 1.16W
Ferriday U.S.A. **83** 31.38N 91.33W
Ferrières France **15** 48.05N 2.48E
Fès Morocco **50** 34.05N 4.57W
Feshi Zaïre **54** 6.08S 18.12E
Festubert Canada **77** 47.15N 72.40W
Festus U.S.A. **82** 38.13N 90.24W
Feteşti Romania **21** 44.23N 27.50E
Fethiye Turkey **42** 36.37N 29.06E
Fetlar *i.* U.K. **12** 60.37N 0.52W
Feuilles, Rivière aux *r.* Canada **73** 58.47N 70.06W
Fevzipaşa Turkey **42** 37.07N 36.38E
Fianarantsoa Madagascar **57** 21.26S 47.05E
Fichē Ethiopia **49** 9.52N 38.46E
Fidenza Italy **15** 44.52N 10.03E
Fier Albania **19** 40.43N 19.34E
Fife *d.* U.K. **12** 56.10N 3.10W
Fife Ness *c.* U.K. **12** 56.17N 2.36W
Figeac France **17** 44.32N 2.01E
Figueira da Foz Portugal **16** 40.09N 8.51W
Figueres Spain **16** 42.16N 2.57E
Fihaonana Madagascar **57** 18.36S 47.12E
Fiherenana *r.* Madagascar **57** 23.19S 43.37E
Fiji Pacific Oc. **68** 18.00S178.00E
Fīk' Ethiopia **49** 8.10N 42.18E
Filabusi Zimbabwe **56** 20.34S 29.20E
Filey U.K. **10** 54.13N 0.18W
Filiaşi Romania **21** 44.33N 23.31E
Filiatrá Greece **19** 37.09N 21.35E
Filingué Niger **53** 14.21N 3.22E
Filipstad Sweden **23** 59.43N 14.10E
Fillmore Canada **75** 49.50N103.25W
Fillmore Calif. U.S.A. **81** 34.24N118.55W
Fīltu Ethiopia **49** 5.05N 40.42E
Fimi *r.* Zaïre **54** 3.00S 17.00E
Finale Emilia Italy **15** 44.50N 11.17E
Finale Ligure Italy **15** 44.10N 8.20E
Finarwa Ethiopia **49** 13.05N 38.58E
Findhorn *r.* U.K. **12** 57.38N 3.37W
Findlay U.S.A. **84** 41.02N 83.40W
Findlay, Mt. Canada **74** 50.04N116.10W
Finisterre, Cabo de *c.* Spain **16** 42.54N 9.16W
Finke Australia **64** 25.35S134.34E
Finke *r.* Australia **65** 27.00S136.10E
Finland Europe **24** 64.30N 27.00E
Finland, G. of Finland/U.S.S.R. **23** 59.30N 24.00E
Finlay *r.* Canada **74** 57.00N125.05W
Finley Australia **67** 35.40S145.34E
Finmark Canada **76** 48.36N 89.44W
Finn *r.* Rep. of Ire. **13** 54.50N 7.30W
Finnmark *d.* Norway **22** 70.10N 26.00E
Finschhafen P.N.G. **37** 6.35S147.51E
Finse Norway **23** 60.36N 7.30E
Finspång Sweden **23** 58.43N 15.47E
Fiorenzuola d'Arda Italy **15** 44.56N 9.55E
Firat *r.* Turkey *see* Al Furāt *r.* Asia **42**
Firebag *r.* Canada **75** 57.45N111.20W
Firedrake L. Canada **75** 61.25N104.30W
Firenze Italy **18** 43.46N 11.15E
Firenzuola Italy **15** 44.07N 11.23E
Fīrozābād India **41** 27.09N 78.25E
Fīrozpur India **40** 30.55N 74.38E
Fīrozpur Jhirka India **40** 27.48N 76.57E
Firth of Clyde *est.* U.K. **12** 55.35N 4.53W
Firth of Forth *est.* U.K. **12** 56.05N 3.00W
Firth of Lorn *est.* U.K. **12** 56.20N 5.40W
Firth of Tay *est.* U.K. **12** 56.24N 3.08W
Fīrūzābād Iran **43** 28.50N 52.35E
Firyuza U.S.S.R. **28** 37.55N 58.03E
Fish *r.* Namibia **56** 28.07S 17.45E
Fisher U.S.A. **83** 35.30N 90.58W
Fisher Str. Canada **73** 63.00N 84.00W
Fishguard U.K. **11** 51.59N 4.59W
Fiskenaesset Greenland **73** 63.05N 50.40W
Fiskivötn *f.* Iceland **22** 64.50N 20.45W
Fismes France **15** 49.18N 3.41E
Fitzgerald U.S.A. **85** 31.43N 83.16W
Fitz Roy Argentina **93** 47.00S 67.15W
Fitzroy *r.* Australia **62** 17.31S123.35E
Fitzroy Crossing Australia **62** 18.13S125.33E
Fivizzano Italy **15** 44.14N 10.08E
Fizi Zaïre **55** 4.18S 28.56E
Fjällåsen Sweden **22** 67.29N 20.10E

Fjällsjo *r.* Sweden **22** 63.27N 17.06E
Flå Norway **23** 60.25N 9.26E
Flagler U.S.A. **80** 39.18N103.04W
Flagstaff U.S.A. **81** 35.12N111.39W
Flagstaff B. St. Helena **95** 15.55S 5.40W
Flåm Norway **23** 60.50N 7.07E
Flamborough Head U.K. **10** 54.06N 0.05W
Flaming Gorge Resr. U.S.A. **80** 41.15N109.30W
Flandre *f.* Belgium **14** 50.52N 3.00E
Flannan Is. U.K. **12** 58.16N 7.40W
Flåsjön *l.* Sweden **22** 64.06N 15.51E
Flat *r.* Canada **74** 61.51N126.00W
Flathead L. U.S.A. **80** 47.52N114.08W
Flatonia U.S.A. **83** 29.47N 97.06W
Flattery, C. Australia **64** 14.58S145.21E
Flattery, C. U.S.A. **78** 48.23N124.43W
Flatts Village Bermuda **95** 32.19N 64.44W
Flaxton U.S.A. **82** 48.54N102.24W
Fleetwood U.K. **10** 53.55N 3.01W
Flekkefjord *town* Norway **23** 58.17N 6.41E
Flemington U.S.A. **85** 40.31N 74.52W
Flen Sweden **23** 59.04N 16.35E
Flensburg Germany **20** 54.47N 9.27E
Flers France **15** 48.45N 0.34W
Fleur-de-Lys Canada **77** 50.06N 56.08W
Flevoland *d.* Neth. **14** 52.25N 5.30E
Flinders *r.* Australia **64** 17.30S140.45E
Flinders B. Australia **63** 34.23S115.19E
Flinders I. S.A. Australia **66** 33.44S134.30E
Flinders I. Tas. Australia **65** 40.00S148.00E
Flinders Ranges *mts.* Australia **66** 31.25S138.45E
Flinders Reefs Australia **64** 17.37S148.31E
Flin Flon Canada **75** 54.46N101.53W
Flint U.K. **10** 53.15N 3.07W
Flint U.S.A. **84** 43.03N 83.40W
Flint *r.* Ga. U.S.A. **85** 30.52N 84.38W
Flint I. Kiribati **69** 11.26S151.48W
Flinton Australia **65** 27.54S149.34E
Flisa Norway **23** 60.34N 12.06E
Flora U.S.A. **82** 38.40N 88.30W
Florac France **17** 44.19N 3.36E
Florence *see* Firenze Italy **18**
Florence Ala. U.S.A. **85** 34.48N 87.40W
Florence Ariz. U.S.A. **81** 33.02N111.23W
Florence Colo. U.S.A. **80** 38.23N105.08W
Florence Oreg. U.S.A. **80** 43.58N124.07W
Florence S.C. U.S.A. **85** 34.12N 79.44W
Florence, L. Australia **66** 28.52S138.08E
Florencia Colombia **90** 1.37N 75.37W
Florennes Belgium **14** 50.14N 4.35E
Florenville Belgium **14** 49.42N 5.19E
Flores *i.* Indonesia **37** 8.40S121.20E
Flores, Laut *sea* Indonesia **37** 7.00S121.00E
Floreshty U.S.S.R. **21** 47.52N 28.12E
Flores Sea *see* Flores, Laut *sea* Indonesia **37**
Floriano Brazil **91** 6.45S 43.00W
Florianópolis Brazil **94** 27.35S 48.34W
Florida Uruguay **93** 34.06S 56.13W
Florida *d.* U.S.A. **85** 28.00N 82.00W
Florida, Str. of U.S.A. **85** 24.00N 81.00W
Florida B. U.S.A. **85** 25.00N 80.45W
Florida City U.S.A. **85** 25.27N 80.30W
Florida Keys *is.* U.S.A. **85** 24.45N 81.00W
Florina Australia **66** 32.23S139.58E
Flórina Greece **19** 40.48N 21.25E
Florö Norway **23** 61.36N 5.00E
Fluessen *l.* Neth. **14** 52.58N 5.23E
Flushing *see* Vlissingen Neth. **14**
Fly *r.* P.N.G. **64** 8.22S142.23E
Focşani Romania **21** 45.40N 27.12E
Foggia Italy **18** 41.28N 15.33E
Foggo Nigeria **53** 11.21N 9.57E
Fogo Canada **77** 49.43N 54.17W
Fogo I. Canada **77** 49.40N 54.13W
Foix France **17** 42.57N 1.35E
Folda *est.* Nordland Norway **22** 67.36N 14.50E
Folda *est.* N. Trönd. Norway **22** 64.45N 11.20E
Folégandros *i.* Greece **19** 36.35N 24.55E
Foley Botswana **56** 21.34S 27.21E
Foleyet Canada **76** 48.05N 82.26W
Folgares Angola **56** 14.55S 15.03E
Folgefonna *glacier* Norway **23** 60.00N 6.20E
Foligno Italy **18** 42.56N 12.43E
Folkestone U.K. **11** 51.05N 1.11E
Folkston U.S.A. **85** 30.49N 82.02W
Folsom U.S.A. **80** 38.41N121.15W
Fominskoye U.S.S.R. **24** 59.45N 42.03E
Fond du Lac Canada **75** 59.17N106.00W
Fond du Lac U.S.A. **82** 43.48N 88.27W
Fonsagrada Spain **16** 43.08N 7.04W
Fonseca, Golfo de *g.* Honduras **87** 13.10N 87.30W
Fontainebleau France **15** 48.24N 2.42E
Fonte Boa Brazil **90** 2.33S 65.59W
Fontenay France **17** 46.28N 0.48W
Fonuafo'ou *i.* Tonga **69** 18.47S173.58W
Foochow *see* Fuzhou China **33**
Foothills *town* Canada **74** 53.04N116.47W
Forbach France **17** 49.11N 6.54E
Forbes Australia **67** 33.24S148.03E
Forbesganj India **41** 26.18N 87.15E
Forchheim Germany **20** 49.43N 11.04E
Förde Norway **23** 61.27N 5.52E
Ford's Bridge Australia **67** 29.46S145.25E
Fordyce U.S.A. **83** 33.49N 92.25W
Forécariah Guinea **52** 9.28N 13.06W
Forel, Mt. Greenland **73** 67.00N 37.00W
Foreland Pt. U.K. **11** 51.15N 3.47W
Foremost Canada **75** 49.29N111.25W
Forest of Bowland *hills* U.K. **10** 53.57N 2.30W
Forest of Dean *f.* U.K. **11** 51.48N 2.32W
Forfar U.K. **12** 56.38N 2.54W
Forked River *town* U.S.A. **85** 39.51N 74.12W
Forlì Italy **15** 44.13N 12.02E
Forman U.S.A. **82** 46.07N 97.38W
Formby Pt. U.K. **10** 53.34N 3.07W
Formentera *i.* Spain **16** 38.41N 1.30E
Formerie France **15** 49.39N 1.44E
Formiga Brazil **94** 20.30S 45.27W
Formosa Argentina **92** 26.06S 58.14W
Formosa *d.* Argentina **92** 25.00S 60.00W
Formosa *see* Taiwan Asia **33**
Formosa Brazil **91** 15.30S 47.22W
Formosa, Serra *mts.* Brazil **91** 12.00S 55.20W
Fornovo di Taro Italy **15** 44.42N 10.06E
Forres U.K. **12** 57.37N 3.38W
Fors Sweden **23** 60.13N 16.18E
Forsayth Australia **64** 18.35S143.36E
Forssa Finland **23** 60.49N 23.38E
Forst Germany **20** 51.46N 14.39E
Forster Australia **67** 32.12S152.30E
Forsyth U.S.A. **80** 46.16N106.41W
Fort Abbās Pakistan **40** 29.12N 72.52E
Fort Adams U.S.A. **83** 31.05N 91.33W
Fort Albany Canada **76** 52.15N 81.35W
Fortaleza Brazil **91** 3.45S 38.35W
Fort Atkinson U.S.A. **82** 42.56N 88.50W
Fort Augustus U.K. **12** 57.09N 4.41W
Fort Beaufort R.S.A. **56** 32.46S 26.36E
Fort Benning U.S.A. **85** 32.20N 84.58W
Fort Benton U.S.A. **80** 47.49N110.40W
Fort Carnot Madagascar **57** 21.53S 47.28E
Fort Chipewyan Canada **75** 58.42N111.08W
Fort Collins U.S.A. **80** 40.35N105.05W
Fort Coulonge Canada **76** 45.51N 76.44W
Fort-de-France Martinique **87** 14.36N 61.05W
Fort de Possel C.A.R. **53** 5.03N 19.16E
Fort Dodge U.S.A. **82** 42.30N 94.10W
Fort Drum U.S.A. **85** 27.31N 80.49W
Forte dei Marmi Italy **15** 43.57N 10.10E
Fort Erie Canada **76** 42.54N 78.56W
Fortescue *r.* Australia **62** 21.00S116.06E
Fort Frances Canada **76** 48.35N 93.25W
Fort Franklin Canada **72** 65.11N123.45W
Fort Garland U.S.A. **80** 37.26N105.26W
Fort Good Hope Canada **72** 66.16N128.37W
Fort Grahame Canada **74** 56.30N124.35W
Forth *r.* U.K. **12** 56.06N 3.48W
Fort Hancock U.S.A. **81** 31.17N105.53W
Fort Hope Canada **76** 51.32N 88.00W
Fort Klamath U.S.A. **80** 42.42N122.00W
Fort Lallemand Algeria **51** 31.18N 6.20E
Fort Lauderdale U.S.A. **85** 26.08N 80.08W
Fort Liard Canada **74** 60.15N123.28W
Fort Lupton U.S.A. **80** 40.05N104.49W
Fort Mackay Canada **75** 57.12N111.41W
Fort Macleod Canada **74** 49.45N113.30W
Fort MacMahon Algeria **51** 29.46N 1.37E
Fort Madison U.S.A. **82** 40.38N 91.27W
Fort Maguire Malaŵi **55** 13.38S 34.59E
Fort McKenzie Canada **77** 56.50N 68.59W
Fort McMurray Canada **75** 56.45N111.27W
Fort McPherson Canada **72** 67.29N134.50W
Fort Miribel Algeria **51** 29.26N 3.00E
Fort Morgan U.S.A. **80** 40.15N103.48W
Fort Myers U.S.A. **85** 26.39N 81.51W
Fort Nelson Canada **74** 58.49N122.39W
Fort Nelson *r.* Canada **74** 59.30N124.00W
Fort Norman Canada **72** 64.55N125.29W
Fort Peck Dam U.S.A. **80** 47.52N106.38W
Fort Peck Resr. U.S.A. **80** 47.45N106.50W
Fort Pierce U.S.A. **85** 27.28N 80.20W
Fort Portal Uganda **55** 0.40N 30.17E
Fort Providence Canada **74** 61.21N117.39W
Fort Qu'Appelle Canada **75** 50.45N103.50W
Fort Randall U.S.A. **72** 55.10N162.47W
Fort Reliance Canada **75** 63.00N109.20W
Fort Resolution Canada **74** 61.10N113.40W
Fortrose New Zealand **60** 46.34S168.48E
Fortrose U.K. **12** 57.34N 4.09W
Fort Rupert B.C. Canada **74** 50.39N127.27W
Fort Saint Tunisia **51** 30.19N 9.30E
Fort St. John Canada **74** 56.15N120.51W
Fort Sandeman Pakistan **40** 31.20N 69.27E
Fort Saskatchewan Canada **74** 53.40N113.15W
Fort Scott U.S.A. **83** 37.50N 94.42W
Fort Severn Canada **75** 56.00N 87.40W
Fort Shevchenko U.S.S.R. **25** 44.31N 50.15E
Fort Simpson Canada **74** 61.46N121.15E
Fort Smith Canada **75** 60.00N111.51W
Fort Smith *d.* Canada **72** 63.30N118.00W
Fort Smith U.S.A. **83** 35.23N 94.25W
Fort Stockton U.S.A. **83** 30.53N102.53W
Fort Sumner U.S.A. **81** 34.28N104.15W
Fort Thomas U.S.A. **81** 33.02N109.58W
Fortuna Calif. U.S.A. **80** 40.36N124.09W
Fortuna N.Dak. U.S.A. **82** 48.55N103.47W
Fortune B. Canada **77** 47.25N 55.25W
Fort Valley U.S.A. **85** 32.32N 83.56W
Fort Vermilion Canada **74** 58.24N116.00W
Fort Wayne U.S.A. **84** 41.05N 85.08W
Fort William U.K. **12** 56.49N 5.07W
Fort Worth U.S.A. **83** 32.45N 97.20W
Fort Yates U.S.A. **82** 46.05N100.38W
Forty Mile *town* Canada **72** 64.24N140.31W
Fort Yukon U.S.A. **72** 66.35N145.20W
Foshan China **33** 23.08N113.08E
Fossano Italy **15** 44.33N 7.43E
Foster Australia **67** 38.39S146.12E
Fostoria U.S.A. **84** 41.10N 83.25W
Fougamou Gabon **54** 1.10S 10.31E
Fougères France **15** 48.21N 1.12W
Foula *i.* U.K. **12** 60.08N 2.05W
Foulness I. U.K. **11** 51.35N 0.55E
Foulwind, C. New Zealand **60** 41.45S171.30E
Foumban Cameroon **53** 5.43N 10.50E
Fountain U.S.A. **80** 38.41N104.42W
Fourmies France **14** 50.01N 4.02E
Foúrnoi *i.* Greece **19** 37.34N 26.30E
Fouta Djalon *f.* Guinea **52** 11.30N 12.30W
Foveaux Str. New Zealand **60** 46.40S168.00E
Fowey U.K. **11** 50.20N 4.39W
Fowler U.S.A. **80** 38.08N104.01W
Fowlers B. Australia **65** 31.59S132.27E
Fowlerton U.S.A. **83** 28.28N 98.48W
Fox Creek *town* Canada **74** 54.26N116.55W
Foxe Basin *b.* Canada **73** 67.30N 79.00W
Foxe Channel Canada **73** 65.00N 80.00W
Foxe Pen. Canada **73** 65.00N 76.00W
Fox Glacier *town* New Zealand **60** 43.28S170.01E
Foxton New Zealand **60** 40.27S175.18E
Fox Valley *town* Canada **75** 50.29N109.28W
Foyle *r.* U.K. **13** 55.00N 7.20W
Foyle, Lough U.K. **13** 55.05N 7.10W
Foz do Cunene Angola **54** 17.15S 11.48E
Foz do Iguaçu Brazil **94** 25.33S 54.31W
Franca Brazil **94** 20.33S 47.27W
Francavilla Fontana Italy **19** 40.31N 17.35E
France Europe **17** 47.00N 2.00E
Frances Australia **66** 36.41S140.59E
Frances *r.* Canada **74** 60.16N129.10W
Frances L. Canada **74** 61.23N129.30W
Frances Lake *town* Canada **74** 61.15N129.12W
Francesville U.S.A. **84** 40.59N 86.54W
Franceville Gabon **54** 1.38S 13.31E
Franche-Comté *d.* France **17** 47.10N 6.00E
Francia Uruguay **93** 32.33S 56.37W
Francistown Botswana **56** 21.12S 27.29E
François L. Canada **74** 54.00N125.40W
Franeker Neth. **14** 53.13N 5.31E
Frankfort R.S.A. **56** 27.15S 28.30E
Frankfort Kans. U.S.A. **82** 39.42N 96.25W
Frankfort Ky. U.S.A. **84** 38.11N 84.53W
Frankfurt *Brandenburg* Germany **20** 52.20N 14.32E
Frankfurt *Hessen* Germany **20** 50.06N 8.41E
Frankland *r.* Australia **63** 34.58S116.49E
Franklin Ky. U.S.A. **85** 36.42N 86.35W
Franklin La. U.S.A. **83** 29.48N 91.30W
Franklin N.H. U.S.A. **84** 43.27N 71.39W
Franklin Tex. U.S.A. **83** 31.02N 96.29W
Franklin W.Va. U.S.A. **84** 38.39N 79.20W
Franklin B. Canada **72** 70.00N126.30W
Franklin D. Roosevelt L. U.S.A. **80** 48.20N118.10W
Franklin Harbour Australia **66** 33.42S136.56E
Franklin I. Antarctica **96** 76.10S168.30E
Frankston Australia **65** 38.08S145.07E
Fransfontein Namibia **56** 20.12S 15.01E
Frantsa Iosifa, Zemlya *is.* U.S.S.R. **28** 81.00N 54.00E
Franz Canada **76** 48.28N 84.25W
Franz Josef Land *is. see* Frantsa Iosifa, Zemlya *ya* U.S.S.R. **28**
Fraser *r.* B.C. Canada **74** 49.07N123.11W
Fraser *r.* Nfld. Canada **77** 56.35N 61.55W
Fraser, I. Australia **64** 25.15S153.10E
Fraser Basin *f.* Canada **74** 54.29N124.00W
Fraserburg R.S.A. **56** 31.55S 21.29E
Fraserburgh U.K. **12** 57.42N 2.00W
Fraser Plateau *f.* Canada **74** 52.52N124.00W
Fraustro Mexico **83** 25.51N101.04W
Fray Bentos Uruguay **93** 33.08S 58.18W
Fray Marcos Uruguay **93** 34.11S 55.44W
Frederica U.S.A. **85** 39.01N 75.28W
Fredericia Denmark **23** 55.35N 9.46E
Frederick Md. U.S.A. **85** 39.23N 77.25W
Frederick Okla. U.S.A. **83** 34.23N 99.01W
Frederick S.Dak. U.S.A. **82** 45.50N 98.30W
Frederick Hills Australia **64** 12.41S136.00E
Fredericksburg Tex. U.S.A. **83** 30.17N 98.52W
Fredericksburg Va. U.S.A. **79** 38.18N 77.30W
Frederick Sd. U.S.A. **74** 57.00N133.00W
Fredericton Canada **77** 45.58N 66.39W
Frederikshåb Greenland **73** 62.05N 49.30W
Frederikshavn Denmark **23** 57.26N 10.32E
Fredonia Kans. U.S.A. **83** 37.32N 95.49W
Fredonia N.Y. U.S.A. **84** 42.27N 79.22W
Fredrika Sweden **22** 64.05N 18.24E
Fredrikstad Norway **23** 59.13N 10.57E
Freehold U.S.A. **85** 40.16N 74.17W
Freels, C. Canada **77** 49.15N 53.28W
Freelton Canada **76** 43.22N 80.02W
Freeman U.S.A. **82** 43.21N 97.26W
Freeport Bahamas **87** 26.30N 78.45W
Freeport N.S. Canada **77** 44.17N 66.19W
Freeport Ill. U.S.A. **82** 42.17N 89.38W
Freeport N.Y. U.S.A. **85** 40.40N 73.35W
Freeport Tex. U.S.A. **83** 28.58N 95.22W
Freetown Sierra Leone **52** 8.30N 13.17W
Freiberg Germany **20** 50.54N 13.20E
Freiburg Germany **20** 48.00N 7.52E
Freilingen Germany **14** 50.33N 7.50E
Freising Germany **20** 48.24N 11.45E
Freistadt Austria **20** 48.31N 14.31E
Fréjus France **17** 43.26N 6.44E
Fremantle Australia **63** 32.07S115.44E
Fremont Calif. U.S.A. **80** 37.34N122.01W
Fremont Nebr. U.S.A. **82** 41.26N 96.30W
Fremont Ohio U.S.A. **84** 41.21N 83.08W
Frenchglen U.S.A. **80** 42.48N118.56W
French I. Australia **67** 38.20S145.20E
Frenchman Butte *town* Canada **75** 53.35N109.38W
Frenda Algeria **51** 35.04N 1.03E
Freren Germany **14** 52.29N 7.32E
Fresco *r.* Brazil **91** 7.10S 52.30W
Fresco Ivory Coast **52** 5.03N 5.31W
Freshford Rep. of Ire. **13** 52.44N 7.23W
Fresnillo Mexico **86** 23.10N102.53W
Fresno U.S.A. **80** 36.45N119.45W
Frewena Australia **64** 19.25S135.25E
Fria Guinea **52** 10.27N 13.38W
Fria, C. Namibia **56** 18.25S 12.01E
Frias Argentina **92** 28.40S 65.10W
Fribourg Switz. **20** 46.50N 7.10E
Friedberg Hessen Germany **20** 50.20N 8.45E
Friedrichshafen Germany **20** 47.39N 9.29E
Friesland *d.* Neth. **14** 53.05N 5.45E
Friesoythe Germany **14** 53.02N 7.52E
Frio, Cabo *c.* Brazil **94** 22.59S 42.00W
Friuli-Venezia Giulia *d.* Italy **15** 46.15N 12.45E
Frobisher B. Canada **73** 63.00N 66.45W
Frobisher Bay *town* Canada **73** 63.45N 68.30W
Frobisher L. Canada **75** 56.25N108.20W
Frohavet *est.* Norway **22** 63.55N 9.05E
Froid U.S.A. **80** 48.20N104.30W
Frolovo U.S.S.R. **25** 49.45N 43.40E
Frome *r.* Australia **66** 29.49S138.40E
Frome U.K. **11** 51.16N 2.17W
Frome, L. Australia **66** 30.48S139.48E
Frome Downs *town* Australia **66** 31.13S139.46E
Frontera Mexico **86** 18.32N 92.38W
Frosinone Italy **18** 41.36N 13.21E
Fröya *i.* Norway **22** 63.45N 8.45E
Frunze U.S.S.R. **30** 42.53N 74.46E
Frunzovka U.S.S.R. **21** 47.19N 29.44E
Frýdek-Místek Czech. **21** 49.41N 18.22E
Fu'an China **33** 27.04N119.37E
Fuchū Japan **35** 35.40N139.29E
Fuchuan China **33** 24.50N111.16E
Fuchun Jiang *r.* China **33** 30.05N120.00E
Fuding China **33** 27.18N120.12E
Fuefuki *r.* Japan **35** 35.33N138.28E
Fuente-obejuna Spain **16** 38.15N 5.25W
Fuentes de Oñoro Spain **16** 40.33N 6.52W
Fuerte *r.* Mexico **81** 25.50N109.25W
Fuerteventura *i.* Canary Is. **50** 28.20N 14.10W
Fuga *i.* Phil. **33** 18.53N121.22E
Fuglö *i.* Faroe Is. **8** 62.22N 6.15W
Fugou China **32** 34.04N114.23E
Fugu China **32** 39.02N111.03E
Fuji Japan **35** 35.09N138.39E
Fuji *r.* Japan **35** 35.07N138.38E
Fujian *d.* China **33** 26.00N118.00E
Fu Jiang *r.* China **33** 30.02N106.20E
Fujieda Japan **35** 34.52N138.16E
Fujin China **31** 47.15N131.59E
Fujinomiya Japan **35** 35.12N138.38E
Fuji san *mtn.* Japan **35** 35.22N138.44E
Fujisawa Japan **35** 35.21N139.29E
Fuji-yoshida Japan **35** 35.38N138.42E
Fukui Japan **31** 36.04N136.12E
Fukuoka Japan **31** 33.39N130.21E
Fukuroi Japan **35** 34.45N137.55E
Fūlādī, Kūh-e *mtn.* Afghan. **40** 34.38N 67.32E
Fulda Germany **20** 50.35N 9.45E
Fulda *r.* Germany **20** 50.33N 9.41E
Fuling China **33** 29.40N107.20E
Fulton Mo. U.S.A. **82** 38.52N 91.57W
Fulton N.Y. U.S.A. **84** 43.20N 76.26W
Fumay France **14** 49.59N 4.42E
Funabashi Japan **35** 35.42N139.59E
Funafuti Tuvalu **68** 8.31S179.13E
Funan Gaba Ethiopia **49** 4.22N 37.58E
Funchal Madeira Is. **95** 32.40N 16.55W
Fundão Portugal **16** 40.08N 7.30W
Fundy, B. of Canada **77** 45.00N 66.00W
Funing China **33** 23.37N105.36E
Funiu Shan *mts.* China **32** 33.40N112.20E
Funtua Nigeria **53** 11.34N 7.18E
Fuping China **32** 38.52N114.12E
Fuqing China **33** 25.43N119.22E
Furancungo Mozambique **55** 14.51S 33.38E
Fūrg Iran **43** 28.19N 55.10E
Furnas, Reprêsa de *resr.* Brazil **94** 20.45S 46.00W
Furneaux Group *is.* Australia **65** 40.15S148.15E
Furqlus Syria **44** 34.38N 37.08E
Fürstenau Germany **14** 52.32N 7.41E
Fürstenwalde Germany **20** 52.22N 14.04E
Fürth Germany **20** 49.28N 11.00E
Furu-tone *r.* Japan **35** 35.58N139.51E
Fusagasugá Colombia **90** 4.22N 74.21W
Fushun China **32** 41.50N123.55E
Fusong China **31** 42.17N127.19E
Fusui China **33** 22.35N107.57E
Fuwah Egypt **44** 31.12N 30.33E
Fu Xian Liaoning China **32** 39.35N122.07E
Fu Xian Shaanxi China **32** 36.00N109.20E
Fuxin China **32** 42.08N121.45E
Fuyang Anhui China **32** 32.52N115.52E
Fuyang Zhejiang China **33** 30.03N119.57E
Fuyang He *r.* China **32** 38.10N116.08E
Fuyu China **31** 45.12N124.49E
Fuyuan Heilongjiang China **31** 48.20N134.18E
Fuyuan Yunnan China **33** 25.40N104.14E
Fuzhou Fujian China **33** 26.09N119.21E
Fuzhou Jiangxi China **33** 28.01N116.13E
Fyn *i.* Denmark **23** 55.20N 10.30E
Fyne, Loch U.K. **12** 55.55N 5.23W

G

Ga Ghana **52** 9.48N 2.28W
Gaalkacyo Somali Rep. **45** 6.49N 47.23E
Gabela Angola **54** 10.52S 14.24E
Gabès Tunisia **51** 33.53N 10.07E
Gabès, Golfe de *g.* Tunisia **51** 34.00N 10.25E
Gabir Sudan **49** 8.35N 24.40E
Gabon Africa **54** 0.00 12.00E
Gabon *r.* Gabon **54** 0.15N 10.00E
Gaborone Botswana **56** 24.45S 25.55E
Gabras Sudan **49** 10.16N 26.14E
Gabrovo Bulgaria **19** 42.52N 25.19E
Gacé France **15** 48.48N 0.18E
Gach Sārān Iran **43** 30.13N 50.49E
Gada Nigeria **53** 13.50N 5.40E
Gādarwāra India **41** 22.55N 78.47E
Gäddede Sweden **22** 64.30N 14.15E
Gadra Pakistan **40** 25.40N 70.37E
Gadsden U.S.A. **85** 34.00N 86.00W
Gaeta Italy **18** 41.13N 13.35E
Gaeta, Golfo di *g.* Italy **18** 41.05N 13.30E
Gaferut *i.* Caroline Is. **37** 9.14N145.23E
Gaffney U.S.A. **85** 35.03N 81.40W
Gafsa Tunisia **51** 34.25N 8.48E
Gagarin U.S.S.R. **24** 55.38N 35.00E
Gagnoa Ivory Coast **52** 6.04N 5.55W
Gagnon Canada **77** 51.53N 68.10W
Gaibānda Bangla. **41** 25.19N 89.33E
Gaillac France **17** 43.54N 1.53E
Gaillon France **15** 49.10N 1.20E
Gainesville Fla. U.S.A. **85** 29.37N 82.21W
Gainesville Ga. U.S.A. **85** 34.17N 83.50W
Gainesville Mo. U.S.A. **83** 36.36N 92.26W
Gainesville Tex. U.S.A. **83** 33.37N 97.08W
Gainsborough U.K. **10** 53.23N 0.46W
Gairdner *r.* Australia **63** 34.20S119.30E
Gairdner, L. Australia **66** 31.30S136.00E
Gairloch U.K. **12** 57.43N 5.40W
Gaithersburg U.S.A. **85** 39.09N 77.12W
Gai Xian China **32** 40.25N122.15E
Galana *r.* Kenya **55** 3.12S 40.09E
Galangue Angola **54** 13.40S 16.00E
Galapagos, Islas *is.* Pacific Oc. **69** 0.30S 90.30W
Galashiels U.K. **12** 55.37N 2.49W
Galaţi Romania **21** 45.27N 27.59E
Galatina Italy **19** 40.10N 18.10E
Galdhöpiggen *mtn.* Norway **23** 61.37N 8.17E
Galeana Mexico **83** 24.50N100.04W
Galeh Dār Iran **43** 27.36N 52.42E
Galena Alas. U.S.A. **72** 64.43N157.00W
Galena Md. U.S.A. **85** 39.20N 75.55W
Galesburg U.S.A. **82** 40.57N 90.22W
Galich U.S.S.R. **24** 58.20N 42.12E
Galicia *d.* Spain **16** 43.00N 8.00W
Galilee, L. Australia **64** 22.21S145.48E
Galiuro Mts. U.S.A. **81** 32.40N110.20W
Gallarate Italy **15** 45.40N 8.47E
Gallatin U.S.A. **85** 36.22N 86.28W
Galle Sri Lanka **39** 6.01N 80.13E
Gállego *r.* Spain **16** 41.40N 0.55W
Gallegos *r.* Argentina **93** 51.35S 69.00W
Galley Head Rep. of Ire. **13** 51.32N 8.57W
Galliate Italy **15** 45.29N 8.42E
Gallinas, Punta *c.* Colombia **90** 12.20N 71.30W
Gallipoli Italy **19** 40.02N 18.01E
Gallipoli *see* Gelibolu Turkey **19**
Gallipolis U.S.A. **84** 38.49N 82.14W
Gällivare Sweden **22** 67.07N 20.45E
Gällö Sweden **22** 62.56N 15.15E
Galloway *f.* U.K. **12** 55.00N 4.28W
Gallup U.S.A. **81** 35.32N108.44W
Galong Australia **67** 34.37S148.34E
Galston U.K. **12** 55.36N 4.23W
Galty Mts. Rep. of Ire. **13** 52.20N 8.10W
Galva U.S.A. **82** 41.10N 90.03W
Galveston U.S.A. **83** 29.18N 94.48W
Galveston B. U.S.A. **83** 29.36N 94.57W
Galvez Argentina **92** 32.03S 61.14W
Galway Rep. of Ire. **13** 53.17N 9.04W
Galway *d.* Rep. of Ire. **13** 53.25N 9.00W
Galway B. Rep. of Ire. **13** 53.12N 9.07W
Gam *r.* Vietnam **33** 18.47N105.40E
Gamagōri Japan **35** 34.50N137.14E
Gamawa Nigeria **53** 12.10N 10.31E
Gamba China **41** 28.18N 88.32E
Gambēla Ethiopia **49** 8.18N 34.37E
Gambia Africa **52** 13.10N 16.00W
Gambia *r.* Gambia **52** 13.28N 15.55W
Gambier, Îles *is.* Pacific Oc. **69** 23.10S135.00W
Gambier I. Australia **66** 35.12S136.32E
Gambo Canada **77** 48.46N 54.14W
Gamboli Pakistan **40** 29.50N 68.26E
Gamboma Congo **54** 1.50S 15.58E
Gamboula C.A.R. **53** 4.05N 15.10E
Gamia Benin **53** 10.24N 2.45E
Gamlakarleby *see* Kokkola Finland **22**
Gamleby Sweden **23** 57.54N 16.24E
Gamo Gofa *d.* Ethiopia **49** 6.00N 37.00E
Ganado U.S.A. **81** 35.43N109.33W
Gananoque Canada **76** 44.20N 76.10W
Ganbashao China **33** 26.37N107.41E
Ganda Angola **54** 12.58S 14.39E
Gandajika Zaïre **54** 6.46S 23.58E
Gandak *r.* India **41** 25.40N 85.13E
Gāndarbal Jammu & Kashmir **40** 34.14N 74.47E
Gandāva Pakistan **40** 28.37N 67.29E
Gander Canada **77** 48.57N 54.34W
Gander *r.* Canada **77** 49.15N 54.30W
Gander L. Canada **77** 48.55N 54.40W
Gandevi India **40** 20.49N 73.00E
Gāndhi Sāgar *resr.* India **40** 24.18N 75.21E
Gandía Spain **16** 38.59N 0.11W
Gandou Congo **54** 2.25N 17.25E
Ganga *r.* India **41** 23.22N 90.32E
Gangāpur Rāj. India **40** 26.29N 76.43E
Gangāpur Rāj. India **40** 25.13N 74.16E
Gangara Niger **53** 14.35N 8.40E
Gāngārāmpur India **41** 25.24N 88.31E
Gangdhār India **40** 23.57N 75.37E
Gangdisê Shan *mts.* China **41** 31.15N 82.00E
Ganges *r. see* Ganga *r.* India **41**
Gangotri India **41** 30.56N 79.02E
Gangtok India **41** 27.20N 88.37E
Gangu China **32** 34.30N105.30E
Gan Jiang *r.* China **33** 29.10N116.00E
Ganmain Australia **67** 34.47S147.01E
Gannat France **17** 46.06N 3.11E
Gannett Peak *mtn.* U.S.A. **80** 43.11N109.39W
Ganquan China **32** 36.19N109.19E

Gansu d. China 30 36.00N103.00E
Ganta Liberia 52 7.15N 8.59W
Gantheaume, C. Australia 66 36.05S137.27E
Ganye Nigeria 53 8.24N 12.02E
Ganyu China 32 34.50N119.07E
Ganzhou China 33 25.49N114.50E
Gao Mali 52 16.19N 0.09W
Gao d. Mali 53 17.20N 1.25E
Gao'an China 33 28.25N115.22E
Gaohe China 33 22.46N112.57E
Gaolan China 32 36.23N103.55E
Gaolou Ling mtn. China 33 24.47N106.48E
Gaomi China 32 36.23N119.44E
Gaoping China 32 35.48N112.55E
Gaotai China 30 39.20N 99.58E
Gaoua Burkina 52 10.20N 3.09W
Gaoual Guinea 52 11.44N 13.14W
Gaoxiong Taiwan 33 22.40N120.18E
Gaoyou China 32 32.40N119.30E
Gaoyou Hu l. China 32 32.50N119.25E
Gaozhou China 33 21.58N110.59E
Gap France 17 44.33N 6.05E
Gar China 41 32.11N 79.59E
Gara, Lough Rep. of Ire. 13 53.57N 8.27W
Garah Australia 67 29.04S149.38E
Garanhuns Brazil 91 8.53S 36.28W
Garba C.A.R. 49 9.12N 20.30E
Gārbosh, Kūh-e mtn. Iran 43 32.36N 50.02E
Gard r. France 17 43.52N 4.40E
Garda Italy 15 45.34N 10.42E
Garda, Lago di l. Italy 15 45.40N 10.40E
Gardelegen Germany 20 52.31N 11.23E
Garden City Ala. U.S.A. 85 34.01N 86.55W
Garden City Kans. U.S.A. 83 37.58N100.53W
Garden Reach India 41 22.33N 88.17E
Gardēz Afghan. 40 33.37N 69.07E
Gardiner U.S.A. 80 45.02N110.42W
Gardnerville U.S.A. 80 38.56N119.45W
Gardone Val Trompia Italy 15 45.41N 10.11E
Garessio Italy 15 44.12N 8.02E
Garet el Djenoun mtn. Algeria 51 25.05N 5.25E
Garhākota India 41 23.46N 79.09E
Garhi Khairo Pakistan 40 28.04N 67.59E
Garibaldi Prov. Park Canada 74 49.50N122.40W
Garies R.S.A. 56 30.34S 18.00E
Garigliano r. Italy 18 41.13N 13.45E
Garissa Kenya 55 0.27S 39.49E
Garko Nigeria 53 11.45N 8.53E
Garland Tex. U.S.A. 83 32.54N 96.39W
Garland Utah U.S.A. 80 41.45N112.10W
Garlasco Italy 15 45.12N 8.55E
Garlin France 17 43.34N 0.15W
Garm Āb Afghan. 40 32.14N 65.01E
Garmisch Partenkirchen Germany 20 47.30N 11.05E
Garmsār Iran 43 35.15N 52.21E
Garnett U.S.A. 82 38.17N 95.14W
Garo Hills India 41 25.45N 90.30E
Garonne r. France 17 45.00N 0.37W
Garoua Cameroon 53 9.17N 13.22E
Garoua Boulaï Cameroon 53 5.54N 14.33E
Garrison U.S.A. 83 31.49N 94.30W
Garrison Resr. U.S.A. 82 48.00N102.30W
Garron Pt. U.K. 13 55.03N 5.57W
Garry L. Canada 73 66.00N100.00W
Garson Canada 76 46.34N 80.52W
Garub Namibia 56 26.33S 16.00E
Garut Indonesia 37 7.15S107.55E
Garvão Portugal 16 37.42N 8.21W
Garve U.K. 12 57.37N 4.41W
Garvie Mts. New Zealand 60 45.15S169.00E
Garwa India 41 24.11N 83.49E
Gary U.S.A. 84 41.34N 87.20W
Garyarsa China 30 31.30N 80.40E
Gar Zangbo r. China 41 32.25N 79.40E
Garzón Colombia 90 2.14N 75.37W
Gas City U.S.A. 84 40.28N 85.37W
Gascogne, Golfe de g. France 17 44.00N 2.40W
Gascony, G. of see Gascogne, Golfe de France 17
Gascoyne r. Australia 62 25.00S113.40E
Gascoyne Junction Australia 62 25.02S115.15E
Gash r. Ethiopia see Qāsh r. Sudan 48
Gashua Nigeria 53 12.53N 11.02E
Gaspé Canada 77 48.50N 64.30W
Gaspé, Cap de c. Canada 77 48.45N 64.09W
Gaspé, Péninsule de pen. Canada 77 48.30N 65.00W
Gaspésie Prov. Park Canada 77 48.50N 65.45W
Gassol Nigeria 53 8.34N 10.25E
Gastonia U.S.A. 85 35.14N 81.12W
Gastre Argentina 93 42.17S 69.15W
Gata, Cabo de c. Spain 16 36.45N 2.11W
Gata, Sierra de mts. Spain 16 40.20N 6.30W
Gatas, Akrotírion c. Cyprus 44 34.33N 33.03E
Gatchina U.S.S.R. 24 59.32N 30.05E
Gatehouse of Fleet U.K. 12 54.53N 4.12W
Gateshead U.K. 10 54.57N 1.35W
Gatesville U.S.A. 83 31.26N 97.45W
Gatineau Canada 77 45.29N 75.38W
Gatineau r. Canada 77 45.27N 75.40W
Gatineau N.C.C. Park Canada 77 45.30N 75.52W
Gattinara Italy 15 43.37N 8.22E
Gatton Australia 65 27.32S152.18E
Gatun L. Panama 87 9.20N 80.00W
Gauchy France 15 49.49N 3.13E
Gauer L. Canada 75 57.00N 97.50W
Gauhāti India 41 26.11N 91.44E
Gaurela India 41 22.45N 81.54E
Gauri Sankar mtn. China / Nepal 41 27.57N 86.21E
Gavá Spain 16 41.18N 2.00E
Gavāter Iran 43 25.10N 61.31E
Gāv Koshī Iran 43 28.39N 57.13E
Gävle Sweden 23 60.40N 17.10E
Gävleborg d. Sweden 23 61.30N 16.15E
Gávrion Greece 19 37.52N 24.46E
Gawachab Namibia 56 27.03S 17.50E
Gāwilgarh Hills India 40 21.30N 77.00E
Gawler Australia 66 34.38S138.44E
Gawler Ranges mts. Australia 66 32.30S136.00E
Gaya India 41 24.47N 85.00E
Gaya Niger 53 11.53N 3.31E
Gayndah Australia 64 25.37S151.36E
Gayny U.S.S.R. 24 60.17N 54.15E
Gaysin U.S.S.R. 21 48.50N 29.29E
Gayvoron U.S.S.R. 21 48.20N 29.52E
Gaza see Ghazzah Egypt 44
Gaza d. Mozambique 57 23.20S 32.35E
Gaza Strip f. Egypt 44 31.32N 34.23E
Gaziantep Turkey 42 37.04N 37.21E
Gbanhui Ivory Coast 52 8.12N 3.02W
Gboko Nigeria 53 7.22N 8.58E
Gcuwa R.S.A. 56 32.20S 28.09E
Gdańsk Poland 21 54.22N 18.38E
Gdansk, G. of Poland 21 54.45N 19.15E
Gdov U.S.S.R. 24 58.48N 27.52E
Gdynia Poland 21 54.31N 18.30E
Gebe i. Indonesia 37 0.05S129.20E
Gebze Turkey 42 40.48N 29.26E
Gech'a Ethiopia 49 7.31N 35.22E
Gedera Israel 44 31.48N 34.46E
Gediz r. Turkey 19 38.37N 26.47E
Gedser Denmark 23 54.35N 11.57E
Geel Belgium 14 51.10N 5.00E
Geelong Australia 66 38.10S144.26E
Gê'gyai China 41 32.25N 84.05E
Gehua P.N.G. 64 10.20S150.25E
Geidam Nigeria 53 12.55N 11.55E
Geikie r. Canada 75 57.45N103.52W
Geilenkirchen Germany 14 50.58N 6.08E
Geilo Norway 23 60.31N 8.12E
Gejiu China 30 23.25N103.05E
Gela Italy 18 37.03N 14.15E
Geladī Ethiopia 45 6.58N 44.30E
Gelai mtn. Tanzania 55 2.37S 36.07E
Gelderland d. Neth. 14 52.05N 6.00E
Geldermalsen Neth. 14 51.53N 5.17E
Geldern Germany 14 51.31N 6.19E
Geldrop Neth. 14 51.26N 5.31E
Geleen Neth. 14 50.58N 5.51E
Gélengdeng Chad 53 10.56N 15.32E
Gelibolu Turkey 19 40.25N 26.31E
Gelligaer U.K. 11 51.40N 3.18W
Gelsenkirchen Germany 14 51.30N 7.05E
Gem Canada 74 50.58N112.11W
Gemas Malaysia 36 2.35N102.35E
Gembloux Belgium 14 50.34N 4.42E
Gemena Zaïre 54 3.14N 19.48E
Gemerek Turkey 42 39.13N 36.05E
Gemlik Turkey 42 40.26N 29.10E
Gemona del Friuli Italy 15 46.16N 13.09E
Genalē r. Ethiopia 49 4.15N 42.10E
Genappe Belgium 14 50.37N 4.25E
Gendringen Neth. 14 51.52N 6.26E
General Acha Argentina 93 37.20S 64.35W
General Alvear Buenos Aires Argentina 93 36.00S 60.00W
General Alvear Mendoza Argentina 93 34.59S 67.42W
General Belgrano Argentina 93 35.45S 58.30W
General Campos Argentina 93 31.30S 58.25W
General Conesa Argentina 93 36.30S 57.19W
General Guido Argentina 93 36.40S 57.45W
General Lavalle Argentina 93 36.22S 56.55W
General Madariaga Argentina 93 37.00S 57.05W
General Paz Argentina 93 35.32S 58.18W
General Pico Argentina 93 35.38S 63.46W
General Roca Argentina 93 39.02S 67.33W
General Santos Phil. 37 6.05N125.15E
Geneseo Ill. U.S.A. 82 41.27N 90.09W
Geneseo N.Y. U.S.A. 84 42.46N 77.49W
Geneva see Genève Switz. 20
Geneva Nebr. U.S.A. 82 40.32N 97.36W
Geneva N.Y. U.S.A. 84 42.53N 76.59W
Geneva Ohio U.S.A. 84 41.48N 80.57W
Geneva, L. see Léman, Lac l. Switz. 20
Genève Switz. 20 46.13N 6.09E
Genichesk U.S.S.R. 25 46.10N 34.49E
Genil r. Spain 16 37.42N 5.20W
Genk Belgium 14 50.58N 5.34E
Gennep Neth. 14 51.43N 5.58E
Gennes France 15 47.20N 0.14W
Genoa Australia 67 37.29S149.35E
Genoa see Genova Italy 15
Genoa U.S.A. 82 41.27N 97.44W
Genoa, G. of see Genova, Golfo di g. Italy 15
Genova Italy 15 44.24N 8.54E
Genova, Golfo di g. Italy 15 44.12N 8.55E
Gent Belgium 14 51.02N 3.42E
Gentilly Canada 77 46.24N 72.17W
Geographe B. Australia 63 33.35S115.15E
George r. Australia 66 28.24S136.39E
George r. Canada 73 58.30N 66.00W
George R.S.A. 56 33.57S 22.27E
George, L. N.S.W. Australia 67 35.07S149.22E
George, L. S.A. Australia 66 37.26S140.00E
George, L. Uganda 55 0.00 30.10E
George, L. Fla. U.S.A. 85 29.17N 81.36W
George B. Canada 77 45.50N 61.45W
George's Cove Canada 77 52.40N 55.50W
Georgetown Ascension 95 7.56S 14.25W
Georgetown Qld. Australia 64 18.18S143.33E
George Town Tas. Australia 65 41.04S146.48E
Georgetown Canada 77 46.11N 62.32W
Georgetown Cayman Is. 87 19.20N 81.23W
Georgetown Gambia 52 13.31N 14.50W
Georgetown Guyana 90 6.46N 58.10W
George Town Malaysia 36 5.30N100.16E
Georgetown Del. U.S.A. 85 38.42N 75.23W
Georgetown S.C. U.S.A. 85 33.23N 79.18W
Georgetown Tex. U.S.A. 83 30.38N 97.41W
George V Land f. Antarctica 96 69.00S145.00E
Georgia d. U.S.A. 85 32.50N 83.15W
Georgia, Str. of Canada 74 49.25N124.00W
Georgian B. Canada 76 45.15N 80.45W
Georgina r. Australia 64 23.12S139.33E
Georgiu-Dezh U.S.S.R. 25 51.00N 39.30E
Georgiyevsk U.S.S.R. 25 44.10N 43.30E
Gera Germany 20 50.51N 12.11E
Geraardsbergen Belgium 14 50.47N 3.53E
Geral de Goiás, Serra mts. Brazil 91 13.00S 45.40W
Geraldine New Zealand 60 44.05S171.15E
Geral do Paraná, Serra mts. Brazil 91 14.40S 47.30W
Geraldton Australia 63 28.49S114.36E
Geraldton Canada 76 49.44N 86.59W
Gerede Turkey 42 40.48N 32.13E
Gereshk Afghan. 40 31.48N 64.34E
Gérgal Spain 16 37.07N 2.31W
Gering U.S.A. 82 41.50N103.40W
Gerlach U.S.A. 80 40.40N119.21W
Gerlachovsky mtn. Czech. 21 49.10N 20.05E
Germany Europe 20 51.00N 10.00E
Germiston R.S.A. 56 26.14S 28.10E
Gerolstein Germany 14 50.14N 6.40E
Gerringong Australia 67 34.45S150.50E
Gêrzê China 41 32.16N 84.12E
Gescher Germany 14 51.58N 7.00E
Getafe Spain 16 40.18N 3.44W
Gete r. Belgium 14 50.58N 5.07E
Gethsémani Canada 77 50.13N 60.40W
Gettysburg S.Dak. U.S.A. 82 45.01N 99.57W
Gevān Iran 43 26.03N 57.17E
Gevelsberg Germany 14 51.20N 7.20E
Geysdorp R.S.A. 56 26.31S 25.17E
Geyser U.S.A. 80 47.16N110.30W
Geyve Turkey 42 40.32N 30.18E
Ghābat al 'Arab Sudan 49 9.02N 29.29E
Ghadaf, Wādī al r. Jordan 44 31.46N 36.50E
Ghadāmis Libya 51 30.08N 9.30E
Ghaddūwah Libya 51 26.26N 14.18E
Ghāghra r. India 41 25.47N 84.37E
Ghana Africa 52 8.00N 1.00W
Ghanzi Botswana 56 21.42S 21.39E
Ghanzi d. Botswana 56 21.44S 21.38E
Gharb al Istiwā'īyah d. Sudan 49 5.25N 29.00E
Ghardaïa Algeria 51 32.29N 3.40E
Gharghoda India 41 22.10N 83.21E
Ghārib, Jabal mtn. Egypt 44 28.06N 32.54E
Gharo Pakistan 40 24.44N 67.35E
Gharyān Libya 51 32.10N 13.01E
Gharyān d. Libya 51 30.35N 12.00E
Ghāt Libya 51 24.58N 10.11E
Ghātsīla India 41 22.36N 86.29E
Ghazāl, Bahr al r. Sudan 49 9.31N 30.25E
Ghāziābād India 41 28.40N 77.26E
Ghāzīpur India 41 25.35N 83.34E
Ghazlūna Pakistan 40 31.24N 67.49E
Ghaznī Afghan. 40 33.33N 68.26E
Ghaznī d. Afghan. 40 32.45N 68.30E
Ghaznī r. Afghan. 40 32.35N 67.58E
Ghazzah Egypt 44 31.30N 34.28E
Ghedi Italy 15 45.24N 10.16E
Gheorghe-Gheorghiu-Dej Romania 21 46.14N 26.44E
Gheorgheni Romania 21 46.43N 25.36E
Gherla Romania 21 47.02N 23.55E
Ghotki Pakistan 40 28.01N 69.19E
Ghowr d. Afghan. 40 34.00N 64.15E
Ghubaysh Sudan 49 12.09N 27.21E
Ghudāf, Wādī al r. Iraq 42 32.54N 43.33E
Ghūrīān Afghan. 40 34.21N 61.30E
Gia Dinh Vietnam 34 10.54N106.43E
Gibb River town Australia 62 16.29S126.20E
Gibeon Namibia 56 25.09S 17.44E
Gibraltar Europe 16 36.07N 5.22W
Gibraltar, Str. of Africa / Europe 16 36.00N 5.25W
Gibraltar Pt. U.K. 10 53.05N 0.20E
Gibson Australia 63 33.39S121.48E
Gibson Desert Australia 62 23.10S125.35E
Gīda Ethiopia 49 9.40N 35.16E
Giddings U.S.A. 83 30.11N 96.56W
Gien France 15 47.41N 2.37E
Giessen Germany 20 50.35N 8.42E
Gieten Neth. 14 53.01N 6.45E
Gifford r. Canada 73 70.21N 83.05W
Gifford U.S.A. 80 48.20N118.08W
Gifhorn Germany 20 52.29N 10.33E
Gifu Japan 35 35.25N136.45E
Gifu d. Japan 35 35.32N137.15E
Giganta, Sierra de la mts. Mexico 81 25.30N111.15W
Gigantes, Llanos de los f. Mexico 81 30.00N105.00W
Gigha i. U.K. 12 55.41N 5.44W
Giglio i. Italy 18 42.21N 10.53E
Gijón Spain 16 43.32N 5.40W
Gila r. U.S.A. 81 32.43N114.33W
Gila Bend U.S.A. 81 32.57N112.43W
Gila Bend Mts. U.S.A. 81 33.10N113.10W
Gilbert r. Australia 64 16.35S141.15E
Gilbert Islands Kiribati 68 2.00S175.00E
Gildford U.S.A. 80 48.34N110.18W
Gilé Mozambique 55 16.10S 38.17E
Gilgandra Australia 67 31.42S148.40E
Gil Gil r. Australia 67 29.10S148.50E
Gilgil Kenya 55 0.29S 36.19E
Gilgit Jammu & Kashmir 38 35.54N 74.20E
Gilgunnia Australia 67 32.25S146.04E
Gill, Lough Rep. of Ire. 13 54.15N 8.14W
Gilles, L. Australia 66 32.50S136.45E
Gillette U.S.A. 80 44.18N105.30W
Gillingham Kent U.K. 11 51.24N 0.33E
Gill Pt. c. St. Helena 95 15.59S 5.38W
Gilmour Canada 76 44.48N 77.37W
Gilo r. Ethiopia 49 8.10N 33.15E
Gimli Canada 75 50.39N 97.00W
Gingin Australia 63 31.21S115.42E
Gīnīr Ethiopia 49 7.07N 40.46E
Ginzo de Limia Spain 16 42.03N 7.47W
Gióna mtn. Greece 19 38.38N 22.14E
Girardot Colombia 90 4.19N 74.47W
Girdle Ness U.K. 12 57.06N 2.02W
Giresun Turkey 42 40.55N 38.25E
Gīr Hills India 40 21.10N 71.00E
Giri r. Zaïre 54 0.30N 17.58E
Girīdīh India 41 24.11N 86.18E
Girilambone Australia 67 31.14S146.55E
Girna r. India 40 21.08N 75.19E
Girona Spain 16 41.59N 2.49E
Gironde r. France 17 45.35N 1.00W
Girvan U.K. 12 55.15N 4.51W
Girwa r. India 41 27.20N 81.25E
Gisborne New Zealand 60 38.41S178.02E
Gisborne d. New Zealand 60 38.20S177.45E
Gisors France 15 49.17N 1.47E
Gitega Burundi 55 3.25S 29.58E
Giulianova Italy 18 42.45N 13.57E
Giurgiu Romania 21 43.52N 25.58E
Giv'atayim Israel 44 32.04N 34.49E
Givet France 17 50.08N 4.49E
Gīzāb Afghan. 40 33.23N 65.55E
Gizhiga U.S.S.R. 29 62.00N160.34E
Gizhiginskaya Guba g. U.S.S.R. 29 61.00N158.00E
Giżycko Poland 21 54.03N 21.47E
Gjerstad Norway 23 58.54N 9.00E
Gjirokastër Albania 19 40.05N 20.10E
Gjoa Haven town Canada 73 68.39N 96.08W
Gjövik Norway 23 60.48N 10.42E
Glace Bay town Canada 77 46.12N 59.57W
Glacier Nat. Park Canada 74 51.15N117.30W
Glacier Peak mtn. U.S.A. 80 48.07N121.06W
Gladewater U.S.A. 83 32.33N 94.56W
Gladmar Canada 75 49.12N104.31W
Gladstone Qld. Australia 64 23.52S151.16E
Gladstone S.A. Australia 66 33.17S138.22E
Gladstone Mich. U.S.A. 84 45.52N 87.02W
Gladstone N.J. U.S.A. 85 40.43N 74.40W
Glafsfjorden l. Sweden 23 59.34N 12.37E
Glåma r. Norway 23 59.15N 10.55E
Glamoč Yugo. 19 44.03N 16.51E
Glan r. Germany 14 49.46N 7.43E
Glanaman U.K. 11 51.49N 3.54W
Glandorf Germany 14 52.05N 8.00E
Glasco Kans. U.S.A. 82 39.22N 97.50W
Glasgow U.K. 12 55.52N 4.15W
Glasgow Ky. U.S.A. 85 36.59N 85.56W
Glasgow Mont. U.S.A. 80 48.12N106.38W
Glassboro U.S.A. 85 39.42N 75.07W
Glastonbury U.K. 11 51.09N 2.42W
Glazov U.S.S.R. 24 58.09N 52.42E
Gleisdorf Austria 20 47.06N 15.44E
Glen R.S.A. 56 28.57S 26.19E
Glen Affric f. U.K. 12 57.15N 5.03W
Glénans, Îles de is. France 17 47.43N 3.57W
Glenarm U.K. 13 54.57N 5.58W
Glenburnie Australia 66 37.49S140.56E
Glen Burnie U.S.A. 85 39.10N 76.37W
Glencoe Australia 66 37.41S140.05E
Glen Coe f. U.K. 12 56.40N 5.03W
Glencoe U.S.A. 82 44.45N 94.10W
Glen Cove U.S.A. 85 40.52N 73.37W
Glendale Ariz. U.S.A. 81 33.32N112.11W
Glendale Calif. U.S.A. 81 34.10N118.17W
Glendale Oreg. U.S.A. 80 42.44N123.26W
Glen Davis Australia 67 33.07S150.22E
Glendive U.S.A. 80 47.06N104.43W
Glenelg r. Australia 66 38.03S141.00E
Glengarriff Rep. of Ire. 13 51.45N 9.33W
Glen Garry f. Highland U.K. 12 57.03N 5.04W
Glen Head Rep. of Ire. 13 54.44N 8.46W
Glen Helen town Australia 64 23.15S132.35E
Glen Innes Australia 67 29.42S151.45E
Glen Mòr f. U.K. 12 57.15N 4.30W
Glenmora U.S.A. 83 30.59N 92.35W
Glenmorgan Australia 65 27.19S149.40E
Glen Moriston U.K. 12 57.09N 4.50W
Glenns Ferry U.S.A. 80 42.57N115.18W
Glenrock U.S.A. 80 42.52N105.52W
Glenrothes U.K. 12 56.12N 3.10W
Glenroy Australia 62 17.23S126.01E
Glens Falls town U.S.A. 84 43.19N 73.39W
Glenshee f. U.K. 12 56.45N 3.25W
Glen Spean f. U.K. 12 56.53N 4.40W
Glenwood Ark. U.S.A. 83 34.20N 93.33W
Glenwood Iowa U.S.A. 82 41.03N 95.45W
Glenwood Oreg. U.S.A. 80 45.39N123.16W
Glenwood Springs town U.S.A. 80 39.33N107.19W
Glittertind mtn. Norway 23 61.39N 8.33E
Gliwice Poland 21 50.17N 18.40E
Globe U.S.A. 81 33.24N110.47W
Głogów Poland 20 51.40N 16.06E
Glotovo U.S.S.R. 24 63.25N 49.28E
Gloucester Australia 67 31.59S151.58E
Gloucester U.K. 11 51.52N 2.15W
Gloucester U.S.A. 84 42.41N 70.39W
Gloucester City U.S.A. 85 39.54N 75.07W
Gloucestershire d. U.K. 11 51.45N 2.00W
Głubczyce Poland 21 50.13N 17.49E
Glückstadt Germany 20 53.47N 9.25E
Glusha U.S.S.R. 21 53.03N 28.55E
Gmünd Austria 20 48.47N 14.59E
Gnarp Sweden 23 62.03N 17.16E
Gnesta Sweden 23 59.03N 17.18E
Gniewkowo Poland 21 52.24N 18.25E
Gniezno Poland 21 52.32N 17.32E
Gnjilane Yugo. 19 42.28N 21.58E
Gnosjö Sweden 23 57.22N 13.44E
Gnowangerup Australia 63 33.57S117.58E
Gnuca Australia 63 31.08S117.24E
Goa d. India 38 15.30N 74.00E
Goageb Namibia 56 26.45S 17.18E
Goālpāra India 41 26.10N 90.37E
Goat Fell mtn. U.K. 12 55.37N 5.12W
Goba Ethiopia 49 7.02N 40.00E
Goba Mozambique 57 26.11S 32.08E
Gobabis Namibia 56 22.28S 18.58E
Gobi des. Asia 32 45.00N108.00E
Goch Germany 14 51.41N 6.09E
Gochas Namibia 56 24.50S 18.48E
Godalming U.K. 11 51.11N 0.37W
Godar Pakistan 40 28.10N 63.14E
Godāvari r. India 39 16.40N 82.15E
Godbout Canada 77 49.19N 67.37W
Goderich Canada 76 43.45N 81.43W
Goderville France 15 49.39N 0.22E
Godhavn Greenland 73 69.20N 53.30W
Godhra India 40 22.45N 73.38E
Godoy Cruz Argentina 93 32.55S 68.50W
Gods r. Canada 75 56.22N 92.51W
Gods L. Canada 75 54.45N 94.00W
Godthåb Greenland 73 64.10N 51.40W
Goéland, Lac au l. Canada 76 49.47N 76.41W
Goélands, Lac aux l. Canada 77 55.25N 64.20W
Goes Neth. 14 51.30N 3.54E
Gogama Canada 76 47.35N 81.35W
Gogeh Ethiopia 49 8.12N 38.27E
Gogonou Benin 53 10.50N 2.50E
Gogra r. see Ghāghra India 41
Gogrial Sudan 49 8.32N 28.07E
Goha Ethiopia 49 10.25N 34.38E
Gohad India 41 26.26N 78.27E
Goiana Brazil 91 7.30S 35.00W
Goiânia Brazil 91 16.43S 49.18W
Goiás Brazil 91 15.57S 50.07W
Goiás d. Brazil 91 15.00S 48.00W
Goichran India 41 31.04N 78.07E
Goito Italy 15 45.15N 10.40E
Gojam d. Ethiopia 49 11.10N 37.00E
Gojeb r. Ethiopia 49 7.10N 37.27E
Gojō Japan 35 34.21N135.42E
Gojra Pakistan 40 31.09N 72.41E
Gökçeada i. Turkey 19 40.10N 25.51E
Göksun Turkey 42 38.03N 36.30E
Gokteik Burma 39 22.26N 97.00E
Gokwe Zimbabwe 56 18.14S 28.54E
Gol Norway 23 60.42N 8.57E
Gola Gokaran Nath India 41 28.05N 80.28E
Golan Heights mts. Syria 44 32.55N 35.42E
Golconda U.S.A. 80 40.57N117.30W
Goldap Poland 21 54.19N 22.19E
Gold Beach town U.S.A. 80 42.25N124.25W
Golden Canada 74 51.20N117.00W
Golden Rep. of Ire. 13 52.30N 7.59W
Golden U.S.A. 80 39.46N105.13W
Golden B. New Zealand 60 40.45S172.50E
Goldendale U.S.A. 80 45.49N120.50W
Golden Hinde mtn. Canada 74 49.40N125.44W
Golden Ridge town Australia 63 30.51S121.42E
Golden Vale f. Rep. of Ire. 13 52.30N 8.07W
Goldfield U.S.A. 80 37.42N117.14W
Goldfields Canada 75 59.28N108.31W
Goldpines Canada 76 50.45N 93.05W
Goldsand L. Canada 75 56.58N101.02W
Goldsboro U.S.A. 85 35.23N 78.00W
Goldsworthy Australia 62 20.20S119.30E
Goleniów Poland 20 53.36N 14.50E
Golets Skalisty mtn. U.S.S.R. 29 56.00N130.40E
Golfito Costa Rica 87 8.42N 83.10W
Golfo degli Aranci town Italy 18 41.00N 9.38E
Goliad U.S.A. 83 28.40N 97.23W
Golling Austria 20 47.36N 13.10E
Golmud China 30 36.22N 94.55E
Golovanevsk U.S.S.R. 21 48.25N 30.30E
Golpāyegān Iran 43 33.23N 50.18E
Golspie U.K. 12 57.58N 3.58W
Goma Zaïre 55 1.37S 29.10E
Gomang Co l. China 41 31.10N 89.10E
Gombe Nigeria 53 10.17N 11.20E
Gombe r. Tanzania 55 4.43S 31.30E
Gomel U.S.S.R. 21 52.25N 31.00E
Gomera i. Canary Is. 50 28.08N 17.14W
Gómez Palacio Mexico 83 25.34N103.30W
Gomīshān Iran 43 37.04N 54.06E
Gompa Jammu & Kashmir 40 35.02N 77.20E
Gonaïves Haiti 87 19.29N 72.42W
Gonâve, Golfe de la g. Haiti 87 19.20N 73.00W
Gonâve, Île de la i. Haiti 87 18.50N 73.00W
Gonbad-e Kāvūs Iran 43 37.15N 55.11E
Gonda India 41 27.08N 81.56E
Gondal India 40 21.58N 70.48E
Gonder Ethiopia 49 12.39N 37.29E
Gonder d. Ethiopia 49 12.30N 37.30E
Gondia India 41 21.27N 80.12E
Gongbo'gyamda China 41 29.56N 93.23E
Gonggar China 41 29.15N 90.50E
Gongga Shan mtn. China 30 29.30N101.30E
Gongola d. Nigeria 53 8.40N 11.30E
Gongola r. Nigeria 53 9.30N 12.06E
Gongolgon Australia 67 30.22S146.56E
Goñi Uruguay 93 33.31S 56.24W
Goniri Nigeria 53 11.30N 12.15E
Gonzaga Italy 15 44.57N 10.49E
Gonzales U.S.A. 83 29.30N 97.27W
Good Hope, C. of R.S.A. 56 34.21S 18.28E
Good Hope Mtn. Canada 74 51.09N124.10W
Gooding U.S.A. 80 42.56N114.43W
Goodland U.S.A. 82 39.21N101.43W

Goodooga Australia 67 29.08S147.30E
Goodsprings U.S.A. 81 35.50N115.26W
Goole U.K. 10 53.42N 0.52W
Goolgowi Australia 67 33.59S145.42E
Goolma Australia 67 32.21S149.20E
Gooloogong Australia 67 33.36S148.27E
Goolwa Australia 66 35.31S138.45E
Goomalling Australia 63 31.19S116.49E
Goombalie Australia 67 29.59S145.24E
Goondiwindi Australia 67 28.30S150.17E
Goongarrie Australia 63 30.03S121.09E
Goor Neth. 14 52.16N 6.33E
Goose r. Canada 77 53.18N 60.23W
Goose Bay town Canada 77 53.19N 60.24W
Goose L. U.S.A. 80 41.57N120.25W
Gopālganj Bangla. 41 23.01N 89.50E
Gopālganj India 41 26.28N 84.26E
Göppingen Germany 20 48.43N 9.39E
Gorakhpur India 41 26.45N 83.22E
Goras India 40 25.32N 76.56E
Gordon r. Australia 63 34.12S117.00E
Gordon U.S.A. 82 42.48N102.12W
Gordon Downs town Australia 62 18.43S128.33E
Gordon L. Canada 74 63.05N113.11W
Gordonvale Australia 64 17.05S145.47E
Goré Chad 53 7.57N 16.31E
Gorē Ethiopia 49 8.08N 35.33E
Gore New Zealand 60 46.06S168.58E
Gorgān Iran 43 36.50N 54.29E
Gorgān r. Iran 43 37.00N 54.00E
Gorgol d. Mauritania 50 15.45N 13.00W
Gori U.S.S.R. 43 41.59N 44.05E
Gorinchem Neth. 14 51.50N 4.59E
Gorizia Italy 18 45.58N 13.37E
Gorki see Gor'kiy U.S.S.R. 24
Gor'kiy U.S.S.R. 24 56.20N 44.00E
Gorkovskoye Vodokhranilishche resr. U.S.S.R. 24 56.49N 43.00E
Görlitz Germany 20 51.09N 15.00E
Gorlovka U.S.S.R. 25 48.17N 38.05E
Gorna Oryakhovitsa Bulgaria 19 43.07N 25.40E
Gorno Altaysk U.S.S.R. 28 51.59N 85.56E
Gorno Filinskoye U.S.S.R. 28 60.06N 69.58E
Gornyatskiy U.S.S.R. 24 67.30N 64.03E
Goroch'an mtn. Ethiopia 49 9.22N 37.04E
Gorodenka U.S.S.R. 21 48.40N 25.30E
Gorodishche B.S.S.R. U.S.S.R. 21 53.18N 26.00E
Gorodishche B.S.S.R. U.S.S.R. 21 53.45N 29.45E
Gorodnitsa U.S.S.R. 21 50.50N 27.19E
Gorodnya U.S.S.R. 21 51.54N 31.37E
Gorodok U.S.S.R. 21 49.48N 23.39E
Goroka P.N.G. 37 6.02S145.22E
Goroke Australia 66 36.43S141.30E
Gorokhov U.S.S.R. 21 50.30N 24.46E
Gorongosa r. Mozambique 57 20.29S 34.36E
Gorontalo Indonesia 37 0.33N123.05E
Gort Rep. of Ire. 13 53.04N 8.49W
Goryn r. U.S.S.R. 21 52.08N 27.17E
Gorzów Wielkopolski Poland 20 52.42N 15.12E
Gosford Australia 67 33.25S151.18E
Goslar Germany 20 51.54N 10.25E
Gospić Yugo. 20 44.34N 15.23E
Gosport U.K. 11 50.48N 1.08W
Gossi Mali 52 15.49N 1.17W
Gossinga Sudan 49 8.39N 25.59E
Gostivar Yugo. 19 41.47N 20.24E
Gostynin Poland 21 52.26N 19.29E
Göta r. Sweden 23 57.42N 11.52E
Göta Kanal Sweden 23 58.50N 13.58E
Göteborg Sweden 23 57.43N 11.58E
Göteborg och Bohus d. Sweden 23 58.30N 11.30E
Gotemba Japan 35 35.18N138.56E
Götene Sweden 23 58.32N 13.29E
Gotha Germany 20 50.57N 10.43E
Gothenburg see Göteborg Sweden 23
Gothenburg U.S.A. 82 40.56N100.09W
Gothèye Niger 53 13.51N 1.31E
Gotland d. Sweden 23 57.30N 18.30E
Gotland i. Sweden 23 57.30N 18.33E
Göttingen Germany 20 51.32N 9.57E
Gouda Neth. 14 52.01N 4.43E
Gough I. Atlantic Oc. 95 40.20S 10.00W
Gouin, Résr. Canada 76 48.38N 74.54W
Goulburn Australia 67 34.47S149.43E
Goulburn r. Australia 67 36.08S144.30E
Goulburn Is. Australia 64 11.33S133.26E
Goulimime Morocco 50 28.56N 10.04W
Goundam Mali 52 17.27N 3.39W
Gourdon France 17 44.45N 1.22E
Gouré Niger 53 13.59N 10.15E
Gourma-Rharous Mali 52 16.58N 1.50W
Gournay France 15 49.29N 1.44E
Gouro Chad 51 19.33N 19.33E
Governador Valadares Brazil 94 18.51S 42.00W
Govind Balabh Pant Sāgar resr. India 41 24.05N 82.50E
Govind Sāgar resr. India 40 31.20N 76.45E
Gowanda U.S.A. 84 42.28N 78.57W
Gowd-e Zereh des. Afghan. 43 30.00N 62.00E
Gower pen. U.K. 11 51.37N 4.10W
Gowmal r. Afghan. see Gumal r. Pakistan 40
Gowmal Kalay Afghan. 40 32.29N 68.55E
Goya Argentina 92 29.10S 59.20W
Goyder r. Australia 64 12.38S135.11E
Goz Béïda Chad 49 12.13N 21.25E
Gozo i. Malta 18 36.03N 14.16E
Graaff Reinet R.S.A. 56 32.15S 24.31E
Gračac Yugo. 20 44.18N 15.51E
Grace, L. Australia 63 33.18S118.15E
Gracias á Dios, Cabo c. Honduras/Nicaragua 87 15.00N 83.10W
Grado Italy 15 45.40N 13.23E
Grado Spain 16 43.23N 6.04W
Grafton Australia 67 29.40S152.56E
Grafton N.Dak. U.S.A. 82 48.25N 97.25W
Grafton Wisc. U.S.A. 82 43.20N 87.58W
Grafton W.Va. U.S.A. 84 39.21N 80.03W
Graham r. Canada 74 56.31N122.17W
Graham U.S.A. 83 33.06N 98.35W
Graham, Mt. U.S.A. 81 32.42N109.52W
Graham I. Canada 74 53.40N132.30W
Graham Land f. Antarctica 96 67.00S 60.00W
Grahamstown R.S.A. 56 33.18S 26.30E
Graiguenamanagh Rep. of Ire. 13 52.33N 6.57W
Grajaú r. Brazil 91 3.41S 44.48W
Grampian d. U.K. 12 57.22N 2.35W
Grampian Mts. U.K. 12 56.55N 4.00W
Grampians mts. Australia 66 37.12S142.34E
Granada Nicaragua 87 11.58N 85.59W
Granada Spain 16 37.10N 3.35W
Granby Canada 77 45.23N 72.44W
Gran Canaria i. Canary Is. 50 28.00N 15.30W
Gran Chaco f. S. America 92 22.00S 60.00W
Grand r. Canada 76 42.51N 79.34W
Grand r. S.Dak. U.S.A. 82 45.40N100.32W
Grand Bahama I. Bahamas 87 26.40N 78.20W
Grand Bank town Canada 77 47.06N 55.47W
Grand Bassam Ivory Coast 52 5.14N 3.45W
Grand Canal see Da Yunhe canal China 32
Grand Canyon f. U.S.A. 81 36.10N112.45W
Grand Canyon town U.S.A. 81 36.03N112.09W
Grand Canyon Nat. Park U.S.A. 81 36.15N112.58W
Grand Cayman i. Cayman Is. 87 19.20N 81.30W
Grand Centre Canada 75 54.25N110.13W
Grand Cess Liberia 52 4.40N 8.12W
Grand Couronne France 15 49.21N 1.00E
Grande r. Bolivia 92 15.10S 64.55W
Grande r. Bahia Brazil 91 11.05S 43.09W
Grande r. Minas Gerais Brazil 92 20.00S 51.00W
Grande, Bahía b. Argentina 93 51.30S 67.30W
Grande, Ilha i. Brazil 94 23.07S 44.16W
Grande, Sierra mts. Mexico 81 29.35N104.55W
Grande Cascapédia Canada 77 48.19N 65.54W
Grande Comore see Njazídja i. Comoros 55
Grande do Gurupá, Ilha i. Brazil 91 1.00S 51.30W
Grande Prairie Canada 74 55.15N118.50W
Grand Erg de Bilma des. Niger 53 18.30N 14.00E
Grand Erg Occidental des. Algeria 50 30.10N 0.20E
Grand Erg Oriental des. Algeria 51 30.00N 7.00E
Grande Rivière town Canada 77 48.24N 64.30W
Grandes, Salinas f. Argentina 92 29.37S 64.56W
Grandes Bergeronnes Canada 77 48.15N 69.33W
Grande Vallée Canada 77 49.14N 65.08W
Grand Falls town N.B. Canada 77 46.55N 67.45W
Grand Falls town Nfld. Canada 77 48.56N 55.40W
Grand Forks Canada 74 49.00N118.30W
Grand Forks U.S.A. 82 47.55N 97.03W
Grand Fougeray France 15 47.44N 1.44W
Grand Island town U.S.A. 82 40.55N 98.21W
Grand Junction U.S.A. 80 39.05N108.33W
Grand L. N.B. Canada 77 45.38N 67.38W
Grand L. Nfld. Canada 77 49.00N 57.25W
Grand L. U.S.A. 84 45.15N 67.50W
Grand Lahou Ivory Coast 52 5.09N 5.01W
Grand Manan I. Canada 77 44.40N 66.50W
Grand Marais U.S.A. 82 47.45N 90.20W
Grand' Mère Canada 77 46.37N 72.41W
Grandois Canada 77 51.07N 55.46W
Grândola Portugal 16 38.10N 8.34W
Grand Passage N. Cal. 68 18.45S163.10E
Grand Prairie town U.S.A. 83 32.45N 96.59W
Grand Rapids town Canada 75 53.08N 99.20W
Grand Rapids town Mich. U.S.A. 84 42.57N 85.40W
Grand Rapids town Minn. U.S.A. 82 47.14N 93.31W
Grand Récif de Cook reef N. Cal. 68 19.25S163.50E
Grand St. Bernard, Col du pass Italy/Switz. 15 45.52N 7.11E
Grand Teton mtn. U.S.A. 80 43.44N110.48W
Grand Teton Nat. Park U.S.A. 80 43.30N110.37W
Grand Traverse B. U.S.A. 84 45.02N 85.30W
Grand Valley Canada 76 43.54N 80.19W
Grand Valley town U.S.A. 80 39.27N108.03W
Grandville U.S.A. 84 42.54N 85.48W
Grangemouth U.K. 12 56.01N 3.44W
Granger U.S.A. 80 41.35N109.58W
Grängesberg Sweden 23 60.05N 14.59E
Grangeville U.S.A. 80 45.56N116.07W
Granite City U.S.A. 82 38.43N 90.04W
Granite Falls town U.S.A. 82 44.49N 95.31W
Granite Peak town Australia 62 25.38S121.21E
Granite Peak mtn. U.S.A. 78 45.10N109.50W
Granity New Zealand 60 41.38S171.51E
Granja Brazil 91 3.06S 40.50W
Gränna Sweden 23 58.01N 14.28E
Granollers Spain 16 41.37N 2.18E
Granön Sweden 22 64.15N 19.19E
Gran Paradiso mtn. Italy 15 45.31N 7.15E
Grant Mich. U.S.A. 84 43.20N 85.49W
Grant Nebr. U.S.A. 82 40.50N101.56W
Grant City U.S.A. 82 40.29N 94.25W
Grantham U.K. 10 52.55N 0.39W
Grantown-on-Spey U.K. 12 57.20N 3.38W
Grant Range mts. U.S.A. 80 38.25N115.30W
Grants U.S.A. 81 35.09N107.52W
Grants Pass town U.S.A. 80 42.26N123.19W
Grantsville U.S.A. 84 38.55N 81.07W
Granville France 15 48.50N 1.35W
Granville N.Dak. U.S.A. 82 48.16N100.47W
Granville L. Canada 75 56.18N100.30W
Gras, Lac de l. Canada 72 64.30N110.30W
Graskop R.S.A. 56 24.55S 30.50E
Grasse France 17 43.40N 6.56E
Grasset, L. Canada 76 49.55N 78.00W
Grass Valley town Calif. U.S.A. 80 39.13N121.04W
Grass Valley town Oreg. U.S.A. 80 45.22N120.47W
Grates Pt. Canada 77 48.09N 52.57W
Grave Neth. 14 51.45N 5.45E
Grave, Pointe de c. France 17 45.35N 1.04W
Gravelbourg Canada 75 49.53N106.34W
Gravenhurst Canada 76 44.55N 79.22W
Gravesend Australia 67 29.35S150.20E
Gravesend U.K. 11 51.27N 0.24E
Gray France 17 47.27N 5.35E
Grayling U.S.A. 84 44.40N 84.43W
Grays U.K. 11 51.29N 0.20E
Graz Austria 20 47.05N 15.22E
Grdelica Yugo. 19 42.54N 22.04E
Great Abaco I. Bahamas 87 26.25N 77.10W
Great Artesian Basin f. Australia 64 26.30S143.02E
Great Australian Bight Australia 63 33.10S129.30E
Great B. U.S.A. 85 39.30N 74.23W
Great Barrier I. New Zealand 60 36.15S175.30E
Great Barrier Reef f. Australia 64 16.30S146.30E
Great Basin f. U.S.A. 80 40.35N116.00W
Great Bear L. Canada 72 66.00N120.00W
Great Bend town U.S.A. 82 38.22N 98.46W
Great Bitter L. see Murrah al Kubrá, Al Buḩayrah al h5ayrah al Egypt 44
Great Blasket I. Rep. of Ire. 13 52.05N 10.32W
Great Coco i. Burma 34 14.06N 93.21E
Great Divide Basin f. U.S.A. 80 42.00N108.10W
Great Dividing Range mts. Australia 67 29.00S152.00E
Great Driffield U.K. 10 54.01N 0.26W
Greater Antilles is. C. America 87 17.00N 70.00W
Greater London d. U.K. 11 51.31N 0.06W
Greater Manchester d. U.K. 10 53.30N 2.18W
Great Exuma i. Bahamas 87 23.00N 76.00W
Great Falls town U.S.A. 80 47.30N111.17W
Great Inagua I. Bahamas 87 21.00N 73.20W
Great Indian Desert see Thar Desert India/Pakistan 40
Great Karoo f. R.S.A. 56 32.40S 22.20E
Great Kei r. R.S.A. 56 32.39S 28.23E
Great L. Australia 65 41.50S146.43E
Great Malvern U.K. 11 52.07N 2.19W
Great Namaland f. Namibia 56 25.30S 17.20E
Great Nicobar i. India 34 7.00N 93.45E
Great Ouse r. U.K. 10 52.47N 0.23E
Great Ruaha r. Tanzania 55 7.55S 37.52E
Great Salt L. U.S.A. 80 41.10N112.30W
Great Salt Lake Desert U.S.A. 80 40.40N113.30W
Great Sand Hills Canada 75 50.35N109.05W
Great Sandy Desert Australia 62 20.30S123.35E
Great Sandy Desert see An Nafūd des. Saudi Arabia 42
Great Sea Reef Fiji 68 16.25S179.20E
Great Slave L. Canada 74 61.23N115.38W
Great Smoky Mountain Nat. Park U.S.A. 85 35.56N 82.48W
Great Sound b. Bermuda 95 32.18N 64.60W
Great Victoria Desert Australia 63 29.00S127.30E
Great Whernside mtn. U.K. 10 54.09N 1.59W
Great Yarmouth U.K. 11 52.40N 1.45E
Great Zimbabwe ruins Zimbabwe 56 20.30S 30.30E
Gréboun, Mont mtn. Niger 51 20.01N 8.35E
Gredos, Sierra de mts. Spain 16 40.18N 5.20W
Greece Europe 19 39.00N 22.00E
Greeley U.S.A. 80 40.25N104.42W
Green r. U.S.A. 80 38.11N109.53W
Green B. U.S.A. 82 45.00N 87.30W
Green Bay town U.S.A. 82 44.30N 88.01W
Greenbush Minn. U.S.A. 82 48.42N 96.11W
Greenbushes Australia 63 33.50S116.00E
Greencastle Ind. U.S.A. 84 39.39N 86.51W
Greene U.S.A. 84 42.20N 75.46W
Greeneville U.S.A. 85 36.10N 82.50W
Greenfield Ill. U.S.A. 82 39.21N 90.21W
Greenfield Iowa U.S.A. 82 41.18N 94.28W
Greenfield Mo. U.S.A. 83 37.25N 93.51W
Greenhills Australia 63 31.58S117.01E
Greening Canada 76 48.08N 74.55W
Greenland N. America 73 68.00N 45.00W
Greenlaw U.K. 12 55.43N 2.28W
Greenock U.K. 12 55.57N 4.45W
Greenore Pt. Rep. of Ire. 13 52.14N 6.19W
Greenough r. Australia 63 29.22S114.34E
Green River town Utah U.S.A. 80 38.59N110.10W
Green River town Wyo. U.S.A. 80 41.32N109.28W
Greensboro N.C. U.S.A. 85 36.04N 79.47W
Greensburg Ind. U.S.A. 84 39.20N 85.29W
Greenvale Australia 64 18.57S144.53E
Greenvale Canada 74 55.03N129.33W
Greenville Liberia 52 5.01N 9.03W
Greenville Ala. U.S.A. 85 31.50N 86.40W
Greenville Mich. U.S.A. 84 43.11N 85.13W
Greenville Miss. U.S.A. 83 33.25N 91.05W
Greenville Mo. U.S.A. 83 37.08N 90.27W
Greenville N.C. U.S.A. 85 35.36N 77.23W
Greenville S.C. U.S.A. 85 34.52N 82.25W
Greenville Tex. U.S.A. 83 33.08N 96.07W
Greenwich Conn. U.S.A. 85 41.05N 73.37W
Greenwood Miss. U.S.A. 83 33.31N 90.11W
Greenwood S.C. U.S.A. 85 34.11N 82.10W
Gregory r. Australia 64 17.53S139.17E
Gregory U.S.A. 82 43.14N 99.26W
Gregory, L. S.A. Australia 66 28.55S139.00E
Gregory L. W.A. Australia 62 20.10S127.20E
Gregory Range mts. Australia 64 19.00S143.05E
Greifswald Germany 20 54.06N 13.24E
Gremikha U.S.S.R. 24 68.03N 39.38E
Grenå Denmark 23 56.25N 10.53E
Grenada C. America 87 12.07N 61.40W
Grenade France 17 43.47N 1.10E
Grenfell Australia 67 33.53S148.11E
Grenoble France 17 45.11N 5.43E
Grenville, C. Australia 64 12.00S143.13E
Gresik Indonesia 37 7.12S112.38E
Gretna U.K. 12 55.00N 3.04W
Gretna U.S.A. 83 29.55N 90.03W
Greven Germany 14 52.07N 7.38E
Grevenbroich Germany 14 51.07N 6.33E
Grevesmühlen Germany 20 53.51N 11.10E
Grey r. New Zealand 60 42.28S171.13E
Grey, C. Australia 64 13.00S136.40E
Greybull U.S.A. 80 44.30N108.03W
Grey Is. Canada 77 50.50N 55.37W
Greymouth New Zealand 60 42.28S171.12E
Grey Range mts. Australia 65 27.30S143.59E
Greystones Rep. of Ire. 13 53.09N 6.04W
Greytown R.S.A. 56 29.04S 30.36E
Griffin U.S.A. 79 33.15N 84.17W
Griffith Australia 67 34.18S146.04E
Griggsville U.S.A. 82 39.42N 90.43W
Grignan France 17 44.25N 4.54E
Grigoriopol U.S.S.R. 21 47.08N 29.18E
Grim, C. Australia 65 40.45S144.45E
Grimari C.A.R. 49 5.44N 20.03E
Grimsby Canada 76 43.12N 79.34W
Grimsby U.K. 10 53.35N 0.05W
Grimstad Norway 23 58.20N 8.36E
Grimsvötn mtn. Iceland 22 64.30N 17.10W
Grindavik Iceland 22 63.50N 22.27W
Grindsted Denmark 23 55.45N 8.56E
Grinnell U.S.A. 82 41.45N 92.43W
Griqualand East f. R.S.A. 56 30.40S 29.10E
Griqualand West f. R.S.A. 56 28.50S 23.30E
Griva U.S.S.R. 24 60.35N 50.58E
Grobina U.S.S.R. 23 56.33N 21.10E
Groblershoop R.S.A. 56 28.55S 20.59E
Grodno U.S.S.R. 21 53.40N 23.50E
Grodzisk Poland 20 52.14N 16.22E
Grodzyanka U.S.S.R. 21 53.30N 28.41E
Groenlo Neth. 14 52.02N 6.36E
Groix, Île de i. France 17 47.38N 3.26W
Gronau Germany 14 52.14N 7.02E
Grong Norway 22 64.27N 12.19E
Groningen Neth. 14 53.13N 6.35E
Groningen d. Neth. 14 53.15N 6.45E
Groom U.S.A. 83 35.12N101.06W
Groot r. C.P. r. R.S.A. 56 33.58S 25.03E
Groote Eylandt i. Australia 64 14.00S136.40E
Grootfontein Namibia 56 19.32S 18.07E
Groot Karasberge mts. Namibia 56 27.20S 18.50E
Grootlaagte r. Botswana 56 20.58S 21.42E
Groot Swartberge mts. R.S.A. 56 33.20S 22.00E
Grossenbrode Germany 20 54.23N 11.07E
Grossenhain Germany 20 51.17N 13.31E
Grosseto Italy 18 42.46N 11.08E
Gross Glockner mtn. Austria 20 47.05N 12.50E
Groswater B. Canada 77 54.20N 57.30W
Grote Nete r. Belgium 14 51.07N 4.20E
Groundhog r. Canada 76 49.40N 82.06W
Grouse Creek town U.S.A. 80 41.22N113.53W
Grover City U.S.A. 81 35.07N120.37W
Groves U.S.A. 83 29.57N 93.55W
Groveton Tex. U.S.A. 83 31.03N 95.08W
Groznyy U.S.S.R. 25 43.21N 45.42E
Grudziądz Poland 21 53.29N 18.45E
Grumeti r. Tanzania 55 2.05S 33.45E
Grünau Namibia 56 27.44S 18.18E
Grundarfjördhur town Iceland 22 64.55N 23.20W
Grundy U.S.A. 85 37.13N 82.08W
Grungedal Norway 23 59.44N 7.43E
Gruzinskaya S.S.R. d. U.S.S.R. 25 42.00N 43.30E
Gryazovets U.S.S.R. 24 58.52N 40.12E
Gryfice Poland 20 53.56N 15.12E
Guachipas Argentina 92 25.31S 65.31W
Guacuí Brazil 94 20.44S 41.40W
Guadalajara Mexico 86 20.30N103.20W
Guadalajara Spain 16 40.37N 3.10W
Guadalcanal i. Solomon Is. 68 9.32S160.12E
Guadalete r. Spain 16 36.37N 6.15W
Guadalmena r. Spain 16 38.00N 3.50W
Guadalquivir r. Spain 16 36.50N 6.20W
Guadalupe Mexico 83 25.41N100.15W
Guadalupe, Isla de i. Mexico 81 29.00N118.15W
Guadalupe, Sierra de mts. Spain 16 39.30N 5.25W
Guadarrama r. Spain 16 39.55N 4.10W
Guadarrama, Sierra de mts. Spain 16 41.00N 3.50W
Guadeloupe i. Leeward Is. 87 16.20N 61.40W
Guadiana r. Portugal 16 37.10N 7.36W
Guadix Spain 16 37.19N 3.08W
Guafo, Golfo de g. Chile 93 43.35S 74.15W
Guainía r. Colombia 90 2.01N 67.07W
Guaíra Brazil 92 24.04S 54.15W
Guajará Mirim Brazil 90 10.48S 65.22W
Guajira, Península de la pen. Colombia 90 12.00N 72.00W
Gualeguay Argentina 93 33.10S 59.20W
Gualeguay r. Argentina 93 33.18S 59.38W
Gualeguaychu Argentina 93 33.00S 58.30W
Guam i. Northern Marianas 37 13.30N144.40E
Guamal Colombia 90 9.10N 74.15W
Guanajuato Mexico 86 21.00N101.16W
Guanajuato d. Mexico 86 21.00N101.00W
Guanare Venezuela 90 9.04N 69.45W
Guanarito Venezuela 90 8.43N 69.12W
Guane Cuba 87 22.13N 84.07W
Guang'an China 33 30.30N106.35E
Guangchang China 33 26.50N116.16E
Guangdong d. China 33 23.00N113.00E
Guanghan China 33 30.59N104.15E
Guanghua China 32 32.26N111.41E
Guangji China 33 29.42N115.39E
Guangming Ding mtn. China 33 30.09N118.11E
Guangnan China 33 24.03N105.03E
Guangrao China 32 37.04N118.22E
Guangxi Zhuangzu d. China 33 23.30N109.00E
Guangyuan China 32 32.29N105.55E
Guangze China 33 27.27N117.23E
Guangzhou China 33 23.08N113.20E
Guanling China 33 25.57N105.38E
Guantánamo Cuba 87 20.09N 75.14W
Guan Xian Shandong China 32 36.29N115.25E
Guan Xian Sichuan China 39 30.59N103.40E
Guanyun China 32 34.17N119.15E
Guaporé r. Bolivia/Brazil 92 12.00S 65.15W
Guaqui Bolivia 92 16.35S 68.51W
Guarabira Brazil 91 6.46S 35.25W
Guarapuava Brazil 94 25.22S 51.28W
Guaratinguetá Brazil 94 22.49S 45.09W
Guarda Portugal 16 40.32N 7.17W
Guardavalle Italy 19 38.30N 16.30E
Guardo Spain 16 42.47N 4.50W
Guareim r. Uruguay see Quarí r. Brazil 93
Guasave Mexico 81 25.34N108.27W
Guasipati Venezuela 90 7.28N 61.54W
Guastalla Italy 15 44.55N 10.39E
Guatemala C. America 87 15.40N 90.00W
Guatemala town Guatemala 86 14.38N 90.22W
Guatemala Basin Pacific Oc. 69 12.00N 95.00W
Guatemala Trench Pacific Oc. 69 15.00N 93.00W
Guatire Venezuela 90 10.28N 66.32W
Guaviare r. Colombia 90 4.00N 67.35W
Guaxupé Brazil 94 21.17S 46.44W
Guayaquil Ecuador 90 2.13S 79.54W
Guayaquil, Golfo de g. Ecuador 90 3.00S 80.35W
Guaymallén Argentina 93 32.54S 68.47W
Guaymas Mexico 81 27.56N110.54W
Guayquiraró r. Argentina 93 30.25S 59.36W
Guba Zaïre 54 10.40S 26.26E
Gubakha U.S.S.R. 24 58.55N 57.30E
Gubeikou China 32 40.41N117.09E
Gubin Poland 20 51.59N 14.42E
Gubio Nigeria 53 12.31N 12.44E
Guchab Namibia 56 19.40S 17.47E
Gucheng China 32 37.20N115.57E
Gúdar, Sierra de mts. Spain 16 40.27N 0.42W
Gudbrandsdalen f. Norway 23 61.30N 10.00E
Gudvangen Norway 23 60.52N 6.50E
Guecho Spain 16 43.21N 3.01W
Guékédou Guinea 52 8.35N 10.11W
Guelma Algeria 51 36.28N 7.26E
Guelph Canada 76 43.34N 80.16W
Guelta Zemmur W. Sahara 50 25.15N 12.20W
Guéméné-sur-Scorff France 17 48.04N 3.13W
Guera d. Chad 53 11.22N 18.00E
Guérard, Lac l. Canada 77 56.20N 65.35W
Guéret France 17 46.10N 1.52E
Guernica Spain 16 43.19N 2.40W
Guernsey i. U.K. 11 49.27N 2.35W
Guerra Mozambique 55 13.05S 35.12E
Guerrero d. Mexico 86 18.00N100.00W
Guiana S. America 91 3.40N 53.00W
Guiana Highlands S. America 90 4.00N 59.00W
Guichón Uruguay 93 32.21S 57.12W
Guidimaka d. Mauritania 50 15.20N 12.00W
Guiding China 33 26.32N107.15E
Guidong China 33 26.12N114.00E
Guiers, Lac de l. Senegal 52 16.12N 15.50W
Gui Jiang r. China 33 23.25N111.20E
Guildford Australia 63 31.55S115.55E
Guildford U.K. 11 51.14N 0.35W
Guilin China 33 25.20N110.10E
Guillaume-Delisle, Lac l. Canada 76 56.20N 75.50W
Guimarães Brazil 91 2.08S 44.36W
Guimarães Portugal 16 41.27N 8.18W
Guimeng Ding mtn. China 32 35.34N117.50E
Guinan China 30 35.20N100.50E
Guinea Africa 52 10.30N 11.30W
Guinea, G. of Africa 53 3.00N 3.00E
Guinea Basin f. Atlantic Oc. 95 0.00 5.00W
Guinea Bissau Africa 52 11.30N 15.00W
Güines Cuba 87 22.50N 82.02W
Guingamp France 17 48.34N 3.09W
Guinguinéo Senegal 52 14.20N 15.57W
Guiping China 33 23.20N110.02E
Guir, Hammada du f. Morocco/Algeria 50 31.00N 3.20W

Güiria Venezuela 90 10.37N 62.21W
Guiscard France 15 49.39N 3.03E
Guise France 15 49.54N 3.38E
Guiuan Phil. 37 11.02N125.44E
Guixi China 33 28.12N117.10E
Gui Xian China 33 23.02N109.40E
Guiyang China 33 26.31N106.39E
Guizhou d. China 33 27.00N107.00E
Gujarat d. India 40 22.20N 70.30E
Gūjar Khān Pakistan 40 33.16N 73.19E
Gujrānwāla Pakistan 40 32.26N 74.33E
Gujrāt Pakistan 40 32.34N 74.05E
Gulang Gansu China 32 37.30N102.54E
Gulargambone Australia 67 31.21S148.32E
Gulbarga India 38 17.22N 76.47E
Gulfport U.S.A. 83 30.22N 89.06W
Gulgong Australia 67 32.20S149.49E
Gulin China 33 28.07N105.51E
Gulistān Pakistan 40 30.36N 66.35E
Gull Lake town Canada 75 50.08N108.27W
Gulma Nigeria 53 12.41N 4.24E
Gulshad U.S.S.R. 30 46.37N 74.22E
Gulu Uganda 55 2.46N 32.21E
Guluy Ethiopia 48 14.43N 36.45E
Gulwe Tanzania 55 6.27S 36.27E
Gumal r. Pakistan 40 32.08N 69.50E
Gumel Nigeria 53 12.39N 9.23E
Gumla India 41 23.03N 84.33E
Gummersbach Germany 14 51.03N 7.32E
Gum Spring town U.S.A. 85 37.47N 77.54W
Gümüşhane Turkey 42 40.26N 39.26E
Guna India 40 24.39N 77.19E
Gunbar Australia 67 34.04S145.25E
Gundagai Australia 67 35.07S148.05E
Gundlupet India 38 11.48N 76.41E
Gungu Zaïre 54 5.43S 19.20E
Gunisao r. Canada 75 53.54N 97.58W
Gunisao L. Canada 75 53.33N 96.15W
Gunnedah Australia 67 30.59S150.15E
Gunning Australia 67 34.46S149.17E
Gunnison r. U.S.A. 80 39.03N108.35W
Gunnison Colo. U.S.A. 80 38.33N106.56W
Gunnison Utah U.S.A. 80 39.09N111.49W
Guntersville U.S.A. 85 34.20N 86.18W
Guntersville L. U.S.A. 85 34.45N 86.03W
Guntūr India 39 16.20N 80.27E
Gunungsitoli Indonesia 36 1.17N 97.37E
Gunupur India 41 19.05N 83.49E
Günzburg Germany 20 48.27N 10.16E
Guochengyi China 32 36.14N104.52E
Gurais Jammu & Kashmir 40 34.38N 74.50E
Gura Portiţei f. Romania 21 44.40N 29.00E
Gurban Obo China 32 43.05N112.27E
Gurdāspur Jammu & Kashmir 40 32.02N 75.31E
Gurgaon India 40 28.28N 77.02E
Gurgueia r. Brazil 91 6.45S 43.35W
Gurha India 40 25.14N 71.45E
Gurskøy i. Norway 22 62.16N 5.42E
Guruè Mozambique 57 15.30S 36.58E
Gürün Turkey 42 38.44N 37.15E
Gurupá Brazil 91 1.25S 51.39W
Gurupi r. Brazil 91 1.13S 46.06W
Guru Sikhar mtn. India 40 24.39N 72.46E
Guruve Zimbabwe 56 16.42S 30.40E
Gurvan Sayhan Uul mts. Mongolia 32 43.45N103.30E
Guryev U.S.S.R. 25 47.08N 51.59E
Gusau Nigeria 53 12.12N 6.40E
Gusev U.S.S.R. 21 54.32N 22.12E
Gusong China 33 28.25N105.12E
Guspini Italy 18 39.32N 8.38E
Gustav Holm, Kap c. Greenland 73 67.00N 34.00W
Güstrow Germany 20 53.48N 12.11E
Gütersloh Germany 20 51.54N 8.22E
Guthrie Ky. U.S.A. 85 36.40N 87.10W
Guthrie Okla. U.S.A. 83 35.53N 97.25W
Guyana S. America 90 4.40N 59.00W
Guyang China 32 41.03N110.03E
Guymon U.S.A. 83 36.41N101.29W
Guyra Australia 67 30.14S151.40E
Guyuan Hebei China 32 41.40N115.41E
Guyuan Ningxia Huizu China 32 36.00N106.25E
Guzhen Anhui China 32 33.19N117.19E
Guzman, Laguna de l. Mexico 81 31.25N107.25W
Gwa Burma 39 17.36N 94.35E
Gwabegar Australia 67 30.34S149.00E
Gwadabawa Nigeria 53 13.23N 5.15E
Gwādar Pakistan 40 25.07N 62.19E
Gwagwada Nigeria 53 10.15N 7.15E
Gwai Zimbabwe 56 19.15S 27.42E
Gwai r. Zimbabwe 56 17.59S 26.55E
Gwalior India 41 26.13N 78.10E
Gwanda Zimbabwe 56 20.59S 29.00E
Gwane Zaïre 49 4.43N 25.50E
Gwasero Nigeria 53 9.30N 8.30E
Gweebarra B. Rep. of Ire. 13 54.52N 8.28W
Gwent d. U.K. 11 51.44N 3.00W
Gweru Zimbabwe 56 19.25S 29.50E
Gwydir r. Australia 67 29.35S148.45E
Gwynedd d. U.K. 10 53.00N 4.00W
Gyaca China 41 29.05N 92.55E
Gyandzha U.S.S.R. 43 40.39N 46.20E
Gyangrang China 41 30.47N 85.09E
Gyangzê China 41 28.57N 89.38E
Gyaring Co l. China 41 31.05N 88.00E
Gydanskiy Poluostrov pen. U.S.S.R. 28 70.00N 78.30E
Gyimda China 41 31.03N 97.18E
Gyirong China 41 29.00N 85.15E
Gympie Australia 64 26.11S152.40E
Gyöngyös Hungary 21 47.47N 19.56E
Győr Hungary 21 47.41N 17.40E
Gypsum Pt. Canada 74 61.53N114.35W
Gypsumville Canada 75 51.45N 98.35W

H

Haan Germany 14 51.10N 7.02E
Ha'apai Group is. Tonga 69 19.50S174.30W
Haapajärvi Finland 22 63.45N 25.20E
Haapamäki Finland 22 62.15N 24.28E
Haapavesi Finland 22 64.08N 25.22E
Haapsalu U.S.S.R. 23 58.56N 23.33E
Hā Arava r. Israel/Jordan 44 30.30N 35.10E
Haarlem Neth. 14 52.22N 4.38E
Haarlem R.S.A. 56 33.46S 23.28E
Hab r. Pakistan 40 24.53N 66.41E
Habahe China 30 47.53N 86.12E
Ḥabarūt Yemen 38 17.18N 52.44E
Habaswein Kenya 55 1.06N 39.26E
Habay-la-Neuve Belgium 14 49.45N 5.38E
Ḥabbān Yemen 45 14.21N 47.05E
Hab Chauki Pakistan 40 25.01N 66.53E
Habiganj Bangla. 41 24.23N 91.25E
Habikino Japan 35 34.33N135.37E
Habo Sweden 23 57.55N 14.04E
Hachinohe Japan 31 40.30N141.30E
Hachiōji Japan 35 35.39N139.20E
Hack, Mt. Australia 66 30.44S138.45E
Hadāli Pakistan 40 32.18N 72.12E
Hadano Japan 35 35.22N139.14E
Ḥadāribah, Ra's al c. Sudan 48 22.04N 36.54E
Ḥadbaram Oman 45 17.27N 55.15E
Ḥadd, Ra's al c. Oman 43 22.32N 59.49E
Haddington U.K. 12 55.57N 2.47W
Hadejia Nigeria 53 12.30N 10.03E
Hadejia r. Nigeria 53 12.47N 10.44E
Hadera Israel 44 32.26N 34.55E
Haderslev Denmark 23 55.15N 9.30E
Hadībōh Yemen 45 12.39N 54.02E
Hadjer Mornou mtn. Chad 48 17.12N 23.08E
Ha Dong Vietnam 33 20.40N105.58E
Ḥaḍramawt f. Yemen 45 16.30N 49.30E
Hadsten Denmark 23 56.20N 10.03E
Hadsund Denmark 23 56.43N 10.07E
Haedo, Cuchilla de mts. Uruguay 93 31.50S 56.10W
Haegeland Norway 23 58.15N 7.50E
Haeju N. Korea 31 38.04N125.40E
Haena Hawaiian Is. 69 22.14N159.34W
Ḥafar al Bāṭin Saudi Arabia 43 28.28N 46.00E
Hāfizābād Pakistan 40 32.04N 73.41E
Hafnarfjördhur town Iceland 22 64.04N 21.58W
Haft Gel Iran 43 31.28N 49.35E
Hagen Germany 14 51.22N 7.27E
Hagerman U.S.A. 81 33.07N104.20W
Hagerstown U.S.A. 84 39.39N 77.43W
Hagersville Canada 76 42.58N 80.03W
Hagfors Sweden 23 60.02N 13.42E
Ha Giang Vietnam 33 22.50N105.00E
Hags Head Rep. of Ire. 13 52.56N 9.29W
Hague, Cap de la c. France 15 49.44N 1.56W
Haguenau France 17 48.49N 7.47E
Hai'an Shan mts. China 33 23.00N115.30E
Haicheng China 32 40.52N122.48E
Hai Duong Vietnam 34 20.56N106.21E
Haifa see Hefa Israel 44
Haifeng China 33 22.58N115.20E
Haikang China 33 20.55N110.04E
Haikou China 33 20.03N110.27E
Ḥā'il Saudi Arabia 42 27.31N 41.45E
Hailākāndi India 41 24.41N 92.34E
Hailar China 31 49.15N119.41E
Hailong China 32 42.39N125.49E
Hailsham U.K. 11 50.52N 0.17E
Hailun China 31 47.29N126.58E
Hailuoto i. Finland 22 65.02N 24.42E
Haimen China 33 28.41N121.30E
Hainan d. China 33 19.00N109.30E
Hainaut d. Belgium 14 50.30N 3.45E
Haines Alas. U.S.A. 74 59.11N135.23W
Haines Oreg. U.S.A. 80 44.55N117.56W
Haines Junction Canada 74 60.45N137.30W
Haining China 33 30.30N120.35E
Haiphong Vietnam 33 20.48N106.40E
Haiti C. America 87 19.00N 73.00W
Haiyang China 32 36.46N121.09E
Haiyuan China 32 36.35N105.40E
Ḥajar Banga Sudan 49 11.30N 23.00E
Hajdúböszörmény Hungary 21 47.41N 21.30E
Hajdúszoboszló Hungary 21 47.27N 21.24E
Hājīpur India 41 25.41N 85.13E
Hakkâri Turkey 43 37.36N 43.45E
Hakodate Japan 31 41.46N140.44E
Hakupu Niue 68 19.07S169.51W
Hala Pakistan 40 25.49N 68.25E
Ḥalab Syria 42 36.14N 37.10E
Ḥalabjah Iraq 43 35.10N 45.59E
Ḥalā'ib Sudan 48 22.13N 36.38E
Ḥalbā Lebanon 44 34.34N 36.05E
Halberstadt Germany 20 51.54N 11.04E
Halden Norway 23 59.09N 11.23E
Haldia India 41 22.05N 88.03E
Haldwāni India 41 29.13N 79.31E
Haleyville U.S.A. 85 34.12N 87.38W
Half Assini Ghana 52 5.04N 2.53W
Halfmoon Bay town Canada 74 49.31N123.54W
Halfmoon Bay town New Zealand 60 46.45S168.08E
Haliburton Canada 76 45.03N 78.03W
Haliburton Highlands Canada 76 45.20N 78.00W
Halifax Canada 77 44.39N 63.36W
Halifax U.K. 10 53.43N 1.51W
Halifax U.S.A. 85 36.46N 78.57W
Halīl r. Iran 38 27.35N 58.44E
Halkett, C. U.S.A. 72 71.00N152.00W
Halkirk U.K. 12 58.30N 3.30W
Halladale r. U.K. 12 58.34N 3.54W
Halland d. Sweden 23 56.45N 13.00E
Halle Belgium 14 50.45N 4.14E
Halle Germany 20 51.28N 11.58E
Hällefors Sweden 23 59.47N 14.30E
Hallingdal f. Norway 23 60.30N 9.00E
Hall Is. Pacific Oc. 68 8.37N152.00E
Hall Lake town Canada 73 68.40N 81.30W
Hällnäs Sweden 22 64.19N 19.38E
Hall Pen. Canada 73 63.30N 66.00W
Hallsberg Sweden 23 59.04N 15.07E
Hall's Creek town Australia 62 18.13S127.39E
Hallstavik Sweden 23 60.03N 18.36E
Hallstead U.S.A. 84 41.58N 75.45W
Halmahera i. Indonesia 37 0.45N128.00E
Halmstad Sweden 23 56.39N 12.50E
Halsa Norway 22 63.03N 8.14E
Hälsingborg Sweden 23 56.03N 12.42E
Haltern Germany 14 51.45N 7.10E
Haltia Tunturi mtn. Finland 22 69.17N 21.21E
Haltwhistle U.K. 10 54.58N 2.27W
Ham France 15 49.45N 3.04E
Ḥamad, Wādī al r. Saudi Arabia 42 25.49N 36.37E
Hamada f. see Drâa, Hamada du f. W. Sahara 50
Hamadān Iran 43 34.47N 48.33E
Ḥamādat Marzūq f. Libya 51 26.00N 12.30E
Ḥamāh Syria 44 35.09N 36.44E
Hamakita Japan 35 34.48N137.47E
Hamamatsu Japan 35 34.42N137.44E
Hamar Norway 23 60.48N 11.06E
Hamaröy Norway 22 68.05N 15.40E
Ḥamāṭah, Jabal mtn. Egypt 42 24.11N 35.01E
Hamborn Germany 14 51.29N 6.46E
Hamburg Germany 20 53.33N 10.00E
Hamburg R.S.A. 56 33.17S 27.27E
Hamburg N.J. U.S.A. 85 41.09N 74.35W
Hamburg N.Y. U.S.A. 76 42.43N 78.50W
Hamburg Penn. U.S.A. 85 40.34N 75.59W
Häme d. Finland 23 61.20N 24.30E
Hämeenlinna Finland 23 61.00N 24.27E
Hamelin B. Australia 63 34.10S115.00E
Hameln Germany 20 52.06N 9.21E
Hamer Koke Ethiopia 49 5.12N 36.45E
Hamersley Range mts. Australia 62 22.00S118.00E
Hamhŭng N. Korea 31 39.54N127.35E
Hami China 30 42.40N 93.30E
Hamilton Australia 66 37.45S142.04E
Hamilton r. Australia 65 27.12S135.28E
Hamilton Bermuda 95 32.18N 64.48W
Hamilton Canada 76 43.15N 79.50W
Hamilton New Zealand 60 37.46S175.18E
Hamilton U.K. 12 55.46N 4.10W
Hamilton Mont. U.S.A. 80 46.15N114.09W
Hamilton Ohio U.S.A. 84 39.23N 84.33W
Hamilton Tex. U.S.A. 83 31.42N 98.07W
Hamley Bridge town Australia 66 34.21S138.41E
Hamlin Tex. U.S.A. 83 32.53N100.08W
Hamm Germany 14 51.40N 7.49E
Hammamet, Golfe de g. Tunisia 51 36.05N 10.40E
Hammam Lif Tunisia 51 36.44N 10.20E
Ḥammār, Hawr al l. Iraq 43 30.50N 47.00E
Hammerdal Sweden 22 63.35N 15.20E
Hammerfest Norway 22 70.40N 23.42E
Hammond Australia 66 32.33S138.20E
Hammond La. U.S.A. 83 30.30N 90.28W
Hammond N.Y. U.S.A. 84 44.27N 75.42W
Hammonton U.S.A. 85 39.38N 74.48W
Hamoir Belgium 14 50.25N 5.32E
Hamoyet, Jabal mtn. Sudan 48 17.33N 38.00E
Hampshire d. U.K. 11 51.03N 1.20W
Hampton S.C. U.S.A. 85 32.52N 81.06W
Hampton Va. U.S.A. 85 37.02N 76.23W
Hamra, Saguia el wadi W. Sahara 50 27.15N 13.21W
Ḥamrīn, Jabal mts. Iraq 43 34.40N 44.10E
Hāmūn-e Jaz Mūrīān l. Iran 38 27.20N 58.55E
Hana Hawaiian Is. 69 20.45N155.59W
Hanang mtn. Tanzania 55 4.30S 35.21E
Hancheng China 32 35.29N110.30E
Hancock Mich. U.S.A. 84 47.08N 88.34W
Handa Japan 35 34.53N136.56E
Handa Somali Rep. 45 10.39N 51.08E
Handan China 32 36.37N114.26E
Handeni Tanzania 55 5.25S 38.04E
HaNegev des. Israel 44 30.42N 34.55E
Hanford U.S.A. 81 36.20N119.39W
Hanga Roa I. de Pascua 69 27.09S109.26W
Hanggin Houqi China 32 40.50N107.06E
Hanggin Qi China 32 39.56N108.54E
Hangö Finland 23 59.50N 22.57E
Hangu China 32 39.11N117.45E
Hangu Pakistan 40 33.32N 71.04E
Hangzhou China 33 30.14N120.08E
Hangzhou Wan b. China 33 30.25N121.00E
Hanjiang China 33 25.30N119.14E
Hankey R.S.A. 56 33.50S 24.52E
Hankinson U.S.A. 82 46.04N 96.55W
Hanksville U.S.A. 80 38.21N110.44W
Hānle Jammu & Kashmir 41 32.48N 79.00E
Hanmer Springs town New Zealand 60 42.31S172.50E
Hann, Mt. Australia 62 15.55S125.57E
Hanna Canada 75 51.38N111.54W
Hannaford U.S.A. 82 47.19N 98.11W
Hannah B. Canada 76 51.20N 80.00W
Hannibal Mo. U.S.A. 79 39.41N 91.25W
Hannover Germany 20 52.23N 9.44E
Hannut Belgium 14 50.40N 5.05E
Hanöbukten b. Sweden 23 55.45N 14.30E
Hanoi Vietnam 33 21.01N105.53E
Hanover Canada 76 44.09N 81.02W
Hanover R.S.A. 56 31.04S 24.25E
Hanover Penn. U.S.A. 85 39.48N 76.59W
Hanover, Isla i. Chile 93 50.57S 74.40W
Han Pijesak Yugo. 19 44.04N 18.59E
Hānsdiha India 41 24.36N 87.05E
Hanshou China 33 28.55N111.58E
Han Shui r. China 33 30.32N114.20E
Hānsi Haryana India 40 29.06N 75.58E
Hansi Himachal P. India 41 32.27N 77.50E
Hanson, L. Australia 66 31.02S136.13E
Hantengri Feng mtn. China 30 42.09N 80.12E
Han Ul China 32 45.10N119.48E
Hanyang China 33 30.42N113.50E
Hanyin China 32 32.53N108.37E
Hanzhong China 32 33.08N107.04E
Haouach, Ouadi wadi Chad 51 16.45N 19.35E
Haparanda Sweden 22 65.50N 24.10E
Happy Valley town Canada 77 53.16N 60.14W
Hapsu N. Korea 31 41.12N128.48E
Hāpur India 41 28.43N 77.47E
Ḥaql Saudi Arabia 44 29.14N 34.56E
Ḥaraḍ Saudi Arabia 43 24.12N 49.08E
Harare Zimbabwe 57 17.49S 31.04E
Har-Ayrag Mongolia 32 45.42N109.14E
Haraze Chad 49 9.55N 20.48E
Harbin China 31 45.45N126.41E
Harborcreek U.S.A. 76 42.10N 79.57W
Harbour Deep town Canada 77 50.22N 56.27W
Harbour Grace town Canada 77 47.42N 53.13W
Harburg Germany 20 53.27N 9.58E
Harda India 40 22.20N 77.06E
Hardangerfjorden est. Norway 23 60.10N 6.00E
Hardangerjökulen mtn. Norway 23 60.33N 7.26E
Hardanger Vidda f. Norway 23 60.20N 7.30E
Hardeeville U.S.A. 85 32.18N 81.05W
Hardenberg Neth. 14 52.36N 6.40E
Harderwijk Neth. 14 52.21N 5.37E
Harding R.S.A. 56 30.34S 29.52E
Hardman U.S.A. 80 45.10N119.40W
Hardoi India 41 27.25N 80.07E
Hardwār India 41 29.58N 78.10E
Hardwicke B. Australia 66 34.52S137.10E
Hardy U.S.A. 83 36.19N 91.29W
Hare B. Canada 77 51.18N 55.50W
Haren Germany 14 52.48N 7.15E
Hārer Ethiopia 49 9.20N 42.10E
Hārergē d. Ethiopia 49 8.00N 41.00E
Harfleur France 15 49.30N 0.12E
Hargeysa Somali Rep. 45 9.31N 44.02E
Har Hu l. China 30 38.20N 97.40E
Hari r. Indonesia 36 1.00S104.15E
Harīpur Pakistan 40 33.59N 72.56E
Harīrūd r. Afghan. 38 35.42N 61.12E
Harlan U.S.A. 82 41.39N 95.19W
Harlech U.K. 10 52.52N 4.08W
Harlem U.S.A. 80 48.32N108.47W
Harlingen Neth. 14 53.10N 5.25E
Harlingen U.S.A. 83 26.11N 97.42W
Harlow U.K. 11 51.47N 0.08E
Harlowton U.S.A. 80 46.26N109.50W
Harnai Pakistan 40 30.06N 67.56E
Harnātānr India 41 27.19N 84.01E
Harney Basin f. U.S.A. 80 43.15N120.40W
Harney L. U.S.A. 80 43.14N119.07W
Härnösand Sweden 22 62.37N 17.55E
Har Nuur l. Mongolia 30 48.00N 93.25E
Haroldswick U.K. 8 60.47N 0.50W
Harper Liberia 52 4.25N 7.43W
Harrai India 41 22.37N 79.13E
Harricana r. Canada 76 51.10N 79.45W
Harrigan, C. Canada 77 55.50N 60.21W
Harrington Australia 67 31.50S152.43E
Harrington U.S.A. 85 38.56N 75.35W
Harrington Harbour Canada 77 50.31N 59.30W
Harris Canada 75 51.44N107.35W
Harris i. U.K. 12 57.50N 6.55W
Harris, L. Australia 66 31.08S135.14E
Harris, Sd. of U.K. 12 57.43N 7.05W
Harrisburg Ill. U.S.A. 83 37.44N 88.33W
Harrisburg Oreg. U.S.A. 80 44.16N123.10W
Harrisburg Penn. U.S.A. 84 40.16N 76.52W
Harrismith Australia 63 32.55S117.50E
Harrismith R.S.A. 56 28.15S 29.07E
Harrison Ark. U.S.A. 83 36.14N 93.07W
Harrison Nebr. U.S.A. 82 42.41N103.53W
Harrison, C. Canada 77 54.55N 57.55W
Harrison L. Canada 74 49.33N121.50W
Harrisonville U.S.A. 82 38.39N 94.21W
Harrodsburg U.S.A. 85 37.46N 84.51W
Harrogate U.K. 10 53.59N 1.32W
Harrow U.K. 11 51.35N 0.21W
Harstad Norway 22 68.48N 16.30E
Harsūd India 40 22.06N 76.44E
Hart, L. Australia 66 31.08S136.24E
Hartford U.S.A. 84 41.45N 72.42W
Hartland Canada 77 46.18N 67.32W
Hartland U.K. 11 50.59N 4.29W
Hartland Pt. U.K. 11 51.01N 4.32W
Hartlepool U.K. 10 54.42N 1.11W
Hartley Bay town Canada 74 53.27N129.18W
Hartola Finland 23 61.35N 26.01E
Hartshorne U.S.A. 83 34.51N 95.33W
Harts Range town Australia 64 23.06S134.55E
Hartsville U.S.A. 85 34.23N 80.05W
Hārūnābād Pakistan 40 29.37N 73.08E
Har Us Nuur l. Mongolia 30 48.10N 92.10E
Hārūt r. Afghan. 40 31.35N 61.18E
Harvey Australia 63 33.06S115.50E
Harvey Ill. U.S.A. 82 41.37N 87.39W
Harvey N.Dak. U.S.A. 82 47.47N 99.56W
Harwich U.K. 11 51.56N 1.18E
Haryana d. India 40 29.15N 76.30E
Ḥasā, Wādī al r. Jordan 44 31.01N 35.29E
Ḥasa Oasis see Aḥsā', Wāḥat al oasis Saudi Arabia 43
Hasdo r. India 41 21.44N 82.44E
Hase r. Germany 14 52.42N 7.17E
Haselünne Germany 14 52.40N 7.30E
Hasenkamp Argentina 93 31.30S 59.50W
Hashābah Sudan 48 14.19N 32.19E
Ḥasharūd Iran 43 37.29N 47.05E
Hashimoto Japan 35 34.19N135.37E
Haskell U.S.A. 83 33.10N 99.44W
Haslemere U.K. 11 51.05N 0.41W
Hasselt Belgium 14 50.56N 5.20E
Hassi bel Guebbour Algeria 51 28.30N 6.41E
Hassi er Rmel well Algeria 51 32.57N 3.11E
Hassi Messaoud Algeria 51 31.43N 6.03E
Hassi Tagsist well Algeria 50 25.20N 1.35E
Hässleholm Sweden 23 56.09N 13.46E
Hastings Australia 67 38.18S145.12E
Hastings New Zealand 60 39.39S176.52E
Hastings U.K. 11 50.51N 0.36E
Hastings Nebr. U.S.A. 82 40.35N 98.23W
Hatanbulag Mongolia 32 43.08N109.05E
Hatch U.S.A. 81 32.40N107.09W
Hatches Creek town Australia 64 20.56S135.12E
Hatfield Australia 66 33.53S143.47E
Hatfield U.K. 11 51.46N 0.13W
Hāthras India 41 27.36N 78.03E
Hātia I. Bangla. 41 22.40N 90.55E
Ha Tinh Vietnam 34 18.21N105.55E
Hatta India 41 24.07N 79.36E
Hattah Australia 66 34.52S142.23E
Hattem Neth. 14 52.29N 6.06E
Hatteras, C. U.S.A. 85 35.13N 75.32W
Hattiesburg U.S.A. 83 31.19N 89.16W
Hattingen Germany 14 51.24N 7.09E
Hatton U.S.A. 80 46.46N118.49W
Hatutu i. Is. Marquises 69 7.56S140.38W
Hatvan Hungary 21 47.40N 19.41E
Hauge Norway 23 58.18N 6.15E
Haugesund Norway 23 59.25N 5.18E
Haugsdorf Austria 20 48.42N 16.05E
Hauraki G. New Zealand 60 36.30S175.00E
Haut Atlas mts. Morocco 50 31.30N 7.00W
Haute Kotto d. C.A.R. 49 7.15N 23.30E
Haute Maurice Prov. Park Canada 76 48.38N 74.30W
Haute-Normandie d. France 15 49.30N 1.00E
Hauterive Canada 77 49.11N 68.16W
Haut Mbomou d. C.A.R. 49 6.25N 26.10E
Hautmont France 14 50.16N 3.52E
Hauts Bassins d. Burkina 52 10.45N 4.30W
Hauts Plateau f. Morocco/Algeria 50 34.00N 0.10W
Haut Zaïre d. Zaïre 55 2.00N 27.00E
Havana see La Habana Cuba 87
Havant U.K. 11 50.51N 0.59W
Havel r. Germany 20 52.51N 11.57E
Havelange Belgium 14 50.23N 5.14E
Havelberg Germany 20 52.50N 12.04E
Havelock New Zealand 60 41.17S173.46E
Haverfordwest U.K. 11 51.48N 4.59W
Haverhill U.K. 11 52.06N 0.27E
Havlíčkuv Brod Czech. 20 49.38N 15.35E
Havre U.S.A. 80 48.33N109.41W
Havre de Grace U.S.A. 85 39.33N 76.06W
Havre St. Pierre Canada 77 50.15N 63.36W
Hawaii d. U.S.A. 78 21.00N156.00W
Hawaii i. Hawaii U.S.A. 78 19.30N155.30W
Hawaiian Is. U.S.A. 78 21.00N157.00W
Hawdon North, L. Australia 66 37.09S139.54E
Hawea, L. New Zealand 60 44.30S169.15E
Hawera New Zealand 60 39.35S174.19E
Hawick U.K. 12 55.25N 2.47W
Hawke B. New Zealand 60 39.18S177.15E
Hawker Australia 66 31.53S138.25E
Hawker Gate Australia 66 29.46S141.00E
Hawke's Bay d. New Zealand 60 39.00S176.35E
Hawkesbury Canada 77 45.36N 74.37W
Ḥawrān, Wādī r. Iraq 42 33.57N 42.35E
Ḥawsh 'Īsá Egypt 44 30.55N 30.17E
Hawthorne U.S.A. 80 38.32N118.38W
Hay Australia 67 34.31S144.31E
Hay r. Australia 64 25.00S138.00E
Hay r. Canada 74 60.49N115.52W
Haya r. Japan 35 35.30N138.26E
Hayange France 17 49.20N 6.02E
Haybān Sudan 45 11.13N 30.31E
Hayden U.S.A. 81 33.00N110.47W
Hayes r. Canada 75 57.03N 92.09W
Hayes Creek town Australia 62 13.27S131.25E
Hay-on-Wye U.K. 11 52.04N 3.09W
Hay River town Canada 74 60.51N115.44W
Hays U.S.A. 82 38.53N 99.20W
Hayward U.S.A. 82 46.02N 91.26W
Haywards Heath f. U.K. 11 51.00N 0.05E
Hazārān, Kūh-e mtn. Iran 43 29.30N 57.18E
Hazard U.S.A. 85 37.14N 83.11W
Hazārībāgh India 41 23.59N 85.21E
Hazelton Canada 74 55.20N127.42W
Hazelton U.S.A. 82 46.29N100.17W
Hazen U.S.A. 80 39.34N119.03W
Hazlehurst Ga. U.S.A. 85 31.53N 82.34W
Hazlehurst Miss. U.S.A. 83 31.52N 90.24W
Hazleton U.S.A. 84 40.58N 75.59W
Healdsburg U.S.A. 80 38.37N122.52W
Healesville Australia 67 37.40S145.31E
Healy U.S.A. 72 63.52N148.58W
Heanor U.K. 10 53.01N 1.20W
Hearne L. Canada 74 62.20N113.10W
Hearst Canada 76 49.40N 83.41W
Heathcote Australia 67 36.54S144.42E
Hebei d. China 32 39.00N116.00E
Hebel Australia 67 28.55S147.49E
Heber Springs town U.S.A. 83 35.30N 92.02W
Hebi China 32 35.57N114.05E
Hebrides, Sea of the U.K. 8 57.00N 7.20W
Hebron Canada 73 58.05N 62.30W
Hebron see Al Khalīl Jordan 44

Hebron N.Dak. U.S.A. 82 46.54N102.03W
Hebron Nebr. U.S.A. 82 40.10N 97.35W
Heby Sweden 23 59.56N 16.53E
Hecate Str. Canada 74 53.00N131.00W
Hechi China 33 24.42N108.02E
Hechtel Belgium 14 51.07N 5.22E
Hechuan China 33 30.05N106.14E
Hecla U.S.A. 82 45.53N 98.09W
Hede Sweden 23 62.25N 13.30E
Hedemora Sweden 23 60.17N 15.59E
Hedi Shuiku resr. China 33 21.50N110.19E
Hedley U.S.A. 83 34.52N100.39W
Hedmark d. Norway 23 61.20N 11.30E
Heemstede Neth. 14 52.21N 4.38E
Heerde Neth. 14 52.23N 6.02E
Heerenveen Neth. 14 52.57N 5.55E
Heerlen Neth. 14 50.53N 5.59E
Hefa Israel 44 32.49N 34.59E
Hefei China 33 31.50N117.16E
Hegang China 31 47.36N130.30E
Heide Germany 20 54.12N 9.06E
Heidelberg Germany 20 49.25N 8.42E
Heidelberg C.P. R.S.A. 56 34.05S 20.58E
Heilbron R.S.A. 56 27.16S 27.57E
Heilbronn Germany 20 49.08N 9.14E
Heilongjiang d. China 31 47.15N128.50E
Heiloo Neth. 14 52.37N 4.43E
Heinola Finland 23 61.13N 26.02E
Heinsberg Germany 14 51.04N 6.06E
Heishan China 32 41.40N122.03E
Heishui China 32 42.03N119.21E
Heishuisi China 32 36.01N108.56E
Hejaz f. see Al Ḥijāz f. Saudi Arabia 42
Hejian China 32 38.26N116.05E
Hejiang China 33 28.48N105.47E
Hekinan Japan 35 34.51N136.58E
Hekla, Mt. Iceland 22 64.00N 19.45W
Hekou China 39 22.39N103.57E
Helagsfjället mtn. Sweden 22 62.58N 12.25E
Helan China 32 38.35N106.16E
Helan Shan mts. China 32 38.40N106.00E
Helena U.S.A. 80 46.36N112.01W
Helen Reef i. Caroline Is. 37 2.43N131.46E
Helensburgh U.K. 12 56.01N 4.44W
Helensville New Zealand 60 36.40S174.27E
Hellendoorn Neth. 14 52.24N 6.29E
Hellenthal Germany 14 50.28N 6.25E
Hellesylt Norway 23 62.05N 6.54E
Hellevoetsluis Neth. 14 51.49N 4.08E
Hellín Spain 16 38.31N 1.43W
Helmand d. Afghan. 40 31.15N 64.00E
Helmand r. Asia 40 31.12N 61.34E
Helmond Neth. 14 51.28N 5.40E
Helmsdale U.K. 12 58.07N 3.40W
Helmsdale r. U.K. 12 58.05N 3.39W
Helsingfors see Helsinki Finland 23
Helsingör Denmark 23 56.02N 12.37E
Helsinki Finland 23 60.08N 25.00E
Helston U.K. 11 50.07N 5.17W
Helvecia Argentina 93 31.06S 60.05W
Hemaruka Canada 75 51.48N111.10W
Hemel Hempstead U.K. 11 51.46N 0.28W
Hemingford U.S.A. 82 42.19N103.04W
Hempstead N.Y. U.S.A. 85 40.42N 73.37W
Hempstead Tex. U.S.A. 83 30.06N 96.05W
Hemse Sweden 23 57.14N 18.22E
Hemsedal Norway 23 60.52N 8.34E
Henan d. China 32 34.00N114.00E
Henares r. Spain 16 40.26N 3.35W
Henbury Australia 64 24.35S133.15E
Hendaye France 17 43.22N 1.46W
Henderson Ky. U.S.A. 85 37.50N 87.35W
Henderson N.C. U.S.A. 85 36.20N 78.26W
Henderson Nev. U.S.A. 81 36.02N114.59W
Henderson Tex. U.S.A. 83 32.09N 94.48W
Henderson I. Pacific Oc. 69 24.20S128.20W
Hendrik Verwoerd Dam R.S.A. 56 30.37S 25.29E
Hendrina R.S.A. 56 26.09S 29.42E
Hengelo Neth. 14 52.16N 6.46E
Hengshan Hunan China 33 27.14N112.52E
Hengshan Shaanxi China 32 37.57N109.11E
Hengshui China 32 37.40N115.48E
Heng Xian China 33 22.35N109.26E
Hengyang China 33 26.52N112.35E
Hénin-Beaumont France 14 50.25N 2.55E
Henlopen, C. U.S.A. 85 38.48N 75.05W
Hennebont France 17 47.48N 3.16W
Henrietta Maria, C. Canada 76 55.00N 82.15W
Henryetta U.S.A. 83 35.27N 95.59W
Henryville Canada 77 45.08N 73.11W
Hentiesbaai Namibia 56 22.10S 14.19E
Henty Australia 67 35.30S147.03E
Henzada Burma 34 17.36N 95.26E
Heppner U.S.A. 80 45.21N119.33W
Hepu China 33 21.31N109.10E
Heqing China 39 26.34N100.12E
Herāt Afghan. 40 34.20N 62.12E
Herāt d. Afghan. 40 34.10N 62.30E
Herceg-Novi Yugo. 19 42.27N 18.32E
Hereford U.K. 11 52.04N 2.43W
Hereford Md. U.S.A. 85 39.35N 76.40W
Hereford Tex. U.S.A. 83 34.49N102.24W
Hereford and Worcester d. U.K. 11 52.08N 2.30W
Herentals Belgium 14 51.12N 4.42E
Herford Germany 20 52.07N 8.40E
Herington U.S.A. 82 38.40N 96.57W
Hermannsburg Australia 64 23.56S132.46E
Hermanus R.S.A. 56 34.24S 19.16E
Hermidale Australia 67 31.33S146.44E
Hermiston U.S.A. 80 45.51N119.17W
Hermosillo Mexico 81 29.04N110.58W
Herne Germany 14 51.32N 7.12E
Herne Bay town U.K. 11 51.23N 1.10E
Herning Denmark 23 56.08N 8.59E
Heron Bay town Canada 76 48.40N 86.25W
Herrera del Duque Spain 16 39.10N 5.03W
Herstal Belgium 14 50.14N 5.38E
Herten Germany 14 51.36N 7.08E
Hertford U.K. 11 51.48N 0.05W
Hertfordshire d. U.K. 11 51.51N 0.05W
Hervey B. Australia 64 25.00S153.00E
Herzliyya Israel 44 32.10N 34.50E
Hesbaye f. Belgium 14 50.32N 5.07E
Hesel Germany 14 53.19N 7.35E
Heshui China 32 35.43N108.07E
Heshun China 32 37.19N113.34E
Hessen d. Germany 20 50.30N 9.15E
Hesso Australia 66 32.08S137.58E
Hetou China 33 21.05N109.44E
Hettinger U.S.A. 82 46.00N102.39W
Hetzerath Germany 14 49.54N 6.50E
Hewett, C. Canada 73 70.20N 68.00W
Hexham U.K. 10 54.58N 2.06W
Hexi China 33 24.51N117.13E
He Xian China 33 24.25N111.31E
Hexigten Qi China 32 43.17N117.24E
Heysham U.K. 10 54.03N 2.53W
Heyuan China 33 23.42N114.48E
Heywood Australia 66 38.08S141.38E
Heywood U.K. 10 53.36N 2.13W
Heze China 32 35.12N115.15E
Hezhang China 33 27.08N104.43E
Hiawatha Kans. U.S.A. 82 39.51N 95.32W
Hiawatha Utah U.S.A. 80 39.29N111.01W
Hibbing U.S.A. 82 47.25N 92.55W
Hickman, Mt. Canada 74 57.11N131.10W
Hickory U.S.A. 85 35.44N 81.23W
Hicks Bay town New Zealand 60 37.35S178.18E
Hickson L. Canada 75 56.17N104.25W
Hicksville U.S.A. 85 40.46N 73.32W
Hidalgo d. Mexico 86 20.50N 98.30W
Hidalgo Nuevo León Mexico 83 25.59N100.27W
Hidalgo Tamaulipas Mexico 86 24.15N 99.26W
Hidalgo del Parral Mexico 81 26.56N105.40W
Hieradhsvotn r. Iceland 22 65.45N 18.50W
Hierro i. Canary Is. 50 27.45N 18.00W
Higashimatsuyama Japan 35 36.02N139.24E
Higashimurayama Japan 35 35.46N139.29E
Higashiōsaka Japan 35 34.39N135.35E
Higgins U.S.A. 83 36.07N100.02W
Higginsville Australia 63 31.46S121.43E
High Hill r. Canada 75 55.52N 94.42W
Highland d. U.K. 12 57.42N 5.00W
Highland town U.S.A. 85 41.43N 73.58W
High Level Canada 74 58.31N117.08W
Highmore U.S.A. 82 44.31N 99.27W
High Peak mtn. U.K. 10 53.22N 1.48W
High Point town U.S.A. 85 35.58N 80.00W
High Prairie Canada 74 55.30N116.30W
Highrock L. Man. Canada 75 55.45N100.30W
Highrock L. Sask. Canada 75 57.04N105.30W
High Willhays mtn. U.K. 11 50.41N 4.00W
High Wycombe U.K. 11 51.38N 0.46W
Hiiumaa i. U.S.S.R. 23 58.52N 22.40E
Híjar Spain 16 41.10N 0.27W
Ḥijāz, Jabal al mts. Saudi Arabia 48 19.45N 41.55E
Hikone Japan 35 35.15N136.15E
Hikurangi New Zealand 60 35.36S174.17E
Hikurangi mtn. New Zealand 60 37.50S178.10E
Hikutavake Niue 68 18.57S169.53W
Hilden Germany 14 51.10N 6.56E
Hildesheim Germany 20 52.09N 9.58E
Hill City Kans. U.S.A. 82 39.22N 99.51W
Hill City Minn. U.S.A. 82 46.59N 93.44W
Hillegom Neth. 14 52.19N 4.35E
Hill End Australia 67 33.01S149.26E
Hill Island L. Canada 75 60.30N109.50W
Hillsboro Oreg. U.S.A. 80 45.31N122.59W
Hillsboro Tex. U.S.A. 83 32.01N 97.08W
Hillsdale U.S.A. 84 41.56N 84.37W
Hillsport Canada 76 49.27N 85.34W
Hillston Australia 67 33.30S145.33E
Hilo Hawaii U.S.A. 78 19.42N155.04W
Hilton U.S.A. 76 43.17N 77.48W
Hilton Head I. U.S.A. 85 32.12N 80.45W
Hiltrup Germany 14 51.55N 7.36E
Hilversum Neth. 14 52.14N 5.12E
Himachal Pradesh d. India 40 32.05N 77.15E
Himalaya mts. Asia 41 29.00N 84.30E
Himanka Finland 22 64.04N 23.39E
Himarë Albania 19 40.07N 19.44E
Himatnagar India 40 23.36N 72.57E
Ḥimş Syria 44 34.44N 36.43E
Hinchinbrook I. Australia 64 18.23S146.17E
Hinckley U.K. 11 52.33N 1.21W
Hindaun India 40 26.43N 77.01E
Hindmarsh, L. Australia 66 36.03S141.53E
Hindubāgh Pakistan 40 30.49N 67.45E
Hindu Kush mts. Asia 38 36.40N 70.00E
Hindupur India 38 13.49N 77.29E
Hines Creek town Canada 74 56.20N118.40W
Hinganghāt India 41 20.34N 78.50E
Hingol r. Pakistan 40 25.23N 65.28E
Hingoli India 40 19.43N 77.09E
Hinnöy i. Norway 22 68.35N 15.50E
Hinojosa Spain 16 38.30N 5.17W
Hinsdale Mont. U.S.A. 80 48.24N107.05W
Hinton Canada 74 53.25N117.34W
Hipólito Mexico 83 25.41N101.26W
Hippolytushoef Neth. 14 52.57N 4.58E
Hirakata Japan 35 34.48N135.38E
Hirākud India 41 21.31N 83.57E
Hirākud resr. India 41 21.31N 83.52E
Hirāpur India 41 24.22N 79.13E
Hiratsuka Japan 35 35.19N139.21E
Hirmand r. see Helmand r. Iran 40
Hirok Sāmi Pakistan 40 26.02N 63.25E
Hiroshima Japan 31 34.23N132.27E
Hirson France 14 49.56N 4.05E
Hîrşova Romania 21 44.41N 27.57E
Hirtshals Denmark 23 57.35N 9.58E
Hisai Japan 35 34.40N136.28E
Hisār India 40 29.10N 75.43E
Ḥismá f. Saudi Arabia 44 28.45N 35.56E
Hispaniola i. C. America 87 19.00N 71.00W
Hisua India 41 24.50N 85.25E
Ḥisyah Syria 44 34.24N 36.45E
Hīt Iraq 42 33.38N 42.50E
Hitchin U.K. 11 51.57N 0.16W
Hitra i. Norway 22 63.37N 8.46E
Hiva Oa i. Îs. Marquises 69 9.45S139.00W
Hixon Canada 74 53.27N122.36W
Hjälmaren l. Sweden 23 59.15N 15.45E
Hjalmar L. Canada 75 61.33N109.25W
Hjörring Denmark 23 57.28N 9.59E
Hlotse Lesotho 56 28.52S 28.02E
Ho Ghana 52 6.38N 0.38E
Hòa Bình Vietnam 33 20.40N105.17E
Hoare B. Canada 73 65.20N 62.30W
Hoarusib r. Namibia 56 19.04S 12.33E
Hobart Australia 65 42.54S147.18E
Hobart Ind. U.S.A. 84 41.32N 87.14W
Hobart Okla. U.S.A. 83 35.01N 99.06W
Hobbs U.S.A. 83 32.42N103.08W
Hoboken Belgium 14 51.11N 4.21E
Hoboken U.S.A. 85 40.45N 74.03W
Hobq Shamo des. China 32 40.00N109.00E
Hobro Denmark 23 56.38N 9.48E
Hobyo Somali Rep. 45 5.20N 48.30E
Ho Chi Minh Vietnam 34 10.46N106.43E
Hockley U.S.A. 83 30.02N 95.51W
Hodal India 40 27.54N 77.22E
Hodgson Canada 75 51.13N 97.34W
Hod HaSharon Israel 44 32.15N 34.55E
Hodh ech Chargui d. Mauritania 52 19.00N 7.15W
Hodh el Gharbi d. Mauritania 52 16.30N 10.00W
Hódmezövásárhely Hungary 19 46.26N 20.21E
Hodna, Monts du mts. Algeria 51 35.50N 4.50E
Hoek van Holland Neth. 14 51.59N 4.08E
Hof Germany 20 50.19N 11.56E
Höfn Iceland 22 64.16N 15.10W
Hofors Sweden 23 60.33N 16.17E
Hofsjökull mtn. Iceland 22 64.50N 19.00W
Hofsos Iceland 22 65.53N 19.26W
Höganäs Sweden 23 56.12N 12.33E
Hogeland U.S.A. 80 48.51N108.39W
Hogem Ranges f. Canada 74 55.40N126.00W
Hohhot China 32 40.42N111.38E
Hoh Tolgoin Sum China 32 44.27N112.41E
Hoi An Vietnam 34 15.54N108.19E
Hoima Uganda 55 1.25N 31.22E
Hojāi India 41 26.00N 92.51E
Hokitika New Zealand 60 42.42S170.59E
Hokkaidō i. Japan 31 43.30N143.20E
Hokksund Norway 23 59.47N 9.59E
Hola Kenya 55 1.29S 40.02E
Holbaek Denmark 23 55.43N 11.43E
Holbrook Australia 67 35.46S147.20E
Holbrook U.S.A. 81 34.54N110.10W
Holdrege U.S.A. 82 40.26N 99.22W
Holguín Cuba 87 20.54N 76.15W
Höljes Sweden 23 60.54N 12.36E
Hollabrunn Austria 20 48.34N 16.05E
Holland Mich. U.S.A. 84 42.46N 86.06W
Holland N.Y. U.S.A. 76 42.38N 78.33W
Holly Kans. U.S.A. 83 38.03N102.07W
Hollywood U.S.A. 85 26.01N 80.09W
Holman Island town Canada 72 70.43N117.43W
Holmavik Iceland 22 65.43N 21.39W
Holmer, Lac l. Canada 77 54.10N 71.44W
Holmestrand Norway 23 59.29N 10.18E
Holmön i. Sweden 22 63.47N 20.53E
Holmsund Sweden 22 63.41N 20.20E
Holon Israel 44 32.01N 34.46E
Holroyd r. Australia 64 14.10S141.36E
Holstebro Denmark 23 56.21N 8.38E
Holstein Canada 76 44.02N 80.42W
Holsteinsborg Greenland 73 66.55N 53.30W
Holsworthy U.K. 11 50.48N 4.21W
Holt U.K. 10 52.55N 1.04E
Holten Neth. 14 52.18N 6.26E
Holwerd Neth. 14 53.22N 5.54E
Holy Cross U.S.A. 72 62.12N159.47W
Holyhead U.K. 10 53.18N 4.38W
Holyhead B. U.K. 10 53.22N 4.40W
Holy I. England U.K. 10 55.41N 1.47W
Holy I. Wales U.K. 10 53.15N 4.38W
Holyoke Colo. U.S.A. 82 40.35N102.18W
Holywood U.K. 13 54.38N 5.50W
Hombori Mali 52 15.20N 1.38W
Home B. Canada 73 69.00N 66.00W
Home Hill town Australia 64 19.40S147.25E
Homer Alas. U.S.A. 72 59.40N151.37W
Homer La. U.S.A. 83 32.48N 93.04W
Homer Tunnel New Zealand 60 44.40S168.15E
Homestead U.S.A. 85 25.29N 80.29W
Homoine Mozambique 57 23.45S 35.09E
Homoljske Planina f. Yugo. 21 44.20N 21.45E
Honda Colombia 90 5.15N 74.50W
Hondeklipbaai R.S.A. 56 30.19S 17.12E
Hondo r. Mexico 87 18.33N 88.22W
Hondo U.S.A. 83 29.21N 99.09W
Honduras C. America 87 14.30N 87.00W
Honduras, G. of Carib. Sea 87 16.20N 87.30W
Honfleur France 15 49.25N 0.14E
Hong'an China 33 31.18N114.33E
Hòn Gay Vietnam 33 21.01N107.02E
Hong Hà r. Vietnam 34 20.15N106.36E
Honghu China 33 29.42N113.26E
Hong Hu l. China 33 29.50N113.15E
Hongjiang China 33 27.08N109.54E
Hongjian Nur l. China 32 39.09N109.56E
Hong Kong Asia 33 22.15N114.15E
Hongor Mongolia 32 45.45N112.56E
Hongshui He r. China 33 23.20N110.04E
Hongtong China 32 36.15N111.37E
Honguedo, Détroit d' str. Canada 77 49.25N 64.00W
Hongze China 32 33.18N118.51E
Hongze Hu l. China 32 33.15N118.40E
Honiton U.K. 11 50.48N 3.13W
Honkajoki Finland 23 62.00N 22.15E
Honokaa Hawaiian Is. 69 20.05N155.28W
Honokahua Hawaiian Is. 69 21.00N156.39W
Honolulu Hawaii U.S.A. 78 21.19N157.50W
Honshū i. Japan 31 36.00N138.00E
Hood Pt. Australia 63 34.23S119.34E
Hood Range mts. Australia 67 28.35S144.30E
Hoogeveen Neth. 14 52.44N 6.29E
Hoogezand Neth. 14 53.10N 6.47E
Hooghly r. India 41 21.55N 88.05E
Hoogstade Belgium 14 50.59N 2.42E
Hooker U.S.A. 83 36.52N101.13W
Hook Head Rep. of Ire. 13 52.07N 6.55W
Hoopa U.S.A. 80 41.03N123.40W
Hoopeston U.S.A. 82 40.28N 87.41W
Hoopstad R.S.A. 56 27.48S 25.52E
Hoorn Neth. 14 52.38N 5.03E
Hoover Dam U.S.A. 81 36.00N114.27W
Hope U.S.A. 83 33.40N 93.36W
Hope, L. S.A. Australia 66 28.23S139.19E
Hope, L. W.A. Australia 63 32.31S120.25E
Hopedale Canada 77 55.50N 60.10W
Hopefield R.S.A. 56 33.04S 18.19E
Hopetoun Vic. Australia 66 35.43S142.20E
Hopetoun W.A. Australia 63 33.57S120.05E
Hopetown R.S.A. 56 29.37S 24.04E
Hopkins r. Australia 66 38.25S142.00E
Hopkins, L. Australia 62 24.15S128.50E
Hopkinsville U.S.A. 85 36.50N 87.30W
Hopland U.S.A. 80 38.58N123.07W
Hoquiam U.S.A. 80 46.59N123.53W
Hordaland d. Norway 23 60.30N 6.30E
Horde Germany 14 51.29N 7.30E
Hörh Uul mts. Mongolia 32 42.20N105.30E
Horinger China 32 40.23N111.53E
Horizonte Mexico 83 25.50N103.48W
Horlick Mts. Antarctica 96 86.00S102.00W
Hormuz, Str. of Asia 43 26.35N 56.20E
Horn Austria 20 48.40N 15.40E
Horn r. Canada 74 61.30N118.01W
Horn, C. see Hornos, Cabo de c. S. America 93
Hornavan l. Sweden 22 66.10N 17.30E
Horncastle U.K. 10 53.13N 0.08W
Horndal Sweden 23 60.18N 16.25E
Hornell U.S.A. 84 42.19N 77.39W
Hornell L. Canada 74 62.20N119.25W
Hornepayne Canada 76 49.14N 84.48W
Hornindal Norway 23 61.58N 6.31E
Horn Mts. Canada 74 62.15N119.15W
Hornos, Cabo de c. S. America 93 55.47S 67.00W
Hornsby Australia 67 33.11S151.06E
Hornsea U.K. 10 53.55N 0.10W
Hořovice Czech. 20 49.50N 13.54E
Horqin Zuoyi Houqi China 32 42.57N122.21E
Horqin Zuoyi Zhongqi China 32 44.08N123.18E
Horru China 41 30.30N 91.32E
Horse Creek town U.S.A. 80 41.25N105.11W
Horsens Denmark 23 55.52N 9.52E
Horsham Australia 66 36.45S142.15E
Horsham U.K. 11 51.04N 0.20W
Horta wadi Chad 48 17.15N 21.52E
Horten Norway 23 59.25N 10.30E
Horton r. Canada 72 70.00N127.00W
Horton L. Canada 72 67.30N122.28W
Hosa'ina Ethiopia 49 7.38N 37.52E
Hose, Pegunungan mts. Malaysia 36 1.30N114.10E
Hoshāb Pakistan 40 26.01N 63.56E
Hoshangābād India 41 22.45N 77.43E
Hoshiārpur India 40 31.32N 75.54E
Hôsh 'Isa Egypt 44 30.55N 30.17E
Hoskins P.N.G. 61 5.30S150.27E
Hospitalet de Llobregat Spain 16 41.20N 2.06E
Hoste, Isla i. Chile 93 55.10S 69.00W
Hotan China 30 37.07N 79.57E
Hotazel R.S.A. 56 27.16S 22.57E
Hotham r. Australia 63 32.58S116.22E
Hotham, Mt. Australia 67 36.58S147.11E
Hoting Sweden 22 64.07N 16.10E
Hotin Gol China 32 38.58N104.14E
Hot Springs town Ark. U.S.A. 83 34.30N 93.02W
Hot Springs town S.Dak. U.S.A. 82 43.26N103.29W
Hottah L. Canada 72 65.04N118.29W
Houailou N. Cal. 68 21.17S165.38E
Houdan France 15 48.47N 1.36E
Houffalize Belgium 14 50.08N 5.50E
Houghton L. U.S.A. 84 44.16N 84.48W
Houghton-le-Spring U.K. 10 54.51N 1.28W
Houlton U.S.A. 84 46.08N 67.51W
Houma China 32 35.36N111.21E
Houma U.S.A. 83 29.36N 90.43W
Houndé Burkina 52 11.34N 3.31W
Hourn, Loch U.K. 12 57.06N 5.33W
Houston Mo. U.S.A. 83 37.22N 91.58W
Houston Tex. U.S.A. 83 29.46N 95.22W
Hovd Mongolia 30 46.40N 90.45E
Hove U.K. 11 50.50N 0.10W
Hovlya U.S.S.R. 25 49.19N 44.01E
Hövsgöl Mongolia 32 43.36N109.40E
Hövsgöl Nuur l. Mongolia 30 51.00N100.30E
Howa, Ouadi see Howar, Wādī Chad 48
Howar, Wādī Sudan 48 17.30N 27.08E
Howard L. Canada 75 62.15N105.57W
Howe, C. Australia 67 37.30S149.59E
Howick Canada 77 45.11N 73.51W
Howitt, Mt. Australia 67 37.15S146.40E
Howrah India 41 22.35N 88.20E
Howth Head Rep. of Ire. 13 53.22N 6.03W
Hoy i. U.K. 12 58.51N 3.17W
Höyanger Norway 23 61.13N 6.05E
Hoyos Spain 16 40.09N 6.45W
Hradec Králové Czech. 20 50.13N 15.50E
Hron r. Czech. 21 47.49N 18.45E
Hrubieszów Poland 21 50.49N 23.55E
Hrvatska d. Yugo. 21 45.10N 15.30E
Hsenwi Burma 34 23.18N 97.58E
Hsipaw Burma 34 22.42N 97.21E
Hsuphāng Burma 34 20.18N 98.42E
Huab r. Namibia 56 20.55S 13.28E
Huabei Pingyuan f. China 32 35.00N115.30E
Huachi China 32 36.32N108.14E
Huacho Peru 90 11.05S 77.36W
Huachuca City U.S.A. 81 31.34N110.21W
Huade China 32 41.57N114.04E
Hua Hin Thailand 34 12.34N 99.58E
Huahine i. Îs. de la Société 69 16.45S151.00W
Huai'an Hebei China 32 40.40N114.18E
Huai'an Jiangsu China 32 33.29N119.15E
Huaibei China 32 33.58N116.50E
Huaide China 32 43.25N124.50E
Huai He r. China 32 32.58N118.18E
Huaiji China 33 23.58N112.10E
Huailai China 32 40.25N115.27E
Huainan China 32 32.39N117.01E
Huaining China 33 30.21N116.42E
Huairen China 32 39.50N113.07E
Huairou China 32 40.20N116.37E
Huaiyang China 32 33.47N114.59E
Huaiyuan China 32 32.57N117.12E
Huajuápan Mexico 86 17.50N 97.48W
Hualian Taiwan 33 24.00N121.39E
Huallaga r. Peru 90 5.02S 75.30W
Huamanrazo mtn. Peru 90 12.54S 75.04W
Huambo Angola 54 12.47S 15.44E
Huambo d. Angola 54 12.30S 15.45E
Huanan China 31 46.13N130.31E
Huancané Peru 90 15.10S 69.44W
Huancapi Peru 90 13.35S 74.05W
Huancavelica Peru 90 12.45S 75.03W
Huancayo Peru 90 12.05S 75.12W
Huangchuan China 33 32.07N115.02E
Huanggang China 33 30.33N114.59E
Huanggang Shan mtn. China 33 27.50N117.47E
Huang Hai b. N. Korea 32 39.30N123.40E
Huang He r. China 32 38.00N118.40E
Huanghe Kou est. China 32 37.54N118.48E
Huanghua China 32 38.22N117.20E
Huangling China 32 35.36N109.17E
Huangpi China 33 30.52N114.22E
Huangping China 33 26.54N107.53E
Huangshi China 33 30.10N115.04E
Huang Xian China 32 37.38N120.30E
Huangyan China 33 28.42N121.25E
Huan Jiang r. China 32 35.13N108.00E
Huanren China 32 41.16N125.21E
Huanta Peru 90 12.54S 74.13W
Huánuco Peru 90 9.55S 76.11W
Huaráz Peru 90 9.33S 77.31W
Huarmey Peru 90 10.05S 78.05W
Huascaran mtn. Peru 90 9.08S 77.36W
Huasco Chile 92 28.28S 71.14W
Huatabampo Mexico 81 26.50N109.38W
Huatong China 32 40.03N121.56E
Hua Xian Guangdong China 33 23.22N113.12E
Hua Xian Shaanxi China 32 34.31N109.46E
Huayuan China 33 28.37N109.28E
Hubei d. China 33 31.00N112.00E
Hubli India 38 15.20N 75.14E
Hückelhoven Germany 14 51.04N 6.10E
Hucknall U.K. 10 53.03N 1.12W
Huddersfield U.K. 10 53.38N 1.49W
Huddinge Sweden 23 59.14N 17.59E
Hudiksvall Sweden 23 61.44N 17.07E
Hudson r. U.S.A. 84 40.42N 74.02W
Hudson N.Y. U.S.A. 84 42.15N 73.47W
Hudson Wyo. U.S.A. 80 42.54N108.35W
Hudson B. Canada 73 58.00N 86.00W
Hudson Bay town Canada 75 52.52N102.25W
Hudson Highlands U.S.A. 85 41.24N 74.15W
Hudson Hope Canada 74 56.03N121.59W
Hudson Mts. Antarctica 96 76.00S 99.00W
Hudson Str. Canada 73 62.00N 70.00W
Hue Vietnam 34 16.28N107.40E
Huedin Romania 21 46.52N 23.02E
Huehuetenango Guatemala 86 15.19N 91.26W
Huelva Spain 16 37.15N 6.56W
Huelva r. Spain 16 37.25N 6.00W
Huércal-Overa Spain 16 37.23N 1.56W
Huesca Spain 16 42.02N 0.25W
Ḥufrat an Naḥās Sudan 49 9.45N 24.19E
Hugh r. Australia 64 25.01S134.01E
Hughenden Australia 64 20.51S144.12E
Hughes Australia 65 30.40S129.32E
Hughes U.S.A. 72 66.03N154.16W
Hugo U.S.A. 83 34.01N 95.31W
Hugoton U.S.A. 83 37.11N101.21W
Hugou China 32 33.22N117.07E
Hui'an China 33 25.02N118.48E
Huiarau Range mts. New Zealand 60 38.20S177.15E
Huikou China 33 29.49N116.15E
Huíla d. Angola 54 15.10S 15.30E
Huilai China 33 23.03N116.17E
Huimin China 32 37.30N117.29E
Huining China 32 35.42N105.06E
Huisne r. France 15 47.59N 0.11E
Huixtla Mexico 86 15.09N 92.30W
Huizen Neth. 14 52.18N 5.12E
Huizhou China 33 23.05N114.29E

ntsi Botswana **56** 24.02S 21.48E
yfā' Saudi Arabia **42** 26.00N 40.47E
Czech. **21** 49.19N 17.28E
Canada **77** 45.26N 75.45W
Germany **14** 51.23N 6.30E
Neth. **14** 51.18N 4.01E
fred Sweden **23** 57.29N 15.50E
Nur *l.* China **31** 49.00N117.27E
ān Egypt **44** 29.51N 31.20E
aitá Brazil **90** 7.31S 63.02W
ansdorp R.S.A. **56** 34.02S 24.45E
aydah Sudan **48** 14.22N 22.31E
ber *r.* U.K. **10** 53.40N 0.12W
berside *d.* U.K. **10** 53.48N 0.35W
ble U.S.A. **83** 30.00N 95.16W
boldt Canada **75** 52.12N105.07W
boldt U.S.A. **83** 35.49N 88.55W
boldt *r.* U.S.A. **80** 40.02N118.31W
e, L. Australia **67** 36.06S147.05E
edān Iran **43** 25.24N 59.39E
enné Czech. **21** 48.56N 21.55E
phreys Peak *mtn.* U.S.A. **81** 20N111.40W
Libya **51** 29.07N 15.56E
aflói *b.* Iceland **22** 65.45N 20.50W
an *d.* China **33** 27.30N111.30E
dred Mile House *town* Canada **74** 38N121.18W
edoara Romania **21** 45.45N 22.54E
gary Europe **21** 47.30N 19.00E
gerford Australia **66** 29.00S144.26E
gerford U.K. **11** 51.25N 1.30W
gfou Hsü *i.* Taiwan **33** 22.03N121.33E
gnam N. Korea **31** 39.49N127.40E
g Yen Vietnam **33** 20.38N106.05E
sberge *mts.* Namibia **56** 27.40S 17.12E
se *r.* Neth. **14** 53.20N 6.18E
srück *mts.* Germany **14** 49.44N 7.05E
stanton U.K. **10** 52.57N 0.30E
e *r.* Germany **20** 52.30N 8.19E
er *r.* Australia **67** 32.50S151.42E
er I. Australia **65** 40.30S144.46E
er I. Canada **74** 51.55N128.00W
er Island Ridge Pacific Oc. **68** 30S175.00E
ingdon U.K. **11** 52.20N 0.11W
ingdon Penn. U.S.A. **84** 40.29N 78.01W
ington Ind. U.S.A. **84** 40.54N 85.30W
ington N.Y. U.S.A. **85** 40.51N 73.25W
ington Oreg. U.S.A. **80** 44.21N117.16W
ington Utah U.S.A. **80** 39.20N110.58W
ington W.Va. U.S.A. **85** 38.24N 82.26W
ington Beach *town* U.S.A. **81** 39N118.01W
ly New Zealand **60** 37.35S175.10E
ly U.K. **12** 57.27N 2.47W
tsville Canada **76** 45.20N 79.13W
tsville Ala. U.S.A. **85** 34.44N 86.35W
tsville Tex. U.S.A. **83** 30.43N 95.33W
vani *r.* Mozambique **57** 15.41S 30.38E
yuan China **32** 39.45N113.35E
n Pen. P.N.G. **37** 6.00S147.00E
nville Australia **65** 43.01S147.01E
shan China **33** 31.24N116.20E
Qi China **32** 42.44N121.44E
tin Sum China **32** 40.19N103.02E
ock U.S.A. **85** 38.38N 75.52W
nāgai Pakistan **40** 28.18N 64.26E
n S.Dak. U.S.A. **82** 44.22N 98.13W
n, L. Canada / U.S.A. **84** 44.30N 82.15W
so Ethiopia **49** 9.38N 41.38E
avík Iceland **22** 66.03N 17.21W
evig Faroe Is. **8** 61.49N 6.41W
Romania **21** 46.40N 28.04E
kvarna Sweden **23** 57.48N 14.16E
um Germany **20** 54.29N 9.04E
chinson R.S.A. **56** 31.30S 23.10E
chinson U.S.A. **83** 38.05N 97.56W
ig U.S.A. **83** 33.02N 92.11W
o He *r.* China **32** 39.10N117.12E
Yanchi *l.* China **32** 39.24N105.01E
Belgium **14** 50.31N 5.14E
i. Yugo. **19** 43.10N 16.45E
a *r.* Iceland **22** 64.33N 21.45W
nge Zimbabwe **56** 18.20S 26.29E
nge Nat. Park Zimbabwe **56** 19.00S 30E
ng Ho *r. see* Huang He *r.* China **32**
nnis U.S.A. **82** 41.59N101.44W
gas Nuur *l.* Mongolia **30** 49.30N 93.35E
aburg U.S.A. **74** 55.15N132.50W
e U.K. **10** 53.26N 2.06W
en Australia **63** 32.27S118.53E
erābād India **39** 17.22N 78.26E
erābād Pakistan **40** 25.22N 68.22E
esville U.S.A. **80** 40.31N124.00W
res France **17** 43.07N 6.08E
res, Îles d' *is.* France **17** 43.01N 6.25E
nd *r.* Canada **74** 59.50N128.10W
nd, Mt. Australia **67** 30.09S152.25E
nd Post Canada **74** 57.40N128.10W
estad Norway **23** 61.10N 5.18E
dman Peak U.S.A. **80** 43.50N114.10W
ham U.S.A. **80** 46.18N107.14W
he Kent U.K. **11** 51.04N 1.05E
inkää Finland **23** 60.38N 24.52E

ro Madagascar **57** 23.06S 46.40E
niţa *r.* Romania **21** 44.41N 27.52E
Connacht *f.* Rep. of Ire. **13** 53.21N 9.22W
Romania **21** 47.09N 27.38E

Iauaretê Brazil **90** 0.36N 69.12W
Iaupolo P.N.G. **64** 9.34S150.30E
Ibadan Nigeria **53** 7.23N 3.56E
Ibagué Colombia **90** 4.25N 75.20W
Ibar *r.* Yugo. **19** 43.44N 20.44E
Ibaraki Japan **35** 34.49N135.34E
Ibarra Ecuador **90** 0.23N 78.05W
Ibb Yemen **45** 13.58N 44.11E
Ibba Sudan **49** 4.48N 29.06E
Ibba *wadi* Sudan **49** 7.09N 28.41E
Ibbenbüren Germany **14** 52.17N 7.44E
Iberville Canada **77** 45.18N 73.14W
Ibi *r.* Japan **35** 35.03N136.42E
Ibi Nigeria **53** 8.11N 9.44E
Ibiapaba, Serra da *mts.* Brazil **91** 5.30S 41.00W
Ibicaraí Brazil **91** 14.52S 39.37W
Ibicuy Argentina **93** 33.45S 59.13W
Ibina *r.* Zaïre **55** 1.00N 28.40E
Ibitinga Brazil **94** 21.43S 48.47W
Ibiza *i.* Spain **16** 39.00N 1.23E
Ibiza *town* Spain **16** 38.55N 1.30E
Ibotirama Brazil **91** 12.13S 43.12W
Ibrah, Wadi Sudan **49** 10.36N 25.05E
'Ibrī Oman **45** 23.14N 56.30E
Ibshawāy Egypt **44** 29.21N 30.40E
Içá *r.* Brazil **90** 3.07S 67.58W
Ica Peru **90** 14.02S 75.48W
Içana Brazil **90** 0.21N 67.19W
Içana *r.* Brazil **90** 0.00 67.10W
Iceland Europe **22** 64.45N 18.00W
Ichchāpuram India **41** 19.07N 84.42E
Ichihara Japan **35** 35.31N140.05E
Ichikawa Japan **35** 35.44N139.55E
Ichinomiya Japan **35** 35.18N136.48E
Icoraci Brazil **91** 1.16S 48.28W
Icy Str. U.S.A. **74** 58.20N135.30W
Idabel U.S.A. **83** 33.54N 94.50W
Ida Grove U.S.A. **82** 42.21N 95.28W
Idah Nigeria **53** 7.05N 6.45E
Idaho *d.* U.S.A. **80** 44.58N115.56W
Idaho Falls *town* U.S.A. **80** 43.30N112.02W
Idar India **40** 23.50N 73.00E
Idar-Oberstein Germany **14** 49.43N 7.19E
Ideles Algeria **51** 23.49N 5.55E
Idfū Egypt **42** 24.58N 32.50E
Ídhi Óros *mtn.* Greece **19** 35.13N 24.45E
Ídhra *i.* Greece **19** 37.20N 23.32E
Idiofa Zaïre **54** 4.58S 19.38E
Idmū Egypt **44** 28.09N 30.41E
Idre Sweden **23** 61.52N 12.43E
Ieper Belgium **14** 50.51N 2.53E
Ierápetra Greece **19** 35.00N 25.45E
Iesi Italy **18** 43.32N 13.15E
Iesolo Italy **15** 45.32N 12.38E
Ifakara Tanzania **55** 8.09S 36.41E
Ifalik *is.* Caroline Is. **37** 7.15N144.27E
Ifanadiana Madagascar **57** 21.19S 47.39E
Ife Oyo Nigeria **53** 7.33N 4.34E
Iferouâne Niger **53** 19.04N 8.24E
Iga *r.* Japan **35** 34.45N136.01E
Igatpuri India **40** 19.42N 73.33E
Iggesund Sweden **23** 61.38N 17.04E
Iglesias Italy **18** 39.18N 8.32E
Igli Algeria **50** 30.27N 2.18W
Igloolik Island *town* Canada **73** 69.05N 81.25W
Ignace Canada **76** 49.30N 91.40W
Iğneada Burnu *c.* Turkey **19** 41.50N 28.05E
Igoumenítsa Greece **19** 39.32N 20.14E
Igra U.S.S.R. **24** 57.31N 53.09E
Iguaçu *r.* Brazil **94** 25.33S 54.35W
Iguaçu, Saltos do *f.* Brazil / Argentina **94** 25.35S 54.22W
Iguala Mexico **86** 18.21N 99.31W
Igualada Spain **16** 41.35N 1.37E
Iguassu Falls *see* Iguaçu, Saltos do *f.* Brazil / Argentina **94**
Iguatu Brazil **91** 6.22S 39.20W
Iguéla Gabon **54** 1.57S 9.22E
Ihiala Nigeria **53** 5.51N 6.52E
Ihosy Madagascar **57** 22.24S 46.08E
Ihosy *r.* Madagascar **57** 21.58S 43.38E
Ii *r.* Finland **22** 65.19N 25.20E
Iida Japan **35** 35.31N137.50E
Iīdaan Somali Rep. **45** 6.03N 49.01E
Iisalmi Finland **22** 63.34N 27.11E
Ijebu Ode Nigeria **53** 6.47N 3.54E
Ijill, Kediet *mtn.* Mauritania **50** 22.38N 12.33W
IJmuiden Neth. **14** 52.28N 4.37E
IJssel *r.* Zuid Holland Neth. **14** 51.54N 4.32E
IJssel *r.* Overijssel Neth. **14** 52.34N 5.50E
IJsselmeer *l.* Neth. **14** 52.45N 5.20E
Ijuí Brazil **94** 28.23S 53.55W
Ijzendijke Neth. **14** 51.19N 3.37E
Ijzer *r.* Belgium **14** 51.09N 2.44E
Ikaría *i.* Greece **19** 37.35N 26.10E
Ikdū Egypt **44** 31.18N 30.18E
Ikela Zaïre **54** 1.06S 23.04E
Ikelemba Congo **54** 1.15N 16.38E
Ikelemba *r.* Zaïre **54** 0.08N 18.19E
Ikerre Nigeria **53** 7.30N 5.14E
Ikopa *r.* Madagascar **57** 16.29S 46.43E
Ila Nigeria **53** 8.01N 4.55E
Ilagan Phil. **37** 17.07N121.53E
Īlām Iran **43** 33.27N 46.27E
Ilām Nepal **41** 26.55N 87.56E
Ilan Taiwan **33** 24.45N121.44E
Ilangali Tanzania **55** 6.50S 35.06E
Ilaro Nigeria **53** 6.53N 3.03E
Iława Poland **21** 53.37N 19.33E
Ilebo Zaïre **54** 4.20S 20.35E
Ilek *r.* U.S.S.R. **25** 51.30N 54.00E
Ileret Kenya **55** 4.22N 36.13E
Ilerh, Oued *wadi* Algeria **51** 20.59N 2.14E
Ilesha Oyo Nigeria **53** 7.39N 4.45E
Ilford Canada **75** 56.04N 95.35W
Ilfracombe Australia **64** 23.30S144.30E

Ilfracombe U.K. **11** 51.13N 4.08W
Ilhabela Brazil **94** 23.47S 45.20W
Ilha Grande, Baía da *b.* Brazil **94** 23.09S 44.30W
Ilha Grande, Reprêsa *resr.* Brazil **94** 23.10S 53.40W
Ilhéus Brazil **91** 14.50S 39.06W
Ili *r.* U.S.S.R. **30** 45.00N 74.20E
Ilia Romania **21** 45.56N 22.39E
Iliamna L. U.S.A. **72** 59.30N155.00W
Ilich U.S.S.R. **30** 40.50N 68.29E
Iligan Phil. **37** 8.12N124.13E
Ilintsy U.S.S.R. **21** 49.08N 29.11E
Ilion U.S.A. **84** 43.01N 75.02W
Ilkley U.K. **10** 53.56N 1.49W
Illapel Chile **92** 31.38S 71.10W
Ille-et-Vilaine *d.* France **15** 48.10N 1.30W
Illéla Niger **53** 14.30N 5.09E
Iller *r.* Germany **20** 48.23N 9.58E
Illeret Kenya **49** 4.19N 36.13E
Illiers France **15** 48.18N 1.15E
Illinois *d.* U.S.A. **82** 40.30N 89.30W
Illinois *r.* U.S.A. **82** 38.58N 90.27W
Illizi Algeria **51** 26.29N 8.28E
Ilmajoki Finland **22** 62.44N 22.34E
Ilminster U.K. **11** 50.55N 2.56W
Ilo Peru **92** 17.38S 71.20W
Iloilo Phil. **37** 10.45N122.33E
Ilorin Nigeria **53** 8.32N 4.34E
Īlubabor *d.* Ethiopia **49** 7.50N 34.55E
Imala Mozambique **55** 14.39S 39.34E
Imandra U.S.S.R. **24** 67.53N 33.30E
Imandra, Ozero *l.* U.S.S.R. **24** 67.30N 32.45E
Imbābah Egypt **44** 30.05N 31.12E
Imese Zaïre **54** 2.07N 18.06E
Īmī Ethiopia **49** 6.28N 42.18E
Immingham U.K. **10** 53.37N 0.12W
Immokalee U.S.A. **85** 26.25N 81.26W
Imo *d.* Nigeria **53** 5.30N 7.20E
Imola Italy **15** 44.21N 11.42E
Imperatriz Brazil **91** 5.32S 47.28W
Imperia Italy **15** 43.53N 8.01E
Imperial Calif. U.S.A. **81** 32.51N115.34W
Imperial Nebr. U.S.A. **82** 40.31N101.39W
Imperial Dam U.S.A. **81** 32.55N114.30W
Imperial Valley *f.* U.S.A. **81** 32.50N115.30W
Impfondo Congo **54** 1.36N 17.58E
Imphāl India **39** 24.47N 93.55E
Imroz *i. see* Gökçeada *i.* Turkey **19**
Ina Japan **35** 35.50N137.57E
Ina *r.* Japan **35** 34.43N135.28E
In Abbangarit *well* Niger **53** 17.49N 6.15E
Inaccessible I. Tristan da Cunha **95** 37.19S 12.44W
I-n-Amguel Algeria **51** 23.40N 5.08E
Inangahua Junction New Zealand **60** 41.53S171.58E
Inanwatan Indonesia **37** 2.08S132.10E
Inarajan Guam **68** 13.16N144.45E
Inari *l.* Finland **22** 69.00N 28.00E
Inari *town* Finland **22** 68.54N 27.01E
Inazawa Japan **35** 35.15N136.47E
I-n-Belbel Algeria **50** 27.54N 1.10E
Inca Spain **16** 39.43N 2.54E
Incesu Turkey **42** 38.39N 35.12E
Inchiri *d.* Mauritania **50** 20.10N 15.00W
Inch'on S. Korea **31** 37.30N126.38E
Indals *r.* Sweden **22** 62.30N 17.20E
Indaw Burma **34** 23.40N 94.46E
Independence Calif. U.S.A. **80** 36.48N118.12W
Independence Kans. U.S.A. **83** 37.13N 95.42W
Independence Mo. U.S.A. **82** 39.05N 94.24W
Inderborskiy U.S.S.R. **25** 48.32N 51.44E
India Asia **39** 23.00N 78.30E
Indiana *d.* U.S.A. **84** 40.00N 86.15W
Indiana *town* U.S.A. **84** 40.37N 79.09W
Indianapolis U.S.A. **84** 39.45N 86.10W
Indian Cabins Canada **74** 59.52N117.02W
Indian Harbour Canada **77** 54.25N 57.20W
Indian Head Canada **75** 50.32N103.40W
Indianola U.S.A. **82** 41.22N 93.34W
Indian River B. U.S.A. **85** 38.36N 75.05W
Indiga U.S.S.R. **24** 67.40N 49.00E
Indigirka *r.* U.S.S.R. **29** 71.00N148.45E
Indija Yugo. **21** 45.03N 20.05E
Indio U.S.A. **81** 33.43N116.13W
Indonesia Asia **36** 6.00S118.00E
Indore India **40** 22.43N 75.50E
Indragiri *r.* Indonesia **36** 0.30S103.08E
Indramayu Indonesia **37** 6.22S108.20E
Indrāvati *r.* India **41** 18.44N 80.16E
Indre *r.* France **17** 47.16N 0.19W
Indus *r.* Pakistan **40** 24.20N 67.47E
Inebolu Turkey **42** 41.57N 33.45E
Inegöl Turkey **42** 40.06N 29.31E
I-n-Eker Algeria **51** 24.01N 5.05E
I-n-Ezzane *well* Algeria **51** 23.29N 11.15E
Infiesto Spain **16** 43.21N 5.21W
I-n-Gall Niger **53** 16.47N 6.56E
Ingatestone U.K. **11** 51.41N 0.22E
Ingende Zaïre **54** 0.17S 18.58E
Ingenika *r.* Canada **74** 56.43N125.07W
Ingersoll Canada **76** 43.02N 80.53W
Inggen China **32** 41.35N104.47E
Ingham Australia **64** 18.35S146.12E
Ingleborough *mtn.* U.K. **10** 54.10N 2.23W
Inglewood *Qld* Australia **67** 28.25S151.02E
Inglewood Vic. Australia **66** 36.33S143.53E
Inglewood Canada **76** 43.47N 79.56W
Inglewood New Zealand **60** 39.09S174.12E
Inglewood U.S.A. **81** 33.58N118.21W
Ingolstadt Germany **20** 48.46N 11.27E
Ingomar Australia **66** 29.38S134.48E
Ingulets U.S.S.R. **25** 47.43N 33.16E
Ingwiller France **17** 48.52N 7.29E
Inhambane Mozambique **57** 23.51S 35.29E

Inhambane *d.* Mozambique **57** 22.20S 34.00E
Inhaminga Mozambique **57** 18.24S 35.00E
Inharrime Mozambique **57** 24.29S 35.01E
Inhassoro Mozambique **57** 21.32S 35.10E
Inirida *r.* Colombia **90** 3.59N 67.45W
Inishbofin *i.* Galway Rep. of Ire. **13** 53.38N 10.14W
Inisheer *i.* Rep. of Ire. **13** 53.04N 9.32W
Inishmaan *i.* Rep. of Ire. **13** 53.06N 9.36W
Inishmore *i.* Rep. of Ire. **13** 53.08N 9.43W
Inishowen Pen. Rep. of Ire. **13** 55.08N 7.20W
Inishturk *i.* Rep. of Ire. **13** 53.43N 10.08W
Injune Australia **64** 25.51S148.34E
Inklin Canada **74** 58.56N133.05W
Inklin *r.* Canada **74** 58.50N133.10W
Inn *r.* Europe **20** 48.33N 13.26E
Innaminka Australia **65** 27.43S140.46E
Inner Hebrides *is.* U.K. **12** 56.50N 6.45W
Inner Mongolia *d. see* Nei Monggol *d.* China **32**
Inner Sd. U.K. **12** 57.30N 5.55W
Innisfail Australia **64** 17.32S146.02E
Innisfail Canada **74** 52.00N113.57W
Innsbruck Austria **20** 47.17N 11.25E
Innset Norway **22** 68.41N 18.50E
Inongo Zaïre **54** 1.55S 18.20E
Inowrocław Poland **21** 52.49N 18.12E
I-n-Salah Algeria **51** 27.13N 2.28E
Insein Burma **34** 16.54N 96.08E
In Tasik *well* Mali **53** 18.03N 2.00E
Interlaken Switz. **20** 46.42N 7.52E
International Falls *town* U.S.A. **82** 48.38N 93.26W
Intracoastal Waterway *canal* U.S.A. **83** 28.45N 95.40W
Intute Mozambique **55** 14.08S 39.55E
Inukjuac Canada **73** 58.25N 78.18W
Inuvik Canada **72** 68.16N133.40W
Inuvik *d.* Canada **72** 68.00N130.00W
Inuyama Japan **35** 35.23N136.56E
Inveraray U.K. **12** 56.24N 5.05W
Inverbervie U.K. **12** 56.51N 2.17W
Invercargill New Zealand **60** 46.26S168.21E
Inverell Australia **67** 29.46S151.10E
Invergordon U.K. **12** 57.42N 4.10W
Inverness U.K. **12** 57.27N 4.15W
Inverurie U.K. **12** 57.17N 2.23W
Inverway Australia **62** 17.49S129.40E
Investigator Group *is.* Australia **66** 33.45S134.30E
Investigator Str. Australia **66** 35.25S137.10E
Invinheima *r.* Brazil **92** 22.52S 53.20W
Inya U.S.S.R. **28** 50.24N 86.47E
Inyangani *mtn.* Zimbabwe **57** 18.18S 32.50E
Inyonga Tanzania **55** 6.43S 32.02E
Inzia *r.* Zaïre **54** 3.47S 17.57E
Ioánnina Greece **19** 39.39N 20.49E
Iola U.S.A. **83** 37.55N 95.24W
Iona *i.* U.K. **12** 56.20N 6.25W
Iongo Angola **54** 9.11S 17.45E
Ionia U.S.A. **84** 42.58N 85.06W
Ionian Is. *see* Iónioi Nísoi *is.* Greece **19**
Ionian Sea Med. Sea **19** 38.30N 18.45E
Iónioi Nísoi *is.* Greece **19** 38.45N 20.00E
Íos *i.* Greece **19** 36.42N 25.20E
Iowa *d.* U.S.A. **82** 42.00N 93.30W
Iowa *r.* U.S.A. **82** 41.10N 91.02W
Iowa City U.S.A. **82** 41.40N 91.32W
Iowa Falls *town* U.S.A. **82** 42.31N 93.16W
Ipatovo U.S.S.R. **25** 45.44N 42.56E
Ipiales Colombia **90** 0.52N 77.38W
Ipiaú Brazil **91** 14.07S 39.43W
Ipixuna Brazil **90** 7.00S 71.30W
Ipoh Malaysia **36** 4.36N101.02E
Ippa *r.* U.S.S.R. **21** 52.13N 29.08E
Ippy C.A.R. **49** 6.15N 21.12E
Ipswich Australia **67** 27.38S152.40E
Ipswich U.K. **11** 52.04N 1.09E
Ipu Brazil **91** 4.23S 40.44W
Ipuh Indonesia **36** 2.58S101.28E
Iquique Chile **92** 20.13S 70.10W
Iquitos Peru **90** 3.51S 73.13W
Irago-suidō *str.* Japan **35** 34.35N137.00E
Iráklion Greece **19** 35.20N 25.08E
Iran Asia **43** 32.00N 54.30E
Iran, Pegunungan *mts.* Indonesia / Malaysia **36** 3.20N115.00E
Īrānshahr Iran **43** 27.14N 60.42E
Irapuato Mexico **86** 20.40N101.40W
Iraq Asia **42** 33.00N 44.00E
Irauen, Wādī Libya **51** 26.28N 12.00E
Irayel U.S.S.R. **24** 64.23N 55.25E
Irazú *mtn.* Costa Rica **87** 9.59N 83.52W
Irbid Jordan **44** 32.33N 35.51E
Irbīl Iraq **43** 36.12N 44.01E
Irebu Zaïre **54** 0.37S 17.45E
Ireland I. Bermuda **95** 32.19N 64.51W
Irharhar, Oued *wadi* Algeria **51** 23.45N 5.55E
Irian Jaya *d.* Indonesia **37** 4.00S138.00E
Iriba Chad **48** 15.07N 22.15E
Irié Guinea **52** 8.15N 9.10W
Iringa Tanzania **55** 7.49S 35.39E
Iringa *d.* Tanzania **55** 8.30S 35.00E
Iriomote jima *i.* Japan **31** 24.30N124.00E
Iriri *r.* Brazil **91** 3.50S 52.40W
Irish Sea U.K. / Rep. of Ire. **13** 53.30N 5.40W
Irkutsk U.S.S.R. **30** 52.18N104.15E
Iron Baron Australia **66** 32.59S137.09E
Iron Gate *f.* Romania / Yugo. **21** 44.40N 22.30E
Iron Knob Australia **66** 32.44S137.08E
Iron Mountain *town* U.S.A. **84** 45.51N 88.03W
Iron Mts. Rep. of Ire. **13** 54.10N 7.56W
Iron River *town* U.S.A. **82** 46.05N 88.38W
Irons U.S.A. **84** 44.08N 85.55W
Ironton U.S.A. **84** 38.32N 82.40W
Ironwood U.S.A. **84** 46.25N 90.08W
Iroquois Falls *town* Canada **76** 48.40N 80.40W
Irosin Phil. **37** 12.45N124.02E
Irō-zaki *c.* Japan **35** 34.36N138.51E

Irpen U.S.S.R. **21** 50.31N 30.29E
Irrapatana Australia **66** 29.03S136.28E
Irrawaddy *d.* Burma **34** 17.00N 95.00E
Irrawaddy *r.* Burma **34** 15.50N 95.00E
Irrawaddy Delta Burma **34** 16.45N 95.00E
Irsha *r.* U.S.S.R. **21** 50.45N 29.30E
Irthing *r.* U.K. **9** 54.55N 2.50W
Irtysh *r.* U.S.S.R. **28** 61.00N 68.40E
Iruma *r.* Japan **35** 35.57N139.30E
Irumu Zaïre **55** 1.29N 29.48E
Irún Spain **16** 43.20N 1.48W
Irvine U.K. **12** 55.37N 4.40W
Irvinestown U.K. **13** 54.29N 7.40W
Irving U.S.A. **83** 32.49N 96.56W
Irwin, Pt. Australia **63** 35.03S116.20E
Is, Jabal *mtn.* Sudan **48** 22.03N 35.28E
Isa Nigeria **53** 13.14N 6.24E
Isaac *r.* Australia **64** 22.52S149.20E
Isabelia, Cordillera *mts.* Nicaragua **87** 13.30N 85.00W
Ísafjördhur *town* Iceland **22** 66.05N 23.06W
Isaka Tanzania **55** 3.52S 32.54E
Isaka Bandundu Zaïre **54** 2.35S 18.48E
Isaka Equateur Zaïre **54** 1.49S 20.50E
Īsa Khel Pakistan **40** 32.41N 71.17E
Isakogorka U.S.S.R. **24** 64.23N 40.31E
Isangi Zaïre **54** 0.48N 24.03E
Isar *r.* Germany **20** 48.48N 12.57E
Isbergues France **14** 50.38N 2.24E
Ischia *i.* Italy **18** 40.43N 13.54E
Ise Japan **35** 34.29N136.42E
Iseo, Lago d' *l.* Italy **15** 45.43N 10.04E
Isère *r.* France **17** 45.02N 4.54E
Iserlohn Germany **14** 51.23N 7.42E
Isernia Italy **18** 41.36N 14.14E
Ise-wan *b.* Japan **35** 34.45N136.40E
Iseyin Nigeria **53** 7.59N 3.36E
Isfahan *see* Eşfahān Iran **38**
Ishim U.S.S.R. **28** 56.10N 69.30E
Ishim *r.* U.S.S.R. **28** 57.50N 71.00E
Ishinomaki Japan **31** 38.25N141.18E
Ishpeming U.S.A. **84** 46.29N 87.40W
Ishurdi Bangla. **41** 24.09N 89.03E
Isigny France **15** 49.18N 1.06W
Isiolo Kenya **55** 0.20N 37.36E
Isipingo Beach *town* R.S.A. **56** 30.00S 30.57E
Isiro Zaïre **55** 2.50N 27.40E
Iskenderun Turkey **42** 36.37N 36.08E
Iskenderun Körfezi *g.* Turkey **42** 36.40N 35.50E
Iskilip Turkey **42** 40.45N 34.28E
Iskŭr *r.* Bulgaria **19** 43.42N 24.27E
Isla *r.* U.K. **12** 56.32N 3.22W
Islāmābād Pakistan **40** 33.40N 73.10E
Islāmkot Pakistan **40** 24.42N 70.11E
Islāmpur Bihār India **41** 25.09N 85.12E
Islāmpur W. Bengal India **41** 26.16N 88.12E
Island L. Australia **66** 31.30S136.40E
Island L. Canada **75** 53.47N 94.25W
Island Magee *pen.* U.K. **13** 54.48N 5.44W
Islands, B. of Canada **77** 49.10N 58.15W
Islands, B. of New Zealand **60** 35.15S174.15E
Islay *i.* U.K. **12** 55.45N 6.20W
Isle *r.* France **17** 45.02N 0.08W
Isle of Portland *f.* U.K. **11** 50.32N 2.25W
Isle of Wight *d.* U.K. **11** 50.40N 1.17W
Isleta U.S.A. **81** 34.55N106.42W
Ismael Cortinas Uruguay **93** 33.58S 57.06W
Ismay U.S.A. **80** 46.30N104.48W
Isnā Egypt **42** 25.16N 32.30E
Isoka Zambia **55** 10.06S 32.39E
Isola della Scala Italy **15** 45.16N 11.00E
Isparta Turkey **42** 37.46N 30.32E
Ispica Italy **18** 36.46N 14.55E
Ispikān Pakistan **40** 26.14N 62.12E
Israel Asia **44** 32.00N 34.50E
Israelite B. Australia **63** 33.40S123.55E
Israelite Bay *town* Australia **63** 33.37S123.48E
Issia Ivory Coast **52** 6.33N 6.33W
Issoire France **17** 45.33N 3.15E
Is-sur-Tille France **17** 47.30N 5.10E
Issyk Kul *l.* U.S.S.R. **30** 43.30N 77.20E
Istanbul Turkey **19** 41.02N 28.58E
Istanbul Boğazi *str.* Turkey **19** 41.07N 29.04E
Isthmus of Kra Thailand **34** 10.20N 99.10E
Istiaía Greece **19** 38.57N 23.09E
Istok Yugo. **19** 42.47N 20.29E
Istra *pen.* Yugo. **20** 45.12N 13.55E
Itabaiana Brazil **91** 7.20S 35.20W
Itabira Brazil **94** 19.39S 43.14W
Itabirito Brazil **94** 20.21S 43.45W
Itabuna Brazil **91** 14.48S 39.18W
Itacajuna *r.* Brazil **91** 5.20S 49.08W
Itacoatiara Brazil **90** 3.06S 58.22W
Itagüí Colombia **90** 6.10N 75.36W
Itaí Brazil **94** 23.23S 49.05W
Itaim *r.* Brazil **91** 6.43S 42.48W
Itaipu, Reprêsa *resr.* Brazil / Paraguay **94** 24.30S 54.20W
Itaituba Brazil **91** 4.17S 55.59W
Itajaí Brazil **94** 26.50S 48.39W
Itajubá Brazil **94** 22.24S 45.25W
Itaka Tanzania **55** 8.51S 32.48E
Italy Europe **18** 43.00N 12.00E
Itami Japan **35** 34.46N135.25E
Itapecerica Brazil **94** 20.28S 45.09W
Itapecuru Mirim Brazil **91** 3.24S 44.20W
Itaperuna Brazil **94** 21.14S 41.51W
Itapetinga Brazil **91** 15.17S 40.16W
Itapetininga Brazil **94** 23.36S 48.07W
Itapeva Brazil **94** 23.59S 48.59W
Itapicuru *r.* Brazil **91** 11.50S 37.30W
Itapira Brazil **94** 22.24S 46.56W
Itaqui Brazil **94** 29.07S 56.33W
Itārsi India **41** 22.37N 77.45E
Itatiba Brazil **94** 22.59S 46.51W
Itatinga Brazil **94** 23.06S 48.36W
Itatuba Brazil **90** 5.40S 63.20W

Itaúna Brazil 94 20.04S 44.14W
Itboyat i. Phil. 33 20.45N121.50E
Ithaca U.S.A. 84 42.26N 76.30W
Itháki Greece 19 38.23N 20.42E
Itimbiri r. Zaïre 54 2.02N 22.47E
Itmurinkol, Ozero l. U.S.S.R. 25 49.30N 52.17E
Itō Japan 35 34.58N139.05E
Itoko Zaïre 54 1.00S 21.45E
Iton r. France 15 49.09N 1.12E
Itsa Egypt 44 29.14N 30.47E
Ittel, Oued wadi Algeria 51 34.18N 6.02E
Itu Brazil 94 23.17S 47.18W
Ituí r. Brazil 90 4.38S 70.19W
Ituiutaba Brazil 94 19.00S 49.25W
Ituri r. Zaïre 55 1.45N 27.06E
Iturup i. U.S.S.R. 31 44.00N147.30E
Ituverava Brazil 94 20.22S 47.48W
Ituxi r. Brazil 90 7.20S 64.50W
Ityāy al Bārūd Egypt 44 30.53N 30.40E
Itzehoe Germany 20 53.56N 9.32E
Ivaí r. Brazil 94 23.20S 53.23W
Ivalo Finland 22 68.42N 27.30E
Ivalo r. Finland 22 68.43N 27.36E
Ivanhoe Australia 66 32.56S144.22E
Ivanhoe U.S.A. 82 44.28N 96.12W
Ivano-Frankovsk U.S.S.R. 21 48.55N 24.42E
Ivanovo B.S.S.R. U.S.S.R. 21 52.10N 25.13E
Ivanovo R.S.F.S.R. U.S.S.R. 24 57.00N 41.00E
Ivdel U.S.S.R. 24 60.45N 60.30E
Ivenets U.S.S.R. 21 53.50N 26.40E
Ivigtût Greenland 73 61.10N 48.00W
Ivindo Gabon 54 0.02S 12.13E
Ivittuut see Ivigtût Greenland 73
Iviza i. see Ibiza i. Spain 16
Ivohibe Madagascar 57 22.29S 45.52E
Ivory Coast Africa 52 8.00N 5.30W
Ivrea Italy 15 45.28N 7.52E
Ivujivik Canada 73 62.24N 77.55W
Ivybridge U.K. 11 50.24N 3.56W
Iwata Japan 35 34.42N137.48E
Iwo Nigeria 53 7.38N 4.11E
Ixiamas Bolivia 92 13.45S 68.09W
Izabal, Lago de l. Guatemala 87 15.30N 89.00W
Izberbash U.S.S.R. 25 42.31N 47.52E
Izhevsk U.S.S.R. 24 56.49N 53.11E
Izhma U.S.S.R. 24 65.03N 53.48E
Izhma r. U.S.S.R. 24 65.16N 53.18E
Izmail U.S.S.R. 21 45.20N 28.50E
Izmir Turkey 19 38.24N 27.09E
Izmir Körfezi g. Turkey 19 38.30N 26.45E
Izmit Turkey 42 40.48N 29.55E
Izozog, Bañados de f. Bolivia 92 18.30S 62.05W
Izozog Marshes f. see Izozog, Bañados de f. Bolivia 92
Izu-hantō pen. Japan 35 34.53N138.55E
Izumi Japan 35 34.29N135.26E
Izumi-ōtsu Japan 35 34.30N135.24E
Izumi-sano Japan 35 34.25N135.19E
Izumo r. Japan 35 34.38N136.33E
Izyaslav U.S.S.R. 21 50.10N 26.46E
Izyum U.S.S.R. 25 49.12N 37.19E

J

Jaba Ethiopia 49 6.17N 35.12E
Jabal, Bahr al r. Sudan 49 9.30N 30.30E
Jabal al Awliyā' Sudan 48 15.14N 32.30E
Jabal Dūd Sudan 49 13.22N 33.09E
Jabalón r. Spain 16 38.55N 4.07W
Jabalpur India 41 23.10N 79.57E
Jabālyah Egypt 44 31.32N 34.29E
Jabbān, Arḍ al f. Jordan 44 32.08N 36.35E
Jabiru Australia 64 12.39S132.55E
Jabjabah, Wādī Egypt 48 22.37N 33.17E
Jablah Syria 44 35.22N 35.56E
Jablonec nad Nisou Czech. 20 50.44N 15.10E
Jabori Pakistan 40 34.36N 73.16E
Jaboticabal Brazil 94 21.15S 48.17W
Jabrat Sa'īd wells Sudan 48 16.06N 31.50E
Jaca Spain 16 42.34N 0.33W
Jacareí Brazil 94 23.17S 45.57W
Jackman U.S.A. 84 45.38N 70.16W
Jackson Ky. U.S.A. 85 37.32N 83.24W
Jackson Mich. U.S.A. 84 42.15N 84.24W
Jackson Miss. U.S.A. 83 32.18N 90.12W
Jackson Mo. U.S.A. 83 37.23N 89.40W
Jackson Ohio U.S.A. 84 39.03N 82.40W
Jackson Tenn. U.S.A. 83 35.37N 88.49W
Jackson Wyo. U.S.A. 80 43.29N110.38W
Jackson Bay town Canada 74 50.32N125.57W
Jacksonville Fla. U.S.A. 85 30.20N 81.40W
Jacksonville Ill. U.S.A. 82 39.44N 90.14W
Jacksonville N.C. U.S.A. 85 34.45N 77.26W
Jacksonville Tex. U.S.A. 83 31.58N 95.17W
Jacksonville Beach town U.S.A. 85 30.18N 81.24W
Jacobābād Pakistan 40 28.17N 68.26E
Jacobina Brazil 91 11.13S 40.30W
Jacob Lake town U.S.A. 81 36.41N112.14W
Jacques Cartier, Détroit de str. Canada 77 50.00N 63.30W
Jacques Cartier, Mt. Canada 77 48.59N 65.57W
Jacuí r. Brazil 94 29.56S 51.13W
Jacundá r. Brazil 91 1.57S 50.26W
Jaddi, Rās c. Pakistan 40 25.14N 63.31E
Jade Germany 14 53.21N 8.11E
Jadebusen b. Germany 14 53.30N 8.12E
Jādū Libya 51 31.57N 12.01E
Jaén Peru 90 5.21S 78.28W
Jaén Spain 16 37.46N 3.48W
Jāfarābād India 40 20.52N 71.22E
Jaffa see Tel Aviv-Yafo Israel 44
Jaffa, C. Australia 66 36.58S139.39E
Jaffna Sri Lanka 39 9.38N 80.02E
Jagādhri India 40 30.10N 77.18E
Jāgan Pakistan 40 28.05N 68.30E
Jagatsingpur India 41 20.16N 86.10E
Jagdalpur India 41 19.04N 82.02E
Jaggang China 41 32.52N 79.45E
Jagtiāl India 41 18.48N 78.56E
Jaguarão Brazil 94 32.30S 53.25W
Jahānābād India 41 25.13N 84.59E
Jahrom Iran 43 28.30N 53.30E
Jailolo Indonesia 37 1.05N127.29E
Jainti India 41 26.42N 89.36E
Jaintiāpur Bangla. 41 25.08N 92.07E
Jaipur India 40 26.53N 75.50E
Jāis India 41 26.15N 81.32E
Jaisalmer India 40 26.55N 70.54E
Jājarkot Nepal 41 28.42N 82.14E
Jajawijaya Mts. Asia 37 4.20S139.10E
Jajjha Pakistan 40 28.45N 70.34E
Jājpur India 41 20.51N 86.20E
Jakarta Indonesia 37 6.08S106.45E
Jakarta d. Indonesia 37 6.10S106.48E
Jakhāu India 40 23.13N 68.43E
Jäkkvik Sweden 22 66.23N 17.00E
Jakobstad see Pietarsaari Finland 22
Jal U.S.A. 83 32.07N103.12W
Jalālābād Afghan. 40 34.26N 70.28E
Jalālah al Baḥrīyah, Jabal mts. Egypt 44 29.20N 32.12E
Jalālat al Qiblīyah, Jabal al mts. Egypt 44 28.42N 32.23E
Jalālpur India 41 26.19N 82.44E
Jalapa Mexico 86 19.45N 96.48W
Jālaun India 41 26.09N 79.21E
Jaldak Afghan. 40 31.58N 66.44E
Jalesar India 41 27.29N 78.19E
Jaleswar India 41 21.49N 87.13E
Jālgaon Mahār. India 40 21.01N 75.34E
Jālgaon Mahār. India 40 21.03N 76.32E
Jalingo Nigeria 53 8.54N 11.21E
Jalisco d. Mexico 86 21.00N103.00W
Jālna India 40 19.50N 75.53E
Jalón r. Spain 16 41.47N 1.02W
Jālor India 40 25.21N 72.37E
Jalpaiguri India 41 26.31N 88.44E
Jālū Libya 51 29.02N 21.33E
Jaluit i. Pacific Oc. 68 6.00N169.35E
Jalūlā Iraq 43 34.16N 45.10E
Jamaame Somali Rep. 55 0.04N 42.46E
Jamaari Nigeria 53 11.44N 9.53E
Jamaica C. America 87 18.00N 77.00W
Jamālpur Bangla. 41 24.55N 89.56E
Jamālpur India 41 25.18N 86.30E
Jamanxim r. Brazil 91 4.43S 56.18W
Jambes Belgium 14 50.28N 4.52E
Jambi Indonesia 36 1.36S103.39E
Jambi d. Indonesia 36 2.00S102.30E
Jambusar India 40 22.03N 72.48E
James r. S.Dak. U.S.A. 82 42.55N 97.28W
James r. Va. U.S.A. 85 36.57N 76.26W
James B. Canada 76 53.30N 80.00W
James Bay Prov. Park Canada 76 51.30N 79.00W
Jamestown Australia 66 33.12S138.38E
Jamestown St. Helena 95 15.56S 5.44W
Jamestown N.Dak. U.S.A. 82 46.54N 98.42W
Jamestown N.Y. U.S.A. 84 42.06N 79.14W
Jamestown Tenn. U.S.A. 85 36.24N 84.58W
Jamjodhpur India 40 21.54N 70.01E
Jammerbugt b. Denmark 23 57.20N 9.30E
Jammu Jammu & Kashmir 40 32.42N 74.52E
Jammu & Kashmir Asia 40 34.45N 76.00E
Jāmnagar India 40 22.28N 70.04E
Jamnotri India 41 31.01N 78.27E
Jampang Kulon Indonesia 37 7.18S106.33E
Jāmpur Pakistan 40 28.45N 70.36E
Jamsah Egypt 44 27.39N 33.35E
Jämsänkoski Finland 23 61.55N 25.11E
Jamshedpur India 41 22.48N 86.11E
Jämtland d. Sweden 22 63.00N 14.30E
Jamūi India 41 24.55N 86.13E
Jamuna r. Bangla. 41 23.51N 89.45E
Jand Pakistan 40 33.26N 72.01E
Janda, Laguna de la l. Spain 16 36.15N 5.50W
Jandiāla India 40 31.33N 75.02E
Jándula r. Spain 16 38.08N 4.08W
Janesville U.S.A. 82 42.42N 89.02W
Jangamo Mozambique 57 24.06S 35.21E
Jangipur India 41 24.28N 88.04E
Janin Jordan 44 32.28N 35.18E
Jan Kempdorp R.S.A. 56 27.55S 24.48E
Jan Mayen i. Arctic Oc. 96 71.00N 9.00W
Januária Brazil 94 15.28S 44.23W
Janūb Dārfūr d. Sudan 49 11.45N 25.00E
Janūb Kurdufān d. Sudan 49 11.10N 30.00E
Janzé France 15 47.58N 1.30W
Jaora India 40 23.38N 75.08E
Japan Asia 31 36.00N136.00E
Japan, Sea of Asia 31 40.00N135.00E
Japan Trench Pacific Oc. 68 33.00N142.00E
Japla India 41 24.33N 84.01E
Japurá r. Brazil 90 3.00S 64.50W
Jarales U.S.A. 81 34.37N106.46W
Jarama r. Spain 16 40.27N 3.32W
Jarānwāla Pakistan 40 31.20N 73.26E
Jarash Jordan 44 32.17N 35.54E
Jardee Australia 63 34.18S116.04E
Jardine r. Australia 64 11.07S142.30E
Jardines de la Reina is. Cuba 87 20.30N 79.00W
Jardinópolis Brazil 94 20.59S 47.48W
Jargeau France 15 47.52N 2.07E
Jāria Jhānjail Bangla. 41 25.02N 90.39E
Jaridih India 41 23.38N 86.04E
Jarocin Poland 21 51.59N 17.31E
Jarosław Poland 21 50.02N 22.42E
Jarrāḥī r. Iran 43 30.40N 48.23E
Jartai China 32 39.45N105.46E
Jartai Yanchi l. China 32 39.43N105.41E
Jarud Qi China 32 44.30N120.35E
Järvenpää Finland 23 60.28N 25.06E
Jarvis Canada 76 42.53N 80.06W
Jarvis I. Pacific Oc. 68 0.23S160.02W
Jasdan India 40 22.02N 71.12E
Jāsk Iran 43 25.40N 57.45E
Jasło Poland 21 49.45N 21.29E
Jasper Canada 74 52.55N118.05W
Jasper Ala. U.S.A. 85 33.48N 87.18W
Jasper Fla. U.S.A. 85 30.31N 82.58W
Jasper Tex. U.S.A. 83 30.55N 94.01W
Jasper Nat. Park Canada 74 52.50N118.08W
Jasra India 41 25.17N 81.48E
Jastrebarsko Yugo. 20 45.40N 15.39E
Jastrowie Poland 20 53.26N 16.49E
Jászberény Hungary 21 47.30N 19.55E
Jataí Brazil 94 17.58S 51.45W
Jāti Pakistan 40 24.21N 68.16E
Jatibarang Indonesia 37 6.26S108.18E
Jatinegara Indonesia 37 6.12S106.51E
Játiva Spain 16 39.00N 0.32W
Jatni India 41 20.10N 85.42E
Jaú Brazil 94 22.11S 48.35W
Jauja Peru 90 11.50S 75.15W
Jaunjelgava U.S.S.R. 24 56.34N 25.02E
Jaunpur India 41 25.44N 82.41E
Java i. see Jawa i. Indonesia 37
Javari r. Peru 90 4.30S 71.20W
Java Sea see Jawa, Laut sea Indonesia 36
Java Trench f. Indonesia 36 10.00S110.00E
Jawa i. Indonesia 37 7.25S110.00E
Jawa, Laut sea Indonesia 36 5.00S111.00E
Jawa Barat d. Indonesia 37 7.10S107.00E
Jawa Tengah d. Indonesia 37 7.49S110.35E
Jawa Timur d. Indonesia 37 8.42S113.10E
Jayah, Wādī al see Hā 'Arava Jordan/Israel 44
Jayapura Indonesia 37 2.28S140.38E
Jaynagar India 41 26.32N 86.07E
Jazirah Doberai f. Indonesia 37 1.10S132.30E
Jazzīn Lebanon 44 33.32N 35.34E
Jean U.S.A. 81 35.46N115.20W
Jeanerette U.S.A. 83 29.55N 91.40W
Jean Marie River town Canada 72 61.32N120.40W
Jebāl Bārez, Kūh-e mts. Iran 43 28.40N 58.10E
Jebba Nigeria 53 9.11N 4.49E
Jebri Pakistan 40 27.18N 65.44E
Jedburgh U.K. 12 55.29N 2.33W
Jedda see Jiddah Saudi Arabia 48
Jedrzejów Poland 21 50.39N 20.18E
Jefferson, Mt. Nev. U.S.A. 80 38.46N116.55W
Jefferson, Mt. Oreg. U.S.A. 80 44.40N121.47W
Jefferson City U.S.A. 82 38.34N 92.10W
Jeffersonville U.S.A. 84 38.16N 85.45W
Jega Nigeria 53 12.12N 4.23E
Jēkabpils U.S.S.R. 24 56.28N 25.58E
Jelenia Góra Poland 20 50.55N 15.45E
Jelgava U.S.S.R. 23 56.39N 23.42E
Jelli Sudan 49 5.22N 31.48E
Jember Indonesia 37 8.07S113.45E
Jena Germany 20 50.56N 11.35E
Jena U.S.A. 83 31.41N 92.08W
Jenbach Austria 20 47.24N 11.47E
Jenolan Caves town Australia 67 33.53S150.03E
Jepara Indonesia 37 6.32S110.40E
Jeparit Australia 66 36.09S141.59E
Jeppo Finland 22 63.24N 22.37E
Jequié Brazil 91 13.52S 40.06W
Jequitinhonha r. Brazil 94 16.46S 39.45W
Jerada Morocco 50 34.17N 2.13W
Jerantut Malaysia 36 3.56N102.22E
Jérémie Haiti 87 18.40N 74.09W
Jerez Spain 16 38.20N 6.45W
Jerez de la Frontera Spain 16 36.41N 6.08W
Jericho see Arīḥā Jordan 44
Jerilderie Australia 67 35.23S145.41E
Jerome U.S.A. 80 42.43N114.31W
Jerramungup Australia 63 33.57S118.53E
Jersey i. U.K. 11 49.13N 2.08W
Jersey City U.S.A. 85 40.44N 74.04W
Jerseyville U.S.A. 82 39.07N 90.20W
Jerusalem see Yerushalayim Israel/Jordan 44
Jervis B. Australia 67 35.05S150.44E
Jesenice Yugo. 18 46.27N 14.04E
Jessore Bangla. 41 23.10N 89.13E
Jesup U.S.A. 85 31.36N 81.54W
Jesús Carranza Mexico 86 17.26N 95.02W
Jetmore U.S.A. 83 38.03N 99.54W
Jetpur India 40 21.44N 70.37E
Jever Germany 14 53.34N 7.54E
Jevnaker Norway 23 60.15N 10.28E
Jewett Tex. U.S.A. 83 31.22N 96.09W
Jeypore India 41 18.51N 82.35E
Jeziorak, Jezioro l. Poland 21 53.40N 19.04E
Jhābua India 40 22.46N 74.36E
Jhajha India 41 24.46N 86.22E
Jhal Pakistan 40 28.17N 67.27E
Jhālakāti Bangla. 41 22.39N 90.12E
Jhālawār India 40 24.36N 76.09E
Jhal Jhao Pakistan 40 26.18N 65.35E
Jhālod India 40 23.06N 74.09E
Jhang Sadar Pakistan 40 31.16N 72.20E
Jhānsi India 41 25.26N 78.35E
Jharia India 41 23.45N 86.24E
Jhārsuguda India 41 21.51N 84.02E
Jhawāni Nepal 41 27.35N 84.38E
Jhelum Pakistan 40 32.56N 73.44E
Jhelum r. Pakistan 40 31.12N 72.08E
Jhinkpāni India 41 22.25N 85.47E
Jhok Rind Pakistan 40 31.27N 70.26E
Jhūnjhunu India 40 28.08N 75.24E
Jiaganj India 41 24.14N 88.16E
Jialing Jiang r. China 33 29.30N106.35E
Jiamusi China 31 46.50N130.21E
Ji'an China 33 27.03N115.00E
Jianchang China 32 40.50N119.50E
Jiange China 32 32.04N105.26E
Jiangling China 33 30.20N112.14E
Jiangmen China 33 22.31N113.08E
Jiangshan China 33 28.43N118.39E
Jiangsu d. China 32 33.00N119.30E
Jiangxi d. China 33 27.00N115.30E
Jiangyou China 33 31.47N104.45E
Jianhe China 33 26.39N108.35E
Jian'ou China 33 27.04N118.17E
Jianping China 32 41.23N119.40E
Jianshi China 33 30.42N109.20E
Jianyang Fujian China 33 27.19N118.01E
Jianyang Sichuan China 33 30.25N104.32E
Jiaochangba Sichuan China 32 32.05N103.43E
Jiaohe China 31 43.42N127.19E
Jiaolai He r. China 32 43.48N123.00E
Jiaoling China 33 24.40N116.10E
Jiaonan China 32 35.53N119.58E
Jiao Xian China 32 36.16N120.00E
Jiaozou China 32 35.11N113.27E
Jiashan China 32 32.49N118.01E
Jiawang China 32 34.27N117.27E
Jiaxian China 32 38.02N110.29E
Jiaxing China 33 30.52N120.45E
Jiayi Taiwan 33 23.30N120.24E
Jiazi China 33 22.57N116.01E
Jiddah Saudi Arabia 48 21.30N 39.10E
Jiddat al Ḥarāsīs f. Oman 45 19.45N 56.30E
Jiepai China 33 31.11N113.42E
Jiexi China 33 23.26N115.52E
Jiexiu China 32 37.00N111.55E
Jieyang China 33 23.29N116.19E
Jihlava Czech. 20 49.24N 15.35E
Jijel Algeria 51 36.48N 5.46E
Jijiga Ethiopia 45 9.22N 42.47E
Jilib Somali Rep. 55 0.28N 42.50E
Jilin China 31 43.53N126.35E
Jilin d. China 31 44.50N125.00E
Jilong Taiwan 33 25.09N121.45E
Jima Ethiopia 49 7.36N 36.50E
Jimbe Angola 54 10.20S 16.40E
Jiménez Mexico 86 27.08N104.55W
Jimeta Nigeria 53 9.19N 12.25E
Jimo China 32 36.23N120.27E
Jinan China 32 36.40N117.01E
Jind India 40 29.19N 76.19E
Jindabyne Australia 67 36.24S148.37E
Jing'an China 33 28.52N115.22E
Jingbian China 32 37.33N108.36E
Jingchuan China 32 35.15N107.22E
Jingde China 33 30.19N118.31E
Jingdezhen China 33 29.14N117.14E
Jingellic Australia 67 35.54S147.44E
Jinggu Gansu China 32 35.05N103.41E
Jinggu Yunnan China 39 23.29N100.19E
Jinghai China 33 23.02N116.31E
Jing He r. China 32 34.26N109.00E
Jinghong China 30 21.59N100.49E
Jingmen China 33 31.02N112.06E
Jingning China 32 35.30N105.45E
Jingou China 32 41.37N120.33E
Jingtai China 32 37.10N104.08E
Jingxi China 33 23.03N106.36E
Jing Xian China 33 26.35N109.41E
Jingyuan Gansu China 32 36.40N104.40E
Jingyuan Ningxia Huizu China 32 35.29N106.20E
Jinhua China 33 29.05N119.40E
Jining Nei Monggol China 31 40.56N113.00E
Jining Shantung China 32 35.22N116.45E
Jinja Uganda 55 0.27N 33.10E
Jinotepe Nicaragua 87 11.50N 86.10W
Jinsha Jiang r. China 39 26.30N101.40E
Jinshi China 33 29.35N111.56E
Jintang China 33 30.51N104.27E
Jinxi Fujian China 33 26.12N117.34E
Jinxi Liaoning China 32 40.48N120.46E
Jinxian China 33 28.13N116.34E
Jin Xian Liaoning China 32 41.10N121.20E
Jin Xian Liaoning China 32 39.06N121.49E
Jinxiang China 32 35.08N116.20E
Jinzhou China 32 41.06N121.05E
Jipijapa Ecuador 90 1.23S 80.35W
Jire Somali Rep. 45 5.22N 48.05E
Jirjā Egypt 48 26.20N 31.53E
Jishui China 33 27.13N115.07E
Jitarning Australia 63 32.48S117.57E
Jiu r. Romania 19 43.44N 23.52E
Jiuding Shan mtn. China 33 31.36N103.54E
Jiudongshan China 33 23.44N117.32E
Jiujiang China 33 29.39N116.02E
Jiulian Shan mts. China 33 24.40N115.00E
Jiuling Shan mts. China 33 28.40N114.45E
Jiulong Jiang r. China 33 24.30N117.47E
Jiuzhou Jiang r. China 33 21.25N109.58E
Jixi China 31 45.17N131.00E
Ji Xian Henan China 32 35.25N114.05E
Ji Xian Tianjin China 32 40.03N117.24E
Jīzān Saudi Arabia 48 16.54N 42.32E
Jīzl, Wādī al r. Saudi Arabia 42 25.37N 38.20E
João Pessoa Brazil 91 7.06S 34.53W
Jódar Spain 16 37.50N 3.21W
Jodhpur India 40 26.17N 73.02E
Jodiya India 40 22.42N 70.18E
Jodoigne Belgium 14 50.45N 4.52E
Joensuu Finland 24 62.35N 29.46E
Joetsu Japan 35 37.07N138.15E
Jogdor China 32 42.30N115.52E
Johannesburg R.S.A. 56 26.11S 28.04E
Johi Pakistan 40 26.41N 67.37E
John Day U.S.A. 80 44.25N118.57W
John Day r. U.S.A. 80 45.44N120.39W
John O'Groats U.K. 12 58.39N 3.02W
Johnson U.S.A. 83 37.34N101.45W
Johnson City Tenn. U.S.A. 85 36.20N 82.2
Johnsons Crossing Canada 74 60.29N133.18W
Johnston, L. Australia 63 32.25S120.30E
Johnstone Str. Canada 74 50.28N126.00W
Johnston I. Pacific Oc. 68 16.45N169.32W
Johnstown Penn. U.S.A. 84 40.20N 78.55W
Johor Baharu Malaysia 36 1.29N103.40E
Joigny France 15 48.00N 3.20E
Joinville Brazil 94 26.20S 48.49W
Joinville France 17 48.27N 5.08E
Jokkmokk Sweden 22 66.37N 19.50E
Jökulsá á Brú r. Iceland 22 65.33N 14.23W
Jökulsá á Fjöllum r. Iceland 22 66.05N 16.32W
Jolfa Iran 43 32.40N 51.39E
Joliet U.S.A. 82 41.32N 88.05W
Joliette Canada 77 46.02N 73.27W
Jolo i. Phil. 37 5.55N121.20E
Jolo town Phil. 37 6.03N121.00E
Jombang Indonesia 37 7.30S112.21E
Jombo r. Angola 54 10.20S 16.37E
Jomda China 39 31.30N 98.16E
Jonava U.S.S.R. 23 55.05N 24.17E
Jonê China 32 34.35N103.32E
Jonesboro Ark. U.S.A. 83 35.50N 90.42W
Jonesboro La. U.S.A. 83 32.15N 92.43W
Jones Sd. Canada 73 76.00N 85.00W
Jönköping Sweden 23 57.47N 14.11E
Jönköping d. Sweden 23 57.30N 14.30E
Joplin U.S.A. 83 37.06N 94.31W
Jora India 41 26.20N 77.49E
Jordan Asia 42 31.00N 36.00E
Jordan r. see Al Urdunn r. Asia 44
Jordan Mont. U.S.A. 80 47.19N106.55W
Jordan Valley town U.S.A. 80 42.58N117.0
Jorhāt India 39 26.45N 94.13E
Jörn Sweden 22 65.04N 20.02E
Jos Nigeria 53 9.54N 8.53E
José de San Martín Argentina 93 44.04S 70.26W
José Enrique Rodó Uruguay 93 33.41S 57.34W
Joseph, Lac l. Canada 77 52.45N 65.15W
Joseph Bonaparte G. Australia 62 14.00S128.30E
Joseph City U.S.A. 81 34.57N110.20W
Joshimath India 41 30.34N 79.34E
Jos Plateau f. Nigeria 53 10.00N 9.00E
Jotunheimen mts. Norway 23 61.38N 8.18
Joué-lès-Tours France 15 47.21N 0.40E
Joure Neth. 14 52.59N 5.49E
Joverega Botswana 56 19.08S 24.15E
Jowai India 41 25.27N 92.12E
Juan Aldama Mexico 83 24.19N103.21W
Juan B. Arruabarrena Argentina 93 30.25S 58.15W
Juan de Fuca, Str. of Canada/U.S.A. 74 48.15N124.00W
Juan de Nova i. Madagascar 57 17.03S 42.45E
Juan Fernández, Islas is. Pacific Oc. 69 34.20S 80.00W
Juárez Argentina 93 37.40S 59.48W
Juárez Chihuahua Mexico 81 30.20N108.03
Juárez Coahuila Mexico 83 27.37N100.44W
Juárez, Sierra de mts. Mexico 81 32.00N115.45W
Juàzeiro Brazil 91 9.25S 40.30W
Juàzeiro do Norte Brazil 91 7.10S 39.18W
Jūbā Sudan 49 4.51N 31.37E
Jūbāl, Maḍīq str. Egypt 44 27.40N 33.55E
Jubal, Str. of see Jūbāl, Maḍīq str. Egypt 44
Jubba r. Somali Rep. 55 0.20S 42.40E
Jubilee Downs town Australia 62 18.22S125.17E
Juby, Cap c. Morocco 50 27.58N 12.55W
Júcar r. Spain 16 39.10N 0.15W
Juchitán Mexico 86 16.27N 95.05W
Judenburg Austria 20 47.10N 14.40E
Judith Basin f. U.S.A. 80 47.10N109.58W
Juist Germany 14 53.41N 7.01E
Juist i. Germany 14 53.43N 7.00E
Juiz de Fora Brazil 94 21.47S 43.23W
Jujuy d. Argentina 92 23.00S 66.00W
Juklegga mtn. Norway 23 61.03N 8.13E
Juliaca Peru 90 15.29S 70.09W
Julia Creek town Australia 64 20.39S141.4
Juliana Kanaal canal Neth. 14 51.00N 5.48E
Julianehåb Greenland 73 60.45N 46.00W
Jülich Germany 14 50.55N 6.21E
Jullundur India 40 31.20N 75.35E
Jumboo Somali Rep. 55 0.12S 42.38E
Jumet Belgium 14 50.27N 4.27E
Jumilla Spain 16 38.28N 1.19W
Jumla Nepal 41 29.17N 82.13E
Jumna r. see Yamuna India 41
Junāgadh India 40 21.31N 70.28E
Junan China 32 35.11N118.50E
Junction U.S.A. 83 30.29N 99.46W
Junction B. Australia 64 11.50S134.15E
Junction City Kans. U.S.A. 82 39.02N 96.5
Junction City Oreg. U.S.A. 80 44.13N123.1
Jundah Australia 64 24.50S143.02E
Jundiaí Brazil 94 23.10S 46.54W
Juneau U.S.A. 74 58.26N134.30W
Junee Australia 67 34.51S147.40E
Jungfrau mtn. Switz. 17 46.30N 8.00E
Junggar Pendi f. Asia 30 44.20N 86.30E
Junglinster Lux. 14 49.41N 6.13E
Jungshāhi Pakistan 40 24.51N 67.46E
Junín Argentina 93 34.35S 60.58W
Junín de los Andes Argentina 93 39.57S 71.05W
Juniville France 15 49.24N 4.23E

ah Lebanon 44 33.59N 35.38E
n China 33 28.08N104.29E
h, Jabal mts. Egypt 44 28.52N 34.15E
r India 40 19.12N 73.53E
li d. Sudan 49 7.30N 32.30E
le Sweden 22 63.40N 16.55E
ra U.S.A. 80 43.46N118.05W
an China 32 32.40N111.18E
r r. Canada 77 49.29N 63.32W
r U.S.A. 85 26.57N 80.08W
Sudan 49 7.45N 28.00E
nts. Europe 17 46.55N 6.45E
U.K. 12 55.58N 5.55W
Sd. of U.K. 12 56.00N 5.45W
o Colombia 90 7.07N 77.46W
rakowska mts. Poland 21 50.30N
0E
n Ul Shan mts. China 41 34.00N 91.00E
la U.S.S.R. 23 56.58N 23.42E
r. Brazil 90 2.33S 65.50W
na Brazil 92 12.50S 58.58W
na r. Brazil 91 7.20S 57.30W
Brazil 91 2.09S 56.04W
y France 17 47.49N 5.54E
r. Brazil 90 2.35S 67.00W
lpa Honduras 87 14.45N 86.12W
d pen. see Jylland pen. Denmark 23
China 32 35.23N116.06E
n Iran 43 28.10N 53.52E
yā Lebanon 44 33.14N 35.20E
d pen. Denmark 23 56.00N 9.15E
kylä Finland 22 62.14N 25.44E

n. Asia 30 35.53N 76.32E
Nigeria 53 11.35N 4.10E
ong Uganda 55 3.28N 34.08E
stad see Cape Town R.S.A. 56
Guinea 52 10.08N 11.49W
na i. Indonesia 37 5.25S122.00E
a Sierra Leone 52 9.40N 11.36W
le Uganda 55 1.13S 30.00E
ega Falls f. Uganda 55 2.17N 31.46E
ega Falls Nat. Park Uganda 55 2.15N
5E
lo Zaïre 55 6.02S 27.00E
mbare Zaïre 55 4.40S 27.41E
nga Zambia 56 17.36S 26.45E
a Nigeria 53 7.50N 6.07E
akagami r. Canada 84 50.20N 84.20W
da Zaïre 54 6.10S 24.29E
Kūh mts. Iran 43 33.00N 47.00E
ābīyah Sudan 49 13.39N 24.05E
l Afghan. 40 34.31N 69.12E
l d. Afghan. 40 34.45N 69.15E
mpo Zambia 54 13.35S 24.10E
mpo r. Zambia 54 14.17S 23.15E
ngo Zaïre 54 7.22S 25.34E
nzo Zaïre 55 6.41S 27.49E
udia, Ra's c. Tunisia 51 35.14N 11.10E
d Gonbad Iran 43 37.02N 59.46E
l see Kābol Afghan. 40
mbu Zaïre 54 4.07S 26.17E
nda Zaïre 55 12.27S 29.15E
ndi Zaïre 55 10.07S 27.13E
e Zambia 55 14.27S 28.25E
ā Kūh mts. Iran 43 29.30N 61.20E
chh, G. of India 40 22.40N 69.30E
in d. Burma 34 26.00N 97.30E
iry U.S.S.R. 28 53.07N 76.08E
isi Ethiopia 49 9.39N 37.50E
ney r. Afghan. 40 31.20N 65.47E
Ghana 52 6.08N 0.51W
i r. C.A.R. 53 3.28N 16.05E
India 40 23.18N 72.20E
a Australia 66 33.58S137.14E
li Mali 52 10.38N 5.45W
ka U.S.A. 82 43.50N101.31W
ma Zimbabwe 56 18.23S 29.52E
na Nigeria 53 10.28N 7.25E
na d. Nigeria 53 11.00N 7.35E
na r. Nigeria 53 8.45N 5.45E
qlī Sudan 49 11.01N 29.43E
sam mtn. China 39 28.30N 96.45E
herom U.S.S.R. 24 64.42N 55.59E
i Mauritania 50 16.09N 13.30W
é Cameroon 53 10.05N 14.28E
ong N. Korea 31 37.59N126.30E
chan Nigeria 53 9.38N 8.20E
ine Senegal 52 14.08N 15.34W
Kingi Sudan 49 9.16N 24.25E
évs, Ákra c. Greece 19 38.11N 24.30E
ad Dawwār Egypt 44 31.08N 30.08E
al Baṭṭīkh Egypt 44 31.24N 31.44E
ash Shaykh Egypt 44 31.07N 30.56E
az Zayyāt Egypt 44 30.50N 30.49E
Salīm Egypt 44 31.09N 30.07E
r. Uganda 55 1.40N 32.07E
e Zambia 55 15.40S 28.13E
e r. Zambia 55 15.53S 28.55E
e Dam Zambia 55 15.40S 27.10E
e Nat. Park Zambia 54 15.30S 25.35E
nzo Uganda 55 1.05S 30.26E
Bandoro C.A.R. 53 7.00N 19.10E
n Pakistan 40 34.47N 73.32E
n U.S.S.R. 28 39.45N 64.32E
rlyk U.S.S.R. 21 49.50N 30.50E
znagar India 41 19.18N 79.50E
ra d. Tanzania 55 2.00S 31.20E
man Turkey 42 40.08N 43.07E
shima Japan 31 31.37N130.32E
l U.S.S.R. 19 45.54N 28.11E

Kahama Tanzania 55 3.48S 32.38E
Kahayan r. Indonesia 36 3.20S114.04E
Kahemba Zaïre 54 7.20S 19.00E
Kahntah r. Canada 74 58.15N120.55W
Kahnūj Iran 43 27.55N 57.45E
Kahoolawe i. Hawaiian Is. 69 20.33N156.37W
Kahraman Maraş Turkey 42 37.34N 36.54E
Kai, Kepulauan is. Indonesia 37 5.45S132.55E
Kaiama Nigeria 53 9.37N 4.03E
Kaiapoi New Zealand 60 43.23S172.39E
Kaiedin Sudan 49 9.45N 32.11E
Kaifeng China 32 34.46N114.22E
Kaikohe New Zealand 60 35.25S173.49E
Kaikoura New Zealand 60 42.24S173.41E
Kaikoura Range mts. New Zealand 60
42.00S173.40E
Kailahun Sierra Leone 52 8.21N 10.21W
Kaili China 33 26.35N107.55E
Kailu China 32 43.35N121.12E
Kailua Hawaiian Is. 69 21.24N157.44W
Kaimana Indonesia 37 3.39S133.44E
Kaimanawa Mts. New Zealand 60
39.10S176.15E
Kainantu P.N.G. 37 6.16S145.50E
Kainji Resr. Nigeria 53 10.00N 4.35E
Kaintragarh India 41 20.47N 84.40E
Kaipara Harbour New Zealand 60
36.30S174.00E
Kaiserslautern Germany 14 49.27N 7.47E
Kaitaia New Zealand 60 35.08S173.18E
Kaithal India 40 29.48N 76.23E
Kaitum r. Sweden 22 67.30N 21.05E
Kaiwi Channel Hawaiian Is. 69
21.15N157.30W
Kaiyuan China 32 42.45N123.50E
Kaizuka Japan 35 34.27N135.21E
Kajaani Finland 22 64.14N 27.41E
Kajabbi Australia 64 20.02S140.02E
Kajiado Kenya 55 1.50S 36.48E
Kajo Kaji Sudan 49 3.53N 31.40E
Kajuru Nigeria 53 10.19N 7.40E
Kākā Sudan 49 10.36N 32.11E
Kakamas R.S.A. 56 28.44S 20.35E
Kakamega Kenya 55 0.21N 34.47E
Kakamigahara Japan 35 35.28N136.48E
Kākdwīp India 41 21.53N 88.11E
Kakegawa Japan 35 34.46N138.01E
Kakenge Zaïre 54 4.51S 21.55E
Kakhovskoye Vodokhranilishche resr.
U.S.S.R. 25 47.33N 34.40E
Kākī Iran 43 28.19N 51.34E
Kākināda India 39 16.59N 82.20E
Kakisa r. Canada 74 61.03N117.10W
Kakisa L. Canada 74 60.55N117.40W
Kakonko Tanzania 55 3.19S 30.54E
Kakuma Kenya 55 3.38N 34.48E
Kakuto Uganda 55 0.54S 31.26E
Kala r. Finland 22 64.17N 23.55E
Kālābāgh Pakistan 40 32.58N 71.34E
Kalabahi Indonesia 37 8.13S124.31E
Kalabáka Greece 19 39.42N 21.43E
Kalabity Australia 66 31.53S140.18E
Kalabo Zambia 54 14.58S 22.33E
Kalach-na-Donu U.S.S.R. 25 48.43N 43.31E
Kaladan r. Burma 34 20.09N 92.55E
Kalahari Desert Botswana 56 23.30S 22.00E
Kalahari Gemsbok Nat. Park R.S.A. 56
25.45S 20.25E
Kalajoki Finland 22 64.15N 23.57E
Kalakan U.S.S.R. 29 55.10N116.45E
Kalámai Greece 19 37.02N 22.05E
Kalamazoo U.S.A. 84 42.17N 85.36W
Kalamb India 40 18.56N 73.55E
Kalamera Tanzania 55 2.07S 33.43E
Kalamurra, L. Australia 66 28.00S138.00E
Kalandula Angola 54 9.06S 16.11E
Kalannie Australia 63 30.21S117.04E
Kalanshiyū, Sarīr des. Libya 51 27.00N
21.30E
Kalarash U.S.S.R. 21 47.18N 28.16E
Kalāt Pakistan 40 29.02N 66.35E
Kalb, Ra's al c. Yemen 45 14.02N 48.41E
Kalbarri Australia 63 27.40S114.12E
Kalchās Pakistan 40 29.21N 69.42E
Kalecik Turkey 42 40.06N 33.22E
Kalehe Zaïre 55 2.05S 28.53E
Kalemie Zaïre 55 5.57S 29.10E
Kalgan r. Australia 63 34.55S117.58E
Kalgoorlie Australia 63 30.49S121.29E
Kaliakra, Nos c. Bulgaria 19 43.23N 28.29E
Kalianda Indonesia 36 5.50S105.45E
Kalima Zaïre 54 2.35S 26.34E
Kalimantan d. Indonesia 36 1.00S113.00E
Kalimantan f. Indonesia 36 0.05N112.30E
Kalimantan Barat d. Indonesia 36
0.30N110.00E
Kalimantan Selatan d. Indonesia 36
2.30S115.30E
Kalimantan Tengah d. Indonesia 36
2.00S113.30E
Kalimantan Timur d. Indonesia 36
2.20N116.30E
Kálimnos i. Greece 19 37.00N 27.00E
Kālimpong India 41 27.04N 88.29E
Kaliningrad U.S.S.R. 23 54.43N 20.30E
Kalinkovichi U.S.S.R. 21 52.10N 29.13E
Kalinovka U.S.S.R. 21 49.29N 28.30E
Kalisat Indonesia 37 8.02S113.50E
Kāli Sindh r. India 40 25.32N 76.17E
Kalispell U.S.A. 80 48.12N114.19W
Kalisz Poland 21 51.46N 18.02E
Kaliua Tanzania 55 5.08S 31.50E
Kalix r. Sweden 22 65.50N 23.11E
Kalkar Germany 14 51.45N 6.17E
Kalkfontein Botswana 56 22.08S 20.54E
Kalkrand Namibia 56 24.05S 17.34E
Kallsjön l. Sweden 22 63.35N 13.00E
Kalmar Sweden 23 56.40N 16.22E

Kalmar d. Sweden 23 57.20N 16.00E
Kalmarsund str. Sweden 23 56.40N 16.25E
Kalmthout Belgium 14 51.23N 4.28E
Kalmykovo U.S.S.R. 25 49.02N 51.55E
Kālna India 41 23.13N 88.22E
Kalo P.N.G. 64 10.05S147.45E
Kalocsa Hungary 21 46.32N 18.59E
Kaloko Zaïre 54 6.47S 25.47E
Kālol Gujarat India 40 22.36N 73.27E
Kālol Gujarat India 40 23.15N 72.29E
Kalole Zaïre 55 3.40S 27.22E
Kalomo Zambia 54 16.55S 26.29E
Kalonje Zambia 55 12.21S 31.06E
Kālpi India 41 26.07N 79.44E
Kāl Qal 'eh Afghan. 40 32.38N 62.32E
Kalsö i. Faroe Is. 8 62.19N 6.42W
Kalsūbai mtn. India 40 19.36N 73.43E
Kaltag U.S.A. 72 64.20N158.44W
Kaluga U.S.S.R. 24 54.31N 36.16E
Kālu Khuhar Pakistan 40 25.08N 67.46E
Kalumburu Australia 62 14.14S126.38E
Kalundborg Denmark 23 55.41N 11.06E
Kalush U.S.S.R. 21 49.02N 24.20E
Kalutara Sri Lanka 39 6.35N 79.58E
Kalyān India 40 19.15N 73.09E
Kama r. U.S.S.R. 24 55.30N 52.00E
Kamakura Japan 35 35.19N139.33E
Kamālia Pakistan 40 30.44N 72.39E
Kamanashi r. Japan 35 35.33N138.28E
Kamanjab Namibia 56 19.39S 14.50E
Kamarsuk Canada 77 56.18N 61.38W
Kamba Nigeria 53 11.52N 3.42E
Kamba Zaïre 54 4.00S 22.22E
Kambalda Australia 63 31.12S121.40E
Kambar Pakistan 40 27.36N 68.00E
Kambarka U.S.S.R. 24 56.18N 54.13E
Kambia Sierra Leone 52 9.09N 12.53W
Kamchatka, Poluostrov pen. U.S.S.R. 29
56.00N160.00E
Kamen mtn. U.S.S.R. 29 68.40N 94.20E
Kamenets Podolskiy U.S.S.R. 21 48.40N
26.36E
Kamenka R.S.F.S.R. U.S.S.R. 24 65.55N
44.02E
Kamenka R.S.F.S.R. U.S.S.R. 24 53.10N
44.05E
Kamenka Bugskaya U.S.S.R. 21 50.07N
24.30E
Kamen Kashirskiy U.S.S.R. 21 51.32N 24.59E
Kamen-na-Obi U.S.S.R. 28 53.46N 81.18E
Kamenskoye U.S.S.R. 29 62.31N165.15E
Kamensk-Shakhtinskiy U.S.S.R. 25 48.20N
40.16E
Kamensk-Ural'skiy U.S.S.R. 28 56.29N
61.49E
Kāmet mtn. India/China 41 30.54N 79.37E
Kameyama Japan 35 34.51N136.27E
Kamiah U.S.A. 80 46.14N116.02W
Kamieskroon R.S.A. 56 30.12S 17.53E
Kamilukuak L. Canada 75 62.22N101.40W
Kamina Zaïre 54 8.46S 24.58E
Kaminak L. Canada 75 62.10N 95.00W
Kamloops Canada 74 50.40N120.20W
Kamloops Plateau f. Canada 74
50.00N120.20W
Kamo r. Japan 35 35.00N139.52E
Kāmoke Pakistan 40 31.58N 74.13E
Kamp Germany 14 50.14N 7.37E
Kampa Indonesia 36 1.46S105.26E
Kampala Uganda 55 0.19N 32.35E
Kampar r. Indonesia 36 0.20N102.55E
Kampen Neth. 14 52.33N 5.55E
Kampene Zaïre 54 3.36S 26.40E
Kamphaeng Phet Thailand 34 16.28N 99.31E
Kamp-Lintfort Germany 14 51.34N 6.38E
Kâmpóng Cham Cambodia 34 11.59N105.26E
Kâmpóng Chhnăng Cambodia 34
12.16N104.39E
Kâmpóng Saôm Cambodia 36 10.38N103.30E
Kâmpóng Thum Cambodia 34 12.42N104.52E
Kâmpôt Cambodia 34 10.37N104.11E
Kampti Burkina 52 10.07N 3.22W
Kampuchea see Cambodia Asia 34
Kamsack Canada 75 51.34N101.54W
Kamskoye Vodokhranilishche resr. U.S.S.R.
24 58.55N 56.20E
Kāmthi India 41 21.14N 79.12E
Kamyshin U.S.S.R. 25 50.05N 45.24E
Kana r. Zimbabwe 56 18.30S 26.50E
Kanaaupscow r. Canada 76 53.40N 77.10W
Kanafis Sudan 49 9.48N 25.40E
Kanagawa d. Japan 35 35.25N139.10E
Kanairiktok r. Canada 77 55.05N 60.20W
Kananga Zaïre 54 5.53S 22.26E
Kanash U.S.S.R. 24 55.30N 47.27E
Kanaudi India 41 23.36N 81.23E
Kanawha r. U.S.A. 84 38.50N 82.08W
Kanazawa Japan 31 36.35N136.38E
Kanchanaburi Thailand 34 14.02N 99.28E
Kānchenjunga mtn. Nepal/India 41 27.44N
88.11E
Kānchipuram India 39 12.50N 79.44E
Kandāhu Pakistan 40 27.33N 69.24E
Kandalaksha U.S.S.R. 24 67.09N 32.31E
Kandalakshskaya Guba g. U.S.S.R. 24 66.30N
34.00E
Kandangan Indonesia 36 2.50S115.15E
Kandavu i. Fiji 68 19.05S178.15E
Kandavu Passage Fiji 68 18.45S178.00E
Kandhkot Pakistan 40 28.14N 69.11E
Kandi Benin 53 11.05N 2.59E
Kāndi India 41 23.57N 88.02E
Kandiāro Pakistan 40 27.04N 68.13E
Kandira Turkey 42 41.05N 30.08E
Kandla India 40 23.00N 70.10E
Kandos Australia 67 32.53S149.59E
Kandrāch Pakistan 40 25.29N 65.29E
Kandreho Madagascar 57 17.29S 46.06E

Kandy Sri Lanka 39 7.18N 80.43E
Kane U.S.A. 84 41.40N 78.49W
Kanem d. Chad 53 15.10N 15.30E
Kanevka U.S.S.R. 24 67.08N 39.50E
Kang Botswana 56 23.43S 22.51E
Kangaba Mali 52 11.56N 8.25W
Kangān Iran 43 27.50N 52.07E
Kangar Malaysia 36 6.28N100.10E
Kangaroo I. Australia 66 35.50S137.06E
Kangding China 30 30.05N102.04E
Kangean, Kepulauan is. Indonesia 37
7.00S115.30E
Kangerlussuaq see Söndreströmfjord
Greenland 73
Kangiqsujuaq Canada 73 61.30N 72.00W
Kangirsuk Canada 73 60.01N 70.01W
Kangle China 32 35.16N103.39E
Kangmar Xizang China 41 28.30N 89.45E
Kangmar Xizang China 41 30.45N 85.43E
Kango Gabon 54 0.15N 10.14E
Kangping China 32 42.45N123.20E
Kangrinboqê Feng mtn. China 41 31.05N
81.21E
Kangto mtn. China 41 27.54N 92.32E
Kanhar r. India 41 24.28N 83.08E
Kani Ivory Coast 52 8.34N 6.35W
Kaniama Zaïre 54 7.32S 24.11E
Kanin, Poluostrov pen. U.S.S.R. 24 68.00N
45.00E
Kaningo Kenya 55 0.52S 38.31E
Kanin Nos, Mys c. U.S.S.R. 24 68.38N 43.20E
Kaniva Australia 66 36.33S141.17E
Kanjiža Yugo. 21 46.04N 20.04E
Kankakee U.S.A. 82 41.08N 87.52W
Kankan Gabon 54 0.03S 12.14E
Kankan Guinea 52 10.22N 9.11W
Kānker India 41 20.17N 81.29E
Kankossa Mauritania 50 15.58N 11.31W
Kannack Vietnam 34 14.07N108.36E
Kannapolis U.S.A. 85 35.30N 80.36W
Kannauj India 41 27.04N 79.55E
Kannod India 40 22.40N 76.44E
Kano r. Japan 35 35.05N138.52E
Kano Nigeria 53 12.00N 8.31E
Kano d. Nigeria 53 12.00N 9.00E
Kanona Zambia 55 13.03S 30.37E
Kanowna Australia 63 30.36S121.36E
Kānpur India 41 26.28N 80.21E
Kansas d. U.S.A. 82 38.30N 99.00W
Kansas r. U.S.A. 82 39.07N 94.36W
Kansas City Kans. U.S.A. 82 39.07N 94.39W
Kansas City Mo. U.S.A. 82 39.05N 94.35W
Kansenia Zaïre 54 10.19S 26.02E
Kansk U.S.S.R. 29 56.11N 95.20E
Kansŏng S. Korea 31 38.20N128.28E
Kantābānji India 41 20.29N 82.55E
Kantché Niger 53 13.31N 8.30E
Kantemirovka U.S.S.R. 25 49.40N 39.52E
Kantō d. Japan 35 35.35N139.30E
Kantōheiya f. Japan 35 36.02N140.10E
Kantō-sanchi mts. Japan 35 36.00N138.35E
Kanye Botswana 56 24.58S 25.17E
Kanyu Botswana 56 20.05S 24.39E
Kao i. Tonga 69 19.40S175.01W
Kaoko Veld f. Namibia 56 18.30S 13.30E
Kaolack Senegal 52 14.09N 16.08W
Kaoma Zambia 54 14.55S 24.58E
Kapaa Hawaiian Is. 69 22.05N159.19W
Kapadvanj India 40 23.01N 73.04E
Kapanga Zaïre 54 8.22S 22.37E
Kapchagay U.S.S.R. 30 43.51N 77.14E
Kapenguria Kenya 55 1.13N 35.07E
Kapfenberg Austria 20 47.27N 15.18E
Kapiri Mposhi Zambia 55 13.59S 28.40E
Kapiskau Canada 76 52.20N 82.01W
Kapiskau r. Canada 76 52.20N 83.40W
Kapit Malaysia 36 2.01N112.56E
Kapiti I. New Zealand 60 40.50S174.50E
Kapoeta Sudan 49 4.47N 33.35E
Kapongolo Zaïre 55 7.51S 28.12E
Kaposvár Hungary 19 46.22N 17.47E
Kappar Pakistan 40 25.19N 62.42E
Kapps Namibia 56 22.22S 17.52E
Kapsabet Kenya 55 0.12N 35.05E
Kaptai Bangla. 41 22.21N 92.17E
Kapuas r. Indonesia 36 0.13S109.12E
Kapunda Australia 66 34.21S138.54E
Kapūrthala India 40 31.23N 75.23E
Kapuskasing Canada 76 49.25N 82.30W
Kaputar, Mt. Australia 67 30.20S150.10E
Kapuvár Hungary 21 47.36N 17.02E
Kara U.S.S.R. 28 69.12N 65.00E
Kara-Bogaz Gol, Zaliv b. U.S.S.R. 43 41.20N
53.40E
Karabük Turkey 42 41.12N 32.36E
Karabutak U.S.S.R. 28 49.55N 60.05E
Karāchi Pakistan 40 24.52N 67.03E
Karād India 38 17.17N 74.12E
Karaganda U.S.S.R. 28 49.53N 73.07E
Karaginskiy, Ostrov i. U.S.S.R. 29
59.00N165.00E
Karakas U.S.S.R. 30 48.20N 83.30E
Karakelong i. Indonesia 37 4.20N126.50E
Karakoram Pass Asia 39 35.33N 77.51E
Karakoram Range mts. Jammu & Kashmir 38
35.30N 76.30E
Karakoro r. Mauritania 50 14.43N 12.03W
Karaköse see Ağri Turkey 25
Karakumskiy Kanal canal U.S.S.R. 43 37.30N
65.48E
Karakumy, Peski f. U.S.S.R. 43 37.45N
60.00E
Karakuwisa Namibia 56 18.56S 19.43E
Karaman Turkey 42 37.11N 33.13E
Karamay China 30 45.48N 84.30E
Karamea New Zealand 60 41.15S172.07E
Karamea Bight b. New Zealand 60
41.15S171.30E

Karamürsel Turkey 42 40.42N 29.37E
Karand Iran 43 34.16N 46.15E
Kāranja India 41 20.29N 77.29E
Karanjia India 41 21.47N 85.58E
Karasburg Namibia 56 28.00S 18.46E
Karasjok Norway 22 69.27N 25.30E
Karasuk U.S.S.R. 28 53.45N 78.01E
Karatau, Khrebet mts. U.S.S.R. 25 44.15N
52.10E
Karatobe U.S.S.R. 25 49.44N 53.30E
Karaton U.S.S.R. 25 46.26N 53.32E
Karauli India 40 26.30N 77.01E
Karawa Zaïre 54 3.12N 20.20E
Karazhal U.S.S.R. 28 48.00N 70.55E
Karbalā' Iraq 43 32.37N 44.03E
Karcag Hungary 21 47.19N 20.56E
Kardhítsa Greece 19 39.22N 21.59E
Kärdla U.S.S.R. 23 59.00N 22.42E
Kareli India 41 22.55N 79.04E
Karema Tanzania 55 6.50S 30.25E
Karen d. Burma 34 17.30N 97.45E
Karen India 39 12.50N 92.55E
Karepino U.S.S.R. 24 61.05N 58.02E
Karesuando Finland 22 68.25N 22.30E
Kargasok U.S.S.R. 28 59.07N 80.58E
Kargi Kenya 55 2.31N 37.34E
Kargil Jammu & Kashmir 40 34.34N 76.06E
Kargopol U.S.S.R. 24 61.32N 38.59E
Kari Nigeria 53 11.17N 10.35E
Kariba Zimbabwe 56 16.32S 28.50E
Kariba, L. Zimbabwe/Zambia 56 16.50S
28.00E
Kariba Dam Zimbabwe/Zambia 56 16.15S
28.55E
Karibib Namibia 56 21.56S 15.52E
Kārikāl India 39 10.58N 79.50E
Karimama Benin 53 12.02N 3.15E
Karīmganj India 41 24.52N 92.20E
Karin Somali Rep. 45 10.51N 45.45E
Karis Finland 23 60.05N 23.40E
Karisimbi, Mt. Zaïre/Rwanda 55 1.31S 29.25E
Kariya Japan 35 34.59N136.59E
Kariyangwe Zimbabwe 56 17.57S 27.30E
Karkaralinsk U.S.S.R. 28 49.21N 75.27E
Karkar I. P.N.G. 37 4.40S146.00E
Karkas, Kūh-e mtn. Iran 43 33.25N 51.40E
Karkheh r. Iran 43 31.45N 47.52E
Karkinitskiy Zaliv g. U.S.S.R. 25 45.50N
32.45E
Karkoo Australia 66 34.02S135.44E
Karlino Poland 20 54.03N 15.51E
Karl-Marx-Stadt See Chemnitz Germany 20
Karlovac Yugo. 18 45.30N 15.34E
Karlovy Vary Czech. 20 50.14N 12.53E
Karlsborg Sweden 23 58.32N 14.31E
Karlshamn Sweden 23 56.10N 14.51E
Karlskoga Sweden 23 59.20N 14.31E
Karlskrona Sweden 23 56.10N 15.35E
Karlsruhe Germany 20 49.00N 8.24E
Karlstad Sweden 23 59.22N 13.30E
Karlstad U.S.A. 82 48.35N 96.31W
Karmah Sudan 48 19.38N 30.25E
Karmöy i. Norway 23 59.15N 5.15E
Karnafuli Resr. Bangla. 39 22.40N 92.05E
Karnāl India 40 29.41N 76.59E
Karnāli r. Nepal 41 28.45N 81.16E
Karnaphuli Resr. Bangla. 41 22.30N 92.20E
Karnataka d. India 38 14.45N 76.00E
Karnes City U.S.A. 83 28.53N 97.54W
Karnobat Bulgaria 19 42.40N 27.00E
Kärnten d. Austria 20 46.50N 13.50E
Karoi Zimbabwe 56 16.51S 29.39E
Karokh Afghan. 40 34.28N 62.35E
Karonga Malaŵi 55 9.54S 33.55E
Karonie Australia 63 30.58S122.32E
Karoonda Australia 66 35.09S139.54E
Karor Pakistan 40 31.13N 70.57E
Karora Sudan 48 17.42N 38.22E
Karos Dam R.S.A. 56 28.27S 21.39E
Karpach U.S.S.R. 21 48.00N 27.10E
Kárpathos Greece 19 35.30N 27.14E
Kárpathos i. Greece 19 35.35N 27.08E
Karpineny U.S.S.R. 21 46.46N 28.18E
Karpinsk U.S.S.R. 24 59.48N 59.59E
Karpogory U.S.S.R. 24 64.01N 44.30E
Karragullen Australia 63 32.05S116.03E
Karratha Australia 62 20.44S116.50E
Karridale Australia 63 34.12S115.04E
Kars Turkey 42 40.35N 43.05E
Karsakpay U.S.S.R. 28 47.47N 66.43E
Kärsämäki Finland 22 63.58N 25.46E
Kārsava U.S.S.R. 24 56.45N 27.40E
Karskoye More sea U.S.S.R. 28 73.00N
65.00E
Kartaly U.S.S.R. 28 53.06N 60.37E
Karufa Indonesia 37 3.50S133.27E
Karumba Australia 64 17.28S140.50E
Kārūn r. Iran 43 30.25N 48.12E
Karunga Kenya 49 1.09S 36.49E
Karungi Sweden 22 66.03N 23.55E
Karungu Kenya 55 0.50S 34.09E
Karviná Czech. 21 49.50N 18.30E
Kasai r. Zaïre 54 3.10S 16.13E
Kasai Occidental d. Zaïre 54 5.00S 21.30E
Kasai Oriental d. Zaïre 54 5.00S 24.00E
Kasaji Zaïre 54 10.22S 23.27E
Kasama Zambia 55 10.10S 31.11E
Kasane Botswana 56 17.48S 25.09E
Kasanga Tanzania 55 8.27S 31.10E
Kāsaragod India 38 12.30N 75.00E
Kasba India 41 25.51N 87.33E
Kasba L. Canada 75 60.20N102.10W
Kasempa Zambia 54 13.28S 25.48E
Kasese Uganda 55 0.07N 30.06E
Kāsganj India 41 27.49N 78.39E
Kāshān Iran 43 33.59N 51.31E
Kashi China 30 39.29N 76.02E
Kashin U.S.S.R. 24 57.22N 37.39E

Kashīpur India **41** 29.13N 78.57E
Kashiwa Japan **35** 35.52N139.59E
Kāshmar Iran **43** 35.12N 58.26E
Kashmor Pakistan **40** 28.26N 69.35E
Kasia India **41** 26.45N 83.55E
Kasimov U.S.S.R. **24** 54.55N 41.25E
Kaskaskia *r.* U.S.A. **83** 37.59N 89.56W
Kaskattama *r.* Canada **75** 57.03N 90.07W
Kaskinen Finland **22** 62.23N 21.13E
Kaskö *see* Kaskinen Finland **22**
Kaslo Canada **74** 49.55N117.00W
Kasongo Zaïre **54** 4.32S 26.33E
Kasongo-Lunda Zaïre **54** 6.30S 16.47E
Kásos *i.* Greece **19** 35.22N 26.56E
Kassalā Sudan **48** 15.28N 36.24E
Kassalā *d.* Sudan **48** 15.30N 35.00E
Kassel Germany **20** 51.18N 9.30E
Kastamonu Turkey **42** 41.22N 33.47E
Kastoría Greece **19** 40.32N 21.15E
Kasugai Japan **35** 35.14N136.58E
Kasukabe Japan **35** 35.58N139.45E
Kasulu Tanzania **55** 4.34S 30.06E
Kasungu Malaŵi **55** 13.04S 33.29E
Kasūr Pakistan **40** 31.07N 74.27E
Kataba Zambia **54** 16.12S 25.05E
Katako Kombe Zaïre **54** 3.27S 24.21E
Katangi India **41** 23.27N 79.47E
Katanning Australia **63** 33.42S117.33E
Katanti Zaïre **55** 2.19S 27.08E
Katarniān Ghāt India **41** 28.20N 81.09E
Katchall *i.* India **39** 7.57N 93.22E
Katete Zambia **55** 14.08S 31.50E
Katha Burma **34** 24.11N 95.20E
Katherine Australia **64** 14.29S132.20E
Kāthgodām India **41** 29.16N 79.32E
Kathla India **40** 32.00N 76.47E
Kathmandu Nepal **41** 27.42N 85.20E
Kathor India **40** 21.18N 72.57E
Kathua Jammu & Kashmir **40** 32.22N 75.31E
Kati Mali **52** 12.41N 8.04W
Katihār India **41** 25.32N 87.35E
Katima Rapids *f.* Zambia **54** 17.15S 24.20E
Katiola Ivory Coast **52** 8.10N 5.10W
Kātlang Pakistan **40** 34.22N 72.05E
Kātol India **41** 21.16N 78.35E
Katonah U.S.A. **85** 41.16N 73.41W
Katonga *r.* Uganda **55** 0.03N 30.15E
Katoomba Australia **67** 33.42S150.23E
Katopa Zaïre **54** 2.45S 25.06E
Katowice Poland **21** 50.15N 18.59E
Kātrīnā, Jabal *mtn.* Egypt **44** 28.30N 33.57E
Katrine, Loch U.K. **12** 56.15N 4.30W
Katrineholm Sweden **23** 59.00N 16.12E
Katsina Nigeria **53** 13.00N 7.32E
Katsina *d.* Nigeria **53** 12.25N 7.55E
Katsina Ala Nigeria **53** 7.10N 9.30E
Katsina Ala *r.* Nigeria **53** 7.50N 8.58E
Katsura *r.* Japan **35** 34.53N135.42E
Katsuura Japan **35** 35.08N140.18E
Kattegat *str.* Denmark / Sweden **23** 57.00N 11.20E
Katul, Jabal *mtn.* Sudan **48** 14.16N 29.23E
Katumba Zaïre **54** 7.45S 25.18E
Kātwa India **41** 23.39N 88.08E
Katwijk aan Zee Neth. **14** 52.13N 4.27E
Kauai *i.* Hawaii U.S.A. **78** 22.05N159.30W
Kaub Germany **14** 50.07N 7.50E
Kaufbeuren Germany **20** 47.53N 10.37E
Kauhajoki Finland **22** 62.26N 22.11E
Kauhava Finland **22** 63.06N 23.05E
Kaukauna U.S.A. **82** 44.20N 88.16W
Kaukauveld *mts.* Namibia **56** 20.00S 20.15E
Kauliranta Finland **22** 66.26N 23.40E
Kaumba Zaïre **54** 8.26S 24.40E
Kaunas U.S.S.R. **23** 54.54N 23.54E
Kaura Namoda Nigeria **53** 12.39N 6.38E
Kautokeino Norway **22** 69.00N 23.02E
Kavála Greece **19** 40.56N 24.24E
Kāvali India **39** 14.55N 80.01E
Kavarna Bulgaria **19** 43.26N 28.22E
Kavimba Botswana **56** 18.05S 24.34E
Kavkaz U.S.S.R. **25** 45.20N 36.39E
Kavkazskiy Khrebet *mts.* U.S.S.R. **25** 43.00N 44.00E
Kavungo Angola **54** 11.28S 23.01E
Kaw Guiana **91** 4.29N 52.02W
Kawachi-nagano Japan **35** 34.25N135.32E
Kawagoe Japan **35** 35.55N139.29E
Kawaguchi Japan **35** 35.48N139.43E
Kawambwa Zambia **55** 9.47S 29.10E
Kawardha India **41** 22.01N 81.15E
Kawasaki Japan **35** 35.32N139.43E
Kawerau New Zealand **60** 38.05S176.42E
Kawhia New Zealand **60** 38.04S174.49E
Kawm Sudan **49** 13.31N 22.50E
Kawthaung Burma **34** 10.09N 98.33E
Kaya Burkina **52** 13.04N 1.04W
Kayah *d.* Burma **34** 19.15N 97.30E
Kayambi Zambia **55** 9.26S 32.01E
Kayan *r.* Indonesia **36** 2.47N117.46E
Kaycee U.S.A. **80** 43.43N106.38W
Kayenta U.S.A. **80** 36.44N110.17W
Kayes Congo **54** 4.25S 11.41E
Kayes Mali **52** 14.26N 11.28W
Kayes *d.* Mali **52** 14.00N 10.55W
Kayonza Rwanda **49** 1.53S 30.31E
Kayseri Turkey **42** 38.42N 35.28E
Kaysville U.S.A. **80** 41.02N111.56W
Kazachye U.S.S.R. **29** 70.46N136.15E
Kazakhskaya S.S.R. *d.* U.S.S.R. **25** 48.00N 52.30E
Kazakhskiy Zaliv *b.* U.S.S.R. **25** 42.43N 52.30E
Kazan U.S.S.R. **24** 55.45N 49.10E
Kazanlŭk Bulgaria **19** 42.38N 25.26E
Kazatin U.S.S.R. **21** 49.41N 28.49E
Kazaure Nigeria **53** 12.40N 8.25E
Kazbek *mtn.* U.S.S.R. **25** 42.42N 44.30E
Kāzerūn Iran **43** 29.35N 51.39E
Kazhim U.S.S.R. **24** 60.18N 51.34E
Kazima C.A.R. **49** 5.16N 26.11E
Kazincbarcika Hungary **21** 48.16N 20.37E
Kazo Japan **35** 36.07N139.36E
Kazumba Zaïre **54** 6.30S 22.02E
Kbal Dâmrei Cambodia **34** 14.03N105.20E
Kéa *i.* Greece **19** 37.36N 24.20E
Kearney U.S.A. **82** 40.42N 99.05W
Keban Turkey **42** 38.48N 38.45E
K'ebelē Ethiopia **49** 12.52N 40.40E
Kebili Tunisia **51** 33.42N 8.58E
Kebnekaise *mtn.* Sweden **22** 67.53N 18.33E
K'ebrī Dehar Ethiopia **45** 6.47N 44.17E
Kebumen Indonesia **37** 7.40S109.41E
Kech *r.* Pakistan **40** 26.00N 62.44E
Kechika *r.* Canada **74** 59.36N127.05W
Kecskemét Hungary **21** 46.54N 19.42E
Kedada Ethiopia **49** 5.20N 36.00E
Kedainiai U.S.S.R. **23** 55.17N 24.00E
Kedgwick Canada **77** 47.39N 67.21W
Kediri Indonesia **37** 7.45S112.01E
Kédougou Senegal **52** 12.35N 12.09W
Keefers Canada **74** 50.00N121.40W
Keele Peak *mtn.* Canada **72** 63.15N129.50W
Keene U.S.A. **84** 42.56N 72.17W
Keepit, L. Australia **67** 30.52S150.30E
Keer-Weer, C. Australia **64** 13.58S141.30E
Keetmanshoop Namibia **56** 26.34S 18.07E
Keewatin Canada **76** 49.46N 94.34W
Keewatin *d.* Canada **73** 65.00N 90.00W
Kefa *d.* Ethiopia **49** 7.00N 36.30E
Kefallinía *i.* Greece **19** 38.15N 20.33E
Kefar Sava Israel **44** 32.11N 34.54E
Keffi Nigeria **53** 8.52N 7.53E
Keflavík Iceland **22** 64.01N 22.35W
K'eftya Ethiopia **48** 13.56N 37.13E
Keg River *town* Canada **74** 57.54N117.07W
Kehsi Mānsām Burma **34** 21.56N 97.51E
Keighley U.K. **10** 53.52N 1.54W
Keila U.S.S.R. **23** 59.18N 24.29E
Keimoes R.S.A. **56** 28.41S 20.58E
Keitele *l.* Finland **22** 62.55N 26.00E
Keith Australia **66** 36.06S140.22E
Keith U.K. **12** 57.32N 2.57W
Keith Arm *b.* Canada **72** 65.20N122.15W
Kekri India **40** 25.58N 75.09E
Kelang Malaysia **36** 2.57N101.24E
Kelberg Germany **14** 50.17N 6.56E
Kelem Ethiopia **49** 4.48N 36.06E
Kelkit *r.* Turkey **42** 40.46N 36.32E
Kelle Congo **54** 0.05S 14.33E
Keller U.S.A. **80** 48.03N118.40W
Kellerberrin Australia **63** 31.38S117.43E
Kellett, C. Canada **72** 71.59N125.34W
Kelloselkä Finland **24** 66.55N 28.50E
Kells Meath Rep. of Ire. **13** 53.44N 6.53W
Kelme U.S.S.R. **23** 55.38N 22.56E
Kélo Chad **53** 9.21N 15.50E
Kelowna Canada **74** 49.50N119.25W
Kelso U.K. **12** 55.36N 2.26W
Kelso Calif. U.S.A. **81** 35.01N115.39W
Kelso Wash. U.S.A. **80** 46.09N122.54W
Keluang Malaysia **36** 2.01N103.18E
Kelvedon U.K. **11** 51.50N 0.43E
Kelvington Canada **75** 52.10N103.30W
Kem U.S.S.R. **24** 64.58N 34.39E
Kema Indonesia **37** 1.22N125.08E
Ke Macina Mali **52** 14.05N 5.20W
Kemah Turkey **42** 39.35N 39.02E
Kemaliye Turkey **42** 39.16N 38.29E
Kemano Canada **74** 53.35N128.00W
Kembolcha Ethiopia **49** 11.02N 39.43E
Kemerovo U.S.S.R. **28** 55.25N 86.10E
Kemi Finland **22** 65.49N 24.32E
Kemi *r.* Finland **22** 65.47N 24.30E
Kemijärvi Finland **22** 66.36N 27.24E
Kemmerer U.S.A. **80** 41.48N110.32W
Kempen *f.* Belgium **14** 51.05N 5.00E
Kemp Land *f.* Antarctica **96** 69.00S 57.00E
Kempsey Australia **67** 31.05S152.50E
Kempt, Lac *l.* Canada **76** 47.25N 74.30W
Kempten Germany **20** 47.44N 10.19E
Ken *r.* India **41** 25.46N 80.31E
Kenai U.S.A. **72** 60.33N151.15W
Kenamuke Swamp Sudan **49** 5.55N 33.48E
Kenaston Canada **75** 51.30N106.18W
Kendai India **41** 22.45N 82.37E
Kendal Indonesia **37** 6.56S110.14E
Kendal U.K. **10** 54.19N 2.44W
Kendall Australia **67** 31.28S152.40E
Kendall U.S.A. **76** 43.20N 78.02W
Kendari Indonesia **37** 3.57S122.36E
Kendenup Australia **63** 34.28S117.35E
Kendrāpāra India **41** 20.30N 86.25E
Kendrick U.S.A. **80** 46.37N116.39W
Kenebri Australia **67** 30.45S149.02E
Kenema Sierra Leone **52** 7.57N 11.11W
Kenge Zaïre **54** 4.56S 17.04E
Kengeja Tanzania **55** 5.24S 39.45E
Keng Tung Burma **34** 21.16N 99.39E
Kenhardt R.S.A. **56** 29.21S 21.08E
Kenilworth U.K. **11** 52.22N 1.35W
Kenitra Morocco **50** 34.20N 6.34W
Kenli China **32** 37.35N118.34E
Kenmare Rep. of Ire. **13** 51.53N 9.36W
Kenmare U.S.A. **80** 48.40N102.05W
Kenmore U.S.A. **76** 42.58N 78.53W
Kennebec *r.* U.S.A. **84** 44.00N 69.50W
Kenner U.S.A. **83** 29.59N 90.15W
Kennet *r.* U.K. **11** 51.28N 0.57W
Kennett Square U.S.A. **85** 39.51N 75.43W
Kennewick U.S.A. **80** 46.12N119.07W
Kenogami *r.* Canada **76** 50.24N 84.20W
Keno Hill *town* Canada **72** 63.58N135.22W
Kenora Canada **76** 49.47N 94.29W
Kenosha U.S.A. **82** 42.35N 87.49W
Kenozero, Ozero *l.* U.S.S.R. **24** 62.20N 37.00E
Kent *d.* U.K. **11** 51.12N 0.40E
Kent Ohio U.S.A. **84** 41.10N 81.20W
Kent Tex. U.S.A. **81** 31.04N104.13W
Kent Wash. U.S.A. **80** 47.23N122.14W
Kentau U.S.S.R. **30** 43.28N 68.36E
Kentland U.S.A. **84** 40.46N 87.26W
Kenton U.S.A. **84** 40.38N 83.38W
Kent Pen. Canada **72** 68.30N107.00W
Kentucky *d.* U.S.A. **85** 37.30N 85.15W
Kentucky *r.* U.S.A. **85** 38.40N 85.09W
Kentucky L. U.S.A. **83** 36.25N 88.05W
Kentville Canada **77** 45.05N 64.30W
Kenya Africa **55** 1.00N 38.00E
Kenya, Mt. Kenya **55** 0.10S 37.19E
Keokuk U.S.A. **82** 40.24N 91.24W
Keonjhargarh India **41** 21.38N 85.35E
Kepi Indonesia **37** 6.32S139.19E
Kepno Poland **21** 51.17N 17.59E
Keppel B. Australia **64** 23.21S150.55E
Kerala *d.* India **38** 10.30N 76.30E
Kerang Australia **66** 35.42S143.59E
Kerch U.S.S.R. **25** 45.22N 36.27E
Kerchenskiy Proliv *str.* U.S.S.R. **25** 45.15N 36.35E
Kerema P.N.G. **37** 7.59S145.46E
Keren Ethiopia **48** 15.46N 38.28E
Kericho Kenya **55** 0.22S 35.19E
Kerinci, Gunung *mtn.* Indonesia **36** 1.45S101.20E
Kerio *r.* Kenya **55** 3.00N 36.14E
Kerkebet Ethiopia **48** 16.13N 37.30E
Kerkenna, Îles *is.* Tunisia **51** 34.44N 11.12E
Kerki R.S.F.S.R. U.S.S.R. **24** 63.40N 54.00E
Kerki Tk.S.S.R. U.S.S.R. **28** 37.53N 65.10E
Kérkira Greece **19** 39.37N 19.50E
Kérkira *i.* Greece **19** 39.35N 19.50E
Kerkrade Neth. **14** 50.52N 6.02E
Kermadec Is. Pacific Oc. **68** 30.00S178.30W
Kermadec Trench Pacific Oc. **68** 33.30S176.00W
Kermān Iran **43** 30.18N 57.05E
Kermānshāh Iran **43** 34.19N 47.04E
Keme Körfezi *g.* Turkey **19** 36.52N 27.53E
Kermit U.S.A. **83** 31.51N103.06W
Kerouane Guinea **52** 9.16N 9.00W
Kerpen Germany **14** 50.52N 6.42E
Kerrobert Canada **75** 51.55N109.08W
Kerrville U.S.A. **83** 30.03N 99.08W
Kerry *d.* Rep. of Ire. **13** 52.07N 9.35W
Kerry Head Rep. of Ire. **13** 52.24N 9.56W
Kerulen *r.* Mongolia **31** 48.45N117.00E
Kesagami L. Canada **76** 50.23N 80.15W
Keşan Turkey **19** 40.50N 26.39E
Keshod India **40** 21.18N 70.15E
Keskal India **41** 20.03N 81.34E
Keski-Suomi *d.* Finland **22** 62.30N 25.30E
Keswick U.K. **10** 54.35N 3.09W
Keszthely Hungary **21** 46.46N 17.15E
Ketapang Jawa Indonesia **37** 6.56S113.14E
Ketapang Kalimantan Indonesia **36** 1.50S110.02E
Ketchikan U.S.A. **74** 55.25N131.40W
Ketchum U.S.A. **80** 43.41N114.22W
Kete Krachi Ghana **52** 7.50N 0.03W
Keti Bandar Pakistan **40** 24.08N 67.27E
Ketrzyn Poland **21** 54.06N 21.23E
Kettering U.K. **11** 52.24N 0.44W
Kettering U.S.A. **84** 39.41N 84.10W
Kettle *r.* Canada **75** 56.55N 89.25W
Kettle Falls *town* U.S.A. **80** 48.36N118.03W
Keweenaw B. U.S.A. **84** 46.46N 88.26W
Keweenaw Pen. U.S.A. **84** 47.10N 88.30W
Key, Lough Rep. of Ire. **13** 54.00N 8.15W
Keyala Sudan **49** 4.27N 32.52E
Key Harbour Canada **76** 45.52N 80.42W
Keynsham U.K. **11** 51.25N 2.30W
Key West U.S.A. **85** 24.33N 81.48W
Kezhma U.S.S.R. **29** 58.58N101.08E
Kežmarok Czech. **21** 49.08N 20.25E
Kgalagadi *d.* Botswana **56** 25.00S 21.30E
Kgatleng *d.* Botswana **56** 24.20S 26.20E
Khaanziir, Ras *c.* Somali Rep. **45** 10.55N 45.47E
Khabarovsk U.S.S.R. **31** 48.32N135.08E
Khairāgarh India **41** 21.25N 80.58E
Khairpur Punjab Pakistan **40** 29.35N 72.14E
Khairpur Sind Pakistan **40** 27.32N 68.46E
Khajrāho India **41** 24.50N 79.58E
Khalatse Jammu & Kashmir **40** 34.20N 76.49E
Khalkhāl Iran **43** 37.36N 48.36E
Khalkís Greece **19** 38.27N 23.36E
Khalmer Yu U.S.S.R. **24** 67.58N 64.48E
Khālsar Jammu & Kashmir **41** 34.31N 77.41E
Khalturin U.S.S.R. **24** 58.38N 48.50E
Khalūf Oman **38** 20.31N 58.04E
Khambhāliya India **40** 22.12N 69.39E
Khambhāt, G. of India **40** 20.30N 71.45E
Khāmgaon India **40** 20.41N 76.34E
Khamkeut Laos **34** 18.14N104.44E
Khānaqīn Iraq **43** 34.22N 45.22E
Khandela India **40** 27.36N 75.30E
Khandwa India **40** 21.50N 76.20E
Khāneh Khvodī Iran **43** 36.05N 56.04E
Khānewāl Pakistan **40** 30.18N 71.56E
Khāngarh Punjab Pakistan **40** 29.55N 71.10E
Khāngarh Punjab Pakistan **40** 28.22N 71.43E
Khanh Hung Vietnam **34** 9.36N105.55E
Khaniá Greece **19** 35.30N 24.02E
Khanka, Ozero *l.* U.S.S.R. **31** 45.00N132.30E
Khanna India **40** 30.42N 76.14E
Khānozai Pakistan **40** 30.37N 67.19E
Khānpur Pakistan **40** 28.39N 70.39E
Khanty-Mansiysk U.S.S.R. **28** 61.00N 69.00E
Khān Yūnus Egypt **44** 31.21N 34.18E
Khapalu Jammu & Kashmir **40** 35.10N 76.20E
Khapcheranga U.S.S.R. **31** 49.46N112.20E
Kharagpur India **41** 22.20N 87.20E
Khārān *r.* Iran **43** 27.37N 58.48E
Khārān Pakistan **40** 28.35N 65.25E
Khargon India **40** 21.49N 75.36E
Khāriān Pakistan **40** 32.49N 73.52E
Khariār Road *town* India **41** 20.54N 82.31E
Khārijah, Al Wāḥāt al *oasis* Egypt **42** 24.55N 30.35E
Kharkov U.S.S.R. **25** 50.00N 36.15E
Khār Kūh *mtn.* Iran **43** 31.37N 53.47E
Kharovsk U.S.S.R. **24** 59.67N 40.07E
Khartoum *see* Al Kharṭūm Sudan **48**
Kharutayuvam U.S.S.R. **24** 66.51N 59.31E
Khasavyurt U.S.S.R. **25** 43.16N 46.36E
Khāsh Afghan. **40** 31.31N 62.52E
Khāsh *r.* Afghan. **40** 31.11N 61.50E
Khāsh Iran **43** 28.14N 61.15E
Khāsh, Dasht-e *des.* Afghan. **40** 31.50N 62.30E
Khashgort U.S.S.R. **24** 65.25N 65.40E
Khashm al Qirbah Sudan **48** 14.58N 35.55E
Khaskovo Bulgaria **19** 41.57N 25.33E
Khatanga U.S.S.R. **29** 71.50N102.31E
Khatangskiy Zaliv *g.* U.S.S.R. **29** 75.00N112.10E
Khāvda India **40** 23.51N 69.43E
Khawr Barakah *r.* Sudan **48** 18.13N 37.35E
Khemisset Morocco **50** 33.50N 6.03W
Khemmarat Thailand **34** 16.00N105.10E
Khenchela Algeria **51** 35.26N 7.08E
Khenifra Morocco **50** 33.00N 5.40W
Khersān *r.* Iran **43** 31.29N 48.53E
Kherson U.S.S.R. **25** 46.39N 32.38E
Kherwāra India **40** 23.59N 73.35E
Khetia India **40** 21.40N 74.35E
Khewāri Pakistan **40** 26.36N 68.52E
Khíos Greece **19** 38.23N 26.07E
Khíos *i.* Greece **19** 38.23N 26.04E
Khipro Pakistan **40** 25.50N 69.22E
Khiva U.S.S.R. **43** 41.25N 60.49E
Khmelnik U.S.S.R. **21** 49.36N 27.59E
Khmelnitskiy U.S.S.R. **21** 49.25N 26.49E
Khodorov U.S.S.R. **21** 49.20N 24.19E
Khogali Sudan **49** 6.08N 27.47E
Khok Kloi Thailand **34** 8.19N 98.18E
Kholm U.S.S.R. **24** 57.10N 31.11E
Kholmogory U.S.S.R. **24** 63.51N 41.46E
Khomas-Hochland *mts.* Namibia **56** 22.50S 16.25E
Khondmāl Hills India **41** 20.15N 84.00E
Khonu U.S.S.R. **29** 66.29N143.12E
Khoper *r.* U.S.S.R. **25** 49.35N 42.17E
Khorāl India **40** 26.30N 71.14E
Khorixas Namibia **56** 20.24S 14.58E
Khorog U.S.S.R. **30** 37.32N 71.32E
Khorramābād Iran **43** 33.29N 48.21E
Khorramshahr Iran **43** 30.26N 48.09E
Khotimsk U.S.S.R. **21** 53.24N 32.36E
Khotin U.S.S.R. **21** 48.30N 26.31E
Khouribga Morocco **50** 32.54N 6.57W
Khowai India **41** 24.06N 91.38E
Khowrnag, Kūh-e *mtn.* Iran **43** 32.10N 54.38E
Khowst Afghan. **40** 33.22N 69.57E
Khoyniki U.S.S.R. **21** 51.54N 30.00E
Khudzhand U.S.S.R. **30** 40.14N 69.40E
Khugiāni Afghan. **40** 31.33N 66.15E
Khūgīānī Sānī Afghan. **40** 31.31N 66.12E
Khūiāla India **40** 27.15N 70.25E
Khuis Botswana **56** 26.37S 21.45E
Khulga *r.* U.S.S.R. **24** 63.33N 61.53E
Khulna Bangla. **41** 22.48N 89.33E
Khumbur Khule Ghar *mtn.* Afghan. **40** 33.05N 69.00E
Khunti India **41** 23.05N 85.17E
Khurai India **41** 24.03N 78.19E
Khurda India **41** 20.11N 85.37E
Khurīyā Murīyā, Jazā'ir *is.* Oman **38** 17.30N 56.00E
Khurja India **41** 28.15N 77.51E
Khurli Pakistan **40** 28.59N 65.52E
Khurr, Wādī al *r.* Iraq **45** 31.02N 42.00E
Khurra Bārīk *r.* Iraq **42** 32.00N 44.15E
Khushāb Pakistan **40** 32.18N 72.21E
Khust U.S.S.R. **21** 48.11N 23.19E
Khuwayy Sudan **49** 13.05N 29.14E
Khuzdār Pakistan **40** 27.48N 66.37E
Khvājeh Ra'ūf Afghan. **40** 33.19N 64.43E
Khvor Iran **43** 33.47N 55.06E
Khvormuj Iran **43** 28.40N 51.20E
Khvoy Iran **43** 38.32N 45.02E
Khyber Pass Afghan. / Pakistan **40** 34.06N 71.05E
Kiama Australia **67** 34.41S150.49E
Kibali *r.* Zaïre **55** 3.37N 28.38E
Kibamba Zaïre **54** 4.53S 26.33E
Kibar India **41** 32.20N 78.01E
Kibenga Zaïre **54** 7.55S 17.35E
Kibombo Zaïre **54** 3.58S 25.57E
Kibondo Tanzania **55** 3.35S 30.41E
Kibre Mengist Ethiopia **49** 5.52N 39.00E
Kibungu Rwanda **55** 2.10S 30.31E
Kibwesa Tanzania **55** 6.30S 29.57E
Kibwezi Kenya **55** 2.28S 37.57E
Kichiga U.S.S.R. **29** 59.50N163.27E
Kicking Horse Pass Canada **74** 51.27N116.25W
Kidal Mali **53** 18.27N 1.25E
Kidderminster U.K. **11** 52.24N 2.13W
Kidete Morogoro Tanzania **55** 6.39S 36.42E
Kidsgrove U.K. **10** 53.06N 2.15W
Kiel Germany **20** 54.20N 10.08E
Kielce Poland **21** 50.52N 20.37E
Kielder *resr.* U.K. **10** 55.12N 2.30W
Kieler Bucht *b.* Germany **20** 54.30N 10.30E
Kiev *see* Kiyev U.S.S.R. **21**
Kiffa Mauritania **50** 16.38N 11.28W
Kigali Rwanda **55** 1.59S 30.05E
Kiglapatt, C. Canada **77** 57.05N 61.05W
Kigoma Tanzania **55** 4.52S 29.36E
Kigoma *d.* Tanzania **55** 4.45S 30.00E
Kigosi *r.* Tanzania **55** 4.37S 31.29E
Kiiminkin *r.* Finland **22** 65.12N 25.18E
Kikinda Yugo. **21** 45.51N 20.30E
Kikládhes *is.* Greece **19** 37.00N 25.00E
Kikongo Zaïre **54** 4.16S 17.11E
Kikori P.N.G. **37** 7.25S144.13E
Kikori *r.* P.N.G. **37** 7.10S144.05E
Kikwit Zaïre **54** 5.02S 18.51E
Kil Sweden **23** 59.30N 13.19E
Kilafors Sweden **23** 61.14N 16.34E
Kila Kila P.N.G. **37** 9.31S147.10E
Kilchu N. Korea **31** 40.55N129.21E
Kilcoy Australia **65** 26.57S152.33E
Kilcullen Rep. of Ire. **13** 53.08N 6.46W
Kildare Rep. of Ire. **13** 53.10N 6.55W
Kildare *d.* Rep. of Ire. **13** 53.10N 6.50W
Kildonan Zimbabwe **56** 17.22S 30.33E
Kilfinan U.K. **12** 55.58N 5.18W
Kilgore U.S.A. **83** 32.23N 94.53W
Kilifi Kenya **55** 3.30S 39.50E
Kilimanjaro *d.* Tanzania **55** 3.45S 37.40E
Kilimanjaro *mtn.* Tanzania **55** 3.02S 37.20E
Kilindoni Tanzania **55** 7.55S 39.39E
Kilingi-Nõmme U.S.S.R. **23** 58.09N 24.58E
Kilis Turkey **42** 36.43N 37.07E
Kiliya U.S.S.R. **21** 45.30N 29.16E
Kilkee Rep. of Ire. **13** 52.41N 9.40W
Kilkenny Rep. of Ire. **13** 52.39N 7.16W
Kilkenny *d.* Rep. of Ire. **13** 52.35N 7.15W
Kilkieran B. Rep. of Ire. **13** 53.20N 9.42W
Kilkís Greece **19** 40.59N 22.51E
Killala B. Rep. of Ire. **13** 54.15N 9.10W
Killard Pt. U.K. **13** 54.19N 5.31W
Killarney Australia **67** 28.18S152.15E
Killarney Man. Canada **75** 49.12N 99.42W
Killarney Rep. of Ire. **13** 52.04N 9.32W
Killary Harbour *est.* Rep. of Ire. **13** 53.38N 9.56W
Killdeer U.S.A. **80** 47.22N102.45W
Killeen U.S.A. **83** 31.08N 97.44W
Killin U.K. **12** 56.29N 4.19W
Killíni *mtn.* Greece **19** 37.56N 22.22E
Killorglin Rep. of Ire. **13** 52.07N 9.45W
Killybegs Rep. of Ire. **13** 54.38N 8.27W
Killyleagh U.K. **13** 54.24N 5.39W
Kilmarnock U.K. **12** 55.37N 4.30W
Kilmichael Pt. Rep. of Ire. **13** 52.44N 6.09W
Kilmore Australia **67** 37.18S144.58E
Kilninver U.K. **12** 56.21N 5.30W
Kilombero *r.* Tanzania **55** 8.30S 37.28E
Kilosa Tanzania **55** 6.49S 37.00E
Kilronan Rep. of Ire. **13** 53.08N 9.41W
Kilrush Rep. of Ire. **13** 52.39N 9.30W
Kilsyth U.K. **12** 55.59N 4.04W
Kilvo Sweden **22** 66.50N 21.04E
Kilwa Kivinje Tanzania **55** 8.45S 39.21E
Kilwa Masoko Tanzania **55** 8.55S 39.31E
Kimaan Indonesia **37** 7.54S138.51E
Kimba Australia **66** 33.09S136.25E
Kimball U.S.A. **82** 41.14N103.40W
Kimberley Canada **74** 49.40N115.59W
Kimberley R.S.A. **56** 28.44S 24.44E
Kimberley Plateau Australia **62** 17.20S127.20E
Kimito *i.* Finland **23** 60.10N 22.30E
Kimparana Mali **52** 12.52N 4.59W
Kimry U.S.S.R. **24** 56.51N 37.20E
Kimsquit Canada **74** 52.45N126.57W
Kinabalu *mtn.* Malaysia **36** 6.10N116.40E
Kincaid Canada **75** 49.39N107.00W
Kincardine Canada **76** 44.11N 81.38W
Kindersley Canada **75** 51.27N109.10W
Kindia Guinea **52** 10.03N 12.49W
Kindu Zaïre **54** 3.00S 25.56E
Kinel U.S.S.R. **24** 53.17N 50.42E
Kineshma U.S.S.R. **24** 57.28N 42.08E
Kingaroy Australia **64** 26.33S151.50E
King City U.S.A. **81** 36.13N121.08W
Kingcome Inlet *town* Canada **74** 50.58N125.15W
King Edward *r.* Australia **62** 14.12S126.34E
King George Is. Canada **76** 57.20N 78.25W
King George Sd. Australia **63** 35.03S117.5
King I. Australia **65** 39.50S144.00E
King I. Canada **74** 52.10N127.40W
King Leopold Range *mts.* Australia **62** 17.00S125.30E
Kingman Ariz. U.S.A. **81** 35.12N114.04W
Kingman Kans. U.S.A. **83** 37.39N 98.07W
Kingman Reef Pacific Oc. **68** 6.24N162.22W
Kingoonya Australia **66** 30.54S135.18E
Kingri Pakistan **40** 30.27N 69.49E
Kings *r.* U.S.A. **81** 36.03N119.49W
Kingsbridge U.K. **11** 50.17N 3.46W
Kings Canyon Australia **64** 24.15S131.33E
Kings Canyon Nat. Park U.S.A. **80** 36.48N118.30W
Kingsclere U.K. **11** 51.20N 1.14W
Kingscote Australia **66** 35.40S137.38E
King Sd. Australia **62** 17.00S123.30E
Kingsdown Kent U.K. **11** 51.21N 0.17E
Kingsley Dam U.S.A. **78** 41.15N101.30W
King's Lynn U.K. **10** 52.45N 0.25E
Kingsmill Group *is.* Kiribati **68** 1.00S175.00
Kings Peaks *mts.* U.S.A. **80** 40.46N110.23W
Kingsport U.S.A. **85** 36.33N 82.34W
Kingston Canada **76** 44.14N 76.30W
Kingston Jamaica **87** 17.58N 76.48W
Kingston New Zealand **60** 45.20S168.43E
Kingston N.Y. U.S.A. **77** 41.56N 74.00W
Kingston W.Va. U.S.A. **85** 37.58N 81.19W
Kingston S.E. Australia **66** 36.50S139.50E
Kingston upon Hull U.K. **10** 53.45N 0.20W
Kingstown St. Vincent **87** 13.12N 61.14W
Kingstree U.S.A. **85** 33.40N 79.50W
Kingsville U.S.A. **83** 27.31N 97.52W
Kingswood Avon U.K. **11** 51.27N 2.29W
Kings Worthy U.K. **11** 51.06N 1.18W

ington U.K. **11** 52.12N 3.02W
ingurutik *r.* Canada **77** 56.49N 62.00W
ingussie U.K. **12** 57.05N 4.04W
ng William I. Canada **73** 69.00N 97.30W
ng William's Town R.S.A. **56** 32.52S 27.23E
nloch Rannoch U.K. **12** 56.42N 4.11W
inna Sweden **23** 57.30N 12.41E
innairds Head U.K. **12** 57.42N 2.00W
innegad Rep. of Ire. **13** 53.28N 7.08W
ino *r.* Japan **35** 34.13N135.09E
inross U.K. **12** 56.13N 3.27W
insale Rep. of Ire. **13** 51.42N 8.32W
inshasa Zaïre **54** 4.18S 15.18E
insley U.S.A. **83** 37.55N 99.25W
ntyre *pen.* U.K. **12** 55.35N 5.35W
nuso Canada **74** 55.25N115.25W
nvara Rep. of Ire. **13** 53.08N 8.56W
nyeti *mtn.* Sudan **49** 3.57N 32.54E
nzia Zaïre **54** 3.36S 18.26E
owa Kans. U.S.A. **83** 37.01N 98.29W
owa Okla. U.S.A. **83** 34.43N 95.54W
parissía Greece **19** 37.15N 21.40E
pawa, Lac *l.* Canada **76** 47.00N 79.00W
pengere Range *mts.* Tanzania **55** 9.15S 34.15E
pili Tanzania **55** 7.30S 30.39E
pini Kenya **55** 2.31S 40.32E
ppure *mtn.* Rep. of Ire. **13** 53.11N 6.20W
pungo Angola **54** 14.49S 14.34E
pushi Zaïre **55** 11.46S 27.15E
rby U.S.A. **80** 43.49N108.10W
rbyville U.S.A. **83** 30.40N 93.54W
rcheimbolanden Germany **14** 49.39N 8.00E
rensk U.S.S.R. **29** 57.45N108.00E
rgiziya Step *f.* U.S.S.R. **25** 50.00N 57.10E
rgizskaya S.S.R. *d.* U.S.S.R. **30** 41.30N 75.00E
rgiz Steppe *see* Kirgiziya Step *f.* U.S.S.R. **25**
ri Zaïre **54** 1.23S 19.00E
ribati Pacific Oc. **68** 6.00S170.00W
rikkale Turkey **42** 39.51N 33.32E
rillov U.S.S.R. **24** 59.53N 38.21E
rínia Cyprus **44** 35.20N 33.20E
ritimati *i.* Kiribati **69** 1.52N157.20W
rkby Lonsdale U.K. **10** 54.13N 2.36W
rkby Stephen U.K. **10** 54.27N 2.23W
rkcaldy U.K. **12** 56.07N 3.10W
rkcudbright U.K. **12** 54.50N 4.03W
rkenes Norway **22** 69.40N 30.03E
rkland Ariz. U.S.A. **81** 34.26N112.43W
rkland Wash. U.S.A. **80** 47.41N122.12W
rkland Lake *town* Canada **76** 48.15N 80.00W
rklareli Turkey **19** 41.44N 27.12E
rkpatrick, Mt. Antarctica **96** 85.00S170.00E
rksville U.S.A. **82** 40.12N 92.35W
rkük Iraq **43** 35.28N 44.26E
rkwall U.K. **12** 58.59N 2.58W
rkwood R.S.A. **56** 33.25S 25.24E
rkwood U.S.A. **82** 38.35N 90.24W
n Germany **14** 49.47N 7.28E
ov R.S.F.S.R. U.S.S.R. **24** 58.38N 49.38E
ov R.S.F.S.R. U.S.S.R. **24** 53.59N 34.20E
ovakan U.S.S.R. **43** 40.49N 44.30E
ovo-Chepetsk U.S.S.R. **24** 58.40N 50.02E
ovograd U.S.S.R. **25** 48.31N 32.15E
ovsk U.S.S.R. **24** 67.37N 33.39E
ovskiy U.S.S.R. **29** 54.25N155.37E
riemuir Canada **75** 51.56N110.20W
riemuir U.K. **12** 56.41N 3.01W
s U.S.S.R. **24** 59.21N 52.10E
sanoy U.S.S.R. **25** 51.29N 52.30E
şehir Turkey **42** 39.09N 34.08E
thar Range *mts.* Pakistan **40** 27.15N 67.00E
una Sweden **22** 67.51N 20.16E
a Sweden **23** 57.59N 15.37E
aga Tanzania **55** 4.26S 34.26E
angani Zaïre **54** 0.33N 25.14E
antu Zaïre **54** 5.07S 15.05E
aran Indonesia **36** 2.47N 99.29E
arazu Japan **35** 35.23N139.55E
elevsk U.S.S.R. **28** 54.01N 86.41E
hanganj India **41** 26.07N 87.56E
hangarh Rāj. India **40** 27.52N 70.34E
hangarh Rāj. India **40** 26.34N 74.52E
hinev U.S.S.R. **21** 47.00N 28.50E
hiwada Japan **35** 34.28N135.22E
horganj Bangla. **41** 24.26N 90.46E
htwār Jammu & Kashmir **40** 33.19N 75.46E
i Kenya **55** 0.40S 34.44E
ju Tanzania **55** 7.23S 39.20E
kitto L. Canada **75** 54.16N 98.34W
körös Hungary **21** 46.38N 19.17E
kunfélegyháza Hungary **21** 46.43N 19.52E
kunhalas Hungary **21** 46.26N 19.30E
ovodsk U.S.S.R. **25** 43.56N 42.44E
maayo Somali Rep. **55** 0.25S 42.31E
o Japan **35** 35.02N136.45E
o sammyaku *mts.* Japan **35** 35.42N137.50E
samos Greece **19** 35.30N 23.38E
sidougou Guinea **52** 9.48N 10.08W
simmee U.S.A. **85** 28.20N 81.24W
sissing L. Canada **75** 55.10N101.20W
sū, Jabal *mtn.* Sudan **48** 21.35N 25.09E
na *r. see* Krishna *r.* India **38**
umu Kenya **55** 0.07S 34.47E
várda Hungary **21** 48.13N 22.05E
Mali **52** 13.04N 9.29W
b U.S.S.R. **28** 39.08N 66.51E
bu Zaïre **54** 6.31S 26.40E
kyūshū Japan **31** 33.52N130.49E
le Kenya **55** 1.01N 35.01E
Carson U.S.A. **82** 38.46N102.48W
hener Australia **63** 31.01S124.20E
hener Canada **76** 43.27N 80.30W
higama *r.* Canada **76** 51.12N 78.55W
um Uganda **55** 3.17N 32.54E

Kíthira Greece **19** 36.09N 23.00E
Kíthira *i.* Greece **19** 36.15N 23.00E
Kíthnos *i.* Greece **19** 37.25N 24.25E
Kitikmeot *d.* Canada **72** 80.00N105.00W
Kitimat Canada **74** 54.05N128.38W
Kitinen *r.* Finland **22** 67.20N 27.27E
Kitsman U.S.S.R. **21** 48.30N 25.50E
Kittakittaooloo, L. Australia **66** 28.09S138.09E
Kittanning U.S.A. **84** 40.49N 79.32W
Kittery U.S.A. **84** 43.05N 70.45W
Kittilä Finland **22** 67.40N 24.54E
Kitui Kenya **55** 1.22S 38.01E
Kitunda Tanzania **55** 6.48S 33.17E
Kitwe Zambia **55** 12.50S 28.04E
Kiumbi Zaïre **54** 5.31S 26.34E
Kiunga Kenya **55** 1.46S 41.30E
Kivijärvi *l.* Finland **22** 63.10N 25.09E
Kivik Sweden **23** 55.41N 14.15E
Kivu *d.* Zaïre **55** 3.00S 27.00E
Kivu, L. Rwanda / Zaïre **55** 2.00S 29.10E
Kiyev U.S.S.R. **21** 50.28N 30.29E
Kiyevskoye Vodokhranilishche *resr.* U.S.S.R. **21** 51.00N 30.25E
Kizel U.S.S.R. **24** 59.01N 57.42E
Kizema U.S.S.R. **24** 61.12N 44.52E
Kizil *r.* Turkey **42** 41.45N 35.57E
Kizlyar U.S.S.R. **25** 43.51N 46.43E
Kizlyarskiy Zaliv *b.* U.S.S.R. **25** 44.33N 47.00E
Kizu *r.* Japan **35** 34.53N135.42E
Kizyl-Arvat U.S.S.R. **43** 39.00N 56.23E
Kizyl Atrek Turkey **43** 37.37N 54.49E
Kladno Czech. **20** 50.10N 14.05E
Klagenfurt Austria **20** 46.38N 14.20E
Klaipeda U.S.S.R. **23** 55.43N 21.07E
Klakah Indonesia **37** 7.55S113.12E
Klaksvig Faroe Is. **8** 62.13N 6.34W
Klamath *r.* U.S.A. **80** 41.33N124.04W
Klamath Falls *town* U.S.A. **80** 42.14N121.47W
Klamath Mts. U.S.A. **80** 41.40N123.20W
Klamono Indonesia **37** 1.08S131.28E
Klar *r.* Sweden **23** 59.23N 13.32E
Klatovy Czech. **20** 49.24N 13.18E
Klawer R.S.A. **56** 31.48S 18.34E
Klawock U.S.A. **74** 55.33N133.06W
Kleena Kleene Canada **74** 51.58N124.50W
Kleinsee R.S.A. **56** 29.41S 17.04E
Klerksdorp R.S.A. **56** 26.51S 26.38E
Klevan U.S.S.R. **21** 50.44N 25.50E
Kleve Germany **14** 51.47N 6.11E
Klickitat U.S.A. **80** 45.49N121.09W
Klimovichi U.S.S.R. **21** 53.36N 31.58E
Klimpfjäll Sweden **22** 65.04N 14.52E
Klin U.S.S.R. **24** 56.20N 36.45E
Klinaklini *r.* Canada **74** 51.21N125.40W
Klintehamn Sweden **23** 57.24N 18.12E
Klintsy U.S.S.R. **21** 52.45N 32.15E
Klipdale R.S.A. **56** 34.18S 19.58E
Klippan Sweden **23** 56.08N 13.06E
Klipplaat R.S.A. **56** 33.01S 24.19E
Kłobuck Poland **21** 50.55N 18.57E
Kłodzko Poland **20** 50.27N 16.39E
Klöfta Norway **23** 60.04N 11.09E
Klondike Canada **72** 64.02N139.24W
Kluane Nat. Park Canada **74** 60.32N139.40W
Kluczbork Poland **21** 50.59N 18.13E
Klukwan U.S.A. **74** 59.25N135.55W
Klungkung Indonesia **37** 8.32S115.25E
Knaresborough U.K. **10** 54.01N 1.29W
Knight Inlet *f.* Canada **74** 50.45N125.40W
Knighton U.K. **11** 52.21N 3.02W
Knin Yugo. **20** 44.02N 16.10E
Knockadoon Head Rep. of Ire. **13** 51.52N 7.52W
Knockalongy *mtn.* Rep. of Ire. **13** 54.12N 8.45W
Knockmealdown Mts. Rep. of Ire. **13** 52.15N 7.55W
Knokke Belgium **14** 51.21N 3.17E
Knolls U.S.A. **80** 40.44N113.18W
Knossos *site* Greece **19** 35.20N 25.10E
Knox, C. Canada **74** 54.11N133.04W
Knox City U.S.A. **83** 33.25N 99.49W
Knoxville U.S.A. **85** 36.00N 83.57W
Knutsford U.K. **10** 53.18N 2.22W
Knyazhevo U.S.S.R. **24** 59.40N 43.51E
Knysna R.S.A. **56** 34.02S 23.03E
Kobar Sink *f.* Ethiopia **48** 14.00N 40.30E
Kōbe Japan **35** 34.41N135.10E
København Denmark **23** 55.43N 12.34E
Koblenz Germany **14** 50.21N 7.36E
Kobowen Swamp Sudan **49** 5.38N 33.54E
Kobrin U.S.S.R. **21** 52.16N 24.22E
Kobroor *i.* Indonesia **37** 6.10S134.30E
Kočani Yugo. **19** 41.55N 22.24E
Kočevje Yugo. **18** 45.38N 14.52E
Kochi India **38** 9.56N 76.15E
Kochkoma U.S.S.R. **24** 64.03N 34.14E
Kochmes U.S.S.R. **24** 66.12N 60.48E
Kodaira Japan **35** 35.44N139.29E
Kodari Nepal **41** 27.56N 85.56E
Kodarma India **41** 24.28N 85.36E
Kodiak U.S.A. **72** 57.49N152.30W
Kodiak I. U.S.A. **72** 57.00N153.50W
Kodima U.S.S.R. **24** 62.24N 43.57E
Kodinār India **40** 20.47N 70.42E
Kodok Sudan **49** 9.53N 32.07E
Kodyma U.S.S.R. **21** 48.06N 29.04E
Koekelare Belgium **14** 51.08N 2.59E
Koekenaap R.S.A. **56** 31.30S 18.18E
Koersel Belgium **14** 51.04N 5.19E
Koës Namibia **56** 25.58S 19.07E
Koffiefontein R.S.A. **56** 29.24S 25.00E
Köflach Austria **20** 47.04N 15.05E
Koforidua Ghana **52** 6.01N 0.12W
Kōfu Japan **35** 35.39N138.35E
Koga Tanzania **55** 6.10S 32.21E

Kogaluk *r.* Canada **77** 56.12N 61.45W
Köge Denmark **23** 55.27N 12.11E
Köge Bugt *b.* Greenland **73** 65.00N 40.30W
Kohak Pakistan **40** 25.44N 62.33E
Kohāt Pakistan **40** 33.35N 71.26E
Kohima India **39** 25.40N 94.08E
Kohler Range *mts.* Antarctica **96** 77.00S110.00W
Kohtla-Järve U.S.S.R. **24** 59.28N 27.20E
Koidu Sierra Leone **52** 8.41N 10.55W
Koito *r.* Japan **35** 35.21N139.52E
Kojonup Australia **63** 33.50S117.05E
Kokand U.S.S.R. **30** 40.33N 70.55E
Kokas Indonesia **37** 2.45S132.26E
Kokchetav U.S.S.R. **28** 53.18N 69.25E
Kokemäki Finland **23** 61.15N 22.21E
Kokenau Indonesia **37** 4.42S136.25E
Kokka Sudan **48** 20.00N 30.35E
Kokkola Finland **22** 63.50N 23.07E
Koko Sokoto Nigeria **53** 11.27N 4.35E
Kokoda P.N.G. **64** 8.50S147.45E
Kokomo U.S.A. **84** 40.30N 86.09W
Kokpekty U.S.S.R. **30** 48.45N 82.25E
Koksoak *r.* Canada **73** 58.30N 68.15W
Kokstad R.S.A. **56** 30.32S 29.25E
Kokuora U.S.S.R. **29** 71.33N144.50E
Kolāchi *r.* Pakistan **40** 26.25N 67.50E
Kolahun Liberia **52** 8.24N 10.02W
Kolaka Indonesia **37** 4.04S121.38E
Kola Pen. *see* Kolskiy Poluostrov *pen.* U.S.S.R. **24**
Kolār India **39** 13.10N 78.10E
Kolāras India **41** 25.14N 77.36E
Kolari Finland **22** 67.20N 23.48E
Kolāyat India **40** 27.50N 72.57E
Kolbio Kenya **55** 1.11S 41.10E
Kolda Senegal **52** 12.56N 14.55W
Kolding Denmark **23** 55.31N 9.29E
Kole H.Zaïre Zaïre **54** 2.07N 25.26E
Kole K.Oriental Zaïre **54** 3.28S 22.29E
Kolepom *i. see* Yos Sudarsa, Pulau *i.* Indonesia **37**
Kolguyev, Ostrov *i.* U.S.S.R. **24** 69.00N 49.00E
Kolhāpur India **38** 16.43N 74.15E
Kolia Ivory Coast **52** 9.46N 6.28W
Kolín Czech. **20** 50.02N 15.10E
Kolka U.S.S.R. **23** 57.45N 22.35E
Kolki U.S.S.R. **21** 51.09N 25.40E
Kollam India **38** 8.53N 76.38E
Köln Germany **14** 50.56N 6.57E
Kolno Poland **21** 53.25N 21.56E
Koło Poland **21** 52.12N 18.37E
Kołobrzeg Poland **20** 54.10N 15.35E
Kologriv U.S.S.R. **24** 58.49N 44.19E
Kolokani Mali **52** 13.35N 7.45W
Kololo Ethiopia **49** 7.29N 41.58E
Kolomna U.S.S.R. **24** 55.05N 38.45E
Kolomyya U.S.S.R. **21** 48.31N 25.00E
Kolondiéba Mali **52** 11.05N 6.54W
Kolosib India **41** 24.14N 92.42E
Kolpashevo U.S.S.R. **28** 58.21N 82.59E
Kolpino U.S.S.R. **24** 59.44N 30.39E
Kolskiy Poluostrov *pen.* U.S.S.R. **24** 67.00N 38.00E
Kolsva Sweden **23** 59.36N 15.50E
Koluszki Poland **21** 51.44N 19.49E
Kolvereid Norway **22** 64.53N 11.35E
Kolwezi Zaïre **54** 10.44S 25.28E
Kolyma *r.* U.S.S.R. **29** 68.50N161.00E
Kolymskiy, Khrebet *mts* U.S.S.R. **29** 63.00N160.00E
Kom *r.* Cameroon **54** 2.20N 10.38E
Kom Kenya **55** 1.06N 38.00E
Koma Ethiopia **49** 8.25N 36.53E
Komadugu Gana *r.* Nigeria **53** 13.06N 12.23E
Komadugu Yobe *r.* Niger / Nigeria **53** 13.43N 13.19E
Komagane Japan **35** 35.43N137.55E
Komaga-take *mtn.* Japan **35** 35.47N137.48E
Komaki Japan **35** 35.17N136.55E
Komandorskiye Ostrova *is.* U.S.S.R. **68** 55.00N167.00E
Komárno Czech. **21** 47.45N 18.09E
Komarom Hungary **21** 47.44N 18.08E
Komatipoort R.S.A. **57** 25.25S 31.55E
Komba Zaïre **54** 2.52N 24.03E
Komló Hungary **21** 46.12N 18.16E
Kommunarsk U.S.S.R. **25** 48.30N 38.47E
Kommunizma, Pik *mtn.* U.S.S.R. **30** 38.39N 72.01E
Komotiní Greece **19** 41.07N 25.26E
Komrat U.S.S.R. **21** 46.18N 28.40E
Komsberg *mtn.* R.S.A. **56** 32.40S 20.48E
Komsomolets, Ostrov *i.* U.S.S.R. **29** 80.20N 96.00E
Komsomolets, Zaliv *g.* U.S.S.R. **25** 45.17N 53.30E
Komsomolsk-na-Amure U.S.S.R. **29** 50.32N136.59E
Kōnan Japan **35** 35.20N136.53E
Konar *r.* Afghan. **40** 34.26N 70.32E
Konārak India **41** 19.54N 86.07E
Konar-e Khās Afghan. **40** 34.39N 70.54E
Konch India **41** 25.59N 79.09E
Kondagaon India **41** 19.36N 81.40E
Kondakovo U.S.S.R. **29** 69.38N152.00E
Kondinin Australia **63** 32.33S118.13E
Kondoa Tanzania **55** 4.54S 35.49E
Kondopoga U.S.S.R. **24** 62.12N 34.17E
Kondratyevo U.S.S.R. **29** 57.22N 98.15E
Kondut Australia **63** 30.44S117.06E
Koné N. Cal. **68** 21.04S164.52E
Kōng *r.* Cambodia **34** 13.32N105.57E
Kong Ivory Coast **52** 8.54N 4.36W
Kong Christian den IX Land *f.* Greenland **73** 68.20N 37.00W

Kong Frederik den VI Kyst *f.* Greenland **73** 63.00N 44.00W
Kong Haakon VII Hav *sea* Antarctica **96** 65.00S 25.00E
Kongolo Zaïre **55** 5.20S 27.00E
Kongor Sudan **49** 7.10N 31.21E
Kongsberg Norway **23** 59.39N 9.39E
Kongsvinger Norway **23** 60.12N 12.00E
Kongur Shan *mtn.* China **30** 38.40N 75.30E
Kongwa Tanzania **55** 6.13S 36.28E
Konin Poland **21** 52.13N 18.16E
Konjic Yugo. **21** 43.39N 17.57E
Könkämä *r.* Sweden / Finland **22** 68.29N 22.30E
Konkouré *r.* Guinea **52** 9.55N 13.45W
Konongo Ghana **52** 6.38N 1.12W
Konosha U.S.S.R. **24** 60.58N 40.08E
Kōnosu Japan **35** 36.03N139.31E
Konotop U.S.S.R. **25** 51.15N 33.14E
Końskie Poland **21** 51.12N 20.26E
Konstanz Germany **20** 47.40N 9.10E
Kontagora Nigeria **53** 10.24N 5.22E
Kontcha Cameroon **53** 7.59N 12.15E
Kontiomäki Finland **24** 64.21N 28.10E
Kontum Vietnam **34** 14.23N108.00E
Kontum, Plateau du *f.* Vietnam **34** 14.00N108.00E
Konya Turkey **42** 37.51N 32.30E
Konz Germany **14** 49.42N 6.34E
Konza Kenya **55** 1.45S 37.07E
Koolkootinnie L. Australia **66** 27.58S137.47E
Koolyanobbing Australia **63** 30.48S119.29E
Koondrook Australia **66** 35.39S144.11E
Koongawa Australia **66** 33.11S135.52E
Koorawatha Australia **67** 34.02S148.33E
Koorda Australia **63** 30.50S117.51E
Kootenay L. Canada **74** 49.45N117.00W
Kootenay Nat. Park Canada **74** 51.00N116.00W
Kootjieskolk R.S.A. **56** 31.14S 20.18E
Kopāganj India **41** 26.01N 83.34E
Kopargaon India **40** 19.53N 74.29E
Kópavogur Iceland **22** 64.06N 21.53W
Koper Yugo. **20** 45.33N 13.44E
Kopervik Norway **23** 59.17N 5.18E
Kopet Dag, Khrebet *mts.* U.S.S.R. **43** 38.00N 58.00E
Köping Sweden **23** 59.31N 16.00E
Kopparberg *d.* Sweden **23** 60.50N 15.00E
Koppom Sweden **23** 59.43N 12.09E
Koprivnica Yugo. **20** 46.10N 16.50E
Kopychintsy U.S.S.R. **21** 49.10N 25.58E
Kor *r.* Iran **43** 29.40N 53.17E
Koraput India **41** 18.49N 82.43E
Koratla India **41** 18.49N 78.43E
Korba India **41** 22.21N 82.41E
Korbach Germany **20** 51.16N 8.53E
Korçë Albania **19** 40.37N 20.45E
Korčula *i.* Yugo. **19** 42.56N 16.53E
Kord Küy Iran **43** 36.48N 54.07E
Korea Str. S. Korea / Japan **31** 35.00N129.20E
Korem Ethiopia **49** 12.30N 39.30E
Korets U.S.S.R. **21** 50.39N 27.10E
Korhogo Ivory Coast **52** 9.22N 5.31W
Korim Indonesia **37** 0.58S136.10E
Korinthiakós Kólpos *g.* Greece **19** 38.15N 22.30E
Kórinthos Greece **19** 37.56N 22.55E
Kōriyama Japan **31** 37.23N140.22E
Korma U.S.S.R. **21** 53.08N 30.47E
Körmend Hungary **20** 47.01N 16.37E
Kornat *i.* Yugo. **18** 43.48N 15.20E
Korneshty U.S.S.R. **21** 47.21N 28.00E
Kornsjö Norway **23** 58.57N 11.39E
Koro *i.* Fiji **68** 17.22S179.25E
Koro Ivory Coast **52** 8.36N 7.28W
Koro Mali **52** 14.01N 2.58W
Korocha U.S.S.R. **25** 50.50N 37.13E
Korogwe Tanzania **55** 5.10S 38.35E
Koroit Australia **66** 38.17S142.26E
Korong Vale *town* Australia **66** 36.22S143.45E
Koror *i.* Belau **37** 7.30N134.30E
Koro Sea Fiji **68** 18.00S179.00E
Korosten U.S.S.R. **21** 51.00N 28.30E
Korostyshev U.S.S.R. **21** 50.19N 29.03E
Koro Toro Chad **53** 16.05N 18.30E
Korrat *i.* Yugo. **20** 43.48N 15.20E
Korsör Denmark **23** 55.20N 11.09E
Korsze Poland **21** 54.10N 21.09E
Kortrijk Belgium **14** 50.49N 3.17E
Koryakskiy Khrebet *mts.* U.S.S.R. **29** 62.20N171.00E
Koryazhma U.S.S.R. **24** 61.19N 47.12E
Kos *i.* Greece **19** 36.48N 27.10E
Kosa Ethiopia **49** 7.51N 36.51E
Kościan Poland **20** 52.06N 16.38E
Kościerzyna Poland **21** 54.08N 18.00E
Kosciusko U.S.A. **83** 32.58N 89.35W
Kosciusko, Mt. Australia **67** 36.28S148.17E
Kosha Sudan **48** 20.49N 30.32E
Koshk-e Kohneh Afghan **43** 34.52N 62.29E
Košice Czech. **21** 48.44N 21.15E
Koski Finland **23** 60.39N 23.09E
Koslan U.S.S.R. **24** 63.29N 48.59E
Kosovska-Mitrovica Yugo. **19** 42.54N 20.51E
Kossanto Senegal **52** 13.12N 11.56W
Kossovo U.S.S.R. **21** 52.40N 25.18E
Kosta Sweden **23** 56.51N 15.23E
Koster R.S.A. **56** 25.51S 26.52E
Kostopol U.S.S.R. **21** 50.51N 26.22E
Kostroma U.S.S.R. **24** 57.46N 40.59E
Kostrzyn Poland **20** 52.24N 17.11E
Kostyukovichi U.S.S.R. **21** 53.20N 32.01E
Kosyu U.S.S.R. **24** 65.36N 59.00E
Koszalin Poland **20** 54.12N 16.09E
Kota Madhya P. India **41** 22.18N 82.02E
Kota Rāj. India **40** 25.11N 75.50E
Kota Baharu Malaysia **36** 6.07N102.15E

Kota Belud Malaysia **36** 6.00N116.00E
Kotabumi Indonesia **36** 4.52S104.59E
Kot Addu Pakistan **40** 30.28N 70.58E
Kota Kinabalu Malaysia **36** 5.59N116.04E
Kotelnich U.S.S.R. **24** 58.20N 48.10E
Kotelnikovo U.S.S.R. **25** 47.39N 43.08E
Kotel'nyy, Ostrov *i.* U.S.S.R. **29** 75.30N141.00E
Kotka Finland **24** 60.26N 26.55E
Kot Kapūra India **40** 30.35N 74.49E
Kotlas U.S.S.R. **24** 61.15N 46.28E
Kotli Jammu & Kashmir **40** 33.31N 73.55E
Kotlik U.S.A. **72** 63.02N163.33W
Kotor Yugo. **19** 42.28N 18.47E
Kotovsk M.S.S.R. U.S.S.R. **21** 46.50N 28.31E
Kotovsk Ukr.S.S.R. U.S.S.R. **21** 47.42N 29.30E
Kot Pūtli India **40** 27.43N 76.12E
Kotra India **40** 24.22N 73.10E
Kotri Pakistan **40** 25.22N 68.18E
Kotri Allāhrakhio Pakistan **40** 24.24N 67.50E
Kottagūdem India **39** 17.32N 80.39E
Kotto *r.* C.A.R. **49** 4.14N 22.02E
Kotuy *r.* U.S.S.R. **29** 71.40N103.00E
Kotzebue U.S.A. **72** 66.51N162.40W
Kotzebue Sd. U.S.A. **72** 66.20N163.00W
Kouango C.A.R. **49** 4.58N 20.00E
Koudougou Burkina **52** 12.15N 2.21W
Kouibli Ivory Coast **52** 7.09N 7.16W
Kouki C.A.R. **53** 7.09N 17.13E
Koúklia Cyprus **44** 34.42N 32.34E
Koula Moutou Gabon **54** 1.12S 12.29E
Koulikoro Mali **52** 12.55N 7.31W
Koumac N. Cal. **68** 20.33S164.17E
Koumankou Mali **52** 11.58N 6.06W
Koumbal C.A.R. **49** 9.26N 22.39E
Koumbia Burkina **52** 11.18N 3.38W
Koumbia Guinea **52** 11.54N 13.40W
Koumbisaleh *site* Mauritania **50** 15.55N 8.05W
Koumongou Togo **52** 10.10N 0.29E
Koumra Chad **53** 8.56N 17.32E
Koupéla Burkina **52** 12.09N 0.22W
Kouroussa Guinea **52** 10.40N 9.50W
Kousseri Chad **53** 12.05N 14.56E
Koutiala Mali **52** 12.20N 5.23W
Kouto Ivory Coast **52** 9.53N 6.25W
Kouvola Finland **24** 60.54N 26.45E
Kouyou *r.* Congo **54** 0.40S 16.37E
Kovdor U.S.S.R. **24** 67.33N 30.30E
Kovel U.S.S.R. **21** 51.12N 24.48E
Kovpyta U.S.S.R. **21** 51.22N 30.51E
Kovrov U.S.S.R. **24** 56.23N 41.21E
Kovzha *r.* U.S.S.R. **24** 61.05N 36.27E
Kowanyama Australia **64** 15.29S141.44E
Kowloon Hong Kong **33** 22.19N114.12E
Kowt-e 'Ashrow Afghan. **40** 34.27N 68.48E
Koyukuk *r.* U.S.A. **72** 64.50N157.30W
Kozan Turkey **42** 37.27N 35.47E
Kozáni Greece **19** 40.18N 21.48E
Kozelets U.S.S.R. **21** 50.54N 31.09E
Kozhikode India **38** 11.15N 75.45E
Kozhim U.S.S.R. **24** 65.45N 59.30E
Kozhposelok U.S.S.R. **24** 63.10N 38.10E
Kpandu Ghana **52** 7.02N 0.17E
Kpessi Togo **53** 8.07N 1.17E
Krabi Thailand **34** 8.08N 98.52E
Krâchéh Cambodia **34** 12.30N106.00E
Kragan Indonesia **37** 6.40S111.33E
Kragerö Norway **23** 58.52N 9.25E
Kragujevac Yugo. **19** 44.01N 20.55E
Kraków Poland **21** 50.03N 19.55E
Kraljevo Yugo. **19** 43.44N 20.41E
Kramatorsk U.S.S.R. **25** 48.43N 37.33E
Kramer U.S.A. **82** 48.20N100.42W
Kramfors Sweden **22** 62.55N 17.50E
Kranj Yugo. **20** 46.15N 14.21E
Kranskop R.S.A. **56** 28.58S 30.52E
Krapkowice Poland **21** 50.29N 17.56E
Krasavino U.S.S.R. **24** 60.58N 46.25E
Krasilov U.S.S.R. **21** 49.39N 26.59E
Kraskino U.S.S.R. **31** 42.42N130.48E
Krasnaya Gora U.S.S.R. **21** 53.00N 31.36E
Kraśnik Poland **21** 50.56N 22.13E
Krasnodar U.S.S.R. **25** 45.02N 39.00E
Krasnograd U.S.S.R. **25** 49.22N 35.28E
Krasnokamsk U.S.S.R. **24** 58.05N 55.49E
Krasnoperekopsk U.S.S.R. **25** 45.56N 33.47E
Krasnoselkup U.S.S.R. **28** 65.45N 82.31E
Krasnoturinsk U.S.S.R. **24** 59.46N 60.10E
Krasnoufimsk U.S.S.R. **24** 56.40N 57.49E
Krasnouralsk U.S.S.R. **28** 58.25N 60.00E
Krasnovishersk U.S.S.R. **24** 60.25N 57.02E
Krasnovodsk U.S.S.R. **43** 40.01N 53.00E
Krasnovodskiy Poluostrov *pen.* U.S.S.R. **43** 40.30N 53.10E
Krasnovodskiy Zaliv *g.* U.S.S.R. **43** 39.50N 53.15E
Krasnoyarsk U.S.S.R. **29** 56.05N 92.46E
Krasnyy Yar U.S.S.R. **25** 46.32N 48.21E
Kratovo Yugo. **19** 42.05N 22.11E
Krawang Indonesia **37** 6.15S107.15E
Krefeld Germany **14** 51.20N 6.32E
Kremenchug U.S.S.R. **25** 49.03N 33.25E
Kremenchugskoye Vodokhranilishche *resr.* U.S.S.R. **25** 49.20N 32.30E
Kremenets U.S.S.R. **21** 50.05N 25.48E
Kremmling U.S.A. **80** 40.03N106.24W
Krems Austria **20** 48.25N 15.36E
Krestovka U.S.S.R. **24** 66.24N 52.31E
Kretinga U.S.S.R. **23** 55.53N 21.13E
Kribi Cameroon **53** 2.56N 9.56E
Krichev U.S.S.R. **21** 53.40N 31.44E
Krishna *r.* India **39** 16.00N 81.00E
Krishnanagar India **41** 23.24N 88.30E
Kristiansand Norway **23** 58.10N 8.00E
Kristianstad Sweden **23** 56.02N 14.08E
Kristianstad *d.* Sweden **23** 56.15N 13.35E
Kristiansund Norway **22** 63.07N 7.45E
Kristiinankaupunki Finland **23** 62.17N 21.23E

Kristinehamn Sweden **23** 59.20N 14.07E
Kristinestad *see* Kristiinankaupunki Finland **23**
Kristinovka U.S.S.R. **21** 48.50N 29.58E
Kríti *i.* Greece **19** 35.15N 25.00E
Kritikón Pélagos *sea* Greece **19** 36.00N 25.00E
Krivaja *r.* Yugo. **21** 44.27N 18.09E
Krivoy Rog U.S.S.R. **25** 47.55N 33.24E
Krk *i.* Yugo. **20** 45.04N 14.36E
Krnov Czech. **21** 50.05N 17.41E
Kroken Norway **22** 65.23N 14.15E
Krokom Sweden **22** 63.20N 14.30E
Krông Kaôh Kông Cambodia **34** 11.37N102.59E
Kronoberg *d.* Sweden **23** 56.45N 14.15E
Kronprins Olav Kyst *f.* Antarctica **96** 69.00S 42.00E
Kronshtadt U.S.S.R. **24** 60.00N 29.40E
Kroonstad R.S.A. **56** 27.38S 27.12E
Kropotkin U.S.S.R. **25** 45.25N 40.35E
Krosno Poland **21** 49.42N 21.46E
Krotoszyn Poland **21** 51.42N 17.26E
Kroya Indonesia **37** 7.37S109.13E
Kruger Nat. Park R.S.A. **57** 24.10S 31.36E
Krugersdorp R.S.A. **56** 26.06S 27.46E
Krujë Albania **19** 41.30N 19.48E
Krumbach Germany **20** 48.14N 10.22E
Krung Thep *see* Bangkok Thailand **34**
Krupki U.S.S.R. **21** 54.19N 29.05E
Kruševac Yugo. **21** 43.34N 21.20E
Krym *pen.* U.S.S.R. **25** 45.30N 34.00E
Krymsk U.S.S.R. **25** 44.56N 38.00E
Krzyz Poland **20** 52.54N 16.01E
Ksar el Boukhari Algeria **51** 35.53N 2.45E
Ksar-el-Kebir Morocco **50** 35.01N 5.54W
Ksar Rhilane Tunisia **51** 33.00N 9.38E
Ksel, Djebel *mtn.* Algeria **51** 33.44N 1.10E
Kuala Dungun Malaysia **36** 4.47N103.26E
Kualakapuas Indonesia **36** 3.01S114.21E
Kuala Lipis Malaysia **36** 4.11N102.00E
Kuala Lumpur Malaysia **36** 3.08N101.42E
Kuala Trengganu Malaysia **36** 5.10N103.10E
Kuancheng China **32** 40.36N118.27E
Kuandang Indonesia **37** 0.53N122.58E
Kuandian China **32** 40.47N124.43E
Kuantan Malaysia **36** 3.50N103.19E
Kuba U.S.S.R. **43** 41.23N 48.33E
Kuban *r.* U.S.S.R. **25** 45.20N 37.17E
Kubbum Sudan **49** 11.47N 23.47E
Kuchaiburi India **41** 22.16N 86.10E
Kuchāman India **40** 27.09N 74.52E
Kuching Malaysia **36** 1.32N110.20E
Kūchnay Darvīshān Afghan. **40** 30.59N 64.11E
Kūd Jammu & Kashmir **40** 33.05N 75.17E
Kudat Malaysia **36** 6.45N116.47E
Kudus Indonesia **37** 6.46S110.48E
Kufstein Austria **20** 47.36N 12.11E
Kūhpāyeh Iran **43** 32.42N 52.25E
Kūhrān, Kūh-e *mtn.* Iran **43** 26.46N 58.15E
Kuito Angola **54** 12.25S 16.58E
Kuiu I. U.S.A. **74** 56.40N134.00W
Kuivaniemi Finland **22** 65.35N 25.11E
Kuke Botswana **56** 23.19S 24.29E
Kukerin Australia **63** 33.11S118.03E
Kukës Albania **19** 42.05N 20.24E
Kukshi India **40** 22.12N 74.45E
Kūl *r.* Iran **43** 28.00N 55.45E
Kula Turkey **42** 38.33N 28.38E
Kulāchi Pakistan **40** 31.56N 70.27E
Kulakshi U.S.S.R. **25** 47.09N 55.22E
Kulal, Mt. Kenya **55** 2.44N 36.56E
Kulaura Bangla. **41** 24.30N 92.03E
Kuldīga U.S.S.R. **23** 56.58N 21.59E
Kulgera Australia **64** 25.50S133.18E
Kulin Australia **63** 32.40S118.10E
Kulja Australia **63** 30.28S117.17E
Kulkyne *r.* Australia **67** 30.16S144.12E
Kulpara Australia **66** 34.07S137.59E
Kulsary U.S.S.R. **25** 46.59N 54.02E
Kulu India **40** 31.58N 77.07E
Kulu Turkey **25** 39.06N 33.02E
Kulunda U.S.S.R. **28** 52.34N 78.58E
Kulwin Australia **66** 35.02S142.40E
Kulyab U.S.S.R. **30** 37.55N 69.47E
Kuma *r.* U.S.S.R. **25** 44.40N 46.55E
Kumagaya Japan **35** 36.08N139.23E
Kumai Indonesia **36** 2.45S111.44E
Kumamoto Japan **31** 32.50N130.42E
Kumanovo Yugo. **19** 42.08N 21.40E
Kumara New Zealand **60** 42.38S171.11E
Kumarl Australia **63** 32.47S121.33E
Kumasi Ghana **52** 6.45N 1.35W
Kumba Cameroon **53** 4.39N 9.26E
Kumbakonam India **39** 10.59N 79.24E
Kum Dag U.S.S.R. **43** 39.14N 54.33E
Kumdah Saudi Arabia **45** 20.23N 45.05E
Kumertau U.S.S.R. **24** 52.48N 55.46E
Kumi Uganda **55** 1.26N 33.54E
Kumla Sweden **23** 59.08N 15.08E
Kumon Range *mts.* Burma **34** 26.30N 97.15E
Kunashir *i.* U.S.S.R. **31** 44.25N146.00E
Kunchha Nepal **41** 28.08N 84.22E
Kundam India **41** 23.13N 80.21E
Kundelungu Mts. Zaïre **55** 9.30S 27.50E
Kundiān Pakistan **40** 32.27N 71.28E
Kundip Australia **63** 33.44S120.11E
Kundla India **40** 21.20N 71.18E
Kungälv Sweden **23** 57.52N 11.58E
Kungsbacka Sweden **23** 57.29N 12.04E
Kungu Zaïre **54** 2.47N 19.12E
Kungur U.S.S.R. **24** 57.27N 56.50E
Kuningan Indonesia **37** 7.02S108.30E
Kunkuri India **41** 22.45N 83.57E
Kunlong Burma **34** 23.25N 98.39E
Kunlun Shan *mts.* China **30** 36.40N 88.00E
Kunming China **30** 25.04N102.41E
Kunö *i.* Faroe Is. **8** 62.20N 6.39W
Kunsan S. Korea **31** 35.57N126.42E
Kunshan China **33** 31.24N121.08E
Kuntair Gambia **52** 13.36N 16.20W
Kununoppin Australia **63** 31.09S117.53E
Kununurra Australia **61** 15.42S128.50E
Kunyo Ethiopia **45** 6.20N 42.32E
Kuolayarvi U.S.S.R. **22** 66.58N 29.12E
Kuopio Finland **24** 62.51N 27.30E
Kupa *r.* Yugo. **20** 45.30N 16.20E
Kupang Indonesia **37** 10.13S123.38E
Kupreanof I. U.S.A. **74** 56.50N133.30W
Kupyansk U.S.S.R. **25** 49.41N 37.37E
Kuqa China **30** 41.43N 82.58E
Kura *r.* U.S.S.R. **43** 39.18N 49.22E
Kuraymah Sudan **48** 18.33N 31.51E
Kurchum U.S.S.R. **30** 48.35N 83.39E
Kurdistan *f.* Asia **43** 37.00N 43.30E
Kŭrdzhali Bulgaria **19** 41.38N 25.21E
Kuressaare U.S.S.R. **23** 58.12N 22.30E
Kurgaldzhino U.S.S.R. **28** 50.35N 70.03E
Kurgan U.S.S.R. **28** 55.20N 65.20E
Kurīgrām Bangla. **41** 25.49N 89.39E
Kurikka Finland **22** 62.37N 22.25E
Kuril Ridge Pacific Oc. **68** 46.10N152.30E
Kurilskiye Ostrova *is.* U.S.S.R. **31** 46.00N150.30E
Kuril Trench Pacific Oc. **68** 46.00N155.00E
Kuring Kuru Namibia **56** 17.36S 18.36E
Kurlovski U.S.S.R. **24** 55.26N 40.40E
Kurmuk Sudan **49** 10.33N 34.17E
Kurnool India **39** 15.51N 78.01E
Kurow New Zealand **60** 44.44S170.28E
Kurram Pakistan **40** 30.06N 66.31E
Kurri Kurri Australia **67** 32.49S151.29E
Kurseong India **41** 26.53N 88.17E
Kursk U.S.S.R. **25** 51.45N 36.14E
Kurškiy Zaliv *b.* U.S.S.R. **23** 55.00N 21.00E
Kuršumlija Yugo. **19** 43.09N 21.16E
Kūrtī Sudan **48** 18.07N 31.33E
Kuru Finland **23** 61.52N 23.44E
Kuru Sudan **49** 7.43N 26.31E
Kuruman R.S.A. **56** 27.28S 23.25E
Kuruman *r.* R.S.A. **56** 26.53S 20.38E
Kurur, Jabal *mtn.* Sudan **48** 20.31N 31.32E
Kusatsu Japan **35** 35.02N135.57E
Kusel Germany **14** 49.32N 7.21E
Kushālgarh India **40** 23.10N 74.27E
Kushchevskaya U.S.S.R. **25** 46.34N 39.39E
Kushida *r.* Japan **35** 34.36N136.34E
Kushiro Japan **31** 42.58N144.24E
Kushka U.S.S.R. **43** 35.14N 62.15E
Kushtia Bangla. **41** 23.55N 89.07E
Kusiyāra *r.* Bangla. **41** 24.36N 91.44E
Kuskokwim B. U.S.A. **72** 59.45N162.25W
Kuskokwim Mts. U.S.A. **72** 62.50N156.00W
Kusma Nepal **41** 28.13N 83.41E
Kustanay U.S.S.R. **28** 53.15N 63.40E
Küstenkanal Germany **14** 53.05N 7.46E
Kūstī Sudan **49** 13.10N 32.40E
Kütahya Turkey **42** 39.25N 29.56E
Kutaisi U.S.S.R. **25** 42.15N 42.44E
Kutiyāna India **40** 21.38N 69.59E
Kutná Hora Czech. **20** 49.57N 15.16E
Kutno Poland **21** 52.15N 19.23E
Kutu Zaïre **54** 2.42S 18.09E
Kutubdia I. Bangla. **41** 21.50N 91.52E
Kutum Sudan **48** 14.12N 24.40E
Kutztown U.S.A. **85** 40.31N 75.47W
Kuujjuaq Canada **73** 58.10N 68.15W
Kuusamo Finland **24** 65.57N 29.15E
Kuvango Angola **54** 14.28S 16.25E
Kuwait Asia **43** 29.20N 47.40E
Kuwait *town see* Al Kuwayt Kuwait **43**
Kuwana Japan **35** 35.04N136.42E
Kuybyshev U.S.S.R. **24** 53.10N 50.15E
Kuybyshevskoye Vodokhranilishche *resr.* U.S.S.R. **24** 55.00N 49.00E
Kuyeda U.S.S.R. **24** 56.25N 55.33E
Kuzey Anadolu Dağlari *mts.* Turkey **42** 40.32N 38.00E
Kuznetsk U.S.S.R. **24** 53.08N 46.36E
Kuzomen U.S.S.R. **24** 66.15N 36.51E
Kuzreka U.S.S.R. **24** 66.35N 34.48E
Kvaenangen *est.* Norway **22** 69.50N 21.30E
Kwale Kenya **55** 4.20S 39.25E
Kwamouth Zaïre **54** 3.11S 16.16E
Kwangju S. Korea **31** 35.07N126.52E
Kwango *r.* Zaïre **54** 3.20S 17.23E
Kwara *d.* Nigeria **53** 8.20N 5.35E
Kwatisore Indonesia **37** 3.18S134.50E
Kwa Zulu *f.* R.S.A. **56** 27.30S 32.00E
Kwekwe Zimbabwe **56** 18.59S 29.46E
Kweneng *d.* Botswana **56** 24.30S 25.40E
Kwenge *r.* Zaïre **54** 4.53S 18.47E
Kwethluk U.S.A. **72** 60.49N161.27W
Kwidzyn Poland **21** 53.45N 18.56E
Kwigillingok U.S.A. **72** 59.51N163.08W
Kwiguk U.S.A. **72** 62.45N164.28W
Kwilu *r.* Zaïre **54** 3.18S 17.22E
Kwinana Australia **63** 32.15S115.48E
Kwoka *mtn.* Indonesia **37** 1.30S132.30E
Kyabé Chad **53** 9.28N 18.54E
Kyabram Australia **67** 36.18S145.05E
Kyaiklat Burma **34** 16.25N 95.42E
Kyaikto Burma **34** 17.16N 97.01E
Kyaka Tanzania **55** 1.16S 31.27E
Kyakhta U.S.S.R. **30** 50.22N106.30E
Kyalite Australia **66** 34.57S143.31E
Kyancutta Australia **66** 33.08S135.34E
Kyaukpadaung Burma **34** 20.50N 95.08E
Kyaukpyu Burma **34** 19.20N 93.33E
Kybybolite Australia **66** 36.54S140.58E
Kychema U.S.S.R. **24** 65.32N 42.42E
Kyle of Lochalsh *town* U.K. **12** 57.17N 5.43W
Kyll *r.* Germany **14** 49.48N 6.42E
Kyllburg Germany **14** 50.03N 6.36E
Kyluchevskaya *mtn.* U.S.S.R. **29** 56.00N160.30E
Kyneton Australia **66** 37.14S144.28E
Kynuna Australia **64** 21.35S141.55E
Kyoga, L. Uganda **55** 1.30N 33.00E
Kyogle Australia **67** 28.36S152.59E
Kyong Burma **34** 20.49N 96.40E
Kyonpyaw Burma **34** 17.18N 95.12E
Kyotera Uganda **55** 0.40S 31.31E
Kyōto Japan **35** 35.00N135.45E
Kyōto *d.* Japan **35** 34.55N135.35E
Kyrön *r.* Finland **22** 63.14N 21.45E
Kyrta U.S.S.R. **24** 64.02N 57.40E
Kyūshū *i.* Japan **31** 32.50N130.50E
Kyushu Palau Ridge Pacific Oc. **68** 15.00N135.00E
Kyustendil Bulgaria **19** 42.18N 22.39E
Kywong Australia **67** 35.01S146.45E
Kyyjärvi Finland **22** 63.02N 24.34E
Kyzyl U.S.S.R. **30** 51.42N 94.28E
Kyzyl Kum, Peski *f.* U.S.S.R. **28** 42.00N 64.30E
Kzyl Orda U.S.S.R. **28** 44.52N 65.28E

L

Laas Caanood Somali Rep. **45** 8.26N 47.24E
Laas Dawaco Somali Rep. **45** 10.22N 49.03E
Laas Dhaareed Somali Rep. **45** 10.10N 46.01E
Laas Qoray Somali Rep. **45** 11.10N 48.16E
La Asunción Venezuela **90** 11.06N 63.53W
Laâyoune *see* El Aaiún W. Sahara **50**
La Baleine *r.* Canada **73** 58.00N 57.50W
La Banda Argentina **92** 27.44S 64.15W
La Bañeza Spain **16** 42.17N 5.55W
Labao Indonesia **37** 8.12S122.49E
La Barca Mexico **86** 20.20N102.33W
La Barge U.S.A. **80** 42.16N110.12W
La Bassée France **14** 50.32N 2.49E
La Baule France **17** 47.18N 2.23W
Labbezanga Mali **52** 14.57N 0.42E
Labe *r.* Czech. *see* Elbe *r.* Germany **20**
Labé Guinea **52** 11.17N 12.11W
La Belle U.S.A. **85** 26.43N 81.27W
Laberge, L. Canada **74** 61.11N135.12W
Labinsk U.S.S.R. **25** 44.39N 40.44E
La Blanquilla *i.* Venezuela **87** 11.53N 64.38W
Labouheyre France **17** 44.13N 0.55W
Laboulaye Argentina **93** 34.05S 63.25W
Labrador *f.* Canada **77** 53.00N 62.00W
Labrador Basin *f.* Atlantic Oc. **95** 55.00N 45.00W
Labrador City Canada **77** 52.57N 66.54W
Labrador Sea Canada / Greenland **73** 57.00N 53.00W
Lábrea Brazil **90** 7.16S 64.47W
Labrit France **17** 44.07N 0.33W
Labuan Indonesia **37** 6.25S105.49E
Labuan *i.* Malaysia **36** 5.20N115.15E
Labuha Indonesia **37** 0.37S127.29E
Labutta Burma **34** 16.09N 94.46E
Labyrinth, L. Australia **66** 30.43S135.07E
Lac *d.* Chad **53** 13.30N 14.35E
La Calera Chile **93** 32.47S 71.12W
La Capelle France **14** 49.59N 3.57E
La Carlota Argentina **93** 33.25S 63.18W
La Carolina Spain **16** 38.16N 3.36W
Lacaune France **17** 43.42N 2.41E
La Ceiba Honduras **87** 15.45N 86.45W
Lacepede B. Australia **66** 36.47S139.45E
Lac Giao Vietnam **34** 12.41N108.02E
Lacha, Ozero *l.* U.S.S.R. **24** 61.25N 39.00E
La Charité France **17** 47.11N 3.01E
La Chartre France **15** 47.44N 0.35E
La Chaux-de-Fonds Switz. **20** 47.07N 6.51E
Lach Dera *r.* Somali Rep. **55** 0.01S 42.45E
Lachhmangarh India **40** 27.49N 75.02E
Lachine Canada **77** 45.26N 73.40W
Lachlan *r.* Australia **66** 34.21S143.58E
Lachute Canada **77** 45.38N 74.20W
Lackan Resr. Rep. of Ire. **13** 53.09N 6.31W
Lackawanna U.S.A. **84** 42.49N 78.49W
Lac la Biche *town* Canada **75** 54.46N111.58W
Lac la Ronge Prov. Park Canada **75** 55.14N104.45W
La Cocha Argentina **92** 27.45S 65.35W
Lacombe Canada **74** 52.30N113.44W
La Concepción Venezuela **90** 10.25N 71.41W
La Concordia Mexico **86** 16.05N 92.38W
La Coruña Spain **16** 43.22N 8.24W
Lac Rémi *town* Canada **77** 46.01N 74.47W
La Crosse Kans. U.S.A. **82** 38.32N 99.18W
La Crosse Wisc. U.S.A. **82** 43.48N 91.15W
La Cruz Mexico **81** 27.50N105.11W
La Cruz Uruguay **93** 33.56S 56.15W
Ladākh Range *mts.* Jammu & Kashmir **41** 34.15N 78.00E
La Demanda, Sierra de *mts.* Spain **16** 42.10N 3.20W
Ladismith R.S.A. **56** 33.29S 21.15E
Ladispoli Italy **18** 41.56N 12.05E
Lādīz Iran **43** 28.57N 61.18E
Lādnun India **40** 27.39N 74.23E
Ladoga *l. see* Ladozhskoye Ozero *l.* U.S.S.R. **24**
La Dorada Colombia **90** 5.27N 74.40W
Ladozhskoye Ozero *l.* U.S.S.R. **24** 61.00N 32.00E
La Dura Mexico **81** 28.22N109.33W
Ladushkin U.S.S.R. **21** 54.30N 20.05E
Ladva Vetka U.S.S.R. **24** 61.16N 34.23E
Ladybrand R.S.A. **56** 29.11S 27.26E
Ladysmith Canada **74** 49.58N123.49W
Ladysmith R.S.A. **56** 28.32S 29.47E
Ladysmith U.S.A. **82** 45.27N 91.07W
Lae P.N.G. **37** 6.45S146.30E
Lae Thailand **34** 19.25N101.00E
Laesö *i.* Denmark **23** 57.16N 11.01E
La Estrada Spain **16** 42.40N 8.30W
La Fayette Ga. U.S.A. **85** 34.42N 85.18W
Lafayette Ind. U.S.A. **84** 40.25N 86.54W
Lafayette La. U.S.A. **83** 30.14N 92.01W
La Fère France **15** 49.40N 3.22E
La Ferté-Bernard France **15** 48.11N 0.40E
La Ferté-Gaucher France **15** 48.47N 3.18E
La Ferté-Macé France **15** 48.36N 0.22W
La Ferté-St. Aubin France **15** 47.43N 1.56E
Lafia Nigeria **53** 8.35N 8.34E
Lafiagi Nigeria **53** 8.50N 5.23E
La Flèche France **15** 47.42N 0.05W
Lafollette U.S.A. **85** 36.23N 84.09W
Laforest Canada **76** 47.04N 81.12W
La Fregeneda Spain **16** 40.58N 6.54W
La Fuente de San Esteban Spain **16** 40.48N 6.15W
Lagan *r.* U.K. **13** 54.37N 5.44W
Lågen *r.* Akershus Norway **23** 60.10N 11.28E
Lågen *r.* Vestfold Norway **23** 59.03N 10.05E
Laghouat Algeria **51** 33.49N 2.55E
Lago Dilolo *town* Angola **54** 11.27S 22.03E
Lagos Mexico **86** 21.21N101.55W
Lagos Nigeria **53** 6.27N 3.28E
Lagos *d.* Nigeria **53** 6.32N 3.30E
Lagos Portugal **16** 37.05N 8.40W
La Goulette Tunisia **51** 36.49N 10.18E
La Grande *r.* Canada **76** 53.50N 79.00W
La Grande U.S.A. **80** 45.20N118.05W
La Grande Résr. 3 Canada **76** 53.35N 74.55W
La Grande Résr. 2 Canada **76** 53.35N 77.10W
La Grande Résr. 4 Canada **76** 53.50N 73.30W
Lagrange Australia **62** 18.46S121.49E
La Grange U.S.A. **85** 33.02N 85.02W
La Guaira Venezuela **90** 10.38N 66.55W
La Guerche-de-Bretagne France **15** 47.56N 1.14W
Laguna Brazil **92** 28.29S 48.47W
Laguna Dam U.S.A. **81** 32.55N114.25W
Lagunas Chile **92** 20.59S 69.37W
Lagunas Peru **90** 5.10S 73.35W
La Habana Cuba **87** 23.07N 82.25W
Lahad Datu Malaysia **36** 5.05N118.20E
La Harpe U.S.A. **82** 40.35N 90.57W
Lahat Indonesia **36** 3.46S103.32E
La Haye-du-Puits France **15** 49.18N 1.33W
Laḥij Yemen **45** 13.04N 44.53E
Lāhījān Iran **43** 37.12N 50.00E
Lahn *r.* Germany **14** 50.18N 7.36E
Lahnstein Germany **14** 50.17N 7.38E
Laholm Sweden **23** 56.31N 13.02E
Lahore Pakistan **40** 31.35N 74.18E
Lahri Pakistan **40** 29.11N 68.13E
Lahti Finland **23** 60.58N 25.40E
Laï Chad **53** 9.22N 16.14E
Laiagam P.N.G. **37** 5.31S143.39E
Laibin China **33** 23.42N109.16E
Lai Chau Vietnam **34** 22.04N103.12E
L'Aigle France **15** 48.45N 0.38E
Laignes France **15** 47.50N 4.22E
Laihia Finland **22** 62.58N 22.01E
Laingsburg R.S.A. **56** 33.11S 20.49E
Lainio *r.* Sweden **22** 67.28N 22.50E
Lairg U.K. **12** 58.01N 4.25W
Laisamis Kenya **55** 1.38N 37.47E
Laissac France **17** 44.23N 2.49E
Laitila Finland **23** 60.53N 21.41E
Laiyuan China **32** 39.19N114.41E
Laizhou Wan *b.* China **32** 37.30N119.30E
Lajes Brazil **94** 27.48S 50.20W
La Junta U.S.A. **80** 37.59N103.33W
Lakaband Pakistan **40** 31.00N 69.30E
Lak Bor *r.* Kenya **49** 1.18N 40.40E
Lak Bor *r.* Somali Rep. **55** 0.32N 42.05E
Lake Biddy *town* Australia **63** 33.01S118.51E
Lake Boga *town* Australia **66** 35.27S143.39E
Lake Brown *town* Australia **63** 30.57S118.19E
Lake Cargelligo *town* Australia **67** 33.19S146.23E
Lake Charles *town* U.S.A. **83** 30.13N 93.12W
Lake City U.S.A. **85** 30.12N 82.39W
Lake District *f.* U.K. **10** 54.30N 3.10W
Lake George *town* Colo. U.S.A. **80** 38.58N105.23W
Lake Grace *town* Australia **63** 33.06S118.28E
Lake Harbour *town* Canada **73** 62.50N 69.50W
Lake King *town* Australia **63** 33.05S119.40E
Lakeland *town* U.S.A. **85** 28.02N 81.59W
Lake Mead Nat. Recreation Area U.S.A. **81** 36.00N114.30W
Lake Nash *town* Australia **64** 21.00S137.55E
Lakepa Niue **68** 19.01S169.49W
Lake Placid *town* U.S.A. **84** 44.17N 73.59W
Lake River *town* Canada **76** 54.30N 82.30W
Lakes Entrance *town* Australia **67** 37.53S147.59E
Lakeshore U.S.A. **80** 37.15N119.12W
Lakeside Utah U.S.A. **80** 41.13N112.54W
Lake Superior Prov. Park Canada **76** 47.30N 84.50W
Lakeview U.S.A. **80** 42.11N120.21W
Lake Village U.S.A. **83** 33.20N 91.17W
Lakewood N.J. U.S.A. **85** 40.06N 74.12W
Lakewood N.Mex. U.S.A. **81** 32.39N104.39W
Lakewood Ohio U.S.A. **84** 41.29N 81.50W
Lākheri India **40** 25.40N 76.10E
Lakhimpur India **41** 27.57N 80.46E
Lakhnādon India **41** 22.36N 79.36E
Lakhpat India **40** 23.49N 68.47E
Lakonikós Kólpos *g.* Greece **19** 36.35N 22.42E
Lakota Ivory Coast **52** 5.50N 5.30W
Lakota U.S.A. **82** 48.02N 98.21W
Laksefjorden *est.* Norway **22** 70.58N 27.00E
Lakselv Norway **22** 70.03N 24.55E
Lakshadweep Is. Indian Oc. **38** 11.00N 72.00E
Lala India **41** 24.25N 92.40E
Lāla Mūsa Pakistan **40** 32.42N 73.58E
Lalaua Mozambique **55** 14.20S 38.30E
Lālehzār, Kūh-e *mtn.* Iran **43** 29.26N 56.48E
Lālganj India **41** 25.52N 85.11E
Lalibela Ethiopia **49** 12.02N 39.02E
La Libertad El Salvador **87** 13.28N 89.20W
Lalín Spain **16** 42.40N 8.05W
La Línea Spain **16** 36.10N 5.21W
Lalitpur India **41** 24.41N 78.25E
Lalitpur Nepal **41** 27.41N 85.20E
Lālmanir Hāt Bangla. **41** 25.54N 89.27E
La Loche Canada **75** 56.29N109.27W
La Loche, Lac *l.* Canada **75** 56.25N109.30W
La Loupe France **15** 48.28N 1.01E
La Louvière Belgium **14** 50.29N 4.11E
Lālpur India **40** 22.12N 69.58E
Lālsot India **40** 26.34N 76.20E
Lamar U.S.A. **82** 38.05N102.37W
Lambaréné Gabon **54** 0.40S 10.15E
Lambasa Fiji **68** 16.25S179.24E
Lambayeque Peru **90** 6.36S 79.50W
Lambay I. Rep. of Ire. **13** 53.29N 6.01W
Lambert's Bay *town* R.S.A. **56** 32.06S 18.16E
Lamé Chad **53** 9.14N 14.33E
Lame Nigeria **53** 10.27N 9.12E
Lamego Portugal **16** 41.05N 7.49W
Lameroo Australia **66** 35.20S140.33E
La Mesa Calif. U.S.A. **81** 32.46N117.01W
Lamesa Tex. U.S.A. **83** 32.44N101.57W
Lamía Greece **19** 38.53N 22.25E
Lammermuir Hills U.K. **12** 55.51N 2.40W
Lammhult Sweden **23** 57.09N 14.35E
Lamongan Indonesia **37** 7.05S112.26E
Lamont U.S.A. **80** 42.12N107.28W
Lamotrek *i.* Caroline Is. **37** 7.28N146.23E
Lamotte-Beuvron France **15** 47.37N 2.01E
La Moure U.S.A. **82** 46.21N 98.18W
Lampa Peru **90** 15.10S 70.30W
Lampasas U.S.A. **83** 31.04N 98.12W
Lampazos Mexico **83** 27.00N100.30W
Lampedusa *i.* Italy **18** 35.30N 12.35E
Lampeter U.K. **11** 52.06N 4.06W
Lampione *i.* Italy **18** 35.33N 12.18E
Lamu Kenya **55** 2.20S 40.54E
La Mure France **17** 44.54N 5.47E
Lanai *i.* Hawaiian Is. **69** 20.50N156.55W
Lanai City Hawaiian Is. **69** 20.50N156.55W
La Nao, Cabo de Spain **16** 38.42N 0.15E
Lanark U.K. **12** 55.41N 3.47W
Lancang Jiang *r.* China *see* Mekong *r.* Asia **34**
Lancashire *d.* U.K. **10** 53.53N 2.30W
Lancaster Canada **77** 45.08N 74.30W
Lancaster U.K. **10** 54.03N 2.48W
Lancaster Calif. U.S.A. **81** 34.42N118.08W
Lancaster N.Y. U.S.A. **76** 42.54N 78.40W
Lancaster Ohio U.S.A. **84** 39.43N 82.37W
Lancaster Penn. U.S.A. **85** 40.02N 76.19W
Lancaster S.C. U.S.A. **85** 34.43N 80.47W
Lancaster Tex. U.S.A. **83** 32.36N 96.46W
Lancaster Sd. Canada **73** 74.00N 85.00W
Lancelin Australia **63** 31.01S115.19E
Lanchow *see* Lanzhou China **32**
Lancun China **32** 36.24N120.10E
Landau Bayern Germany **20** 48.40N 12.43E
Landay Afghan. **40** 30.31N 63.47E
Landeck Austria **20** 47.09N 10.35E
Landen Belgium **14** 50.46N 5.04E
Lander *r.* Australia **64** 20.25S132.00E
Lander U.S.A. **80** 42.50N108.44W
Landerneau France **17** 48.27N 4.16W
Landisville U.S.A. **85** 39.31N 74.55W
Landor Australia **62** 25.06S116.50E
Landrecies France **14** 50.08N 3.40E
Land's End *c.* U.K. **11** 50.03N 5.45W
Landshut Germany **20** 48.31N 12.10E
Landskrona Sweden **23** 55.52N 12.50E
Lanett U.S.A. **85** 32.52N 85.12W
Langå Denmark **23** 56.23N 9.55E
La'nga Co *l.* China **41** 30.45N 81.15E
Langadhás Greece **19** 40.45N 23.04E
Langanes *c.* Iceland **22** 66.30N 14.30W
Langao China **32** 33.22N109.04E
Langdon U.S.A. **82** 48.46N 98.22W
Langeais France **15** 47.20N 0.24E
Langeland *i.* Denmark **23** 55.00N 10.50E
Längelmävesi *l.* Finland **23** 61.32N 24.22E
Langeoog *i.* Germany **14** 53.46N 7.30E
Langesund Norway **23** 59.00N 9.45E
Langholm U.K. **12** 55.09N 3.00W
Langjökull *ice cap* Iceland **22** 63.43N 20.03W
Langkawi *i.* Malaysia **36** 6.20N 99.30E
Langlade Canada **76** 48.14N 76.00W
Langon France **17** 44.33N 0.14W
Langöy *i.* Norway **22** 68.45N 15.00E
Langres France **17** 47.53N 5.20E
Langsa Indonesia **36** 4.28N 97.59E
Langshan China **32** 41.02N107.27E
Lang Shan *mts.* China **32** 41.30N107.10E
Lang Son Vietnam **33** 21.49N106.45E
Langtry U.S.A. **83** 29.48N101.34W
Languedoc-Roussillon *d.* France **17** 43.50N 3.30E
Langxi China **33** 31.08N119.10E
Lannion France **17** 48.44N 3.27W
Lanoraie Canada **77** 45.58N 73.13W
Lansdale U.S.A. **85** 40.15N 75.17W
Lansdowne India **41** 29.50N 78.41E
L'Anse au Loup Canada **77** 51.34N 56.48W
Lansing U.S.A. **84** 42.44N 84.34W
Lanslebourg France **15** 45.17N 6.52E
Lantewa Nigeria **53** 12.15N 11.45E
Lanxi China **33** 29.17N119.31E
Lanzarote *i.* Canary Is. **50** 29.00N 13.40W
Lanzhou China **32** 36.01N103.46E
Lanzo Torinese Italy **15** 45.16N 7.28E
Laoag Phil. **37** 18.14N120.36E
Lào Cai Vietnam **34** 22.30N104.00E

:hang China 33 25.12N104.35E
ıa He r. China 32 43.30N120.42E
s d. Rep. of Ire. 13 53.00N 7.20W
un Shan mtn. China 32 33.45N111.38E
France 15 49.34N 3.37E
ıa U.S.A. 76 45.35N 88.40W
'rotava Canary Is. 95 28.26N 16.30W
roya Peru 90 11.36S 75.54W
s Asia 34 18.30N104.00E
alma i. Canary Is. 50 28.50N 18.00W
alma Spain 16 37.23N 6.33W
ampa d. Argentina 93 37.00S 66.00W
aragua Venezuela 90 6.53N 63.22W
az Entre Ríos Argentina 93 30.45S 59.38W
'az Mendoza Argentina 93 33.28S 67.34W
'az Bolivia 92 16.30S 68.09W
'az d. Bolivia 92 16.00S 68.10W
'az Mexico 81 24.10N110.18W
'az, Bahía de b. Mexico 81 15N110.30W
edrera Colombia 90 1.18S 69.43W
eer U.S.A. 84 43.03N 83.09W
eña, Sierra de mts. Spain 16 42.30N 0W
erouse Str. U.S.S.R. 29 45.50N142.30E
ine U.S.A. 80 43.40N121.30W
njärvi Finland 23 60.38N 26.13E
land f. Sweden/Finland 22 68.10N 24.10E
'lata Argentina 93 34.55S 57.57W
lata Md. U.S.A. 85 38.32N 76.59W
lata Mo. U.S.A. 82 40.02N 92.29W
lata, Río de est. Argentina/Uruguay 93 15S 56.45W
ointe, Lac l. Canada 77 53.32N 68.56W
oajärvi l. Finland 22 63.08N 23.40E
oeenranta Finland 24 61.04N 28.05E
oi d. Finland 22 67.20N 26.00E
tevykh, More sea U.S.S.R. 29 30N125.00E
ua Finland 22 62.57N 23.00E
'ush U.S.A. 80 47.55N124.38W
uiaca Argentina 92 22.05S 65.36W
quila Italy 18 42.22N 13.25E
iran 43 27.37N 54.16E
Australia 66 38.01S144.26E
che Morocco 50 35.12N 6.10W
amie U.S.A. 80 41.19N105.35W
amie Mts. U.S.A. 80 42.00N105.40W
oro Sweden 23 57.47N 18.47E
che, Col de France/Italy 15 44.25N 6.53E
edo U.S.A. 83 27.31N 99.30W
edo Sd. Canada 74 52.30N128.53W
geau Chad 53 17.55N 19.07E
gs U.K. 12 55.48N 4.52W
ang Indonesia 36 1.35S119.25E
Rioja Argentina 92 29.25S 66.50W
'ioja d. Argentina 92 29.00S 66.00W
ioja d. Spain 16 42.15N 2.25W
sa Greece 19 39.36N 22.24E
k r. U.K. 11 52.26N 0.20E
kāna Pakistan 40 27.33N 68.13E
kspur U.S.A. 80 39.13N104.54W
naca see Lárnax Cyprus 44
nax Cyprus 44 34.54N 33.39E
ne U.K. 13 54.51N 5.49W
Robla Spain 16 42.50N 5.41W
Roche Belgium 14 50.11N 5.35E
Rochelle France 17 46.10N 1.10W
Roche-sur-Yon France 17 46.40N 1.25W
Roda Spain 16 39.13N 2.10W
Romana Dom. Rep. 87 18.27N 68.57W
Ronge Canada 75 55.06N105.17W
Ronge, Lac l. Canada 72 55.07N105.15W
oquebrou France 17 44.58N 2.11E
imah Australia 64 15.35S133.12E
vik Norway 23 59.04N 10.00E
Sagra mtn. Spain 16 37.58N 2.35W
Salle U.S.A. 82 41.20N 89.06W
Animas U.S.A. 80 38.04N103.13W
Sarre Canada 76 48.45N 79.15W
Casitas, Cerro mtn. Mexico 81 .32N109.59W
Cruces U.S.A. 81 32.23N106.29W
Cuevas Mexico 83 29.38N101.19W
Seine, Baie de France 17 49.40N 0.30W
Serena Chile 92 29.54S 71.16W
Seyne France 17 43.06N 5.53E
Flores Argentina 93 36.02S 59.07W
h-e Joveyn Afghan. 40 31.43N 61.37E
Heras Argentina 93 32.50S 68.50W
hio Burma 34 22.58N 96.51E
hkar Gāh Afghan. 40 31.30N 64.21E
Lomitas Argentina 92 24.43S 60.35W
Marismas f. Spain 16 37.00N 6.15W
somption r. Canada 77 45.43N 73.29W
Palmas de Gran Canaria Canary Is. 50 .08N 15.27W
Palomas Mexico 81 31.44N107.37W
Perlas, Archipelago de Panama 87 8.45N .30W
Spezia Italy 15 44.07N 9.49E
Piedras Uruguay 93 34.44S 56.13W
Plumas Argentina 93 43.40S 67.15W
say France 15 48.26N 0.30W
sen Peak mtn. U.S.A. 80 40.29N121.31W
ssomption Canada 77 45.50N 73.25W
t Chance U.S.A. 80 39.45N103.36W
t Mountain L. Canada 75 51.05N105.10W
toursville Gabon 54 0.50S 12.47E
tovo i. Yugo. 19 42.45N 16.52E
Tres Vírgenes, Volcán mtn. Mexico 81 .27N112.37W
trup Germany 14 52.48N 7.55E
Suze France 15 47.54N 0.02E
Vegas Nev. U.S.A. 81 36.11N115.08W
Vegas N.Mex. U.S.A. 81 35.36N105.13W
acunga Ecuador 90 0.58S 78.36W
Tagua Colombia 90 0.03S 74.40W

Latakia see Al Lādhiqīyah Syria 44
Latambar Pakistan 40 33.07N 70.52E
Late i. Tonga 69 18.49S174.40W
Lātēhar India 41 23.45N 84.30E
La Teste-de-Buch France 17 44.38N 1.09W
Lathen Germany 14 52.54N 7.20E
Lāthi India 40 21.43N 71.23E
Latina Italy 18 41.28N 12.52E
Latisana Italy 15 45.47N 13.00E
La Tortuga i. Venezuela 90 11.00N 65.20W
La Trobe, Mt. Australia 67 39.03S146.25E
La Tuque Canada 77 47.27N 72.47W
Latviyskaya S.S.R. d. U.S.S.R. 23 56.45N 23.00E
Lau Nigeria 53 9.14N 11.15E
Lauchhammer Germany 20 51.30N 13.48E
Lauenburg Germany 20 53.22N 10.33E
Laughlen, Mt. Australia 64 23.23S134.23E
Lau Group is. Fiji 68 19.00S178.30W
Launceston Australia 65 41.25S147.07E
Launceston U.K. 11 50.38N 4.21W
La Unión Chile 93 40.15S 73.02W
La Unión Spain 16 37.38N 0.53W
Laura Australia 66 33.08S138.19E
La Urbana Venezuela 90 7.08N 66.56W
Laurel Del. U.S.A. 85 38.33N 75.34W
Laurel Miss. U.S.A. 83 31.42N 89.08W
Laurel Mont. U.S.A. 80 45.40N108.46W
Laurencekirk U.K. 12 56.50N 2.29W
Laurens U.S.A. 85 34.29N 82.01W
Laurentides mts. Canada 77 46.25N 73.28W
Laurentides Prov. Park Canada 77 47.30N 71.30W
Laurieton Australia 67 31.38S152.46E
Laurinburg U.S.A. 85 34.46N 79.29W
Lausanne Switz. 20 46.32N 6.39E
Laut i. Indonesia 36 3.45S116.20E
Lautaro Chile 93 38.31S 72.27W
Lauterecken Germany 14 49.39N 7.36E
Lautoka Fiji 68 17.37S177.27E
Lavagh More mtn. Rep. of Ire. 13 54.45N 8.07W
Lava Hot Springs town U.S.A. 80 42.37N112.01W
Laval Canada 77 45.35N 73.45W
Laval France 15 48.04N 0.45W
La Vega Dom. Rep. 87 19.15N 70.33W
La Vela Venezuela 90 11.27N 69.34W
La Vérendrye Prov. Park Canada 76 47.32N 77.00W
Laverne U.S.A. 83 36.43N 99.54W
Laverton Australia 63 28.49S122.25E
Lavia Finland 23 61.36N 22.36E
Lavik Norway 23 61.06N 5.30E
Lavras Brazil 94 21.15S 44.59W
Lávrion Greece 19 37.44N 24.04E
Lawra Ghana 52 10.40N 2.49W
Lawrence New Zealand 60 45.55S169.42E
Lawrence Kans. U.S.A. 82 38.58N 95.14W
Lawrence Mass. U.S.A. 84 42.42N 71.09W
Lawrenceburg U.S.A. 85 35.16N 87.20W
Lawrenceville Canada 77 45.25N 72.19W
Lawton Okla. U.S.A. 83 34.37N 98.25W
Lawz, Jabal al mtn. Saudi Arabia 44 28.40N 35.20E
Laxå Sweden 23 58.59N 14.37E
Laysan i. Hawaiian Is. 68 25.46N171.44W
Laytonville U.S.A. 80 39.41N123.29W
Lazio d. Italy 18 42.20N 12.00E
Lead U.S.A. 82 44.21N103.46W
Leader Canada 75 50.53N109.31W
Leadhills U.K. 12 55.25N 3.46W
Leamington U.S.A. 80 39.31N112.17W
Learmonth Australia 62 22.13S114.04E
Leavenworth U.S.A. 82 39.19N 94.55W
Lebak Phil. 37 6.32N124.03E
Lebango Congo 54 0.24N 14.44E
Lebanon Asia 44 34.00N 36.00E
Lebanon Ind. U.S.A. 84 40.02N 87.28W
Lebanon Kans. U.S.A. 82 39.49N 98.33W
Lebanon Ky. U.S.A. 85 37.33N 85.15W
Lebanon Mo. U.S.A. 83 37.41N 92.40W
Lebanon Oreg. U.S.A. 80 44.32N122.54W
Lebanon Penn. U.S.A. 84 40.20N 76.25W
Lebanon Tenn. U.S.A. 85 36.11N 86.19W
Lebec U.S.A. 81 34.50N118.52W
Lebesby Norway 22 70.34N 27.00E
Le Blanc France 17 46.37N 1.03E
Łebork Poland 21 54.33N 17.44E
Lebrija Spain 16 36.55N 6.10W
Lebu Chile 93 37.37S 73.39W
Le Bugue France 17 44.55N 0.56E
Le Cateau France 14 50.07N 3.33E
Le Catelet France 14 50.00N 3.12E
Lecce Italy 19 40.21N 18.11E
Lecco Italy 15 45.51N 9.23E
Lech r. Germany 20 48.45N 10.51E
Lechang China 33 25.08N113.20E
Le Chesne France 14 49.31N 4.46E
Lechiguanas, Islas de las is. Argentina 93 33.26S 59.42W
Le Creusot France 17 46.48N 4.27E
Lectoure France 17 43.56N 0.38E
Ledbury U.K. 11 52.03N 2.25W
Ledesma Spain 16 41.05N 6.00W
Le Dorat France 17 46.14N 1.05E
Leduc Canada 74 53.20N113.30W
Lee r. Rep. of Ire. 13 51.53N 8.25W
Leech L. U.S.A. 82 47.09N 94.23W
Leedey U.S.A. 83 35.52N 99.21W
Leeds U.K. 10 53.48N 1.34W
Leeds U.S.A. 85 33.32N 86.31W
Leek U.K. 10 53.07N 2.02W
Leer Germany 14 53.14N 7.27E
Leesburg Fla. U.S.A. 85 28.49N 81.54W
Leeston New Zealand 60 43.46S172.18E
Leeton Australia 67 34.33S146.24E
Leeuwarden Neth. 14 53.12N 5.48E

Leeuwin, C. Australia 63 34.22S115.08E
Leeward Is. C. America 87 18.00N 61.00W
Lefroy, L. Australia 63 31.15S121.40E
Legazpi Phil. 37 13.10N123.45E
Legges Tor mtn. Australia 65 41.32S147.40E
Legget U.S.A. 80 39.52N123.34W
Leghorn see Livorno Italy 18
Legion Mine Zimbabwe 56 21.23S 28.33E
Legionowo Poland 21 52.25N 20.56E
Legnago Italy 15 45.11N 11.18E
Legnano Italy 15 45.36N 8.54E
Legnica Poland 20 51.12N 16.10E
Le Grand-Lucé France 15 47.52N 0.28E
Le Grand-Quevilly France 15 49.25N 1.02E
Leh Jammu & Kashmir 41 34.10N 77.35E
Le Havre France 15 49.30N 0.06E
Lehrte Germany 20 52.22N 9.59E
Lehututu Botswana 56 23.54S 21.52E
Leiah Pakistan 40 30.58N 70.56E
Leibnitz Austria 20 46.48N 15.32E
Leicester U.K. 11 52.39N 1.09W
Leicestershire d. U.K. 11 52.29N 1.10W
Leichhardt r. Australia 64 17.35S139.48E
Leiden Neth. 14 52.10N 4.30E
Leie r. Belgium 14 51.03N 3.44E
Leifeng China 33 25.35N118.17E
Leigh Creek r. Australia 66 29.49S138.10E
Leigh Creek town Australia 66 30.31S138.25E
Leighton Buzzard U.K. 11 51.55N 0.39W
Leikanger Norway 23 61.10N 6.52E
Leinster Australia 63 27.59S120.30E
Leipzig Germany 20 51.20N 12.20E
Leiria Portugal 16 39.45N 8.48W
Lei Shui r. China 33 26.57N112.33E
Leithbridge Canada 74 49.40N112.45W
Leitrim d. Rep. of Ire. 13 54.08N 8.00W
Leiyang China 33 26.30N112.42E
Leizhou Bandao pen. China 33 21.00N110.00E
Lek r. Neth. 14 51.55N 4.29E
Leksvik Norway 22 63.40N 10.40E
Leland U.S.A. 83 33.24N 90.54W
Leland Lakes Canada 75 60.00N110.59W
Lelchitsy U.S.S.R. 21 51.48N 28.20E
Leleque Argentina 93 42.24S 71.04W
Leling China 32 37.45N117.13E
Le Lion-d'Angers France 15 47.38N 0.43W
Le Lude France 15 47.39N 0.09E
Lelystad Neth. 14 52.32N 5.29E
Léman, Lac l. Switz. 20 46.30N 6.30E
Le Mans France 15 48.01N 0.10E
Le Mars U.S.A. 82 42.47N 96.10W
Leme Brazil 94 22.10S 47.23W
Le Merlerault France 15 48.42N 0.18E
Lemesós Cyprus 44 34.40N 33.03E
Lemgo Germany 20 52.02N 8.54E
Lemhi Range mts. U.S.A. 80 44.30N113.25W
Lemmer Neth. 14 52.50N 5.43E
Lemmon U.S.A. 82 45.56N102.10W
Lemsid W. Sahara 50 26.32N 13.49W
Lemvig Denmark 23 56.32N 8.18E
Lena U.S.A. 83 31.47N 92.48W
Lena r. U.S.S.R. 29 72.00N127.10E
Lenakel Vanuatu 68 19.32S169.16E
Lendery U.S.S.R. 24 63.24N 31.04E
Lendinara Italy 15 45.05N 11.36E
Lengerich Germany 14 52.12N 7.52E
Lengoue r. Congo 54 1.15S 16.42E
Lenina, Kanal canal U.S.S.R. 25 43.46N 45.00E
Lenina, Pik mtn. U.S.S.R. 30 40.14N 69.40E
Leninakan U.S.S.R. 43 40.47N 43.49E
Leningrad U.S.S.R. 24 59.55N 30.25E
Leninogorsk U.S.S.R. 28 50.23N 83.32E
Leninsk U.S.S.R. 25 48.42N 45.14E
Leninsk Kuznetskiy U.S.S.R. 28 54.44N 86.13E
Lenkoran U.S.S.R. 43 38.45N 48.50E
Lenmalu Indonesia 37 1.58S130.00E
Lenne r. Germany 14 51.24N 7.30E
Lenoir U.S.A. 85 35.56N 81.31W
Lenora U.S.A. 82 39.38N100.03W
Lenore L. Canada 75 52.30N105.00W
Lens France 14 50.26N 2.50E
Lentini Italy 18 37.17N 15.00E
Lenvik Norway 22 69.22N 18.10E
Léo Burkina 52 11.05N 2.06W
Leoben Austria 20 47.23N 15.06E
Leominster U.K. 11 52.15N 2.43W
Leominster U.S.A. 84 42.32N 71.45W
León Mexico 86 21.10N101.42W
León d. Mexico 83 25.00N100.20W
León Nicaragua 87 12.24N 86.52W
León Spain 16 42.35N 5.34W
Leon U.S.A. 82 40.44N 93.45W
Leonardtown U.S.A. 85 38.17N 76.38W
Leonardville Namibia 56 23.21S 18.47E
Leonárison Cyprus 44 35.28N 34.08E
Leongatha Australia 67 38.29S145.57E
Leonora Australia 63 28.54S121.20E
Leopoldina Brazil 94 21.30S 42.38W
Leopoldsburg Belgium 14 51.08N 5.13E
Leovo U.S.S.R. 21 46.29N 28.12E
Lepel U.S.S.R. 24 54.48N 28.40E
Leping China 33 28.58N117.08E
L'Epiphanie Canada 77 45.51N 73.30W
Le Puy France 17 45.03N 3.54E
Le Quesnoy France 14 50.15N 3.39E
Lerbäck Sweden 23 58.56N 15.02E
Léré Chad 53 9.41N 14.17E
Lerici Italy 15 44.04N 9.55E
Lerma Spain 16 42.02N 3.46W
Leross Canada 75 51.17N103.53W
Le Roy Kans. U.S.A. 83 38.05N 95.38W
Le Roy Mich. U.S.A. 84 44.03N 85.29W
Le Roy N.Y. U.S.A. 76 42.59N 77.59W
Lerwick U.K. 12 60.09N 1.09W
Les Andelys France 15 49.15N 1.25E
Les Cayes Haiti 87 18.15N 73.46W

Leschenault, C. Australia 63 31.50S115.23E
Les Ecrins mtn. France 17 44.50N 6.20E
Leshan China 33 29.30N103.45E
Leshukonskoye U.S.S.R. 24 64.55N 45.50E
Lesjaskog Norway 23 62.15N 8.22E
Leskovac Yugo. 19 43.00N 21.56E
Leslie Ark. U.S.A. 83 35.50N 92.34W
Lesotho Africa 56 29.00S 28.00E
Lesozavodsk U.S.S.R. 31 45.30N133.29E
Les Pieux France 15 49.35N 1.50W
Les Riceys France 15 47.59N 4.22E
Les Sables d'Olonne France 17 46.30N 1.47W
Lessay France 15 49.14N 1.30W
Lesser Antilles is. C. America 87 13.00N 65.00W
Lesser Slave L. Canada 74 55.30N115.25W
Lesser Sunda Is. see Nusa Tenggara is. Indonesia 36
Lessines Belgium 14 50.43N 3.50E
Lesti r. Finland 22 64.04N 23.38E
Le Sueur U.S.A. 82 44.27N 93.54W
Lésvos i. Greece 19 39.10N 26.16E
Leszno Poland 20 51.51N 16.35E
Letchworth U.K. 11 51.58N 0.13W
Lethbridge Canada 72 49.43N112.48W
Lethem Guyana 90 3.18N 59.46W
Leti, Kepulauan is. Indonesia 37 8.20S128.00E
Letiahau r. Botswana 56 21.16S 24.00E
Leticia Colombia 90 4.09S 69.57W
Leting China 32 39.26N118.56E
Letohatchee U.S.A. 85 32.08N 86.30W
Le Tréport France 17 50.04N 1.22E
Letterkenny Rep. of Ire. 13 54.56N 7.45W
Leuk Switz. 15 46.19N 7.38E
Leuser mtn. Indonesia 36 3.50N 97.10E
Leuven Belgium 14 50.53N 4.45E
Leuze Hainaut Belgium 14 50.36N 3.37E
Leuze Namur Belgium 14 50.34N 4.53E
Levanger Norway 22 63.45N 11.19E
Levanto Italy 15 44.10N 9.38E
Levelland U.S.A. 83 33.35N102.23W
Lévêque, C. Australia 62 16.25S123.00E
Le Verdon France 17 45.33N 1.04W
Leverkusen Germany 14 51.02N 6.59E
Levice Czech. 21 48.13N 18.37E
Levin New Zealand 60 40.37S175.18E
Lévis Canada 77 46.49N 71.11W
Lévka Cyprus 44 35.06N 32.51E
Levkás Greece 19 38.50N 20.41E
Levkás i. Greece 19 38.44N 20.37E
Levkosía Cyprus 44 35.11N 33.23E
Lewes U.K. 11 50.53N 0.02E
Lewes U.S.A. 85 38.47N 75.08W
Lewis i. U.K. 12 58.10N 6.40W
Lewis Pass f. New Zealand 60 42.30S172.15E
Lewisporte Canada 77 49.15N 55.04W
Lewis Range mts. U.S.A. 80 48.30N113.15W
Lewiston Idaho U.S.A. 80 46.25N117.01W
Lewiston Maine U.S.A. 84 44.06N 70.13W
Lewistown Mont. U.S.A. 80 47.04N109.26W
Lewistown Penn. U.S.A. 84 40.36N 77.31W
Lexington Ky. U.S.A. 85 38.03N 84.30W
Lexington Miss. U.S.A. 83 33.07N 90.03W
Lexington Nebr. U.S.A. 82 40.47N 99.45W
Lexington Oreg. U.S.A. 80 45.27N119.41W
Leyburn U.K. 10 54.19N 1.50W
Leydsdorp R.S.A. 56 23.59S 30.32E
Leyte i. Phil. 37 10.40N124.50E
Lezignan France 17 43.12N 2.46E
Lhari China 41 30.47N 93.24E
Lhasa China 41 29.39N 91.06E
Lhasa He r. China 41 29.21N 90.45E
Lhazê China 41 29.10N 87.45E
Lhazhong China 41 32.02N 86.34E
Lhokseumawe Indonesia 36 5.09N 97.09E
Lhozhag China 41 28.23N 90.49E
Lhuntsi Dzong Bhutan 41 27.39N 91.09E
Lhünzê China 41 28.26N 92.27E
Lhünzhub China 41 30.00N 91.12E
Li Thailand 34 17.50N 98.55E
Liancheng China 33 25.47N116.48E
Liangcheng China 32 40.31N112.29E
Liangdang China 32 33.59N106.23E
Lianjiang Fujian China 33 26.10N119.33E
Lianjiang Guangdong China 33 21.33N110.19E
Lianshan China 33 24.37N112.02E
Lianshui China 32 33.46N119.18E
Lian Xian China 33 24.52N112.27E
Lianyungang China 32 34.36N119.10E
Liaocheng China 32 36.25N115.58E
Liaodong Bandao pen. China 32 40.00N122.20E
Liaodong Wan b. China 32 40.00N121.00E
Liao He r. China 32 40.40N122.20E
Liaoning d. China 32 41.40N121.20E
Liaoyang China 32 41.17N123.13E
Liaoyuan China 32 42.50N125.08E
Liard r. Canada 74 61.51N121.18W
Liāri Pakistan 40 25.41N 66.29E
Liart France 15 49.46N 4.20E
Libby U.S.A. 80 48.23N115.33W
Libenge Zaïre 54 3.39N 18.39E
Liberal U.S.A. 83 37.02N100.55W
Liberdade Brazil 94 22.01S 44.22W
Liberec Czech. 20 50.48N 15.05E
Liberia Africa 52 6.30N 9.30W
Liberia Costa Rica 87 10.39N 85.28W
Liberty Tex. U.S.A. 83 30.03N 94.47W
Lībīyah, Aş Şahrā' al des. Africa 42 24.00N 25.30E
Libo China 33 25.25N107.53E
Libourne France 17 44.55N 0.14W
Libramont Belgium 14 49.56N 5.22E
Libreville Gabon 54 0.25N 9.30E
Libya Africa 51 26.30N 17.00E
Libyan Desert see Lībīyah, Aş Şahrā' al a-' al Africa 42

Libyan Plateau see Ad Diffah f. Africa 42
Licantén Chile 93 34.59S 72.00W
Licata Italy 18 37.07N 13.58E
Lichfield U.K. 11 52.40N 1.50W
Lichinga Mozambique 55 13.09S 35.17E
Lichtenburg R.S.A. 56 26.08S 26.09E
Lichtenvoorde Neth. 14 51.59N 6.32E
Lichuan Hubei China 33 30.18N108.51E
Lichuan Jiangxi China 33 27.22N116.59E
Lida U.S.A. 80 37.29N117.29W
Lida U.S.S.R. 21 53.50N 25.19E
Lidköping Sweden 23 58.30N 13.10E
Liechtenstein Europe 20 47.08N 9.35E
Liège Belgium 14 50.38N 5.35E
Liège d. Belgium 14 50.32N 5.35E
Lien-Huong Vietnam 34 11.13N108.48E
Lienz Austria 20 46.50N 12.47E
Liepāja U.S.S.R. 23 56.31N 21.01E
Lier Belgium 14 51.08N 4.35E
Lierneux Belgium 14 50.18N 5.50E
Liești Romania 21 45.38N 27.32E
Liévin France 14 50.27N 2.49E
Lièvre, Rivière du r. Canada 77 45.31N 75.26W
Liffey r. Rep. of Ire. 13 53.21N 6.14W
Liffré France 15 48.13N 1.30W
Lifou, Île i. N. Cal. 68 20.53S167.13E
Lightning Ridge town Australia 67 29.27S148.00E
Liguria d. Italy 15 42.25N 8.40E
Ligurian Sea Med. Sea 18 43.30N 9.00E
Lihou Reef and Cays Australia 64 17.25S151.40E
Lihue Hawaiian Is. 69 21.59N159.23W
Lihula U.S.S.R. 23 58.41N 23.50E
Lijiang China 39 26.50N100.15E
Lijin China 32 37.29N118.16E
Likasi Zaïre 54 10.58S 26.50E
Likati Zaïre 54 3.21N 23.53E
Likona r. Congo 54 0.11N 16.25E
Likouala r. Congo 54 0.51S 17.17E
Liku Niue 68 19.03S169.48W
Lille France 14 50.39N 3.05E
Lille Baelt str. Denmark 23 55.20N 9.45E
Lillebonne France 15 49.31N 0.33E
Lillehammer Norway 23 61.08N 10.30E
Lillers France 14 50.34N 2.29E
Lillesand Norway 23 58.15N 8.24E
Lilleström Norway 23 59.57N 11.05E
Lillhärdal Sweden 23 61.51N 14.04E
Lillooet Canada 74 50.42N121.56W
Lillooet r. Canada 74 49.15N121.57W
Lilongwe Malaŵi 55 13.58S 33.49E
Liloy Phil. 37 8.08N122.40E
Lilydale Australia 66 32.58S139.59E
Lim r. Yugo. 19 43.45N 19.13E
Lima Peru 90 12.06S 77.03W
Lima r. Portugal 16 41.40N 8.50W
Lima Sweden 23 60.56N 13.26E
Lima Mont. U.S.A. 80 44.38N112.36W
Lima Ohio U.S.A. 84 40.43N 84.06W
Limassol see Lemesós Cyprus 44
Limavady U.K. 13 55.03N 6.57W
Limay r. Argentina 93 39.02S 68.07W
Limbang Malaysia 36 4.50N115.00E
Limbdi India 40 22.34N 71.48E
Limbe Cameroon 53 4.01N 9.12E
Limbourg Belgium 14 50.36N 5.57E
Limburg d. Belgium 14 50.36N 5.57E
Limburg d. Neth. 14 51.15N 5.45E
Limeira Brazil 94 22.34S 47.25W
Limerick Rep. of Ire. 13 52.40N 8.37W
Limerick d. Rep. of Ire. 13 52.40N 8.37W
Limfjorden str. Denmark 23 56.55N 9.10E
Liminka Finland 22 64.49N 25.24E
Limmen Bight Australia 64 14.45S135.40E
Límnos i. Greece 19 39.55N 25.14E
Limoges France 17 45.50N 1.15E
Limogne France 17 44.24N 1.46E
Limón Costa Rica 87 10.00N 83.01W
Limon U.S.A. 80 39.16N103.41W
Limone Piemonte Italy 15 44.12N 7.34E
Limousin d. France 17 45.45N 1.30E
Limpopo r. Mozambique 57 25.14S 33.33E
Linah Saudi Arabia 43 28.48N 43.45E
Linakhamari U.S.S.R. 24 69.39N 31.21E
Linares Chile 93 35.51S 71.36W
Linares Mexico 83 24.52N 99.34W
Linares Spain 16 38.05N 3.38W
Lincang China 30 24.00N100.10E
Lincheng China 32 37.26N114.34E
Lincoln Argentina 93 34.55S 61.30W
Lincoln New Zealand 60 43.38S172.29E
Lincoln U.K. 10 53.14N 0.32W
Lincoln Ill. U.S.A. 82 40.10N 89.21W
Lincoln Nebr. U.S.A. 82 40.48N 96.42W
Lincoln N.H. U.S.A. 84 44.03N 71.40W
Lincoln City U.S.A. 80 44.59N124.00W
Lincoln Sea Greenland 96 82.00N 55.00W
Lincolnshire d. U.K. 10 53.14N 0.32W
Lincoln Wolds hills U.K. 10 53.22N 0.08W
Lindeman Group is. Australia 64 20.28S149.05E
Linden Ala. U.S.A. 83 32.18N 87.47W
Lindesnes c. Norway 23 58.00N 7.02E
Líndhos Greece 19 36.05N 28.02E
Lindi Tanzania 55 10.00S 39.41E
Lindi r. Zaïre 54 0.30N 25.06E
Lindsay Canada 76 44.21N 78.44W
Lindsay U.S.A. 81 36.12N119.05W
Line Is. Pacific Oc. 69 3.00S155.00W
Linfen China 32 36.07N111.34E
Lingao China 33 19.54N109.40E
Lingayen Phil. 37 16.02N120.14E
Lingbo Sweden 23 61.03N 16.41E
Lingchuan China 33 25.25N110.20E
Lingen Germany 14 52.32N 7.19E
Lingga i. Indonesia 36 0.20S104.30E

Lingling China 33 26.12N111.30E
Lingshan China 33 22.17N109.27E
Lingshui China 33 18.31N110.00E
Linguère Senegal 52 15.22N 15.11W
Linhai China 33 28.49N121.08E
Linhe China 32 40.50N107.30E
Linköping Sweden 23 58.25N 15.37E
Linnhe, Loch U.K. 12 56.35N 5.25W
Linosa i. Italy 18 35.52N 12.50E
Linquan China 32 33.03N115.17E
Linru China 32 34.12N112.45E
Lins Brazil 94 21.40S 49.44W
Linshui China 33 30.18N106.55E
Lintan China 32 34.33N103.40E
Lintao China 32 35.20N104.00E
Linton Ind. U.S.A. 84 39.01N 87.10W
Linton N.Dak. U.S.A. 82 46.16N100.14W
Lintong China 32 34.24N109.13E
Lintorf Germany 14 51.19N 6.50E
Linxe France 17 43.56N 1.10W
Linxi China 32 43.31N118.02E
Linxia China 32 35.30N103.10E
Lin Xian China 32 37.57N110.57E
Linyi Shandong China 32 35.08N118.20E
Linyi Shanxi China 32 35.12N110.45E
Linz Austria 20 48.19N 14.18E
Linz Germany 14 50.34N 7.19E
Lion, Golfe du g. France 17 43.12N 4.15E
Lions, G. of see Lion, Golfe du g. France 17
Liouesso Congo 54 1.12N 15.47E
Lipéité Congo 54 3.09N 17.22E
Lipetsk U.S.S.R. 24 52.37N 39.36E
Liphook U.K. 11 51.05N 0.49W
Liping China 33 26.16N109.08E
Lipkany U.S.S.R. 21 48.18N 26.48E
Lipova Romania 21 46.05N 21.40E
Lipovets U.S.S.R. 21 49.11N 29.01E
Lippe r. Germany 14 51.38N 6.37E
Lippstadt Germany 20 51.41N 8.20E
Liptovský Mikuláš Czech. 21 49.06N 19.37E
Liptrap, C. Australia 67 38.53S145.55E
Lipu China 33 24.28N110.12E
Lira Uganda 55 2.15N 32.55E
Liranga Congo 54 0.43S 17.32E
Liri r. Italy 18 41.12N 13.45E
Liria Spain 16 39.37N 0.35W
Liria Sudan 49 4.38N 32.05E
Lisala Zaïre 54 2.13N 21.37E
Lisboa Portugal 16 38.44N 9.08W
Lisbon see Lisboa Portugal 16
Lisbon N.Dak. U.S.A. 82 46.27N 97.41W
Lisburn U.K. 13 54.30N 6.03W
Lisburne, C. U.S.A. 72 69.00N165.50W
Liscannor B. Rep. of Ire. 13 52.55N 9.24W
Lishi China 32 37.30N111.07E
Lishui China 33 28.28N119.59E
Lisianski i. Hawaiian Is. 68 26.04N173.58W
Lisichansk U.S.S.R. 25 48.53N 38.25E
Lisieux France 15 49.09N 0.14E
Liskeard U.K. 11 50.27N 4.29W
Lismore N.S.W. Australia 67 28.48S153.17E
Lismore Vic. Australia 66 37.58S143.22E
Lismore Rep. of Ire. 13 52.08N 7.57W
Liss U.K. 11 51.03N 0.53W
Lisse Neth. 14 52.18N 4.33E
Listowel Rep. of Ire. 13 52.27N 9.30W
Litang China 33 23.09N109.09E
Litang Qu r. China 39 28.09N101.30E
Litchfield Ill. U.S.A. 82 39.11N 89.40W
Litchfield Minn. U.S.A. 82 45.08N 94.31W
Litchfield Nebr. U.S.A. 82 41.09N 99.09W
Lithgow Australia 67 33.30S150.09E
Lititz U.S.A. 85 40.09N 76.18W
Litovskaya S.S.R. d. U.S.S.R. 21 54.30N 24.00E
Little Andaman i. India 34 10.40N 92.24E
Little Belt Mts. U.S.A. 80 46.45N110.35W
Little Cayman i. Cayman Is. 87 19.40N 80.00W
Little Coco i. Burma 34 13.59N 93.12E
Little Colorado r. U.S.A. 81 36.11N111.48W
Little Current r. Canada 76 50.00N 84.35W
Little Current town Canada 84 45.58N 81.56W
Little Falls town Minn. U.S.A. 82 45.59N 94.21W
Little Falls town N.Y. U.S.A. 84 43.03N 74.52W
Littlefield U.S.A. 83 33.55N102.20W
Littlefork U.S.A. 82 48.24N 93.33W
Little Grand Rapids town Canada 75 52.05N 95.29W
Littlehampton U.K. 11 50.48N 0.32W
Little Inagua i. Bahamas 87 21.30N 73.00W
Little Karoo f. R.S.A. 56 33.40S 21.40E
Little Lake town U.S.A. 81 35.58N117.53W
Little Mecatina r. Canada 77 50.28N 59.35W
Little Missouri r. U.S.A. 82 47.30N102.25W
Little Nicobar i. India 39 7.20N 93.40E
Little Ouse r. U.K. 11 52.34N 0.20E
Little Quill L. Canada 75 51.55N104.05W
Little Rann of Kachchh f. India 40 23.25N 71.30E
Little Rock town U.S.A. 83 34.44N 92.15W
Little Smoky r. Canada 74 55.42N117.38W
Littleton Colo. U.S.A. 80 39.37N105.01W
Little Topar Australia 66 31.44S142.14E
Liuba China 32 33.37N106.55E
Liucheng China 33 24.39N109.14E
Liuchong He r. China 33 26.50N106.04E
Liuli Tanzania 55 11.07S 34.34E
Liulin China 32 37.26N110.52E
Liuzhou China 33 24.19N109.12E
Livarot France 15 49.01N 0.09E
Live Oak U.S.A. 85 30.19N 82.59W
Livermore, Mt. U.S.A. 81 30.39N104.11W
Liverpool Australia 67 33.57S150.52E
Liverpool Canada 77 44.02N 64.43W
Liverpool U.K. 10 53.25N 3.00W
Liverpool, C. Canada 73 73.38N 78.06W
Liverpool B. U.K. 10 53.30N 3.10W
Liverpool Range mts. Australia 67 31.45S150.45E
Livingston U.K. 12 55.54N 3.31W
Livingston Mont. U.S.A. 80 45.40N110.34W
Livingston Tex. U.S.A. 83 30.43N 94.56W
Livingstone see Maramba Zambia 56
Livingstonia Malaŵi 55 10.35S 34.10E
Livo r. Finland 22 65.24N 26.48E
Livorno Italy 18 43.33N 10.18E
Liwale Tanzania 55 9.47S 38.00E
Liwan Sudan 49 4.55N 35.41E
Li Xian Gansu China 32 34.11N105.02E
Li Xian Hunan China 33 29.38N111.45E
Liyujiang China 33 25.59N113.12E
Lizard U.K. 11 49.58N 5.12W
Lizard I. Australia 64 14.39S145.28E
Lizard Pt. U.K. 11 49.57N 5.15W
Ljubljana Yugo. 18 46.04N 14.28E
Ljugarn Sweden 23 57.19N 18.42E
Ljungan r. Sweden 23 62.19N 17.23E
Ljungby Sweden 23 56.50N 13.56E
Ljungdalen Sweden 22 62.54N 12.45E
Ljusdal Sweden 23 61.50N 16.05E
Ljusnan r. Sweden 23 61.12N 17.08E
Ljusne Sweden 23 61.13N 17.08E
Llandeilo U.K. 11 51.54N 4.00W
Llandovery U.K. 11 51.59N 3.49W
Llandrindod Wells U.K. 11 52.15N 3.23W
Llandudno U.K. 10 53.19N 3.49W
Llanelli U.K. 11 51.41N 4.11W
Llanes Spain 16 43.25N 4.45W
Llangadfan U.K. 11 52.41N 3.28W
Llangollen U.K. 10 52.58N 3.10W
Llanidloes U.K. 11 52.28N 3.31W
Llanos f. S. America 90 7.30N 70.00W
Llanwrtyd Wells U.K. 11 52.06N 3.39W
Lleida Spain 16 41.37N 0.38E
Llerena Spain 16 38.14N 6.00W
Lloret de Mar Spain 16 41.41N 2.53E
Lloret de Mar Spain 16 41.41N 2.53E
Lloydminster Canada 75 53.17N110.00W
Loange r. Zaïre 54 4.18S 20.05E
Lobatse Botswana 56 25.12S 25.39E
Löbau Germany 20 51.05N 14.40E
Lobaye r. C.A.R. 53 3.40N 18.35E
Lobería Argentina 93 38.08S 58.48W
Lobito Angola 54 12.20S 13.34E
Lobonäs Sweden 23 61.33N 15.20E
Lobos Argentina 93 35.10S 59.05W
Locarno Switz. 20 46.10N 8.48E
Lochboisdale town U.K. 12 57.09N 7.19W
Lochem Neth. 14 52.10N 6.25E
Loches France 17 47.08N 1.00E
Lochgilphead U.K. 12 56.02N 5.26W
Lochinver U.K. 12 58.09N 5.15W
Lochmaddy town U.K. 12 57.36N 7.10W
Lochnagar mtn. U.K. 12 56.57N 3.15W
Lochranza U.K. 12 55.42N 5.18W
Loch Raven Resr. U.S.A. 85 39.27N 76.36W
Lochy, Loch U.K. 12 56.58N 4.55W
Lock Australia 66 33.34S135.46E
Lockeport Canada 77 43.42N 65.07W
Lockerbie U.K. 12 55.07N 3.21W
Lockhart Australia 67 35.16S146.42E
Lockhart U.S.A. 83 29.53N 97.41W
Lockhart, L. Australia 63 33.27S119.00E
Lockhart River town Australia 64 12.58S143.29E
Lock Haven U.S.A. 84 41.08N 77.27W
Lockport U.S.A. 84 43.11N 78.39W
Loc Ninh Vietnam 34 11.51N106.35E
Lodalskåpa mtn. Norway 23 61.47N 7.13E
Loddon r. Australia 66 35.40S143.59E
Lodeynoye Pole U.S.S.R. 24 60.43N 33.30E
Lodge Grass U.S.A. 80 45.19N107.22W
Lodhrān Pakistan 40 29.32N 71.38E
Lodi Italy 15 45.19N 9.30E
Lodi Calif. U.S.A. 80 38.08N121.16W
Lodja Zaïre 54 3.29S 23.33E
Lodwar Kenya 55 3.06N 35.38E
Łódź Poland 21 51.49N 19.28E
Loei Thailand 34 17.32N101.34E
Lofoten Vesterålen is. Norway 22 68.15N 13.50E
Log U.S.S.R. 25 49.28N 43.51E
Loga Niger 53 13.40N 3.15E
Logan N.Mex. U.S.A. 81 35.22N103.25W
Logan Utah U.S.A. 80 41.44N111.50W
Logan, Mt. Canada 74 60.34N140.24W
Logansport U.S.A. 84 40.45N 86.25W
Loge r. Angola 54 7.52S 13.08E
Logone r. Cameroon/Chad 53 12.10N 15.00E
Logone Occidental d. Chad 53 8.40N 15.50E
Logone Oriental d. Chad 53 8.10N 16.00E
Logoysk U.S.S.R. 21 54.08N 27.42E
Logroño Spain 16 42.28N 2.26W
Lögstör Denmark 23 56.58N 9.15E
Lohārdaga India 41 23.26N 84.41E
Lohāru India 40 28.27N 75.49E
Lohja Finland 23 60.15N 24.05E
Lohjanjärvi l. Finland 23 60.15N 23.55E
Loikaw Burma 34 19.40N 97.17E
Loimaa Finland 23 60.51N 23.03E
Loir r. France 15 47.29N 0.32W
Loire r. France 15 47.18N 2.00W
Loiret d. France 15 47.55N 2.20E
Loir-et-Cher d. France 15 47.30N 1.30E
Loja Ecuador 90 3.59S 79.16W
Loja Spain 16 37.10N 4.09W
Loka Sudan 49 4.16N 31.01E
Loka Zaïre 54 0.20N 17.57E
Löken Norway 23 59.48N 11.29E
Loken tekojärvi resr. Finland 22 67.55N 27.40E
Lokeren Belgium 14 51.06N 3.59E
Lokichar Kenya 55 2.23N 35.39E
Lokitaung Kenya 55 4.15N 35.45E
Lokka Finland 22 67.49N 27.44E
Lökken Denmark 23 57.22N 9.43E
Lökken Norway 22 63.06N 9.43E
Loknya U.S.S.R. 24 56.49N 30.00E
Lokoja Nigeria 53 7.49N 6.44E
Lokolo r. Zaïre 54 0.45S 19.36E
Lokoro r. Zaïre 54 1.40S 18.29E
Lol r. Sudan 49 9.11N 29.12E
Lolland i. Denmark 23 54.46N 11.30E
Lom Bulgaria 21 43.49N 23.13E
Lom Norway 23 61.50N 8.33E
Loma U.S.A. 80 47.57N110.30W
Lomami r. Zaïre 54 0.45N 24.10E
Lomas de Zamora Argentina 93 34.46S 58.24W
Lombardia d. Italy 15 45.25N 10.00E
Lombok i. Indonesia 36 8.30S116.20E
Lombok, Selat str. Indonesia 37 8.38S115.40E
Lomé Togo 53 6.10N 1.21E
Lomela Zaïre 54 2.15S 23.15E
Lomela r. Zaïre 54 0.14S 20.45E
Lomié Cameroon 53 3.09N 13.35E
Lomme France 14 50.38N 2.59E
Lommel Belgium 14 51.15N 5.18E
Lomond Canada 74 50.21N112.39W
Lomond, Loch U.K. 12 56.07N 4.36W
Lompoc U.S.A. 81 34.38N120.27W
Łomża Poland 21 53.11N 22.04E
Londinières France 15 49.50N 1.24E
London Canada 76 42.58N 81.15W
London Kiribati 69 1.58N157.28W
London U.K. 11 51.32N 0.06W
Londonderry U.K. 13 55.00N 7.21W
Londonderry d. U.K. 13 55.00N 7.00W
Londonderry, C. Australia 62 13.58S126.55E
Londonderry, Isla i. Chile 93 55.03S 70.40W
Londrina Brazil 92 23.30S 51.13W
Lone Pine U.S.A. 81 36.36N118.04W
Longa r. Angola 54 16.15S 19.07E
Longa, Proliv str. U.S.S.R. 29 70.00N178.00E
Long'an China 33 23.11N107.41E
Longarone Italy 15 46.16N 12.18E
Long Beach town Calif. U.S.A. 81 33.46N118.11W
Long Beach town N.Y. U.S.A. 85 40.35N 73.41W
Long Branch U.S.A. 85 40.18N 74.00W
Longchamps Belgium 14 50.05N 5.42E
Longchang China 33 29.18N105.20E
Longchuan China 33 24.12N115.25E
Long Creek town U.S.A. 80 44.43N119.06W
Long Eaton U.K. 10 52.54N 1.16W
Longford Rep. of Ire. 13 53.44N 7.48W
Longford d. Rep. of Ire. 13 53.42N 7.45W
Longhua Hebei China 32 41.17N117.37E
Long I. Bahamas 87 23.00N 75.00W
Long I. Canada 76 54.55N 79.30W
Long I. U.S.A. 84 40.46N 73.00W
Longido Tanzania 55 2.43S 36.41E
Longiram Indonesia 36 0.05S115.45E
Long Jiang r. China 33 24.12N109.30E
Long L. Canada 76 49.30N 86.50W
Longlac town Canada 76 49.45N 86.25W
Longli China 33 26.29N107.59E
Longlin China 33 24.43N105.26E
Longmont U.S.A. 80 40.10N105.06W
Longnan China 33 24.54N114.47E
Longnawan Indonesia 36 1.54N114.53E
Longniddry U.K. 12 55.58N 2.53W
Long Point B. Canada 76 42.40N 80.14W
Long Pt. Canada 76 42.33N 80.04W
Longquan China 33 28.05N119.07E
Long Range Mts. Nfld. Canada 77 50.00N 57.00W
Long Range Mts. Nfld. Canada 77 48.00N 58.30W
Longreach Australia 64 23.26S144.15E
Longsheng China 33 25.59N110.01E
Longs Peak U.S.A. 80 40.15N105.37W
Longtown U.K. 10 55.01N 2.58W
Longué France 15 47.23N 0.06W
Longueuil Canada 77 45.32N 73.30W
Longuyon France 14 49.27N 5.35E
Longview Tex. U.S.A. 83 32.30N 94.44W
Longview Wash. U.S.A. 80 46.08N122.57W
Longwood St. Helena 95 15.57S 5.42W
Longwy France 14 49.32N 5.46E
Longxi China 32 34.59N104.45E
Long Xian China 32 34.52N106.50E
Long Xuyen Vietnam 34 10.23N105.23E
Longyan China 33 25.10N117.02E
Longzhou China 33 22.24N106.50E
Lonigo Italy 15 45.23N 11.23E
Löningen Germany 14 52.44N 7.46E
Lönsdal Norway 22 66.46N 15.26E
Lonsdale, L. Australia 66 37.05S142.15E
Lons-le-Saunier France 17 46.40N 5.33E
Looc Phil. 37 12.20N122.05E
Looe U.K. 11 50.51N 4.26W
Lookout, C. U.S.A. 85 34.35N 76.32W
Loolmalassin mtn. Tanzania 55 3.00S 35.45E
Loop Head Rep. of Ire. 13 52.33N 9.56W
Lopari Zaïre 49 1.15N 19.59E
Lopari r. Zaïre 54 1.20N 20.22E
Lop Buri Thailand 34 14.49N100.37E
Lopez, C. Gabon 54 0.36S 8.40E
Lopi Congo 54 2.57N 16.47E
Lop Nur l. China 30 40.30N 90.30E
Lopphavet est. Norway 22 70.30N 20.00E
Lopydino U.S.S.R. 24 61.10N 52.02E
Lora, Hāmūn-i- l. Pakistan 40 29.20N 64.50E
Lora Creek r. Australia 66 28.10S135.22E
Lorain U.S.A. 84 41.28N 82.11W
Loralai Pakistan 40 30.22N 68.36E
Lorca Spain 16 37.40N 1.41W
Lord Howe I. Pacific Oc. 68 31.28S159.09E
Lord Howe Rise Pacific Oc. 68 29.00S162.30E
Lordsburg U.S.A. 81 32.21N108.43W
Lorena Brazil 94 22.44S 45.07W
Lorengau P.N.G. 37 2.01S147.15E
Lorenzo Geyres Uruguay 93 32.05S 57.55W
Loreto Brazil 91 7.05S 45.09W
Loreto Italy 18 43.26N 13.36E
Loreto Mexico 81 26.01N111.21W
Lorian Swamp Kenya 55 0.35N 39.40E
Lorient France 17 47.45N 3.21W
Lormes France 15 47.17N 3.49E
Lorne Australia 66 38.34S144.01E
Lorraine d. France 17 49.00N 6.20E
Lorris France 15 47.53N 2.31E
Lorup Germany 14 52.58N 7.39E
Los Alamos Mexico 83 28.40N103.30W
Los Alamos U.S.A. 81 35.53N106.19W
Los Andes Chile 93 32.50S 70.37W
Los Angeles Chile 93 37.28S 72.21W
Los Angeles U.S.A. 78 34.00N118.17W
Los Bajios Mexico 81 28.31N108.25W
Los Banos U.S.A. 80 37.04N120.51W
Los Blancos Argentina 92 23.40S 62.35W
Los Blancos Spain 16 37.37N 0.48W
Los Canarreos, Archipiélago de Cuba 87 21.40N 82.30W
Los Herreras Mexico 83 25.55N 99.24W
Lošinj i. Yugo. 18 44.36N 14.20E
Losinovka U.S.S.R. 21 50.50N 31.57E
Los Llanos de Aridane Canary Is. 95 28.39N 17.54W
Los Lunas U.S.A. 81 34.48N106.44W
Los Mochis Mexico 86 25.45N108.57W
Los Olivos U.S.A. 81 34.40N120.06W
Los Roques is. Venezuela 90 12.00N 67.00W
Lossiemouth U.K. 12 57.43N 3.18W
Lost Cabin U.S.A. 80 43.19N107.36W
Los Teques Venezuela 90 10.25N 67.01W
Los Vilos Chile 92 31.55S 71.31W
Lot r. France 17 44.17N 0.22E
Lota Chile 93 37.05S 73.10W
Lothian d. U.K. 12 55.50N 3.00W
Lotoi r. Zaïre 54 1.30S 18.30E
Lotsani r. Botswana 56 22.42S 28.11E
Lötschberg Tunnel Switz. 17 46.25N 7.53E
Lotuke mtn. Sudan 49 4.07N 33.48E
Louang Namtha Laos 34 20.57N101.25E
Louangphrabang Laos 34 19.53N102.10E
Loubomo Congo 54 4.09S 12.40E
Loudéac France 17 48.11N 2.45W
Loudima Congo 54 4.06S 13.05E
Loué France 15 48.00N 0.09W
Louga Senegal 52 15.37N 16.13W
Loughborough U.K. 10 52.47N 1.11W
Loughrea Rep. of Ire. 13 53.12N 8.35W
Loughros More B. Rep. of Ire. 13 54.48N 8.32W
Louisburgh Rep. of Ire. 13 53.46N 9.49W
Louiseville Canada 77 46.14N 72.56W
Louisiade Archipelago is. P.N.G. 64 11.00S153.00E
Louisiana d. U.S.A. 83 30.60N 92.30W
Louis Trichardt R.S.A. 56 23.03S 29.54E
Louisville Ky. U.S.A. 84 38.13N 85.48W
Louisville Miss. U.S.A. 83 33.07N 89.03W
Louis XIV, Pointe c. Canada 76 54.35N 79.50W
Loukhi U.S.S.R. 24 66.05N 33.04E
Loukouo Congo 54 3.38S 14.39E
Loulé Portugal 16 37.08N 8.02W
Loum Cameroon 53 4.46N 9.45E
Lourches France 14 50.19N 3.20E
Lourdes France 17 43.06N 0.02W
Louth Australia 67 30.34S145.09E
Louth d. Rep. of Ire. 13 53.55N 6.30W
Louth U.K. 10 53.23N 0.00
Louviers France 15 49.13N 1.10E
Louvigné-du-Désert France 15 48.29N 1.08W
Lövånger Sweden 22 64.22N 21.18E
Lovat r. U.S.S.R. 24 58.06N 31.37E
Lovech Bulgaria 19 43.08N 24.44E
Loveland U.S.A. 80 40.24N105.05W
Lovell U.S.A. 80 44.50N108.24W
Lovelock U.S.A. 80 40.11N118.28W
Love Point town U.S.A. 85 39.02N 76.18W
Lovere Italy 15 45.49N 10.04E
Lovington U.S.A. 83 32.57N103.21W
Lovoi r. Zaïre 55 8.14S 26.40E
Lovozero U.S.S.R. 24 68.01N 35.08E
Lovrin Romania 21 45.58N 20.48E
Lovua r. Zaïre 54 6.08S 20.35E
Lowa Zaïre 54 1.24S 25.51E
Lowa r. Kivu Zaïre 54 1.25S 25.55E
Lowell U.S.A. 84 42.39N 71.18W
Lower Arrow L. Canada 74 49.40N118.05W
Lower California pen. see Baja California pen. Mexico 86
Lower Egypt see Mişr Baḩrī f. Egypt 44
Lower Hutt New Zealand 60 41.13S174.55E
Lower Lough Erne U.K. 13 54.28N 7.48W
Lower Post Canada 74 59.55N128.30W
Lower Red L. U.S.A. 82 48.00N 94.50W
Lowestoft U.K. 11 52.29N 1.44E
Lowgar d. Afghan. 40 34.10N 69.20E
Łowicz Poland 21 52.06N 19.55E
Lowrah r. Afghan. see Pishīn Lora r. Pakistan 40
Loxton Australia 66 34.38S140.38E
Loyalty Is. see Loyauté, Îles is. N. Cal. 68
Loyauté, Îles is. N. Cal. 68 21.00S167.00E
Loyoro Uganda 55 3.22N 34.16E
Loznica Yugo. 19 44.32N 19.13E
Lua r. Zaïre 54 2.45N 18.28E
Luabo Mozambique 57 18.30S 36.10E
Luachimo Angola 54 7.25S 20.43E
Lualaba r. Zaïre 54 0.18N 25.32E
Luama r. Zaïre 55 4.45S 26.55E
Luampa Zambia 54 15.04S 24.20E
Lu'an China 33 31.47N116.30E
Luancheng Guang. Zhuang. China 33 22.48N108.55E
Luancheng Hebei China 32 37.53N114.39E
Luanda Angola 54 8.50S 13.20E
Luanda d. Angola 54 9.00S 13.20E
Luando Game Res. Angola 54 11.00S 17.4
Luanginga r. Zambia 54 15.11S 23.05E
Luangwa r. Central Zambia 55 15.32S 30.2
Luan He r. China 32 39.25N119.10E
Luanping China 32 40.55N117.17E
Luanshya Zambia 55 13.09S 28.24E
Luan Xian China 32 39.45N118.44E
Luapula r. Zambia 55 9.25S 28.36E
Luarca Spain 16 43.33N 6.31W
Luau Angola 54 10.41S 22.09E
Lubalo Angola 54 9.13S 19.21E
Lubango Angola 54 14.52S 13.30E
Lubao Zaïre 54 5.19S 25.43E
Lubbock U.S.A. 83 33.35N101.51W
Lubeck Australia 66 36.47S142.38E
Lübeck Germany 20 53.52N 10.40E
Lubefu r. Zaïre 54 4.05S 23.00E
Lubenka U.S.S.R. 25 50.22N 54.13E
Lubersac France 17 45.27N 1.24E
Lubia Angola 54 11.01S 17.06E
Lubika Zaïre 55 7.50S 29.12E
Lubilash r. Zaïre 54 4.59S 23.25E
Lubin Poland 20 51.24N 16.13E
Lublin Poland 21 51.18N 22.31E
Lubliniec Poland 21 50.40N 18.41E
Lubny U.S.S.R. 25 50.01N 33.00E
Lubudi Zaïre 54 9.57S 25.59E
Lubudi r. K.Occidental Zaïre 54 4.00S 21.2
Lubudi r. Shaba Zaïre 54 9.13S 25.40E
Lubumbashi Zaïre 55 11.44S 27.29E
Lubutu Zaïre 54 0.48S 26.19E
Lucas González Argentina 93 32.25S 59.3
Lucca Italy 15 43.50N 10.29E
Luce B. U.K. 12 54.45N 4.47W
Lucena Phil. 37 13.56N121.37E
Lucena Spain 16 37.25N 4.29W
Lucena del Cid Spain 16 40.09N 0.17W
Lučenec Czech. 21 48.20N 19.40E
Lucera Italy 18 41.30N 15.20E
Lucerne U.S.A. 80 48.12N120.36W
Lucero Mexico 81 30.49N106.30W
Lucin U.S.A. 80 41.22N113.55W
Lucindale Australia 66 36.59S140.25E
Lucira Angola 54 13.51S 12.31E
Luckeesarai India 41 25.11N 86.05E
Luckenwalde Germany 20 52.05N 13.11E
Lucknow India 41 26.51N 80.55E
Lucy Creek town Australia 64 22.25S136.2
Lüda see Dalian China 32
Lüdenscheid Germany 14 51.13N 7.36E
Lüderitz Namibia 56 26.37S 15.09E
Ludhiāna India 40 30.55N 75.51E
Lüdinghausen Germany 14 51.46N 7.27E
Ludington U.S.A. 84 43.58N 86.27W
Ludlow U.K. 11 52.23N 2.42W
Ludogorie mts. Bulgaria 21 43.45N 27.00E
Luduş Romania 21 46.29N 24.05E
Ludvika Sweden 23 60.09N 15.11E
Ludwigsburg Germany 20 48.53N 9.11E
Ludwigshafen Germany 20 49.29N 8.27E
Luebo Zaïre 54 5.16S 21.27E
Luena Angola 54 11.46S 19.55E
Luena r. Angola 54 12.30S 22.37E
Luena Zaïre 54 9.27S 25.47E
Luena Zambia 55 10.40S 30.21E
Luena r. Western Zambia 54 14.47S 23.05E
Luengue r. Angola 54 16.58S 21.15E
Luenha r. Mozambique 57 16.29S 33.40E
Lüeyang China 32 33.20N106.03E
Lufeng China 33 23.01N115.35E
Lufira r. Zaïre 54 8.15S 26.30E
Lufkin U.S.A. 79 31.21N 94.47W
Luga U.S.S.R. 24 58.42N 29.49E
Lugano Switz. 15 46.01N 8.58E
Lugano, Lago di l. Switz./Italy 15 46.00N 9.00E
Lugansk U.S.S.R. 25 48.35N 39.20E
Luganville Vanuatu 68 15.32S167.08E
Lugela Mozambique 57 16.25S 36.42E
Lugenda r. Mozambique 55 11.23S 38.30E
Luginy U.S.S.R. 21 51.05N 28.21E
Lugnaquilla Mtn. Rep. of Ire. 13 52.58N 6.2
Lugo Italy 15 44.25N 11.54E
Lugo Spain 16 43.00N 7.33W
Lugoj Romania 21 45.42N 21.56E
Luiana Angola 54 17.08S 22.59E
Luiana r. Angola 54 17.28S 23.02E
Luilaka r. Zaïre 54 0.15S 19.00E
Luilu r. Zaïre 54 6.22S 23.53E
Luino Italy 15 46.00N 8.44E
Luiro r. Finland 22 67.18N 27.28E
Luisa Zaïre 54 7.15S 22.27E
Lujiang China 33 31.14N117.17E
Lukala Zaïre 54 5.23S 13.02E
Lukanga Swamp f. Zambia 55 14.15S 27.3
Lukenie r. Zaïre 54 2.43S 18.12E
Lukka Sudan 48 14.33N 23.42E
Łuków Poland 21 51.56N 22.23E
Lukoyanov U.S.S.R. 24 55.03N 44.29E
Lukuga r. Zaïre 55 5.37S 26.58E
Lukula r. Zaïre 54 4.15S 17.59E
Lukulu Zambia 54 14.35S 23.25E
Lukumbule Tanzania 55 11.34S 37.24E
Lule r. Sweden 22 65.35N 22.03E
Luleå Sweden 22 65.34N 22.10E
Lüleburgaz Turkey 19 41.25N 27.23E
Lüliang Shan mts. China 32 37.00N111.20E
Lulonga r. Zaïre 54 0.42N 18.26E
Lulu r. Zaïre 54 1.18N 23.42E
Lulua r. Zaïre 54 5.03S 21.07E
Lumai Angola 54 13.13S 21.13E
Lumajangdong Co l. China 41 34.02N 81.40

Lumbala Kaquengue Angola 54 12.37S 22.33E
Lumbala N'guimbo Angola 54 14.02S 21.35E
Lumberton Miss. U.S.A. 83 31.00N 89.27W
Lumberton N.Mex. U.S.A. 80 36.55N106.56W
Lumsden New Zealand 60 45.44S168.26E
.ūnāvāda India 40 23.08N 73.37E
.und Sweden 23 55.42N 13.11E
.und Nev. U.S.A. 80 38.52N115.00W
.und Utah U.S.A. 80 38.01N113.28W
.unda Norte d. Angola 54 8.30S 19.00E
.unda Sul d. Angola 54 11.00S 20.00E
.undazi Zambia 55 12.19S 33.11E
.undi r. Zimbabwe 57 21.20S 32.23E
.undy i. U.K. 11 51.10N 4.41W
.une r. U.K. 10 54.03N 2.49W
.üneburg Germany 20 53.15N 10.24E
.ünen Germany 14 51.37N 7.31E
unéville France 17 48.36N 6.30E
unga r. Zambia 54 14.28S 26.27E
unge Angola 54 12.13S 16.07E
unggar China 41 31.10N 84.01E
ungwebungu r. Zambia 54 14.20S 23.15E
ūni India 40 26.00N 73.00E
ūni r. India 40 24.41N 71.15E
uninets U.S.S.R. 21 52.18N 26.50E
uning U.S.A. 80 38.30N118.10W
ūnkaransar India 40 28.32N 73.50E
uocheng China 33 24.47N108.54E
uodian China 33 25.29N106.39E
uoding China 33 22.44N111.32E
uofo Zaïre 55 0.12S 29.15E
uogosanto Italy 18 41.02N 9.12E
uohe China 32 33.30N114.04E
uo He r. China 32 34.40N110.15E
uonan China 32 34.06N110.10E
uoyang China 32 34.48N112.25E
upilichi Mozambique 55 11.45S 35.15E
uquan China 39 25.35N102.30E
ūrah r. Afghan. 40 31.20N 65.45E
ure France 17 47.42N 6.30E
urgan U.K. 13 54.28N 6.21W
urio Mozambique 55 13.30S 40.30E
urio r. Mozambique 55 13.32S 40.31E
usaka Zambia 55 15.20S 28.14E
usambo Zaïre 54 4.59S 23.26E
uscar Canada 74 53.05N117.26W
Shan mtn. China 32 36.18N118.03E
ishi China 32 34.04N111.02E
ushnje Albania 19 40.56N 19.42E
ushoto Tanzania 55 4.48S 38.20E
ishun China 32 38.42N121.15E
usk U.S.A. 80 42.46N104.27W
ita see Lüda China 32
ton U.K. 11 51.53N 0.25W
tsk U.S.S.R. 21 50.42N 25.15E
tterworth U.K. 11 52.28N 1.12W
ud r. Somali Rep. 45 10.25N 51.05E
uq Somali Rep. 55 3.56N 42.32E
verne U.S.A. 82 43.39N 96.13W
vua r. Zaïre 55 6.45S 27.00E
wegu r. Tanzania 55 8.30S 37.28E
wingu Zambia 55 10.13S 30.05E
xembourg d. Belgium 14 49.58N 5.30E
xembourg Europe 14 49.50N 6.15E
xembourg town Lux. 14 49.37N 6.08E
xi China 33 28.17N110.10E
xor see Al Uqşur Egypt 42
za U.S.S.R. 24 60.41N 47.12E
za r. U.S.S.R. 24 60.45N 46.25E
zarches France 15 49.07N 2.25E
zern Switz. 20 47.03N 8.17E
zhai China 33 24.29N109.29E
zhou China 33 28.48N105.23E
ziânia Brazil 91 16.18S 47.57W
zon i. Phil. 37 17.50N121.00E
zon Str. Pacific Oc. 37 20.20N122.00E
ov U.S.S.R. 21 49.50N 24.00E
antonde Uganda 55 0.26S 31.08E
bster U.K. 12 58.18N 3.18W
cksele Sweden 22 64.36N 18.40E
denburg R.S.A. 56 25.06S 30.27E
ell I. Canada 74 52.40N131.35W
me B. U.K. 11 50.40N 2.55W
me Regis U.K. 11 50.44N 2.57W
mington U.K. 11 50.46N 1.32W
na r. Poland 21 54.37N 21.14E
nchburg U.S.A. 85 37.24N 79.10W
nden Canada 76 43.14N 80.09W
ndhurst Australia 66 30.19S138.24E
ndonville U.S.A. 76 43.19N 78.23W
ngdal Norway 23 58.08N 7.05E
ngen Norway 22 69.36N 20.10E
ngen est. Norway 22 69.35N 20.20E
nn U.S.A. 84 42.28N 70.57W
nn Canal U.S.A. 74 58.38N135.08W
nn Lake town Canada 75 56.51N101.03W
nton U.K. 11 51.14N 3.50W
nx Canada 76 50.08N 85.55W
on France 17 45.46N 4.50E
ons Australia 66 30.34S133.50E
ons r. Australia 62 25.02S115.09E
sefjorden est. Norway 23 59.00N 6.14E
sekil Sweden 23 58.16N 11.26E
sva U.S.S.R. 24 58.07N 57.49E
syanka U.S.S.R. 21 49.16N 30.49E
syye Gory U.S.S.R. 25 51.32N 44.48E
tham St. Anne's U.K. 10 53.45N 3.01W
ubar U.S.S.R. 21 49.58N 27.41E
ubech U.S.S.R. 21 51.42N 30.41E
ubertsy U.S.S.R. 24 55.38N 37.58E
ubeshov U.S.S.R. 21 51.42N 25.32E
ushcha U.S.S.R. 21 52.28N 26.41E

M

Ma r. Vietnam 33 19.48N105.55E
Ma, Oued el- wadi Mauritania 50 24.30N 9.10W
Maamakeogh mtn. Rep. of Ire. 13 54.17N 9.29W
Maamturk Mts. Rep. of Ire. 13 53.32N 9.42W
Ma'ān Jordan 44 30.11N 35.43E
Ma'anshan China 33 31.47N118.33E
Maarianhamina Finland 23 60.06N 19.57E
Maas r. Neth. 14 51.44N 4.42E
Maaseik Belgium 14 51.08N 5.48E
Maassluis Neth. 14 51.58N 4.12E
Maastricht Neth. 14 50.51N 5.42E
Maave Mozambique 57 21.06S 34.48E
Maaza Plateau Egypt 44 27.39N 31.45E
Mabalane Mozambique 57 23.49S 32.36E
Mablethorpe U.K. 10 53.21N 0.14E
Mabrouk Mali 52 19.29N 1.15W
Macá mtn. Chile 93 45.06S 73.12W
Macaé Brazil 94 22.21S 41.48W
Macalister r. Australia 67 37.55S146.50E
Macapá Brazil 91 0.04N 51.04W
Macarthur Australia 66 38.01S142.01E
Macau Asia 33 22.11N113.33E
Macau Brazil 91 5.05S 36.37W
Macclesfield U.K. 10 53.16N 2.09W
Macdiarmid Canada 76 49.27N 88.08W
Macdoel U.S.A. 80 41.50N122.00W
Macdonald, L. Australia 62 23.30S129.00E
Macdonnell Ranges mts. Australia 64 23.45S133.20E
Macduff U.K. 12 57.40N 2.29W
Macedon, Mt. Australia 67 37.27S144.34E
Macedonia see Makedonija d. Yugo. 19
Maceió Brazil 91 9.40S 35.44W
Macenta Guinea 52 8.31N 9.32W
Macerata Italy 18 43.18N 13.30E
MacFarlane r. Canada 75 59.12N107.58W
Macfarlane, L. Australia 66 31.55S136.42E
Macgillycuddy's Reeks mts. Rep. of Ire. 13 52.00N 9.43W
Machado Brazil 94 21.39S 45.33W
Machala Ecuador 90 3.20S 79.57W
Machattie, L. Australia 64 24.50S139.48E
Machece Mozambique 57 19.17S 35.33E
Macheke Zimbabwe 57 18.08S 31.49E
Macheng China 33 31.11N115.02E
Machevna U.S.S.R. 29 60.46N171.40E
Machias Maine U.S.A. 84 44.43N 67.28W
Machichi r. Canada 75 57.03N 92.06W
Machida Japan 35 35.32N139.27E
Machilīpatnam India 39 16.13N 81.12E
Machiques Venezuela 90 10.04N 72.37W
Machiya r. Japan 35 35.01N136.42E
Machrihanish U.K. 12 55.25N 5.44W
Machynlleth U.K. 11 52.35N 3.51W
Maciá Argentina 93 32.11S 59.25W
Macia Mozambique 57 25.03S 33.10E
Macintyre r. Australia 67 28.50S150.50E
Mackay Australia 64 21.09S149.11E
MacKay U.S.A. 80 43.55N113.37W
Mackay, L. Australia 62 22.30S149.10E
Mackenzie r. Australia 64 22.48S149.15E
Mackenzie r. Canada 72 69.20N134.00W
Mackenzie King I. Canada 72 77.30N112.00W
Mackenzie Mts. Canada 72 64.00N130.00W
Mackinaw City U.S.A. 84 45.47N 84.43W
Mackinnon Road town Kenya 55 3.50S 39.03E
Macklin Canada 75 52.20N109.56W
Macksville Australia 67 30.43S152.55E
Maclean Australia 65 29.27S153.14E
Maclear R.S.A. 56 31.04S 28.21E
Macleay r. Australia 67 30.52S153.01E
MacLeod, L. Australia 62 24.10S113.35E
Maçobere Mozambique 57 21.14S 32.50E
Macomer Italy 18 40.16N 8.45E
Mâcon France 17 46.18N 4.50E
Macon Ga. U.S.A. 85 32.49N 83.37W
Macon Mo. U.S.A. 82 39.44N 92.28W
Macquarie r. Australia 67 30.07S147.24E
Macquarie, L. Australia 67 33.05S151.35E
Macquarie-Balleny Ridge Pacific Oc. 68 58.00S160.00E
Macquarie I. Pacific Oc. 68 54.29S158.58E
Macquarie Marshes Australia 67 30.50S147.32E
MacRobertson Land f. Antarctica 96 69.30S 64.00E
Macroom Rep. of Ire. 13 51.54N 8.58W
Macumba r. Australia 65 27.55S137.15E
Ma'dabā Jordan 44 31.44N 35.48E
Madagascar Africa 57 17.00S 46.00E
Madang P.N.G. 37 5.14S145.45E
Madaoua Niger 53 14.05N 6.27E
Mādārīpur Bangla. 41 23.10N 90.12E
Madawaska U.S.A. 84 47.21N 68.20W
Madeira r. Brazil 90 3.20S 59.00W
Madeira i. Madeira Is. 95 32.45N 17.00W
Madeira, Arquipélago da is. Atlantic Oc. 95 32.45N 17.00W
Madeira Is. see Madeira, Arquipélago da is. Atlantic Oc. 95
Madeleine, Îles de la is. Canada 77 47.20N 61.50W
Madera U.S.A. 80 36.57N120.03W
Madera, Sierra de la mts. Mexico 81 30.20N109.00W
Madgaon India 38 15.26N 73.50E
Madhubani India 41 26.22N 86.05E
Madhupur India 41 24.16N 86.39E
Madhya Pradesh d. India 41 23.30N 78.30E
Madibira Tanzania 55 8.13S 34.47E
Madigan G. Australia 66 28.55S137.48E
Madill U.S.A. 83 34.06N 96.46W
Madīnat ash Sha'b Yemen 45 12.50N 44.56E
Madison Fla. U.S.A. 79 30.29N 83.39W
Madison Ind. U.S.A. 84 38.46N 85.22W
Madison N.J. U.S.A. 85 40.46N 74.25W
Madison S.Dak. U.S.A. 82 44.00N 97.07W
Madison Tenn. U.S.A. 85 36.16N 86.44W
Madison Wisc. U.S.A. 82 43.05N 89.22W
Madison W.Va. U.S.A. 85 38.03N 81.50W
Madison Junction U.S.A. 80 44.39N110.51W
Madisonville Ky. U.S.A. 85 37.20N 87.30W
Madisonville Tex. U.S.A. 83 30.57N 95.55W
Madiun Indonesia 37 7.37S111.33E
Madoc Canada 76 44.30N 77.28W
Mado Gashi Kenya 55 0.40N 39.11E
Madoi China 30 34.28N 98.56E
Madonna di Campiglio Italy 15 46.14N 10.49E
Madrakah, Ra's al c. Oman 38 19.00N 57.50E
Madras India 39 13.05N 80.18E
Madras U.S.A. 80 44.38N121.08W
Madre, Laguna b. Mexico 83 25.00N 97.40W
Madre, Laguna b. U.S.A. 83 27.00N 97.35W
Madre, Sierra mts. Mexico / Guatemala 86 15.20N 92.20W
Madre de Dios r. Bolivia 90 10.24S 65.30W
Madre del Sur, Sierra mts. Mexico 86 17.00N100.00W
Madre Occidental, Sierra mts. Mexico 81 25.00N105.00W
Madre Oriental, Sierra mts. Mexico 83 28.10N102.10W
Madrid Spain 16 40.25N 3.43W
Madrid d. Spain 16 40.45N 3.40W
Madukani Tanzania 55 3.57S 35.49E
Madura i. Indonesia 37 7.02S113.22E
Madurai India 39 9.55N 78.07E
Mae Klong r. Thailand 34 13.21N100.00E
Mae Sot Thailand 34 16.40N 98.35E
Maestra, Sierra mts. Cuba 87 20.10N 76.30W
Maevatanana Madagascar 57 16.56S 46.49E
Maewo i. Vanuatu 68 15.10S168.10E
Mafeking Canada 75 52.43N100.59W
Mafeteng Lesotho 56 29.51S 27.13E
Maffra Australia 67 37.58S146.59E
Mafia I. Tanzania 55 7.50S 39.50E
Mafikeng R.S.A. 56 25.52S 25.36E
Mafra Portugal 16 38.56N 9.20W
Magadan U.S.S.R. 29 59.38N150.50E
Magadi Kenya 55 1.53S 36.18E
Magallanes, Estrecho de str. Chile 93 53.00S 71.00W
Magalluf Spain 16 39.30N 2.31E
Magangué Colombia 90 9.14N 74.46W
Magazine U.S.A. 83 35.10N 93.40W
Magburaka Sierra Leone 52 8.44N 11.57W
Magdalena Argentina 93 35.04S 57.32W
Magdalena Bolivia 92 13.50S 64.08W
Magdalena r. Colombia 90 10.56N 74.58W
Magdalena Mexico 81 30.38N110.59W
Magdalena, Isla i. Chile 93 44.42S 73.10W
Magdalena, Llano de la f. Mexico 81 24.55N111.40W
Magdalene mtn. Malaysia 36 4.25N117.55E
Magdeburg Germany 20 52.08N 11.36E
Magé Brazil 94 22.37S 43.03W
Magee U.S.A. 83 31.52N 89.44W
Magelang Indonesia 37 7.28S110.11E
Magellan's Str. see Magallanes, Estrecho de str. Chile 93
Magenta Italy 15 45.28N 8.53E
Magenta, L. Australia 63 33.26S119.10E
Mageröya i. Norway 22 71.03N 25.45E
Maggiorasca, Monte mtn. Italy 15 44.33N 9.29E
Maggiore, Lago l. Italy 15 46.00N 8.40E
Maghāghah Egypt 44 28.39N 30.50E
Magherafelt U.K. 13 54.45N 6.38W
Magna U.S.A. 80 40.42N112.06W
Magnetic I. Australia 64 19.08S146.50E
Magnitogorsk U.S.S.R. 24 53.28N 59.06E
Magnolia Ark. U.S.A. 83 33.16N 93.14W
Magnolia Miss. U.S.A. 83 31.09N 90.28W
Magnolia Tex. U.S.A. 83 30.13N 95.45W
Magny-en-Vexin France 15 49.09N 1.47E
Magog Canada 77 45.16N 72.09W
Magoye Zambia 55 16.00S 27.38E
Magpie r. Canada 77 50.18N 64.28W
Magrath Canada 74 49.25N112.50W
Magude Mozambique 57 25.01S 32.39E
Magué Mozambique 55 15.46S 31.42E
Maguse River town Canada 75 61.20N 94.25W
Magwe Burma 34 20.08N 95.00E
Magwe d. Burma 34 23.00N 95.00E
Mahābād Iran 43 36.44N 45.44E
Mahābhārat Range mts. Nepal 41 28.00N 84.30E
Mahabo Madagascar 57 20.23S 44.40E
Mahadday Weyne Somali Rep. 55 2.58N 45.32E
Mahādeo Hills India 41 22.15N 78.30E
Mahagi Zaïre 55 2.16N 30.59E
Mahajamba r. Madagascar 57 15.33S 47.08E
Mahājan India 40 28.47N 73.50E
Mahajanga Madagascar 57 15.43S 46.19E
Mahajilo r. Madagascar 57 19.42S 45.22E
Mahalapye Botswana 56 23.04S 26.47E
Maḩallāt Iran 43 33.54N 50.28E
Mahānadi India 41 20.19N 86.45E
Mahānadi r. India 39 20.17N 86.43E
Mahanoro Madagascar 57 19.54S 48.48E
Mahārājpur India 41 25.01N 79.44E
Mahārāshtra d. India 40 19.40N 76.00E
Mahāsamund India 41 21.06N 82.06E
Maha Sarakham Thailand 34 15.50N103.47E
Mahavavy r. Madagascar 57 15.57S 45.54E
Mahbés W. Sahara 50 27.13N 9.44W
Mahd adh Dhahab Saudi Arabia 42 23.30N 40.52E
Mahdia Guyana 90 5.10N 59.12W
Mahendraganj India 41 25.20N 89.45E
Mahenge Tanzania 55 8.46S 36.38E
Mahi r. India 40 22.30N 72.58E
Mahia Pen. New Zealand 60 39.10S177.50E
Mahmūdābād India 41 27.18N 81.07E
Mahmūd-e 'Erāqī Afghan. 40 35.01N 69.20E
Mahnomen U.S.A. 82 47.19N 96.01W
Maho Sri Lanka 39 7.49N 80.17E
Mahoba India 41 25.17N 79.52E
Mahón Spain 16 39.55N 4.18E
Mahone B. Canada 77 44.30N 64.15W
Mahroni India 41 24.35N 78.43E
Mahuva India 40 21.05N 71.48E
Maiäo i. Îs. de la Société 69 17.23S150.37W
Maidenhead U.K. 11 51.32N 0.44W
Maidstone U.K. 11 51.17N 0.32E
Maiduguri Nigeria 53 11.53N 13.16E
Maignelay France 15 49.33N 2.31E
Maihar India 41 24.16N 80.45E
Maikala Range mts. India 41 21.45N 81.00E
Maiko r. Zaïre 54 0.15N 25.35E
Main r. Germany 20 50.00N 8.19E
Main Camp Kiribati 69 2.01N157.25W
Main Centre Canada 75 50.38N107.20W
Main Channel str. Canada 76 45.22N 81.50W
Mai Ndombe l. Zaïre 54 2.00S 18.20E
Maine d. U.S.A. 84 45.15N 69.15W
Mainland i. Orkney Is. U.K. 12 59.00N 3.10W
Mainoru Australia 64 14.02S134.05E
Mainpuri India 41 27.14N 79.01E
Maintenon France 15 48.35N 1.35E
Maintirano Madagascar 57 18.03S 44.01E
Mainz Germany 20 50.00N 8.16E
Maípo mtn. Argentina 93 34.10S 69.50W
Maipú Argentina 93 36.52S 57.54W
Maiquetía Venezuela 90 10.03N 66.57W
Maiskhāl I. Bangla. 41 21.36N 91.56E
Maitland N.S.W. Australia 67 32.33S151.33E
Maitland S.A. Australia 66 34.21S137.42E
Maizhokunggar China 41 29.50N 91.44E
Majeigha Sudan 49 11.33N 24.40E
Majene Indonesia 36 3.33S118.59E
Majī Ethiopia 49 6.11N 35.38E
Majiahewan China 32 37.12N105.48E
Majiang China 33 26.30N107.35E
Majorca i. see Mallorca i. Spain 16
Majrūr Sudan 48 14.01N 30.27E
Majuba Hill R.S.A. 56 27.26S 29.48E
Majuro i. Pacific Oc. 68 7.09N171.12E
Makabana Congo 54 3.25S 12.41E
Makale Indonesia 36 3.06S119.53E
Makalu mtn. China / Nepal 41 27.54N 87.06E
Makarikha U.S.S.R. 24 66.17N 58.28E
Makaryev U.S.S.R. 24 57.52N 43.40E
Makasar, Selat str. Indonesia 36 3.00S118.00E
Makassar Str. see Makasar, Selat str. Indonesia 36
Makat U.S.S.R. 25 47.38N 53.16E
Makaw Burma 34 26.27N 96.42E
Makay, Massif du mts. Madagascar 57 21.15S 45.15E
Makaya Zaïre 54 3.22S 18.02E
Makedonija d. Yugo. 19 41.35N 21.30E
Makefu Niue 68 19.01S169.55W
Makeni Sierra Leone 52 8.57N 12.02W
Makere Tanzania 55 4.15S 30.26E
Makeyevka U.S.S.R. 25 48.01N 38.00E
Makgadikgadi Salt Pan f. Botswana 56 20.50S 25.45E
Makhachkala U.S.S.R. 25 42.59N 47.30E
Makham Thailand 34 12.40N102.12E
Makhfar al Quwayrah Jordan 44 29.49N 35.18E
Makhrūq, Wādī al r. Jordan 44 31.30N 37.10E
Makinsk U.S.S.R. 28 52.40N 70.28E
Makkah Saudi Arabia 48 21.26N 39.49E
Makkovik Canada 77 55.00N 59.10W
Makó Hungary 21 46.13N 20.30E
Mako Senegal 52 13.00N 12.26W
Makokou Gabon 54 0.38N 12.47E
Makoua Congo 54 0.01S 15.40E
Makrai India 40 22.04N 77.06E
Makran f. Asia 43 26.30N 61.20E
Makrāna India 40 27.03N 74.43E
Makrān Coast Range mts. Pakistan 40 25.30N 64.30E
Maksamaa Finland 22 63.14N 22.05E
Makuliro Tanzania 55 9.34S 37.26E
Makurdi Nigeria 53 7.44N 8.35E
Māl India 41 26.52N 88.44E
Malabo Equat. Guinea 53 3.45N 8.48E
Malacca see Melaka Malaysia 36
Malacca, Str. of Indian Oc. 36 3.00N100.30E
Malad City U.S.A. 80 42.12N112.15W
Málaga Spain 16 36.43N 4.25W
Malaga U.S.A. 81 32.14N104.04W
Malaimbandy Madagascar 57 20.20S 45.36E
Malaita Solomon Is. 68 9.00S161.00E
Malakāl Sudan 49 9.31N 31.39E
Malakand Pakistan 40 34.34N 71.56E
Malam Chad 49 11.27N 20.59E
Malang Indonesia 37 7.59S112.45E
Malangwa Nepal 41 26.52N 85.34E
Malanje Angola 54 9.36S 16.21E
Malanje d. Angola 54 8.40S 16.50E
Mälaren l. Sweden 23 59.30N 17.12E
Malartic Canada 76 48.09N 78.09W
Malatya Turkey 42 38.22N 38.18E
Malaut India 40 30.11N 74.30E
Malaŵi Africa 55 12.00S 34.00E
Malaŵi, L. Africa 55 12.00S 34.30E
Malaya Vishera U.S.S.R. 24 58.53N 32.08E
Malāyer Iran 43 34.19N 48.51E
Malaysia Asia 36 5.00N110.00E
Malazgirt Turkey 42 39.09N 42.31E
Malbaie r. Canada 77 47.40N 70.05W
Malbaie, Baie de b. Canada 77 48.35N 64.16W
Malbooma Australia 66 30.41S134.11E
Malbork Poland 21 54.02N 19.01E
Malcolm Australia 63 28.56S121.30E
Malcolm, Pt. Australia 63 33.47S123.44E
Malden Mo. U.S.A. 83 36.34N 89.57W
Malden I. Kiribati 69 4.03S154.49W
Maldives Indian Oc. 38 6.20N 73.00E
Maldon U.K. 11 51.43N 0.41E
Maldonado Uruguay 94 34.57S 54.59W
Male Italy 15 46.21N 10.55E
Maléa, Ákra c. Greece 19 36.27N 23.11E
Malebo Pool f. Zaïre 54 4.15S 15.25E
Mālegaon India 40 20.33N 74.32E
Malek Sudan 49 6.04N 31.36E
Malek Dīn Afghan. 40 32.25N 68.04E
Malekula i. Vanuatu 68 16.15S167.30E
Malema Mozambique 55 14.55S 37.09E
Malenga U.S.S.R. 24 63.50N 36.50E
Māler Kotla India 40 30.32N 75.53E
Malesherbes France 15 48.18N 2.25E
Malgomaj l. Sweden 22 64.47N 16.12E
Malheur L. U.S.A. 80 43.20N118.45W
Mali Africa 52 17.30N 2.30E
Mali r. Burma 34 25.43N 97.29E
Malik, Wādī al Sudan 48 18.02N 30.58E
Malili Indonesia 37 2.38S121.06E
Malin U.S.S.R. 21 50.48N 29.08E
Malinau Indonesia 36 3.35N116.38E
Malindi Kenya 55 3.14S 40.08E
Malingping Indonesia 37 6.45S106.01E
Malin Head Rep. of Ire. 13 55.23N 7.24W
Malin More Rep. of Ire. 13 54.42N 8.48W
Malipo China 33 23.11N104.41E
Malita Phil. 37 6.19N125.39E
Māliya India 40 23.05N 70.46E
Malkāpur India 40 20.53N 76.12E
Mallacoota Australia 67 37.34S149.43E
Mallacoota Inlet b. Australia 67 37.34S149.43E
Mallaig U.K. 12 57.00N 5.50W
Mallawī Egypt 44 27.44N 30.50E
Mallorca i. Spain 16 39.35N 3.00E
Mallow Rep. of Ire. 13 52.08N 8.39W
Malm Norway 22 64.04N 11.12E
Malmberget Sweden 22 67.10N 20.40E
Malmédy Belgium 14 50.25N 6.02E
Malmesbury R.S.A. 56 33.28S 18.43E
Malmö Sweden 23 55.36N 13.00E
Malmöhus d. Sweden 23 55.45N 13.30E
Malmyzh U.S.S.R. 24 56.34N 50.41E
Maloja Switz. 15 46.24N 9.41E
Malolos Guam 68 13.18N144.46E
Malone U.S.A. 84 44.51N 74.17W
Malonga Zaïre 54 10.26S 23.10E
Malorita U.S.S.R. 21 51.50N 24.08E
Målöy Norway 23 61.56N 5.07E
Malozemelskaya Tundra f. U.S.S.R. 24 67.40N 50.10E
Malpas Australia 66 34.44S140.43E
Malta Europe 18 35.55N 14.25E
Malta Mont. U.S.A. 80 48.21N107.52W
Malta Channel Med. Sea 18 36.20N 14.45E
Maltby U.K. 10 53.25N 1.12W
Malton U.K. 10 54.09N 0.48W
Maluku d. Indonesia 37 4.00S129.00E
Maluku, Laut sea Pacific Oc. 37
Malumfashi Nigeria 53 11.48N 7.36E
Malundo Angola 54 14.51S 22.00E
Malung Sweden 23 60.40N 13.44E
Malūţ Sudan 49 10.26N 32.12E
Malvinas, Islas see Falkland Is. Atlantic Ocean 93
Mama U.S.S.R. 29 58.20N112.55E
Mamadysh U.S.S.R. 24 55.43N 51.20E
Mamaia Romania 21 44.15N 28.37E
Mambasa Zaïre 55 1.20N 29.05E
Mamberamo r. Indonesia 37 1.45S137.25E
Mambéré r. C.A.R. 53 3.30N 16.08E
Mambilima Falls town Zambia 55 10.32S 28.45E
Mamers France 15 48.21N 0.23E
Mamfe Cameroon 53 5.46N 9.18E
Mamonovo U.S.S.R. 21 54.30N 19.59E
Mamore r. Bolivia 92 12.00S 65.15W
Mamou Guinea 52 10.24N 12.05W
Mampika Congo 54 2.58S 14.38E
Mampikony Madagascar 57 16.06S 47.38E
Mampong Ghana 52 7.06N 1.24W
Mamry, Jezioro l. Poland 21 54.08N 21.42E
Mamuju Indonesia 36 2.41S118.55E
Ma'mūn Sudan 49 12.15N 22.41E
Man Ivory Coast 52 7.31N 7.37W
Man Jammu & Kashmir 41 33.51N 78.32E
Man, Isle of U.K. 10 54.15N 4.30W
Mana r. Guiana 91 5.35N 53.55W
Mana Hawaiian Is. 69 22.02N156.46W
Manacapuru Brazil 90 3.16S 60.37W
Manacor Spain 16 39.32N 3.12E
Manado Indonesia 37 1.30N124.58E
Managua Nicaragua 87 12.06N 86.18W
Managua, Lago de l. Nicaragua 87 12.10N 86.30W
Manahawkin U.S.A. 85 39.42N 74.16W
Manakara Madagascar 57 22.08S 48.01E
Manāli India 40 32.16N 77.10E
Manambao r. Madagascar 57 17.43S 43.57E
Mananara Madagascar 57 16.10S 49.46E
Mananara r. Madagascar 57 23.21S 47.42E
Manangatang Australia 66 35.02S142.54E
Mananjary Madagascar 57 21.13S 48.20E
Manankoro Mali 52 10.25N 7.26W
Manantali, Lac de l. Mali 52 13.00N 10.20W
Manantenina Madagascar 57 24.17S 47.19E
Manapouri, L. New Zealand 60 45.30S167.00E
Manār r. India 40 18.39N 77.44E
Manāslu mtn. Nepal 41 28.33N 84.35E

Manasquan U.S.A. 85 40.07N 74.03W
Manau P.N.G. 37 8.02S148.00E
Manaus Brazil 90 3.06S 60.00W
Manāwar India 40 22.14N 75.05E
Manawatu-Wanganui *d.* New Zealand 60 39.00S175.25E
Mancelona U.S.A. 84 44.54N 85.03W
Manche *d.* France 15 49.00N 1.10W
Mancherāl India 41 18.52N 79.26E
Manchester U.K. 10 53.30N 2.15W
Manchester Conn. U.S.A. 84 41.47N 72.31W
Manchester N.H. U.S.A. 84 42.59N 71.28W
Manchurian Plain *f. see* Dongbei Pingyuan *f.* China 31
Mand *r.* Iran 43 28.09N 51.16E
Manda Iringa Tanzania 55 10.30S 34.37E
Manda Mbeya Tanzania 55 7.59S 32.27E
Manda, Jabal *mtn.* Sudan 49 8.39N 24.27E
Mandabe Madagascar 57 21.03S 44.55E
Mandal Norway 23 58.02N 7.27E
Mandala Peak Indonesia 37 4.45S140.15E
Mandalay Burma 34 21.58N 96.04E
Mandalay *d.* Burma 34 22.00N 96.00E
Mandalgovi Mongolia 32 45.40N106.10E
Mandals *r.* Norway 23 58.02N 7.28E
Mandan U.S.A. 82 46.50N100.54W
Mandara Mts. Nigeria / Cameroon 53 10.30N 13.30E
Mandasor India 40 24.04N 75.04E
Mandeb, Bāb el *str.* Asia 49 13.00N 43.10E
Mandel Afghan. 40 33.17N 61.52E
Mandera Kenya 55 3.55N 41.50E
Mandi India 40 31.42N 76.55E
Mandiana Guinea 52 10.37N 8.39W
Mandi Būrewāla Pakistan 40 30.09N 72.41E
Mandi Dabwāli India 40 29.58N 74.42E
Mandji Gabon 54 1.37S 10.53E
Mandla India 41 22.36N 80.23E
Mandora Australia 62 19.45S120.50E
Mandoto Madagascar 57 19.34S 46.17E
Mandra Pakistan 40 33.22N 73.14E
Mandritsara Madagascar 57 15.50S 48.49E
Māndu India 40 22.22N 75.23E
Mandurah Australia 63 32.31S115.41E
Manduria Italy 19 40.24N 17.38E
Māndvi India 40 22.50N 69.22E
Mandya India 38 12.33N 76.54E
Måne *r.* Norway 23 59.55N 8.48E
Manendragarh India 41 23.13N 82.13E
Manerbio Italy 15 45.21N 10.08E
Manevichi U.S.S.R. 21 51.19N 25.35E
Manfredonia Italy 18 41.38N 15.54E
Manfredonia, Golfo di *g.* Italy 18 41.35N 16.05E
Mangaia I. Cook Is. 69 21.56S157.56W
Mangaldai India 41 26.26N 92.02E
Mangalia Romania 21 43.50N 28.35E
Mangalore India 38 12.54N 74.51E
Mangando Angola 54 8.02S 17.08E
Mangareva *i.* Pacific Oc. 69 23.07S134.57W
Mangawān India 41 24.41N 81.33E
Mangaweka New Zealand 60 38.49S175.48E
Mangeigne Chad 49 10.31N 21.19E
Mangnai China 30 37.52N 91.26E
Mango Togo 52 10.23N 0.30E
Mangochi Malaŵi 55 14.29S 35.15E
Mangoky *r.* Madagascar 57 21.29S 43.41E
Mangombe Zaïre 55 1.23S 26.50E
Mangonui New Zealand 60 35.00S173.34E
Mangoro *r.* Madagascar 57 20.00S 48.45E
Māngrol India 40 21.07N 70.07E
Mangueira, L. Brazil 94 33.06S 52.48W
Mangum U.S.A. 83 34.53N 99.30W
Mangyshlak, Poluostrov *pen.* U.S.S.R. 25 44.00N 52.30E
Manhattan U.S.A. 82 39.11N 96.35W
Manhiça Mozambique 57 25.24S 32.49E
Manhuaçu Brazil 94 20.16S 42.01W
Manhumirim Brazil 94 20.22S 41.57W
Mania *r.* Madagascar 57 19.42S 45.22E
Maniago Italy 15 46.10N 12.43E
Maniamba Mozambique 55 12.30S 35.05E
Manica Mozambique 57 19.00S 33.00E
Manica *d.* Mozambique 57 20.00S 34.00E
Manicoré Brazil 90 5.49S 61.17W
Manicouagan *r.* Canada 77 49.15N 68.20W
Manicouagan, Résr. Canada 77 51.20N 68.48W
Maniitsoq *see* Sukkertoppen Greenland 73
Mānikganj Bangla. 41 23.19N 87.03E
Mānikpur India 41 25.04N 81.07E
Manila Phil. 37 14.36N120.59E
Manila U.S.A. 80 40.59N109.43W
Manildra Australia 67 33.12S148.41E
Manilla Australia 67 30.45S150.45E
Maningory *r.* Madagascar 57 17.13S 49.28E
Manipur *d.* India 39 25.00N 93.40E
Manisa Turkey 19 38.37N 27.28E
Manistee U.S.A. 84 44.14N 86.20W
Manistee *r.* U.S.A. 84 44.14N 86.20W
Manistique U.S.A. 84 45.58N 86.17W
Manitoba *d.* Canada 75 55.00N 96.00W
Manitoba, L. Canada 75 51.00N 98.45W
Manitoulin I. Canada 76 45.45N 82.30W
Manitowoc U.S.A. 82 44.06N 87.40W
Maniwaki Canada 76 46.23N 75.58W
Manizales Colombia 90 5.03N 75.32W
Manja Madagascar 57 21.26S 44.20E
Manjakandriana Madagascar 57 18.55S 47.47E
Mānjhand Pakistan 40 25.55N 68.14E
Manjīl Iran 43 36.44N 49.29E
Manjimup Australia 63 34.14S116.06E
Mankato U.S.A. 82 44.10N 94.01W
Mankera Pakistan 40 31.23N 71.26E
Mankono Ivory Coast 52 8.01N 6.09W
Manly Australia 67 33.47S151.17E
Manmād India 40 20.15N 74.27E
Mann *r.* Australia 67 29.38S152.21E
Mann *r.* Australia 64 12.20S134.07E
Mān Na Burma 34 23.27N 97.14E
Manna Indonesia 36 4.27S102.55E
Mannahill Australia 66 32.26S139.59E
Mannar Sri Lanka 39 8.59N 79.54E
Mannar, G. of India / Sri Lanka 39 8.20N 79.00E
Mannessier, Lac *l.* Canada 77 55.28N 70.38W
Mannheim Germany 20 49.30N 8.28E
Mannin B. Rep. of Ire. 13 53.28N 10.06W
Manning Canada 74 56.53N117.39W
Manning U.S.A. 85 33.42N 80.12W
Mannu *r.* Sardegna Italy 18 39.16N 9.00E
Mannum Australia 66 34.50S139.20E
Mano Sierra Leone 52 8.04N 12.02W
Manoharpur India 41 22.23N 85.12E
Manokwari Indonesia 37 0.53S134.05E
Manombo Madagascar 57 22.57S 43.28E
Manono Zaïre 55 7.18S 27.24E
Manorhamilton Rep. of Ire. 13 54.18N 8.10W
Manosque France 17 43.50N 5.47E
Manouane *r.* Canada 77 49.29N 71.13W
Manouane, Lac *l.* Canada 77 50.40N 70.45W
Mānpur India 41 20.22N 80.43E
Manresa Spain 16 41.43N 1.50E
Mānsa Gujarat India 40 23.26N 72.40E
Mānsa Punjab India 40 29.59N 75.23E
Mansa Zambia 55 11.10S 28.52E
Mānsehra Pakistan 40 34.20N 73.12E
Mansel I. Canada 73 62.00N 80.00W
Mansfield U.K. 10 53.08N 1.12W
Mansfield La. U.S.A. 83 32.02N 93.43W
Mansfield Mass. U.S.A. 84 42.02N 71.13W
Mansfield Ohio U.S.A. 84 40.46N 82.31W
Manso *r.* Brazil 92 11.59S 50.25W
Mansôa Guinea Bissau 52 12.08N 15.18W
Manta Ecuador 90 0.59S 80.44W
Mantaro *r.* Peru 90 12.00S 74.00W
Manteca U.S.A. 80 37.48N121.13W
Mantes France 15 49.00N 1.41E
Mantiqueira, Serra da *mts.* Brazil 94 22.25S 45.00W
Mantova Italy 15 45.09N 10.47E
Mänttä Finland 23 62.02N 24.38E
Manturovo U.S.S.R. 24 58.20N 44.42E
Mäntyluoto Finland 23 61.35N 21.29E
Manú Peru 90 12.14S 70.51W
Manua Is. Samoa 68 14.13S169.35W
Manuel Benavides Mexico 83 29.05N103.55W
Manui *i.* Indonesia 37 3.35S123.08E
Manukau New Zealand 60 36.59S174.53E
Manukau Harbour *est.* New Zealand 60 37.10S174.00E
Manunda Creek *r.* Australia 66 32.50S138.58E
Manus *i.* P.N.G. 37 2.00S147.00E
Manville U.S.A. 80 42.47N104.37W
Manyane Botswana 56 23.23S 21.44E
Manyara, L. Tanzania 55 3.40S 35.50E
Manych *r.* U.S.S.R. 25 47.14N 40.20E
Manych Gudilo, Ozero *l.* U.S.S.R. 25 46.20N 42.45E
Manyinga *r.* Zambia 56 13.28S 24.25E
Manyoni Tanzania 55 5.46S 34.50E
Mānzai Pakistan 40 30.07N 68.52E
Manzanares Spain 16 39.00N 3.23W
Manzanillo Cuba 87 20.21N 77.21W
Manzano Mts. U.S.A. 81 34.48N106.12W
Manzhouli China 31 49.36N117.28E
Manzil Pakistan 40 29.15N 63.05E
Manzilah, Buḩayrat al *l.* Egypt 44 31.20N 32.00E
Manzini Swaziland 56 26.29S 31.24E
Mao Chad 53 14.06N 15.11E
Maobitou *c.* Taiwan 33 22.00N120.45E
Maoke, Pegunungan *mts.* Indonesia 37 4.00S137.30E
Maokui Shan *mtn.* China 32 33.55N111.33E
Maoming China 33 21.50N110.58E
Maoniu Shan *mtn.* China 32 33.00N103.56E
Mapai Mozambique 57 22.51S 32.00E
Mapam Yumco *l.* China 41 30.40N 81.20E
Mapi Indonesia 37 7.06S139.23E
Mapia, Kepulauan *is.* Indonesia 37 1.00N134.15E
Mapimí, Bolsóne de *des.* Mexico 83 27.30N103.15W
Mapinhane Mozambique 57 22.19S 35.03E
Mapire Venezuela 90 7.46N 64.41W
Maple Creek *town* Canada 75 49.55N109.27W
Maprik P.N.G. 37 3.38S143.02E
Mapuera *r.* Brazil 91 2.00S 55.40W
Maputo Mozambique 57 25.58S 32.35E
Maputo *d.* Mozambique 57 26.00S 32.30E
Maqnā Saudi Arabia 44 28.26N 34.44E
Maqu China 39 34.05N102.15E
Maquan He *r.* China 41 29.35N 84.10E
Maquela do Zombo Angola 54 6.06S 15.12E
Maquinchao Argentina 93 41.15S 68.44W
Maquoketa U.S.A. 82 42.04N 90.40W
Mar, Serra do *mts.* Brazil 94 23.00S 44.40W
Mara Tanzania 55 1.30S 34.31E
Mara *d.* Tanzania 55 1.45S 34.30E
Mara *r.* Tanzania 55 1.30S 33.52E
Maraā Brazil 90 1.50S 65.22W
Maraa Tahiti 69 17.46S149.34W
Marabá Brazil 91 5.23S 49.10W
Marabastad R.S.A. 56 23.58S 29.21E
Maracaibo Venezuela 90 10.44N 71.37W
Maracaibo, Lago de *l.* Venezuela 90 9.50N 71.30W
Maracaju, Serra de *mts.* Brazil 94 21.38S 55.10W
Maracay Venezuela 90 10.20N 67.28W
Marādah Libya 51 29.14N 19.13E
Maradi Niger 53 13.29N 7.10E
Maradi *d.* Niger 53 14.00N 8.10E
Marāgheh Iran 43 37.25N 46.13E
Maragogipe Brazil 91 12.48S 38.59W
Marahuaca, Cerro *mtn.* Venezuela 90 3.37N 65.25W
Marajó, Ilha de *i.* Brazil 91 1.00S 49.40W
Maralal Kenya 55 1.15N 36.48E
Maralinga Australia 63 30.13S131.32E
Maramba Zambia 54 17.40S 25.50E
Maramsilli Resr. India 41 20.32N 81.41E
Mārān, Koh-i- *mtn.* Pakistan 40 29.33N 66.53E
Marana U.S.A. 81 32.27N111.13W
Marand Iran 43 38.25N 45.50E
Maranhão *d.* Brazil 91 6.00S 45.30W
Maranoa *r.* Australia 65 27.55S148.30E
Marañón *r.* Peru 90 4.40S 73.20W
Marão Mozambique 57 24.21S 34.07E
Marapi *mtn.* Indonesia 36 0.20S100.45E
Mărăşeşti Romania 21 45.52N 27.14E
Marathón Greece 19 38.10N 23.59E
Marathon Tex. U.S.A. 83 30.12N103.15W
Maratua *i.* Indonesia 36 2.10N118.35E
Marāveh Tappeh Iran 43 37.55N 55.57E
Marav L. Pakistan 40 29.04N 69.18E
Marawī Sudan 48 18.29N 31.49E
Marbella Spain 16 36.31N 4.53W
Marble Bar Australia 62 21.16S119.45E
Marburg Germany 20 50.49N 8.36E
Marcaria Italy 15 45.07N 10.32E
March U.K. 11 52.33N 0.05E
Marche Belgium 14 50.13N 5.21E
Marche *d.* Italy 18 43.35N 13.00E
Marchena Spain 16 37.20N 5.24W
Mar Chiquita *l.* Argentina 92 30.42S 62.36W
Marcos Paz Argentina 93 34.49S 58.51W
Marcounda C.A.R. 53 7.37N 16.59E
Marcq-en-Baroeul France 14 50.40N 3.01E
Marcus Hook U.S.A. 85 39.49N 75.25W
Marcus I. Pacific Oc. 68 24.18N153.58E
Mardān Pakistan 40 34.12N 72.02E
Mar del Plata Argentina 93 38.00S 57.32W
Marden U.K. 11 51.11N 0.30E
Mardie Australia 62 21.14S115.57E
Mardin Turkey 42 37.19N 40.43E
Maré, Île *i.* N. Cal. 68 21.30S168.00E
Maree, Loch U.K. 12 57.41N 5.28W
Mareeba Australia 64 17.00S145.26E
Marettimo *i.* Italy 18 37.58N 12.05E
Marfa U.S.A. 83 30.18N104.01W
Margai Caka *l.* China 39 35.11N 86.57E
Margaret *r.* Australia 66 29.26S137.00E
Margaret Bay *town* Canada 74 51.20N127.20W
Margaret L. Canada 74 58.56N115.25W
Margaret River *town* W. Aust. Australia 62 18.38S126.52E
Margaret River *town* W. Aust. Australia 63 33.57S115.04E
Margarita, Isla de *i.* Venezuela 90 11.00N 64.00W
Margate R.S.A. 56 30.51S 30.22E
Margate U.K. 11 51.23N 1.24E
Mārgow, Dasht-e *des.* Afghan. 40 30.45N 63.10E
Maria Elena Chile 92 22.21S 69.40W
María Grande Argentina 93 31.40S 59.55W
Maria I. Australia 64 14.52S135.40E
Mariana Brazil 94 20.23S 43.23W
Marianao Cuba 87 23.03N 82.29W
Mariana Ridge Pacific Oc. 68 17.00N146.00E
Mariana Trench Pacific Oc. 68 16.00N148.00E
Marianna Ark. U.S.A. 83 34.46N 90.46W
Marianna Fla. U.S.A. 85 30.45N 85.15W
Mariánské Lázně Czech. 20 49.59N 12.43E
Marias *r.* U.S.A. 80 47.56N110.30W
Maribo Denmark 23 54.46N 11.31E
Maribor Yugo. 20 46.35N 15.40E
Marico *r.* R.S.A. 56 24.12S 26.57E
Maricopa U.S.A. 81 35.03N119.24W
Marīdī Sudan 49 4.55N 29.28E
Marīdī *r.* Sudan 49 6.55N 29.00E
Marié *r.* Brazil 90 0.27S 66.26W
Marieburg Belgium 14 50.07N 4.30E
Marie-Galante *i.* Guadeloupe 87 15.54N 61.11W
Mariehamn *see* Maarianhamina Finland 23
Mariemberg Neth. 14 52.32N 6.35E
Mariental Namibia 56 24.38S 17.58E
Mariestad Sweden 23 58.43N 13.51E
Marietta Ga. U.S.A. 85 33.57N 84.34W
Marietta Ohio U.S.A. 84 39.26N 81.27W
Marieville Canada 77 45.26N 73.10W
Mariga *r.* Nigeria 53 9.37N 5.55E
Marijampolė U.S.S.R. 23 54.33N 23.21E
Marília Brazil 94 22.13S 50.20W
Marín Spain 16 42.23N 8.42W
Marina di Ravenna Italy 15 44.29N 12.17E
Marineland U.S.A. 85 29.39N 81.13W
Marinette U.S.A. 82 45.06N 87.38W
Maringá Brazil 94 23.36S 52.02W
Maringa Zaïre 49 1.14N 20.00E
Maringa *r.* Zaïre 54 1.13N 19.50E
Maringue Mozambique 57 17.55S 34.24E
Marinha Grande Portugal 16 39.45N 8.55W
Marion Ill. U.S.A. 83 37.44N 88.56W
Marion Ind. U.S.A. 84 40.33N 85.40W
Marion Iowa U.S.A. 82 42.02N 91.36W
Marion Ohio U.S.A. 84 40.35N 83.08W
Marion S.C. U.S.A. 85 34.11N 79.23W
Marion Va. U.S.A. 85 36.51N 81.30W
Marion, L. U.S.A. 85 33.30N 80.25W
Marion Bay *town* Australia 66 35.13S137.00E
Marion Reef Australia 64 19.10S152.17E
Mariposa U.S.A. 80 37.29N119.58W
Mariscal Estigarribia Paraguay 94 22.03S 60.35W
Maritsa *r.* Turkey 19 41.00N 26.15E
Mariupol' U.S.S.R. 25 47.05N 37.34E
Marka Somali Rep. 55 1.42N 44.47E
Markaryd Sweden 23 56.26N 13.36E
Marked Tree U.S.A. 83 35.32N 90.25W
Marken *i.* Neth. 14 52.28N 5.03E
Markerwaard *f.* Neth. 14 52.30N 5.15E
Market Drayton U.K. 10 52.55N 2.30W
Market Harborough U.K. 11 52.29N 0.55W
Market Rasen U.K. 10 53.24N 0.20W
Market Weighton U.K. 10 53.52N 0.04W
Markha *r.* U.S.S.R. 29 63.37N119.00E
Markham Canada 76 43.52N 79.16W
Markham, Mt. Antarctica 96 83.00S164.00E
Marks U.S.S.R. 25 51.43N 46.45E
Marla Australia 65 27.22S133.48E
Marla Australia 64 27.22S133.48E
Marlborough Australia 64 22.51S149.50E
Marlborough U.K. 11 51.26N 1.44W
Marle France 15 49.44N 3.46E
Marlette U.S.A. 84 43.20N 83.04W
Marlin U.S.A. 83 31.18N 96.53W
Marlo Australia 67 37.50S148.35E
Marmara *i.* Turkey 19 40.38N 27.37E
Marmara, Sea of *see* Marmara Denizi *sea* Turkey 19
Marmara Denizi *sea* Turkey 19 40.45N 28.15E
Marmaris Turkey 19 36.50N 28.17E
Marmarth U.S.A. 82 46.18N103.54W
Marmion L. Canada 76 48.55N 91.25W
Marmolada *mtn.* Italy 15 46.26N 11.51E
Marne *d.* France 15 48.55N 4.10E
Marne *r.* France 15 48.50N 2.25E
Marnoo Australia 66 36.40S142.55E
Maroantsetra Madagascar 57 15.26S 49.44E
Marobi Pakistan 40 32.36N 69.52E
Marolambo Madagascar 57 20.02S 48.07E
Maromme France 15 49.28N 1.02E
Marondera Zimbabwe 57 18.11S 31.31E
Maroni *r.* Guiana 91 5.30N 54.00W
Maroochydore Australia 65 26.40S153.07E
Maroua Cameroon 53 10.35N 14.20E
Marovoay Madagascar 57 16.06S 46.39E
Marquard R.S.A. 56 28.39S 27.25E
Marquesas Is. *see* Marquises, Îles *is.* Pacific Oc. 69
Marquette U.S.A. 84 46.33N 87.23W
Marquises, Îles *is.* Pacific Oc. 69 9.00S139.30W
Marra Australia 66 31.11S144.03E
Marra *r.* Australia 67 30.05S147.05E
Marracuene Mozambique 57 25.44S 32.41E
Marradi Italy 15 44.04N 11.37E
Marrah, Jabal *mtn.* Sudan 49 13.10N 24.22E
Marrakech Morocco 50 31.49N 8.00W
Marrawah Australia 65 40.55S144.42E
Marree Australia 66 29.40S138.04E
Marromeu Mozambique 57 18.20S 35.56E
Marrupa Mozambique 55 13.10S 37.30E
Marsá al Burayqah Libya 48 30.25N 19.35E
Marsabit Kenya 55 2.20N 37.59E
Marsala Italy 18 37.48N 12.27E
Marsá Maṭrūḩ Egypt 42 31.21N 27.14E
Marsden Australia 67 33.46S147.35E
Marseille France 17 43.18N 5.22E
Marseille-en-Beauvaisis France 15 49.35N 1.57E
Marsfjället *mtn.* Sweden 22 65.05N 15.28E
Marshall Liberia 52 6.10N 10.23W
Marshall Ark. U.S.A. 83 35.55N 92.38W
Marshall Minn. U.S.A. 82 44.27N 95.47W
Marshall Mo. U.S.A. 82 39.07N 93.12W
Marshall Tex. U.S.A. 83 32.33N 94.23W
Marshall Is. Pacific Oc. 68 10.00N172.00E
Marshalltown U.S.A. 82 42.03N 92.55W
Marshyhope Creek *r.* U.S.A. 85 38.32N 75.45W
Martaban Burma 34 16.32N 97.35E
Martaban, G. of Burma 34 15.10N 96.30E
Martapura Indonesia 36 3.22S114.56E
Marte Nigeria 53 12.23N 13.46E
Martelange Belgium 14 49.50N 5.44E
Martés, Sierra *mts.* Spain 16 39.10N 1.00W
Marthaguy Creek *r.* Australia 67 30.16S147.35E
Martha's Vineyard *i.* U.S.A. 84 41.25N 70.40W
Martigny Switz. 20 46.07N 7.05E
Martin Czech. 21 49.05N 18.55E
Martin U.S.A. 82 43.10N101.44W
Martina Franca Italy 19 40.42N 17.21E
Martinique *i.* Windward Is. 87 14.40N 61.00W
Martin L. U.S.A. 85 32.50N 85.55W
Martin Pt. U.S.A. 72 70.10N143.50W
Martinsburg W.Va. U.S.A. 84 39.27N 77.58W
Martins Ferry *town* U.S.A. 84 40.07N 80.45W
Martinsville Ind. U.S.A. 84 39.25N 86.25W
Martinsville Va. U.S.A. 85 36.43N 79.53W
Martin Vaz *is.* Atlantic Oc. 95 20.30S 28.51W
Marton New Zealand 60 40.04S175.25E
Martos Spain 16 37.44N 3.58W
Martre, Lac la *l.* Canada 74 63.15N116.55W
Martti Finland 22 67.28N 28.28E
Marudi Malaysia 36 4.15N114.19E
Ma'rūf Afghan. 40 31.34N 67.03E
Marula Zimbabwe 56 20.26S 28.06E
Marum Neth. 14 53.06N 6.16E
Marvejols France 17 44.33N 3.18E
Marvel Loch *town* Australia 63 31.31S119.30E
Mārwār India 40 25.44N 73.36E
Mary U.S.S.R. 28 37.42N 61.54E
Maryborough Qld. Australia 64 25.32S152.36E
Maryborough Vic. Australia 66 37.05S143.47E
Marydale R.S.A. 56 29.24S 22.06E
Mary Frances L. Canada 75 63.19N106.13W
Maryland *d.* U.S.A. 84 39.00N 76.45W
Maryland Beach *town* U.S.A. 85 38.26N 74.59W
Maryport U.K. 10 54.43N 3.30W
Mary's Harbour Canada 77 52.18N 55.51W
Marystown Canada 77 47.11N 55.10W
Marysvale U.S.A. 80 38.27N112.11W
Marysville Kans. U.S.A. 82 39.51N 96.39W
Maryvale Australia 64 24.41S134.04E
Maryville Mo. U.S.A. 82 40.21N 94.52W
Maryville Tenn. U.S.A. 85 35.45N 83.59W
Marzūq Libya 51 25.55N 13.55E
Marzūq, Ṣaḩrā' *des.* Libya 51 24.30N 13.00E
Masāhim, Kūh-e *mtn.* Iran 43 30.26N 55.08E
Masai Steppe *f.* Tanzania 55 4.30S 37.00E
Masaka Uganda 55 0.20S 31.46E
Masan S. Korea 31 35.10N128.35E
Masasi Tanzania 55 10.43S 38.48E
Masba Nigeria 53 10.35N 13.01E
Masbate *i.* Phil. 37 12.00N123.30E
Mascara Algeria 50 35.24N 0.08E
Maseru Lesotho 56 29.18S 27.28E
Mashhad Iran 43 36.16N 59.34E
Māshkai *r.* Pakistan 40 26.02N 65.19E
Māshkel *r.* Pakistan 40 28.02N 63.25E
Māshkel, Hāmūn-i- *l.* Pakistan 40 28.15N 63.00E
Mashki Chāh Pakistan 40 29.01N 62.27E
Mashonaland *f.* Zimbabwe 57 18.20S 32.00E
Mashūray Afghan. 40 32.12N 68.21E
Masi Norway 22 69.26N 23.40E
Masīlah, Wādī al *f.* Yemen 45 15.10N 51.08E
Masi-Manimba Zaïre 54 4.47S 17.54E
Masindi Uganda 55 1.41N 31.45E
Maşīrah *i.* Oman 38 20.30N 58.50E
Maşīrah, Khalīj *b.* Oman 45 20.10N 58.10E
Masjed Soleymān Iran 43 31.59N 49.18E
Mask, Lough Rep. of Ire. 13 53.38N 9.22W
Maskinongé Canada 77 46.35N 73.30W
Mason Tex. U.S.A. 83 30.45N 99.14W
Mason City U.S.A. 82 43.09N 93.12W
Maspalomas Canary Is. 95 27.42N 15.34W
Masqaṭ Oman 43 23.36N 58.37E
Massa Italy 15 44.02N 10.09E
Massachusetts *d.* U.S.A. 84 42.15N 71.50W
Massakory Chad 53 13.02N 15.43E
Massa Marittima Italy 18 43.03N 10.53E
Massangena Mozambique 57 21.31S 33.03E
Massangulo Mozambique 57 13.54S 35.24E
Massarosa Italy 15 43.52N 10.20E
Massena U.S.A. 84 44.56N 74.54W
Massenya Chad 53 11.21N 16.09E
Masset Canada 74 54.00N132.09W
Massif Central *mts.* France 17 45.00N 3.30E
Massillon U.S.A. 84 40.48N 81.32W
Massinga Mozambique 57 23.20S 35.25E
Massingir Mozambique 57 23.49S 32.04E
Masterton New Zealand 60 40.57S175.39E
Mastung Pakistan 40 29.48N 66.51E
Mastūrah Saudi Arabia 42 23.06N 38.50E
Masvingo Zimbabwe 56 20.10S 30.49E
Maşyāf Syria 44 35.03N 36.21E
Matabeleland *f.* Zimbabwe 56 19.50S 28.15E
Matachewan Canada 76 47.56N 80.39W
Matadi Zaïre 54 5.50S 13.36E
Matagami Canada 76 49.45N 77.34W
Matagami, L. Canada 76 49.50N 77.40W
Matagorda B. U.S.A. 83 28.35N 96.20W
Matakana Australia 67 32.59S145.53E
Matakana I. New Zealand 60 37.35S176.15E
Matala Angola 54 14.45S 15.02E
Matam Senegal 50 15.40N 13.15W
Matamata New Zealand 60 37.49S175.46E
Matameye Niger 53 13.26N 8.28E
Matamoros Coahuila Mexico 83 25.32N103.15W
Matamoros Tamaulipas Mexico 83 25.53N 97.30W
Ma'ṭan Bishrah *well* Libya 48 22.58N 22.39E
Matandu *r.* Tanzania 55 8.44S 39.22E
Matane Canada 77 48.51N 67.32W
Matang China 33 29.30N113.08E
Matankari Niger 53 13.47N 4.00E
Matanzas Cuba 87 23.04N 81.35W
Mataram Indonesia 37 8.36S116.07E
Matarani Peru 92 16.58S 72.07W
Mataranka Australia 62 14.56S133.07E
Mataró Spain 16 41.32N 2.27E
Matatiele R.S.A. 56 30.19S 28.48E
Matatula, C. Samoa 68 14.15S170.35W
Mataura *r.* New Zealand 60 46.34S168.45E
Matautu W. Samoa 68 13.57S171.56W
Matavera Rarotonga Cook Is. 68 21.13S159.44W
Matawai New Zealand 60 38.21S177.32E
Maţāy Egypt 44 28.25N 30.46E
Matehuala Mexico 86 23.40N100.40W
Mateke Hills Zimbabwe 56 21.48S 31.00E
Matera Italy 19 40.41N 16.36E
Matetsi Zimbabwe 56 18.17S 25.57E
Matfors Sweden 23 62.21N 17.02E
Mathews Peak *mtn.* Kenya 55 1.18N 37.20E
Mathis U.S.A. 83 28.06N 97.50W
Mathoura Australia 67 35.49S144.54E
Mathura India 41 27.30N 77.41E
Mati Phil. 37 6.55N126.15E
Matias Barbosa Brazil 94 21.52S 43.21W
Matipó Brazil 94 20.16S 42.17W
Mātli Pakistan 40 25.02N 68.39E
Matlock U.K. 10 53.09N 1.32W
Matochkin Shar U.S.S.R. 28 73.15N 56.35E
Mato Grosso *d.* Brazil 92 13.00S 55.00W
Mato Grosso *town* Brazil 92 15.05S 59.57W
Mato Grosso, Planalto do *f.* Brazil 92 16.00S 54.00W
Mato Grosso do Sul *d.* Brazil 92 20.00S 54.30W
Matope Malaŵi 55 15.20S 34.57E
Matopo Hills Zimbabwe 56 20.45S 28.30E
Matosinhos Portugal 16 41.11N 8.42W
Maṭraḩ Oman 43 23.37N 58.33E
Matsena Nigeria 53 13.13N 10.04E
Matsiatra *r.* Madagascar 57 21.25S 45.33E
Matsubara Japan 35 34.34N135.33E
Matsudo Japan 35 35.47N139.54E

atsue Japan **31** 35.29N133.00E
atsusaka Japan **35** 34.34N136.32E
atsuyama Japan **31** 33.50N132.47E
attagami *r.* Canada **76** 50.43N 81.29W
attawa Canada **76** 46.19N 78.42W
attawamkeag U.S.A. **84** 45.31N 68.21W
atterhorn *mtn.* Italy / Switz. **15** 45.58N 7.38E
atterhorn *mtn.* U.S.A. **80** 41.49N115.23W
atthews Ridge *town* Guyana **90** 7.30N 60.10W
atthew Town Bahamas **87** 20.57N 73.40W
attice Canada **76** 49.39N 83.20W
attmar Sweden **22** 63.19N 13.45E
attoon U.S.A. **82** 39.29N 88.21W
atua Indonesia **36** 2.58S110.52E
aturín Venezuela **90** 9.45N 63.10W
aua Mozambique **57** 13.53S 37.10E
au Aimma India **41** 25.42N 81.55E
aubeuge France **14** 50.17N 3.58E
audaha India **41** 25.41N 80.07E
aude Australia **66** 34.27S144.21E
aués Brazil **91** 3.24S 57.42W
auganj India **41** 24.41N 81.53E
aui *i.* Hawaii U.S.A. **78** 20.45N156.15W
aulvi Bāzār Bangla. **41** 24.29N 91.42E
aumee U.S.A. **84** 41.34N 83.41W
aumee *r.* U.S.A. **84** 41.40N 83.35W
aumere Indonesia **37** 8.35S122.13E
aun Botswana **56** 19.52S 23.40E
aunaloa Hawaiian Is. **69** 21.08N157.13W
auna Loa *mtn.* Hawaiian Is. **69** 19.29N155.36W
aunath Bhanjan India **41** 25.57N 83.33E
au Rānīpur India **41** 25.15N 79.08E
aurice, L. Australia **65** 29.28S130.58E
aurice Nat. Park Canada **77** 46.42N 73.00W
auritania Africa **50** 20.00N 10.00W
auston U.S.A. **82** 43.48N 90.05W
avinga Angola **54** 15.47S 20.21E
avuradonha Mts. Zimbabwe **57** 16.30S 31.20E
awjib, Wādī al *r.* Jordan **44** 31.28N 35.34E
awlaik Burma **34** 23.50N 94.30E
axcanú Mexico **86** 20.35N 89.59W
axville Canada **77** 45.17N 74.51W
ay, C. U.S.A. **85** 38.58N 74.55W
aya Spain **16** 43.12N 1.29W
ayaguana I. Bahamas **87** 22.30N 73.00W
ayagüez Puerto Rico **87** 18.13N 67.09W
ayāmey Iran **43** 36.27N 55.40E
aya Mts. Belize **87** 16.30N 89.00W
aybole U.K. **12** 55.21N 4.41W
aych'ew Ethiopia **45** 13.02N 39.34E
aydena Australia **65** 42.45S146.38E
aydh Somali Rep. **45** 10.57N 47.06E
ayen Germany **14** 50.19N 7.14E
ayenne France **15** 48.18N 0.37W
ayenne *d.* France **15** 48.05N 0.40W
ayenne *r.* France **15** 47.30N 0.37W
ayerthorpe Canada **74** 53.57N115.08W
ayfield U.S.A. **83** 36.44N 88.38W
aykop U.S.S.R. **25** 44.37N 40.48E
aymyo Burma **34** 22.05N 96.28E
aynooth Rep. of Ire. **13** 53.23N 6.37W
ayo *r.* Mexico **81** 26.45N109.47W
ayo *d.* Rep. of Ire. **13** 53.47N 9.07W
ayo, Plains of *f.* Rep. of Ire. **13** 53.46N .05W
ayo Daga Nigeria **53** 6.59N 11.25E
ayo Landing Canada **72** 63.45N135.45W
ayor I. New Zealand **60** 37.15S176.15E
ayotte, Île *i.* Comoros **55** 12.50S 45.10E
ay Pen Jamaica **87** 17.58N 77.14W
ays Landing U.S.A. **85** 39.27N 74.44W
aysville U.S.A. **84** 38.38N 83.46W
ayumba Gabon **54** 3.23S 10.38E
ayville N.Dak. U.S.A. **82** 47.30N 97.19W
ayville N.Y. U.S.A. **76** 42.15N 79.30W
azabuka Zambia **55** 15.50S 27.47E
azagão Brazil **91** 0.07S 51.17W
azamba Mozambique **57** 18.32S 34.50E
azamet France **17** 43.30N 2.24E
azán Peru **90** 3.15S 73.00W
azarredo Argentina **93** 47.00S 66.45W
azarrón Spain **16** 37.38N 1.19W
azatenango Guatemala **86** 14.31N 91.30W
azatlán Mexico **81** 23.13N106.25W
žeikiai U.S.S.R. **23** 56.19N 22.20E
azirbe U.S.S.R. **23** 57.41N 22.21E
azowe *r.* Mozambique **57** 16.32S 33.25E
azowe Zimbabwe **57** 17.30S 30.58E
zu Liedao *is.* China **31** 26.12N120.00E
zunga Zimbabwe **56** 21.45S 29.52E
zurski, Pojezierze *lakes* Poland **21** 53.50N 1.00E
abane Swaziland **56** 26.19S 31.08E
agne Mauritania **50** 16.06N 14.47W
Baiki C.A.R. **53** 3.53N 18.01E
ala C.A.R. **49** 7.48N 20.51E
ala Zambia **55** 8.50S 31.24E
ale Uganda **55** 1.04N 34.12E
almayo Cameroon **53** 3.35N 11.31E
amba Bay *town* Tanzania **55** 11.18S 34.50E
andaka Zaïre **54** 0.03N 18.21E
anza Congo Angola **54** 6.18S 14.16E
arara Uganda **55** 0.36S 30.40E
ari *r.* C.A.R. **49** 4.34N 22.43E
eya Tanzania **55** 8.54S 33.29E
eya *d.* Tanzania **55** 8.30S 32.30E
inda Congo **54** 2.11S 12.55E
ogo Tanzania **55** 7.26S 33.26E
omou *d.* C.A.R. **49** 5.10N 23.00E
omou *r.* C.A.R. **49** 4.08N 22.26E
oro Sudan **49** 6.18N 28.45E
our Senegal **52** 14.22N 16.54W
out Mauritania **50** 16.02N 12.35W
ridge *r.* Angola **54** 7.12S 12.55E
ua Fiji **68** 16.48S178.37E
Mbuji Mayi Zaïre **54** 6.08S 23.39E
Mbulamuti Uganda **55** 0.50N 33.05E
Mbura Tanzania **55** 11.14S 35.25E
Mbutha Fiji **68** 16.39S179.50E
Mbuzi Zambia **55** 12.20S 32.17E
McAlester U.S.A. **83** 34.56N 95.46W
McAllen U.S.A. **83** 26.12N 98.15W
McArthur *r.* Australia **64** 15.54S136.40E
McBride Canada **74** 53.20N120.10W
McCamey U.S.A. **83** 31.08N102.13W
McClintock Canada **75** 57.50N 94.10W
McClintock Channel Canada **73** 71.20N102.00W
McClure Str. Canada **72** 74.30N116.00W
McComb U.S.A. **83** 31.14N 90.27W
McConaughy, L. U.S.A. **82** 41.15N102.00W
McConnel Creek *town* Canada **74** 56.53N126.30W
McCook U.S.A. **82** 40.12N100.38W
McDermitt U.S.A. **80** 41.59N117.36W
McDouall Peak Australia **66** 29.51S134.55E
McGrath U.S.A. **72** 62.58N155.40W
McGregor U.S.A. **82** 46.36N 93.19W
McHenry U.S.A. **82** 42.21N 88.16W
Mchinja Tanzania **55** 9.44S 39.45E
Mchinji Malaŵi **55** 13.48S 32.55E
McIlwraith Range *mts.* Australia **64** 14.00S143.10E
McKeesport U.S.A. **84** 40.21N 79.52W
McKenzie U.S.A. **83** 36.08N 88.31W
McKinley, Mt. U.S.A. **72** 63.00N151.00W
McKinney U.S.A. **83** 33.12N 96.37W
McKittrick U.S.A. **81** 35.18N119.37W
McLaughlin U.S.A. **82** 45.49N100.49W
McLennan Canada **74** 55.42N116.50W
McLeod *r.* Canada **74** 54.08N115.42W
McLeod B. Canada **75** 62.53N110.00W
Mcleod Lake *town* Canada **74** 54.58N123.00W
M'Clintock Canada **74** 60.35N134.25W
McMinnville Oreg. U.S.A. **80** 45.13N123.12W
McMinnville Tenn. U.S.A. **85** 35.40N 85.49W
McNary U.S.A. **81** 34.04N109.51W
McPherson U.S.A. **82** 38.22N 97.40W
McPherson Range *mts.* Australia **67** 28.15S153.00E
Mdantsane R.S.A. **56** 32.54S 27.24E
Mead, L. U.S.A. **81** 36.05N114.25W
Meade U.S.A. **83** 37.17N100.20W
Meadow Lake *town* Canada **75** 54.07N108.20W
Meadville U.S.A. **84** 41.38N 80.09W
Mealhada Portugal **16** 40.22N 8.27W
Meander River *town* Canada **74** 59.02N117.42W
Mearim *r.* Brazil **91** 3.20S 44.20W
Meath *d.* Rep. of Ire. **13** 53.32N 6.40W
Meaux France **15** 48.58N 2.54E
Mécatina, Cap *c.* Canada **77** 50.45N 59.01W
Mecca *see* Makkah Saudi Arabia **48**
Mecca U.S.A. **81** 33.35N116.03W
Mechanicsville U.S.A. **85** 38.26N 76.44W
Mechelen Belgium **14** 51.01N 4.28E
Mecheria Algeria **50** 33.33N 0.17W
Mecklenburger Bucht *b.* Germany **20** 54.05N 11.00E
Mecklenburg-Vorpommern *d.* Germany **20** 53.30N 13.15E
Meconta Mozambique **55** 15.00S 39.50E
Mecufi Mozambique **55** 13.20S 40.32E
Meda Portugal **16** 40.58N 7.16W
Medan Indonesia **36** 3.35N 98.39E
Mede Italy **15** 45.06N 8.44E
Médéa Algeria **51** 36.15N 2.48E
Mededsiz *mtn.* Turkey **42** 37.33N 34.38E
Medegue Gabon **54** 0.37N 10.08E
Medellín Colombia **90** 6.15N 75.36W
Medemblik Neth. **14** 52.48N 5.06E
Médenine Tunisia **51** 33.21N 10.30E
Mederdra Mauritania **52** 17.02N 15.41W
Medford Oreg. U.S.A. **80** 42.19N122.52W
Medford Wisc. U.S.A. **82** 45.09N 90.20W
Medgidia Romania **21** 44.15N 28.16E
Medi Sudan **49** 5.04N 30.44E
Media U.S.A. **85** 39.54N 75.23W
Mediaş Romania **21** 46.10N 24.21E
Medicina Italy **15** 44.28N 11.38E
Medicine Bow Mts. U.S.A. **80** 41.10N106.10W
Medicine Bow Peak *mtn.* U.S.A. **80** 41.21N106.19W
Medicine Hat Canada **75** 50.03N110.40W
Medicine Lake *town* U.S.A. **80** 48.30N104.30W
Medicine Lodge U.S.A. **83** 37.17N 98.35W
Medina *see* Al Madīnah Saudi Arabia **42**
Medina N.Dak. U.S.A. **82** 46.54N 99.18W
Medina N.Y. U.S.A. **84** 43.14N 78.23W
Medina del Campo Spain **16** 41.20N 4.55W
Medina de Ríoseco Spain **16** 41.53N 5.03W
Mêdog China **30** 29.19N 95.19E
Medstead Canada **75** 53.19N108.02W
Medveditsa *r.* U.S.S.R. **25** 49.35N 42.45E
Medvezhyegorsk U.S.S.R. **24** 62.56N 34.28E
Medvin U.S.S.R. **21** 49.25N 30.48E
Medway *r.* U.K. **11** 51.24N 0.31E
Medzhibozh U.S.S.R. **21** 49.29N 27.28E
Meeberrie Australia **62** 26.58S115.51E
Meekatharra Australia **62** 26.35S118.30E
Meeker U.S.A. **80** 40.02N107.55W
Meer Belgium **14** 51.27N 4.46E
Meerhusener Moor *f.* Germany **14** 53.36N 7.33E
Meerut India **41** 28.59N 77.42E
Mēga Ethiopia **49** 4.07N 38.16E
Mégara Greece **19** 38.00N 23.21E
Megasini *mtn.* India **41** 21.38N 86.21E
Meghalaya *d.* India **41** 25.30N 91.00E
Meghna *r.* Bangla. **41** 22.50N 90.50E
Mégiscane *r.* Canada **76** 48.36N 76.00W
Mehadia Romania **21** 44.55N 22.22E
Mehar Pakistan **40** 27.11N 67.49E
Mehekar India **40** 20.09N 76.34E
Mehidpur India **40** 23.49N 75.40E
Mehndāwal India **41** 26.59N 83.07E
Mehsāna India **40** 23.36N 72.24E
Mehtar Lām Afghan. **40** 34.39N 70.10E
Meiktila Burma **34** 20.53N 95.50E
Meiningen Germany **20** 50.34N 10.25E
Meishan China **33** 30.02N103.50E
Meissen Germany **20** 51.10N 13.28E
Mei Xian China **33** 24.20N116.15E
Meiyino Sudan **49** 6.12N 34.40E
Mekatina Canada **76** 46.58N 84.05W
Mekdela Ethiopia **49** 11.28N 39.23E
Mek'elē Ethiopia **49** 13.33N 39.30E
Mekerrhane, Sebkha *f.* Algeria **50** 26.22N 1.20E
Mekhtar Pakistan **40** 30.28N 69.22E
Meknès Morocco **50** 33.53N 5.37W
Mekong *r.* Asia **34** 10.00N106.40E
Mekong Delta Vietnam **34** 10.00N105.40E
Mekongga *mtn.* Indonesia **37** 3.39S121.15E
Mékôngk *r.* Kampuchea *see* Mekong *r.* Asia **34**
Mékrou *r.* Benin **53** 12.20N 2.47E
Melaka Malaysia **36** 2.11N102.16E
Melanesia *is.* Pacific Oc. **68** 5.00N165.00E
Melbourne Australia **67** 37.45S144.58E
Melbourne U.S.A. **85** 28.04N 80.38W
Mélé C.A.R. **49** 9.46N 21.33E
Melegnano Italy **15** 45.21N 9.19E
Meleuz U.S.S.R. **24** 52.58N 55.56E
Mélèzes, Rivière aux *r.* Canada **77** 57.40N 69.29W
Melfi Chad **53** 11.04N 18.03E
Melfi Italy **18** 40.59N 15.39E
Melilla Morocco **50** 35.17N 2.57W
Melilla Spain **16** 35.17N 2.57W
Melipilla Chile **93** 33.42S 71.13W
Melitopol U.S.S.R. **25** 46.51N 35.22E
Melk Austria **20** 48.14N 15.20E
Mellen U.S.A. **82** 46.20N 90.40W
Mellerud Sweden **23** 58.42N 12.28E
Mellit Sudan **48** 14.08N 25.33E
Melmore Pt. Rep. of Ire. **13** 55.15N 7.49W
Melnik Bulgaria **19** 41.30N 23.22E
Mělník Czech. **20** 50.20N 14.29E
Melo Uruguay **94** 32.22S 54.10W
Melrhir, Chott *f.* Algeria **51** 34.20N 6.20E
Melrose U.K. **12** 55.36N 2.43W
Melrose Mont. U.S.A. **80** 45.37N112.41W
Melrose N.Mex U.S.A. **81** 34.26N103.38W
Melstone U.S.A. **80** 46.36N107.52W
Meltaus Finland **22** 66.54N 25.22E
Melton Australia **67** 37.41S144.36E
Melton Mowbray U.K. **10** 52.46N 0.53W
Melun France **15** 48.32N 2.40E
Melvich U.K. **12** 58.33N 3.55W
Melville Canada **75** 50.55N102.48W
Melville, C. Australia **64** 14.11S144.30E
Melville, L. Canada **77** 53.45N 59.30W
Melville B. Australia **64** 12.10S136.32E
Melville Hills Canada **72** 69.20N122.00W
Melville I. Australia **64** 11.30S131.00E
Melville I. Canada **72** 75.30N110.00W
Melville Pen. Canada **73** 68.00N 84.00W
Melvin, Lough Rep. of Ire. / U.K. **13** 54.26N 8.12W
Melzo Italy **15** 45.30N 9.25E
Mêmar Co *l.* China **41** 34.10N 82.15E
Memba Mozambique **57** 14.16S 40.30E
Memboro Indonesia **36** 9.22S119.32E
Memmingen Germany **20** 47.59N 10.11E
Memphis *ruins* Egypt **44** 29.52N 31.12E
Memphis Tenn. U.S.A. **83** 35.08N 90.03W
Mena U.S.A. **83** 34.35N 94.15W
Mena U.S.S.R. **21** 51.30N 32.15E
Menai Str. U.K. **10** 53.17N 4.20W
Ménaka Mali **51** 15.55N 2.24E
Mènam Khong *r.* Laos *see* Mekong *r.* Asia **34**
Menarandra *r.* Madagascar **57** 25.17S 44.30E
Menard U.S.A. **83** 30.55N 99.47W
Menawashei Sudan **49** 12.40N 24.59E
Mendawai *r.* Indonesia **36** 3.17S113.20E
Mende France **17** 44.32N 3.30E
Mendebo Mts. Ethiopia **49** 7.00N 39.30E
Mendi P.N.G. **37** 6.13S143.39E
Mendip Hills U.K. **11** 51.15N 2.40W
Mendocino, C. U.S.A. **80** 40.25N124.25W
Mendooran Australia **67** 31.48S149.08E
Mendoza Argentina **93** 32.54S 68.50W
Mendoza *d.* Argentina **93** 34.30S 68.00W
Mendung Indonesia **36** 0.31N103.12E
Mene Grande Venezuela **90** 9.51N 70.57W
Menemen Turkey **42** 38.34N 27.03E
Menen Belgium **14** 50.48N 3.07E
Menfi Italy **18** 37.36N 12.59E
Mengcheng China **32** 33.16N116.33E
Mengzi China **39** 23.20N103.21E
Menihek Lakes Canada **77** 54.00N 66.35W
Menindee Australia **66** 32.23S142.30E
Menindee L. Australia **66** 32.21S142.20E
Menominee U.S.A. **82** 45.07N 87.37W
Menomonie U.S.A. **82** 44.53N 91.55W
Menongue Angola **54** 14.40S 17.41E
Menorca *i.* Spain **16** 40.00N 4.00E
Mentawai, Kepulauan *is.* Indonesia **36** 2.50S 99.00E
Mentekab Malaysia **36** 3.29N102.21E
Mentok Indonesia **36** 2.04S105.12E
Menton France **17** 43.47N 7.30E
Menyapa, Gunung *mtn.* Indonesia **36** 1.00N116.20E
Menzel Bourguiba Tunisia **51** 37.10N 9.48E
Menzies Australia **63** 29.41S121.02E
Menzies, Mt. Antarctica **96** 71.50S 61.00E
Meppel Neth. **14** 52.42N 6.12E
Meppen Germany **14** 52.42N 7.17E
Mer France **15** 47.42N 1.30E
Merano Italy **18** 46.41N 11.10E
Merauke Indonesia **64** 8.30S140.22E
Merbein Australia **66** 34.11S142.04E
Mercato Saraceno Italy **15** 43.57N 12.12E
Merced U.S.A. **80** 37.18N120.29W
Mercedes Buenos Aires Argentina **93** 34.40S 59.25W
Mercedes Corrientes Argentina **92** 29.15S 58.05W
Mercedes San Luis Argentina **93** 33.40S 65.30W
Mercedes Uruguay **93** 33.16S 58.01W
Mercy, C. Canada **73** 65.00N 63.30W
Mere U.K. **11** 51.05N 2.16W
Meredith Australia **66** 37.50S144.05E
Meredith, L. U.S.A. **83** 35.36N101.42W
Mereeg Somali Rep. **45** 3.47N 47.18E
Merefa U.S.S.R. **25** 49.49N 36.05E
Mereke C.A.R. **49** 7.34N 23.09E
Mergenevo U.S.S.R. **25** 49.59N 51.19E
Mergui Burma **34** 12.26N 98.38E
Mergui Archipelago *is.* Burma **34** 11.15N 98.00E
Meribah Australia **66** 34.42S140.53E
Meriç *r.* Turkey **19** 40.52N 26.12E
Mérida Mexico **87** 20.59N 89.39W
Mérida Spain **16** 38.55N 6.20W
Mérida Venezuela **90** 8.24N 71.08W
Mérida, Cordillera de *mts.* Venezuela **90** 8.30N 71.00W
Meridian U.S.A. **83** 32.22N 88.42W
Mérignac France **17** 44.50N 0.42W
Merigur Australia **66** 34.21S141.23E
Merikarvia Finland **23** 61.51N 21.30E
Merimbula Australia **67** 36.52S149.55E
Merino Australia **66** 37.45S141.35E
Merir *i.* Caroline Is. **37** 4.19N132.18E
Merirumã Brazil **91** 1.15N 54.50W
Merizo Guam **68** 13.16N144.40E
Merksem Belgium **14** 51.14N 4.25E
Merlo Argentina **93** 34.40S 58.45W
Merredin Australia **63** 31.29S118.16E
Merrick *mtn.* U.K. **12** 55.08N 4.29W
Merrill Oreg. U.S.A. **80** 42.01N121.36W
Merrill Wisc. U.S.A. **82** 45.11N 89.41W
Merriman U.S.A. **82** 42.55N101.42W
Merritt Canada **74** 50.10N120.45W
Merriwa Australia **67** 32.08S150.20E
Mersa Fatma Ethiopia **48** 14.55N 40.20E
Mersch Lux. **14** 49.44N 6.05E
Mersea I. U.K. **11** 51.47N 0.58E
Merseburg Germany **20** 51.22N 12.00E
Mersey *r.* U.K. **10** 53.22N 2.37W
Merseyside *d.* U.K. **10** 53.28N 3.00W
Mersin Turkey **42** 36.47N 34.37E
Mersing Malaysia **36** 2.25N103.50E
Merta India **40** 26.39N 74.02E
Merta Road *town* India **40** 26.43N 73.55E
Merthyr Tydfil U.K. **11** 51.45N 3.23W
Mértola Portugal **16** 37.38N 7.40W
Merton U.K. **11** 51.25N 0.12W
Mertzon U.S.A. **83** 31.16N100.49W
Méru France **15** 49.14N 2.08E
Meru *mtn.* Tanzania **55** 3.15S 36.44E
Méry France **15** 48.30N 3.53E
Merzifon Turkey **42** 40.52N 35.28E
Merzig Germany **14** 49.26N 6.39E
Mesa U.S.A. **81** 33.25N111.50W
Mesagne Italy **19** 40.33N 17.49E
Meslay-du-Maine France **15** 47.57N 0.33W
Mesocco Switz. **15** 46.23N 9.14E
Mesolóngion Greece **19** 38.23N 21.23E
Mesopotamia *f.* Iraq **43** 33.30N 44.30E
Messalo *r.* Mozambique **55** 11.38S 40.27E
Messina Italy **18** 38.13N 15.34E
Messina R.S.A. **56** 22.20S 30.03E
Messina, Stretto di *str.* Italy **18** 38.10N 15.35E
Messíni Greece **19** 37.03N 22.00E
Messiniakós, Kólpos *g.* Greece **19** 36.50N 22.05E
Mesta *r.* Bulgaria *see* Néstos *r.* Greece **19**
Mestre Italy **15** 45.29N 12.15E
Meta *r.* Venezuela **90** 6.10N 67.30W
Metán Argentina **92** 25.30S 65.00W
Metangula Mozambique **55** 12.41S 34.51E
Metković Yugo. **19** 43.03N 17.38E
Metlakatla U.S.A. **74** 55.09N131.35W
Métsovon Greece **19** 39.46N 21.11E
Metz France **17** 49.07N 6.11E
Meulaboh Indonesia **36** 4.10N 96.09E
Meulan France **15** 49.01N 1.54E
Meuse *r.* Belgium *see* Maas *r.* Neth. **14**
Mexia U.S.A. **83** 31.41N 96.29W
Mexicali Mexico **81** 32.40N115.29W
Mexico C. America **86** 20.00N100.00W
México *d.* Mexico **86** 19.45N 99.30W
Mexico Mo. U.S.A. **82** 39.10N 91.53W
Mexico, G. of N. America **86** 25.00N 90.00W
Mexico City *see* Ciudad de México Mexico **86**
Meydān Kalay Afghan. **40** 32.25N 66.44E
Meydān Khvolah Afghan. **40** 33.36N 69.51E
Meymaneh Afghan. **38** 35.54N 64.43E
Mezen U.S.S.R. **24** 65.50N 44.20E
Mezen *r.* U.S.S.R. **24** 65.50N 44.18E
Mézenc, Mont *mtn.* France **17** 44.54N 4.11E
Mezenskaya Guba *g.* U.S.S.R. **24** 66.30N 44.00E
Mezökövesd Hungary **21** 47.50N 20.34E
Mezzolombardo Italy **15** 46.13N 11.05E
Mhow India **40** 22.33N 75.46E
Miahuatlán Mexico **86** 16.20N 96.36W
Miājlar India **40** 26.15N 70.23E
Miami Fla. U.S.A. **85** 25.45N 80.15W
Miami Okla. U.S.A. **83** 36.53N 94.53W
Miami Tex. U.S.A. **83** 35.42N100.38W
Miami Beach *town* U.S.A. **85** 25.47N 80.07W
Miāndow Āb Iran **43** 36.57N 46.06E
Miandrivazo Madagascar **57** 19.31S 45.28E
Mīāneh Iran **43** 37.23N 47.45E
Miang, Phukao *mtn.* Thailand **34** 16.55N101.00E
Miāni India **40** 21.51N 69.23E
Miāni Hōr *b.* Pakistan **40** 25.34N 66.19E
Miānwāli Pakistan **40** 32.35N 71.33E
Mianyang Hubei China **33** 30.25N113.30E
Mianyang Sichuan China **33** 31.26N104.45E
Miao'er Shan *mtn.* China **33** 25.50N110.22E
Miaoli Taiwan **33** 24.34N120.48E
Miarinarivo Madagascar **57** 18.57S 46.55E
Miass U.S.S.R. **28** 55.00N 60.00E
Mibu *r.* Japan **35** 35.49N137.57E
Mica R.S.A. **56** 24.09S 30.49E
Micang Shan *mts.* China **32** 32.40N107.28E
Michael, L. Canada **77** 54.32N 58.15W
Michalovce Czech. **21** 48.45N 21.55E
Michelson, Mt. U.S.A. **72** 69.19N144.17W
Michigan *d.* U.S.A. **84** 44.00N 85.00W
Michigan, L. U.S.A. **84** 44.00N 87.00W
Michigan City U.S.A. **84** 41.43N 86.54W
Michipicoten Canada **76** 47.59N 84.55W
Michipicoten I. Canada **76** 47.40N 85.50W
Michoacán *d.* Mexico **86** 19.20N101.00W
Michurin Bulgaria **19** 42.09N 27.51E
Michurinsk U.S.S.R. **24** 52.54N 40.30E
Micronesia *is.* Pacific Oc. **68** 8.00N160.00E
Midale Canada **75** 49.22N103.27W
Mid Atlantic Ridge *f.* Atlantic Oc. **95** 20.00N 45.00W
Middelburg Neth. **14** 51.30N 3.36E
Middelburg C.P. R.S.A. **56** 31.29S 25.00E
Middelburg Trans. R.S.A. **56** 25.45S 29.27E
Middelharnis Neth. **14** 51.46N 4.09E
Middenmeer Neth. **14** 52.51N 4.59E
Middleboro Canada **75** 49.01N 95.21W
Middlebury U.S.A. **84** 44.01N 73.10W
Middle I. Australia **63** 34.07S123.12E
Middle Loup *r.* U.S.A. **82** 41.17N 98.23W
Middleport N.Y. U.S.A. **76** 43.13N 78.29W
Middlesboro U.S.A. **85** 36.37N 83.43W
Middlesbrough U.K. **10** 54.34N 1.13W
Middleton Canada **77** 44.57N 65.04W
Middleton Reef Pacific Oc. **68** 29.28S159.06E
Middletown Del. U.S.A. **85** 39.25N 75.47W
Middletown Ind. U.S.A. **84** 39.31N 84.13W
Middletown N.Y. U.S.A. **85** 41.27N 74.25W
Mid Glamorgan *d.* U.K. **11** 51.38N 3.25W
Midi-Pyrénées *d.* France **17** 44.10N 2.00E
Midland Canada **76** 44.45N 79.53W
Midland Mich. U.S.A. **84** 43.38N 84.14W
Midland Tex. U.S.A. **83** 32.00N102.05W
Midland Junction Australia **63** 31.54S115.57E
Midleton Rep. of Ire. **13** 51.55N 8.10W
Midnapore India **41** 22.26N 87.20E
Midongy-Sud Madagascar **57** 23.35S 47.01E
Midway Is. Hawaiian Is. **68** 28.15N177.25W
Midwest U.S.A. **80** 43.25N106.16W
Midwest City U.S.A. **83** 35.27N 97.24W
Midyan *f.* Saudi Arabia **44** 27.50N 35.30E
Midye Turkey **19** 41.37N 28.07E
Midžor *mtn.* Yugo. **19** 43.23N 22.42E
Mie *d.* Japan **35** 34.42N136.08E
Miechów Poland **21** 50.23N 20.01E
Miedzychód Poland **20** 52.36N 15.55E
Mielec Poland **21** 50.18N 21.25E
Mienga Angola **54** 17.16S 19.50E
Mieres Spain **16** 43.15N 5.46W
Migang Shan *mtn.* China **32** 35.32N106.13E
Miguel Hidalgo, Presa *resr.* Mexico **81** 26.41N108.19W
Migyaunglaung Burma **34** 14.40N 98.09E
Mijares *r.* Spain **16** 39.58N 0.01W
Mikhaylov U.S.S.R. **24** 54.14N 39.00E
Mikhaylovgrad Bulgaria **19** 43.25N 23.11E
Mikhaylovka U.S.S.R. **25** 50.05N 43.15E
Miki Japan **35** 34.48N134.59E
Mikínai Greece **19** 37.44N 22.45E
Mikindani Tanzania **55** 10.16S 40.05E
Mikkeli Finland **24** 61.44N 27.15E
Mikkwa *r.* Canada **74** 58.25N114.46W
Míkonos *i.* Greece **19** 37.29N 25.25E
Mikumi Tanzania **55** 7.22S 37.00E
Mikun U.S.S.R. **24** 62.20N 50.01E
Milagro Ecuador **90** 2.11S 79.36W
Milan *see* Milano Italy **15**
Milan Mo. U.S.A. **82** 40.12N 93.07W
Milange Mozambique **55** 16.09S 35.44E
Milano Italy **15** 45.28N 9.10E
Milâs Turkey **19** 37.18N 27.48E
Milbank U.S.A. **82** 45.14N 96.38W
Milbanke Sd. Canada **74** 52.18N128.33W
Mildenhall U.K. **11** 52.20N 0.30E
Mildura Australia **66** 34.14S142.13E
Miles Australia **64** 26.40S150.11E
Miles City U.S.A. **80** 46.25N105.51W
Milford Del. U.S.A. **85** 38.55N 75.25W
Milford Utah U.S.A. **80** 38.24N113.01W
Milford Haven *town* U.K. **11** 51.43N 5.02W
Milford Sound *town* New Zealand **60** 44.41S167.56E
Miliana Algeria **51** 27.21N 2.28E
Miling Australia **63** 30.27S116.20E
Milk *r.* U.S.A. **80** 48.05N106.15W
Millau France **17** 44.06N 3.05E
Millbrook U.S.A. **85** 41.47N 73.42W
Mille Lacs, Lac des *l.* Canada **76** 48.45N 90.35W
Mille Lacs L. U.S.A. **82** 46.10N 93.45W
Miller *r.* Australia **66** 30.05S136.07E
Millerovo U.S.S.R. **25** 48.55N 40.25E
Millersburg Mich. U.S.A. **84** 45.21N 84.02W
Milleur Pt. U.K. **12** 55.01N 5.07W
Millicent Australia **66** 37.36S140.22E
Millington U.S.A. **85** 39.16N 75.50W
Millinocket U.S.A. **84** 45.39N 68.43W
Millmerran Australia **65** 27.51S151.17E

Millom U.K. **10** 54.13N 3.16W
Mills L. Canada **74** 61.30N118.10W
Millville U.S.A. **85** 39.24N 75.02W
Milne Inlet *town* Canada **73** 72.30N 80.59W
Milo *r.* Guinea **52** 11.05N 9.05W
Milos Greece **19** 36.45N 24.27E
Mílos *i.* Greece **19** 36.40N 24.26E
Milparinka Australia **66** 29.45S141.55E
Milton Australia **67** 35.19S150.24E
Milton Canada **76** 43.31N 79.53W
Milton Del. U.S.A. **85** 38.47N 75.19W
Milton Keynes U.K. **11** 52.03N 0.42W
Miltou Chad **53** 10.10N 17.30E
Miluo China **33** 28.50N113.05E
Milwaukee U.S.A. **82** 43.02N 87.55W
Milwaukie U.S.A. **80** 45.27N122.38W
Milyatino U.S.S.R. **24** 54.30N 34.20E
Mim Ghana **52** 6.55N 2.34W
Miminiska L. Canada **76** 51.32N 88.33W
Mina U.S.A. **80** 38.24N118.07W
Mīnā 'al Aḥmadī Kuwait **38** 29.04N 48.08E
Mīnāb Iran **43** 27.07N 57.05E
Mīnā Baranis Egypt **48** 23.55N 35.28E
Minaki Canada **76** 50.00N 94.48W
Minas Uruguay **93** 34.23S 55.14W
Minas Basin *b.* Canada **77** 45.20N 64.00W
Minas Channel *str.* Canada **77** 45.15N 64.45W
Minas de Corrales Uruguay **93** 31.35S 55.28W
Minas de Ríotinto Spain **16** 37.41N 6.37W
Minas Gerais *d.* Brazil **94** 18.00S 45.00W
Minatitlán Mexico **86** 17.59N 94.32W
Minbu Burma **34** 20.09N 94.52E
Mindanao *i.* Phil. **37** 7.30N125.00E
Mindanao Sea Phil. **37** 9.10N124.25E
Minden Germany **20** 52.18N 8.54E
Minden U.S.A. **83** 32.37N 93.17W
Mindif Cameroon **53** 10.25N 14.23E
Mindiptana Indonesia **37** 5.45S140.22E
Mindona L. Australia **66** 33.09S142.09E
Mindoro *i.* Phil. **37** 13.00N121.00E
Mindoro Str. Pacific Oc. **37** 12.30N120.10E
Mindra *mtn.* Romania **21** 45.20N 23.32E
Minehead U.K. **11** 51.12N 3.29W
Mineola U.S.A. **83** 32.40N 95.29W
Minerva Australia **64** 24.00S148.05E
Mingan Canada **77** 50.18N 64.02W
Mingary Australia **66** 32.09S140.46E
Mingela Australia **64** 19.53S146.40E
Mingenew Australia **63** 29.11S115.26E
Mingin Burma **34** 22.52N 94.39E
Mingin Range *mts.* Burma **34** 24.00N 95.45E
Minhe China **32** 36.12N102.59E
Minidoka U.S.A. **80** 42.46N113.30W
Minigwal, L. Australia **63** 29.35S123.12E
Min Jiang *r.* China **33** 26.06N119.15E
Minlaton Australia **66** 34.46S137.37E
Minna Nigeria **53** 9.39N 6.32E
Minneapolis Kans. U.S.A. **82** 39.08N 97.42W
Minneapolis Minn. U.S.A. **82** 44.59N 93.13W
Minnedosa Canada **75** 50.14N 99.51W
Minnesota *d.* U.S.A. **82** 46.00N 94.00W
Minnesota *r.* U.S.A. **82** 44.54N 93.10W
Minnesota Lake *town* U.S.A. **82** 43.51N 93.50W
Minnipa Australia **66** 32.51S135.09E
Minnitaki L. Canada **76** 50.00N 91.50W
Mino Japan **35** 35.34N136.56E
Miño *r.* Spain **16** 41.50N 8.52W
Minobu-sanchi *mts.* Japan **35** 35.05N138.15E
Mino-kamo Japan **35** 35.26N137.01E
Mino-mikawa-kōgen *mts.* Japan **35** 35.16N137.10E
Minorca *i. see* Menorca *i.* Spain **16**
Minot U.S.A. **82** 48.16N101.19W
Minqin China **32** 38.42N103.11E
Minsen Germany **14** 53.44N 7.59E
Min Shan *mts.* China **32** 32.40N104.40E
Minsk U.S.S.R. **21** 53.51N 27.30E
Minto, L. Canada **73** 51.00N 73.37W
Minto, Lac *l.* Canada **76** 57.15N 74.50W
Minturno Italy **18** 41.15N 13.45E
Minūf Egypt **44** 30.28N 30.56E
Min Xian China **32** 34.26N104.02E
Minyā al Qamḥ Egypt **44** 30.31N 31.21E
Minyar U.S.S.R. **24** 55.06N 57.29E
Miquelon Canada **76** 49.25N 76.32W
Mira Italy **15** 45.26N 12.08E
Mīrābād Afghan. **40** 30.25N 61.50E
Miracema Brazil **94** 21.22S 42.09W
Mirah, Wādī al *r.* Iraq **42** 32.27N 41.21E
Miraj India **38** 16.51N 74.42E
Miramichi B. Canada **77** 47.08N 65.08W
Mīram Shāh Pakistan **40** 33.01N 70.04E
Mīrān Pakistan **40** 31.24N 70.43E
Miranda de Ebro Spain **16** 42.41N 2.57W
Miranda do Douro Portugal **16** 41.30N 6.16W
Mirande France **17** 43.31N 0.25E
Mirandela Portugal **16** 41.28N 7.10W
Mirando City U.S.A. **83** 27.26N 99.00W
Mirandola Italy **15** 44.53N 11.04E
Mīr Bachcheh Kūt Afghan. **40** 34.45N 69.08E
Mirbāṭ Oman **38** 17.00N 54.45E
Mirecourt France **17** 48.18N 6.08E
Miri Malaysia **36** 4.28N114.00E
Miriam Vale *town* Australia **64** 24.20S151.34E
Mirim, L. Brazil **94** 33.10S 53.30W
Mirintu Creek *r.* Australia **66** 28.58S143.18E
Mironovka U.S.S.R. **21** 49.40N 30.59E
Miroşi Romania **21** 44.25N 24.58E
Mīrpur Jammu & Kashmir **40** 33.15N 73.55E
Mīrpur Batoro Pakistan **40** 24.44N 68.16E
Mīrpur Khās Pakistan **38** 25.33N 69.05E
Mīrpur Sakro Pakistan **40** 24.33N 67.37E
Miryeny U.S.S.R. **21** 47.00N 29.06E
Mirzāpur India **41** 25.09N 82.35E
Miscou I. Canada **77** 47.57N 64.33W
Mishawaka U.S.A. **84** 41.38N 86.10W
Mishima Japan **35** 35.07N138.55E
Mishkino U.S.S.R. **24** 55.34N 56.00E
Misima I. P.N.G. **64** 10.40S152.45E
Misiones *d.* Argentina **92** 27.00S 54.40W
Miskī Sudan **48** 14.51N 24.13E
Miskolc Hungary **21** 48.07N 20.47E
Mismār Sudan **48** 18.13N 35.38E
Misool *i.* Indonesia **37** 1.50S130.10E
Misr al Jadīdah Egypt **44** 30.06N 31.20E
Miṣrātah Libya **51** 32.23N 15.06E
Miṣrātah *d.* Libya **51** 30.30N 17.00E
Miṣr Baḥrī *f.* Egypt **44** 30.30N 31.00E
Missinaibi *r.* Canada **76** 50.44N 81.29W
Mission U.S.A. **82** 43.18N100.40W
Mississauga Canada **76** 43.35N 79.37W
Mississippi *d.* U.S.A. **83** 32.40N 90.00W
Mississippi *r.* U.S.A. **83** 29.00N 89.15W
Mississippi Delta U.S.A. **83** 29.10N 89.15W
Mississippi Sd. U.S.A. **83** 30.15N 88.40W
Missoula U.S.A. **80** 46.52N114.01W
Missouri *d.* U.S.A. **82** 38.30N 92.00W
Missouri *r.* U.S.A. **82** 38.50N 90.08W
Missouri Valley *town* U.S.A. **82** 41.33N 95.53W
Mistake Creek *town* Australia **62** 17.06S129.04E
Mistassini Canada **77** 48.54N 72.13W
Mistassini *r.* Canada **77** 48.53N 72.14W
Mistassini, Lac *l.* Canada **77** 51.15N 73.10W
Mistassini Prov. Park Canada **77** 51.30N 73.20W
Mistastin Canada **77** 55.55N 63.30W
Mistinibi, L. Canada **77** 55.55N 64.10W
Mistretta Italy **18** 37.56N 14.22E
Mitchell Australia **64** 26.29S147.58E
Mitchell *r.* Qld. Australia **64** 15.12S141.35E
Mitchell *r.* Vic. Australia **67** 37.53S147.41E
Mitchell Oreg. U.S.A. **80** 44.34N120.09W
Mitchell S.Dak. U.S.A. **82** 43.40N 98.00W
Mitchell, Mt. U.S.A. **85** 35.47N 82.16W
Mitchelstown Rep. of Ire. **13** 52.16N 8.17W
Mīt Ghamr Egypt **44** 30.43N 31.16E
Mithapur India **40** 22.25N 69.00E
Mithi Pakistan **40** 24.44N 69.48E
Mitilíni Greece **19** 39.06N 26.34E
Mitla, Mamarr *pass* Egypt **44** 30.00N 32.53E
Mitla Pass *see* Mitla, Mamarr *pass* Egypt **44**
Mitsinjo Madagascar **57** 16.01S 45.52E
Mits'iwa Ethiopia **48** 15.36N 39.29E
Mits'iwa Channel Ethiopia **48** 15.30N 40.00E
Mittagong Australia **67** 34.27S150.25E
Mittellandkanal Germany **14** 52.24N 7.52E
Mitú Colombia **90** 1.08N 70.03W
Mitumba, Monts *mts.* Zaïre **55** 3.00S 28.30E
Mitwaba Zaïre **55** 8.32S 27.20E
Mitzic Gabon **54** 0.48N 11.30E
Miura Japan **35** 35.08N139.37E
Miya *r.* Japan **35** 34.32N136.44E
Miyako jima *i.* Japan **31** 24.45N125.25E
Miyakonojō Japan **31** 31.43N131.02E
Miyazaki Japan **31** 31.58N131.50E
Mizdah Libya **51** 31.26N 12.59E
Mizen Head Rep. of Ire. **13** 51.27N 9.50W
Mizil Romania **21** 45.00N 26.26E
Mizoch U.S.S.R. **21** 50.30N 25.50E
Mizoram *d.* India **39** 23.40N 92.40E
Mizpe Ramon Israel **44** 30.36N 34.48E
Mizukaidō Japan **35** 36.01N139.59E
Mizunami Japan **35** 35.22N137.15E
Mjölby Sweden **23** 58.19N 15.08E
Mjösa *l.* Norway **23** 60.40N 11.00E
Mkata Tanga Tanzania **55** 5.47S 38.18E
Mkushi Zambia **55** 13.40S 29.26E
Mkuze R.S.A. **57** 27.10S 32.00E
Mkwaja Tanzania **55** 5.46S 38.51E
Mkwiti Tanzania **55** 10.27S 39.18E
Mladá Boleslav Czech. **20** 50.26N 14.55E
Mława Poland **21** 53.06N 20.23E
Mljet *i.* Yugo. **19** 42.45N 17.30E
Mneni Zimbabwe **56** 20.38S 30.03E
Moab U.S.A. **80** 38.35N109.33W
Moa I. Australia **64** 10.12S142.16E
Moama Australia **67** 36.05S144.50E
Moamba Mozambique **57** 25.35S 32.13E
Moanda Gabon **54** 1.25S 13.18E
Moapa U.S.A. **81** 36.40N114.39W
Moatize Mozambique **57** 16.10S 33.40E
Moba Zaïre **55** 7.03S 29.42E
Mobara Japan **35** 35.25N140.18E
Mobaye C.A.R. **49** 4.19N 21.11E
Moberly U.S.A. **82** 39.25N 92.26W
Mobert Canada **76** 48.41N 85.40W
Mobile U.S.A. **83** 30.42N 88.05W
Mobile B. U.S.A. **83** 30.25N 88.00W
Mobridge U.S.A. **82** 45.32N100.26W
Mobutu Sese Seko, L. *see* Albert, L. Uganda / Zaïre **55**
Moçambique *town* Mozambique **55** 15.00S 40.47E
Mocimboa da Praia Mozambique **55** 11.19S 40.19E
Mocimboa do Ruvuma Mozambique **55** 11.05S 39.15E
Moclips U.S.A. **80** 47.14N124.13W
Mococa Brazil **94** 21.28S 47.00W
Moctezuma Mexico **81** 30.10N106.28W
Mocuba Mozambique **55** 16.52S 37.02E
Modane France **17** 45.12N 6.40E
Modāsa India **40** 23.28N 73.18E
Modder *r.* R.S.A. **56** 29.03S 23.56E
Modena Italy **15** 44.39N 10.55E
Modena U.S.A. **80** 37.48N113.57W
Modesto U.S.A. **80** 37.39N121.00W
Modica Italy **18** 36.51N 14.51E
Modjamboli Zaïre **54** 2.28N 22.06E
Moe Australia **67** 38.10S146.15E
Moebase Mozambique **57** 17.04S 38.41E
Moelv Norway **23** 60.56N 10.42E
Moffat U.K. **12** 55.20N 3.27W
Moga India **40** 30.48N 75.10E
Mogadishu *see* Muqdisho Somali Rep. **55**
Mogaung Burma **34** 25.15N 96.54E
Mogi das Cruzes Brazil **94** 23.33S 46.14W
Mogi-Guaçu Brazil **94** 20.55S 48.06W
Mogilev U.S.S.R. **21** 53.54N 30.20E
Mogilev Podolskiy U.S.S.R. **21** 48.29N 27.49E
Mogilno Poland **21** 52.40N 17.58E
Mogi-Mirim Brazil **94** 22.29S 46.55W
Mogincual Mozambique **55** 15.33S 40.29E
Mogliano Veneto Italy **15** 45.33N 12.14E
Mogok Burma **34** 23.00N 96.30E
Mogollon Rim *f.* U.S.A. **81** 32.30N111.00W
Mogumber Australia **63** 31.01S116.02E
Mohács Hungary **21** 45.59N 18.42E
Mohammedia Morocco **50** 33.44N 7.24W
Mohana India **41** 25.54N 77.45E
Mohawk Ariz. U.S.A. **81** 32.41N113.47W
Mohéli *see* Mwali *i.* Comoros **55**
Mohon France **15** 49.45N 4.44E
Mohoro Tanzania **55** 8.09S 39.07E
Mohoru Kenya **55** 1.01S 34.07E
Moi Norway **23** 58.28N 6.32E
Moincêr China **41** 31.10N 80.52E
Moindi Gabon **54** 3.24S 11.43E
Mointy U.S.S.R. **28** 47.10N 73.18E
Mo-i-Rana Norway **22** 66.19N 14.10E
Mõisaküla U.S.S.R. **23** 58.06N 25.11E
Moisdon France **15** 47.37N 1.22W
Moisie *r.* Canada **77** 50.13N 66.02W
Moissac France **17** 44.07N 1.05E
Moïssala Chad **53** 8.20N 17.40E
Mojave U.S.A. **81** 35.03N118.10W
Mojave Desert U.S.A. **81** 35.00N117.00W
Mojokerto Indonesia **37** 7.25S112.31E
Mokameh India **41** 25.24N 85.55E
Mokau New Zealand **60** 38.41S174.37E
Mokmer Indonesia **37** 1.13S136.13E
Mokpo S. Korea **31** 34.50N126.25E
Mol Belgium **14** 51.11N 5.09E
Molchanovo U.S.S.R. **28** 57.39N 83.45E
Mold U.K. **10** 53.10N 3.08W
Moldavskaya S.S.R. *d.* U.S.S.R. **21** 47.30N 28.30E
Molde Norway **22** 62.44N 7.08E
Molepolole Botswana **56** 24.26S 25.34E
Molfetta Italy **19** 41.12N 16.36E
Molihong Shan *mtn.* China **32** 42.11N124.43E
Molina de Aragón Spain **16** 40.50N 1.54W
Moline U.S.A. **82** 41.30N 90.30W
Molinella Italy **15** 44.37N 11.40E
Molino Lacy Mexico **81** 30.05N114.24W
Moliro Zaïre **55** 8.11S 30.29E
Molise *d.* Italy **18** 41.40N 15.00E
Mollendo Peru **92** 17.02S 72.01W
Mölndal Sweden **23** 57.39N 12.01E
Molodechno U.S.S.R. **21** 54.16N 26.50E
Molokai *i.* Hawaii U.S.A. **78** 21.20N157.00W
Molong Australia **67** 33.08S148.53E
Molopo *r.* R.S.A. **56** 28.30S 20.22E
Moloundou Cameroon **54** 2.55N 12.01E
Molson L. Canada **75** 54.12N 96.45W
Molt U.S.A. **82** 46.22N102.20W
Molteno R.S.A. **56** 31.23S 26.21E
Moluccas *is.* Indonesia **37** 4.00S128.00E
Molucca Sea *see* Maluku, Laut *sea* Pacific Oc. **37**
Moma Mozambique **55** 16.40S 39.10E
Mombasa Kenya **55** 4.04S 39.40E
Momi Zaïre **55** 1.42S 27.03E
Mommark Denmark **20** 54.55N 10.03E
Mompós Colombia **90** 9.15N 74.29W
Mon *d.* Burma **34** 16.45N 97.25E
Møn *i.* Denmark **23** 55.00N 12.20E
Mona *i.* Puerto Rico **87** 18.06N 67.54W
Monaco Europe **17** 43.40N 7.25E
Monadhliath Mts. U.K. **12** 57.09N 4.08W
Monaghan Rep. of Ire. **13** 54.15N 6.58W
Monaghan *d.* Rep. of Ire. **13** 54.10N 7.00W
Monahans U.S.A. **83** 31.36N102.54W
Monarch Mt. Canada **74** 51.55N125.57W
Monastir Tunisia **51** 35.35N 10.50E
Moncalieri Italy **15** 45.00N 7.40E
Monchegorsk U.S.S.R. **24** 67.55N 33.01E
Mönchen-Gladbach Germany **14** 51.12N 6.25E
Monchique Portugal **16** 37.19N 8.33W
Monclova Mexico **83** 26.54N101.25W
Moncton Canada **77** 46.06N 64.47W
Mondo Tanzania **55** 5.00S 35.54E
Mondoubleau France **15** 47.59N 0.54E
Mondovì Italy **15** 44.24N 7.50E
Mondrain I. Australia **63** 34.08S122.15E
Monessen U.S.A. **84** 40.08N 79.54W
Monet Canada **76** 48.10N 75.40W
Monett U.S.A. **83** 36.55N 93.55W
Monfalcone Italy **18** 45.49N 13.32E
Monforte Spain **16** 42.32N 7.30W
Monga Zaïre **49** 4.12N 22.49E
Mongala *r.* Zaïre **54** 1.58N 19.55E
Mongalla Sudan **49** 5.12N 31.46E
Mong Cai Vietnam **33** 21.36N107.55E
Mongers L. Australia **63** 29.15S117.05E
Monghyr India **41** 25.23N 86.28E
Mongo Chad **53** 12.14N 18.45E
Mongolia Asia **30** 46.30N104.00E
Mongororo Chad **49** 12.01N 22.28E
Mongu Zambia **54** 15.10S 23.09E
Monifieth U.K. **12** 56.29N 2.50W
Monitor Range *mts.* U.S.A. **80** 38.45N116.30W
Monkoto Zaïre **49** 1.38S 20.39E
Monmouth U.K. **11** 51.48N 2.43W
Monmouth Ill. U.S.A. **82** 40.54N 90.39W
Monmouth Oreg. U.S.A. **80** 44.51N123.14W
Monocacy *r.* U.S.A. **85** 39.13N 77.27W
Mono L. U.S.A. **80** 38.00N119.00W
Monopoli Italy **19** 40.56N 17.19E
Monor Hungary **21** 47.21N 19.27E
Monreal del Campo Spain **16** 40.47N 1.20W
Monroe La. U.S.A. **83** 32.33N 92.07W
Monroe Mich. U.S.A. **84** 41.56N 83.21W
Monroe N.C. U.S.A. **85** 35.00N 80.35W
Monroe N.Y. U.S.A. **85** 41.20N 74.11W
Monroe Wisc. U.S.A. **82** 42.36N 89.38W
Monroe City U.S.A. **82** 39.39N 91.44W
Monroeville U.S.A. **85** 31.32N 87.21W
Monrovia Liberia **52** 6.20N 10.46W
Mons Belgium **14** 50.27N 3.57E
Monselice Italy **15** 45.14N 11.45E
Mönsterås Sweden **23** 57.02N 16.26E
Montabaur Germany **14** 50.27N 7.51E
Montagnana Italy **15** 45.14N 11.28E
Montague Canada **77** 46.10N 62.39W
Montalbán Spain **16** 40.50N 0.48W
Montalto di Castro Italy **18** 42.21N 11.37E
Montana Switz. **15** 46.18N 7.29E
Montana *d.* U.S.A. **80** 47.14N109.26W
Montargis France **15** 48.00N 2.44E
Montauban France **17** 44.01N 1.20E
Montbard France **15** 47.37N 4.20E
Montbéliard France **17** 47.31N 6.48E
Montbrison France **17** 45.37N 4.04E
Montceau-les-Mines France **17** 46.40N 4.22E
Mont Cenis, Col du *pass* France **17** 45.15N 6.55E
Montcornet France **15** 49.41N 4.01E
Mont de Marsan *town* France **17** 43.54N 0.30W
Montdidier France **15** 49.39N 2.34E
Monte Alegre *town* Brazil **91** 2.01S 54.04W
Monte Azul *town* Brazil **94** 15.53S 42.53W
Montebello Canada **77** 45.39N 74.56W
Monte Carlo Monaco **17** 43.44N 7.25E
Monte Caseros Argentina **93** 30.15S 57.38W
Montecatini Terme Italy **15** 43.53N 10.46E
Montecristo *i.* Italy **18** 42.20N 10.19E
Montego Bay *town* Jamaica **87** 18.27N 77.56W
Montélimar France **17** 44.33N 4.45E
Montemor-o-Velho Portugal **16** 40.10N 8.41W
Montenegro *see* Crna Gora *d.* Yugo. **19**
Montepuez Mozambique **57** 13.09S 39.33E
Montereau France **15** 48.22N 2.57E
Monterey Calif. U.S.A. **80** 36.37N121.55W
Monterey B. U.S.A. **80** 36.45N121.55W
Montería Colombia **90** 8.45N 75.54W
Montero Bolivia **92** 17.20S 63.15W
Monteros Argentina **92** 27.10S 65.30W
Monterrey Mexico **83** 25.40N100.19W
Monte Santu, Capo di *c.* Italy **18** 40.05N 9.44E
Montes Claros Brazil **94** 16.45S 43.52W
Montevideo Uruguay **93** 34.53S 56.11W
Montevideo U.S.A. **82** 44.57N 95.43W
Montezuma U.S.A. **83** 37.36N100.26W
Montfort-sur-Meu France **15** 48.08N 1.57W
Montgomery U.K. **11** 52.34N 3.09W
Montgomery Ala. U.S.A. **85** 32.22N 86.20W
Montguyon France **17** 45.13N 0.11W
Monthey Switz. **15** 46.15N 6.57E
Monthois France **15** 49.19N 4.43E
Monticello Ark. U.S.A. **83** 33.38N 91.47W
Monticello Miss. U.S.A. **83** 31.33N 90.07W
Monticello Utah U.S.A. **80** 37.52N109.21W
Montichiari Italy **15** 45.25N 10.23E
Montiel, Campo de *f.* Spain **16** 38.46N 2.44W
Montigny-le-Roi France **17** 48.00N 5.30E
Montijo Portugal **16** 38.42N 8.59W
Montijo Dam Spain **16** 38.52N 6.20W
Montilla Spain **16** 37.36N 4.40W
Montivilliers France **15** 49.33N 0.12E
Mont Joli *town* Canada **77** 48.35N 68.14W
Mont Laurier *town* Canada **76** 46.33N 75.31W
Mont Louis *town* Canada **77** 49.15N 65.46W
Montluçon France **17** 46.20N 2.36E
Montmagny Canada **77** 46.59N 70.33W
Montmédy France **14** 49.31N 5.21E
Montmirail France **15** 48.52N 3.32E
Montmorillon France **17** 46.26N 0.52E
Montmort France **15** 48.55N 3.49E
Monto Australia **64** 24.52S151.07E
Montoro Spain **16** 38.02N 4.23W
Montpelier Idaho U.S.A. **80** 42.20N111.20W
Montpelier Vt. U.S.A. **84** 44.16N 72.35W
Montpellier France **17** 43.36N 3.53E
Montreal Canada **77** 45.30N 73.36W
Montreal *r.* Canada **76** 47.13N 84.40W
Montreal L. Canada **75** 54.20N105.40W
Montreal Lake *town* Canada **75** 54.03N105.46W
Montréal-Nord Canada **77** 45.36N 73.38W
Montrejeau France **17** 43.05N 0.33E
Montreuil France **17** 50.28N 1.46E
Montreux Switz. **20** 46.27N 6.55E
Montrichard France **15** 47.21N 1.11E
Montrose U.K. **12** 56.43N 2.29W
Montrose Colo. U.S.A. **80** 38.29N107.53W
Montserrat *i.* Leeward Is. **87** 16.45N 62.14W
Montserrat, Serra de *mts.* Spain **16** 41.20N 1.00E
Mont Tremblant Prov. Park Canada **76** 46.30N 74.30W
Monument Valley *f.* U.S.A. **80** 36.50N110.20W
Monveda Zaïre **54** 2.57N 21.27E
Monywa Burma **34** 22.05N 95.15E
Monza Italy **15** 45.35N 9.16E
Monze Zambia **55** 16.16S 27.28E
Monzón Spain **16** 41.52N 0.10E
Moolawatana Australia **66** 29.55S139.43E
Mooloogool Australia **62** 26.06S119.05E
Moomba Australia **65** 28.08S140.16E
Moomin Creek *r.* Australia **67** 29.35S148.45E
Moonbi Range *mts.* Australia **67** 31.00S151.10E
Moonie Australia **65** 27.40S150.19E
Moonie *r.* Australia **65** 29.30S148.40E
Moonta Australia **66** 34.04S137.37E
Moora Australia **63** 30.40S116.01E
Moorarie Australia **62** 25.56S117.35E
Moorcroft U.S.A. **80** 44.16N104.57W
Moore *r.* Australia **63** 31.22S115.29E
Moore, L. Australia **63** 29.30S117.30E
Mooréa *i.* Îs. de la Société **69** 17.32S149.50
Moorfoot Hills U.K. **12** 55.43N 3.03W
Moorhead U.S.A. **82** 46.53N 96.45W
Moornanyah L. Australia **66** 33.02S143.58E
Mooroopna Australia **67** 36.24S145.22E
Moose Creek *town* Canada **77** 45.15N 74.5
Moosehead L. U.S.A. **84** 45.40N 69.40W
Moose Jaw Canada **75** 50.23N105.32W
Moose Lake *town* U.S.A. **82** 46.26N 92.45W
Moosomin Canada **75** 50.07N101.40W
Moosonee Canada **76** 51.17N 80.39W
Mootwingee Australia **66** 31.52S141.14E
Mopanzhang China **32** 33.07N117.22E
Mopêia Velha Mozambique **57** 17.58S 35.4
Mopti Mali **52** 14.29N 4.10W
Mopti *d.* Mali **50** 15.30N 3.40W
Moqor Afghan. **40** 32.55N 67.40E
Moquegua Peru **92** 17.20S 70.55W
Mora Cameroon **53** 11.02N 14.07E
Mora Spain **16** 39.41N 3.46W
Mora Sweden **23** 61.00N 14.33E
Mora U.S.A. **82** 45.53N 93.18W
Morādābād India **41** 28.50N 78.47E
Morafenobe Madagascar **57** 17.49S 44.45E
Moralana Australia **66** 31.42S138.12E
Moramanga Madagascar **57** 18.56S 48.12E
Morar, Loch U.K. **12** 56.56N 4.00W
Morava *r.* Czech. **21** 48.10N 16.59E
Morava *r.* Yugo. **21** 44.43N 21.02E
Moravské Budějovice Czech. **20** 49.03N 15.49E
Morawhanna Guyana **90** 8.17N 59.44W
Moray Firth *est.* U.K. **12** 57.35N 5.15W
Morbach Germany **14** 49.49N 7.05E
Morbegno Italy **15** 46.08N 9.34E
Morcenx France **17** 44.02N 0.55W
Morden Australia **66** 30.30S142.23E
Morden Canada **75** 49.11N 98.05W
Mordovo U.S.S.R. **25** 52.06N 40.45E
Moreau *r.* U.S.A. **82** 45.18N100.43W
Morecambe U.K. **10** 54.03N 2.52W
Morecambe B. U.K. **10** 54.05N 3.00W
Moree Australia **67** 29.29S149.53E
Morée France **15** 47.55N 1.15E
Morehead U.S.A. **85** 38.11N 83.27W
Morehead City U.S.A. **85** 34.43N 76.44W
Morelia Mexico **86** 19.40N101.11W
Morella Spain **16** 40.37N 0.06W
Morelos *d.* Mexico **86** 18.40N 99.00W
Morena India **41** 26.30N 78.09E
Morena, Sierra *mts.* Spain **16** 38.10N 5.00W
Morenci U.S.A. **81** 33.05N109.22W
Moreno Mexico **81** 28.29N110.41W
Möre og Romsdal *d.* Norway **22** 63.00N 9.0
Moresby I. Canada **74** 52.30N131.40W
Moreton I. Australia **65** 27.10S153.25E
Morez France **17** 46.31N 6.02E
Mórfou Cyprus **44** 35.12N 33.00E
Mórfou, Kólpos *b.* Cyprus **44** 35.15N 32.50E
Morgan Australia **66** 34.02S139.40E
Morgan U.S.A. **83** 32.01N 97.37W
Morgan City U.S.A. **83** 29.42N 91.12W
Morganfield U.S.A. **85** 37.41N 87.55W
Morgantown U.S.A. **84** 39.38N 79.57W
Morghāb *r.* Afghan. **38** 36.50N 63.00E
Moriki Nigeria **53** 12.55N 6.30E
Morin Heights Canada **77** 45.54N 74.21W
Morioka Japan **31** 39.43N141.08E
Morisset Australia **67** 33.06S151.29E
Moriyama Japan **35** 35.04N135.59E
Morlaix France **17** 48.35N 3.50W
Mormon Range *mts.* U.S.A. **80** 37.08N114.20W
Mornington I. Australia **64** 16.33S139.24E
Mornington Mission Australia **64** 16.40S139.10E
Morobe P.N.G. **37** 7.45S147.35E
Morocco Africa **50** 32.30N 5.00W
Moro G. Phil. **37** 6.30N123.20E
Morogoro Tanzania **55** 6.47S 37.40E
Morogoro *d.* Tanzania **55** 8.30S 37.00E
Moroleón Mexico **86** 20.08N101.12W
Morombe Madagascar **57** 21.45S 43.22E
Morón Argentina **93** 34.39S 58.37W
Morón Cuba **87** 22.08N 78.39W
Mörön Mongolia **30** 49.36N100.08E
Morón Spain **16** 37.06N 5.28W
Morondava Madagascar **57** 20.17S 44.17E
Moroni Comoros **55** 11.40S 43.19E
Morotai *i.* Indonesia **37** 2.10N128.30E
Moroto Uganda **55** 2.32N 34.41E
Moroto, Mt. Uganda **55** 2.30N 34.46E
Morpeth U.K. **10** 55.10N 1.40W
Morrilton U.S.A. **83** 35.09N 92.45W
Morrinsville New Zealand **60** 37.39S175.32E
Morris Minn. U.S.A. **82** 45.35N 95.55W
Morristown Ariz. U.S.A. **81** 33.51N112.37W
Morristown N.J. U.S.A. **85** 40.48N 74.29W
Morristown S.Dak. U.S.A. **82** 45.56N101.43W
Morristown Tenn. U.S.A. **85** 36.13N 83.18W
Morrumbene Mozambique **57** 23.41S 35.25E
Morsbach Germany **14** 50.52N 7.44E
Morsi India **41** 21.21N 78.00E
Mortagne France **15** 48.32N 0.33E
Mortain France **15** 48.39N 0.56W
Mortara Italy **15** 45.15N 8.44E
Mortes *r.* Brazil **94** 21.09S 45.06W
Mortes *r. see* Manso *r.* Brazil **92**
Mortlake *town* Australia **66** 38.05S142.48E
Morundah Australia **67** 34.56S146.18E
Moruya Australia **67** 35.56S150.06E

rven Australia 64 26.25S147.05E
rvern f. U.K. 12 56.37N 5.45W
rvi India 40 22.49N 70.50E
rwell Australia 67 38.14S146.25E
rzhovets i. U.S.S.R. 24 66.45N 42.30E
sby Norway 23 58.14N 7.54E
scow U.S.A. 80 46.44N117.00W
scow see Moskva U.S.S.R. 24
sel r. Germany 14 50.23N 7.37E
selle r. see Mosel r. France/Lux. 14
ses Lake town U.S.A. 80 47.08N119.17W
sgiel New Zealand 60 45.53S170.22E
shi Tanzania 55 3.20S 37.21E
sjöen Norway 22 65.50N 13.10E
skenes Norway 22 67.55N 13.00E
skenesöy i. Norway 22 67.55N 13.00E
skva U.S.S.R. 24 55.45N 37.42E
skva r. U.S.S.R. 24 55.08N 38.50E
squera Colombia 90 2.30N 78.29W
squero U.S.A. 81 35.47N103.58W
squitia Plain Honduras 87 15.00N 84.00W
squitos, Costa de f. Nicaragua 87 13.00N
.00W
squitos, Golfo de los g. Panama 87 9.00N
.00W
ss Norway 23 59.26N 10.42E
ssaka Congo 54 1.20S 16.44E
ssburn New Zealand 60 45.41S168.15E
sselbaai R.S.A. 56 34.11S 22.08E
ssendjo Congo 54 2.52S 12.46E
ssgiel Australia 67 33.18S144.05E
ssman Australia 64 16.28S145.22E
ssoró Brazil 91 5.10S 37.18W
ssuril Mozambique 57 14.58S 40.42E
ss Vale town Australia 67 34.33S150.24E
st Czech. 20 50.31N 13.39E
staganem Algeria 50 35.56N 0.05E
star Yugo. 19 43.20N 17.50E
sting, Kap c. Greenland 73 64.00N 41.00W
stiska U.S.S.R. 21 49.48N 23.05E
sul see Al Mawşil Iraq 42
tagua r. Guatemala 87 15.56N 87.45W
tala Sweden 23 58.33N 15.03E
th India 41 25.43N 78.57E
therwell U.K. 12 55.48N 4.00W
tihāri India 41 26.39N 84.55E
tloutse r. Botswana 56 22.15S 29.00E
tol U.S.S.R. 21 52.25N 25.05E
tou China 32 32.17N120.35E
tril Spain 16 36.44N 3.37W
tt U.S.A. 80 46.22N102.20W
tueka New Zealand 60 41.08S173.01E
tu Iti i. Îs. de la Société 69 16.15S151.50W
tutapu Niue 68 19.02S169.52W
uali Congo 54 0.10N 15.33E
uchalagane r. Canada 77 53.32N 69.00W
údhros Greece 19 39.52N 25.16E
udjéria Mauritania 50 17.53N 12.20W
uhoun r. Burkina see Black Volta r. Ghana
2
uila Gabon 54 1.50S 11.02E
uka C.A.R. 49 7.16N 21.52E
ulamein Australia 66 35.03S144.05E
ulhoulé Djibouti 49 12.36N 43.12E
ulins France 17 46.34N 3.20E
ulins-la-Marche France 15 48.39N 0.29E
ulmein Burma 34 16.55N 97.49E
ulouya, Oued r. Morocco 50 35.05N 2.25W
ultrie U.S.A. 85 31.11N 83.47W
ultrie, L. U.S.A. 85 33.20N 80.05W
und City U.S.A. 82 40.07N 95.14W
undou Chad 53 8.36N 16.02E
undsville U.S.A. 84 39.54N 80.44W
undville U.S.A. 83 32.59N 87.38W
untain Ash U.K. 11 51.42N 3.22W
untain City U.S.A. 80 41.50N115.58W
untain Home Ark. U.S.A. 83 36.20N
2.23W
untain Home Idaho U.S.A. 80
3.08N115.41W
untain Nile r. see Jabal, Bahr al r. Sudan 49
untain Village U.S.A. 72 62.05N163.44W
unt Airy town Md. U.S.A. 85 39.23N 77.09W
unt Airy town N.C. U.S.A. 85 36.31N
0.38W
ount Barker town S.A. Australia 66
5.06S138.52E
ount Barker town W.A. Australia 63
4.36S117.37E
ount Beauty town Australia 67
6.43S147.11E
ount Bellew town Rep. of Ire. 13 53.28N
3.30W
ount Carmel town Ill. U.S.A. 82 38.25N
7.46W
ount Darwin town Zimbabwe 57 16.46S
1.36E
ount Drysdale town Australia 67
1.11S145.51E
ount Eba town Australia 66 30.12S135.33E
ount Fletcher town R.S.A. 56 30.41S 28.30E
ount Gambier town Australia 66
7.51S140.50E
ount Hagen town P.N.G. 37 5.54S144.13E
ount Holly town U.S.A. 85 39.59N 74.47W
ount Hope town N.S.W. Australia 67
2.49S145.48E
ount Hope town S.A. Australia 66
4.07S135.23E
ount Hopeless town Australia 66
9.42S139.41E
ount Isa town Australia 64 20.50S139.29E
ount Lofty Range mts. Australia 66
4.40S139.03E
ount Magnet town Australia 63
8.06S117.50E
ount Manara town Australia 66
2.28S143.59E
Mountmellick Rep. of Ire. 13 53.08N 7.21W
Mount Morgan town Australia 64
23.39S150.23E
Mount Murchison town Australia 66
31.23S143.42E
Mount Pleasant town Canada 76 43.05N
80.19W
Mount Pleasant town Mich. U.S.A. 84 43.36N
84.46W
Mount Pleasant town S.C. U.S.A. 85 32.48N
79.54W
Mount Pleasant town Tex. U.S.A. 83 33.09N
94.58W
Mount Robson town Canada 74
52.56N119.15W
Mount's B. U.K. 11 50.05N 5.25W
Mount Sterling town U.S.A. 85 38.03N 83.56W
Mount Vernon town Australia 62
24.09S118.10E
Mount Vernon town Ill. U.S.A. 82 38.19N
88.52W
Mount Vernon town N.Y. U.S.A. 85 40.54N
73.50W
Mount Vernon town Wash. U.S.A. 80
48.25N122.20W
Mount Walker town Australia 63
27.47S152.32E
Mount Willoughby Australia 66
27.58S134.08E
Moura Australia 64 24.33S149.58E
Moura Brazil 90 1.27S 61.38W
Moura Chad 48 13.47N 21.13E
Mourdi, Dépression de f. Chad 48 18.10N
23.00E
Mourdiah Mali 52 14.35N 7.25W
Mourne r. U.K. 9 54.50N 7.29W
Mourne Mts. U.K. 13 54.10N 6.02W
Mouscron Belgium 14 50.46N 3.10E
Moussoro Chad 53 13.41N 16.31E
Moxico Angola 54 11.50S 20.05E
Moxico d. Angola 54 13.00S 21.00E
Moy r. Rep. of Ire. 13 54.10N 9.09W
Moyale Kenya 55 3.31N 39.04E
Moyamba Sierra Leone 52 8.04N 12.03W
Moyen Atlas mts. Morocco 50 33.30N 5.00W
Moyen-Chari d. Chad 53 9.20N 17.35E
Moyeni Lesotho 56 30.24S 27.41E
Moyie Canada 74 49.17N115.50W
Moyobamba Peru 90 6.04S 76.56W
Moyowosi r. Tanzania 55 4.59S 30.58E
Mozambique Africa 57 17.30S 35.45E
Mozambique Channel Indian Oc. 57 16.00S
42.30E
Mozdok U.S.S.R. 25 43.45N 44.43E
Mozyr U.S.S.R. 21 52.02N 29.10E
Mpala Zaïre 55 6.45S 29.31E
M'Pama r. Congo 54 0.59S 15.40E
Mpanda Tanzania 55 6.21S 31.01E
Mpésoba Mali 52 12.31N 5.39W
Mphoengs Zimbabwe 56 21.10S 27.51E
Mpika Zambia 55 11.52S 31.30E
Mponela Malaŵi 55 13.32S 33.43E
Mporokoso Zambia 55 9.22S 30.06E
M'Pouya Congo 54 2.38S 16.08E
Mpunde mtn. Tanzania 55 6.12S 33.48E
Mpwapwa Tanzania 55 6.23S 36.38E
M'qoun, Irhil mtn. Morocco 50 31.31N 6.25W
Mrhila, Djebel mtn. Tunisia 51 35.25N 9.14E
Msaken Tunisia 51 35.42N 10.33E
Mseleni R.S.A. 57 27.21S 32.33E
Msingu Tanzania 55 4.52S 39.08E
Msta r. U.S.S.R. 24 58.28N 31.20E
Mtakuja Tanzania 55 7.21S 30.37E
Mtama Tanzania 55 10.20S 39.19E
Mtito Andei Kenya 55 2.32S 38.10E
Mtsensk U.S.S.R. 24 53.18N 36.35E
Mtwara Tanzania 55 10.17S 40.11E
Mtwara d. Tanzania 55 10.00S 38.30E
Muaná Brazil 91 1.32S 49.13W
Muangangia Angola 54 13.33S 18.04E
Muang Chiang Rai Thailand 34 19.56N 99.51E
Muang Khammouan Laos 34 17.22N104.50E
Muang Khon Kaen Thailand 34
16.25N102.52E
Muang Lampang Thailand 34 18.16N 99.30E
Muang Lamphun Thailand 34 18.36N 99.02E
Muang Nakhon Phanom Thailand 34
17.22N104.45E
Muang Nakhon Sawan Thailand 34
15.42N100.04E
Muang Nan Thailand 34 18.47N100.50E
Muang Ngoy Laos 34 20.43N102.41E
Muang Pak Lay Laos 34 18.12N101.25E
Muang Phaya Thailand 34 19.10N 99.55E
Muang Phetchabun Thailand 34
16.25N101.08E
Muang Phichit Thailand 34 16.29N100.21E
Muang Phitsanulok Thailand 34
16.45N100.18E
Muang Phrae Thailand 34 18.07N100.09E
Muang Sakon Nakhon Thailand 34
17.10N104.08E
Muang Sing Laos 34 21.11N101.09E
Muang Soum Laos 34 18.46N102.36E
Muang Ubon Thailand 34 15.15N104.50E
Muar Malaysia 36 2.01N102.35E
Muara Brunei 36 5.01N115.01E
Muara Indonesia 36 0.32S101.20E
Muarakaman Indonesia 36 0.02S116.45E
Muaratewe Indonesia 36 0.57S114.53E
Muāri, Rās c. Pakistan 40 24.49N 66.40E
Mubende Uganda 55 0.30N 31.24E
Mubi Nigeria 53 10.16N 13.17E
Mucanona Angola 54 8.13S 16.39E
Muchea Australia 63 31.36S115.57E
Muchinga Mts. Zambia 55 12.15S 31.00E
Muck i. U.K. 12 56.50N 6.14W
Mucojo Mozambique 55 12.05S 40.26E
Muconda Angola 54 10.31S 21.20E
Mudanjiang China 31 44.36N129.42E
Mudgee Australia 67 32.37S149.36E
Mudon Burma 34 16.15N 97.44E
Mudyuga U.S.S.R. 24 63.45N 39.29E
Muèda Mozambique 55 11.40S 39.31E
Muene Quibau Angola 54 11.27S 19.14E
Mufulira Zambia 55 12.30S 28.12E
Mufu Shan mts. China 33 29.30N114.45E
Muganskaya Ravnina f. U.S.S.R. 43 39.40N
48.30E
Mughshin, Wādī Oman 45 19.44N 55.15E
Mugía Spain 16 43.06N 9.14W
Muğla Turkey 19 37.12N 28.22E
Muhamdi India 41 27.57N 80.13E
Muḩammad, Ra's c. Egypt 44 27.42N 34.13E
Mühldorf Germany 20 48.15N 12.32E
Mühlhausen Germany 20 51.12N 10.27E
Mühlig Hofmann fjella mts. Antarctica 96
72.30S 5.00E
Muhola Finland 22 63.20N 25.05E
Muhos Finland 22 64.48N 25.59E
Muhu i. U.S.S.R. 23 58.32N 23.20E
Muhuru Kenya 49 1.01S 34.07E
Muhu Väin str. U.S.S.R. 23 58.45N 23.30E
Mui Ca Mau c. Vietnam 34 8.30N104.35E
Muine Bheag town Rep. of Ire. 13 52.42N
6.58W
Muir, L. Australia 63 34.30S116.30E
Mukachevo U.S.S.R. 21 48.26N 22.45E
Mukah Malaysia 36 2.56N112.02E
Mukandwara India 40 24.49N 75.59E
Mukawa P.N.G. 64 9.48S150.00E
Mukeriān India 40 31.57N 75.37E
Mukinbudin Australia 63 30.52S118.08E
Muko r. Japan 35 34.41N135.23E
Mukoba Zaïre 54 6.50S 20.50E
Mukongo Zaïre 54 6.32S 23.30E
Muktsar India 40 30.28N 74.31E
Mukwela Zambia 54 17.00S 26.40E
Mūl India 41 20.04N 79.40E
Mula r. India 40 19.35N 74.50E
Mūla r. Pakistan 40 27.57N 67.37E
Mulanje Mts. Malaŵi 55 15.57S 35.33E
Mulchén Chile 93 37.43S 72.14W
Mulde r. Germany 20 51.10N 12.48E
Mulgathing Australia 66 30.15S134.00E
Mulgrave Canada 77 45.37N 61.23W
Mulhacén mtn. Spain 16 37.04N 3.22W
Mülheim N.-Westfalen Germany 14 51.25N
6.50E
Mülheim N.-Westfalen Germany 14 50.58N
7.00E
Mulhouse France 17 47.45N 7.21E
Mull i. U.K. 12 56.28N 5.56W
Mull, Sd. of str. U.K. 12 56.32N 5.55W
Mullaghanattin mtn. Rep. of Ire. 13 51.56N
9.51W
Mullaghareirk Mts. Rep. of Ire. 13 52.19N
9.06W
Mullaghmore mtn. U.K. 13 54.51N 6.51W
Mullaley Australia 67 31.06S149.55E
Mullen U.S.A. 82 42.03N101.01W
Mullengudgery Australia 67 31.40S147.23E
Mullens U.S.A. 85 37.35N 81.25W
Mullet Pen. Rep. of Ire. 13 54.12N 10.04W
Mullewa Australia 63 28.33S115.31E
Mullingar Rep. of Ire. 13 53.31N 7.21W
Mull of Galloway c. U.K. 12 54.39N 4.52W
Mull of Kintyre c. U.K. 12 55.17N 5.45W
Mullovka U.S.S.R. 24 54.12N 49.26E
Mullumbimby Australia 67 28.32S153.30E
Mulobezi Zambia 56 16.49S 25.09E
Muloorina Australia 66 29.10S137.51E
Multai India 41 21.46N 78.15E
Multān Pakistan 40 30.11N 71.29E
Multyfarnham Rep. of Ire. 13 53.37N 7.25W
Mulyungarie Australia 66 31.30S140.45E
Mumbwa Zambia 55 14.57S 27.01E
Mun r. Thailand 34 15.15N104.50E
Mun, Jabal mtn. Sudan 48 14.08N 22.42E
Muna i. Indonesia 37 5.00S122.30E
Munābāo India 40 25.45N 70.17E
Munan Pass China/Vietnam 33
22.06N106.46E
Münchberg Germany 20 50.11N 11.47E
München Germany 20 48.08N 11.35E
Muncho Lake town Canada 74
59.00N125.50W
Muncie U.S.A. 84 40.11N 85.23W
Mundaring Weir Australia 63 31.59S116.13E
Münden Germany 20 51.25N 9.39E
Mundiwindi Australia 62 23.50S120.07E
Mundo r. Spain 16 38.20N 1.50W
Mundra India 40 22.51N 69.44E
Mungari Mozambique 57 17.12S 33.31E
Mungbere Zaïre 55 2.40N 28.25E
Mungeli India 41 22.04N 81.41E
Mungeranie Australia 66 28.00S138.36E
Mungindi Australia 67 28.58S148.56E
Munhango Angola 54 12.10S 18.36E
Munich see München Germany 20
Muniz Freire Brazil 94 20.25S 41.23W
Munkfors Sweden 23 59.50N 13.32E
Munning r. Australia 67 31.50S152.30E
Münster N.-Westfalen Germany 14 51.58N
7.37E
Muntadgin Australia 63 31.41S118.32E
Muong Hinh Vietnam 33 19.49N105.03E
Muonio Finland 22 67.57N 23.42E
Muonio r. Finland/Sweden 22 67.10N 23.40E
Mupa Angola 56 16.07S 15.45E
Mupa r. Mozambique 57 19.07S 35.50E
Muping China 32 37.23N121.35E
Muqaddam, Wādī Sudan 48 18.04N 31.30E
Muqdisho Somali Rep. 55 2.02N 45.21E
Mur r. Austria see Mura r. Yugo. 20
Mura r. Yugo. 20 46.18N 16.53E
Murallón mtn. Argentina/Chile 93 49.48S
73.25W
Muranga Kenya 55 0.43S 37.10E
Murashi U.S.S.R. 24 59.20N 48.59E
Murchison Australia 67 36.36S145.14E
Murchison r. Australia 62 27.30S114.10E
Murchison New Zealand 60 41.48S172.20E
Murcia Spain 16 37.59N 1.08W
Murcia d. Spain 16 38.15N 1.50W
Murdo U.S.A. 82 43.53N100.43W
Mureş r. Romania 21 46.16N 20.10E
Muret France 17 43.28N 1.19E
Murewa Zimbabwe 57 17.40S 31.47E
Murfreesboro U.S.A. 85 35.50N 86.25W
Murgha Faqīrzai Pakistan 40 31.03N 67.48E
Murgha Kibzai Pakistan 40 30.44N 69.25E
Murgon Australia 64 26.15S151.57E
Murguía Spain 16 42.57N 2.49W
Muri Cook Is. 68 21.14S159.43W
Muria, Gunung mtn. Indonesia 37
6.39S110.51E
Muriaé Brazil 94 21.08S 42.33W
Müritzsee l. Germany 20 52.25N 12.45E
Murjek Sweden 22 66.29N 20.50E
Murliganj India 41 25.54N 86.59E
Murmansk U.S.S.R. 24 68.59N 33.08E
Murnei Sudan 49 12.57N 22.52E
Murom U.S.S.R. 24 55.04N 42.04E
Muroran Japan 31 42.21N140.59E
Murrah al Kubrá, Al Buḩayrah al l. Egypt 44
30.20N 32.20E
Murra Murra Australia 67 28.18S146.48E
Murray r.S.A. Australia 66 35.23S139.20E
Murray r.W.A. Australia 63 32.35S115.46E
Murray r. Canada 74 56.11N120.45W
Murray Ky. U.S.A. 83 36.37N 88.19W
Murray Utah U.S.A. 80 40.40N111.53W
Murray, L. P.N.G. 37 7.00S141.30E
Murray, L. U.S.A. 85 34.04N 81.23W
Murray Bridge town Australia 66
35.10S139.17E
Murrayville Australia 66 35.16S141.14E
Murree Pakistan 40 33.54N 73.24E
Murringo Australia 67 34.19S148.36E
Murrumbidgee r. Australia 66 34.38S143.10E
Murrumburrah Australia 67 34.33S148.21E
Murrurundi Australia 67 31.47S150.51E
Murshidābād India 41 24.11N 88.16E
Murtoa Australia 66 36.40S142.31E
Murud mtn. Malaysia 36 3.45N115.30E
Murwāra India 41 23.51N 80.24E
Murwillumbah Australia 67 28.20S153.24E
Muş Turkey 42 38.45N 41.30E
Mūsá, Jabal mtn. Egypt 44 28.31N 33.59E
Musadi Zaïre 54 2.31S 22.50E
Mūsa Khel Pakistan 40 32.38N 71.44E
Mūsa Khel Bāzār Pakistan 40 30.52N 69.49E
Musala mtn. Bulgaria 19 42.11N 23.35E
Mūsā Qal 'eh Afghan. 40 32.05N 64.51E
Mūsā Qal 'eh r. Afghan. 40 32.22N 64.46E
Musay'īd Qatar 43 24.47N 51.36E
Mūsāzai Pakistan 40 30.23N 66.32E
Muscat see Masqaţ Oman 43
Muscatine U.S.A. 82 41.25N 91.03W
Musgrave Australia 64 14.47S143.30E
Musgrave Ranges mts. Australia 62
26.10S131.50E
Mushie Zaïre 54 2.59S 16.55E
Mushima Zambia 56 14.13S 25.05E
Mushin Nigeria 53 6.33N 3.22E
Musi r. Indonesia 36 2.20S104.57E
Muskegon U.S.A. 84 43.13N 86.15W
Muskegon r. U.S.A. 84 43.13N 86.16W
Muskegon Heights town U.S.A. 84 43.03N
86.16W
Muskogee U.S.A. 83 35.45N 95.22W
Muskoka, L. Canada 76 45.00N 79.25W
Muskwa r. Alta. Canada 74 56.16N114.06W
Muskwa r. B.C. Canada 74 58.47N122.48W
Musoma Tanzania 55 1.31S 33.48E
Mussari Angola 56 13.07S 17.56E
Musselburgh U.K. 12 55.57N 3.04W
Musselkanaal Neth. 14 52.57N 7.01E
Musselshell r. U.S.A. 80 47.21N107.58W
Mussende Angola 54 10.33S 16.02E
Musserra Angola 54 7.31S 13.02E
Mustahil Ethiopia 45 5.12N 44.17E
Mustāng Nepal 41 29.11N 83.57E
Mustjala U.S.S.R. 23 58.28N 22.14E
Muswellbrook Australia 67 32.17S150.55E
Mūţ Egypt 48 25.29N 28.59E
Mut Turkey 42 36.38N 33.27E
Mutala Mozambique 57 15.54S 37.51E
Mutalau Niue 68 18.58S169.50W
Mutanda Zambia 54 12.23S 26.16E
Mutare Zimbabwe 57 18.59S 32.40E
Mutoko Zimbabwe 57 17.23S 32.13E
Mutooroo Australia 66 32.30S140.58E
Mutoray U.S.S.R. 29 61.20N100.32E
Mutshatsha Zaïre 54 10.39S 24.27E
Mutton Bay town Canada 77 50.47N 59.02W
Muwale Tanzania 55 6.22S 33.46E
Muxima Angola 54 9.33S 13.58E
Muya U.S.S.R. 29 56.28N115.50E
Muyinga Burundi 55 2.48S 30.21E
Muynak U.S.S.R. 28 43.46N 59.00E
Muzaffarābād Jammu & Kashmir 40 34.22N
73.28E
Muzaffargarh Pakistan 40 30.04N 71.12E
Muzaffarnagar India 41 29.28N 77.41E
Muzaffarpur India 41 26.07N 85.24E
Muzhi U.S.S.R. 24 65.25N 64.40E
Muzoka Zambia 56 16.43S 27.18E
Muztag mtn. China 30 36.25N 87.25E
Mvadhi Gabon 54 1.13N 13.10E
Mvolo Sudan 49 6.03N 29.56E
Mvomero Tanzania 55 6.18S 37.26E
Mvuma Zimbabwe 56 19.16S 30.30E
Mvurwi Range mts. Zimbabwe 56 17.10S
30.45E
Mwali i. Comoros 55 12.22S 43.45E
Mwanza Tanzania 55 2.30S 32.54E
Mwanza d. Tanzania 55 3.00S 32.30E
Mwanza Zaïre 54 7.51S 26.43E
Mwaya Mbeya Tanzania 55 9.33S 33.56E
Mweka Zaïre 54 4.51S 21.34E
Mwene Ditu Zaïre 54 7.04S 23.27E
Mwenezi r. Mozambique 57 22.42S 31.45E
Mwenezi Zimbabwe 56 21.22S 30.45E
Mweru, L. Zaïre/Zambia 55 9.00S 28.40E
Mwingi Kenya 55 1.00S 38.04E
Mwinilunga Zambia 54 11.44S 24.24E
Mya, Oued wadi Algeria 51 31.40N 5.15E
Myanaung Burma 39 18.25N 95.10E
Myanma see Burma Asia 34
Myaungmya Burma 34 16.33N 94.55E
Myingyan Burma 34 21.22N 95.28E
Myinkyado Burma 34 20.56N 96.42E
Myinmu Burma 34 21.58N 95.43E
Myitkyinā Burma 34 25.24N 97.25E
Mymensingh Bangla. 41 24.45N 90.24E
Myrdal Norway 23 60.44N 7.08E
Myrdalsjökull ice cap Iceland 22 63.40N
19.06W
Myrtle Beach town U.S.A. 85 33.42N 78.54W
Myrtle Creek town U.S.A. 80 43.01N123.17W
Myrtleford Australia 67 36.35S146.44E
Myrtle Point town U.S.A. 80 43.04N124.08W
Myślenice Poland 21 49.51N 19.56E
Mysore India 38 12.18N 76.37E
My Tho Vietnam 34 10.27N106.20E
Mytishchi U.S.S.R. 24 55.54N 37.47E
Mziha Tanzania 55 5.53S 37.48E
Mzimba Malaŵi 55 12.00S 33.39E

N

Naab r. Germany 20 49.01N 12.02E
Naalehu Hawaiian Is. 69 19.04N155.35W
Na'ām r. Sudan 49 6.48N 29.57E
Naantali Finland 23 60.27N 22.02E
Naas Rep. of Ire. 13 53.13N 6.41W
Näätämö r. Norway 22 69.40N 29.30E
Nababeep R.S.A. 56 29.36S 17.44E
Nabadwīp India 41 23.25N 88.22E
Nabari r. Japan 35 34.45N136.01E
Naberezhnyye Chelny U.S.S.R. 24 55.42N
52.20E
Nabeul Tunisia 51 36.28N 10.44E
Nābha India 40 30.22N 76.09E
Nabingora Uganda 55 0.31N 31.11E
Nabi Shu'ayb, Jabal an mtn. Yemen 45 15.17N
43.59E
Naboomspruit R.S.A. 56 24.31S 28.24E
Nabq Egypt 44 28.04N 34.26E
Nābulus Jordan 44 32.13N 35.16E
Nacala Mozambique 57 14.34S 40.41E
Nacchio Ethiopia 49 7.30N 40.15E
Nachikapau L. Canada 77 56.44N 68.00W
Nachingwea Tanzania 55 10.21S 38.46E
Nāchna India 40 27.30N 71.43E
Naco Mexico 81 31.20N109.56W
Nacogdoches U.S.A. 83 31.36N 94.39W
Nadiād India 40 22.42N 72.52E
Nador Morocco 50 35.12N 2.55W
Nadūshan Iran 43 32.03N 53.33E
Nadvoitsy U.S.S.R. 24 63.56N 34.20E
Nadvornaya U.S.S.R. 21 48.37N 24.30E
Nadym U.S.S.R. 28 65.25N 72.40E
Naenwa India 40 25.46N 75.51E
Naeröy Norway 22 64.48N 11.17E
Naestved Denmark 23 55.14N 11.46E
Nafada Nigeria 53 11.08N 11.20E
Nafishah Egypt 44 30.34N 32.15E
Naft-e Safīd Iran 43 31.38N 49.20E
Nāg Pakistan 40 27.24N 65.08E
Naga Phil. 37 13.36N123.12E
Nāgāland d. India 39 26.10N 94.30E
Nagambie Australia 67 36.48S145.12E
Nagano Japan 31 36.39N138.10E
Nagano d. Japan 35 35.33N137.50E
Nagaoka Japan 31 37.30N138.50E
Nāgappattinam India 39 10.45N 79.50E
Nagara r. Japan 35 35.01N136.43E
Nagar Pārkar Pakistan 40 24.22N 70.45E
Nagarzê China 41 28.58N 90.24E
Nagasaki Japan 31 32.45N129.52E
Nāgaur India 40 27.12N 73.44E
Nāgāvali r. India 41 18.13N 83.56E
Nagda India 40 23.27N 75.25E
Nagele Neth. 14 52.39N 5.43E
Nāgercoil India 38 8.11N 77.30E
Nagichot Sudan 49 4.16N 33.34E
Nagina India 41 29.27N 78.27E
Nagles Mts. Rep. of Ire. 13 52.06N 8.26W
Nagorskoye U.S.S.R. 24 58.18N 50.50E
Nagoya Japan 35 35.10N136.55E
Nāgpur India 41 21.09N 79.06E
Nagqên China 39 32.15N 96.13E
Nagqu China 41 31.30N 92.00E
Nagykanizsa Hungary 21 46.27N 17.01E
Naha Japan 31 26.10N127.40E
Nāhan India 41 30.33N 77.18E
Nahanni Butte town Canada 74
61.02N123.20W
Nahariyya Israel 44 33.01N 35.05E
Nahāvand Iran 43 34.13N 48.23E
Nahe r. Germany 14 49.58N 7.54E
Nahr al Furāt r. Asia 43 31.00N 47.27E
Nahunta U.S.A. 85 31.12N 82.00W
Nai Ga Burma 34 27.48N 97.30E

Naiman Qi China **32** 42.53N120.40E
Nain Canada **77** 57.00N 61.40W
Nā'īn Iran **43** 32.52N 53.05E
Naini Tāl India **41** 29.23N 79.27E
Nainpur India **41** 22.26N 80.07E
Nairn U.K. **12** 57.35N 3.52W
Nairobi Kenya **55** 1.17S 36.50E
Naita *mtn.* Ethiopia **49** 5.31N 35.18E
Naivasha Kenya **55** 0.44S 36.26E
Najd *f.* Saudi Arabia **42** 25.00N 45.00E
Naj 'Hammādi Egypt **42** 26.04N 32.13E
Najrān *see* Abā as Su'ūd Saudi Arabia **45**
Nāka Khārari Pakistan **40** 25.15N 66.44E
Nakambe *r.* Burkina *see* White Volta *r.* Ghana **52**
Nakape Sudan **49** 5.47N 28.38E
Nakatsugawa Japan **35** 35.29N137.30E
Nak'fa Ethiopia **48** 16.43N 38.32E
Nakhichevan U.S.S.R. **43** 39.12N 45.24E
Nakhodka U.S.S.R. **31** 42.53N132.54E
Nakhola India **41** 26.07N 92.11E
Nakhon Pathom Thailand **34** 13.50N100.01E
Nakhon Ratchasima Thailand **34** 14.58N102.06E
Nakhon Si Thammarat Thailand **34** 8.24N 99.58E
Nakhtarana India **40** 23.20N 69.15E
Nakina Canada **76** 50.10N 86.40W
Nakło Poland **21** 53.08N 17.35E
Naknek U.S.A. **72** 58.45N157.00W
Nakop Namibia **56** 28.05S 19.57E
Nakskov Denmark **23** 54.50N 11.09E
Näkten *l.* Sweden **22** 65.50N 14.35E
Nakuru Kenya **55** 0.16S 36.04E
Nāl *r.* Pakistan **40** 26.02N 65.19E
Nalbāri India **41** 26.26N 91.30E
Nalchik U.S.S.R. **25** 43.31N 43.38E
Nalón *r.* Spain **16** 43.35N 6.06W
Nālūt Libya **51** 31.52N 10.59E
Namacurra Mozambique **55** 17.35S 37.00E
Namakī *r.* Iran **43** 31.02N 55.20E
Namanga Kenya **55** 2.33S 36.48E
Namangan U.S.S.R. **30** 40.59N 71.41E
Namanyere Tanzania **55** 7.34S 31.00E
Namapa Mozambique **57** 13.48S 39.44E
Namaponda Mozambique **57** 15.51S 39.52E
Namari Senegal **50** 15.05N 13.39W
Namarroi Mozambique **57** 15.58S 36.55E
Namatele Tanzania **55** 10.01S 38.26E
Namba Angola **54** 11.32S 15.33E
Nambala Zambia **56** 15.07S 27.02E
Nambour Australia **65** 26.36S152.59E
Nambucca Heads *town* Australia **67** 30.38S152.59E
Namco China **41** 30.53N 91.06E
Nam Co *l.* China **41** 30.45N 90.30E
Nam Dinh Vietnam **33** 20.21N106.09E
Namecala Mozambique **57** 12.50S 39.38E
Nametil Mozambique **57** 15.41S 39.30E
Namib Desert Namibia **56** 23.00S 15.20E
Namibe Angola **54** 15.10S 12.10E
Namibe *d.* Angola **54** 15.30S 12.30E
Namibia Africa **56** 21.30S 16.45E
Namīn Iran **43** 38.25N 48.30E
Namlea Indonesia **37** 3.15S127.07E
Namling China **41** 29.40N 89.03E
Namoi *r.* Australia **67** 30.14S148.28E
Namonuito *i.* Pacific Oc. **68** 8.46N150.02E
Namous, Oued *wadi* Algeria **50** 30.28N 0.14W
Nampa Canada **74** 56.02N117.07W
Nampa U.S.A. **80** 43.44N116.34W
Nam Phan *f.* Vietnam **34** 10.40N106.00E
Nam Phong Thailand **34** 16.45N102.52E
Namp'o N. Korea **31** 38.40N125.30E
Nampula Mozambique **57** 15.09S 39.14E
Nampula *d.* Mozambique **57** 15.00S 39.00E
Namsen *r.* Norway **22** 64.27N 12.19E
Namsos Norway **22** 64.28N 11.30E
Namtu Burma **34** 23.04N 97.26E
Namu Canada **74** 51.52N127.41W
Namuchabawashan *mtn.* China **39** 29.30N 95.10E
Namungua Mozambique **55** 13.11S 40.30E
Namur Belgium **14** 50.28N 4.52E
Namur *d.* Belgium **14** 50.20N 4.45E
Namur Canada **77** 45.54N 74.56W
Namutoni Namibia **56** 18.48S 16.58E
Namwala Zambia **54** 15.44S 26.25E
Nanaimo Canada **74** 49.10N124.00W
Nanango Australia **65** 26.42S151.58E
Nanchang China **33** 28.37N115.57E
Nancheng China **33** 27.35N116.33E
Nanchong China **33** 30.53N106.05E
Nanchuan China **33** 29.12N107.30E
Nancy France **17** 48.42N 6.12E
Nanda Devi *mtn.* India **41** 30.23N 79.59E
Nandan China **33** 24.59N107.32E
Nānded India **40** 19.09N 77.20E
Nandewar Range *mts.* Australia **67** 30.20S150.45E
Nāndgaon India **40** 20.19N 74.39E
Nandi Fiji **68** 17.48S177.25E
Nandu Jiang *r.* China **33** 20.04N110.20E
Nandurbār India **40** 21.22N 74.15E
Nandyāl India **39** 15.29N 78.29E
Nanfeng China **33** 27.10N116.24E
Nanga Eboko Cameroon **53** 4.41N 12.21E
Nānga Parbat *mtn.* Jammu & Kashmir **38** 35.10N 74.35E
Nangapinoh Indonesia **36** 0.20S111.44E
Nangola Mali **52** 12.41N 6.35W
Nangqên China **30** 32.15N 96.13E
Nangrūl Pīr India **40** 20.19N 77.21E
Nang Xian China **41** 29.03N 93.12E
Nanhui China **33** 31.03N121.46E
Nanjiang China **32** 32.21N106.50E
Nanjing China **33** 32.02N118.52E
Nanking *see* Nanjing China **33**
Nanling China **33** 30.56N118.19E
Nan Ling *mts.* China **33** 25.10N110.00E
Nannine Australia **62** 26.53S118.20E
Nanning China **33** 22.48N108.18E
Nannup Australia **63** 33.57S115.42E
Nanortalik Greenland **73** 60.09N 45.15W
Nānpāra India **41** 27.52N 81.30E
Nanpi China **32** 38.02N116.42E
Nanping Fujian China **33** 26.38N118.10E
Nanpu Xi *r.* China **33** 26.38N118.10E
Nanri *i.* China **33** 25.13N119.30E
Nansei shotō *is.* Japan **31** 26.30N125.00E
Nansei-Shotō Trench Pacific Oc. **68** 25.00N129.00E
Nanshan *is.* S. China Sea **36** 10.30N116.00E
Nantes France **15** 47.14N 1.35W
Nanteuil-le-Haudouin France **15** 49.08N 2.48E
Nanticoke U.S.A. **84** 41.12N 76.00W
Nanton Canada **74** 50.21N113.46W
Nantong China **32** 32.02N120.55E
Nantou Taiwan **33** 23.54N120.41E
Nantua France **20** 46.09N 5.37E
Nantucket I. U.S.A. **84** 41.16N 70.03W
Nantucket Sd. U.S.A. **84** 41.30N 70.15W
Nantwich U.K. **10** 53.05N 2.31W
Nanumea *i.* Tuvalu **68** 5.40S176.10E
Nanwan Shuiku *resr.* China **33** 32.05N113.55E
Nanxi China **33** 28.52N104.59E
Nan Xian China **33** 29.22N112.25E
Nanxiong China **33** 25.10N114.16E
Nanyang China **32** 33.07N112.30E
Nanzhang China **33** 31.47N111.42E
Naococane, Lac *l.* Canada **77** 52.50N 70.40W
Naogaon Bangla. **41** 24.47N 88.56E
Naokot Pakistan **40** 24.51N 69.27E
Napa U.S.A. **80** 38.18N122.17W
Napadogan Canada **77** 46.24N 67.01W
Napè Laos **34** 18.18N105.07E
Napier New Zealand **60** 39.29S176.58E
Napierville Canada **77** 45.11N 73.25W
Naples *see* Napoli Italy **18**
Naples Fla. U.S.A. **85** 26.09N 81.48W
Napo China **33** 23.23N105.48E
Napo *r.* Peru **90** 3.30S 73.10W
Napoleon U.S.A. **84** 41.24N 84.09W
Napoli Italy **18** 40.50N 14.14E
Napoli, Golfo di *g.* Italy **18** 40.42N 14.15E
Naqb Ishtar Jordan **44** 30.00N 35.30E
Nara Japan **35** 34.41N135.50E
Nara *d.* Japan **35** 34.27N135.55E
Nara Mali **50** 15.13N 7.20W
Nāra Pakistan **40** 24.07N 69.07E
Naracoorte Australia **66** 36.58S140.46E
Naradhan Australia **67** 33.39S146.20E
Naraini India **41** 25.11N 80.29E
Naran Mongolia **32** 45.20N113.41E
Narathiwat Thailand **34** 6.25N101.48E
Nara Visa U.S.A. **83** 35.37N103.06W
Nārāyanganj Bangla. **41** 23.37N 90.30E
Narbada *r. see* Narmada *r.* India **40**
Narbonne France **17** 43.11N 3.00E
Nardò Italy **19** 40.11N 18.02E
Narembeen Australia **63** 32.04S118.23E
Nares Str. Canada **73** 78.30N 75.00W
Naretha Australia **63** 31.01S124.50E
Nāri *r.* Pakistan **40** 29.10N 67.50E
Naria U.S.A. **41** 23.18N 90.25E
Narita Japan **35** 35.47N140.19E
Narmada *r.* India **40** 21.40N 73.00E
Nārnaul India **40** 28.03N 76.06E
Nāro, Koh-i- *mtn.* Pakistan **40** 29.15N 63.30E
Narodichi U.S.S.R. **21** 51.11N 29.01E
Narodnaya *mtn.* U.S.S.R. **24** 65.00N 61.00E
Narok Kenya **55** 1.04S 35.54E
Narooma Australia **67** 36.15S150.06E
Narrabri Australia **67** 30.20S149.49E
Narrabri West Australia **67** 30.22S149.47E
Narran *r.* Australia **67** 29.45S147.20E
Narrandera Australia **67** 34.36S146.34E
Narran L. Australia **67** 29.40S147.25E
Narrogin Australia **63** 32.58S117.10E
Narromine Australia **67** 32.17S148.20E
Narsimhapur India **41** 22.57N 79.12E
Narsingdi Bangla. **41** 23.55N 90.43E
Narsinghgarh India **40** 23.42N 77.06E
Narubis Namibia **56** 26.56S 18.36E
Narva U.S.S.R. **24** 59.22N 28.17E
Narvik Norway **22** 68.26N 17.25E
Narwāna India **40** 29.37N 76.07E
Naryan Mar U.S.S.R. **24** 67.37N 53.02E
Naryilco Australia **66** 28.41S141.50E
Naryn U.S.S.R. **28** 41.24N 76.00E
Nasa *mtn.* Norway **22** 66.29N 15.23E
Nasarawa Nigeria **53** 8.35N 7.44E
Naseby New Zealand **60** 45.01S170.09E
Nashua Iowa U.S.A. **82** 42.57N 92.32W
Nashua Mont. U.S.A. **80** 48.08N106.22W
Nashua N.H. U.S.A. **84** 42.46N 71.27W
Nashville U.S.A. **85** 36.10N 86.50W
Našice Yugo. **21** 45.29N 18.06E
Näsijärvi *l.* Finland **23** 61.37N 23.42E
Nāsik India **40** 19.59N 73.48E
Nāṣir Sudan **49** 8.36N 33.04E
Nāṣir, Buḩayrat *l.* Egypt **48** 22.40N 32.00E
Nasīrābād India **40** 26.18N 74.44E
Nasīrābād Pakistan **40** 28.23N 68.24E
Naskaupi *r.* Canada **77** 53.45N 60.50W
Naṣr Egypt **44** 30.36N 30.23E
Nass *r.* Canada **74** 55.00N129.50W
Nassau Bahamas **87** 25.05N 77.21W
Nassau *i.* Cook Is. **68** 11.33S165.25W
Nasser, L. *see* Nāṣir, Buḩayrat *l.* Egypt **48**
Nassian Ivory Coast **52** 8.33N 3.18W
Nässjö Sweden **23** 57.39N 14.41E
Nastapoca *r.* Canada **76** 56.55N 76.33W
Nastapoka Is. Canada **76** 57.00N 77.00W
Nata Botswana **56** 20.12S 26.12E
Natal Brazil **91** 5.46S 35.15W
Natal Indonesia **36** 0.35N 99.07E
Natal *d.* R.S.A. **56** 28.30S 30.30E
Natanes Plateau *f.* U.S.A. **81** 33.35N110.15W
Naṭanz Iran **43** 33.30N 51.57E
Natashquan Canada **77** 50.11N 61.49W
Natashquan *r.* Canada **77** 50.06N 61.49W
Natchez U.S.A. **83** 31.34N 91.23W
Natchitoches U.S.A. **83** 31.46N 93.05W
Nathalia Australia **67** 36.02S145.14E
Nāthdwāra India **40** 24.56N 73.49E
National City U.S.A. **81** 32.40N117.06W
Natitingou Benin **53** 10.17N 1.19E
Natoma U.S.A. **82** 39.11N 99.01W
Natron, L. Tanzania **55** 2.18S 36.05E
Naṭrūn, Wādī an *f.* Egypt **44** 30.25N 30.18E
Natuna Besar *i.* Indonesia **36** 4.00N108.20E
Naturaliste, C. Australia **63** 33.32S115.01E
Naubinway U.S.A. **84** 46.05N 85.27W
Naumburg Germany **20** 51.09N 11.48E
Nā'ūr Jordan **44** 31.53N 35.50E
Nauroz Kalāt Pakistan **40** 28.47N 65.38E
Nauru Pacific Oc. **68** 0.32S166.55E
Naushahro Fīroz Pakistan **40** 26.50N 68.07E
Naustdal Norway **23** 61.31N 5.43E
Nauta Peru **90** 4.30S 73.40W
Nautanwa India **41** 27.26N 83.25E
Nautla Mexico **86** 20.13N 96.47W
Nava Mexico **83** 28.25N100.46W
Nava *r.* Zaïre **55** 1.45N 27.06E
Navalmoral de la Mata Spain **16** 39.54N 5.33W
Navan Rep. of Ire. **13** 53.39N 6.42W
Navāpur India **40** 21.15N 73.55E
Navarra *d.* Spain **16** 42.40N 1.45W
Navarre Australia **66** 36.54S143.09E
Navarro Argentina **93** 35.00S 59.10W
Navasota U.S.A. **83** 30.23N 96.05W
Naver *r.* U.K. **12** 58.32N 4.14W
Navlya U.S.S.R. **24** 52.51N 34.30E
Navoi U.S.S.R. **28** 40.04N 65.20E
Navojoa Mexico **81** 27.06N109.26W
Návpaktos Greece **19** 38.24N 21.49E
Návplion Greece **19** 37.33N 22.47E
Navrongo Ghana **52** 10.51N 1.03W
Navsāri India **40** 20.57N 72.59E
Nawā Syria **44** 32.53N 36.03E
Nawābganj Bangla. **41** 24.36N 88.17E
Nawābganj India **41** 26.56N 81.13E
Nawābshāh Pakistan **40** 26.15N 68.25E
Nawāda India **41** 24.53N 85.32E
Nāwah Afghan. **40** 32.19N 67.53E
Nawākot Nepal **41** 27.55N 85.10E
Nawa Kot Pakistan **40** 28.20N 71.22E
Nawalgarh India **40** 27.51N 75.16E
Nawāpāra India **41** 20.58N 81.51E
Naxi China **33** 28.44N105.27E
Náxos Greece **19** 37.06N 25.23E
Náxos *i.* Greece **19** 37.03N 25.30E
Nayāgarh India **41** 20.08N 85.06E
Nayak Afghan. **40** 34.44N 66.57E
Nayarit *d.* Mexico **86** 21.30N104.00W
Nāy Band Iran **43** 27.23N 52.38E
Nāy Band Iran **43** 32.20N 57.34E
Nāy Band, Kūh-e *mtn.* Iran **43** 32.25N 57.30E
Nazaré Brazil **91** 13.00S 39.00W
Nazarovka U.S.S.R. **24** 54.19N 41.20E
Nazas *r.* Mexico **86** 25.34N103.25W
Nazca Peru **90** 14.53S 74.54W
Nazerat Israel **44** 32.41N 35.16E
Nazilli Turkey **42** 37.55N 28.20E
Nazinon *r.* Burkina *see* Red Volta *r.* Ghana **52**
Nāzir Hāt Bangla. **41** 22.38N 91.47E
Nazrēt Ethiopia **49** 8.32N 39.22E
Nazuo China **33** 24.06N105.19E
Nchanga Zambia **55** 12.30S 27.55E
Ncheu Malaŵi **55** 14.50S 34.45E
N'dalatando Angola **54** 9.12S 14.54E
Ndali Benin **53** 9.53N 2.45E
Ndasegera *mtn.* Tanzania **55** 1.58S 35.41E
Ndélé C.A.R. **49** 8.24N 20.39E
Ndélélé Cameroon **53** 4.03N 14.55E
N'Dendé Gabon **54** 2.20S 11.23E
Ndikiniméki Cameroon **53** 4.46N 10.49E
N'Djamena Chad **53** 12.10N 14.59E
Ndjolé Gabon **54** 0.07S 10.45E
Ndola Zambia **56** 12.58S 28.39E
Ndoro Gabon **54** 0.24S 12.34E
Ndrhamcha, Sebkha de *f.* Mauritania **50** 18.45N 15.48W
Ndungu Tanzania **55** 4.25S 38.04E
Nea *r.* Norway **22** 63.15N 11.00E
Neagh, Lough U.K. **13** 54.36N 6.25W
Neale, L. Australia **64** 24.21S130.04E
Néa Páfos Cyprus **44** 34.45N 32.25E
Neápolis Greece **19** 36.30N 23.04E
Neath U.K. **11** 51.39N 3.49W
Nebit-Dag U.S.S.R. **43** 39.31N 54.24E
Nebraska *d.* U.S.A. **82** 41.50N100.06W
Nebraska City U.S.A. **82** 40.41N 95.52W
Nebrodi, Monti *mts.* Italy **18** 37.53N 14.32E
Nechako *r.* Canada **74** 53.30N122.44W
Neches *r.* U.S.A. **83** 29.55N 93.50W
Neckar *r.* Germany **20** 49.32N 8.26E
Necochea Argentina **93** 38.31S 58.46W
Necuto Angola **54** 4.55S 12.38E
Nêdong China **41** 29.14N 91.48E
Nedroma Algeria **50** 35.00N 1.44W
Needles U.S.A. **81** 34.51N114.37W
Neepawa Canada **75** 50.13N 99.29W
Neerpelt Belgium **14** 51.13N 5.28E
Nefta Tunisia **51** 33.52N 7.33E
Neftegorsk U.S.S.R. **25** 44.21N 39.44E
Nefyn U.K. **10** 52.55N 4.31W
Negara Indonesia **37** 8.21S114.35E
Negaunee U.S.A. **84** 46.31N 87.37W
Negele Ethiopia **49** 5.20N 39.36E
Negev *des. see* HaNegev *des.* Israel **44**
Negoiu *mtn.* Romania **21** 45.36N 24.32E
Negomano Mozambique **55** 11.26S 38.30E
Negombo Sri Lanka **39** 7.13N 79.50E
Negotin Yugo. **21** 44.14N 22.33E
Negrais, C. Burma **34** 16.00N 94.12E
Negritos Peru **90** 4.42S 81.18W
Negro *r.* Argentina **93** 40.50S 63.00W
Negro *r.* Brazil **90** 3.00S 59.55W
Negro *r.* Uruguay **93** 33.27S 58.20W
Negro, Baia del *b.* Somali Rep. **45** 7.52N 49.50E
Negros *i.* Phil. **37** 10.00N123.00E
Negru-Vodă Romania **21** 43.50N 28.12E
Neijiang China **33** 29.29N105.03E
Nei Monggol *d.* China **32** 41.50N 112.30E
Neisse *r.* Poland/Germany **20** 52.05N 14.42E
Neiva Colombia **90** 2.58N 75.15W
Nejanilini L. Canada **75** 59.33N 97.48W
Nejo Ethiopia **49** 9.30N 35.30E
Nek'emtē Ethiopia **49** 9.02N 36.31E
Neksö Denmark **23** 55.04N 15.09E
Nelidovo U.S.S.R. **24** 56.13N 32.46E
Neligh U.S.A. **82** 42.08N 98.02W
Nelkan U.S.S.R. **29** 57.40N136.04E
Nelligen Australia **67** 35.39S150.06E
Nellore India **39** 14.29N 80.00E
Nelson Australia **66** 38.04S141.05E
Nelson Canada **74** 49.30N117.20W
Nelson *r.* Canada **75** 57.04N 92.30W
Nelson New Zealand **60** 41.18S173.17E
Nelson U.K. **10** 53.50N 2.14W
Nelson U.S.A. **81** 35.30N113.16W
Nelson, C. Australia **66** 38.27S141.35E
Nelson, Estrecho *str.* Chile **93** 51.33S 74.40W
Nelson Bay *town* Australia **67** 32.43S152.08E
Nelson Forks Canada **74** 59.30N124.00W
Nelson-Marlborough *d.* New Zealand **60** 41.40S173.40E
Nelspoort R.S.A. **56** 32.07S 23.00E
Nelspruit R.S.A. **56** 25.27S 30.58E
Néma Mauritania **50** 16.40N 7.15W
Neman *r.* U.S.S.R. **23** 55.18N 21.23E
Nembe Nigeria **53** 4.32N 6.25E
Nemours France **15** 48.16N 2.41E
Nenagh Rep. of Ire. **13** 52.52N 8.13W
Nenana U.S.A. **72** 64.35N149.20W
Nene *r.* U.K. **10** 52.49N 0.12E
Nenjiang China **31** 49.10N125.15E
Neodesha U.S.A. **83** 37.25N 95.41W
Neosho U.S.A. **83** 36.52N 94.22W
Neosho *r.* U.S.A. **82** 35.48N 95.18W
Nepal Asia **41** 28.00N 84.00E
Nepālganj Nepal **41** 28.03N 81.38E
Nepa Nagar India **40** 21.28N 76.23E
Nephi U.S.A. **80** 39.43N111.50W
Nephin Beg *mtn.* Rep. of Ire. **13** 54.02N 9.38W
Nephin Beg Range *mts.* Rep. of Ire. **13** 54.00N 9.37W
Nera *r.* Italy **18** 42.33N 12.43E
Nérac France **17** 44.08N 0.20E
Nerekhta U.S.S.R. **24** 57.30N 40.40E
Néret, Lac *l.* Canada **77** 54.45N 70.50W
Neretva *r.* Yugo. **19** 43.02N 17.28E
Neriquinha Angola **56** 15.50S 21.40E
Nero Deep Pacific Oc. **37** 12.40N145.50E
Néronde France **17** 45.50N 4.14E
Nerva Spain **16** 37.42N 6.30W
Nes Neth. **14** 53.27N 5.46E
Nesbyen Norway **23** 60.34N 9.09E
Nesle France **15** 49.46N 2.51E
Nesna Norway **22** 66.13N 13.04E
Nesöy *i.* Norway **22** 66.35N 12.40E
Ness, Loch U.K. **12** 57.16N 4.30W
Nestaocano *r.* Canada **77** 48.40N 73.25W
Nesterov U.S.S.R. **21** 50.04N 24.00E
Néstos *r.* Greece **19** 40.51N 24.48E
Nesttun Norway **23** 60.19N 5.20E
Nesvizh U.S.S.R. **21** 53.16N 26.40E
Netanya Israel **44** 32.20N 34.51E
Netcong U.S.A. **85** 40.54N 74.42W
Netherlands Europe **14** 52.00N 5.30E
Netherlands Antilles S. America **87** 12.30N 69.00W
Neto *r.* Italy **19** 39.12N 17.08E
Netrakona Bangla. **41** 24.53N 90.43E
Nettilling L. Canada **73** 66.30N 70.40W
Neubrandenburg Germany **20** 53.33N 13.16E
Neuchâtel Switz. **20** 47.00N 6.56E
Neuchâtel, Lac de *l.* Switz. **20** 46.55N 6.55E
Neuenhaus Germany **14** 52.30N 6.58E
Neufchâteau Belgium **14** 49.51N 5.26E
Neufchâtel France **15** 49.44N 1.26E
Neuillé-Pont-Pierre France **15** 47.33N 0.33E
Neumarkt Germany **20** 49.16N 11.28E
Neumünster Germany **20** 54.06N 9.59E
Neuquén Argentina **93** 39.00S 68.05W
Neuquén *d.* Argentina **93** 38.30S 70.00W
Neuquén *r.* Argentina **93** 39.02S 68.07W
Neuruppin Germany **20** 52.55N 12.48E
Neuse *r.* U.S.A. **85** 35.06N 76.30W
Neusiedler See *l.* Austria **20** 47.52N 16.45E
Neuss Germany **14** 51.12N 6.42E
Neustadt Bayern Germany **20** 49.44N 12.11E
Neustrelitz Germany **20** 53.22N 13.05E
Neuvic France **17** 45.23N 2.16E
Neuwied Germany **14** 50.26N 7.28E
Nevada U.S.A. **83** 37.51N 94.22W
Nevada *d.* U.S.A. **80** 39.50N116.10W
Nevada, Sierra *mts.* Spain **16** 37.04N 3.20W
Nevada, Sierra *mts.* U.S.A. **78** 37.30N119.00W
Nevanka U.S.S.R. **29** 56.31N 98.57E
Nevel U.S.S.R. **24** 56.00N 29.59E
Nevers France **17** 47.00N 3.09E
Nevertire Australia **67** 31.52S147.47E
Nevinnomyssk U.S.S.R. **25** 44.38N 41.59E
Nevşehir Turkey **42** 38.38N 34.43E
Newala Tanzania **55** 10.56S 39.15E
New Albany Ind. U.S.A. **84** 38.17N 85.50W
New Albany Miss. U.S.A. **83** 34.29N 89.00W
New Amsterdam Guyana **91** 6.18N 57.30W
New Angledool Australia **67** 29.06S147.57E
Newark Del. U.S.A. **85** 39.41N 75.45W
Newark N.J. U.S.A. **85** 40.44N 74.11W
Newark N.Y. U.S.A. **84** 43.03N 77.06W
Newark Ohio U.S.A. **84** 40.03N 82.25W
Newark-on-Trent U.K. **10** 53.06N 0.48E
New Athens U.S.A. **82** 38.19N 89.53W
New Bedford U.S.A. **84** 41.38N 70.56W
Newberg U.S.A. **80** 45.18N122.58W
New Bern U.S.A. **85** 35.05N 77.04W
Newberry Mich. U.S.A. **84** 46.22N 85.30W
Newberry S.C. U.S.A. **85** 34.17N 81.39W
Newbiggin-by-the-Sea U.K. **10** 55.11N 1.30W
New Braunfels U.S.A. **83** 29.42N 98.08W
New Britain *i.* P.N.G. **61** 6.00S150.00E
New Brunswick *d.* Canada **77** 46.50N 66.00W
New Brunswick U.S.A. **85** 40.29N 74.27W
Newburgh U.S.A. **85** 41.30N 74.00W
Newbury U.K. **11** 51.24N 1.19W
New Bussa Nigeria **53** 9.53N 4.29E
New Caledonia *is. see* Nouvelle Calédonie *is.* Pacific Oc. **68**
Newcastle Australia **67** 32.55S151.46E
Newcastle N.B. Canada **77** 47.00N 65.34W
Newcastle Ont. Canada **76** 43.55N 78.35W
Newcastle R.S.A. **56** 27.44S 29.55E
Newcastle U.K. **13** 54.13N 5.53W
New Castle Penn. U.S.A. **84** 41.00N 80.22W
Newcastle Wyo. U.S.A. **80** 43.50N104.11W
Newcastle B. Australia **64** 10.50S142.37E
Newcastle Emlyn U.K. **11** 52.02N 4.29W
Newcastle-under-Lyme U.K. **10** 53.02N 2.15W
Newcastle upon Tyne U.K. **10** 54.58N 1.36W
Newcastle Waters *town* Australia **64** 17.24S133.24E
Newcastle West Rep. of Ire. **13** 52.26N 9.04W
New City U.S.A. **85** 41.09N 73.59W
Newdegate Australia **63** 33.06S119.01E
New Delhi India **40** 28.36N 77.12E
New Denver Canada **74** 50.00N117.25W
New England U.S.A. **82** 46.32N102.52W
New England Range *mts.* Australia **67** 30.30S151.50E
Newenham, C. U.S.A. **72** 58.37N162.12W
Newent U.K. **11** 51.56N 2.24W
Newfane U.S.A. **76** 43.17N 78.43W
New Forest *f.* U.K. **11** 50.50N 1.35W
Newfoundland *d.* Canada **77** 54.00N 60.10W
Newfoundland *i.* Canada **77** 48.30N 56.00W
New Freedom U.S.A. **85** 39.44N 76.42W
New Galloway U.K. **12** 55.05N 4.09W
Newgate Canada **74** 49.01N115.08W
New Glasgow Canada **77** 45.35N 62.39W
New Guinea *i.* Austa. **37** 5.00S140.00E
New Hampshire *d.* U.S.A. **84** 43.35N 71.40W
New Hanover *i.* Pacific Oc. **61** 2.00S150.00E
Newhaven U.K. **11** 50.47N 0.04E
New Haven U.S.A. **84** 41.18N 72.55W
New Hebrides Basin Pacific Oc. **68** 16.00S162.00E
New Holland U.S.A. **85** 40.06N 76.05W
New Iberia U.S.A. **83** 30.00N 91.49W
New Ireland *i.* P.N.G. **61** 2.30S151.30E
New Jersey *d.* U.S.A. **85** 40.15N 74.30W
New Liskeard Canada **76** 47.31N 79.41W
New London Conn. U.S.A. **84** 41.21N 72.06W
New London Minn. U.S.A. **82** 45.18N 94.56W
Newman Australia **62** 23.22S119.43E
Newman U.S.A. **81** 31.55N106.20W
Newman, Mt. Australia **62** 23.15S119.33E
Newmarket Rep. of Ire. **13** 52.13N 9.00W
Newmarket U.K. **11** 52.15N 0.23E
Newmarket on Fergus Rep. of Ire. **13** 52.46N 8.55W
New Martinsville U.S.A. **84** 39.39N 80.52W
New Meadows U.S.A. **80** 44.58N116.32W
New Mexico *d.* U.S.A. **80** 33.30N106.00W
New Milford Conn. U.S.A. **85** 41.35N 73.25W
Newnan U.S.A. **85** 33.23N 84.48W
New Norcia Australia **63** 30.58S116.15E
New Norfolk Australia **65** 42.46S147.02E
New Orleans U.S.A. **83** 29.58N 90.07W
New Philadelphia U.S.A. **84** 40.31N 81.28W
New Plymouth New Zealand **60** 39.03S174.04E
Newport Mayo Rep. of Ire. **13** 53.53N 9.34W
Newport Tipperary Rep. of Ire. **13** 52.42N 8.25W
Newport Dyfed U.K. **11** 52.01N 4.51W
Newport Essex U.K. **11** 51.58N 0.13E
Newport Gwent U.K. **11** 51.34N 2.59W
Newport Hants. U.K. **11** 50.43N 1.18W
Newport Ark. U.S.A. **83** 35.35N 91.16W
Newport Maine U.S.A. **84** 44.50N 69.17W
Newport N.H. U.S.A. **84** 43.21N 72.09W
Newport Oreg. U.S.A. **80** 44.38N124.03W
Newport R.I. U.S.A. **84** 41.13N 71.18W
Newport News U.S.A. **85** 36.59N 76.26W
New Providence I. Bahamas **87** 25.25N 78.35W
Newquay U.K. **11** 50.24N 5.06W
New Quay U.K. **11** 52.13N 4.22W
New Radnor U.K. **11** 52.15N 3.10W
New Rochelle U.S.A. **85** 40.55N 73.47W
New Rockford U.S.A. **82** 47.41N 99.15W
New Romney U.K. **11** 50.59N 0.58E
New Ross Rep. of Ire. **13** 52.24N 6.57W
Newry U.K. **13** 54.11N 6.21W
New Scone U.K. **12** 56.25N 3.25W
New Smyrna Beach *town* U.S.A. **85** 29.01N 80.56W
New South Wales *d.* Australia **67** 32.40S147.40E

ewton Ill. U.S.A. 82 38.59N 88.10W
ewton Iowa U.S.A. 82 41.42N 93.03W
ewton Kans. U.S.A. 83 38.03N 97.21W
ewton Miss. U.S.A. 83 32.19N 89.10W
ewton N.J. U.S.A. 85 41.03N 74.45W
ewton Abbot U.K. 11 50.32N 3.37W
ewton Aycliffe U.K. 10 54.36N 1.34W
ewtonmore U.K. 12 57.04N 4.08W
ewton Stewart U.K. 12 54.57N 4.29W
ewtown U.K. 11 52.31N 3.19W
ewtownabbey U.K. 13 54.39N 5.57W
ewtownards U.K. 13 54.35N 5.41W
ewtown Butler U.K. 13 54.12N 7.22W
ewtown St. Boswells U.K. 12 55.35N 2.40W
ewtownstewart U.K. 13 54.43N 7.25W
ew Waterford Canada 77 46.15N 60.05W
ew Westminster Canada 74 49.10N 122.52W
ew York U.S.A. 85 40.40N 73.50W
ew York d. U.S.A. 84 43.00N 75.00W
ew York State Barge Canal U.S.A. 76 43.05N 78.43W
ew Zealand Austa. 60 41.00S 175.00E
ew Zealand Plateau Pacific Oc. 68 50.00S 170.00E
eya U.S.S.R. 24 58.18N 43.40E
eyagawa Japan 35 34.46N 135.38E
eyrīz Iran 43 29.12N 54.17E
eyshābūr Iran 43 36.13N 58.49E
ezhin U.S.S.R. 21 51.03N 31.54E
gala Nigeria 53 12.21N 14.10E
gambwe Rapids f. Zambia 54 17.08S 24.10E
gami, L. Botswana 56 20.32S 22.38E
gamiland d. Botswana 56 19.40S 22.00E
gamiland f. Botswana 56 20.00S 22.30E
gamring China 41 29.14N 87.10E
gangla Ringco l. China 41 31.40N 83.00E
ganglong Kangri mtn. China 41 32.40N 81.00E
ganglong Kangri mts. China 41 32.15N 82.00E
gangzê Co l. China 41 31.00N 87.00E
ganjuk Indonesia 37 7.36S 111.56E
'Gao Congo 54 2.28S 15.40E
gaoundéré Cameroon 53 7.20N 13.35E
gara-Binsam Congo 54 1.36N 13.30E
gardiam C.A.R. 49 9.00N 20.58E
garuawahia New Zealand 60 37.40S 175.09E
garuroro r. New Zealand 60 39.34S 176.54E
gatangiia Rarotonga Cook Is. 68 21.14S 159.44W
gau i. Fiji 68 18.02S 179.18E
gauruhoe mtn. New Zealand 60 39.10S 175.35E
gawi Indonesia 37 7.23S 111.22E
gaya mtn. C.A.R. 49 9.18N 23.28E
g'iro, Mt. Kenya 55 2.06N 36.44E
'Giva Angola 56 17.03S 15.47E
goc Linh mtn. Vietnam 34 15.04N 107.59E
goma Zambia 54 16.04S 26.06E
gomba Tanzania 55 8.16S 32.51E
gomeni Kenya 55 3.00S 40.11E
gong Kenya 55 1.22S 36.40E
gonye Falls f. Zambia 54 16.35S 23.39E
gorongoro Crater f. Tanzania 55 3.13S 35.32E
gouo, Mont mtn. C.A.R. 49 7.55N 24.38E
gozi Burundi 55 2.52S 29.50E
guigmi Niger 53 14.00N 13.11E
guru Nigeria 53 12.53N 10.30E
guruka Tanzania 55 5.08S 30.58E
gwaketse d. Botswana 56 25.10S 25.00E
gwerere Zambia 55 15.18S 28.20E
haccongo Mozambique 57 24.18S 35.14E
hachengue Mozambique 57 22.52S 35.10E
handugue r. Mozambique 57 18.47S 34.30E
ha Trang Vietnam 34 12.15N 109.10E
hill Australia 66 36.20S 141.40E
hulunbuy Australia 64 12.11S 136.46E
hungo Angola 56 13.17S 20.06E
afounké Mali 50 15.56N 4.00W
agara Canada 76 43.05N 79.20W
agara Falls town Canada 76 43.06N 79.04W
agara Falls town U.S.A. 84 43.06N 79.02W
ah Malaysia 36 3.52N 113.44E
amey Niger 53 13.32N 2.05E
amey d. Niger 53 14.00N 1.40E
anforando Guinea 52 9.37N 10.36W
angara Zaïre 55 3.47N 27.54E
a-Nia Zaïre 55 1.30N 27.41E
apa, Gunung mtn. Indonesia 36 .45N 117.30E
as i. Indonesia 36 1.05N 97.30E
assa d. Mozambique 55 13.00S 36.30E
caragua C. America 87 13.00N 85.00W
caragua, Lago de l. Nicaragua 87 11.30N 85.30W
castro Italy 18 38.58N 16.16E
ce France 17 43.42N 7.16E
chelino Italy 15 44.59N 7.38E
cholson Australia 62 18.02S 128.54E
cholson r. Australia 64 17.31S 139.36E
cholson L. Canada 75 62.40N 102.35W
cobar Is. India 34 8.00N 93.30E
colet Canada 77 46.13N 72.37W
colet r. Canada 77 46.14N 72.39W
colls Town Bahamas 87 25.08N 78.00W
cosia see Levkosía Cyprus 44
coya, Golfo de g. Costa Rica 87 9.30N 85.00W
coya, Península de pen. Costa Rica 87 10.30N 85.30W
d r. Norway 23 58.24N 8.48E
da r. Poland 21 50.18N 20.52E
do, Sierra de mts. Mexico 81 29.30N 107.00W
dzica Poland 21 53.22N 20.26E
ederösterreich d. Austria 20 48.20N 15.50E
edersachsen d. Germany 14 52.55N 7.40E
Niekerkshoop R.S.A. 56 29.19S 22.48E
Niéllé Ivory Coast 52 10.05N 5.28W
Nienburg Germany 20 52.38N 9.13E
Niéré Chad 48 14.30N 21.09E
Niers r. Neth. 14 51.43N 5.56E
Nieuw Nickerie Surinam 91 5.57N 56.59W
Nieuwpoort Belgium 14 51.08N 2.45E
Niğde Turkey 42 37.58N 34.42E
Niger d. Nigeria 53 9.50N 6.00E
Niger r. Nigeria 53 4.15N 6.05E
Niger Delta Nigeria 53 4.00N 6.10E
Nigeria Africa 53 9.00N 9.00E
Nightcaps New Zealand 60 45.58S 168.02E
Nightingale I. Tristan da Cunha 95 37.28S 12.32W
Nihing r. Pakistan 40 26.00N 62.44E
Nihoa i. Hawaiian Is. 68 23.03N 161.55W
Niigata Japan 31 37.58N 139.02E
Niihau i. Hawaiian Is. 69 21.55N 160.10W
Niiza Japan 35 35.48N 139.34E
Nijmegen Neth. 14 51.50N 5.52E
Nikel U.S.S.R. 22 69.20N 30.00E
Nikiniki Indonesia 62 9.49S 124.29E
Nikki Benin 53 9.55N 3.18E
Nikolayev U.S.S.R. 25 46.57N 32.00E
Nikolayevskiy U.S.S.R. 25 50.05N 45.32E
Nikolayevsk-na-Amure U.S.S.R. 29 53.20N 140.44E
Nikolsk U.S.S.R. 24 59.33N 45.30E
Nikopol U.S.S.R. 25 47.34N 34.25E
Niksar Turkey 42 40.35N 36.59E
Nikshahr Iran 43 26.14N 60.15E
Nikšić Yugo. 19 42.48N 18.56E
Nikumaroro i. Kiribati 68 4.40S 174.32W
Nil, An r. Egypt 44 31.30N 30.25E
Nila i. Indonesia 37 6.45S 129.30E
Nile r. see Nil, An r. Egypt 44
Nile Delta Egypt 44 31.00N 31.00E
Niles Mich. U.S.A. 84 41.51N 86.15W
Nilgiri India 41 21.28N 86.46E
Nilgiri Hills India 38 11.30N 77.30E
Nimach India 40 24.28N 74.52E
Nimai r. Burma 34 25.44N 97.30E
Nimba, Mt. Guinea 52 7.35N 8.28W
Nimbin Australia 67 28.35S 153.12E
Nîmes France 17 43.50N 4.21E
Nim Ka Thāna India 40 27.44N 75.48E
Nimrūz d. Afghan. 40 30.40N 62.15E
Nimule Sudan 49 3.36N 32.03E
Nindigully Australia 67 28.20S 148.47E
Ninety Mile Beach f. Australia 67 38.07S 147.30E
Ninety Mile Beach f. New Zealand 60 34.45S 173.00E
Nineveh ruins Iraq 42 36.24N 43.08E
Ningbo China 33 29.56N 121.32E
Ningde China 33 26.41N 119.32E
Ningdu China 33 26.29N 115.46E
Ninggang China 33 26.45N 113.58E
Ningguo China 33 30.38N 118.58E
Ningming China 33 22.04N 107.02E
Ningnan China 30 27.03N 102.46E
Ningqiang China 32 32.49N 106.13E
Ningwu China 32 38.59N 112.12E
Ningxia Huizu d. China 32 37.00N 105.00E
Ning Xian China 32 35.27N 107.50E
Ningxiang China 33 28.15N 112.33E
Ninh Binh Vietnam 34 20.14N 106.00E
Ninove Belgium 14 50.50N 4.02E
Niobrara U.S.A. 82 42.45N 98.02W
Niobrara r. U.S.A. 82 42.45N 98.00W
Nioki Zaïre 54 2.43S 17.41E
Nioro Mali 50 15.12N 9.35W
Nioro du Rip Senegal 52 13.40N 15.50W
Niort France 17 46.19N 0.27W
Niout well Mauritania 50 16.03N 6.52W
Nipāni India 38 16.24N 74.23E
Nipigon Canada 76 49.00N 88.17W
Nipigon, L. Canada 76 49.50N 88.30W
Nipigon B. Canada 76 48.55N 88.00W
Nipissing, L. Canada 76 46.17N 80.00W
Niquelândia Brazil 94 14.27S 48.27W
Nirasaki Japan 35 35.42N 138.27E
Nirmal India 41 19.06N 78.21E
Nirmali India 41 26.19N 86.35E
Nirwāno Pakistan 40 26.22N 62.43E
Niš Yugo. 19 43.20N 21.54E
Nisa Portugal 16 39.31N 7.39W
Nishi China 33 29.54N 110.38E
Nishinomiya Japan 35 34.43N 135.20E
Niskibi r. Canada 75 56.28N 88.10W
Nisko Poland 21 50.35N 22.07E
Nissedal Norway 23 59.10N 8.30E
Nisser l. Norway 23 59.10N 8.30E
Nițā' Saudi Arabia 43 27.13N 48.25E
Nitchequon Canada 77 53.12N 70.47W
Niterói Brazil 94 22.54S 43.06W
Nith r. U.K. 12 55.00N 3.35W
Nitra Czech. 21 48.20N 18.05E
Niue i. Cook Is. 68 19.02S 169.52W
Niut, Gunung mtn. Indonesia 36 1.00N 110.00E
Nivala Finland 22 63.55N 24.58E
Nivelles Belgium 14 50.36N 4.20E
Nixon U.S.A. 83 29.16N 97.46W
Nizāmābād India 39 18.40N 78.05E
Nizgān r. Afghan. 40 33.05N 63.20E
Nizhneangarsk U.S.S.R. 29 55.48N 109.35E
Nizhnekamskoye Vodokhranilishche U.S.S.R. 24 55.45N 53.50E
Nizhne Kolymsk U.S.S.R. 29 68.34N 160.58E
Nizhneudinsk U.S.S.R. 29 54.55N 99.00E
Nizhnevartovsk U.S.S.R. 28 60.57N 76.40E
Nizhniy Tagil U.S.S.R. 24 58.00N 60.00E
Nizhnyaya Tunguska r. U.S.S.R. 29 65.50N 88.00E
Nizhnyaya Tura U.S.S.R. 24 58.40N 59.48E
Nizke Tatry mts. Czech. 21 48.54N 19.40E
Nizza Monferrato Italy 15 44.46N 8.21E
Njazídja i. Comoros 55 11.35S 43.20E
Njombe Tanzania 55 9.20S 34.47E
Njombe r. Tanzania 55 7.02S 35.55E
Njoro Tanzania 55 5.16S 36.30E
Nkalagu Nigeria 53 6.28N 7.46E
Nkawkaw Ghana 52 6.35N 0.47W
Nkayi Zimbabwe 56 19.00S 28.54E
Nkhata Bay town Malaŵi 55 11.37S 34.20E
Nkhotakota Malaŵi 55 12.55S 34.19E
Nkongsamba Cameroon 53 4.59N 9.53E
Nkungwe Mt. Tanzania 55 6.15S 29.54E
Noākhāli Bangla. 41 22.51N 91.06E
Noatak U.S.A. 72 67.34N 162.59W
Noce r. Italy 15 46.09N 11.04E
Nogales Mexico 81 31.20N 110.56W
Nogara Italy 15 45.11N 11.04E
Nogayskiye Step f. U.S.S.R. 25 44.25N 45.30E
Nogent-le-Rotrou France 15 48.19N 0.50E
Nogent-sur-Seine France 15 48.29N 3.30E
Nogoyá Argentina 93 32.22S 59.49W
Noguera Ribagorçana r. Spain 16 41.27N 0.25E
Nohar India 40 29.11N 74.46E
Nohta India 41 23.40N 79.34E
Noire r. Que. Canada 77 45.33N 72.58W
Noirmoutier, Île de i. France 17 47.00N 2.15W
Nojima-zaki c. Japan 35 34.56N 139.53E
Nokha India 40 27.35N 73.29E
Nokia Finland 23 61.28N 23.30E
Nok Kundi Pakistan 40 28.46N 62.46E
Nokomis Canada 75 51.30N 105.00W
Nokou Chad 53 14.35N 14.47E
Nola C.A.R. 53 3.28N 16.08E
Nolinsk U.S.S.R. 24 57.38N 49.52E
Noman L. Canada 75 62.15N 108.55W
Noma Omuramba r. Botswana 56 19.14S 22.15E
Nombre de Dios Mexico 81 28.41N 106.05W
Nome U.S.A. 72 64.30N 165.30W
Nomgon Mongolia 32 42.50N 105.13E
Nomuka Group is. Tonga 69 20.15S 174.46W
Nonancourt France 15 48.47N 1.11E
Nonburg U.S.S.R. 24 65.32N 50.37E
Nong Khai Thailand 34 17.50N 102.46E
Nongoma R.S.A. 57 27.58S 31.35E
Nongpoh India 41 25.54N 91.53E
Nongstoin India 41 25.31N 91.16E
Nonning Australia 66 32.30S 136.30E
Nono Ethiopia 49 8.31N 37.30E
Nonthaburi Thailand 34 13.48N 100.11E
Noojee Australia 67 37.57S 146.00E
Noonamah Australia 62 12.35S 131.03E
Noonan U.S.A. 82 48.54N 103.01W
Noongaar Australia 63 31.21S 118.55E
Noonkanbah Australia 62 18.30S 124.50E
Noonthorangee Range mts. Australia 66 31.00S 142.20E
Noorama Creek r. Australia 67 28.05S 145.55E
Noord Beveland f. Neth. 14 51.35N 3.45E
Noord Brabant d. Neth. 14 51.37N 5.00E
Noord Holland d. Neth. 14 52.37N 4.50E
Noordoost-Polder f. Neth. 14 52.45N 5.45E
Noordwijk Neth. 14 52.16N 4.29E
Noorvik U.S.A. 72 66.50N 161.14W
Noosa Heads town Australia 64 26.23S 153.07E
Nootka I. Canada 74 49.32N 126.42W
Noqui Angola 54 5.51S 13.25E
Nora Sweden 23 59.31N 15.02E
Noranda Canada 76 48.20N 79.00W
Nord d. Burkina 52 13.50N 2.20W
Nord d. France 14 50.17N 3.14E
Nordaustlandet i. Arctic Oc. 96 79.55N 23.00E
Norddeich Germany 14 53.35N 7.10E
Nordegg Canada 74 52.29N 116.05W
Norden Germany 14 53.34N 7.13E
Nordenham Germany 20 53.30N 8.29E
Norderney Germany 14 53.43N 7.09E
Norderney i. Germany 14 53.45N 7.15E
Nordfjord est. Norway 23 61.54N 5.12E
Nordfjordeid Norway 23 61.54N 6.00E
Nordfold Norway 22 67.48N 15.20E
Nordfriesische Inseln is. Germany 20 54.30N 8.00E
Nordhausen Germany 20 51.31N 10.48E
Nordhorn Germany 14 52.27N 7.05E
Nordkapp c. Norway 22 71.11N 25.48E
Nordkinnhalvöya pen. Norway 22 70.55N 27.45E
Nordland d. Norway 22 66.50N 14.50E
Nord-Ostsee-Kanal Germany 20 53.54N 9.12E
Nordreisa Norway 22 69.46N 21.00E
Nordrhein-Westfalen d. Germany 14 51.18N 6.32E
Nord Tröndelag d. Norway 22 64.20N 12.00E
Nordvik U.S.S.R. 29 73.40N 110.50E
Nore Norway 23 60.10N 9.01E
Nore r. Rep. of Ire. 13 52.25N 6.58W
Norfolk d. U.K. 11 52.39N 1.00E
Norfolk Nebr. U.S.A. 82 42.02N 97.25W
Norfolk Va. U.S.A. 85 36.54N 76.18W
Norfolk Broads f. U.K. 10 52.43N 1.35E
Norfolk I. Pacific Oc. 68 29.02S 167.57E
Norfolk Island Ridge Pacific Oc. 68 29.00S 167.00E
Norheimsund Norway 23 60.22N 6.08E
Norilsk U.S.S.R. 29 69.21N 88.02E
Normal U.S.A. 82 40.31N 89.00W
Norman r. Australia 64 17.28S 140.49E
Norman U.S.A. 83 35.13N 97.26W
Normanby r. Australia 64 14.25S 144.08E
Normanby New Zealand 60 39.32S 174.16E
Normanby I. P.N.G. 64 10.05S 151.05E
Normandie, Collines de hills France 15 48.50N 0.40W
Normanton Australia 64 17.40S 141.05E
Norman Wells Canada 72 65.19N 126.46W
Nornalup Australia 63 34.58S 116.49E
Ñorquinco Argentina 93 41.50S 70.55W
Norrahammar Sweden 23 57.42N 14.06E
Norra Kvarken str. Sweden / Finland 22 63.36N 20.43E
Norra Storfjället mtn. Sweden 22 65.52N 15.18E
Norrbotten d. Sweden 22 67.00N 19.50E
Nörresundby Denmark 23 57.04N 9.56E
Norris L. U.S.A. 85 36.18N 83.58W
Norristown U.S.A. 85 40.07N 75.20W
Norrköping Sweden 23 58.36N 16.11E
Norrsundet Sweden 23 60.56N 17.08E
Norrtälje Sweden 23 59.46N 18.42E
Norseman Australia 63 32.15S 121.47E
Norsk U.S.S.R. 29 52.22N 129.57E
Norte d. W. Sahara 50 26.50N 11.15W
Norte, C. Brazil 91 1.40N 49.55W
Norte, Cabo c. I. de Pascua 69 27.03S 109.24W
Norte, Punta c. Argentina 93 36.17S 56.46W
North, C. Canada 77 47.01N 60.28W
Northallerton U.K. 10 54.20N 1.26W
Northam Australia 63 31.41S 116.40E
Northampton Australia 63 28.21S 114.37E
Northampton U.K. 11 52.14N 0.54W
Northampton Penn. U.S.A. 85 40.41N 75.30W
Northamptonshire d. U.K. 11 52.18N 0.55W
North Battleford Canada 75 52.47N 108.17W
North Bay town Canada 76 46.19N 79.28W
North Bend Oreg. U.S.A. 80 43.24N 124.14W
North Berwick U.K. 12 56.04N 2.43W
North Bourke Australia 67 30.01S 145.59E
North C. Antarctica 96 71.00S 166.00E
North C. New Zealand 60 34.28S 173.00E
North Canadian r. U.S.A. 83 35.17N 95.31W
North Caribou L. Canada 76 52.50N 90.50W
North Carolina d. U.S.A. 85 35.30N 80.00W
North Channel str. Canada 76 46.02N 82.50W
North Channel U.K. 13 55.15N 5.52W
North Chicago U.S.A. 82 42.20N 87.51W
North China Plain f. see Huabei Pingyuan f. China 32
Northcliffe Australia 63 34.36S 116.04E
North Dakota d. U.S.A. 82 47.00N 100.00W
North Dorset Downs hills U.K. 11 50.46N 2.25W
North Downs hills U.K. 11 51.18N 0.40E
North East d. Botswana 56 20.45S 27.05E
North East U.S.A. 76 42.13N 79.50W
North Eastern d. Kenya 55 1.00N 40.00E
North Eastern Atlantic Basin f. Atlantic Oc. 95 45.00N 17.00W
North East Pt. Kiribati 69 1.57N 157.16W
Northern d. Ghana 52 9.00N 1.30W
Northern Indian L. Canada 75 57.20N 97.20W
Northern Ireland d. U.K. 13 54.40N 6.45W
Northern Territory d. Australia 64 20.00S 133.00E
North Esk r. U.K. 12 56.45N 2.25W
North Fiji Basin Pacific Oc. 68 17.00S 173.00E
North Foreland c. U.K. 11 51.23N 1.26E
North French r. Canada 76 51.04N 80.46W
North Frisian Is. see Nordfriesische Inseln is. Germany 20
North Head c. Canada 77 53.42N 56.24W
North Henik L. Canada 75 61.45N 97.40W
North Horr Kenya 55 3.19N 37.00E
North I. Kenya 49 4.04N 36.03E
North I. New Zealand 60 39.00S 175.00E
Northiam U.K. 11 50.59N 0.39E
North Knife r. Canada 75 58.53N 94.45W
North Korea Asia 31 40.00N 128.00E
Northland d. New Zealand 60 35.25S 174.00E
North Las Vegas U.S.A. 81 36.12N 115.07W
North Little Rock U.S.A. 83 34.46N 92.14W
North Loup r. U.S.A. 82 41.17N 98.23W
North Mankato U.S.A. 82 44.15N 94.06W
North Nahanni r. Canada 74 62.15N 123.20W
North Ogden U.S.A. 80 41.18N 112.00W
Northome U.S.A. 82 47.52N 94.17W
North Platte U.S.A. 82 41.08N 100.46W
North Platte r. U.S.A. 82 41.15N 100.45W
Northport U.S.A. 85 33.14N 87.33W
North Powder U.S.A. 80 45.13N 117.55W
North Pt. Canada 77 47.05N 64.00W
North Rona i. U.K. 8 59.09N 5.43W
North Ronaldsay i. U.K. 12 59.23N 2.26W
North Saskatchewan r. Canada 75 53.15N 105.06W
North Sea Europe 20 54.00N 4.00E
North Seal r. Canada 75 58.50N 98.10W
North Sporades see Voríai Sporádhes is. Greece 19
North Sydney Canada 77 46.13N 60.15W
North Taranaki Bight b. New Zealand 60 38.45S 174.15E
North Tawton U.K. 11 50.48N 3.55W
North Thompson r. Canada 74 50.40N 120.20W
North Tonawanda U.S.A. 84 43.02N 78.54W
North Twin I. Canada 76 53.20N 80.00W
North Uist i. U.K. 12 57.35N 7.20W
Northumberland d. U.K. 10 55.12N 2.00W
Northumberland, C. Australia 66 38.04S 140.40E
Northumberland Is. Australia 64 21.40S 150.00E
Northumberland Str. Canada 77 46.00N 63.30W
North Wabasca L. Canada 74 56.00N 113.55W
North Walsham U.K. 10 52.49N 1.22E
Northway U.S.A. 72 62.58N 142.00W
North West C. Australia 62 21.48S 114.10E
North West Chile Ridge Pacific Oc. 69 42.00S 90.00W
North Western d. Zambia 56 13.00S 25.00E
North Western Atlantic Basin f. Atlantic Oc. 95 33.00N 55.00W
Northwest Frontier d. Pakistan 40 33.45N 71.00E
North West Highlands U.K. 12 57.30N 5.15W
North West Pt. Kiribati 69 2.02N 157.29W
North West River town Canada 77 53.32N 60.09W
Northwest Territories d. Canada 73 66.00N 95.00W
Northwich U.K. 10 53.16N 2.30W
Northwood Iowa U.S.A. 82 43.27N 93.13W
Northwood N.Dak. U.S.A. 82 47.44N 97.34W
North York Moors hills U.K. 10 54.21N 0.50W
North Yorkshire d. U.K. 10 54.14N 1.14W
Norton Kans. U.S.A. 82 39.50N 99.53W
Norton Sound b. U.S.A. 72 63.50N 164.00W
Nort-sur-Erdre France 15 47.26N 1.30W
Norwalk Conn. U.S.A. 85 41.07N 73.25W
Norwalk Ohio U.S.A. 84 41.14N 82.37W
Norway Europe 22 65.00N 13.00E
Norway House town Canada 75 53.59N 97.50W
Norwegian Dependency Antarctica 96 77.00S 10.00E
Norwegian Sea Europe 96 65.00N 5.00E
Norwich U.K. 11 52.38N 1.17E
Norwood Ohio U.S.A. 84 39.12N 84.21W
Noshul U.S.S.R. 24 60.04N 49.30E
Nosovka U.S.S.R. 21 50.55N 31.37E
Noșratābād Iran 43 29.54N 59.58E
Noss Head U.K. 12 58.28N 3.03W
Nosy Be i. Madagascar 57 13.20S 48.15E
Nosy Boraha i. Madagascar 57 16.50S 49.55E
Nosy Varika Madagascar 57 20.35S 48.32E
Noteć r. Poland 20 52.44N 15.26E
Nothern Marianas is. Pacific Oc. 68 15.00N 145.00E
Noto Italy 18 36.53N 15.05E
Notodden Norway 23 59.34N 9.17E
Notre Dame, Monts mts. Canada 77 48.00N 69.00W
Notre Dame B. Canada 77 49.45N 55.15W
Notre Dame de la Salette Canada 77 45.46N 75.35W
Nottawasaga B. Canada 76 44.40N 80.30W
Nottaway r. Canada 76 51.25N 78.50W
Nottingham U.K. 10 52.57N 1.10W
Nottinghamshire d. U.K. 10 53.10N 1.00W
Notwani r. Botswana 56 23.46S 26.57E
Nouadhibou Mauritania 50 20.54N 17.01W
Nouakchott Mauritania 50 18.09N 15.58W
Nouméa New Caledonia 68 22.16S 166.27E
Nouna Burkina 52 12.44N 3.54W
Noupoort R.S.A. 56 31.11S 24.56E
Nouveau, Lac l. Canada 77 51.59N 68.58W
Nouveau-Comptoir Canada 76 53.02N 78.55W
Nouvelle Anvers Zaïre 54 1.38N 19.10E
Nouvelle Calédonie is. Pacific Oc. 68 21.30S 165.30E
Nouzonville France 15 49.49N 4.45E
Nova Caipemba Angola 54 7.25S 14.36E
Novafeltria Bagnodi Romagna Italy 15 43.53N 12.17E
Nova Friburgo Brazil 94 22.16S 42.32W
Nova Iguaçu Brazil 94 22.45S 43.27W
Nova Lamego Guinea Bissau 52 12.19N 14.11W
Nova Lima Brazil 94 19.59S 43.51W
Novara Italy 15 45.27N 8.37E
Nova Scotia d. Canada 77 45.00N 63.30W
Nova Sofala Mozambique 57 20.09S 34.24E
Novato U.S.A. 80 38.06N 122.34W
Novaya Ladoga U.S.S.R. 24 60.09N 32.15E
Novaya Lyalya U.S.S.R. 28 59.02N 60.38E
Novaya Sibir, Ostrov i. U.S.S.R. 29 75.20N 148.00E
Novaya Ushitsa U.S.S.R. 21 48.50N 27.12E
Novaya Zemlya i. U.S.S.R. 28 74.00N 56.00E
Novelda Spain 16 38.24N 0.45W
Nové Zámky Czech. 21 47.59N 18.11E
Novgorod U.S.S.R. 24 58.30N 31.20E
Novgorod Severskiy U.S.S.R. 24 52.00N 33.15E
Novi di Modena Italy 15 44.54N 10.54E
Novigrad Yugo. 20 45.19N 13.34E
Novi Ligure Italy 15 44.46N 8.47E
Novi Pazar Yugo. 19 43.08N 20.28E
Novi Sad Yugo. 21 45.16N 19.52E
Novoalekseyevka U.S.S.R. 25 46.14N 34.36E
Novoanninskiy U.S.S.R. 25 50.32N 42.42E
Novo Arkhangel'sk U.S.S.R. 21 48.34N 30.50E
Novocherkassk U.S.S.R. 25 47.25N 40.05E
Novofedorovka U.S.S.R. 25 47.04N 35.18E
Novograd Volynskiy U.S.S.R. 21 50.34N 27.32E
Novogrudok U.S.S.R. 21 53.35N 25.50E
Novo Hamburgo Brazil 94 29.37S 51.07W
Novokazalinsk U.S.S.R. 28 45.48N 62.06E
Novokuznetsk U.S.S.R. 28 53.45N 87.12E
Novomoskovsk R.S.F.S.R. U.S.S.R. 24 54.06N 38.15E
Novomoskovsk Ukr.S.S.R. U.S.S.R. 25 48.38N 35.15E
Novorossiysk U.S.S.R. 25 44.44N 37.46E
Novoshakhtinsk U.S.S.R. 25 47.46N 39.55E
Novosibirsk U.S.S.R. 28 55.04N 82.55E
Novosibirskiye Ostrova is. U.S.S.R. 29 76.00N 144.00E
Novouzensk U.S.S.R. 25 50.29N 48.08E
Novo-Vyatsk U.S.S.R. 24 58.30N 49.40E
Novozybkov U.S.S.R. 21 52.31N 31.58E
Novska Yugo. 20 45.21N 16.59E
Nový Jičín Czech. 21 49.36N 18.00E
Novyy Bykhov U.S.S.R. 21 53.20N 30.21E

Novyy Port U.S.S.R. 28 67.38N 72.33E
Nowa Ruda Poland 20 50.34N 16.30E
Nowa Sól Poland 20 51.49N 15.41E
Nowendoc Australia 67 31.35S151.45E
Nowgong Assam India 41 26.21N 92.40E
Nowgong Madhya P. India 41 25.04N 79.27E
Nowingi Australia 66 34.36S142.15E
Nowra Australia 67 35.54S150.36E
Nowrangapur India 41 19.14N 82.33E
Nowshera Pakistan 40 34.01N 71.59E
Nowy Dwór Mazowiecki Poland 21 52.26N 20.43E
Nowy Korczyn Poland 21 50.19N 20.48E
Nowy Sącz Poland 21 49.39N 20.40E
Nowy Targ Poland 21 49.29N 20.02E
Nowy Tomśyl Poland 20 52.20N 16.07E
Now Zād Afghan. 40 32.24N 64.28E
Noxon U.S.A. 80 48.01N115.47W
Noyant France 15 47.31N 0.08E
Noyes I. U.S.A. 74 55.30N133.40W
Noyon France 15 49.35N 3.00E
Nozay France 15 47.34N 1.38W
Nsanje Malaŵi 55 16.55S 35.12E
Nsawam Ghana 52 5.49N 0.20W
Nsok Equat. Guinea 54 1.10N 11.19E
Nsombo Zambia 55 10.50S 29.56E
Nsukka Nigeria 53 6.51N 7.29E
Nuatja Togo 53 6.59N 1.11E
Nubian Desert Sudan 48 20.30N 34.00E
Nueces r. U.S.A. 83 27.50N 97.30W
Nueces Plains f. U.S.A. 83 28.30N 99.15W
Nueltin L. Canada 75 60.30N 99.30W
Nueva Casas Grandes Mexico 81 30.25N107.55W
Nueva Gerona Cuba 87 21.53N 82.49W
Nueva Helvecia Uruguay 93 34.19S 57.13W
Nueva Palmira Uruguay 93 33.53S 58.25W
Nueva Rosita Mexico 83 27.57N101.13W
Nueve de Julio Argentina 93 35.30S 60.50W
Nuevitas Cuba 87 21.34N 77.18W
Nuevo d. Mexico 83 26.00N100.00W
Nuevo, Golfo g. Argentina 93 42.42S 64.35W
Nuevo Berlín Uruguay 93 32.59S 58.03W
Nuevo Laredo Mexico 83 27.30N 99.31W
Nuevo León d. Mexico 86 26.00N 99.00W
Nuevo Rocafuerte Ecuador 90 0.56S 75.24W
Nūh, Rās c. Pakistan 40 25.05N 62.24E
Nui i. Tuvalu 68 7.12S177.10E
Nu Jiang r. China see Salween r. Burma 39
Nukha U.S.S.R. 43 41.12N 47.10E
Nukhaylah Sudan 48 19.03N 26.19E
Nuku'alofa Tonga 69 21.07S175.12W
Nuku Hiva i. Îs. Marquises 69 8.56S140.00W
Nukunonu Pacific Oc. 68 9.10S171.55W
Nulato U.S.A. 72 64.43N158.06W
Nullagine Australia 62 21.56S120.06E
Nullarbor Australia 63 31.26S130.55E
Nullarbor Plain f. Australia 63 31.30S128.00E
Numalla, L. Australia 66 28.45S144.21E
Numan Nigeria 53 9.30N 12.01E
Numazu Japan 35 35.06N138.52E
Numedal f. Norway 23 60.06N 9.06E
Numurkah Australia 67 36.05S145.26E
Nundle Australia 67 31.28S151.08E
Nuneaton U.K. 11 52.32N 1.29W
Nungo Mozambique 57 13.25S 37.45E
Nunivak I. U.S.A. 72 60.00N166.30W
Nunkun mtn. Jammu & Kashmir 40 33.59N 76.01E
Nuoro Italy 18 40.19N 9.20E
Nuqūb Yemen 45 14.59N 45.48E
Nürburg Germany 14 50.20N 6.59E
Nure r. Italy 15 45.03N 9.49E
Nuriootpa Australia 66 34.27S139.02E
Nürnberg Germany 20 49.27N 11.05E
Nurri, Mt. Australia 67 31.44S146.04E
Nusa Tenggara is. Indonesia 36 8.30S118.00E
Nusa Tenggara Barat d. Indonesia 36 8.50S117.30E
Nusa Tenggara Timur d. Indonesia 37 9.30S122.00E
Nusaybin Turkey 42 37.05N 41.11E
Nushki Pakistan 40 29.33N 66.01E
Nutak Canada 77 57.39N 61.50W
Nuuk see Godthåb Greenland 73
Nuwākot Nepal 41 28.08N 83.53E
Nuwaybi'al Muzayyinah Egypt 44 28.58N 34.38E
Nuweveldberge mts. R.S.A. 56 32.15S 21.50E
Nuyts, Pt. Australia 63 35.02S116.32E
Nuyts Archipelago is. Australia 65 32.35S133.17E
Nxaunxau Botswana 56 18.19S 21.04E
Nyaake Liberia 52 4.52N 7.37W
Nyabing Australia 63 33.32S118.09E
Nyahua Tanzania 55 5.25S 33.16E
Nyahururu Falls town Kenya 55 0.04N 36.22E
Nyah West Australia 66 35.11S143.21E
Nyainqêntanglha Feng mtn. China 41 30.27N 90.33E
Nyainqêntanglha Shan mts. China 41 30.00N 90.00E
Nyainrong China 41 32.02N 92.15E
Nyakanazi Tanzania 55 3.05S 31.16E
Nyaksimvol U.S.S.R. 24 62.30N 60.52E
Nyala Sudan 49 12.03N 24.53E
Nyalam China 41 28.12N 85.58E
Nyamandhlovu Zimbabwe 56 19.50S 28.15E
Nyamapanda Zimbabwe 57 16.59S 32.50E
Nyamlell Sudan 49 9.07N 26.58E
Nyamtukusa Tanzania 55 3.03S 32.44E
Nyandoma U.S.S.R. 24 61.33N 40.05E
Nyanga r. Gabon 54 3.00S 10.17E
Nyang Qu r. China 41 29.19N 88.52E
Nyanza d. Kenya 55 0.30S 34.30E
Nyanza Rwanda 55 2.20S 29.42E
Nyashabozh U.S.S.R. 24 65.28N 53.42E
Nyaunglebin Burma 34 17.57N 96.44E
Nyaungu Burma 34 21.12N 94.55E
Nyborg Denmark 23 55.19N 10.48E
Nybro Sweden 23 56.45N 15.54E
Nyda U.S.S.R. 28 66.35N 72.58E
Nyêmo China 41 29.25N 90.15E
Nyeri Kenya 55 0.22S 36.56E
Nyerol Sudan 49 8.41N 32.02E
Nyhammar Sweden 23 60.17N 14.58E
Nyika Plateau f. Malaŵi 55 10.25S 33.50E
Nyima China 41 31.50N 87.48E
Nyimba Zambia 55 14.33S 30.49E
Nyíregyháza Hungary 21 47.59N 21.43E
Nyköbing Falster Denmark 23 54.46N 11.53E
Nyköbing Jylland Denmark 23 56.48N 8.52E
Nyköbing Sjaelland Denmark 23 55.55N 11.41E
Nyköping Sweden 23 58.45N 17.00E
Nylstroom R.S.A. 56 24.42S 28.24E
Nymagee Australia 67 32.05S146.20E
Nymboida Australia 67 29.57S152.32E
Nymboida r. Australia 67 29.39S152.30E
Nymburk Czech. 20 50.11N 15.03E
Nynäshamn Sweden 23 58.54N 17.57E
Nyngan Australia 67 31.34S147.14E
Nyngynderry Australia 66 32.16S143.22E
Nyoma Jammu & Kashmir 41 33.11N 78.38E
Nyong r. Cameroon 53 3.15N 9.55E
Nyons France 17 44.22N 5.08E
Nysa Poland 21 50.29N 17.20E
Nysa Kłodzka r. Poland 21 50.49N 17.50E
Nyssa U.S.A. 80 43.53N117.00W
Nyuksenitsa U.S.S.R. 24 60.24N 44.08E
Nyunzu Zaïre 55 5.55S 28.00E
Nyurba U.S.S.R. 29 63.18N118.28E
Nyuri India 41 27.42N 92.13E
Nzega Tanzania 55 4.13S 33.09E
N'zérékoré Guinea 52 7.49N 8.48W
N'zeto Angola 54 7.13S 12.56E
Nzwani i. Comoros 55 12.12S 44.28E

O

Oahe Resr. U.S.A. 82 45.30N100.25W
Oahu i. Hawaiian Is. 69 21.30N158.00W
Oakbank Australia 66 33.07S140.33E
Oakdale U.S.A. 83 30.49N 92.40W
Oakesdale U.S.A. 80 47.08N117.15W
Oakey Australia 65 27.26S151.43E
Oak Harbour U.S.A. 80 48.18N122.39W
Oak Hill town Fla. U.S.A. 85 28.52N 80.52W
Oakland Calif. U.S.A. 80 37.47N122.13W
Oakland Oreg. U.S.A. 80 43.25N123.18W
Oaklands Australia 67 35.25S146.15E
Oakley U.S.A. 80 42.15N113.53W
Oakover r. Australia 62 20.49S120.40E
Oakridge U.S.A. 80 43.45N122.28W
Oak Ridge town U.S.A. 85 36.02N 84.12W
Oakvale Australia 66 33.01S140.41E
Oakville Canada 76 43.27N 79.41W
Oamaru New Zealand 60 45.07S170.58E
Oates Land f. Antarctica 96 70.00S155.00E
Oaxaca Mexico 86 17.05N 96.41W
Oaxaca d. Mexico 86 17.30N 97.00W
Ob r. U.S.S.R. 24 66.50N 69.00E
Oba Canada 76 49.04N 84.07W
Oba i. Vanuatu 68 15.25S167.50E
Oban U.K. 12 56.26N 5.28W
Oberá Argentina 92 27.30S 55.07W
Oberhausen Germany 14 51.28N 6.51E
Oberlin Kans. U.S.A. 82 39.49N100.32W
Oberon Australia 67 33.41S149.52E
Oberösterreich d. Austria 20 48.15N 14.00E
Obi i. Indonesia 37 1.45S127.30E
Obidos Brazil 91 1.55S 55.31W
Obitsu r. Japan 35 35.24N139.54E
Obo C.A.R. 49 5.24N 26.30E
Obock Djibouti 49 11.59N 43.16E
Obodovka U.S.S.R. 21 48.28N 29.10E
Oboyan U.S.S.R. 25 51.13N 36.17E
Obozerskiy U.S.S.R. 24 63.28N 40.29E
Obregón, Presa resr. Mexico 81 28.00N109.50W
Obruk Platosu f. Turkey 42 38.00N 33.30E
Obskaya Guba g. U.S.S.R. 28 68.30N 74.00E
Ōbu Japan 35 35.00N136.58E
Obuasi Ghana 52 6.15N 1.36W
Obudu Nigeria 53 6.42N 9.07E
Ocala U.S.A. 85 29.11N 82.09W
Ocaña Colombia 90 8.16N 73.21W
Ocaña Spain 16 39.57N 3.30W
Occidental, Cordillera mts. Colombia 90 5.00N 76.15W
Occidental, Cordillera mts. S. America 92 17.00S 69.00W
Ocean City Md. U.S.A. 85 38.20N 75.05W
Ocean City N.J. U.S.A. 85 39.16N 74.36W
Ocean Falls town Canada 74 52.25N127.40W
Ocean I. see Banaba i. Kiribati 68
Oceanside Calif. U.S.A. 81 33.12N117.23W
Oceanside N.Y. U.S.A. 85 40.38N 73.38W
Ochamchire U.S.S.R. 25 42.44N 41.30E
Ochil Hills U.K. 12 56.16N 3.25W
Ochsenfurt Germany 20 49.40N 10.03E
Ockelbo Sweden 23 60.53N 16.43E
Ocmulgee r. U.S.A. 85 31.58N 82.32W
Oconee r. U.S.A. 85 31.58N 82.32W
Oconto U.S.A. 82 44.55N 87.52W
Ocotal Nicaragua 87 13.37N 86.31W
Ocotlán Mexico 86 20.21N102.42W
Octeville France 15 49.37N 1.39W
Ocua Mozambique 57 13.40S 39.46E
Oda Ghana 52 5.55N 0.56W
Oda, Jabal mtn. Sudan 48 20.21N 36.39E
Odádhahraun mts. Iceland 22 65.00N 17.30W
Odawara Japan 35 35.15N139.10E
Odda Norway 23 60.04N 6.33E
Ödeborg Sweden 23 58.33N 12.00E
Odemira Portugal 16 37.36N 8.38W
Ödemiş Turkey 19 38.12N 28.00E
Odense Denmark 23 55.24N 10.23E
Odenwald mts. Germany 20 49.40N 9.20E
Oder r. Germany see Odra r. Poland 20
Oderzo Italy 15 45.47N 12.29E
Odessa Tex. U.S.A. 83 31.51N102.22W
Odessa U.S.S.R. 21 46.30N 30.46E
Odienné Ivory Coast 52 9.36N 7.32W
Odorhei Romania 21 46.18N 25.18E
Odra r. Poland 20 53.30N 14.36E
Odžak Yugo. 21 45.03N 18.18E
Odzi r. Zimbabwe 57 19.46S 32.22E
Oegstgeest Neth. 14 52.12N 4.31E
Oeiras Brazil 91 7.00S 42.07W
Oelrichs U.S.A. 82 43.10N103.13W
Oelwein U.S.A. 82 42.41N 91.55W
Oeno I. Pacific Oc. 69 23.55S130.45W
Ofanto r. Italy 18 41.22N 16.12E
Ofaqim Israel 44 31.19N 34.37E
Offa Nigeria 53 8.09N 4.44E
Offaly d. Rep. of Ire. 13 53.15N 7.30W
Offenbach Germany 20 50.06N 8.46E
Offenburg Germany 20 48.29N 7.57E
Offerdal Sweden 22 63.28N 14.03E
Offranville France 15 49.52N 1.03E
Ofir Portugal 16 41.31N 8.47W
Ofotfjorden est. Norway 22 68.25N 17.00E
Ofu i. Samoa 68 14.11S169.40W
Ogadēn f. Ethiopia 45 7.50N 45.40E
Ōgaki Japan 35 35.21N136.37E
Ogallala U.S.A. 82 41.08N101.43W
Ogbomosho Nigeria 53 8.05N 4.11E
Ogden Iowa U.S.A. 82 42.02N 94.02W
Ogden Utah U.S.A. 80 41.14N111.58W
Ogeechee r. U.S.A. 85 31.51N 81.06W
Ogilvie Mts. Canada 72 65.00N139.30W
Oginskiy, Kanal canal U.S.S.R. 21 52.25N 25.55E
Oglio r. Italy 15 45.02N 10.39E
Ognon r. France 17 47.20N 5.37E
Ogoja Nigeria 53 6.40N 8.45E
Ogoki Canada 76 51.35N 86.00W
Ogoki r. Canada 76 51.35N 86.00W
Ogoki Resr. Canada 76 51.00N 88.15W
Ogooué r. Gabon 54 1.00S 9.05E
Ogosta r. Bulgaria 19 43.44N 23.51E
Ogr Sudan 49 12.02N 27.06E
Ogulin Yugo. 20 45.17N 15.14E
Ogun d. Nigeria 53 6.50N 3.20E
Ohai New Zealand 60 45.56S167.57E
Ohanet Algeria 51 28.40N 8.50E
Ohey Belgium 14 50.26N 5.06E
O'Higgins, Cabo c. I. de Pascua 69 27.05S109.15W
O'Higgins, L. Chile 93 48.03S 73.10W
Ohio d. U.S.A. 84 40.15N 82.45W
Ohio r. U.S.A. 84 36.59N 89.08W
Ōhito Japan 35 34.59N138.56E
Ohře r. Czech. 20 50.32N 14.08E
Ohrid Yugo. 19 41.06N 20.48E
Ohrid, L. Albania/Yugo. 19 41.00N 20.43E
Ōi r. Japan 35 34.45N138.18E
Oil City U.S.A. 84 41.26N 79.42W
Oise d. France 15 49.30N 2.30E
Oise r. France 15 49.00N 2.10E
Oisterwijk Neth. 14 51.34N 5.10E
Ojai U.S.A. 81 34.27N119.15W
Ojocaliente Mexico 86 22.35N102.18W
Ojo de Agua Argentina 92 29.30S 63.44W
Ojos del Salado mtn. Argentina/Chile 92 27.05S 68.05W
Oka Canada 77 45.29N 74.06W
Oka Nigeria 53 7.28N 5.48E
Oka r. U.S.S.R. 24 56.09N 43.00E
Okaba Indonesia 37 8.06S139.46E
Okahandja Namibia 56 21.58S 16.44E
Okanagan L. Canada 74 50.00N119.30W
Okanogan U.S.A. 80 48.39N120.41W
Okanogan r. U.S.A. 80 48.22N119.35W
Okaputa Namibia 56 20.08S 16.58E
Okāra Pakistan 40 30.49N 73.27E
Okarito New Zealand 60 43.14S.170.07
Okaukuejo Namibia 56 19.12S 15.56E
Okavango r. Botswana 56 18.30S 22.04E
Okavango Basin f. Botswana 56 19.30S 22.30E
Okayama Japan 31 34.40N133.54E
Okeechobee U.S.A. 85 27.14N 80.50W
Okeechobee, L. U.S.A. 85 26.55N 80.45W
Okefenokee Swamp f. U.S.A. 85 30.42N 82.20W
Okehampton U.K. 11 50.44N 4.01W
Okere r. Uganda 55 1.37N 33.53E
Okha U.S.S.R. 29 53.35N142.50E
Okhaldhunga Nepal 41 27.19N 86.31E
Okhansk U.S.S.R. 24 57.42N 55.20E
Okhotsk U.S.S.R. 29 59.20N143.15E
Okhotsk, Sea of U.S.S.R. 29 55.00N150.00E
Okhotskiy Perevoz U.S.S.R. 29 61.55N135.40E
Okiep R.S.A. 56 29.36S 17.49E
Oki guntō is. Japan 31 36.30N133.20E
Okinawa jima i. Japan 31 26.30N128.00E
Okino Torishima i. Pacific Oc. 37 20.24N136.02E
Okipoko r. Namibia 56 18.40S 16.03E
Okitipupa Nigeria 53 6.31N 4.50E
Oklahoma d. U.S.A. 83 35.20N 98.00W
Oklahoma City U.S.A. 83 35.28N 97.32W
Okmulgee U.S.A. 83 35.37N 95.58W
Oknitsa U.S.S.R. 21 48.22N 27.30E
Oko, Wādī Sudan 48 21.15N 35.56E
Okola Cameroon 53 4.03N 11.23E
Okolona U.S.A. 83 34.00N 88.45W
Okondja Gabon 54 0.03S 13.45E
Okoyo Congo 54 1.28S 15.00E
Oksskolten mtn. Norway 22 65.59N 14.15E
Oktyabr'sk U.S.S.R. 25 49.30N 57.22E
Oktyabrskiy B.S.S.R. U.S.S.R. 21 52.35N 28.45E
Oktyabrskiy R.S.F.S.R. U.S.S.R. 24 54.30N 53.30E
Oktyabr'skoy Revolyutsii, Ostrov i. U.S.S.R. 29 79.30N 96.00E
Okuru New Zealand 60 43.56S168.55E
Okuta Nigeria 53 9.13N 3.12E
Ola U.S.A. 83 35.02N 93.13W
Ólafsvík Iceland 22 64.53N 23.44W
Olancha U.S.A. 81 36.17N118.01W
Öland i. Sweden 23 56.45N 16.38E
Olary Australia 66 32.18S140.19E
Olascoaga Argentina 93 35.14S 60.37W
Olavarría Argentina 93 36.57S 60.20W
Oława Poland 21 50.57N 17.17E
Olbia Italy 18 40.55N 9.29E
Old Bar Australia 67 31.59S152.35E
Old Crow Canada 72 67.34N139.43W
Oldenburg Nschn. Germany 14 53.08N 8.13E
Oldenburg Sch.-Hol. Germany 20 54.17N 10.52E
Oldenzaal Neth. 14 52.19N 6.55E
Old Forge Penn. U.S.A. 84 41.22N 75.44W
Old Fort r. Canada 75 58.30N110.30W
Old Gumbiro Tanzania 55 10.00S 35.24E
Oldham U.K. 10 53.33N 2.08W
Old Head of Kinsale c. Rep. of Ire. 13 51.37N 8.33W
Oldman r. Canada 75 49.56N111.42W
Old Moolawatana Australia 66 30.04S140.02E
Olds Canada 74 51.50N114.10W
Old Town U.S.A. 84 44.56N 68.39W
Olean U.S.A. 84 42.05N 78.26W
Olecko Poland 21 54.03N 22.30E
Olekma r. U.S.S.R. 29 60.20N120.30E
Olekminsk U.S.S.R. 29 60.25N120.00E
Olema U.S.S.R. 24 64.25N 40.15E
Olenëk U.S.S.R. 29 68.38N112.15E
Olenëk r. U.S.S.R. 29 73.00N120.00E
Olenëkskiy Zaliv g. U.S.S.R. 29 74.00N120.00E
Oléron, Île d' i. France 17 45.55N 1.16W
Oleśnica Poland 21 51.13N 17.23E
Olevsk U.S.S.R. 21 51.12N 27.35E
Olga U.S.S.R. 31 43.46N135.14E
Olga, Mt. Australia 64 25.18S130.44E
Olga L. Canada 76 49.44N 77.18W
Ölgiy Mongolia 30 48.54N 90.00E
Olgopol U.S.S.R. 21 48.10N 29.30E
Olhão Portugal 16 37.01N 7.50W
Olifants r. Namibia 56 25.28S 19.23E
Olifants r. C.P. R.S.A. 56 31.42S 18.10E
Olifants r. Trans. R.S.A. 56 24.08S 32.39E
Ólimbos mtn. Cyprus 44 34.55N 32.52E
Ólimbos Greece 19 35.44N 27.11E
Ólimbos mtn. Greece 19 40.04N 22.20E
Olinda Brazil 91 8.00S 34.51W
Oliva Argentina 92 32.05S 63.35W
Oliva Spain 16 38.58N 0.15W
Olivares Spain 16 39.45N 2.21W
Oliveira Brazil 94 20.39S 44.47W
Olivenza Spain 16 38.41N 7.09W
Olney U.K. 11 52.09N 0.42W
Olney U.S.A. 82 38.45N 88.05W
Olofström Sweden 23 56.16N 14.30E
Olomouc Czech. 21 49.36N 17.16E
Olonets U.S.S.R. 24 61.00N 32.59E
Oloron France 17 43.12N 0.35W
Olosega i. Samoa 68 14.12S169.38W
Olot Spain 16 42.11N 2.30E
Olovyannaya U.S.S.R. 31 50.58N115.35E
Olpe Germany 14 51.02N 7.52E
Olsztyn Poland 21 53.48N 20.29E
Olsztynek Poland 21 53.36N 20.17E
Olt r. Romania 21 43.43N 24.51E
Olteniţa Romania 21 44.05N 26.31E
Olteţ r. Romania 21 44.13N 24.28E
Olympia U.S.A. 80 47.03N122.53W
Olympic Mts. U.S.A. 80 47.50N123.45W
Olympic Nat. Park U.S.A. 80 47.48N123.30W
Olympus mtn. see Ólimbos mtn. Greece 19
Olympus, Mt. U.S.A. 80 47.48N123.43W
Oma China 41 32.30N 83.14E
Omae-zaki c. Japan 35 34.36N138.14E
Omagh U.K. 13 54.36N 7.20W
Omaha U.S.A. 82 41.16N 95.57W
Oman Asia 38 22.30N 57.30E
Oman, G. of Asia 43 25.00N 58.00E
Omarama New Zealand 60 44.29S169.58E
Omaruru Namibia 56 21.25S 15.57E
Omate Peru 92 16.40S 70.58W
Omboué Gabon 54 1.38S 9.20E
Ombrone r. Italy 18 42.40N 11.00E
Ombu China 41 31.20N 86.34E
Omdurman see Umm Durmān Sudan 48
Omegna Italy 15 45.53N 8.24E
Omeo Australia 67 37.05S147.37E
Ometepec Mexico 86 16.41N 98.25W
Om Hājer Ethiopia 48 14.24N 36.46E
Ōmi-hachiman Japan 35 35.08N136.06E
Omineca r. Canada 74 56.05N124.30W
Omitara Namibia 56 22.18S 18.01E
Ōmiya Japan 35 35.54N139.38E
Ommen Neth. 14 52.32N 6.25E
Ömnögovĭ d. Mongolia 32 43.00N105.00E
Omo r. Ethiopia 49 4.51N 36.55E
Omolon r. U.S.S.R. 29 68.50N158.30E
Omsk U.S.S.R. 28 55.00N 73.22E
Omulew r. Poland 21 53.05N 21.32E
Omuramba Omatako r. Namibia 56 18.19S 19.52E
Omuta Japan 31 33.02N130.26E
Oña Spain 16 42.44N 3.25W
Onaga U.S.A. 82 39.29N 96.10W
Onai Angola 56 16.43S 17.33E
Onancock U.S.A. 85 37.43N 75.46W
Oncocua Angola 56 16.40S 13.25E
Onda Spain 16 39.58N 0.16W
Ondangua Namibia 56 17.59S 16.02E
Ondo d. Nigeria 53 7.10N 5.20E
Onega U.S.S.R. 24 63.57N 38.11E
Onega r. U.S.S.R. 24 63.59N 38.11E
Oneida U.S.A. 84 43.06N 75.39W
O'Neill U.S.A. 82 42.27N 98.39W
Onezhskaya Guba b. U.S.S.R. 24 63.55N 37.30E
Onezhskoye Ozero l. U.S.S.R. 24 62.00N 35.30E
Ongerup Australia 63 33.58S118.29E
Ongiyn Gol r. Mongolia 32 43.40N103.45E
Ongniud Qi China 32 43.00N118.43E
Ongole India 39 15.31N 80.04E
Onilahy r. Madagascar 57 23.34S 43.45E
Onitsha Nigeria 53 6.10N 6.47E
Onslow Australia 62 21.41S115.12E
Onslow B. U.S.A. 85 34.20N 77.20W
Onstwedde Neth. 14 53.04N 7.02E
Ontario d. Canada 76 51.00N 88.00W
Ontario Calif. U.S.A. 81 34.04N117.39W
Ontario Oreg. U.S.A. 80 44.02N116.58W
Ontario, L. Canada/U.S.A. 76 43.40N 78.00W
Ontonagon U.S.A. 84 46.52N 89.18W
Oodnadatta Australia 65 27.30S135.27E
Ooldea Australia 65 30.27S131.50E
Oostelijk-Flevoland f. Neth. 14 52.30N 5.40E
Oostende Belgium 14 51.13N 2.55E
Oosterhout Neth. 14 51.38N 4.50E
Oosterschelde est. Neth. 14 51.35N 3.57E
Oosthuizen Neth. 14 52.33N 5.00E
Oostmalle Belgium 14 51.18N 4.45E
Oost Vlaanderen d. Belgium 14 51.00N 3.45E
Oost Vlieland Neth. 14 53.18N 5.04E
Ootsa L. Canada 74 53.50N126.20W
Opaka Bulgaria 19 43.28N 26.10E
Opal Mexico 83 24.18N102.22W
Opala U.S.S.R. 29 51.58N156.30E
Opala Zaïre 54 0.42S 24.15E
Oparino U.S.S.R. 24 59.53N 48.10E
Opasatika Canada 76 49.30N 82.50W
Opasatika r. Canada 76 50.24N 82.26W
Opasquia Canada 75 53.16N 93.34W
Opava Czech. 21 49.56N 17.54E
Opelousas U.S.A. 83 30.32N 92.05W
Opheim U.S.A. 80 48.51N106.24W
Opinaca r. Canada 76 52.20N 78.00W
Opinnagau r. Canada 76 54.12N 82.21W
Opiscotéo, Lac l. Canada 77 53.10N 68.10W
Opochka U.S.S.R. 24 56.41N 28.42E
Opole Poland 21 50.40N 17.56E
Oporto see Porto Portugal 16
Opotiki New Zealand 60 38.00S177.18E
Opp U.S.A. 85 31.16N 86.18W
Oppdal Norway 22 62.36N 9.41E
Oppland d. Norway 23 61.30N 9.00E
Opportunity U.S.A. 80 47.39N117.15W
Opunake New Zealand 60 39.27S173.51E
Ora Italy 15 46.21N 11.18E
Ora Banda Australia 63 30.27S121.04E
Oradea Romania 21 47.03N 21.55E
Öraefajökull mtn. Iceland 22 64.02N 16.39W
Orai India 41 25.59N 79.28E
Oran Algeria 50 35.42N 0.38W
Orán Argentina 92 23.07S 64.16W
Orange Australia 67 33.19S149.10E
Orange France 17 44.08N 4.48E
Orange r. R.S.A. 56 28.38S 16.38E
Orange Tex. U.S.A. 83 30.01N 93.44W
Orange, C. Brazil 91 4.25N 51.32W
Orangeburg U.S.A. 85 33.28N 80.53W
Orange Free State d. R.S.A. 56 28.00S 28.00E
Orangevale U.S.A. 80 38.41N121.13W
Orangeville Canada 76 43.55N 80.06W
Oranienburg Germany 20 52.45N 13.14E
Oranjefontein R.S.A. 56 23.27S 27.40E
Oranjemund Namibia 56 28.35S 16.26E
Orarak Sudan 49 6.15N 32.23E
Oras Phil. 37 12.09N125.22E
Orbetello Italy 18 42.27N 11.13E
Orbost Australia 67 37.42S148.30E
Örbyhus Sweden 23 60.14N 17.42E
Orchies France 14 50.28N 3.15E
Orchila i. Venezuela 87 11.52N 66.10W
Orco r. Italy 15 45.10N 7.52E
Ord r. Australia 62 15.30S128.30E
Ordu Turkey 42 41.00N 37.52E
Orduña Spain 16 43.00N 3.00W
Örebro Sweden 23 59.17N 15.13E
Örebro d. Sweden 23 59.30N 15.00E
Oregon d. U.S.A. 80 43.49N120.36W
Oregon City U.S.A. 80 45.21N122.36W
Öregrund Sweden 23 60.20N 18.26E
Orekhovo-Zuyevo U.S.S.R. 24 55.47N 39.00E
Orel U.S.S.R. 24 52.58N 36.04E
Orem U.S.A. 80 40.19N111.42W
Orenburg U.S.S.R. 24 51.50N 55.00E
Orense Spain 16 42.20N 7.52W
Oressa r. U.S.S.R. 21 52.33N 28.45E
Orestiás Greece 19 41.30N 26.33E
Orfanoú, Kólpos g. Greece 19 40.40N 24.00E
Orford U.S.A. 84 43.54N 72.10W
Orford, Mt. Canada 77 45.18N 72.08W
Orford Ness c. Australia 64 11.22S142.50E
Orford Ness c. U.K. 11 52.05N 1.36E
Orgeyev U.S.S.R. 21 47.24N 28.50E
Orgūn Afghan. 40 32.55N 69.10E
Orick U.S.A. 80 41.17N124.04W
Oriental, Cordillera mts. Bolivia 92 17.00S 65.00W

Oriental, Cordillera *mts.* Colombia **90** 5.00N 74.30W
Origny France **15** 49.54N 3.30E
Orihuela Spain **16** 38.05N 0.56W
Orillia Canada **76** 44.37N 79.25W
Orimattila Finland **23** 60.48N 25.45E
Orinduik Guyana **90** 4.42N 60.01W
Orinoco *r.* Venezuela **90** 9.00N 61.30W
Orinoco, Delta del *f.* Venezuela **90** 9.00N 61.00W
Orissa *d.* India **41** 20.20N 84.00E
Oristano Italy **18** 39.53N 8.36E
Oristano, Golfo di *g.* Italy **18** 39.50N 8.30E
Orizaba Mexico **86** 18.51N 97.08W
Orkanger Norway **22** 63.17N 9.52E
Orkney Is. *d.* U.K. **12** 59.00N 3.00W
Orlândia Brazil **94** 20.55S 47.54W
Orlando U.S.A. **85** 28.33N 81.21W
Orléans Canada **77** 45.28N 75.31W
Orléans France **15** 47.54N 1.54E
Orléans, Canal d' France **15** 47.54N 1.55E
Ormāra Pakistan **40** 25.12N 64.38E
Ormāra, Rās *c.* Pakistan **40** 25.09N 64.35E
Ormoc Phil. **37** 11.00N124.37E
Ormond New Zealand **60** 38.35S177.58E
Ormond Beach *town* U.S.A. **85** 29.26N 81.03W
Ormskirk U.K. **10** 53.35N 2.53W
Orne *d.* France **15** 48.40N 0.05E
Orne *r.* France **15** 49.17N 0.10W
Örnsköldsvik Sweden **22** 63.17N 18.50E
Orobie, Alpi *mts.* Italy **15** 46.03N 10.00E
Orocué Colombia **90** 4.48N 71.20W
Orodara Burkina **52** 11.00N 4.54W
Orogrande U.S.A. **81** 32.23N106.28W
Orohena *mtn.* Tahiti **69** 17.37S149.28W
Oromocto Canada **77** 45.51N 66.29W
Oron Israel **44** 30.55N 35.01E
Oron Nigeria **53** 4.49N 8.15E
Orona *i.* Kiribati **68** 4.29S172.10W
Orono Canada **76** 43.59N 78.37W
Orono U.S.A. **84** 44.53N 68.40W
Orosei Italy **18** 40.23N 9.40E
Orosei, Golfo di *g.* Italy **18** 40.15N 9.45E
Orosháza Hungary **21** 46.34N 20.40E
Orote Pen. Guam **68** 13.26N144.38E
Orotukan U.S.S.R. **29** 62.16N151.43E
Oroville Calif. U.S.A. **80** 39.31N121.33W
Oroville Wash. U.S.A. **80** 48.56N119.26W
Orroroo Australia **66** 32.46S138.39E
Orsa Sweden **23** 61.07N 14.37E
Orsha U.S.S.R. **24** 54.30N 30.23E
Orsières Switz. **15** 46.02N 7.09E
Orsk U.S.S.R. **24** 51.13N 58.35E
Orşova Romania **21** 44.42N 22.22E
Orta Nova Italy **18** 41.19N 15.42E
Orthez France **17** 43.29N 0.46W
Ortigueira Spain **16** 43.41N 7.51W
Ortona Italy **18** 42.21N 14.24E
Ortonville U.S.A. **82** 45.18N 96.28W
Orūmīyeh Iran **43** 37.32N 45.02E
Oruro Bolivia **92** 17.59S 67.09W
Oruro *d.* Bolivia **92** 18.00S 72.30W
Orūzgān Afghan. **40** 32.56N 66.38E
Orūzgān *d.* Afghan. **40** 33.40N 66.00E
Oryakhovo Bulgaria **19** 43.42N 23.58E
Orzinuovi Italy **15** 45.24N 9.55E
Os Norway **22** 62.31N 11.11E
Osa, Península de *pen.* Costa Rica **87** 8.20N 83.30W
Osage *r.* U.S.A. **79** 38.35N 91.57W
Osage Iowa U.S.A. **82** 43.17N 92.49W
Osage Wyo. U.S.A. **80** 43.59N104.25W
Osaka Japan **35** 34.40N135.30E
Osaka *d.* Japan **35** 34.24N135.25E
Osaka-wan *b.* Japan **35** 34.30N135.18E
Osborne U.S.A. **82** 39.26N 98.42W
Osby Sweden **23** 56.22N 13.59E
Osceola Iowa U.S.A. **82** 41.02N 93.46W
Osceola Mo. U.S.A. **83** 38.03N 93.42W
Osen Norway **22** 64.18N 10.32E
Osh U.S.S.R. **28** 40.37N 72.49E
Oshawa Canada **76** 43.53N 78.51W
O shima *i.* Tosan Japan **35** 34.43N139.24E
Oshkosh Nebr. U.S.A. **82** 41.24N102.21W
Oshmyany U.S.S.R. **21** 54.22N 25.52E
Oshnovīyeh Iran **43** 37.03N 45.05E
Oshogbo Nigeria **53** 7.50N 4.35E
Oshtorān, Kūh *mtn.* Iran **43** 33.18N 49.15E
Oshvor U.S.S.R. **24** 66.59N 62.59E
Oshwe Zaïre **54** 3.27S 19.32E
Osiān India **40** 26.43N 72.55E
Osijek Yugo. **19** 45.35N 18.43E
Osipovichi U.S.S.R. **21** 53.19N 28.36E
Oskaloosa U.S.A. **82** 41.18N 92.39W
Oskarshamn Sweden **23** 57.16N 16.26E
Oskol *r.* U.S.S.R. **25** 49.08N 37.10E
Oslo Norway **23** 59.56N 10.45E
Oslofjorden *est.* Norway **23** 59.20N 10.35E
Osmancik Turkey **42** 40.58N 34.50E
Osmaniye Turkey **42** 37.04N 36.15E
Osnabrück Germany **14** 52.17N 8.03E
Osorno Chile **93** 40.35S 73.14W
Osorno Spain **16** 42.24N 4.22W
Osöyra Norway **23** 60.11N 5.30E
Osprey Reef Australia **64** 13.55S146.38E
Oss Neth. **14** 51.46N 5.31E
Ossa *mtn.* Greece **19** 39.47N 22.41E
Ossa, Mt. Australia **65** 41.52S146.04E
Ossabaw I. U.S.A. **85** 31.47N 81.06W
Osse *r.* Nigeria **53** 5.55N 5.15E
Ossining U.S.A. **85** 41.10N 73.52W
Ossokmanuan L. Canada **77** 53.25N 65.00W
Ostashkov U.S.S.R. **24** 57.09N 33.10E
Ostend *see* Oostende Belgium **14**
Oster U.S.S.R. **21** 50.55N 30.53E
Oster *r.* U.S.S.R. **21** 53.47N 31.46E
Osterdal *r.* Sweden **23** 61.03N 14.30E
Österdalen *f.* Norway **23** 61.15N 11.10E
Östergötland *d.* Sweden **23** 58.25N 15.35E
Österö *i.* Faroe Is. **8** 62.16N 6.54W
Osteröy *i.* Norway **23** 60.33N 5.35E
Östersund Sweden **22** 63.10N 14.40E
Östfold *d.* Norway **23** 59.20N 11.10E
Ostfriesische Inseln *is.* Germany **14** 53.45N 7.00E
Östhammar Sweden **23** 60.16N 18.22E
Ostrava Czech. **21** 49.50N 18.15E
Ostróda Poland **21** 53.43N 19.59E
Ostrog U.S.S.R. **21** 50.20N 26.29E
Ostrołeka Poland **21** 53.06N 21.34E
Ostrov U.S.S.R. **24** 57.22N 28.22E
Ostrowiec-Świetokrzyski Poland **21** 50.57N 21.23E
Ostrów Mazowiecka Poland **21** 52.50N 21.51E
Ostrów Wielkopolski Poland **21** 51.39N 17.49E
Ostuni Italy **19** 40.44N 17.35E
Osŭm *r.* Bulgaria **19** 43.41N 24.51E
Ōsumi shotō *is.* Japan **31** 30.30N131.00E
Osuna Spain **16** 37.14N 5.06W
Oswego U.S.A. **84** 43.27N 76.31W
Oswestry U.K. **10** 52.52N 3.03W
Otago *d.* New Zealand **60** 45.10S169.20E
Otago Pen. New Zealand **60** 45.48S170.45E
Otaki New Zealand **60** 40.45S175.08E
Otaru Japan **31** 43.14N140.59E
Otavalo Ecuador **90** 0.14N 78.16W
Otavi Namibia **56** 19.37S 17.21E
Otelec Romania **21** 45.36N 20.50E
Otematata New Zealand **60** 44.37S170.11E
Oti *r.* Ghana **52** 8.43N 0.10E
Otira New Zealand **60** 42.51S171.33E
Otish, Monts *mts.* Canada **77** 52.22N 70.30W
Otisville U.S.A. **85** 41.28N 74.32W
Otiwarongo Namibia **56** 20.30S 16.39E
Otjiwero Namibia **56** 17.59S 13.22E
Otju Namibia **56** 18.15S 13.18E
Otočac Yugo. **20** 44.52N 15.14E
Otog Qi China **32** 39.05N107.59E
Otosquen Canada **75** 53.17N102.01W
Otra *r.* Norway **23** 58.09N 8.00E
Otradnyy U.S.S.R. **24** 53.26N 51.30E
Otranto Italy **19** 40.09N 18.30E
Otranto, Str. of Med. Sea **19** 40.10N 19.00E
Otrokovice Czech. **21** 49.13N 17.31E
Otsego U.S.A. **84** 42.26N 85.42W
Otsego Lake *town* U.S.A. **84** 44.55N 84.41W
Ōtsu Japan **35** 35.02N135.52E
Ōtsuki Japan **35** 35.36N138.57E
Otta Norway **23** 61.46N 9.32E
Ottawa Canada **77** 45.25N 75.43W
Ottawa *r.* Canada **76** 45.23N 73.55W
Ottawa Ill. U.S.A. **82** 41.21N 88.51W
Ottawa Kans. U.S.A. **82** 38.37N 95.16W
Ottawa Is. Canada **73** 59.50N 80.00W
Otter *r.* U.K. **11** 50.38N 3.19W
Otterbäcken Sweden **23** 58.57N 14.02E
Otterburn U.K. **10** 55.14N 2.10W
Otter L. Canada **75** 55.35N104.39W
Otterndorf Germany **20** 53.48N 8.53E
Otteröy *i.* Norway **22** 62.45N 6.50E
Ottosdal R.S.A. **56** 26.48S 26.00E
Ottumwa U.S.A. **82** 41.01N 92.25W
Oturkpo Nigeria **53** 7.13N 8.10E
Otway, C. Australia **66** 38.51S143.34E
Ou *r.* Laos **34** 20.03N102.19E
Ouachita *r.* U.S.A. **83** 31.38N 91.49W
Ouachita, L. U.S.A. **83** 34.40N 93.25W
Ouachita Mts. U.S.A. **83** 34.40N 94.25W
Ouada, Djebel *mtn.* C.A.R. **49** 8.56N 23.26E
Ouadane Mauritania **50** 20.56N 11.37W
Ouadda C.A.R. **49** 8.04N 22.24E
Ouaddaï *d.* Chad **49** 13.00N 21.00E
Ouagadougou Burkina **52** 12.20N 1.40W
Ouahigouya Burkina **52** 13.31N 2.21W
Ouaka *d.* C.A.R. **49** 6.00N 21.00E
Oualâta Mauritania **50** 17.18N 7.02W
Ouallam Niger **53** 14.23N 2.09E
Ouallene Algeria **50** 24.35N 1.17E
Ouanda Djallé C.A.R. **49** 8.54N 22.48E
Ouarane *f.* Mauritania **50** 21.00N 9.30W
Ouararda, Passe de *pass* Mauritania **50** 21.01N 13.03W
Ouareau *r.* Canada **77** 45.56N 73.25W
Ouargla Algeria **51** 31.57N 5.20E
Ouarra *r.* C.A.R. **49** 5.05N 24.26E
Ouarzazate Morocco **50** 30.57N 6.50W
Ouassouas *well* Mali **50** 16.01N 1.26E
Ouddorp Neth. **14** 51.49N 3.57E
Oudenaarde Belgium **14** 50.50N 3.37E
Oudenbosch Neth. **14** 51.35N 4.30E
Oude Rijn *r.* Neth. **14** 52.14N 4.26E
Oudon *r.* France **15** 47.47N 1.02W
Oudtshoorn R.S.A. **56** 33.35S 22.11E
Oued-Zem Morocco **50** 32.55N 6.30W
Ouellé Ivory Coast **52** 7.26N 4.01W
Ouenza Algeria **51** 35.57N 8.07E
Ouessant, Île d' *i.* France **17** 48.28N 5.05W
Ouesso Congo **54** 1.38N 16.03E
Ouezzane Morocco **50** 34.52N 5.35W
Oughter, Lough Rep. of Ire. **13** 54.01N 7.28W
Ouham *r.* Chad **53** 9.15N 18.13E
Ouimet Canada **76** 48.43N 88.35W
Ouistreham France **15** 49.17N 0.15W
Oujda Morocco **50** 34.41N 1.45W
Oulu Finland **22** 65.01N 25.28E
Oulu *d.* Finland **22** 65.00N 27.00E
Oulu *r.* Finland **22** 65.01N 25.25E
Oulujärvi *l.* Finland **22** 64.20N 27.15E
Oum Chalouba Chad **51** 15.48N 20.46E
Oumé Ivory Coast **52** 6.25N 5.23W
Oum er Rbia, Oued *r.* Morocco **50** 33.19N 8.21W
Oumm ed Droûs Guebli, Sebkhet *f.* Mauritania **50** 24.03N 11.45W
Oumm ed Droûs Telli, Sebkhet *f.* Mauritania **50** 24.20N 11.30W
Ounas *r.* Finland **22** 66.30N 25.45E
Oundle U.K. **11** 52.28N 0.28W
Ounianga Kébir Chad **51** 19.04N 20.29E
Our *r.* Lux. **14** 49.53N 6.16E
Ouray U.S.A. **80** 40.06N109.40W
Ourcq *r.* France **15** 49.01N 3.01E
Ouri Chad **51** 21.34N 19.13E
Ourinhos Brazil **94** 23.00S 49.54W
Ouro Fino Brazil **94** 22.16S 46.25W
Ouro Prêto Brazil **94** 20.54S 43.30W
Ourthe *r.* Belgium **14** 50.38N 5.36E
Ouse *r.* Humber. U.K. **10** 53.41N 0.42W
Outardes, Rivière aux *r.* Canada **77** 49.04N 68.25W
Outer Hebrides *is.* U.K. **12** 57.40N 7.35W
Outjo Namibia **56** 20.07S 16.10E
Outlook U.S.A. **80** 48.53N104.47W
Ouyen Australia **66** 35.06S142.22E
Ouzouer-le-Marché France **15** 47.55N 1.32E
Ouzzal, Oued I-n- *wadi* Algeria **51** 20.54N 2.28E
Ovalle Chile **92** 30.36S 71.12W
Ovamboland *f.* Namibia **56** 17.45S 16.00E
Ovar Portugal **16** 40.52N 8.38W
Ovens *r.* Australia **67** 36.20S146.18E
Overath Germany **14** 50.56N 7.18E
Overflakkee *i.* Neth. **14** 51.45N 4.08E
Overijssel *d.* Neth. **14** 52.25N 6.30E
Överkalix Sweden **22** 66.21N 22.56E
Overland Park *town* U.S.A. **82** 38.59N 94.40W
Overton U.S.A. **81** 36.33N114.27W
Övertorneå Sweden **22** 66.23N 23.40E
Ovidiopol U.S.S.R. **21** 46.18N 30.28E
Oviedo Spain **16** 43.21N 5.50W
Ovinishche U.S.S.R. **24** 58.20N 37.00E
Övörhangay *d.* Mongolia **32** 45.00N103.00E
Ovruch U.S.S.R. **21** 51.20N 28.50E
Owaka New Zealand **60** 46.27S169.40E
Owando Congo **54** 0.30S 15.48E
Owatonna U.S.A. **82** 44.06N 93.10W
Owbeh Afghan. **40** 34.22N 63.10E
Owel, Lough Rep. of Ire. **13** 53.34N 7.24W
Owen Falls Dam Uganda **55** 0.30N 33.07E
Owensboro U.S.A. **85** 37.46N 87.07W
Owens L. U.S.A. **81** 36.25N117.56W
Owen Sound *town* Canada **76** 44.34N 80.56W
Owen Stanley Range *mts.* P.N.G. **64** 9.30S148.00E
Owerri Nigeria **53** 5.29N 7.02E
Owl *r.* Canada **75** 57.51N 92.44W
Owo Nigeria **53** 7.10N 5.39E
Owosso U.S.A. **84** 43.00N 84.11W
Owyhee *r.* U.S.A. **80** 43.46N117.02W
Oxelösund Sweden **23** 58.40N 17.06E
Oxford U.K. **11** 51.45N 1.15W
Oxford Md. U.S.A. **85** 38.42N 76.10W
Oxford Penn. U.S.A. **85** 39.47N 75.59W
Oxfordshire *d.* U.K. **11** 51.46N 1.10W
Oxley Australia **66** 34.11S144.10E
Oxnard U.S.A. **81** 34.12N119.11W
Oyapock *r.* Guiana **91** 4.10N 51.40W
Oyem Gabon **54** 1.34N 11.31E
Oyen Canada **75** 51.22N110.28W
Öyer Norway **23** 61.12N 10.22E
Öyeren *l.* Norway **23** 59.48N 11.14E
Oykel *r.* U.K. **12** 57.53N 4.21W
Oymyakon U.S.S.R. **29** 63.30N142.44E
Oyo Nigeria **53** 7.50N 3.55E
Oyo *d.* Nigeria **53** 8.10N 3.40E
Oyonnax France **17** 46.15N 5.40E
Ozamiz Phil. **37** 8.09N123.59E
Ozarichi U.S.S.R. **21** 52.28N 29.12E
Ozark Ala. U.S.A. **85** 31.27N 85.40W
Ozark Ark. U.S.A. **83** 35.29N 93.50W
Ozark Mo. U.S.A. **83** 37.01N 93.12W
Ozark Plateau U.S.A. **83** 37.00N 93.00W
Ózd Hungary **21** 48.14N 20.18E
Ozernoye U.S.S.R. **24** 51.45N 51.29E
Ozersk U.S.S.R. **21** 54.26N 22.00E
Ozinki U.S.S.R. **25** 51.11N 49.43E
Ozona U.S.A. **83** 30.43N101.12W

P

Paamiut *see* Frederikshåb Greenland **73**
Pa-an Burma **34** 16.51N 97.37E
Paarl R.S.A. **56** 33.44S 18.58E
Pabianice Poland **21** 51.40N 19.22E
Pābna Bangla. **41** 24.00N 89.15E
Pacaraima, Sierra *mts.* Venezuela **90** 4.00N 62.30W
Pacasmayo Peru **90** 7.27S 79.33W
Pachmarhi India **41** 22.28N 78.26E
Pāchora India **40** 20.40N 75.21E
Pachuca Mexico **86** 20.10N 98.44W
Pacific-Antarctic Basin Pacific Oc. **69** 58.00S 98.00W
Pacific-Antarctic Ridge Pacific Oc. **69** 57.00S145.00W
Pacific Ocean 69
Pacitan Indonesia **37** 8.12S111.05E
Packsaddle Australia **66** 30.28S141.28E
Packwood U.S.A. **80** 46.36N121.40W
Pacy-sur-Eure France **15** 49.01N 1.23E
Padam Jammu & Kashmir **40** 33.28N 76.53E
Padampur India **41** 20.59N 83.04E
Padang Indonesia **36** 0.55S100.21E
Padangpanjang Indonesia **36** 0.30S100.26E
Padangsidempuan Indonesia **36** 1.20N 99.11E
Padany U.S.S.R. **24** 63.12N 33.20E
Padauari *r.* Brazil **90** 0.15S 64.05W
Paderborn Germany **20** 51.43N 8.44E
Padilla Bolivia **92** 19.19S 64.20W
Padlei Canada **75** 62.10N 97.05W
Padloping Island *town* Canada **73** 67.00N 62.50W
Padova Italy **15** 45.27N 11.52E
Pādra India **40** 22.14N 73.05E
Padrauna India **41** 26.55N 83.59E
Padre I. U.S.A. **83** 27.00N 97.15W
Padstow U.K. **11** 50.33N 4.57W
Padthaway Australia **66** 36.37S140.28E
Padua *see* Padova Italy **15**
Paducah U.S.A. **83** 37.05N 88.36W
Paeroa New Zealand **60** 37.23S175.41E
Pafúri Mozambique **57** 22.27S 31.21E
Pag *i.* Yugo. **20** 44.28N 15.00E
Pagadian Phil. **37** 7.50N123.30E
Pagai Selatan *i.* Indonesia **36** 3.00S100.18E
Pagai Utara *i.* Indonesia **36** 2.42S100.05E
Pagan Burma **34** 21.07N 94.53E
Page U.S.A. **80** 36.57N111.27W
Pager *r.* Uganda **55** 3.05N 32.28E
Paghmān Afghan. **40** 34.36N 68.57E
Pago Pago Samoa **68** 14.16S170.42W
Pagosa Springs *town* U.S.A. **80** 37.16N107.01W
Pagri China **41** 27.45N 89.10E
Paguchi L. Canada **76** 49.38N 91.40W
Pagwa River *town* Canada **76** 50.02N 85.14W
Pahala Hawaii U.S.A. **78** 19.12N155.28W
Pahiatua New Zealand **60** 40.26S175.49E
Paible U.K. **12** 57.35N 7.27W
Paide U.S.S.R. **23** 58.54N 25.33E
Paihia New Zealand **60** 35.16S174.05E
Päijänne *l.* Finland **23** 61.35N 25.30E
Paikü Co *l.* China **41** 28.48N 85.36E
Paimboeuf France **17** 47.14N 2.01W
Painan Indonesia **36** 1.21S100.34E
Painesville U.S.A. **84** 41.43N 81.15W
Pains Brazil **94** 20.23S 45.38W
Paintsville U.S.A. **85** 37.49N 82.48W
Paisley U.K. **12** 55.50N 4.26W
País Vasco *d.* Spain **16** 43.00N 2.30W
Paiton Indonesia **37** 7.42S113.30E
Pajala Sweden **22** 67.11N 23.22E
Pajule Uganda **55** 2.58N 32.53E
Pakaraima Mts. Guyana **90** 5.00N 60.00W
Pakaur India **41** 24.38N 87.51E
Paki Nigeria **53** 11.33N 8.08E
Pakistan Asia **40** 29.00N 67.00E
Pakokku Burma **34** 21.20N 95.10E
Pākpattan Pakistan **40** 30.21N 73.24E
Paks Hungary **21** 46.39N 18.53E
Paktīā *d.* Afghan. **40** 33.25N 69.30E
Pakwach Uganda **55** 2.27N 31.18E
Pakxé Laos **34** 15.07N105.47E
Pala Chad **53** 9.25N 15.05E
Palaiokhóra Greece **19** 35.14N 23.41E
Palaiseau France **15** 48.43N 2.15E
Palamós Spain **16** 41.51N 3.08E
Palana U.S.S.R. **29** 59.05N159.59E
Palangkaraya Indonesia **36** 2.16S113.56E
Palanguinos Spain **16** 42.27N 5.31W
Pālanpur India **40** 24.10N 72.26E
Palapye Botswana **56** 22.33S 27.07E
Palatka U.S.A. **85** 29.38N 81.40W
Palaw Burma **34** 12.58N 98.39E
Palawan *i.* Phil. **36** 9.30N118.30E
Paldiski U.S.S.R. **23** 59.20N 24.06E
Paleleh Indonesia **37** 1.04N121.57E
Palembang Indonesia **36** 2.59S104.50E
Palencia Spain **16** 42.01N 4.34W
Palenque Mexico **86** 17.32N 91.59W
Palermo Italy **18** 38.09N 13.22E
Palestine U.S.A. **83** 31.46N 95.38W
Paletwa Burma **34** 21.25N 92.49E
Pāli India **40** 25.46N 73.20E
Palimé Togo **52** 6.55N 0.38E
Palisades Resr. U.S.A. **80** 43.15N111.05W
Pālitāna India **40** 21.31N 71.50E
Palizada Mexico **86** 18.15N 92.05W
Palk Str. India / Sri Lanka **39** 10.00N 79.40E
Pallës, Bishti i *c.* Albania **19** 41.24N 19.23E
Pallinup *r.* Australia **63** 34.29S118.54E
Palliser, C. New Zealand **60** 41.35S175.15E
Pallu India **40** 28.56N 74.13E
Palma Mozambique **55** 10.48S 40.25E
Palma Spain **16** 39.36N 2.39E
Palma, Bahía de *b.* Spain **16** 39.30N 2.40E
Palma del Río Spain **16** 37.43N 5.17W
Palmanova Italy **15** 45.54N 13.19E
Palmares Brazil **91** 8.41S 35.36W
Palmas, C. Liberia **52** 4.30N 7.55W
Palmas, Golfo di *g.* Italy **18** 39.00N 8.30E
Palm Beach *town* U.S.A. **85** 26.41N 80.02W
Palmeira dos Indios Brazil **91** 9.25S 36.38W
Palmeirinhas, Punta das Angola **54** 9.09S 12.58E
Palmer *r.* Australia **62** 24.46S133.25E
Palmer U.S.A. **72** 61.36N149.07W
Palmer Land Antarctica **96** 74.00S 61.00W
Palmerston New Zealand **60** 45.29S170.43E
Palmerston, C. Australia **64** 21.32S149.29E
Palmerston Atoll Cook Is. **68** 18.04S163.10W
Palmerston North New Zealand **60** 40.20S175.39E
Palmerton U.S.A. **85** 40.48N 75.37W
Palmetto U.S.A. **85** 27.31N 82.32W
Palmi Italy **18** 38.22N 15.50E
Palmira Colombia **90** 3.33N 76.17W
Palm Is. Australia **64** 18.48S146.37E
Palms U.S.A. **84** 43.37N 82.46W
Palm Springs *town* U.S.A. **81** 33.50N116.33W
Palmyra I. Pacific Oc. **68** 5.52N162.05W
Palmyras Pt. India **41** 20.46N 87.02E
Paloh Indonesia **36** 1.46N109.17E
Paloich Sudan **49** 10.28N 32.32E
Palojoensuu Finland **22** 68.17N 23.05E
Palomani *mtn.* Bolivia **92** 14.38S 69.14W
Palopo Indonesia **37** 3.01S120.12E
Palu Turkey **42** 38.43N 39.56E
Palwal India **40** 28.09N 77.20E
Pama Burkina **52** 11.15N 0.44E
Pamanukan Indonesia **37** 6.16S107.46E
Pamekasan Indonesia **37** 7.11S113.30E
Pameungpeuk Indonesia **37** 7.39S107.40E
Pamiers France **17** 43.07N 1.36E
Pamir *mts.* U.S.S.R. **30** 37.50N 73.30E
Pamlico Sd. U.S.A. **85** 35.20N 75.55W
Pampa U.S.A. **83** 35.32N100.58W
Pampas *f.* Argentina **93** 34.00S 64.00W
Pamplona Colombia **90** 7.24N 72.38W
Pamplona Spain **16** 42.49N 1.39W
Pana U.S.A. **82** 39.23N 89.05W
Panaca U.S.A. **80** 37.47N114.23W
Panaji India **38** 15.29N 73.50E
Panama C. America **87** 9.00N 80.00W
Panamá *town* Panama **87** 8.57N 79.30W
Panama Sri Lanka **39** 6.46N 81.47E
Panamá, Golfo de *g.* Panama **87** 8.30N 79.00W
Panama City U.S.A. **85** 30.10N 85.41W
Panamint Range *mts.* U.S.A. **81** 36.30N117.20W
Panaro *r.* Italy **15** 44.55N 11.25E
Panay *i.* Phil. **37** 11.10N122.30E
Pandan Phil. **37** 11.45N122.10E
Pandaria India **41** 22.14N 81.25E
Pandeglang Indonesia **37** 6.19S106.05E
Pāndharkawada India **41** 20.01N 78.32E
Pāndhurna India **41** 21.36N 78.31E
Pando *d.* Bolivia **92** 11.20S 67.40W
Pando Uruguay **93** 34.43S 55.57W
Panevežys U.S.S.R. **23** 55.44N 24.21E
Panfilov U.S.S.R. **30** 44.10N 80.01E
Panga Zaïre **54** 1.51N 26.25E
Pangandaran Indonesia **37** 7.41S108.40E
Pangani Tanga Tanzania **55** 5.21S 39.00E
Pangi Zaïre **54** 3.10S 26.38E
Pangkalpinang Indonesia **36** 2.05S106.09E
Pang Long Burma **39** 23.11N 98.45E
Pangnirtung Canada **73** 66.05N 65.45W
Panīpat India **40** 29.23N 76.58E
Panjāb Afghan. **40** 34.22N 67.01E
Panjgūr Pakistan **40** 26.58N 64.06E
Panjpāi Pakistan **40** 29.55N 66.30E
Pankshin Nigeria **53** 9.22N 9.25E
Panna India **41** 24.43N 80.12E
Pannawonica Australia **62** 21.42S116.22E
Páno Lévkara Cyprus **44** 34.55N 33.10E
Páno Plátres Cyprus **44** 34.53N 32.52E
Panshan China **32** 41.10N122.01E
Pantano del Esla *l.* Spain **16** 41.40N 5.50W
Pantelleria *i.* Italy **18** 36.48N 12.00E
Panton *r.* Australia **62** 17.05S128.46E
Pánuco Mexico **86** 22.03N 98.10W
Panvel India **40** 18.59N 73.06E
Pan Xian China **33** 25.46N104.39E
Panyu China **33** 23.00N113.30E
Paola Italy **18** 39.21N 16.03E
Paola U.S.A. **82** 38.35N 94.53W
Paoua C.A.R. **53** 7.09N 16.20E
Paôy Pêt Thailand **34** 13.41N102.34E
Papa Hawaiian Is. **69** 19.12N155.53W
Pápa Hungary **21** 47.19N 17.28E
Papa Stour *i.* U.K. **8** 60.20N 1.42W
Papa Westray *i.* U.K. **8** 59.22N 2.54W
Papeete Tahiti **69** 17.32S149.34W
Papenburg Germany **14** 53.05N 7.25E
Papenoo Tahiti **69** 17.30S149.25W
Papetoai Îs. de la Société **69** 17.29S149.52W
Paphos *see* Néa Páfos Cyprus **44**
Papigochic *r.* Mexico **81** 29.09N109.40W
Papillion U.S.A. **82** 41.09N 96.04W
Papineau, Lac *l.* Canada **77** 45.48N 74.46W
Papineauville Canada **77** 45.37N 75.01W
Papua, G. of P.N.G. **64** 8.30S145.00E
Papua New Guinea Austa. **61** 6.00S144.00E
Papun Burma **34** 18.05N 97.26E
Papunya Australia **64** 23.15S131.53E
Para *d.* Brazil **91** 4.00S 53.00W
Paraburdoo Australia **62** 23.12S117.40E
Paracatu Brazil **94** 17.14S 46.52W
Paracatu *r.* Brazil **94** 16.30S 45.10W
Paracel Is. S. China Sea **36** 16.20N112.00E
Parachilna Australia **66** 31.09S138.24E
Pārachinār Pakistan **40** 33.54N 70.06E
Paraćin Yugo. **21** 43.52N 21.24E
Pará de Minas Brazil **94** 19.53S 44.35W
Paradip India **41** 20.15N 86.35E
Paradise *r.* Canada **77** 53.23N 57.18W
Paradise Calif. U.S.A. **80** 39.46N121.37W
Paradise Nev. U.S.A. **81** 36.09N115.10W
Paragonah U.S.A. **80** 37.53N112.46W
Paragould U.S.A. **83** 36.03N 90.29W
Paragua *r.* Venezuela **90** 6.55N 62.55W
Paraguaçu *r.* Brazil **91** 12.35S 38.59W
Paraguaná, Península de *pen.* Venezuela **90** 11.50N 69.59W
Paraguarí Paraguay **94** 25.36S 57.06W
Paraguay *r.* Argentina **94** 27.30S 58.50W
Paraguay S. America **94** 23.00S 57.00W
Paraiba *d.* Brazil **91** 7.30S 36.30W
Paraíba *r.* Brazil **94** 21.45S 41.10W
Paraibuna Brazil **94** 23.29S 45.32W
Paraisópolis Brazil **94** 22.33S 45.48W
Parakou Benin **53** 9.23N 2.40E
Paramagudi India **39** 9.33N 78.36E
Paramaribo Surinam **91** 5.52N 55.14W
Paramonga Peru **90** 10.42S 77.50W
Paraná Argentina **93** 31.45S 60.30W
Paraná *r.* Argentina **93** 34.00S 58.30W
Paranã Brazil **91** 12.33S 47.48W
Paraná *d.* Brazil **94** 24.30S 52.00W

Paranã *r.* Brazil **91** 12.30S 48.10W
Paranaguá Brazil **94** 25.32S 48.36W
Paranaíba Brazil **94** 19.44S 51.12W
Paranaíba *r.* Brazil **94** 20.00S 51.00W
Paranapanema *r.* Brazil **94** 22.30S 53.03W
Paranapiacaba, Serra *mts.* Brazil **94** 24.30S 49.15W
Paranavaí Brazil **94** 23.02S 52.36W
Parangaba Brazil **91** 3.45S 38.33W
Paraparaumu New Zealand **60** 40.55S175.00E
Paratoo Australia **66** 32.46S139.40E
Paray-le-Monial France **17** 46.27N 4.07E
Pārbati *r.* India **40** 25.51N 76.36E
Pārbatipur Bangla. **41** 25.39N 88.55E
Parbhani India **40** 19.16N 76.47E
Parchim Germany **20** 53.25N 11.51E
Parczew Poland **21** 51.39N 22.54E
Pārdi India **40** 20.31N 72.57E
Pardo *r.* Bahia Brazil **94** 15.40S 39.38W
Pardo *r.* Mato Grosso Brazil **94** 21.56S 52.07W
Pardo *r.* São Paulo Brazil **94** 20.10S 48.36W
Pardubice Czech. **20** 50.03N 15.45E
Parecis, Serra dos *mts.* Brazil **90** 13.30S 58.30W
Parent Canada **76** 47.55N 74.35W
Parent, Lac *l.* Canada **76** 48.40N 77.03W
Parepare Indonesia **36** 4.03S119.40E
Párga Greece **19** 39.17N 20.23E
Pargas Finland **23** 60.18N 22.18E
Paria, Golfo de *g.* Venezuela **90** 10.30S 62.00W
Paria, Península de *pen.* Venezuela **90** 10.45N 62.30W
Pariaguán Venezuela **90** 8.51N 64.43W
Pariaman Indonesia **36** 0.36S100.09E
Parichi U.S.S.R. **21** 52.48N 29.25E
Parigi Indonesia **37** 0.49S120.10E
Parika Guyana **90** 6.51N 58.25W
Parima, Sierra *mts.* Venezuela **90** 2.30N 64.00W
Parinari Peru **90** 4.35S 74.25W
Paringa Australia **66** 34.10S140.49E
Parintins Brazil **91** 2.36S 56.44W
Paris France **15** 48.52N 2.20E
Paris Kiribati **69** 1.56N157.29W
Paris Ill. U.S.A. **82** 39.35N 87.41W
Paris Ky. U.S.A. **84** 38.13N 84.15W
Paris Tenn. U.S.A. **83** 36.19N 88.20W
Paris Tex. U.S.A. **83** 33.40N 95.33W
Parisienne *d.* France **15** 48.50N 2.20E
Parkano Finland **23** 62.01N 23.01E
Parkbeg Canada **75** 50.28N106.18W
Parker Ariz. U.S.A. **81** 34.09N114.17W
Parker, C. Canada **73** 75.04N 79.40W
Parker Dam U.S.A. **81** 34.18N114.10W
Parkersburg U.S.A. **84** 39.17N 81.33W
Parkes Australia **67** 33.10S148.13E
Park Falls *town* U.S.A. **82** 45.56N 90.32W
Park Forest *town* U.S.A. **82** 41.35N 87.41W
Parkland U.S.A. **80** 47.09N122.26W
Park Range *mts.* U.S.A. **80** 40.00N106.30W
Parkton U.S.A. **85** 39.38N 76.40W
Parlākimidi India **41** 18.46N 84.05E
Parma Italy **15** 44.48N 10.18E
Parma *r.* Italy **15** 44.56N 10.26E
Parma U.S.A. **84** 41.24N 81.44W
Parnaguá Brazil **91** 10.17S 44.39W
Parnaíba Brazil **91** 2.58S 41.46W
Parnaíba *r.* Brazil **91** 2.58S 41.47W
Parnassós *mtn.* Greece **19** 38.33N 22.35E
Parndana Australia **66** 35.44S137.14E
Pärnu U.S.S.R. **23** 58.24N 24.32E
Pärnu *r.* U.S.S.R. **23** 58.23N 24.29E
Pārola India **40** 20.53N 75.07E
Paroo *r.* Australia **66** 31.30S143.34E
Páros *i.* Greece **19** 37.04N 25.11E
Parrakie Australia **66** 35.18S140.12E
Parral Chile **93** 36.09S 71.50W
Parramatta Australia **67** 33.50S150.57E
Parras Mexico **83** 25.30N102.11W
Parras, Sierra de *mts.* Mexico **83** 25.20N102.10W
Parrett *r.* U.K. **11** 51.10N 3.00W
Parry Canada **75** 49.47N104.41W
Parry, C. Greenland **73** 76.50N 71.00W
Parry Is. Canada **73** 76.00N102.00W
Parry Sound *town* Canada **84** 45.21N 80.02W
Parsad India **40** 24.11N 73.42E
Parsęta *r.* Poland **20** 54.12N 15.33E
Parsnip *r.* Canada **74** 55.10N123.02W
Parsons Kans. U.S.A. **83** 37.20N 95.16W
Parthenay France **17** 46.39N 0.14W
Partille Sweden **23** 57.44N 12.07E
Partinico Italy **18** 38.03N 13.07E
Partry Mts. Rep. of Ire. **13** 53.40N 9.30W
Paru *r.* Brazil **91** 1.33S 52.38W
Pārvatīpuram India **41** 18.47N 83.26E
Paryang China **41** 30.04N 83.28E
Parys R.S.A. **56** 26.54S 27.26E
Pasadena Calif. U.S.A. **81** 34.09N118.09W
Pasadena Tex. U.S.A. **83** 29.42N 95.13W
Pasaje Ecuador **90** 3.23S 79.50W
Pasawng Burma **34** 18.52N 97.18E
Pasay Phil. **37** 14.33N121.00E
Pascagoula U.S.A. **83** 30.23N 88.31W
Paşcani Romania **21** 47.15N 26.44E
Pasco U.S.A. **80** 46.14N119.06W
Pascua, Isla de *i.* Pacific Oc. **69** 27.08S109.23W
Pasewalk Germany **20** 53.30N 14.00E
Pasfield L. Canada **75** 58.25N105.20W
Pasinler Turkey **42** 39.59N 41.41E
Pasir Puteh Malaysia **36** 5.50N102.24E
Påskallavik Sweden **23** 57.10N 16.27E
Pasley, C. Australia **63** 33.55S123.30E
Pasmore *r.* Australia **66** 31.07S139.48E
Pasni Pakistan **40** 25.16N 63.28E
Paso de los Libres *town* Argentina **93** 29.45S 57.05W
Paso de los Toros *town* Uruguay **93** 32.49S 56.31W
Paso Robles U.S.A. **81** 35.38N120.41W
Paspébiac Canada **77** 48.01N 65.20W
Pasquia Hills Canada **75** 53.13N102.37W
Pasrūr Pakistan **40** 32.16N 74.40E
Passaic U.S.A. **85** 40.51N 74.08W
Passau Germany **20** 48.35N 13.28E
Passero, C. Italy **18** 36.40N 15.08E
Passo Fundo Brazil **94** 28.16S 52.20W
Passos Brazil **94** 20.45S 46.38W
Pastaza *r.* Peru **90** 4.50S 76.25W
Pasto Colombia **90** 1.12N 77.17W
Pasuquin Phil. **33** 18.25N120.37E
Pasuruan Indonesia **37** 7.38S112.54E
Patagonia *f.* Argentina **93** 42.20S 67.00W
Pātan India **40** 23.50N 72.07E
Patchewollock Australia **66** 35.25S142.14E
Patea New Zealand **60** 39.46S174.29E
Pategi Nigeria **53** 8.44N 5.47E
Pate I. Kenya **55** 2.08S 41.02E
Paternò Italy **18** 37.34N 14.54E
Paterson U.S.A. **85** 40.55N 74.10W
Pathānkot India **40** 32.17N 75.39E
Pathfinder Resr. U.S.A. **80** 42.30N106.50W
Pathiong Sudan **49** 6.46N 30.54E
Pati Indonesia **37** 6.45S111.00E
Patía *r.* Colombia **90** 1.54N 78.30W
Patiāla India **40** 30.19N 76.23E
Pati Pt. Guam **68** 13.36N144.57E
Patkai Hills Burma **34** 26.30N 95.30E
Pátmos *i.* Greece **19** 37.20N 26.33E
Patna India **41** 25.36N 85.07E
Patnāgarh India **41** 20.43N 83.09E
Patos Brazil **91** 6.55S 37.15W
Patos, Lagoa dos *l.* Brazil **94** 31.00S 51.10W
Patos de Minas Brazil **94** 18.35S 46.32W
Patquía Argentina **92** 30.02S 66.55W
Pátrai Greece **19** 38.15N 21.45E
Patraïkós Kólpos *g.* Greece **19** 38.15N 21.35E
Patrasuy U.S.S.R. **24** 63.35N 61.50E
Patrickswell Rep. of Ire. **13** 52.36N 8.43W
Pattani Thailand **34** 6.51N101.16E
Pattaya Thailand **34** 12.57N100.53E
Pattoki Pakistan **40** 31.01N 73.51E
Patuākhāli Bangla. **41** 22.21N 90.21E
Patuca *r.* Honduras **87** 15.50N 84.18W
Pātūr India **40** 20.27N 76.56E
Patuxent *r.* U.S.A. **85** 38.18N 76.25W
Pau France **17** 43.18N 0.22W
Pauillac France **17** 45.12N 0.44W
Paúl do Mar Madeira Is. **95** 32.45N 17.14W
Paulina U.S.A. **80** 44.09N119.58W
Paulistana Brazil **91** 8.09S 41.09W
Paulo Afonso Brazil **91** 9.25S 38.15W
Paulsboro U.S.A. **85** 39.50N 75.15W
Pauls Valley *town* U.S.A. **83** 34.44N 97.13W
Paungde Burma **34** 18.30N 95.30E
Pauni India **41** 20.47N 79.38E
Pauri Madhya P. India **40** 25.32N 77.21E
Pauri Uttar P. India **41** 30.09N 78.47E
Pavia Italy **15** 45.10N 9.10E
Pavilly France **15** 49.34N 0.58E
Pavlodar U.S.S.R. **28** 52.21N 76.59E
Pavlograd U.S.S.R. **25** 48.34N 35.50E
Pavlovo U.S.S.R. **24** 55.58N 43.05E
Pavlovsk U.S.S.R. **25** 50.28N 40.07E
Pavlovskaya U.S.S.R. **25** 46.18N 39.48E
Pavullo nel Frignano Italy **15** 44.20N 10.50E
Pawnee U.S.A. **83** 36.20N 96.48W
Paxoí *i.* Greece **19** 39.12N 20.12E
Paxton U.S.A. **82** 41.07N101.21W
Payette U.S.A. **80** 44.05N116.56W
Payne, L. Canada **73** 59.25N 74.00W
Paynes Find Australia **63** 29.15S117.41E
Paysandú Uruguay **93** 32.19S 58.05W
Pays de Caux *f.* France **15** 49.40N 0.40E
Pays de la Loire *d.* France **17** 47.30N 1.00W
Pazardzhik Bulgaria **19** 42.10N 24.22E
Peace *r.* Canada **74** 59.00N111.25W
Peace River *town* Canada **74** 56.15N117.18W
Peach Springs *town* U.S.A. **81** 35.32N113.25W
Peacock Hills Canada **72** 66.05N110.45W
Peak, The *mtn.* Ascension **95** 7.57S 14.21W
Peake Creek *r.* Australia **66** 28.05S136.07E
Peak Hill *town* N.S.W. Australia **67** 32.47S148.13E
Peak Range *mts.* Australia **64** 23.18S148.30E
Peale, Mt. U.S.A. **80** 38.26N109.14W
Pearl *r.* U.S.A. **83** 30.11N 89.32W
Pearland U.S.A. **83** 29.34N 95.17W
Pearsall U.S.A. **83** 28.53N 99.06W
Peary Land *f.* Greenland **96** 82.00N 35.00W
Pebane Mozambique **57** 17.14S 38.10E
Pebas Peru **90** 3.17S 71.55W
Peć Yugo. **19** 42.40N 20.17E
Pechenga U.S.S.R. **22** 69.28N 31.04E
Pechora U.S.S.R. **24** 65.14N 57.18E
Pechora *r.* U.S.S.R. **24** 68.10N 54.00E
Pechorskaya Guba *g.* U.S.S.R. **24** 69.00N 56.00E
Pechorskoye More *sea* U.S.S.R. **24** 69.00N 55.00E
Pecos U.S.A. **83** 31.25N103.30W
Pecos *r.* U.S.A. **83** 29.42N101.22W
Pécs Hungary **21** 46.05N 18.14E
Peddie R.S.A. **56** 33.12S 27.07E
Pedregulho Brazil **94** 20.15S 47.29W
Pedreiras Brazil **91** 4.32S 44.40W
Pedrinhas Brazil **91** 11.12S 37.41W
Pedro Afonso Brazil **91** 8.59S 48.11W
Pedro de Valdivia Chile **92** 22.36S 69.40W
Pedro Juan Caballero Paraguay **94** 22.30S 55.44W
Peebinga Australia **66** 34.55S140.57E
Peebles U.K. **12** 55.39N 3.12W
Peebles U.S.A. **84** 38.57N 83.14W
Peekskill U.S.A. **85** 41.17N 73.55W
Peel *r.* Canada **72** 68.13N135.00W
Peel U.K. **10** 54.14N 4.42W
Peel Inlet Australia **63** 32.35S115.44E
Peel Pt. Canada **72** 73.22N114.35W
Peene *r.* Germany **20** 53.53N 13.49E
Peera Peera Poolanna L. Australia **64** 26.43S137.42E
Peerless L. Canada **74** 56.37N114.35W
Pegasus B. New Zealand **60** 43.15S173.00E
Pegu Burma **34** 17.20N 96.36E
Pegu *d.* Burma **34** 17.30N 96.30E
Pegunungan Van Rees *mts.* Indonesia **37** 2.35S138.15E
Pegu Yoma *mts.* Burma **34** 18.30N 96.00E
Pehuajó Argentina **93** 35.50S 61.50W
Peikang Taiwan **33** 23.35N120.19E
Peixe Brazil **91** 12.03S 48.32W
Pei Xian China **32** 34.44N116.55E
Pekalongan Indonesia **37** 6.54S109.37E
Pekanbaru Indonesia **36** 0.33N101.20E
Pekin U.S.A. **82** 40.34N 89.40W
Peking *see* Beijing China **32**
Pelabuanratu Indonesia **37** 7.00S106.32E
Pelat, Mont *mtn.* France **17** 44.17N 6.41E
Peleaga *mtn.* Romania **21** 45.22N 22.54E
Peleng *i.* Indonesia **37** 1.30S123.10E
Peleniya U.S.S.R. **21** 47.58N 27.48E
Pelican U.S.A. **74** 57.55N136.10W
Pelkum Germany **14** 51.38N 7.44E
Pello Finland **22** 66.47N 24.00E
Pelly *r.* Canada **72** 62.50N137.35W
Pelly Bay *town* Canada **73** 68.38N 89.45W
Pelly L. Canada **73** 65.59N101.12W
Peloncillo Mts. U.S.A. **81** 32.16N109.00W
Pelotas Brazil **94** 31.45S 52.20W
Pemalang Indonesia **37** 6.53S109.21E
Pematangsiantar Indonesia **36** 2.59N 99.01E
Pemba Mozambique **57** 13.02S 40.30E
Pemba Zambia **55** 16.33S 27.20E
Pemba I. Tanzania **55** 5.10S 39.45E
Pemberton Australia **63** 34.28S116.01E
Pemberton Canada **74** 50.20N122.48W
Pembina *r.* Canada **74** 54.45N114.15W
Pembroke Canada **76** 45.49N 77.07W
Pembroke U.K. **11** 51.41N 4.57W
Pembroke U.S.A. **85** 32.09N 81.39W
Penang *see* Pinang, Pulau *i.* Malaysia **36**
Peñaranda de Bracamonte Spain **16** 40.54N 5.13W
Pen Argyl U.S.A. **85** 40.52N 75.16W
Penarth U.K. **11** 51.26N 3.11W
Peñas, Cabo de *c.* Spain **16** 43.42N 5.52W
Penas, Golfo de *g.* Chile **93** 47.20S 75.00W
Pende *r.* Chad **53** 7.30N 16.20E
Pendembu Eastern Sierra Leone **52** 8.09N 10.42W
Pendine U.K. **11** 51.44N 4.33W
Pendleton U.S.A. **80** 45.40N118.47W
Penedo Brazil **91** 10.16S 36.33W
Penetanguishene Canada **76** 44.47N 79.55W
Penganga *r.* India **41** 19.53N 79.09E
Penge Zaïre **54** 5.31S 24.37E
Penghu Liedao *is.* Taiwan **33** 23.35N119.32E
Pengshui China **33** 29.17N108.13E
Penicuik U.K. **12** 55.49N 3.13W
Peninsular Malaysia *d.* Malaysia **36** 5.00N102.00E
Penneshaw Australia **66** 35.42S137.55E
Pennines, Alpes *mts.* Switz. **15** 46.08N 7.34E
Pennsauken U.S.A. **85** 39.58N 75.04W
Penns Grove U.S.A. **85** 39.43N 75.28W
Pennsylvania *d.* U.S.A. **84** 40.45N 77.30W
Penn Yan U.S.A. **76** 42.40N 77.03W
Penny Highland *mtn.* Canada **73** 67.10N 66.50W
Penobscot *r.* U.S.A. **84** 44.30N 68.50W
Penola Australia **66** 37.23S140.21E
Penong Australia **63** 31.55S133.01E
Penonomé Panama **87** 8.30N 80.20W
Penrhyn Atoll Cook Is. **69** 9.00S158.00W
Penrith Australia **67** 33.47S150.44E
Penrith U.K. **10** 54.40N 2.45W
Penryn U.K. **11** 50.10N 5.07W
Pensacola U.S.A. **83** 30.26N 87.12W
Pensacola Mts. Antarctica **96** 84.00S 45.00W
Penshurst Australia **66** 37.52S142.20E
Pentecost I. Vanuatu **68** 15.42S168.10E
Penticton Canada **74** 49.30N119.30W
Pentland Australia **64** 20.32S145.24E
Pentland Firth *str.* U.K. **12** 58.40N 3.00W
Pentland Hills U.K. **12** 55.50N 3.20W
Penylan L. Canada **75** 61.50N106.20W
Penza U.S.S.R. **24** 53.11N 45.00E
Penzance U.K. **11** 50.07N 5.32W
Penzhinskaya Guba *g.* U.S.S.R. **29** 61.00N163.00E
Peoria Ariz. U.S.A. **81** 33.35N112.14W
Peoria Ill. U.S.A. **82** 40.43N 89.38W
Peper Sudan **49** 7.04N 33.00E
Perabumulih Indonesia **36** 3.29S104.14E
Perche, Collines du *hills* France **15** 48.30N 0.40E
Percival Lakes Australia **62** 21.25S125.00E
Pereira Colombia **90** 4.47N 75.46W
Perekop U.S.S.R. **25** 46.10N 33.42E
Perené *r.* Peru **92** 11.02S 74.19W
Perevolotskiy U.S.S.R. **24** 51.10N 54.15E
Pereyaslav-Khmelnitskiy U.S.S.R. **21** 50.05N 31.28E
Pergamino Argentina **93** 33.53S 60.35W
Pergine Valsugana Italy **15** 46.04N 11.14E
Perham U.S.A. **82** 46.36N 95.34W
Péribonca *r.* Canada **77** 48.45N 72.05W
Pericos Mexico **81** 25.03N107.42W
Périers France **15** 49.11N 1.25W
Périgueux France **17** 45.12N 0.44E
Perija, Sierra de *mts.* Venezuela **90** 10.30N 72.30W
Peri L. Australia **66** 30.44S143.34E
Perm U.S.S.R. **24** 58.01N 56.10E
Pernambuco *d.* Brazil **91** 8.00S 39.00W
Pernatty L. Australia **66** 31.31S137.14E
Pernik Bulgaria **19** 42.35N 23.03E
Perniö Finland **23** 60.12N 23.08E
Péronne France **14** 49.56N 2.57E
Perosa Argentina Italy **15** 44.58N 7.10E
Pérouse, Bahía la *b.* I. de Pascua **69** 27.04S109.20W
Perpendicular, Pt. Australia **67** 35.03S150.50E
Perpignan France **17** 42.42N 2.54E
Perranporth U.K. **11** 50.21N 5.09W
Perry Fla. U.S.A. **85** 30.08N 83.36W
Perry Iowa U.S.A. **82** 41.50N 94.06W
Perry Okla. U.S.A. **83** 36.17N 97.17W
Perryton U.S.A. **83** 36.24N100.48W
Perryville U.S.A. **83** 37.43N 89.52W
Persepolis *ruins* Iran **43** 29.55N 53.00E
Perth Australia **63** 31.58S115.49E
Perth Canada **76** 44.54N 76.15W
Perth U.K. **12** 56.24N 3.28W
Perth Amboy U.S.A. **85** 40.32N 74.17W
Peru S. America **90** 10.00S 75.00W
Peru Ill. U.S.A. **82** 41.19N 89.11W
Peru Basin Pacific Oc. **69** 19.00S 96.00W
Peru-Chile Trench Pacific Oc. **69** 21.00S 72.00W
Perugia Italy **18** 43.06N 12.24E
Péruwelz Belgium **14** 50.32N 3.36E
Pervomaysk U.S.S.R. **21** 48.03N 30.50E
Pervouralsk U.S.S.R. **24** 56.59N 59.58E
Pesaro Italy **15** 43.54N 12.54E
Pescara Italy **18** 42.27N 14.13E
Pescara *r.* Italy **18** 42.28N 14.13E
Pescia Italy **15** 43.54N 10.41E
Peshāwar Pakistan **40** 34.01N 71.33E
Peshīn Jān Afghan. **40** 33.25N 61.28E
Pesqueira Brazil **91** 8.24S 36.38W
Pesqueria *r.* Mexico **83** 25.55N 99.28W
Pessac France **17** 44.48N 0.38W
Peşteana Jiu Romania **21** 44.50N 23.15E
Pestovo U.S.S.R. **24** 58.32N 35.42E
Petah Tiqwa Israel **44** 32.05N 34.53E
Petaluma U.S.A. **80** 38.14N122.39W
Pétange Lux. **14** 49.32N 5.56E
Petare Venezuela **90** 10.31N 66.50W
Petatlán Mexico **86** 17.31N101.16W
Petauke Zambia **55** 14.16S 31.21E
Petawawa Canada **76** 45.54N 77.17W
Peterborough S.A. Australia **66** 33.00S138.51E
Peterborough Vic. Australia **66** 38.36S142.55E
Peterborough Canada **76** 44.19N 78.20W
Peterborough U.K. **11** 52.35N 0.14W
Peterhead U.K. **12** 57.30N 1.46W
Peterlee U.K. **10** 54.45N 1.18W
Petermann Ranges *mts.* Australia **62** 25.00S129.46E
Peter Pond L. Canada **75** 55.55N108.44W
Petersburg Alas. U.S.A. **74** 56.49N132.58W
Petersburg Va. U.S.A. **85** 37.14N 77.24W
Petersburg W.Va. U.S.A. **84** 39.00N 79.07W
Petersfield U.K. **11** 51.00N 0.56W
Petitot *r.* Canada **74** 60.14N123.29W
Petit St. Bernard, Col du *pass* France / Italy **15** 45.40N 6.53E
Petitsikapau L. Canada **77** 54.45N 66.25W
Petlād India **40** 22.30N 72.45E
Petoskey U.S.A. **84** 45.22N 84.59W
Petra *ruins* Jordan **44** 30.19N 35.26E
Petrich Bulgaria **19** 41.25N 23.13E
Petrikov U.S.S.R. **21** 52.09N 28.30E
Petrodvorets U.S.S.R. **24** 59.50N 29.57E
Petrolina Brazil **91** 9.22S 40.30W
Petropavlovsk U.S.S.R. **28** 54.53N 69.13E
Petropavlovsk Kamchatskiy U.S.S.R. **29** 53.03N158.43E
Petrópolis Brazil **94** 22.30S 43.06W
Petroşani Romania **21** 45.25N 23.22E
Petrovaradin Yugo. **21** 45.16N 19.55E
Petrovsk U.S.S.R. **24** 52.20N 45.24E
Petrovsk Zabaykal'skiy U.S.S.R. **29** 51.20N108.55E
Petrozavodsk U.S.S.R. **24** 61.46N 34.19E
Petrus Steyn R.S.A. **56** 27.38S 28.08E
Peureulak Indonesia **36** 4.48N 97.45E
Pevek U.S.S.R. **29** 69.41N170.19E
Pézenas France **17** 43.28N 3.25E
Pezinok Czech. **21** 48.18N 17.17E
Pezmog U.S.S.R. **24** 61.50N 51.45E
Pezu Pakistan **40** 32.19N 70.44E
Pfaffenhofen Germany **20** 48.31N 11.30E
Pfalzel Germany **14** 49.47N 6.41E
Pforzheim Germany **20** 48.53N 8.41E
Phagwāra India **40** 31.13N 75.47E
Phalodi India **40** 27.08N 72.22E
Phangan, Ko *i.* Thailand **36** 9.50N100.00E
Phangnga Thailand **34** 8.29N 98.31E
Phan Rang Vietnam **34** 11.34N109.00E
Phan Thiet Vietnam **34** 11.00N108.06E
Pharenda India **41** 27.06N 83.17E
Phariāro Pakistan **40** 27.12N 68.59E
Phat Diem Vietnam **33** 20.06N106.07E
Phatthalung Thailand **34** 7.38N100.04E
Phelps L. Canada **75** 59.15N103.15W
Phenix City U.S.A. **85** 32.28N 85.01W
Phet Buri Thailand **34** 13.00N 99.58E
Philadelphia Miss. U.S.A. **83** 32.46N 89.07W
Philadelphia Penn. U.S.A. **85** 39.57N 75.07W
Philippeville Belgium **14** 50.12N 4.32E
Philippines Asia **37** 13.00N123.00E
Philippine Sea Pacific Oc. **68** 18.00N135.00E
Philippine Trench Pacific Oc. **68** 9.00N127.00E
Philipstown R.S.A. **56** 30.25S 24.26E
Phillip U.S.A. **82** 44.02N101.40W
Phillip I. Australia **67** 38.29S145.14E
Phillips *r.* Australia **63** 33.55S120.01E
Phillips Maine U.S.A. **84** 44.49N 70.21W
Phillips Wisc. U.S.A. **82** 45.41N 90.24W
Phillipsburg Kans. U.S.A. **82** 39.45N 99.19W
Phillipsburg N.J. U.S.A. **85** 40.42N 75.12W
Phillipson, L. Australia **66** 29.28S134.28E
Phnom Penh Cambodia **34** 11.35N104.55E
Phoenix Ariz. U.S.A. **81** 33.27N112.05W
Phoenix Is. Kiribati **68** 4.00S172.00W
Phoenixville Penn. U.S.A. **85** 40.08N 75.31W
Phon Thailand **34** 15.50N102.35E
Phôngsali Laos **34** 21.40N102.11E
Phou Loi *mtn.* Laos **34** 20.16N103.18E
Phu Huu Vietnam **33** 19.00N105.35E
Phukao Miang *mtn.* Thailand **39** 16.50N101.00E
Phuket Thailand **34** 7.55N 98.23E
Phuket, Ko *i.* Thailand **34** 8.10N 98.20E
Phu Ly Vietnam **33** 20.30N105.58E
Phumi Chuuk Vietnam **34** 10.50N104.28E
Phumi Sâmraông Cambodia **34** 14.12N103.31E
Phu Quoc *i.* Cambodia **34** 10.20N104.00E
Phu Tho Vietnam **34** 21.23N105.13E
Phu Vinh Vietnam **34** 9.57N106.20E
Piacá Brazil **91** 7.42S 47.18W
Piacenza Italy **15** 45.03N 9.42E
Pialba Australia **64** 25.13S152.55E
Pian *r.* Australia **67** 30.03S148.18E
Piana France **17** 42.14N 8.38E
Piangil Australia **65** 35.04S143.20E
Pianoro Italy **15** 44.22N 11.20E
Pianosa *i.* Italy **18** 42.35N 10.05E
Piatra-Neamţ Romania **21** 46.56N 26.22E
Piauí *d.* Brazil **91** 7.45S 42.30W
Piauí *r.* Brazil **91** 6.14S 42.51W
Piave *r.* Italy **15** 45.33N 12.45E
Piawaning Australia **63** 30.51S116.22E
Pibor *r.* Sudan **49** 8.26N 33.13E
Pibor Post Sudan **49** 6.48N 33.08E
Pic *r.* Canada **76** 48.38N 86.25W
Picardie *d.* France **14** 49.47N 3.12E
Pickering U.K. **10** 54.15N 0.46W
Pickle Crow Canada **76** 51.30N 90.04W
Pickwick L. *resr.* U.S.A. **83** 34.55N 88.10W
Picos Brazil **91** 7.05S 41.28W
Picquigny France **15** 49.57N 2.09E
Picton Australia **67** 34.12S150.35E
Picton Canada **76** 44.00N 77.08W
Picton New Zealand **60** 41.17S174.02E
Picún Leufú Argentina **93** 39.30S 69.15W
Pidálion, Akrotírion *c.* Cyprus **44** 34.56N 34.05E
Pidarak Pakistan **40** 25.51N 63.14E
Piedecuesta Colombia **90** 6.59N 73.03W
Piedmont U.S.A. **85** 33.55N 85.39W
Piedras *r.* Peru **90** 12.30S 69.10W
Piedras, Punta *c.* Argentina **93** 35.25S 57.07W
Piedras Negras Mexico **83** 28.40N100.32W
Piedra Sola Uruguay **93** 32.04S 56.21W
Pielavesi Finland **22** 63.14N 26.45E
Pielinen *l.* Finland **24** 63.20N 29.50E
Piemonte *d.* Italy **15** 44.45N 8.00E
Pierce U.S.A. **80** 46.29N115.48W
Pierre U.S.A. **82** 44.22N100.21W
Pierreville Canada **77** 46.04N 72.49W
Piesseville Australia **63** 33.11S117.12E
Piešt'any Czech. **21** 48.36N 17.50E
Pietarsaari Finland **22** 63.40N 22.42E
Pietermaritzburg R.S.A. **56** 29.36S 30.23E
Pietersburg R.S.A. **56** 23.54S 29.27E
Pietrasanta Italy **15** 43.57N 10.14E
Piet Retief R.S.A. **56** 27.00S 30.49E
Pietrosu *mtn.* Romania **21** 47.36N 24.38E
Pietrosul *mtn.* Romania **21** 47.08N 25.11E
Pieve di Cadore Italy **15** 46.26N 12.22E
Pigailoe *i.* Caroline Is. **37** 8.08N146.40E
Pigna Italy **15** 43.56N 7.40E
Pihtipudas Finland **22** 63.23N 25.34E
Pikalevo U.S.S.R. **24** 59.35N 34.07E
Pikangikum Canada **75** 51.49N 94.00W
Pikes Peak *mtn.* U.S.A. **80** 38.51N105.03W
Pikesville U.S.A. **85** 39.25N 77.25W
Piketberg R.S.A. **56** 32.54S 18.43E
Piketon U.S.A. **84** 39.03N 83.01W
Pikeville U.S.A. **85** 37.29N 82.33W
Pila Argentina **93** 36.00S 58.10W
Piła Poland **20** 53.09N 16.44E
Pilar Paraguay **94** 26.52S 58.23W
Pilar do Sul Brazil **94** 23.48S 47.45W
Pilcomayo *r.* Argentina / Paraguay **92** 25.15S 57.43W
Pīlībhīt India **41** 28.38N 79.48E
Pilica *r.* Poland **21** 51.52N 21.17E
Pilliga Australia **67** 30.23S148.55E
Pílos Greece **19** 36.55N 21.40E
Pilot Point *town* U.S.A. **83** 33.24N 96.58W
Pilsum Germany **14** 53.29N 7.06E
Pimba Australia **66** 31.18S136.47E
Pimenta Bueno Brazil **90** 11.40S 61.14W
Pinang, Pulau *i.* Malaysia **36** 5.30N100.10E
Pinarbaşi Turkey **42** 38.43N 36.23E
Pinar del Río Cuba **87** 22.24N 83.42W
Pincher Creek *town* Canada **74** 49.30N113.57W
Píndhos Óros *mts.* Albania / Greece **19** 39.40N 21.00E
Pindiga Nigeria **53** 9.58N 10.53E
Pindi Gheb Pakistan **40** 33.14N 72.16E
Pindwāra India **40** 24.48N 73.04E
Pine *r.* Canada **74** 56.08N120.41W
Pine, C. Canada **77** 46.37N 53.30W
Pine Bluff *town* U.S.A. **83** 34.13N 92.01W

ne Bluffs town U.S.A. 80 41.11N104.04W
ne City U.S.A. 82 45.50N 92.59W
ne Creek town Australia 62 13.51S131.50E
nega U.S.S.R. 24 64.42N 43.28E
nega r. U.S.S.R. 24 63.51N 41.48E
nehouse L. Canada 75 55.32N106.35W
ne Is. U.S.A. 85 26.35N 82.06W
ne Point town Canada 74 60.50N114.28W
ne River town Canada 75 51.45N100.40W
ne River town U.S.A. 82 46.43N 94.24W
nerolo Italy 15 44.53N 7.21E
netown R.S.A. 56 29.49S 30.52E
neville U.S.A. 83 31.19N 92.26W
ney France 15 48.22N 4.20E
ing r. Thailand 34 15.47N100.05E
ingaring Australia 63 34.45S118.34E
ingba China 33 26.25N106.15E
ingdingshan Henan China 32 33.38N113.30E
ingdingshan Liaoning China 32 41.28N124.45E
ingdong Taiwan 33 22.44N120.30E
ingelap i. Pacific Oc. 68 6.15N160.40E
ingelly Australia 63 32.34S117.04E
ingle China 33 24.38N110.38E
ingliang China 32 35.21N107.12E
ingluo China 32 38.56N106.34E
ingnan China 33 23.33N110.23E
ingrup Australia 63 33.33S118.30E
ingtan i. China 33 25.36N119.48E
ingwu China 32 32.25N104.36E
ingxiang Guang. Zhuang. China 33 22.07N106.42E
ingxiang Jiangxi China 33 27.36N113.48E
ingyang China 33 27.40N120.33E
ingyao China 32 37.12N112.08E
ingyi China 32 35.30N117.36E
ingyuan China 33 24.34N115.54E
inhal Brazil 94 22.10S 46.46W
inhel Portugal 16 40.46N 7.04W
ini i. Indonesia 36 0.10N 98.30E
iniós r. Greece 19 39.51N 22.37E
injarra Australia 63 32.37S115.53E
innaroo Australia 66 35.18S140.54E
inos, Isla de i. Cuba 87 21.40N 82.40W
inrang Indonesia 36 3.48S119.41E
ins, Île des i. N. Cal. 68 22.37S167.30E
insk U.S.S.R. 21 52.08N 26.01E
into Argentina 92 29.09S 62.38W
into Butte mtn. Canada 75 49.22N107.25W
inyug U.S.S.R. 24 60.10N 47.43E
iombino Italy 18 42.56N 10.30E
iorini, L. Brazil 90 3.34S 63.15W
iotrków Trybunalski Poland 21 51.25N 19.42E
iove di Sacco Italy 15 45.18N 12.02E
ipār India 40 26.23N 73.32E
iparia India 41 22.45N 78.21E
ipestone r. Ont. Canada 76 52.48N 89.35W
ipestone r. Sask. Canada 75 58.40N105.45W
ipestone U.S.A. 82 43.58N 96.10W
ipinas Argentina 93 35.30S 57.19W
iplān Pakistan 40 32.17N 71.21E
ipmouacane, Résr. Canada 77 49.35N 70.30W
iqua U.S.A. 84 40.08N 84.14W
iracicaba Brazil 94 22.45S 47.40W
iracicaba r. Brazil 94 22.35S 48.14W
iracuruca Brazil 91 3.56S 41.42W
iraeus see Piraiévs Greece 19
iraiévs Greece 19 37.56N 23.38E
iram I. India 40 21.36N 72.41E
irassununga Brazil 94 21.59S 47.25W
irgos Greece 19 37.42N 21.27E
irna Germany 20 50.58N 13.58E
irojpur Bangla. 41 22.34N 89.59E
irot Yugo. 19 43.10N 22.32E
ir Panjāl Range mts. Jammu & Kashmir 40 33.50N 74.30E
iryatin U.S.S.R. 25 50.14N 32.31E
isa Italy 18 43.43N 10.24E
isciotta Italy 18 40.08N 15.12E
isco Peru 90 13.46S 76.12W
isek Czech. 20 49.19N 14.10E
ishan China 30 37.30N 78.20E
ishin Pakistan 40 30.35N 67.00E
ishin Lora r. Pakistan 40 29.09N 64.55E
istoia Italy 15 43.55N 10.54E
isuerga r. Spain 16 41.35N 5.40W
isz Poland 21 53.38N 21.49E
ita Guinea 52 11.05N 12.15W
italito Colombia 90 1.51N 76.01W
itarpunga, L. Australia 66 34.23S143.32E
itcairn I. Pacific Oc. 69 25.04S130.06W
ite r. Sweden 22 65.14N 21.32E
iteå Sweden 22 65.20N 21.30E
itești Romania 21 44.52N 24.51E
ithāpuram India 39 17.07N 82.16E
ithiviers France 15 48.10N 2.15E
ithoragarh India 41 29.35N 80.13E
iti Guam 68 13.28N144.41E
itlochry U.K. 12 56.43N 3.45W
itt I. Canada 74 53.35N129.45W
ittsburg Kans. U.S.A. 83 37.25N 94.42W
ittsburg N.H. U.S.A. 84 45.03N 71.26W
ittsburg Tex. U.S.A. 83 32.60N 94.58W
ittsburgh U.S.A. 84 40.26N 80.00W
ittsfield U.S.A. 84 42.27N 73.15W
ittston U.S.A. 84 41.19N 75.47W
ittsville U.S.A. 85 38.24N 75.52W
ittville U.S.A. 80 41.03N121.20W
iūí Brazil 94 20.28S 45.58W
iura Peru 90 5.15S 80.38W
iuthān Nepal 41 28.06N 82.54E
lacentia Canada 77 47.15N 53.58W
lacentia B. Canada 77 47.15N 54.30W
lain Dealing U.S.A. 83 32.54N 93.42W
lainfield N.J. U.S.A. 85 40.37N 74.26W
lains U.S.A. 80 47.27N114.53W
Plainview U.S.A. 83 34.11N101.43W
Plampang Indonesia 36 8.48S117.48E
Planá Czech. 20 49.52N 12.44E
Plana Cays is. Bahamas 87 21.31N 72.14W
Plantagenet Canada 77 45.32N 75.00W
Plasencia Spain 16 40.02N 6.05W
Plassen Norway 23 61.08N 12.31E
Plaster Rock town Canada 77 46.54N 67.24W
Platani r. Italy 18 37.24N 13.15E
Plate, R. est. see La Plata, Río de Argentina/Uruguay 93
Plateau d. Nigeria 53 8.50N 9.00E
Plati, Ákra c. Greece 19 40.26N 23.59E
Platinum U.S.A. 72 59.00N161.50W
Plato Colombia 90 9.54N 74.46W
Platte r. U.S.A. 82 41.04N 95.53W
Platteville U.S.A. 82 42.44N 90.29W
Plattling Germany 20 48.47N 12.53E
Plattsburgh U.S.A. 84 44.42N 73.28W
Plauen Germany 20 50.29N 12.08E
Plavsk U.S.S.R. 24 53.40N 37.20E
Pleasantville U.S.A. 85 39.23N 74.32W
Pleasonton U.S.A. 83 28.58N 98.29W
Pleiku Vietnam 34 13.57N108.01E
Plenty, B. of New Zealand 60 37.40S176.50E
Plentywood U.S.A. 80 48.47N104.34W
Plesetsk U.S.S.R. 24 62.42N 40.21E
Pleshchenitsy U.S.S.R. 21 54.24N 27.52E
Pleszew Poland 21 51.54N 17.48E
Plétipi, Lac l. Canada 77 51.44N 70.06W
Pleven Bulgaria 19 43.25N 24.39E
Pljevlja Yugo. 19 43.22N 19.22E
Płock Poland 21 52.33N 19.43E
Ploiești Romania 21 44.57N 26.02E
Plomb du Cantal mtn. France 17 45.04N 2.45E
Plombières France 17 47.58N 6.28E
Plön Germany 20 54.09N 10.25E
Plonge, Lac la l. Canada 75 55.05N107.15W
Płońsk Poland 21 52.38N 20.23E
Ploudalmézeau France 17 48.33N 4.39W
Plovdiv Bulgaria 19 42.09N 24.45E
Plumtree Zimbabwe 56 20.30S 27.50E
Plunkett Canada 75 51.56N105.29W
Plymouth U.K. 11 50.23N 4.09W
Plymouth Ind. U.S.A. 84 41.20N 86.19W
Plymouth Wisc. U.S.A. 82 43.44N 87.58W
Plzeň Czech. 20 49.45N 13.22E
Pô Burkina 52 11.11N 1.10W
Po r. Italy 15 44.51N 12.30E
Pobé Benin 53 7.00N 2.56E
Pobeda, Gora mtn. U.S.S.R. 29 65.20N145.50E
Pobla de Segur Spain 16 42.15N 0.58E
Pocahontas Canada 74 53.15N118.00W
Pocahontas Ark. U.S.A. 83 36.16N 90.58W
Pocahontas Iowa U.S.A. 82 42.44N 94.40W
Pocatello U.S.A. 80 42.52N112.27W
Pocklington U.K. 10 53.56N 0.48W
Poços de Caldas Brazil 94 21.48S 46.33W
Poděbrady Czech. 20 50.08N 15.07E
Podgaytsy U.S.S.R. 21 49.19N 25.10E
Podkamennaya Tunguska U.S.S.R. 29 61.45N 90.13E
Podkamennaya Tunguska r. U.S.S.R. 29 61.40N 90.00E
Podolsk U.S.S.R. 24 55.23N 37.32E
Podor Senegal 52 16.35N 15.02W
Podporozhye U.S.S.R. 24 60.55N 34.02E
Pofadder R.S.A. 56 29.08S 19.22E
Pogrebishche U.S.S.R. 21 49.30N 29.15E
Poh Indonesia 37 1.00S122.50E
P'ohang S. Korea 31 36.00N129.26E
Poinsett, C. Antarctica 96 65.35S113.00E
Point Arena f. U.S.A. 80 38.55N123.41W
Pointe-à-Pitre Guadeloupe 87 16.14N 61.32W
Pointe aux Anglais town Canada 77 49.34N 67.10W
Pointe-aux-Trembles town Canada 77 45.39N 73.29W
Pointe-Claire Canada 77 45.26N 73.50W
Pointe Noire town Congo 54 4.46S 11.53E
Point Hope town U.S.A. 72 68.21N166.41W
Point Lookout town Australia 67 30.33S152.20E
Point Pleasant town N.J. U.S.A. 85 40.05N 74.04W
Point Pleasant town W.Va. U.S.A. 84 38.53N 82.07W
Point Samson town Australia 62 20.46S117.10E
Poissy France 15 48.56N 2.03E
Poitiers France 17 46.35N 0.20E
Poitou-Charentes d. France 17 46.00N 0.00
Poix France 15 49.47N 2.00E
Poix-Terron France 15 49.39N 4.39E
Pokaran India 40 26.55N 71.55E
Pokhara Nepal 41 28.12N 83.59E
Poko Zaïre 54 3.08N 26.51E
Pokoinu Rarotonga Cook Is. 68 21.12S159.50W
Polacca U.S.A. 81 35.50N110.23W
Pola de Lena Spain 16 43.10N 5.49W
Polān Iran 43 25.29N 61.15E
Poland Europe 21 52.30N 19.00E
Polatli Turkey 42 39.34N 32.08E
Polch Germany 14 50.18N 7.19E
Polda Australia 66 33.30S135.10E
Pole Zaïre 54 2.51S 23.12E
Polesye f. U.S.S.R. 21 52.15N 28.00E
Poli Cameroon 53 8.30N 13.15E
Policastro, Golfo di g. Italy 18 40.00N 15.35E
Poligny France 17 46.50N 5.42E
Pólis Cyprus 44 35.02N 32.26E
Políyiros Greece 19 40.23N 23.27E
Pollino mtn. Italy 18 39.53N 16.11E
Pollock Reef Australia 63 34.28S123.40E
Polnovat U.S.S.R. 28 63.47N 65.54E
Polonnoye U.S.S.R. 21 50.10N 27.30E
Polotsk U.S.S.R. 24 55.30N 28.43E
Polperro U.K. 11 50.19N 4.31W
Polson U.S.A. 80 47.41N114.09W
Poltava U.S.S.R. 25 49.35N 34.35E
Polunochnoye U.S.S.R. 24 60.52N 60.28E
Polyarnyy U.S.S.R. 24 69.14N 33.30E
Polynesia is. Pacific Oc. 68 4.00S165.00W
Pomarkku Finland 23 61.42N 22.00E
Pombal Brazil 91 6.45S 37.45W
Pombal Portugal 16 39.55N 8.38W
Pomene Mozambique 57 22.53S 35.33E
Pomeroy Wash. U.S.A. 80 46.28N117.36W
Pomona Namibia 56 27.09S 15.18E
Pomona U.S.A. 81 34.04N117.45W
Pompano Beach town U.S.A. 85 26.14N 80.07W
Pompey's Pillar town U.S.A. 80 45.59N107.56W
Ponape i. Pacific Oc. 68 6.55N158.15E
Ponca City U.S.A. 83 36.42N 97.05W
Ponce Puerto Rico 87 18.00N 66.40W
Pondicherry India 39 11.59N 79.50E
Pond Inlet str. Canada 73 72.30N 75.00W
Ponds, I. of Canada 77 53.24N 55.55W
Ponferrada Spain 16 42.32N 6.31W
Pongani P.N.G. 64 9.05S148.35E
Pongo r. Sudan 49 8.52N 27.40E
Pongola r. Mozambique 57 26.13S 32.38E
Ponnāni India 38 10.46N 75.54E
Ponnyadaung Range mts. Burma 34 22.30N 94.20E
Ponoka Canada 74 52.42N113.40W
Ponorogo Indonesia 37 7.51S111.30E
Ponoy U.S.S.R. 24 67.02N 41.03E
Ponoy r. U.S.S.R. 24 67.00N 41.10E
Ponta Grossa Brazil 94 25.00S 50.09W
Pont-à-Mousson France 17 48.55N 6.03E
Ponta Porã Brazil 94 22.27S 55.39W
Pont-Audemer France 15 49.21N 0.31E
Pontax r. Canada 76 51.30N 78.48W
Pont Canavese Italy 15 45.25N 7.36E
Pontchartrain, L. U.S.A. 83 30.10N 90.10W
Pont-d'Ain France 17 46.03N 5.20E
Pontedera Italy 18 43.40N 10.38E
Pontefract U.K. 10 53.42N 1.19W
Ponteix Canada 75 49.49N107.30W
Ponte Nova Brazil 94 20.25S 42.54W
Pontevedra Spain 16 42.25N 8.39W
Pontiac Ill. U.S.A. 82 40.54N 88.36W
Pontiac Mich. U.S.A. 84 42.39N 83.18W
Pontianak Indonesia 36 0.05S109.16E
Pontivy France 17 48.05N 3.00W
Pont l'Évêque France 15 49.18N 0.11E
Pontoise France 15 49.03N 2.05E
Pontorson France 15 48.33N 1.31W
Pontremoli Italy 15 44.22N 9.53E
Pontresina Switz. 15 46.28N 9.53E
Pontrilas U.K. 11 51.56N 2.53W
Pont-sur-Yonne France 15 48.17N 3.12E
Pontypool U.K. 11 51.42N 3.01W
Pontypridd U.K. 11 51.36N 3.21W
Ponziane, Isole is. Italy 18 40.56N 12.58E
Poochera Australia 66 32.42S134.52E
Poole U.K. 11 50.42N 2.02W
Pooncarie Australia 66 33.23S142.34E
Poopelloe L. Australia 66 31.39S144.00E
Poopó, Lago de l. Bolivia 92 19.00S 67.00W
Popayán Colombia 90 2.27N 76.32W
Poperinge Belgium 14 50.51N 2.44E
Popes Creek town U.S.A. 85 38.09N 76.58W
Popilta L. Australia 66 33.09S141.45E
Poplar r. Canada 75 53.00N 97.18W
Poplar U.S.A. 80 48.07N105.12W
Poplar Bluff town U.S.A. 83 36.45N 90.24W
Poplarville U.S.A. 83 30.51N 89.32W
Popocatépetl mtn. Mexico 86 19.02N 98.38W
Popokabaka Zaïre 54 5.41S 16.40E
Popondetta P.N.G. 64 8.45S148.15E
Poprad Czech. 21 49.03N 20.18E
Popricani Romania 21 47.18N 27.31E
Porāli r. Pakistan 40 25.30N 66.25E
Porbandar India 40 21.38N 69.36E
Por Chaman Afghan. 40 33.08N 63.51E
Porcher I. Canada 74 54.00N130.30W
Porcupine r. U.S.A. 72 66.25N145.20W
Porcupine Hills Canada 75 52.30N101.45W
Pordenone Italy 15 45.57N 12.39E
Pori Finland 23 61.29N 21.47E
Porirua New Zealand 60 41.08S174.50E
Porjus Sweden 22 66.57N 19.50E
Porkhov U.S.S.R. 24 57.43N 29.31E
Porkkala Finland 23 59.59N 24.26E
Porlamar Venezuela 90 11.01N 63.54W
Pornic France 17 47.07N 2.05W
Porog U.S.S.R. 24 63.50N 38.32E
Poronaysk U.S.S.R. 29 49.13N142.55E
Porosozero U.S.S.R. 24 62.45N 32.48E
Porretta Terme Italy 15 44.09N 10.59E
Porsangen est. Norway 22 70.58N 25.30E
Porsangerhalvöya pen. Norway 22 70.50N 25.00E
Porsgrunn Norway 23 59.09N 9.40E
Porsuk r. Turkey 42 39.41N 31.56E
Portachuela Bolivia 92 17.21S 63.24W
Portadown U.K. 13 54.25N 6.27W
Portaferry U.K. 13 54.23N 5.33W
Portage Wisc. U.S.A. 82 43.33N 89.28W
Portage la Prairie town Canada 75 49.57N 98.25W
Port Alberni Canada 74 49.14N124.48W
Port Albert Australia 67 38.09S146.40E
Portalegre Portugal 16 39.17N 7.25W
Portales U.S.A. 83 34.11N103.20W
Port Alfred R.S.A. 56 33.36S 26.52E
Port Alice Canada 74 50.25N127.25W
Port Angeles U.S.A. 80 48.07N123.27W
Port Antonio Jamaica 87 18.10N 76.27W
Port Arthur Australia 65 43.08S147.50E
Port Arthur U.S.A. 83 29.55N 93.55W
Port Augusta Australia 66 32.30S137.46E
Port au Port Canada 77 48.33N 58.45W
Port-au-Prince Haiti 87 18.33N 72.20W
Port Austin U.S.A. 84 44.04N 82.59W
Port Bergé Madagascar 57 15.33S 47.40E
Port Blair India 34 11.40N 92.40E
Portbou Spain 16 42.25N 3.09E
Port Bouet Ivory Coast 52 5.14N 3.58W
Port Bradshaw b. Australia 64 12.30S136.42E
Port Broughton Australia 66 33.36S137.56E
Port Campbell Australia 66 38.37S143.04E
Port Canning India 41 22.18N 88.40E
Port Cartier Canada 77 50.01N 66.53W
Port Chalmers New Zealand 60 45.49S170.37E
Port Chester U.S.A. 85 41.00N 73.40W
Port Colborne Canada 76 42.53N 79.14W
Port Coquitlam Canada 74 49.20N122.45W
Port Credit Canada 76 43.33N 79.35W
Port Curtis Australia 64 23.50S151.13E
Port Dalhousie Canada 76 43.12N 79.16W
Port-de-Paix Haiti 87 19.57N 72.50W
Port Dover Canada 76 42.47N 80.12W
Port Edward R.S.A. 56 31.03S 30.13E
Portela Brazil 94 21.38S 41.59W
Port Elizabeth R.S.A. 56 33.57S 25.34E
Port Ellen U.K. 12 55.38N 6.12W
Port-en-Bessin France 15 49.21N 0.45W
Port Erin U.K. 10 54.05N 4.45W
Porter Landing Canada 74 58.46N130.05W
Porterville R.S.A. 56 33.01S 19.00E
Porterville U.S.A. 81 36.04N119.01W
Port Fairy Australia 66 38.23S142.17E
Port Gentil Gabon 54 0.40S 8.46E
Port Germein Australia 66 33.01S138.00E
Port Gibson U.S.A. 83 31.58N 90.58W
Portglenone U.K. 13 54.52N 6.30W
Port Harcourt Nigeria 53 4.43N 7.05E
Port Harrison see Inoucdjouac Canada 73
Port Hawkesbury Canada 77 45.37N 61.21W
Porthcawl U.K. 11 51.28N 3.42W
Port Hedland Australia 62 20.24S118.36E
Port Henry U.S.A. 84 44.03N 73.28W
Porthill U.S.A. 80 49.00N116.30W
Porthmadog U.K. 10 52.55N 4.08W
Port Hope Canada 76 43.57N 78.18W
Port Huron U.S.A. 84 42.59N 82.28W
Portimão Portugal 16 37.08N 8.32W
Port Isaac B. U.K. 11 50.36N 4.50W
Portițel, Gura f. Romania 19 44.40N 29.00E
Port Jervis U.S.A. 85 41.22N 74.40W
Port Keats Australia 62 14.15S129.35E
Port Kembla Australia 67 34.28S150.54E
Port Kenny Australia 66 33.09S134.42E
Portland N.S.W. Australia 67 33.20S150.00E
Portland Vic. Australia 66 38.21S141.38E
Portland Maine U.S.A. 84 43.39N 70.17W
Portland Oreg. U.S.A. 80 45.33N122.36W
Portland Tex. U.S.A. 83 27.53N 97.20W
Portland Pt. Ascension 95 7.58S 14.26W
Port-la-Nouvelle France 17 43.01N 3.03E
Port Laoise Rep. of Ire. 13 53.03N 7.20W
Port Lavaca U.S.A. 83 28.37N 96.38W
Port Lincoln Australia 66 34.43S135.49E
Port Loko Sierra Leone 52 8.50N 12.50W
Port MacDonnell Australia 66 38.03S140.46E
Port Macquarie Australia 67 31.28S152.25E
Port Maitland N.S. Canada 77 43.59N 66.09W
Port Maitland Ont. Canada 76 42.52N 79.34W
Portmarnock Rep. of Ire. 13 53.25N 6.09W
Port Menier Canada 77 49.49N 64.20W
Port Moresby P.N.G. 64 9.30S147.07E
Port Musgrave b. Australia 64 11.59S142.00E
Portnaguiran U.K. 12 58.15N 6.10W
Port Neill Australia 66 34.07S136.20E
Port Nelson Canada 75 57.03N 92.36W
Port Nolloth R.S.A. 56 29.16S 16.54E
Port Norris U.S.A. 85 39.15N 75.02W
Port-Nouveau Québec Canada 73 58.35N 65.59W
Porto Portugal 16 41.09N 8.37W
Pôrto Alegre Brazil 94 30.03S 51.10W
Porto Amboim Angola 54 10.45S 13.43E
Pôrto de Moz Brazil 91 1.45S 52.13W
Porto Esperança Brazil 94 19.36S 57.24W
Pôrto Feliz Brazil 94 23.11S 47.32W
Portoferraio Italy 18 42.49N 10.19E
Port of Ness U.K. 12 58.30N 6.13W
Pôrto Franco Brazil 91 6.21S 47.25W
Port of Spain Trinidad 87 10.38N 61.31W
Porto Grande Brazil 91 0.42N 51.24W
Portogruaro Italy 15 45.47N 12.50E
Pörtom Finland 22 62.42N 21.37E
Portomaggiore Italy 15 44.42N 11.48E
Porto Moniz Madeira Is. 95 32.52N 17.12W
Pôrto Murtinho Brazil 94 21.42S 57.52W
Porton U.K. 11 51.08N 1.44W
Pôrto Nacional Brazil 91 10.42S 48.25W
Porto-Novo Benin 53 6.30N 2.47E
Pôrto Primavera, Reprêsa resr. Brazil 94 21.50S 52.00W
Porto San Giorgio Italy 18 43.11N 13.48E
Porto Santo i. Madeira Is. 50 33.04N 16.20W
Porto Tolle Italy 15 44.56N 12.22E
Porto Torres Italy 18 40.49N 8.24E
Pôrto Valter Brazil 90 8.15S 72.45W
Porto Vecchio France 17 41.35N 9.16E
Pôrto Velho Brazil 90 8.45S 63.54W
Portoviejo Ecuador 90 1.07S 80.28W
Portpatrick U.K. 12 54.51N 5.07W
Port Phillip B. Australia 67 38.05S144.50E
Port Pirie Australia 66 33.11S138.01E
Port Radium Canada 72 66.05N118.02W
Portree U.K. 12 57.24N 6.12W
Port Renfrew Canada 74 48.30N124.20W
Portrush U.K. 13 55.12N 6.40W
Port Said see Būr Sa'īd Egypt 44
Port St. Joe U.S.A. 85 29.49N 85.19W
Port St. Louis France 17 43.25N 4.40E
Port Saunders Canada 77 50.39N 57.18W
Portsea Australia 67 38.19S144.43E
Port Shepstone R.S.A. 56 30.44S 30.27E
Port Simpson Canada 74 54.32N130.25W
Portsmouth U.K. 11 50.48N 1.06W
Portsmouth N.H. U.S.A. 84 43.04N 70.46W
Portsmouth Ohio U.S.A. 84 38.45N 82.59W
Portsmouth Va. U.S.A. 85 36.50N 76.20W
Portsoy U.K. 12 57.41N 2.41W
Port Stanley Canada 84 42.40N 81.13W
Portstewart U.K. 13 55.11N 6.43W
Port Sudan see Būr Sūdān Sudan 48
Port Talbot U.K. 11 51.35N 3.48W
Porttipahdan tekojärvi resr. Finland 22 68.08N 26.40E
Port Townsend U.S.A. 80 48.07N122.46W
Portugal Europe 16 39.30N 8.05W
Portumna Rep. of Ire. 9 53.06N 8.14W
Port Vendres France 17 42.31N 3.06E
Port Victoria Australia 66 34.30S137.30E
Port Wakefield Australia 66 34.12S138.11E
Port Warrender Australia 62 14.30S125.50E
Porvenir Chile 93 53.18S 70.22W
Porz Germany 14 50.53N 7.05E
Posada Italy 18 40.38N 9.43E
Posadas Argentina 92 27.25S 55.48W
Poschiavo Switz. 15 46.18N 10.04E
Posht r. Iran 43 29.09N 58.09E
Poso Indonesia 37 1.23S120.45E
Posse Brazil 94 14.05S 46.22W
Post U.S.A. 83 33.12N101.23W
Postavy U.S.S.R. 24 55.07N 26.50E
Poste-de-la-Baleine town Canada 76 55.20N 77.40W
Poste Maurice Cortier Algeria 50 22.18N 1.05E
Poste Weygand Algeria 50 24.29N 0.40E
Postmasburg R.S.A. 56 28.19S 23.03E
Postojna Yugo. 20 45.47N 14.13E
Postoli U.S.S.R. 21 52.30N 28.00E
Potchefstroom R.S.A. 56 26.42S 27.05E
Poteau U.S.A. 83 35.03N 94.37W
Potenza Italy 18 40.40N 15.47E
Potgietersrus R.S.A. 56 24.11S 29.00E
Poti r. Brazil 91 5.01S 42.48W
Poti U.S.S.R. 25 42.11N 41.41E
Potiskum Nigeria 53 11.40N 11.03E
Potomac r. U.S.A. 85 38.00N 76.18W
Potosí Bolivia 92 19.35S 65.45W
Potosí d. Bolivia 92 21.00S 67.00W
Potosi Cerro mtn. Mexico 83 24.50N100.15W
Pototan Phil. 37 10.54N122.38E
Potsdam Germany 20 52.24N 13.04E
Potsdam U.S.A. 84 44.40N 74.59W
Pottstown U.S.A. 85 40.15N 75.38W
Pouancé France 15 47.47N 1.11W
Poughkeepsie U.S.A. 85 41.43N 73.56W
Pouso Alegre Brazil 94 22.13S 45.49W
Pouté Senegal 50 15.42N 14.10W
Poŭthĭsăt Cambodia 34 12.27N103.50E
Povenets U.S.S.R. 24 62.52N 34.05E
Póvoa de Varzim Portugal 16 41.22N 8.46W
Povorino U.S.S.R. 25 51.12N 42.15E
Powder r. U.S.A. 80 46.44N105.26W
Powder River town U.S.A. 80 43.03N106.58W
Powell U.S.A. 80 44.45N108.46W
Powell, L. U.S.A. 80 37.25N110.45W
Powell River town Canada 74 49.22N124.31W
Powers U.S.A. 76 45.42N 87.31W
Powers Lake town U.S.A. 82 48.34N102.39W
Powys d. U.K. 11 52.26N 3.26W
Poyang Hu l. China 33 29.10N116.20E
Požarevac Yugo. 21 44.38N 21.12E
Poza Rica de Hidalgo Mexico 86 20.34N 97.26W
Poznań Poland 20 52.25N 16.53E
Pozoblanco Spain 16 38.23N 4.51W
Prachin Buri Thailand 34 14.02N101.23E
Prachuap Khiri Khan Thailand 34 11.50N 99.49E
Pradera Colombia 90 3.23N 76.11W
Prades France 17 42.38N 2.25E
Praestö Denmark 23 55.07N 12.03E
Prague see Praha Czech. 20
Praha Czech. 20 50.05N 14.25E
Prainha Amazonas Brazil 90 7.16S 60.23W
Prainha Para Brazil 91 1.48S 53.29W
Prairie City U.S.A. 80 44.28N118.43W
Prairie du Chien town U.S.A. 82 43.03N 91.09W
Prairie Village U.S.A. 82 39.01N 94.38W
Prang Ghana 52 8.02N 0.58W
Pratāpgarh India 40 24.02N 74.47E
Prato Italy 15 43.52N 11.06E
Pratt U.S.A. 83 37.39N 98.44W
Pravia Spain 16 43.30N 6.12W
Predazzo Italy 15 46.19N 11.36E
Pré-en-Pail France 15 48.27N 0.12W
Preesall U.K. 10 53.55N 2.58W
Pregel r. U.S.S.R. 21 54.41N 20.22E
Premer Australia 67 31.26S149.54E
Premier Canada 74 56.04N129.56W
Prentice U.S.A. 82 45.33N 90.17W
Prenzlau Germany 20 53.19N 13.52E
Preparis i. Burma 34 14.51N 93.38E
Přerov Czech. 21 49.27N 17.27E
Prescott Ariz. U.S.A. 81 34.33N112.28W
Prescott Ark. U.S.A. 83 33.48N 93.23W
Presho U.S.A. 82 43.54N100.04W
Presidencia Roque Sáenz Peña Argentina 92 26.50S 60.30W
Presidente Epitácio Brazil 94 21.56S 52.07W
Presidente Hermes Brazil 92 11.17S 61.55W
Presidente Prudente Brazil 94 22.09S 51.24W
Presidio U.S.A. 83 29.33N104.23W
Prešov Czech. 21 49.00N 21.15E

Prespa, L. Albania/Greece/Yugo. **19** 40.53N 21.02E
Presque Isle *town* Maine U.S.A. **84** 46.41N 68.01W
Prestea Ghana **52** 5.26N 2.07W
Presteigne U.K. **11** 52.17N 3.00W
Preston U.K. **10** 53.46N 2.42W
Preston Idaho U.S.A. **80** 42.06N111.53W
Preston Minn. U.S.A. **82** 43.40N 92.04W
Prestonpans U.K. **12** 55.57N 3.00W
Prestwick U.K. **12** 55.30N 4.36W
Prêto *r.* Brazil **94** 22.00S 43.21W
Pretoria R.S.A. **56** 25.43S 28.11E
Préveza Greece **19** 38.58N 20.43E
Prey Vêng Cambodia **34** 11.29N105.19E
Priboj Yugo. **19** 43.35N 19.31E
Příbram Czech. **20** 49.42N 14.00E
Price Md. U.S.A. **85** 39.06N 75.58W
Price Utah U.S.A. **80** 39.36N110.48W
Prichard U.S.A. **83** 30.44N 88.07W
Prieska R.S.A. **56** 29.40S 22.43E
Prijedor Yugo. **19** 44.59N 16.43E
Prikaspiyskaya Nizmennost *f.* U.S.S.R. **25** 47.00N 48.00E
Prilep Yugo. **19** 41.20N 21.32E
Priluki R.S.F.S.R. U.S.S.R. **24** 63.05N 42.05E
Priluki Ukr.S.S.R. U.S.S.R. **25** 50.35N 32.24E
Primorsk R.S.F.S.R. U.S.S.R. **24** 60.18N 28.35E
Primrose L. Canada **75** 54.55N109.45W
Primstal Germany **14** 49.33N 6.59E
Prince Albert Canada **75** 53.12N105.46W
Prince Albert R.S.A. **56** 33.14S 22.02E
Prince Albert Nat. Park Canada **75** 54.00N106.25W
Prince Albert Sd. Canada **72** 70.25N115.00W
Prince Alfred C. Canada **72** 74.30N125.00W
Prince Charles I. Canada **73** 67.50N 76.00W
Prince Edward Island *d.* Canada **77** 46.45N 63.00W
Prince Frederick U.S.A. **85** 38.33N 76.35W
Prince George Canada **74** 53.50N122.50W
Prince of Wales, C. U.S.A. **72** 66.00N168.30W
Prince of Wales I. Australia **64** 10.40S142.10E
Prince of Wales I. Canada **73** 73.00N 99.00W
Prince of Wales I. U.S.A. **74** 55.00N132.30W
Prince Patrick I. Canada **72** 77.00N120.00W
Prince Regent Inlet *str.* Canada **73** 73.00N 90.30W
Prince Rupert Canada **74** 54.09N130.20W
Princess Charlotte B. Australia **64** 14.25S144.00E
Princess Royal I. Canada **74** 53.00N128.40W
Princeton Ind. U.S.A. **84** 38.21N 87.33W
Princeton Ky. U.S.A. **85** 37.06N 87.55W
Princeton Mo. U.S.A. **82** 40.24N 93.35W
Princeton N.J. U.S.A. **85** 40.21N 74.40W
Príncipe *i.* São Tomé & Príncipe **53** 1.37N 7.27E
Príncipe da Beira Brazil **90** 12.23S 64.28W
Prinzapolca Nicaragua **87** 13.19N 83.35W
Priozersk U.S.S.R. **24** 61.01N 30.08E
Pripet Marshes *see* Polesye *f.* U.S.S.R. **21**
Pripyat *r.* U.S.S.R. **21** 51.08N 30.30E
Priština Yugo. **19** 42.39N 21.10E
Pritzwalk Germany **20** 53.09N 12.10E
Privas France **20** 44.44N 4.36E
Privolzhskaya Vozvyshennost *f.* U.S.S.R. **24** 53.15N 45.45E
Prizren Yugo. **19** 42.13N 20.42E
Probolinggo Indonesia **37** 7.45S113.09E
Proddatūr India **39** 14.44N 78.33E
Progreso Mexico **87** 21.20N 89.40W
Prokopyevsk U.S.S.R. **28** 53.55N 86.45E
Prome Burma **34** 18.50N 95.14E
Prophet *r.* Canada **74** 58.48N122.40W
Propriá Brazil **91** 10.15S 36.51W
Proserpine Australia **64** 20.24S148.34E
Prostějov Czech. **21** 49.29N 17.07E
Protection U.S.A. **83** 37.12N 99.29W
Provence-Côte d'Azur *d.* France **17** 43.45N 6.00E
Providence U.S.A. **84** 41.50N 71.25W
Providence Mts. U.S.A. **81** 34.55N115.35W
Providencia, Isla de *i.* Colombia **87** 13.21N 81.22W
Provins France **15** 48.34N 3.18E
Provo U.S.A. **80** 40.14N111.39W
Prozor Yugo. **21** 43.49N 17.37E
Prudhoe Bay *town* U.S.A. **72** 70.20N148.25W
Prüm Germany **14** 50.12N 6.25E
Prüm *r.* Germany **14** 49.50N 6.29E
Pruszcz Gdański Poland **21** 54.17N 18.40E
Pruszków Poland **21** 52.11N 20.48E
Prut *r.* Romania/U.S.S.R. **21** 45.29N 28.14E
Pruzhany U.S.S.R. **21** 52.23N 24.28E
Prydz B. Antarctica **96** 68.30S 74.00E
Pryor U.S.A. **83** 36.19N 95.19W
Przemyśl Poland **21** 49.48N 22.48E
Przeworsk Poland **21** 50.05N 22.29E
Przhevalsk U.S.S.R. **30** 42.31N 78.22E
Psará *i.* Greece **19** 38.34N 25.35E
Psel *r.* U.S.S.R. **25** 49.00N 33.30E
Pskov U.S.S.R. **24** 57.48N 28.00E
Pskovskoye, Ozero *l.* U.S.S.R. **24** 58.00N 27.55E
Ptich U.S.S.R. **21** 52.15N 28.49E
Ptich *r.* U.S.S.R. **21** 52.09N 28.52E
Ptolemais Greece **19** 40.31N 21.41E
Puán Argentina **93** 37.30S 62.45W
Pu'an China **33** 25.47N104.57E
Puapua W. Samoa **68** 13.34S172.12W
Pucallpa Peru **90** 8.21S 74.33W
Pucarani Bolivia **92** 16.23S 68.30W
Pucheng China **33** 27.56N118.32E
Pudasjärvi Finland **22** 65.25N 26.50E
Püdeh Tal *r.* Afghan. **40** 31.00N 61.50E
Pudozh U.S.S.R. **24** 61.50N 36.32E
Pudozhgora U.S.S.R. **24** 62.18N 35.54E
Puebla Mexico **86** 19.03N 98.10W
Puebla *d.* Mexico **86** 18.30N 98.00W
Pueblo U.S.A. **80** 38.16N104.37W
Pueblo Hundido Chile **92** 26.23S 70.03W
Puelches Argentina **93** 38.09S 65.58W
Puelén Argentina **93** 37.32S 67.38W
Puente Alta Chile **93** 33.37S 70.35W
Puente-Genil Spain **16** 37.24N 4.46W
Puerto Aisén Chile **93** 45.27S 72.58W
Puerto Ángel Mexico **86** 15.40N 96.29W
Puerto Armuelles Panama **87** 8.19N 82.15W
Puerto Ayacucho Venezuela **90** 5.39N 67.32W
Puerto Barrios Guatemala **87** 15.41N 88.32W
Puerto Bermúdez Peru **90** 10.20S 75.00W
Puerto Berrío Colombia **90** 6.28N 74.28W
Puerto Cabello Venezuela **90** 10.29N 68.02W
Puerto Cabezas Nicaragua **87** 14.02N 83.24W
Puerto Carreño Colombia **90** 6.08N 67.27W
Puerto Casado Paraguay **92** 22.20S 57.55W
Puerto Coig Argentina **93** 50.54S 69.15W
Puerto Cortés Costa Rica **87** 8.58N 83.32W
Puerto Cortés Honduras **87** 15.50N 87.55W
Puerto de Nutrias Venezuela **90** 8.07N 69.18W
Puerto de Santa María Spain **16** 36.36N 6.14W
Puerto Heath Bolivia **90** 12.30S 68.40W
Puerto Juárez Mexico **87** 21.26N 86.51W
Puerto La Cruz Venezuela **90** 10.14N 64.40W
Puerto Leguízamo Colombia **90** 0.12S 74.46W
Puertollano Spain **16** 38.41N 4.07W
Puerto Lobos Argentina **93** 42.01S 65.04W
Puerto Madryn Argentina **93** 42.46S 65.02W
Puerto Maldonado Peru **90** 12.37S 69.11W
Puerto Melendez Peru **90** 4.30S 77.30W
Puerto Montt Chile **93** 41.28S 73.00W
Puerto Natales Chile **93** 51.44S 72.31W
Puerto Páez Venezuela **90** 6.13N 67.28W
Puerto Peñasco Mexico **81** 31.20N113.33W
Puerto Pinasco Paraguay **94** 22.36S 57.53W
Puerto Plata Dom. Rep. **87** 19.48N 70.41W
Puerto Princesa Phil. **36** 9.46N118.45E
Puerto Quepos Costa Rica **87** 9.28N 84.10W
Puerto Rey Colombia **90** 8.48N 76.34W
Puerto Rico C. America **87** 18.20N 66.30W
Puerto Rico Trench Atlantic Oc. **87** 19.50N 66.00W
Puerto Saavedra Chile **93** 38.47S 73.24W
Puerto Santa Cruz Argentina **93** 50.03S 68.35W
Puerto Sastre Paraguay **94** 22.02S 58.00W
Puerto Siles Bolivia **92** 12.48S 65.05W
Puerto Tejado Colombia **90** 3.16N 76.22W
Puerto Vallarta Mexico **86**
Puerto Varas Chile **93** 41.20S 73.00W
Pugachev U.S.S.R. **24** 52.02N 48.49E
Puglia *d.* Italy **19** 41.00N 16.40E
Puisaye, Collines de la *hills* France **15** 47.34N 3.28E
Pujehun Sierra Leone **52** 7.23N 11.44W
Pukaki, L. New Zealand **60** 44.00S170.10E
Pukatawagan Canada **75** 55.45N101.20W
Pukekohe New Zealand **60** 37.12S174.56E
Pukeuri New Zealand **60** 45.02S171.02E
Pukhovichi U.S.S.R. **21** 53.28N 28.18E
Pula Yugo. **20** 44.52N 13.53E
Pulacayo Bolivia **92** 20.25S 66.41W
Pulaski Tenn. U.S.A. **85** 35.11N 87.02W
Pulaski Va. U.S.A. **85** 37.03N 80.47W
Puławy Poland **21** 51.25N 21.57E
Pulgaon India **41** 20.44N 78.20E
Pulkkila Finland **22** 64.16N 25.52E
Pullman U.S.A. **80** 46.44N117.10W
Pulog *mtn.* Phil. **37** 16.50N120.50E
Pulozero U.S.S.R. **24** 68.22N 33.15E
Pulpito, Punta *c.* Mexico **81** 26.31N111.28W
Pułtusk Poland **21** 52.42N 21.02E
Puma Tanzania **55** 5.02S 34.46E
Puma Yumco *l.* China **41** 28.35N 90.20E
Punaauia Tahiti **69** 17.38S149.36W
Punakha Bhutan **41** 27.37N 89.52E
Puncak Jaya *mtn.* Indonesia **37** 4.00S137.15E
Pūnch Jammu & Kashmir **40** 33.46N 74.06E
Pune India **38** 18.34N 73.58E
Punjab *d.* India **40** 30.45N 75.30E
Punjab *d.* Pakistan **40** 30.25N 72.30E
Puno Peru **90** 15.53S 70.03W
Punta Alta *town* Argentina **93** 38.50S 62.00W
Punta Arenas *town* Chile **93** 53.10S 70.56W
Puntabie Australia **66** 32.15S134.13E
Punta Delgada *town* Argentina **93** 42.43S 63.38W
Punta Gorda *town* Belize **87** 16.10N 88.45W
Punta Gorda *town* U.S.A. **85** 26.56N 82.01W
Puntarenas Costa Rica **87** 10.00N 84.50W
Punto Fijo Venezuela **90** 11.50N 70.16W
Puolanka Finland **22** 64.52N 27.40E
Puqi China **33** 29.40N113.52E
Puquio Peru **90** 14.44S 74.07W
Pur *r.* U.S.S.R. **28** 67.30N 75.30E
Pūranpur India **41** 28.31N 80.09E
Purari *r.* P.N.G. **37** 7.49S145.10E
Purcell U.S.A. **83** 35.01N 97.22W
Purgatoire *r.* U.S.A. **80** 38.04N103.10W
Puri India **41** 19.48N 85.51E
Purísima, Sierra de la *mts.* Mexico **83** 26.28N101.45W
Purli India **40** 18.51N 76.32E
Pūrna *r.* India **40** 19.07N 77.02E
Purnea India **41** 25.47N 87.31E
Purros Namibia **56** 18.38S 12.59E
Purūlia India **41** 23.20N 86.22E
Purus *r.* Brazil **90** 3.58S 61.25W
Purwakarta Indonesia **37** 6.30S107.25E
Purwodadi Indonesia **37** 7.05S110.53E
Purwokerto Indonesia **37** 7.28S109.09E
Purworejo Indonesia **37** 7.45S110.04E
Pusad India **41** 19.54N 77.35E
Pusan S. Korea **31** 35.05N129.02E
Pushkar India **40** 26.30N 74.33E
Pushkin U.S.S.R. **24** 59.43N 30.22E
Pushkino U.S.S.R. **25** 51.16N 47.09E
Püspökladány Hungary **21** 47.19N 21.07E
Pustoshka U.S.S.R. **24** 56.20N 29.20E
Putao Burma **34** 27.22N 97.27E
Putaruru New Zealand **60** 38.03S175.47E
Putian China **33** 25.29N119.04E
Puting, Tanjung *c.* Indonesia **36** 3.35S111.52E
Putoran, Gory *mts.* U.S.S.R. **29** 68.30N 96.00E
Putsonderwater R.S.A. **56** 29.14S 21.50E
Puttalam Sri Lanka **39** 8.02N 79.50E
Puttgarden Germany **20** 54.30N 11.13E
Putumayo *r.* Brazil **90** 3.05S 68.10W
Puulavesi *l.* Finland **23** 61.50N 26.42E
Puyallup U.S.A. **80** 47.11N122.18W
Puyang China **32** 35.40N115.02E
Puy de Dôme *mtn.* France **17** 45.46N 2.56E
Puysegur Pt. New Zealand **60** 46.10S166.35E
Pūzak, Jehīl-e *l.* Afghan. **40** 31.30N 61.45E
Pwani *d.* Tanzania **55** 7.00S 39.00E
Pweto Zaïre **55** 8.27S 28.52E
Pwllheli U.K. **10** 52.53N 4.25W
Pyaozero, Ozero *l.* U.S.S.R. **24** 66.00N 31.00E
Pyapon Burma **34** 16.15N 95.40E
Pyasina *r.* U.S.S.R. **29** 73.10N 84.55E
Pyatigorsk U.S.S.R. **25** 44.04N 43.06E
Pyhä *r.* Finland **22** 64.28N 24.13E
Pyhäjärvi *l.* Oulu Finland **22** 63.35N 25.57E
Pyhäjärvi *l.* Turku-Pori Finland **23** 61.00N 22.20E
Pyhäjoki Finland **22** 64.28N 24.14E
Pyinmana Burma **34** 19.45N 96.12E
Pyŏngyang N. Korea **31** 39.00N125.47E
Pyramid U.S.A. **80** 40.05N119.43W
Pyramid Hill *town* Australia **66** 36.03S144.24E
Pyramid Hills Canada **77** 57.35N 65.00W
Pyramid L. U.S.A. **80** 40.00N119.35W
Pyramids Egypt **48** 29.52N 31.00E
Pyrénées *mts.* France/Spain **17** 42.40N 0.30E
Pyrzyce Poland **20** 53.10N 14.55E
Pytteggja *mtn.* Norway **23** 62.13N 7.42E
Pyu Burma **34** 18.29N 96.26E

Q

Qaanaaq *see* Thule Greenland **73**
Qā'emshahr Iran **43** 36.28N 52.53E
Qagan Nur *l.* China **32** 43.30N114.35E
Qagbasêrag China **41** 30.51N 92.42E
Qagcaka China **41** 32.32N 81.52E
Qahā Egypt **44** 30.17N 31.12E
Qalāt Afghan. **40** 32.07N 66.54E
Qal'at Bīshah Saudi Arabia **48** 19.50N 42.36E
Qal 'eh Kāh Afghan. **40** 32.18N 61.31E
Qal'eh-ye Now Afghan **43** 34.58N 63.04E
Qal'eh-ye Sāber Afghan. **40** 34.02N 69.01E
Qallābāt Sudan **49** 12.58N 36.09E
Qalyūb Egypt **44** 30.11N 31.12E
Qamar, Ghubbat al *b.* Yemen **45** 16.00N 52.30E
Qamdo China **30** 31.11N 97.18E
Qamīnis Libya **48** 31.40N 20.01E
Qamr-ud-dīn Kārez Pakistan **40** 31.39N 68.25E
Qanâtir Muhammad 'Alî Egypt **44** 30.12N 31.08E
Qandahār Afghan. **40** 31.32N 65.30E
Qandahār *d.* Afghan. **40** 31.00N 65.30E
Qandala Somali Rep. **45** 11.23N 49.53E
Qaqortoq *see* Julianehåb Greenland **73**
Qarā, Jabal al *mts.* Oman **45** 17.15N 54.15E
Qârah Egypt **42** 27.37N 26.30E
Qārat Khazzī *hill* Libya **48** 21.26N 24.30E
Qardho Somali Rep. **45** 9.30N 49.03E
Qareh Sū Iran **43** 34.52N 51.25E
Qareh Sū *r.* Iran **43** 35.58N 56.25E
Qarqan He *r.* China **30** 40.56N 86.27E
Qarūn, Birkat *l.* Egypt **44** 29.30N 30.40E
Qaryat al Qaddāḥiyah Libya **51** 31.22N 15.14E
Qāsh *r.* Sudan **48** 16.48N 35.51E
Qasigiannguit *see* Christianshåb Greenland **73**
Qaşr al Farāfirah Egypt **42** 27.15N 28.10E
Qaşr al Qarābūllī Libya **51** 32.45N 13.43E
Qaşr-e Qand Iran **43** 26.13N 60.37E
Qa'ṭabah Yemen **45** 13.51N 44.42E
Qatanā Syria **44** 33.27N 36.04E
Qatar Asia **43** 25.20N 51.10E
Qaṭrānī, Jabal *mts.* Egypt **44** 29.40N 30.36E
Qattara Depression *see* Qaṭṭārah, Munkhafaḍ al *f.* Egypt **42**
Qaṭṭārah, Munkhafaḍ al *f.* Egypt **42** 29.40N 27.30E
Qawz Rajab Sudan **48** 16.04N 35.34E
Qāyen Iran **43** 33.44N 59.07E
Qaysān Sudan **49** 10.45N 34.48E
Qāzigund Jammu & Kashmir **40** 33.38N 75.09E
Qazvīn Iran **43** 36.16N 50.00E
Qeqertarsuaq *see* Godhavn Greenland **73**
Qeqertarsuatsiaat *see* Fiskenaesset Greenland **73**
Qeshm Iran **43** 26.58N 57.17E
Qeshm *i.* Iran **43** 26.48N 55.48E
Qezel Owzan *r.* Iran **43** 36.44N 49.27E
Qezi'ot Israel **44** 30.52N 34.28E
Qian'an China **32** 45.00N124.00E
Qianjiang China **33** 29.28N108.43E
Qianxi China **32** 40.10N118.19E
Qianyang China **33** 27.22N110.14E
Qiaotou China **32** 42.56N118.54E
Qidong Hunan China **33** 26.47N112.07E
Qidong Jiangsu China **33** 31.49N121.40E
Qiemo China **30** 38.08N 85.33E
Qijiang China **33** 29.00N106.40E
Qila Abdullāh Pakistan **40** 30.43N 66.38E
Qila Lādgasht Pakistan **40** 27.54N 62.57E
Qila Saifullāh Pakistan **40** 30.43N 68.21E
Qilian Shan *mts.* China **30** 38.30N 99.20E
Qimantag *mts.* China **30** 37.45N 89.40E
Qimen China **33** 29.50N117.38E
Qinā Egypt **42** 26.10N 32.43E
Qinā, Wādī *r.* Egypt **42** 26.07N 32.42E
Qingdao China **32** 36.02N120.25E
Qinghai *d.* China **41** 34.20N 91.00E
Qinghai Hu *l.* China **30** 36.40N100.00E
Qingjian China **32** 37.02N110.06E
Qingjiang China **33** 28.01N115.30E
Qing Jiang Shuiku *resr.* China **33** 30.00N112.12E
Qinglong Guizhou China **33** 25.47N105.12E
Qinglong Hebei China **32** 40.24N118.53E
Qingshui Jiang *r.* China **33** 28.08N110.06E
Qing Xian China **32** 38.35N116.48E
Qingxu China **32** 37.36N112.21E
Qingyang China **32** 36.03N107.52E
Qingyuan Guangdong China **33** 23.42N113.00E
Qingyuan Jilin China **32** 42.05N125.01E
Qingyuan Zhejiang China **33** 27.37N119.03E
Qing Zang Gaoyuan *f.* China **30** 33.40N 86.00E
Qinhuangdao China **32** 39.52N119.42E
Qin Ling *mts.* China **32** 33.30N109.00E
Qin Xian China **32** 36.45N112.41E
Qinyang China **32** 35.06N112.57E
Qinzhou China **33** 21.58N108.34E
Qionghai China **33** 19.12N110.31E
Qiongshan China **33** 19.59N110.30E
Qiongzhou Haixia *str.* China **33** 20.09N110.20E
Qipanshan China **32** 42.05N117.37E
Qiqihar China **31** 47.23N124.00E
Qira China **30** 37.02N 80.53E
Qiryat Ata Israel **44** 32.48N 35.06E
Qiryat Gat Israel **44** 31.37N 34.47E
Qiryat Shemona Israel **44** 33.13N 35.35E
Qishn Yemen **38** 15.25N 51.40E
Qiuxizhen China **33** 29.54N104.40E
Qi Xian Henan China **32** 35.35N114.08E
Qi Xian Henan China **32** 34.30N114.50E
Qom Iran **43** 34.40N 50.57E
Qonggyai China **41** 29.03N 91.41E
Qornet'es Sauda *mtn.* Lebanon **44** 34.17N 36.04E
Qoṭūr Iran **43** 38.28N 44.25E
Quairading Australia **63** 32.00S117.22E
Quakenbrück Germany **14** 52.41N 7.59E
Quakertown U.S.A. **85** 40.26N 75.21W
Qu'ali China **33** 29.46N117.15E
Quambatook Australia **66** 35.52S143.36E
Quambone Australia **67** 30.54S147.55E
Quang Ngai Vietnam **34** 15.09N108.50E
Quang Tri Vietnam **34** 16.44N107.10E
Quang Yen Vietnam **34** 20.56N106.49E
Quan Long Vietnam **34** 9.11N105.09E
Quannan China **33** 24.45N114.32E
Quantico U.S.A. **85** 38.31N 77.17W
Quanzhou Fujian China **33** 24.57N118.36E
Quanzhou Guang. Zhuang. China **33** 26.00N111.00E
Qu'Appelle *r.* Canada **75** 50.33N101.20W
Quaqtaq Canada **73** 61.05N 69.36W
Quaraí Brazil **93** 30.23S 56.27W
Quaraí *r.* Brazil **93** 30.12S 57.36W
Quarryville U.S.A. **85** 39.54N 76.10W
Quartu Sant'Elena Italy **18** 39.14N 9.11E
Quartzsite U.S.A. **81** 33.40N114.13W
Quatsino Sd. Canada **74** 50.42N127.58W
Qūchān Iran **43** 37.04N 58.29E
Queanbeyan Australia **67** 35.24S149.17E
Québec Canada **77** 46.50N 71.15W
Québec *d.* Canada **77** 51.20N 68.45W
Quebracho Uruguay **93** 31.57S 57.53W
Quedlinburg Germany **20** 51.48N 11.09E
Queen Anne U.S.A. **85** 38.55N 75.57W
Queen Charlotte Canada **74** 53.18N132.04W
Queen Charlotte Is. Canada **74** 53.00N132.00W
Queen Charlotte Sd. Canada **74** 51.30N129.30W
Queen Charlotte Str. Canada **74** 51.00N128.00W
Queen Elizabeth Is. Canada **73** 78.30N 99.00W
Queen Maud G. Canada **73** 68.30N 99.00W
Queen Maud Range *mts.* Antarctica **96** 86.20S165.00W
Queens Channel Australia **62** 14.46S129.24E
Queenscliff Australia **67** 38.17S144.42E
Queensland *d.* Australia **64** 23.30S144.00E
Queenstown Australia **65** 42.07S145.33E
Queenstown New Zealand **60** 45.03S168.41E
Queenstown R.S.A. **56** 31.52S 26.51E
Queenstown U.S.A. **85** 38.59N 76.09W
Queguay Grande *r.* Uruguay **93** 32.09S 58.09W
Queimadas Brazil **91** 10.58S 39.38W
Quela Angola **54** 9.18S 17.05E
Quelimane Mozambique **55** 17.53S 36.57E
Quemado U.S.A. **81** 34.20N108.30W
Quemoy *i.* China **33** 24.30N118.20E
Quentico Prov. Park Canada **76** 48.20N 91.30W
Quequén Argentina **93** 38.34S 58.42W
Querétaro Mexico **86** 20.38N100.23W
Querétaro *d.* Mexico **86** 21.03N100.00W
Querobabi Mexico **81** 30.03N111.01W
Queshan China **32** 32.48N114.01E
Quesnel Canada **74** 53.05N122.30W
Quesnel *r.* Canada **74** 52.58N122.29W
Quetta Pakistan **40** 30.12N 67.00E
Quettehou France **15** 49.36N 1.18W
Quevedo Ecuador **90** 0.59S 79.27W
Quezaltenango Guatemala **86** 14.50N 91.30W
Quezon City Phil. **37** 14.39N121.01E
Quibala Angola **54** 10.48S 14.56E
Quibaxi Angola **54** 8.34S 14.37E
Quibdo Colombia **90** 5.40N 76.38W
Quiberon France **17** 47.29N 3.07W
Quibocolo Angola **54** 6.20S 15.05E
Quicama Nat. Park Angola **54** 9.40S 13.30E
Quiet L. Canada **74** 61.05N133.05W
Quilán, C. Chile **93** 43.16S 74.27W
Quilengues Angola **54** 14.09S 14.04E
Quillabamba Peru **90** 12.50S 72.50W
Quillacollo Bolivia **92** 17.26S 66.17W
Quillota Chile **93** 32.53S 71.16W
Quilpie Australia **64** 26.37S144.15E
Quilpué Chile **93** 33.03S 71.27W
Quimbele Angola **54** 6.29S 16.25E
Quimilí Argentina **92** 27.35S 62.25W
Quimper France **17** 48.00N 4.06W
Quimperlé France **17** 47.52N 3.33W
Quincy Ill. U.S.A. **82** 39.56N 91.23W
Quincy Wash. U.S.A. **80** 47.14N119.51W
Qui Nhon Vietnam **34** 13.47N109.11E
Quintanar de la Orden Spain **16** 39.36N 3.05W
Quintana Roo *d.* Mexico **87** 19.00N 88.00W
Quinter U.S.A. **82** 39.04N100.14W
Quinto Spain **16** 41.25N 0.30W
Quinzau Angola **54** 6.51S 12.46E
Quionga Mozambique **55** 10.37S 40.31E
Quiriguá *ruins* Guatemala **87** 15.20N 89.25W
Quirimbo Angola **54** 10.41S 14.16E
Quirindi Australia **67** 31.30S150.42E
Quiros, C. Vanuatu **68** 14.55S167.01E
Quissanga Mozambique **55** 12.24S 40.33E
Quissico Mozambique **57** 24.42S 34.44E
Quitapa Angola **54** 10.30S 18.16E
Quiterajo Mozambique **55** 11.46S 40.25E
Quito Ecuador **90** 0.14S 78.30W
Qu Jiang *r.* China **33** 30.02N106.20E
Qumigxung China **41** 30.53N 86.38E
Quorn Australia **66** 32.20S138.02E
Qurayyah, Wādī *r.* Egypt **44** 30.26N 34.01E
Qurdūd Sudan **49** 10.17N 29.56E
Qurlurtuuq Canada **72** 67.49N115.12W
Qū' Wishām *f.* Oman **45** 18.55N 55.55E
Qu Xian China **33** 28.59N118.56E
Quxian China **33** 30.50N106.54E
Qūzū China **41** 29.21N 90.39E

R

Raahe Finland **22** 64.41N 24.29E
Raalte Neth. **14** 52.22N 6.17E
Raasay *i.* U.K. **12** 57.25N 6.05W
Rába *r.* Hungary **21** 47.42N 17.38E
Raba Indonesia **36** 8.27S118.45E
Rabak Sudan **49** 13.09N 32.44E
Rabang China **41** 33.03N 80.29E
Rabat Morocco **50** 34.02N 6.51W
Rabbit Flat *town* Australia **62** 20.10S129.53E
Rabbitskin *r.* Canada **74** 61.47N120.42W
Rābor Iran **43** 29.18N 56.56E
Rabyānah Libya **48** 24.14N 21.59E
Rabyānah, Şaḥrā' *f.* Libya **51** 24.30N 21.00E
Racconigi Italy **15** 44.46N 9.46E
Race, C. Canada **77** 46.40N 53.10W
Rach Gia Vietnam **34** 10.02N105.05E
Racibórz Poland **21** 50.06N 18.13E
Racine U.S.A. **82** 42.42N 87.50W
Rădăuţi Romania **21** 47.51N 25.55E
Radebeul Germany **20** 51.06N 13.41E
Radekhov U.S.S.R. **21** 50.18N 24.35E
Radford U.S.A. **85** 37.07N 80.34W
Rādhanpur India **40** 23.50N 71.36E
Radium Hill *town* Australia **66** 32.30S140.32E
Radium Hot Springs *town* Canada **74** 50.48N116.12W
Radom Poland **21** 51.26N 21.10E
Radomir Bulgaria **19** 42.32N 22.56E
Radomsko Poland **21** 51.05N 19.25E
Radomyshl U.S.S.R. **21** 50.30N 29.14E
Radöy *i.* Norway **23** 60.38N 5.05E
Radstock U.K. **11** 51.17N 2.25W
Radstock, C. Australia **66** 33.11S134.21E
Radville Canada **75** 49.27N104.17W
Raḍwá, Jabal *mtn.* Saudi Arabia **42** 24.36N 38.18E
Rae Canada **74** 62.50N116.03W
Rāe Bareli India **41** 26.13N 81.14E
Raeren Germany **14** 50.41N 6.07E
Raeside, L. Australia **63** 29.30S122.00E
Rafaela Argentina **92** 31.16S 61.44W
Rafaḥ Egypt **44** 31.18N 34.15E
Rafai C.A.R. **49** 4.58N 23.56E
Raffili Mission Sudan **49** 6.53N 27.58E
Rafsanjān Iran **38** 30.24N 56.00E
Rafsanjān Iran **43** 30.24N 56.00E
Raga Sudan **49** 8.28N 25.41E
Ragged, Mt. Australia **63** 33.27S123.27E
Ragunda Sweden **22** 63.06N 16.23E
Ragusa Italy **18** 36.56N 14.44E
Raha Indonesia **37** 4.50S122.43E
Raḥá, Ḥarrat ar *f.* Saudi Arabia **44** 28.00N 36.35E
Rahad *r.* Sudan **48** 14.28N 33.31E
Rahad al Bardī Sudan **49** 11.18N 23.53E
Rahīm Ki Bāzār Pakistan **40** 24.19N 69.09E
Rahīmyār Khān Pakistan **40** 28.25N 70.18E
Raiatea *i.* Îs. de la Société **69** 16.50S151.25W

Rāichūr India **38** 16.15N 77.20E
Raiganj India **41** 25.37N 88.07E
Raigarh India **41** 21.54N 83.24E
Rainbow Australia **66** 35.56S142.01E
Rainelle U.S.A. **85** 37.58N 80.47W
Rainier, Mt. U.S.A. **80** 46.52N121.46W
Rainy L. Canada / U.S.A. **76** 48.42N 93.10W
Rainy River *town* Canada **76** 48.43N 94.29W
Raipur India **41** 21.14N 81.38E
Raipur Uplands *mts.* India **41** 20.45N 82.30E
Rairākhol India **41** 21.03N 84.23E
Ra'is Saudi Arabia **42** 23.35N 38.36E
Raisen India **41** 23.20N 77.48E
Raivavae *i.* Pacific Oc. **69** 23.52S147.40W
Rājahmundry India **39** 17.01N 81.52E
Rajāj Sudan **49** 10.55N 24.43E
Rajang *r.* Malaysia **36** 2.10N112.45E
Rājanpur Pakistan **40** 29.06N 70.19E
Rājapālaiyam India **38** 9.26N 77.36E
Rājasthān *d.* India **40** 26.15N 74.00E
Rājasthān Canal India **40** 31.10N 75.00E
Rājbāri Bangla. **41** 23.46N 89.39E
Rāj Gāngpur India **41** 22.11N 84.36E
Rājgarh Madhya P. India **40** 23.56N 76.58E
Rājgarh Rāj. India **40** 27.14N 76.38E
Rājgarh Rāj. India **40** 28.38N 75.23E
Rājkot India **40** 22.18N 70.47E
Rāj-Nāndgaon India **41** 21.06N 81.02E
Rājpīpla India **40** 21.47N 73.34E
Rājpur India **40** 21.56N 75.08E
Rājshāhi Bangla. **41** 24.22N 88.36E
Rājula India **40** 21.01N 71.34E
Rakahanga Atoll Cook Is. **68** 10.03S161.06W
Rakaia New Zealand **60** 43.45S172.01E
Rakaia *r.* New Zealand **60** 43.52S172.13E
Raka Zangbo *r.* China **41** 29.24N 87.58E
Rakhni Pakistan **40** 30.03N 69.55E
Rakhov U.S.S.R. **21** 48.02N 24.10E
Rakhshān *r.* Pakistan **40** 27.10N 63.25E
Rakitnoye U.S.S.R. **21** 51.18N 27.10E
Rakops Botswana **56** 21.00S 24.32E
Rakov U.S.S.R. **21** 53.58N 26.59E
Rakulka U.S.S.R. **24** 62.19N 46.52E
Råkvåg Norway **22** 63.47N 10.10E
Rakvere U.S.S.R. **24** 59.22N 26.28E
Raleigh U.S.A. **85** 35.46N 78.39W
Raleigh B. U.S.A. **85** 35.47N 76.09W
Ralik Chain *is.* Pacific Oc. **68** 8.00N168.00E
Ram *r.* Canada **74** 62.01N123.41W
Rama Nicaragua **87** 12.09N 84.15W
Rāmah Saudi Arabia **43** 25.33N 47.08E
Rām Allāh Jordan **44** 31.55N 35.12E
Ramallo Argentina **93** 33.28S 60.02W
Rāmānuj Ganj India **41** 23.48N 83.42E
Ramat Gan Israel **44** 32.05N 34.48E
Rambau, Lac *l.* Canada **77** 53.40N 70.10W
Rambouillet France **15** 48.39N 1.50E
Rām Dās India **40** 31.58N 74.55E
Rame Head Australia **67** 37.50S149.25E
Rame Head U.K. **11** 50.18N 4.13W
Ramelton Rep. of Ire. **13** 55.02N 7.40W
Rāmgarh Bangla. **41** 22.59N 91.43E
Rāmgarh Bihār India **41** 23.38N 85.31E
Rāmgarh Rāj. India **40** 27.15N 75.11E
Rāmgarh Rāj. India **40** 27.22N 70.30E
Rāmhormoz Iran **43** 31.14N 49.37E
Ramillies Belgium **14** 50.39N 4.56E
Ramingstein Austria **20** 47.04N 13.50E
Ramis *r.* Ethiopia **49** 7.59N 41.34E
Ramla Israel **44** 31.56N 34.52E
Ramlu *mtn.* Ethiopia **49** 13.20N 41.45E
Rāmnagar India **41** 25.17N 83.02E
Ramo Ethiopia **49** 6.50N 41.15E
Ramona Calif. U.S.A. **81** 33.08N116.52W
Ramona Okla. U.S.A. **83** 36.32N 95.55W
Ramore Canada **76** 48.30N 80.25W
Ramos Arizpe Mexico **83** 25.33N100.58W
Rāmpur Himachal P. India **41** 31.27N 77.38E
Rāmpur Uttar P. India **41** 28.49N 79.02E
Rampura India **40** 24.28N 75.26E
Ramree I. Burma **34** 19.06N 93.48E
Ramsey England U.K. **11** 52.27N 0.06W
Ramsey I.o.M. U.K. **10** 54.19N 4.23W
Ramsey L. Canada **76** 47.10N 82.18W
Ramsgate U.K. **11** 51.20N 1.25E
Rāmshīr Iran **43** 30.54N 49.24E
Ramsjö Sweden **23** 62.11N 15.39E
Rāmtek India **41** 21.24N 79.20E
Ramu *r.* P.N.G. **37** 4.00S144.40E
Ramusio, Lac *l.* Canada **77** 55.04N 63.40W
Ranau Malaysia **36** 5.58N116.41E
Rancagua Chile **93** 34.10S 70.45W
Rancheria *r.* Canada **74** 60.13N129.07W
Rānchī India **41** 23.21N 85.20E
Rand Australia **67** 35.34S146.35E
Randalstown U.K. **13** 54.45N 6.20W
Rānder India **40** 21.14N 72.47E
Randers Denmark **23** 56.28N 10.03E
Randolph Kans. U.S.A. **82** 39.27N 96.44W
Randsburg U.S.A. **81** 35.22N117.39W
Randsfjorden *l.* Norway **23** 60.25N 10.24E
Råne *r.* Sweden **22** 65.52N 22.19E
Råneå Sweden **22** 65.52N 22.18E
Rāner India **40** 28.53N 73.17E
Ranfurly New Zealand **60** 45.08S170.08E
Rangdong China **32** 32.51N112.18E
Rangely U.S.A. **80** 40.05N108.48W
Ranger U.S.A. **85** 38.07N 82.10W
Rangia India **41** 26.28N 91.38E
Rangiora New Zealand **60** 43.18S172.38E
Rangiroa *i.* Pacific Oc. **69** 15.00S147.40W
Rangitaiki *r.* New Zealand **60** 37.55S176.50E
Rangkasbitung Indonesia **37** 6.21S106.12E
Rangoon Burma **34** 16.47N 96.10E
Rangpur Bangla. **41** 25.45N 89.15E
Rāniganj India **41** 23.37N 87.08E
Rānīkhet India **41** 29.39N 79.25E
Rāniwāra India **40** 24.45N 72.13E
Rankin Inlet *town* Canada **73** 62.52N 92.00W
Rankins Springs *town* Australia **67** 33.52S146.18E
Rannoch, Loch U.K. **12** 56.41N 4.20W
Rann of Kachchh *f.* India **40** 23.50N 69.50E
Ranohira Madagascar **57** 22.29S 45.24E
Rano Kao *mtn.* I. de Pascua **69** 27.11S109.27W
Ranong Thailand **34** 9.59N 98.40E
Rantauprapat Indonesia **36** 2.05N 99.46E
Rantekombola *mtn.* Indonesia **36** 3.30S119.58E
Rao Co *mtn.* Laos **34** 18.10N105.25E
Raoping China **33** 23.45N117.05E
Raoul *i.* Pacific Oc. **68** 29.15S177.55W
Rapa *i.* Pacific Oc. **69** 27.35S144.20W
Rapallo Italy **15** 44.20N 9.14E
Rāpar India **40** 23.34N 70.38E
Rapid Bay *town* Australia **66** 35.33S138.09E
Rapid City U.S.A. **82** 44.05N103.14W
Raquette Lake *town* U.S.A. **84** 43.49N 74.41W
Rarotonga *i.* Cook Is. **68** 21.14S159.46W
Ra's al Ḥadd *c.* Oman **38** 22.32N 59.49E
Ra's al Khaymah U.A.E. **43** 25.48N 55.56E
Ra's al Unūf Libya **51** 30.31N 18.34E
Ra's an Nabq *town* Egypt **44** 29.36N 34.51E
Ra's an Naqb *town* Jordan **44** 30.30N 35.29E
Ras Dashen *mtn.* Ethiopia **49** 13.20N 38.10E
Rās Ghârib Egypt **44** 28.22N 33.04E
Rashād Sudan **49** 11.51N 31.04E
Rashid Egypt **44** 31.25N 30.25E
Rashid Qal 'eh Afghan. **40** 31.31N 67.31E
Rasht Iran **43** 37.18N 49.38E
Raška Yugo. **19** 43.17N 20.37E
Rās Koh *mtn.* Pakistan **40** 28.50N 65.12E
Rason L. Australia **63** 28.46S124.20E
Rasra India **41** 25.51N 83.51E
Ratak Chain *is.* Pacific Oc. **68** 8.00N172.00E
Ratangarh India **40** 28.05N 74.36E
Rat Buri Thailand **34** 13.30N 99.50E
Ratcatchers L. Australia **66** 32.40S143.13E
Rāth India **41** 25.35N 79.34E
Rathcormack Rep. of Ire. **13** 52.05N 8.18W
Rathdrum Rep. of Ire. **13** 52.56N 6.15W
Rathenow Germany **20** 52.37N 12.21E
Rathlin I. U.K. **13** 55.17N 6.15W
Rath Luirc Rep. of Ire. **13** 52.21N 8.41W
Rathmullen Rep. of Ire. **13** 55.06N 7.32W
Ratlām India **40** 23.19N 75.04E
Ratnāgiri India **38** 16.59N 73.18E
Ratno U.S.S.R. **21** 51.40N 24.32E
Ratodero Pakistan **40** 27.48N 68.18E
Raton U.S.A. **80** 36.54N104.24W
Rattlesnake Range *mts.* U.S.A. **80** 42.45N107.10W
Rattray Head U.K. **12** 57.37N 1.50W
Rättvik Sweden **23** 60.53N 15.06E
Rauch Argentina **93** 36.47S 59.05W
Raufoss Norway **23** 60.43N 10.37E
Raul Soares Brazil **94** 20.04S 42.27W
Rauma Finland **23** 61.08N 21.30E
Rauma *r.* Norway **22** 62.32N 7.43E
Raung, Gunung *mtn.* Indonesia **37** 8.07S114.03E
Raurkela India **41** 22.13N 84.53E
Rautas Sweden **22** 68.00N 19.55E
Ravalgaon India **40** 20.38N 74.25E
Rāvar Iran **43** 31.14N 56.51E
Rava-Russkaya U.S.S.R. **21** 50.15N 23.36E
Ravena U.S.A. **84** 42.29N 73.49W
Ravenna Italy **15** 44.25N 12.12E
Ravensburg Germany **20** 47.47N 9.37E
Ravenshoe Australia **64** 17.37S145.29E
Ravensthorpe Australia **63** 33.35S120.02E
Rāver India **40** 21.15N 76.05E
Ravi *r.* Pakistan **38** 30.30N 72.13E
Rawaki *i.* Kiribati **68** 3.43S170.43W
Rāwalpindi Pakistan **40** 33.36N 73.04E
Rawāndūz Iraq **43** 36.38N 44.32E
Rawdon Canada **77** 46.03N 73.44W
Rawene New Zealand **60** 35.24S173.30E
Rawicz Poland **20** 51.37N 16.52E
Rawlinna Australia **63** 31.00S125.21E
Rawlins U.S.A. **80** 41.47N107.14W
Rawson Argentina **93** 34.40S 60.02W
Raxaul India **41** 26.59N 84.51E
Ray U.S.A. **82** 48.21N103.10W
Ray, C. Canada **77** 47.40N 59.18W
Raya *mtn.* Indonesia **36** 0.45S112.45E
Rāyagada India **41** 19.10N 83.25E
Rāyen Iran **43** 29.34N 57.26E
Raymond Canada **74** 49.30N112.35W
Raymond U.S.A. **80** 46.41N123.44W
Raymond Terrace Australia **67** 32.47S151.45E
Raymondville U.S.A. **83** 26.29N 97.47W
Rayong Thailand **34** 12.43N101.20E
Razan Iran **43** 35.22N 49.02E
Razdelnaya U.S.S.R. **21** 46.50N 30.02E
Razgrad Bulgaria **21** 43.32N 26.30E
Ré, Île de *i.* France **17** 46.10N 1.26W
Reading U.K. **11** 51.27N 0.57W
Reading U.S.A. **85** 40.20N 75.56W
Realicó Argentina **93** 35.02S 64.14W
Reay Forest *f.* U.K. **12** 58.17N 4.48W
Rebecca, L. Australia **63** 30.07S122.32E
Rebi Indonesia **37** 6.24S134.07E
Rebiana Sand Sea *see* Rabyānah, Ṣaḥrā' *f.* Libya **51**
Reboly U.S.S.R. **24** 63.50N 30.49E
Recalde Argentina **93** 36.39S 61.05W
Rechāh Lām Afghan. **40** 34.58N 70.51E
Recherche, Archipelago of the *is.* Australia **63** 34.05S122.45E
Rechitsa U.S.S.R. **21** 52.21N 30.24E
Recife Brazil **91** 8.06S 34.53W
Recklinghausen Germany **14** 51.36N 7.11E
Reconquista Argentina **92** 29.08S 59.38W
Recreo Argentina **92** 29.20S 65.04W
Red *r.* Canada **75** 50.20N 96.50W
Red *r.* U.S.A. **83** 31.00N 91.40W
Red *r. see* Hong Hà *r.* Vietnam **34**
Red Bank U.S.A. **85** 40.21N 74.03W
Red Basin *f. see* Sichuan Pendi *f.* China **33**
Red Bay *town* Canada **77** 51.44N 56.45W
Red Bluff U.S.A. **80** 40.11N122.15W
Redcar U.K. **10** 54.37N 1.04W
Red Cliffs *town* Australia **66** 34.22S142.13E
Red Cloud U.S.A. **82** 40.04N 98.31W
Red Deer Canada **74** 52.20N113.50W
Red Deer *r.* Canada **75** 50.56N109.54W
Redding U.S.A. **80** 40.35N122.24W
Redditch U.K. **11** 52.18N 1.57W
Rede *r.* U.K. **10** 55.08N 2.13W
Redfield U.S.A. **82** 44.53N 98.31W
Redhill *town* Australia **66** 33.34S138.12E
Red Indian L. Canada **77** 48.40N 56.50W
Red L. U.S.A. **79** 48.00N 95.00W
Red Lake *town* Canada **75** 51.03N 93.49W
Redlands U.S.A. **81** 34.03N117.11W
Red Lion U.S.A. **85** 39.54N 76.36W
Red Lodge U.S.A. **80** 45.11N109.15W
Redmond U.S.A. **80** 44.17N121.11W
Red Oak U.S.A. **82** 41.01N 95.14W
Redondela Spain **16** 42.15N 8.38W
Redondo Portugal **16** 38.39N 7.33W
Redondo Beach *town* U.S.A. **81** 33.51N118.23W
Red Rock Canada **74** 53.39N122.41W
Redrock U.S.A. **81** 32.35N111.19W
Redruth U.K. **11** 50.14N 5.14W
Red Sea Africa / Asia **45** 20.00N 39.00E
Redstone Canada **74** 52.13N123.50W
Red Sucker L. Canada **75** 54.09N 93.40W
Red Volta *r.* Ghana **52** 10.32N 0.31W
Redwater Alta. Canada **74** 53.55N113.06W
Red Wing U.S.A. **82** 44.33N 92.31W
Redwood City U.S.A. **80** 37.29N122.13W
Ree, Lough Rep. of Ire. **13** 53.31N 7.58W
Reed City U.S.A. **84** 43.54N 85.31W
Reeder U.S.A. **82** 46.06N102.57W
Reedsport U.S.A. **80** 43.42N124.06W
Reefton New Zealand **60** 42.07S171.52E
Reese *r.* U.S.A. **80** 40.39N116.54W
Reftele Sweden **23** 57.11N 13.35E
Refuge Cove *town* Canada **74** 50.07N124.50W
Refugio U.S.A. **83** 28.18N 97.17W
Rega *r.* Poland **20** 54.10N 15.18E
Regensburg Germany **20** 49.01N 12.07E
Reggane Algeria **50** 26.42N 0.10E
Reggio Calabria Italy **18** 38.07N 15.38E
Reggio Emilia-Romagna Italy **15** 44.40N 10.37E
Reghin Romania **21** 46.47N 24.42E
Regina Canada **75** 50.25N104.39W
Regiwar Pakistan **40** 25.57N 65.44E
Regnéville France **15** 49.01N 1.33W
Rehoboth Namibia **56** 23.19S 17.10E
Rehoboth B. U.S.A. **85** 38.40N 75.06W
Rehoboth Beach *town* U.S.A. **85** 38.43N 75.05W
Rehovot Israel **44** 31.54N 34.46E
Reidsville U.S.A. **85** 36.21N 79.40W
Reigate U.K. **11** 51.14N 0.13W
Reims France **15** 49.15N 4.02E
Reindeer L. Canada **75** 57.15N102.40W
Reinosa Spain **16** 43.01N 4.09W
Reisterstown U.S.A. **85** 39.28N 76.50W
Relizane Algeria **51** 35.45N 0.33E
Remanso Brazil **91** 9.41S 42.04W
Remarkable, Mt. Australia **66** 32.48S138.10E
Rembang Indonesia **37** 6.45S111.22E
Remeshk Iran **43** 26.52N 58.46E
Remich Lux. **14** 49.34N 6.23E
Remiremont France **17** 48.01N 6.35E
Remscheid Germany **14** 51.10N 7.11E
Rena Norway **23** 61.08N 11.22E
Rendsburg Germany **20** 54.19N 9.39E
Renfrew Canada **76** 45.28N 76.41W
Rengat Indonesia **36** 0.26S102.35E
Rengo Chile **93** 34.25S 70.52W
Renheji China **33** 31.56N115.07E
Reni India **40** 28.41N 75.02E
Reni U.S.S.R. **21** 45.28N 28.17E
Renkum Neth. **14** 51.59N 5.46E
Renmark Australia **66** 34.10S140.45E
Rennell Sd. Canada **74** 53.23N132.35W
Renner Springs *town* Australia **64** 18.20S133.48E
Rennes France **15** 48.06N 1.40W
Reno *r.* Italy **15** 44.36N 12.17E
Reno U.S.A. **80** 39.31N119.48W
Renton U.S.A. **80** 47.30N122.11W
Ren Xian China **32** 37.07N114.41E
Réo Burkina **52** 12.20N 2.27W
Repki U.S.S.R. **21** 51.47N 31.06E
Republic Wash. U.S.A. **80** 48.39N118.44W
Republican *r.* U.S.A. **82** 39.03N 96.48W
Republic of Ireland Europe **13** 53.00N 8.00W
Republic of South Africa Africa **56** 28.30S 24.50E
Repulse B. Australia **64** 20.36S148.43E
Repulse Bay *town* Canada **73** 66.35N 86.20W
Requa U.S.A. **80** 41.34N124.05W
Requena Peru **90** 5.05S 73.52W
Requena Spain **16** 39.29N 1.08W
Reserve Canada **75** 52.28N102.39W
Resistencia Argentina **92** 27.28S 59.00W
Reşiţa Romania **21** 45.17N 21.53E
Resolute Canada **73** 74.40N 95.00W
Resolution I. Canada **73** 61.30N 65.00W
Resolution I. New Zealand **60** 45.40S166.30E
Restigouche *r.* Canada **77** 48.04N 66.20W
Rethel France **15** 49.31N 4.22E
Réthimnon Greece **19** 35.22N 24.29E
Reus Spain **16** 41.10N 1.06E
Reusel Neth. **14** 51.21N 5.09E
Reutlingen Germany **20** 48.30N 9.13E
Reutte Austria **20** 47.29N 10.43E
Revda U.S.S.R. **24** 56.49N 59.58E
Revelstoke Canada **74** 51.00N118.00W
Revilla Gigedo, Islas de *is.* Mexico **86** 19.00N111.00W
Revillagigedo I. U.S.A. **74** 55.50N131.20W
Revin France **14** 49.58N 4.40E
Revue *r.* Mozambique **57** 19.58S 34.40E
Rewa India **41** 24.32N 81.18E
Rewāri India **40** 28.11N 76.37E
Rexburg U.S.A. **80** 43.49N111.47W
Rexford U.S.A. **80** 48.53N115.13W
Rey Iran **43** 35.35N 51.27E
Reykjavík Iceland **22** 64.09N 21.58W
Reynosa Mexico **83** 26.07N 98.18W
Rezé France **17** 47.12N 1.34W
Rēzekne U.S.S.R. **24** 56.30N 27.22E
Rhayader U.K. **11** 52.19N 3.30W
Rheden Neth. **14** 52.01N 6.02E
Rhein *r.* Europe **14** 51.53N 6.03E
Rheinbach Germany **14** 50.39N 6.59E
Rheine Germany **14** 52.17N 7.26E
Rheinland-Pfalz *d.* Germany **14** 50.05N 7.09E
Rhenen Neth. **14** 51.58N 5.34E
Rhine *see* Rhein *r.* Europe **14**
Rhinebeck U.S.A. **85** 41.56N 73.55W
Rhinelander U.S.A. **82** 45.39N 89.23W
Rhino Camp *town* Uganda **55** 2.58N 31.20E
Rhir, Cap *c.* Morocco **50** 30.38N 9.55W
Rho Italy **15** 45.32N 9.02E
Rhode Island *d.* U.S.A. **84** 41.40N 71.30W
Rhodes *i. see* Ródhos *i.* Greece **19**
Rhodopi Planina *mts.* Bulgaria **19** 41.35N 24.35E
Rhondda U.K. **11** 51.39N 3.30W
Rhône *r.* France **17** 43.25N 4.45E
Rhône-Alpes *d.* France **17** 45.20N 5.45E
Rhosneigr U.K. **10** 53.14N 4.31W
Rhum *i.* U.K. **12** 57.00N 6.20W
Rhyl U.K. **10** 53.19N 3.29W
Riachão Brazil **91** 7.22S 46.37W
Riāng India **41** 27.32N 92.56E
Riāsi Jammu & Kashmir **40** 33.05N 74.50E
Riau *d.* Indonesia **36** 0.00 102.35E
Riau, Kepulauan *is.* Indonesia **36** 0.50N104.00E
Ribadeo Spain **16** 43.32N 7.04W
Ribarroja, Embalse de *resr.* Spain **16** 41.12N 0.20E
Ribauè Mozambique **55** 14.57S 38.27E
Ribble *r.* U.K. **10** 53.45N 2.44W
Ribe Denmark **23** 55.21N 8.46E
Ribeauvillé France **17** 48.12N 7.19E
Ribécourt France **15** 49.31N 2.55E
Ribeirão Prêto Brazil **94** 21.09S 47.48W
Ribérac France **17** 45.14N 0.22E
Riberalta Bolivia **92** 10.59S 66.06W
Ribnitz-Damgarten Germany **20** 54.15N 12.28E
Ribstone Creek *r.* Canada **75** 52.51N110.05W
Riccione Italy **15** 43.59N 12.39E
Rice U.S.A. **81** 34.06N114.50W
Rice Lake *town* U.S.A. **82** 45.30N 91.43W
Richard's Bay *town* R.S.A. **57** 28.47S 32.06E
Richardson *r.* Canada **75** 58.30N111.30W
Richardson U.S.A. **83** 32.57N 96.44W
Richelieu *r.* Canada **77** 46.03N 73.07W
Richfield Idaho U.S.A. **80** 43.03N114.09W
Richfield Utah U.S.A. **80** 38.46N112.05W
Rich Hill *town* U.S.A. **83** 38.06N 94.22W
Richibucto Canada **77** 46.41N 64.52W
Richland U.S.A. **80** 46.17N119.18W
Richmond Qld. Australia **64** 20.44S143.08E
Richmond Ont. Canada **77** 45.11N 75.50W
Richmond Que. Canada **77** 45.40N 72.09W
Richmond New Zealand **60** 41.20S173.10E
Richmond C.P. R.S.A. **56** 31.24S 23.56E
Richmond U.K. **10** 54.24N 1.43W
Richmond Ind. U.S.A. **84** 39.50N 84.51W
Richmond Utah U.S.A. **80** 41.55N111.48W
Richmond Va. U.S.A. **85** 37.34N 77.27W
Richmond Hill *town* Canada **76** 43.52N 79.27W
Richmond Range *mts.* Australia **67** 29.00S152.48E
Ricobayo, Embalse de *resr.* Spain **16** 41.40N 5.50W
Ridderkerk Neth. **14** 51.53N 4.39E
Rideau *r.* Canada **77** 45.27N 75.42W
Rideau Lakes Canada **76** 44.40N 76.10W
Ridgway U.S.A. **84** 41.26N 78.44W
Riding Mtn. Canada **75** 50.37N 99.50W
Riding Mtn. Nat. Park Canada **75** 50.55N100.25W
Ried Austria **20** 48.13N 13.30E
Riemst Belgium **14** 50.49N 5.38E
Riesa Germany **20** 51.18N 13.18E
Rieti Italy **18** 42.24N 12.53E
Rifle U.S.A. **80** 39.32N107.47W
Rift Valley *d.* Kenya **55** 1.00N 36.00E
Riga U.S.S.R. **23** 56.53N 24.08E
Riga, G. of *see* Rīgas Jūras Līcis *g.* U.S.S.R. **23**
Rīgān Iran **43** 28.40N 58.58E
Rīgas Jūras Līcis *g.* U.S.S.R. **23** 57.30N 23.35E
Rīgestān *f.* Afghan. **40** 30.35N 65.00E
Riggins U.S.A. **80** 45.25N116.19W
Rig Matī Iran **43** 27.40N 58.11E
Rigo P.N.G. **64** 9.50S147.35E
Rigolet Canada **77** 54.20N 58.35W
Riihimäki Finland **23** 60.45N 24.46E
Riiser-Larsenhalvöya *pen.* Antarctica **96** 68.00S 35.00E
Rijeka Yugo. **18** 45.20N 14.25E
Rijssen Neth. **14** 52.19N 6.31E
Rijswijk Neth. **14** 52.03N 4.22E
Riley U.S.A. **80** 43.31N119.28W
Rimah, Wādī ar *r.* Saudi Arabia **42** 26.10N 44.00E
Rimavská Sobota Czech. **21** 48.23N 20.02E
Rimbo Sweden **23** 59.45N 18.22E
Rimini Italy **15** 44.01N 12.34E
Rîmnicu-Sărat Romania **21** 45.24N 27.06E
Rîmnicu-Vîlcea Romania **21** 45.06N 24.22E
Rimouski Canada **77** 48.27N 68.32W
Rinbung China **41** 29.16N 89.54E
Rinconada Argentina **92** 22.26S 66.10W
Rindal Norway **22** 63.04N 9.13E
Ringebu Norway **23** 61.31N 10.10E
Ringerike Norway **23** 60.10N 10.12E
Ringim Nigeria **53** 12.09N 9.08E
Ringköbing Denmark **23** 56.05N 8.15E
Ringling U.S.A. **80** 46.16N110.49W
Ringsted Denmark **23** 55.27N 11.49E
Ringus India **40** 27.21N 75.34E
Ringvassöy *i.* Norway **22** 69.55N 19.10E
Ringwood U.K. **11** 50.50N 1.48W
Riobamba Ecuador **90** 1.44S 78.40W
Rio Branco Brazil **90** 9.59S 67.49W
Rio Bueno Chile **93** 40.20S 72.55W
Rio Casca Brazil **94** 20.13S 42.38W
Rio Claro Brazil **94** 22.19S 47.35W
Río Cuarto Argentina **93** 33.08S 64.20W
Rio de Janeiro Brazil **94** 22.53S 43.17W
Rio de Janeiro *d.* Brazil **94** 22.00S 42.30W
Río Gallegos Argentina **93** 51.37S 69.10W
Río Grande *town* Argentina **93** 53.50S 67.40W
Rio Grande *town* Brazil **94** 32.03S 52.08W
Rio Grande *r.* Mexico / U.S.A. **83** 25.57N 97.09W
Río Grande *r.* Nicaragua **87** 12.48N 83.30W
Rio Grande City U.S.A. **83** 26.23N 98.49W
Rio Grande do Norte *d.* Brazil **91** 6.00S 36.30W
Rio Grande do Sul *d.* Brazil **94** 30.15S 53.30W
Ríohacha Colombia **90** 11.34N 72.58W
Rio Largo Brazil **91** 9.28S 35.50W
Río Negro *d.* Argentina **93** 40.00S 67.00W
Rio Negro Brazil **94** 26.06S 49.48W
Río Negro, Embalse del *resr.* Uruguay **93** 32.45S 56.00W
Rio Novo Brazil **94** 21.15S 43.09W
Rio Piracicaba Brazil **94** 19.54S 43.10W
Rio Pomba Brazil **94** 21.15S 43.12W
Rio Prêto Brazil **94** 22.06S 43.52W
Ríosucio Colombia **90** 7.27N 77.07W
Rio Tercero Argentina **92** 32.10S 64.05W
Rio Verde *town* Brazil **92** 17.50S 50.55W
Ripley N.Y. U.S.A. **84** 42.16N 79.43W
Ripon Canada **77** 45.47N 75.06W
Ripon U.K. **10** 54.08N 1.31W
Rirapora Brazil **94** 17.20S 45.02W
Risbäck Sweden **22** 64.42N 15.32E
Riscle France **17** 43.40N 0.05W
Rishā, Wādī ar *r.* Saudi Arabia **43** 25.40N 44.08E
Rishikesh India **41** 30.07N 78.42E
Rishon LeZiyyon Israel **44** 31.57N 34.48E
Risle *r.* France **15** 49.26N 0.23E
Rison U.S.A. **83** 33.58N 92.11W
Risör Norway **23** 58.43N 9.14E
Rissani Morocco **50** 31.23N 4.09W
Riti Nigeria **53** 7.57N 9.41E
Ritidian Pt. Guam **68** 13.39N144.51E
Ritzville U.S.A. **80** 47.08N118.23W
Riva Italy **15** 45.53N 10.50E
Rivadavia Argentina **92** 24.11S 62.53W
Rivarolo Canavese Italy **15** 45.25N 7.36E
Rivas Nicaragua **87** 11.26N 85.50W
Rivera Uruguay **93** 30.54S 55.31W
River Cess *town* Liberia **52** 5.28N 9.32W
Rivergaro Italy **15** 44.55N 9.36E
Riverhead U.S.A. **84** 40.55N 72.40W
Riverina *f.* Australia **67** 34.30S145.20E
Rivers Canada **75** 50.02N100.12W
Rivers *d.* Nigeria **53** 4.45N 6.35E
Riversdale R.S.A. **56** 34.05S 21.15E
Riverside U.S.A. **81** 33.59N117.22W
Rivers Inlet *town* Canada **74** 51.40N127.20W
Riverton Australia **66** 34.08S138.24E
Riverton Canada **75** 50.59N 96.59W
Riverton New Zealand **60** 46.21S168.01E
Riverton U.S.A. **80** 43.02N108.23W
Riviera di Levante *f.* Italy **15** 44.00N 9.40E
Riviera di Ponente *f.* Italy **15** 43.40N 8.00E
Rivière-du-Loup *town* Canada **77** 47.50N 69.32W
Rivière Pentecôte *town* Canada **77** 49.47N 67.10W
Rivoli Italy **15** 45.04N 7.31E
Riyadh *see* Ar Riyāḍ Saudi Arabia **43**
Rize Turkey **42** 41.03N 40.31E
Rizhao China **32** 35.26N119.27E
Rizokárpason Cyprus **44** 35.35N 34.24E
Rizzuto, Capo *c.* Italy **19** 38.54N 17.06E
Rjukan Norway **23** 59.52N 8.34E
Roa Norway **23** 60.17N 10.37E
Roag, Loch U.K. **12** 58.14N 6.50W
Roanne France **17** 46.02N 4.05E
Roanoke *r.* U.S.A. **85** 35.56N 76.43W
Roanoke Ala. U.S.A. **85** 33.09N 85.24W
Roanoke Va. U.S.A. **85** 37.15N 79.58W
Roanoke Rapids *town* U.S.A. **85** 36.28N 77.40W
Roaring Springs U.S.A. **83** 33.54N100.52W
Robāṭ Iran **43** 30.04N 54.49E
Robe Australia **66** 37.11S139.45E
Robe, Mt. Australia **66** 31.39S141.16E
Robertsganj India **41** 24.42N 83.04E
Robertson R.S.A. **56** 33.48S 19.52E
Robertsport Liberia **52** 6.45N 11.22W
Robertstown Australia **66** 33.59S139.03E
Roberval Canada **77** 48.31N 72.13W
Robin Hood's Bay *town* U.K. **10** 54.26N 0.31W
Robinson *r.* Australia **64** 16.03S137.16E

Robinson Range mts. Australia 62 25.45S119.00E
Robinvale Australia 66 34.37S142.50E
Robledo Spain 16 38.46N 2.26W
Roblin Man. Canada 75 51.17N101.28W
Roboré Bolivia 92 18.20S 59.45W
Robson, Mt. Canada 74 53.10N119.10W
Rocas i. Atlantic Oc. 95 3.50S 33.50W
Roccella Italy 19 38.19N 16.24E
Rocciamelone mtn. Italy 15 45.12N 7.05E
Rocha Uruguay 94 34.30S 54.22W
Rocha da Gale, Barragem resr. Portugal 16 38.20N 7.35W
Rochdale U.K. 10 53.36N 2.10W
Rochechouart France 17 45.49N 0.50E
Rochefort Belgium 14 50.10N 5.13E
Rochefort France 17 45.57N 0.58W
Rochelle U.S.A. 82 41.55N 89.05W
Rocher River town Canada 74 61.23N112.44W
Rochester Australia 67 36.22S144.42E
Rochester Kent U.K. 11 51.22N 0.30E
Rochester Minn. U.S.A. 82 44.01N 92.27W
Rochester N.Y. U.S.A. 84 43.12N 77.37W
Rochfort Bridge Rep. of Ire. 13 53.25N 7.19W
Rock r. Canada 74 60.07N127.07W
Rock U.S.A. 84 46.03N 87.10W
Rockall i. U.K. 8 57.39N 13.44W
Rockall Bank f. Atlantic Oc. 8 57.30N 14.00W
Rockdale U.S.A. 85 39.21N 76.46W
Rockefeller Plateau Antarctica 96 80.00S140.00W
Rockford U.S.A. 82 42.17N 89.06W
Rock Hall U.S.A. 85 39.08N 76.14W
Rockhampton Australia 64 23.22S150.32E
Rock Hill town U.S.A. 85 34.55N 81.01W
Rockingham Australia 63 32.16S115.21E
Rockingham U.S.A. 85 34.56N 79.47W
Rock Island town U.S.A. 82 41.30N 90.34W
Rockland Canada 77 45.32N 75.19W
Rockland Idaho U.S.A. 80 42.34N112.53W
Rockland Maine U.S.A. 84 44.06N 69.06W
Rockland Mich. U.S.A. 84 46.44N 89.12W
Rocklands Resr. Australia 66 37.13S141.52E
Rockport U.S.A. 80 39.45N123.47W
Rock Rapids town U.S.A. 82 43.26N 96.10W
Rock Sound town Bahamas 87 24.54N 76.11W
Rocksprings Tex. U.S.A. 83 30.01N100.13W
Rock Springs Wyo. U.S.A. 80 41.35N109.13W
Rockville U.S.A. 85 39.05N 77.09W
Rockwood Tenn. U.S.A. 85 35.52N 84.40W
Rocky Ford U.S.A. 78 38.03N103.44W
Rocky Gully town Australia 63 34.31S117.01E
Rocky Island L. Canada 76 46.55N 82.55W
Rocky Mount town U.S.A. 85 35.56N 77.48W
Rocky Mountain Foothills f. Canada 74 57.17N123.21W
Rocky Mountain Nat. Park U.S.A. 80 40.19N105.42W
Rocky Mountain Trench f. Canada 74 56.45N124.47W
Rocky Mts. N. America 80 43.21N109.50W
Rocky Pt. Namibia 56 19.00S 12.29E
Rocroi France 14 49.56N 4.31E
Rod Pakistan 40 28.06N 63.12E
Rødby Denmark 23 54.42N 11.24E
Roddickton Canada 77 50.52N 56.08W
Rodel U.K. 12 57.44N 6.58W
Rodeo Mexico 83 25.11N104.34W
Rodez France 17 44.21N 2.34E
Ródhos i. Greece 19 36.12N 28.00E
Ródhos town Greece 19 36.24N 28.15E
Rodonit, Kep-i- c. Albania 19 41.34N 19.25E
Roe, L. Australia 63 30.40S122.10E
Roebourne Australia 62 20.45S117.08E
Roebuck B. Australia 62 19.04S122.17E
Roermond Neth. 14 51.12N 6.00E
Roeselare Belgium 14 50.57N 3.06E
Rogachev U.S.S.R. 21 53.05N 30.02E
Rogaland d. Norway 23 59.00N 6.15E
Rogers, Mt. U.S.A. 85 36.35N 81.32W
Rogerson U.S.A. 80 42.14N114.47W
Roggan r. Canada 76 54.24N 78.05W
Roggan L. Canada 76 54.10N 77.58W
Roggan River town Canada 76 54.24N 78.05W
Roggeveen, Cabo c. I. de Pascua 69 27.06S109.16W
Rogliano France 17 42.57N 9.25E
Rogue r. U.S.A. 80 42.26N124.25W
Rohri Pakistan 40 27.41N 68.54E
Rohtak India 40 28.54N 76.34E
Rojas Argentina 93 34.15S 60.44W
Rokan r. Indonesia 36 2.00N101.00E
Rokel r. Sierra Leone 52 8.36N 12.55W
Rola Co l. China 39 35.26N 88.24E
Röldal Norway 23 59.49N 6.48E
Rolette U.S.A. 82 48.40N 99.51W
Rolla Mo. U.S.A. 83 37.57N 91.46W
Rolla N.Dak. U.S.A. 82 48.52N 99.37W
Rolleston Australia 64 24.25S148.35E
Rolleville Bahamas 87 23.41N 76.00W
Rolvsöya i. Norway 22 70.58N 24.00E
Roma Australia 64 26.35S148.47E
Roma Italy 18 41.54N 12.29E
Roma Sweden 23 57.32N 18.28E
Romain, C. U.S.A. 85 33.00N 79.22W
Romaine r. Canada 77 50.18N 63.47W
Roman Romania 21 46.55N 26.56E
Romang i. Indonesia 37 7.45S127.20E
Romania Europe 21 46.30N 24.00E
Romano, C. U.S.A. 85 25.50N 81.41W
Romans France 17 45.03N 5.03E
Rome see Roma Italy 18
Rome Ga. U.S.A. 85 34.01N 85.02W
Rome N.Y. U.S.A. 84 43.13N 75.27W
Romeo U.S.A. 84 42.47N 83.01W
Romilly France 15 48.31N 3.44E
Romney Marsh f. U.K. 11 51.03N 0.55E
Romorantin France 15 47.22N 1.44E
Rona i. U.K. 12 57.33N 5.58W
Ronan U.S.A. 80 47.32N114.06W
Ronas Hill U.K. 8 60.32N 1.26W
Roncesvalles Spain 16 43.01N 1.19W
Ronda Spain 16 36.45N 5.10W
Rondane mtn. Norway 23 61.55N 9.45E
Rondônia d. Brazil 90 12.10S 62.30W
Rondonópolis Brazil 91 16.29S 54.37W
Rongcheng China 32 37.09N122.23E
Ronge, Lac la l. Canada 75 55.07N104.45W
Rongjiang China 33 25.56N108.31E
Rongxar China 41 28.14N 87.44E
Rong Xian China 33 29.28N104.32E
Roniu mtn. Tahiti 69 17.49S149.12W
Rönne Denmark 23 55.06N 14.42E
Ronneby Sweden 23 56.12N 15.18E
Ronse Belgium 14 50.45N 3.36E
Ronuro r. Brazil 91 11.56S 53.33W
Roof Butte mtn. U.S.A. 81 36.28N109.05W
Roorkee India 41 29.52N 77.53E
Roosendaal Neth. 14 51.32N 4.28E
Roosevelt r. Brazil 90 7.35S 60.20W
Roosevelt U.S.A. 80 40.18N109.59W
Roosevelt I. Antarctica 96 79.00S161.00W
Root r. Canada 74 62.50N123.40W
Ropcha U.S.S.R. 24 62.50N 51.55E
Roper r. Australia 64 14.40S135.30E
Roque Pérez Argentina 93 35.23S 59.22W
Roraima d. Brazil 90 2.00N 62.00W
Roraima, Mt. Guyana 90 5.14N 60.44W
Rorketon Canada 75 51.26N 99.32W
Röros Norway 22 62.35N 11.23E
Rosa, Monte mtn. Italy/Switz. 15 45.56N 7.51E
Rosamond U.S.A. 81 34.52N118.10W
Rosario Argentina 93 32.57S 60.40W
Rosário Brazil 91 3.00S 44.15W
Rosario Mexico 81 23.00N105.52W
Rosario Uruguay 93 34.19S 57.21W
Rosario de la Frontera Argentina 92 25.50S 64.55W
Rosario del Tala Argentina 93 32.20S 59.10W
Rosário do Sul Brazil 94 30.15S 54.55W
Rosarito Mexico 81 28.38N114.04W
Roscoe S.Dak. U.S.A. 82 45.27N 99.20W
Roscoff France 17 48.44N 4.00W
Roscommon Rep. of Ire. 13 53.38N 8.13W
Roscommon d. Rep. of Ire. 13 53.38N 8.11W
Roscrea Rep. of Ire. 13 52.57N 7.49W
Roseau r. Canada 75 49.10N 97.20W
Roseau Dominica 87 15.18N 61.23W
Roseau U.S.A. 82 48.51N 95.46W
Rose Blanche Canada 77 47.37N 58.43W
Rosebud Australia 67 38.21S144.54E
Rosebud r. Canada 74 51.25N112.37W
Roseburg U.S.A. 80 43.13N123.20W
Rose Harbour Canada 74 52.15N131.10W
Rosenberg U.S.A. 83 29.33N 95.48W
Rosenheim Germany 20 47.51N 12.09E
Roses Spain 16 42.19N 3.10E
Rosetown Canada 75 51.33N108.00W
Rosetta R.S.A. 56 29.18S 29.58E
Roseville Calif. U.S.A. 80 38.45N121.17W
Roseville Mich. U.S.A. 76 42.30N 82.56W
Rosières France 15 49.49N 2.43E
Rosignano Marittimo Italy 18 43.24N 10.28E
Roşiori-de-Vede Romania 21 44.07N 25.00E
Rositsa Bulgaria 21 43.57N 27.57E
Roska r. U.S.S.R. 21 49.27N 29.45E
Roskilde Denmark 23 55.39N 12.05E
Roslags-Näsby Sweden 23 59.26N 18.04E
Roslavl U.S.S.R. 24 53.55N 32.53E
Ross New Zealand 60 42.54S170.49E
Rossano Italy 19 39.35N 16.39E
Ross Dependency Antarctica 96 75.00S170.00W
Rossignol, L. Canada 77 44.10N 65.10W
Rossing Namibia 56 22.31S 14.52E
Rossiyskaya S.F.S.R. d. U.S.S.R. 28 62.00N 80.00E
Rosslare Rep. of Ire. 13 52.17N 6.23W
Rosso Mauritania 50 16.30N 15.49W
Ross-on-Wye U.K. 11 51.55N 2.36W
Rossosh U.S.S.R. 25 50.12N 39.35E
Ross River town Canada 74 62.30N131.30W
Rössvatnet l. Norway 22 65.45N 14.00E
Rosta Norway 22 68.59N 19.40E
Rosthern Canada 75 52.40N106.17W
Rostock Germany 20 54.06N 12.09E
Rostov R.S.F.S.R. U.S.S.R. 25 47.15N 39.45E
Rostov R.S.F.S.R. U.S.S.R. 24 57.11N 39.23E
Roswell Ga. U.S.A. 85 34.02N 84.21W
Roswell N.Mex. U.S.A. 81 33.24N104.32W
Rotem Belgium 14 51.04N 5.44E
Rothbury U.K. 10 55.19N 1.54W
Rother r. U.K. 9 50.56N 0.46E
Rotherham U.K. 10 53.26N 1.21W
Rothes U.K. 12 57.31N 3.13W
Rothesay Canada 77 45.23N 66.00W
Rothesay U.K. 12 55.50N 5.03W
Roti i. Indonesia 62 10.30S123.10E
Roto Australia 67 33.04S145.27E
Rotondella Italy 19 40.10N 16.32E
Rotorua New Zealand 60 38.07S176.17E
Rotorua, L. New Zealand 60 38.00S176.00E
Rotterdam Neth. 14 51.55N 4.29E
Rottnest I. Australia 63 32.01S115.28E
Rottweil Germany 20 48.10N 8.37E
Roubaix France 14 50.42N 3.10E
Rouen France 15 49.26N 1.05E
Rouge r. Canada 77 45.39N 74.41W
Rougé France 15 47.47N 1.26W
Rouku P.N.G. 64 8.40S141.35E
Round Mt. Australia 67 30.26S152.15E
Round Pond l. Canada 77 48.10N 56.00W
Roundup U.S.A. 80 46.27N108.33W
Rousay i. U.K. 12 59.10N 3.02W
Rouyn Canada 76 48.20N 79.00W
Rovaniemi Finland 22 66.30N 25.40E
Rovato Italy 15 45.34N 10.00E
Rovereto Italy 15 45.53N 11.02E
Rovigo Italy 15 45.04N 11.47E
Rovinj Yugo. 20 45.06N 13.39E
Rovno U.S.S.R. 21 50.39N 26.10E
Rowena Australia 67 29.49S148.54E
Rowley Shoals f. Australia 62 17.30S119.00E
Roxboro U.S.A. 85 36.24N 79.00W
Roxburgh New Zealand 60 45.33S169.19E
Roxby Downs town Australia 66 30.42S136.46E
Roxen l. Sweden 23 58.30N 15.41E
Roxton Canada 77 45.29N 72.36W
Roy U.S.A. 81 35.57N104.12W
Royale, Isle i. U.S.A. 84 48.00N 89.00W
Royal L. Canada 75 56.00N103.15W
Royal Leamington Spa U.K. 11 52.18N 1.32W
Royal Tunbridge Wells U.K. 11 51.07N 0.16E
Royan France 17 45.37N 1.02W
Roye France 15 49.42N 2.48E
Royston U.K. 11 52.03N 0.01W
Rozhishche U.S.S.R. 21 50.58N 25.15E
Rožňava Czech. 21 48.40N 20.32E
Rtishchevo U.S.S.R. 24 52.16N 43.45E
Ruahine Range mts. New Zealand 60 40.00S176.00E
Ruapehu mtn. New Zealand 60 39.20S175.30E
Ruapuke I. New Zealand 60 46.45S168.30E
Rub 'al Khali des. see Ar Rub 'al Khālī des. Saudi Arabia 38
Rubi r. Zaïre 54 2.50N 24.06E
Rubino Ivory Coast 52 6.04N 4.18W
Rubio Colombia 90 7.42N 72.23W
Rubryn U.S.S.R. 21 51.52N 27.30E
Rubtsovsk U.S.S.R. 28 51.29N 81.10E
Ruby Mts. U.S.A. 80 40.25N115.35W
Rūdān r. Iran 43 27.02N 56.53E
Rudauli India 41 26.45N 81.45E
Rūdbār Afghan. 40 30.09N 62.36E
Rudewa Tanzania 55 6.40S 37.08E
Rudki U.S.S.R. 21 49.40N 23.28E
Rudnaya Pristan U.S.S.R. 31 44.18N135.51E
Rudnichnyy U.S.S.R. 24 59.10N 52.28E
Rudnik Poland 21 50.28N 22.15E
Rudnyy U.S.S.R. 28 53.00N 63.05E
Rudolstadt Germany 20 50.44N 11.20E
Rue France 17 50.15N 1.40E
Rufā'ah Sudan 48 14.46N 33.22E
Ruffec France 17 46.02N 0.12E
Rufiji r. Tanzania 55 8.02S 39.19E
Rufino Argentina 93 34.16S 62.45W
Rufisque Senegal 52 14.43N 17.16W
Rufunsa Zambia 55 15.02S 29.35E
Rugao China 32 32.25N120.40E
Rugby U.K. 11 52.23N 1.16W
Rugby U.S.A. 82 48.22N100.00W
Rügen i. Germany 20 54.30N 13.30E
Ruhr f. Germany 14 51.22N 7.26E
Ruhr r. Germany 14 51.27N 6.41E
Rui'an China 33 26.50N120.40E
Ruijin China 33 25.49N116.00E
Ruinen Neth. 14 52.47N 6.21E
Rukwa d. Tanzania 55 7.05S 31.25E
Rukwa, L. Tanzania 55 8.00S 32.20E
Ruma Yugo. 21 44.59N 19.51E
Rumbek Sudan 49 6.48N 29.41E
Rum Cay i. Bahamas 87 23.41N 74.53W
Rumford U.S.A. 84 44.33N 70.33W
Rummānah Egypt 44 31.01N 32.40E
Runcorn U.K. 10 53.20N 2.44W
Rundvik Sweden 22 63.30N 19.24E
Rungāni Pakistan 40 26.38N 65.43E
Rungwa r. Tanzania 55 7.38S 31.55E
Rungwa Singida Tanzania 55 6.57S 33.35E
Rungwe Mt. Tanzania 55 9.10S 33.40E
Runka Nigeria 53 12.28N 7.20E
Ruoqiang China 30 39.00N 88.00E
Ruo Shui r. China 30 42.15N101.03E
Rūpar India 40 30.58N 76.32E
Rupert r. Canada 76 51.30N 78.45W
Rupununi r. Guyana 90 4.00N 58.30W
Rur r. Neth. 14 51.12N 5.58E
Rurutu i. Pacific Oc. 69 22.25S151.20W
Rusape Zimbabwe 57 18.30S 32.08E
Ruşayriş, Khazzān ar resr. Sudan 49 11.40N 34.20E
Ruse Bulgaria 19 43.50N 25.59E
Rusera India 41 25.45N 86.02E
Rushan China 32 36.54N121.30E
Rushden U.K. 11 52.17N 0.37W
Rush Springs town U.S.A. 83 34.47N 97.58W
Rushworth Australia 67 36.38S145.02E
Russell Canada 77 45.17N 75.17W
Russellkonda India 41 19.56N 84.35E
Russell L. Man. Canada 75 56.15N101.30W
Russell L. N.W.T. Canada 74 63.05N115.44W
Russell Pt. Canada 72 73.30N115.00W
Russell Range mts. Australia 63 33.15S123.30E
Russellville U.S.A. 83 35.17N 93.08W
Russkaya Polyana U.S.S.R. 28 53.48N 73.54E
Rustavi U.S.S.R. 25 41.34N 45.03E
Rustenburg R.S.A. 56 25.39S 27.13E
Ruston U.S.A. 83 32.32N 92.38W
Rutana Burundi 55 3.58S 30.00E
Rutanzige, L. see Edward, L. Uganda/Zaïre 55
Rütenbrock Germany 14 52.51N 7.06E
Ruteng Indonesia 37 8.35S120.28E
Rutenga Zimbabwe 56 21.15S 30.46E
Ruth U.S.A. 80 39.17N114.59W
Ruthin U.K. 10 53.07N 3.18W
Rutland U.S.A. 84 43.36N 72.59W
Rutledge r. Canada 75 61.04N112.00W
Rutledge L. Canada 75 61.33N110.47W
Rutog China 41 33.27N 79.43E
Rutshuru Zaïre 55 1.10S 29.26E
Ruvu Coast Tanzania 55 6.50S 38.42E
Ruvuma r. Mozambique/Tanzania 55 10.30S 40.30E
Ruvuma d. Tanzania 55 10.45S 36.15E
Ruwaybah wells Sudan 48 15.39N 28.45E
Ruwenzori Range mts. Uganda/Zaïre 55 0.30N 30.00E
Ruyigi Burundi 55 3.26S 30.14E
Ruzayevka U.S.S.R. 24 54.04N 44.55E
Ruzitgort U.S.S.R. 24 62.51N 64.52E
Ružomberok Czech. 21 49.06N 19.18E
Rwanda Africa 55 2.00S 30.00E
Ryan, Loch U.K. 12 54.56N 5.02W
Ryasna U.S.S.R. 21 54.00N 31.14E
Ryazan U.S.S.R. 24 54.37N 39.43E
Ryazhsk U.S.S.R. 24 53.40N 40.07E
Rybachiy, Poluostrov pen. U.S.S.R. 24 69.45N 32.30E
Rybachye U.S.S.R. 30 46.27N 81.30E
Rybinskoye Vodokhranilishche resr. U.S.S.R. 24 58.30N 38.25E
Rybnik Poland 21 50.06N 18.32E
Rybnitsa U.S.S.R. 21 47.42N 29.00E
Ryd Sweden 23 56.28N 14.41E
Rye U.K. 11 50.57N 0.46E
Rye r. U.K. 10 54.10N 0.44W
Ryki Poland 21 51.39N 21.56E
Rylstone Australia 67 32.48S149.58E
Ryūgasaki Japan 35 35.54N140.11E
Ryukyu Is. see Nansei shotō is. Japan 31
Rzeszów Poland 21 50.04N 22.00E
Rzhev U.S.S.R. 24 56.15N 34.18E

S

Saa Cameroon 53 4.24N 11.25E
Saale r. Germany 20 51.58N 11.53E
Saanich Canada 74 48.28N123.22W
Saar r. Germany 14 49.43N 6.34E
Saarbrücken Germany 20 49.15N 6.58E
Saarburg Germany 14 49.36N 6.33E
Saaremaa i. U.S.S.R. 23 58.25N 22.30E
Saarijärvi Finland 22 62.43N 25.16E
Saariselkä mts. Finland 22 68.15N 28.30E
Saarland d. Germany 14 49.30N 6.50E
Saba i. Leeward Is. 87 17.42N 63.26W
Šabac Yugo. 21 44.45N 19.41E
Sabadell Spain 16 41.33N 2.07E
Sabah d. Malaysia 36 5.30N117.00E
Sabalān, Kūhhā-ye mts. Iran 43 38.15N 47.50E
Sabana, Archipiélago de Cuba 87 23.30N 80.00W
Sabanalarga 5400/022Yemen 90 10.38N 75.00W
Sab'atayn, Ramlat as f. Yemen/S. Yemen 45 15.30N 46.10E
Sabaudia Italy 18 41.18N 13.01E
Sabbioneta Italy 15 45.00N 10.39E
Sabhā Libya 51 27.02N 14.26E
Sabhā d. Libya 51 27.02N 15.30E
Sabi r. Zimbabwe 57 21.16S 32.20E
Sabinas Mexico 83 27.51N101.07W
Sabinas Hidalgo Mexico 83 26.30N100.10W
Sabine r. U.S.A. 83 30.00N 93.45W
Sabine L. U.S.A. 83 29.50N 93.50W
Sabkhat al Bardawīl l. Egypt 44 31.10N 33.15E
Sablayan Phil. 37 12.50N120.50E
Sable, C. Canada 77 43.25N 65.35W
Sable, C. U.S.A. 85 25.05N 65.50W
Sable I. Canada 73 43.55N 59.50W
Sablé-sur-Sarthe France 15 47.50N 0.20W
Sabon Birni Nigeria 53 13.37N 6.15E
Sabongidda Nigeria 53 6.54N 5.56E
Sabrina Coast f. Antarctica 96 67.00S120.00E
Şabyā Saudi Arabia 48 17.09N 42.37E
Sabzevār Iran 43 36.13N 57.38E
Sacaca Bolivia 92 18.05S 66.25W
Sacajawea mtn. U.S.A. 80 45.15N117.17W
Sacandica Angola 54 5.58S 15.56E
Sac City U.S.A. 82 42.25N 95.00W
Sacedón Spain 16 40.29N 2.44W
Sachigo r. Canada 75 55.00N 89.00W
Sachigo L. Canada 75 53.50N 92.00W
Sachsen d. Germany 20 51.10N 13.15E
Sachsen-Anhalt d. Germany 20 52.05N 11.30E
Sackville Canada 77 45.54N 64.22W
Saco U.S.A. 84 43.29N 70.28W
Sacramento Brazil 94 19.51S 26.47W
Sacramento U.S.A. 80 38.35N121.30W
Sacramento r. U.S.A. 80 38.03N121.56W
Sacramento Mts. U.S.A. 81 33.10N105.50W
Sacramento Valley f. U.S.A. 80 39.15N122.00W
Sádaba Spain 16 42.19N 1.10W
Sadani Tanzania 55 6.00S 38.40E
Sadda Pakistan 40 33.42N 70.20E
Sa Dec Vietnam 34 10.19N105.45E
Sādiqābād Pakistan 40 28.18N 70.08E
Sadiya India 39 27.49N 95.38E
Sādri India 40 25.11N 73.26E
Sadulgarh India 40 29.35N 74.19E
Şafājah des. Saudi Arabia 42 26.30N 39.30E
Şafāniyah Egypt 44 28.49N 30.48E
Şafarābād Iran 43 38.59N 47.25E
Säffle Sweden 23 59.08N 12.56E
Saffron Walden U.K. 11 52.02N 0.15E
Safi Morocco 50 32.20N 9.17W
Safid r. Iran 43 37.23N 50.11E
Safonovo R.S.F.S.R. U.S.S.R. 24 55.08N 33.16E
Safonovo R.S.F.S.R. U.S.S.R. 24 65.40N 48.10E
Saga China 41 29.30N 85.09E
Sagaing Burma 34 22.00N 96.00E
Sagaing d. Burma 34 24.00N 95.00E
Sagala Mali 52 14.09N 6.38W
Sagami r. Japan 35 35.14N139.23E
Sagamihara Japan 35 35.32N139.23E
Sagami-nada b. Japan 35 34.55N139.30E
Sāgar India 41 23.50N 78.43E
Sagara Japan 35 34.41N138.12E
Sage U.S.A. 80 41.49N110.59W
Saginaw U.S.A. 84 43.25N 83.54W
Saginaw B. U.S.A. 84 43.56N 83.40W
Sagiz U.S.S.R. 25 47.31N 54.55E
Sagres Portugal 16 37.00N 8.56W
Saguache U.S.A. 80 38.05N106.08W
Sagua la Grande Cuba 87 22.55N 80.05W
Saguenay r. Canada 77 48.10N 69.43W
Sagunto Spain 16 39.40N 0.17W
Sāgwāra India 40 23.41N 74.01E
Sa'gya China 41 28.55N 88.03E
Sahaba Sudan 48 18.55N 30.28E
Sahagún Spain 16 42.23N 5.02W
Sahand, Kūh-e mtn. Iran 43 37.37N 46.27E
Sahara des. Africa 51 22.30N 3.00E
Sahāranpur India 41 29.58N 77.33E
Saharsa India 41 25.53N 86.36E
Sahaswān India 41 28.05N 78.45E
Sahbā, Wādī as r. Saudi Arabia 43 23.48N 49.50E
Sahel d. Burkina 52 14.00N 0.50W
Sāhibganj India 41 25.15N 87.39E
Sāhīwāl Punjab Pakistan 40 30.40N 73.06E
Sāhīwāl Punjab Pakistan 40 31.58N 72.20E
Sahtaneh r. Canada 74 59.02N122.28W
Sahuarita U.S.A. 81 31.57N110.58W
Saibai i. Australia 64 9.24S142.40E
Sa'īdābād Iran 43 29.28N 55.43E
Saidpur Bangla. 41 25.47N 88.54E
Saidu Pakistan 40 34.45N 72.21E
Saigon see Ho Chi Minh Vietnam 34
Saimaa l. Finland 24 61.20N 28.00E
Saimbeyli Turkey 42 38.07N 36.08E
Saindak Pakistan 40 29.17N 61.34E
St. Abb's Head U.K. 12 55.54N 2.07W
St. Agapit Canada 77 46.34N 71.26W
St. Alban's Canada 77 47.52N 55.51W
St. Albans U.K. 11 51.46N 0.21W
St. Albans Vt. U.S.A. 84 44.49N 73.05W
St. Albert Canada 74 53.37N113.40W
St. Alexis des Monts Canada 77 46.28N 73.08W
St. Amand France 14 50.27N 3.26E
St. Amand-Mont-Rond town France 17 46.43N 2.29E
St. Andrews U.K. 12 56.20N 2.48W
St. Andries Belgium 14 51.12N 3.10E
St. Ann's Bay town Jamaica 87 18.26N 77.12W
St. Anthony Canada 77 51.22N 55.35W
St. Anthony U.S.A. 78 43.59N111.40W
St. Arnaud Australia 66 36.40S143.20E
St. Augustin r. Canada 77 51.14N 58.41W
St. Augustine U.S.A. 85 29.54N 81.19W
St. Augustin Saguenay Canada 77 51.14N 58.39W
St. Austell U.K. 11 50.20N 4.48W
St. Barthélemy Canada 77 46.12N 73.08W
St. Barthélemy i. Leeward Is. 87 17.55N 62.50W
St. Bees Head U.K. 10 54.31N 3.39W
St. Boniface Canada 75 49.55N 97.06W
St. Brides B. U.K. 11 51.48N 5.03W
St. Brieuc France 17 48.31N 2.45W
St. Calais France 15 47.55N 0.45E
St. Casimir Canada 77 46.40N 72.08W
St. Catharines Canada 76 43.10N 79.15W
St. Catherine's Pt. U.K. 11 50.34N 1.18W
St. Céré France 17 44.52N 1.53E
St. Charles Mo. U.S.A. 82 38.47N 90.29W
St. Cloud U.S.A. 82 45.33N 94.10W
St. Croix i. U.S.V.Is. 87 17.45N 64.35W
St. Cyrille de Wendover Canada 77 45.56N 72.26W
St. David's U.K. 11 51.54N 5.16W
St. David's I. Bermuda 95 32.23N 64.42W
St. Denis France 15 48.56N 2.21E
St. Dié France 17 48.17N 6.57E
St. Dizier France 15 48.38N 4.58E
St. Donat Canada 77 46.19N 74.13W
Sainte-Agathe-des-Monts Canada 77 46.03N 74.17W
Sainte Anne de Beaupré Canada 77 47.02N 70.56W
Sainte Anne de la Pérade Canada 77 46.35N 72.12W
Sainte-Anne-des-Monts Canada 77 49.07N 66.29W
Sainte Emelie Canada 77 46.19N 73.39W
St. Elias, Mt. U.S.A. 74 60.18N140.55W
St. Elias Mts. Canada 74 60.30N139.30W
St. Éloi Canada 77 48.02N 69.13W
Sainte Lucie Canada 77 46.07N 74.13W
Sainte Marguerite Canada 77 46.03N 74.05W
Sainte Marguerite r. Canada 77 50.10N 66.40W
Sainte Menehould France 15 49.05N 4.54E
Sainte Mère-Église France 15 49.24N 1.19W
Saintes France 17 45.44N 0.38W
St. Espirit Canada 77 45.56N 73.40W
Sainte-Thérèse-de-Blainville Canada 77 45.39N 73.49W
St. Étienne France 17 45.26N 4.26E
St. Fargeau France 15 47.38N 3.04E
St. Faustin Canada 77 46.07N 74.30W
St. Félix Canada 77 46.10N 73.26W
Saintfield U.K. 13 54.28N 5.50W

Fintan's Canada 77 48.10N 58.50W
Florent France 17 42.41N 9.18E
Florentin France 15 48.00N 3.44E
Flour France 17 45.02N 3.05E
Francis U.S.A. 82 39.47N101.47W
Francisville U.S.A. 83 30.47N 91.23W
Francois r. Canada 77 46.07N 72.55W
Gabriel Canada 77 46.17N 73.23W
Gallen Switz. 20 47.25N 9.23E
Gaudens France 17 43.07N 0.44E
George Australia 65 28.03S148.30E
George Bermuda 95 32.24N 64.42W
George N.B. Canada 77 45.11N 66.57W
George Ont. Canada 76 43.15N 80.15W
George U.S.A. 80 37.06N113.35W
George, C. U.S.A. 85 29.35N 85.04W
Georges Belgium 14 50.37N 5.20E
Georges Canada 77 46.37N 72.40W
George's Grenada 87 12.04N 61.44W
Georges Guiana 91 3.54N 51.48W
George's B. Canada 77 48.20N 59.00W
George's Channel Rep. of Ire./U.K. 13 .30N 6.20W
George's I. Bermuda 95 32.24N 64.42W
Germain France 15 48.53N 2.04E
Germain de Grantham Canada 77 45.50N 2.34W
Gheorghe's Mouth est. Romania 19 .51N 29.37E
Gilles-Croix-de-Vie France 17 46.42N 56W
Girons France 17 42.59N 1.08E
Gotthard Pass Switz. 17 46.30N 8.55E
Govan's Head U.K. 11 51.36N 4.55W
Grégoire Canada 77 46.16N 72.30W
Guillaume d'Upton Canada 77 45.53N 2.46W
Helena i. Atlantic Oc. 95 15.58S 5.43W
Helena B. R.S.A. 56 32.35S 18.05E
Helens U.K. 10 53.28N 2.43W
Helens U.S.A. 80 45.52N122.48W
Helier U.K. 11 49.12N 2.07W
Hilaire-du-Harcouët France 15 48.35N 06W
Hubert Belgium 14 50.02N 5.22E
Hyacinthe Canada 77 45.38N 72.57W
Ignace U.S.A. 84 45.53N 84.44W
Ives U.K. 11 50.13N 5.29W
Jacques Canada 77 45.57N 73.34W
Jean Canada 77 45.18N 73.20W
Jean r. Canada 77 50.17N 64.20W
Jean France 17 45.17N 6.21E
Jean, Lac l. Canada 77 48.35N 72.00W
Jean de Matha Canada 77 46.10N 73.30W
Jean Pied-de-Port France 17 43.10N 14W
Jérôme Canada 77 45.47N 74.00W
John Canada 77 45.16N 66.03W
John r. Canada 77 45.16N 66.04W
John U.S.A. 83 38.00N 98.46W
John, C. Canada 77 50.00N 55.32W
John B. Canada 77 50.40N 57.08W
John's Antigua 87 17.07N 61.51W
John's Canada 77 47.34N 52.43W
Johns U.S.A. 81 34.30N109.22W
Johns r. U.S.A. 85 30.24N 81.24W
Johnsbury U.S.A. 84 44.25N 72.01W
John's Pt. U.K. 13 54.14N 5.39W
Jordi, Golf de g. Spain 16 40.50N 1.10E
Joseph La. U.S.A. 83 31.55N 91.14W
Joseph Mich. U.S.A. 84 42.05N 86.30W
Joseph Mo. U.S.A. 82 39.46N 94.51W
Joseph, L. Canada 76 51.05N 90.35W
Jovite Canada 77 46.07N 74.36W
Jude Canada 77 45.46N 72.59W
Junien France 17 45.53N 0.55E
Just-en-Chaussée France 15 49.30N .26E
Kilda i. U.K. 8 57.55N 8.20W
Kitts-Nevis Leeward Is. 87 17.20N 62.45W
Lambert Canada 77 45.30N 73.30W
Laurent Man. Canada 75 50.24N 97.56W
Laurent Que. Canada 77 45.31N 73.41W
Laurent du Maroni Guiana 91 5.30N 54.02W
Lawrence r. Canada 77 48.45N 68.30W
Lawrence, G. of Canada 77 48.00N 62.00W
Lawrence I. U.S.A. 72 63.00N170.00W
Léonard d'Aston Canada 77 46.06N 72.22W
Lewis Sd. Canada 77 52.20N 55.40W
Lin Canada 77 45.51N 73.45W
Lô France 15 49.07N 1.05W
Louis Senegal 52 16.01N 16.30W
Louis U.S.A. 82 38.38N 90.11W
Louis Park town U.S.A. 82 44.56N 93.22W
Lucia Windward Is. 87 14.05N 61.00W
Lucia, L. R.S.A. 57 28.05S 32.26E
Magnus B. U.K. 8 60.25N 1.35W
Maixent France 17 46.25N 0.12W
Malo France 15 48.39N 2.00W
Malo, Golfe de g. France 17 49.20N 2.00W
-Marc Haiti 87 19.08N 72.41W
Margaret's Hope U.K. 12 58.49N 2.57W
Maries U.S.A. 80 47.19N116.35W
Martin i. Leeward Is. 87 18.05N 63.05W
Martin U.K. 11 49.27N 2.34W
Martin, L. Canada 75 51.37N 98.29W
Martin's i. U.K. 11 49.57N 6.16W
Mary U.K. 11 49.14N 2.10W
Mary Peak Australia 66 31.30S138.35E
Marys Australia 65 41.33S148.12E
Mary's r. Canada 77 45.02N 61.54W
Mary's i. U.K. 11 49.55N 6.16W
Mary's, C. Canada 77 46.49N 54.12W
Mary's B. Canada 77 46.50N 53.47W
Matthew I. U.S.A. 72 60.30N172.45W
St. Maur France 15 48.48N 2.30E
St. Maurice r. Canada 77 46.22N 72.32W
St. Moritz Switz. 20 46.30N 9.51E
St. Nazaire France 17 47.17N 2.12W
St. Neots U.K. 11 52.14N 0.16W
St. Niklaas Belgium 14 51.10N 4.09E
St. Omer France 17 50.45N 2.15E
St. Pacôme Canada 77 47.24N 69.57W
St. Pascal Canada 77 47.32N 69.48W
St. Paul r. Canada 77 51.26N 57.40W
St. Paul Pyr. Or. France 17 42.49N 2.29E
St. Paul Ark. U.S.A. 83 35.50N 93.48W
St. Paul Minn. U.S.A. 82 45.00N 93.10W
St. Paul Nebr. U.S.A. 82 41.13N 98.27W
St. Paul du Nord Canada 77 48.27N 69.15W
St. Paulin Canada 77 46.25N 73.01W
St. Paul Rocks is. Atlantic Oc. 95 1.00N 29.23W
St. Peter U.S.A. 82 44.17N 93.57W
St. Peter Port U.K. 11 49.27N 2.32W
St. Petersburg U.S.A. 85 27.45N 82.40W
St. Pierre Char. Mar. France 17 45.57N 1.19W
St. Pierre S. Mar. France 15 49.48N 0.29E
St. Pierre, Lac l. Canada 77 46.12N 72.52W
St. Pierre and Miquelon is. N. America 77 46.55N 56.10W
St. Pierre-Église France 15 49.40N 1.24W
St. Pölten Austria 20 48.13N 15.37E
St. Polycarpe Canada 77 45.18N 74.18W
St. Quentin France 15 49.51N 3.17E
St. Seine-l'Abbaye France 15 47.26N 4.47E
St. Siméon Canada 77 47.55N 69.58W
St. Stephen Canada 77 45.12N 67.17W
St. Thomas Canada 76 42.47N 81.12W
St. Thomas i. U.S.V.Is. 87 18.22N 64.57W
St. Tropez France 17 43.16N 6.39E
St. Truiden Belgium 14 50.49N 5.11E
St. Valéry France 15 49.52N 0.43E
St. Vallier France 17 45.11N 4.49E
St. Vincent, G. Australia 66 35.00S138.05E
St. Vincent and the Grenadines Windward Is. 87 13.00N 61.15W
St. Vith Belgium 14 50.15N 6.08E
St. Wendel Germany 14 49.27N 7.10E
St. Yrieix France 17 45.31N 1.12E
St. Zénon Canada 77 46.33N 73.49W
Saitama d. Japan 35 35.55N139.00E
Sajama mtn. Bolivia 92 18.06S 69.00W
Saka Kenya 55 0.09S 39.18E
Sakai Japan 35 34.35N135.28E
Sakākah Saudi Arabia 42 29.59N 40.12E
Sakakawea, L. see Garrison Resr. U.S.A. 82
Sakami r. Canada 76 53.40N 76.40W
Sakami, Lac l. Canada 76 53.10N 77.00W
Sâkâne, Erg i-n f. Mali 50 21.00N 1.00W
Sakania Zaïre 55 12.44S 28.34E
Sakarya r. Turkey 42 41.08N 30.36E
Sakété Benin 53 6.45N 2.45E
Sakhalin i. U.S.S.R. 31 50.00N143.00E
Sākhar Afghan. 40 32.57N 65.32E
Sakhi Sarwar Pakistan 40 29.59N 70.18E
Sakht-Sar Iran 43 36.54N 50.41E
Sakoli India 41 21.05N 79.59E
Sakrand Pakistan 40 26.08N 68.16E
Sakri India 40 21.02N 74.40E
Sakrivier R.S.A. 56 30.53S 20.24E
Sakti India 41 22.02N 82.58E
Sakuma Japan 35 35.05N137.48E
Sal r. U.S.S.R. 25 47.33N 40.40E
Sala Ethiopia 48 16.58N 37.27E
Sala Sweden 23 59.55N 16.36E
Salaca r. U.S.S.R. 23 57.45N 24.21E
Salacgriva U.S.S.R. 23 57.45N 24.21E
Salado r. Buenos Aires Argentina 93 35.44S 57.22W
Salado r. Santa Fé Argentina 93 31.40S 60.41W
Salado r. La Pampa Argentina 93 36.15S 66.55W
Salado r. Mexico 83 26.50N 99.17W
Salaga Ghana 52 8.36N 0.32W
Salailua W. Samoa 68 13.42S172.35W
Salālah Oman 38 17.00N 54.04E
Salālah Sudan 48 21.19N 36.13E
Salamanca Spain 16 40.58N 5.40W
Salamat d. Chad 49 11.00N 20.40E
Salāmbek Pakistan 40 28.18N 65.09E
Salamina Colombia 90 5.24N 75.31W
Salām Khān Afghan. 40 31.47N 66.45E
Salani W. Samoa 68 14.02S171.35W
Salatiga Indonesia 37 7.15S110.34E
Salāya India 40 22.19N 69.35E
Sala y Gomez i. Pacific Oc. 69 26.28S105.28W
Salbris France 15 47.26N 2.03E
Salcombe U.K. 11 50.14N 3.47W
Saldaña Spain 16 42.32N 4.48W
Saldanha R.S.A. 56 33.00S 17.56E
Saldanha B. R.S.A. 56 33.05S 17.50E
Saldus U.S.S.R. 23 56.40N 22.30E
Sale Australia 67 38.06S147.06E
Salé Morocco 50 34.04N 6.50W
Salekhard U.S.S.R. 24 66.33N 66.35E
Salelologa W. Samoa 68 13.43S172.13W
Salem India 39 11.38N 78.08E
Salem Ind. U.S.A. 84 38.38N 86.06W
Salem Mo. U.S.A. 83 37.39N 91.32W
Salem N.J. U.S.A. 85 39.34N 75.28W
Salem Oreg. U.S.A. 80 44.57N123.01W
Salem Va. U.S.A. 85 37.17N 80.04W
Sälen Sweden 23 61.10N 13.16E
Salerno Italy 18 40.41N 14.45E
Salerno, Golfo di g. Italy 18 40.30N 14.45E
Salford U.K. 10 53.30N 2.17W
Salgótarján Hungary 21 48.07N 19.48E
Salgueiro Brazil 91 8.04S 39.05W
Salima Malaŵi 55 13.45S 34.29E
Salim's Tanzania 55 10.37S 36.33E
Salina U.S.A. 82 38.50N 97.37W
Salina Cruz Mexico 86 16.11N 95.12W
Salinas Ecuador 90 2.13S 80.58W
Salinas U.S.A. 80 36.40N121.38W
Salinas r. U.S.A. 78 36.45N121.48W
Saline r. U.S.A. 82 38.51N 97.30W
Salinópolis Brazil 91 0.37S 47.20W
Salins France 17 46.56N 5.53E
Salisbury U.K. 11 51.04N 1.48W
Salisbury Md. U.S.A. 85 38.22N 75.36W
Salisbury N.C. U.S.A. 85 35.20N 80.30W
Salisbury Plain f. U.K. 11 51.15N 1.55W
Salisbury Sd. U.S.A. 74 57.30N135.56W
Şalkhad Syria 44 32.29N 36.42E
Sallisaw U.S.A. 83 35.28N 94.47W
Salluit Canada 73 62.10N 75.40W
Sallyāna Nepal 41 28.22N 82.12E
Salmās Iran 43 38.13N 44.50E
Salmi U.S.S.R. 24 61.19N 31.46E
Salmon r. Canada 74 54.03N122.40W
Salmon U.S.A. 80 45.11N113.55W
Salmon r. U.S.A. 80 45.51N116.46W
Salmon Gums Australia 63 32.59S121.39E
Salmon River Mts. U.S.A. 80 44.45N115.30W
Salo Finland 23 60.23N 23.08E
Salò Italy 15 45.36N 10.31E
Salobreña Spain 16 36.45N 3.35W
Salome U.S.A. 81 33.47N113.37W
Salon France 17 43.38N 5.06E
Salonga r. Zaïre 54 0.09S 19.52E
Salonta Romania 21 46.48N 21.40E
Salsk U.S.S.R. 25 46.30N 41.33E
Salso r. Italy 18 37.07N 13.57E
Salsomaggiore Terme Italy 15 44.49N 9.59E
Salt r. U.S.A. 81 33.23N112.18W
Salta Argentina 92 24.47S 65.24W
Salta d. Argentina 92 25.00S 65.00W
Saltdal Norway 22 67.06N 15.25E
Saltee Is. Rep. of Ire. 13 52.08N 6.36W
Saltfjorden est. Norway 22 67.15N 14.10E
Saltfleet U.K. 10 53.25N 0.11E
Salt Fork r. U.S.A. 79 36.41N 97.05W
Saltillo Mexico 83 25.25N101.00W
Salt Lake City U.S.A. 80 40.46N111.53W
Salto Argentina 93 34.17S 60.15W
Salto Brazil 94 23.10S 47.16W
Salto r. Italy 18 42.23N 12.54E
Salto Uruguay 93 31.23S 57.58W
Salto da Divisa Brazil 91 16.04S 40.00W
Salto Grande, Embalse de resr. Argentina/Uruguay 93 31.00S 57.50W
Salton Sea l. U.S.A. 81 33.19N115.50W
Salūmbar India 40 24.08N 74.03E
Saluzzo Italy 15 44.39N 7.29E
Salvador Brazil 91 12.58S 38.29W
Salvador Canada 75 52.12N109.32W
Salversville U.S.A. 85 37.43N 83.06W
Salween r. Burma 34 16.32N 97.35E
Salyany U.S.S.R. 43 39.36N 48.59E
Salzbrunn Namibia 56 24.23S 18.00E
Salzburg Austria 20 47.54N 13.03E
Salzburg d. Austria 20 47.25N 13.15E
Salzgitter Germany 20 52.02N 10.22E
Salzwedel Germany 20 52.51N 11.09E
Sam India 40 26.50N 70.31E
Samalambo Angola 54 14.16S 17.53E
Samālūt Egypt 44 28.18N 30.43E
Samaná Dom. Rep. 87 19.14N 69.20W
Samana Cay i. Bahamas 87 23.05N 73.45W
Samanga Tanzania 55 8.24S 39.18E
Samannūd Egypt 44 30.58N 31.14E
Samar i. Phil. 37 11.45N125.15E
Samara r. U.S.S.R. 24 53.17N 50.42E
Samarai P.N.G. 64 10.37S150.40E
Samarinda Indonesia 36 0.30S117.09E
Samarkand U.S.S.R. 28 39.40N 66.57E
Sāmarrā Iraq 43 34.13N 43.52E
Samāstipur India 41 25.51N 85.47E
Samawāri Pakistan 40 28.34N 66.46E
Samba Zaïre 54 0.14N 21.19E
Sambalpur India 41 21.27N 83.58E
Sambao r. Madagascar 57 16.40S 44.26E
Sambava Madagascar 57 14.16S 50.10E
Sambāza Pakistan 40 31.46N 69.20E
Sambhal India 41 28.35N 78.33E
Sāmbhar India 40 26.55N 75.12E
Sāmbhar L. India 40 26.58N 75.05E
Sambor U.S.S.R. 21 49.31N 23.10E
Samborombón, Bahía b. Argentina 93 36.00S 57.00W
Sambre r. Belgium 14 50.29N 4.52E
Samburu Kenya 55 3.46S 39.17E
Samch'ŏk S. Korea 31 37.30N129.10E
Samdari India 40 25.49N 72.35E
Same Tanzania 55 4.10S 37.43E
Samnū Libya 51 27.16N 14.54E
Samoa is. Pacific Oc. 68 14.20S170.00W
Samoa Is. Pacific Oc. 68 14.00S171.00W
Samobor Yugo. 20 45.48N 15.43E
Samorogouan Burkina 52 11.21N 4.57W
Sámos i. Greece 19 37.44N 26.45E
Samothráki i. Greece 19 40.26N 25.35E
Sampang Indonesia 37 7.13S113.15E
Sampit Indonesia 36 2.34S112.59E
Sam Rayburn Resr. U.S.A. 83 31.27N 94.37W
Samsang China 41 30.22N 82.57E
Sam Son Vietnam 33 19.44N105.53E
Samsun Turkey 42 41.17N 36.22E
Samtredia U.S.S.R. 25 42.10N 42.22E
Samui, Ko i. Thailand 34 9.30N100.00E
Samur r. U.S.S.R. 25 42.00N 48.20E
Samut Prakan Thailand 34 13.32N100.35E
Samut Sakhon Thailand 34 13.31N100.13E
San r. Cambodia 34 13.32N105.57E
San Mali 52 13.21N 4.57W
San r. Poland 21 50.25N 22.20E
Şan'ā' Yemen 45 15.23N 44.14E
Sana see Şan'ā' Yemen 45
Sana r. Yugo. 20 45.03N 16.23E
Sanaba Burkina 52 12.25N 3.47W
Sanaga r. Cameroon 53 3.35N 9.40E
San Ambrosio i. Pacific Oc. 69 26.28S 79.53W
Sānand India 40 22.59N 72.23E
Sanandaj Iran 43 35.18N 47.01E
San Andreas U.S.A. 80 38.12N120.41W
San Andrés, Isla de i. Colombia 87 12.33N 81.42W
San Andrés Tuxtla Mexico 86 18.27N 95.13W
San Angelo U.S.A. 83 31.28N100.26W
San Antonio Chile 93 33.35S 71.38W
San Antonio N.Mex. U.S.A. 81 33.55N106.52W
San Antonio Tex. U.S.A. 83 29.28N 98.31W
San Antonio, C. Cuba 87 21.50N 84.57W
San Antonio, Cabo c. Argentina 93 36.40S 56.42W
San Antonio, Punta c. Mexico 81 29.45N115.41W
San Antonio, Sierra de mts. Mexico 81 30.00N110.10W
San Antonio Abad Spain 16 38.58N 1.18E
San Antonio de Areco Argentina 93 34.16S 59.30W
San Antonio Oeste Argentina 93 40.44S 64.57W
San Augustine U.S.A. 83 31.32N 94.07W
Sanāwad India 40 22.11N 76.04E
San Benedetto Italy 18 42.57N 13.53E
San Benedetto Po Italy 15 45.02N 10.55E
San Benito Guatemala 87 16.55N 89.54W
San Benito U.S.A. 83 26.08N 97.38W
San Bernardino U.S.A. 81 34.06N117.17W
San Bernardo Chile 93 33.36S 70.43W
San Blas, C. U.S.A. 85 29.40N 85.22W
San Bonifacio Italy 15 45.24N 11.16E
San Carlos Chile 93 36.25S 71.58W
San Carlos Mexico 83 29.01N100.51W
San Carlos Nicaragua 87 11.07N 84.47W
San Carlos Phil. 37 15.59N120.22E
San Carlos Venezuela 90 1.55N 67.04W
San Carlos Venezuela 90 9.39N 68.35W
San Carlos de Bariloche Argentina 93 41.08S 71.15W
San Carlos del Zulia Venezuela 90 9.01N 71.55W
Sancerre France 15 47.20N 2.51E
Sancerrois, Collines du hills France 15 47.25N 2.45E
Sancha He r. China 33 26.50N106.04E
San Clemente U.S.A. 81 33.26N117.37W
San Clemente i. U.S.A. 81 32.54N118.29W
San Cristóbal Argentina 92 30.20S 61.41W
San Cristóbal Dom. Rep. 87 18.27N 70.07W
San Cristóbal Venezuela 90 7.46N 72.15W
Sancti Spíritus Cuba 87 21.55N 79.28W
Sand Norway 23 59.29N 6.15E
Sanda i. U.K. 12 55.17N 5.34W
Sandakan Malaysia 36 5.52N118.04E
Sandaré Mali 52 14.40N 10.15W
Sanday i. U.K. 12 59.15N 2.33W
Sandbach U.K. 10 53.09N 2.23W
Sandefjord Norway 23 59.08N 10.14E
Sanders U.S.A. 81 35.13N109.20W
Sanderson U.S.A. 83 30.09N102.24W
Sandersville U.S.A. 85 32.59N 82.49W
Sandgate Australia 67 27.18S153.00E
Sandhornöy i. Norway 22 67.05N 14.10E
Sāndi India 41 27.18N 79.57E
Sandia Peru 90 14.14S 69.25W
San Diego U.S.A. 81 32.43N117.09W
San Diego, C. Argentina 93 54.38S 65.05W
Sandīla India 41 27.05N 80.31E
Sand Lake town Canada 76 47.45N 84.30W
Sandnes Norway 23 58.51N 5.44E
Sandness U.K. 12 60.18N 1.38W
Sandö i. Faroe Is. 8 61.50N 6.45W
Sandoa Zaïre 54 9.41S 22.56E
Sandomierz Poland 21 50.41N 21.45E
San Donà di Piave Italy 15 45.38N 12.34E
Sandover r. Australia 64 21.43S136.32E
Sandoway Burma 34 18.28N 94.20E
Sandown U.K. 11 50.39N 1.09W
Sandpoint town U.S.A. 80 48.17N116.34W
Sandringham U.K. 10 52.50N 0.30E
Sandstone Australia 63 27.59S119.17E
Sandu Shuizu Zizhixian China 33 25.59N107.52E
Sandusky Ohio U.S.A. 84 41.27N 82.42W
Sandveld f. Namibia 56 21.25S 20.00E
Sandviken Sweden 23 60.37N 16.46E
Sandwich B. Canada 77 53.35N 57.15W
Sandwip I. Bangla. 41 22.29N 91.26E
Sandy U.S.A. 80 40.35N111.53W
Sandy B. St. Helena 95 16.02S 5.42W
Sandy Bight b. Australia 63 33.53S123.25E
Sandy C. Australia 64 24.42S153.17E
Sandy Creek town U.S.A. 84 43.39N 76.05W
Sandy Desert Pakistan 40 28.00N 65.00E
Sandy Hook f. U.S.A. 85 40.27N 74.00W
Sandy L. Nfld. Canada 77 49.16N 57.00W
Sandy L. Ont. Canada 75 53.00N 93.00W
Sandy Lake town Ont. Canada 75 53.00N 93.00W
Sandy Lake town Sask. Canada 75 57.00N107.15W
San Enrique Argentina 93 35.47S 60.22W
San Esteban, Isla i. Mexico 81 28.41N112.35W
San Felipe Chile 93 32.45S 70.44W
San Felipe Colombia 90 1.55N 67.06W
San Felipe Mexico 81 31.00N114.52W
San Felipe Venezuela 90 10.25N 68.40W
San Félix i. Pacific Oc. 69 26.23S 80.05W
San Fernando Argentina 93 34.26S 58.34W
San Fernando Chile 93 34.35S 71.00W
San Fernando r. Mexico 83 24.55N 97.40W
San Fernando Phil. 37 16.39N120.19E
San Fernando Spain 16 36.28N 6.12W
San Fernando Trinidad 90 10.16N 61.28W
San Fernando de Apure Venezuela 90 7.35N 67.15W
San Fernando de Atabapo Venezuela 90 4.03N 67.45W
Sanford r. Australia 62 27.22S115.53E
Sanford Fla. U.S.A. 85 28.49N 81.17W
Sanford N.C. U.S.A. 85 35.29N 79.10W
San Francisco Argentina 92 31.29S 62.06W
San Francisco Mexico 81 30.50N112.40W
San Francisco U.S.A. 80 37.48N122.24W
San Francisco r. U.S.A. 81 32.59N109.22W
San Francisco, C. Ecuador 90 0.50N 80.05W
San Francisco del Oro Mexico 81 26.52N105.51W
San Francisco de Macorís Dom. Rep. 87 19.19N 70.15W
Sanga Angola 54 11.09S 15.21E
Sanga-Tolon U.S.S.R. 29 61.44N149.30E
Sang-e Māsheh Afghan. 40 33.08N 67.27E
Sanggan He r. China 32 40.23N115.18E
Sangha r. Congo 54 1.10S 16.47E
Sanghar Pakistan 40 26.02N 68.57E
Sangihe i. Indonesia 37 3.30N125.30E
Sangihe, Kepulauan is. Indonesia 37 2.45N125.20E
San Gil Colombia 90 6.35N 73.08W
San Giovanni in Persiceto Italy 15 44.38N 11.11E
Sangkulirang Indonesia 36 1.00N117.58E
Sāngli India 38 16.55N 74.37E
Sangmélima Cameroon 53 2.55N 12.01E
Sangonera r. Spain 16 37.58N 1.04W
San Gottardo, Passo del pass Switz. 20 46.30N 8.55E
Sangre de Cristo Mts. U.S.A. 80 37.30N105.15W
San Gregorio Uruguay 93 32.37S 55.40W
Sangri China 41 29.18N 92.05E
Sangrūr India 40 30.14N 75.51E
Sangzhi China 33 29.24N110.09E
Sanhala Ivory Coast 52 10.01N 6.48W
San Ignacio Bolivia 92 16.23S 60.59W
San Ignacio Mexico 81 27.27N112.51W
San Ignacio Paraguay 92 26.52S 57.03W
San Ignacio, Laguna l. Mexico 81 26.50N113.11W
San Isidro Argentina 93 34.29S 58.31W
Saniyah, Hawr as l. Iraq 43 31.52N 46.50E
San Javier Argentina 93 30.40S 59.55W
San Javier Bolivia 92 16.22S 62.38W
San Javier Chile 93 35.35S 71.45W
Sanjāwi Pakistan 40 30.17N 68.21E
San Joaquin r. U.S.A. 80 38.03N121.50W
San Jorge, Bahía de b. Mexico 81 31.08N113.15W
San Jorge, Golfo g. Argentina 93 46.00S 66.00W
San José Costa Rica 87 9.59N 84.04W
San José Guatemala 86 13.58N 90.50W
San José Mexico 81 27.32N110.09W
San Jose U.S.A. 80 37.20N121.53W
San José, Isla i. Mexico 81 25.00N110.38W
San José de Chiquitos Bolivia 92 17.53S 60.45W
San José de Feliciano Argentina 93 30.25S 58.45W
San José de Guanipa Venezuela 90 8.54N 64.09W
San José del Cabo town Mexico 81 23.03N109.41W
San José del Guaviare Colombia 90 2.35N 72.38W
San José de Mayo Uruguay 93 34.20S 56.42W
San José de Ocuné Colombia 90 4.15N 70.20W
San Juan Argentina 92 31.30S 68.30W
San Juan d. Argentina 92 31.00S 68.30W
San Juan r. Costa Rica 87 10.50N 83.40W
San Juan Dom. Rep. 87 18.40N 71.05W
San Juan Peru 92 15.20S 75.09W
San Juan Phil. 37 8.25N126.22E
San Juan Puerto Rico 87 18.29N 66.08W
San Juan r. U.S.A. 80 37.18N110.28W
San Juan, C. Argentina 93 54.45S 63.50W
San Juan Bautista Spain 16 39.05N 1.30E
San Juan de Guadalupe Mexico 83 24.38N102.44W
San Juan del Norte Nicaragua 87 10.58N 83.40W
San Juan de los Morros Venezuela 90 9.53N 67.23W
San Juan del Río Durango Mexico 83 24.47N104.27W
San Juan del Río Querétaro Mexico 86 20.23N100.00W
San Juan Mts. U.S.A. 80 37.35N107.10W
San Julián Argentina 93 49.19S 67.40W
San Justo Argentina 93 30.47S 60.35W
Sankh r. India 41 22.15N 84.48E
Sankheda India 40 22.10N 73.35E
Sānkra India 41 20.18N 82.03E
Sankt Niklaus Switz. 15 46.11N 7.48E
Sankuru r. Zaïre 54 4.20S 20.27E
San Lázaro, Cabo c. Mexico 81 24.50N112.18W
San Lázaro, Sierra de mts. Mexico 81 23.20N110.00W
San Leonardo Spain 16 41.49N 3.04W
San Lorenzo Argentina 93 32.45S 60.44W
San Lorenzo mtn. Chile 93 47.37S 72.19W
San Lorenzo Ecuador 90 1.17N 78.50W
San Lorenzo r. Mexico 81 24.15N107.25W
San Lorenzo de El Escorial Spain 16 40.34N 4.08W

Sanlúcar de Barrameda Spain **16** 36.46N 6.21W
Sanlúcar la Mayor Spain **16** 37.26N 6.18W
San Lucas Bolivia **92** 20.06S 65.07W
San Lucas, Cabo *c.* Mexico **81** 22.50N109.55W
San Luis Argentina **93** 33.20S 66.20W
San Luis *d.* Argentina **93** 34.00S 66.00W
San Luis Cuba **87** 20.13N 75.50W
San Luis Obispo U.S.A. **81** 35.17N120.40W
San Luis Potosí Mexico **86** 22.10N101.00W
San Luis Potosí *d.* Mexico **86** 23.00N100.00W
San Luis Rio Colorado Mexico **81** 32.29N114.48W
San Luis Valley *f.* U.S.A. **80** 37.25N106.00W
San Marcos U.S.A. **83** 29.53N 97.57W
San Marino Europe **15** 43.55N 12.27E
San Marino *town* San Marino **15** 43.55N 12.27E
San Martin *r.* Bolivia **92** 12.25S 64.25W
San Mateo U.S.A. **80** 37.35N122.19W
San Matías Bolivia **90** 16.22S 58.24W
San Matías, Golfo *g.* Argentina **93** 41.30S 64.00W
Sanmenxia China **32** 35.45N111.22E
San Miguel *r.* Bolivia **90** 13.52S 63.56W
San Miguel *r.* Bolivia **92** 12.25S 64.25W
San Miguel El Salvador **87** 13.28N 88.10W
San Miguel del Monte Argentina **93** 35.25S 58.49W
San Miguel de Tucumán Argentina **92** 26.49S 65.13W
San Miguelito Panama **87** 9.02N 79.30W
Sanming China **33** 26.25N117.35E
Sannār Sudan **49** 13.33N 33.38E
Sannicandro Italy **18** 41.50N 15.34E
San Nicolas Argentina **93** 33.20S 60.13W
Sanniquellie Liberia **52** 7.24N 8.45W
Sanok Poland **21** 49.35N 22.10E
San Pablo Phil. **37** 13.58N121.10E
San Pedro Buenos Aires Argentina **93** 33.40S 59.41W
San Pedro Jujuy Argentina **92** 24.14S 64.50W
San Pedro Dom. Rep. **87** 18.30N 69.18W
San Pedro Ivory Coast **52** 4.45N 6.37W
San Pedro Sonora Mexico **81** 27.00N109.53W
San Pedro Paraguay **94** 24.08S 57.08W
San Pedro, Punta *c.* Costa Rica **87** 8.38N 83.45W
San Pedro, Sierra de *mts.* Spain **16** 39.20N 6.20W
San Pedro de las Colonais Mexico **83** 25.45N102.59W
San Pedro Mártir, Sierra *mts.* Mexico **81** 30.45N115.30W
San Pedro Sula Honduras **87** 15.26N 88.01W
San Pellegrino Terme Italy **15** 45.50N 9.40E
San Pietro *i.* Italy **18** 39.09N 8.16E
Sanquhar U.K. **12** 55.22N 3.56W
San Quintín Mexico **81** 30.28N115.58W
San Rafael U.S.A. **80** 37.59N122.31W
San Raphael Argentina **93** 34.40S 68.21W
San Remo Italy **15** 43.48N 7.46E
San Salvador Argentina **93** 31.37S 58.30W
San Salvador *i.* Bahamas **87** 24.00N 74.32W
San Salvador El Salvador **87** 13.40N 89.10W
San Salvador de Jujuy Argentina **92** 24.10S 65.20W
San Sebastián Argentina **93** 53.15S 68.30W
San Sebastián Spain **16** 43.19N 1.59W
San Severo Italy **18** 41.40N 15.24E
Sanshui China **33** 23.09N112.52E
San Simon U.S.A. **81** 32.16N109.14W
Santa *r.* Peru **90** 9.00S 78.35W
Santa Ana Argentina **92** 27.20S 65.35W
Santa Ana Bolivia **92** 13.45S 65.35W
Santa Ana El Salvador **87** 14.00N 89.31W
Santa Ana Mexico **81** 30.33N111.07W
Santa Ana U.S.A. **81** 33.44N117.54W
Santa Bárbara Mexico **81** 26.48N105.49W
Santa Barbara U.S.A. **81** 34.25N119.42W
Santa Catarina *d.* Brazil **94** 27.00S 52.00W
Santa Catarina Mexico **83** 25.41N100.28W
Santa Clara Cuba **87** 22.25N 79.58W
Santa Clara Calif. U.S.A. **80** 37.21N121.57W
Santa Clara Utah U.S.A. **80** 37.08N113.39W
Santa Clotilde Peru **90** 2.25S 73.35W
Santa Comba Dão Portugal **16** 40.24N 8.08W
Santa Cruz *d.* Argentina **93** 48.00S 69.30W
Santa Cruz *r.* Argentina **93** 50.03S 68.35W
Santa Cruz Bolivia **92** 17.45S 63.14W
Santa Cruz *d.* Bolivia **92** 17.45S 62.00W
Santa Cruz Madeira Is. **95** 32.41N 16.48W
Santa Cruz U.S.A. **80** 36.58N122.08W
Santa Cruz *i.* U.S.A. **81** 34.01N119.45W
Santa Cruz de Tenerife Canary Is. **50** 28.28N 16.15W
Santa Cruz Is. Solomon Is. **68** 10.30S166.00E
Santa Domingo Mexico **81** 25.32N112.02W
Santa Elena Argentina **93** 31.00S 59.50W
Santa Elena U.S.A. **83** 26.46N 98.30W
Santa Elena, C. Costa Rica **87** 10.54N 85.56W
Santa Fé Argentina **93** 31.40S 60.40W
Santa Fé *d.* Argentina **92** 30.00S 61.00W
Santa Fe U.S.A. **81** 35.42N106.57W
Santa Filomena Brazil **91** 9.07S 45.56W
Santai China **33** 31.10N105.02E
Santa Inés, Isla *i.* Chile **93** 53.40S 73.00W
Santa Isabel Argentina **93** 36.15S 66.55W
Santa Isabel do Morro Brazil **91** 11.36S 50.37W
Sāntalpur India **40** 23.45N 71.10E
Santa Lucía Uruguay **93** 34.27S 56.24W
Santa Lucía *r.* Uruguay **93** 34.48S 56.22W
Santa Lucia Range *mts.* U.S.A. **81** 36.00N121.20W
Santa Margarita, Isla de *i.* Mexico **81** 24.25N111.50W
Santa Margarita, Sierra de *mts.* Mexico **81** 30.00N110.00W
Santa Margherita Ligure Italy **15** 44.20N 9.12E
Santa María Brazil **94** 29.40S 53.47W
Santa Maria U.S.A. **81** 34.57N120.26W
Santa María, Laguna de *l.* Mexico **81** 31.07N107.17W
Santa Maria di Leuca, Capo *c.* Italy **19** 39.47N 18.24E
Santa Maria Madalena Brazil **94** 21.58S 42.02W
Santa Marta Colombia **90** 11.18N 74.10W
Santa Marta, Sierra Nevada de *mts.* Colombia **90** 11.20N 73.00W
Santa Monica U.S.A. **81** 34.01N118.30W
Santana Madeira Is. **95** 32.48N 16.54W
Santana do Livramento Brazil **93** 30.53S 55.31W
Santander Colombia **90** 3.00N 76.25W
Santander Spain **16** 43.28N 3.48W
Santañy Spain **16** 39.20N 3.07E
Santarém Brazil **91** 2.26S 54.41W
Santarém Portugal **16** 39.14N 8.40W
Santa Rosa Argentina **93** 36.00S 64.40W
Santa Rosa Bolivia **90** 10.36S 67.25W
Santa Rosa Brazil **94** 27.52S 54.29W
Santa Rosa Honduras **87** 14.47N 88.46W
Santa Rosa *i.* U.S.A. **81** 33.58N120.06W
Santa Rosa Calif. U.S.A. **80** 38.26N122.34W
Santa Rosa N.Mex. U.S.A. **81** 34.57N104.41W
Santa Rosa, Mt. Guam **68** 13.32N144.55E
Santa Rosa de Cabal Colombia **90** 4.52N 75.37W
Santa Rosalía Mexico **81** 27.19N112.17W
Santa Rosa Range *mts.* U.S.A. **80** 41.00N117.40W
Santa Teresa Mexico **83** 25.19N 97.50W
Santa Vitória do Palmar Brazil **94** 33.31S 53.21W
San Telmo Mexico **81** 31.00N116.06W
Sant Feliu de Guíxols Spain **16** 41.47N 3.02E
Santhià Italy **15** 45.22N 8.10E
Santiago Chile **93** 33.27S 70.40W
Santiago Dom. Rep. **87** 19.30N 70.42W
Santiago Panama **87** 8.08N 80.59W
Santiago *r.* Peru **90** 4.30S 77.48W
Santiago de Compostela Spain **16** 42.52N 8.33W
Santiago de Cuba Cuba **87** 20.00N 75.49W
Santiago del Estero Argentina **92** 27.50S 64.15W
Santiago del Estero *d.* Argentina **92** 27.40S 63.30W
Santiago Vázquez Uruguay **93** 34.48S 56.21W
Sāntipur India **41** 23.15N 88.26E
Santo Amaro Brazil **91** 12.35S 38.41W
Santo André Brazil **94** 23.39S 46.29W
Santo Angelo Brazil **94** 28.18S 54.16W
Santo Antônio do Içá Brazil **90** 3.05S 67.57W
Santo Domingo Dom. Rep. **87** 18.30N 69.57W
Santo Domingo Pueblo U.S.A. **81** 35.31N106.22W
Santoña Spain **16** 43.27N 3.26W
Santos Brazil **94** 23.56S 46.22W
Santos Dumont Brazil **94** 21.30S 43.34W
Santo Tomás Peru **90** 14.34S 72.30W
Santo Tomé Argentina **92** 28.31S 56.03W
Santpoort Neth. **14** 52.27N 4.38E
San Valentín, Cerro *mtn.* Chile **93** 46.40S 73.25W
San Vicente El Salvador **87** 13.38N 88.42W
San Vito al Tagliamento Italy **15** 45.54N 12.52E
Sanyuan China **32** 34.30N108.52E
Sanza Pombo Angola **54** 7.20S 16.12E
São Borja Brazil **94** 28.35S 56.01W
São Caetano do Sul Brazil **94** 23.36S 46.34W
São Carlos Brazil **94** 22.01S 47.54W
São Domingos Guinea Bissau **52** 12.22N 16.08W
São Francisco *r.* Brazil **91** 10.20S 36.20W
São Francisco do Sol Brazil **94** 26.17S 48.39W
São Gabriel Brazil **94** 30.20S 54.19W
São Gonçalo do Sapucaí Brazil **94** 21.54S 45.35W
Sao Hill *town* Tanzania **55** 8.21S 35.10E
São João da Boa Vista Brazil **94** 21.59S 46.45W
São João da Madeira Portugal **16** 40.54N 8.30W
São João del Rei Brazil **94** 21.08S 44.15W
São João do Piauí Brazil **91** 8.21S 42.15W
São Joaquim da Barra Brazil **94** 20.36S 47.51W
São José do Calçado Brazil **94** 21.01S 41.37W
São José do Rio Prêto Brazil **94** 20.50S 49.20W
São José dos Campos Brazil **94** 23.07S 45.52W
São Leopoldo Brazil **94** 29.46S 51.09W
São Lourenço Brazil **94** 22.08S 45.05W
São Luís Brazil **91** 2.34S 44.16W
São Manuel Brazil **94** 22.40S 48.35W
São Manuel *r.* see Teles Pires *r.* Brazil **91**
São Miguel d'Oeste Brazil **94** 26.45S 53.34W
Saona *i.* Dom. Rep. **87** 18.09N 68.42W
Saône *r.* France **20** 45.46N 4.52E
Saoner India **41** 21.23N 78.54E
São Paulo Brazil **94** 23.33S 46.39W
São Paulo *d.* Brazil **94** 22.05S 48.00W
São Paulo de Olivença Brazil **90** 3.34S 68.55W
São Roque Brazil **94** 23.31S 47.09W
São Roque, Cabo de *c.* Brazil **95** 5.00S 35.00W
São Sebastião Brazil **94** 23.48S 45.26W
São Sebastião, Ilha de *i.* Brazil **94** 23.53S 45.17W
São Sebastião do Paraíso Brazil **94** 20.54S 46.59W
São Tiago Brazil **94** 20.54S 44.30W
São Tomé & Príncipe Africa **53** 2.00N 6.40E
Saoura, Oued *wadi* Algeria **50** 28.48N 0.50W
São Vicente Brazil **94** 23.57S 46.23W
São Vicente, Cabo de *c.* Portugal **16** 37.01N 8.59W
São Vicente de Minas Brazil **94** 21.40S 44.26W
Sapé Brazil **91** 7.06S 35.13W
Sapele Nigeria **53** 5.53N 5.41E
Sapelo I. U.S.A. **85** 31.28N 81.15W
Sapporo Japan **31** 43.05N141.21E
Sapri Italy **18** 40.04N 15.38E
Sapt Kosi *r.* Nepal **41** 26.30N 86.55E
Sapu Angola **54** 12.28S 19.26E
Sapulpa U.S.A. **83** 36.00N 96.06W
Saqin Sum China **32** 42.06N111.03E
Saqqārah Egypt **44** 29.51N 31.13E
Saqqez Iran **43** 36.14N 46.15E
Sarāb Iran **43** 37.56N 47.35E
Sarābiyūm Egypt **44** 30.23N 32.17E
Sara Buri Thailand **34** 14.30N100.59E
Sarāi Naurang Pakistan **40** 32.50N 70.47E
Sarajevo Yugo. **21** 43.52N 18.26E
Saranac Lake *town* U.S.A. **76** 44.20N 74.10W
Sarandí del Yi Uruguay **93** 33.21S 55.38W
Sarandí Grande Uruguay **93** 33.44S 56.20W
Sārangarh India **41** 21.36N 83.05E
Sārangpur India **40** 23.34N 76.28E
Saranley Somali Rep. **49** 2.28N 42.08E
Saranpaul U.S.S.R. **24** 64.15N 60.58E
Saransk U.S.S.R. **24** 54.12N 45.10E
Sarapul U.S.S.R. **24** 56.30N 53.49E
Sarar Plain Somali Rep. **45** 9.35N 46.15E
Sarasota U.S.A. **85** 27.20N 82.32W
Sarata U.S.S.R. **21** 46.00N 29.40E
Saratoga U.S.A. **80** 37.16N122.02W
Saratoga Springs U.S.A. **84** 43.05N 73.47W
Saratov U.S.S.R. **25** 51.30N 45.55E
Saravan Laos **34** 15.43N106.24E
Sarawak *d.* Malaysia **36** 2.00N113.00E
Saraychik U.S.S.R. **25** 47.29N 51.42E
Sarbāz Iran **43** 26.39N 61.20E
Sarcelles France **15** 49.00N 2.23E
Sardār Chāh Pakistan **40** 27.58N 64.50E
Sardārpur India **40** 22.39N 74.59E
Sardārshahr India **40** 28.26N 74.29E
Sardegna *d.* Italy **18** 40.05N 9.00E
Sardegna *i.* Italy **18** 40.00N 9.00E
Sardinia *i.* see Sardegna *i.* Italy **18**
Sarek *mtn.* Sweden **22** 67.25N 17.46E
Sareks Nat. Park Sweden **22** 67.15N 17.30E
Sargasso Sea Atlantic Oc. **95** 28.00N 60.00W
Sargodha Pakistan **38** 32.01N 72.40E
Sarh Chad **53** 9.08N 18.22E
Sarhro, Jbel *mts.* Morocco **50** 31.00N 5.55W
Sarī Iran **43** 36.33N 53.06E
Sarikamiş Turkey **42** 40.19N 42.35E
Sarikei Malaysia **36** 2.07N111.31E
Sarina Australia **64** 21.26S149.13E
Sarita U.S.A. **83** 37.13N 97.47W
Sark *i.* U.K. **11** 49.26N 2.22W
Sarlat France **17** 44.53N 1.13E
Sărmasu Romania **21** 46.46N 24.11E
Sarmi Indonesia **37** 1.51S138.45E
Sarmiento Argentina **93** 45.35S 69.05W
Särna Sweden **23** 61.41N 13.08E
Sarnia Canada **76** 42.58N 82.23W
Sarny U.S.S.R. **21** 51.21N 26.31E
Saronno Italy **15** 45.38N 9.02E
Saros Körfezi *g.* Turkey **19** 40.32N 26.25E
Sárospatak Hungary **21** 48.19N 21.34E
Sarpsborg Norway **23** 59.17N 11.07E
Sarrebourg France **17** 48.43N 7.03E
Sarreguemines France **17** 49.06N 7.03E
Sarria Spain **16** 42.47N 7.25W
Sarro Mali **52** 13.40N 5.05W
Sartène France **17** 41.36N 8.59E
Sarthe *d.* France **15** 48.00N 0.05E
Sarthe *r.* France **15** 47.29N 0.30W
Sartilly France **15** 48.45N 1.27W
Sartynya U.S.S.R. **28** 63.22N 63.11E
Şarūr Oman **43** 23.25N 58.10E
Sárvár Hungary **20** 47.15N 16.57E
Saryshagan U.S.S.R. **30** 46.08N 73.32E
Sarzana Italy **15** 44.07N 9.58E
Sasabeneh Ethiopia **45** 7.55N 43.39E
Sasarām India **41** 24.57N 84.02E
Sasebo Japan **31** 33.10N129.42E
Saser *mtn.* Jammu & Kashmir **41** 34.50N 77.50E
Saskatchewan *d.* Canada **75** 55.00N106.00W
Saskatchewan *r.* Canada **75** 53.12N 99.16W
Saskatoon Canada **75** 52.07N106.38W
Sasovo U.S.S.R. **24** 54.21N 41.58E
Sassandra Ivory Coast **52** 4.58N 6.08W
Sassandra *r.* Ivory Coast **52** 5.00N 6.04W
Sassari Italy **18** 40.43N 8.33E
Sassnitz Germany **20** 54.32N 13.40E
Sasso Marconi Italy **15** 44.24N 11.15E
Sassuolo Italy **15** 44.33N 10.47E
Sastown Liberia **52** 4.44N 8.01W
Sasyk, Ozero *l.* U.S.S.R. **21** 45.38N 29.38E
Satadougou Mali **52** 12.30N 11.30W
Satāna India **40** 20.35N 74.12E
Satanta U.S.A. **83** 37.26N100.59W
Sātāra India **38** 17.43N 74.05E
Satīt *r.* Sudan **48** 14.20N 35.50E
Satkānia Bangla. **41** 22.04N 92.03E
Satna India **41** 24.35N 80.50E
Sátoraljaújhely Hungary **21** 48.24N 21.39E
Sātpura Range *mts.* India **40** 21.30N 76.00E
Satu Mare Romania **21** 47.48N 22.52E
Satun Thailand **34** 6.38N100.05E
Sauce Argentina **93** 30.05S 58.45W
Sauda Norway **23** 59.39N 6.20E
Saudi Arabia Asia **42** 26.00N 44.00E
Sauk Centre U.S.A. **82** 45.44N 94.57W
Saulieu France **15** 47.17N 4.14E
Sault Sainte Marie Canada **76** 46.32N 84.20W
Sault Sainte Marie U.S.A. **84** 46.29N 84.22W
Saumarez Reef Australia **64** 21.50S153.40E
Saumlaki Indonesia **64** 7.59S131.22E
Saumur France **15** 47.16N 0.05W
Saurimo Angola **54** 9.38S 20.20E
Sausar India **41** 21.42N 78.52E
Sava *r.* Yugo. **21** 44.50N 20.26E
Savage U.S.A. **80** 47.27N104.21W
Savai'i *i.* W. Samoa **68** 13.36S172.27W
Savalou Benin **53** 7.55N 1.59E
Savanna U.S.A. **82** 42.06N 90.07W
Savannah *r.* U.S.A. **85** 32.02N 80.53W
Savannah Ga. U.S.A. **85** 32.04N 81.05W
Savannah Tenn. U.S.A. **83** 35.14N 88.14W
Savannakhét Laos **34** 16.34N104.48E
Savant L. Canada **76** 50.48N 90.20W
Savant Lake *town* Canada **76** 50.20N 90.40W
Savé Benin **53** 8.04N 2.37E
Save *r.* Mozambique **57** 20.59S 35.02E
Sāveh Iran **43** 35.00N 50.25E
Savelugu Ghana **52** 9.39N 0.48W
Saverdun France **17** 43.14N 1.35E
Savigliano Italy **15** 44.38N 7.40E
Savigny-sur-Braye France **15** 47.53N 0.49E
Savona Italy **15** 44.18N 8.28E
Savonlinna Finland **24** 61.52N 28.51E
Savoonga U.S.A. **72** 63.42N170.27W
Savu Sea *see* Sawu, Laut *sea* Pacific Oc. **37**
Sawai Mādhopur India **40** 25.59N 76.22E
Sawākin Sudan **48** 19.07N 37.20E
Sawatch Range *mts.* U.S.A. **82** 39.10N106.25W
Sawbridgeworth U.K. **11** 51.50N 0.09W
Sawdā', Jabal as *hills* Libya **51** 28.40N 15.00E
Sawdā', Qurnat as *mtn.* Lebanon **44** 34.17N 36.04E
Sawdirī Sudan **48** 14.25N 29.05E
Sawfajjin, Wādī Libya **51** 31.54N 15.07E
Sawhāj Egypt **42** 26.33N 31.42E
Şawqirah, Ghubbat *b.* Oman **45** 18.35N 57.00E
Sawston U.K. **11** 52.07N 0.11E
Sawtell Australia **67** 30.21S153.05E
Sawtooth Mts. U.S.A. **80** 44.03N114.35W
Sawu *i.* Indonesia **37** 10.30S121.50E
Sawu, Laut *sea* Pacific Oc. **37** 9.30S122.30E
Saxmundham U.K. **11** 52.13N 1.29E
Saxon Switz. **15** 46.09N 7.11E
Say Mali **52** 13.50N 4.57W
Say Niger **53** 13.08N 2.22E
Sayama Japan **35** 35.51N139.24E
Şaydā Lebanon **44** 33.32N 35.22E
Sayers Lake *town* Australia **66** 32.46S143.20E
Saynshand Mongolia **32** 44.58N110.12E
Sayula Mexico **86** 19.52N103.36W
Sázava *r.* Czech. **20** 49.53N 14.21E
Sbaa Algeria **50** 28.13N 0.10W
Scafell Pike *mtn.* U.K. **10** 54.27N 3.12W
Scalea Italy **18** 39.49N 15.48E
Scalloway U.K. **12** 60.08N 1.17W
Scammon Bay *town* U.S.A. **72** 61.50N165.35W
Scapa Flow *str.* U.K. **12** 58.53N 3.05W
Scarborough Canada **76** 43.44N 79.16W
Scarborough Tobago **90** 11.11N 60.45W
Scarborough U.K. **10** 54.17N 0.24W
Scenic U.S.A. **80** 43.46N102.32W
Schaerbeek Belgium **14** 50.54N 4.20E
Schaffhausen Switz. **20** 47.42N 8.38E
Schagen Neth. **14** 52.47N 4.47E
Schefferville Canada **73** 54.50N 67.00W
Schelde *r.* Belgium **14** 51.13N 4.25E
Schell Creek Range *mts.* U.S.A. **80** 39.10N114.40W
Schenectady U.S.A. **84** 42.47N 73.53W
Scheveningen Neth. **14** 52.07N 4.16E
Schiedam Neth. **14** 51.55N 4.25E
Schiermonnikoog *i.* Neth. **14** 53.28N 6.15E
Schio Italy **15** 45.43N 11.21E
Schleiden Germany **14** 50.32N 6.29E
Schleswig Germany **20** 54.32N 9.34E
Schleswig-Holstein *d.* Germany **20** 54.00N 10.30E
Schouten, Kepulauan *is.* Indonesia **37** 0.45S135.50E
Schouwen *i.* Neth. **14** 51.42N 3.45E
Schreiber Canada **76** 48.45N 87.20W
Schuler Canada **75** 50.22N110.05W
Schuylkill *r.* U.S.A. **85** 39.53N 75.12W
Schwandorf Germany **20** 49.20N 12.08E
Schwaner, Pegunungan *mts.* Indonesia **36** 0.45S113.20E
Schwarzrand *mts.* Namibia **56** 25.40S 16.53E
Schwarzwald *f.* Germany **20** 48.00N 7.45E
Schwedt Germany **20** 53.04N 14.17E
Schweich Germany **14** 49.50N 6.47E
Schweinfurt Germany **20** 50.03N 10.16E
Schwelm Germany **14** 51.17N 7.18E
Schwerin Germany **20** 53.38N 11.25E
Schwyz Switz. **20** 47.02N 8.40E
Sciacca Italy **18** 37.31N 13.05E
Scilla Italy **18** 38.15N 15.44E
Scilly, Isles of U.K. **11** 49.55N 6.20W
Scobey U.S.A. **80** 48.47N105.25W
Scone Australia **67** 32.01S150.53E
Scotia Calif. U.S.A. **80** 40.26N123.31W
Scotia Ridge *f.* Atlantic Oc. **95** 60.00S 35.00W
Scotia Sea Atlantic Oc. **95** 57.00S 45.00W
Scotland U.K. **12** 55.30N 4.00W
Scotsbluff U.S.A. **82** 41.52N103.40W
Scottburgh R.S.A. **56** 30.17S 30.45E
Scott City U.S.A. **82** 38.29N100.54W
Scott Is. Canada **74** 50.48N128.40W
Scott L. Canada **75** 59.55N106.18W
Scott Reef Australia **62** 14.00S121.50E
Scottsbluff U.S.A. **80** 41.52N103.40W
Scottsboro U.S.A. **83** 34.40N 86.02W
Scottsdale Australia **65** 41.09S147.31E
Scottsdale U.S.A. **81** 33.30N111.56W
Scottsville U.S.A. **83** 36.45N 86.11W
Scranton U.S.A. **84** 41.24N 75.40W
Scugog, L. Canada **76** 44.10N 78.51W
Scunthorpe U.K. **10** 53.35N 0.38W
Scutari, L. Yugo. / Albania **19** 42.10N 19.18E
Seabrook, L. Australia **63** 30.56S119.40E
Seaford U.S.A. **85** 38.39N 75.37W
Seagroves U.S.A. **83** 32.57N102.34W
Seahouses U.K. **10** 55.35N 1.38W
Sea Isle City U.S.A. **85** 39.09N 74.42W
Seal *r.* Canada **75** 59.04N 94.48W
Sea Lake *town* Australia **66** 35.31S142.54E
Seal Bight Canada **77** 52.27N 55.40W
Searchlight U.S.A. **81** 35.28N114.55W
Seascale U.K. **10** 54.24N 3.29W
Seaside Calif. U.S.A. **80** 36.37N121.50W
Seaside Oreg. U.S.A. **80** 46.02N123.55W
Seaton U.K. **11** 50.43N 3.05W
Seattle U.S.A. **80** 47.36N122.20W
Seaview Range *mts.* Australia **64** 18.56S146.00E
Sebastian U.S.A. **85** 27.50N 80.29W
Sebastián Vizcaíno, Bahía *b.* Mexico **81** 28.00N114.30W
Sebba Burkina **52** 13.27N 0.33E
Sebeş Romania **21** 45.58N 23.34E
Sebidiro P.N.G. **37** 9.00S142.15E
Sebinkarahisar Turkey **42** 40.19N 38.25E
Sebou, Oued *r.* Morocco **50** 34.15N 6.40W
Sebring U.S.A. **85** 27.30N 81.28W
Sechura, Desierto de *des.* Peru **90** 6.00S 80.30W
Seclin France **14** 50.34N 3.01E
Sêda *r.* Portugal **16** 38.55N 7.30W
Sedalia U.S.A. **82** 38.42N 93.14W
Sedan France **15** 49.42N 4.57E
Sedan U.S.A. **83** 37.08N 96.11W
Seddon New Zealand **60** 41.40S174.04E
Sedgewick Canada **75** 52.46N111.41W
Sédhiou Senegal **52** 12.44N 15.30W
Sedom Israel **44** 31.04N 35.23E
Seeheim Namibia **56** 26.50S 17.45E
Sées France **15** 48.38N 0.10E
Sefrou Morocco **50** 33.50N 4.50W
Segbwema Sierra Leone **52** 8.00N 11.00W
Seggueur, Oued es *wadi* Algeria **51** 31.44N 2.18E
Ségou Mali **52** 13.28N 6.18W
Ségou *d.* Mali **52** 13.55N 6.20W
Segovia Spain **16** 40.57N 4.07W
Segozero, Ozero *l.* U.S.S.R. **24** 63.15N 33.40E
Segré France **15** 47.41N 0.53W
Segre *r.* Spain **16** 41.25N 0.21E
Séguédine Niger **53** 20.12N 12.59E
Séguéla Ivory Coast **52** 7.58N 6.44W
Seguin U.S.A. **83** 29.34N 97.58W
Segura Portugal **16** 39.50N 6.59W
Segura *r.* Spain **16** 38.07N 0.14W
Segura, Sierra de *mts.* Spain **16** 38.00N 2.50W
Sehore India **40** 23.12N 77.05E
Sehwān Pakistan **40** 26.26N 67.52E
Seiches-sur-le-Loir France **15** 47.35N 0.22W
Seiland *i.* Norway **22** 70.25N 23.10E
Seinäjoki Finland **22** 62.47N 22.50E
Seine *r.* France **15** 49.28N 0.25E
Seine, Baie de la *b.* France **15** 49.25N 0.15E
Seine-et-Marne *d.* France **15** 48.30N 3.00E
Seine-Maritime *d.* France **15** 49.45N 1.00E
Sekayu Indonesia **36** 2.58S103.58E
Seki Japan **35** 35.29N136.55E
Sekoma Botswana **56** 24.41S 23.50E
Sekondi-Takoradi Ghana **52** 4.57N 1.44W
Sek'ot'a Ethiopia **49** 12.38N 39.03E
Seküheh Iran **43** 30.45N 61.29E
Selaru *i.* Indonesia **64** 8.09S131.00E
Selatan, Tanjung *c.* Indonesia **36** 4.20S114.45E
Selatan Natuna, Kepulauan *is.* Indonesia **36** 3.00N108.50E
Selayar *i.* Indonesia **37** 6.07S120.28E
Selbu Norway **22** 63.14N 11.03E
Selby U.K. **10** 53.47N 1.05W
Selby U.S.A. **82** 45.31N100.02W
Selbyville U.S.A. **85** 38.28N 75.13W
Seldovia U.S.A. **72** 59.27N151.43W
Sele *r.* Italy **18** 40.30N 14.50E
Selenga *r.* U.S.S.R. **30** 52.20N106.20E
Selenge Mörön *r.* see Selenga Mongolia **30**
Sélestat France **20** 48.16N 7.28E
Seligman U.S.A. **81** 35.20N112.53W
Sélingue, Lac de *l.* Mali **52** 11.25N 8.15W
Seljord Norway **23** 59.29N 8.37E
Selkirk Man. Canada **75** 50.09N 96.52W
Selkirk Ont. Canada **76** 42.49N 79.56W
Selkirk U.K. **12** 55.33N 2.51W
Selkirk Mts. Canada **74** 50.02N116.20W
Selles-sur-Cher France **15** 47.16N 1.33E
Sells U.S.A. **81** 31.55N111.53W
Selma Ala. U.S.A. **83** 32.25N 87.01W
Selma Calif. U.S.A. **81** 36.34N119.37W
Selmer U.S.A. **83** 35.11N 88.36W
Selseleh ye Safīd Kūh *mts.* Afghan **43** 34.30N 63.30E
Selsey Bill *c.* U.K. **11** 50.44N 0.47W
Selty U.S.S.R. **24** 57.19N 52.12E
Sélune *r.* France **15** 48.35N 1.15W
Selva Argentina **94** 29.50S 62.02W
Selvas *f.* Brazil **90** 6.00S 65.00W
Selwyn L. Canada **75** 60.00N104.30W

Selwyn Mts. Canada **72** 63.00N130.00W
Selwyn Range *mts.* Australia **64** 21.35S140.35E
Seman *r.* Albania **19** 40.53N 19.25E
Semara W. Sahara **50** 26.44N 14.41W
Semarang Indonesia **37** 6.58S110.29E
Sembabule Uganda **55** 0.08S 31.27E
Semeru, Gunung *mtn.* Indonesia **37** 8.04S112.53E
Seminoe Resr. U.S.A. **80** 42.00N106.50W
Seminole U.S.A. **83** 32.43N102.39W
Semiozernoye U.S.S.R. **28** 52.22N 64.06E
Semipalatinsk U.S.S.R. **28** 50.26N 80.16E
Semirom Iran **43** 31.31N 52.10E
Semiyarka U.S.S.R. **28** 50.52N 78.23E
Semliki *r.* Zaïre **55** 1.12N 30.27E
Semmering Pass Austria **20** 47.40N 16.00E
Semnān Iran **43** 35.31N 53.24E
Semois *r.* France **14** 49.53N 4.45E
Semporna Malaysia **36** 4.27N118.36E
Semu *r.* Tanzania **55** 3.57S 34.20E
Semur-en-Auxois France **15** 47.29N 4.20E
Sena Mozambique **55** 17.36S 35.00E
Senador Pompeu Brazil **91** 5.30S 39.25W
Senaja Malaysia **36** 6.49N117.02E
Sena Madureira Brazil **90** 9.04S 68.40W
Senanga Zambia **54** 15.52S 23.19E
Senatobia U.S.A. **83** 34.39N 89.58W
Sendai Tofuku Japan **31** 38.16N140.52E
Sendenhorst Germany **14** 51.52N 7.50E
Sendhwa India **40** 21.41N 75.06E
Sendurjana India **41** 21.32N 78.17E
Seneca Oreg. U.S.A. **80** 44.08N118.58W
Seneca S.C. U.S.A. **85** 34.41N 82.59W
Senegal Africa **52** 14.30N 14.30W
Sénégal *r.* Senegal/Mauritania **52** 16.00N 16.28W
Senekal R.S.A. **56** 28.18S 27.37E
Senhor do Bonfim Brazil **91** 10.28S 40.11W
Senica Czech. **21** 48.41N 17.22E
Senigallia Italy **20** 43.42N 13.14E
Senise Italy **18** 40.09N 16.18E
Senj Yugo. **20** 45.00N 14.58E
Senja *i.* Norway **22** 69.15N 17.20E
Senlis France **15** 49.12N 2.35E
Senmonoron Vietnam **34** 12.27N107.12E
Sennan Japan **35** 34.22N135.17E
Sennen U.K. **11** 50.04N 5.42W
Senneterre Canada **76** 48.25N 77.15W
Sens France **15** 48.12N 3.18E
Senta Yugo. **21** 45.56N 20.04E
Sentinel U.S.A. **81** 32.53N113.12W
Seonāth *r.* India **41** 21.44N 82.28E
Seoni India **41** 22.05N 79.32E
Seoni Mālwa India **41** 22.27N 77.28E
Seorīnārāyan India **41** 21.44N 82.35E
Seoul *see* Sŏul S. Korea **31**
Sepik *r.* P.N.G. **37** 3.54S144.30E
Sepopa Botswana **56** 18.45S 22.11E
Sept Îles *town* Canada **77** 50.12N 66.23W
Sepúlveda Spain **16** 41.18N 3.45W
Seraing Belgium **14** 50.37N 5.33E
Seram *i.* Indonesia **37** 3.10S129.30E
Seram, Laut *sea* Pacific Oc. **37** 2.50S128.00E
Serang Indonesia **37** 6.07S106.09E
Serbia *d. see* Srbija *d.* Yugo. **21**
Serdo Ethiopia **49** 11.59N 41.30E
Seremban Malaysia **36** 2.42N101.54E
Serengeti Nat. Park Tanzania **55** 2.30S 35.00E
Serengeti Plain *f.* Tanzania **55** 3.00S 35.00E
Serenje Zambia **55** 13.12S 30.50E
Sergach U.S.S.R. **24** 55.32N 45.27E
Sergipe *d.* Brazil **91** 11.00S 37.00W
Sergiyevsk U.S.S.R. **24** 53.56N 50.01E
Seria Brunei **36** 4.39N114.23E
Serian Malaysia **36** 1.10N110.35E
Sericho Kenya **49** 1.05N 39.05E
Sérifos *i.* Greece **19** 37.11N 24.31E
Sérigny *r.* Canada **77** 55.59N 68.43W
Serkout, Djebel *mtn.* Algeria **51** 23.40N 6.48E
Serle, Mt Australia **66** 30.34S138.55E
Sermata *i.* Indonesia **37** 8.30S129.00E
Serodino Argentina **93** 32.37S 60.57W
Serov U.S.S.R. **24** 59.42N 60.32E
Serowe Botswana **56** 22.22S 26.42E
Serpa Portugal **16** 37.56N 7.36W
Serpentine *r.* Australia **63** 32.33S115.46E
Serpent's Mouth *str.* Venezuela **90** 9.50N 61.00W
Serpukhov U.S.S.R. **24** 54.53N 37.25E
Serra do Navio Brazil **91** 0.59N 52.03W
Sérrai Greece **19** 41.04N 23.32E
Serra Talhada Brazil **91** 8.01S 38.17W
Serravalle Scrivia Italy **15** 44.43N 8.51E
Serre *r.* France **14** 49.40N 3.22E
Serrinha Brazil **91** 11.38S 38.56W
Seru Ethiopia **49** 7.50N 40.28E
Serui Indonesia **37** 1.53S136.15E
Serule Botswana **56** 21.54S 27.17E
Serviceton Australia **66** 36.22S141.02E
Ses, Munţii *mts.* Romania **21** 47.05N 22.30E
Seseganaga L. Canada **76** 50.00N 90.10W
Sese Is. Uganda **55** 0.20S 32.30E
Sesepe Indonesia **37** 1.30S127.59E
Sesheke Zambia **54** 17.14S 24.22E
Sesia *r.* Italy **15** 45.05N 8.37E
Sesimbra Portugal **16** 38.26N 9.06W
Sestao Spain **16** 43.18N 3.00W
Sestri Levante Italy **15** 44.16N 9.24E
Sète France **17** 43.25N 3.43E
Sete Lagoas Brazil **94** 19.29S 44.15W
Sétif Algeria **51** 36.10N 5.26E
Seto Japan **35** 35.14N137.06E
Settat Morocco **50** 33.04N 7.37W
Setté Cama Gabon **54** 2.32S 9.46E
Settimo Torinese Italy **15** 45.09N 7.46E
Settle U.K. **10** 54.05N 2.18W
Settlement of Edinburgh Tristan da Cunha **95** 37.03S 12.18W
Setúbal Portugal **16** 38.31N 8.54W
Setúbal, Baía de *b.* Portugal **16** 38.20N 9.00W
Seul, Lac *l.* Canada **76** 50.20N 92.30W
Sevagram India **41** 20.45N 78.30E
Sevan, Ozero *l.* U.S.S.R. **43** 40.22N 45.20E
Sevastopol' U.S.S.R. **25** 44.36N 33.31E
Sevenoaks U.K. **11** 51.16N 0.12E
Seven Sisters Peaks *mts.* Canada **74** 54.56N128.10W
Sévérac France **17** 44.20N 3.05E
Severn *r.* Australia **67** 29.08S150.50E
Severn *r.* Canada **75** 56.00N 87.38W
Severn *r.* U.K. **11** 51.50N 2.21W
Severnaya Zemlya *is.* U.S.S.R. **29** 80.00N 96.00E
Severnyy U.S.S.R. **24** 69.55N 49.01E
Severnyy Donets *r.* U.S.S.R. **25** 49.08N 37.28E
Severnyy Dvina *r.* U.S.S.R. **24** 57.03N 24.00E
Severodvinsk U.S.S.R. **24** 64.35N 39.50E
Severomorsk U.S.S.R. **24** 69.05N 33.30E
Sevier *r.* U.S.A. **80** 39.04N113.06W
Sevier L. U.S.A. **80** 38.55N113.09W
Sevilla Spain **16** 37.24N 5.59W
Sèvre-Nantaise *r.* France **17** 47.12N 1.35W
Sèvre Niortaise *r.* France **17** 46.35N 1.05W
Sevrey Mongolia **32** 43.33N102.13E
Sewa *Alas* Sierra Leone **52** 7.15N 12.08W
Seward U.S.A. **72** 60.05N149.34W
Seward Nebr. U.S.A. **82** 40.55N 97.06W
Seward Pen. U.S.A. **72** 65.00N164.10W
Seydhisfjördhur *town* Iceland **22** 65.16N 14.02W
Seylac Somali Rep. **45** 11.21N 43.30E
Seym *r.* U.S.S.R. **25** 51.30N 32.30E
Seymour Australia **67** 37.01S145.10E
Seymour U.S.A. **83** 33.35N 99.16W
Sézanne France **15** 48.44N 3.44E
Sfax Tunisia **51** 34.45N 10.43E
Sfîntu-Gheorghe Romania **21** 45.52N 25.50E
'sGravenhage Neth. **14** 52.05N 4.16E
Shaanxi *d.* China **32** 35.00N108.30E
Shaba *d.* Zaïre **55** 8.00S 27.00E
Shabeelle *r.* Somali Rep. **55** 0.30N 43.10E
Shabunda Zaïre **55** 2.42S 27.20E
Shache China **30** 38.27N 77.16E
Shafter U.S.A. **81** 35.30N119.16W
Shaftesbury U.K. **11** 51.00N 2.12W
Shagamu *r.* Canada **75** 55.50N 86.48W
Shāhābād India **41** 27.39N 79.57E
Shāhāda India **40** 21.28N 74.18E
Shahbā' Syria **44** 32.51N 36.37E
Shāhbandar Pakistan **40** 24.10N 67.54E
Shāhbāz Kalāt Pakistan **40** 26.42N 63.58E
Shahdād Iran **43** 30.27N 57.44E
Shāhdādkot Pakistan **40** 27.51N 67.54E
Shāhdādpur Pakistan **40** 25.56N 68.37E
Shahdol India **41** 23.17N 81.21E
Shāhganj India **41** 26.03N 82.41E
Shāhgarh India **40** 27.07N 69.54E
Shaḩḩāt Libya **48** 32.50N 21.52E
Shāh Jahān, Kūh-e *mts.* Iran **43** 37.00N 58.00E
Shāhjahānpur India **41** 27.53N 79.55E
Shāh Jūy Afghan. **40** 32.31N 67.25E
Shāh Kot Pakistan **40** 31.34N 73.29E
Shāh Kūh *mtn.* Iran **43** 31.38N 59.16E
Shāhpur Pakistan **40** 28.43N 68.25E
Shāhpura India **40** 25.35N 75.00E
Shāhpur Chākar Pakistan **40** 26.09N 68.39E
Shahrak Afghan. **40** 34.06N 64.18E
Shahr-e Bābak Iran **43** 30.08N 55.04E
Shahrestān Afghan. **40** 34.22N 66.47E
Shahrezā Iran **43** 32.00N 51.52E
Shahr Kord Iran **43** 32.40N 50.52E
Shahsavār Iran **43** 36.49N 50.54E
Sha'īb Abā al Qūr *wadi* Saudi Arabia **42** 31.02N 42.00E
Shaikhpura India **41** 25.09N 85.51E
Shājāpur India **40** 23.26N 76.16E
Shakawe Botswana **56** 18.22S 21.50E
Shaker Heights *town* U.S.A. **84** 41.29N 81.36W
Shakhty U.S.S.R. **25** 47.43N 40.16E
Shakhunya U.S.S.R. **24** 57.41N 46.46E
Shaki Nigeria **53** 8.41N 3.24E
Shakshūk Egypt **44** 29.28N 30.42E
Shala Hāyk' *l.* Ethiopia **49** 7.25N 38.30E
Shalingzi China **32** 40.42N114.55E
Shallotte U.S.A. **85** 33.58N 78.25W
Shām, Jabal ash *mtn.* Oman **43** 23.14N 57.17E
Shamāl Dārfūr *d.* Sudan **48** 17.15N 25.30E
Shamāl Kurdūfān *d.* Sudan **48** 14.00N 29.00E
Shāmat al Akbād *des.* Saudi Arabia **42** 28.15N 43.05E
Shāmli India **40** 29.27N 77.19E
Shamokin U.S.A. **84** 40.47N 76.34W
Shamrock U.S.A. **83** 35.13N100.15W
Shamva Zimbabwe **55** 17.20S 31.38E
Shan *d.* Burma **34** 22.00N 98.00E
Shandi Sudan **48** 16.42N 33.26E
Shandong *d.* China **32** 36.00N119.00E
Shandong Bandao *pen.* China **32** 37.00N121.30E
Shangcheng China **33** 31.48N115.24E
Shangdu China **32** 41.33N113.31E
Shanggao China **33** 28.15N114.55E
Shanghai China **33** 31.18N121.50E
Shanghai *d.* China **33** 31.00N121.30E
Shanglin China **33** 23.26N108.36E
Shangqiu China **32** 34.21N115.40E
Shangrao China **33** 28.24N117.56E
Shangshui China **32** 33.31N114.39E
Shang Xian China **32** 33.49N109.56E
Shangyi China **32** 41.06N114.00E
Shangyou Shuiku *resr.* China **33** 25.52N114.21E
Shangyu China **33** 30.01N120.52E
Shanhaiguan China **32** 39.58N119.45E
Shannon *r.* Rep. of Ire. **13** 52.39N 8.43W
Shannon, Mouth of the *est.* Rep. of Ire. **13** 52.29N 9.57W
Shan Plateau Burma **34** 18.50N 98.00E
Shanshan China **30** 42.52N 90.10E
Shantarskiy Ostrova *is.* U.S.S.R. **29** 55.00N138.00E
Shantou China **33** 23.22N116.39E
Shanwa Tanzania **55** 3.09S 33.48E
Shanxi *d.* China **32** 37.00N112.00E
Shanyin China **32** 39.30N112.50E
Shaoguan China **33** 24.53N113.31E
Shaoxing China **33** 30.01N120.40E
Shaoyang China **33** 27.10N111.14E
Shap U.K. **10** 54.32N 2.40W
Shapinsay *i.* U.K. **12** 59.03N 2.51W
Shapur *ruins* Iran **43** 29.42N 51.30E
Shaqrā' Saudi Arabia **43** 25.17N 45.14E
Shaqrā' Yemen **45** 13.21N 45.42E
Sharan Jogīzai Pakistan **40** 31.02N 68.33E
Shark B. Australia **62** 25.30S113.30E
Sharlyk U.S.S.R. **24** 52.58N 54.46E
Sharm ash Shaykh Egypt **44** 27.51N 34.16E
Sharon U.S.A. **84** 41.16N 80.30W
Sharon Springs *town* U.S.A. **82** 38.54N101.45W
Sharq al Istiwā'īyah *d.* Sudan **49** 5.00N 33.00E
Sharqī, Al Jabal ash *mts.* Lebanon **44** 34.00N 36.25E
Sharqīyah, Aş Şaḩrā' ash *des.* Egypt **44** 27.40N 32.00E
Sharya U.S.S.R. **24** 58.22N 45.50E
Shashi *r.* Botswana/Zimbabwe **56** 22.10S 29.15E
Shashi China **33** 30.18N112.20E
Shasta, Mt. U.S.A. **80** 41.20N122.20W
Shatt al Arab *r.* Iraq **43** 30.00N 48.30E
Shaunavon Canada **75** 49.40N108.25W
Shawangunk Mts. U.S.A. **85** 41.35N 74.30W
Shawano U.S.A. **76** 44.46N 88.38W
Shawbridge Canada **77** 45.52N 74.05W
Shaw I. Australia **64** 20.29S149.05E
Shawinigan Canada **77** 46.33N 72.45W
Shawinigan Sud Canada **77** 46.30N 72.45W
Shawnee Okla. U.S.A. **83** 35.20N 96.55W
Sha Xi *r.* China **33** 26.38N118.10E
Sha Xian China **33** 26.27N117.42E
Shayang China **33** 30.42N112.29E
Shay Gap *town* Australia **62** 20.28S120.05E
Shaykh, Jabal ash *mtn.* Lebanon **44** 33.24N 35.52E
Shaykh 'Uthmān Yemen **45** 12.52N 44.59E
Shchara *r.* U.S.S.R. **21** 53.27N 24.45E
Shchelyayur U.S.S.R. **24** 65.16N 53.17E
Shchors U.S.S.R. **21** 51.50N 31.59E
Sheboygan U.S.A. **82** 43.46N 87.36W
Shebshi Mts. Nigeria **53** 8.30N 11.45E
Shediac Canada **77** 46.13N 64.32W
Sheeffry Hills Rep. of Ire. **13** 53.41N 9.42W
Sheelin, Lough Rep. of Ire. **13** 53.48N 7.20W
Sheep Range *mts.* U.S.A. **81** 36.45N115.05W
Sheet Harbour Canada **77** 44.55N 62.32W
Sheffield U.K. **10** 53.23N 1.28W
Sheffield Ala. U.S.A. **85** 34.46N 87.40W
Sheffield Tex. U.S.A. **83** 30.41N101.49W
Shefford U.K. **11** 52.02N 0.20W
Shegaon India **40** 20.47N 76.41E
Shekatika Bay *town* Canada **77** 51.17N 58.20W
Shēkhābād Afghan. **40** 34.05N 68.45E
Shek Hasan Ethiopia **49** 12.09N 35.54E
Shekhūpura Pakistan **40** 31.42N 73.59E
Sheki U.S.S.R. **25** 41.12N 47.10E
Sheksna *r.* U.S.S.R. **24** 60.00N 37.49E
Shelburne N.S. Canada **77** 43.46N 65.19W
Shelburne B. Australia **64** 11.49S143.00E
Shelby Mich. U.S.A. **84** 43.36N 86.22W
Shelby Mont. U.S.A. **80** 48.30N111.51W
Shelbyville Ind. U.S.A. **84** 39.31N 85.46W
Shelbyville Tenn. U.S.A. **85** 35.29N 86.30W
Sheldon Iowa U.S.A. **82** 43.11N 95.51W
Sheldon N.Dak. U.S.A. **82** 46.35N 97.30W
Sheldrake Canada **77** 50.20N 64.51W
Shelikof Str. U.S.A. **72** 58.00N153.45W
Shelley U.S.A. **80** 43.23N112.07W
Shellharbour Australia **67** 34.35S150.52E
Shell Lake *town* Canada **75** 53.18N107.07W
Shelton U.S.A. **80** 47.13N123.06W
Shenandoah *r.* U.S.A. **84** 39.19N 78.12W
Shenandoah Iowa U.S.A. **82** 40.46N 95.22W
Shenandoah Va. U.S.A. **84** 38.29N 78.37W
Shenchi China **32** 39.08N112.10E
Shëngjin Albania **19** 41.49N 19.33E
Shengze China **33** 30.53N120.40E
Shenkursk U.S.S.R. **24** 62.05N 42.58E
Shenmu China **32** 38.54N110.24E
Shennongjia China **33** 31.44N110.44E
Shen Xian China **32** 36.15N115.40E
Shenyang China **32** 41.48N123.27E
Shenzhen China **33** 22.32N114.08E
Sheo India **40** 26.11N 71.15E
Sheoganj India **40** 25.09N 73.04E
Sheopur India **40** 25.40N 76.42E
Shepetovka U.S.S.R. **21** 50.12N 27.01E
Shepherd Is. Vanuatu **68** 16.55S168.36E
Shepparton Australia **67** 36.25S145.26E
Sheppey, Isle of U.K. **11** 51.24N 0.50E
Sherada Ethiopia **49** 7.21N 36.32E
Sherborne U.K. **11** 50.56N 2.31W
Sherbro I. Sierra Leone **52** 7.30N 12.50W
Sherbrooke Canada **77** 45.24N 71.54W
Sherburne U.S.A. **84** 42.41N 75.30W
Sheridan U.S.A. **80** 44.48N106.58W
Sheringa Australia **66** 33.51S135.15E
Sheringham U.K. **10** 52.56N 1.11E
Sherkin I. Rep. of Ire. **13** 51.28N 9.25W
Sherman N.Y. U.S.A. **76** 42.10N 79.36W
Sherman Tex. U.S.A. **83** 33.38N 96.36W
Sherman Mills U.S.A. **84** 45.52N 68.23W
Sherridon Canada **75** 55.07N101.05W
'sHertogenbosch Neth. **14** 51.42N 5.19E
Shesh Gāv Afghan. **40** 33.45N 68.33E
Shetland Is. *d.* U.K. **12** 60.20N 1.15W
Shetpe U.S.S.R. **25** 44.09N 52.06E
Shetrunji *r.* India **40** 21.20N 72.05E
Shevchenko U.S.S.R. **25** 43.37N 51.11E
Shewa *d.* Ethiopia **49** 8.40N 38.00E
Shewa Gimīra Ethiopia **49** 7.00N 35.50E
Sheyang China **32** 33.47N120.19E
Sheyenne *r.* U.S.A. **82** 47.05N 96.50W
Shibām Yemen **45** 15.56N 48.38E
Shibīn al Kawm Egypt **44** 30.33N 31.00E
Shibīn al Qanāţir Egypt **44** 30.19N 31.19E
Shibogama L. Canada **76** 53.35N 88.10W
Shidao China **32** 36.52N122.26E
Shiel, Loch U.K. **12** 56.48N 5.33W
Shiga *d.* Japan **35** 34.55N136.00E
Shigaib Sudan **48** 15.01N 23.36E
Shihpao Shan *mts.* China **33** 30.00N112.00E
Shijiazhuang China **32** 38.03N114.26E
Shijiu Hu *l.* China **33** 31.20N118.48E
Shikārpur Pakistan **40** 27.57N 68.38E
Shikohābād India **41** 27.06N 78.36E
Shikoku *i.* Japan **31** 33.30N133.30E
Shilabo Ethiopia **45** 6.05N 44.48E
Shilka U.S.S.R. **31** 51.55N116.01E
Shilka *r.* U.S.S.R. **31** 53.20N121.10E
Shillington U.S.A. **85** 40.18N 75.58W
Shillong India **41** 25.34N 91.53E
Shilong China **33** 23.02N113.50E
Shima Japan **35** 34.13N136.51E
Shimada Japan **35** 34.49N138.11E
Shima-hantō *pen.* Japan **35** 34.25N136.45E
Shimizu Japan **35** 35.01N138.29E
Shimoda Japan **35** 34.40N138.57E
Shimoga India **38** 13.56N 75.31E
Shimonoseki Japan **31** 33.59N130.58E
Shimpek U.S.S.R. **30** 44.50N 74.10E
Shin, Loch U.K. **12** 58.06N 4.32W
Shindand Afghan. **40** 33.18N 62.08E
Shingleton U.S.A. **84** 46.21N 86.28W
Shinkay Afghan. **40** 31.57N 67.26E
Shīn Naray Afghan. **40** 31.19N 66.43E
Shinshār Syria **44** 34.36N 36.45E
Shinshiro Japan **35** 34.54N137.30E
Shinyanga Tanzania **55** 3.40S 33.20E
Shinyanga *d.* Tanzania **55** 3.30S 33.00E
Ship Bottom U.S.A. **85** 39.39N 74.11W
Shipka Pass Bulgaria **19** 42.45N 25.25E
Shippegan Canada **77** 47.45N 64.42W
Shippensburg U.S.A. **84** 40.03N 77.31W
Shiprock U.S.A. **80** 36.47N108.41W
Shipston on Stour U.K. **11** 52.04N 1.38W
Shiqian China **33** 27.20N108.10E
Shiqiao China **33** 31.19N111.59E
Shiqizhen China **33** 22.22N113.21E
Shiquan China **32** 33.03N108.17E
Shiquan He *r.* China **41** 32.30N 79.40E
Shirakskaya Step *f.* U.S.S.R. **43** 41.40N 46.20E
Shirane san *mtn.* Japan **35** 35.40N138.15E
Shirāz Iran **43** 29.36N 52.33E
Shirbīn Egypt **44** 31.13N 31.31E
Shire *r.* Mozambique **55** 17.46S 35.20E
Shīr Kūh *mtn.* Iran **43** 31.38N 54.07E
Shirpur India **40** 21.21N 74.53E
Shirvān Iran **43** 37.24N 57.55E
Shivpuri India **41** 25.26N 77.39E
Shiwan Dashan *mts.* China **33** 21.48N107.50E
Shiyan Hubei China **32** 32.38N110.47E
Shizuishan China **32** 39.14N106.47E
Shizuoka Japan **35** 34.58N138.23E
Shizuoka *d.* Japan **35** 35.00N138.00E
Shklov U.S.S.R. **21** 54.16N 30.16E
Shkodër Albania **19** 42.03N 19.30E
Shkumbin *r.* Albania **19** 41.01N 19.26E
Shoal C. Australia **63** 33.51S121.10E
Shoalhaven *r.* Australia **67** 34.51S150.40E
Sholāpur India **38** 17.43N 75.56E
Shonai *r.* Japan **35** 35.04N136.50E
Shoshone Calif. U.S.A. **81** 35.58N116.17W
Shoshone Idaho U.S.A. **80** 42.57N114.25W
Shoshone Mts. U.S.A. **80** 39.25N117.15W
Shoshoni U.S.A. **80** 43.14N108.07W
Shostka U.S.S.R. **24** 51.53N 33.30E
Shou Xian China **32** 32.30N116.35E
Shouyang China **32** 37.55N113.10E
Show Low U.S.A. **81** 34.15N110.02W
Shpola U.S.S.R. **21** 49.00N 31.25E
Shreveport U.S.A **83** 32.30N 93.45W
Shrewsbury U.K. **11** 52.42N 2.45W
Shropshire *d.* U.K. **11** 52.35N 2.40W
Shuangliao China **32** 43.28N123.27E
Shuangyashan China **31** 46.37N131.22E
Shubenacadie Canada **77** 45.05N 63.25W
Shubrā al Khaymah Egypt **44** 30.06N 31.15E
Shuicheng China **33** 26.36N104.51E
Shujāābād Pakistan **40** 29.53N 71.18E
Shujālpur India **40** 23.24N 76.43E
Shuksan U.S.A. **80** 48.55N121.43W
Shule China **30** 39.25N 76.06E
Shumagin Is. U.S.A. **72** 55.00N160.00W
Shumerlya U.S.S.R. **24** 55.30N 46.25E
Shumikha U.S.S.R. **28** 55.15N 63.14E
Shumyachi U.S.S.R. **21** 53.52N 32.25E
Shunayn, Sabkhat *f.* Libya **48** 30.10N 21.00E
Shunchang China **33** 26.48N117.47E
Shunde China **33** 22.40N113.20E
Shūr *r.* Kermān Iran **43** 30.45N 57.55E
Shūr *r.* Khorāsān Iran **43** 34.05N 60.22E
Shūr *r.* Kermān Iran **43** 31.14N 55.29E
Shūr *r.* Khorāsān Iran **43** 34.11N 60.07E
Shūrāb Iran **43** 28.09N 60.18E
Shūrāb *r.* Iran **43** 31.30N 55.18E
Shurugwi Zimbabwe **56** 19.40S 30.00E
Shūshtar Iran **43** 32.04N 48.53E
Shuswap L. Canada **74** 50.55N119.03W
Shuwak Sudan **48** 14.23N 35.52E
Shuya U.S.S.R. **24** 56.49N 41.23E
Shwebo Burma **34** 22.35N 95.42E
Shyok Jammu & Kashmir **41** 34.11N 78.08E
Siāhān Range *mts.* Pakistan **40** 27.30N 64.30E
Siālkot Pakistan **40** 32.30N 74.31E
Sian *see* Xi'an China **32**
Siargao *i.* Phil. **37** 9.55N126.05E
Siari Jammu & Kashmir **40** 34.56N 76.44E
Siau *i.* Indonesia **37** 2.42N125.24E
Siauliai U.S.S.R. **23** 55.56N 23.19E
Sibasa R.S.A. **56** 22.56S 30.28E
Šibenik Yugo. **18** 43.45N 15.55E
Siberut *i.* Indonesia **36** 1.30S 99.00E
Sibi Pakistan **40** 29.33N 67.53E
Sibiti Congo **54** 3.40S 13.24E
Sibiti *r.* Tanzania **55** 3.47S 34.45E
Sibiu Romania **19** 45.47N 24.09E
Sibley U.S.A. **82** 43.25N 95.43W
Sibolga Indonesia **36** 1.42N 98.48E
Sibu Malaysia **36** 2.18N111.49E
Sibut C.A.R. **53** 5.46N 19.06E
Sicasica Bolivia **92** 17.22S 67.45W
Siccus *r.* Australia **66** 31.26S139.30E
Sichuan *d.* China **30** 30.30N103.00E
Sichuan Pendi *f.* China **33** 31.00N106.00E
Sicilia *d.* Italy **18** 37.30N 14.00E
Sicilia *i.* Italy **18** 37.30N 14.00E
Sicily *i. see* Sicilia *i.* Italy **18**
Sicuani Peru **90** 14.21S 71.13W
Sidamo *d.* Ethiopia **49** 4.30N 39.00E
Sidaouet Niger **53** 18.34N 8.03E
Sidhi India **41** 24.25N 81.53E
Sidhpur India **40** 23.55N 72.23E
Sīdī Barrānī Egypt **42** 31.38N 25.58E
Sidi bel Abbès Algeria **50** 35.12N 0.38W
Sidi Ifni Morocco **50** 29.24N 10.12W
Sidi-Kacem Morocco **50** 34.15N 5.39W
Sīdī Sālim Egypt **44** 31.16N 30.47E
Sidi Smaïl Morocco **50** 32.49N 8.30W
Sidlaw Hills U.K. **12** 56.31N 3.10W
Sidley, Mt. Antarctica **96** 77.30S125.00W
Sidmouth U.K. **11** 50.40N 3.13W
Sidney Canada **74** 48.39N123.24W
Sidney Mont. U.S.A. **80** 47.43N104.09W
Sidney Nebr. U.S.A. **82** 41.09N102.59W
Sidney Ohio U.S.A. **84** 40.16N 84.10W
Sidon *see* Şaydā Lebanon **44**
Sidra, G. of *see* Surt, Khalīj *g.* Libya **51**
Siedlce Poland **21** 52.10N 22.18E
Sieg *r.* Germany **14** 50.49N 7.11E
Siegburg Germany **14** 50.48N 7.13E
Siegen Germany **14** 50.52N 8.02E
Siemiatycze Poland **21** 52.26N 22.53E
Siĕmréab Cambodia **34** 13.21N103.50E
Siena Italy **18** 43.19N 11.20E
Sieradz Poland **21** 51.36N 18.45E
Sierck-les-Bains France **14** 49.28N 6.20E
Sierpc Poland **21** 52.52N 19.41E
Sierra Blanca *town* U.S.A. **81** 31.11N105.12W
Sierra Colorada Argentina **93** 40.35S 67.50W
Sierra Leone Africa **52** 9.00N 12.00W
Sierra Mojada *town* Mexico **83** 27.17N103.42W
Sierra Nevada *mts.* U.S.A. **80** 37.45N119.30W
Sierre Switz. **15** 46.18N 7.32E
Sifeni Ethiopia **49** 12.20N 40.24E
Sífnos *i.* Greece **19** 36.59N 24.60E
Sig Algeria **50** 35.32N 0.11W
Sig U.S.S.R. **24** 65.31N 34.16E
Sighetul Marmaţiei Romania **21** 47.56N 23.54E
Sighişoara Romania **21** 46.13N 24.49E
Sigli Indonesia **36** 5.23N 95.57E
Siglufjördhur Iceland **22** 66.12N 18.55W
Signy France **15** 49.42N 4.25E
Sigüenza Spain **16** 41.04N 2.38W
Siguiri Guinea **52** 11.28N 9.07W
Sihor India **40** 21.42N 71.58E
Sihorā India **41** 23.29N 80.07E
Siikā *r.* Finland **22** 64.50N 24.44E
Siirt Turkey **42** 37.56N 41.56E
Sikanni Chief *r.* Canada **74** 58.20N121.50W
Sīkar India **40** 27.37N 75.09E
Sikasso Mali **52** 11.18N 5.38W
Sikasso *d.* Mali **52** 11.20N 6.05W
Sikeston U.S.A. **83** 36.53N 89.35W
Sikhote Alin *mts.* U.S.S.R. **31** 44.00N135.00E
Síkinos *i.* Greece **19** 36.39N 25.06E
Sikkim *d.* India **41** 27.30N 88.30E
Sil *r.* Spain **16** 42.24N 7.15W
Silchar India **39** 24.49N 92.47E
Silcox Canada **75** 57.12N 94.10W
Silet Algeria **51** 22.39N 4.35E
Silgarhi-Doti Nepal **41** 29.16N 80.58E
Silghāt India **41** 26.37N 92.56E
Silifke Turkey **42** 36.22N 33.57E
Siliguri India **41** 26.42N 88.26E
Siling Co *l.* China **41** 31.45N 88.50E
Silistra Bulgaria **19** 44.07N 27.17E
Siljan *l.* Sweden **23** 60.50N 14.45E
Silkeborg Denmark **23** 56.10N 9.34E
Sille-le-Guillaume France **15** 48.12N 0.08E
Sillil Somali Rep. **45** 10.59N 43.31E
Silloth U.K. **10** 54.53N 3.25W
Silogui Indonesia **36** 1.10S 98.46E
Silsbee U.S.A **83** 30.21N 94.11W
Silvassa India **40** 20.17N 73.00E
Silver Bow U.S.A. **80** 46.00N112.40W
Silver City U.S.A. **81** 32.46N108.17W
Silver Creek *town* U.S.A. **76** 42.33N 79.10W
Silver Lake *town* U.S.A. **80** 43.08N120.56W
Silver Spring *town* U.S.A. **85** 39.02N 77.03W

Silverstone U.K. **11** 52.05N 1.03W
Silverthrone Mtn. Canada **74** 51.31N126.06W
Silverton Australia **66** 31.53S141.13E
Silverton U.S.A. **80** 45.01N122.47W
Silvi Italy **18** 42.34N 14.05E
Simanggang Malaysia **36** 1.10N111.32E
Simàrd, Lac *l.* Canada **76** 47.40N 78.40W
Simav *r.* Turkey **19** 40.24N 28.31E
Simba Kenya **55** 2.10S 37.37E
Simba Zaïre **54** 0.36N 22.55E
Simcoe Canada **76** 42.50N 80.18W
Simcoe, L. Canada **76** 44.25N 79.20W
Simdega India **41** 22.37N 84.31E
Simenga U.S.S.R. **29** 62.42N108.25E
Simeria Romania **19** 45.51N 23.01E
Simeulue *i.* Indonesia **36** 2.30N 96.00E
Simferopol' U.S.S.R. **25** 44.57N 34.05E
Simikot Nepal **41** 29.58N 81.51E
Simitli Bulgaria **19** 41.51N 23.09E
Simiyu *r.* Tanzania **55** 2.32S 33.25E
Simla India **40** 31.06N 77.09E
Simleul Silvaniei Romania **21** 47.14N 22.48E
Simmern Germany **14** 49.59N 7.32E
Simo *r.* Finland **22** 65.37N 25.03E
Simojärvo *l.* Finland **22** 66.06N 27.03E
Simon, Lac *l.* Canada **77** 45.58N 75.05W
Simon's Town R.S.A. **56** 34.12S 18.26E
Simoom Sound *town* Canada **72** 50.45N126.45W
Simplon Pass Switz. **17** 46.15N 8.03E
Simplon Tunnel Italy/Switz. **18** 46.20N 8.05E
Simpson Desert Australia **64** 25.00S136.50E
Simrishamn Sweden **23** 55.33N 14.20E
Simuco Mozambique **55** 14.00S 40.35E
Sînâ', Shibh Jazîrat *pen.* Egypt **44** 29.00N 34.00E
Sinadhago Somali Rep. **45** 5.22N 46.22E
Sinai *see* Sînâ', Shibh Jazîrat *pen.* Egypt **44**
Sinaloa *d.* Mexico **81** 25.00N107.30W
Sinaloa *r.* Mexico **81** 25.18N108.30W
Sinan China **33** 27.51N108.24E
Sînâwin Libya **51** 31.02N 10.36E
Sincelejo Colombia **90** 9.17N 75.23W
Sinclair U.S.A. **80** 41.47N107.07W
Sinclair Mills Canada **74** 54.05N121.40W
Sind *r.* India **41** 26.26N 79.13E
Sindara Gabon **54** 1.07S 10.41E
Sindari India **40** 25.35N 71.55E
Sindh *d.* Pakistan **40** 26.45N 69.00E
Sindhūli Garhi Nepal **41** 27.16N 85.58E
Sindri India **41** 23.45N 86.42E
Sines Portugal **16** 37.58N 8.52W
Sinfra Ivory Coast **52** 6.35N 5.56W
Singālila *mtn.* India **41** 27.13N 88.01E
Singapore Asia **36** 1.20N103.45E
Singapore *town* Singapore **36** 1.20N103.45E
Singaraja Indonesia **37** 8.06S115.07E
Singatoka Fiji **68** 18.08S177.30E
Sing Buri Thailand **34** 14.56N100.21E
Singida Tanzania **55** 4.45S 34.42E
Singida *d.* Tanzania **55** 6.00S 34.30E
Singing India **39** 28.53N 94.47E
Singitikós Kólpos *g.* Greece **19** 40.12N 24.00E
Singkaling Hkāmti Burma **39** 26.00N 95.42E
Singkang Indonesia **37** 4.09S120.02E
Singkawang Indonesia **36** 0.57N108.57E
Singkep *i.* Indonesia **36** 0.30S104.20E
Singleton Australia **67** 32.33S151.11E
Singoli India **40** 25.00N 75.25E
Singosan N. Korea **31** 38.50N127.27E
Sinj Yugo. **19** 43.42N 16.38E
Sinjah Sudan **49** 13.09N 33.56E
Sinkāt Sudan **48** 18.50N 36.50E
Sinnar India **40** 19.51N 74.00E
Sînnicolau Mare Romania **19** 46.05N 20.38E
Sinnūris Egypt **44** 29.25N 30.52E
Sinop Turkey **42** 42.02N 35.09E
Sinsheim Germany **20** 49.15N 8.53E
Sintang Indonesia **36** 0.03N111.31E
Sint Eustatius *i.* Leeward Is. **87** 17.33N 63.00W
Sint Maarten *i. see* St. Martin *i.* Leeward Is. **87**
Sinton U.S.A. **83** 29.41N 95.58W
Sinŭiju N. Korea **31** 40.04N124.25E
Sinyavka U.S.S.R. **21** 52.58N 26.30E
Sinyukha *r.* U.S.S.R. **21** 48.03N 30.51E
Siocon Phil. **37** 7.42N122.08E
Siófok Hungary **21** 46.54N 18.04E
Sion Switz. **15** 46.14N 7.21E
Sioux City U.S.A. **82** 42.30N 96.23W
Sioux Falls *town* U.S.A. **82** 43.32N 96.44W
Sioux Lookout *town* Canada **76** 50.06N 91.55W
Siphaqeni R.S.A. **56** 31.05S 29.29E
Siping Hubei China **33** 31.58N111.10E
Siping Jilin China **32** 43.10N124.24E
Sipiwesk L. Canada **75** 55.05N 97.35W
Sipura *i.* Indonesia **36** 2.10S 99.40E
Sira *r.* Norway **23** 58.17N 6.24E
Siracusa Italy **18** 37.05N 15.17E
Sirājganj Bangla. **41** 24.27N 89.43E
Sirakoro Mali **52** 12.41N 9.14W
Sirasso Ivory Coast **52** 9.16N 6.06W
Sirē Ethiopia **49** 9.00N 36.55E
Sir Edward Pellew Group *is.* Australia **64** 15.40S136.48E
Siret *r.* Romania **19** 45.28N 27.56E
Sirha Nepal **41** 26.39N 86.12E
Sirḥān, Wādī as *f.* Saudi Arabia **42** 31.00N 37.30E
Sir James MacBrien, Mt. Canada **74** 62.07N127.41W
Sir Joseph Banks Group *is.* Australia **66** 34.35S136.12E
Sirohi India **40** 24.53N 72.52E
Sironj India **41** 24.06N 77.42E
Síros *i.* Greece **19** 37.26N 24.56E
Sirrah, Wādī as *r.* Saudi Arabia **43** 23.10N 44.22E
Sirsa India **40** 29.32N 75.02E
Sisak Yugo. **18** 45.30N 16.21E
Sisaket Thailand **34** 15.08N104.18E
Sishen R.S.A. **56** 27.46S 22.59E
Sisimiut *see* Holsteinsborg Greenland **73**
Sisipuk L. Canada **75** 55.45N101.50W
Sisŏphŏn Cambodia **34** 13.37N102.58E
Sisseton U.S.A. **82** 45.40N 97.03W
Sissonne France **15** 49.34N 3.54E
Sisteron France **17** 44.16N 5.56E
Sitāmarhi India **41** 26.36N 85.29E
Sitāpur India **41** 27.34N 80.41E
Sitka U.S.A. **74** 57.05N135.20W
Sittang *r.* Burma **34** 17.25N 96.50E
Sittard Neth. **14** 51.00N 5.52E
Sittwe Burma **34** 20.09N 92.50E
Situbondo Indonesia **37** 7.40S114.01E
Siuruan *r.* Finland **22** 65.20N 25.55E
Sīvan *r.* Iran **43** 29.50N 52.47E
Sivas Turkey **42** 39.44N 37.01E
Sivomaskinskiy U.S.S.R. **24** 66.45N 62.44E
Sivrihisar Turkey **42** 39.29N 31.32E
Sīwah Egypt **42** 29.12N 25.31E
Sīwah, Wāḥat *oasis* Egypt **42** 29.10N 25.40E
Siwalik Range *mts.* India **41** 31.15N 77.45E
Siwān India **41** 26.13N 84.22E
Siwa Oasis *see* Sīwah, Wāḥat *oasis* Egypt **42**
Sixmilecross U.K. **13** 54.34N 7.08W
Siya U.S.S.R. **24** 63.38N 41.40E
Sjaelland *i.* Denmark **23** 55.30N 11.45E
Sjötorp Sweden **23** 58.50N 13.59E
Skagafjördhur *est.* Iceland **22** 65.55N 19.35W
Skagen Denmark **23** 57.44N 10.36E
Skagerrak *str.* Denmark/Norway **23** 57.45N 8.55E
Skagway U.S.A. **74** 59.23N135.20W
Skaill U.K. **12** 58.56N 2.43W
Skála Oropoú Greece **19** 38.20N 23.46E
Skala Podolskaya U.S.S.R. **21** 48.51N 26.11E
Skalat U.S.S.R. **21** 49.20N 25.59E
Skanderborg Denmark **23** 56.02N 9.56E
Skånevik Norway **23** 59.44N 5.59E
Skara Sweden **23** 58.22N 13.25E
Skaraborg *d.* Sweden **23** 58.20N 13.30E
Skarnes Norway **23** 60.15N 11.41E
Skarżysko-Kamienna Poland **21** 51.08N 20.53E
Skeena *r.* Canada **74** 54.09N130.02W
Skeena Mts. Canada **74** 57.00N128.30W
Skegness U.K. **10** 53.09N 0.20E
Skellefte *r.* Sweden **22** 64.42N 21.06E
Skellefteå Sweden **22** 64.46N 20.57E
Skelleftehamn Sweden **22** 64.41N 21.14E
Skelmersdale U.K. **10** 53.34N 2.49W
Skene Sweden **23** 57.29N 12.38E
Skerries Rep. of Ire. **13** 53.35N 6.07W
Skhíza *i.* Greece **19** 36.42N 21.45E
Ski Norway **23** 59.43N 10.50E
Skiddaw *mtn.* U.K. **10** 54.40N 3.09W
Skidel U.S.S.R. **21** 53.37N 24.19E
Skien Norway **23** 59.12N 9.36E
Skierniewice Poland **21** 51.58N 20.08E
Skikda Algeria **51** 36.53N 6.54E
Skipness U.K. **12** 56.45N 5.22W
Skipton U.K. **10** 53.57N 2.01W
Skíros Greece **19** 38.53N 24.33E
Skíros *i.* Greece **19** 38.50N 24.33E
Skive Denmark **23** 56.34N 9.02E
Skjálfanda Fljót *r.* Iceland **22** 65.55N 17.30W
Skjálfandi *est.* Iceland **22** 66.08N 17.38W
Skjönsta Norway **22** 67.12N 15.45E
Skoghall Sweden **23** 59.19N 13.26E
Skole U.S.S.R. **21** 49.00N 23.30E
Skopje Yugo. **19** 41.58N 21.27E
Skotterud Norway **23** 59.59N 12.07E
Skövde Sweden **23** 58.24N 13.50E
Skovorodino U.S.S.R. **29** 54.00N123.53E
Skreia Norway **23** 60.39N 10.56E
Skull Rep. of Ire. **13** 51.32N 9.33W
Skuodas U.S.S.R. **23** 56.16N 21.32E
Skutskär Sweden **23** 60.38N 17.25E
Skvira U.S.S.R. **21** 49.42N 29.40E
Skye *i.* U.K. **12** 57.20N 6.15W
Slagelse Denmark **23** 55.24N 11.22E
Słalowa Wola Poland **21** 50.40N 22.05E
Slamet *mtn.* Indonesia **37** 7.14S109.10E
Slaney *r.* Rep. of Ire. **13** 52.21N 6.30W
Slantsy U.S.S.R. **24** 59.09N 28.09E
Slatina Romania **19** 44.26N 24.23E
Slaton U.S.A. **83** 33.26N101.39W
Slave *r.* Canada **74** 61.18N113.39W
Slavgorod B.S.S.R. U.S.S.R. **21** 53.25N 31.00E
Slavgorod R.S.F.S.R. U.S.S.R. **28** 53.01N 78.37E
Slavuta U.S.S.R. **21** 50.20N 26.58E
Slavyansk U.S.S.R. **25** 48.51N 37.36E
Sławno Poland **20** 54.22N 16.40E
Sleaford U.K. **10** 53.00N 0.22W
Sleaford B. Australia **66** 35.00S136.50E
Sleat, Sd. of *str.* U.K. **12** 57.05N 5.48W
Sledge U.S.A. **83** 34.26N 90.13W
Sledmere U.K. **10** 54.04N 0.35W
Sleeper Is. Canada **76** 56.50N 80.30W
Sleetmute U.S.A. **72** 61.40N157.11W
Sliedrecht Neth. **14** 51.48N 4.46E
Slieve Aughty Mts. Rep. of Ire. **13** 53.05N 8.31W
Slieve Bloom Mts. Rep. of Ire. **13** 53.03N 7.35W
Slieve Callan *mtn.* Rep. of Ire. **13** 52.51N 9.18W
Slieve Donard *mtn.* U.K. **13** 54.11N 5.56W
Slieve Gamph *mts.* Rep. of Ire. **13** 54.06N 8.52W
Slievekimalta *mtn.* Rep. of Ire. **13** 52.45N 8.17W
Slieve Mish *mts.* Rep. of Ire. **13** 52.48N 9.48W
Slieve Miskish *mts.* Rep. of Ire. **13** 51.41N 9.56W
Slievenamon *mtn.* Rep. of Ire. **13** 52.25N 7.34W
Slieve Snaght *mtn.* Donegal Rep. of Ire. **13** 55.12N 7.20W
Sligo Rep. of Ire. **13** 54.17N 8.28W
Sligo *d.* Rep. of Ire. **13** 54.10N 8.35W
Sligo B. Rep. of Ire. **13** 54.18N 8.40W
Slite Sweden **23** 57.43N 18.48E
Sliven Bulgaria **19** 42.41N 26.19E
Sloan U.S.A. **82** 42.14N 96.14W
Slobodka U.S.S.R. **21** 47.56N 29.18E
Slobodskoy U.S.S.R. **24** 58.42N 50.10E
Slonim U.S.S.R. **21** 53.05N 25.21E
Slough U.K. **11** 51.30N 0.35W
Slovechna *r.* U.S.S.R. **21** 51.41N 29.41E
Slovechno U.S.S.R. **21** 51.23N 28.20E
Slovenija *d.* Yugo. **18** 46.10N 14.45E
Slovenjgradec Yugo. **18** 46.31N 15.05E
Slovensko *d.* Czech. **21** 48.25N 19.20E
Słubice Poland **20** 52.20N 14.32E
Sluch *r.* U.S.S.R. **21** 52.08N 27.31E
Sluis Neth. **14** 51.18N 3.23E
Slunj Yugo. **20** 45.07N 15.35E
Słupsk Poland **21** 54.28N 17.01E
Slurry R.S.A. **56** 25.48S 25.49E
Slutsk U.S.S.R. **21** 53.02N 27.31E
Slyne Head Rep. of Ire. **13** 53.25N 10.12W
Slyudyanka U.S.S.R. **30** 51.40N103.40E
Smallwood Resr. Canada **77** 54.00N 64.00W
Smeaton Canada **75** 53.30N104.49W
Smederevo Yugo. **19** 44.40N 20.56E
Smela U.S.S.R. **25** 49.15N 31.54E
Smilde Neth. **14** 52.58N 6.28E
Smilovichi U.S.S.R. **21** 53.45N 28.00E
Smith Canada **74** 55.10N114.00W
Smith Arm *b.* Canada **72** 66.15N124.00W
Smithers Canada **74** 54.45N127.10W
Smithfield R.S.A. **56** 30.11S 26.31E
Smiths Falls *town* Canada **76** 44.54N 76.01W
Smithton Australia **65** 40.52S145.07E
Smithtown Australia **67** 31.03S152.53E
Smoky *r.* Canada **74** 56.10N117.21W
Smoky Bay *town* Australia **66** 32.22S133.56E
Smoky C. Australia **67** 30.55S153.05E
Smoky Hill *r.* U.S.A. **82** 39.03N 96.48W
Smöla *i.* Norway **22** 63.20N 8.00E
Smolensk U.S.S.R. **24** 54.49N 32.04E
Smolevichi U.S.S.R. **21** 54.00N 28.01E
Smólikas *mtn.* Greece **19** 40.06N 20.55E
Smolyan Bulgaria **19** 41.34N 24.45E
Smorgon U.S.S.R. **21** 54.28N 26.20E
Smyrna U.S.A. **85** 39.18N 75.36W
Snaefell *mtn.* Iceland **22** 64.48N 15.34W
Snaefell *mtn.* U.K. **10** 54.16N 4.28W
Snake *r.* Idaho U.S.A. **78** 43.50N117.05W
Snake *r.* Wash. U.S.A. **80** 46.12N119.02W
Snake Range *mts.* U.S.A. **80** 39.00N114.15W
Snake River *town* U.S.A. **80** 44.10N110.40W
Snake River Plain *f.* U.S.A. **80** 43.00N113.00W
Snåsa Norway **22** 64.15N 12.23E
Snåsavatn *l.* Norway **22** 64.05N 12.00E
Sneek Neth. **14** 53.03N 5.40E
Sneem Rep. of Ire. **13** 51.50N 9.54W
Sneeuwberg *mtn.* R.S.A. **56** 32.30S 19.09E
Śniardwy, Jezioro *l.* Poland **21** 53.46N 21.44E
Snina Czech. **21** 48.59N 22.07E
Snizort, Loch U.K. **12** 57.35N 6.30W
Snöhetta *mtn.* Norway **23** 62.20N 9.17E
Snov *r.* U.S.S.R. **21** 51.45N 31.45E
Snowbird L. Canada **75** 60.45N103.00W
Snowdon *mtn.* U.K. **10** 53.05N 4.05W
Snowdrift Canada **75** 62.24N110.44W
Snowdrift *r.* Canada **75** 62.24N110.44W
Snowflake U.S.A. **81** 34.30N110.05W
Snow Hill *town* U.S.A. **85** 38.11N 75.23W
Snowy *r.* Australia **67** 37.48S148.30E
Snowy *r.* Australia **67** 37.49S148.30E
Snowy Mts. Australia **67** 36.30S148.20E
Snyatyn U.S.S.R. **21** 48.30N 25.50E
Snyder U.S.A. **83** 32.44N100.05W
Soacha Colombia **90** 4.35N 74.13W
Soalala Madagascar **57** 16.06S 45.20E
Soanierana-Ivongo Madagascar **57** 16.55S 49.35E
Soasiu Indonesia **37** 0.40N127.25E
Soavinandriana Madagascar **57** 19.09S 46.45E
Sob *r.* U.S.S.R. **21** 48.42N 29.17E
Sobat *r.* Sudan **49** 9.30N 31.30E
Sobernheim Germany **14** 49.47N 7.40E
Soboko C.A.R. **49** 6.49N 24.50E
Sobradinho, Reprêsa de *resr.* Brazil **91** 10.00S 42.30W
Sobral Brazil **91** 3.45S 40.20W
Sochi U.S.S.R. **25** 43.35N 39.46E
Société, Îles de la *is.* Pacific Oc. **69** 17.00S150.00W
Society Is. *see* Société, Îles de la *is.* Pacific Oc. **69**
Socorro Colombia **90** 6.30N 73.16W
Socorro U.S.A. **81** 34.04N106.54W
Socorro, Isla *i.* Mexico **86** 18.45N110.58W
Socotra *i. see* Suquṭrá *i.* Yemen **45**
Socuéllamos Spain **16** 39.16N 2.47W
Sodankylä Finland **22** 67.29N 26.32E
Söderhamn Sweden **23** 61.18N 17.03E
Söderköping Sweden **23** 58.29N 16.18E
Södermanland *d.* Sweden **23** 59.10N 16.35E
Södertälje Sweden **23** 59.12N 17.37E
Sodium R.S.A. **56** 30.10S 23.08E
Sodo Ethiopia **49** 6.52N 37.47E
Södra Vi Sweden **23** 57.45N 15.48E
Soest Germany **14** 51.34N 8.06E
Sofala Australia **67** 33.05S149.42E
Sofala *d.* Mozambique **57** 19.00S 34.39E
Sofia *see* Sofiya Bulgaria **19**
Sofia *r.* Madagascar **57** 15.27S 47.23E
Sofiya Bulgaria **19** 42.41N 23.19E
Sofiysk U.S.S.R. **29** 52.19N133.55E
Sofporog U.S.S.R. **24** 65.47N 31.30E
Sogamoso Colombia **90** 5.43N 72.56W
Sögel Germany **14** 52.51N 7.31E
Sognefjorden *est.* Norway **23** 61.06N 5.10E
Sogn og Fjordane *d.* Norway **23** 61.30N 6.50E
Söğüt Turkey **42** 40.02N 30.10E
Sog Xian China **41** 31.51N 93.40E
Sohāgpur India **41** 22.42N 78.12E
Soignies Belgium **14** 50.35N 4.04E
Soissons France **15** 49.23N 3.20E
Sojat India **40** 25.55N 73.40E
Sokal U.S.S.R. **21** 50.30N 24.10E
Söke Turkey **19** 37.46N 27.26E
Sokodé Togo **53** 8.59N 1.11E
Sokol U.S.S.R. **24** 59.28N 40.04E
Sokółka Poland **21** 53.25N 23.31E
Sokolo Mali **52** 14.53N 6.11W
Sokolov Czech. **20** 50.09N 12.40E
Sokoto Nigeria **53** 13.02N 5.15E
Sokoto *d.* Nigeria **53** 11.50N 5.05E
Sokoto *r.* Nigeria **53** 13.05N 5.13E
Solbad Hall Austria **20** 47.17N 11.31E
Solec Kujawski Poland **21** 53.06N 18.14E
Soledad Venezuela **90** 8.10N 63.34W
Solesmes France **14** 50.12N 3.32E
Solginskiy U.S.S.R. **24** 61.07N 41.30E
Solheim Norway **23** 60.53N 5.27E
Soligalich U.S.S.R. **24** 59.02N 42.15E
Solihull U.K. **9** 52.26N 1.47W
Solikamsk U.S.S.R. **24** 59.40N 56.45E
Sol-Iletsk U.S.S.R. **24** 51.09N 55.00E
Solingen Germany **14** 51.10N 7.05E
Sollefteå Sweden **22** 63.12N 17.20E
Sollentuna Sweden **23** 59.28N 17.54E
Sóller Spain **16** 39.47N 2.41E
Sollia Norway **23** 61.47N 10.24E
Solola Somali Rep. **49** 0.08N 41.30E
Solomon Is. Pacific Oc. **68** 8.00S160.00E
Solomons U.S.A. **85** 38.21N 76.29W
Solomon Sea Pacific Oc. **61** 7.00S150.00E
Solon U.S.A. **84** 44.57N 69.52W
Solon Springs U.S.A. **82** 46.22N 91.48W
Solothurn Switz. **20** 47.13N 7.32E
Solovetskiye, Ostrova *is.* U.S.S.R. **24** 65.05N 35.30E
Šolta *i.* Yugo. **18** 43.23N 16.17E
Solṭānābād Iran **43** 36.25N 58.02E
Soltau Germany **20** 52.59N 9.49E
Sölvesborg Sweden **23** 56.03N 14.33E
Solway Firth *est.* U.K. **10** 54.50N 3.30W
Solwezi Zambia **54** 12.11S 26.23E
Solzach *r.* Austria **20** 48.35N 13.30E
Soma Turkey **19** 39.11N 27.36E
Somabhula Zimbabwe **56** 19.40S 29.38E
Somali Republic Africa **45** 5.30N 47.00E
Sombor Yugo. **19** 45.48N 19.08E
Sombrerete Mexico **86** 23.38N103.39W
Somerset *d.* U.K. **11** 51.09N 3.00W
Somerset Ky. U.S.A. **85** 37.05N 84.38W
Somerset East R.S.A. **56** 32.43S 25.33E
Somerset I. Bermuda **95** 32.18N 64.53W
Somerset I. Canada **73** 73.00N 93.30W
Somers Point *town* U.S.A. **85** 39.20N 74.36W
Somerville N.J. U.S.A. **85** 40.34N 74.37W
Somes *r.* Hungary **21** 48.40N 22.30E
Somme *r.* France **17** 50.01N 1.40E
Sommen *l.* Sweden **23** 58.01N 15.15E
Sompeta India **41** 18.56N 84.36E
Sompuis France **15** 48.41N 4.23E
Son *r.* India **41** 25.42N 84.52E
Sonāmarg Jammu & Kashmir **40** 34.18N 75.18E
Sonāmura India **41** 23.29N 91.17E
Sŏnbong N. Korea **31** 42.19N130.24E
Sönderborg Denmark **23** 54.55N 9.47E
Sondershausen Germany **20** 51.22N 10.52E
Söndreströmfjord Greenland **73** 66.30N 50.52W
Sondrio Italy **15** 46.10N 9.52E
Sonepur India **41** 20.50N 83.55E
Songa *r.* Norway **23** 59.45N 7.59E
Song-Cau Vietnam **34** 13.27N109.13E
Songea Tanzania **55** 10.42S 35.39E
Songhua Jiang *r.* China **31** 47.46N132.30E
Songjiang China **33** 31.01N121.20E
Songkhla Thailand **34** 7.12N100.35E
Songololo Zaïre **54** 5.40S 14.05E
Songpan China **32** 32.36N103.36E
Songtao Miaozu Zizhixian China **33** 28.12N109.12E
Song Xian China **32** 34.02N111.48E
Sonid Youqi China **32** 42.44N112.40E
Sonid Zuoqi China **32** 43.58N113.59E
Sonīpat India **40** 28.59N 77.01E
Son La Vietnam **34** 21.20N103.55E
Sonmiāni Pakistan **40** 25.26N 66.36E
Sonmiāni B. Pakistan **40** 25.15N 66.30E
Sonneberg Germany **20** 50.22N 11.10E
Sonoita Mexico **81** 31.51N112.50W
Sonora *d.* Mexico **81** 29.30N110.40W
Sonora *r.* Mexico **81** 28.50N111.33W
Sonora U.S.A. **83** 30.34N100.39W
Sonsorol *i.* Caroline Is. **37** 5.20N132.13E
Son Tay Vietnam **33** 21.15N105.17E
Sopi Indonesia **37** 2.40N128.28E
Sopo *r.* Sudan **49** 8.51N 26.11E
Sopot Poland **21** 54.28N 18.34E
Sopotskin U.S.S.R. **21** 53.49N 23.42E
Soppero Sweden **22** 68.07N 21.40E
Sopron Hungary **20** 47.41N 16.36E
Sop's Arm *town* Canada **77** 49.46N 56.56W
Sopur Jammu & Kashmir **40** 34.18N 74.28E
Sorada India **41** 19.45N 84.26E
Sorel Canada **77** 46.03N 73.06W
Sörfjorden Norway **22** 66.29N 13.20E
Sörfold Norway **22** 67.30N 15.30E
Sorgono Italy **18** 40.01N 9.06E
Soria Spain **16** 41.46N 2.28W
Soriano Uruguay **93** 33.24S 58.19W
Sor Kvalöy *i.* Norway **22** 69.40N 18.30E
Sörli Norway **22** 64.15N 13.50E
Sor Mertvyy Kultuk *f.* U.S.S.R. **25** 45.30N 54.00E
Soro India **41** 21.17N 86.40E
Sorocaba Brazil **94** 23.29S 47.27W
Sorochinsk U.S.S.R. **24** 52.29N 53.15E
Soroki U.S.S.R. **21** 48.08N 28.12E
Sorol *i.* Caroline Is. **37** 8.09N140.25E
Soron India **41** 27.53N 78.45E
Sorong Indonesia **37** 0.50S131.17E
Soroti Uganda **55** 1.40N 33.37E
Söröya *i.* Norway **22** 70.35N 22.30E
Sorraia *r.* Portugal **16** 39.00N 8.51W
Sorrento Italy **18** 40.37N 14.22E
Sör-Rondane *mts.* Antarctica **96** 72.30S 22.00E
Sorsele Sweden **22** 65.30N 17.30E
Sortavala U.S.S.R. **24** 61.40N 30.40E
Sortland Norway **22** 68.44N 15.25E
Sör Tröndelag *d.* Norway **22** 63.00N 10.20E
Sorūbī Afghan. **40** 34.36N 69.43E
Sosnogorsk U.S.S.R. **24** 63.32N 53.55E
Sosnovo U.S.S.R. **24** 60.33N 30.11E
Sosnovyy U.S.S.R. **24** 66.01N 32.40E
Sosnowiec Poland **21** 50.18N 19.08E
Sosva U.S.S.R. **24** 59.10N 61.50E
Sosyka U.S.S.R. **25** 46.11N 38.49E
Sotik Kenya **55** 0.40S 35.08E
Sotra *i.* Norway **23** 60.15N 5.10E
Sotteville France **15** 49.25N 1.06E
Soubré Ivory Coast **52** 5.50N 6.35W
Souderton U.S.A. **85** 40.19N 75.19W
Soufflay Congo **54** 2.00N 14.54E
Souflión Greece **19** 41.12N 26.18E
Souk Ahras Algeria **51** 36.17N 7.57E
Souk-el-Arba-du-Rharb Morocco **50** 34.43N 6.01W
Sŏul S. Korea **31** 37.30N127.00E
Sources, Mont-aux- *mtn.* Lesotho **56** 28.44S 28.52E
Soure Portugal **16** 40.04N 8.38W
Souris *r.* Canada **75** 49.39N 99.34W
Souris Man. Canada **75** 49.38N100.15W
Souris P.E.I. Canada **77** 46.21N 62.15W
Sous, Oued *wadi* Morocco **50** 30.27N 9.31W
Sousa Brazil **91** 6.41S 38.14W
Sous le Vent, Îles *is.* Îs. de la Société **69** 16.30S151.30W
Sousse Tunisia **51** 35.48N 10.38E
Soustons France **17** 43.45N 1.19W
South Alligator *r.* Australia **64** 12.53S132.29E
Southampton Canada **76** 44.29N 81.23W
Southampton U.K. **11** 50.54N 1.23W
Southampton I. Canada **73** 64.30N 84.00W
South Aulatsivik I. Canada **77** 56.45N 61.30W
South Australia *d.* Australia **66** 30.00S137.00E
South Bend Ind. U.S.A. **84** 41.40N 86.15W
South Bend Wash. U.S.A. **80** 46.40N123.48W
South Boston U.S.A. **85** 36.42N 78.58W
South Branch U.S.A. **84** 44.29N 83.36W
South Carolina *d.* U.S.A. **85** 34.00N 81.00W
South Cerney U.K. **11** 51.40N 1.55W
South China Sea Asia **36** 12.30N115.00E
South Dakota *d.* U.S.A. **82** 45.00N100.00W
South Dorset Downs *hills* U.K. **11** 50.40N 2.25W
South Downs *hills* U.K. **11** 50.04N 0.34W
South East *d.* Botswana **56** 25.00S 25.45E
South East C. Australia **65** 43.38S146.48E
South Eastern Atlantic Basin *f.* Atlantic Oc. **95** 20.00S 0.00
South East Head *c.* Ascension **95** 7.58S 14.18W
South East Is. Australia **63** 34.23S123.30E
South East Pt. Kiribati **69** 1.40N157.10W
Southend-on-Sea U.K. **11** 51.32N 0.43E
Southern *d.* Zambia **56** 16.30S 26.40E
Southern Alps *mts.* New Zealand **60** 43.20S170.45E
Southern Cross Australia **63** 31.14S119.16E
Southern Indian L. Canada **75** 57.10N 98.40W
Southern Lueti *r.* Zambia **56** 16.15S 23.12E
Southern Ocean Pacific Oc. **68** 44.00S130.00E
Southern Pines U.S.A. **85** 35.12N 79.23W
Southern Uplands *hills* U.K. **12** 55.30N 3.30W
South Esk *r.* U.K. **12** 56.43N 2.32W
South Esk Tablelands *f.* Australia **62** 20.50S126.40E
Southey Canada **75** 50.56N104.30W
South Fiji Basin Pacific Oc. **68** 27.00S176.00E
South Georgia *i.* Atlantic Oc. **95** 54.50S 36.00W
South Glamorgan *d.* U.K. **11** 51.27N 3.22W
South-haa U.K. **12** 60.34N 1.17W
South Hātia I. Bangla. **41** 22.19N 91.07E
South Haven U.S.A. **84** 42.25N 86.16W
South Henik L. Canada **75** 61.30N 97.30W
South Honshu Ridge Pacific Oc. **68** 22.00N141.00E
South Horr Kenya **55** 2.10N 36.45E
South I. Kenya **55** 2.36N 36.38E
South I. New Zealand **60** 43.00S171.00E
South Knife *r.* Canada **75** 58.55N 94.37W
South Korea Asia **31** 36.00N128.00E
South Lake Tahoe *town* U.S.A. **80** 38.57N119.57W
Southland *d.* New Zealand **60** 45.40S168.00E
South Loup *r.* U.S.A. **82** 41.04N 98.40W

uth Molton U.K. 11 51.01N 3.50W
uth Nahanni *r.* Canada 74 61.03N123.21W
uth Orkney Is. Atlantic Oc. 95 60.50S 5.00W
uth Platte *r.* U.S.A. 82 41.07N100.42W
uthport Qld. Australia 67 27.58S153.20E
uthport Tas. Australia 65 43.25S146.59E
uthport U.K. 10 53.38N 3.01W
uthport U.S.A. 85 33.55N 78.00W
uth River *town* U.S.A. 85 40.27N 74.23W
uth Ronaldsay *i.* U.K. 12 58.47N 2.56W
uth Sandwich Is. Atlantic Oc. 95 57.00S 7.00W
uth Sandwich Trench *f.* Atlantic Oc. 95 7.00S 25.00W
uth Saskatchewan *r.* Canada 75 3.15N105.05W
uth Seal *r.* Canada 75 58.48N 98.08W
uth Shields U.K. 10 55.00N 1.24W
uth Sioux City U.S.A. 82 42.28N 96.24W
uth Tasmania Ridge *f.* Pac. Oc./Ind. Oc. 68 6.00S147.00E
uth Thompson *r.* Canada 74 0.40N120.20W
uth Tucson U.S.A. 81 32.12N110.58W
uth Twin I. Canada 76 53.00N 79.50W
uth Tyne *r.* U.K. 12 54.59N 2.08W
uth Uist *i.* U.K. 12 57.15N 7.20W
uth Wabasca L. Canada 74 5.54N113.45W
uthwest C. New Zealand 60 47.15S167.30E
uth Western Pacific Basin Pacific Oc. 69 9.00S148.00W
uth West Peru Ridge Pacific Oc. 69 20.00S 2.00W
uth West Pt. *c.* Kiribati 69 1.52N157.33W
uth West Pt. *c.* St. Helena 95 16.00S 5.48W
uth Windham U.S.A. 84 43.44N 70.26W
uthwold U.K. 11 52.19N 1.41E
uth Yorkshire *d.* U.K. 10 53.28N 1.25W
utpansberg *mts.* R.S.A. 56 22.58S 29.50E
vetsk Lit.S.S.R. U.S.S.R. 23 55.05N 21.53E
vetsk R.S.F.S.R. U.S.S.R. 24 57.39N 48.59E
vetskaya Gavan U.S.S.R. 29 8.57N140.16E
weto R.S.A. 56 26.16S 27.51E
yo Angola 54 6.12S 12.25E
yopa Mexico 81 28.47N109.39W
zh *r.* U.S.S.R. 21 51.57N 30.48E
a Belgium 14 50.29N 5.52E
ain Europe 16 40.00N 4.00W
alding Australia 66 33.29S138.40E
alding U.K. 10 52.47N 0.09W
alding U.S.A. 82 41.41N 98.22W
andau Germany 20 52.32N 13.13E
anish Fork U.S.A. 80 40.07N111.39W
arks U.S.A. 80 39.32N119.45W
arrows Point *town* U.S.A. 85 39.13N 6.26W
arta Ga. U.S.A. 85 33.17N 82.58W
arta N.J. U.S.A. 85 41.02N 74.38W
arta Wisc. U.S.A. 82 43.57N 90.47W
artanburg U.S.A. 85 34.56N 81.57W
árti Greece 19 37.04N 22.28E
artivento, Capo *c.* Calabria Italy 18 37.55N 6.04E
artivento, Capo *c.* Sardegna Italy 18 8.53N 8.50E
átha, Ákra *c.* Greece 19 35.42N 23.43E
atsizi Plateau Wilderness Prov. Park anada 74 57.13N127.53W
earman U.S.A. 83 36.12N101.12W
eculator U.S.A. 84 43.30N 74.17W
eke G. Tanzania 55 2.20S 33.30E
ence Bay *town* Canada 73 69.30N 93.20W
encer Idaho U.S.A. 80 44.21N112.11W
encer Iowa U.S.A. 82 43.09N 95.09W
encer S.Dak. U.S.A. 82 43.44N 97.36W
encer, C. Australia 66 35.18S136.53E
encer G. Australia 66 34.00S137.00E
ences Bridge *town* Canada 74 0.25N121.20W
errin Mts. U.K. 13 54.49N 7.06W
étsai *i.* Greece 19 37.15N 23.10E
ey *r.* U.K. 12 57.40N 3.06W
eyer Germany 20 49.18N 8.26E
iekeroog *i.* Germany 14 53.48N 7.45E
ilimbergo Italy 15 46.07N 12.54E
ilsby U.K. 10 53.10N 0.06E
ina *ruins* Italy 15 44.42N 12.08E
inazzola Italy 18 40.58N 16.06E
in Büldak Afghan. 40 31.01N 66.24E
irit River *town* Canada 74 55.45N118.50W
išská Nova Ves Czech. 21 48.57N 20.34E
ithead *str.* U.K. 11 50.45N 1.05W
itsbergen *is.* Arctic Oc. 96 78.00N 17.00E
ittal an der Drau Austria 20 46.48N 13.30E
lit Yugo. 19 43.32N 16.27E
lit L. Canada 75 56.08N 96.15W
offord U.S.A. 83 29.11N100.25W
okane U.S.A. 80 47.40N117.23W
okane *r.* U.S.A. 80 47.44N118.20W
ooner U.S.A. 82 45.50N 91.53W
ratly *i.* S. China Sea 36 8.45N111.54E
ray U.S.A. 80 44.50N119.48W
ree *r.* Germany 20 52.32N 13.15E
ringbok R.S.A. 56 29.40S 17.50E
ringdale Canada 77 49.30N 56.04W
ringer U.S.A. 80 36.22N104.36W
ringerville U.S.A. 81 34.08N109.17W
ringfield New Zealand 60 43.20S171.56E
ringfield Colo. U.S.A. 83 37.24N102.37W
ringfield Ill. U.S.A. 82 39.49N 89.39W
ringfield Mass. U.S.A. 84 42.07N 72.35W
ringfield Miss. U.S.A. 79 37.11N 93.19W
ringfield Mo. U.S.A. 83 37.14N 93.17W
ringfield Ohio U.S.A. 84 39.55N 83.48W
ringfield Oreg. U.S.A. 80 44.03N123.01W
Springfield Tenn. U.S.A. 85 36.30N 86.54W
Springfield Vt. U.S.A. 84 43.18N 72.29W
Springfontein R.S.A. 56 30.15S 25.41E
Spring Grove U.S.A. 85 39.52N 76.52W
Springhill Canada 77 45.39N 64.03W
Springs *town* R.S.A. 56 26.16S 28.27E
Springsure Australia 64 24.07S148.05E
Spring Valley *town* U.S.A. 82 43.41N 92.23W
Springville Utah U.S.A. 80 40.10N111.37W
Spry U.S.A. 80 37.55N112.28W
Spurn Head U.K. 10 53.35N 0.08E
Spuzzum Canada 74 49.37N121.23W
Squamish Canada 74 49.45N123.10W
Squaw Rapids *town* Canada 75 53.41N103.20W
Squillace Italy 19 38.46N 16.31E
Sragen Indonesia 37 7.24S111.00E
Srbija *d.* Yugo. 19 44.30N 20.30E
Srednekolymsk U.S.S.R. 29 67.27N153.35E
Sredne Russkaya Vozvyshennost *f.* U.S.S.R. 24 53.00N 37.00E
Sredne Sibirskoye Ploskogor'ye *f.* U.S.S.R. 29 66.00N108.00E
Srê Moat Cambodia 34 13.15N107.10E
Srêpôk *r.* Cambodia 34 13.33N106.16E
Sretensk U.S.S.R. 31 52.15N117.52E
Sri Düngargarh India 40 28.05N 74.00E
Sri Gangānagar India 40 29.55N 73.52E
Srikākulam India 39 18.18N 83.54E
Sri Lanka Asia 39 7.30N 80.50E
Sri Mohangarh India 40 27.17N 71.14E
Srinagar Jammu & Kashmir 40 34.05N 74.49E
Sripur Bangla. 41 24.12N 90.29E
Srirampur India 40 19.30N 74.30E
Srnetica Yugo. 19 44.26N 16.40E
Staaten *r.* Australia 64 16.24S141.17E
Stadskanaal Neth. 14 53.02N 6.55E
Stadtkyll Germany 14 50.21N 6.32E
Stadtlohn Germany 14 52.00N 6.58E
Staffa *i.* U.K. 12 56.26N 6.21W
Stafford U.K. 10 52.49N 2.09W
Stafford U.S.A. 85 38.09N 76.51W
Staffordshire *d.* U.K. 10 52.40N 1.57W
Staines U.K. 11 51.26N 0.31W
Stainforth U.K. 10 53.37N 1.01W
Stakhanov U.S.S.R. 25 48.34N 38.40E
Stalina Kanal *canal* U.S.S.R. 24 64.33N 34.48E
Stamford U.K. 11 52.39N 0.28W
Stamford Conn. U.S.A. 85 41.03N 73.32W
Stamford N.Y. U.S.A. 84 42.25N 74.37W
Stamford Tex. U.S.A. 83 32.57N 99.48W
Stanberry U.S.A. 82 40.13N 94.35W
Standerton R.S.A. 56 26.57S 29.14E
Stanger R.S.A. 56 29.20S 31.17E
Stanley Canada 72 55.45N104.55W
Stanley Falkland Is. 93 51.42W 57.51W
Stanley U.K. 10 54.53N 1.42W
Stanley Idaho U.S.A. 80 44.13N114.35W
Stanley Wisc. U.S.A. 82 44.58N 90.56W
Stanley Mission Canada 75 55.27N104.33W
Stanovoy Khrebet *mts.* U.S.S.R. 29 56.00N125.40E
Stanthorpe Australia 67 28.37S151.52E
Stanton U.S.A. 83 32.08N101.48W
Stapleton U.S.A. 82 41.29N100.31W
Starachowice Poland 21 51.03N 21.04E
Stara Dorogi U.S.S.R. 21 53.02N 28.18E
Stara Planina *mts.* Bulgaria 19 42.50N 24.30E
Staraya Russa U.S.S.R. 24 58.00N 31.22E
Staraya Sinyava U.S.S.R. 21 49.38N 27.39E
Stara Zagora Bulgaria 19 42.26N 25.37E
Starbuck I. Kiribati 69 5.37S155.55W
Stargard Szczeciński Poland 20 53.21N 15.01E
Staritsa U.S.S.R. 24 56.29N 34.59E
Starke U.S.A. 85 29.55N 82.06W
Starkville U.S.A. 83 33.28N 88.48W
Starnberg Germany 20 48.00N 11.20E
Starobin U.S.S.R. 21 52.40N 27.29E
Starogard Gdański Poland 21 53.59N 18.33E
Starokonstantinov U.S.S.R. 21 49.48N 27.10E
Start Pt. U.K. 11 50.13N 3.38W
Staryy Oskol U.S.S.R. 25 51.20N 37.50E
State College U.S.A. 84 40.48N 77.52W
Staten I. *see* Estados, Isla de los *i.* Argentina 93
Statesville U.S.A. 85 35.46N 80.54W
Staunton U.S.A. 85 38.09N 79.04W
Stavanger Norway 23 58.58N 5.45E
Stavelot Belgium 14 50.23N 5.54E
Staveren Neth. 14 52.53N 5.21E
Stavropol' U.S.S.R. 25 45.03N 41.59E
Stavropolskaya Vozvyshennost *mts.* U.S.S.R. 25 45.00N 42.30E
Stawell Australia 66 37.06S142.52E
Stawiski Poland 21 53.23N 22.09E
Stayton U.S.A. 80 44.48N122.48W
Steamboat Springs *town* U.S.A. 80 40.29N106.50W
Steele U.S.A. 82 46.51N 99.55W
Steelpoort R.S.A. 56 24.44S 30.13E
Steelton U.S.A. 84 40.14N 76.49W
Steenbergen Neth. 14 51.36N 4.19E
Steenvoorde France 14 50.49N 2.35E
Steenwijk Neth. 14 52.47N 6.07E
Steep Rock Lake *town* Canada 76 48.50N 91.38W
Steiermark *d.* Austria 20 47.10N 15.10E
Steilloopbrug R.S.A. 56 23.26S 28.37E
Steinbach Canada 75 49.32N 96.41W
Steinkjer Norway 22 64.00N 11.30E
Steinkopf R.S.A. 56 29.16S 17.41E
Stella R.S.A. 56 26.32S 24.51E
Stellarton Canada 77 45.34N 62.40W
Stellenbosch R.S.A. 56 33.56S 18.51E
Stenay France 15 49.29N 5.11E
Stendal Germany 20 52.36N 11.52E
Stenträsk Sweden 22 66.20N 19.50E
Stepan U.S.S.R. 21 51.09N 26.18E
Stepanakert U.S.S.R. 43 39.48N 46.45E
Stephens Passage *str.* U.S.A. 74 57.50N133.50W
Stephenville Canada 77 48.33N 58.35W
Stephenville U.S.A. 83 32.13N 98.12W
Stepnyak U.S.S.R. 28 52.52N 70.49E
Steps Pt. *c.* Samoa 68 14.22S170.45W
Sterkstroom R.S.A. 56 31.32S 26.31E
Sterling Colo. U.S.A. 80 40.37N103.13W
Sterling Ill. U.S.A. 82 41.48N 89.43W
Sterling Mich. U.S.A. 84 44.02N 84.02W
Sterlitamak U.S.S.R. 24 53.40N 55.59E
Šternberk Czech. 21 49.44N 17.18E
Stettler Canada 74 52.19N112.40W
Steuben U.S.A. 84 46.12N 86.27W
Steubenville U.S.A. 84 40.22N 80.39W
Stevenage U.K. 11 51.54N 0.11W
Stevenson L. Canada 75 53.56N 96.09W
Stevens Point *town* U.S.A. 82 44.32N 89.33W
Stevenston U.K. 12 55.39N 4.45W
Stewart Canada 74 55.56N130.01W
Stewart I. New Zealand 60 47.00S168.00E
Stewart River *town* Canada 72 63.19N139.26W
Steynsburg R.S.A. 56 31.17S 25.48E
Steyr Austria 20 48.04N 14.25E
Stikine *r.* Canada/U.S.A. 74 56.40N132.30W
Stikine Mts. Canada 72 59.00N129.00W
Stikine Plateau *f.* Canada 74 58.45N130.00W
Stiklestad Norway 22 63.48N 11.22E
Stilbaai R.S.A. 56 34.22S 21.22E
Stillwater U.S.A. 83 36.07N 97.04W
Stillwater Range *mts.* U.S.A. 80 39.50N118.15W
Stilton U.K. 11 52.29N 0.17W
Stimson Canada 76 48.58N 80.36W
Stinchar *r.* U.K. 12 55.06N 5.00W
Stînisoara, Munţii *mts.* Romania 21 47.10N 26.00E
Štip Yugo. 19 41.44N 22.12E
Stirling U.K. 12 56.07N 3.57W
Stirling Range *mts.* Australia 63 34.23S117.50E
Stjernöya *i.* Norway 22 70.17N 22.40E
Stjördalshalsen Norway 22 63.29N 10.51E
Stockaryd Sweden 23 57.18N 14.35E
Stockbridge U.K. 11 51.07N 1.30W
Stockdale U.S.A. 83 29.14N 97.58W
Stockerau Austria 20 48.23N 16.13E
Stockett U.S.A. 80 47.21N111.10W
Stockholm Sweden 23 59.20N 18.03E
Stockholm *d.* Sweden 23 59.40N 18.10E
Stockinbingal Australia 67 34.03S147.53E
Stockport U.K. 10 53.25N 2.11W
Stocksbridge U.K. 10 53.30N 1.36W
Stockton Calif. U.S.A. 80 37.57N121.17W
Stockton Kans. U.S.A. 82 39.26N 99.16W
Stockton-on-Tees U.K. 10 54.34N 1.20W
Stoeng Trêng Cambodia 34 13.31N105.59E
Stoffberg R.S.A. 56 25.25S 29.49E
Stoke-on-Trent U.K. 10 53.01N 2.11W
Stokes Bay *town* Canada 76 44.58N 81.18W
Stokhod *r.* U.S.S.R. 21 51.52N 25.38E
Stokksund Norway 22 64.03N 10.05E
Stolac Yugo. 19 43.05N 17.58E
Stolberg Germany 14 50.47N 6.12E
Stolbtsy U.S.S.R. 21 53.30N 26.44E
Stolin U.S.S.R. 21 51.52N 26.51E
Stone U.K. 10 52.55N 2.10W
Stone Harbor U.S.A. 85 39.03N 74.45W
Stonehaven U.K. 12 56.58N 2.13W
Stony I. Canada 77 53.00N 55.48W
Stony Rapids *town* Canada 75 59.16N105.50W
Stooping *r.* Canada 76 52.08N 82.00W
Stora Lulevatten *l.* Sweden 22 67.10N 19.16E
Stora Sjöfallets Nat. Park Sweden 22 67.44N 18.16E
Storavan *l.* Sweden 22 65.40N 18.15E
Storby Finland 23 60.13N 19.34E
Stord *i.* Norway 23 59.53N 5.25E
Store Baelt *str.* Denmark 23 55.30N 11.00E
Stor Elvdal Norway 23 61.32N 11.02E
Stören Norway 22 63.03N 10.18E
Storlien Sweden 22 63.20N 12.05E
Storm Lake *town* U.S.A. 82 42.39N 95.10W
Stornoway U.K. 12 58.12N 6.23W
Storozhevsk U.S.S.R. 24 62.00N 52.20E
Storozhinets U.S.S.R. 21 48.11N 25.40E
Storsjön *l.* Sweden 22 63.10N 14.20E
Storuman Sweden 22 65.06N 17.06E
Storuman *l.* Sweden 22 65.10N 16.40E
Stouffville Canada 76 43.59N 79.15W
Stoughton U.S.A. 82 42.55N 89.13W
Stour *r.* Dorset U.K. 11 50.43N 1.47W
Stour *r.* Kent U.K. 11 51.19N 1.22E
Stour *r.* Suffolk U.K. 11 51.56N 1.03E
Stourport-on-Severn U.K. 11 52.21N 2.16W
Stowmarket U.K. 11 52.11N 1.00E
Stow on the Wold U.K. 11 51.55N 1.42W
Strabane U.K. 13 54.50N 7.30W
Stradbally Laois Rep. of Ire. 13 53.01N 7.09W
Stradbroke I. Australia 65 27.38S153.45E
Stradella Italy 15 45.05N 9.18E
Straelen Germany 14 51.27N 6.14E
Strahan Australia 65 42.08S145.21E
Strakonice Czech. 20 49.16N 13.55E
Stralsund Germany 20 54.18N 13.06E
Strand R.S.A. 56 34.07S 18.50E
Stranda Norway 22 62.19N 6.58E
Strangford Lough U.K. 13 54.28N 5.35W
Strangways Australia 66 29.08S136.35E
Stranraer U.K. 12 54.54N 5.02W
Strasbourg France 17 48.35N 7.45E
Strasburg N.Dak. U.S.A. 82 46.08N100.10W
Stratford Australia 67 37.57S147.05E
Stratford Canada 76 43.22N 80.57W
Stratford New Zealand 60 39.20S174.18E
Stratford Tex. U.S.A. 83 36.20N102.04W
Stratford-upon-Avon U.K. 11 52.12N 1.42W
Strathalbyn Australia 66 35.16S138.54E
Strathclyde *d.* U.K. 12 55.45N 4.45W
Strathcona Prov. Park Canada 74 49.38N125.40W
Strathmore *f.* Tayside U.K. 12 56.44N 2.45W
Strathspey *f.* U.K. 12 57.25N 3.25W
Stratton U.S.A. 82 39.18N102.36W
Straubing Germany 20 48.53N 12.35E
Straumnes *c.* Iceland 22 66.30N 23.05W
Strawn U.S.A. 83 32.33N 98.30W
Streaky B. Australia 66 32.36S134.08E
Streaky Bay *town* Australia 66 32.48S134.13E
Streator U.S.A. 82 41.07N 88.53W
Street U.K. 11 51.07N 2.43W
Streeter U.S.A. 82 46.39N 99.21W
Streetsville Canada 76 43.35N 79.42W
Stresa Italy 15 45.53N 8.32E
Stretton Australia 63 32.30S117.42E
Strimon *r.* Greece 19 40.47N 23.51E
Stromboli *i.* Italy 18 38.48N 15.14E
Stromeferry U.K. 12 57.21N 5.34W
Stromness U.K. 12 58.57N 3.18W
Strömö *i.* Faroe Is. 8 62.08N 7.00W
Strömsbruk Sweden 23 61.53N 17.19E
Strömstad Sweden 23 58.56N 11.10E
Strömsund Sweden 22 63.51N 15.35E
Strömsvattudal *f.* Sweden 22 64.15N 15.00E
Strongfield Canada 75 51.20N106.36W
Stronsay *i.* U.K. 12 59.07N 2.36W
Stroud Australia 67 32.25S151.58E
Stroud U.K. 11 51.44N 2.12W
Struan Australia 66 37.08S140.49E
Struer Denmark 23 56.29N 8.37E
Struga Yugo. 19 41.10N 20.41E
Struma *r.* Bulgaria *see* Strimon *r.* Greece 19
Strumica Yugo. 19 41.26N 22.39E
Strydenburg R.S.A. 56 29.56S 23.39E
Stryker U.S.A. 80 48.40N114.44W
Stryy U.S.S.R. 21 49.16N 23.51E
Strzelecki Creek *r.* Australia 66 29.37S139.59E
Strzelno Poland 21 52.38N 18.11E
Stuart Fla. U.S.A. 85 27.12N 80.16W
Stuart Nebr. U.S.A. 82 42.36N 99.08W
Stuart Creek *town* Australia 66 29.43S137.01E
Stuart L. Canada 74 54.30N124.30W
Stuart Range *mts.* Australia 66 29.10S134.56E
Stuart Town Australia 67 32.51S149.08E
Stupart *r.* Canada 75 56.00N 93.22W
Sturgeon Bay *town* U.S.A. 82 44.50N 87.23W
Sturgeon Falls *town* Canada 76 46.22N 79.55W
Sturgeon L. Ont. Canada 76 50.00N 90.40W
Sturgis U.S.A. 82 44.25N103.31W
Sturminster Newton U.K. 11 50.56N 2.18W
Sturt B. Australia 66 35.24S137.32E
Sturt Creek *r.* Australia 62 20.08S127.24E
Sturt Desert Australia 66 28.30S141.12E
Sturt Plain *f.* Australia 64 17.00S132.48E
Stutterheim R.S.A. 56 32.32S 27.25E
Stuttgart Germany 20 48.47N 9.12E
Stviga *r.* U.S.S.R. 21 52.04N 27.54E
Stykkishólmur Iceland 22 65.06N 22.48W
Styr *r.* U.S.S.R. 21 52.07N 26.35E
Suao Taiwan 33 24.36N121.51E
Subarnarekha *r.* India 41 21.34N 87.24E
Subay', 'Urūq *f.* Saudi Arabia 48 22.15N 43.05E
Subei Guangai Zongqu *canal* China 32 34.06N120.19E
Subotica Yugo. 19 46.04N 19.41E
Suceava Romania 21 47.39N 26.19E
Suck *r.* Rep. of Ire. 13 53.16N 8.04W
Suckling, Mt. P.N.G. 64 9.45S148.55E
Sucre Bolivia 92 19.02S 65.17W
Sucuriu *r.* Brazil 94 20.44S 51.40W
Sudan Africa 48 14.30N 29.00E
Sudan U.S.A. 83 34.04N102.32W
Sudbury Canada 76 46.30N 81.00W
Sudbury U.K. 11 52.03N 0.45E
Sudety *mts.* Czech./Poland 20 50.30N 16.30E
Sudirman, Pegunungan *mts.* Indonesia 37 3.50S136.30E
Sud Ouest *d.* Burkina 52 10.45N 3.10W
Sueca Spain 16 39.12N 0.21W
Suez *see* As Suways Egypt 44
Suez, G. of *see* Suways, Khalīj as *g.* Egypt 44
Suez Canal *see* Suways, Qanāt as *canal* Egypt 44
Şufaynah Saudi Arabia 42 23.09N 40.32E
Suffolk *d.* U.K. 11 52.16N 1.00E
Suffolk U.S.A. 85 36.44N 76.37W
Şuḩār Oman 43 24.23N 56.43E
Sühbaatar *d.* Mongolia 32 45.30N114.00E
Suhl Germany 20 50.37N 10.43E
Sui Pakistan 40 28.37N 69.19E
Suibin China 31 47.19N131.49E
Suichang China 33 28.36N119.16E
Suichuan China 33 26.24N114.31E
Suide China 32 37.35N110.08E
Suihua China 31 46.39N126.59E
Suileng China 31 47.15N127.05E
Suining Jiangsu China 32 33.54N117.56E
Suining Sichuan China 33 30.31N105.32E
Suipacha Argentina 93 34.47S 59.40W
Suippes France 15 49.08N 4.32E
Suir *r.* Rep. of Ire. 13 52.17N 7.00W
Suita Japan 35 34.45N135.32E
Sui Xian Henan China 32 34.25N115.04E
Sui Xian Hubei China 33 31.45N113.30E
Suiyang Guizhou China 33 27.57N107.11E
Suizhong China 32 40.25N120.25E
Suj China 32 42.02N107.58E
Sūjāngarh India 40 27.42N 74.28E
Sujāwal Pakistan 40 24.36N 68.05E
Sukabumi Indonesia 37 6.55S106.50E
Sukadana Indonesia 36 1.15S110.00E
Sukaraja Indonesia 36 2.23S110.35E
Sukhinichi U.S.S.R. 24 54.07N 35.21E
Sukhona *r.* U.S.S.R. 24 61.30N 46.28E
Sukhumi U.S.S.R. 25 43.01N 41.01E
Sukkertoppen Greenland 73 65.40N 53.00W
Sukkur Pakistan 40 27.42N 68.52E
Sukoharjo Indonesia 37 7.40S110.50E
Sula *i.* Norway 23 61.08N 4.55E
Sula, Kepulauan *is.* Indonesia 37 1.50S125.10E
Sulaimān Range *mts.* Pakistan 40 30.00N 69.50E
Sulak *r.* U.S.S.R. 25 43.18N 47.35E
Sulawesi *i.* Indonesia 37 2.00S120.30E
Sulawesi Selatan *d.* Indonesia 37 3.45S120.30E
Sulawesi Utara *d.* Indonesia 37 1.45S120.30E
Sulechów Poland 20 52.06N 15.37E
Sulejów Poland 21 51.22N 19.53E
Sulina Romania 19 45.08N 29.40E
Sulitjelma Norway 22 67.10N 16.05E
Sullana Peru 90 4.52S 80.39W
Sullivan U.S.A. 82 38.13N 91.10W
Sully France 15 47.46N 2.22E
Sulmona Italy 18 42.04N 13.57E
Sulphur U.S.A. 83 34.31N 96.58W
Sultan Canada 76 47.36N 82.47W
Sultan Hamud Kenya 55 2.02S 37.20E
Sultānpur India 41 26.16N 82.04E
Sulu Archipelago Phil. 37 5.30N121.00E
Sulūq Libya 51 31.40N 20.15E
Sulu Sea Pacific Oc. 37 8.00N120.00E
Sumatera *i.* Indonesia 36 2.00S102.00E
Sumatera Barat *d.* Indonesia 36 1.00S100.00E
Sumatera Selatan *d.* Indonesia 36 3.00S104.00E
Sumatera Utara *d.* Indonesia 36 2.00N 99.00E
Sumatra *see* Sumatera *i.* Indonesia 36
Sumatra U.S.A. 80 46.38N107.31W
Sumba *i.* Indonesia 36 9.30S119.55E
Sumbar *r.* U.S.S.R. 43 38.00N 55.20E
Sumbawa *i.* Indonesia 36 8.45S117.50E
Sumbawanga Tanzania 55 7.58S 31.36E
Sumbe Angola 54 11.11S 13.52E
Sumburgh Head U.K. 12 59.51N 1.16W
Sumedang Indonesia 37 6.54S107.55E
Šumen Bulgaria 19 43.15N 26.55E
Sumenep Indonesia 37 7.01S113.51E
Sumgait U.S.S.R. 43 40.35N 49.38E
Summerland Canada 74 49.32N119.41W
Summerside Canada 77 46.24N 63.47W
Summerville Ga. U.S.A. 85 34.29N 85.21W
Summerville S.C. U.S.A. 85 33.02N 80.11W
Šumperk Czech. 20 49.58N 16.58E
Sumprabum Burma 34 26.33N 97.34E
Sumuştā al Waqf Egypt 44 28.55N 30.51E
Sumy U.S.S.R. 25 50.55N 34.49E
Sunām India 40 30.08N 75.48E
Sunāmganj Bangla. 41 25.04N 91.24E
Sunart, Loch U.K. 12 56.43N 5.45W
Sunburst U.S.A. 80 48.53N111.55W
Sunbury Australia 67 37.36S144.45E
Sunda, Selat *str.* Indonesia 36 6.00S105.50E
Sundance U.S.A. 80 44.24N104.23W
Sundarbans *f.* India/Bangla. 41 21.45N 89.00E
Sundargarh India 41 22.07N 84.02E
Sundays *r.* R.S.A. 56 33.43S 25.50E
Sunderland U.K. 10 54.55N 1.22W
Sundsvall Sweden 23 62.23N 17.18E
Sungai Kolok Thailand 34 6.02N101.58E
Sungaipakning Indonesia 36 1.19N102.00E
Sungaipenuh Indonesia 36 2.00S101.28E
Sungguminasa Indonesia 36 5.14S119.27E
Sungurlu Turkey 42 40.10N 34.23E
Sunjikāy Sudan 49 12.20N 29.46E
Sunne Sweden 23 59.50N 13.09E
Sunnyside U.S.A. 80 46.20N120.00W
Suntar U.S.S.R. 29 62.10N117.35E
Suntsar Pakistan 40 25.31N 62.00E
Sun Valley *town* U.S.A. 78 43.42N114.21W
Sunwu China 31 49.40N127.10E
Sunyani Ghana 52 7.22N 2.18W
Suoyarvi U.S.S.R. 24 62.02N 32.20E
Supaul India 41 26.07N 86.36E
Superior Mont. U.S.A. 80 47.12N114.53W
Superior Wisc. U.S.A. 82 46.42N 92.05W
Superior Wyo. U.S.A. 80 41.46N108.58W
Superior, L. Canada/U.S.A. 84 48.00N 88.00W
Suphan Buri Thailand 34 14.14N100.07E
Suphan Buri *r.* Thailand 34 13.34N100.15E
Süphan Dagi *mtn.* Turkey 25 38.55N 42.55E
Süphan Daglari *mtn.* Turkey 42 38.55N 42.55E
Suqian China 32 33.59N118.25E
Suquţrá *i.* Yemen 45 12.30N 54.00E
Şūr Lebanon 44 33.16N 35.12E
Şūr Oman 43 22.23N 59.32E
Sur *d.* W. Sahara 50 23.40N 14.15W
Sur, Cabo *c.* I. de Pascua 69 27.12S109.26W
Sur, Punta *c.* Argentina 93 36.53S 56.41W
Sura U.S.S.R. 24 53.52N 45.45E
Sūrāb Pakistan 40 28.29N 66.16E
Surabaya Indonesia 37 7.14S112.45E
Surakarta Indonesia 37 7.32S110.50E
Şūrān Syria 44 35.18N 36.44E
Šurany Czech. 21 48.06N 18.14E
Surat Australia 65 27.09S149.05E
Surat India 40 21.12N 72.50E
Sūratgarh India 40 29.18N 73.54E
Surat Thani Thailand 34 9.09N 99.23E
Surazh U.S.S.R. 21 53.00N 32.22E
Süre *r.* Lux. 14 49.43N 6.31E
Sureau, Lac *l.* Canada 77 53.10N 70.50W
Surendranagar India 40 22.42N 71.41E
Surfer's Paradise Australia 67 27.58S153.26E

Surgut U.S.S.R. **28** 61.13N 73.20E
Sūri India **41** 23.55N 87.32E
Surigao Phil. **37** 9.47N125.29E
Surin Thailand **34** 14.58N103.33E
Surinam S. America **91** 4.00N 56.00W
Suriname *r.* Surinam **91** 5.52N 55.14W
Surrey *d.* U.K. **11** 51.16N 0.30W
Surt Libya **51** 31.13N 16.35E
Surt, Khalīj *g.* Libya **51** 31.45N 17.50E
Surtanāhu Pakistan **40** 26.22N 70.00E
Surtsey *i.* Iceland **22** 63.18N 20.30W
Surud Ad *mtn.* Somali Rep. **45** 10.41N 47.18E
Suruga-wan *b.* Japan **35** 34.45N138.30E
Susa Italy **15** 45.08N 7.03E
Susanino U.S.S.R. **29** 52.46N140.09E
Susanville U.S.A. **80** 40.25N120.39W
Susquehanna *r.* U.S.A. **85** 39.33N 76.05W
Sussex N.J. U.S.A. **85** 41.13N 74.36W
Sussex Wyo. U.S.A. **80** 43.42N106.19W
Sutak Jammu & Kashmir **41** 33.12N 77.28E
Sutherland Australia **67** 34.02S151.04E
Sutherland R.S.A. **56** 32.23S 20.38E
Sutherlin U.S.A. **80** 43.25N123.19W
Sutlej *r.* Pakistan **40** 29.23N 71.02E
Sutton *r.* Canada **76** 55.22N 83.48W
Sutton England U.K. **11** 51.22N 0.12W
Sutton Nebr. U.S.A. **82** 40.36N 97.52W
Sutton W. Va. U.S.A. **84** 38.41N 80.43W
Sutton in Ashfield U.K. **10** 53.08N 1.16W
Suva Fiji **68** 18.08S178.25E
Suwa Ethiopia **48** 14.16N 41.10E
Suwałki Poland **21** 54.07N 22.56E
Suwanee *r.* U.S.A. **85** 29.18N 83.09W
Suways, Khalīj as *g.* Egypt **44** 28.48N 33.00E
Suways, Qanāt as *canal* Egypt **44** 30.40N 32.20E
Suwon S. Korea **31** 37.16N126.59E
Suzhou China **33** 31.22N120.45E
Suzuka Japan **35** 34.51N136.35E
Suzuka *r.* Japan **35** 34.54N136.39E
Suzuka-sammyaku *mts.* Japan **35** 35.00N136.20E
Suzzara Italy **15** 45.00N 10.45E
Svalyava U.S.S.R. **21** 48.33N 23.00E
Svanvik Norway **22** 69.25N 30.00E
Svappavaara Sweden **22** 67.39N 21.04E
Svarhofthalvöya Norway **22** 70.35N 26.00E
Svartenhuk Halvo *c.* Greenland **73** 71.55N 55.00W
Svartisen *mtn.* Norway **22** 66.40N 13.56E
Svatovo U.S.S.R. **25** 49.24N 38.11E
Svay Riĕng Cambodia **34** 11.05N105.48E
Svedala Sweden **23** 55.30N 13.14E
Sveg Sweden **23** 62.02N 14.21E
Svelgen Norway **23** 61.47N 5.15E
Svendborg Denmark **23** 55.03N 10.37E
Svenstrup Denmark **23** 56.59N 9.52E
Sverdlovsk U.S.S.R. **24** 56.52N 60.35E
Svetlograd U.S.S.R. **25** 45.25N 42.58E
Svetogorsk U.S.S.R. **24** 61.07N 28.50E
Svetozarevo Yugo. **19** 43.58N 21.16E
Svinö *i.* Faroe Is. **8** 62.17N 6.18W
Svir *r.* U.S.S.R. **24** 60.09N 32.15E
Svishtov Bulgaria **19** 43.36N 25.23E
Svisloch U.S.S.R. **21** 53.28N 29.00E
Svitavy Czech. **20** 49.45N 16.27E
Svobodnyy U.S.S.R. **31** 51.24N128.05E
Svolvaer Norway **22** 68.15N 14.40E
Swaffham U.K. **11** 52.38N 0.42E
Swain Reefs Australia **64** 21.40S152.15E
Swains I. Samoa **68** 11.03S171.06W
Swakop *r.* Namibia **56** 22.38S 14.32E
Swakopmund Namibia **56** 22.40S 14.34E
Swale *r.* U.K. **10** 54.05N 1.20W
Swan *r.* Australia **63** 32.03S115.45E
Swanage U.K. **11** 50.36N 1.59W
Swan Hill *town* Australia **66** 35.23S143.37E
Swan Hills Canada **74** 54.42N115.24W
Swan L. Canada **75** 52.30N100.45W
Swan River *town* Canada **74** 52.10N101.17W
Swansea Australia **65** 42.08S148.00E
Swansea U.K. **11** 51.37N 3.57W
Swastika Canada **76** 48.07N 80.06W
Swatow *see* Shantou China **33**
Swaziland Africa **56** 26.30S 32.00E
Sweden Europe **22** 63.00N 16.00E
Swedru Ghana **52** 5.31N 0.42W
Sweetwater U.S.A. **83** 32.28N100.25W
Swidnica Poland **20** 50.51N 16.29E
Swiebodzin Poland **20** 52.15N 15.32E
Świetokrzyskie, Góry *mts.* Poland **21** 51.00N 20.30E
Swift Current *town* Canada **75** 50.17N107.50W
Swilly, Lough Rep. of Ire. **13** 55.10N 7.32W
Swindon U.K. **11** 51.33N 1.47W
Świnoujście Poland **20** 53.55N 14.18E
Switzerland Europe **17** 47.00N 8.00E
Swords Rep. of Ire. **9** 53.27N 6.15W
Syderö *i.* Faroe Is. **8** 61.30N 6.50W
Sydney Australia **67** 33.55S151.10E
Sydney Canada **77** 46.09N 60.11W
Sydney Mines *town* Canada **77** 46.14N 60.14W
Sydprövén Greenland **73** 60.30N 45.35W
Syktyvkar U.S.S.R. **24** 61.42N 50.45E
Sylacauga U.S.A. **85** 33.10N 86.15W
Sylhet Bangla. **41** 24.54N 91.52E
Sylt *i.* Germany **20** 54.50N 8.20E
Sylte Norway **22** 62.31N 7.07E
Sylvan Lake *town* Canada **74** 52.20N114.10W
Syracuse Kans. U.S.A. **83** 37.59N101.45W
Syracuse N.Y. U.S.A. **84** 43.03N 76.09W
Syr Darya *r.* U.S.S.R. **28** 46.00N 61.12E
Syria Asia **42** 35.00N 38.00E
Syriam Burma **36** 16.45N 96.17E
Syrian Desert *see* Bādiyat ash Shām *des.* Asia **42**
Syzran U.S.S.R. **24** 53.10N 48.29E
Szarvas Hungary **21** 46.52N 20.34E
Szczecin Poland **20** 53.25N 14.32E
Szczecinek Poland **20** 53.42N 16.41E
Szczytno Poland **21** 53.34N 21.00E
Szécsény Hungary **21** 48.06N 19.31E
Szeged Hungary **19** 46.16N 20.08E
Székesfehérvár Hungary **21** 47.12N 18.25E
Szekszárd Hungary **19** 46.22N 18.44E
Szentes Hungary **21** 46.39N 20.16E
Szolnok Hungary **21** 47.10N 20.12E
Szombathely Hungary **20** 47.12N 16.38E
Sztutowo Poland **21** 54.20N 19.15E

T

Tabagne Ivory Coast **52** 7.59N 3.04W
Ṭābah Saudi Arabia **42** 27.02N 42.10E
Tabarka Tunisia **51** 36.56N 8.43E
Ṭabas Khorāsān Iran **43** 32.48N 60.14E
Ṭabas Khorāsān Iran **43** 33.36N 56.55E
Tabasco *d.* Mexico **86** 18.30N 93.00W
Tābask, Kūh-e *mtn.* Iran **43** 29.51N 51.52E
Tabelbala Algeria **50** 29.24N 3.15W
Taber Canada **74** 49.47N112.08W
Tabili Zaïre **55** 0.04N 28.01E
Table B. R.S.A. **56** 33.52S 18.26E
Tábor Czech. **20** 49.25N 14.41E
Tabora Tanzania **55** 5.02S 32.50E
Tabora *d.* Tanzania **55** 5.30S 32.50E
Tabou Ivory Coast **52** 4.28N 7.20W
Tabrīz Iran **43** 38.05N 46.18E
Tabuaeran *i.* Kiribati **69** 3.52N159.20W
Tabūk Saudi Arabia **44** 28.23N 36.36E
Tabulam Australia **67** 28.50S152.35E
Ṭabūt Yemen **45** 15.57N 52.09E
Tachia Taiwan **33** 24.21N120.37E
Tachikawa Japan **35** 35.42N139.25E
Tacloban Phil. **37** 11.15N124.59E
Tacna Peru **92** 18.01S 70.15W
Tacoma U.S.A. **80** 47.15N122.27W
Tacora *mtn.* Chile **92** 17.40S 69.45W
Tacuarembó Uruguay **93** 31.44S 55.59W
Tademaït, Plateau du *f.* Algeria **51** 28.30N 2.15E
Tadjetaret, Oued Algeria **51** 21.00N 7.30E
Tadjmout Algeria **51** 25.30N 3.42E
Tadjoura, Golfe de *g.* Djibouti **45** 11.42N 43.00E
Tadmor New Zealand **60** 41.26S172.47E
Tadmur Syria **42** 34.36N 38.15E
Tadoule L. Canada **75** 58.36N 98.20W
Tadoussac Canada **77** 48.09N 69.43W
Tadzhikskaya S.S.R. *d.* U.S.S.R. **30** 39.00N 70.30E
Taegu S. Korea **31** 35.52N128.36E
Taejŏn S. Korea **31** 36.20N127.26E
Tafalla Spain **16** 42.31N 1.40W
Tafassasset, Oued *wadi* Niger **51** 22.00N 9.55E
Tafassasset, Ténéré du *des.* Niger **53** 21.00N 11.00E
Taffanel, Lac *l.* Canada **77** 53.22N 70.56W
Tafí Viejo Argentina **92** 26.45S 65.15W
Tafraout Morocco **50** 29.40N 8.58W
Taftān, Kūh-e *mtn.* Iran **43** 28.38N 61.08E
Taga W. Samoa **68** 13.47S172.30W
Taganrog U.S.S.R. **25** 47.14N 38.55E
Taganrogskiy Zaliv *g.* U.S.S.R. **25** 47.00N 38.30E
Tagant *d.* Mauritania **50** 18.30N 10.30W
Tagant *f.* Mauritania **50** 18.20N 11.00W
Tagaytay City Phil. **37** 14.07N120.58E
Tagbilaran Phil. **37** 9.38N123.53E
Tagish Canada **74** 60.19N134.16W
Tagliamento *r.* Italy **15** 45.38N 13.06E
Taglio di Po Italy **15** 45.00N 12.12E
Tagounit Morocco **50** 29.58N 5.36W
Tagula I. P.N.G. **64** 11.30S153.30E
Tagum Phil. **37** 7.33N125.53E
Tagus *r.* Portugal / Spain *see* Tejo *r.* Portugal **16**
Tahaa *i.* Īs. de la Société **69** 16.38S151.30W
Tahara Japan **35** 34.40N137.16E
Tahat *mtn.* Algeria **51** 23.18N 5.32E
Tahe China **31** 52.35N124.48E
Tahiti *i.* Īs. de la Société **69** 17.37S149.27W
Tahiti, Archipel de *is.* Īs. de la Société **69** 17.00S149.35W
Tahlequah U.S.A. **83** 35.55N 94.58W
Tahoe, L. U.S.A. **80** 39.07N120.03W
Tahoua Niger **53** 14.57N 5.16E
Tahoua *d.* Niger **53** 15.38N 4.50E
Ṭahṭā Egypt **42** 26.46N 31.30E
Tahuna Indonesia **37** 3.37N125.29E
Taï Ivory Coast **52** 5.52N 7.28W
Tai'an China **32** 36.16N117.13E
Taiarapu, Presqu'île de *pen.* Tahiti **69** 17.47S149.14W
Taibai China **32** 36.08N108.41E
Taibai Shan *mtn.* China **32** 33.55N107.45E
Taibus Qi China **32** 41.55N115.23E
Taidong Taiwan **33** 22.49N121.10E
Taigu China **32** 37.23N112.34E
Taihang Shan *mts.* China **32** 36.00N113.35E
Taihape New Zealand **60** 39.40S175.48E
Taihe Anhui China **32** 33.10N115.36E
Taihe Jiangxi China **33** 26.48 114.56E
Tai Hu *l.* China **33** 31.15N120.10E
Tailai China **31** 46.23N123.24E
Tailem Bend *town* Australia **66** 35.14S139.29E
Tain U.K. **12** 57.48N 4.04W
Tainan Taiwan **33** 23.01N120.12E
Taínaron, Ákra *c.* Greece **19** 36.22N 22.28E
Tai-o-haé Īs. Marquises **69** 8.55S140.04W
Taipei Taiwan **33** 25.05N121.30E
Taiping Anhui China **33** 30.18N118.06E
Taiping Malaysia **36** 4.54N100.42E
Taishan China **33** 22.10N112.57E
Taito, Península de *pen.* Chile **93** 46.30S 74.25W
Taitze He *r.* China **32** 41.07N122.43E
Taivalkoski Finland **22** 65.34N 28.15E
Taiwan Asia **33** 24.00N121.00E
Taiwan Str. China / Taiwan **33** 24.30N119.30E
Taiyuan China **32** 37.48N112.33E
Taiyue Shan *mts.* China **32** 36.40N112.00E
Taizhong Taiwan **33** 24.11N120.40E
Taizhou China **32** 32.22N119.58E
Ta'izz Yemen **45** 13.35N 44.02E
Tajarḥī Libya **51** 24.21N 14.28E
Tajimi Japan **35** 35.19N137.08E
Tajitos Mexico **81** 30.58N112.18W
Tajo *r.* Spain *see* Tejo *r.* Portugal **16**
Tajrīsh Iran **43** 35.48N 51.20E
Tajuna *r.* Spain **16** 40.10N 3.35W
Tak Thailand **34** 16.51N 99.08E
Takaka New Zealand **60** 40.51S172.48E
Takalar Indonesia **36** 5.29S119.26E
Takamatsu Japan **31** 34.20N134.01E
Takapuna New Zealand **60** 36.48S174.47E
Takarazuka Japan **35** 34.49N135.21E
Takatsuki Japan **35** 34.51N135.37E
Tākestān Iran **43** 36.02N 49.40E
Takêv Cambodia **34** 11.00N104.46E
Takhādīd *well* Iraq **43** 29.59N 44.30E
Takla L. Canada **74** 55.15N125.45W
Taklimakan Shamo *des.* China **30** 38.10N 82.00E
Taku *r.* Canada / U.S.A. **74** 58.30N133.50W
Talā Egypt **44** 30.41N 30.56E
Tala Uruguay **93** 34.21S 55.46W
Talagang Pakistan **40** 32.55N 72.25E
Talagante Chile **93** 33.40S 70.56W
Talāja India **40** 21.21N 72.03E
Tālāla India **40** 21.02N 70.32E
Talangbetutu Indonesia **36** 2.48S104.42E
Talara Peru **90** 4.38S 81.18W
Talasskiy Alatau *mts.* U.S.S.R. **30** 42.20N 73.20E
Talata Mafara Nigeria **53** 12.37N 6.05E
Talaud, Kepulauan *is.* Indonesia **37** 4.20N126.50E
Talavera de la Reina Spain **16** 39.58N 4.50W
Talawdī Sudan **49** 10.38N 30.23E
Talbragar *r.* Australia **67** 32.12S148.37E
Talca Chile **93** 35.26S 71.40W
Talcahuano Chile **93** 36.43S 73.07W
Tālcher India **41** 20.57N 85.13E
Taldom U.S.S.R. **24** 56.49N 37.30E
Taldy Kurgan U.S.S.R. **30** 45.02N 78.23E
Taleex *well* Somali Rep. **45** 9.12N 48.23E
Talia Australia **66** 33.16S134.53E
Taliabu *i.* Indonesia **37** 1.50S124.55E
Tali Post Sudan **49** 5.54N 30.47E
Talkeetna U.S.A. **72** 62.20N150.09W
Ṭalkhā Egypt **44** 31.04N 31.22E
Tallahassee U.S.A. **85** 30.26N 84.19W
Tallangatta Australia **67** 36.14S147.19E
Tallard France **17** 44.28N 6.03E
Tallinn U.S.S.R. **23** 59.22N 24.48E
Tall Kalakh Syria **44** 34.40N 36.18E
Tall Kūshik Syria **42** 36.48N 42.04E
Tall Salḥab Syria **44** 35.15N 36.22E
Tallulah U.S.A. **83** 32.25N 91.11W
Talmont France **17** 46.28N 1.36W
Talnoye U.S.S.R. **21** 48.55N 30.40E
Taloda India **40** 21.34N 74.13E
Talofofo Guam **68** 13.21N144.45E
Talsi U.S.S.R. **23** 57.15N 22.36E
Taltal Chile **92** 25.24S 70.29W
Talvik Norway **22** 70.05N 22.52E
Talwood Australia **67** 28.29S149.25E
Talyawalka *r.* Australia **66** 31.49S143.25E
Tama *r.* Japan **35** 35.32N139.47E
Tamala Australia **62** 26.42S113.47E
Tamale Ghana **52** 9.26N 0.49W
Tamanar Morocco **50** 31.00N 9.35W
Tamanrasset Algeria **51** 22.47N 5.31E
Tamanrasset, Oued *wadi* Algeria **50** 21.24N 1.00E
Tamanthi Burma **34** 25.19N 95.18E
Tamar *r.* U.K. **11** 50.28N 4.13W
Tamaské Niger **53** 14.55N 5.55E
Tamaulipas *d.* Mexico **83** 24.30N 98.50W
Tamazunchale Mexico **86** 21.16N 98.47W
Tambacounda Senegal **52** 13.45N 13.40W
Tambara Mozambique **55** 16.42S 34.17E
Tambar Springs *town* Australia **67** 31.20S149.50E
Tambellup Australia **63** 34.03S117.36E
Tambo Australia **64** 24.53S146.15E
Tambo *r.* Australia **67** 37.51S147.48E
Tambohorano Madagascar **57** 17.30S 43.58E
Tambor Mexico **81** 25.08N105.27W
Tambov U.S.S.R. **24** 52.44N 41.28E
Tambre *r.* Spain **16** 42.50N 8.55W
Tambura Sudan **49** 5.36N 27.28E
Tamchaket Mauritania **50** 17.25N 10.40W
Tâmega *r.* Portugal **16** 41.04N 8.17W
Tamil Nadu *d.* India **39** 11.15N 79.00E
Ṭāmiyah Egypt **44** 29.29N 30.58E
Tamkuhi India **41** 26.41N 84.11E
Tam Ky Vietnam **34** 15.34N108.29E
Tammisaari Finland **23** 59.58N 23.26E
Tampa U.S.A. **85** 27.58N 82.38W
Tampa B. U.S.A. **85** 27.45N 82.35W
Tampere Finland **23** 61.30N 23.45E
Tampico Mexico **86** 22.18N 97.52W
Tamri Morocco **50** 30.43N 9.43W
Tamsagbulag Mongolia **31** 47.10N117.21E
Tamworth Australia **67** 31.07S150.57E
Tamworth U.K. **11** 52.38N 1.42W
Tana *r.* Kenya **55** 2.32S 40.32E
Tana Norway **22** 70.26N 28.14E
Tana *r.* Norway **22** 69.45N 28.15E
Tana *i.* Vanuatu **68** 19.30S169.20E
Tanacross U.S.A. **72** 63.12N143.30W
Tanafjorden Norway **22** 70.54N 28.40E
T'ana Hāyk' *l.* Ethiopia **49** 12.00N 37.20E
Tanahgrogot Indonesia **36** 1.55S116.12E
Tanahmerah Indonesia **37** 6.08S140.18E
Tanakpur India **41** 29.05N 80.07E
Tanami Desert Australia **62** 19.50S130.50E
Tanana U.S.A. **72** 65.11N152.10W
Tanana *r.* U.S.A. **72** 65.09N151.55W
Tananarive *see* Antananarivo Madagascar **57**
Tanaro *r.* Italy **15** 45.01N 8.46E
Tānda India **41** 26.33N 82.39E
Tanda Ivory Coast **52** 7.48N 3.10W
Tandaltī Sudan **49** 13.01N 31.50E
Țăndărei Romania **21** 44.38N 27.40E
Tandil Argentina **93** 37.18S 59.10W
Tandjilé *d.* Chad **53** 9.45N 16.28E
Tando Ādam Pakistan **40** 25.46N 68.40E
Tando Allāhyār Pakistan **40** 25.28N 68.43E
Tando Bāgo Pakistan **40** 24.47N 68.58E
Tando Muhammad Khan Pakistan **40** 25.08N 68.32E
Tandou L. Australia **66** 32.38S142.05E
Tandula Tank *resr.* India **41** 20.40N 81.12E
Taneytown U.S.A. **85** 39.40N 77.10W
Tanezrouft *des.* Algeria **50** 22.25N 0.30E
Tanga Tanzania **55** 5.07S 39.05E
Tanga *d.* Tanzania **55** 5.20S 38.30E
Tangalla Sri Lanka **39** 6.02N 80.47E
Tanganyika, L. Africa **55** 6.00S 29.30E
Tanger Morocco **50** 35.48N 5.45W
Tanggo China **41** 31.37N 93.18E
Tanggu China **32** 39.01N117.43E
Tanggula Shan *mts.* China **41** 33.00N 90.00E
Tanggula Shankou *pass* China **41** 32.45N 92.24E
Tanggulashanqu China **41** 34.10N 92.23E
Tanghe China **32** 32.41N112.49E
Tāngi India **41** 19.57N 85.30E
Tangi Pakistan **40** 34.18N 71.40E
Tangier *see* Tanger Morocco **50**
Tangmarg Jammu & Kashmir **40** 34.02N 74.26E
Tangra Yumco *l.* China **41** 31.00N 86.15E
Tangshan China **32** 39.32N118.08E
Tangtse Jammu & Kashmir **41** 34.02N 78.11E
Tanguiéta Benin **53** 10.37N 1.18E
Tanimbar, Kepulauan *is.* Indonesia **37** 7.50S131.30E
Tanishpa *mtn.* Pakistan **40** 31.10N 68.24E
Tanjay Phil. **37** 9.31N123.10E
Tanjona Ankaboa *c.* Madagascar **57** 21.57S 43.16E
Tanjona Bobaomby *c.* Madagascar **57** 11.57S 49.17E
Tanjona Masoala *c.* Madagascar **57** 15.59S 50.13E
Tanjona Vilanandro *c.* Madagascar **57** 16.11S 44.27E
Tanjona Vohimena *c.* Madagascar **57** 25.36S 45.08E
Tanjung Indonesia **36** 2.10S115.25E
Tanjungbalai Indonesia **36** 2.59N 99.46E
Tanjungkarang Indonesia **36** 5.28S105.16E
Tanjungpandan Indonesia **36** 2.44S107.36E
Tanjungredeb Indonesia **36** 2.09N117.29E
Tānk Pakistan **40** 32.13N 70.23E
Tankapirtti Finland **22** 68.16N 27.20E
Tännäs Sweden **23** 62.27N 12.40E
Tannin Canada **76** 49.40N 91.00W
Tannu Ola *mts.* U.S.S.R. **29** 51.00N 93.30E
Tannūrah, Ra's *c.* Saudi Arabia **45** 26.39N 50.10E
Tano *r.* Ghana **52** 5.07N 2.54W
Tanout Niger **53** 14.55N 8.49E
Ṭanṭā Egypt **44** 30.48N 31.00E
Tanzania Africa **55** 5.00S 35.00E
Tao'an China **32** 45.20N122.48E
Taole China **32** 38.50N106.40E
Taoudenni Mali **52** 22.45N 4.00W
Tapachula Mexico **86** 14.54N 92.15W
Tapajós *r.* Brazil **91** 2.25S 54.40W
Tapaktuan Indonesia **36** 3.30N 97.10E
Tapalquén Argentina **93** 36.20S 60.02W
Tapanahoni *r.* Surinam **91** 4.20N 54.25W
Tapanlieh Taiwan **33** 21.58N120.47E
Tapanui New Zealand **60** 45.57S169.16E
Tapauá *r.* Brazil **90** 5.40S 64.20W
Tapeta Liberia **52** 6.25N 8.47W
Tapirapecó, Serra *mts.* Venezuela / Brazil **90** 1.00N 64.30W
Tāplejung Nepal **41** 27.21N 87.40E
Tapolca Hungary **21** 46.53N 17.27E
Tāpti *r.* India **40** 21.05N 72.40E
Tapurucuara Brazil **90** 0.24S 65.02W
Taquari *r.* Brazil **94** 19.00S 57.27W
Taquaritinga Brazil **94** 21.23S 48.33W
Tar *r.* U.S.A. **85** 35.33N 77.05W
Tara U.S.S.R. **28** 56.55N 74.24E
Tara *r.* U.S.S.R. **28** 56.30N 74.40E
Tara *r.* Yugo. **19** 43.23N 18.47E
Tarabine, Oued Ti-n- *wadi* Algeria **51** 21.16N 7.24E
Tarabuco Bolivia **92** 19.10S 64.57W
Ṭarābulus Lebanon **44** 34.27N 35.50E
Ṭarābulus *d.* Libya **51** 32.40N 13.15E
Ṭarābulus *f.* Libya **51** 31.00N 13.30E
Ṭarābulus *town* Libya **51** 32.58N 13.12E
Tarago Australia **67** 35.05S149.10E
Tarakan Indonesia **36** 3.20N117.38E
Taranaki *d.* New Zealand **60** 39.00S174.30E
Tarancón Spain **16** 40.01N 3.01W
Taranto Italy **19** 40.28N 17.14E
Taranto, Golfo di *g.* Italy **19** 40.00N 17.20E
Tarapacá Colombia **90** 2.52S 69.44W
Tarapoto Peru **90** 6.31S 76.23W
Tarashcha U.S.S.R. **21** 49.35N 30.20E
Tarasovo U.S.S.R. **24** 66.14N 46.43E
Tarauacá Brazil **90** 8.10S 70.46W
Tarauacá *r.* Brazil **90** 6.42S 69.48W
Taravao, Isthme de Tahiti **69** 17.43S149.19W
Tarawa *i.* Kiribati **68** 1.25N173.00E
Tarawera New Zealand **60** 39.02S176.36E
Tarbagatay, Khrebet *mts.* U.S.S.R. **30** 47.00N 83.00E
Tarbat Ness *c.* U.K. **12** 57.52N 3.46W
Tarbert Rep. of Ire. **13** 52.34N 9.24W
Tarbert Strath. U.K. **12** 55.51N 5.25W
Tarbert W. Isles U.K. **12** 57.54N 6.49W
Tarbes France **17** 43.14N 0.05E
Tarcento Italy **15** 46.13N 13.13E
Tarcoola S.A. Australia **66** 30.41S134.33E
Tarcoon Australia **67** 30.19S146.43E
Tarcutta Australia **67** 35.17S147.45E
Taree Australia **67** 31.54S152.26E
Tarella Australia **66** 30.55S143.06E
Tärendö Sweden **22** 67.10N 22.38E
Ṭarfā, Wādī aṭ *r.* Egypt **44** 28.36N 30.50E
Tarfaya Morocco **50** 27.58N 12.55W
Tarhjicht Morocco **50** 29.05N 9.24W
Tarifa Spain **16** 36.01N 5.36W
Tarija Bolivia **92** 21.31S 64.45W
Tarija *d.* Bolivia **92** 21.40S 64.20W
Tarīm Yemen **45** 16.03N 49.00E
Tarim He *r.* China **30** 41.00N 83.30E
Tarīn Kowt Afghan. **40** 32.52N 65.38E
Taritatu *r.* Indonesia **37** 2.54S138.27E
Tarka La *mtn.* Bhutan **41** 27.05N 89.40E
Tarkwa Ghana **52** 5.16N 1.59W
Tarlac Phil. **37** 15.29N120.35E
Tarm Denmark **23** 55.55N 8.32E
Tarma Peru **90** 11.28S 75.41W
Tarn *r.* France **17** 44.15N 1.15E
Tärnaby Sweden **22** 65.43N 15.16E
Tarnak *r.* Afghan. **40** 31.26N 65.31E
Tarnica *mtn.* Poland **21** 49.05N 22.44E
Tarnobrzeg Poland **21** 50.35N 21.41E
Tarnów Poland **21** 50.01N 20.59E
Taro *r.* Italy **15** 45.00N 10.15E
Taroom Australia **64** 25.39S149.49E
Taroudannt Morocco **50** 30.31N 8.55W
Tarpon Springs *town* U.S.A. **85** 28.08N 82.45W
Tarragona Spain **16** 41.07N 1.15E
Tarran Hills Australia **67** 32.27S146.27E
Tarrytown U.S.A. **85** 41.05N 73.52W
Tarso Ahon *mtn.* Chad **53** 20.23N 18.18E
Tarso Ouri *mtn.* Chad **53** 21.25N 18.56E
Tarsus Turkey **42** 36.52N 34.52E
Tartagal Argentina **92** 22.32S 63.50W
Tartu U.S.S.R. **24** 58.20N 26.44E
Ṭarṭūs Syria **44** 34.55N 35.52E
Tarutino U.S.S.R. **21** 46.09N 29.04E
Tarutung Indonesia **36** 2.01N 98.54E
Tashan China **32** 40.51N120.56E
Tashauz U.S.S.R. **28** 41.49N 59.58E
Tashi Gang Dzong Bhutan **41** 27.19N 91.34E
Tashkent U.S.S.R. **30** 41.16N 69.13E
Tasiilaq *see* Ammassalik Greenland **73**
Tasikmalaya Indonesia **37** 7.20S108.16E
Tåsjön Sweden **22** 64.15N 15.47E
Tasman B. New Zealand **60** 41.00S173.15E
Tasmania *d.* Australia **65** 42.00S147.00E
Tasman Mts. New Zealand **60** 41.00S172.40E
Tasman Pen. Australia **65** 43.08S147.51E
Tasman Sea Pacific Oc. **68** 38.00S162.00E
Tassili-n-Ajjer *f.* Algeria **51** 26.05N 7.00E
Tassili oua-n-Ahaggar *f.* Algeria **51** 20.30N 5.00E
Tataa, Pt. Tahiti **69** 17.33S149.36W
Tatabánya Hungary **21** 47.34N 18.26E
Tatarsk U.S.S.R. **28** 55.14N 76.00E
Tatarskiy Proliv *g.* U.S.S.R. **29** 47.40N141.00E
Tateyama Japan **35** 34.59N139.52E
Tathlina L. Canada **74** 60.32N117.32W
Tathra Australia **67** 36.44S149.58E
Tatinnai L. Canada **75** 60.55N 97.40W
Tatnam, C. Canada **75** 57.16N 91.00W
Tatong Australia **67** 36.46S146.03E
Tatta Pakistan **40** 24.45N 67.55E
Tatvan Turkey **42** 38.31N 42.15E
Tau *i.* Samoa **68** 14.15S169.30W
Taubaté Brazil **94** 23.00S 45.36W
Taulihawa Nepal **41** 27.32N 83.05E
Taumarunui New Zealand **60** 38.53S175.16E
Taumaturgo Brazil **90** 8.57S 72.48W
Taung R.S.A. **56** 27.32S 24.46E
Taungdwingyi Burma **34** 20.00N 95.30E
Taung-gyi Burma **34** 20.49N 97.01E
Taungup Burma **34** 18.51N 94.14E
Taunoa Tahiti **69** 17.45S149.21W
Taunsa Pakistan **40** 30.42N 70.39E
Taunton U.K. **11** 51.01N 3.07W
Taunus *mts.* Germany **20** 50.07N 7.48E
Taupo New Zealand **60** 38.42S176.06E
Taupo, L. New Zealand **60** 38.45S175.30E
Taurage U.S.S.R. **23** 55.15N 22.17E
Tauranga New Zealand **60** 37.42S176.11E
Taureau, Résr. Canada **77** 46.45N 73.50W
Taurianova Italy **18** 38.21N 16.01E
Taurus Mts. *see* Toros Dağlari *mts.* Turkey **42**
Tautira Tahiti **69** 17.45S149.10W
Tavani Canada **75** 62.10N 93.30W
Tavda U.S.S.R. **28** 58.04N 65.12E
Tavda *r.* U.S.S.R. **28** 57.40N 67.00E
Taveta Kenya **55** 3.23S 37.42E
Taveuni *i.* Fiji **68** 16.56S179.58W
Tavira Portugal **16** 37.07N 7.39W
Tavistock U.K. **11** 50.33N 4.09W
Tavoy Burma **34** 14.02N 98.12E

'aw r. U.K. 11 51.05N 4.05W
'awas City U.S.A. 84 44.16N 83.33W
'awau Malaysia 36 4.16N117.54E
'awitawi i. Phil. 37 5.10N120.05E
'awkar Sudan 48 18.26N 37.44E
'awu Taiwan 33 22.22N120.54E
'āwurghā', Sabkhat f. Libya 51 31.10N 15.15E
'ay r. U.K. 12 56.21N 3.18W
ay, L. Australia 63 33.00S120.52E
ay, Loch U.K. 12 56.32N 4.08W
ayabamba Peru 90 8.15S 77.15W
ayan Indonesia 36 0.02S110.05E
ayeegle Somali Rep. 45 4.02N 44.36E
aylor Tex. U.S.A. 83 30.34N 97.25W
aylor, Mt. U.S.A. 81 35.14N107.37W
aylors Island town U.S.A. 85 38.28N 76.18W
aymā' Saudi Arabia 42 27.37N 38.30E
aymyr, Ozero l. U.S.S.R. 29 74.20N101.00E
aymyr, Poluostrov pen. U.S.S.R. 29 75.30N 99.00E
ay Ninh Vietnam 34 11.21N106.02E
ayport U.K. 12 56.27N 2.53W
ayshet U.S.S.R. 29 55.56N 98.01E
ayside d. U.K. 12 56.35N 3.28W
aytay Phil. 36 10.47N119.32E
az r. U.S.S.R. 28 67.30N 78.50E
aza Morocco 50 34.16N 4.01W
azenakht Morocco 50 30.35N 7.12W
azin L. Canada 75 59.40N109.00W
āzirbū Libya 48 25.45N 21.00E
azovskiy U.S.S.R. 28 67.28N 78.43E
bilisi U.S.S.R. 43 41.43N 44.48E
chad, Lac see Chad, L. Africa 53
chamba Togo 53 9.05N 1.27E
chibanga Gabon 54 2.52S 11.07E
chien Liberia 52 6.00N 8.10W
chigaï, Plateau du f. Niger/Chad 53 21.30N 14.50E
cholliré Cameroon 53 8.25N 14.10E
czew Poland 21 54.06N 18.47E
e Anau New Zealand 60 45.25S167.43E
e Anau, L. New Zealand 60 45.10S167.15E
eaneck U.S.A. 85 40.53N 74.01W
eapa Mexico 86 17.33N 92.57W
e Araroa New Zealand 60 37.38S178.25E
ébessa Sumatra Utara Algeria 51 35.22N 8.08E
ebingtinggi Indonesia 36 3.20N 99.08E
ebingtinggi Sumatra Selatan Indonesia 36 3.37S103.09E
ebulos Mta mtn. U.S.S.R. 25 42.34N 45.17E
echiman Ghana 52 7.36N 1.55W
ecuci Romania 21 45.49N 27.27E
edesa Ethiopia 49 5.07N 37.45E
ees r. U.K. 10 54.35N 1.11W
efé Brazil 90 3.24S 64.45W
efé r. Brazil 90 3.35S 64.47W
egal Indonesia 37 6.52S109.07E
egelen Neth. 14 51.20N 6.08E
egina Nigeria 53 10.06N 6.11E
ego Australia 67 28.48S146.47E
egouma well Niger 53 15.33N 9.19E
egucigalpa Honduras 87 14.05N 87.14W
eguidda I-n-Tessoum Niger 53 17.21N 6.32E
ehamiyam Sudan 48 18.20N 36.32E
ehata Bangla. 41 23.43N 88.32E
ehini Ivory Coast 52 9.39N 3.32W
ehrān Iran 43 35.40N 51.26E
ehri India 41 30.23N 78.29E
ehuacán Mexico 86 18.30N 97.26W
ehuantepec Mexico 86 16.21N 95.13W
ehuantepec, Golfo de g. Mexico 86 16.00N 95.00W
ehuantepec, Istmo de f. Mexico 86 17.00N 94.30W
ifi r. U.K. 11 52.05N 4.41W
eignmouth U.K. 11 50.33N 3.30W
eixeiras Brazil 94 20.37S 42.52W
ejakula Indonesia 37 8.09S115.19E
ejo r. Portugal 16 39.00N 8.57W
e Kaha New Zealand 60 37.44S177.52E
ekamah U.S.A. 82 41.47N 96.13W
ekapo, L. New Zealand 60 43.35S170.30E
ekax Mexico 87 20.12N 89.17W
ekezē r. Ethiopia see Satīt r. Sudan 48
ekirdag Turkey 19 40.59N 27.30E
ekkali India 41 18.37N 84.14E
ekouiat, Oued wadi Algeria 51 22.20N 2.30E
ekro well Chad 48 19.30N 20.58E
e Kuiti New Zealand 60 38.20S175.10E
el r. India 41 20.50N 83.54E
ela Honduras 87 15.56N 87.25W
elavi U.S.S.R. 43 41.56N 45.30E
el Aviv-Yafo Israel 44 32.05N 34.46E
ele r. Zaïre 54 2.48N 24.00E
elegraph Creek town Canada 74 57.55N131.10W
elemark d. Norway 23 59.40N 8.30E
eleneshty U.S.S.R. 21 47.35N 28.17E
eles Pires r. Brazil 91 7.20S 57.30W
elfer Australia 62 21.42S122.13E
elford U.K. 11 52.42N 2.30W
elfs Austria 20 47.19N 11.04E
elgte Germany 14 51.59N 7.46E
elimélé Guinea 52 10.54N 13.02W
ell Atlas mts. Algeria 51 36.00N 1.00E
ell City U.S.A. 85 37.56N 86.46W
eller U.S.A. 72 65.16N166.22W
elpos-Iz mtn. U.S.S.R. 24 63.56N 59.02E
elsen Argentina 93 42.25S 67.00W
elšiai U.S.S.R. 23 55.59N 22.15E
elukbetung Indonesia 36 5.28S105.16E
eluk Intan Malaysia 36 4.00N101.00E
ema Ghana 52 5.41N 0.01W
emagami, L. Canada 76 47.00N 80.05W
e Manga mtn. Rarotonga Cook Is. 68 21.13S159.45W
Temaverachi, Sierra mts. Mexico 81 29.30N109.30W
Tembo Aluma Angola 54 7.42S 17.15E
Teme r. U.K. 11 52.10N 2.13W
Temir U.S.S.R. 25 49.09N 57.06E
Temirtau U.S.S.R. 28 50.05N 72.55E
Témiscaming Canada 76 46.44N 79.05W
Temora Australia 67 34.27S147.35E
Tempe U.S.A. 81 33.25N111.56W
Tempino Indonesia 36 1.55S103.23E
Tempio Italy 18 40.54N 9.06E
Temple U.S.A. 83 31.06N 97.21W
Temple B. Australia 64 12.10S143.04E
Templemore Rep. of Ire. 13 52.48N 7.51W
Templin Germany 20 53.07N 13.30E
Temuco Chile 93 38.44S 72.36W
Tenabo Mexico 86 20.03N 90.14W
Tenaha U.S.A. 83 31.57N 94.15W
Tenasserim Burma 34 12.05N 99.00E
Tenasserim d. Burma 34 13.00N 99.00E
Tenby U.K. 11 51.40N 4.42W
Tendaho Ethiopia 49 11.48N 40.52E
Tende France 17 44.05N 7.36E
Tende, Col de pass France/Italy 15 44.09N 7.34E
Ten Degree Channel Indian Oc. 34 10.00N 93.00E
Tendrara Morocco 50 33.04N 1.59W
Tenenkou Mali 52 14.25N 4.58W
Tenerife i. Canary Is. 50 28.10N 16.30W
Ténès Algeria 51 36.31N 1.18E
Teng r. Burma 34 19.50N 97.40E
Tengchong China 39 25.02N 98.28E
Tengger Shamo des. China 32 39.00N104.10E
Tengiz, Ozero l. U.S.S.R. 28 50.30N 69.00E
Teng Xian China 32 35.08N117.20E
Tenke Zaïre 54 10.34S 26.07E
Tenkodogo Burkina 52 11.47N 0.19W
Tennant Creek town Australia 64 19.31S134.15E
Tennessee d. U.S.A. 85 35.50N 85.30W
Tennessee r. U.S.A. 85 37.04N 88.33W
Tenosique Mexico 86 17.29N 91.26W
Tenryū Japan 35 34.52N137.49E
Tenryū r. Japan 35 34.39N137.47E
Tensift, Oued r. Morocco 50 32.02N 9.22W
Tenterfield Australia 67 29.01S152.04E
Teófilo Otoni Brazil 94 17.52S 41.31W
Tepa Indonesia 37 7.52S129.31E
Tepa Pt. Niue 68 19.07S169.56W
Tepelenë Albania 19 40.18N 20.01E
Tepic Mexico 86 21.30N104.51W
Teplice Czech. 20 50.40N 13.50E
Ter r. Spain 16 42.02N 3.10E
Téra Niger 52 14.01N 0.45E
Tera r. Portugal 16 38.55N 8.01W
Teramo Italy 18 42.40N 13.43E
Terang Australia 66 38.13S142.56E
Tercan Turkey 42 39.47N 40.23E
Terebovlya U.S.S.R. 21 49.18N 25.44E
Terekhova U.S.S.R. 21 52.13N 31.28E
Teresina Brazil 91 5.09S 42.46W
Teresópolis Brazil 94 22.26S 42.59W
Terevaka mtn. I. de Pascua 69 27.05S109.23W
Tergnier France 15 49.39N 3.18E
Terhazza Mali 52 23.45N 4.59W
Termez U.S.S.R. 28 37.15N 67.15E
Termination I. Australia 63 34.25S121.53E
Termini Italy 18 37.59N 13.42E
Términos, Laguna de b. Mexico 86 18.30N 91.30W
Termoli Italy 18 41.58N 14.59E
Ternate Indonesia 37 0.48N127.23E
Terneuzen Neth. 14 51.20N 3.50E
Terni Italy 18 42.34N 12.44E
Ternopol U.S.S.R. 21 49.35N 25.39E
Terra Bella U.S.A. 81 35.58N119.03W
Terrace Canada 74 54.31N128.35W
Terracina Italy 18 41.17N 13.15E
Terralba Italy 18 39.43N 8.38E
Terrassa Spain 16 41.34N 2.00E
Terre Adélie f. Antarctica 96 80.00S140.00E
Terrebonne Canada 77 45.42N 73.38W
Terre Haute U.S.A. 84 39.27N 87.24W
Terrenceville Canada 77 47.42N 54.43W
Terry U.S.A. 80 46.47N105.19W
Terschelling i. Neth. 14 53.25N 5.25E
Teruel Spain 16 40.21N 1.06W
Tervola Finland 22 66.05N 24.48E
Tešanj Yugo. 21 44.37N 18.00E
Tesaret, Oued wadi Algeria 51 25.32N 2.52E
Teslin Canada 74 60.10N132.43W
Teslin r. Canada 74 61.34N134.54W
Teslin L. Canada 74 60.15N132.57W
Tessalit Mali 52 20.12N 1.00E
Tessaoua Niger 53 13.46N 7.55E
Tessy-sur-Vire France 15 48.58N 1.04W
Test r. U.K. 11 50.55N 1.29W
Têt r. France 17 42.43N 3.00E
Tetachuck L. Canada 74 53.18N125.55W
Tete Mozambique 57 16.10S 33.30E
Tete d. Mozambique 55 15.30S 33.00E
Teterev r. U.S.S.R. 21 51.03N 30.30E
Teterow Germany 20 53.46N 12.34E
Teteven Bulgaria 19 42.55N 24.16E
Tethul r. Canada 74 60.35N112.12W
Tetiaora i. Îs. de la Société 69 17.05S149.32W
Tetiyev U.S.S.R. 21 49.22N 29.40E
Tétouan Morocco 50 35.34N 5.23W
Tetovo Yugo. 19 42.01N 20.58E
Tetuan see Tétouan Morocco 50
Teulada Italy 18 38.58N 8.46E
Teun i. Indonesia 37 6.59S129.08E
Teuva Finland 22 62.29N 21.44E
Tevere r. Italy 18 41.45N 12.16E
Teverya Israel 44 32.48N 35.32E
Teviot r. U.K. 12 55.36N 2.27W
Teviotdale f. U.K. 10 55.26N 2.46W
Teviothead U.K. 12 55.20N 2.56W
Tewkesbury U.K. 11 51.59N 2.09W
Texarkana Ark. U.S.A. 83 33.26N 94.02W
Texarkana Tex. U.S.A. 83 33.26N 94.03W
Texarkana, L. U.S.A. 83 33.16N 94.14W
Texas Australia 67 28.50S151.09E
Texas d. U.S.A. 83 31.30N100.00W
Texas City U.S.A. 83 29.23N 94.54W
Texel i. Neth. 14 53.05N 4.47E
Texoma, L. U.S.A. 83 33.55N 96.37W
Texon U.S.A. 83 31.13N101.43W
Teyvareh Afghan. 40 33.21N 64.25E
Tezpur India 41 26.38N 92.48E
Tha-anne r. Canada 75 60.31N 94.37W
Thabana Ntlenyana mtn. Lesotho 56 29.28S 29.17E
Thabazimbi R.S.A. 56 24.36S 27.23E
Thādiq Saudi Arabia 43 25.18N 45.52E
Thai Binh Vietnam 33 20.30N106.26E
Thailand Asia 34 17.00N101.30E
Thailand, G. of Asia 34 11.00N101.00E
Thai Nguyen Vietnam 33 21.46N105.52E
Thak Pakistan 40 30.32N 70.13E
Thal Pakistan 40 33.22N 70.33E
Thal Desert Pakistan 40 31.30N 71.40E
Thale Luang l. Thailand 34 7.40N100.20E
Thallon Australia 67 28.39S148.49E
Thamarīt Oman 38 17.39N 54.02E
Thames r. Canada 76 42.19N 82.28W
Thames New Zealand 60 37.08S175.35E
Thames r. U.K. 11 51.30N 0.05E
Thāna India 40 19.12N 72.58E
Thāna Pakistan 40 28.55N 63.45E
Thanh Hóa Vietnam 33 19.47N105.49E
Thanjāvūr India 39 10.46N 79.09E
Thāno Bula Khān Pakistan 40 25.22N 67.50E
Tharād India 40 24.24N 71.38E
Thar Desert Pakistan/India 40 28.00N 72.00E
Thargomindah Australia 65 27.59S143.45E
Tharrawaddy Burma 34 17.37N 95.48E
Tharthār, Wādī ath r. Iraq 42 34.18N 43.07E
Thásos Greece 19 40.47N 24.42E
Thásos i. Greece 19 40.40N 24.39E
Thatcher U.S.A. 81 32.51N109.56W
Thaton Burma 34 16.50N 97.21E
Thaungdut Burma 34 24.26N 94.45E
Thayer U.S.A. 83 36.31N 91.33W
Thayetmyo Burma 34 19.20N 95.10E
Thazi Burma 34 20.51N 96.05E
Thebes ruins Egypt 42 25.41N 32.40E
The Bight town Bahamas 87 24.19N 75.24W
The Cherokees, L. O' U.S.A. 83 36.45N 94.50W
The Cheviot mtn. U.K. 10 55.29N 2.10W
The Cheviot Hills U.K. 10 55.22N 2.24W
The Coorong g. Australia 66 36.00S139.30E
The Dalles town U.S.A. 80 45.36N121.10W
Thedford U.S.A. 82 41.59N100.35W
The Everglades f. U.S.A. 85 26.00N 80.40W
The Fens f. U.K. 11 55.10N 4.13W
The Gulf Asia 43 27.00N 50.00E
The Hague see 'sGravenhage Neth. 14
Thekulthili L. Canada 75 61.03N110.00W
The Little Minch str. U.K. 12 57.40N 6.45W
Thelon r. Canada 73 64.23N 96.15W
The Machers f. U.K. 12 54.45N 4.28W
The Minch str. U.K. 12 58.10N 5.50W
The Needles c. U.K. 11 50.39N 1.35W
Theodore Australia 64 24.57S150.05E
Theodore Roosevelt L. U.S.A. 81 33.30N110.57W
Theog India 40 31.07N 77.21E
The Pas Canada 75 53.50N101.15W
The Pennines hills U.K. 10 55.40N 2.20W
Thérain r. France 15 49.15N 2.27E
Theresa U.S.A. 84 44.13N 75.48W
The Rhinns f. U.K. 12 54.50N 5.02W
Thermaïkós Kólpos g. Greece 19 40.10N 23.00E
Thermopolis U.S.A. 80 43.39N108.13W
Thermopylae, Pass of Greece 19 38.47N 22.34E
The Rock town Australia 67 35.16S147.07E
The Salt L. Australia 66 30.05S142.10E
The Snares is. New Zealand 68 48.00S166.30E
The Solent str. U.K. 11 50.45N 1.20W
The Sound str. Denmark/Sweden 23 55.35N 12.40E
Thessalon Canada 76 46.20N 83.30W
Thessaloníki Greece 19 40.38N 22.56E
Thetford U.K. 11 52.25N 0.44E
Thetford Mines town Canada 77 46.06N 71.18W
The Twins town Australia 66 30.00S135.16E
The Wash b. U.K. 10 52.55N 0.15E
The Weald f. U.K. 11 51.05N 0.20E
Thibodaux U.S.A. 83 29.48N 90.49W
Thicket Portage Canada 75 55.19N 97.42W
Thief River Falls town U.S.A. 82 48.07N 96.10W
Thiene Italy 15 45.42N 11.29E
Thiers France 17 45.51N 3.33E
Thiès Senegal 52 14.50N 16.55W
Thika Kenya 55 1.04S 37.04E
Thimbu Bhutan 41 27.28N 89.39E
Thingvallavatn l. Iceland 22 64.10N 21.10W
Thionville France 17 49.22N 6.11E
Thíra i. Greece 19 36.24N 25.27E
Thirsk U.K. 10 54.15N 1.20W
Thiruvananthapuram India 38 8.41N 76.57E
Thisted Denmark 23 56.57N 8.42E
Thistilfjördhur b. Iceland 22 66.11N 15.20W
Thistle I. Australia 66 35.00S136.09E
Thívai Greece 19 38.21N 23.19E
Thjórsá r. Iceland 22 63.53N 20.38W
Thoa r. Canada 75 60.31N109.47W
Thoen Thailand 34 17.41N 99.14E
Tholen i. Neth. 14 51.34N 4.07E
Thomas U.S.A. 84 39.09N 79.30W
Thomaston U.S.A. 85 32.55N 84.20W
Thomasville Ala. U.S.A. 83 31.55N 87.51W
Thomasville Fla. U.S.A. 85 30.50N 83.59W
Thompson Canada 75 55.45N 97.52W
Thompson Utah U.S.A. 80 38.58N109.43W
Thompson Landing Canada 75 62.56N110.40W
Thompsonville U.S.A. 84 44.32N 85.57W
Thomson r. Australia 64 25.11S142.53E
Thonburi Thailand 34 13.43N100.27E
Thórisvatn l. Iceland 22 64.15N 18.50W
Thorshavn Faroe Is. 8 62.02N 6.47W
Thorshöfn Iceland 22 66.12N 15.17W
Thouars France 17 46.59N 0.13W
Thowa r. Kenya 49 1.33S 40.03E
Thrapston U.K. 11 52.24N 0.32W
Three Forks U.S.A. 80 45.54N111.33W
Three Hills town Canada 74 51.43N113.15W
Three Kings Is. New Zealand 68 34.09S172.09E
Three Rivers town Australia 62 25.07S119.09E
Three Rivers town U.S.A. 83 28.28N 98.11W
Three Sisters Mt. U.S.A. 80 44.10N121.46W
Thuin Belgium 14 50.21N 4.20E
Thul Pakistan 40 28.14N 68.46E
Thule Greenland 73 77.30N 69.29W
Thun Switz. 20 46.46N 7.38E
Thunder Bay town Canada 76 48.25N 89.14W
Thunder Hills Canada 75 54.30N106.00W
Thung Song Thailand 34 8.10N 99.41E
Thunkar Bhutan 41 27.55N 91.00E
Thuringen d. Germany 20 50.50N 11.35E
Thüringer Wald mts. Germany 20 50.40N 10.50E
Thurles Rep. of Ire. 13 52.41N 7.50W
Thurloo Downs town Australia 66 29.18S143.30E
Thursday I. Australia 68 10.35S142.13E
Thursday Island town Australia 64 10.34S142.14E
Thurso U.K. 12 58.35N 3.32W
Thurso r. U.K. 8 58.35N 3.32W
Thury-Harcourt France 15 48.59N 0.29W
Thysville Zaïre 54 5.15S 14.52E
Tiandong China 33 23.36N107.08E
Tian'e China 33 25.00N107.10E
Tian Head Canada 74 53.47N133.06W
Tianjin China 32 39.07N117.08E
Tianjin d. China 32 39.30N117.20E
Tianjun China 30 37.16N 98.52E
Tianlin China 33 24.18N106.13E
Tianmen China 33 30.40N113.25E
Tian Shan mts. Asia 30 42.00N 80.30E
Tianshui China 32 34.25N105.58E
Tiantai China 33 29.09N121.02E
Tianyang China 33 23.45N106.54E
Tiarei Tahiti 69 17.32S149.20W
Tiaret Algeria 51 35.28N 1.21E
Tiavea W. Samoa 68 13.57S171.28W
Tibasti, Sarīr des. Libya 51 24.00N 17.00E
Tibati Cameroon 53 6.25N 12.33E
Tiber r. see Tevere r. Italy 18
Tiberias see Teverya Israel 44
Tiberias, L. see Yam Kinneret l. Israel 44
Tibesti mts. Chad 53 21.00N 17.30E
Tibet d. see Xizang d. China 41
Tibetan Plateau see Qing Zang Gaoyuan f. China 30
Tibooburra Australia 66 29.28S142.04E
Tiburón, Isla Mexico 81 29.00N112.20W
Tîchît Mauritania 50 18.28N 9.30W
Tichla W. Sahara 50 21.35N 14.58W
Ticino r. Italy 15 45.09N 9.12E
Ticonderoga U.S.A. 84 43.51N 73.26W
Tidaholm Sweden 23 58.11N 13.57E
Tidikelt f. Algeria 51 27.00N 1.30E
Tidirhine, Jbel mtn. Morocco 50 34.50N 4.30W
Tidjikdja Mauritania 50 18.29N 11.31W
Tiel Neth. 14 51.53N 5.26E
Tieling China 32 42.13N123.48E
Tielt Belgium 14 51.00N 3.20E
Tienen Belgium 14 50.49N 4.56E
Tiénigbé Ivory Coast 52 8.11N 5.43W
Tientsin see Tianjin China 32
Tierp Sweden 23 60.20N 17.30E
Tierra Amarilla U.S.A. 80 36.42N106.33W
Tierra Blanca Mexico 86 18.28N 96.12W
Tierra del Fuego d. Argentina 93 54.30S 67.00W
Tierra del Fuego i. Argentina/Chile 93 54.00S 69.00W
Tietar r. Spain 16 39.50N 6.00W
Tietê Brazil 94 23.04S 47.41W
Tifton U.S.A. 85 31.27N 83.31W
Tiger U.S.A. 80 48.42N117.24W
Tiger Hills Canada 75 49.25N 99.30W
Tigil U.S.S.R. 29 57.49N158.40E
Tiglit Morocco 50 28.31N 10.15W
Tignère Cameroon 53 7.23N 12.37E
Tignish Canada 77 46.57N 64.02W
Tigray d. Ethiopia 48 14.10N 39.35E
Tigre r. Venezuela 90 9.20N 62.30W
Tigris r. see Dijlah r. Asia 43
Tih, Jabal at f. Egypt 44 28.50N 34.00E
Tihāmah f. Saudi Arabia 48 19.00N 41.00E
Tijuana Mexico 81 32.32N117.01W
Tikamgarh India 41 24.44N 78.50E
Tikaré Burkina 52 13.16N 1.44W
Tikhoretsk U.S.S.R. 25 45.52N 40.07E
Tikhvin U.S.S.R. 24 59.35N 33.29E
Tikitiki New Zealand 60 37.47S178.25E
Tiksha U.S.S.R. 24 64.04N 32.35E
Tiksi U.S.S.R. 29 71.40N128.45E
Tilburg Neth. 14 51.34N 5.05E
Tilbury U.K. 11 51.28N 0.23E
Tilemsi, Vallée du f. Mali 52 16.15N 0.02E
Tilghman U.S.A. 85 38.42N 76.20W
Tilhar India 41 27.59N 79.44E
Till r. Northum. U.K. 10 55.41N 2.12W
Tillabéri Niger 53 14.28N 1.27E
Tillamook U.S.A. 80 45.27N123.51W
Tílos i. Greece 19 36.25N 27.25E
Tilpa Australia 66 30.57S144.24E
Timanskiy Kryazh mts. U.S.S.R. 24 66.00N 49.00E
Timaru New Zealand 60 44.23S171.41E
Timashevsk U.S.S.R. 25 45.38N 38.56E
Timbákion Greece 19 35.04N 24.46E
Timbédra Mauritania 50 16.17N 8.16W
Timber Creek town Australia 62 15.38S130.28E
Timboon Australia 66 38.32S143.02E
Timbuktu see Tombouctou Mali 52
Timimoun Algeria 50 29.15N 0.15E
Timimoun, Sebkha de f. Algeria 50 29.10N 0.05E
Timiris, Cap c. Mauritania 52 19.23N 16.32W
Timiş r. Yugo./Romania 21 44.49N 20.28E
Timişoara Romania 21 45.47N 21.15E
Timişul r. Yugo. 19 44.49N 20.28E
Timmins Canada 76 48.28N 81.25W
Timok r. Yugo. 19 44.13N 22.40E
Timor i. Indonesia 62 9.30S125.00E
Timor Sea Austa. 62 11.00S127.00E
Timor Timur d. Indonesia 37 9.00S125.00E
Timpahute Range mts. U.S.A. 80 37.38N115.34W
Tinahely Rep. of Ire. 13 52.48N 6.19W
Tindouf Algeria 50 27.42N 8.09W
Tindouf, Sebkha de f. Algeria 50 27.45N 7.30W
Tingha Australia 67 29.58S151.16E
Tingo María Peru 90 9.09S 75.56W
Tingping China 33 26.10N110.17E
Tingréla Ivory Coast 52 10.26N 6.20W
Tingri China 41 28.30N 86.34E
Tingsryd Sweden 23 56.32N 14.59E
Tinguipaya Bolivia 92 19.11S 65.51W
Tinkisso r. Guinea 52 11.25N 9.05W
Tinnenburra Australia 67 28.40S145.30E
Tinnoset Norway 23 59.43N 9.02E
Tínos i. Greece 19 37.36N 25.08E
Tinsukia India 39 27.30N 95.22E
Tintinara Australia 66 35.52S140.04E
T'i'o Ethiopia 48 14.40N 40.15E
Tioman, Pulau i. Malaysia 36 2.45N104.10E
Tionaga Canada 76 48.05N 82.00W
Tione di Trento Italy 15 46.02N 10.43E
Tipperary Rep. of Ire. 13 52.29N 8.10W
Tipperary d. Rep. of Ire. 13 52.37N 7.55W
Tirān, Jazirat Saudi Arabia 44 27.56N 34.34E
Tiranë Albania 19 41.20N 19.48E
Tirano Italy 15 46.12N 10.10E
Tiraspol U.S.S.R. 21 46.50N 29.38E
Tirat Karmel Israel 44 32.46N 34.58E
Tirebolu Turkey 42 41.02N 38.49E
Tiree i. U.K. 12 56.30N 6.50W
Tîrgovişte Romania 21 44.56N 25.27E
Tîrgu-Jiu Romania 21 45.03N 23.17E
Tîrgu-Lăpuş Romania 21 47.27N 23.52E
Tîrgu Mureş Romania 21 46.33N 24.34E
Tîrgu-Neamţ Romania 21 47.12N 26.22E
Tîrgu-Ocna Romania 21 46.15N 26.37E
Tîrgu-Secuiesc Romania 21 46.00N 26.08E
Tiris Zemmour d. Mauritania 50 24.00N 9.00W
Tirnavos Greece 19 39.45N 22.17E
Tirodi India 41 21.41N 79.42E
Tirol d. Austria 20 47.15N 11.20E
Tir Pol Afghan. 43 34.38N 61.19E
Tirso r. Italy 18 39.52N 8.33E
Tiruchchirāppalli India 39 10.50N 78.43E
Tirunelveli India 38 8.45N 77.43E
Tirupati India 39 13.39N 79.25E
Tiruppur India 38 11.05N 77.20E
Tisa r. Yugo. 21 45.09N 20.16E
Tis'ah Egypt 44 30.02N 32.35E
Tisdale Canada 75 52.51N104.04W
Tisza r. Hungary see Tisa r. Yugo. 21
Tit Algeria 51 22.58N 5.11E
Titicaca, L. Bolivia/Peru 92 16.00S 69.00W
Titikaveka Rarotonga Cook Is. 68 21.16S159.45W
Titiwa Nigeria 53 12.14N 12.53E
Titlagarh India 41 20.18N 83.09E
Titograd Yugo. 19 42.30N 19.16E
Titovo Užice Yugo. 21 43.52N 19.51E
Titov Veles Yugo. 19 41.43N 21.49E
Titran Norway 22 63.42N 8.22E
Ti Tree Australia 64 22.06S133.17E
Titule Zaïre 54 3.17N 25.32E
Titusville Fla. U.S.A. 85 28.37N 80.50W
Titusville Penn. U.S.A. 84 41.38N 79.41W
Tiuni India 41 30.57N 77.51E
Tivaouane Senegal 52 14.57N 16.49W
Tiverton U.K. 11 50.54N 3.30W
Tivoli Italy 18 41.58N 12.48E
Tizimín Mexico 87 21.10N 88.09W
Tizi Ouzou Algeria 51 36.44N 4.05E
Tiznit Morocco 50 29.43N 9.44W
Tjeuke Meer l. Neth. 14 52.55N 5.51E
Tjörn i. Sweden 23 58.00N 11.38E
Tlaxcala d. Mexico 86 19.45N 98.20W
Tlemcen Algeria 50 34.53N 1.19W
Tmassah Libya 51 26.22N 15.48E
Tni Haïa well Algeria 50 24.15N 2.45W
Toab U.K. 12 59.53N 1.16W
Toamasina Madagascar 57 18.10S 49.23E
Toano Italy 15 44.23N 10.34E
Toanoano Tahiti 69 17.52S149.12W
Toba Japan 35 34.29N136.51E
Toba, Danau l. Indonesia 36 2.45N 98.50E

Toba Kākar Range *mts.* Pakistan **40** 31.15N 68.00E
Tobar U.S.A. **80** 40.53N114.54W
Toba Tek Singh Pakistan **40** 30.58N 72.29E
Tobelo Indonesia **37** 1.45N127.59E
Tobermory Canada **76** 45.14N 81.36W
Tobermory U.K. **12** 56.37N 6.04W
Tobi *i.* Caroline Is. **37** 3.01N131.10E
Tobin L. Canada **75** 53.40N103.35W
Toboali Indonesia **36** 3.00S106.30E
Tobol *r.* U.S.S.R. **28** 58.15N 68.12E
Tobolsk U.S.S.R. **28** 58.15N 68.12E
Tobruk *see* Ţubruq Libya **48**
Tobseda U.S.S.R. **24** 68.34N 52.16E
Tocantinópolis Brazil **91** 6.20S 47.25W
Tocantins *d.* Brazil **91** 10.15S 48.30W
Tocantins *r.* Brazil **91** 1.50S 49.15W
Toccoa U.S.A. **85** 34.34N 83.21W
Töcksfors Sweden **23** 59.30N 11.50E
Tocopilla Chile **92** 22.05S 70.12W
Tocorpuri *mtn.* Bolivia / Chile **92** 22.26S 67.53W
Tocumwal Australia **67** 35.51S145.34E
Tocuyo *r.* Venezuela **90** 11.03N 68.23W
Todenyang Kenya **55** 4.34N 35.52E
Todos Santos Mexico **81** 23.27N110.13W
Tofua *i.* Tonga **69** 19.45S175.05W
Togian, Kepulauan *is.* Indonesia **37** 0.20S122.00E
Togo Africa **52** 8.00N 1.00E
Toi Niue **68** 18.58S169.52W
Toijala Finland **23** 61.10N 23.52E
Toili Indonesia **37** 1.25S122.23E
Tojg Afghan. **40** 32.04N 61.48E
Tokaj Hungary **21** 48.08N 21.27E
Tokala *mtn.* Indonesia **37** 1.36S121.41E
Tokat Turkey **42** 40.20N 36.35E
Tokelau Is. Pacific Oc. **68** 9.00S171.45W
Toki Japan **35** 35.21N137.11E
Toki *r.* Japan **35** 35.12N136.52E
Tokmak U.S.S.R. **30** 42.49N 75.15E
Tokoname Japan **35** 34.53N136.51E
Tokoroa New Zealand **60** 38.13S175.53E
Tokuno shima *i.* Japan **31** 27.40N129.00E
Tōkyō Japan **35** 35.42N139.46E
Tōkyō-wan *b.* Japan **35** 35.25N139.45E
Tolaga Bay *town* New Zealand **60** 38.22S178.18E
Tolbukhin Bulgaria **19** 43.34N 27.52E
Toledo Spain **16** 39.52N 4.02W
Toledo U.S.A. **84** 41.40N 83.35W
Toledo, Montes de *mts.* Spain **16** 39.35N 4.30W
Toledo Bend Resr. U.S.A. **83** 31.46N 93.25W
Toliara Madagascar **57** 23.21S 43.40E
Tolmezzo Italy **15** 46.24N 13.01E
Tolo, Teluk *g.* Indonesia **37** 2.00S122.30E
Tolosa Spain **16** 43.09N 2.04W
Tolstyy-Les U.S.S.R. **21** 51.24N 29.48E
Tolti Jammu & Kashmir **40** 35.02N 76.06E
Toluca Mexico **86** 19.20N 99.40W
Toluca *mtn.* Mexico **86** 19.10N 99.40W
Tol'yatti U.S.S.R. **24** 53.32N 49.24E
Tomah U.S.A. **82** 43.59N 90.30W
Tomar Portugal **16** 39.36N 8.25W
Tomás Gomensoro Uruguay **93** 30.26S 57.26W
Tomaszów Lubelski Poland **21** 50.28N 23.25E
Tomaszów Mazowiecki Poland **21** 51.32N 20.01E
Tombe Sudan **49** 5.49N 31.41E
Tombigbee *r.* U.S.A. **83** 31.04N 87.58W
Tombos Brazil **94** 20.53S 42.03W
Tombouctou Mali **52** 16.49N 2.59W
Tombouctou *d.* Mali **52** 19.35N 3.20W
Tombua Angola **54** 15.55S 11.51E
Tomé Chile **93** 36.37S 72.57W
Tomelilla Sweden **23** 55.33N 13.57E
Tomelloso Spain **16** 39.09N 3.01W
Tomingley Australia **67** 32.06S148.15E
Tomini Indonesia **37** 0.31N120.30E
Tomini, Teluk *g.* Indonesia **37** 0.30S120.45E
Tominian Mali **52** 13.17N 4.35W
Tomintoul U.K. **12** 57.15N 3.24W
Tomkinson Ranges *mts.* Australia **62** 26.11S129.05E
Tom Price Australia **62** 22.49S117.51E
Tomra China **41** 30.52N 87.30E
Tomra Norway **22** 62.34N 6.55E
Tomsk U.S.S.R. **28** 56.30N 85.05E
Toms River *town* U.S.A. **85** 39.57N 74.12W
Tonalá Mexico **86** 16.08N 93.41W
Tonalea U.S.A. **81** 36.20N110.58W
Tonasket U.S.A. **80** 48.42N119.26W
Tonawanda U.S.A. **76** 43.01N 78.53W
Tonbridge U.K. **11** 51.12N 0.16E
Tondano Indonesia **37** 1.19N124.56E
Tönder Denmark **23** 54.56N 8.54E
Tondibi Mali **52** 16.39N 0.14W
Tondoro Namibia **56** 17.45S 18.50E
Tone *r.* Japan **35** 35.44N140.51E
Tonga Pacific Oc. **69** 20.00S175.00W
Tonga Sudan **49** 9.28N 31.03E
Tongaat R.S.A. **56** 29.34S 31.07E
Tong'an China **33** 24.44N118.09E
Tongatapu *i.* Tonga **69** 21.10S175.10W
Tongatapu Group *is.* Tonga **69** 21.10S175.10W
Tonga Trench *f.* Pacific Oc. **68** 20.00S173.00W
Tongchuan China **32** 35.05N109.10E
Tongeren Belgium **14** 50.47N 5.28E
Tongguan Hunan China **33** 28.27N112.48E
Tongguan Shaanxi China **32** 34.32N110.26E
Tonghai China **39** 24.07N102.45E
Tonghua China **31** 41.40N126.52E
Tongking, G. of China / Vietnam **34** 20.00N108.00E
Tongliao China **32** 43.40N122.20E
Tongling China **33** 30.55N117.42E
Tonglu China **33** 29.49N119.40E
Tongo Australia **66** 30.30S143.47E
Tongoa *i.* Vanuatu **68** 16.54S168.34E
Tongobory Madagascar **57** 23.32S 44.20E
Tongoy Chile **92** 30.15S 71.30W
Tongren China **33** 27.41N109.08E
Tongsa Dzong Bhutan **41** 27.31N 90.30E
Tongtianheyan China **41** 33.50N 92.19E
Tongue U.K. **12** 58.28N 4.25W
Tongue *r.* U.S.A. **80** 46.24N105.25W
Tongwei China **32** 35.18N105.10E
Tong Xian China **32** 39.52N116.45E
Tongxin China **32** 36.59N105.50E
Tongyu China **32** 44.48N123.06E
Tongzi China **33** 28.08N106.49E
Tonj Sudan **49** 7.17N 28.45E
Tonk India **40** 26.10N 75.47E
Tonkābon Iran **43** 36.49N 50.54E
Tônlé Sap *l.* Cambodia **34** 12.50N104.15E
Tonnerre France **15** 47.51N 3.59E
Tonopah U.S.A. **80** 38.04N117.14W
Tonota Botswana **56** 21.28S 27.24E
Tons *r.* India **41** 25.17N 82.04E
Tönsberg Norway **23** 59.17N 10.25E
Tonstad Norway **23** 58.40N 6.43E
Tonto Basin *town* U.S.A. **81** 33.55N111.18W
Toobeah Australia **67** 28.22S149.50E
Toodyay Australia **63** 31.35S116.26E
Tooele U.S.A. **80** 40.32N112.18W
Toolondo Australia **66** 36.55S142.00E
Toowoomba Australia **65** 27.35S151.54E
Topeka U.S.A. **82** 39.03N 95.41W
Topko *mtn.* U.S.S.R. **29** 57.20N138.10E
Topley Canada **74** 54.32N126.05W
Toplița Romania **21** 46.55N 25.21E
Topock U.S.A. **81** 34.44N114.27W
Topolovgrad Bulgaria **19** 42.05N 26.20E
Topozero, Ozero *l.* U.S.S.R. **24** 65.45N 32.00E
Toppenish U.S.A. **80** 46.23N120.19W
Tor Ethiopia **49** 7.53N 33.40E
Tora-Khem U.S.S.R. **29** 52.31N 96.13E
Torbat-e Ḩeydarīyeh Iran **43** 35.16N 59.13E
Torbat-e Jām Iran **43** 35.15N 60.37E
Tördal Norway **23** 59.10N 8.45E
Tordesillas Spain **16** 41.30N 5.00W
Töre Sweden **22** 65.54N 22.39E
Töreboda Sweden **23** 58.43N 14.08E
Torgau Germany **20** 51.34N 13.00E
Torhout Belgium **14** 51.04N 3.06E
Toride Japan **35** 35.53N140.04E
Torino Italy **15** 45.04N 7.40E
Torit Sudan **49** 4.24N 32.34E
Tormes *r.* Spain **16** 41.18N 6.29W
Torne *r.* Sweden *see* Tornio *r.* Finland **22**
Torneträsk Sweden **22** 68.15N 19.30E
Torneträsk *l.* Sweden **22** 68.20N 19.10E
Tornio Finland **22** 65.52N 24.10E
Tornio *r.* Finland **22** 65.53N 24.07E
Tornquist Argentina **93** 38.06S 62.14W
Toro Spain **16** 41.31N 5.24W
Toronaíos Kólpos *g.* Greece **19** 40.05N 23.38E
Toronto Canada **76** 43.42N 79.25W
Toropets U.S.S.R. **24** 56.30N 31.40E
Tororo Uganda **55** 0.42N 34.13E
Toros Daglari *mts.* Turkey **42** 37.15N 34.15E
Torquay Australia **66** 38.20S144.20E
Torquay U.K. **11** 50.27N 3.31W
Torrance U.S.A. **81** 33.50N118.19W
Torreblanca Spain **16** 40.14N 0.12E
Torre de Moncorvo Portugal **16** 41.10N 7.03W
Torrelavega Spain **16** 43.21N 4.00W
Torremolinos Spain **16** 36.38N 4.30W
Torrens, L. Australia **66** 31.00S137.50E
Torrens Creek *r.* Australia **64** 22.22S145.09E
Torrens Creek *town* Australia **64** 20.50S145.00E
Torreón Mexico **83** 25.33N103.26W
Torre Pellice Italy **15** 44.49N 9.13E
Torres Str. Australia **64** 10.00S142.20E
Torres Vedras Portugal **16** 39.05N 9.15W
Torrevieja Spain **16** 37.59N 0.40W
Torrey U.S.A. **80** 38.18N111.25W
Torridge *r.* U.K. **11** 51.01N 4.12W
Torridon U.K. **12** 57.23N 5.31W
Torridon, Loch U.K. **12** 57.35N 5.45W
Torriglia Italy **15** 44.31N 9.10E
Torrington Wyo. U.S.A. **80** 42.04N104.11W
Torsby Sweden **23** 60.08N 13.00E
Tortola *i.* B.V.Is. **87** 18.28N 64.40W
Tortona Italy **15** 44.54N 8.52E
Tortosa Spain **16** 40.49N 0.31E
Tortue, Île de la *i.* Cuba **87** 20.05N 72.57W
Toruń Poland **21** 53.01N 18.35E
Tory I. Rep. of Ire. **13** 55.16N 8.13W
Tory Sd. Rep. of Ire. **13** 55.14N 8.15W
Torzhok U.S.S.R. **24** 57.02N 34.51E
Toscana *d.* Italy **18** 43.35N 11.10E
Tosen Norway **22** 65.16N 12.50E
Tosno U.S.S.R. **24** 59.38N 30.46E
Tostado Argentina **92** 29.15S 61.45W
Totana Spain **16** 37.46N 1.30W
Tôtes France **15** 49.41N 1.03E
Totma U.S.S.R. **24** 59.59N 42.44E
Totora Bolivia **92** 17.42S 65.09W
Tottenham Australia **67** 32.14S147.24E
Tottori Japan **31** 35.32N134.12E
Touba Ivory Coast **52** 8.22N 7.42W
Toubkal *mtn.* Morocco **50** 31.03N 7.57W
Toucy France **15** 47.44N 3.18E
Tougan Burkina **52** 13.05N 3.04W
Touggourt Algeria **51** 33.06N 6.04E
Tougué Guinea **52** 11.25N 11.50W
Toul France **17** 48.41N 5.54E
Toulnustouc *r.* Canada **77** 49.35N 68.25W
Toulon France **17** 43.07N 5.53E
Toulouse France **17** 43.33N 1.24E
Toummo Niger **51** 22.45N 14.08E
Tounassine, Hamada *des.* Algeria **50** 28.36N 5.00W
Toungoo Burma **34** 18.57N 96.26E
Touques *r.* France **15** 49.22N 0.06E
Tourassine *well* Mauritania **50** 24.40N 11.20W
Tourcoing France **14** 50.44N 3.09E
Tournai Belgium **14** 50.36N 3.23E
Tournon France **17** 45.04N 4.50E
Tournus France **17** 46.33N 4.55E
Tours France **15** 47.23N 0.42E
Toury France **15** 48.11N 1.56E
Touwsrivier *town* R.S.A. **56** 33.20S 20.02E
Towcester U.K. **11** 52.07N 0.56W
Tower U.S.A. **82** 47.47N 92.19W
Towner U.S.A. **82** 48.21N100.25W
Townsend, Mt. Australia **67** 36.24S148.15E
Townshend I. Australia **64** 22.15S150.30E
Townsville Australia **64** 19.13S146.48E
Towrzī Afghan. **40** 30.11N 65.59E
Towson U.S.A. **85** 39.24N 76.36W
Towyn U.K. **11** 52.37N 4.08W
Toyah U.S.A. **83** 31.19N103.47W
Toyama Japan **31** 36.42N137.14E
Toyo *r.* Japan **35** 34.47N137.20E
Toyohashi Japan **35** 34.46N137.23E
Toyokawa Japan **35** 34.49N137.24E
Toyota Japan **35** 35.05N137.09E
Tozeur Tunisia **51** 33.55N 8.08E
Traben-Trarbach Germany **14** 49.57N 7.07E
Trabzon Turkey **42** 41.00N 39.43E
Tracadie Canada **77** 47.31N 64.54W
Tracy Canada **77** 46.01N 73.09W
Tracy U.S.A. **82** 44.14N 95.37W
Trade Town Liberia **52** 5.43N 9.56W
Trafalgar, Cabo *c.* Spain **16** 36.11N 6.02W
Traiguén Chile **93** 38.15S 72.41W
Trail Canada **74** 49.05N117.40W
Trajanova Vrata *pass* Bulgaria **19** 42.13N 23.58E
Trakt U.S.S.R. **24** 62.40N 51.26E
Tralee Rep. of Ire. **13** 52.16N 9.42W
Tralee B. Rep. of Ire. **13** 52.18N 9.55W
Tranås Sweden **23** 58.03N 14.59E
Trang Thailand **34** 7.35N 99.35E
Trangan *i.* Indonesia **37** 6.30S134.15E
Trangie Australia **67** 32.03S148.01E
Trani Italy **18** 41.17N 16.26E
Tranoroa Madagascar **57** 24.42S 45.04E
Tranqueras Uruguay **93** 31.12S 55.45W
Transkei Africa **56** 31.30S 29.00E
Transkei *f.* R.S.A. **56** 32.12S 28.20E
Transvaal *d.* R.S.A. **56** 24.30S 29.30E
Transylvanian Alps *see* Carpații Meridionalimts. *mts.* Romania **19**
Trapani Italy **18** 38.02N 12.30E
Traralgon Australia **67** 38.12S146.32E
Traryd Sweden **23** 56.35N 13.45E
Trarza *d.* Mauritania **50** 18.00N 14.50W
Trarza *f.* Mauritania **50** 18.00N 15.00W
Trasimeno, Lago *l.* Italy **18** 43.09N 12.07E
Trat Thailand **34** 12.14N102.33E
Traunstein Germany **20** 47.52N 12.38E
Travellers L. Australia **66** 33.18S142.00E
Travers, Mt. New Zealand **60** 42.05S172.45E
Traverse City U.S.A. **84** 44.46N 85.38W
Travnik Yugo. **19** 44.14N 17.40E
Trayning Australia **63** 31.09S117.46E
Trbovlje Yugo. **20** 46.10N 15.03E
Trebbia *r.* Italy **15** 45.04N 9.41E
Třebíč Czech. **20** 49.13N 15.55E
Trebinje Yugo. **19** 42.43N 18.20E
Trebišov Czech. **21** 48.40N 21.47E
Třeboň Czech. **20** 49.01N 14.50E
Trecate Italy **15** 45.26N 8.44E
Tredegar U.K. **11** 51.47N 3.16W
Tregaron U.K. **11** 52.14N 3.56W
Tregosse Islets and Reefs Australia **64** 17.41S150.43E
Tréguier France **17** 48.47N 3.16W
Treinta-y-Tres Uruguay **94** 33.16S 54.17W
Treis Germany **14** 50.10N 7.20E
Trélazé France **15** 47.27N 0.28W
Trelew Argentina **93** 43.15S 65.20W
Trelleborg Sweden **23** 55.22N 13.10E
Trélon France **14** 50.04N 4.05E
Tremadog B. U.K. **10** 52.52N 4.14W
Tremblant, Mont *mtn.* Canada **77** 46.16N 74.35W
Tremp Spain **16** 42.10N 0.52E
Trena Ethiopia **49** 10.45N 40.38E
Trenčín Czech. **21** 48.54N 18.04E
Trenggalek Indonesia **37** 8.01S111.38E
Trenque Lauquen Argentina **93** 35.56S 62.43W
Trent *r.* U.K. **10** 53.41N 0.41W
Trentino-Alto Adige *d.* Italy **15** 46.30N 11.20E
Trento Italy **15** 46.04N 11.08E
Trenton Canada **76** 44.06N 77.35W
Trenton Mo. U.S.A. **82** 40.05N 93.37W
Trenton Nebr. U.S.A. **82** 40.11N101.01W
Trenton N.J. U.S.A. **85** 40.15N 74.43W
Trepassey Canada **73** 46.44N 53.22W
Tres Árboles Uruguay **93** 32.24S 56.43W
Tres Arroyos Argentina **93** 38.26S 60.17W
Três Corações Brazil **94** 21.44S 45.15W
Três Lagoas Brazil **94** 20.46S 51.43W
Três Marias, Représa *resr.* Brazil **94** 18.15S 45.15W
Três Pontas Brazil **94** 21.23S 45.29W
Três Rios Brazil **94** 22.07S 43.12W
Treuchtlingen Germany **20** 48.57N 10.55E
Treviglio Italy **15** 45.31N 9.35E
Treviso Italy **15** 45.40N 12.14E
Tribulation, C. Australia **64** 16.03S145.30E
Tribune U.S.A. **82** 38.28N101.45W
Trida Australia **67** 33.00S145.01E
Trier Germany **14** 49.45N 6.39E
Trieste Italy **18** 45.40N 13.47E
Triglav *mtn.* Yugo. **18** 46.21N 13.50E
Trikala Greece **19** 39.34N 21.46E
Trikomon Cyprus **44** 35.17N 33.53E
Triman Pakistan **40** 29.38N 69.05E
Trincomalee Sri Lanka **39** 8.34N 81.13E
Trinidad Bolivia **92** 14.47S 64.47W
Trinidad Colombia **90** 5.25N 71.40W
Trinidad Cuba **87** 21.48N 80.00W
Trinidad Uruguay **93** 33.32S 56.54W
Trinidad U.S.A. **80** 37.10N104.31W
Trinidad & Tobago S. America **87** 10.30N 61.20W
Trinity *r.* U.S.A. **83** 29.55N 94.45W
Trinity B. Australia **64** 16.26S145.26E
Trinity B. Canada **77** 48.00N 53.40W
Trinity Range *mts.* U.S.A. **80** 40.13N119.12W
Trinkitat Sudan **48** 18.41N 37.43E
Trino Italy **15** 45.12N 8.18E
Tripoli *see* Ţarābulus Lebanon **44**
Tripoli *see* Ţarābulus Libya **51**
Trípolis Greece **19** 37.31N 22.21E
Tripolitania *f. see* Ţarābulus *f.* Libya **51**
Tripp U.S.A. **82** 43.13N 97.58W
Tripura *d.* India **41** 23.50N 92.00E
Tristan da Cunha *i.* Atlantic Oc. **95** 37.50S 12.30W
Trivandrum *see* Thiruvananthapuram India **38**
Trnava Czech. **21** 48.23N 17.35E
Troarn France **15** 49.11N 0.11W
Trobriand Is. P.N.G. **64** 8.35S151.05E
Troglav *mtn.* Yugo. **19** 43.57N 16.36E
Troisdorf Germany **14** 50.50N 7.07E
Trois-Rivières *town* Canada **77** 46.21N 72.34W
Troitsk U.S.S.R. **28** 54.08N 61.33E
Troitsko-Pechorsk U.S.S.R. **24** 62.40N 56.08E
Troitskoye R.S.F.S.R. U.S.S.R. **24** 52.18N 56.26E
Troitskoye UKr.S.S.R. U.S.S.R. **21** 47.38N 30.19E
Trölladyngja *mtn.* Iceland **22** 64.54N 17.16W
Trollhättan Sweden **23** 58.16N 12.18E
Trollheimen *mts.* Norway **22** 62.50N 9.15E
Troms *d.* Norway **22** 69.20N 19.30E
Tromsö Norway **22** 69.42N 19.00E
Trondheim Norway **22** 63.36N 10.23E
Trondheimsfjorden *est.* Norway **22** 63.40N 10.30E
Troödos *mts.* Cyprus **44** 34.57N 32.50E
Troon U.K. **12** 55.33N 4.40W
Tropic U.S.A. **80** 37.37N112.05W
Trosh U.S.S.R. **24** 66.24N 56.08E
Trostan *mtn.* N. Ireland **13** 55.03N 6.10W
Trostyanets U.S.S.R. **21** 48.35N 29.10E
Trout *r.* Canada **74** 61.19N119.51W
Trout Creek *town* Canada **76** 45.56N 79.24W
Trout L. N.W.T. Canada **74** 60.35N121.10W
Trout L. Ont. Canada **76** 51.13N 93.20W
Trout River *town* Canada **77** 49.29N 58.08W
Trouville France **15** 49.22N 0.55E
Trowbridge U.K. **11** 51.18N 2.12W
Troy Ala. U.S.A. **85** 31.49N 86.00W
Troy Mo. U.S.A. **82** 38.59N 90.59W
Troy Mont. U.S.A. **80** 48.28N115.53W
Troy N.Y. U.S.A. **84** 42.43N 73.40W
Troy Ohio U.S.A. **84** 40.02N 84.12W
Troyes France **15** 48.18N 4.05E
Troy Peak *mtn.* U.S.A. **80** 38.19N115.30W
Trpanj Yugo. **19** 43.00N 17.17E
Truchas Peak *mtn.* U.S.A. **81** 35.58N105.39W
Truckee U.S.A. **80** 39.20N120.11W
Trujillo Honduras **87** 15.55N 86.00W
Trujillo Peru **90** 8.06S 79.00W
Trujillo Spain **16** 39.28N 5.53W
Trujillo Venezuela **90** 9.20N 70.37W
Truk Is. Pacific Oc. **68** 7.23N151.46E
Trundle Australia **67** 32.54S147.35E
Trung-Luong Vietnam **34** 13.55N109.15E
Trunmore B. Canada **77** 53.48N 57.10W
Truro Australia **66** 34.23S139.09E
Truro Canada **77** 45.22N 63.16W
Truro U.K. **11** 50.17N 5.02W
Trustrup Denmark **23** 56.21N 10.47E
Truth or Consequences U.S.A. **81** 33.08N107.15W
Trysil Norway **23** 61.19N 12.16E
Trysil *r.* Norway **23** 61.03N 12.30E
Trzemeszno Poland **21** 52.35N 17.50E
Tsaratanana Madagascar **57** 16.47S 47.39E
Tsaratanana, Massif de *mts.* Madagascar **57** 14.00S 49.00E
Tsau Botswana **56** 20.10S 22.29E
Tsavo Nat. Park Kenya **55** 2.45S 38.45E
Tselinograd U.S.S.R. **28** 51.10N 71.28E
Tses Namibia **56** 25.58S 18.08E
Tsévié Togo **53** 6.28N 1.15E
Tshabong Botswana **56** 26.03S 22.25E
Tshane Botswana **56** 24.02S 21.54E
Tshela Zaïre **54** 4.57S 12.57E
Tshesebe Botswana **56** 20.45S 27.31E
Tshikapa Zaïre **54** 6.28S 20.48E
Tshofa Zaïre **54** 5.13S 25.20E
Tshopo *r.* Zaïre **54** 0.30N 25.07E
Tshuapa *r.* Zaïre **54** 0.14S 20.45E
Tsihombé Madagascar **57** 25.18S 45.29E
Tsimlyansk U.S.S.R. **25** 47.40N 42.06E
Tsimlyanskoye Vodokhranilishche *resr.* U.S.S.R. **25** 48.00N 43.00E
Tsinan *see* Jinan China **32**
Tsingtao *see* Qingdao China **32**
Tsiribihina Madagascar **57** 19.42S 44.31E
Tsiroanomandidy Madagascar **57** 18.46S 46.02E
Tsivilsk U.S.S.R. **24** 55.50N 47.28E
Tsivory Madagascar **57** 24.04S 46.05E
Tskhinvali U.S.S.R. **25** 42.14N 43.58E
Tsna *r.* B.S.S.R. U.S.S.R. **21** 52.10N 27.03E
Tsna *r.* R.S.F.S.R. U.S.S.R. **24** 54.45N 41.54E
Tsobis Namibia **56** 19.27S 17.30E
Tso Morīri *l.* Jammu & Kashmir **41** 32.54N 78.20E
Tsu Japan **35** 34.43N136.31E
Tsuchiura Japan **35** 36.05N140.12E
Tsudakhar U.S.S.R. **25** 42.20N 47.11E
Tsumeb Namibia **56** 19.12S 17.43E
Tsuru Japan **35** 35.30N138.56E
Tsushima Japan **35** 35.10N136.43E
Tsushima *i.* Japan **31** 34.30N129.20E
Tuam Rep. of Ire. **13** 53.32N 8.52W
Tuamotu, Îles *is.* Pacific Oc. **69** 17.00S142.00W
Tuapa Niue **68** 18.59S169.54W
Tuapse U.S.S.R. **25** 44.06N 39.05E
Tuatapere New Zealand **60** 46.08S167.41E
Tubac U.S.A. **81** 31.37N111.03W
Tuba City U.S.A. **81** 36.08N111.14W
Tuban Indonesia **37** 6.55S112.01E
Tubarão Brazil **94** 28.30S 49.01W
Ţubayq, Jabal aţ *mts.* Saudi Arabia **44** 29.30N 37.15E
Tubbercurry Rep. of Ire. **13** 54.03N 8.45W
Tübingen Germany **20** 48.32N 9.04E
Ţubjah, Wādī *r.* Saudi Arabia **42** 25.35N 38.22E
Ţubruq Libya **48** 32.06N 23.58E
Tubuai *i.* Pacific Oc. **69** 23.23S149.27W
Tubuai Is. Pacific Oc. **69** 23.00S150.00W
Tucacas Venezuela **90** 10.48N 68.19W
Tuchola Poland **21** 53.35N 17.50E
Tuckerton U.S.A. **85** 39.36N 74.20W
Tucson U.S.A. **81** 32.13N110.58W
Tucumán *d.* Argentina **92** 26.30S 65.20W
Tucumcari U.S.A. **81** 35.10N103.44W
Tucupita Venezuela **90** 9.02N 62.04W
Tucuruí Brazil **91** 3.42S 49.44W
Tucuruí, Reprêsa de *resr.* Brazil **91** 4.35S 49.33W
Tudela Spain **16** 42.04N 1.37W
Tufi P.N.G. **64** 9.05S149.20E
Tugela R.S.A. **56** 29.10S 31.25E
Tuguegarao Phil. **37** 17.36N121.44E
Tugur U.S.S.R. **29** 53.44N136.45E
Tuineje Canary Is. **95** 28.18N 14.03W
Tukangbesi, Kepulauan *is.* Indonesia **37** 5.30S124.00E
Tukayyid *well* Iraq **43** 29.47N 45.36E
Ţūkh Egypt **44** 30.21N 31.12E
Tūkrah Libya **51** 32.32N 20.34E
Tuktoyaktuk Canada **72** 69.27N133.00W
Tukums U.S.S.R. **23** 57.00N 23.10E
Tukuyu Tanzania **55** 9.20S 33.37E
Tula Mexico **86** 23.00N 99.43W
Tula U.S.S.R. **24** 54.11N 37.38E
Tūlāk Afghan. **40** 33.58N 63.44E
Tulare U.S.A. **81** 36.13N119.21W
Tulare L. *resr.* U.S.A. **81** 36.03N119.49W
Tularosa U.S.A. **81** 33.04N106.01W
Tulcan Ecuador **90** 0.50N 77.48W
Tulcea Romania **19** 45.10N 28.50E
Tulchin U.S.S.R. **21** 48.40N 28.49E
Tulemalu L. Canada **75** 62.58N 99.25W
Tuli Zimbabwe **56** 21.50S 29.15E
Tuli *r.* Zimbabwe **56** 21.49S 29.00E
Tulia U.S.A. **83** 34.32N101.46W
Ţūlkarm Jordan **44** 32.19N 35.02E
Tullahoma U.S.A. **85** 35.21N 86.12W
Tullamore Australia **67** 32.39S147.39E
Tullamore Rep. of Ire. **13** 53.17N 7.31W
Tulle France **17** 45.16N 1.46E
Tullins France **17** 45.18N 5.29E
Tullow Rep. of Ire. **13** 52.49N 6.45W
Tully Australia **64** 17.55S145.59E
Tully U.S.A. **84** 42.47N 76.06W
Tuloma *r.* U.S.S.R. **24** 68.56N 33.00E
Tulsa U.S.A. **83** 36.09N 95.58W
Tulsequah Canada **74** 58.39N133.35W
Tuluá Colombia **90** 4.05N 76.12W
Tulumbasy U.S.S.R. **24** 57.27N 57.40E
Tulun U.S.S.R. **29** 54.32N100.35E
Tulungagung Indonesia **37** 8.03S111.54E
Tulu Welel *mtn.* Ethiopia **49** 8.53N 34.47E
Tum Indonesia **37** 3.28S130.21E
Tumaco Colombia **90** 1.51N 78.46W
Tumba Sweden **23** 59.12N 17.49E
Tumba, L. Zaïre **54** 0.45S 18.00E
Tumbarumba Australia **67** 35.49S148.01E
Tumbes Peru **90** 3.37S 80.27W
Tumbler Ridge Canada **74** 55.20N120.49W
Tumby Bay *town* Australia **66** 34.20S136.05E
Tumd Youqi China **32** 40.33N110.30E
Tumd Zuoqi China **32** 40.42N111.08E
Tumeremo Venezuela **90** 7.18N 61.30W
Tummel, Loch U.K. **12** 56.43N 3.55W
Tump Pakistan **40** 26.07N 62.22E
Tumsar India **41** 21.23N 79.44E
Tumuc Humac Mts. S. America **91** 2.20N 54.50W
Tumut Australia **67** 35.20S148.14E
Tunari *mtn.* Bolivia **92** 17.18S 66.22W
Tūnat al Jabal Egypt **44** 27.46N 30.44E
Tunceli Turkey **42** 39.07N 39.34E
Tuncurry Australia **67** 32.17S152.29E
Tundubai *well* Sudan **48** 18.31N 28.33E
Tunduma Tanzania **55** 9.19S 32.47E
Tunduru Tanzania **55** 11.08S 37.21E
Tundzha *r.* Bulgaria **19** 41.40N 26.34E
Tungabhadra *r.* India **38** 16.00N 78.15E
Tungaru Sudan **49** 10.14N 30.42E
Tungchiang Taiwan **33** 22.28N120.26E
Tungsten Canada **74** 62.00N128.15W
Tungsten U.S.A. **80** 40.48N118.08W
Tunica U.S.A. **83** 34.41N 90.23W
Tunis Tunisia **51** 36.47N 10.10E

unisia Africa 51 34.00N 9.00E
unja Colombia 90 5.33N 73.23W
unnsjöen *l.* Norway 22 64.45N 13.25E
unungayualok I. Canada 77 56.05N 61.05W
unuyán *r.* Argentina 93 33.33S 67.30W
unxi China 33 29.41N118.22E
uoy-Khaya U.S.S.R. 29 62.33N111.25E
upã Brazil 94 21.57S 50.28W
upelo U.S.A. 83 34.16N 88.43W
upinambaranas, Ilha *f.* Brazil 91 3.00S 58.00W
upiza Bolivia 92 21.27S 65.43W
uquan China 32 45.22N121.41E
úquerres Colombia 90 1.06N 77.37W
ura India 41 25.31N 90.13E
ura Tanzania 55 5.30S 33.50E
ura U.S.S.R. 29 64.05N100.00E
urabah Saudi Arabia 48 21.13N 41.39E
urangi New Zealand 60 38.59S175.48E
urbaco Colombia 90 10.20N 75.25W
urbanovo U.S.S.R. 24 60.05N 50.46E
urbat Pakistan 40 25.59N 63.04E
urbo Colombia 90 8.06N 76.44W
urda Romania 21 46.34N 23.47E
urek Poland 21 52.02N 18.30E
urgeon *r.* Canada 76 50.00N 78.54W
ŭrgovishte Bulgaria 19 43.14N 26.37E
urgutlu Turkey 19 38.30N 27.43E
urhal Turkey 42 40.23N 36.05E
üri U.S.S.R. 23 58.48N 25.26E
uria *r.* Spain 16 39.27N 0.19W
uriaçu Brazil 91 1.41S 45.21W
uriaçu *r.* Brazil 91 1.36S 45.19W
urin Canada 74 49.59N112.35W
urin *see* Torino Italy 15
urka U.S.S.R. 21 49.10N 23.02E
urkana, L. Kenya 55 4.00N 36.00E
urkestan *f.* U.S.S.R. 30 43.17N 68.16E
urkey Asia 42 39.00N 35.00E
urkey U.S.A. 83 34.23N100.54W
urkey Creek *town* Australia 62 17.04S128.15E
urkmenskaya S.S.R. *d.* U.S.S.R. 28 40.00N 60.00E
urks Is. Turks & Caicos Is. 87 21.30N 71.10W
urku Finland 23 60.27N 22.17E
urku-Pori *d.* Finland 23 61.00N 22.35E
urkwel *r.* Kenya 55 3.08N 35.39E
urnagain *r.* Canada 74 59.06N127.35W
urnberry Canada 75 53.25N101.45W
urneffe Is. Belize 87 17.30N 87.45W
urner U.S.A. 80 48.51N108.24W
urnhout Belgium 14 51.19N 4.57E
urnu Măgurele Romania 19 43.43N 24.53E
urnu Roşu, Pasul *pass* Romania 19 45.37N 24.17E
urnu-Severin Romania 19 44.37N 22.39E
uron *r.* Australia 67 33.03S149.33E
uron U.S.A. 83 37.48N 98.26W
urov U.S.S.R. 21 52.04N 27.40E
urpan China 30 42.55N 89.06E
urpan Pendi *f.* China 30 43.40N 89.00E
urquino *mtn.* Cuba 87 20.05N 76.50W
urriff U.K. 12 57.32N 2.28W
urtkul U.S.S.R. 43 41.30N 61.00E
urtle Lake *town* N.Dak. U.S.A. 82 47.31N100.53W
urtle Lake *town* Wisc. U.S.A. 82 45.23N 92.09W
urtle Mtn. Canada / U.S.A. 75 49.05N 99.45W
urukhansk U.S.S.R. 29 65.21N 88.05E
urya *r.* U.S.S.R. 21 51.48N 24.52E
uscaloosa U.S.A. 85 33.12N 87.33W
uscarora U.S.A. 80 41.19N116.14W
uscola Ill. U.S.A. 82 39.48N 88.17W
uscola Tex. U.S.A. 83 32.12N 99.48W
uticorin India 39 8.48N 78.10E
utóia Brazil 91 2.45S 42.16W
utrakan Bulgaria 19 44.02N 26.40E
uttle U.S.A. 82 47.09N100.00W
uttlingen Germany 20 47.59N 8.49E
utuala Indonesia 37 8.24S127.15E
utubu Tanzania 55 5.28S 32.43E
utuila *i.* Samoa 68 14.18S170.42W
uţūn Egypt 44 29.09N 30.46E
uul Gol *r.* Mongolia 30 48.53N104.35E
uvalu Pacific Oc. 68 8.00S178.00E
uwayq, Jabal *mts.* Saudi Arabia 45 23.30N 46.20E
uxpan Mexico 86 21.00N 97.23W
uxtla Gutiérrez Mexico 86 16.45N 93.09W
uy Spain 16 42.03N 8.39W
uyen Quang Vietnam 33 21.48N105.21E
uz Gölü *l.* Turkey 42 38.45N 33.24E
uz Khurmātū Iraq 43 34.53N 44.38E
uzla Yugo. 19 44.33N 18.41E
vaerå Faroe Is. 8 61.34N 6.48W
vedestrand Norway 23 58.37N 8.55E
veitsund Norway 23 59.01N 8.32E
ver U.S.S.R. 24 56.47N 35.57E
weed *r.* U.K. 12 55.46N 2.00W
weed Heads *town* Australia 67 28.13S153.33E
weedsmuir Prov. Park Canada 74 52.55N126.20W
wentynine Palms U.S.A. 81 34.08N116.03W
win Bridges *town* U.S.A. 80 45.33N112.20W
win Falls *town* U.S.A. 80 42.34N114.28W
wins Creek *r.* Australia 66 29.10S139.27E
win Valley *town* U.S.A. 82 47.16N 96.16W
wizel New Zealand 60 44.15S170.06E
wofold B. Australia 67 37.06S149.55E
wo Harbors *town* U.S.A. 82 47.02N 91.40W
wyford U.K. 11 51.01N 1.19W
ler Minn. U.S.A. 82 44.17N 96.08W
ler Tex. U.S.A. 83 32.21N 95.18W
ndinskiy U.S.S.R. 29 55.11N124.34E
ne *r.* U.K. 10 55.00N 1.25W
Tyne and Wear *d.* U.K. 10 54.57N 1.35W
Tynemouth U.K. 10 55.01N 1.24W
Tynset Norway 23 62.17N 10.47E
Tyre *see* Şūr Lebanon 44
Tyrifjorden *l.* Norway 23 60.02N 10.08E
Tyron U.S.A. 85 35.13N 82.14W
Tyrone *d.* U.K. 13 54.35N 7.15W
Tyrone U.S.A. 84 40.40N 78.14W
Tyrrel Canada 75 54.35N 99.10W
Tyrrell *r.* Australia 66 35.28S142.55E
Tyrrell, L. Australia 66 35.22S142.50E
Tyrrhenian Sea Med. Sea 18 40.00N 12.00E
Tysnesöy *i.* Norway 23 60.00N 5.35E
Tyumen U.S.S.R. 28 57.11N 65.29E
Tywi *r.* U.K. 11 51.46N 4.22W
Tzaneen R.S.A. 56 23.49S 30.10E

U

Ua Huka *i.* Îs. Marquises 69 8.55S139.32W
Ua Pu *i.* Îs. Marquises 69 9.25S140.00W
Uatumã *r.* Brazil 91 2.30S 57.40W
Uaupés Brazil 90 0.07S 67.05W
Uaupés *r.* Brazil 90 0.00S 67.10W
Ubá Brazil 94 21.08S 42.59W
Ubangi *r.* Congo / Zaïre 54 0.25S 17.40E
Ubatuba Brazil 94 23.26S 45.05W
Ubauro Pakistan 40 28.10N 69.44E
Ubayyiḍ, Wādī al *r.* Iraq 42 32.04N 42.17E
Ubeda Spain 16 38.01N 3.22W
Uberaba Brazil 94 19.47S 47.57W
Uberlândia Brazil 94 18.57S 48.17W
Ubombo R.S.A. 57 27.35S 32.05E
Ubort *r.* U.S.S.R. 21 52.06N 28.28E
Ubundu Zaïre 54 0.24S 25.28E
Ucayali *r.* Peru 90 4.40S 73.20W
Uch Pakistan 40 29.14N 71.03E
Udaipur India 40 24.35N 73.41E
Udalguri India 41 26.46N 92.08E
Udaquiola Argentina 93 36.35S 58.30W
Udaypur Nepal 41 26.54N 86.32E
Uddevalla Sweden 23 58.21N 11.55E
Uddjaur *l.* Sweden 22 65.55N 17.49E
Udhampur Jammu & Kashmir 40 32.56N 75.08E
Udine Italy 15 46.03N 13.15E
Udipi India 38 13.21N 74.45E
Udon Thani Thailand 34 17.25N102.45E
Uele *r.* Zaïre 49 4.09N 22.26E
Uelzen Germany 20 52.58N 10.34E
Ueno Japan 35 34.45N136.08E
Uere *r.* Zaïre 49 3.42N 25.24E
Ufa U.S.S.R. 24 54.45N 55.58E
Ufa *r.* U.S.S.R. 24 54.45N 56.00E
Uffculme U.K. 11 50.45N 3.19W
Ugab *r.* Namibia 56 21.12S 13.37E
Ugalla *r.* Tanzania 55 5.43S 31.10E
Uganda Africa 55 2.00N 33.00E
Ugep Nigeria 53 5.48N 8.05E
Ughelli Nigeria 53 5.33N 6.00E
Uglegorsk U.S.S.R. 29 49.01N142.04E
Uglovka U.S.S.R. 24 58.13N 33.30E
Ugoma *mtn.* Zaïre 55 4.00S 28.45E
Ugra *r.* U.S.S.R. 24 54.30N 36.10E
Uherske Hradiště Czech. 21 49.05N 17.28E
Uig U.K. 12 57.35N 6.22W
Uíge Angola 54 7.40S 15.09E
Uíge *d.* Angola 54 7.00S 15.30E
Uil U.S.S.R. 25 49.08N 54.43E
Uil *r.* U.S.S.R. 25 48.33N 52.25E
Uinta Mts. U.S.A. 80 40.45N110.05W
Uitenhage R.S.A. 56 33.46S 25.23E
Uithuizen Neth. 14 53.24N 6.41E
Uivlleq *see* Nanortalik Greenland 73
Ujhāni India 41 28.01N 79.01E
Uji *r.* Japan 35 34.53N135.48E
Ujiji Tanzania 55 4.55S 29.39E
Ujjain India 40 23.11N 75.46E
Ujpest Hungary 21 47.33N 19.05E
Ujście Poland 20 53.04N 16.43E
Ujung Pandang Indonesia 36 5.09S119.28E
Uka U.S.S.R. 29 57.50N162.02E
Ukerewe I. Tanzania 55 2.00S 33.00E
Ukhta U.S.S.R. 24 63.33N 53.44E
Ukiah U.S.A. 80 39.09N123.13W
Ukmerge U.S.S.R. 24 55.14N 24.49E
Ukrainskaya S.S.R. *d.* U.S.S.R. 21 49.45N 27.00E
Uku Angola 54 11.24S 14.15E
Ukwi Botswana 56 23.22S 20.30E
Ulaanbaatar Mongolia 30 47.54N106.52E
Ulaangom Mongolia 30 49.59N 92.00E
Ulamba Zaïre 54 9.07S 23.40E
Ulan Bator *see* Ulaanbaatar Mongolia 30
Ulansuhai Nur *l.* China 32 40.56N108.49E
Ulan-Ude U.S.S.R. 30 51.55N107.40E
Ulan Ul Hu *l.* China 39 34.45N 90.25E
Ulcinj Yugo. 19 41.55N 19.11E
Ulenia, L. Australia 66 29.57S142.24E
Ulhāsnagar India 40 19.13N 73.07E
Uliastay Mongolia 30 47.42N 96.52E
Ulindi *r.* Zaïre 54 1.38S 25.55E
Ulla *r.* Spain 16 42.38N 8.45W
Ulladulla Australia 67 35.21S150.25E
Ullånger Sweden 22 62.58N 18.16E
Ullapool U.K. 12 57.54N 5.10W
Ullswater *l.* U.K. 10 54.34N 2.52W
Ulm Germany 20 48.24N 10.00E
Ulongwé Mozambique 55 14.34S 34.21E
Ulricehamn Sweden 23 57.47N 13.25E
Ulsan S. Korea 31 35.32N129.21E
Ulsberg Norway 22 62.45N 9.59E
Ultima Australia 66 35.30S143.20E
Ulu Sudan 49 10.43N 33.29E
Ulúa *r.* Honduras 87 15.50N 87.38W
Uluguru Mts. Tanzania 55 7.05S 37.40E
Uluru *mtn.* Australia 64 25.20S131.01E
Ulverston U.K. 10 54.13N 3.07W
Ulverstone Australia 65 41.09S146.10E
Ul'yanovsk U.S.S.R. 24 54.19N 48.22E
Ulysses U.S.A. 83 37.35N101.22W
Umaisha Nigeria 53 8.01N 7.12E
Umala Bolivia 92 17.21S 68.00W
Uman U.S.S.R. 21 48.45N 30.10E
Umaria India 41 23.32N 80.50E
Umarkot Pakistan 40 25.22N 69.44E
Umbria *d.* Italy 18 42.55N 12.10E
Ume *r.* Sweden 22 63.47N 20.16E
Ume *r.* Zimbabwe 56 17.00S 28.22E
Umeå Sweden 22 63.45N 20.20E
Umfors Sweden 22 65.56N 15.00E
Umfuli *r.* Zimbabwe 56 17.32S 29.23E
Umiat U.S.A. 72 69.25N152.20W
Umm-al-Qaywayn U.A.E. 43 25.32N 55.34E
Umm Badr Sudan 48 14.14N 27.57E
Umm Bel Sudan 49 13.32N 28.04E
Umm Durmān Sudan 48 15.37N 32.59E
Umm el Faḥm Israel 44 32.31N 35.09E
Umm Kuwaykah Sudan 49 12.49N 31.52E
Umm Lajj Saudi Arabia 42 25.03N 37.17E
Umm Qurayn Sudan 49 9.58N 28.55E
Umm Ruwābah Sudan 49 12.54N 31.13E
Umm Shalil Sudan 49 10.51N 23.42E
Umm Shanqah Sudan 49 13.14N 27.14E
Umniati Zimbabwe 56 18.41S 29.45E
Umniati *r.* Zimbabwe 56 17.32S 29.23E
Umrer India 41 20.51N 79.20E
Umreth India 40 22.42N 73.07E
Umtata R.S.A. 56 31.35S 28.47E
Umuahia Nigeria 53 5.31N 7.26E
Umzimkulu R.S.A. 56 30.15S 29.56E
Umzimvubu R.S.A. 56 31.37S 29.32E
Una India 40 20.49N 71.02E
Una *r.* Yugo. 19 45.16N 16.55E
Unalakleet U.S.A. 72 63.53N160.47W
'Unayzah Jordan 44 30.29N 35.48E
'Unayzah Saudi Arabia 43 26.05N 43.57E
'Unayzah, Jabal *mtn.* Iraq 42 32.15N 39.19E
Uncia Bolivia 92 18.27S 66.37W
Uncompahgre Peak U.S.A. 80 38.04N107.28W
Uncompahgre Plateau *f.* U.S.A. 80 38.30N108.25W
Underberg R.S.A. 56 29.46S 29.26E
Underbool Australia 66 35.10S141.50E
Undu, C. Fiji 68 16.08S179.57W
Unecha U.S.S.R. 21 52.52N 32.42E
Ungarie Australia 67 33.38S147.00E
Ungava, Péninsule d' *pen.* Canada 73 60.00N 74.00W
Ungava B. Canada 73 59.00N 67.30W
União Brazil 91 4.35S 42.52W
União da Vitória Brazil 94 26.13S 51.05W
Unimak I. U.S.A. 72 54.50N164.00W
Unini Peru 90 10.41S 73.59W
Union Miss U.S.A. 83 32.34N 89.14W
Union S.C. U.S.A. 85 34.42N 81.37W
Union City Tenn. U.S.A. 83 36.26N 89.03W
Uniondale R.S.A. 56 33.39S 23.07E
Union Gap U.S.A. 80 46.34N120.34W
Union of Soviet Socialist Republics Europe / Asia 21 50.00N 28.00E
Union Springs *town* U.S.A. 85 32.08N 85.44W
Uniontown U.S.A. 84 39.54N 79.44W
Unionville U.S.A. 82 40.29N 93.01W
United Arab Emirates Asia 43 24.00N 54.00E
United Kingdom Europe 9 55.00N 2.00W
United States of America N. America 78 39.00N100.00W
Unity Canada 75 52.27N109.10W
University Park *town* U.S.A. 81 32.17N106.45W
Unjha India 40 23.48N 72.24E
Unna Germany 14 51.32N 7.41E
Unnão India 41 26.32N 80.30E
Unst *i.* U.K. 12 60.45N 0.55W
Ünye Turkey 42 41.09N 37.15E
Upata Venezuela 90 8.02N 62.25W
Upemba, L. Zaïre 54 8.35S 26.28E
Upemba Nat. Park Zaïre 54 9.00S 26.30E
Upernavik Greenland 73 72.50N 56.00W
Upington R.S.A. 56 28.26S 21.12E
Upleta India 40 21.44N 70.17E
Upolu *i.* W. Samoa 68 13.55S171.45W
Upolu Pt. Hawaiian Is. 69 20.16N155.51W
Upper Arrow L. Canada 74 50.30N117.50W
Upper East *d.* Ghana 52 10.40N 0.20W
Upper Egypt *see* Aş Şa'īd *f.* Egypt 42
Upper Hutt New Zealand 60 41.07S175.04E
Upper Klamath L. U.S.A. 80 42.23N122.55W
Upper Laberge Canada 74 60.54N135.12W
Upper Lough Erne N. Ireland 13 54.13N 7.32W
Upper Red L. U.S.A. 82 48.05N 94.50W
Upper Tean U.K. 10 52.57N 1.59W
Upper Volta *see* Burkina Africa 52
Upper West *d.* Ghana 52 10.25N 2.00W
Upper Yarra Resr. Australia 67 37.43S145.56E
Uppsala Sweden 23 59.52N 17.38E
Uppsala *d.* Sweden 23 60.10N 17.50E
Upshi Jammu & Kashmir 41 33.50N 77.49E
Upton Canada 77 45.39N 72.41W
Upton U.S.A. 80 44.06N104.38W
Uqlat aş Şuqūr Saudi Arabia 42 25.50N 42.12E
Ur *ruins* Iraq 43 30.55N 46.07E
Uracoa Venezuela 90 9.03N 62.27W
Uraga-suido *str.* Japan 35 35.10N139.42E
Ural *r.* U.S.S.R. 25 47.00N 52.00E
Uralla Australia 67 30.40S151.31E
Ural Mts. *see* Ural'skiye Gory *mts.* U.S.S.R. 24
Ural'sk U.S.S.R. 25 51.19N 51.20E
Ural'skiye Gory *mts.* U.S.S.R. 24 60.00N 59.00E
Urana Australia 67 35.21S146.19E
Urana, L. Australia 67 35.21S146.19E
Urandangi Australia 64 21.36S138.18E
Uranium City Canada 75 59.28N108.40W
Urapunga Australia 64 14.41S134.34E
Uraricoera *r.* Brazil 90 3.10N 60.30W
Urawa Japan 35 35.51N139.39E
Uray U.S.S.R. 28 60.11N 65.00E
Urbana U.S.A. 82 40.07N 88.12W
Urbino Italy 18 43.43N 12.38E
Urcos Peru 90 13.40S 71.38W
Urda U.S.S.R. 25 48.44N 47.30E
Urdzhar U.S.S.R. 28 47.06N 81.33E
Ure *r.* U.K. 10 54.05N 1.20W
Urechye U.S.S.R. 21 52.59N 27.50E
Uren U.S.S.R. 24 57.30N 45.50E
Urengoy U.S.S.R. 28 65.59N 78.30E
Ures Mexico 86 29.26N110.24W
Urfa Turkey 42 37.08N 38.45E
Ürgüp Turkey 42 38.39N 34.55E
Uribia Colombia 90 11.43N 72.16W
Urisino Australia 66 29.44S143.49E
Urjala Finland 23 61.05N 23.32E
Urk Neth. 14 52.40N 5.36E
Urlingford Rep. of Ire. 13 52.44N 7.35W
Urmia, L. *see* Daryācheh-ye Orūmīyeh *l.* Iran 43
Ursus Poland 21 52.12N 20.53E
Uruaçu Brazil 91 14.30S 49.10W
Uruapan Mexico 86 19.26N102.04W
Urubamba Peru 90 13.20S 72.07W
Urubamba *r.* Peru 90 10.43S 73.55W
Urucará Brazil 91 2.32S 57.45W
Uruçui Brazil 91 7.14S 44.33W
Uruguaiana Brazil 93 29.45S 57.05W
Uruguay *r.* Argentina / Uruguay 93 34.00S 58.30W
Uruguay S. America 94 33.15S 56.00W
Ürümqi China 30 43.43N 87.38E
Urun P.N.G. 64 8.36S147.15E
Urunga Australia 67 30.30S152.28E
Urup *r.* U.S.S.R. 25 44.59N 41.12E
Urzhum U.S.S.R. 24 57.08N 50.00E
Urziceni Romania 19 44.43N 26.38E
Usa *r.* U.S.S.R. 24 65.58N 56.35E
Uşak Turkey 42 38.42N 29.25E
Usakos Namibia 56 22.02S 15.35E
Usambara Mts. Tanzania 55 4.45S 38.25E
Ushant *i. see* Ouessant, Île d' *i.* France 17
Ush-Tobe U.S.S.R. 30 45.15N 77.59E
Ushuaia Argentina 93 54.47S 68.20W
Ushumun U.S.S.R. 29 52.48N126.27E
Usisya Malaŵi 55 11.10S 34.12E
Usk *r.* U.K. 11 51.34N 2.59W
Uskedal Norway 23 59.56N 5.52E
Üsküdar Turkey 19 41.00N 29.03E
Usman U.S.S.R. 25 52.02N 39.43E
Usovo U.S.S.R. 21 51.20N 28.01E
Uspenskiy U.S.S.R. 28 48.41N 72.43E
Ussuriysk U.S.S.R. 31 43.48N131.59E
Ustaoset Norway 23 60.30N 8.04E
Ustica *i.* Italy 18 38.42N 13.11E
Ust'-Ilga U.S.S.R. 29 54.59N105.00E
Ústí nad Labem Czech. 20 50.41N 14.00E
Ust Ishim U.S.S.R. 28 57.45N 71.05E
Ustka Poland 20 54.35N 16.50E
Ust'kamchatsk U.S.S.R. 29 56.14N162.28E
Ust-Kamenogorsk U.S.S.R. 28 50.00N 82.40E
Ust Kulom U.S.S.R. 24 61.34N 53.40E
Ust Kut U.S.S.R. 29 56.40N105.50E
Ust Lyzha U.S.S.R. 24 65.45N 56.38E
Ust'Maya U.S.S.R. 29 60.25N134.28E
Ust Nem U.S.S.R. 24 61.38N 54.50E
Ust Olenëk U.S.S.R. 29 72.59N120.00E
Ust-Omchug U.S.S.R. 29 61.08N149.38E
Ust Port U.S.S.R. 28 69.44N 84.23E
Ust Tapsuy U.S.S.R. 24 62.25N 61.42E
Ust'Tsilma U.S.S.R. 24 65.28N 53.09E
Ust-Tungir U.S.S.R. 29 55.25N120.15E
Ust Ura U.S.S.R. 24 63.06N 44.41E
Ust Vaga U.S.S.R. 24 62.42N 42.45E
Ust Vym U.S.S.R. 24 62.15N 50.25E
Ustyurt, Plato *f.* U.S.S.R. 25 43.30N 55.00E
Usu China 30 44.27N 84.37E
Usumacinta *r.* Mexico 86 18.22N 92.40W
U.S. Virgin Is. C. America 87 18.30N 65.00W
Ut U.S.S.R. 21 52.18N 31.10E
Utah *d.* U.S.A. 80 39.37N112.28W
Utah L. U.S.A. 80 40.13N111.49W
'Uta Vava'u Tonga 69 18.35S174.00W
'Utaybah, Buḥayrat al *l.* Syria 44 33.31N 36.37E
Utembo *r.* Angola 54 17.03S 22.00E
Utengule Tanzania 55 8.55S 35.43E
Utete Tanzania 55 8.00S 38.49E
Uthal Pakistan 40 25.48N 66.37E
Utiariti Brazil 90 13.02S 58.17W
Utica Kans. U.S.A. 82 38.39N100.10W
Utica N.Y. U.S.A. 84 43.05N 75.14W
Utiel Spain 16 39.33N 1.13W
Utikuma L. Canada 74 55.50N115.30W
Utopia Australia 64 22.14S134.33E
Utraula India 41 27.19N 82.25E
Utrecht Neth. 14 52.04N 5.07E
Utrecht *d.* Neth. 14 52.04N 5.10E
Utrecht R.S.A. 56 27.38S 30.19E
Utrera Spain 16 37.10N 5.47W
Utsjoki Finland 22 69.53N 27.00E
Utsunomiya Japan 31 36.33N139.52E
Utta U.S.S.R. 25 46.24N 46.01E
Uttaradit Thailand 34 17.38N100.05E
Uttarkāshi India 41 30.44N 78.27E
Uttar Pradesh *d.* India 41 26.30N 81.30E
Uturoā Îs. de la Société 69 16.44S151.25W
Uummanarsuaq *see* Farvel, Kap *c.* Greenland 73
Uusikaupunki Finland 23 60.48N 21.25E
Uusimaa *d.* Finland 23 60.30N 25.00E
Uvalde U.S.A. 83 29.13N 99.47W
Uvarovichi U.S.S.R. 21 52.35N 30.44E
Uvat U.S.S.R. 28 59.10N 68.49E
Uvéa, Île *i.* N. Cal. 68 20.30S166.35E
Uvinza Tanzania 55 5.08S 30.23E
Uvira Zaïre 55 3.22S 29.06E
Uvs Nuur *l.* Mongolia 30 50.30N 92.30E
Uwajima Japan 31 33.13N132.32E
Uwayl Sudan 49 8.46N 27.24E
'Uwaynāt, Jabal al *mtn.* Libya / Sudan 48 21.54N 24.58E
Uxin Qi China 32 38.30N108.53E
Uyo Nigeria 53 5.01N 7.56E
Uyuni Bolivia 92 20.28S 66.50W
Uyuni, Salar de *f.* Bolivia 92 20.20S 67.42W
Uzbekskaya S.S.R. *d.* U.S.S.R. 28 42.00N 63.00E
Uzda U.S.S.R. 21 53.28N 27.11E
Uzh *r.* U.S.S.R. 21 51.15N 30.12E
Uzhgorod U.S.S.R. 21 48.38N 22.15E

V

Vaagö *i.* Faroe Is. 8 62.03N 7.14W
Vaal *r.* R.S.A. 56 29.04S 23.37E
Vaala Finland 22 64.26N 26.48E
Vaal Dam R.S.A. 56 26.51S 28.08E
Vaasa Finland 22 63.06N 21.36E
Vaasa *d.* Finland 22 62.50N 22.50E
Vác Hungary 21 47.49N 19.10E
Vadodara India 38 22.19N 73.14E
Vado Ligure Italy 15 44.17N 8.27E
Vadsö Norway 22 70.05N 29.46E
Vaduz Liech. 20 47.08N 9.32E
Vaeröy *i.* Norway 22 67.40N 12.40E
Vaga *r.* U.S.S.R. 24 62.45N 42.48E
Vågåmo Norway 23 61.53N 9.06E
Vaggeryd Sweden 23 57.30N 14.07E
Váh *r.* Czech. 21 47.40N 17.50E
Vahsel B. Antarctica 96 77.00S 38.00W
Vaiea Niue 68 19.08S169.53W
Vaihu I. de Pascua 69 27.10S109.22W
Vaijāpur India 40 19.55N 74.44E
Vailly-sur-Aisne France 15 49.25N 3.31E
Vairao Tahiti 69 17.48S149.17W
Vaitupu *i.* Tuvalu 68 7.28S178.41E
Vakaga C.A.R. 49 9.50N 22.30E
Vakarai Sri Lanka 39 8.08N 81.26E
Vålådalen Sweden 22 63.09N 13.00E
Valavsk U.S.S.R. 21 51.40N 28.38E
Valcheta Argentina 93 40.40S 66.10W
Valdagno Italy 15 45.39N 11.18E
Valday U.S.S.R. 24 57.59N 33.10E
Valdayskaya Vozvyshennost *mts.* U.S.S.R. 24 57.10N 33.00E
Valdemārpils U.S.S.R. 23 57.22N 22.35E
Valdemarsvik Sweden 23 58.12N 16.36E
Valdepeñas Spain 16 38.46N 3.24W
Valdés, Pen. Argentina 93 42.30S 64.00W
Val des Bois Canada 77 45.54N 75.35W
Valdez U.S.A. 72 61.07N146.17W
Val d'Isère France 15 45.27N 6.59E
Valdivia Chile 93 39.46S 73.15W
Val d'Oise *d.* France 15 49.10N 2.10E
Val d'Or *town* Canada 76 48.07N 77.47W
Valdosta U.S.A. 85 30.51N 83.51W
Valença Bahia Brazil 91 13.22S 39.06W
Valença R. de Janeiro Brazil 94 22.14S 43.45W
Valença Portugal 16 42.02N 8.38W
Valence France 17 44.56N 4.54E
Valencia Spain 16 39.29N 0.24W
Valencia *d.* Spain 16 39.30N 0.40W
Valencia Venezuela 90 10.14N 67.59W
Valencia, Golfo de *g.* Spain 16 39.38N 0.20W
Valencia de Alcántara Spain 16 39.25N 7.14
Valenciennes France 14 50.22N 3.32E
Valentine Nebr. U.S.A. 82 42.52N100.30W
Valentine N.Mex. U.S.A. 81 30.34N104.29W
Vale of Evesham *f.* U.K. 11 52.05N 1.55W
Vale of Pewsey *f.* U.K. 11 51.21N 1.45W
Vale of York *f.* U.K. 10 54.12N 1.25W
Valera Venezuela 90 9.21N 70.38W
Valga U.S.S.R. 24 57.44N 26.00E
Valinco, Golfe de *g.* France 17 41.40N 8.50E
Valjevo Yugo. 21 44.16N 19.56E
Valkeakoski Finland 23 61.16N 24.02E
Valkenswaard Neth. 14 51.21N 5.27E
Valladolid Mexico 87 20.41N 88.12W
Valladolid Spain 16 41.39N 4.45W
Vall de Uxó *town* Spain 16 39.49N 0.15W
Valle Norway 23 59.12N 7.32E
Valle d'Aosta *d.* Italy 15 45.45N 7.25E
Valle de la Pascua Venezuela 90 9.15N 66.00W
Valledupar Colombia 90 10.31N 73.16W
Valle Edén Uruguay 93 31.50S 56.09W
Vallegrande Bolivia 92 18.29S 64.06W
Valle Hermoso Mexico 83 25.39N 97.52W
Vallenar Chile 92 28.35S 70.46W
Valletta Malta 18 35.53N 14.31E
Valley City U.S.A. 82 46.57N 97.58W
Valley Falls *town* U.S.A. 80 42.29N120.16W
Valleyfield Canada 77 45.15N 74.08W
Valley Stream *town* U.S.A. 85 40.40N 73.42W
Valleyview Canada 74 55.04N117.17W
Vallgrund *i.* Finland 22 63.12N 21.14E
Valls Spain 16 41.18N 1.15E
Val Marie Canada 75 49.14N107.44W
Valmiera U.S.S.R. 24 57.32N 25.29E
Valnera *mtn.* Spain 16 43.10N 3.40W

Valognes France **15** 49.31N 1.28W
Valparaíso Chile **93** 33.02S 71.38W
Valparaíso Mexico **86** 22.46N103.34W
Valparaiso U.S.A. **85** 30.30N 86.31W
Vals, Tanjung *c.* Indonesia **37** 8.30S137.30E
Valverde Dom. Rep. **87** 19.37N 71.04W
Valverde del Camino Spain **16** 37.35N 6.45W
Vammala Finland **23** 61.20N 22.54E
Vamsadhāra *r.* India **41** 18.21N 84.08E
Van Turkey **42** 38.28N 43.20E
Van Blommestein Meer, W.J. *resr.* Surinam **91** 4.45N 55.05W
Van Buren Ark. U.S.A. **83** 35.26N 94.21W
Van Buren Mo. U.S.A. **83** 37.00N 91.01W
Vancouver Canada **74** 49.20N123.10W
Vancouver U.S.A. **80** 45.39N122.40W
Vancouver I. Canada **74** 49.45N126.00W
Vandalia Ill. U.S.A. **82** 38.58N 89.06W
Vandalia Mo. U.S.A. **82** 39.19N 91.29W
Vanderbilt U.S.A. **84** 45.09N 84.39W
Vanderlin I. Australia **64** 15.44S137.02E
Van Diemen, C. Australia **64** 16.31S139.41E
Van Diemen G. Australia **64** 11.50S132.00E
Vandry Canada **77** 47.50N 73.34W
Vänern *l.* Sweden **23** 59.00N 13.15E
Vänersborg Sweden **23** 58.22N 12.19E
Vang Norway **23** 61.10N 8.40E
Vanga Kenya **55** 4.37S 39.13E
Vangaindrano Madagascar **57** 23.21S 47.36E
Van Gölü *l.* Turkey **42** 38.35N 42.52E
Vanier Canada **77** 45.26N 75.40W
Vanimo P.N.G. **37** 2.40S141.17E
Vankarem U.S.S.R. **29** 67.50N175.51E
Vankleek Hill *town* Canada **77** 45.31N 74.39W
Vanna *i.* Norway **22** 70.10N 19.40E
Vännäs Sweden **22** 63.58N 19.48E
Vannes France **17** 47.40N 2.44W
Vanrhynsdorp R.S.A. **56** 31.37S 18.42E
Vansbro Sweden **23** 60.31N 14.13E
Vantaa Finland **23** 60.13N 25.01E
Van Tassell U.S.A. **80** 42.40N104.02W
Vanthali India **40** 21.29N 70.20E
Vanua Levu *i.* Fiji **68** 16.33S179.15E
Vanua Mbalavu *i.* Fiji **68** 17.40S178.57W
Vanuatu Pacific Oc. **68** 16.00S167.00E
Van Wert U.S.A. **84** 40.53N 84.36W
Vanzylsrus R.S.A. **56** 26.51S 22.03E
Vapnyarka U.S.S.R. **21** 48.31N 28.44E
Var *r.* France **20** 43.39N 7.11E
Varades France **15** 47.23N 1.02W
Varallo Italy **15** 45.49N 8.15E
Varāmīn Iran **43** 35.20N 51.39E
Vārānasi India **41** 25.20N 83.00E
Varangerfjorden *est.* Norway **22** 70.00N 30.00E
Varangerhalvöya *pen.* Norway **22** 70.25N 29.30E
Varaždin Yugo. **18** 46.18N 16.20E
Varazze Italy **15** 44.22N 8.34E
Varberg Sweden **23** 57.06N 12.15E
Vardak *d.* Afghan. **40** 34.15N 68.30E
Vardar *r.* Yugo. *see* Axiós *r.* Greece **19**
Varde Denmark **23** 55.38N 8.29E
Varel Germany **14** 53.24N 8.08E
Varennes Canada **77** 45.41N 73.26W
Varennes France **17** 46.19N 3.24E
Varese Italy **15** 45.48N 8.48E
Varese Ligure Italy **15** 44.22N 9.37E
Varginha Brazil **94** 21.33S 45.25W
Varkhān *r.* Afghan. **40** 32.55N 65.30E
Varley Australia **63** 32.48S119.31E
Värmland *d.* Sweden **23** 59.55N 13.00E
Varna Bulgaria **21** 43.13N 27.57E
Värnamo Sweden **23** 57.11N 14.02E
Várpalota Hungary **21** 47.12N 18.09E
Vartofta Sweden **23** 58.06N 13.40E
Varzo Italy **15** 46.12N 8.15E
Varzy France **15** 47.21N 3.23E
Vasa *see* Vaasa Finland **22**
Vasai India **40** 19.21N 72.48E
Vashka *r.* U.S.S.R. **24** 64.55N 45.50E
Vasilkov U.S.S.R. **21** 50.12N 30.15E
Vaslui Romania **21** 46.38N 27.44E
Västerås Sweden **23** 59.37N 16.33E
Västerbotten *d.* Sweden **22** 64.50N 18.10E
Västerdal *r.* Sweden **23** 60.33N 15.08E
Västernorrland *d.* Sweden **22** 63.20N 17.30E
Västervik Sweden **23** 57.45N 16.38E
Västmanland *d.* Sweden **23** 59.50N 16.15E
Vasto Italy **18** 42.07N 14.42E
Vatan France **17** 47.05N 1.48E
Vatican City Europe **18** 41.54N 12.27E
Vatiua Mozambique **57** 14.15S 37.22E
Vatnajökull *mts.* Iceland **22** 64.20N 17.00W
Vatneyri Iceland **22** 65.36N 23.59W
Vatomandry Madagascar **57** 19.20S 48.59E
Vatra Dornei Romania **21** 47.21N 25.21E
Vättern *l.* Sweden **23** 58.30N 14.30E
Vaughan Canada **76** 43.50N 79.32W
Vaughn Mont. U.S.A. **80** 47.35N111.34W
Vaughn N.Mex. U.S.A. **81** 34.36N105.13W
Vaupés *r.* Colombia **90** 0.20N 69.00W
Vava'u Group *is.* Tonga **69** 18.40S174.00W
Vavuniya Sri Lanka **39** 8.45N 80.30E
Växjö Sweden **23** 56.52N 14.49E
Vaygach U.S.S.R. **28** 70.28N 58.59E
Vaygach, Ostrov *i.* U.S.S.R. **24** 70.00N 59.00E
Vecht *r.* Neth. **14** 52.39N 6.01E
Vecsés Hungary **21** 47.26N 19.19E
Veddige Sweden **23** 57.16N 12.19E
Veendam Neth. **14** 53.08N 6.52E
Veenendaal Neth. **14** 52.03N 5.32E
Vega *i.* Norway **22** 65.39N 11.50E
Vega U.S.A. **83** 35.15N102.26W
Veghel Neth. **14** 51.37N 5.35E
Vegreville Canada **74** 53.30N112.05W
Veinticinco de Mayo Argentina **93** 35.25S 60.11W
Vejen Denmark **23** 55.29N 9.09E
Vejer Spain **16** 36.15N 5.59W
Vejle Denmark **23** 55.42N 9.32E
Velddrif R.S.A. **56** 32.47S 18.09E
Vélez Málaga Spain **16** 36.48N 4.05W
Vélez Rubio Spain **16** 37.41N 2.05W
Velhas *r.* Brazil **94** 17.20S 44.55W
Velikiye-Luki U.S.S.R. **24** 56.19N 30.31E
Velikiy Ustyug U.S.S.R. **24** 60.48N 45.15E
Veliko Tŭrnovo Bulgaria **19** 43.04N 25.39E
Velizh U.S.S.R. **24** 55.36N 31.13E
Velletri Italy **18** 41.41N 12.47E
Vellore India **39** 12.56N 79.09E
Velsen Neth. **14** 52.28N 4.39E
Velsk U.S.S.R. **24** 61.05N 42.06E
Veluwe *f.* Neth. **14** 52.17N 5.45E
Vemdalen Sweden **22** 62.29N 13.55E
Venado Tuerto Argentina **93** 33.45S 61.56W
Venaria Italy **15** 45.08N 7.38E
Vence France **15** 43.43N 7.07E
Venda Africa **56** 22.40S 30.40E
Vendas Novas Portugal **16** 38.41N 8.27W
Vendeuvre-sur-Barse France **15** 48.14N 4.28E
Vendôme France **15** 47.48N 1.04E
Veneto *d.* Italy **15** 45.25N 11.50E
Venev U.S.S.R. **24** 54.22N 38.15E
Venezia Italy **15** 45.26N 12.20E
Venezuela S. America **90** 7.00N 65.20W
Venezuela, Golfo de *g.* Venezuela **90** 11.30N 71.00W
Venezuelan Basin *f.* Carib. Sea. **95** 14.30N 68.00W
Vengurla India **38** 15.52N 73.38E
Veniaminof Mtn. U.S.A. **72** 56.05N159.20W
Venice *see* Venezia Italy **15**
Venice U.S.A. **85** 27.05N 82.26W
Venice, G. of Med. Sea **20** 45.20N 13.00E
Venlo Neth. **14** 51.22N 6.10E
Venraij Neth. **14** 51.32N 5.58E
Vent, Îles du *is.* Îs. de la Société **69** 17.30S149.30W
Venta *r.* U.S.S.R. **23** 57.24N 21.33E
Ventersdorp R.S.A. **56** 26.19S 26.48E
Ventimiglia Italy **15** 43.47N 7.36E
Ventnor U.K. **11** 50.35N 1.12W
Ventspils U.S.S.R. **23** 57.24N 21.36E
Ventuari *r.* Venezuela **90** 4.00N 67.35W
Venus B. Australia **67** 38.40S145.43E
Vera Argentina **94** 29.31S 60.30W
Vera Spain **16** 37.15N 1.51W
Veracruz Mexico **86** 19.11N 96.10W
Veracruz *d.* Mexico **86** 18.00N 95.00W
Verāval India **40** 20.54N 70.22E
Verbania Italy **15** 45.56N 8.33E
Vercelli Italy **15** 45.19N 8.26E
Verde *r.* Argentina **93** 42.10S 65.03W
Verde *r.* Brazil **92** 19.11S 50.44W
Verden Germany **20** 52.55N 9.13E
Verdon *r.* France **17** 43.42N 5.39E
Verdun Canada **77** 45.28N 73.35W
Verdun Meuse France **17** 49.10N 5.24E
Vereeniging R.S.A. **56** 26.40S 27.55E
Vergelee R.S.A. **56** 25.46S 24.09E
Verín Spain **16** 41.55N 7.26W
Verkhniy Baskunchak U.S.S.R. **25** 48.14N 46.44E
Verkhniy Lyulyukary U.S.S.R. **24** 65.45N 64.28E
Verkhniy Shar U.S.S.R. **24** 68.21N 50.45E
Verkhniy Ufaley U.S.S.R. **24** 56.05N 60.14E
Verkhnyaya Taymyra *r.* U.S.S.R. **29** 74.10N 99.50E
Verkhnyaya Tura U.S.S.R. **24** 58.22N 59.50E
Verkhovye U.S.S.R. **24** 52.49N 37.14E
Verkhoyansk U.S.S.R. **29** 67.25N133.25E
Verkhoyanskiy Khrebet *mts.* U.S.S.R. **29** 66.00N130.00E
Vermenton France **15** 47.40N 3.42E
Vermilion Canada **75** 53.22N110.51W
Vermilion U.S.A. **84** 41.24N 82.21W
Vermilion Bay *town* Canada **76** 49.51N 93.24W
Vermilion Chutes Canada **74** 58.22N114.51W
Vermillion U.S.A. **82** 42.48N 96.55W
Vermont *d.* U.S.A. **84** 43.50N 72.45W
Vernal U.S.A. **80** 40.27N109.32W
Verneuil France **15** 48.44N 0.56E
Vernon Canada **74** 50.20N119.15W
Vernon France **15** 49.05N 1.29E
Vernon U.S.A. **83** 34.09N 99.17W
Vero Beach *town* U.S.A. **85** 27.39N 80.24W
Véroia Greece **19** 40.31N 22.12E
Verona Italy **15** 45.27N 10.59E
Verónica Argentina **93** 35.24S 57.22W
Verrès Italy **15** 45.40N 7.42E
Versailles France **15** 48.48N 2.08E
Versailles U.S.A. **85** 38.02N 84.45W
Vert, Cap *c.* Senegal **52** 14.45N 17.25W
Vertou France **17** 47.10N 1.28W
Vertus France **15** 48.54N 4.00E
Verviers Belgium **14** 50.36N 5.52E
Vervins France **15** 49.50N 3.54E
Vesanto Finland **22** 62.56N 26.25E
Veselí nad Lužnicí Czech. **20** 49.11N 14.43E
Vesle *r.* France **15** 49.23N 3.38E
Vesoul France **20** 47.38N 6.09E
Vest-Agder *d.* Norway **23** 58.30N 7.10E
Vestfjorden *est.* Norway **22** 68.10N 15.00E
Vestfold *d.* Norway **23** 59.20N 10.10E
Vestmanhavn Faroe Is. **8** 62.09N 7.11W
Vestmannaeyjar *is.* Iceland **22** 63.30N 20.20W
Vestvågöy *i.* Norway **22** 68.10N 13.50E
Vesuvio *mtn.* Italy **18** 40.48N 14.25E
Vesyegonsk U.S.S.R. **24** 58.38N 37.19E
Veszprém Hungary **21** 47.06N 17.55E
Vésztö Hungary **21** 46.55N 21.16E
Vetka U.S.S.R. **21** 52.35N 31.13E
Vetlanda Sweden **23** 57.26N 15.04E
Vetluga U.S.S.R. **24** 57.50N 45.42E
Vetluga *r.* U.S.S.R. **24** 56.18N 46.19E
Vettore, Monte *mtn.* Italy **18** 42.50N 13.18E
Veurne Belgium **14** 51.04N 2.40E
Vevelstad Norway **22** 65.43N 12.30E
Vézelise France **17** 48.29N 6.05E
Vézère *r.* France **17** 44.53N 0.55E
Vezhen *mtn.* Bulgaria **19** 42.45N 24.22E
Viacha Bolivia **90** 16.40S 68.17W
Viadana Italy **15** 44.56N 10.31E
Viadikavkaz U.S.S.R. **25** 43.02N 44.43E
Viana Brazil **91** 3.13S 45.00W
Viana Portugal **16** 38.20N 8.00W
Viana do Castelo Portugal **16** 41.41N 8.50W
Viangchan *see* Vientiane Laos **34**
Viar *r.* Spain **16** 37.45N 5.54W
Viareggio Italy **15** 43.52N 10.14E
Viborg Denmark **23** 56.26N 9.24E
Vibo Valentia Italy **18** 38.40N 16.06E
Vibraye France **15** 48.03N 0.44E
Vic Spain **16** 41.56N 2.16E
Vicente López Argentina **93** 34.32S 58.29W
Vicenza Italy **15** 45.33N 11.32E
Vichada *r.* Colombia **90** 4.58N 67.35W
Vichuga U.S.S.R. **24** 57.12N 41.50E
Vichy France **17** 46.07N 3.25E
Vicksburg U.S.A. **83** 32.14N 90.56W
Viçosa Alagoas Brazil **91** 9.22S 36.10W
Viçosa Minas Gerais Brazil **94** 20.45S 42.53W
Victor Harbor Australia **66** 35.36S138.35E
Victoria Argentina **93** 32.40S 60.10W
Victoria *d.* Australia **67** 37.20S145.00E
Victoria *r.* Australia **62** 15.12S129.43E
Victoria Canada **74** 48.30N123.25W
Victoria Chile **93** 38.13S 72.20W
Victoria Guinea **52** 10.50N 14.32W
Victoria U.S.A. **83** 28.48N 97.00W
Victoria, L. Africa **55** 1.00S 33.00E
Victoria, L. Australia **66** 34.00S141.15E
Victoria, Mt. Burma **34** 21.12N 93.55E
Victoria, Mt. P.N.G. **64** 8.55S147.35E
Victoria Beach *town* Canada **75** 50.43N 96.33W
Victoria de las Tunas Cuba **87** 20.58N 76.59W
Victoria Falls *f.* Zimbabwe/Zambia **56** 17.58S 25.45E
Victoria I. Canada **72** 71.00N110.00W
Victoria L. Australia **66** 32.29S143.22E
Victoria Nile *r.* Uganda **55** 2.14N 31.20E
Victoria River *town* Australia **62** 15.36S131.06E
Victoria River Downs *town* Australia **64** 16.24S131.00E
Victoriaville Canada **77** 46.03N 71.58W
Victoria West R.S.A. **56** 31.24S 23.07E
Victorica Argentina **93** 36.15S 65.25W
Vidalia U.S.A. **85** 32.14N 82.24W
Videle Romania **21** 44.16N 25.31E
Viderö *i.* Faroe Is. **8** 62.21N 6.30W
Vidin Bulgaria **21** 43.58N 22.51E
Vidisha India **41** 23.32N 77.49E
Viedma Argentina **93** 40.50S 63.00W
Viedma, L. Argentina **93** 49.40S 72.30W
Vienna *see* Wien Austria **20**
Vienna Md. U.S.A. **85** 38.29N 75.49W
Vienna S.Dak. U.S.A. **82** 44.42N 97.30W
Vienna Va. U.S.A. **85** 38.54N 77.16W
Vienne France **17** 45.32N 4.54E
Vienne *r.* France **17** 47.13N 0.05W
Vientiane Laos **34** 17.59N102.38E
Vieques *i.* Puerto Rico **87** 18.08N 65.30W
Viersen Germany **14** 51.16N 6.22E
Vierwaldstätter See *l.* Switz. **20** 47.10N 8.50E
Vierzon France **15** 47.14N 2.03E
Vietnam Asia **34** 15.00N108.30E
Viet Tri Vietnam **33** 21.20N105.26E
Vieux-Condé France **14** 50.29N 3.31E
Vigan Phil. **37** 17.35N120.23E
Vigevano Italy **15** 45.19N 8.51E
Vignemale, Pic de *mtn.* France **17** 42.46N 0.08W
Vigo Spain **16** 42.15N 8.44W
Vigrestad Norway **23** 58.34N 5.42E
Vihāri Pakistan **40** 30.02N 72.21E
Vihowa Pakistan **40** 31.08N 70.30E
Vijāpur India **40** 23.35N 72.45E
Vijayawāda India **39** 16.34N 80.40E
Vik Norway **22** 65.19N 12.10E
Vikajärvi Finland **22** 66.37N 26.12E
Vikeke Indonesia **37** 8.42S126.30E
Vikersund Norway **23** 59.59N 10.02E
Vikna *i.* Norway **22** 64.52N 10.57E
Vikulovo U.S.S.R. **28** 56.51N 70.30E
Vila Vanuatu **68** 17.44S168.19E
Vila da Maganja Mozambique **55** 17.25S 37.32E
Vila Franca Portugal **16** 38.57N 8.59W
Vilaine *r.* France **17** 47.30N 2.25W
Vilanculos Mozambique **57** 21.59S 35.16E
Vilanova i la Geltrú Spain **16** 41.13N 1.43E
Vila Real Portugal **16** 41.17N 7.45W
Vila Real de Santo António Portugal **16** 37.12N 7.25W
Vila Velha Brazil **94** 20.20S 40.17W
Vila Verissimo Sarmento Angola **54** 8.08S 20.38E
Vileyka U.S.S.R. **21** 54.30N 26.50E
Vilhelmina Sweden **22** 64.37N 16.39E
Vilhena Brazil **90** 12.40S 60.08W
Viliga Kushka U.S.S.R. **29** 61.35N156.55E
Viljandi U.S.S.R. **24** 58.22N 25.30E
Vilkavišhkis U.S.S.R. **21** 54.39N 23.02E
Vil'kitskogo, Proliv *str.* U.S.S.R. **29** 77.57N102.30E
Vilkovo U.S.S.R. **21** 45.28N 29.32E
Villa Angela Argentina **92** 27.34S 60.45W
Villa Bella Bolivia **92** 10.23S 65.24W
Villablino Spain **16** 42.57N 6.19W
Villacañas Spain **16** 39.38N 3.20W
Villach Austria **20** 46.37N 13.51E
Villa Clara Argentina **93** 31.46S 58.50W
Villa Constitución Argentina **93** 33.14S 60.21W
Villa de Santiago Mexico **83** 25.26N100.09W
Villa Dolores Argentina **92** 31.58S 65.12W
Villafranca di Verona Italy **15** 45.21N 10.50E
Villagarcía Spain **16** 42.35N 8.45W
Villaguay Argentina **93** 31.55S 59.00W
Villahermosa Mexico **86** 18.00N 92.53W
Villa Hernandarias Argentina **93** 31.15S 59.58W
Villa Huidobro Argentina **93** 34.50S 64.34W
Villaines-la-Juhel France **15** 48.21N 0.17W
Villajoyosa Spain **16** 38.31N 0.14W
Villalba Spain **16** 43.18N 7.41W
Villa María Argentina **92** 32.25S 63.15W
Villa Montes Bolivia **92** 21.15S 63.30W
Villanueva de la Serena Spain **16** 38.58N 5.48W
Villaputzu Italy **18** 39.28N 9.35E
Villarrica Chile **93** 39.15S 72.15W
Villarrica Paraguay **94** 25.45S 56.28W
Villarrobledo Spain **16** 39.16N 2.36W
Villa San José Argentina **93** 32.12S 58.15W
Villasayas Spain **16** 41.24N 2.39W
Villavicencio Colombia **90** 4.09N 73.38W
Villaviciosa Spain **16** 43.29N 5.26W
Villazón Bolivia **92** 22.06S 65.36W
Villedieu France **15** 48.50N 1.13W
Villefranche France **17** 46.00N 4.43E
Villena Spain **16** 38.39N 0.52W
Villenauxe-la-Grande France **15** 48.35N 3.33E
Villeneuve France **17** 44.25N 0.43E
Villeneuve d'Ascq France **14** 50.37N 3.10E
Villeneuve-St. Georges France **15** 48.44N 2.27E
Villeneuve-sur-Yonne France **15** 48.05N 3.18E
Villers-Bocage France **15** 49.05N 0.39W
Villers-Cotterêts France **15** 49.15N 3.04E
Villers-sur-Mer France **15** 49.21N 0.02W
Villeurbanne France **20** 45.46N 4.54E
Vilnius U.S.S.R. **21** 54.40N 25.19E
Vilvoorde Belgium **14** 50.56N 4.25E
Vilyuy *r.* U.S.S.R. **29** 64.20N126.55E
Vilyuysk U.S.S.R. **29** 63.46N121.35E
Vimianzo Spain **16** 43.07N 9.02W
Vimmerby Sweden **23** 57.40N 15.51E
Vimoutiers France **15** 48.55N 0.12E
Vina *r.* Chad **53** 7.43N 15.30E
Viña del Mar Chile **93** 33.02S 71.34W
Vinaroz Spain **16** 40.30N 0.27E
Vincennes France **15** 48.51N 2.26E
Vincennes U.S.A. **82** 38.41N 87.32W
Vindel *r.* Sweden **22** 63.54N 19.52E
Vindeln Sweden **22** 64.12N 19.44E
Vinderup Denmark **23** 56.29N 8.47E
Vindhya Range *mts.* India **40** 22.45N 75.30E
Vineland U.S.A. **85** 39.29N 75.02W
Vingåker Sweden **23** 59.02N 15.52E
Vinh Vietnam **34** 18.42N105.41E
Vinh Long Vietnam **34** 10.15N105.59E
Vinita U.S.A. **83** 36.39N 95.09W
Vînju Mare Romania **21** 44.26N 22.52E
Vinkovci Yugo. **19** 45.17N 18.38E
Vinnitsa U.S.S.R. **21** 49.11N 28.30E
Vinson Massif Antarctica **96** 78.00S 85.00W
Vintar Phil. **33** 18.16N120.40E
Vinton U.S.A. **82** 42.10N 92.01W
Vioolsdrif R.S.A. **56** 28.45S 17.33E
Vipava Yugo. **20** 45.51N 13.58E
Virac Phil. **37** 13.35N124.15E
Viramgām India **40** 23.07N 72.02E
Viranşehir Turkey **42** 37.13N 39.45E
Virden Canada **75** 49.51N100.55W
Vire France **17** 48.50N 0.53W
Vire *r.* France **15** 49.20N 0.53W
Vírgenes, C. Argentina **93** 52.00S 68.50W
Virgin Gorda *i.* B.V.Is. **87** 18.30N 64.26W
Virginia U.S.A. **82** 47.31N 92.32W
Virginia *d.* U.S.A. **85** 37.30N 78.45W
Virginia Beach *town* U.S.A. **85** 36.51N 75.59W
Virginia City Mont. U.S.A. **80** 45.18N111.56W
Virginia City Nev. U.S.A. **80** 39.19N119.39W
Virovitica Yugo. **21** 45.51N 17.23E
Virrat Finland **22** 62.14N 23.47E
Virserum Sweden **23** 57.19N 15.35E
Virton Belgium **14** 49.35N 5.32E
Virtsu U.S.S.R. **23** 58.34N 23.31E
Virunga Nat. Park Zaïre **55** 0.30S 29.15E
Vis Yugo. **18** 43.03N 16.21E
Vis *i.* Yugo. **18** 43.03N 16.10E
Visalia U.S.A. **81** 36.20N119.18W
Visayan Sea Phil. **37** 11.35N123.51E
Visby Sweden **23** 57.38N 18.18E
Visconde do Rio Branco Brazil **94** 21.00S 42.51W
Viscount Melville Sd. Canada **72** 74.30N104.00W
Visé Belgium **14** 50.44N 5.42E
Višegrad Yugo. **19** 43.47N 19.20E
Viseu Brazil **91** 1.12S 46.07W
Viseu Portugal **16** 40.40N 7.55W
Viseu de Sus Romania **21** 47.44N 24.22E
Vishākhapatnam India **39** 17.42N 83.24E
Visnagar India **40** 23.42N 72.33E
Viso, Monte *mtn.* Italy **15** 44.38N 7.05E
Visp Switz. **15** 46.18N 7.53E
Vista U.S.A. **81** 33.12N117.15W
Vistula *r. see* Wisła *r.* Poland **21**
Vitarte Peru **90** 12.03S 76.51W
Vitebsk U.S.S.R. **24** 55.10N 30.14E
Viterbo Italy **18** 42.26N 12.07E
Viti Levu *i.* Fiji **68** 18.00S178.00E
Vitim U.S.S.R. **29** 59.28N112.35E
Vitim *r.* U.S.S.R. **29** 59.30N112.36E
Vitória Espírito Santo Brazil **94** 20.19S 40.21W
Vitoria Spain **16** 42.51N 2.40W
Vitória da Conquista Brazil **91** 14.53S 40.52W
Vitré France **15** 48.07N 1.12W
Vitry-le-François France **15** 48.44N 4.35E
Vitteaux France **15** 47.24N 4.30E
Vittoria Italy **18** 36.57N 14.21E
Vittorio Veneto Italy **15** 45.59N 12.18E
Vivonne Bay *town* Australia **66** 35.58S137.10E
Vizcaíno, Desierto de *des.* Mexico **81** 27.40N114.40W
Vizcaíno, Sierra *mts.* Mexico **81** 27.20N114.30W
Vizianagaram India **39** 18.07N 83.30E
Vizinga U.S.S.R. **24** 61.06N 50.05E
Vjosë *r.* Albania **19** 40.39N 19.20E
Vlaardingen Neth. **14** 51.55N 4.20E
Vladimir U.S.S.R. **24** 56.08N 40.25E
Vladimirets U.S.S.R. **21** 51.28N 26.03E
Vladimir Volynskiy U.S.S.R. **21** 50.51N 24.19E
Vladivostok U.S.S.R. **31** 43.09N131.53E
Vlasenica Yugo. **21** 44.11N 18.56E
Vlieland *i.* Neth. **14** 53.15N 5.00E
Vlissingen Neth. **14** 51.27N 3.35E
Vlorë Albania **19** 40.28N 19.27E
Vltava *r.* Czech. **20** 50.22N 14.28E
Voerde Germany **14** 51.37N 6.39E
Vogelkop *f. see* Jazirah Doberai *f.* Indonesia **37**
Voghera Italy **15** 44.59N 9.01E
Voh N. Cal. **68** 20.58S164.42E
Vohibinany Madagascar **57** 18.49S 49.04E
Vohimarina Madagascar **57** 13.21S 50.02E
Vohipeno Madagascar **57** 22.22S 47.51E
Voi Kenya **55** 3.23S 38.35E
Voiron France **17** 45.22N 5.35E
Volborg U.S.A. **80** 45.50N105.40W
Volcano Is. Japan **68** 25.00N141.00E
Volda Norway **23** 62.09N 6.06E
Volga *r.* U.S.S.R. **25** 45.45N 47.50E
Volgograd U.S.S.R. **25** 48.45N 44.30E
Volgogradskoye Vodokhranilishche *resr.* U.S.S.R. **25** 51.00N 46.05E
Volkhov U.S.S.R. **24** 59.54N 32.47E
Volkhov *r.* U.S.S.R. **24** 60.15N 32.15E
Völklingen Germany **20** 49.15N 6.50E
Volkovysk U.S.S.R. **21** 53.10N 24.28E
Vollenhove Neth. **14** 52.41N 5.59E
Volnovakha U.S.S.R. **25** 47.36N 37.32E
Volochanka U.S.S.R. **29** 70.59N 94.18E
Volochisk U.S.S.R. **21** 49.34N 26.10E
Volodarsk U.S.S.R. **24** 56.14N 43.10E
Vologda U.S.S.R. **24** 59.10N 39.55E
Volokolamsk U.S.S.R. **24** 56.02N 35.56E
Vólos Greece **19** 39.22N 22.57E
Volovets U.S.S.R. **21** 48.44N 23.14E
Volsk U.S.S.R. **24** 52.04N 47.22E
Volta *d.* Ghana **52** 7.30N 0.25E
Volta *r.* Ghana **52** 5.50N 0.41E
Volta-Noire *d.* Burkina **52** 12.30N 3.25W
Volta Noire *d.* Ghana **52** 12.30N 3.25W
Volta Redonda Brazil **94** 22.31S 44.05W
Volterra Italy **18** 43.24N 10.51E
Voltri Italy **15** 44.26N 8.45E
Volturno *r.* Italy **18** 41.02N 13.56E
Volzhskiy U.S.S.R. **25** 48.48N 44.45E
Vondrozo Madagascar **57** 22.49S 47.20E
Voorburg Neth. **14** 52.05N 4.22E
Vopnafjördhur *est.* Iceland **22** 65.50N 14.30W
Vopnafjördhur *town* Iceland **22** 65.46N 14.50W
Vorarlberg *d.* Austria **20** 47.15N 9.55E
Vordingborg Denmark **23** 55.01N 11.55E
Voríai Sporádhes *is.* Greece **19** 39.00N 24.00E
Vorkuta U.S.S.R. **24** 67.27N 64.00E
Vormsi *i.* U.S.S.R. **23** 59.00N 23.20E
Voronezh U.S.S.R. **25** 51.40N 39.13E
Voronovo U.S.S.R. **21** 54.09N 25.19E
Vosges *mts.* France **20** 48.10N 7.00E
Voss Norway **23** 60.39N 6.26E
Vostochno Sibirskoye More *sea* U.S.S.R. **29** 73.00N160.00E
Vostochnyy Sayan *mts.* U.S.S.R. **30** 51.30N102.00E
Vostok I. Kiribati **69** 10.05S152.23W
Votkinsk U.S.S.R. **24** 57.02N 53.59E
Votkinskoye Vodokhranilishche *resr.* U.S.S.R. **24** 57.00N 55.00E
Votuporanga Brazil **92** 20.26S 49.53W
Vouga *r.* Portugal **16** 40.41N 8.38W
Vouillé France **17** 46.38N 0.10E
Voulou C.A.R. **49** 8.33N 22.36E
Vouziers France **15** 49.24N 4.42E
Voves France **15** 48.16N 1.37E
Voxna Sweden **23** 61.20N 15.30E
Voxna *r.* Sweden **23** 61.17N 16.26E
Voyvozh U.S.S.R. **24** 64.19N 55.12E
Vozhega U.S.S.R. **24** 60.25N 40.11E
Voznesensk U.S.S.R. **25** 47.34N 31.21E
Vrangelya, Ostrov *i.* U.S.S.R. **29** 71.00N180.00
Vranje Yugo. **19** 42.34N 21.52E
Vratsa Bulgaria **19** 43.12N 23.33E
Vrbas *r.* Yugo. **19** 45.06N 17.29E
Vrede R.S.A. **56** 27.24S 29.09E
Vredendal R.S.A. **56** 31.40S 18.28E
Vresse Belgium **14** 49.53N 4.57E
Vries Neth. **14** 53.06N 6.35E
Vrindāvan India **41** 27.35N 77.42E
Vrnograč Yugo. **18** 45.10N 15.56E
Vršac Yugo. **21** 45.08N 21.18E
Vryburg R.S.A. **56** 26.57S 24.42E
Vught Neth. **14** 51.39N 5.18E
Vukovar Yugo. **21** 45.21N 19.00E
Vung Tau Vietnam **34** 10.21N107.04E

ära India 40 21.07N 73.24E
atka r. U.S.S.R. 28 55.40N 51.40E
atskiye Polyany U.S.S.R. 24 56.14N 51.08E
azma U.S.S.R. 24 55.12N 34.17E
azniki U.S.S.R. 24 56.14N 42.08E
borg U.S.S.R. 24 60.45N 28.41E
chegda r. U.S.S.R. 24 61.15N 46.28E
chodné Beskydy mts. Europe 21 49.30N 2.00E
gozero, Ozero l. U.S.S.R. 24 63.30N 34.30E
nwy, L. U.K. 10 52.46N 3.30W
shka U.S.S.R. 43 39.19N 54.10E
shniy-Volochek U.S.S.R. 24 57.34N 34.23E
egra U.S.S.R. 24 61.04N 36.27E

W

a Ghana 52 10.07N 2.28W
al r. Neth. 14 51.45N 4.40E
alwijk Neth. 14 51.42N 5.04E
bag P.N.G. 37 5.28S143.40E
basca r. Canada 74 58.22N115.20W
bash U.S.A. 82 40.47N 85.48W
bash r. U.S.A. 82 37.46N 88.02W
bē Mena r. Ethiopia 49 6.20N 40.41E
beno U.S.A. 82 45.27N 88.38W
bera Ethiopia 49 6.25N 40.45E
bē Shebelē r. Ethiopia see Shabeelle r. Somali Rep. 45
brzeźno Poland 21 53.17N 18.57E
bush City Canada 77 52.53N 66.50W
co U.S.A. 83 31.55N 97.08W
couno r. Canada 77 50.50N 65.58W
d Pakistan 40 27.21N 66.22E
d Bandah Sudan 49 13.06N 27.57E
ddān Libya 51 29.10N 16.08E
ddeneilanden is. Neth. 14 53.20N 5.00E
ddenzee b. Neth. 14 53.15N 5.05E
ddikee Australia 66 33.18S136.12E
ddington, Mt. Canada 74 51.23N125.15W
dena U.S.A. 82 46.26N 95.08W
d Hāmid Sudan 48 16.30N 32.48E
dhurst U.K. 11 51.03N 0.21E
dī Halfā' Sudan 42 21.56N 31.20E
dī Mūsā town Jordan 44 30.19N 35.29E
d Madanī Sudan 48 14.24N 33.32E
d Nimr Sudan 48 14.32N 32.08E
afrah Kuwait 43 28.39N 47.56E
geningen Neth. 14 51.58N 5.39E
ger B. Canada 73 65.26N 88.40W
ger Bay town Canada 73 65.55N 90.40W
gga Wagga Australia 67 35.07S147.24E
gin Australia 63 33.18S117.21E
gon Mound town U.S.A. 81 36.01N104.42W
h Pakistan 40 33.48N 72.42E
hai Indonesia 37 2.48S129.30E
hat Salīmah Sudan 48 21.22N 29.19E
hiawa Hawaiian Is. 69 21.30N158.01W
hiba Sands des. Oman 38 21.56N 58.55E
hpeton U.S.A. 82 46.16N 96.36W
iau New Zealand 60 42.39S173.03E
idhān India 41 24.04N 82.20E
idhofen Austria 20 47.58N 14.47E
igeo i. Indonesia 37 0.05S130.30E
ihi New Zealand 60 37.24S175.50E
ikato d. New Zealand 60 38.15S175.10E
ikato r. New Zealand 60 37.19S174.50E
ikerie Australia 66 34.11S139.59E
ikokopu New Zealand 60 39.05S177.50E
ikouaiti New Zealand 60 45.36S170.41E
iluku Hawaiian Is. 69 20.53N156.30W
imakariri r. New Zealand 60 43.23S172.40E
imate New Zealand 60 44.45S171.03E
imea Hawaiian Is. 69 20.01N155.41W
inganga r. India 41 18.50N 79.55E
ingapu Indonesia 37 9.30S120.10E
inwright Canada 75 52.49N110.52W
inwright U.S.A. 72 70.39N160.00W
iouru New Zealand 60 39.39S175.40E
ipara New Zealand 60 43.03S172.45E
ipawa New Zealand 60 39.56S176.35E
ipiro New Zealand 60 38.02S178.21E
ipu New Zealand 60 35.59S174.26E
ipukurau New Zealand 60 40.00S176.33E
irau r. New Zealand 60 41.32S174.08E
iroa New Zealand 60 39.03S177.25E
itaki r. New Zealand 60 44.56S171.10E
itara New Zealand 60 38.59S174.13E
iuku New Zealand 60 37.15S174.44E
jir Kenya 55 1.46N 40.05E
ka Ethiopia 49 7.07N 37.26E
ka Zaïre 54 0.48S 20.10E
katipu, L. New Zealand 60 45.10S168.30E
kayama Japan 35 34.13N135.11E
kefield Canada 77 45.38N 75.56W
kefield U.K. 10 53.41N 1.31W
ke I. Pacific Oc. 68 19.17N166.36E
kema Burma 34 16.36N 95.11E
kkanai Japan 31 45.26N141.43E
kre Indonesia 37 0.30S131.05E
kuach, L. Canada 77 55.37N 67.40W
lamba Zambia 55 13.27S 28.44E
lbrzych Poland 20 50.48N 16.19E
lcha Australia 67 31.00S151.36E
lcheren f. Neth. 14 51.32N 3.35E
lcz Poland 20 53.17N 16.28E
ldbröl Germany 14 50.52N 7.34E
ldeck Germany 20 51.12N 9.04E
lden U.S.A. 80 40.34N106.11W
ldorf U.S.A. 85 38.37N 76.54W
ldport U.S.A. 80 44.26N124.04W
Waldron U.S.A. 83 34.54N 94.05W
Wales d. U.K. 11 52.30N 3.45W
Wales U.S.A. 82 47.13N 91.41W
Walgett Australia 67 30.03S148.10E
Walikale Zaïre 55 1.29S 28.05E
Walker U.S.A. 82 47.06N 94.35W
Walker L. U.S.A. 80 38.44N118.43W
Wall U.S.A. 80 43.59N102.14W
Wallace Idaho U.S.A. 80 47.28N115.55W
Wallace Nebr. U.S.A. 82 40.50N101.10W
Wallaceburg Canada 76 42.36N 82.23W
Wallachia f. Romania 21 44.35N 25.00E
Wallambin, L. Australia 63 30.58S117.30E
Wallangarra Australia 67 28.51S151.52E
Wallaroo Australia 66 33.57S137.36E
Walla Walla Australia 67 35.48S146.52E
Walla Walla U.S.A. 80 46.08N118.20W
Wallis, Îles is. Pacific Oc. 68 13.16S176.15W
Wallkill r. U.S.A. 85 41.51N 74.03W
Wallowa U.S.A. 80 45.34N117.32W
Wallowa Mts. U.S.A. 80 45.10N117.30W
Wallsend Australia 67 32.55S151.40E
Walmsley L. Canada 75 63.25N108.36W
Walpole Australia 63 34.57S116.44E
Walsall U.K. 11 52.36N 1.59W
Walsenburg U.S.A. 80 37.37N104.47W
Walterboro U.S.A. 85 32.54N 80.21W
Walton on the Naze U.K. 11 51.52N 1.17E
Walton on the Wolds U.K. 10 52.49N 0.49W
Walvis B. R.S.A. 56 22.55S 14.30E
Walvisbaai R.S.A. 56 22.57S 14.30E
Walvis Bay d. R.S.A. 56 22.56S 14.35E
Walvis Bay town see Walvisbaai R.S.A. 56
Walvis Ridge f. Atlantic Oc. 95 28.00S 4.00E
Wamanfo Ghana 52 7.16N 2.44W
Wamba Kenya 55 0.58N 37.19E
Wamba Nigeria 53 8.57N 8.42E
Wamba Zaïre 55 2.10N 27.59E
Wamba r. Zaïre 54 4.35S 17.15E
Wami r. Tanzania 55 6.10S 38.50E
Wamsasi Indonesia 37 3.27S126.07E
Wan Indonesia 64 8.23S137.55E
Wāna Pakistan 40 32.17N 69.35E
Wanaaring Australia 66 29.42S144.14E
Wanaka New Zealand 60 44.42S169.08E
Wanaka, L. New Zealand 60 44.30S169.10E
Wan'an China 33 26.27N114.46E
Wanapiri Indonesia 37 4.30S135.50E
Wanapitei r. Canada 76 46.02N 80.51W
Wanapitei L. Canada 76 46.45N 80.45W
Wanbi Australia 66 34.46S140.19E
Wandana Australia 66 32.04S133.45E
Wandoan Australia 64 26.09S149.51E
Wanganella Australia 67 35.13S144.53E
Wanganui New Zealand 60 39.56S175.00E
Wangaratta Australia 67 36.22S146.20E
Wangary Australia 66 34.30S135.26E
Wangdu China 32 38.43N115.09E
Wangdu Phodrang Bhutan 41 27.29N 89.54E
Wangerooge i. Germany 14 53.50N 7.50E
Wanghai Shan mtn. China 32 41.40N121.43E
Wangianna Australia 66 29.42S137.32E
Wangjiang China 33 30.07N116.41E
Wangpan Yang b. China 33 30.30N121.30E
Wangyuanqiao China 32 38.24N106.16E
Wani India 41 20.04N 78.57E
Wānkāner India 40 22.37N 70.56E
Wanle Weyne Somali Rep. 45 2.38N 44.55E
Wannian China 33 28.42N117.03E
Wanning China 33 18.48N110.22E
Wānow Afghan. 40 32.38N 65.54E
Wantage U.K. 11 51.35N 1.25W
Wanxian China 33 30.52N108.20E
Wanyang Shan mts. China 33 26.01N113.48E
Wanyuan China 32 32.04N108.02E
Wanzai China 33 28.06N114.27E
Wāpi India 40 20.22N 72.54E
Wapiti r. Canada 74 55.05N118.18W
Wappingers Falls U.S.A. 85 41.36N 73.55W
Wārāh Pakistan 40 27.27N 67.48E
Warangal India 39 18.00N 79.35E
Waranga Resr. Australia 67 36.32S145.04E
Wārāseoni India 41 21.45N 80.02E
Waratah B. Australia 65 38.55S146.04E
Warburton r. Australia 65 27.55S137.15E
Warburton Range mts. S.A. Australia 66 30.30S134.32E
Warburton Range mts. W.A. Australia 62 26.09S126.38E
Ward Rep. of Ire. 13 53.26N 6.20W
Warden R.S.A. 56 27.49S 28.57E
Wardenburg Germany 14 53.04N 8.11E
Wardha India 41 20.45N 78.37E
Wardha r. India 41 19.38N 79.48E
Ward Hill U.K. 8 58.54N 3.20W
Wardlow Canada 75 50.54N111.33W
Waren Germany 20 53.31N 12.40E
Warendorf Germany 14 51.57N 8.00E
Warialda Australia 67 29.33S150.36E
Wark Forest hills U.K. 10 55.06N 2.24W
Warkopi Indonesia 37 1.12S134.09E
Warkworth New Zealand 60 36.24S174.40E
Warley U.K. 11 52.29N 2.02W
Warmbad Namibia 56 28.26S 18.41E
Warminster U.K. 11 51.12N 2.11W
Warm Springs town U.S.A. 80 39.39N114.49W
Warner Robins U.S.A. 85 32.35N 83.37W
Waroona Australia 63 32.51S115.50E
Warracknabeal Australia 66 36.15S142.28E
Warragul Australia 67 38.11S145.55E
Warrakalanna, L. Australia 66 28.13S139.23E
Warrambool r. Australia 67 30.04S147.38E
Warrego r. Australia 67 30.24S145.18E
Warrego Range mts. Australia 64 24.55S146.20E
Warren Australia 67 31.44S147.53E
Warren Ark. U.S.A. 83 33.37N 92.04W
Warren Mich. U.S.A. 84 42.28N 83.01W
Warren Minn. U.S.A. 82 48.12N 96.46W
Warren Ohio U.S.A. 84 41.15N 80.49W
Warren Penn. U.S.A. 84 41.51N 79.08W
Warrenpoint U.K. 13 54.06N 6.15W
Warrensburg Mo. U.S.A. 82 38.46N 93.44W
Warrenton R.S.A. 56 28.07S 24.49E
Warri Nigeria 53 5.36N 5.46E
Warrina Australia 66 28.10S135.49E
Warriner Creek r. Australia 66 29.15S137.03E
Warrington U.K. 10 53.25N 2.38W
Warrington U.S.A. 83 30.23N 87.16W
Warrnambool Australia 66 38.23S142.03E
Warroad U.S.A. 82 48.54N 95.19W
Warrumbungle Range mts. Australia 67 31.20S149.00E
Warsaw see Warszawa Poland 21
Warsaw Ind. U.S.A. 84 41.13N 85.52W
Warshiikh Somali Rep. 45 2.19N 45.50E
Warszawa Poland 21 52.15N 21.00E
Warta r. Poland 20 52.45N 15.09E
Warud India 41 21.28N 78.16E
Warwick Australia 67 28.12S152.00E
Warwick U.K. 11 52.17N 1.36W
Warwick N.Y. U.S.A. 85 41.16N 74.22W
Warwickshire d. U.K. 11 52.13N 1.30W
Wasatch Plateau f. U.S.A. 80 39.20N111.30W
Wasco Calif. U.S.A. 81 35.36N119.20W
Wasco Oreg. U.S.A. 80 45.35N120.42W
Washburn N.Dak. U.S.A. 82 47.17N101.02W
Washburn Wisc. U.S.A. 82 46.41N 90.52W
Washburn L. Canada 72 70.03N106.50W
Wāshim India 40 20.06N 77.09E
Washington U.K. 10 54.55N 1.30W
Washington d. U.S.A. 80 47.43N120.00W
Washington D.C. U.S.A. 85 38.55N 77.00W
Washington Ga. U.S.A. 85 33.43N 82.46W
Washington Ind. U.S.A. 84 38.40N 87.10W
Washington Iowa U.S.A. 82 41.18N 91.42W
Washington N.C. U.S.A. 85 35.33N 77.04W
Washington Utah U.S.A. 80 37.08N113.30W
Washington Va. U.S.A. 84 38.43N 78.10W
Washington Crossing U.S.A. 85 40.18N 74.52W
Wāshuk Pakistan 40 27.44N 64.48E
Wasian Indonesia 37 1.51S133.21E
Wasior Indonesia 37 2.38S134.27E
Wasiri Indonesia 37 7.30S126.30E
Waskaganish Canada 76 51.29N 78.45W
Waskesiu L. Canada 75 53.56N106.10W
Wassenaar Neth. 14 52.10N 4.26E
Wassy France 15 48.30N 4.59E
Waswanipi Lac l. Canada 76 49.35N 76.40W
Watampone Indonesia 37 4.33S120.20E
Watchet U.K. 11 51.10N 3.20W
Waterbury U.S.A. 84 41.33N 73.03W
Waterbury L. Canada 75 58.16N105.00W
Waterford Rep. of Ire. 13 52.16N 7.08W
Waterford d. Rep. of Ire. 13 52.10N 7.40W
Waterford Harbour est. Rep. of Ire. 13 52.12N 6.56W
Waterloo Ork. Belgium 14 50.44N 4.24E
Waterloo Canada 76 43.28N 80.31W
Waterloo Que. Canada 77 45.21N 72.31W
Waterloo Iowa U.S.A. 82 42.30N 92.20W
Waterton Glacier International Peace Park U.S.A. / Canada 80 48.47N113.45W
Watertown N.Y. U.S.A. 84 43.59N 75.55W
Watertown S.Dak. U.S.A. 82 44.54N 97.07W
Watervale Australia 66 33.58S138.39E
Water Valley town U.S.A. 83 34.09N 89.38W
Waterville Rep. of Ire. 13 51.50N 10.11W
Waterville Maine U.S.A. 84 44.33N 69.38W
Waterville Wash. U.S.A. 80 47.39N120.04W
Watford U.K. 11 51.40N 0.25W
Watford City U.S.A. 82 47.48N103.17W
Wa'th Sudan 49 7.24N 28.58E
Wathaman L. Canada 75 56.55N103.43W
Watonga U.S.A. 83 35.51N 98.25W
Watrous Canada 75 51.40N105.28W
Watsa Zaïre 55 3.03N 29.29E
Watson Canada 75 52.07N104.31W
Watson Lake town Canada 74 60.06N128.49W
Watsonville U.S.A. 80 36.55N121.45W
Wattiwarriganna Creek r. Australia 66 28.57S136.10E
Wau P.N.G. 37 7.22S146.40E
Wauchope N.S.W. Australia 67 31.27S152.43E
Wauchope N.T. Australia 64 20.39S134.13E
Waukaringa Australia 66 32.18S139.27E
Waukegan U.S.A. 82 42.22N 87.50W
Waukesha U.S.A. 82 43.01N 88.14W
Waukon U.S.A. 82 43.16N 91.29W
Wauneta U.S.A. 82 40.25N101.23W
Waurika U.S.A. 83 34.10N 98.00W
Wausau U.S.A. 82 44.58N 89.40W
Wautoma U.S.A. 82 44.05N 89.17W
Wauwatosa U.S.A. 82 43.04N 88.02W
Wave Hill town Australia 62 17.29S130.57E
Waveney r. U.K. 11 52.29N 1.46E
Waverly Ill. U.S.A. 82 39.36N 89.57W
Waverly Iowa U.S.A. 82 42.44N 92.29W
Wavre Belgium 14 50.43N 4.37E
Wāw Sudan 49 7.42N 28.00E
Wāw al Kabīr Libya 51 25.20N 16.43E
Waxahachie U.S.A. 83 32.24N 96.51W
Waxweiler Germany 14 50.08N 6.20E
Way, L. Australia 62 26.47S120.21E
Waycross U.S.A. 85 31.12N 82.22W
Wayne N.J. U.S.A. 85 40.03N 75.23W
Waynesboro Ga. U.S.A. 85 33.04N 82.01W
Waynesboro Penn. U.S.A. 84 39.45N 77.35W
Waynesboro Va. U.S.A. 85 38.04N 78.53W
Waynesville U.S.A. 85 35.30N 82.58W
Waynoka U.S.A. 83 36.35N 98.53W
Wazay Afghan. 40 33.22N 69.26E
Waziers France 14 50.24N 3.05E
Wazīrābād Pakistan 40 32.27N 74.07E
Wear r. U.K. 10 54.55N 1.21W
Weatherford Okla. U.S.A. 83 35.32N 98.42W
Weatherford Tex. U.S.A. 83 32.46N 97.48W
Webster N.Y. U.S.A. 76 43.13N 77.26W
Webster Wisc. U.S.A. 82 45.53N 92.22W
Webster City U.S.A. 82 42.28N 93.49W
Webster Groves U.S.A. 82 38.35N 90.21W
Weda Indonesia 37 0.30N127.52E
Weddell Sea Antarctica 96 70.00S 40.00W
Wedderburn Australia 66 36.26S143.39E
Wedgeport Canada 77 43.44N 65.59W
Wedmore U.K. 11 51.14N 2.50W
Wedza Zimbabwe 57 18.37S 31.33E
Weeho r. Canada 74 63.20N115.10W
Weelde Belgium 14 51.25N 5.00E
Weemelah Australia 67 29.02S149.15E
Weert Neth. 14 51.14N 5.40E
Wee Waa Australia 67 30.34S149.27E
Wegorzyno Poland 20 53.32N 15.33E
Wegrów Poland 21 52.25N 22.01E
Weichang China 32 41.56N117.34E
Weiden in der Oberpfalz Germany 20 49.40N 12.10E
Weifang China 32 36.40N119.10E
Weihai China 32 37.28N122.05E
Wei He r. Shaanxi China 32 34.27N109.30E
Wei He r. Shandong China 32 36.47N115.42E
Weilmoringle Australia 67 29.16S146.55E
Weimar Germany 20 50.59N 11.20E
Weinan China 32 34.25N109.30E
Weipa Australia 64 12.41S141.52E
Weir r. Australia 67 29.10S149.06E
Weiser U.S.A. 80 44.37N116.58W
Weishan Hu l. China 32 34.40N117.25E
Weishi China 32 34.24N114.14E
Weissenfels Germany 20 51.12N 11.58E
Wei Xian China 32 36.21N114.56E
Weixin China 33 27.48N105.05E
Weiya China 30 41.50N 94.24E
Weizhou i. China 33 21.01N109.03E
Wejherowo Poland 21 54.37N 18.15E
Wekusko Canada 75 54.45N 99.45W
Weldiya Ethiopia 49 11.50N 39.36E
Weldon U.S.A. 81 35.40N118.20W
Welega d. Ethiopia 49 9.40N 35.50E
Welkom R.S.A. 56 27.59S 26.42E
Welland Canada 76 42.59N 79.14W
Welland r. U.K. 10 52.53N 0.00
Wellesley Is. Australia 64 16.42S139.30E
Wellin Belgium 14 50.05N 5.07E
Wellingborough U.K. 11 52.18N 0.41W
Wellington N.S.W. Australia 67 32.33S148.59E
Wellington S.A. Australia 66 35.21S139.23E
Wellington New Zealand 60 41.17S174.47E
Wellington d. New Zealand 60 40.00S175.30E
Wellington Shrops. U.K. 11 52.42N 2.31W
Wellington Somerset U.K. 11 50.58N 3.13W
Wellington Kans. U.S.A. 83 37.16N 97.24W
Wellington Nev. U.S.A. 80 38.45N119.22W
Wellington, Isla i. Chile 93 49.30S 75.00W
Wells U.K. 11 51.12N 2.39W
Wells Nev. U.S.A. 80 41.07N114.58W
Wellsboro U.S.A. 84 41.45N 77.18W
Wells Gray Prov. Park Canada 74 52.30N120.15W
Wells L. Canada 75 57.15N101.00W
Wells-next-the-Sea U.K. 10 52.57N 0.51E
Wellsville Mo. U.S.A. 82 39.04N 91.34W
Wellton U.S.A. 81 32.40N114.08W
Welmel r. Ethiopia 49 6.00N 40.20E
Welo d. Ethiopia 49 11.30N 40.00E
Wels Austria 20 48.10N 14.02E
Welshpool U.K. 11 52.40N 3.09W
Welwyn Garden City U.K. 11 51.48N 0.13W
Wem U.K. 10 52.52N 2.45W
Wembere r. Tanzania 55 4.07S 34.15E
Wenatchee U.S.A. 80 47.25N120.19W
Wenchang China 33 19.37N110.43E
Wenchi Ghana 52 7.40N 2.06W
Wendel U.S.A. 80 40.20N120.14W
Wendo Ethiopia 49 6.40N 38.27E
Wendover U.S.A. 80 40.44N114.02W
Wenebegon L. Canada 76 47.25N 83.05W
Wengfengzhen China 32 34.56N104.38E
Wenlock r. Australia 64 12.02S141.55E
Wenquan China 41 33.13N 91.50E
Wenshan China 33 23.20N104.11E
Wensleydale f. U.K. 10 54.19N 2.04W
Wentworth Australia 66 34.06S141.56E
Wen Xian China 32 32.52N104.40E
Wenzhou China 33 28.02N120.40E
Weott U.S.A. 80 40.19N123.54W
Wepener R.S.A. 56 29.43S 27.01E
Werda Botswana 56 25.15S 23.16E
Werder well Ethiopia 45 6.58N 45.21E
Werdohl Germany 14 51.16N 7.47E
Were Ilu Ethiopia 49 10.37N 39.28E
Weri Indonesia 37 3.10S132.30E
Werne Germany 14 51.39N 7.36E
Werra r. Germany 20 51.26N 9.39E
Werribee Australia 67 37.54S144.40E
Werris Creek town Australia 67 31.20S150.41E
Wesel Germany 14 51.39N 6.37E
Weser r. Germany 20 53.15N 8.30E
Weslaco U.S.A. 83 26.09N 97.59W
Wesleyville Canada 77 49.09N 53.34W
Wesleyville U.S.A. 76 42.08N 80.01W
Wessel, C. Australia 64 10.59S136.46E
Wessel Is. Australia 64 11.30S136.25E
Wessington U.S.A. 82 44.27N 98.42W
Wessington Springs town U.S.A. 82 44.05N 98.34W
West U.S.A. 83 31.48N 97.06W
West B. U.S.A. 83 29.15N 94.57W
West Bank Jordan 44 32.00N 35.25E
West Bend U.S.A. 82 43.25N 88.11W
West Bengal d. India 41 23.00N 88.00E
West Bromwich U.K. 11 52.32N 2.01W
Westbrook U.S.A. 84 43.41N 70.21W
West Burra i. U.K. 8 60.05N 1.21W
West Caroline Basin Pacific Oc. 68 5.00N139.00E
West Chester U.S.A. 85 39.58N 75.36W
West Coast d. New Zealand 60 43.15S170.10E
West Des Moines U.S.A. 82 41.35N 93.43W
Westende Belgium 14 51.10N 2.46E
Western d. Ghana 52 6.00N 2.40W
Western d. Kenya 55 0.30N 34.30E
Western d. Zambia 56 16.00S 23.45E
Western Australia d. Australia 62 24.20S122.30E
Western Ghāts mts. India 38 15.30N 74.30E
Western Isles d. U.K. 12 57.40N 7.10W
Western Sahara Africa 50 25.00N 13.30W
Western Samoa Pacific Oc. 68 13.55S172.00W
Westerschelde est. Neth. 14 51.25N 3.40E
Westerstede Germany 14 53.15N 7.56E
Westerwald f. Germany 14 50.40N 8.00E
West Falkland i. Falkland Is. 93 51.40W 60.00W
West Felton U.K. 10 52.49N 2.58W
Westfield Mass. U.S.A. 84 42.07N 72.45W
Westfield N.J. U.S.A. 85 40.39N 74.21W
Westfield N.Y. U.S.A. 76 42.19N 79.35W
Westfield Penn. U.S.A. 84 41.55N 77.32W
West Frankfort U.S.A. 83 37.54N 88.55W
West Frisian Is. see Waddeneilanden Neth. 20
West Glamorgan d. U.K. 11 51.42N 3.47W
Westhope U.S.A. 82 48.55N101.01W
West Indies is. C. America 95 21.00N 74.00W
West Lafayette U.S.A. 84 40.26N 86.56W
West Linton U.K. 12 55.45N 3.21W
Westlock Canada 74 54.09N113.55W
Westmeath d. Rep. of Ire. 13 53.30N 7.30W
West Memphis U.S.A. 83 35.08N 90.11W
West Midlands d. U.K. 11 52.28N 1.50W
Westminster U.S.A. 85 39.35N 77.00W
Westmoreland Australia 64 17.18S138.12E
West Nicholson Zimbabwe 56 21.06S 29.25E
Weston Malaysia 36 5.14N115.35E
Weston-Super-Mare U.K. 11 51.20N 2.59W
West Palm Beach town U.S.A. 85 26.42N 80.05W
West Plains town U.S.A. 83 36.44N 91.51W
West Point town U.S.A. 83 33.36N 88.39W
Westport New Zealand 60 41.46S171.38E
Westport Rep. of Ire. 13 53.48N 9.32W
Westport Conn. U.S.A. 85 41.09N 73.22W
Westport Wash. U.S.A. 80 46.53N124.06W
Westray Canada 75 53.36N101.24W
Westray i. U.K. 12 59.18N 2.58W
West Road r. Canada 74 53.18N122.53W
West Siberian Plain f. see Zapadno-Sibirskaya Ravnina f. U.S.S.R. 28
West Sussex d. U.K. 11 50.58N 0.30W
West Terschelling Neth. 14 53.22N 5.13E
West Virginia d. U.S.A. 84 38.45N 80.30W
West Vlaanderen d. Belgium 14 51.00N 3.00E
West Wyalong Australia 67 33.54S147.12E
West Yellowstone U.S.A. 80 44.30N111.05W
West York U.S.A. 85 39.57N 76.46W
West Yorkshire d. U.K. 10 53.45N 1.40W
Wetar i. Indonesia 37 7.45S126.00E
Wetaskiwin Canada 74 52.55N113.24W
Wetteren Belgium 14 51.00N 3.51E
Wetzlar Germany 20 50.33N 8.30E
Wewak P.N.G. 37 3.35S143.35E
Wewoka U.S.A. 83 35.09N 96.30W
Wexford Rep. of Ire. 13 52.20N 6.28W
Wexford d. Rep. of Ire. 13 52.20N 6.25W
Wexford B. Rep. of Ire. 13 52.27N 6.18W
Weyburn Canada 75 49.41N103.52W
Weyib r. Ethiopia 49 4.11N 42.09E
Weymouth U.K. 11 50.36N 2.28W
Weymouth, C. Australia 64 12.32S143.36E
Whakatane New Zealand 60 37.56S177.00E
Whalan r. Australia 67 29.10S148.42E
Whale Cove town Canada 75 62.11N 92.36W
Whalsay i. U.K. 12 60.22N 0.59W
Whangarei New Zealand 60 35.43S174.20E
Wharfe r. U.K. 10 53.50N 1.07W
Wharfedale f. U.K. 10 54.00N 1.55W
Wharton U.S.A. 83 29.19N 96.06W
Whataroa New Zealand 60 43.16S170.22E
Wheatland U.S.A. 80 42.03N104.57W
Wheaton Md. U.S.A. 85 39.03N 77.03W
Wheaton Minn. U.S.A. 82 45.48N 96.30W
Wheeler r. Que. Canada 77 58.05N 67.12W
Wheeler r. Sask. Canada 75 57.25N105.30W
Wheeler Peak mtn. Nev. U.S.A. 80 38.59N114.19W
Wheeler Peak mtn. N.Mex. U.S.A. 80 36.34N105.25W
Wheeler Ridge town U.S.A. 81 35.06N119.01W
Wheeler Springs town U.S.A. 81 34.30N119.18W
Wheeling U.S.A. 84 40.05N 80.43W
Whernside mtn. U.K. 10 54.14N 2.25W
Whidbey Is. Australia 66 34.50S135.00E
Whiskey Gap town Canada 74 49.00N113.03W
Whitburn U.K. 12 55.52N 3.41W
Whitby Canada 76 43.52N 78.56W
Whitby U.K. 10 54.29N 0.37W
Whitchurch Shrops. U.K. 10 52.58N 2.42W
White r. Ark. U.S.A. 83 33.53N 91.10W
White r. Ind. U.S.A. 84 38.29N 87.45W
White r. S.Dak. U.S.A. 82 43.48N 99.22W
White r. Utah U.S.A. 78 40.04N109.41W

White, L. Australia 62 21.05S129.00E
White B. Canada 77 50.00N 56.30W
White Cliffs *town* Australia 66 30.51S143.05E
Whitefish U.S.A. 80 48.25N114.20W
Whitefish B. U.S.A. 84 46.32N 84.45W
Whitefish L. Canada 75 62.41N106.48W
Whitehall Mont. U.S.A. 80 45.52N112.06W
Whitehall Wisc. U.S.A. 82 44.22N 91.19W
Whitehaven U.K. 10 54.33N 3.35W
Whitehorse Canada 74 60.43N135.03W
White L. U.S.A. 83 29.45N 92.30W
Whitemark Australia 65 40.07S148.00E
White Mountain Peak U.S.A. 80 37.38N118.15W
White Mts. Calif. U.S.A. 80 37.30N118.15W
Whitemud *r.* Canada 74 56.41N117.15W
White Nile *r. see* Abyaḑ, Al Baḩr al *r.* Sudan 48
White Otter L. Canada 76 49.09N 91.50W
White Plains *town* Liberia 52 6.28N 10.40W
White Plains *town* U.S.A. 85 41.02N 73.46W
Whitesand *r.* Canada 75 51.34N101.55W
White Sea *see* Beloye More *sea* U.S.S.R. 24
Whiteshell Prov. Park. Canada 75 50.00N 95.25W
Whitetail U.S.A. 80 48.54N105.10W
White Volta *r.* Ghana 52 9.13N 1.15W
Whitewater Baldy *mtn.* U.S.A. 81 33.20N108.39W
Whitfield Australia 67 36.49S146.22E
Whithorn U.K. 12 54.44N 4.25W
Whitianga New Zealand 60 36.50S175.42E
Whiting U.S.A. 85 39.57N 74.23W
Whitley Bay *town* U.K. 10 55.03N 1.25W
Whitney Canada 76 45.30N 78.14W
Whitney, Mt. U.S.A. 81 36.35N118.18W
Whitstable U.K. 11 51.21N 1.02E
Whitsunday I. Australia 64 20.17S148.59E
Whittier U.S.A. 72 60.46N148.41W
Whittlesea Australia 67 37.31S145.08E
Whitton U.K. 10 53.42N 0.39W
Wholdaia L. Canada 75 60.43N104.20W
Whyalla Australia 66 33.02S137.35E
Wichita U.S.A. 83 37.41N 97.20W
Wichita Falls *town* U.S.A. 83 33.54N 98.30W
Wick U.K. 12 58.26N 3.06W
Wickenburg U.S.A. 81 33.58N112.44W
Wickepin Australia 63 32.45S117.31E
Wicklow Rep. of Ire. 13 52.59N 6.03W
Wicklow *d.* Rep. of Ire. 13 52.59N 6.25W
Wicklow Head Rep. of Ire. 13 52.58N 6.00W
Wicklow Mts. Rep. of Ire. 13 53.06N 6.20W
Widgiemooltha Australia 63 31.30S121.34E
Widnes U.K. 10 53.22N 2.44W
Wiehl Germany 14 50.57N 7.32E
Wieluń Poland 21 51.14N 18.34E
Wien Austria 20 48.13N 16.22E
Wiener Neustadt Austria 20 47.49N 16.15E
Wieprz *r.* Poland 21 51.34N 21.49E
Wiesbaden Germany 20 50.05N 8.15E
Wigan U.K. 10 53.33N 2.38W
Wight, Isle of U.K. 9 50.40N 1.17W
Wigton U.K. 10 54.50N 3.09W
Wigtown U.K. 12 54.47N 4.26W
Wigtown B. U.K. 12 54.47N 4.15W
Wilber U.S.A. 82 40.29N 96.58W
Wilcannia Australia 66 31.33S143.24E
Wildhorn *mtn.* Switz. 17 46.22N 7.22E
Wildon Austria 20 46.53N 15.31E
Wildrose U.S.A. 82 48.38N103.11W
Wildspitze *mtn.* Austria 20 46.55N 10.55E
Wildwood U.S.A. 85 38.59N 74.49W
Wilgena Australia 66 30.46S134.44E
Wilhelm, Mt. P.N.G. 37 6.00S144.55E
Wilhelm II Land Antarctica 96 68.00S 89.00E
Wilhelmshaven Germany 14 53.32N 8.07E
Wilkes-Barre U.S.A. 84 41.15N 75.50W
Wilkesboro U.S.A. 85 36.08N 81.09W
Wilkes Land *f.* Antarctica 96 69.00S120.00E
Wilkie Canada 75 52.25N108.43W
Wilkie Canada 72 52.27N108.42W
Wilkinsburg U.S.A. 84 40.27N 79.53W
Wilkinson Lakes Australia 65 29.40S132.39E
Willandra Billabong *r.* Australia 66 33.08S144.06E
Willard N.Mex. U.S.A. 81 34.36N106.02W
Willemstad Neth. Antilles 90 12.12N 68.56W
Willeroo Australia 62 15.17S131.35E
William, Mt. Australia 66 37.20S142.41E
William Creek *town* Australia 66 28.52S136.18E
Williams Australia 63 33.01S116.45E
Williams *r.* Australia 63 32.59S116.24E
Williamsburg U.S.A. 85 37.17N 76.43W
Williams Lake *town* Canada 74 52.08N122.10W
Williamson U.S.A. 85 37.42N 82.16W
Williamsport Penn. U.S.A. 84 41.14N 77.00W
Williamston U.S.A. 85 35.53N 77.05W
Williamstown N.J. U.S.A. 85 39.41N 75.00W
Willis Group *is.* Australia 64 16.18S150.00E
Williston R.S.A. 56 31.21S 20.53E
Williston U.S.A. 82 48.09N103.37W
Williston L. Canada 74 55.40N123.40W
Willits U.S.A. 80 39.25N123.21W
Willmar U.S.A. 82 45.07N 95.03W
Willmore Wilderness Park Canada 74 53.45N119.00W
Willochra Australia 66 32.12S138.10E
Willochra *r.* Australia 66 31.57S137.52E
Willow U.S.A. 72 61.42N150.08W
Willow Grove U.S.A. 85 40.08N 75.06W
Willow L. Canada 74 62.10N119.08W
Willowmore R.S.A. 56 33.18S 23.28E
Willow Ranch U.S.A. 80 41.55N120.21W
Willow River *town* Canada 74 54.06N122.28W
Willunga Australia 66 35.18S138.33E
Wilmette U.S.A. 82 42.04N 87.43W
Wilmington Del. U.S.A. 85 39.44N 75.33W
Wilmington N.C. U.S.A. 85 34.14N 77.55W
Wilmslow U.K. 10 53.19N 2.14W
Wilpena *r.* Australia 66 31.13S139.25E
Wilson N.C. U.S.A. 85 35.43N 77.56W
Wilson N.Y. U.S.A. 76 43.19N 78.50W
Wilson's Promontory *c.* Australia 67 39.06S146.23E
Wilton *r.* Australia 64 14.45S134.33E
Wilton U.K. 11 51.05N 1.52W
Wilton N.Dak. U.S.A. 82 47.10N100.47W
Wiltshire *d.* U.K. 11 51.20N 0.34W
Wiltz Lux. 14 49.59N 5.53E
Wiluna Australia 62 26.36S120.13E
Wimmera *r.* Australia 66 36.05S141.56E
Winam *b.* Kenya 55 0.15S 34.30E
Winburg R.S.A. 56 28.30S 27.01E
Wincanton U.K. 11 51.03N 2.24W
Winchester U.K. 11 51.04N 1.19W
Winchester Ky. U.S.A. 85 38.00N 84.10W
Winchester Va. U.S.A. 84 39.11N 78.10W
Winchester Wyo. U.S.A. 80 43.51N108.10W
Windermere *l.* U.K. 10 54.20N 2.56W
Windfall Canada 74 54.12N116.13W
Windhoek Namibia 56 22.34S 17.06E
Windom U.S.A. 82 43.52N 95.07W
Windorah Australia 64 25.26S142.39E
Wind River Range *mts.* U.S.A. 80 43.05N109.25W
Windsor Australia 67 33.38S150.47E
Windsor Nfld. Canada 77 48.58N 55.40W
Windsor N.S. Canada 77 44.59N 64.08W
Windsor Ont. Canada 76 42.18N 83.01W
Windsor Que. Canada 77 45.34N 72.00W
Windsor U.K. 11 51.29N 0.38W
Windward Is. C. America 87 13.00N 60.00W
Windward Passage *str.* Carib. Sea 87 20.00N 74.00W
Winfield Kans. U.S.A. 83 37.15N 96.59W
Wingen Australia 67 31.43S150.54E
Wingham Australia 67 31.50S152.20E
Wingham Canada 76 43.53N 81.19W
Winifred U.S.A. 80 47.34N109.23W
Winisk Canada 76 55.20N 85.15W
Winisk *r.* Canada 76 55.00N 85.20W
Winisk L. Canada 76 53.00N 88.00W
Winkler Canada 75 49.11N 97.56W
Winneba Ghana 52 5.22N 0.38W
Winnebago, L. U.S.A. 82 44.00N 88.25W
Winnemucca U.S.A. 78 40.58N117.45W
Winnemucca L. U.S.A. 80 40.09N119.20W
Winner U.S.A. 82 43.22N 99.51W
Winnfield U.S.A. 83 31.55N 92.38W
Winnipeg Canada 75 49.53N 97.09W
Winnipeg *r.* Canada 75 50.38N 96.19W
Winnipeg, L. Canada 75 52.00N 97.00W
Winnipegosis, L. Canada 75 52.30N100.00W
Winnsboro La. U.S.A. 83 32.10N 91.43W
Winnsboro S.C. U.S.A. 85 34.22N 81.05W
Winona Kans. U.S.A. 82 39.04N101.15W
Winona Minn. U.S.A. 82 44.03N 91.39W
Winona Miss. U.S.A. 83 33.29N 89.44W
Winooski U.S.A. 84 44.29N 73.11W
Winschoten Neth. 14 53.07N 7.02E
Winsford U.K. 10 53.12N 2.31W
Winslow Ariz. U.S.A. 81 35.01N110.42W
Winslow Maine U.S.A. 84 44.32N 69.38W
Winston U.S.A. 80 46.28N111.38W
Winston-Salem U.S.A. 85 36.05N 80.18W
Winsum Neth. 14 53.20N 6.31E
Winter Haven U.S.A. 85 28.02N 81.46W
Winterset U.S.A. 82 41.20N 94.01W
Winterswijk Neth. 14 51.58N 6.44E
Winterthur Switz. 20 47.30N 8.45E
Winthrop Minn. U.S.A. 82 44.32N 94.22W
Winthrop Wash. U.S.A. 80 48.29N120.11W
Winton Australia 64 22.22S143.00E
Winton New Zealand 60 46.10S168.20E
Winton U.S.A. 80 41.45N109.10W
Wirrabara Australia 66 33.03S138.18E
Wirraminna Australia 66 31.11S136.04E
Wirrappa Australia 66 31.28S137.00E
Wirrega Australia 66 36.11S140.37E
Wirrida, L. Australia 66 29.45S134.39E
Wirulla Australia 66 32.24S134.33E
Wisbech U.K. 11 52.39N 0.10E
Wisconsin *d.* U.S.A. 82 44.30N 90.00W
Wisconsin *r.* U.S.A. 82 43.00N 91.15W
Wisconsin Dells U.S.A. 82 43.38N 89.46W
Wisconsin Rapids *town* U.S.A. 82 44.24N 89.50W
Wisdom U.S.A. 80 45.37N113.27W
Wisła *r.* Poland 21 54.23N 18.52E
Wismar Germany 20 53.54N 11.28E
Wisner U.S.A. 82 41.59N 96.55W
Wisznice Poland 21 51.48N 23.12E
Witchekan L. Canada 75 53.25N107.35W
Witham *r.* U.K. 10 52.56N 0.04E
Withernsea U.K. 10 53.43N 0.02E
Witkowo Poland 21 52.27N 17.47E
Witney U.K. 11 51.47N 1.29W
Witsand R.S.A. 56 34.23S 20.49E
Witten Germany 14 51.26N 7.19E
Wittenberg Germany 20 51.53N 12.39E
Wittenberge Germany 20 52.59N 11.45E
Wittenoom Australia 62 22.19S118.21E
Wittlich Germany 14 49.59N 6.54E
Witu Kenya 55 2.22S 40.20E
Witvlei Namibia 56 22.25S 18.29E
Wiveliscombe U.K. 11 51.02N 3.20W
Wkra *r.* Poland 21 52.27N 20.44E
Władysławowo Poland 21 54.49N 18.25E
Włocławek Poland 21 52.39N 19.01E
Włodawa Poland 21 51.33N 23.31E
Wodonga Australia 67 36.08S146.09E
Woerden Neth. 14 52.07N 4.55E
Wohutun China 32 43.40N123.30E
Wokam *i.* Indonesia 37 5.45S134.30E
Woking Canada 74 55.35N118.50W
Woking U.K. 11 51.20N 0.34W
Woleai *i.* Pacific Oc. 68 7.21N143.52E
Wolf *r.* U.S.A. 82 44.07N 88.43W
Wolf Creek *town* U.S.A. 80 46.50N112.20W
Wolfenbüttel Germany 20 52.10N 10.33E
Wolf Point *town* U.S.A. 80 48.05N105.39W
Wolfsberg Austria 20 46.51N 14.51E
Wolfsburg Germany 20 52.27N 10.49E
Wolin Poland 20 53.51N 14.38E
Wollaston L. Canada 75 58.15N103.20W
Wollaston Pen. Canada 72 70.00N115.00W
Wollongong Australia 67 34.25S150.52E
Wolmaransstad R.S.A. 56 27.11S 25.58E
Wołomin Poland 21 52.21N 21.14E
Wolseley Australia 66 36.21S140.55E
Wolvega Neth. 14 52.53N 6.00E
Wolverhampton U.K. 11 52.35N 2.06W
Womelsdorf U.S.A. 85 40.22N 76.11W
Wondai Australia 64 26.19S151.52E
Wongan Hills *town* Australia 63 30.55S116.41E
Wonogiri Indonesia 37 7.48S110.52E
Wonosari Indonesia 37 7.55S110.39E
Wonosobo Indonesia 37 7.21S109.56E
Wŏnsan N. Korea 31 39.07N127.26E
Wonthaggi Australia 67 38.38S145.37E
Woocalla Australia 66 31.44S137.10E
Woodbine U.S.A. 85 39.14N 74.49W
Woodbridge U.K. 11 52.06N 1.19E
Woodbridge U.S.A. 85 38.39N 77.15W
Wood Buffalo Nat. Park Canada 74 59.00N113.41W
Woodburn Australia 67 29.04S153.21E
Woodbury U.S.A. 85 39.50N 75.10W
Wooded Bluff *f.* Australia 67 29.22S153.22E
Woodenbong Australia 67 28.28S152.35E
Woodland U.S.A. 80 38.41N121.46W
Woodlark I. P.N.G. 64 9.05S152.50E
Wood Mts. Canada 75 49.14N106.20W
Woodroffe, Mt. Australia 64 26.20S131.45E
Woods, L. Australia 64 17.50S133.30E
Woods, L. of the Canada / U.S.A. 76 49.15N 94.45W
Woodside Australia 67 38.31S146.52E
Woods L. Canada 77 54.40N 64.21W
Woodstock Canada 76 43.08N 80.45W
Woodstock U.K. 11 51.51N 1.20W
Woodstown U.S.A. 85 39.39N 75.20W
Woodville New Zealand 60 40.20S175.52E
Woodward U.S.A. 83 36.26N 99.24W
Wooler U.K. 10 55.33N 2.01W
Woolgoolga Australia 67 30.07S153.12E
Wooltana Australia 66 30.28S139.26E
Woomera Australia 66 31.11S136.54E
Woonsocket U.S.A. 84 42.00N 71.31W
Wooramel Australia 62 25.42S114.20E
Wooramel *r.* Australia 62 25.47S114.10E
Woorong, L. Australia 66 29.24S134.06E
Worcester R.S.A. 56 33.39S 19.25E
Worcester U.K. 11 52.12N 2.12W
Worcester U.S.A. 84 42.16N 71.48W
Workington U.K. 10 54.39N 3.34W
Worksop U.K. 10 53.19N 1.09W
Workum Neth. 14 53.00N 5.26E
Worland U.S.A. 80 44.01N107.57W
Worms Germany 20 49.38N 8.23E
Worthing U.K. 11 50.49N 0.21W
Worthington Minn. U.S.A. 82 43.37N 95.36W
Worthington Ohio U.S.A. 84 40.03N 83.03W
Worthville U.S.A. 84 38.38N 85.05W
Wosi Indonesia 37 0.15S128.00E
Wour Chad 53 21.21N 15.57E
Woutchaba Cameroon 53 5.13N 13.05E
Wowoni *i.* Indonesia 37 4.10S123.10E
Wragby U.K. 10 53.17N 0.18E
Wrangel I. *see* Vrangelya, Ostrov *i.* U.S.S.R. 29
Wrangell U.S.A. 74 56.28N132.23W
Wrangell Mts. U.S.A. 72 62.00N143.00W
Wrangle U.K. 10 53.03N 0.09E
Wrath, C. U.K. 12 58.37N 5.01W
Wray U.S.A. 82 40.05N102.13W
Wrecks, B. of Kiribati 69 1.52N157.17W
Wrexham U.K. 10 53.05N 3.00W
Wrigley Canada 72 63.16N123.39W
Wrocław Poland 21 51.05N 17.00E
Wronki Poland 20 52.43N 16.23E
Września Poland 21 52.20N 17.34E
Wubin Australia 63 30.06S116.38E
Wuchang China 33 30.21N114.19E
Wucheng China 32 37.12N116.04E
Wuchuan Guangdong China 33 21.21N110.40E
Wuchuan Nei Monggol China 32 41.08N111.24E
Wuda China 32 39.40N106.40E
Wuday 'ah Saudi Arabia 45 16.05N 47.05E
Wudham 'Alwā' Oman 43 23.48N 57.33E
Wudinna Australia 66 33.03S135.28E
Wudu China 32 33.24N104.50E
Wufeng China 33 30.12N110.36E
Wugang China 33 26.42N110.31E
Wugong Shan *mts.* China 33 27.15N114.00E
Wuhai China 32 39.50N106.40E
Wuhan China 33 30.37N114.19E
Wuhu China 33 31.25N118.25E
Wūjang China 41 33.38N 79.55E
Wu Jiang *r.* China 33 29.41N107.24E
Wukari Nigeria 53 7.57N 9.42E
Wulian China 32 35.45N119.12E
Wuliang Shan *mts.* China 30 24.27N100.43E
Wum Cameroon 53 6.25N 10.03E
Wumbulgal Australia 67 34.25S146.16E
Wuming China 33 23.10N108.16E
Wuning China 33 29.17N115.05E
Wunnummin L. Canada 76 52.50N 89.20W
Wun Rog Sudan 49 9.00N 28.21E
Wuppertal Germany 14 51.15N 7.10E
Wuppertal R.S.A. 56 32.16S 19.12E
Wuqi China 32 37.03N108.14E
Wuqiao China 32 37.38N116.22E
Wuqing China 32 39.19N117.05E
Wurno Nigeria 53 13.20N 5.28E
Würzburg Germany 20 49.48N 9.57E
Wusong China 33 31.20N121.30E
Wutongqiao China 33 29.20N103.48E
Wuwei China 32 38.00N102.59E
Wuxi Jiangsu China 33 31.34N120.20E
Wuxi Sichuan China 33 31.28N109.36E
Wuxing China 33 30.59N120.04E
Wuyi Shan *mts.* China 33 27.00N117.00E
Wuyuan China 32 41.06N108.16E
Wuzhan China 31 50.14N125.18E
Wuzhi Shan *mts.* China 33 18.50N109.30E
Wuzhou China 33 23.28N111.21E
Wyalkatchem Australia 63 31.21S117.22E
Wyalong Australia 67 33.55S147.17E
Wyandotte U.S.A. 84 42.11N 83.10W
Wyandra Australia 65 27.15S146.00E
Wyangala Resr. Australia 67 33.58S148.55E
Wyara, L. Australia 66 28.42S144.16E
Wycheproof Australia 66 36.04S143.14E
Wye U.K. 11 51.11N 0.56E
Wye *r.* U.K. 11 51.37N 2.40W
Wymondham U.K. 11 52.34N 1.07E
Wynbring Australia 65 30.33S133.32E
Wyndham Australia 62 15.29S128.05E
Wynne U.S.A. 83 35.14N 90.47W
Wyoming *d.* U.S.A. 80 43.10N107.36W
Wyong Australia 67 33.17S151.25E
Wyszków Poland 21 52.36N 21.28E
Wytheville U.S.A. 85 36.57N 81.07W

X

Xa Cassau Angola 54 9.02S 20.17E
Xagquka China 41 31.50N 92.46E
Xainza China 41 30.56N 88.40E
Xaitongmoin China 41 29.22N 88.15E
Xai-Xai Mozambique 57 25.05S 33.38E
Xalin *well* Somali Rep. 45 9.08N 48.47E
Xam Nua Laos 34 20.25N104.10E
Xangdoring China 41 32.06N 82.02E
Xangongo Angola 54 16.31S 15.00E
Xanten Germany 14 51.40N 6.29E
Xánthi Greece 19 41.07N 24.55E
Xarardheere Somali Rep. 45 4.32N 47.53E
Xar Hudag China 32 45.07N114.28E
Xar Moron He *r.* China 32 43.30N120.42E
Xassengue Angola 54 10.26S 18.32E
Xau, L. Botswana 56 21.15S 24.50E
Xebert China 32 44.02N122.00E
Xenia U.S.A. 84 39.41N 83.56W
Xequessa Angola 54 16.47S 19.05E
Xhora R.S.A. 56 31.58S 28.40E
Xiachuan *i.* China 33 21.40N112.37E
Xiaguan China 30 25.33N100.09E
Xiamen China 33 24.30N118.08E
Xi'an China 32 34.11N108.55E
Xianfeng China 33 29.41N109.02E
Xiangcheng China 32 33.50N113.29E
Xiangfan China 32 32.04N112.05E
Xiangfen China 32 35.52N111.24E
Xiang Jiang *r.* China 33 28.49N112.30E
Xiangkhoang Laos 34 19.21N103.23E
Xiangquan He *r.* China 41 31.45N 78.40E
Xiangshan China 33 29.29N121.51E
Xiangtan China 33 27.50N112.49E
Xiangtang China 33 28.26N115.58E
Xiangyin China 33 28.40N112.53E
Xiangyuan China 32 36.32N113.02E
Xiangzhou China 33 23.58N109.41E
Xianju China 33 28.51N120.44E
Xianning China 33 29.53N114.13E
Xian Xian China 32 38.12N116.07E
Xianyang China 32 34.20N108.40E
Xianyou China 33 25.28N118.50E
Xiao Hinggan Ling *mts.* China 31 48.40N128.30E
Xiaojiang China 33 27.34N120.27E
Xiaojiao China 32 38.24N113.42E
Xiaowutai Shan *mtn.* China 32 39.57N114.59E
Xiapu China 33 26.58N119.57E
Xiayang China 33 26.45N117.58E
Xichang China 30 27.53N102.18E
Xichou China 33 23.27N104.40E
Xichuan China 32 33.15N111.27E
Xifeng China 33 27.06N106.44E
Xigazê China 30 29.18N 88.50E
Xiheying China 32 39.53N114.42E
Xiji China 32 35.52N105.35E
Xi Jiang *r.* China 33 22.23N113.20E
Xiliao He *r.* China 32 43.48N123.00E
Xilin China 33 24.30N105.03E
Ximeng China 39 22.45N 99.29E
Xin'anjiang China 33 29.27N119.14E
Xin'anjiang Shuiku *resr.* China 33 29.32N119.00E
Xincheng Guang. Zhuang. China 33 24.04N108.40E
Xincheng Ningxia Huizu China 32 38.33N106.10E
Xincheng Shanxi China 32 37.57N112.35E
Xindu China 33 30.50N104.12E
Xinfeng Guangdong China 33 24.04N114.12E
Xinfeng Jiangxi China 33 25.27N114.58E
Xing'an China 33 25.35N110.32E
Xingcheng China 32 40.37N120.43E
Xinghua China 32 32.51N119.50E
Xingkai Hu *l. see* Khanka, Ozero U.S.S.R. / China 31
Xingren China 33 25.26N105.14E
Xingshan China 33 31.10N110.51E
Xingtai China 32 37.04N114.26E
Xingu *r.* Brazil 91 1.40S 52.15W
Xing Xian China 32 38.31N111.04E
Xingyi China 33 25.00N104.59E
Xinhe Hebei China 32 37.22N115.14E
Xinhe Xin. Uygur China 30 41.34N 82.38E
Xinhua China 33 27.45N111.18E
Xining China 30 36.35N101.55E
Xinji China 32 35.17N115.35E
Xinjiang-Uygur *d.* China 30 41.15N 87.00E
Xinjie China 32 39.15N109.36E
Xinjin Liaoning China 32 39.27N121.48E
Xinjin Sichuan China 33 30.30N103.47E
Xinle China 32 38.15N114.40E
Xinlitun China 32 42.00N122.09E
Xinmin China 32 42.01N122.48E
Xinning China 33 26.31N110.48E
Xinshao China 33 27.20N111.26E
Xin Xian China 32 38.24N112.47E
Xinxiang China 32 35.12N113.57E
Xinyang China 32 32.08N114.04E
Xinyi Guangdong China 33 22.21N110.57E
Xinyi Jiangsu China 32 34.20N118.30E
Xinyu China 33 27.50N114.55E
Xinzheng China 32 34.25N113.46E
Xinzhu Taiwan 33 24.50N120.58E
Xiping Henan China 32 33.23N114.02E
Xiping Zhejiang China 33 28.27N119.29E
Xique Xique Brazil 91 10.47S 42.44W
Xi Ujimqin Qi China 32 44.32N117.40E
Xiuning China 33 29.48N118.20E
Xiushan China 33 28.27N108.59E
Xiushui China 33 29.01N114.37E
Xixabangma Feng *mtn.* China 41 28.21N 85.47E
Xixia China 32 33.30N111.30E
Xizang *d.* China 41 31.45N 87.00E
Xorkol China 30 39.04N 91.05E
Xuancheng China 33 30.59N118.40E
Xuang *r.* Laos 34 19.59N102.20E
Xuanhan China 33 31.25N107.38E
Xuanhua China 32 40.30N115.00E
Xuanwei China 33 26.16N104.01E
Xuchang China 32 34.02N113.50E
Xuddur Somali Rep. 45 4.10N 43.53E
Xuefeng Shan *mts.* China 33 27.30N111.00
Xueshuiwen China 31 49.15N129.39E
Xugou China 32 34.40N119.26E
Xunyang China 32 32.48N109.27E
Xupu China 33 27.54N110.35E
Xushui China 32 39.01N115.39E
Xuwen China 33 20.25N110.20E
Xuyong China 33 28.17N105.21E
Xuzhou China 32 34.14N117.20E

Y

Ya Gabon 54 1.17S 14.14E
Ya'an China 39 30.00N102.59E
Yaapeet Australia 66 35.48S142.07E
Yabassi Cameroon 53 4.30N 9.55E
Yabēlo Ethiopia 49 4.54N 38.05E
Yablonovyy Khrebet *mts.* U.S.S.R. 29 53.20N115.00E
Yabrai Shan *mts.* China 32 39.50N103.30E
Yabrai Yanchang China 32 39.24N102.43E
Yabrūd Syria 44 33.58N 36.40E
Yacheng China 33 18.35N109.13E
Yacuiba Bolivia 92 22.00S 63.25W
Yādgir India 38 16.46N 77.08E
Yadong China 41 27.29N 88.54E
Yagaba Ghana 52 10.13N 1.14W
Yagoua Cameroon 53 10.23N 15.13E
Yagra China 41 31.32N 82.27E
Yahagi *r.* Japan 35 34.50N136.59E
Yahisuli Zaïre 54 0.08S 24.04E
Yahuma Zaïre 54 1.06N 23.10E
Yaizu Japan 35 34.52N138.20E
Yajua Nigeria 53 11.27N 12.49E
Yakchāl Afghan. 40 31.47N 64.41E
Yakima U.S.A. 80 46.36N120.31W
Yakmach Pakistan 40 28.45N 63.51E
Yakutat U.S.A. 72 59.33N139.44W
Yakutat U.S.A. 74 59.29N139.49W
Yakutat B. U.S.A. 74 59.29N139.49W
Yakutsk U.S.S.R. 29 62.10N129.20E
Yala Thailand 34 6.32N101.19E
Yalgoo Australia 63 28.20S116.41E
Yalinga C.A.R. 49 6.31N 23.15E
Yallourn Australia 67 38.09S146.22E
Yalong Jiang *r.* China 30 26.35N101.44E
Yalta U.S.S.R. 25 44.30N 34.09E
Yalu Jiang *r.* China 32 40.10N124.25E
Yalutorovsk U.S.S.R. 28 56.41N 66.12E
Yamal, Poluostrov *pen.* U.S.S.R. 28 70.20N 70.00E
Yamanashi Japan 35 35.40N138.40E
Yamanashi *d.* Japan 35 35.30N138.35E
Yamandjo Zaïre 54 1.38N 23.27E
Yaman Tau *mtn.* U.S.S.R. 24 54.20N 58.10E
Yamaska Canada 77 46.01N 72.55W
Yamaska *r.* Canada 77 46.06N 72.56W
Yamato Japan 35 35.29N139.29E
Yamato-takada Japan 35 34.31N135.45E
Yamba N.S.W. Australia 67 29.26S153.22E
Yamba S.A. Australia 66 34.15S140.54E
Yambéring Guinea 52 11.49N 12.18W
Yambio Sudan 49 4.34N 28.23E
Yambol Bulgaria 19 42.28N 26.30E
Yamdena *i.* Indonesia 37 7.30S131.00E
Yamenyingzi China 32 42.23N121.03E
Yamethin Burma 34 20.24N 96.08E
Yam Kinneret *l.* Israel 44 32.49N 35.36E

UNITED KINGDOM
NORTHERN IRELAND
REPUBLIC OF IRELAND
ENGLAND
WALES
FRANCE
IRISH SEA
North Channel
St. George's Channel
Bristol Channel
English Channel
Dogger Bank
Channel Islands (U.K.)
Isle of Man
Isle of Wight
Isles of Scilly
London
Dublin
Belfast
Paris
Birmingham
Liverpool
Manchester
Leeds
Sheffield
Cardiff
Bristol
Newcastle upon Tyne
Cork
Limerick
Galway
Rennes
Le Havre
Caen
Rouen
Lille
Cherbourg
Brest
Le Mans
Orléans
Relief
Feet Metres
16404 5000
9843 3000
6562 2000
3281 1000
1640 500
656 200
0 Sea Level
Land Dep 656 200
13123 4000
22966 7000
Scale 1:4 000 000
0 20 40 60 80 100 Miles
0 40 80 120 160 Kms.
Conic Projection
© Collins ○ Longman Atlases Cbii

ENGLAND AND WALES

Scale 1:2 000 000
0 10 20 30 40 50 Miles
0 20 40 60 80 Kms.
Lambert Conformal Conic Projection
Relief
Feet Metres
3281 1000
1640 500
656 200
328 100
0 Sea Level
66 20
164 50
328 100
656 200
N O R T H
S E A
I R I S H
S E A
NORTHERN IRELAND
North Channel
ISLE OF MAN
S C O T L A N D
Edinburgh
Glasgow
Newcastle upon Tyne
Sunderland
Middlesbrough
Stockton-on-Tees
Carlisle
Scarborough
York
Leeds
Bradford
Kingston upon Hull
Blackpool
Preston
Liverpool
Birkenhead
Manchester
Warrington
Stockport
Sheffield
Stoke-on-Trent
Nottingham
Derby
Lincoln
Grantham
LINCOLNSHIRE
HUMBERSIDE
NORTH YORKSHIRE
LANCASHIRE
CUMBRIA
NORTHUMBERLAND
DURHAM
CHESHIRE
DERBYSHIRE
NOTTINGHAMSHIRE
CLWYD
GWYNEDD
BORDERS
Cumbrian Mts.
Cheviot Hills
North York Moors
Lake District
Anglesey
Caernarfon Bay
Flamborough Head
The Wash

EVERETT LIBRARY
J04904F1848

ART FRAUD DETECTIVE

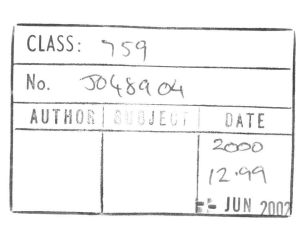

ANNA NILSEN

KINGFISHER

For Elaine
From ATB

KINGFISHER
Kingfisher Publications Plc
New Penderel House
283-288 High Holborn
London WC1V 7HZ

First published in 2000
2 4 6 8 10 9 7 5 3 1

1TR/0100/TWP/MAR(MAR)/150NMA

A CIP catalogue record of this book is available from the British Library.

ISBN 0 7534 0478 8

Printed in Singapore

Author and forgery artwork: Anna Nilsen
Editor: Camilla Reid
Senior Designer: Sarah Goodwin
DTP: Nicky Studdart
Production Controller: Caroline Jackson
Illustrator: Andy Parker

The Publishers would also like to thank the following:
Sinead and Rowan Derbyshire, Elaine Ward,
Erika Langmuir and Suzie Burt.

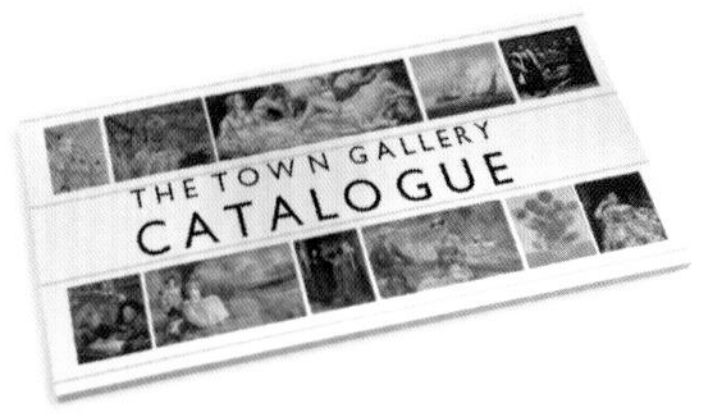
THE TOWN GALLERY
CATALOGUE

THE MYSTERY CALLER

At the Town Gallery Mr Bassett, the old security guard, receives a phone call from someone with a strange, muffled voice. It looks like the gallery may have a bit of a problem…

RING! RING!

ZZZZ

Hello?

Mr Bassett? I have some very important information that could save your gallery from total disaster!

What the…! Who is this?

You silly old fool, call yourself a security guard?! Under your nose, THIRTY of your paintings have been stolen – by four notorious gangs of forgers – and replaced by cunning FAKES! If you want to catch the forgers and stop the real paintings being sold on the black market…

…you'd better find the fakes, FAST! You want to know who I am? All I can tell you is that I am a member of one of the gangs but I've had enough of life as a criminal. Out of all the forgers, I was the only one who refused to get involved in the Town Gallery job. 3

For my own safety, I'm keeping my identity secret and staying in disguise until those devious villains are locked up behind bars. However, if you're smart, you may be able to work out my identity. Oh, one last thing… each gang member, apart from me, has forged exactly TWO paintings!

…and then the line went dead.
This is a catastrophe for the Town Gallery! If we go to the experts for help, people will find out that our paintings aren't the real thing – we'll have to close down and the masterpieces will be lost forever.

But, hang on… if I had a fast-working private detective to search the gallery and find the forgeries, we could be saved. And I've got an idea! How about…
YOU?

FACTS FOR THE DETECTIVE

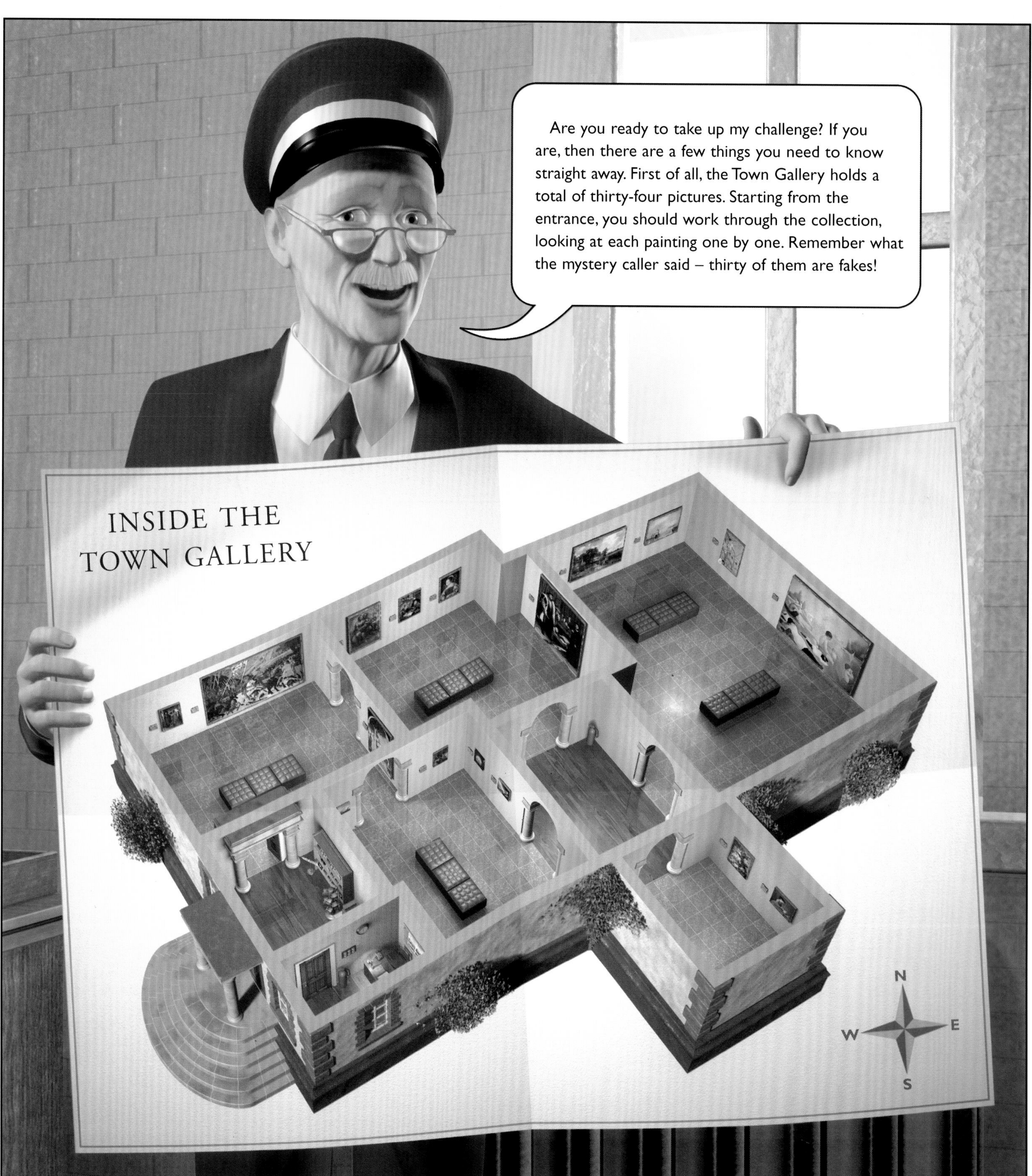

Are you ready to take up my challenge? If you are, then there are a few things you need to know straight away. First of all, the Town Gallery holds a total of thirty-four pictures. Starting from the entrance, you should work through the collection, looking at each painting one by one. Remember what the mystery caller said – thirty of them are fakes!
INSIDE THE TOWN GALLERY
N
E
S
W

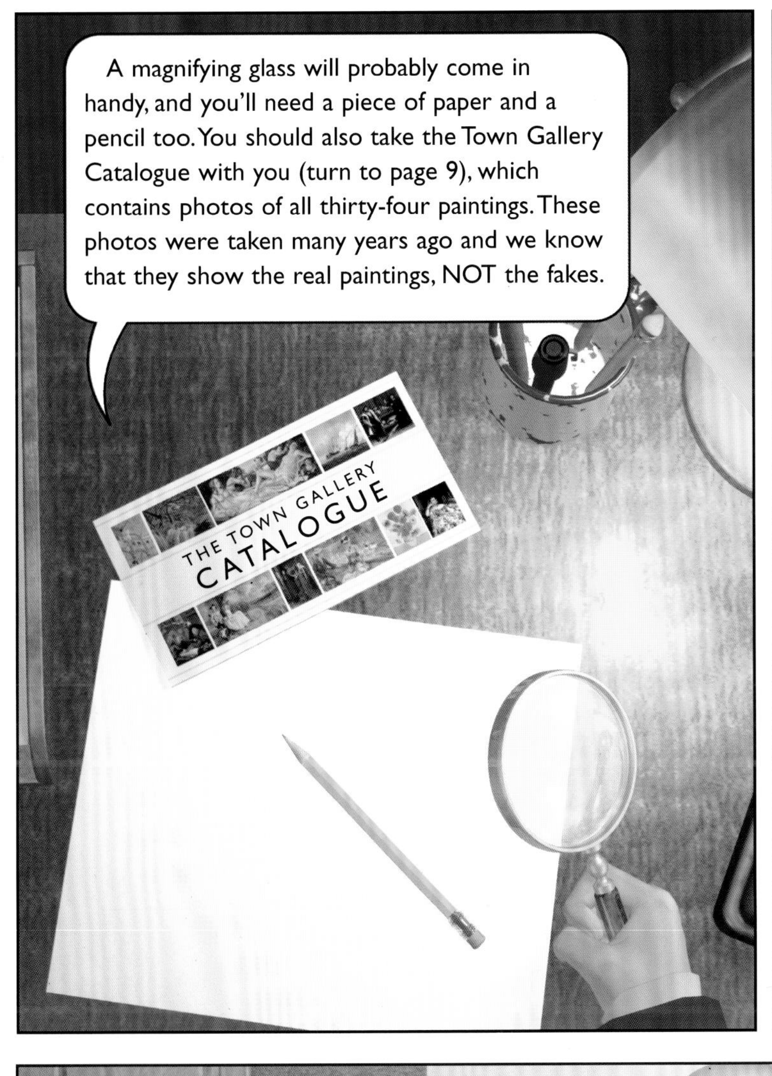
A magnifying glass will probably come in handy, and you'll need a piece of paper and a pencil too. You should also take the Town Gallery Catalogue with you (turn to page 9), which contains photos of all thirty-four paintings. These photos were taken many years ago and we know that they show the real paintings, NOT the fakes.
THE TOWN GALLERY CATALOGUE

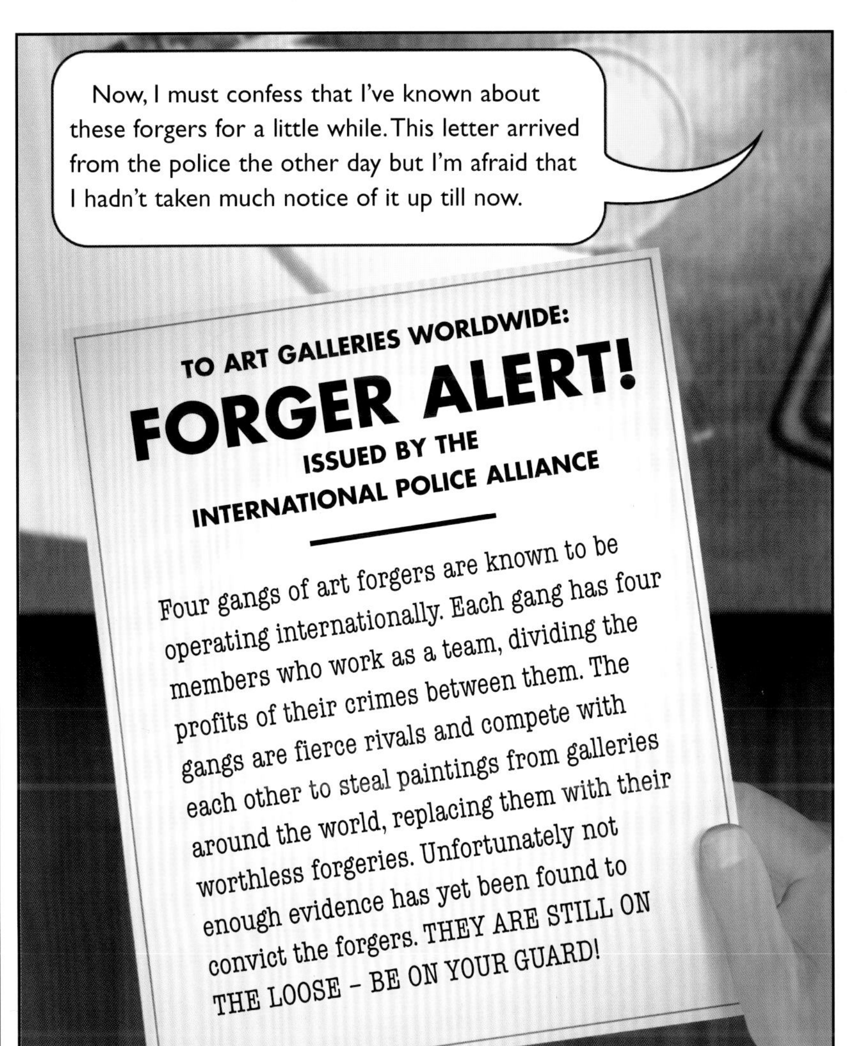
Now, I must confess that I've known about these forgers for a little while. This letter arrived from the police the other day but I'm afraid that I hadn't taken much notice of it up till now.

TO ART GALLERIES WORLDWIDE:

FORGER ALERT!

ISSUED BY THE INTERNATIONAL POLICE ALLIANCE

Four gangs of art forgers are known to be operating internationally. Each gang has four members who work as a team, dividing the profits of their crimes between them. The gangs are fierce rivals and compete with each other to steal paintings from galleries around the world, replacing them with their worthless forgeries. Unfortunately not enough evidence has yet been found to convict the forgers. THEY ARE STILL ON THE LOOSE – BE ON YOUR GUARD!

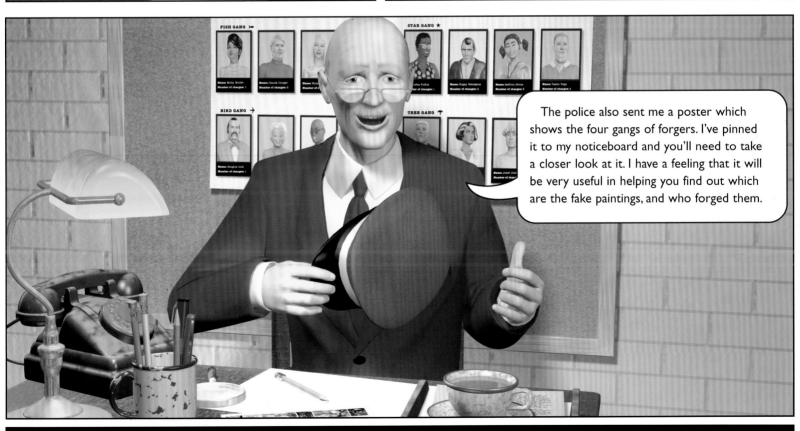

The police also sent me a poster which shows the four gangs of forgers. I've pinned it to my noticeboard and you'll need to take a closer look at it. I have a feeling that it will be very useful in helping you find out which are the fake paintings, and who forged them.

Turn to the next page to see the poster close up...

ART FRAUD

ISSUED TO ART GALLERIES WORLDWIDE BY THE INTERNATIONAL POLICE ALLIANCE

Each gang of forgers is secretly proud of its work and stamps all its fakes with one particular symbol, hidden somewhere in the painting. The International Police Alliance has also discovered that each forger makes a set number of deliberate, tiny changes to every painting

FISH GANG 

Name: Molly Mullet
Number of changes: 1

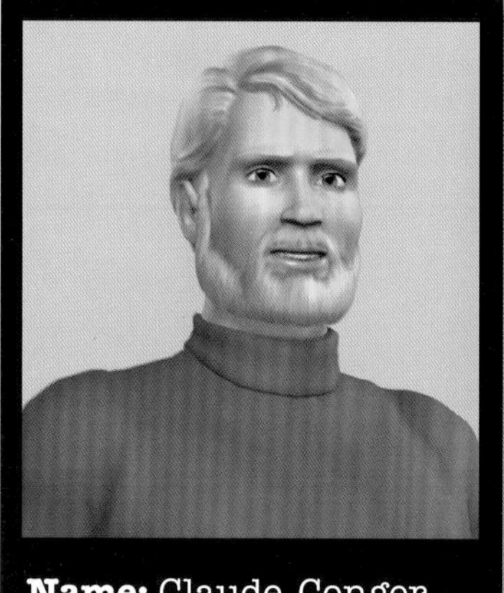

Name: Claude Conger
Number of changes: 2

Name: Bonnie Barracuda
Number of changes: 3

Name: Attila Anchovy
Number of changes: 4

BIRD GANG

Name: Genghis Gull
Number of changes: 1

Name: Lizzie Lapwing
Number of changes: 2

Name: Hawley Hornbill
Number of changes: 3

Name: Imelda Ibis
Number of changes: 4

A HELPING HAND

Back in the office, Mr Bassett has some last minute advice for you…

Have you examined every picture from top to bottom? Do you know which are the fakes and which are the real paintings? Maybe you want to go back and look at the paintings one more time? Try spotting the symbol first, then look for the changes. Remember that there should be only two artists in each box on your chart – if there are more, then you may have missed some changes.

If you're still stuck, don't worry, help is at hand! While you've been busy, I've been doing a bit of detective work myself and have drawn up my own chart. If you need to compare notes, you can use your magnifying glass to check my list.
THE TOWN GALLERY
CATALOGUE

NUMBER OF CHANGES / GANG SYMBOL	FISH GANG	BIRD GANG	STAR GANG	TREE GANG
1	RAPHAEL Molly Mullet	TER BRUGGHEN Genghis Gull	VAN OS Portia Pollux	PERRONNEAU Filippi Fig
	CHARDIN Molly Mullet	MONET Genghis Gull	DELAROCHE Portia Pollux	CONSTABLE Filippi Fig
2	TURNER Claude Conger	PIERO DELLA F. Lizzie Lapwing	VERMEER Bugsy Betelgeux	REMBRANDT Annie Apricot
	VAN GOGH Claude Conger	STEENWYCK Lizzie Lapwing	WATTEAU Bugsy Betelgeux	GAINSBOROUGH Annie Apricot
3	BOTTICELLI Bonnie Barracuda	HOLBEIN Hawley Hornbill	MASSYS Saffron Sirius	VAN EYCK Josef Juniper
	AVERCAMP Bonnie Barracuda	DE HOOCH Hawley Hornbill	INGRES Saffron Sirius	SEURAT Josef Juniper
4	MARINUS Attila Anchovy		GOSSAERT Vasile Vega	UCCELLO Salome Spruce
	ROUSSEAU Attila Anchovy		DEGAS Vasile Vega	BRUEGHEL Salome Spruce

REAL PAINTINGS (no changes)	1. LEONARDO	2. VAN DE VELDE	3. MORISOT	4. PICASSO

Finally, when your chart matches mine, it's time to call in the police. If you have got the facts straight, you should be able to prove which fifteen forgers are guilty and identify the mystery caller. I hope you did a good job because the future of the gallery rests in your hands!
SUSPECTS

Turn to the next page to see if you have succeeded in bringing the forgers to justice!

THE MOMENT OF TRUTH

VAN EYCK
3 changes
Josef Juniper

BOTTICELLI
3 changes
Bonnie Barracuda

MASSYS
3 changes
Saffron Sirius

AVERCAMP
3 changes
Bonnie Barracuda

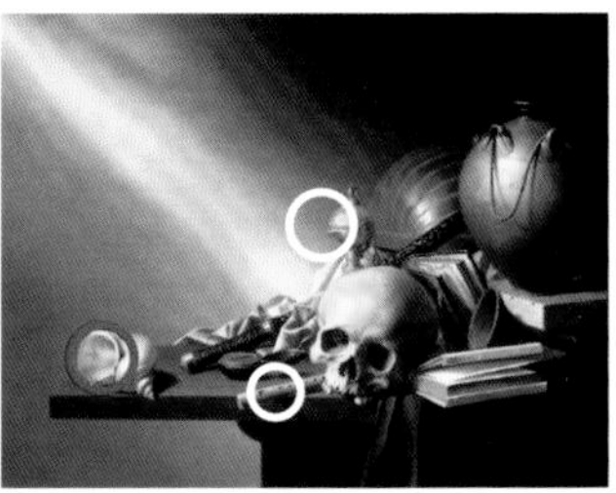

STEENWYCK
2 changes
Lizzie Lapwing

PIERO DELLA F.
2 changes
Lizzie Lapwing

RAPHAEL
1 change
Molly Mullet

GOSSAERT
4 changes
Vasile Vega

HOLBEIN
3 changes
Hawley Hornbill

TER BRUGGHEN
1 change
Genghis Gull

VAN DE VELDE
No changes

UCCELLO
4 changes
Salome Spruce

LEONARDO
No changes

MARINUS
4 changes
Attila Anchovy

BREUGHEL
4 changes
Salome Spruce

REMBRANDT
2 changes
Annie Apricot

Bonnie Barracuda
Molly Mullet
Salome Spruce
Annie Apricot
Portia Pollux
Vasile Vega
Claude Conger
Attila Anchovy
Josef Juniper
Filippi Fig
Saffron Sirius
Bugsy Betelgeux

VERMEER
2 changes ★
Bugsy Betelgeux

PERRONNEAU
1 change
Filippi Fig

VAN OS
1 change ★
Portia Pollux

TURNER
2 changes
Claude Conger

DEGAS
4 changes ★
Vasile Vega

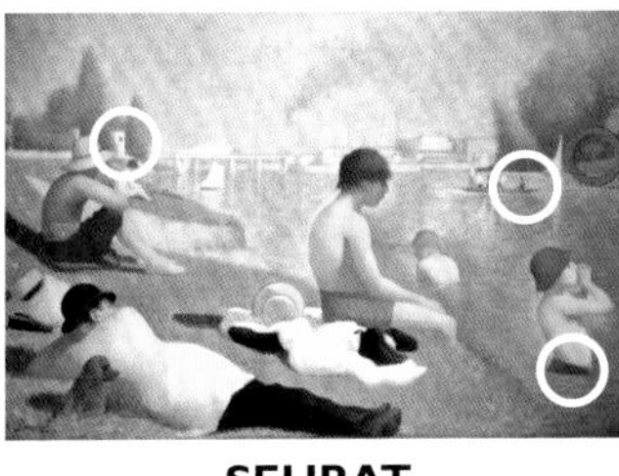

SEURAT
3 changes
Josef Juniper

DE HOOCH
3 changes
Hawley Hornbill

GAINSBOROUGH
2 changes
Annie Apricot

DELAROCHE
1 change ★
Portia Pollux

INGRES
3 changes ★
Saffron Sirius

MONET
1 change
Genghis Gull

VAN GOGH
2 changes
Claude Conger

CHARDIN
1 change
Molly Mullet

WATTEAU
2 changes ★
Bugsy Betelgeux

CONSTABLE
1 change
Filippi Fig

MORISOT
No changes

ROUSSEAU
4 changes
Attila Anchovy

PICASSO
No changes

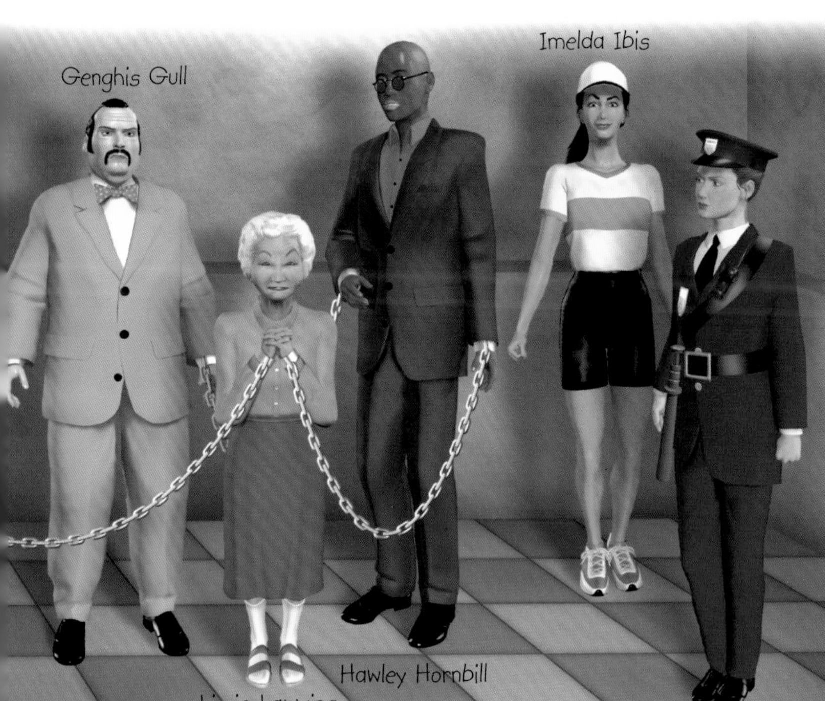
Genghis Gull
Imelda Ibis
Hawley Hornbill
Lizzie Lapwing

Congratulations! You are a top Art Fraud Detective! As you will know by now, the paintings by Leonardo, Van de Velde, Morisot and Picasso are the real masterpieces. And yes, Imelda Ibis is the mystery caller – it was she who tipped us off about the crimes of her fellow forgers. The police have agreed that, unlike the fifteen guilty forgers, she will not be jailed. And finally, the pictures will be returned, the gallery is saved and it's all thanks to you!

GOODBYE!

GLOSSARY OF ART TERMS

CANVAS
Until the 15th century, pictures were usually painted on wooden panels. Gradually artists began painting on canvas, a specially prepared cotton fabric. The canvas is stretched on a wooden frame, then painted with a primer to stop the material absorbing too much paint.

CARTOON
A full-size drawing done in preparation for a painting. The term comes from the Italian word *cartone,* which is used to describe a large sheet of paper.

CLASSICAL
The term used to describe painting or sculpture that is inspired by the pure, simple art of Ancient Greece and Rome.

COMPOSITION
The arrangement of objects in a painting or drawing.

CUBISM
A revolutionary art movement, started at the beginning of the 20th century by Picasso and Braque. Cubism aimed to represent reality in a new way.

FORESHORTENING
In perspective, the technique used to paint an object so that it appears to be three-dimensional.

GOTHIC
A term that describes a style of decorative, courtly painting found in Europe in the late 14th to mid 15th centuries.

IMPRESSIONISM
An art movement of the 19th century. The name comes from Monet's painting, *Impression: Sunrise,* which was exhibited in Paris in 1874 with works by Renoir, Sisley, Cézanne and Pissarro. These artists wanted to capture the atmosphere and feeling of scenes, rather than recording their accurate, factual details.

The Graham Family *by Hogarth is a family portrait.*

LANDSCAPE
A painting of a natural or imaginary outdoor scene.

OIL PAINT
All paint is made up of powdered pigment (the colour), mixed in a liquid called a medium. The medium of oil paint is oil, hence the name. It can be applied with a palette knife or a brush and first became popular in the 1400s.

The Umbrellas *by Renoir is an Impressionist work.*

PATRON
A person or a group of people who buy or commission art. Some of the most important Renaissance patrons belonged to the wealthy Medici family, a powerful family of bankers who controlled the Italian city of Florence.

PERSPECTIVE
Perspective is a drawing system designed to help a flat, two-dimensional picture look three-dimensional. Faraway objects appear to be smaller than those in the foreground and all parallel lines travelling away from the viewer appear to meet in the distance at a single 'vanishing point'. The use of perspective is first seen in paintings of the 15th century.

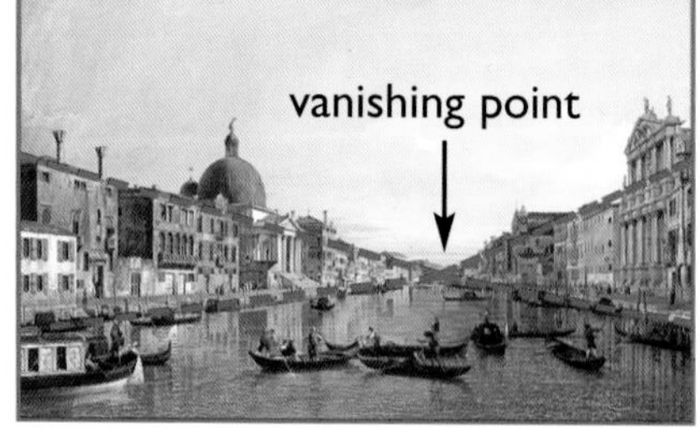
vanishing point

This painting of Venice by Canaletto makes good use of perspective.

PORTRAIT
A picture of a person, usually drawn from life. A portrait can include just the head and shoulders of one person or it can show the full figures of a group of people.

RENAISSANCE
The word renaissance means 'rebirth'. The term is now used to describe an important art movement that took place during the 15th and 16th centuries. During this time, artists started to take a great interest in Classical art, and focused on humans as the subject for their paintings and sculptures. Artists such as Raphael, Leonardo da Vinci and Michelangelo studied anatomy, perspective and science, all of which gave their art a new, realistic quality. Although the Renaissance started in Italy, it soon spread across Europe.

ROCOCO
The term given to a style of painting popular in France during the reign of Louis XV (1715–74). These decorative paintings were delicately coloured and light-hearted in atmosphere.

STILL LIFE
A painting or drawing of a static object or group of static objects, such as pots, utensils, fruit or flowers.

TEMPERA
Paint that is made by mixing powdered pigment with a medium of egg. It was the main kind of paint used on wooden panels up until the 15th century.

WATERCOLOUR
Paint that mixes pigment with water.